Caravan Sites 2006

Garlieston Caravan Club Site, Dumfries & Galloway

This year's *Caravan Sites*, sponsored by the Caravan Club, is the most comprehensive guide of its kind. It is compiled in assoociation with IPC Media's ***Caravan*** magazine and contains details of no fewer than 3450 sites for tourers, motor caravans and caravan holiday-homes. Some of the sites also accept tents.

The Caravan Club spends millions of pounds each year adding to and improving its sites network. It aims to provide members and non-members with a choice of the top locations with quality facilities.

Having more sites across the UK and Ireland than any other club, it can offer its members an unrivalled choice of location. The club has about 200 quality sites at value-for-money prices in a friendly holiday atmosphere. It welcomes tourer and motor caravanners and trailer tenters, and a number of club sites accommodate tent campers, too.

The Caravan Club has a site to match every mood and lifestyle from the fully-equipped Spirit parks for all the family, to the Discovery city sites of London and Edinburgh to its Get Away sites in the most beautiful, remote spots of Scotland and Wales.

For more information about club sites and membership, visit the website, www.caravanclub.co.uk, or call 0800 521161, quoting 'IPC06'.

■ Hopefully, your favourite site is included in this guide. You might like to vote for the site in a competition being run by ***Caravan*** magazine, which is published monthly. To enter, visit www.caravanmagazine.co.uk before 31 January 2006. You could win a portable satellite TV system.

KEY TO SYMBOLS & ABBREVIATIONS

✿ Touring caravan site open all year.
🐕 Dogs allowed, under control at all times.
🛒 Shop on site/nearby (may not be open all year; check with site if not indicated).
🔌 Mains electricity hook-ups for touring units.
♿ Some facilities provided for disabled visitors.
⌀ Gas piped to caravan holiday-homes.
T Touring caravans (number of pitches shown).
MC Motor caravans (number of pitches shown).
S Caravan holiday-homes (number for which park is licensed).
H Caravan holiday-homes for hire (number is shown).

BH&HPA and/or **NCC** indicate that the park owner(s) is a member of the British Holiday & Home Parks Association and/or the National Caravan Council. In consultation with the tourist boards, these two organisations have established the British Graded Holiday Parks Scheme, under which tourist board inspectors visit sites anonymously and award stars – from one to five – to indicate the *quality* of the facilities provided, not the *range*. Gradings awarded are signified by star symbols, e.g. ✰✰✰✰✰

The initials **CaSSOA** denote membership of the Caravan Storage Site Owners' Association. The figure in brackets at the start of most entries states the number of miles the park is from the town/village under which heading the park is listed.

■ We accept no responsibility for information given in error to us by any of the listed sites.

■ Inclusion in the guide does not imply recommendation by the publisher.

Caravan Sites 2006

Caravan

Motor Caravan MAGAZINE

PARK HOME & HOLIDAY CARAVAN

CARAVAN SITES 2006 is an IPC Focus Network annual guide, published by IPC Country & Leisure Media Ltd, part of IPC Media Ltd
© Copyright 2006
IPC Media Ltd

Motor Caravan Magazine, Caravan and Park Home & Holiday Caravan are IPC Focus Network magazines

Production editor Roger White
Database manager Martine Derwish
Front cover design Sarah Collins
Group advertisement manager Chris Williams
Advertisement sales Jill Kelf
Advertisement production manager Gina Mitchell
Publisher Joanna Pieters

Editorial and advertisement departments
Caravan Sites, IPC Media Ltd, Leon House, 233 High Street, Croydon, Surrey CR9 1HZ
☎ 020 8726 8000 fax 020 8726 8299
Origination CTT, Units C/D, Sutherland House, Sutherland Road, London E14 6BU
Printer Stones, Unit 10, Acre Estate, Wildmere Road, Banbury, Oxon OX16 3ES

FRONT COVER Main picture shows the Caravan Club's site at Coed Helen, Caernarfon, Gwynedd. The smaller illustrations are of the club's site at Dunnet Bay, Thurso, Highland (top) and of Seafield Caravan Park, Seahouses, Northumberland (bottom).

The best magazines, whatever your lifestyle

For buying information, top tips and technical help, **Caravan, Motor Caravan Magazine** and **Park Home & Holiday Caravan** are all you need — every month!

YOUR COLOUR-CODED SITE FINDER

REGIONS AND COUNTRIES

CUMBRIA

Alston

(2m). Horse & Wagon Caravan Park, Nentsbury, Alston, Cumbria CA9 3LH. 01434 382805. Owner: Mr W Patterson. The Mimosa Motel, 24a Lonsdale Road, Blackpool FY1 6EE. On A689, 3m E of Alston. Quiet, country location in an Area of Outstanding Natural Beauty. Golf, fishing, horse riding, lead mining centre and England's highest narrow-gauge railway nearby. Open March 1-October 31. **BHHPA. 10T. 10MC. 33S. 2H.** 🛱 🕿

(2m). Hudgill Caravan Park, South Hudgill, Alston, Cumbria CA9 3LG. 01434 381731. Owner: John Watson. Lease holders: Hudgill Caravan Company. Fishing, golf course, 2m to shops, PO, doctor etc. 5 mins walk to PH/hotel. Horse riding, Pennine walk. Nenthead mines and museum. Kilhope museum. Scenic routes. Open April 1-October 31. **2T. 5MC. 90S. 1H.** 🛱 🕿

Ambleside

(6.5m). Greenhowe Caravan Park, Great Langdale, Ambleside, Cumbria LA22 9JU. 01539 437231/0500 131232. Owner: G A Holden. M6, J36 to Ambleside. Left at traffic lights, follow B5343 to Langdale. Site 6.5m on right-hand side. David Bellamy Silver Conservation Award. Open March 1-November 15. ☆☆☆ **BH&HPA. 46H.** 🛱 🕿 ⊘

(0.25m). Hawkshead Hall, Hawkshead Hall Farm, Hawkshead, Ambleside, Cumbria LA22 0NN. 01539 436221. Owner: M Brass. 5m S of Ambleside on left-hand side. Open March 1-November 15. **3T. 5MC. 5S.** 🛱

(1.5m). Skelwith Fold Caravan Park, Ambleside, Cumbria LA22 0HX. 01539 432277. info@skelwith.com. www.skelwith. com. Owner: Mr Wild. c/o Moss Wood Caravan Park, Crimbles Lane, Cockerham, Lancaster LA2 0ES. Leave M6 J36 and take A591 to Ambleside. Follow A593 for Coniston at Clappersgate turn left onto B5286. Park 1.5m from Ambleside, 3m from Hawkshead. Peaceful setting in 130 acres of natural woodland, home to red squirrels, red and roe deer, badgers, rabbits and pole cats. Suitable base for walking the fells or exploring Lake District. David Bellamy Gold Conversation Award. Open March 1-November 15. ☆☆☆☆☆ **BH&HPA. 150T. 150MC. 300S.** 🛱 🕿 & 🕿

The Croft Caravan & Camp Site, North Lonsdale Road, Hawkshead, Ambleside, Cumbria LA22 0NX. 01539 436374. enquiries@hawkshead-croft.com. www.hawkshead-croft.com. Owner: W Barr. 5m from Ambleside on B5286 at Hawkshead village. Rose Award 2005. Showers, shaving and hair-dryer

points. TV room. Laundry Shops in village also Beatrix Potter gallery and Wordsworth's Grammar school. Open March-November. ☆☆☆☆ **BH&HPA. 15T. 10MC. 20H.** 🛱 🕿 &

Appleby-in-Westmorland

(6m). Chapel Farm Caravan Park, Little Asby, Appleby-in-Westmorland, Cumbria CA16 6QE. 01539 623665. beverley @chapelfarmpark.co.uk. www.chapelfarmcaravanpark.co.uk. Owner: Mrs B Williams. M6, J38. Take A685 towards Kirkby Stephen for 5m, take left turn at sign for Gt Asby, follow road over fells to T-junction, turn right then next right. Children's play area. Games room with snooker and pool table. Table tennis. Tennis court. Bottled gas. Nearest PH 3.5m. Open March 1-November 14. **BH&HPA. 50S. 2H.** 🛱 🕿

(3m). Wild Rose Park, Ormside, Appleby-in-Westmorland, Cumbria CA16 6EJ. 01768 351077. sites@wildrose.co.uk. www.wildrose.co.uk. Owner: Heather Stephenson. Via B6260 from town centre, in 1.5m turn left. Follow signs. Recreation room. Heated outdoor swimming and paddling pools. TV. Play areas with safety surfaces. Laundrette. Off licence. Restaurant. Takeaway. Indoor nursery. Licensed mini-market. Pitch and putt. Reduced facilities in winter. Mountain views. Golf course 5m. ☆☆☆☆ **BH&HPA. 184T. 90MC. 240S.** ✿ 🛱 🕿 & 🕿

Askham-in-Furness

(0.25m). Marsh Farm Caravan Site, Askham-in-Furness, Cumbria LA16 7AW. 01229 462321. Owner: Mr T Johnson. Off A595, at Askam-in-Furness over railway crossing, down to shore and over cattle grid on the right. Open April-October. **BH&HPA. 20T. 15MC.** 🛱

Barrow-in-Furness

(5m). Beacon Point Caravan Park, Rampside, Barrow-in-Furness, Cumbria. 01229 822449/824793. Owner: B Middleton. Off A5087 Ulverston to Rampside. Open January 3-October 16. **68S. 6H.** 🛱

(3.5m). Griffin Head Caravan Park, 157-159 Ainslie Street, Barrow-in-Furness, Cumbria LA14 5BB. 01229 824793. Owner: B Middleton. Open January 1-November 30. **63S. 6H.** 🛱

(5m). South End Caravan Park, Walney Island, Barrow-in-Furness, Cumbria LA14 3YQ. 01229 472823/471556. www. walney-island-caravan-park.co.uk. Owner: Kath Mulgrew. Take exit 36 from M6, A590 to Barrow. From Ramsden Square follow Walney signs, 3m S of Bridge. Gas supplies. Family-run park with indoor swimming pool and clubhouse. Close to beach. Open March 1-October 31. **BH&HPA. NCC. 30T. 10MC. 100S.** 🛱 🕿 & 🕿

(4m). Whitehall Caravan Park, Whitehall, Coast Road, Barrow-in-Furness, Cumbria. 01229 822449/824793. Owner: Mr B & M L Middleton. A590. Open January 1-end November. **BH&HPA. 51S. 3H.** 🛱

Brampton

(7m). Cairndale Caravan Site, Cumwhitton, Heads Nook, Brampton, Cumbria CA8 9BZ. 01768 896280. Owner: Mr S F Irving. Country park off A69 at Warwick Bridge, follow road to Corby-Cumwhitton, turn L at Cumwhitton village. Calor Gas. Golf, fishing, cinema, shopping centre, PO, PHs, restaurant, doctors within 6-9m. Open March 1-October 31. ☆☆☆ **BH&HPA. 5T. 15S. 3H.** 🛱 🕿

(0.5m). Irthing Vale Caravan Park, Old Church Lane, Brampton, Cumbria CA8 2AA. 01697 73600. glennwndrby@aol.com. www.ukparks.co.uk/irthingvale. Owner: Mrs O R Campbell. On A6071 Longtown to Brampton.

Amenities include showers, shaver points, washing machine, dryer, iron. David Bellamy Gold Conservation Award. Open March 1-October 31. **BH&HPA. 20T. 20MC. 24S. 1H.** 🐕 🏠 🎣

Carlisle

(6m). Camelot Caravan Park, Sandysike, Longtown, Carlisle, Cumbria CA6 5SZ. *01228 791248.* Owner: Mrs M Fyles-Lee. On A7. 1m S of Longtown, 4m N from J44, M6. Sheltered, level site suitable for Hadrian's Wall, historic Carlisle, north lakes, Borders and Gretna. AA 3 pennants. Dog exercising field. Ice-cream shop. 5 tent pitches. Open March 1-October 31. **15T. MC.** 🐕 🏠 🎣

(4m). Dalston Hall Caravan Park, Dalston Hall, Carlisle, Cumbria CA5 7JX. *01228 710165.* Owner: Nigel, Pauline & NIcola Farthing. Off M6 exit 42 to Dalston Village on B5299, direction Carlisle 1m N of Dalston. Small, family-run park set in 94 acres of wooded park and within easy reach of the Lake District, Solway Firth and Border Counties. 9-hole golf course. Clubhouse. Laundry. Playground. Hot showers. Fishing. Hard-standings. Open March 1-October 31. ☆☆ **BH&HPA. 40T. 40MC. 17S.** 🐕 🏠 🎣

(4m). Dandy Dinmont Caravan & Camping Site, Blackford, Carlisle, Cumbria CA6 4EA. *01228 674611.* dandydinmont@btopenworld.com. www.caravan-camping-carlisle.itgo.com. Owner: Mrs B Inglis. Leave M6 J44. Take A7 Galashiels road, park is about 1.5m N on the R after Blackford village sign. Suitable base for visiting Carlisle. Only 45 minutes from Lake District. Suitable overnight halt. Superstore, PO, horse riding within 2m. Golf, hospital within 4m. Open March 1-October 31. ☆☆☆☆ **BH&HPA. 27T. MC.** 🐕 🏠

(6.5m). Englethwaite Hall Caravan Club Site, Armathwaite, Carlisle, Cumbria CA4 9SY. *01228 560202.* www.caravanclub.co.uk. Owner: The Caravan Club. East Grinstead House, East Grinstead, West Sussex RH19 1UA. See website for standard directions to site. A tranquil site, located in the Eden Valley. Dog walk and exercise field on site. Non-members welcome. Motorhome service point. Suitable for walkers. All hard-standings, part sloping, Calor Gas, Campingaz, information room, storage. Open March-November. **NCC. 63T. MC.** 🐕 🏠

(10m). Glendale Caravan Park, Port Carlisle, Carlisle, Cumbria CA5 5DJ. *01697 351317.* Owner: Wryeside Caravans. Cottage Caravan Park, Port Carlisle, Carlisle, Cumbria CA5 5DJ. On B5307. Licensed club, dancing weekends. Bar meals. Games room. Play area. Hot showers. Laundry. Open March-November. **5T. MC. 160S.** 🐕 🏠 🎣

(11m). Greenfield Park, Kirkpatrick Fleming, Gretna, Carlisle, Cumbria DG11 3AU. *01461 800685.* Owner: Grace Horsfall & Tracie Flannigan. 74 Melbourne Avenue, Eastriggs, Annan, Dumfriesshire DG12 6PJ. M74, J21. Pets at owners' discretion. Nearby facilities include swimming pool, putting green, sports and leisure centre, cinema, golf courses, paint ball shooting. Shops, doctors in Gretna 4m. **30T. MC.** 🐕 🏠 🎣

(6m). Greenhallows Caravan Site, Broadfield, Southwaite, Carlisle, Cumbria CA4 0PT. *01697 473458.* Owner: Mr H Martin. Children allowed. Open March 1-October 31. **NCC. 10S.** 🐕 🐾 ⚓

Hylton Park Holiday Centre, Eden Street, Silloth, Carlisle, Cumbria CA7 4AY. *01697 331707.* enquiries@stanwix.com. www.stanwix.com. Owner: E & R H Stanwix. On A596 at Wigton take B5302 to Silloth. Entering Silloth follow signs to Hylton Park, 0.5m. Suitable base to tour lakes and Scottish Border. Sister park to Stanwix, 0.5m away. Full facilities available to Hylton Park holidaymakers. AA 4 pennants. 18-hole golf course 1m. Open March 1-October 31. **93T. MC. 213S.** 🐕 🏠 ♿

(2.5m). Mayfair Caravan Park, Beckfoot, Silloth, Carlisle, Cumbria CA5 4LA. *01697 331382.* Owner: Mr R G Edwards. Entrance on B5300 Maryport to Silloth. Overlooking Solway Firth. Lake District within easy reach. Champion golf course 2m. Open April 1-October 31. **35S.** 🐕 🏠

(8m). Oakbank Lakes Country Park, Longtown, Carlisle, Cumbria CA5 5NA. *01228 791108.* Owner: M T Powell. 60-acre site with four lakes with carp and trout. Salmon and sea fishing available. Bird sanctuary. Game bird breeding unit. **BH&HPA. 12T. 12MC.** ❀ 🐕 🏠 ♿

(4m). Orton Grange Caravan Park, Wigton Road, Carlisle, Cumbria CA5 6LA. *01228 710252.* chbarton@bartonpark home.freeserve.co.uk.www.barton-parkhomes.co.uk. Owner: Barton Park Homes Ltd. Westgate, Morecambe, Lancs LA3 3BA. On A595. Camping accessory shop. Outdoor heated pool. TV lounge. Pay-phone. Automated laundry. Play area. Hard-standings. Dishwashing sinks. Children allowed. ☆☆☆☆ **BH&HPA. 50T. MC. 4H.** ❀ 🐕 🏠 🎣 ⚓

(7m). Skiddaw View Holiday Park, Bothel, Bassenthwaite, Carlisle, Cumbria CA7 2JG. *01697 320919.* office@skiddaw view.com. www.skiddawview.co.uk. Owner: Mr P Carr. Off A591, near J with A595. SP 'Sunderland Village'. 7m to Cockermouth. Laundry, tourist info, public phone, play area. Shops etc 7m. ☆☆☆ **BH&HPA. 20T. 91S. 21H.** ❀ 🐕 🏠

(4.5m). Tarnside Caravan Park, Tarns, Silloth, Carlisle, Cumbria CA21 2YI. *01697 331377.* Owner: Mrs M L Wise. Open March 1-October 31. **4T. 21S.** 🐕

Cockermouth

(2m). Brigham Caravan Park, Brigham, Cockermouth, Cumbria CA13 0XH. *01900 821820/07860 827979.* Owners: North Lakes Leisure. 66 Leighton Beck Road, Slackhead, Milnthorpe, Cumbria LA7 7AZ. Turn L off A66, 2m W of Cockermouth. SP Brigham & Broughton Cross. Bear R with the road and then immediately left. Park is 50yd on R. Dogs on lead. Suitable base for exploring the beauties of the Lake District, within easy reach of Keswick, Buttermere and Bassenthwaite Lake, etc. Fishing, golf, horse riding close by. New and used static caravans for sale. Open March 1-November 30. **62S.** 🐕

(1m). Graysonside Farm, Lorton Road, Cockermouth, Cumbria CA13 9TQ. *01900 822351.* janette@graysonside. freeserve.co.uk. www.graysonside.co.uk. Owner: Andrew & Janette Likeman. Off B5292, 2m from A66. Suitable base for touring the lakes and western coast. Views of the Lorton/Buttermere fells. Dogs allowed on request only. Open April-November. **5T. 5MC.** 🐕 🏠

(4m). Wheatsheaf Inn, Low Lorton, Cockermouth, Cumbria CA13 9UW. *01900 85268/85199.* thewheatsheaflorton@tiscali. co.uk. www.wheatsheafinnlorton.co.uk. Owner: Mr M Cockbain & Miss J Williams. On B5289 towards Buttermere and Loweswater. Open March-November. **10T. MC. 20S.** 🐕 🏠

(4.5m). Whinfell Caravan Park, Lorton Vale, Cockermouth, Cumbria CA13 0RQ. *01900 85260.* r.a.mcclellan@talk21.co.uk. Owner: Mr R A McClellan. Off B5289 through Low Lorton, SP. Small, secluded park, well-placed for western lakes and fells and set in tranquil Vale of Lorton. 3m to nearest lake. 4m to Cockermouth. Open March 1-October 31. **5T. 5MC. 19S.** 🐕 🏠

CUMBRIA

(0.25m). Wyndham Hall Caravan Park, Old Keswick Road, Cockermouth, Cumbria CA13 9SF. *01900 822571/825238.* www.wyndhamholidaypark.co.uk. On old A66 Keswick to Cockermouth, turn R at Castle Inn sign (end of Bassenthwaite Lake) then bear L to Embleton-Cockermouth, entrance on L on outskirts of Cockermouth. Licensed club. Pool tables, table tennis etc. 10 Log cabins for hire. Children's play area. Shower block for tourers. Tents and tourers welcome. Caravans for sale. Nearby swimming pool and sports centre. Open March 1-November 1. **30T. MC. 70S. 20H.** ⛺ 🔌 🛒

Coniston

(3m). Hoathwaite Farm, Torver, Coniston, Cumbria LA21 8AX. *01539 441349.* Owner: Mrs J Wilson. A590, 3m S of Coniston on Torver road turn left at green railings. Turn left again over first cattle grid. Farm site with basic facilities, near lake. Open seasonally for static vans. **5T. 5MC. 29S.** ✿ ⛺

(1.25m). Park Coppice Caravan Club Site, Coniston, Cumbria LA21 8AY. *01539 441555.* www.caravanclub.co.uk. Owner: The Caravan Club. East Grinstead House, East Grinstead, West Sussex RH19 1UA. See website for standard directions to site. Set in 63 acres of National Trust woodland with facilities for youngsters, including junior orienteering, nature trail and toddler's play area. Nearby lake offers sailing and watersports. Advance booking essential. Non-members and tent campers welcome. Toilet block and laundry facilities. Motorhome service point. Fishing. Suitable base for walking. Open March-November. ✰✰✰✰✰ **NCC. 280T. MC.** ⛺ 🔌 ♿ 🛒

Dent

(4m). Ewegales Farm Caravan Site, Ewegales Farm, Dent, Cumbria. *01539 625440.* Owner: Mr J W Akriag. Leave M6 at J37 on to A684 to Sedbergh. Site 4m E of Dent. Shower. Flat field by river; good for fishing. **5T. 6MC. 3S.** ✿ ⛺

High Laning Caravan Park, High Laning, Dent, Cumbria LA10 5QJ. *01539 625239.* info@highlaning.co.uk. www.highlaning.co.uk. Owner: Mrs M Taylor. M6, J37 SP Sedbergh A684. Dent is a further 5m from Sedbergh. Adjacent to Dent, picturesque, historic, cobbled village in Yorkshire Dales National Park. **25T. MC. 4H.** ✿ ⛺ 🔌 ♿ 🛒

Egremont

(2.25m). Lakeland View, Nethertown, Egremont, Cumbria CA22 2UH. *01946 825768.* Owners: Forest Mere Lodges Ltd. The Lodge, Chester Road, Delamere, Northwich, Cheshire CW8 2HB. Leave A595 for Egremont town. Take road to Nethertown from town centre. Nethertown 2.25m away. Country club with facilities close by. **BH&HPA. 20T. 10MC. 30S. 5H.** ✿ 🔌 🛒

Grange-over-Sands

(4m). Greaves Farm Caravan Park, Field Broughton, Grange-over-Sands, Cumbria LA11 6HU. *01539 536329/536587.* Owner: Mrs E Rigg. Prospect House, Barber Green, Grange-over-Sands, Cumbria LA11 6HU. M6, J36 follow A590 signed Barrow. About 1m before Newby Bridge, L at cross roads Cartmel/Staveley. Site 1m on L before church. Small, quiet, family-run, grassy site. Suitable base for exploring the lakes. Personal supervision. Booking essential. Calor Gas. AA 3 pennants. Open March-October. ✰✰✰✰ **BH&HPA. 3T. 18S. 2H.** ⛺ 🔌

(1m). High Fell Gate Farm, Cartmel, Grange-over-Sands, Cumbria LA11 7QA. *01539 536931.* Owner: Miss A Rigg. Off B5277 Grange to Cartmel Road. Showers. Open March 1-October 31. **BH&HPA. 12T. MC. 12S.** ⛺

(3.5m). Lakeland Leisure Park, Moor Lane, Flookburgh, Grange-over-Sands, Cumbria LA11 7LT. *01539 559005.* oewebmaster@bourne-leisure.co.uk. www.lakelandleisurepark.com. Owner: Bourne Leisure Ltd. One Park Lane, Hemel Hempstead, Herts HP2 4YL. M6, J36 on to A590. Turn L on to A6/A590 for Barrow-In-Furness. B5277 through Grange-over-Sands, then Allithwaite and into Flookburgh. Turn L at the village square and travel 1m down this road to the park. Laundrette. Convenience store. Entertainment complex, arcade, restaurant. Indoor and outdoor heated pools. Tennis courts. Pony-trekking, stables on park. Rose Award and David Bellamy Gold Conservation Award. Open April-November. ✰✰✰✰ **BH&HPA. NCC. 100T. MC. 695S. 138H.** ⛺ 🔌 ♿ 🛒

(0.5m). Lingwood Park, Middle Fellgate Farm, Cartmel Road, Grange-over-Sands, Cumbria LA11 7QA. *015395 32271.* Turn R off B5277 SP Cartmel Road. In 0.5m call at Middle Fellgate Farm. Site entrance further 200yd on R. Open March 1-January 10. **5T. 5MC.** ⛺ 🔌

(2.5m). Meathop Fell Caravan Club Site, Grange-over-Sands, Cumbria LA11 6RB. *01539 532912.* www.caravanclub.co.uk. Owner: The Caravan Club. East Grinstead House, East Grinstead, West Sussex RH19 1UA. See website for standard directions to site. Suitable base from which to explore north Lancashire and southern Lake District. Gas. Advance booking essential bank holidays, Christmas and New Year. Motorhome service point, playground. Non-members welcome. Toilet blocks with privacy cubicles, laundry facilities and baby/toddler washroom. Golf nearby. Suitable for families. ✰✰✰✰✰ **NCC. 130T. MC.** ✿ ⛺ 🔌 ♿

(4.5m). Oak Head Caravan Park, Ayside, Grange-over-Sands, Cumbria LA11 6JA. *01539 531475.* Owner: Mr A S N Scott. M6, 36,14m on A590 to Newby Bridge. 2m to Lake Windermere. 4.5m to Grange-over-Sands railway station. Garage, shops, fishing all within 1-2m. Open March 1-October 31. **30T. 60MC. 71S.** ⛺ 🔌 ♿

(5m). Whitestone Caravan Park, Ayside, Grange-over-Sands, Cumbria LA11 6JD. *01539 531770.* iainsmith@clara.net. www.whitestonecaravanpark.co.uk. Owner: Mrs N M Smith. On A590. No tourers. Gas supplies. Open March 1-November 15. **BH&HPA. 80S.** ⛺

Holmrook

(2m). Saltcoats Caravan Site, Saltcoats, Holmrook, Cumbria CA19 1YY. *01229 717241.* Owner: W J & E Jackson. Bottled gas. Children's play area. Laundry. Open March 1-November 14. **BH&HPA. 10T. MC. 6S. 5H.** ⛺

(2m). Seven Acres Caravan & Camping Park, Holmrook, Cumbria CA19 1YD. *01946 725480.* 1m S of Gosforth on A595 west Cumbria coast road. Flat, grassy, sheltered park. Laundrette. Payphones. Playground. Gas sales. Golf, fell walking, mountain climbing, fishing, boating, rambling, horse riding all available nearby. PO, shops, pubs, restaurants and cafes in Gosforth. Open March-October. **BH&HPA. 39T. MC. 14S.** ⛺ 🔌

(2.5m). The Old Post Office Camp Site, Santon Bridge, Holmrook, Cumbria CA19 1UY. *01946 726286.* Owner: B J Thwaites. A595 to Holmrook, 2.5m to Santon Bridge, over bridge from Bridge Inn. Small, level touring site beside the river Irt. Fishing on site. Mobile shop daily. Bridge Inn/hotel nearby. Close to miniature railway and ancient castle. 2.5m from Wasdale Lake, 5m from sea, golf and doctor. 3m from PO, shops, riding, diving. Mobile van daily. Laundry, washer, dryer now available. Open March 1-November 14. **5T. MC.** ⛺ 🔌 ♿ 🛒

Please mention Caravan Sites 2006 when replying to advertisers

Kendal

(3m). Ashes - Exclusively Adult Caravan Park, New Hutton, Kendal, Cumbria LA8 0AS. *01539 731833.* info@ashescaravanpark.co.uk. www.ashescaravanpark.co.uk. Owners: Mr & Mrs I W Mason. From M6 J37, take A684 to Kendal for 2m. Turn L at crossroads to New Hutton village. Site on R in 0.75m. Small, friendly touring park in peaceful countryside with rural views. Suitable for relaxing weekends, holidays exploring lakes and Yorkshire Dales, and as an overnight halt. Adults only, 18 years and over. Open March 1-November 15. ✰✰✰✰✰ **BH&HPA. 24T. MC.** 🐕 ◨ ♿

(2m). Camping & Caravanning Club Site - Kendal, Millcrest, Shap Road, Kendal, Cumbria LA9 6NY. *01539 741363/0870 243 3331.* www.campingandcaravanningclub.co.uk. Owner: Camping & Caravanning Club. Greenfields House, Westwood Way, Coventry CV4 8JH. 1.5m N of Kendal; on R of A6. N of nameplate 'Skelsmergh'. Good base for Lake District, a few miles from Kendal. All units accepted. Non-members welcome. Site shop. Special deals for families and backpackers. Open March-October. ✰✰✰✰ **50T. 50MC.** 🐕 ◨ ♿

(2.5m). Camping & Caravanning Park - Windermere, Ashes Lane, Staveley, Kendal, Cumbria LA8 9JS. *01539 821119/0870 2433331.* www.campingandcaravanningclub.co.uk. Owners: The Camping & Caravanning Club. Greenfields House, Westwood Way, Coventry CV4 8JH. Signed off A591. 0.75m from roundabout with B5284 towards Windermere. Site overlooks fells of southern Lakes. Set in 22 acres and located 5m S of Windermere, close to village of Staveley. Non-members welcome. All unit accepted. Special deals available for families and backpackers. On-site facilities: licensed bar, take-away, dedicated packbackers facilities, laundry, toilet and showers, play area and dog walk. Fishing, golf, horse riding and water sports available locally (3-5m). Open March-January. ✰✰✰✰✰ **250T. 250MC. 71S.** 🐕 ◨ ♿ ♨ ⊘

(5m). Ings Mill Park, Ings, Kendal, Cumbria LA8 9QF. *01539 821426.* Owner: Mr & Mrs S J Cowperthwaite. On A591, 2m from Windermere. Dogs at site owner's discretion. Small, family-run riverside park, landscaped. Fishing, sailing, golf, horse-riding nearby. Village inn and shop walking distance. Open mid March-mid November. **BH&HPA. 63S. 1H.** 🐕

(9m). Lambhowe Caravan Park, Crosthwaite, Kendal, Cumbria LA8 8JE. *01539 568483.* Owner: Lambhowe Caravan Park Ltd. Laverock Bungalow, Mealbank, Kendal LA8 9DJ. On A5074, Lyth Valley to Bowness opposite Damson Dene Hotel. 15 mins to Lake Windermere. Open March 1-November 16. **14T. 14MC. 111S.** 🐕 ◨

(3m). Low Park Wood Caravan Club Site, Sedgwick, Kendal, Cumbria LA8 0JZ. *01539 560186.* www.caravanclub.co.uk. Owner: The Caravan Club. East Grinstead House, East Grinstead, West Sussex RH19 1UA. See website for standard directions to site. Peaceful location on National Trust land, with several walks from site. River fishing (permits available). Gas. Advance booking essential weekends, bank holidays, July/August. Dog walk. Non-members welcome. Toilet blocks with laundry facilities. Motorhome service point. Suitable for families. Open March-November. ✰✰✰✰ **NCC. 161T. MC.** 🐕 ◨

(5m). Millbrook Caravan Park, Endmoor, Kendal, Cumbria LA8 0HJ. *01539 567624.* info@millbrookcaravanpark.co.uk. www.millbrookcaravanpark.co.uk. Owner: M E Hutchings & Partners. 2m from M6, J36 follow A65 sign for Kendal and Endmoor. Leisure/sports centre, Brewery Art Centre, shopping centre in Kendal (5m). PO in Endmoor. Doctor in Milnthorpe 3m. Open March 1-October 31. **BH&HPA. 7T. 59S.** 🐕 ◨ ♿ ♨

(3m). Pound Farm Caravan Park, Crook, Kendal, Cumbria LA8 8JZ. *01539 821220.* www.lakelandleisureestates.co.uk. Owners: P T & C Morgan. M6, J36 follow A591 to roundabout. Exit roundabout on to B5284, Pound Farm 1.8m on L. Sheltered park 5m from Lake Windermere. Newly developed pitches for lodges. Golf, cinema and town for shopping 3m. Open March 1-November 14. **BH&HPA. 10T. 10MC. 14S.** 🐕 ◨ ♿ ⊘

(3m). Ratherheath Lane Caravan Park, Chain House, Kendal, Cumbria LA8 8JU. *01539 821154.* ratherheath@lakedistrictcaravan.co.uk. www.lakedistrictcaravans.co.uk. Owner: David Wilson. Exit M6, J36 follow A591 for Windermere. Take B5284 to Crook. Park is 1.5m on the right. Small site. Open March 1-November 15. ✰✰✰ **BH&HPA. 8T. MC. 4S. 8H.** ◨

(6m). Sampool Caravan Site, Levens, Kendal, Cumbria LA8 8EQ. *01539 552265.* Owner: Mr A & I Dobson & Son. On A590. No tents. Fishing on site. Village and PO 2m, doctor 4m, golf course 6m. AA 2 pennants. Open March 15-October 31. **BH&HPA. NCC. 15T. MC. 180S.** 🐕 ◨ ♨

(6m). Waters Edge Caravan Park, Crooklands, Kendal, Cumbria LA7 7NN. *01539 567708.* www.watersedge.co.uk. Owner: Water's Edge Caravan Park Ltd. 0.75m from M6 J36, follow A65 Kirkby Lonsdale and then A65 Crooklands at roundabout; site is on right-hand side before Crooklands hotel. Family-run park with modern facilities. Easy access to Lakes, Yorkshire. Reception lounge and licensed bar. Open countryside. Nearby fishing, tennis, riding, etc. Open March 1-November 14. ✰✰✰✰ **BH&HPA. 30T. MC. 19H.** 🐕 ◨ ♿ ♨

Keswick

(4m). Bridge End Farm, Thirlmere, Keswick, Cumbria CA12 4TG. *01768 772166.* Owner: Mr S Robinson. 4m S of Keswick on the A591 Keswick-Amblesia road. Small site on working hill farm. Suitable base for walking in central Lake District. Open March 1-October 31. **NCC. 15T. MC. 13S. 1H.** 🐕 ◨

(3m). Burns Farm Caravan & Camping Site, St Johns-in-the-Vale, Keswick, Cumbria CA12 4RR. *01768 779777.* Owner: Mrs Linda Lamb. Small, quiet site with views, 15m from M6 j40, take A66 Keswick, 2nd left past Threlkeld village, SP Castlerigg-Stone Circle and Burns Farm caravan site. Facilities block. 3 cottages for hire. AA 3 pennants. Open March-November. **32T. MC.** 🐾 🔌 ♿

(0.5m). Camping & Caravanning Club Site - Derwentwater, Derwentwater Caravan Park, Crow Park Road, Keswick, Cumbria CA12 5EN. 01768 772579/0870 243 3331. www.campingandcaravanningclub.co.uk. Owner: Camping & Caravanning Club. Greenfields House, Westwood Way, Coventry CV4 8JH. From M6 J40 follow A66 for 13m, SP Keswick/Workington. At roundabout SP Keswick turn L. At T junction turn L to Keswick town centre. At mini roundabout turn R. Take road to R of church. Site on L. Within the heart of the Lake District National Park, beside the peace of Lake Derwentwater. Non-members welcome. Caravans and motor caravans only (no tents). All-services pitches available. No awnings permitted. Golf, pony trekking, rock climbing, paragliding and swimming are all available in the area. Special deals available for families and backpackers. Open March-November. ✰✰✰✰ **44T. 44MC. 161S.** 🐾 🔌 ♿ ⌀

(0.5m). Camping & Caravanning Club Site - Keswick, Crow Park Road, Keswick, Cumbria CA12 5EP. 01768 772392. www.campingandcaravanningclub.co.uk. Owners: Camping & Caravanning Club. Greenfields House, Westwood Way, Coventry CV4 8JH. Off A66, follow signs for Keswick. Turn L at roundabout, turn left at T-junction. At mini-roundabout turn R, take road to R of church. Turn R up narrow lane, after rugby club. Woodland park with lake frontage and jetty. Some hardstanding. Non-members welcome. All units accepted. Special deals available for families and backpackers. David Bellamy Gold Conservation Award. Open February-November. ✰✰✰✰ **250T. 250MC.** 🐾 🔌 ♿ 🛁

(1.5m). Castlerigg Hall Caravan & Camping Park, Castlerigg Hall, Keswick, Cumbria CA12 4TE. 017687 74499. info@castlerigg.co.uk. www.castlerigg.co.uk. Owner: Mrs B & Mr D D Jackson. Turn R off A591 Keswick to Ambleside. Spectacular views of lakes and mountains. Laundrette. Tea room. Fully-serviced pitches available. Open mid March-mid November. ✰✰✰✰ **BH&HPA. 53T. MC. 24S. 7H.** 🐾 🔌 ♿ 🛁

(2m). Dalebottom Farm Caravan & Camping Park, Naddle, Keswick, Cumbria CA12 4TF. 017687 72176. Owner: Messrs Kitching. 2m S of Keswick on A591 Windermere road. In the heart of Lakeland. Open March 1-November 1. **30T. MC. 30S. 5H.** 🐕 🔌 🛁

(5m). Herdwick Croft, Ouse Bridge, Bassenthwaite, Keswick, Cumbria. 01768 776605. stayinthelakes@btconnect.com. www.stayinthelakes.co.uk. Owner: Mr W Wilson. Off A591, north end of Bassenthwaite lake. Quiet site. All pitches serviced. New shower and toilet block. Golf, riding. animal farm. Open Easter-November. **10T. MC. 40S. 2H.** 🐾 🔌

(6m). High Close Holiday Home Park, Bassenthwaite, Keswick, Cumbria CA12 4QX. 01768 776300. highclose@aol.com. www.highclose.com. Owner: Mr J L Gattward. From the M6, turn off at Penrith, follow Keswick A60, at major roundabout take Carlisle A591, turn into and through Bassenthwaite Village onto Park Wood. High Close is 0.5m on your right-hand side. Open March 1-November 15. **BH&HPA. 70S.** 🐾

Lakeside Holiday Park, off Crowpark Road, Keswick, Cumbria CA125EW. 01768 772878. welcome@lakesideholidaypark.co.uk. www.lakesideholidaypark.co.uk. Park Managers: Sean & Christine Mills. 5 mins walk from main street and town centre – on the lakeshore – level ground. From the M6 J40 take the A66 into town centre, follow caravan and camping signs. Quiet park. Suitable base for surfing, sailing, walking. Children allowed. Open March-November. ✰✰✰✰ **BH&HPA. 29S. 11H.**

(3m). Lane Foot Camp Site, Lane Foot Farm, Thornthwaite, Keswick, Cumbria CA12 5RZ. 01768 778315. Owner: Mr A L Gaskell. Off A66 Keswick to Cockermouth. Country site. Open Easter-October. **10T. 10MC.** 🐾

(1m). Low Briery Village, Penrith Road, Keswick, Cumbria CA12 4RN. 01768 772044. www.keswick.uk.com. Owner: Grey Abbey Properties Ltd. Border House, Coach Road, Whitehaven, Cumbria CA28 9DF. Just upriver from Keswick on eastern side. Access off interchange A66 and Keswick access road. Open April-October. ✰✰✰ **45S. 32H.** 🐾

(4m). Low Manesty Caravan Club Site, Manesty, Keswick, Cumbria CA12 5UG. 01768 777275. www.caravanclub.co.uk. Owner: The Caravan Club. East Grinstead House, East Grinstead, West Sussex RH19 1UA. See website for standard directions to site. 2m from Borrowdale. Set in National Trust woodland, close to Derwentwater with views over fells. Suitable location for lakes and walking. Own sanitation required. Advance booking advised and essential bank holidays, June to end September and late October. Non-members admitted. Motorhome service point. Fishing and water sports. Some hard-standing, steel awning pegs required. Calor Gas and Campingaz, dog walk nearby. Quiet off-peak. NCN cycle route within 5m. Recycling facilities. Open March-November. **NCC. 60T. MC.** 🐾 🔌 🛁

(8.5m). North Lakes Caravan Park, Bewaldeth, Bassenthwaite Lake, Keswick, Cumbria CA13 9SY. 01768 776510. info@northlakesholidays.co.uk. www.northlakesholidays.co.uk. Owner: Messrs J A & P R Frew. On A591. 8.5m N of Keswick. 30-acre, quiet park in northern end of the Lake District. Bar. Laundry. Facilities block. Coarse fishing lake. Open March 1-November 14. **145T. MC. 80S.** 🐾 🔌

(2.5m). Scotgate Holiday Park, Braithwaite, Keswick, Cumbria CA12 5TF. 01768 778343. info@scotgateholidaypark.co.uk. www.scotgateholidaypark.co.uk. Owner: Mr Stuart. 2.5m W of Keswick, just off A66 on B592 entrance to Braithwaite village. Games room. Licensed shop and restaurant. 7 chalets for hire. ✰✰✰✰ **BH&HPA. 15T. 150MC. 28H.** ✿ 🐾 🔌 🛁

(1m). The Burnside Caravan Park, Underskiddaw, Keswick, Cumbria CA12 4PF. 01768 772950. Owner: David Bynon. Close to the roundabout on the J of A66 and A591. Open March-November. **25T. MC.** 🐾 🔌

(5m). Thirlspot Farm, Thirlmere, Keswick, Cumbria CA12 4TW. 01768 772551/72224. enquiries@thirlspot-caravans.co.uk. www.thirlspot-caravans.co.uk. Owner: Mr S Gaskell. 4 Fisher Place, Thirlmere, Keswick, Cumbria CA12 4TW. Situated on A591 between Grasmere and Keswick, near Thirlmere lake. In the heart of the Lake District. On a small hill farm at the foot of Helvellyn. Walks and forest trail nearby. **5MC. 4H.** ✿ 🐾

(6m). Trafford Caravan Site, Low Wood, Bassenthwaite, Keswick, Cumbria CA12 4QH. *01768 776298.* Owner: Mrs M J Trafford & Mrs M A Hewson. On A591. Quiet, lakeland park on Carlisle road. 6m from roundabout outside Keswick. Situated at the foot of Skiddaw with beautiful views all round. Level site suitable for disabled people and wheelchairs. Open April 1-31 October. **12T. MC. 50S. 3H. ✝ ☎ & ⚑**

Kirkby Lonsdale

(0.5m). Woodclose Caravan Park, Casterton, Kirkby Lonsdale, Cumbria LA6 2SE. *01524 271597.* info@wood closepark.com. www.woodclosepark.com. Owner: Lake District Estates Co Ltd. 13 Maude Street, Kendal, Cumbria LA9 4QQ. M6, J36 then A65, 0.5m SE of Kirkby Lonsdale. Quiet, rural site within easy driving distance of the Lake District, Yorkshire Dales and seaside. Park is well established, spreading over 9 acres and in a priviledged location in an Area of Outstanding Natural Beauty. Children's play area on site. Private and secluded, yet only a short stroll from Kirkby Lonsdale. Golf, fishing, horse riding, leisure club. Open March 1-November 1. ✭✭✭✭ **BH&HPA. 17T. MC. 54S. ✝ ☎ & ⚑**

Kirkby Stephen

Augill House Farm Caravan Park, Brough, Kirkby Stephen, Cumbria. Mrs Atkinson. Pleasant site with good access off the A66. Chemical toilet emptying point. Showers, shaver points. Play area. **25S. 2H. ✝ ☎**

(4m). Bowber Head Caravan Site, Ravenstonedale, Kirkby Stephen, Cumbria CA17 4NL. *01539 623254.* enquiries@bow berhead.co.uk. www.bowberhead.co.uk. Owner: Mr W & Mrs C Hamer. 4.5m S of Kirkby Stephen, SP off the A683. Suitable centre for lakes and the dales. Views of Wildboar and the Howgill Fells. TV hook-ups. Bottled gas available. Payphone. Dogs allowed under control. Camping and Caravanning Club listed. Classic coach service operated from site. **5T. 2MC. 16S. ✿ ✝ ☎**

(1m). Pennine View Caravan & Camping Park, Station Road, Kirkby Stephen, Cumbria CA17 4SZ. *01768 371717.* Owner: Mr & Mrs C Sim. M6, J38 follow A685 for 11m, site on R. A66 at Brough follow A685 for 5m site on L. Open March-October. ✭✭✭✭✭**BH&HPA. 43T. ✝ ☎ &**

Lamplugh

> **Dockray Meadow Caravan Club Site, Lamplugh, Cumbria CA14 4SH.** *01946 861357.* www.caravan-club.co.uk. Owner: The Caravan Club. East Grinstead House, East Grinstead, West Sussex RH19 1UA. See website for standard directions to site. 4m from Ennerdale Bridge. Conveniently set on N edge of Lake District with mountain walks off site. All hard-standings. Gas. Advance booking essential bank holidays. No sanitation. Motorhome service point. Non-members welcome. Fishing nearby. Good for walking. Part sloping, steel awning pegs required, Calor Gas and Campingaz. Information room, dog walk nearby. Quiet off-peak, NCN cycle route within 5m. Open March-November. **NCC. 53T. MC. ✝ ☎**

Inglenook Caravan Park, Lamplugh, Cumbria CA14 4SH. *01946 861240.* mesicp@fsbdial.co.uk. inglenookcaravanpark. co.uk. Owner: Mr & Mrs John Hoey. Leave A66 at Cockermouth on to A5086 to Lamplugh. Left past Lamplugh Tip PH. Site 0.5m on right. 7m from Cockermouth. Flat site with tarmac and gravel roads. Fishing and horse riding nearby. Beach 10m. Play area. Rose Award. ✭✭✭✭ **BH&HPA. 12T. 5MC. 40S. 8H. ✿ ✝ ☎ & ⚑**

Maryport

(3m). Blue Dial Farm, Allonby, Maryport, Cumbria CA15 6PB. *01900 881277.* Owner: Bluedial Caravans. Situated on the B5300, 3m N of Maryport, 25m from Lake District. Allonby 1.5m. Dogs allowed under supervision and kept on leads. Open March-October. **BH&HPA. 182S. ✝ ☎ ⚑**

(5m). Dickinson Place Caravan Site, Allonby, Maryport, Cumbria CA15 6QE. *01900 881440.* enquiries@dickinson place.co.uk. www.dickinsonplace.co.uk. Owner: Mr J Williamson. On B5300 Maryport to Silloth. Showers. Hot and cold water. Calor Gas available. Open March-November. **BH&HPA. 5T. MC. 15S. ✝ ☎**

(5m). Fellview Caravan Park, Allonby, Maryport, Cumbria CA15 6QD. *01900 881526.* Owner: Mr R W Watson. On B5300 Maryport to Silloth. Open March 1-November 14. **21S. ✝**

(6m). Manor House Caravan Park , Edderside Road, Allonby, Maryport, Cumbria CA15 6RA. *01900 881236.* holidays@ manorhousepark.co.uk. www.manorhousepark.co.uk. Owner: Simon Brooks. From Maryport, take A596, pick up the B5300 to Allonby. 1m after Allonby take a right turn to Edderside. Licensed club. Sauna and fitness room. Laundrette. Open March 1-November 15. ✭✭✭ **BH&HPA. 20T. 3MC. 150S. 3H. ✝ ☎**

(5m). Spring Lea Caravan Park, Allonby, Maryport, Cumbria CA15 6QF. *01900 881331.* mail@springlea.co.uk. www. springlea.co.uk. Owner: Mr J Williamson. Situated midway between Maryport and Silloth on B5300. Open March-October. ✭✭✭✭ **BH&HPA. 35T. MC. 95S. 3H. ✝ ☎ &**

(5m). Vicarage Field Caravan Park, Beach Road, Allonby, Maryport, Cumbria CA15 6PE. *01772 612987.* Owner: Richard Cole. Silloth 7m. Fell walking, golf, fishing, wind surfing and ponytrekking all within easy reach. Laundry, showers, telephone, play area, bar and restaurant adjacent to site. Open March 1-November 15. **NCC. 80S. ✝ & ⚑**

(5m). Westville Caravan Park, Allonby, Maryport, Cumbria CA15 6QA. *01900 881392.* Owner: Barry & Anita Craggs. A594 from Cockermouth to Maryport. A596 and then B5300 coast road to Allonby. Site in centre of village. 150yd to the PO. Golf course 3m, fishing 5m. Shop and cafe on site. Toilets/showers, games room, play area. Street lighting. Two PHs within 300yd. Restaurant 200yd, swimming pool, beach 100yd away. Open March 1-November 14. **T. MC. 56S. ✝ ☎**

Millom

(1m). Butterflowers Holiday Homes, Port Haverigg, Millom, Cumbria LA18 4HB. *01229 772880.* office@butterflowers.net. www.butterflowers.net. Follow signs from Harbour Hotel past the Beach Cafe, the entrance is on the right before the Inshore Rescue. Indoor swimming pool. **BH&HPA. 70T. 50MC. 79S. ✿ ✝ ☎ ⚑**

(0.5m). Port Haverigg Holiday Village, Haverigg, Millom, Cumbria LA18 4EY. *01229 774228.* Owner: Butterflowers Holiday Homes. Licensed club. Water sports. Moorings. Trout fishing. Open February 10-January 10. **131S. ✝**

Milnthorpe

(2.5m). Fell End Caravan Park, Slackhead Road, Hale, Milnthorpe, Cumbria LA7 7BS. *01539 562122.* enquiries@ southlakeland-caravans.co.uk. www.southlakeland-caravans. co.uk. Owner: South Lakeland Caravans Ltd. South Lakeland House, A6, Yealand Redmayne, Nr Carnforth, Lancs LA5 9RN. Off M6 junction 35, off A6 at sign marked 'Sites'. Next to wildlife oasis just past Cumbria border sign. Follow brown signs. Close to Silverdale/Arnside area of outstanding natural beauty. Beautifully developed and landscaped park incorporating natural features including woodlands and limestone pavements. Shop, bar, restaurant. Shops 2m, Golf course 3m. Cinema 15m. ☆☆☆☆☆ BH&HPA. 80T. 80MC. 216S. ✿ ⚑ ☺ & ⚏

(2m). Hall More Caravan Park, Hale, Milnthorpe, Cumbria LA7 7BP. 01524 781695. enquiries@southlakeland-caravans. co.uk. www.southlakeland-caravans.co.uk. Owner: South Lakeland Caravans Ltd. South Lakeland House, A6, Yealand Redmayne, Nr Carnforth, Lancs LA5 9RN. M6, J35. Follow A6 towards Milnthorpe for 4m. Take the first L marked Arnside with tourism signs for sites. Follow the unclassified road and the park is less than 1m. Pony trekking available. TV hook-ups. 3-acre trout lake on premises. Close to Silverdale/Arnside, Area of Outstanding Natural Beauty. Good base for walking and exploring. Shops 2m, golf course 3m, cycle hire 5m, cinema 15m. Open March-December for holiday homes; open March-November for tourers. BH&HPA. 34T. 34MC. 60S. ⚏ ☺

(3m). Millness Hill Holiday Park, Crooklands, Milnthorpe, Cumbria LA7 7NU. 01539 567306. Owner: K I & E J Fairall. Situated by J36 of M6. A65 to Kirkby Lonsdale left at 1st roundabout, site 100yd on the left. Open March 1-January 15. BH&HPA. 15T. 30S. 14H. ⚏ ☺

(2.5m). Silver Ridge Caravan Park, Hale, Milnthorpe, Cumbria LA7 7BW. 01539 563198. Owner: Arthur Holgate & Son Ltd. Turn off A6 opposite Kings Arms, 4m N from M6 J35. New caravan sales. Open February 1-November 30. BH&HPA. 125S. ⚏

Penrith

(8m). 'Hopkinsons' Whitbarrow Hall Caravan Park, Berrier, Penrith, Cumbria CA11 0XB. 01768 483456. www.hopkinsons-caravanpark.co.uk. Owner: Mr T A & Mrs M Hopkinson. 0.5m off the A66, SP for Hutton Roof. Bar. Laundrette. Showers. Kitchen for campers' use. Calor Gas stockist. AA 3 pennants. Dogs must be on leads. Strict 5mph speed limit. Open March 1-October 31. 80T. MC. 167S. ⚏ ☺ & ⚏

(7m). Beckses Caravan Park, Penruddock, Penrith, Cumbria CA11 0RX. 01768 483224. Owner: Mr John Teasdale. M6, J40 take A66 (SP Keswick). Continue for about 6m, then turn R on to B5288 (SP Greystoke). Beckses Park is 150yd on the R. Small, pleasant site on the edge of Lake District National Park. AA 3-pennants. English Lakes member. Open Easter-October 31. 23T. MC. 12S. 5H. ⚏ ☺

(7m). Cove Caravan Park, Ullswater, Watermillock, Penrith, Cumbria CA11 0LS. 01768 486549. info@cove-park.co.uk. www.cove-park.co.uk. Owner: Mr L Wride. From M6 J40, A66 Keswick, roundabout A594 to Ullswater. T Junction, right, Brackenrigg Inn - right. Cove Park is 1.5m on left. RAC appointed. Peaceful park sheltered by nearby fells and overlooking Lake Ullswater. Well maintained. David Bellamy Gold Conversation award. Shop next door, lake 1.5m. Open March-November. ☆☆☆☆☆ BH&HPA. 35T. 35MC. 38S. 1H. ⚏ ☺ & ⚏

(9m). Cross Fell Caravan & Camping Park, The Fox Inn, Ousby, Penrith, Cumbria CA10 1QA. 01768 881374. info@crossfell.biz. www.crossfell.biz. Owner: Mr & Mrs R G Thomas. 9 miles NE of Penrith. Leave M6 J40 on to A686, Alston road. Take second right, 1.5m after Langwathby. site is 2m at Ousby. Flat, well-drained site. Behind village Inn. Beautiful countryside. Open March 1-January 10. 7T. 2MC. 29S. 1H. ⚏ ☺

(7m). Dunroamin, Cross Dormont, Howtown, Penrith, Cumbria CA10 2NA. 017684 86537. enquiries@crossdormont. co.uk. Owner: Mr A K & Mrs A C Bell. 2m from Pooley Bridge on the Howtown road, SP. Open April-October. 6T. MC. 14S. ⚏

(8m). Eden Valley Holidays, Newby End Farm, Newby, Penrith, Cumbria CA10 3EX. 01931 714 338. davidjones newby@ukonline.co.uk. www.newbyandfarm.co.uk. Owners: Jenny & David Jones. Open April-October. 12T. MC. ⚏ ☺

(4m). Flusco Wood, Flusco. Penrith, Cumbria CA11 0JB. 01768 480020. admin@fluscowood.co.uk. www.fluscowood. co.uk. From M6 J40 travel 3m W on A66. Flusco signed to right, 1m. Quiet, secluded park with serviced grassed and hard-standing pitches in woodland clearings. Centrally heated amenity building with laundry, drying room, boot wash, dishwasher and free hot water. Pine holiday lodges for sale. David Bellamy Gold Conservation Award. Open Easter-November for tourers; open all year for lodges. ☆☆☆☆☆ BH&HPA. 60T. MC. ⚏ ☺ &

(9m). Gill Head Caravan & Camping Park, Gill Head Farm, Troutbeck, Penrith, Cumbria CA11 0ST. 01768 779652. Owner: Mrs J Wilson. Midway between Penrith and Keswick on A66, take A5091 (Ullswater Road). First right 200yd from junction, site is first on R. Quiet, level site with views of Northern Fells. Open Easter-November. 25T. 10MC. 17S. ⚏ ☺ ⚏

(14m). Gillside Caravan & Camping Site, Gillside, Glenridding, Penrith, Cumbria CA11 0QQ. 01768 482346. gillside@btconnect.com. www.gillsidecaravanandcampingsite.co.uk. Owner: Messrs Lightfoot. Take the A592 to Glenridding, SP for Gillside Camping first L after Travellers Rest. Situated at the foot of Helvellyn and 5mins walk from Lake Ullswater. Bunkhouse accommodation. Open March-November. 5T. 5MC. 25S. 5H. ⚏ ☺ ⚏

(4m). Hillcroft Park, Roe Head Lane, Pooley Bridge, Penrith, Cumbria CA10 2LT. 01768 486363. Owner: Lakeland Leisure Estates Ltd. PO Box 22, Windermere, Cumbria LA23 1GE. Off A592. Go through Pooley Bridge, bear R at the church, then straight across the crossroads towards Roe Head. Park on L. Elevated location with magnificent views. Ideal for fell walking, sailing, windsurfing and canoeing. Boat hire nearby. Dogs allowed if kept on leads. Pooley Bridge 250yd, shops, PO etc. Open March 2-November 11. BH&HPA. 6T. 10MC. 200S. ⚏ ☺ & ⚏

Hole House Farm, Pooley Bridge, Penrith, Cumbria. 01768 486325. Owner: Mr W H Coulston. Open March 1-October 31. 5T. 1MC. 53S. 2H. ⚏

(9m). Hutton Moor End Caravan and Camping Site, Troutbeck, Penrith, Cumbria CA11 0SX. 01768 779615. info@huttonmoorend.co.uk. www.huttonmoorend.co.uk. Owner: Mr & Mrs J D Bennett. On A66 9.5m W of M6 J40, turn L for Wallthwaite, site SP. Quiet site for family and walkers. Laundry room, sale of Calor Gas. Golf course just down the road. David Bellamy Silver Conservation Award. Open April-November. BH&HPA. 15T. 4MC. 15S. 1H. ⚏ ☺ & ⚏

(7m). Knotts Hill Chalet & Caravan Site, Watermillock, Penrith, Cumbria CA11 0JR. 01768 486309. holidays@ knottshill.co.uk. www.knottshill.co.uk. Owner: Allen (Park Foot) Ltd. Pooley Bridge, Penrith, Cumbria. From J40 M6 follow A592 to Gowbarrow Lodge. Turn R, site 0.5m on R. Situated in 40 acres of hill and woodland. Holiday caravans for sale with views of Lake Ullswater. Open March 1-October 31. BH&HPA. 30S. ⚏ &

Low Moor, Kirkby Thore, Penrith, Cumbria CA10 1XG. *01768 361231.* www.lowmoorpark.co.uk. Owner: Mrs M Farrell. On A66 Appleby (5m) to Penrith, trans-Pennine route. Open country and all-round views. Local authority approved criteria. Open April/Easter-October. **BH&HPA. 12T. MC. 17S. 3H. ⛺ ☎**

(2m). Lowther Holiday Park, Eamont Bridge, Penrith, Cumbria CA10 2JB. *01768 863631.* alan@lowther-holiday park.co.uk. www.lowther-holidaypark.co.uk. J40, take A66 E then A6 S. AA 4 pennants. Fishing on site, golf 3m, PO and doctors/hospital 2m. Open March-November. ☆☆☆☆ **BH&HPA. 196T. MC. 375S. ⛺ ☎ ⛓ 🛒**

(9m). Melmerby Caravan Park, Melmerby, Penrith, Cumbria CA10 1HE. *01768 881311.* eric.carson@ntlworld.net. www.melmerbycaravanpark.co.uk. Owner: Mrs Susan Carson. On A686 Alston to Penrith. Calor Gas stockist. Chemical toilet emptying point. Laundry. PH, restaurant and bakery 2 mins walk from park. Suitable base for walking and touring. Open March 17-November 26. ☆☆☆☆ **BH&HPA. 5T. 5MC. 40S. 1H. ⛺ ☎ 🛒**

(2m). Oaklands Caravan Site, Great Strickland, Penrith, Cumbria CA10 3DH. *01931 712371.* Owner: Mr N R Thompson. Off A6. Club. Private for residents, golf course nearby. Open March 1-October 31. **20T. MC. 50S. 5H. ⛺ ☎**

(6m). Park Foot Caravan & Camping Park, Howtown Road, Pooley Bridge, Penrith, Cumbria CA10 2NA. *01768 486309.* park.foot@talk21.com. www.parkfootullswater.co.uk. Owner: Allen (Parkfoot) Ltd. M6 J40, A66 Keswick/Ullswater, take A592 Ullswater. At Pooley Bridge take Howtown road 1m on L. Views of Lake Ullswater, with access. Licensed bar, restaurant and takeaway, entertainment. Laundry, car wash, public phone, children's club during summer school holidays. Sailing, windsurfing, canoeing, fishing, walking, ponytrekking, tennis, bike hire, shop and 2 play areas. Calor Gas. RAC 3 pennants. Open March-October. **BH&HPA. 32T. 30MC. 130S. 12H. ⛺ ☎ ⛓ 🛒**

(1m). Southwaite Green Mill Country Park, Eamont Bridge, Penrith, Cumbria CA10 2BY. john heath@ hpcv.fsnet.co.uk. Owner: Mr J Heath. From Penrith on A6, follow signs for Shap and Kendal, turn R at Crown Hotel in Eamont Bridge on B5320. After about 300yd turn R, go down lane for 800yd for entrance to site. **BH&HPA. NCC. 32S. ⛺ ∅**

(2m). Stonefold Caravan Park, Newbiggin, Stainton, Penrith, Cumbria CA11 0HP. *01768 866383.* gill@stonefold. co.uk. www.stonefold.co.uk. Owner: Mrs Gill Harrington. Leave M6 J40 and take A66 Keswick road, turn right at sign for Newbiggin and Stonefold is 1 min drive on the L. Set in a panoramic position overlooking the Eden Valley, with the Pennine Hills in the background. Holiday cottages to let, sleep 2-3. Open Easter-October. **BH&HPA. 15T. MC. ⛺ ☎ ⛓**

(18m). Tebay Caravan Site, Orton, Penrith, Cumbria CA10 3SB. *01539 624511.* caravans@westmorland.com. www.westmorland.com. Owners: Westmorland Ltd. Site is next to Westmorland's picturesque northbound Tebay Services on M6, easily reached from southbound carriageway using the link road between the two service areas. Hard-standings, dog walk, Shops and cafe on service area 500yd; iscount vouchers for meals in the cafe, hotel restaurant and farm shop produce. Open March-October. ☆☆☆☆ **BH&HPA. 35T. 35MC. ⛺ ☎ ⛓ 🛒**

Thacka Lea Caravan Park, Thacka Lane, Penrith, Cumbria CA11 9HX. *01768 863319.* Owner: Mr Atkinson. Off A6. Open March 1-October 31. **25T. 15MC. ⛺ ☎**

(5m). Thanet Well Caravan Park, Greystoke, Penrith, Cumbria CA11 0XX. *01768 484262.* Owner: Mr G & S Cannon. Off M6 J41, B5305. 6m towards Wigton turn left for Lamonby, follow caravan signs. Gas sales. Nearest town, golf 15 mins. Swimming nearby. Good walking. Open March 15-October 31. **BH&HPA. 18T. 2MC. 60S. ⛺ ☎ 🛒**

(6m). The Quiet Caravan & Camping Site, Watermillock, Ullswater, Penrith, Cumbria CA11 0LS. *01768 486337.* info@thequietsite.co.uk. www.thequietsite.co.uk. Owner: Daniel Holder. M6, J40. A66 to Keswick. A592 to Ullswater. Turn R at lake, turn R at Brackerrigg Inn. Site on after 1.5m. Family-run site in pleasant location. Large adventure playground. Caravan and motor caravan storage available. Open March 1-November 14. ☆☆☆☆☆ **BH&HPA. NCC. 60T. 40MC. 23S. 2H. ⛺ ☎ 🛒**

(7m). Ullswater Caravan Camping & Marine Park, Watermillock, Penrith, Cumbria CA11 0LR. 01768 486666. info@uccmp.co.uk. www.uccmp.co.uk. Owner: Messrs Dobinson. From the M6, J40, on to the A592, turn right SP Longthwaite and Watermillock Church. At telephone box. Playground. Bar. Games and TV room. Shop. Lake access 1m. Fishing, boating. Suitable location for touring the lakes. Open March-November. **BH&HPA. 40T. 115MC. 55S. 6H.** 🐕 🔌 ♿ 🔋

(5m). Waterfoot Caravan Park, Ullswater, Pooley Bridge, Penrith, Cumbria CA11 0JF. 01768 486302. enquiries@water footpark.co.uk. www.waterfootpark.co.uk. Owner: Lake District Estates Co Ltd. 13 Maude Street, Kendal, Cumbria. Take J40, M6, join A66 for about 1m, then take the A592, park is on the right-hand side. Parkland site in grounds of a Georgian mansion. Site is well laid out with serviced static caravan pitches and a suitable touring area with a mix of hardstandings lawn areas for awnings or recreation. Children's play area on site. Walking distance of Ullswater Steamers' Pier for cruises on Lake Ullswater. Private boat launch and dinghy storage facilities. Water sports nearby. Fishing, golf, cinema, shopping, lake cruises. Open March-November 14. ☆☆☆☆☆ **BH&HPA. NCC. 38T. MC. 143S.** 🐕 🔌 ♿ 🔋

(10m). White Horse Caravan Site, Kings Meaburn, Penrith, Cumbria CA10 3BU. 01931 714226. Owner: Mrs R J S Addison. Keld Farm, Kings Meaburn, Penrith, Cumbria CA10 3BS. Off the A66 turn left (or right) at south end of Temple Sowerby, SP for Morland; about 1.5m turn left at T-junction, next right, SP for King's Meaburn; 1.5m into village, park behind White Horse Inn, which is adjacent to park. Small shop with PO in PH. Caravan owners able to fly-fish on nearby river Lyvennet. Open March 1-November 14. **4T. 30S.** 🐕 🔌 ♿

Ravenglass

(0.25m). Camping & Caravanning Club Site - Ravenglass, Ravenglass, Cumbria CA18 1SR. 01229 717250/0870 2433331. www.campingandcaravanning club.co.uk. Owner:Camping & Caravanning Club. Greenfields House, Westwood Way, Coventry CV4 8JH. Leave A595 SP to Ravenglass. Turn left at 30mph sign into private road. Site entrance is 25yd on left-hand side, set in 5 acres of mature woodland which was once part of the Muncaster Castle Estate. Suitable base for walking on Cumbria's western coast. On-site facilities include toilet, showers, laundry, washing-up sinks and a play area. All unit types accepted. Non-members welcome. Special deals for families and backpackers. Open March-mid November. ☆☆☆ **60T. 60MC.** 🐕 🔌 🔋

Seascale

(6m). Church Stile Camp Site, Wasdale, Seascale, Cumbria CA20 1ET. 01946 726252. churchstile@campfarm.fsnet.co.uk. www.churchsite.com. Owner: Mr Alan John & Mrs Ruth Knight. Off A595. 4m E of Gosforth to Nether Wasdale site by church. Suitable for climbing. Views, pretty little village. Good for families and couples. Fell walking near lake. Sheltered, family site. Two inns serving bar meals. No touring caravans. Shower block newly refurbished. Open mid March-October 31. **BH&HPA. 15MC. 34S.** 🐕 🔌 ♿

Sedbergh

(5m). Conder Farm, Dent, Sedbergh, Cumbria LA10 5QT. 01539 625277. Owner: M J W Hodgkinson. Turn in Sedbergh (J37, M6) Dent 5.5m. From Sedbergh turn right at George and Dragon (Dent), from Hawes turn left at George and Dragon. Small, family site of 1.5 acres. Quiet with good views. Shop 500yd. Open March-November. **7T. 7MC.** ✿ 🐕 🔌

(2.5m). Cross Hall Farm Caravan Site, Cautley, Sedbergh, Cumbria LA10 5LY. 015396 20668. crosshall@btopenworld.com. www.dalescaravanpark.co.uk. Owner: Mr T R Harper. Off A683 to Kirkby Stephen and Brough overlooking Howgill Fells and 1.5m to Cautley Spout. Quiet, family park at foot of Howgill Fells. Walking, flora and fauna. Shopping 2.5m, golf course 4m. Fell walking from site. Open April-October. **5T. 3MC. 15S. 3H.** 🐕 🔌

(2m). Lincoln's Inn Caravan Site, Firbank, Sedbergh, Cumbria LA10 5EE. 01539 620567. Owner: Mrs M B Airey. Off A684. Open March 1-October 31. **2MC. 3S. 2H.** 🐕

(0.5m). Pinfold Caravan Park, Garedale Road, Sedbergh, Cumbria LA10 5SL. 01539 620576. Owner: Mrs S Maloney. J37, M6 follow A694 Hawes through Sedburgh turn right after Police Station over Dales Bridge. Park on left. Village 0.5m. Mobile shop calls. Open March 1-January 4. **22T. 6MC. 56S.** 🐕 🔌

Yore House Farm Caravan & Camping Park, Yore House, Lunds, Sedbergh, Cumbria LA10 5PX. 01969 667358. Owner: Jim & Liz Pedley. 6m Hawes, 10m Sedberge on A684 near Moorcock pub. Quiet, farm site beside river Ure. Close to N Yorkshire border. Open April-October. **7T. MC.** 🐕

Silloth

(1m). Moordale Park, Blitterlees, Silloth, Cumbria CA7 4JZ. 01697 331375. manda@moordalepark.com. www.moordale park.com. Owner: A & M Ruckledge. On B5300 Maryport to Silloth. Quiet site adjacent Silloth golf course and beach. Soutable base for touring southern Scotland and northern lakes. Tents welcome. Fishing, sailing, horse riding, walking, cycling close by. Open March-October. **12T. 12MC. 106S.** 🐕 🔌

(3m). Rowanbank Caravan Park, Beckfoot, Silloth, Cumbria CA7 4LA. 01697 331653. Owner: Terry/Kay Watson. On B5300 Silloth to Maryport coast road. SP within village of Beckfoot. Small, family-run site with all modern facilities. Set in quiet countryside right next to unspoilt Solway beaches. Open March-November. **BH&HPA. 25T. MC. 25S. 1H.** 🐕 🔌

(0.5m). Seacote Caravan Park, Skinburness Road, Silloth, Cumbria CA5 4QJ. 01697 331121/01697 331031. Owner: Broughton Farm Caravans Ltd. Broughton Farm, Llangennith, Gower, Swansea, West Glamorgan SA3 1JP. 22m SW from Carlisle A595, A596, B5302,18m NW of Keswick from M6, J41, B5305, B5302. Level, peaceful site adjacent to Solway coast. Caravan sales. Children allowed. Open March 1-November 15. ☆☆☆ **BH&HPA. NCC. 16T. 77S. 1H.** 🐕 🔌

(1m). Stanwix Park Holiday Centre, Greenrow, Silloth, Cumbria CA7 4HH. 01697 332666. enquiries@ stanwix.com. www.stanwix.com. Owner: E & R H Stanwix. On A596 at Wigton take B5302 to Silloth. On entering Silloth follow signs to Stanwix Park, about 1m. Caravans for hire. Tents and touring caravans welcome. Indoor leisure centre, pool, gym etc. Ten-pin bowling, family entertainment, bars, disco and cabaret. Golf, fishing, bowling, tennis and shops. Suitable base for exploring Lakes and Carlisle. Open all year except Christmas Day. ☆☆☆☆☆ **BH&HPA. NCC. 121T. MC. 221S77H.** ✿ 🐕 🔌 ♿ 🔋

(1m). **Tanglewood Caravan Park, Causeway Head, Silloth, Cumbria CA7 4PE.** *01697 331253.* michael-tanglewood@hotmail.com. www.tanglewoodcaravanpark.co.uk. Owner: N M & G E Bowman. On B5302. 4m on from Abbeytown, on left before Silloth. Play area. Off-licence. Bottled gas. Pets allowed (free of charge). Laundrette. Clubhouse. Modern, fully-serviced caravans with colour TV. Brochure with tariff available. Golf course, shops, PO, doctor available within 2m. Open Easter-October. ☆☆☆ **BH&HPA. 21T. MC. 60S. 5H.** ⚑ ◪

Silloth-on-Solway

(0.5m). **Solway Holiday Village, Skinburness Drive, Silloth-on-Solway, Cumbria CA7 4QQ.** *01697 331236/01697 331111.* solway@ haganspleisure.co.uk. www.haganspleisure.co.uk. Owner: Hagans Leisure Group. 184 Templepatrick Road, Ballyclare, Co Antrim, N Ireland BT39 0RA. Junction M6, J44 to Wigton on A595/596, follow Silloth sign, take B5302 end of Wigton bypass, park is 10yd on R. Located in the unspoiled seaside Victorian town of Silloth-on-Solway, this 120-acre family park has something for everyone. Facilities include indoor heated pool, children's club, licensed bars with live entertainment, indoor and outdoor play areas, tennis, golf and much more. Open March-November. ☆☆ **BH&HPA. NCC. 90T. 80MC. 185S. 55H.** ⚑ ◪ ▣

St Bees

Seacote Park, The Beach, St Bees, Cumbria CA27 0ES. *01946 822777.* reception@seacote.com. www.seacote.com. Owner: Milburns. Seacote Hotel and Holiday Parks, The Beach, St Bees, Cumbria CA27 0ES. From M6 J40. A66 W then A595 to Whitehaven (4m) then B5345 to St Bees. Adjoining mile-long beach. Restaurant and bar. Clifftop walks, golf course close by. Children welcome. Fishing. PO and shops in St Bees village. Fringe of Lake District. ☆☆☆☆ **BH&HPA. 42T. 42MC. 205S. 75H.** ✿ ⚑ ◪ ⅙ ▣

Ulverston

(0.25m). **Bardsea Leisure Park, Priory Road, Ulverston, Cumbria LA12 9QE.** *01229 584712.* reception@bardsea leisure.co.uk. Owner: Mr & Mrs T & G Varley. Access via A590 and A5087, Ulverston to Barrow. Fishing on site. Golf course, beach 1m. ☆☆☆☆ **BH&HPA. 85T. MC. 88S.** ✿ ⚑ ◪ ▣

(3m). **Black Beck Caravan Park, Bouth, Nr Newby Bridge, Ulverston, Cumbria LA12 8JN.** *01229 861274.* reception@blackbeck.com. Owner: Mr P Kay. M6, J36,A590 for Barrow and South Lakes. After Newby Bridge booth crossroads

turn R, then L, first R. Small hire fleet now available. Zoo, activity centre, swimming, baths, cinema. Open March 1-November 15. ☆☆☆☆☆ **55T. 10MC. 305S. 3H.** ⚑ ◪ ⅙ ▣

(8.5m). **Crake Valley Holiday Park, Water Yeat, Blawith, Ulverston, Cumbria LA12 8DL.** *01229 885203.* crakevalley@coniston1.fslife.co.uk. www.crakevalley.co.uk. Owner: Mr & Mrs I Chesters. On A5084 between Greenodd and Torver. Adjacent to southern end of Coniston Water in a quiet, rural situation, consisting of 10 holiday caravans and 5 timber lodges. Open March-January. ☆☆☆☆☆ **BH&HPA. 15H.** ⚑

(4m). **Meadowlands Caravan Site, Coast Road, Roosebeck, Ulverston, Cumbria.** *01229 869398.* Owner: Mrs W J Inman & Sons. On A5087. Flat, seaside site. Showers. Gas sales. Play area. Open March 1-October 31. **T. MC. 98S.** ⚑

Whicham

Silecroft Camping & Caravan Park, Silecroft, Whicham, Cumbria LA18 4NX. *01229 772659.* silecroftpark@aol.com. www.caravanholidayhomes.com. Owner: Mr & Mrs A Vaughan. A591 to Greenodd, take A5092 to coast road, follow signs. 3.5m from Millom. Golf course 100yd from beach. 1m from mountains. Indoor swimming pool. Open March 1-October 31. ☆☆☆ **BH&HPA. 40T. 20MC. 124S. 4H.** ⚑ ▣ ▣

Wigton

(3.5m). **Blaithwaite Christian Centre, Blaithwaite House, Wigton, Cumbria CA7 0AZ.** *01697 342319.* manager@blaith waite.co.uk. www.blaithwaite.co.uk. Owner: Rev D C Donald. Off A595. Showers. Games room and field. Open Easter-October. **44T. MC.** ▣

(5m). **Clea Hall Holiday Park, Nr Caldbeck, Westward, Wigton, Cumbria CA7 8NQ.** *01697 342880.* Owner: Mr & Mrs G Kennedy. Bona-Vista, Clea Hall Holiday Park. Turn off M6 J 41, B5305, SP Wigton. Through Hutton-in-the-Forest, Unthank, past left turning for Hesket Newmarket and through Sebergham, left turning B5299 to Caldbeck, second crossroads turn right for 1.5m, SP Westward, Wigton. ☆☆☆☆☆ **BH&HPA. 18T. MC. 110S. 3H.** ✿ ⚑ ◪ ⅙ ▣

(10m). **Cottage & Glendale Caravan Park, Port Carlisle, Wigton, Cumbria CA7 5DJ.** *01697 351317.* Owner: Wyreside Caravans. From Carlisle head W on A595. Bear right at roundabout on to B5307. After 1m fork right to Burgh By Sands, follow for 10m to Port Carlisle. Parks on left, SP. Licensed club. Laundry and shop on site. Fishing in 500yd. Club with entertainment and bingo. PO 1m. Doctor and hospital close by. Open March-November. **7T. MC. 57S. 2H.** ⚑ ▣

(6m). Larches Caravan Park, Mealsgate, Wigton, Cumbria CA7 1LQ. 01697 371379. melarches@btinternet.com. www. larchescaravanpark.com. Owner: Ethel Elliott. A595, 0.5m SW Mealsgate village on near side of road. Quiet park, suitable for couples. No ball games allowed. Adults only. Open March 1-October 31. **73T. MC. 100S. 2H.** 🏕🏤♿🛒

(5m). The Beeches Caravan Park, Gilcrux, Wigton, Cumbria CA7 2QX. 01697 321555. holiday@thebeechescaravanpark. com. www.thebeechescaravanpark.com. Owner: Mr & Mrs T H Airey. Off A595 turn into B5301. Holiday caravans set in landscaped park in quiet country village. Shop, laundry room on site, village PH nearby. Play area. Suitable base for touring north and west lakes, Solway coast. 25 mins Keswick. Trout fishing, horse riding in village. Golf courses nearby. **BH&HPA. 27S. 12H.** ⚘🏕♿🛒

Windermere

(1.5m). Barker Knott, Winster Road, Windermere, Cumbria LA23 3JU. 01539 442692. On A5074 1.5m from Bowness-on-Windermere. Farm site. Open Easter-November 15. **30S.** 🏕

Braithwaite Fold Caravan Club Site, Glebe Road, Bowness-on-Windermere, Windermere, Cumbria LA23 3GZ. 01539 442177. www.caravanclub.co.uk. Owner: The Caravan Club. East Grinstead House, East Grinstead, West Sussex RH19 1UA. See website for standard directions to site. Managed by Caravan Club on behalf of South Lakeland District Council, this site is close to the shores of Lake Windermere and within easy walking distance of the town. Windermere has an excellent sailing centre from which to enjoy sailing, windsurfing and canoeing; visitors can hire equipment and take instruction. All hard-standing pitches, toilet block, laundry facilities, Motorhome waste point, vegetable preparation area and dog walk. Open March-November. **NCC. 66T. MC.** 🏕🏤♿

(0.25m). Fallbarrow Caravan Park, Rayrigg Road, Windermere, Cumbria LA23 3DL. 01539 444422. enquiries@southlakeland-caravans.co.uk. www.southlakeland-caravans.co.uk. Owner: South Lakeland Caravans Ltd. South Lakeland House, Main A6, Yealand Redmayne, Carnforth, Lancs LA5 9RN. M6, J36 follow A591 to Windermere until you reach the town centre. Turn L following sign for Bowness 1.5m. At Bowness turn R at mini-roundabout SP Keswick, Steamboat Museum. Park is 300yd on the L. Lakeside park with multi hook-up pitches. Boat launching and Boathouse PH with beer garden, bar meals and family room. Takeaway, cafe, restaurant, shop, children's play area. Shops 400yd. Cinema and boating 800yd. Cycle hire 1m. Gym, swimming 3m. Golf 4m. Open March-October. ✩✩✩✩✩ **BH&HPA. 38T. MC. 261S. 92H.** 🏕🏤♿🛒⊘

(3m). Hill of Oaks & Blakeholme Caravan Estate, Windermere, Cumbria LA12 8NR. 01539 531578. enquiries@hillofoaks.co.uk. www.hillofoaks.co.uk. Owners: Lake District Estates Co Ltd. 13 Maude Street, Kendal, Cumbria LA9 4QD. M6, J36, travel towards Newby Bridge A590, turn R at roundabout A591 towards Bowness for 3m. 0.75m private lake frontage. Boat launching. Lakeside park welcomes touring caravans, motorhomes and caravan holidays. Fully-stocked shop and information on site. Children's play area. Fishing from the shores (appropriate licence available locally). David Bellamy Gold Conservation Award. Fishing, golf, water sports (sailing, windsurfing, canoeing). Open March 1-November 14. ✩✩✩✩✩ **BH&HPA. NCC. 43T. MC. 215S.** 🏕🏤♿🛒⊘

(2.5m). Limefitt Park, Patterdale Road, Windermere, Cumbria LA23 1PA. 01539 432564. enquiries@southlakeland-caravans.co.uk. www.southlakeland-caravans.co.uk. Owner: South Lakeland Caravans Ltd. South Lakeland House, Main A6, Yealand Redmayne, Carnforth, Lancs LA5 9RN. M6, J36 follow SPs 'South Lakes', then 'Windermere'. 0.5m beyond Windermere turn R at mini roundabout taking A592. Patterdale Road, SP 'Ullswater' Limefitt is 2m on R. Spectacular lakeland valley location. 10 mins drive Lake Windermere. Tourers and family campers welcome, friendly Lakeland PH with bar meals, campers' kitchen. Shops, cinema 3m. Sailing, fishing, swimming, boat launch nearby. Open March-October for tourers; open March-January for holiday caravans. ✩✩✩✩✩ **BH&HPA. 72T. 72MC. 72S. 10H.** 🏤♿⊘

(5m). Park Cliffe Estate Camping and Caravan Site, Birks Road, Tower Wood, Windermere, Cumbria LA23 3PG. 01539 531344. info@parkcliffe.co.uk. www.parkcliffe.co.uk. Owner: Mr F W Holgate. Off A592 Newby Bridge to Bowness-in-Windermere. Laundrette. Drying room. Playground. Cafe, bar and takeaway. Off licence. Windermere, cinema, golf 4m. Kendal 15m. Open March 1-mid November. ✩✩✩✩✩ **BH&HPA. 70T. 70MC. 56S.** 🏕🏤♿🛒

(2m). White Cross Bay Leisure Park & Marina, Ambleside Road, Troutbeck Bridge, Windermere, Cumbria LA23 1LF. 01539 443937. enquiries@southlakeland-caravans.co.uk. www.southlakeland-caravans.co.uk. Owner: South Lakeland Caravans. South Lakeland House, A6, Yealand Redmayne, Nr Carnforth, Lancs LA5 9RN. From J36 M6 follow signs to Windermere then A591 to Ambleside, park 2m from Windermere. Restaurant, bar, fast food, tennis court, marina, indoor pool, play area and games room. Shopping, cinema, boating 2m. Golf course 7m. Open March 1-November 14. ✩✩✩✩✩ **BH&HPA. NCC. 25T. 25MC. 332S. 172H.** 🏕🏤♿🛒

BEDFORDSHIRE

Bedford

Riverside Holiday Home Park, Oakley Road, Pavenham, Bedford, Bedfordshire MR43 7PL. 01582 490079. Owner: Luton Caravan Centre. **5T. 55S.**

Biggleswade

(6m). Three Star Park Mobile Homes, Bedford Road, Lower Stondon, Biggleswade, Bedfordshire. 01462 813695. Owner: Mr A J Binks. On A600. Club. No children. **T. MC.** 🏕🛒

Dunstable

(5m). Woodlands Caravan Site, 24 Byslips Road, Studham, Dunstable, Bedfordshire LU6 2ND. 01582 872761. Owner: Mrs S Luak. J9 M1 (5 mins). Whipsnade Zoo (3 mins), London Gliding club (5 mins), Herts Showground (10 mins), Woburn Safari Park (30 mins), Mentmore Towers (30 mins), near Ashridge walking area. Open April-October. **20T. MC.** 🏕🏤

Pavenham

(1m). Riverside Caravan Park, Oakley Road, Pavenham, Bedfordshire MR43 7PL. 01234 825726. Open March-end October. **5T. 55S.** 🏤

Ridgmont

Rose and Crown, 89 High Street, Ridgmont, Bedfordshire MK43 0TY. 01525 280245. Owner: N C McGregor. 3m NE of Woburn on A507, 3m from J13 on M1. Flat, well-drained site close to Woburn Abbey and Safari Park. 5m from Milton Keynes. **10T. MC.** ⚘🏕🛒

CAMBRIDGESHIRE

Bourn

The Fox, Old North Road, Bourn, Cambridgeshire CB3 7UF. *01954 719264.* Owner: R Crouch. Situated on main A1198 crossroad with B1046. 9m N of Royston. Bar, beer garden and restaurant. Shower. ✿ ⊨ ◨

Cambridge

(3m). Camping & Caravanning Club Site - Cambridge, 19 Cabbage Moor, Great Shelford, Cambridge, Cambridgeshire CB2 5NB. *01223 841185.* www.campingandcaravanningclub.co.uk. Owner: Camping & Caravanning Club. Greenfields House, Westwood Way, Coventry CV4 8JH. M11, J11 on to A1309 SP Cambridge. At third set of lights turn R, SP 'Skelford'. After 0.5m follow sign on L, pointing along lane. Suitable base for exploring city and surrounding attractions. Plenty of space for children's ball games, play area. All units accepted. Non-members welcome. Special deals available for families and backpackers. Open March-October. ✰✰✰✰ **120T. 120MC. ⊨ ◨ ♿**

(2.5m). Cherry Hinton Caravan Club Site, Lime Kiln Road, Cherry Hinton, Cambridge, Cambridgeshire CB1 8NQ. *01223 244088.* www.caravanclub.co.uk. Owner: The Caravan Club. East Grinstead House, East Grinstead, West Sussex RH19 1UA. See website for standard directions to site. Imaginatively landscaped site ideally located for exploring Cambridge. Dog walk on site. Non-members and tent campers welcome. Advance booking essential Bank Holidays and weekends June-August. Some pitches limited in size and shape. MV service point. Shops, garage, PO, doctor etc within 1m. Fishing, golf within 10m. Open March-January. ✰✰✰✰✰ **NCC. 60T. MC. ⊨ ◨ ♿**

(5m). Highfield Farm Touring Park, Long Road, Comberton, Cambridge, Cambridgeshire CB3 7DG. *01223 262308.* enquiries@highfieldfarmtouringpark.co.uk www.highfieldfarm touringpark.co.uk. Owner: Mr & Mrs B H Chapman. From Cambridge take A428 (Bedford) and A1303 for 3m then follow signs for Comberton. From M11 leave J12 take A603 (Sandy) then B1046 to Comberton. Laundry facilities. Iron. Hair-dryers. Shaver points. Baby changing facilities. Washing-up sinks. Public telephone. Postbox. Hard-standings. Golf course, PO, shops, doctor available nearby. Open April 1-October 31. ✰✰✰✰✰ **BH&HPA. 60T. 60MC. ⊨ ◨ ♿**

(8m). Roseberry Tourist Park, Earith Road, Willingham, Cambridge, Cambridgeshire CB4 5LT. *01954 260346.* Owner: Mrs Isobel Cuthbert. From A14 take B1050 at Bar Hill. Site 1m N of Willingham on L of B1050. 9-acre orchard site amid pear trees. Ideal for touring Cambridge, Ely or St Ives en route to Felixstowe or Harwich Ferry. Hard-standings. Golf/fishing nearby. Shops 1m. **BH&HPA. 80T. MC. ✿ ⊨ ◨**

(6m). Stanford Park, Weirs Road, Burwell, Cambridge, Cambridgeshire CB5 0BP. *01638 741547/07802 439997.* enquiries@stanfordcaravanpark.co.uk. www.stanfordcaravan park.co.uk. Owner: Mr J Stanford. Caravan site signs at main junctions in village. Quiet site, suitable base for exploring Cambridge and Newmarket. Phone. Gas. Shaver points. Hairdryers. Playground. Laundry room. Shops, restaurants only 15mins walk. RAC appointed. AA 4 pennants. ✰✰✰ **BH&HPA. 100T. 10MC. ✿ ⊨ ◨**

(4m). Toad's Acre Park Home Estate, Mills Lane, Longstanton, Cambridge, Cambridgeshire CB4 5DF. *01954 780939.* Owner: Mr Smith. A14, turn off at Bar Hill (about 1.5m). Dogs allowed with tourers only. **12T. 8MC. 4H. ✿ ◨**

Ely

(10m). Mepal Outdoor Centre, Chatteris Road, Mepal, Ely, Cambridgeshire CB6 2AZ. *01354 692251.* North west from Ely on A142. No entry after 6pm except by prior arrangement. Water sports centre. Play park. **27T. MC. ✿ ◨ ♿**

(4m). Riverside Caravan & Camping Park, 21 New River Bank, Littleport, Ely, Cambridgeshire CB7 4TA. *01353 860255.* riversideccp@btopenworld.com. www.riversideccp. co.uk. Owners: Vanessa & Steve Wood. A10 northbound past Littleport, cross river Ouse. Turn R at roundabout. Site 1m on L. Quiet riverside site. Calor Gas sales. Fishing adjacent. Good PH 400yd, village 10 mins walk. **BH&HPA. 37T. MC. 12S. 4H. ✿ ⊨ ◨ ♨**

(2m). Two Acres Caravan Park, Ely Road, Little Thetford, Ely, Cambridgeshire CB6 3HH. *01353 648870.* Owner: Mrs Maguire. Adjacent to A10 at Little Thetford junction. Small family-run site within easy reach of Cambridge, Newmarket, Norfolk Broads, the fens and east coast. Open February 8-January 6. **BH&HPA. 36T. MC. ⊨ ◨ ♿**

Fenstanton

(0.5m). Crystal Lakes Touring Caravan & Rally Park, Low Road, Fenstanton, Cambridgeshire PE18 9HU. *01480 497728.* Owner: Scenic Estates Ltd. Fenstanton is situated just off A14 between Cambridge and Huntingdon, 8m from top of M11, S; and 8m from A1 at A14 junction, N. 8m from A45. Secluded site just outside village of Fenstanton. Spacious shower facilities. Fishing on site, car boot fair every Sunday. Children's indoor and outdoor activity centre available in winter 2005. Open March-October. ✰ **BH&HPA. 72T. MC. ⊨ ◨ ♿**

Fowlmere

Appleacre Park, London Road, Fowlmere, Cambridgeshire SG8 7RU. *01763 208229/208354.* www.ukparks.co.uk/ appleacre. Owner: Mr T Bearpark. 9m S of Cambridge on B1368 through Fowlmere village, entrance on left. 3m to Imperial War Museum, Duxford. **BH&HPA. 20T. MC. ✿ ⊨ ◨**

Huntingdon

(2m). Houghton Mill Caravan Club Site, Mill Street, Houghton, Huntingdon, Cambridgeshire PE17 2AZ. *01480 466716.* www.caravanclub.co.uk. Owner: The Caravan Club. East Grinstead House, East Grinstead, West Sussex RH19 1UA. See website for standard directions to site. Set on the bank of the river Great Ouse with spectacular views across the river to the National Trust's Houghton Mill. Non-members and tent campers welcome. Toilet blocks with privacy cubicles and laundry facilities. Dog walk nearby, fishing and with 5m of NCN cycle route. Open March-October. **NCC. 65T. MC. ⊨ ◨ ♿**

(6m). Old Manor Caravan Park, Church Road, Grafham, Huntingdon, Cambridgeshire PE28 0BB. *01480 810264.* camping@old-manor.co.uk. www.old-manor.co.uk. Owner: DP & CG Howes. From A14 turn off at Ellington, 5m W of Huntingdon, and follow camping and caravan signs for 2.5m to Grafham. From A1 turn off at Buckden, 4m S of Huntingdon, and follow camping and caravan signs for 2.5m to Grafham. 26 tent pitches, 7 hard-standing pitches. Heated outdoor swimming pool (end May-September). Gas. Laundry room. Deep freezer. Solar heated shower block with shaver points. Dishwashing room. Open all year except Christmas and New Year. ✩✩✩✩ BH&HPA. 58T. 20MC. ✿ ⊁ ⊟ & ⅃

(0.3m). Park Lane Touring Caravan Park, Park Lane, Godmanchester, Huntingdon, Cambridgeshire PE29 2AF. *01480 453740.* Owner: C Birch. 11 The Avenue, Park Lane, Godmanchester. From A14 T-road turn off at sign Huntingdon to Godmanchester. Follow signs on lamp-post in Godmanchester, turn at Black Bull PH. On-site phone. Fishing nearby. ✩✩✩ BH&HPA. 50T. MC. ✿ ⊁ ⊟ &

(5m). Quiet Waters Caravan Park, Hemingford Abbots, Huntingdon, Cambridgeshire PE28 9AJ. *01480 463405.* quiet waters.park@btopenworld.com. www.quietwaterscaravanpark. co.uk. Owner: W H Hutson & Son Ltd. A14, J25. 1m off A14, 5m from Huntingdon, 13m from Cambridge. Riverside park. Angling on site. Open April-October. ✩✩✩✩ BH&HPA. 20T. 9S. ⊁ ⊟ & ∅

Stroud Hill Park, Fen Road, Pidley, Huntingdon, Cambridgeshire PE28 3D. *01487 741333.* stroudhillpark@ btconnect.com. www.stroudhillpark.co.uk. Caravan Club affiliated site. Quiet, rural site. Toilet blocks and laundrette. Shop, cafe, bar and restaurant on site. Good area for walking. Fishing and golf nearby. Peaceful off-peak. ✩✩✩✩✩ NCC. 54T. MC. ✿ ⊁ ⊟ & ⅃

(2m). The Willows Caravan Park, Bromholme Lane, Brampton, Huntingdon, Cambridgeshire PE28 4NE. *01480 437566.* willows@willows33.freeserve.co.uk. www.willowscar avanpark.com. Owner: Stephen A Carter. c/o 2 Werthiem Way, Stuckeley Meadows, Huntingdon, Cambs PE29 6UQ. Leave A1 N join B1514, SP Brampton, follow signs for Huntingdon. Leave A1 S join A14 then B1514 signs for Huntingdon. Park on R turn opposite country park. PH/restaurant, boating, fishing and attractive walks, historical Huntingdon town, Country park and Grafham Water nearby. Dogs allowed under strict supervision. Shop nearby. Tents welcome. Children's playground (under-7s). Washing machine. AA 3 pennants. **40T. 15MC.** ✿ ⊁ ⊟ &

(2m). Wyton Lakes Holiday Park, Wyton Lakes, Banks End Wyton, Huntingdon, Cambridgeshire PE28 2AA. *01480 412715.* loupeter@supanet.com. www.wytonlakes.com. Owners: Louise & Peter Bates. A14, exit 23, follow A141 to March. At fourth roundabout take A1123 to St Ives. 1m down pass Hartford Marina. Wyton Lakes is next door on right-hand side. Adult park. Quality fishing on site. Boating, golfing, riding, water skiing all nearby. Restaurants, shops, pubs within 1m. Doctor, PO within 2m. Rural retreat with river frontage, woodland and lakes. Each pitch with electric and water. Free showers, some hard-standings. Marina next door. Open April 1-October 31. ✩✩✩ BH&HPA. 40T. 40MC. ⊁ ⊟ &

Littleport

(5m). Willetts Riverside Caravans, 20 Sandhill, Littleport, Cambridgeshire CB6 1NT. *01353 860680.* Owner: Mr A & J M Willett. 'Anglebay' The Moors, Littleport, Ely, Cambridgeshire. Off A10 Ely to Downham Market. Open April 1-October 31. **46S. 5H.** ⊁

March

(5m). Floods Ferry Marina Park, Staffurths Bridge, March, Cambridgeshire PE15 0YP. *01354 677302.* Owners: Mr T Quinn, Mr J Quinn and Mrs A Quinn. A141 bypass of March town, turn for Floods Ferry for 3m. Look for brown signs. Tranquil park in heart of Fenland, on site marina, fishing, licensed clubhouse with bar food and occasional live music, all touring pitches, on river bank. ✩✩✩ BH&HPA. 18T. 18MC. ✿ ⊁ ⊟ &

Peterborough

(2m). Ferry Meadows Caravan Club Site, Ham Lane, Peterborough, Cambridgeshire PE2 5UU. *01733 233526.* www.caravanclub.co.uk. Owner: The Caravan Club. East Grinstead House, East Grinstead, West Sussex RH19 1UA. See website for standard directions to site. Family site, level and open, located in country park with water sports, golf, fishing and cycling facilities. Non-members and tent campers welcome. Dogs must be exercised off site. Advance booking essential bank holidays. Motorhome service point. Grass and hard-standing pitches. ✩✩✩✩ NCC. 254T. MC. ✿ ⊁ ⊟ &

(9m). Sacrewell Farm and Country Centre, Thornhaugh, Peterborough, Cambridgeshire PE8 6HJ. *01780 782254.* info@sacrewell.fsnet.co.uk. www.sacrewell.org.uk. Owners: William Scott Abbott Trust. Off A47, just E of A1/A47 junction near Wansford, Peterborough. Farm and country centre admission included in caravan fees: working watermill, bygones, animals. Children's play area. Farm trail. Nearest village with PHs, PO, doctor within 1m. NCC. 40T. ✿ ⊁ ⊟ & ⅃

(8m). Yarwell Mill Caravan Park, Mill Lane, Yarwell, Peterborough, Cambridgeshire PE8 6PS. *01780 782344.* Owner: Mr & Mrs Usher. Cranham Farm, The Chase, Upminster, Essex RM14 3YB. Off A1 and A47 intersection. At Wansford church follow Yarwell signs. Boating and fishing on site. River Nene flows through site. Old stone town of Stamford 6m. Nene Way walks lead from site. Local shop, PO, doctor, medical centre within 1m. Open March 1-October 31. ✩✩✩ BH&HPA. 120T. MC. 24S. ⊁ ⊟ &

St Neots

(0.5m). Camping & Caravanning Club Site - St Neots, Hardwick Road, Eynesbury, St Neots, Cambridgeshire PE19 2PR. *01480 474404/0870 243 3331.* www.campingandcaravanningclub.co.uk. Owner: Camping & Caravanning Club. Greenfield House, Westwood Way, Coventry CV4 8JH. From A1 take A428 to Cambridge, second roundabout left to Tesco's, past sport centre, site SP. On the banks of the Great Ouse. Suitable for boating and fishing. St Neots within easy reach. Non-members welcome and may join at site. All units accepted. Some all-weather pitches available. Facilities nearby: shops, PHs, restaurants, doctors, dentist in St Neots. Fishing is available from this site. Paxton Pits Nature Reserve, for birdwatchers, is just 2m away. Special deals available for families and backpackers. Open March-October. ✩✩✩ 180T. 180MC. ⊁ ⊟ &

Willingham

(0.25m). Alwyn Tourist Park, Over Road, Willingham, Cambridgeshire CB4 5EU. *01954 260977.* Owner: Mr & Mrs P & D Pickering. 9m from Cambridge. M11 to A14 to B1050. Open March 1-October 31. NCC. 84T. MC. ⊁ ⊟

Wisbech

(10m). Pisces Caravan Park & Fishery, Bedford Bank West, Welney, Wisbech, Cambridgeshire PE14 9TB. *01354 610257.* www.ukparks.co.uk/pisces. Owner: C & J R Shelton. On A1101 in Welney Village turn down the river bank opposite the Parish Hall with river on left. Park is 0.5m down lane. Peaceful site. No children under 10 allowed. 4 lakes for fishing. Sales of new and used holiday caravans. Open March-November. BH&HPA. 25S. 5H. ⊁ &

Sheriff Hutton Club Site

Norwich Club Site

award-winning sites
and great services

Our 95 Club sites are well equipped, in great locations with excellent facilities and a legendary reputation for cleanliness. Non-members are welcome and all visitors receive free vouchers for discounts on local attractions, but why not also benefit from reduced site fees with excellent value for money membership at only £30⁺.

NOW ONLY A CLICK AWAY:
www.campingandcaravanningclub.co.uk

It has never been easier to join our Club. Great value caravanning is only a click away.

Find & book YOUR ideal site with our SiteFinder

Call for YOUR UK Club Sites Guide today.

FREE GUIDE
to nearly 100 Club sites
024 7647 5442
PLEASE QUOTE REF 0331

TO JOIN WITH YOUR CREDIT CARD DETAILS
TELEPHONE NOW ON: 024 7647 5442
⁺Cost is £30, plus a £5 joining fee which is waived if you pay by Direct Debit. **PLEASE QUOTE REF 0331**

The Camping and Caravanning Club

The friendly Club

To request your free information pack call the number above. We will use details you provide for servicing your enquiry and informing you of member services. We will disclose your information to our service providers only for these purposes and will not keep it beyond a reasonable period of time.

GREAT SITES AND GREAT SERVICES FOR OVER 100 YEARS

ESSEX

Bradwell-on-Sea

Eastland Meadows Country Park, East End Road, Bradwell-on-Sea, Essex CM0 7PP. *01621 776577.* enquiries@eastland meadows.co.uk. www.eastlandmeadows.co.uk. Owner: Janice Gledhill & James Harvard. Take A turn off the A12 through Banbury. Take B1018 to Latchingdon, bear left at roundabout onto Bradwell through Mayland, Steeple, St Lawrence on to Bradwell, turn right at garage then left at church; site is 0.5m along on left. In the heart of the countryside, yet close to the sea. Small wildlife on the park; pick your own fruit. Open March-January 2nd. ✫✫✫ **BH&HPA. 12T. MC. 140S.** ⚊ ⊞

Brentwood

> **(5m). Camping & Caravanning Club Site - Kelvedon Hatch, Warren Lane, Doddinghurst, Brentwood, Essex CM15 0JG.** *01277 372773/0870 243 3331.* www.campingandcaravanningclub.co.uk. Owner: Camping & Caravanning Club. Greenfields House, Westwood Way, Coventry CV4 8JH. M25, J28, Brentwood 2m L on A128, SP Ongar. After 3m turn R, SP. Between London and Chelmsford with plenty of sporting activities within easy reach. Peaceful site surrounded by trees. Caravans, motor caravans and tents accepted. Non-members welcome. Area for ball games available with volleyball net. Special deals available for families and backpackers. Open March-October. ✫✫✫ **90T. 90MC.** ⚊ ⊞ ♿

Brightlingsea

Lakeside Touring Caravan Park, Promenade Way, Brightlingsea, Essex CO7 0HH. *01206 303421.* Owner: Brightlingsea Town Council. 50yd from town. Open March 1-October 31. **50T. MC. 240S.** ⚊

Burnham-on-Crouch

(1.5m). Creeksea Place Caravan Park, Ferry Road, Burnham-on-Crouch, Essex CM0 8PJ. *01621 782675/782387.* Owner: Mr R Bertorelli & Mrs C Lindsey. Off B1010. Open March-November. **BH&HPA. 50T. MC. 100S.** ⚊ ⊞ ⧆

Millfields Caravan Site, Playing Field, Burnham-on-Crouch, Essex. *01621 854477.* Owner: Maldon District Council. Princes Road, Maldon, Essex CM9 7AL. Open April 1-October 31. **70S.** ⚊

(0.5m). Sea End Caravan Park, Sea End Boathouse, Burnham-on-Crouch, Essex CM0 8AN. *01621 782063.* ricoltd@aol.com. www.riceandcole.co.uk. Owner: Rice & Cole Ltd. At end of Burnham High Street, turn R into Belvedere Road. Follow road for about 0.5m along sea wall. 10 mins walk to town. Open March 1-November 30. **BH&HPA. 180S.** ⚊

Canvey Island

Thorney Bay Park Ltd, Thorney Bay Road, Canvey Island, Essex SS8 0DB. *01268 691500.* sally@thorneybaypark. fsnet.co.uk. Owner: Thorney Bay Park Ltd. On the B1014. Open March-November. **15T. 10MC. 1200S.** ⚊ ⊞ ⧆

Clacton-on-Sea

(3m). Ashley Holiday Park, London Road, Little Clacton, Clacton-on-Sea, Essex CO16 9RN. *01255 860200.* Owner: Mr A Lee & Mrs M Lee. On A133 Colchester to Clacton. Quiet, family park suitable for long weekends. Open April-October. **BH&HPA. 10T. 118S.** ⊞

(3m). Firs Caravan Park, London Road, Little Clacton, Clacton-on-Sea, Essex CO16 9RN. *01255 860279.* Owner: Mr I Senchell. On A133 Little Clacton to Clacton-on-Sea. Club. Friendly, family-run park. Owner-occupiers only. Discounts given on new caravan sales. Write for brochure. Open late March-mid October. **BH&HPA. 224S.** ⧆

> **(2m). Highfield Holiday Park, London Road, Clacton-on-Sea, Essex CO16 9QY.** *0871 664 9746.* highfield.holi daypark@park-resorts.com. www.park-resorts.com. Owner: Park Resorts Ltd. 3rd Floor, Swan Court, Waterhouse Street, Hemel Hempstead, Herts HP1 1FN. Follow A12 to Colchester and take A120 Harwich road, leading to A133 direct to Clacton-on-Sea. Highfield is situated on B1441, on left. Heated oudoor pool, water resorts programme, children's club. Family evening entertainmnent. All-weather sports court, adventure playground, amusements, shop, laundrette, cafe and takeaway, pool, darts. Clacton pier: amusements, stalls and shops. Open April-October. **BH&HPA. NCC. 742S. 157H.**

(5m). Hutleys Caravan Park, St Osyth Beach, St Osyth, Clacton-on-Sea, Essex CO16 8TB. *01255 820712.* office@hut leys.co.uk. hutleyscaravans.co.uk. Owner: Alan Hutley & Gill Went. A12 to Colchester. A120 to Clacton then A133 to Clacton. On to St Osyth. Adjacent to beach. Indoor heated swimming pool. Open March 1-November 1. **BH&HPA. 19T. MC. 750S.** ⚊ ⊞ ♿ ⧆

(4m). Martello Beach Holiday Park, Jaywick, Clacton-on-Sea, Essex CO15 2LF. *0871 664 9782.* martello.beach@park-resorts.com. www.park-resorts.com. Owner: Park Resorts Ltd. 3rd Floor, Swan Court, Waterhouse Street, Hemel Hempstead, Herts HP1 1FN. Follow A12 from London to Colchester. Take A133 to Clacton-on-sea. Turn R on to B1077. Continue for 1.5m then turn L on to Jaywick lane. Continue for 3m then follow signs for the park. Outdoor heated pool, on site store, cafe, children's clubs, amusements, multi-sports court. Outdoor play area, amily entertainment. Clacton-on-sea pier: amusements, stalls and fun fair. Open April-October. **BH&HPA. NCC. 367S. 39H.** ⛺ 🏕

(4m). Oaklands Holiday Village, Colchester Road, St Osyth, Clacton-on-Sea, Essex CO16 8HW. *01255 820432.* info@cinqueportsleisure.com. www.cinqueports leisure.com. Owners: Cinque Ports Leisure Ltd. Coghurst Hall Holiday Village, Ivyhouse Lane, Ore, Hastings, East Sussex TN35 4NP. B1027 from Colchester on main road, 100yd before St Osyth turning. Fishing lake. Family club/bar. Children's club. Open March-October. **BH&HPA. NCC. 400S.** ⛺

(6m). St Osyth Beach Holiday Park, Beach Road, St Osyth Beach, Clacton-on-Sea, Essex CO16 8SG. *01255 820247/01255 820782 (sales).* info@cinqueports leisure.com. www.cinqueportsleisure.com. Owner: Cinque Ports Leisure Ltd. Coghurst Hall Holiday Village, Ivyhouse Lane, Ore, Hastings, East Sussex TN35 4NP. Off B1027. Owners only park. Takeaway. Laundrette. Convenience store. Evening entertainment. Children's club and playpark. Indoor swimming pool. Family club. Fishing lake. All-weather sports pitch. Boat storage area. Open March-October. **BH&HPA. NCC. 504S.** ⛺ 🏕

(1m). Sacketts Grove, Jaywick Lane, Clacton-on-Sea, Essex CO16 7BD. *01255 427765.* Owner: TST (Parks) Ltd. Off A133 and B1027. Riding school on site. Club. Swimming pool. Takeaway. Golf course nearby. PO, doctors, etc less than 1m. Open Easter-October. **BH&HPA. NCC. 50T. MC. 140S. 1H.** ⛺ 🏕

(2m). Silver Dawn Touring Park, Jaywick Lane, Clacton-on-Sea, Essex CO16 8BB. *01255 421856.* Owner: Mr & Mrs S R Bartlett. Off B1027. David Bellamy Silver Conservation Award. Open April 1-September 30. **BH&HPA. 30T. MC. 56S.** ⛺ 🚫

(3m). Tower Holiday Park, Jaywick, Clacton-on-Sea, Essex CO15 2LF. *0870 442 9290.* holidays@gbholidayparks.co.uk. www.gbholidayparks.co.uk. Owner: GB Holiday Parks Ltd. 6 Leylands Park, Nobs Crook, Colden Common, Winchester SO21 1TH. A12-A120-A133 to Clacton, turn right at Clacton seafront. Follow road signs to and through Jaywick. Tower Holiday Park is on outskirts of Clacton-on-Sea, with superb sandy beaches within walking distance and easy reach of fun packed pier, theatres and beautiful gardens. Outdoor heated pool, direct access to beach, children's outdoor play area, riding stables and golf nearby. Amusement centre. Family entertainment, cabaret, etc. Open March-October. ✩✩ **BH&HPA. NCC. 100T. MC. 277S. 35H.** 🚫 🏕

(1m). Valley Farm Holiday Park, Valley Road, Clacton-on-Sea, Essex CO15 6LY. *0871 664 9788.* valley.farm@park-resorts.com. www.park-resorts.com. Owners: Park Resorts Ltd. 3rd floor, Swan Court, Waterhouse Street, Hemel Hempstead, Herts HP1 1FN. Follow A12 to Colchester then take A120 and A133 to Clacton. On entering town, SP for B1032 towards Frinton. Valley is 1m from the town on your L. Indoor pool and heated outdoor pool, soft play area, children's clubs, evening entertainment, amusements, crazy golf, store, laundrette. Clacton Pier with amusements, stalls and funfair. Open April-October. **BH&HPA. NCC. 733S. 54H.** ⛺ 🚫

(4m). Weeley Bridge Caravan Park, Clacton Road, Weeley, Clacton-on-Sea, Essex CO16 9DH. 0871 664 9797. weeley.bridge@park-resorts.com. www.park-resorts.com. Owner: Park Resorts Ltd. 3rd Floor, Swan Court, Waterhouse Street, Hemel Hempstead, Herts HP1 1FN. Follow A12 to Colchester. Take A120 then A133 to Weeley roundabout. Take 2nd exit at Weeley roundabout towards train station. The holiday park is about 0.5m on right-hand side. Outdoor pool, laundrette, bar, outdoor adventure playground, multi-sports court, amusements, children's clubs, family evening entertainment. Horse riding 2m, sea fishing 4m. Open April-October. ✩✩✩ **BH&HPA. NCC. 268S. 12H.** ⛺ 🏕

Colchester

(8m). Bentley Country Park, Flag Hill, Gt Bentley, Colchester, Essex CO7 8RF. *01255 820517.* Owner: Mrs J A Harries. On B1027 Colchester to Clacton back road. Pinelog Leisure Centre nearby with spa, sauna, gym and pool. Fishing available nearby. Open March 1-October 31. **320S.** ⛺ 🏕

(0.75m). Colchester Camping & Caravan Park, Cymbeline Way, Lexden, Colchester, Essex CO3 4AG. *01206 545551.* enquiries@colchestercamping.co.uk. www.colchestercamping. co.uk. Owner: D M & S G Thorp. At junction of A12 and A133 Colchester Central, follow tourist signs. Colchester 5 mins by car, 30 mins walk Colchester. Caravan Club affiliated site. Non-members and tent campers welcome. Suitable touring base for East Anglia and Constable country; stopover for ferry ports. Heated shower block. Secure storage available. Shop on site, golf course nearby. ✩✩✩✩ **BH&HPA. CaSSOA. 165T. MC.** ♿ ⛺ 🚫 ♿ 🏕

(7m). Coopers Beach Holiday Park, East Mersea, Mersea Island, Colchester, Essex CO5 8TN. *0871 664 9731.* coopers. beach@park-resorts.com. www.park-resorts.com. Owners: Park Resorts Ltd. 3rd Floor, Swan Court, Waterhouse Street, Hemel Hempstead, Herts HP1 1FN. Take A12 towards Colchester. Follow signs to Colchester Zoo; look for signs to Mersea Island. Follow the Mersea road on to the Island. Bear L into East Mersea. Park is on R 50yd from PO. Outdoor heated pool, tennis court, restaurant and takeaway, laundrette, multi-sports court, bar, entertainment. Pony trekking 7m. Open April-October. ✩✩✩ **BH&HPA. NCC. 577S. 35H.** ⛺

(8m). Fen Farm, East Mersea, Colchester, Essex CO5 8UA. *01206 383275.* fenfarm@talk21.com. mersea-island.com/fen farm. Owner: Mr & Mrs R Lord. Off B1025, take left fork over causeway, follow road to Dog and Pheasant PH, 1st turning right. Quiet, rural site, close to beach and country park. Village shop and PO 1m. Supermarket, doctor 4m. Showers. Shaver

Waldegraves Holiday Park
Mersea Island, Colchester, Essex CO5 8SE
Tel: 01206 382898 Fax: 01206 385359
Ideal quiet family park, grassland surrounded by trees and lakes. Safe, private beach. 65 miles from London
Family entertainment • Licensed Bar & Restaurant • Children's play area and games room • Pitch & Putt
Heated Swimming Pool • Golf driving range • Fishing & Boating Lakes • Luxury Holiday Homes for hire and sale.
Email –@waldegraves.co.uk Web site – http://www.waldegraves.co.uk

points. Electric hook ups, play area. Shower for people with disability. Laundry room and iron. Mobile shop calls. Safe swimming. Open March-November. ✩✩✩ **BH&HPA. 85T. 10MC. 85S.** 🅷 🅿 ♿

(10m). Seaview Holiday Park, Seaview Avenue, West Mersea, Colchester, Essex CO5 8DA. *01206 382534.* Owner: Glynian (Leisure Parks) Ltd. B1025 Colchester to Mersea. Laundry and showers. Bottled gas supplies. Open March 1- October 31. **120T. MC. 250S.** 🅷 🅿 ♿ 🅻

(10m). Waldegraves Holiday Park, Mersea Island, Colchester, Essex CO5 8SE. *01206 382898.* holidays@walde graves.co.uk. www.waldegraves.co.uk. Owner: Mr D Lord. Off B1025 from Colchester, follow tourist signs on island. Rose Award. Private beach, golf, pitch and putt, fishing, heated pool. Shopping, restaurants nearby. Open March-November. ✩✩✩ **BH&HPA. NCC. 60T. 60MC. 225S. 25H.** 🅷 🅿 ♿ 🅻

Harlow

(3m). Roydon Mill Leisure Park, Roydon, Harlow, Essex CM19 5EJ. *01279 792777.* reception@roydonpark.com. www.roydonpark.com. Owners: Global Enterprises Ltd. Follow tourist board signs from A414 between A10 and Harlow, or from B181. Only 35 mins from London by rail. Limited facilities for the disabled visitors. Open all year for tourers; open March 1-October 31, then weekends November and December for holiday homes. ✩✩✩ **BH&HPA. 70T. 70MC. 90S. 3H.** ⚙ 🅿

Harwich

(1m). Dovercourt Caravan Park, Low Road, Dovercourt, Harwich, Essex CO12 3TZ. *01255 243433.* enquiries@dover courtcp.com. www.dovercourtcp.com. Owner: Hammerton Leisure Ltd. Off A120 Colchester to Harwich. Turn R at Ramsey roundabout, then R, at mini roundabout after 1m, L at next, park is 1m on L. Cafe. Supermarket. Amusement arcade. Playground. Bars. Club. Entertainment. Ballroom. Heated swimming pool. Near sandy beach. Golf, shopping centre within 2m. Open March 1-October 31. **NCC. 50T. 20MC. 600S. 30H.** 🅷 🅿 ♿ 🅻

(1m). Greenacres Caravan Park, Low Road, Dovercourt, Harwich, Essex CO12 3TS. *01255 502657.* Owner: Mr B R Mathews. Off A120 to Dovercourt, 1m SW Dovercourt town centre. Club. Open March 4-October 31. **BH&HPA. 4T. 4MC. 91S. 2H.** 🅷

Hockley

(4m). The Dome Village, Lower Road, Hockley, Essex SS5 5LU. *01702 230278.* hab@domevillage.net. Owner: H & M Baker. 3m E of Hullbridge. Doctor's clinic. PH with food. Residents association hall. Touring caravan storage. PO and general store on site. Children allowed. **10T.** ⚙ 🅷 ♿ 🅻

Loughton

Debden House Camp Site, Debden Green, Loughton, Essex 1G10 2PA. *020 8508 3008.* Off A121. M25 exit J26, A121 to Loughton, left A1168, second left Pyrles Lane, T-junction right then second left. M11, 2m. London Tube 1.5m. Central line to Debden. Access from site into Epping Forest. Bottled gas sales. Laundry and cafe on site. Open April 1-October 31. ✩✩ **125T. 100MC.** 🅷 🅿 🅻

(3m). Elm's Caravan and Camping Park, Lippitt's Hill, Loughton, Essex IG10 4AW. *0208 502 5652.* info@theelms campsite.co.uk. www.theelmscampsite.co.uk. Owner: Terence & Patricia Farr. J26, M25 and head towards Waltham Abbey. Proceed for 1m to a road junction and turn L towards Waltham

Cross and Chingford. Continue to the traffic lights and turn L on to the A112 toward Chingford. Proceed for just over 1m to the Plough PH and turn L at PH. Continue for 0.75m and branch R into Lippitts Hill. The Elms is at the top of the hill on the L. Riding, tennis, boating, restaurants, PH, fishing, golf, swimming, shops, payphone. Open March 1- October 31. ✩✩✩ **BH&HPA. NCC. 50T. 4S. 1H.** 🅿 🅻

Maldon

(3m). Barrow Marsh Caravan Park, Mill Beach, Goldhanger Road, Heybridge, Maldon, Essex CM9 4RA. *01621 852859/ Mobile: 0776 2001231.* Owner: J D & P D Wakelin. On north side of B1026 which runs from Maldon (3m) via Heybridge (2m) to Goldhanger (2m). 200yd from Blackwater estuary and shop. Dogs allowed on leads with tourers. 2m from shops in Heybridge. 200yd to beach and shop in Summer. 100yd to nearest PH. Open March-November. ✩✩ **NCC. 6T. 5MC. 120S. 4H.** 🅷 🅿 ♿

Manningtree

(2m). Strangers Home Inn, The Street, Bradfield, Manningtree, Essex CO11 2US. *01255 870304.* camping@ strangershome.com. www.strangershome.com. Owner: Lin & Bob Dale. On the A120 Colchester to Harwich turn N at Horsley Cross onto B1035 for 1.5m then right to Bradfield and site. Suitable stopover for travelling to and from Harwich ferries. Open March 1-October 31. **75T. 25MC.** 🅷 🅿 🅻

Rochford

(4m). Riverside Village Holiday Park, Creeksea Ferry Road, Wallasea Island, Rochford, Essex SS4 2EY. *01702 258297.* Owner: K Parkes. A127, Rochford, Ashington to Wallasea or A130, Hullbridge, Ashingdon, Canewdon and Wallasea. Flat, well-cut parkland with trees and lakes, suitable for walking, bird-watching, windsurfing and boating. Ferry to Burnham. PH and restaurant adjoining. Open March 1-November 1. ✩✩✩ **BH&HPA. 60T. MC. 180S.** 🅷 🅿 🅻

Southminster

Waterside Holiday Park, Main Road, St Lawrence Bay, Southminster, Essex CM0 7LY. *0871 664 9794.* waterside.holi daypark@park-resorts.com. www.park-resorts.com. Owner: Park Resorts Ltd. 3rd Floor, Swan Court, Waterhouse Street, Hemel Hempstead, Herts HP1 1FN. A12 towards Chelmsford take the A414 to Maldon. Follow signs to Latchingdon on B1010. Drive through village and follow signs for St Lawrence. Pick up signs for Waterside Holiday Park. Indoor swimming pool, sauna and jacuzzi, cafe, fast food takeaway, outdoor play area, amusements, PH, family evening. Open April-October. **BH&HPA. NCC. 220S. 15H.** 🅷

St Lawrence Bay

St Lawrence Holiday Home Park, 10 Main Road, St Lawrence Bay, Essex CM0 7LY. *01621 779434.* gary.duce@btinternet.com. www.slcaravans.co.uk. Owner: St Lawrence Caravans Ltd. Off B1021 at Latchingdon, follow brown and white tourism signs on road to Bradwell. At St Lawrence Bay turn L into Main Road, park about 1m on R. David Bellamy Silver Conservation Award. Welcome Host. Driving range 3m. Golf, cinema 8m. Shopping centre 11m. Open March 1-November 30. ✫ **BH&HPA. 200S.** ⊨ ⅃

St Osyth

(6m). Seawick Holiday Village, Beach Road, St Osyth, Essex CO16 8SG. *01255 820416.* info@cinqueportsleisure.com. www.cinqueportsleisure.com. Owner: Cinque Port Leisure Ltd. Coghurst Hall Holiday Village, Ivyhouse Lane, Ore, Hastings, East Sussex TN35 4NP. Off B1027. Flat ground. 3-bedroom chalet adapted for disabled users available for hire. 500yd from beach. Heated indoor pool. Entertainment and leisure centre, gym, sauna and spa bath. Dogs allowed in owner-occupied holiday homes. Open March 1-October 31. **BH&HPA. NCC. 525S. 124H.** ⅃

The Orchards Holiday Village, Point Clear, St Osyth, Essex CO16 8LJ. *01255 821489.* oewebmaster@bourne-leisure. co.uk. www.orchardsholidayvillage.co.uk. Owne: Bourne Leisure Ltd. One Park Lane, Hemel Hempstead, Herts HP2 4YL. From Clacton-on-Sea, take B1027 out of Clacton (SP Colchester), turn L after the 'Save' petrol station, then over the crossroads in St Osyth. Follow signs to Point Clear. Travel 3m to the park entrance. Indoor and outdoor swimming pool, bowling greens and multi-sports area. Family entertainment. Children's clubs. Two mini markets, bakery, fishing lakes, golf course. Owners executive health suite. 7m to shopping centre/cinema. Open March-October. ✫✫✫✫ **BH&HPA. NCC. 15T. MC. 1284S. 260H.** ⊨ ⅃ ⅃

Walton-on-the-Naze

(0.25m). Naze Marine Holiday Park, Hall Lane, Walton-on-the-Naze, Essex CO14 8HL. *0871 664 9755.* naze.marine@park-resorts.com. www.park-resorts.com. Owner: Park Resorts Ltd. 3rd Floor, Swan Court, Waterhouse Street, Hemel Hempstead, Herts, HP1 1FN. Take A12 to Colchester - follow A120 Harwich Road as far as A133. On the A133 take the B1033 all the way to Walton Seafront. Park is on left-hand side. Heated outdoor pool, water resorts programme, children's clubs, family entertainment, amusements, adventure playground, laundrette, cafe, takeaway, shop. Open April-October. ✫✫ **BH&HPA. NCC. 602S. 65H.** ⊨

(0.5 m). Southcliffe Trailer Park, Woodberry Way, Walton-on-the-Naze, Essex CO14 8EP. *01255 677568.* Owner: Southcliff Trailer Co Ltd. 8 Southview Drive, Walton-on-the Naze, Essex CO14 8EP. Open March 1-October 31. **36S.** ⊨

(1m). Willow Caravan Park, High Tree Lane, Walton-on-the-Naze, Essex CO14 8HU. *01255 675828.* Owner: B R & P E Mathews. On B1034. Club. Open March 1-October 31. **5T. MC. 80S. 20H.**

West Mersea

Firs Chase Caravan Park, Firs Chase, West Mersea, Essex. *01206 382855.* Owner: Mr W Simmons. Turn right when over bridge to Mersea. Open March 15-October 31. **230S.** ⊨

(1m). Seaview Holiday Park, Seaview Avenue, West Mersea, Essex CO5 8DA. *01206 382534.* Owner: Seaview Holiday Park Ltd. Manager: Roy Evenden. Open March 15-January 14. **BH&HPA. 120T. 120MC. 250S.** ⊨ ⅃ ⅃

Wickford

(3m). Hayes Farm Caravan Park, Hayes Chase, Burnham Road, Battlesbridge, Wickford, Essex SS11 7QT. *01245 320309.* Owner: Hammerton Leisure Ltd. Off A132 Wickford to South Woodham Ferrers. Club. Bar. Entertainment. Playground. Adjacent river Crouch and boating. Open April 1-October 31. **NCC. 70T. MC. 300S.** ⊨ ⅃ ⅃

HERTFORDSHIRE

Baldock

Ashridge Farm Caravan Club Site, Ashwell Street, Ashwell, Baldock, Hertfordshire SG7 5QF. *01462 742527.* www.caravanclub.co.uk. Owner: The Caravan Club. East Grinstead House, East Grinstead, West Sussex RH19 1UA. See website for standard directions to site. Members only. Small, pretty site with many trees and shrubs. Toilet blocks, laundry facilities and motorhome service point. Suitable for walking and within 5m of NCN cycle route. Facilities for disabled visitors. Peaceful off-peak. **NCC. T. MC.** ✿ ⊨ ⅃ ⅃

Hemel Hempstead

(2m). Breakspear Way Caravan Club Site, Buncefield Lane, Breakspear Way, Hemel Hempstead, Hertfordshire HP2 4TZ. *01442 268466.* www.caravan club.co.uk. Owner: The Caravan Club. East Grinstead House, East Grinstead, West Sussex RH19 1UA. See web-site for directions. Quiet site convenient for London and M1. Advance booking advised. Non-members welcome. Some hard-standings. Calor Gas and Campingaz, play equipment. Toilet blocks. Limited laundry facilities. Motorhome service point. Restaurant, golf and fishing nearby. NCN cycle route in 5m. ✫✫✫ **NCC. 60T. MC.** ✿ ⊨ ⅃ ⅃

Hertford

Bayford Wood, Bayford, Hertford, Hertfordshire. *01992 511215.* Owner: Mr R Orme. Off B158, SP Bayford. **3T. 1MC. 120S.** ✿

(1m). Camping & Caravanning Club Site - Hertford, Mangrove Road, Hertford, Hertfordshire SG13 8QF. *01992 586696/0870 2433331.* www.campingandcaravan ningclub.co.uk. Owner: Camping & Caravanning Club. Greenfields House, Westwood Way, Coventry CV4 8JH. From A1, avoid town centre signs at Hertford and follow A414. From A10 take A414 to Hertford, cross first round-about, then 1st L into Mangrove Road. Site on L. Sports field. Non-members welcome. Local attractions: Lea Valley Park, Paradise Wildlife Park and gardens of Benington Lordship. David Bellamy Gold Conservation Award. Special deals for families and backpackers. All types of units accepted. ✫✫✫✫ **250T. 250MC.** ✿ ⊨ ⅃ ⅃

Hoddesdon

(1m). Lee Valley Caravan Park, Essex Road, Dobbs Weir, Hoddesdon, Hertfordshire EN11 0AS. *01992 462090.* info@leevalleypark.org.uk. www.leevalleypark.com. Owner: Lee Valley Regional Park. Bulls Cross, Enfield, Middlesex EN2 9HG. 1.75m E of A10. Take Hoddesdon exit from A10. Follow Dinant Link Road and Essex Road. Riverside setting; good fishing and walking. Boating and shop nearby. Open Easter-October 31. ✫✫✫✫ **NCC. 100T. 100MC. 100S.** ⊨ ⅃ ⅃

Waltham Cross

(2m). Camping & Caravanning Club Site - Theobalds Pk, Theobalds Park, Bulls Cross Ride, Waltham Cross, Hertfordshire EN7 5HS. *01992 620604/0870 2433331.* www.campingandcaravanningclub.co.uk. Owner: Camping & Caravanning Club. Greenfields House, Westwood Way, Coventry CV4 8JH. Park located in Hertfordshire just 13m from Central London, 10mins drive from M25, leaving at J25. A10 towards London keep in R lane, R at first lights, R at T-junction, R behind dog kennels. Site 250yd towards top of lane on R. Space for children's games. Non-members welcome. Site is tree screened, wildlife on site. Recreation hall and play area on site. Special deals available for families and backpackers. Open March-October. ☆☆☆ **90T. 90MC.** ⚲ ⌂

Welwyn Garden City

(2m). Commons Wood Caravan Club Site, Ascots Lane, Welwyn Garden City, Hertfordshire AL7 4HJ. *01707 260786.* www.caravanclub.co.uk. Owner: The Caravan Club. East Grinstead House, East Grinstead, West Sussex RH19 1UA. See website for standard directions to site. Members only. Pleasantly green, flat and rural site within easy reach of London by public transport. Toilet blocks. Privacy cubicles. Laundry facilities. Veg prep. Motorhome service point. Golf, fishing and water sports nearby. **NCC. 74T. 74MC.** ✿ ⚲ ⌂ ♿

NORFOLK

Attleborough

(0.50m). Oak Tree Caravan Park, Norwich Road, Attleborough, Norfolk NR17 2JX. *01953 455565.* oaktree.cp@virgin.net. www.oaktree-caravan-park.co.uk. Owner: Mr & Mrs D A M Birkinshaw. Turn right off the A11 (Thetford-Norwich road), SP Attleborough, in 2m continue through Attleborough, passing the Sainsbury's supermarket, fork left immediately past the church at T junction, and the caravan site can be seen on the right-hand side in about 0.5m. ☆☆☆☆ **BH&HPA. 30T. 30MC.** ✿ ⚲ ⌂

Bacton

Cable Gap Holiday Park, Coast Road, Bacton, Norfolk NR12 0EW. *01692 650667.* holidays@cablegap.co.uk. www.ukparks.co.uk/cablegap. Owner: Mr & Mrs A P Epton. Park is situated between the sea and the countryside. Rose Award. Contact brochure line on 0800 0686870. Open mid February-November. ☆☆☆☆☆ **BH&HPA. 65S. 25H.** ⚲ ⚓

Castaways Holiday Park, Paston Road, Bacton, Norfolk NR12 0JB. *01692 650436/650418.* castaways.bacton@ic24.net. www.castawaysholidaypark.co.uk. Owner: Richard & Anna Hollis. Park is located on the B1159 Mundesley to Bacton road and is 5m from North Walsham. Situated in the quiet village of Bacton, with direct access to a fine sandy beach and well situated for discovering all of Norfolk and The Norfolk Broads. Modern caravans, pine lodges and flats. Licensed club, entertainment, children's play area. Pets are welcome. Open March 1-January 1. ☆☆☆☆ **BH&HPA. 35H.** ⚲ ♿ ⚓ ⌀

(1m). Red House Chalet and Caravan Park, Paston Road, Bacton, Norfolk NR12 0JB. *01692 650815.* kayloveday@btconnect.com. Located on the B1159 Bacton to Mundesley road. Caravans, chalets and flats on a small, quiet, family-run coastal park with direct access to the beach via steps. Good location for sea fishing, nearby golf course, horse riding and fishing lakes. Suitable base for touring the Broads and north Norfolk. Open March-January. **BH&HPA. 25H.** ⚲ ♿ ⚓

Cromer

(1m). Brownsells Cliff Caravan Site, East Runton, Cromer, Norfolk. *01263 512695.* Owner: Mr J Brownsell. Located on the A149 Sheringham to Cromer road. Open April 1-October 3. **8S.** ⚲

Cable Gap Holiday Park
Coast Rd, Bacton, Norfolk NR12 0EW
Tel:01692 650667 www.cablegap.org.uk

Cable Gap Holiday park is a friendly family owned park that takes pride in providing first class facilities. Our caravans have achieved the highest Tourist Board grading and the coveted Rose Award for many years. We also have a silver David Bellamy Conservation Award.

FOREST PARK
Outstanding Natural Beauty
Cromer

Set in 90 Acres of glorious natural woodlands where wildlife abounds and Rhododendrons flourish. Forest Park is a top quality David Bellamy Gold Award winning Touring and Holiday Home haven.

◆ OVER 200 ELECTRIC HOOK-UP & OVER 70 NON-ELECTRIC PITCHES
◆ INDOOR HEATED SWIMMING POOL
◆ FIRST RATE HAIR SALON WITH EXPERIENCED STYLIST
◆ THE FORESTERS CLUBHOUSE & RESTAURANT, SERVING REAL ALE,
DELICIOUS FOOD & OF COURSE OUR LEGENDARY SUNDAY CARVERY
◆ A SUPERB WELL STOCKED SHOP   ◆ MILES OF WOODLAND WALKS
◆ INDIVIDUAL HOLIDAY HOME PLOTS SET IN BEAUTIFUL WOODLANDS
◆ A LARGE SELECTION OF NEW & USED HOLIDAY HOMES
FOREST PARK CARAVAN SITE LTD, NORTHREPPS ROAD, CROMER, NORFOLK. NR27 0JR
TEL: 01263 513290   FAX: 01263 511992
E-MAIL: forestpark@netcom.co.uk   WEBSITE: www.forest-park.co.uk

Please mention Caravan Sites 2006 when replying to advertisers

(3m). Camping & Caravanning Club Site - West Runton, Holgate Lane, West Runton, Cromer, Norfolk NR27 9NW. *01263 837544/0870 2433331.* www. campingandcaravanningclub.co.uk. Owner: Camping & Caravanning Club. Greenfields House, Westwood Way, Coventry CV4 8JH. From King's Lynn on A148 towards Cromer, turn L at Roman Camp Inn. Site track on R at Crest of Hill, 0.5m to site. 1m from sea and sandy beaches, 3m to Cromer where golf and fishing are available. All units accepted. Non-members welcome. Visit nearby Cromer with its church tower and lighthouse. Seal reserve at Blakeney Point and the Shire Horse Centre at West Runton. Panoramic views of the surrounding countryside can be enjoyed from site. Special deals available for families and backpackers. Open March-October. ☆☆☆☆ **200T. 200MC.** 🔧 🔌 ♿

(1m). Forest Park Caravan Site, Northrepps Road, Cromer, Norfolk NR27 0JR. *01263 513290.* forestpark@netcom.co.uk. www.forest-park.co.uk. Owner: Forest Park Caravan Site Ltd. Off B1159. Indoor heated pool. Laundrette. Clubhouse. Hair salon. Adjacent to Cromer Golf Course. David Bellamy Gold Conservation Award. Golf course 0.5m. Cinema, shopping centre 1m. Open March 15-January 15. ☆☆☆ **BH&HPA. 350T. 50MC. 400S.** 🔧 🔌 ♿ 🏪

(1m). Gap Caravan Site, Beach Road, East Runton, Cromer, Norfolk. *01263 513292.* www.northnorfolk.co.uk/gapcaravan park. Owner: Mr W R Babbage. The Old Vicarage, 42 Cromwell Road, Cromer, Norfolk NR27 0BE. On A149 Cromer to Sheringham. Close to shops and beach. Open Easter-end October. **178S. 5H.** 🔌 🏪

(1m). Gold Coast Caravan Park, Coast Road, East Runton, Cromer, Norfolk NR27 9PX. *01263 513626.* timothyhay@ aol.com. Owner: Mr T L Hay. Cliff House Holiday Park, Minsmere Road, Dunwich, Saxmundham, Suffolk IP17 3DQ. On A149. Travel on coast road when leaving Cromer, and park can be found on the right just after leaving East Runton. Open March-October. **62S.** 🔧

(1m). Hazelbury Caravan Park, Cliff Lane, East Runton, Cromer, Norfolk NR27 9NH. *01263 513256.* timothyhay@ aol.com. Owner: T L Hay. Cliff House, Minsmere Road, Dunwich, Suffolk IP17 3DQ. Park located off the Cromer to Sheringham coast road at East Runton. Direct sea views. All caravans plumbed in and connected to mains. Cinema, supermarket 1m. Golf course in Cromer, Sherington and West Runton. Open March-October 31. **140S.** 🔧

(2m). Incleboro Fields Caravan Club Site, Station Close, West Runton, Cromer, Norfolk NR27 9QG. *01263 837419.* www.caravanclub.co.uk. Owner: The Caravan Club. East Grinstead House, East Grinstead, West Sussex RH19 1UA. See website for standard directions to site. Members only. Located in a hillside area of 21 acres with sea views, woodlands, walks and wild flowers. 1m from sea. 9-hole golf course adjacent. Play area. Dog walk. Toilet blocks. Privacy cubicles. Laundry facilities. Baby/toddler washroom. Veg prep. Motorhome service point. Family site. Open March-October. **NCC. 260T. MC.** 🔧 🔌 ♿

(2m). Ivy Farm Holiday Park, 1 High Street, Overstrand, Cromer, Norfolk NR27 0PS. *01263 579239.* www.ivy-farm.co.uk. Owner: W Reynolds. On A148 between Cromer and Mundesley. Family run for over 50 years, set in heart of 'Poppyland' in quiet conservation area of Overstrand. 2 mins to beach and village shops, PH, cafe. Golf and fishing nearby. Open March 20-October 31. ☆☆☆ **20T. 5MC. 129S. 11H.** 🔧 🔌

(1.5m). Laburnum Caravan Park, Water Lane, West Runton, Cromer, Norfolk NR27 9QP. *01263 837473.* Owner: Mr & Mrs M F Randell. Ravensfield, Knapton Grove, North Walsham, Norfolk NR28 0RS. Turn N off A149 Sheringham to Cromer. Manager: Mr B Hollis. Open March-October. **BH&HPA. 6T. MC. 166S. 8H.** 🔧 🔌

(1m). Love's Site, East Runton, Cromer, Norfolk. Owner: Mr F Love. Open March-September. **2T. 8S. 8H.** 🔧 🔌

(1m). Manor Farm Caravan Site, East Runton, Cromer, Norfolk NR27 9PR. *01263 512858.* manor-farm@ukf.net. www.manorfarmcaravansite.co.uk. Owner: Mr S T Holliday. 1m W of Cromer turn off A148 at brown and white Manor Farm signs. Secluded, family-run site on traditional mixed farm. Showers, washbasins, shaver points. Hair-dryer points. Laundry and washing-up sinks. Calor Gas. Two supermarkets in 0.25m. No motorcycles. Open Easter-September 30. **110T. 30MC.** 🔧 🔌 ♿

Pinewood Caravan Park, Holt Road, Cromer, Norfolk NR27 9JN. *01263 512140.* Owner: Mr C & M R Forster. On A148 Holt to Cromer. Heated pool. Open Easter-November. **153S.**

(0.5m). Seacroft Camping Park, Runton Road, Cromer, Norfolk NR27 9NH. *01263 511722.* www.ukparks.co.uk/seacroft. Owner: Epton Leisure Ltd. On A149 coast road. Showers. Heated swimming pool. Takeaway. Restaurant. Bar snacks. Playground. Laundry. Open March 20-October 31. ☆☆☆☆ **BH&HPA. 120T. MC.** 🔧 🔌 ♿ 🏪

(1m). Seaview Caravan Park, Beach Road, East Runton, Cromer, Norfolk NR27 9PA. *01263 514569.* info@seaviewcaravanpark.net. www.seaviewcaravanpark.net. Owner: Mr & Mrs M Ashwell. Beach Road is a turning off A149 in centre of village. Letting caravans. Laundry, games room, tea garden, beach kiosk. Steps to beach from site entrance. Golf course, cinema and shops within 2 miles. No dogs allowed in hire caravans. Open March 24-October 30. ✰✰✰ **BH&HPA. 53S. 6H.** 🅃

(3m). Sixacres, Roughton, Cromer, Norfolk. *01263 511620.* Owner: Mr S Marston. On A140 Norwich to Cromer. Open March 1-January 4. **BH&HPA. 45S.** 🅃

(1m). The Poplars Caravan Park, Brick Lane, East Runton, Cromer, Norfolk NR27 9PL. *01263 512892.* Owner: R C & B E Verlander. A149 Sheringham to Cromer. Family-run park. Coastal village set on edge of woodlands in peaceful grounds. 8 chalets for hire. Open March-November. **BH&HPA. NCC. 90S. 8H.** 🅃

> **(1m). Woodhill Park, East Runton, Cromer, Norfolk NR27 9PX.** *01263 512242.* info@woodhill-park.com. www.woodhill-park.com. Owner: Blue Sky Leisure, Timewell Properties Ltd. Clifftop location with sandy beach below between Cromer and Sheringham on A149. Quiet site. Rose Award. David Bellamy Gold Conservation Award. Open March 20-October 31. ✰✰✰✰ **BH&HPA. NCC. 220T. 69MC. 62S. 16H.** 🅃 🖳 ♿ 🖳

(4m). Woodland Caravan Park, Trimingham, Cromer, Norfolk NR11 8AL. *01263 833144/570208.* Owner: Mrs J Harrison. On B1159 south-east of Cromer. Leisure pool, sauna, bar, restaurant complex. Open April 1-October 31. ✰✰✰ **BH&HPA. 115T. MC. 154S.** 🅃 🖳 ♿ 🖳

(0.5m). Wyndham Park Caravan Site, East Runton, Cromer, Norfolk NR27 9NH. *01263 512304.* Owner: G Bullimore & J Barrell. 0.5m W of Cromer on A149 Cromer/Sheringham coast road. Clifftop position. Paddling pool, sand pit, swings, barbecue area. Dog walk. Open Easter-October 31. **150S. 7H.** 🅃 🖳

Diss

(1.5m). The Willows Caravan & Camping Park, Diss Road, Scole, Diss, Norfolk IP21 4DH. *01379 740271.* mshaw@thewillowspark.co.uk. www.thewillowspark.co.uk. Owner: M Shaw. 1.5m E of Diss on A1066, 250yd from Scole A140 roundabout. On Norfolk/Suffolk county boundary. Level, peaceful site on the banks of the river Waveney, surrounded by conservation area. Walking distance to historical Saxon village of Scole. Fishing, golf driving range and golf course nearby. Open March-October. **32T. MC.** 🅃 🖳

(8m). Waveney Valley Holiday Park, Air Station Farm, Pulham St Mary, Diss, Norfolk IP21 4QF. *01379 741690/741228.* Owner: Mr E Wall. Leave A140 for Dickleburgh, travel 2m E to Rushall. Large level site. Shaver points. Outdoor swimming pool. Laundry room. Licensed bar. Restaurant. Horse riding on site. Fishing locally. **25T. MC. 4S. 4H.** ♿ 🅃 🖳 🖳

Fakenham

(0.75m). Fakenham Racecourse Caravan & Camping Site, The Racecourse, Fakenham, Norfolk NR21 7NY. *01328 862388.* caravan@fakenhamracecourse.co.uk. www.fakenhamracecourse.co.uk. Manager: David Hunter. From Norwich A1067. At roundabout follow brown signs to Racecourse Caravan/Camping. From A1065 and A148 on approach to Fakenham follow signs as above. Caravan Club affiliated site. Suitable base for visiting Norfolk's coastal resorts, stately homes, wildlife and other attractions. Sports centre adjacent. Dog walk. Free access to racing for caravan/camping guests. Non-Caravan Club members and tents welcome. Toilet blocks with showers, privacy cubicles. Laundry facilities. Veg prep. Motorhome service point. Bar and restaurant at sports centre on site. Golf, fishing, tennis. ✰✰✰ **120T. MC.** ♿ 🅃 🖳 🖳

(3m). Little Snoring Caravan Park, Holt Road, Little Snoring, Fakenham, Norfolk NR21 0AX. *01328 878335.* Owner: Mr & Mrs Young. On A148 Cromer to Fakenham. **27T. MC.** ♿ 🅃 🖳 🖳

(7m). Old Brick Kilns Caravan & Camping Park, Little Barney Lane, Barney, Fakenham, Norfolk NR21 0NL. *01328 878305.* oldbrickkilns@aol.com. www.old-brick-kilns.co.uk. Owners: Alison & John Strahan. Off A148, at B1354 to Aylsham follow brown Tourist Board signs to Barney. Quiet, family park for discerning caravanner or camper. Mostly flat, open or shaded all weather pitches. Modern facilities. Family games areas. Licensed restaurant. Fishing pond. AA 4 pennants. David Bellamy Gold Conservation Award. Open February 20-January 6. ✰✰✰✰✰ **BH&HPA. 60T. 60MC.** 🅃 🖳 ♿ 🖳

Great Yarmouth

(4m). Beach Estate Caravan Park, Estate Office, Long Beach, Hemsby-on-Sea, Great Yarmouth, Norfolk NR29 4JD. *01493 730023.* info@long-beach.co.uk. www.long-beach.co.uk. Owner: J M Groat. At end of Beach Road Hemsby off B1159. Close to sandy beach. Well lit. Mains electrics, showers, deep sinks. Licensed club. Open mid March-November 7. **3T. MC. 100S.** 🖳

> **Breydon Water Holiday Park, Burgh Castle, Great Yarmouth, Norfolk NR31 9QB.** *0871 664 9710.* breydon.water@park-resorts.com. www.park-resorts.com. Owner: Park Resorts Ltd. 3rd floor, Swan Court, Waterhouse Street, Hemel Hempstead, Herts, HP1 1FN. From Great Yarmouth on A12 towards Lowestoft go straight over 2 roundabouts. Take next exit and turn L at bottom of slip road. At roundabout take 1st exit and straight over next. Turn L at next T-junction and R at next. Park is 0.5m from here. Yare village: heated outdoor pool, water resorts programme, Free children's clubs, tennis court, amusements, laundrette, shop, restaurant and takeaway, free family evening entertainment, indoor pool, adventure playground, crazy golf, gym, solarium, laundrette, fish and chip shop, Open April-October. ✰✰✰ **BH&HPA. NCC. 329S. 49H.** 🅃 🖳

  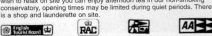

(7m). Broad Farm Camping and Touring Caravan Site, Flegburgh, Great Yarmouth, Norfolk. *01493 369273*. Owner: Mrs L Shingles. On A1064 Caister to Acle. Open May 24-September 8. **500T. MC. 6H.** 🐕 🏢

Broadlands Caravan Club Site, Johnson Street, Ludham, Great Yarmouth, Norfolk NR29 5NY. *01692 630357*. www.caravanclub.co.uk. Owner: The Caravan Club. East Grinstead House, East Grinstead, West Sussex RH19 1UA. See website for standard directions to site. Quiet, open site in the centre of the Broads. Toilet blocks, laundry facilities, baby and toddler washroom and motorhome service point. Playground and boules pitch. Fishing and water sports nearby. Suitable for families. Open March-October. **NCC. 110T. MC.** 🐕 🏢 ♿

(12m). Bureside Holiday Park, Boundary Farm, Oby, Great Yarmouth, Norfolk NR29 3BW. *01493 369233*. Owner: D F Cooke. Close to river and near Thurnemouth. Heated swimming pool, launching slipway and fishing. Play area. Open end-May Bank Holiday-mid-September. **85T. MC. 45S.** 🐕

(5m). Burgh Castle Marina, Butt Lane, Burgh Castle, Great Yarmouth, Norfolk NR31 9PZ. *01493 780331*. info@burgh castlemarina.co.uk. www.burghcastlemarina.co.uk. Owner: Mr R D Wright. Off A143 Yarmouth to Beccles 3m W of Gorleston-on-Sea. Follow signs for marina to Betton. Turn R after 1m for Burgh Castle. Park entrance on left-hand side, another 0.75m. Pontoon moorings. Slipway. Generous space, quiet, rural setting. Views and walks to Roman ruins and bird reserves. Riverside PH and restaurant. Swimming pool. Information and exhibition centre with permanent displays of Roman ruins and marshland heritage. Visiting displays throughout season. Golf course 3m. David Bellamy Gold Conservation Award. Accessibility category 1 award. Green Tourism Business Scheme Silver award. Open March 1-January 31. ☆☆☆☆ **BH&HPA. 45T. 30MC. 230S. 3H.** 🏢 ♿

(3m). Caister Beach Holiday Park, Branford Road, Caister-on-Sea, Great Yarmouth, Norfolk NR30 5NE. *01493 720278*. 5stars@caister.freeserve.co.uk. caister-beach-holiday-park. co.uk. From London M11/A11 to Norwich then A47 to Acle, A1064. From Kings Lynn A47. From Kent M25, A12, A149. . Alongside miles of sandy beach and ideally located near all the local attractions. Club. Golf course 1m, shopping centre, cinema 3m, Pleasurewood Hills Theme Park 8m. Rose Award. Open March-November. ☆☆☆☆☆ **BH&HPA. NCC. 197S. 108H.** 🦺

(3m). Caister Holiday Park, Caister-on-Sea, Great Yarmouth, Norfolk NR30 5NQ. *01493 720405*. oewebmaster@bourne-leisure.co.uk. www.caisterholidaypark.com. Owner: Bourne Leisure Ltd. 1 Park Lane, Hemel Hempstead, Hertfordshire HP2 4YL. A47 into Great Yarmouth and at first roundabout as you enter town take second exit continuing on A47 for 0.5m. At next roundabout take exit towards Caister on A149. Follow by-pass around Caister taking first exit at first roundabout, second exit at second roundabout and third exit at third roundabout. Caister Park is 1m along on the left hand side. Indoor pool. Ten-pin bowling. Mini golf. Laundrette. Shops. Restaurants and takeaways. Children's clubs. Daytime and evening entertainment. Direct beach access, abseiling, fun palace, bouncy castle, kiddy cars. Open March-October. ☆☆☆ **BH&HPA. NCC. 908. 566H.** 🐕 ♿ 🦺 ∅

(3m). California Cliffs Holiday Park, Rottenstone Lane, Scratby, Great Yarmouth, Norfolk NR29 3QU. *0871 664 9716*. california.cliffs@park-resorts.com. www.park-resorts. com. Owner: Park Resorts Ltd. 3rd Floor, Swan Court, Waterhouse Street, Hemel Hempstead, Herts HP1 1FN. From Great Yarmouth take A149 N towards Caister. Take first exit at first roundabout. Just after stadium take 2nd exit at 2nd roundabout on to B1159 and 2nd exit at third roundabout. Turn R at Wheelstop Steak House and follow road to Rottenstone Lane. Turn L here and park is a little way down on L. Indoor and outdoor pool complex. Crazy golf. Laundrette. Shops. Restaurant and takeaway. Free children's club. Free evening entertainment for all the family. Adults-only bar. Open April-October. ☆☆☆☆ **BH&HPA. NCC. 603S. 60H.** 🐕 ♿ 🦺

(10m). Causeway Cottage Caravan Park, Bridge Road, Potter Heigham, Great Yarmouth, Norfolk NR29 5JB. 01692 670238/0786 797 4143. Owner: Trevor & Sue Chaplin. Causeway Cottage Caravan Park, Potter Heigham, Norfolk NR29 5JB. Off A149 at Potter Heigham. Holiday caravans and touring meadow. Small, family site 250yd from river, shops, PHs and entertainment. Fishing, boating. All modern conveniences. Beach 6m. Buses pass park. Gas bottle agent. Open March 15-October 7. **BH&HPA. NCC. 5T. 5MC. 9S. 9H. ⛺ 🔌 ⌀**

(4m). Cherry Tree Holiday Park, Mill Road, Burgh Castle, Great Yarmouth, Norfolk NR31 9QR. 01493 782214. A47 towards Great Yarmouth. At end of dual carriageway take 3rd exit off roundabout and follow A12 towards Gorleston, then take A143 towards Beccles. At Bradwell turn R into New Road, SP Burgh Castle & Belton. Follow road, taking 1st R into Stepshort then turn 1st R into Mill Road. Cherry Tree is on the L. Indoor pool and bubble spa, lounge bar, restaurant/coffee shop, bars, cabaret room, amusement arcade, snooker, putting green. Heated outdoor pool. Laundrette, chip shop, crazy golf, football pitch, picnic area. Open April-October. ☆☆☆☆ **BH&HPA. NCC. 17T. MC. 395S. 90H. ⛺ 🔌 ♿ 🐾 ⌀**

(6m). Clippesby Holidays, Clippesby Hall, Clippesby, Great Yarmouth, Norfolk NR29 3BL. 01493 367800. holidays@clippesby.com. www.clippesby.com. Owner: Lindsay Family. In Norfolk Broads National Park between Acle and Potter Heigham off B1152, turning opposite Clippesby Village sign. Permineter parking. Woodland and parkland setting in 6 different areas. Quiet, family-owned. Grassy, sheltered. Surrounded by rivers, broads, nature reserves and tourist attractions. Lots to do. David Bellamy Gold Conservation Award. Norfolk Broads 2m. Norwich 8m. Great Yarmouth 9m. Open Easter-October. ☆☆☆☆ **BH&HPA. 100T. MC. 17H. ⛺ 🔌 ♿ 🐾**

(6m). Drewery's Caravan Park, California Road, California, Great Ormesby, Great Yarmouth, Norfolk NR29 3QW. 01493 730845. Owner: Mrs E Tuddenham & Mr M Drewery. Off B1159. Laundrette. Clubhouse. Amusements. Close to beach. Open Easter-October 31. **15T. MC. 74S. 10H. ⛺ 🐾 ⌀**

(2m). Eastern Beach Caravan Park, Manor Road, Caister-on-Sea, Great Yarmouth, Norfolk. 01493 720367. Owner: Jill Bramwich. On A47 to A149. Licensed club. Beachside. Children's play area. Arcade. Open Easter-October 30. ☆☆☆☆ **BH&HPA. 56H. ⛺ 🐾 ⌀**

(2m). Elm Beach Caravan Park, Manor Road, Caister-on-Sea, Great Yarmouth, Norfolk. 01493 721630. enquiries@elmbeachcaravanpark.com. www.elmbeachcaravanpark.com. Owner: Mr F Hayes. Off A149 Stalham to Yarmouth. Adjoining sandy beach. Pets allowed. Quiet park. Manager: Mr T Bolger. Open March-January. ☆☆☆ **28S. 30H. ⛺ ⌀**

(3m). Grasmere Caravan Park, Bultitudes Loke, Caister-on-Sea, Great Yarmouth, Norfolk NR30 5DH. 01493 720382. Owner: D J & L D Peers. A149 from Great Yarmouth enter Caister at roundabout. Past Yarmouth Stadium. After 0.5m turn sharp L just before bus stop. Quiet, family site. No on-site entertainment. 250yd to shops. Shower block. Laundry. Shaver points. Open April-October. ☆☆☆ **BH&HPA. 46T. MC. 54S. 9H. 🔌 ♿**

(1.5m). Great Yarmouth Racecourse Caravan Club Site, Jellicoe Road, Great Yarmouth, Norfolk NR30 4AU. 01493 855223. www.caravanclub.co.uk. Owner: The Caravan Club. East Grinstead House, East Grinstead, West Sussex RH19 1UA. See website for standard directions to site. Open site in excellent position next to racecourse and golf course. 300yd from seafront, at quieter, northern end. Dogs must be exercised off site. Advance booking essential bank holidays. Non-members welcome. Toilet blocks. Privacy cubicles. Laundry facilities. Veg prep. Motorhome service point. Play area. Golf, fishing and water sports nearby. Cycle route 5m. Open March-November. ☆☆☆☆ **NCC. 115T. MC. ⛺ 🔌 ♿**

(5m). Green & Beach Farm Caravan Parks, Scratby, Great Yarmouth, Norfolk NR29 3NW. 01493 730440. www.greenfarmcaravanpark.com. Owner: Mr L C Fowler. On A149 and B1159. Two clubs and two indoor swimming pools. 2 mins beach. Amusements. Shops, PO. Open April 1-October 31. ☆☆☆☆☆ **BH&HPA. 87T. MC. 65S. 50H. ⛺ 🔌**

(5m). Green Farm Caravan Park, Scratby, California, Great Yarmouth, Norfolk NR29 3NW. 01493 730440. Owner: Mr G T B Fowler. North on coast from Great Yarmouth. Open March 26-October 31. ☆☆☆☆☆ **50T. 50MC. 150S. 150H. ⛺ 🔌 🐾**

(4m). Hopton Holiday Village, Warren Lane, Hopton on Sea, Great Yarmouth, Norfolk NR31 9BW. 01502 730143. oeweb master@bourne-leisure.co.uk. www.hoptonholidayvillage.com. Owner: Bourne Leisure Ltd. One Park Lane, Hemel Hempstead, Herts HP2 4YL. Off A12 between Lowestoft and Great Yarmouth. Heated indoor and outdoor swimming pool. Club. Entertainment. Mini market. Laundrette. Direct beach access. Multi sports, soft play area, 9-hole golf course, bowling green, crazy golf, bouncy castle. Restaurants. Open March-October. ☆☆☆☆ **BH&HPA. NCC. 1025S. 350H. ⛺ ♿**

(4m). Liffens Park, Burgh Castle, Great Yarmouth, Norfolk NR31 9QB. 01493 780357. www.liffens.co.uk. Owner: Mr P Liffen. From Great Yarmouth follow signs for Beccles. Look for left turn, sign for Burgh Castle 2m and follow to T-junction right. Follow tourist sign for Liffens. 2 Bars with entertainment. Two heated pools. Amusements. Restaurant. Chip shop. Family park. Crazy golf, play area. Open Easter-October for hire caravans; open Easter-end December for owner-occupiers. ☆☆☆☆ **BH&HPA. 150T. 150MC. 150S. 35H. ⛺ 🔌 ♿ 🐾 ⌀**

(4m). Liffens Welcome Holiday Centre, Butt Lane, Burgh Castle, Great Yarmouth, Norfolk NR31 9PU. 01493 780481. www.liffens.co.uk. Owner: Mr Liffen. From Great Yarmouth to Beccles A143 road turn right for Burgh Castle. 0.5m turn right we are 0.5m on right. Family-run holiday centre close Great Yarmouth, great facilities. Gym, solarium, indoor pool, bar, play area. Open March 31-October 30. ☆☆☆☆ **BH&HPA. 150T. 150MC. 140S. 30H. ⛺ 🔌 ♿ 🐾**

Please mention Caravan Sites 2006 when replying to advertisers

(5m). Long Beach Caravan Park, Estate Office, Long Beach, Hemsby, Great Yarmouth, Norfolk NR29 4JD. *01493 730023.* info@long-beach.co.uk. www.long-beach.co.uk. Owner: Long Beach Estates. Turn E off B1159 Hemsby on Beach Road. Then 2nd left (Kings Lake), SP Long Beach. Club. Laundrette. Cafe. Supermarket. Private sandy beach. Open mid March-November. **20T. MC. 130S. 12H.** 🐕 🔲 🛴

(6m). Newport Caravan Park, Newport, Hemsby, Great Yarmouth, Norfolk NR29 4NW. *01493 730405.* Owner: Newport Caravan Park (Norfolk) Ltd. On B1159 coast road between Great Yarmouth and Cromer, 6m N of Great Yarmouth. Close to beach. Licensed club with entertainment. Restaurant, chippy, play area and amusements. Open April-October. ✰✰✰ **BH&HPA. 90T. MC. 26S. 26H.** 🔲 🛴 ⌀

(12m). Norfolk Broads Caravan Park, Bridge Road, Potter Heigham, Great Yarmouth, Norfolk NR29 5JB. *01692 670461.* Owner: BRCP Ltd. On A149 Cromer to Great Yarmouth. 300yd from river in Broads village of Potter Heigham. Electric gates at entrance. Golf courses, Norfolk Broads, beach, shopping in Norwich, swimming, boat hire. Open March 19-October 31 for holiday homes. ✰✰✰✰ **BH&HPA. 50S.** 🐕 ⅂

(4m). Rose Farm Touring and Camping Park, Stepshort, Belton, Great Yarmouth, Norfolk NR31 9JS. *01493 780896.* www.rosefarmtouringpark.co.uk. Owner: Sue & Tore Myhra. From A143 turn into new road, SP Belton and Burgh Castle first R at Stepshort, site first on R. Gorleston 2m. Showers, laundry, recreation room. Calor Gas. Swings. AA 3 pennants. **BH&HPA. 60T. MC.** ✿ 🐕 🔲 🛴

(5m). Scratby Hall Caravan Park, Scratby, Great Yarmouth, Norfolk NR29 3PH. *01493 730283.* Owner: Mrs B Rawnsley. Off B1159. Rural, level and grassy. Laundrette. Games room. Play area. Gas supplies. Washing-up and food prep room. Open Easter-mid October. ✰✰✰✰ **BH&HPA. 108T. MC.** 🐕 🔲 ⅂

(6m). Sea Field Caravan Park, Newport, Hemsby, Great Yarmouth, Norfolk. *01493 730221.* Owner: P Bammant. Open March-October. **T. 310S.** 🔲 🛴

Seabreeze Caravan Park, Newport, Hemsby, Great Yarmouth, Norfolk. *01493 730869/730221.* Owner: T Bammant & Co. Off A11 and A12. Club. Open March-October. **288S.** 🛴

(1m). Seashore Holiday Park, North Denes, Great Yarmouth, Norfolk NR30 4HG. *01493 332634.* oewebmaster@bourne-leisure.co.uk. www.seashoreholidaypark.com. Owner: Bourne Leisure Ltd. 1 Park Lane, Hemel Hempstead, Hertfordshire HP2 4YL. From Gt Yarmouth A149 N towards Caister. R at 2nd set of traffic lights, SP to seafront and racecourse. Continue to sea and turn L. Seashore is on L. Next to racecourse, beach frontage. Fun pool. Adventure playground. Mini golf. On site shops and bakery. Children's club. Family entertainment. Sports and leisure programme, indoor soft play area. Racecourse 3mins from park. Shops 1m. Open April-October for hire caravans, March-November for owner-occupiers. ✰✰✰ **BH&HPA. NCC. 800S. 585H.** 🐕 ♿ 🛴 ⌀

(6m). Summerfields Holiday Park, Beach Road, Scratby, Great Yarmouth, Norfolk NR29 3NW. *01493 731419.* 6m from Great Yarmouth on A149-B1159. Free indoor pool and spa bath, sauna, solarium, show bar, cabaret club, bars, entertainment, eating area, takeaway, play area, amusement arcade, snooker and Busy Bee club.Open Easter-November. ✰✰✰ **BH&HPA. NCC. 65S. 50H.** 🐕 🛴

(4m). The Grange Touring Park, Ormesby St Margaret, Great Yarmouth, Norfolk NR29 3QC. *01493 730306/730023.* info@grangetouring.co.uk. www.grangetouring.co.uk. On B1159 N of Caister-on-Sea. Laundry. Licensed bar. Telephone for August bookings. Gas. 1m to beach and close to Norfolk Broads. Open March-October. ✰✰✰✰ **BH&HPA. 70T. MC.** 🐕 🔲

(3m). The Tower, Off Covent Garden Road, Ormesby Road, Caister-on-Sea, Great Yarmouth, Norfolk NR30 5QJ. *01493 728280.* Owner: Mr D Taylor. Off A149. Open March-October. **79S.** 🐕 🛴

(1m). Vauxhall Holiday Park, 2 Acle New Road, Great Yarmouth, Norfolk NR30 1TB. *01493 857231.* vauxhall.holidays@virgin.net. www.vauxhall-holiday-park.co.uk. Owner: Mr S G Biss. On A47 Norwich to Gt Yarmouth. Free entertainment. Heated indoor pool. Disco. Games room. Club. Adventure playground. Laundrette. Restaurant. Takeaways. Arcade. Supermarket. Multi-sport arena. Open May-September. ✰✰✰✰ **BH&HPA. 255T. 450H.** 🔲 ♿ 🛴

(12m). Waxham Sands Holiday Park, Warren Farm, Horsey, Great Yarmouth, Norfolk NR29 4EJ. *01692 598325.* Owner: CL Associates (Inc). On B1159 coast road between Sea Palling and Winterton. 12m up coast from Great Yarmouth, 22m from Cromer and 22m E of Norwich. Quiet, farm site bordering National Trust and marshland. Own beach. Showers. Open May 26-September 30. **200T. 30MC.** 🐕 ♿ 🛴

(4m). Wild Duck Holiday Park, Howards Common, Belton, Great Yarmouth, Norfolk NR31 9NE. *01493 781587.* oewebmaster@bourne-leisure.co.uk. www.wildduckholidaypark.com. Owner: Bourne Leisure Ltd. 1 Park Lane, Hemel Hempstead,

Please visit the Caravan Club website: www.caravanclub.co.uk

Hertfordshire HP2 4YL. A47 to Gt Yarmouth then A143 for Beccles. 2-3m turn R, SP Belton & Burgh Castle. Follow road to T-junction and turn left. Park is 200yd on right. Set in 98 acres of woodland. Heated indoor pool. Bar and cafe. New Jamboree club, visiting cabarets, games room, amusement arcade, take-away, tennis court. Children Tiger club, playground, crazy golf, bike hire, mini bowling. Golf nearby. Open March-November. ✰✰✰✰ BH&HPA. NCC. 100T. MC. 463S. 120H. ♈ ⚑ ♿ 🅿 ⚓

Harleston

(2m). Little Lakeland Caravan Park, Wortwell, Harleston, Norfolk IP20 0EL. 01986 788646. information@littlelakeland.co.uk. www.littlelakeland.co.uk. Owner: Jean & Peter Leatherbarrow. Turn off A143 (Diss to Bungay) at roundabout SP Wortwell. In village turn R 350yd past Bell PH. Quiet, family touring park with fishing lake and library. Modern toilet block. AA Award for Environment. Open March 15-October 31. ✰✰✰✰ BH&HPA. 40T. MC. 20S. 1H. ♈ 🅿 ♿ ⚓

(2m). Waveney Valley Lakes Caravan Park, Wortwell, Harleston, Norfolk IP20 0EJ. 01986 788676. enquiries. wvl@talk21.com. www.waveneyvalleylakes.com. Owner: Mike Davis. On A143 Diss to Bungay. Turn off into Wortwell village. Access road between two bungalows. Peaceful 60-acre site with 11 lakes. Shop and tackle shop on site. Fishing on site. Dogs allowed in privately owned caravans only. David Bellamy Gold Conservation Award. Golf 10m. Cinema, coast 20m. BH&HPA. 90S. ✿ ♈ ⚓

Holt

(5m). Friary Farm Caravan Park, Cley Road, Blakeney, Holt, Norfolk NR25 7NW. 01263 740393. friary.farm@virgin.net. www.friaryfarm.co.uk. Owner: Mr Hiles, Miss Manklow. Site entrance opposite Blakeney Church on A149. Park offers peace and quiet in north Norfolk countryside. Suitable for sailing, bird watching and walking. Under personal management of owner. Open March 20-October 31. ✰✰✰✰ BH&HPA. 192S. ♈

(3m). Kelling Heath Holiday Park, Weybourne, Holt, Norfolk NR25 7HW. 01263 588181. info@kellingheath.co.uk. www.kellingheath.co.uk. Owner: Blue Sky Leisure, Timewell Properties Ltd. From A148 turn N at site sign at Bodham. From A149 turn S at Weybourne Church. 250-acre estate of woodland and heathland. Nature trails and woodland walks. Health club. Bars and restaurants. Rose award. David Bellamy Gold Conservation Award. Open February 14-December 16. ✰✰✰✰✰ BH&HPA. NCC. 275T. 25MC. 427S. 36H. ♈ 🅿 ♿ ⚓

Hunstanton

Manor Park Holiday Village, Manor Road, Hunstanton, Norfolk PE36 5AZ. 01485 532300. www.manor-park.co.uk. Owner: Mr J Isherwood. On A149. Club. Swimming pool. Laundrette. Dogs allowed except in hire caravans. Local shops 0.5m. 9-hole golf course nearby. Open March 1-October 31. ✰✰✰✰ 64T. 850S. 66H. 🅿

Seagate Touring Caravan Park, South Beach, Hunstanton, Norfolk. 01485 32610. Owner: King's Lynn, W. Norfolk Borough Council. 165S.

(0.5m). Searles Leisure Resort, South Beach, Hunstanton, Norfolk PE36 5BB. 01485 534211. bookings@searles.co.uk. www.searles.co.uk. Owner: Searles Ltd. On B1161 off A149, 14m N of Kings Lynn. 200yd from Award beach. Indoor and outdoor pools. Air-conditioned club and health club. Tennis courts. Hire shop. Environmental award park. 9-hole golf course and driving range, fishing lake, hair and beauty salon. Children's soft play area. Colour brochure on request. Open mid March-mid November. ✰✰✰✰✰ BH&HPA. 150T. 25MC. 400S. 200H. ♈ 🅿 ♿ ⚓

Southend Caravan Park, Hunstanton, Norfolk PE36 5AR. 01485 533676. Owner: Mr M F & R Brook. 200yd from town in Southend Road. Open March 1-November 30. BH&HPA. 60S. ♈

(3m). Sunnymead Holiday Park, Holme-next-Sea, Hunstanton, Norfolk PE36 6LH. 01485 525381. Owner: Mr & Mrs T O'Callaghan. Off the A149. Rose Award Park and caravans. Open mid-March to end-October. ✰✰✰✰ BH&HPA. 14H. ♈ ♿

(3m). White Horse Inn, Holme-next-the-Sea, Hunstanton, Norfolk. 01485 525512. Owner: Mrs S Middleton. Located off the A149. Open March 20-October 31. 64S. ♈

King's Lynn

(10.5m). Diglea Caravan & Camping Park, Beach Road, Snettisham, King's Lynn, Norfolk PE31 7RA. 01485 541367. Owner: Mrs M Carter. Take A149 King's Lynn to Hunstanton road. After about 10.5m turn left at sign marked 'Snettisham Beach'. Site on left in 1.5m. Situated on the west Norfolk coast. Friendly, family-run park in a peaceful rural setting. 0.25m from beach. RSPB reserve close by. Facilities include showers and hair-dryer and shaver points. Washing-up facility, laundrette. Children's playground, clubhouse open lunch time and evenings. Open April 1-October 31. ✰✰✰ BH&HPA. 200T. MC. 150S. ♈ 🅿

Please mention Caravan Sites 2006 when replying to advertisers

(15m). **Heacham Beach Holiday Park, South Beach Road, Heacham, King's Lynn, Norfolk PE31 7BD.** *0871 664 9743.* heacham.beach@park-resorts.com. www.park-resorts.com. Owner: Park Resorts Ltd. 3rd Floor, Swan Court, Waterhouse Street, Hemel Hempstead, Herts, HP1 1FN. Off A149 from Kings Lynn to Hunstanton. Heacham first village after Snettisham. Turn L at sign for Heacham beach and fork L about 1m along this road. Indoor pool. Sports resorts programme court. Laundrette. On-site store. Free children's club. Tavern with family entertainment. Open April-October. ✰✰✰ **BH&HPA. NCC. 430S. 30H.** ⵌ

(2.5m). **King's Lynn Caravan & Camping Park, Parkside House, New Road, North Runcton, King's Lynn, Norfolk PE33 0QR.** *01553 840004.* klynn-campsite@hotmail.com. Owner: Paul & Clare Yallop. 1.5m from the A17, A10, A47, A149 main King's Lynn Hardwick roundabout, on the R of the A47 going towards Swaffham. Well situated for King's Lynn, inland market towns and the north Norfolk coast. Park is in 3.5 acres of pleasant parkland. Good local PHs, Tesco's 1.5m. 30 tent pitches. Clubs welcome. Fishing, golf course nearby. PO and shop 1m, doctor 2m. ✰✰✰ **BH&HPA. 5T. 5MC.** ✿ ⵌ ▣

Manor Park Touring Caravans, Manor Farm, Tattersett, King's Lynn, Norfolk PE31 8RS. *01485 529269.* Owner: Alistair Wagg. From King's Lynn A148 Fakenham (4m). 2m from East Rudham on A148 with PO, shops, butcher, PH. Doctors 5m to Fakenham or Massingham. Open March-October. ✰✰✰ **NCC. 32T.** ⵌ ▣ ♿

(9m). **Pentney Park Caravan & Camping Site, Gayton Road, Pentney, King's Lynn, Norfolk PE32 1HU.** *01760 337479.* holidays@pentney.demon.co.uk. www.pentney_park.co.uk. Owners: Bryan and Hilary Webster. On the A47 Swaffham to King's Lynn road. At junction with B1153. Indoor and outdoor heated swimming pools, games room, laundrette. Spar shop, cafe/bar. Play area, games room. Miniature railway. Fishing within 1m. Open all year except for four weeks from January 15. ✰✰✰✰ **BH&HPA. NCC. 200T. MC. 16S. 4H.** ⵌ ▣ ♿ ▟

(14m). **Pioneer Holiday Park, South Beach Road, Heacham, King's Lynn, Norfolk PE31 7BB.** *01485 570372.* Owner: Mrs T M Norris. From King's Lynn pick up A149, SP to Hunstanton, pick up sign to Heacham Beaches turn left into South Beach Road. Quiet, family-run park. Sites available. Open March-October. **BH&HPA. NCC. 298S.** ⵌ

(16m). **Rickels Caravan & Camping Park, Bircham Road, Stanhoe, King's Lynn, Norfolk PE31 8PU.** *01485 518671.* Owner: Heather Crown. From Kings Lynn A148 to Hillington L on to B1153, fork R on B1155 site on L 100yd over crossroads. Quiet, friendly, family-run site. Open April-October. ✰✰✰ **30T. MC.** ⵌ ▣

(12m). **Seashore Holiday Park, North Beach, Heacham, King's Lynn, Norfolk.** *01485 570565.* Owners: Palm Beach Holiday Parks. North Beach, Heacham, Kings Lynn, Norfolk. On A149 King's Lynn to Hunstanton. Drive through village followng North beach signs. Swimming pool. Laundrette. Shopping 0.5m. Golf course 4m. Open mid March-November 1. **BH&HPA. 106S.** ⵌ ✎

(7m). **Snettisham Caravan Park, Snettisham Beach, Snettisham, King's Lynn, Norfolk PE31 7RB.** *01485 542499/543973.* Owner: Melrose Stores Ltd. Situated 7m from King's Lynn on the A149, 6m from Hunstanton. Private beach. Club. Next to RSPB bird reserve and coastal park. Open March 25-October 25. **BH&HPA. 200S.** ⵌ ♿ ▟

(16m). **The Chequers Inn, Thornham, King's Lynn, Norfolk PE36 6LY.** *01485 512229.* Owner: Mr & Mrs P Newman. On A149 from King's Lynn and Cromer. **7T. 7MC.** ✿ ⵌ

Mundesley

(0.5m). **Kiln Cliffs Caravan Park, Cromer Road, Mundesley, Norfolk NR11 8DE.** *01263 720449.* Owner: Mr & Mrs J Malone. On B1159 Mundesley to Cromer. Peaceful, clifftop site with private access to sandy beach, no bar or clubhouse. Well behaved pets welcome. Discounts for off-peak bookings. Open March 15-November 17. **BH&HPA. 153S. 14H.** ⵌ ♿ ▟

(0.5m). **Sandy Gulls Cliff Top Touring Park, Cromer Road, Mundesley, Norfolk NR11 8DF.** *01263 720513.* Owner: Mr R Shreeve. On A148 Cromer to Mundesley coast road. Clifftop location overlooking sea within easy reach of Norfolk Broads National Park. Close to Sheringham, Cromer, Great Yarmouth and Norwich, also 3 golf courses and indoor bowls. Calor Gas. No teenaged children allowved. Open March-November. ✰✰✰ **BH&HPA. 30T. 30MC. 100S. 2H.** ⵌ ♿ ♿

North Walsham

(0.5m). **North Walsham Chalet and Caravan Park, Bacton Road, North Walsham, Norfolk NR28 0RA.** *01692 501070.* Owner: Mr S Moir & Mrs M Stokes. On B1150, opposite Blue Bell pub on Mundesley side of North Walsham. Heated swimming pool, clubhouse, country club and restaurant. Laundry room. Caravan sales. Open March 1-January 5. ✰✰✰ **BH&HPA. 106S.** ⵌ ♿

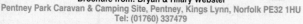

EAST ANGLIA

(1m). **Two MillsTouring Park, Yarmouth Road, North Walsham, Norfolk NR28 9NA.** *01692 405829.* enquiries@ twomills.co.uk. www.twomills.co.uk. Owner: Barbara & Ray Barnes. From N Walsham follow old Yarmouth road 1m SE past police station and hospital to park on L opposite Scarborough Hill hotel. Adults only. 2 dogs per pitch. Shops, doctors, PO etc within 1m. David Bellamy Gold Conservation Award. AA 4 pennants. Open March 1-January 3. ✰✰✰✰✰ **BH&HPA. 55T. MC.** ♪ 🖲 🔌

Norwich

(18m). **Applewood Camping and Caravan Park, The Grove, Banham, Norwich, Norfolk NR16 2HB.** *01953 887771.* info@banhamzoo.co.uk. www.banhamzoo.co.uk. Owner: Mr M Goymour. Between Attleborough and Diss. Choice of restaurants. Hairdressing. Craft courtyard and access to Banham Zoo. Clothes washing and drying. Bottled gas. Local PH and PO. Open March-October; open November and December for special events. ✰✰✰✰ **BH&HPA. 100T. MC.** ♪ 🖲 🔌 🧺

(0.5m). **Camping & Caravanning Club Site - Norwich, Martineau Lane, Norwich, Norfolk NR1 2HX.** *01603 620060/0870 243 3331.* www.campingandcaravanning club.co.uk. Owner: Camping & Caravanning Club. Greenfields House, Westwood Way, Coventry CV4 8JH. From A47, join the A146 towards city centre. L at lights to next lights, under Low Bridge to The Cock PH, turn L. Site 150yd on R. A 2.5-acre site overlooking beautiful open countryside with some shade. Within easy reach of the Norfolk Broads. Non-members welcome. All units accepted. 2mins to PH/restaurant. 5mins walk to local shops and bus into city every 20mins. Norwich city 30mins walk away. Fishing in season. Special deals available for families and backpackers. Open March-October. ✰✰✰ **50T. 50MC.** ♪ 🖲

(9m). **Haveringland Hall Park, Cawston, Norwich, Norfolk NR10 4PN.** *01603 871302.* info@haveringlandhall.co.uk. www.haveringlandhall.co.uk. Owner: Mr Hopkins. Take B1149 N from Norwich to Holt. 2m after Horsford, turn L SP Eastgate. At the Ratcatcher PH turn L for 800yd until park's lodge gates on your L. Follow concrete road for 800yd to reception on L. In 120-acre estate with woods and parkland with 12-acre fishing lake. In different areas of the estate are 2 permanent residential parks and a holiday park for tourers, tents and privately owned static caravans. Static Caravan Hire. New development of timber-clad holiday lodges for sale in arboretum area. Open mid March-end October. ✰✰✰ **BH&HPA. 20T. 6MC. 100S. 3H.** ♪ 🖲 🌀

GOLDEN BEACH HOLIDAY CENTRE
Sea Palling, Norwich, Norfolk
Tel: Hickling (01692) 598269 Fax: 598693

A lovely quiet park situated in a small unspoiled village just behind sand dunes which border miles of golden beaches with excellent sea fishing, therefore making it the ideal location for family holidays and weekends. The Norfolk Broads with its numerous boating, fishing and wildlife attractions are only 4 miles away. We accommodate 102 fully serviced static holiday caravans plus a touring caravan and tenting section. Our facilities include a children's play area, residents' lounge bar, restaurant, shop and laundrette.

**LUXURY SELF CATERING
HOLIDAY HOMES AVAILABLE FOR HIRE AND SALE**
Write or phone for free colour brochure

(4m). **Norfolk Showground Caravan Club Site, Long Lane, Bawburgh, Norwich, Norfolk NR9 3LX.** *01603 742708.* www.caravanclub.co.uk. Owner: The Caravan Club. East Grinstead House, East Grinstead, West Sussex RH19 1UA. See website for standard directions to site. Secluded site adjacent to extensive country parkland and within easy travelling distance of Norwich. Toilet blocks with privacy cubicles and laundry facilities. Motorhome service point. Golf and fishing nearby, dog walk on site. Non-members are welcome. Facilities for disabled. Open March-October. ✰✰✰ **NCC. 60T. MC.** ♪ 🖲 🔌

Pampas Lodge Holiday Park, The Street, Haddiscoe, Norwich, Norfolk NR14 6AA. *01502 677265.* pampas@glob-alnet.co.uk. Owner: CJC & VJ Shirley. Park is located 5m N of Beccles and 10m SW of Great Yarmouth on the A143.Suitable Broads holiday centre. Fishing and golf course nearby. Shops and PO 2m away. Doctor 5m. Open March-October. **BH&HPA. 54T. MC.** ♪ 🖲 🔌

(15m). **Reedham Ferry Touring Park, Reedham Ferry, Acle, Norwich, Norfolk NR13 3HA.** *01493 700429.* reed hamferry @aol.com. www.archerstouringpark.co.uk. Owner: Mr D Archer. Located off the A47 to Acle. Reedham is well-signposted from Acle, 7m S. Flat, landscaped site adjacent to a 17th-century pub. Modern toilet facilities. Tumble dryer. Barbecue. Fishing close by. Moorings and slipway for trailed boats. Open Easter-October. ✰✰✰ **10T. 10MC.** ♪ 🖲 🔌

(7m). **Swans Harbour, Barford Road, Marlingford, Norwich, Norfolk NR9 4BE.** *01603 759658.* info@swans harbour.co.uk. www.swansharbour.co.uk. Owner: Mr & Mrs Morter. Style House, Style Loke, Barford, Norwich NR9 4BE. Turn right off the B1108 (Norwich-Watton) in Barford, SP for Marlingford. After 350yd turn right at T-junction. Site on left hand side after 0.75m (immediately past river bridge). Fishing and golf close by. Shop 0.5m away. **NCC. 25T. MC.** ❀ ♪ 🖲 🔌

(20m). **The Dower House Touring Park, East Harling, Norwich, Norfolk NR16 2SE.** *01953 717314.* info@dower house.co.uk. www.dowerhouse.co.uk. Owner: D Bushell. From Thetford take the A1066 E for 5m, fork left at Camping and East Harling sign, site on left-hand side after 2m, in Thetford Forest. Family-run touring park set deep in forest. David Bellamy Gold Conservation Award. Open mid March-end September. ✰✰✰✰ **BH&HPA. 100T. 100MC.** ♪ 🖲 🔌 🧺

(24m). **Walcott Caravan & Chalet Park, Walcott-on-Sea, Coast Road, Norwich, Norfolk NR12 0AP.** *01692 650020.* park@triciamccarthy.com. Owner: Mrs P M McCarthy. Six miles from North Walsham and/or Stalham. Park is adjacent to a beach. Good beach fishing. Post Office and general store plus a mini supermarket, next to site. Wonderful seaviews. Nearest doctor is at Stalham. Open March 20-October 31. **27S.** ♪ 🧺

(7m). **Woodland View Mobile Home Park, Stratton Strawless Hall, Stratton Strawless, Norwich, Norfolk NR10 5LT.** *01603 754315.* Owner: P C Waller. A140. Past Norwich Airport for five miles, signposted Stratton Strawless. On right hand side of the main A140, turn into entrance by white hall and follow road to park office. On the main bus route, and within easy reach of coast, broads and all attractions of Norwich city. **5T.** ❀ ♪ 🖲

Sandringham

Camping & Caravanning Club Site - Sandringham, The Sandringham Estate, Double Lodges, Sandringham, Norfolk PE35 6EA. *01485 542555/0870 2433331.* www.campingandcaravanningclub.co.uk. Owner: Camping & Caravanning Club. Greenfields House, Westwood Way, Coventry CV4 8JH. From A148 turn L on to B1440 signed West Newton. Follow signs to site or take A149 turning L and follow signs to site. 7.5m from Kings Lynn. Site nestles among trees of the Royal Sandringham Estate. Site just a few miles from the beach. All units accepted. Non-members welcome. Sandringham House, grounds and museum are worth a visit. The historic port of Kings Lynn is within easy reach. The area has some of the most unspoilt country in the UK. Special deals available for families and backpackers. David Bellamy Gold Conservation Award. Open February-November. ☆☆☆☆☆ **275T. 275MC.** 🔭 🖗 🕹 🔋

(1.5m). The Sandringham Estate Caravan Club Site, Glucksburg Woods, Sandringham, Norfolk PE35 6EZ. *01553 631614.* www.caravanclub.co.uk. Owner: The Caravan Club. East Grinstead House, East Grinstead, West Sussex RH19 1UA. See website for standard directions to site. Re-developed to offer full facilities, while retaining its rural charm. Surrounded by 600-acre Sandringham Estate Country Park. Play area. Dog walk. Restricted use of barbecues. Advance booking essential bank holidays and July and August. Non-members admitted. Toilet blocks. Privacy cubicles. Hard-standings. Laundry facilities. Baby snd toddler washroom. Veg prep. Motorhome service point. Playground. Good area for walking. Shop 150yd from site within the estate. Open March-January. ☆☆☆☆☆ **NCC. 129T. MC.** 🔭 🖗 🕹

Sheringham

(0.75m). Beeston Regis Caravan and Camping Park, Cromer Road, West Runton, Cromer, Sheringham, Norfolk NR27 9NG. *01263 823614/0700 Beeston.* info@beestonregis.co.uk. www.beestonregis.co.uk. Owner: The Beeston Group. On A149 Cromer to Sheringham road, from Sheringham proceed to West Runton. The entrance is on the left-hand side after 0.75m. Caravan outfits must proceed over the railway line to site's main entrance. Open March 20-October 31. **219T. 30MC. 260S. 4H.** 🔭 🖗 🕹 🔋 🖉

Snaefell Caravan Site, Holway Road, Sheringham, Norfolk NR26 8HN. *01263 823198.* Owner: Mr A G & F P Sadler. Open April 1-October 31. **10T. MC. 140S. 12H.** 🔭

(3m). Weybourne Hall Holiday Park, Weybourne Holt, Sheringham, Norfolk. *01263 70255.* Owner: Peter, Sheila & Debbie Watson. On A149 Blakeley to Sheringham. Open March-October. **50S. 5H.** 🔭

(2m). Woodland Caravan Park, Holt Road, Upper Sheringham, Sheringham, Norfolk NR26 8TU. *01263 823802/824383.* Off A148. Quiet park situated in pleasant wooded surroundings. Full facilities. Chemical toilet emptying point. Indoor heated 25-metre swimming pool with gymnasium, saunas and steam rooms. Six-rink indoor bowling green. Open March-October. ☆☆☆☆ **BH&HPA. 225T. MC. 151S.** 🔭 🖗 🔋

Stalham

(4m). Golden Beach Holiday Centre, Beach Road, Sea Palling, Stalham, Norfolk NR12 0AL. *01692 598269.* Owner: Mr & Mrs D Waller. On B1159 Stalham to Sea Palling, turn left down beach road. Site is on left. Licensed bar and restaurant on site. PO 500yd, beach 200yd. Broads 4m. Norwich, Great Yarmouth or Cromer all within 15m. Bus service to Norwich. Open March-November. ☆☆☆ **BH&HPA. NCC. 37T. MC. 102S. 9H.** 🔭 🖗 🕹 🔋

Swaffham

(0.5m). Breckland Meadows Touring Park, Lynn Road, Swaffham, Norfolk PE37 7PT. *01760 721246.* info@breckland meadows.co.uk. www.brecklandmeadows.co.uk. Owner: Alan Edwards & Marianne Downes. Take Swaffam turn-off from the A47 between King's Lynn and Norwich. Small, friendly and very clean. 3-acre site about 0.5m W of Swaffham with walkway adjacent linking with Peddars Way. Central for touring Norfolk. Heated amenity block with free showers. Hard-standings available. 3 AA pennants. **BH&HPA. 45T. MC.** ✿ 🔭 🖗 🕹

Thetford

Brick Kiln Farm Caravan Park, Swaffham Road, Ashill, Thetford, Norfolk IP25 7BT. *01760 441300.* brick.kiln@ btclick.com. http://home.btclick.com/brick.kiln. Owner: Spaul's Caravans. 4m from both Watton and Swaffham. Set in 15 acres of farmland with large wooded area, suitable for walking. Suitable location for touring Norfolk, the coast and Thetford forest. Swimming pool, golf courses and fishing close by. ☆☆☆☆ **45T. MC.** ✿ 🔭 🖗 🕹 🔋

Lowe Caravan Park, Ashdale, Hills Road, Saham Hills, Thetford, Norfolk IP25 7EZ. *01953 881051.* Owner: Chris Lowe. 2.5m from Watton. Small friendly park mainly suited to the over-50s. Open all year except Christmas and New Year. ✰✰✰✰ **20T. 5MC. 4H.** ⍩ ▣

The Covert Caravan Club Site, High Ash, Hillborough, Thetford, Norfolk IP26 5BZ. *01842 878356.* Owner: The Caravan Club. East Grinstead House, East Grinstead, West Sussex RH19 1UA. See website for standard directions to site. Located 7.5m from Swaffham. Site is set in Forestry Commission woodland, and is a quiet, secluded site with pitching areas in little open glades, suitabel for the wildlife observer. Dog walk. Own sanitation required. Restricted use of barbecues. Advance booking essential for bank holidays. Non-members are welcome. No toilet block. Motorhome service point. Open March-October. **NCC. 104T. MC.** ⍩ ▣

(5m). Thorpe Woodland Caravan & Camping Site, Forestry Commission (Forest Holidays), Shadwell, Thetford, Norfolk IP24 2RX. *01842 751042.* fe.holidays@forestry.gsi.gov.uk. www.forestholidays.co.uk. Owner: Forestry Commission (Forest Holidays). 231 Corstorphine Road, Edinburgh EH12 7AT. Off the A1066 Thetford to Diss road. After 5m bear left to East Harling. The site is 0.25m on the left-hand side. Secluded site set in Thetford Forest Park and well located for visiting the Norfolk Broads. No toilet facilties. Brochure request line: 01313 340066. Open March-October. **BH&HPA. 138T. MC.** ⍩ ▣ ▟

(10m). Warren House Caravan Site, Brandon Road, Methwold, Thetford, Norfolk IP26 4RL. *01366 728238.* Owner: Mrs J Scarrott. Site is located 1m from Methwold on the B1112 road towards Brandon, 5m. Quiet site surrounded by forestry. Open March-October. **40T. MC.** ⍩

Trimingham

(1m). Trimingham House Caravan Park, Cromer Road, Trimingham, Norfolk NR11 8DX. *01263 720421.* Owner: M J Gardner. On the B1159. 6m from Cromer. Club. Laundrette. Heated pool. Indoor health suite. Children's pool. American hot tub. Live entertainment. Beach access. Open March 1-January 15. **164S. 16H.** ⍩ ▟

Wells-next-the-Sea

(0.5m). Orchard Caravan Park, Burnt Street, Wells-next-the-Sea, Norfolk NR23 1HN. *01328 710394.* orchardcaravans@aol.com. www.orchardcaravansnorfolk.ltd.uk. Owner: Orchard Caravans. Gt Eastern Way, Wells-next-the-Sea, Norfolk NR23 1LY. The Park is located just 5 mins from town centre. Open March 1-January 31. **BH&HPA. 50S.** ⍩

(0.75m). Pinewoods Holiday Park, Beach Road, Wells-next-the-Sea, Norfolk NR23 1DR. *01328 710439.* holiday@pinewoods.co.uk. www.pinewoods.co.uk. Owner: Pinewoods Partnership. Off the A149 and B1105 at Wells Quay. Good facilities on the north Norfolk coast beside a national nature reserve. Suitably placed to explore. Boating, pitch and putt, laundrette, and coffee shop/takeaway. 2 mins to safe, sandy beach. Cinema, golf courses 10m, shopping centre 30m. Open March 15-October 31; open March 15-January 2 for winterised homes. ✰✰✰✰ **BH&HPA. 150T. 541S. 28H.** ⍩ ▣ ▟

SUFFOLK

Beccles

(6m). Waveney River Centre, Staithe Road, Burgh St Peter, Beccles, Suffolk NR34 0BT. *01502 677343.* info@waveneyrivercentre.co.uk. www.waveneyrivercentre.co.uk. Manager: Mr James Knight. Follow brown signs from A143 at Haddiscoe. Turn down Wiggs Road. After 2.3m turn L into Burgh Road, site is another 2m. (Site is 4m from A143). Indoor leisure centre with swimming pool and spa, restaurant and PH. Adjacent to river Waveney, fishing during open season, rowing boats and day boats for hire. Play area, well-stocked shop. Launderette. Golf course 6m. Open March-November. ✰✰✰✰ **BH&HPA. 18T. 14MC. 41S. 13H.** ▣ ▟

Brandon

(3m). Poppyfields Caravan Park, Thetford Road, Santon Downham, Brandon, Suffolk IP27 0TU. *01842 815053.* Owner: Pratt Developments Unlimited. Holdens Caravan Park, Bracklesham Lane, Bracklesham, Chichester, West Sussex PO20 8JG. Follow A11 to Thetford, follow Thetford Ring Road, turn L along B1107 to Brandon. Park entrance is on R before turning to Santon Downham. Forest park on the Norfolk/Suffolk border. Peaceful, secluded setting where deer roam. Telephone for free brochure 01243 670207. Demonstration caravans available for inspection at the park. Horse racing, golf, country pursuits and mountain bike trails all nearby. Ancient cathedral town of Bury St Edmunds and Norfolk Broads within easy reach. Open March-December. **100S.** ⍩

Bungay

(0.3m). Outney Meadow Caravan Park, Bungay, Suffolk NR35 1HG. *01986 892338.* www.outneymeadow.co.uk. Owner: Mr A Hancy. Off A143 between Bungay golf course and river Waveney. Canoe trail. Bike hire, fishing and golf. Open March-October. ✰✰✰ **BH&HPA. 45T. MC.** ⍩ ▣

Bury St Edmunds

(1m). Round Plantation Caravan Club Site, Brandon Road, Mildenhall, Bury St Edmunds, Suffolk IP28 7JE. *01638 713089.* www.caravanclub.co.uk. Owner: The Caravan Club. East Grinstead House, East Grinstead, West Sussex RH19 1UA. See website for standard directions to site. Pleasant, landscaped site in woodland setting. which attracts all kinds of birds. Own sanitation required. Good for walking, dog walk on site. Peaceful off-peak. Non-members welcome. Open March-September. **NCC. 100T. MC.** ⍩ ▣

(4m). The Dell Caravan & Camping Park. Beyton Road, Thurston, Bury St Edmunds, Suffolk IP31 3RB. *01359 270121.* thedellcaravanpark@btinternet.com. Owner: Mr & Mrs Derek Webber. Follow A14E from Bury St Edmunds to Thurston (SP). Midway between Cambridge and Ipswich. 1hr from coast. Family-run site with facilities for disabled people and children. Suitable base for touring East Anglia. Quiet friendly site, with children's play area and new heated toilet block. Facilities in Bury St Edmunds (4m). Good PH and restaurants in village. AA 4 pennants. ✰✰✰✰ **BH&HPA. 100T. MC. 2H.** ❖ ⍩ ▣ ⛨ ▟

Eye

(5m). Honeypot Camp & Caravan Park, Wortham, Eye, Suffolk IP22 1PW. *01379 783312.* honeypotcamping@talk21.com. www.honeypotcamping.co.uk. Owner: C M P Smith. Off A143. Quiet, rural site, established 1970. Well grassed and free draining. Under personal supervision of the owner for over 30 years. Showers, adventure playground. Bressingham steam museum 1m. Landscaped country park with lakeside pitches with fishing on site. Open Mayday weekend-September 22. **35T. MC.** 🛏 🔌 🦮

Felixstowe

(1m). Felixstowe Beach Holiday Village, Walton Avenue, Felixstowe, Suffolk IP11 2HA. *01394 283393.* info@cinqueportsleisure.com. www.cinqueportsleisure.com. Owners: Cinque Ports Leisure Ltd. Coghurst Hall Holiday Village, Ivyhouse Lane, Ore, Hastings, East Sussex TN35 4NP. Off A14. Felixstowe is 200yd down from 2nd roundabout, SP. Indoor pool, children's facilities. Golf, birdwatching, fishing, walking. Open March 1-January 14. **BH&HPA. NCC. 310S. 40H.** 🛏 🦮 🦮

(1m). Languard Caravan Site, Manor Terrace, Felixstowe, Suffolk IP11 2EL. *01394 279850.* Owner: Mr D P Bewers. Off A14 Ipswich to Felixstowe. Open April 1-October 31. **BH&HPA. 32S.** 🛏

(1m). Peewit Caravans Ltd, Walton Avenue, Felixstowe, Suffolk IP11 2HB. *01394 284511.* peewitpark@aol.com. www.peewitcaravanpark.co.uk. Owner: R M Smith. A14 to Felixstowe Port roundabout. Entrance to park on L, 100yd along Walton Avenue towards Town Centre. Laundry, children's play area, bowls green. Boules/petanque. Shops nearby. Town centre 1m, seafront 900yd. Open Easter (or April 1)-October 31. ✰✰✰✰ **BH&HPA. 60T. MC. 210S. 1H.** 🛏 🔌 ♿

(1m). Suffolk Sands Holiday Park, Carr Road, Felixstowe, Suffolk IP11 2TS. *01394 273434.* info@cinqueportsleisure.com. www.cinqueportsleisure.com. Owner: Cinque Ports Leisure Ltd. Coghurst Hall Holiday Village, Ivyhouse Lane, Ore, Hastings, East Sussex TN35 4NP. Off A14, just S of Felixstowe. On the seafront. Family entertainment. Licensed club. Laundrette. Dogs charged for. Open Easter-October 31. **BH&HPA. NCC. 50T. 49MC. 334S.** 🛏 🔌 ♿ 🦮

Hadleigh

(4m). Polstead Caravan & Camping Park, Holt Road, Polstead Heath, Hadleigh, Suffolk CO6 5BZ. *01787 211969.* jim-morton@tesco.net. www.polsteadtouring.co.uk. Owner: C & J Walker. Between Boxford and Hadleigh on A1071, opposite 'The Brewers Arms' Inn. Set in 3.5 acres of level landscaped grounds. Adults only. Hard-standings, dog walk area. Suitable base for touring Constable country. Golf and fishing nearby. ✰✰✰✰ **BH&HPA. 30T. MC.** ✿ 🛏 🔌 ♿ 🦮

Ipswich

(3m). Low House Touring Caravan Centre, Bucklesham Road, Foxhall, Ipswich, Suffolk IP10 0AU. *01473 659437.* low.house@btopenworld.com. www.travelengland.org.uk. Owner: Mr J E Booth. Turn off A14 Ipswich ring road S via slip road on to A1156 go over bridge 2nd right and site is on left, SP. 3.5 acres of lawns and trees. Between Felixstowe and Ipswich. Fully equipped heated shower block. Pets corner, play area and Calor Gas sales. Mobile shop Thursday mornings. ✰✰✰ **30T. MC.** ✿ 🛏 🔌

(4m). Orwell Meadows Leisure Park, Priory Lane, Nacton, Ipswich, Suffolk IP10 0JS. *01473 726666.* recept@orwellmeadows.co.uk. Owner: Mr & Mrs D Miles. 1m from A14 Ipswich bypass follow sign for Ransomes Europark and Orwell Country Park. Showers. Swimming pool. Clubhouse. Family-run site adjacent to country park. Open March 1-January 16. ✰✰✰✰ **BH&HPA. 80T. MC. 6S. 8H.** 🛏 🔌 ♿ 🦮

(4m). Priory Park, Ipswich, Suffolk IP10 0JT. *01473 727393.* enquiries@priory-park.com. www.priory-park.com. Owner: Priory Park Ltd. Leave A14 Ipswich southern bypass at Nacton interchange. Follow signs towards Ipswich town centre. After 300yd turn L and follow road into Priory Park. Set in 100 acres of landscaped parkland with panoramic estuary views. 9-hole golf course, tennis courts, heated outdoor swimming pool, bar and restaurant. Doctor, dentist, hospital, shops 2m. Sainsbury's 1.5m. **BH&HPA. 120T. MC. 160S.** ✿ 🛏 🔌 🖋

(4.5m). The Oaks Caravan Park, Chapel Road, Bucklesham, Ipswich, Suffolk IP10 0BJ. *01394 448837.* oakscaravanpark@aol.com. www.oakscaravanpark.co.uk. Owner: Lee Brown. A14 E towards Felixstowe exit left, SP Bucklesham/Brightwell, continue for about 1m, turn right to Kirton, site is on the right-hand side. Over-18s only. Very quiet in countryside. Facilities include barbecues, quoits, boules, hot and cold washing-up sinks. Patio area, local fishing lake, pay and display golf, cycle hire. Restaurants and PHs nearby. Open April-October. ☆☆☆☆ **100T. MC.** 🐕 🔌

(5m). Woolverstone Marina, Woolverstone, Ipswich, Suffolk IP9 1AS. *01473 780206/354.* Owner: Marina Developments Ltd. Off B1456. Rural site in parkland on the banks of river Orwell. Restaurant and club. Chandlery and provisions. Laundrette. Open April 1-October 31. **2T. MC. 28S.** 🐕 🌊

Leiston

(2m). Cliff House Caravan Park, Sizewell, Leiston, Suffolk IP16 4TU. *01728 830724.* Owner: G E Gooderham. Bar. Restaurant. Games room. Laundrette. Open March 1-November 30. **60T. MC. 62S.** 🐕 🔌 🌊

Lowestoft

(2m). Azure Seas Caravan Park, The Street, Corton, Lowestoft, Suffolk NR32 5HN. *01502 731403.* infoazure seas@aol.com. Owners: Airstream Leisure Ltd. Off the A12 two miles north of Lowestoft on to Corton Long Lane, left then immediately right. Close to Pleasurewood Hills American theme park. Adjoining beach. Gas. Shops near. Booking advisable July and August. Open March-October. **50T. 50MC. 70H.** 🐕 🔌 ♿

(2m). Beach Farm Residential & Holiday Park, Arbor Lane, Pakefield, Lowestoft, Suffolk NR33 7BD. *01502 572794.* beachfarmpark@aol.com. www.beachfarmpark.co.uk. Owner: Mr G Westgate. On the A12 Kessingland to Yarmouth road. Off Pakefield roundabout (Water Tower). Few minutes' walk from sea. Licensed clubroom. Laundry. Swimming pool. 5 mins from large supermarket. Peaceful, sheltered site. Seasonal entertainment, takeaway food. Open March-October. ☆☆☆ **BH&HPA. 6T. MC. 32S. 10H.** 🐕 🔌 ♿

(1.5m). Broad View Caravans, Marsh Road, Oulton Broad, Lowestoft, Suffolk NR33 9JY. *01502 565587.* Owner: P C & P Goodwin. On the edge of The Broads, withabout 40 moorings. Fishing available. Open April 1-October 31. **15T. MC. 46S. 5H.** 🐕 🔌 🌊

(2m). Broadland Sands Holiday Park, Coast Road, Corton, Lowestoft, Suffolk NR32 5LG. *01502 730939.* www.broad landsands.co.uk. Owner: Ladycroft Ltd. Central Administration Office, Lakeside Holiday Park, Westfield Road, Burnham on Sea, Somerset TA8 2AE. 46 level acres. Heated pool with 45ft flume. Children's pool. Large, walled sun terrace. Refurbished family club complex with live entertainment. Tennis. Playground. Pitch and putt etc. Takeaway. Restaurant. Conservatory, sports bar with TV. Arcade. Private beach access. Open March 1-October 31. ☆☆☆☆ **386S. 65H.** ♿ 🌊

(4m). Camping & Caravanning Club Site - Kessingland, Suffolk Wildlife Park, Whites Lane, Kessingland, Lowestoft, Suffolk NR33 7TF. *01502 742040/0870 2433331.* www.campingandcaravanning club.co.uk. Owner: Camping & Caravanning Club. Greenfields House, Westwood Way, Coventry CV4 8JH. Follow Wildlife Park signs off the A12 from Lowestoft towards London. After leaving A12 at roundabout, turn R to site entrance. Adjacent to Suffolk Wildlife Park and within easy reach of east coast resorts. All units accepted. Non-members welcome. Great Yarmouth and Lowestoft are close by. Special deals available for families and backpackers. Open March-October. ☆☆☆☆ **90T. 90MC.** 🐕 🔌 ♿

(2m). Carlton Manor, Chapel Road, Carlton Colville, Lowestoft, Suffolk NR33 8BL. *01502 566511.* Owner: The Braithwaite Family. Situated on the A146. Facilities include restaurant, bar, disco, and playground. Open April-October. **80T. 10MC.** 🐕 🔌

(3.5m). Chestnut Farm Caravan Site, Gisleham, Lowestoft, Suffolk NR33 8EE. *01502 740227.* Owner: Mr N D Collen. West off the A12 at southern roundabout on to Kessingland bypass, opposite Suffolk Wildlife Park, SP Rushmere, Mutford and Gisleham, then second turning on left, then 1st drive on left. AA 2 pennants. Open Easter-October. **NCC. 20T. 20MC.** 🐕 🔌

(4m). Heathland Beach Caravan Park, London Road, Kessingland, Lowestoft, Suffolk NR33 7PJ. *01502 740337.* heathlandbeach@btinternet.co. www.heathlandbeach.co.uk. Owner: Reader Family. Park is located on the A12. Facilities include three heated outdoor pools. Tennis. Play area for children. Private beach access. Bar. Fishing available. Open April 1-October 31. ☆☆☆☆☆ **BH&HPA. 63T. MC. 180S. 6H.** 🐕 🔌 ♿ 🌊

Please mention Caravan Sites 2006 when replying to advertisers

(4m). Kessingland Beach Holiday Park, Kessingland Beach, Lowestoft, Suffolk NR33 7RN. *0871 6649749.* kessingland.beach@park-resorts.com. www.park-resorts.com. Owner: Park Resorts Ltd. 3rd Floor, Swan Court, Waterhouse Street, Hemel Hempstead, Herts HP1 1FN. Kessingland is on A12 Ipswich to Lowestoft Road. About 4m S of Lowestoft, take Kessingland beach exit from roundabout near wildlife park on to Whites Lane. Follow road for about 1.5m to the beach. Park is 400yd further on. Indoor and outdoor heated pools. Laundrette. Tennis courts. Free children's club. Free evening entertainment for all the family. Amusements. Takeaway and restaurant. Open Easter-October. ☆☆☆ **BH&HPA. NCC. 90T. MC. 368S. 97H.** ⊮ ⊡ ⊾

North Denes Caravan Park, Lowestoft, Suffolk NR32 1WX. *01502 573197.* Owner: Waveney District Council. Off A12. Inquiries to the manager. No booking necessary. Open April 1-October 15. **500T. MC. 300S. 30H.** ⊮ ⊾ ⊡

(1.5m). Pakefield Caravan Park, Arbor Lane, Lowestoft, Suffolk NR33 7BQ. *01502 561136.* Owner: Normanhurst Enterprises Ltd. Quiet, select site situated on a cliff with a family clubhouse, heated outdoor pool, shop, laundry and play area. Open March 1-November 30. ☆☆☆ **BH&HPA. 372S. 21H.** ⊮ ⊾

(5m). White House Beach Caravan Club Site, Kessingland, Lowestoft, Suffolk NR33 7RW. *01502 740278.* www.caravanclub.co.uk. Owner: The Caravan Club. East Grinstead House, East Grinstead, West Sussex RH19 1UA. See website for standard directions to site. Members only. Adjacent to beach and well located for touring the Norfolk Broads. Dog walk. No awnings on seafront pitches. Shop in village. Toilet blocks. Privacy cubicles. Laundry facilities. Veg Prep. Motorhome service point. Gas. Playframe. Water sports. Suitable for families. Open March-October. **NCC. 115T. MC.** ⊮ ⊡ ⊾

(3m). White House Farm Caravan Site, Gisleham, Lowestoft, Suffolk NR33 8DX. *01502 740248.* Owner: Mr B G Collen. From London-1st exit off roundabout at Kessingland, signposted Gisleham, follow road bearing right at junction, site 200yd on right. From Lowestoft, exit to Gisleham at 'Safeways' roundabout 1.5m left at church, site 300yd on left. Calor Gas. Farm walks, play area, fishing close by. Shops, PO 0.75m. Open April 1-October 31. **40T. 10MC.** ⊮ ⊡

(2m). Wy-wurry Caravan Park, Bakers Score, The Street, Corton, Lowestoft, Suffolk NR32 5HY. *01502 730427.* Owner: Mr R G Coleman. Off A12 Lowestoft to Yarmouth. Adults-only park. Open April 1-January 6. **2S. 8H.** ⊮ ⊾

Nayland

(6m). Rushbanks Farm, Wiston, Nayland, Suffolk CO6 4NA. *01206 262350/01787 375691.* Owner: Mr G F Bates. Rushbanks Farm, Bures Road, Colchester, Essex. 2m off A134 of Nayland and 7m from Colchester. Unspoilt riverside site on north bank of river Stour suitable for fishing and boating (no engines). Open April-October. **10T. MC.** ⊮

Saxmundham

(0.5m). Carlton Park Caravan Site, Saxmundham, Suffolk IP17 1AT. *01728 604413.* Owner: Saxmundham & District Sports & Recreational Club. On B1121, signed in both directions from the A12. Showers/toilets on site. 0.5 m to shops, supermarket, doctors and PO. Open April 1-October 31. **75T.** ⊮ ⊡

Cliff House Holiday Park, Minsmere Road, Dunwich, Saxmundham, Suffolk IP17 3DQ. *01728 648282.* info@cliff householidays.co.uk. www.cliffhouseholidays.co.uk. Owner: Beeston Group. From A12 at Yoxford turn off to Westleton. Turning left at T-junction. Turn right to Dunwich Heath and after 1.5m turn right again. Park is 0.75m on the left. 6m from Southwold. Country house in 30-acres of woodland, beach frontage between Southwold, 8m, and Aldeburgh, adjoining National Trust and RSPB. Free house bar and informal restaurant. Shower block. Games room and playground. Open March 1-October 31. ☆☆☆☆ **BH&HPA. 87T. 87MC. 93S.** ⊮ ⊡ ⊾ ⊾

(6m). Haw-Wood Farm Caravan Park, Haw -Wood Farm, Darsham, Saxmundham, Suffolk IP17 3QT. *01986 784248.* Owner: Mr A Blois. Off A12. Turn right off A12 1.5m N of Darsham level crossing at Little Chef. Park 0.5m on R. The perfect site for discovering the Suffolk coast and countryside. Quiet site with showers and play area. Managers: Tony & Mavis Wiggins. Fishing and golf nearby. 3m to nearest shop. Little Chef 0.5m, nearest PH about 1.5m. Darsham station 2m. Open April 1-October 31. **BH&HPA. 100T. MC. 55S.** ⊮ ⊡

(2m). Marsh Farm, Sternfield, Saxmundham, Suffolk IP17 1HW. *01728 602168.* Owner: Mrs M Bloomfield. From A12 after Farnham take 1st R, SP Aldeburgh A1094. In 1.5m turn L sp Sternfield proceed 1m then follow farm signs. 16-acre site in tranquil rural setting. Toilet and showers block, chemical toilet emptying point. Coarse fishing lakes adjoining. Close to Snape Maltings and Aldeburgh. **45T. MC.** ⊕ ⊮ ⊡ ⊾

(1m). Whitearch Touring Caravan Park, Main Road, Benhall, Saxmundham, Suffolk IP17 1NA. *01728 604646.* Owner: Mr & Mrs Rowe. Rosebank, Curlew Green, Kelsale, Saxmundham, Suffolk IP17 2RA. J A12 and B1121. Showers. Play area. One-acre coarse fishing lake. Tennis court. 40 pitches electric hook-ups, TV points. Laundry room. Open April-October. ✰✰✰ **40T. MC.** 🛱 🕿 🕭 🕭

Shotley

Shotley Caravan Park, Gate Farm Road, Shotley, Suffolk IP9 1QH. *01473 787421.* phammond3@ntlworld.com. Owner: Mrs J A Hammond. 49 Cuckfield Avenue, Ipswich, Suffolk IP3 8SA. A45 to Ipswich, take B1456 to Shotley through village of Shotley Gate Farm road on left. 9-acre site overlooking the river Orwell with walks along the river. Shop and PO in village, 7mins walk. Rallies welcome. Suitable site for the over-50s, 9-hole putting green, fishing electric hook-up points. Open March 1-October 31. **30T. 10MC.** 🛱 🕿

Southwold

(1m). Harbour Caravan Park, Ferry Road, Southwold, Suffolk IP18 6ND. *01502 722486.* Owner: Waveney District Council. A12 Lowestoft Road take A1095 to Southwold follow signposts to harbour, park is on the right at the end of Ferry Road. Open April 1-October 31. **200T. 200S.** 🛱 🕭

Stowmarket

(2m). Orchard View Caravan Park, Stowupland Service Station, Thorney Green, Stowupland, Stowmarket, Suffolk IP14 4BJ. *01449 612326.* Owner: Mr I D & B G Leeks. Driftway, Saxham Street, Stowupland, Stowmarket, Suffolk. 1m off A14 on A1120 at rear of service station. Quiet, level site, good touring area. Showers. Shop with fresh milk and groceries open 14 hours a day (7 days a week). Camping & Caravanning Club listed. Open April 1-September 30. **8T. MC.** 🕿 🕭

Sudbury

(2m). Willowmere, Bures Road, Little Cornard, Sudbury, Suffolk CO10 0NN. *01787 375559.* Owner: Mrs A Wilson. Off B1508. 1m out of Sudbury. Fishing on site. Golf, horse-riding 2m. Open Easter-October. ✰✰✰ **BH&HPA. 36T. MC.** 🛱 🕿 🕭

Theberton

(1m). Cakes & Ale Caravan Park, Theberton, Suffolk IP16 4TE. *01728 831655.* Owner: Mr Peter Little. Leave A12 turn on to B1121 to Saxmundham. Turn E on to B1119 towards Leiston. After 3m turn N to Theberton and follow camping park signs. 2m W of Minsmere bird sanctuary. Convenient Aldeburgh, Dunwich, Southwold. Quiet, well-maintained grounds and facilities. Most sites hard-standing superpitches. Laundry. Club. Tennis courts. Play area. Recreation area with golf driving range and practice nets. AA 3 pennants. Open Easter-October 31. **50T. 50MC. 200S. 3H.** 🛱 🕿 🕭

Woodbridge

(6m). Forest Camping, in Rendlesham Forest Centre, Tangham Campsite, Butley, Woodbridge, Suffolk IP12 3NF. *01394 450707.* admin@forestcamping.co.uk. www.forestcamping.co.uk. Owner: Mrs C M Lummis. Off B1084 between Woodbridge and Orford. Follow Rendlesham Forest Centre tourist brown signs. Shower block. Spacious site in centre of Forestry Commission forest. Riding cycle trail. Miles of walks in the forest. Space for children to play. Open April 1-October 31. ✰✰✰ **BH&HPA. 90T. MC.** 🛱 🕿 🕭 🕭

(4m). Moon and Sixpence, Newbourn Road, Waldringfield, Woodbridge, Suffolk IP12 4PP. *01473 736650.* moonsix@dircon.co.uk. www.moonsix.dircon.co.uk. Turn off Ipswich eastern bypass A12 taking minor road towards Waldringfield. Park is SP. AA 5 pennants. Bathrooms, lounge bar and restaurant. 2-acre deep water lake with private fishing from mid September to mid October; sandy beach. Adventure play area. 3 hard tennis courts, volley and basket ball, petanque, golf practice. Quietness essential from 9pm to 8am. 18-hole golf 0.5m. Sailing, water sports 2m. Indoor pool 4m. Open March 1-January 15; open April 1-October 31 for smaller park. **90T. 90MC. 250S.** 🛱 🕿 🕭

(6m). St Margarets House, Shottisham, Woodbridge, Suffolk IP12 3HD. *01394 411247.* ken.norton@virgin.net. Owner: Mr K Norton. Off A12 to Bawdsey B1083. Left at Shottisham, T-junction. Site on left 100m past Sorrel Horse Inn. Grassy, well drained, flat, sheltered and very quiet site. In a designated area of outstanding natural beauty, 2m from river Deben and 3.5m from the sea. Good walking, cycling country with fishing, boating, swimming pool, tennis, bowling, golf and horse riding within 5m. Booking advisable. Open April-October. **25T. 10MC.** 🛱 🕿

(7m). The Sandlings Centre, Lodge Road, Hollesley, Woodbridge, Suffolk IP12 3RR. *01394 411422.* mja@sandlings.co.uk. www.sandlings.co.uk. Owner: Mr M J & W A Adams. Birch House, Lodge Road, Hollesley, Woodbridge, Suffolk. B1083 to Shottisham village. Turn L at T junction, 1.5m on L. All mains services. Golf, sailing, fishing nearby. Open March 1-January 15. **BH&HPA. 59S.** 🛱

Please mention Caravan Sites 2006 when replying to advertisers

GLOUCESTERSHIRE

Bourton-on-the-Water
(2.5m). Folly Farm, Notgrove, Bourton-on-the-Water, Gloucestershire GL54 3BY. *01451 820285.* j.kenwright@virgin.net. www.cotswoldcamping.net. Owner: S A Kenwright. 2.5m from Bourton on the Water on the A436. Suitable for walkers and cyclists. Site is in an Area of Outstanding Natural Beauty and is deliberately basic with its facilities – i.e. no floodlights, playgrounds, shops but there are showers, toilets, chemical toilet emptying points. Situated close to Stow-on-the-Wold. Open March-October. **20T. MC.** ⚑ 🚻 ♿

(4.5m). Notgrove Caravan Club Site, Cheltenham Road, Bourton-on-the-Water, Gloucestershire GL54 3BU. *01451 850249.* www.caravanclub.co.uk. Owner: The Caravan Club. East Grinstead House, London Road, East Grinstead, West Sussex RH19 1UA. See website for standard directions to site. Caravan Club members only. Site high up in the Cotswolds surrounded by open countryside and superb views. Chemical toilet emptying point. No toilet block. Motorhome service point. Some hardstandings, gas dog walk on site, storage pitches. Peaceful off peak. Open March-October. **NCC. 72T. MC.** ⚑ 🚻

Cheltenham
(3m). Cheltenham Parks, Briarfields, Gloucester Road, Cheltenham, Gloucestershire GL51 0SX. *01242 235324.* carol.carline@haulfryn.co.uk. www.haulfryn.co.uk. Owner: Haulfryn Group. Willows Riverside Park, Maidenhead Road, Windsor Berkshire SL4 5TR. From the M5 J11, follow the A40 towards Cheltenham for about 1m, taking first exit off the roundabout into Gloucester Road, B4063 and Briarfields will be found on the left-hand side. New site, 6 acres of level, grassy, landscaped grounds. Suitable base for touring the Cotswolds. **BH&HPA. NCC. 72T. MC.** ✿ ⚑ 🚻 ♿

(1.25m). Cheltenham Racecourse Caravan Club Site, Prestbury Park, Cheltenham, Gloucestershire GL50 4SH. *01242 523102.* www.caravanclub.co.uk. Owner: The Caravan Club. East Grinstead House, London Road, East Grinstead, West Sussex RH19 1UA. See website for standard directions to site. A sophisticated location set on the edge of Cheltenham with panoramic views of the Cleeve Hills. Dog walk. Non-members welcome. Toilet block. Laundry facilities. Vegetable preparation area. Motorhome service point. Open April-October. **NCC. 69T. MC.** ⚑ 🚻

(3.5m). Oxbutts Park, Off Station Road, Woodmancote, Cheltenham, Gloucestershire GL52 4HN. *01242 674372.* Owner: A S Loveridge. Park in located in countryside within walking distance of shops. **80T.** ⚑ 🚻 ♿ 🛒

(2m). Stansby Park, The Reddings, Cheltenham, Gloucestershire GL51 6RS. *01242 235324.* briarfields@haulfryn.co.uk. www.haulfryn.co.uk. Owner: Haulfryn Group Ltd. Willows Riverside Park, Maidenhead Road, Windsor Berkshire SL4 5TR. From M5 J11 follow the A40 to Cheltenham, at first roundabout turn right and follow signs to park. Limited facilities for disabled people. Open January 30-December 31. **BH&HPA. NCC. 30T. MC.** ✿ ⚑ 🚻 ♿ ∅

Cirencester
(1m). Cirencester Park Caravan Club Site, Stroud Road, Cirencester, Gloucestershire GL7 1UT. *01285 651546.* www.thecaravanclub.co.uk. Owner: The Caravan Club. East Grinstead House, East Grinstead, West Sussex RH19 1UA. See website for standard directions to site. Caravan Club members only. Set in l grade 1 listed parkland, and forming part of the Bathurst Estate, this site is peaceful, level, with many mature trees and within walking distance of Cirencester. Toilet blocks, laundry facilities, baby and toddler washroom and motorhome service point. Playground, boules pitch and dog walk on site. Fishing, golf, watersports and NCN cycle route nearby. Open March-January. **NCC. 220T. MC.** ⚑ 🚻 ♿

Ermin Farm, Preston, Cirencester, Gloucestershire. *01285 860270.* Owner: Mr F Glass. **25T. 6MC. 2H.** ⚑

(4m). Hoburne Cotswold, Broadway Lane, South Cerney, Cirencester, Gloucestershire GL7 5UQ. *01285 860216.* enquiries@hoburne.com. www.hoburne.com. Owner: Hoburne Ltd. 261 Lymington Road, Highcliffe, Christchurch, Dorset BH23 5EE. Clearly SP from A419 Cirencester road. 21 chalets and 41 lodges. Licensed club and seasonal entertainment. Outdoor pool and new indoor leisure pool. New family-style restaurant. Fishing. Tennis. Laundrette. Adventure playground. Themed pub style bar with mini ten-pin bowling. Open end February-October. ✰✰✰✰ **BH&HPA. NCC. 302T. MC. 218S. 40H.** 🚻 ♿ 🛒

(2m). Mayfield Park, Cheltenham Road, Perrotts Brook, Cirencester, Gloucestershire GL7 7BH. *01285 831301.* mayfield-park@cirencester.fsbusiness.co.uk. www.mayfieldpark.co.uk. Owners: Jan & Adrian Yates & June & Peter Rathbone. On A435, 2m from Cirencester and 13m Cheltenham. Leave new bypass at Burford Road junction. Turn towards Cirencester and follow brown camping and caravan signs. A mixture of grass and hard-standing pitches. Small shop with off-sales and a selection of takeaway meals. Chemical toilet emptyingl point. Modern amenity block with free showers. Laundry room, tumble and spin dryers. Calor Gas and Campingaz stocked. New gravel area for winter use. ✰✰✰✰ **BH&HPA. 36T. MC. 2H.** ✿ ⚑ 🚻 🛒

Coleford
(1.5m). Eastville Caravan Park, Coopers Road, Christchurch, Coleford, Gloucestershire GL16 7AP. *01594 834956.* Owner: Mrs L Taylor & Mr I Taylor. From Ross-on-Wye follow the B4234 to the village of Christchurch turn left into Coopers Road, park on left-hand side. From Gloucester follow the B4136 to Five Acres crossroad turn right to Berry Hill, just past shops on right turn into Belmont Road, follow this on to Coopers Road, park on left. Situated in the Forest of Dean. Free seasonal swimming pool. Dogs allowed with permission. **BH&HPA. 8H.** ✿ 🛒

(2m). Forest of Dean Forestry Commission Sites, Christchurch, Bracelands Drive, Coleford, Gloucestershire GL16 7NN. *0131 314 6505.* fe.holidays@forestry.gsi.gov.uk. www.forestholidays.co.uk. Owner: Forestry Commission (Forest Holidays). 231 Corstophine Road, Edinburgh EH12 7ATN of Coleford on the minor road to Symonds Yat. Three sites: Christchurch, Bracelands and Woodlands. Reception at Christchurch. Set in the heart of the Forest of Dean, suitable for Symonds Yat. Dogs welcome except at Christchurch. Brochure request line: 0131 334 0066. Open March-November. ✰✰✰✰ **BH&HPA. 890T. MC.** 🚻 ♿ 🛒

Dursley

(5m). Hogsdown Farm Caravan & Camping Site, Lower Wick, Dursley, Gloucestershire GL11 6DS. *01453 810224.* Owner: Mrs Jenny Smith. Off A38, between J13 and J14, M5. Halfway between Bristol and Gloucester, SP. Excellent walking and touring country on edge of Cotswold Hills. Tents also available. Fishing and golf nearby. **40T. 12MC. 3H. ✿ ⅓ 🗗 ⅃**

Forthampton

(1.25m). The Lower Lode Inn, Forthampton, Gloucestershire GL19 4RE. *01684 293224.* Owner: Mr J & Mrs L Harwood. From Tewkesbury, A438 to Ledbury over Mythe Bridge. 2.5m to 2nd on left turn sp Forthampton. Turn left at top, travel out of village. At crossroads go straight over (no-through road). **5T. 5MC. ✿ ⅓ 🗗 ఈ**

Gloucester

(6m). Gables Farm, Moreton Valence, Gloucester, Gloucestershire GL2 7ND. *01452 720331.* Owner: Mrs D M Dickenson. M5, J12 then 1.5m S on A38 and J13 then 1.5m N on A38. No shop but essentials available within 3m. Open March-November. **20T. 10MC. ⅓ 🗗**

(2m). Riverside Caravan Park, The George Inn, Nr Dursley, Gloucester, Gloucestershire GL2 7AL. *01453 890270.* Owner: Mr & Mrs E Hogben. A38 Bristol to Gloucester, exit M5 J13 or 14. Pub/restaurant on site. Summer barbecues. Children's play area. Birds and animals pets corner. Toilet/shower block. Storage available. **27T. MC. ✿ ⅓ 🗗**

(5m). The Red Lion Caravan Site, Wainlode Hill, Norton, Gloucester, Gloucestershire GL2 9LW. *01452 730251/01299 400787.* Owner: G A Skilton. From Tewkesbury travel 3m S on A38, then turn R on to B4213. After 3m turn L to Wainlode Hill. On banks of the river Severn. Shaver points. Hair-dryers. Fishing. AA and RAC approved. ✩✩✩ **109T. MC. 40S. 4H. ✿ ⅓ 🗗 ఈ ⅃**

Lechlade

(0.25m). Bridge House Campsite, Bridge House, Lechlade, Gloucestershire GL7 3AG. *01367 252348.* Owner: R Cooper. On A361, 0.25m S of Lechlade. Shops, PO, doctor, restaurants and PHs all within 0.25m. Fishing nearby. Open March 1-October 31. **BH&HPA. 6T. 10MC. ⅓ 🗗 ఈ**

(0.5m). St Johns Priory Parks Ltd, Faringdon Road, Lechlade, Gloucestershire GL7 3EZ. *01367 252360.* Owner: Mr T C Worsfold. 0.5m on left Lechlade to Faringdon A417. Bank of Thames adjoining famous Trout Inn. Pets welcome. Open March 1-October 31 for holiday homes; open all year for tourers. **BH&HPA. NCC. 25T. 25MC. 87S. ✿ ⅓ 🗗 ⌀**

The Red Lion Caravan & Camping Park and Riverside Inn Pub

Wainlode Hill, Norton, Gloucester GL2 9LW
Tel: 01452 730251 or 01299 400787

From Tewkesbury travel 3 miles south on A38 then turn right onto B4213. Approx 3 miles turn left to Wainlode Hill.

109 pitches, some electric, open all year round.

Toilet, shower block.

Beautiful River Severn bank location with old worldie Pub which do great meals.

Nearby towns:
Gloucester, Cheltenham, Tewkesbury.

Moreton-in-Marsh

Cross Hands Inn, Salford Hill, A44, Moreton-in-Marsh, Gloucestershire GL56 0SP. *01608 643106.* crosshandsinn@hotmail.com. www.crosshandsinn.co.uk. Owner: Mr Graham & Mrs Denise Povey. On A44, junction with A436. 3.5m from Chipping Norton. Panoramic views with adjacent Coaching Inn with good food and friendly atmosphere, (new dining room and facilities block). Nearest newsagents, supermarket and petrol 3.5m. Also PO, doctor, dentis, small hospital, small play area for children. Discounts for rallies. **18T. MC. ✿ ⅓ 🗗**

(0.5m). Moreton-in-Marsh Caravan Club Site, Bourton Road, Moreton-in-Marsh, Gloucestershire GL56 0BT. *01608 650519.* www.caravanclub.co.uk. Owner: The Caravan Club. East Grinstead House, East Grinstead, West Sussex RH19 1UA. See website for standard directions to site. This attractive site is within walking distance of Moreton-in-the-Marsh. Surrounded by picturesque Cotswold villages. Advance booking essential. Dog walk on site. Non-members welcome. Toilet blocks. Privacy cubicles. Laundry facilities. Baby/toddler washroom. Veg prep. MV service point. Hard-standings. Play equipment. Boules pitch. Fishing locally. Suitable for families. Shops within 0.25m. ✩✩✩✩✩ **NCC. 182T. MC. ✿ ⅓ 🗗 ఈ**

Slimbridge

(0.5m). Tudor Caravan Park, Shepherds Patch, Slimbridge, Gloucestershire GL2 7BP. *01453 890483.* info@tudorcaravanpark.co.uk. www.tudorcaravanpark.com. Owner: Keith, Joan and Robin Fairall. M5 J13, on to A38, follow signs for Slimbridge WWT Wetlands Centre. 1.5m off A38 at rear of Tudor Arms PH. Quiet, family-run park adjacent to bird sanctuary and Gloucester to Sharpness Canal. Separate area for adults only. David Bellamy Gold Conservation Award. PH and restaurant adjoining. Fishing. Tearoom and small convenience shop adjacent. Golf course nearby. AA 3 pennants. **BH&HPA. 75T. MC. ✿ ⅓ 🗗**

Tewkesbury

(6m). Brooklands Farm, Alderton, Tewkesbury, Gloucestershire GL20 8NX. *01242 620259.* Owner: S M Greener. M5 exit 9 then the A46 Evesham Road to Teddington roundabout, follow Stow road B4077 for 3m past roundabout. Site signed on right. Small lake on site with coarse fishing. Large games room. Play area. Open March 16-January 16. **BH&HPA. 80T. MC. ⅓ 🗗 ⅃**

(6m). Camping & Caravanning Club Site - Winchcombe, Brooklands Farm, Alderton, Tewkesbury, Gloucestershire GL20 8NX. *01242 620259/0870 243 3331.* www.campingandcaravanning club.co.uk. Owner: Camping & Caravanning Club.Greenfields House, Westwood Way, Coventry CV4 8JH. On A46 from Tewkesbury keep straight on at roundabout and take B4077 to Stow on the Wold, site on R in 3m. Site is set in countryside with its own fishing lake. Non-members welcome. All units accepted. 80 pitches set in 20 acres. A visit to nearby Cheltenham, with its fine shopping, is worthwhile. David Bellamy Gold Conservation Award. Village of Winchcombe, with its antique shops and tearooms, is close to the site. Plenty of space for childrens' ball games. Special deals available for families and backpackers. Open March-January. ✩✩✩ **80T. 80MC. ⅓ 🗗 ఈ**

(1.5m). Croft Farm Leisure & Water Park, Bredons Hardwick, Tewkesbury, Gloucestershire GL20 7EE. *01684 772321.* alan@croftfarmleisure. www.croftfarmleisure.co.uk. Owner: Alan Newell. Take Bredon Road out of Tewkesbury on B4080. 1.5m on L. Touring caravan and camping site with own water sports lake and fitness centre. Luxury facilities. Winter storage. Tuition available in windsurfing, sailing and canoeing. Open March 1-December 31. ✩✩✩ **BH&HPA. CaSSOA. 76T. 76MC.** ⌂ ⌕ &

(2m). Dawleys Caravan Park, Owls Lane, Shuthonger, Tewkesbury, Gloucestershire GL20 6EQ. *01684 292622.* www.ukparks.co.uk/dawleys. M50 J1, take A38 S towards Tewkesbury-turn R after 1m. Quiet site in rural surroundings. Good walk and fishing nearby. Suitable for touring the Cotswolds, Malvern and Vale of Evesham. Special offers for 7 nights. Golf, fishing, cinema, swimming pool, shopping all within 2m. Park Manager: Richard Harrison. Open Easter-September 30 for tourers; open March 15-December 31 for owner-occupied holiday caravans. **BH&HPA. 20T. MC. 89S.** ⌂ ⌕

(3m). Fleet Close Caravan Park, Twyning, Tewkesbury, Gloucestershire. *01684 292787.* Owner: Mr & Mrs Kostiuk. Off A38. Open April 1-September 30. **8S.**

(0.25m). Mill Avon Holiday Park, Gloucester Road, Tewkesbury, Gloucestershire GL20 5SW. *01684 296876.* Owner: Mr L Stamp. On the A38, S of town centre. Fishing. Shops 5 mins walk. Four golf courses within 15 mins drive. Slipway for small boats. Golf course 0.5m, cinema 0.75m. Open March 1-October 31. **BH&HPA. 10T. MC. 24S.** ⌂ ⌕

(2m). Sunset View Touring Tent & Caravan Park & Ostrich Farm, Church Lane End, Twyning, Tewkesbury, Gloucestershire GL20 6EH. *01684 292145.* cheryl@golden springs.freeserve.co.uk. Owner: Mr & Mrs A B Goulstone. N of Tewkesbury on the A38, almost opposite Crown Inn turn right. Site 200yd on right. Two level acres. Quiet, family-run site. Horse riding, fishing and golf nearby; PH with restaurant within 5mins walk. Ostrich meat and eggs on sale at site. **25T. MC.** ✿ ⌂ ⌕ &

Tewkesbury Abbey Caravan Club Site, Gander Lane, Tewkesbury, Gloucestershire GL20 5PG. *01684 294035.* www.caravanclub.co.uk. Owner: The Caravan Club. East Grinstead House, East Grinstead, West Sussex RH19 1UA. M5, leave at J9 onto A438 SP Tewkesbury at traffic lights keep right and continue straight. In town centre at crossroads keep left, in 200yd turn left into Gander Lane, site on left. Site is almost in the shadow of the ancient abbey and a short walk from town centre. Dog walk. Tent campers welcome. Advance booking advisable. Non-members welcome. Toilet blocks, privacy cubicles. Laundry facilities. Motorhome service point. Veg prep. Golf and fishing nearby. Suitable for families. Shop 0.25m away. Good walking, cycling nearby. Open April-October. ✩✩✩ **NCC. 170T. MC.** ⌂ ⌕ &

HEREFORDSHIRE

Bromyard

(1m). Rock Farm Caravan Park, Tenbury Wells Road, Bromyard, Herefordshire HR7 4LP. *01885 482630/07970 425770 (mobile).* rjharperio@hotmail.com. Owner: Mr Richard Harper. Take Tenbury road out of Bromyard, 1m and park is on right. Well situated for walking, fishing, golf, bowls, tennis, archery or exploring the heart of the country.Open February 4-January 4. **BH&HPA. 6T. 4MC. 50S. 1H.** ⌂ ⌕

(2.5m). Saltmarshe Castle Caravan Park, Bromyard, Herefordshire HR7 4PN. *01885 483207.* Owner: Mr & Mrs H Weekers. On Bromyard to Stourport road B4203, 2.5m from Bromyard. Licensed club. Open March 15-October 31. **10T. MC. 240S. 3H.** ⌂ ⌕ & ⌿

Hereford

(4m). Cuckoos Corner, Moreton-on-Lugg, Hereford, Herefordshire HR4 8AH. *01432 760234.* cuckoos.corner@lc24.net. www.caravancampsites.co.uk. Owner: Mrs J M James. Easily accessible off A49. N of Hereford. Family site, with games room, shower block. Archery, croquet. Takeaway food, PH and shop 0.5m. **10T. 5MC. 1S.** ✿ ⌂ ⌕ &

Hereford Racecourse, Roman Road, Hereford, Herefordshire HR4 9QU. *01432 272364.* Off A49 on A4103. On outskirts of Cathedral City of Hereford. Free access to racing if staying on site night before and night after race day. Advance booking advised bank holidays. Open April-September. **60T. MC.** ⌂ ⌕ ⌿

(5m). Lucksall Caravan & Camping Park, Mordiford, Hereford, Herefordshire HR1 4LP. *01432 870213.* enquiries@lucksallpark.co.uk. www.lucksallpark.co.uk. Owner: Orleton Rise Park Ltd. Off B4224. Between Hereford and Ross on Wye. 9m from Ross-on-Wye. Bordered by river Wye, flat, spacious and peaceful. Showers. Fishing, shop on site. Canoes for hire. Open March 1-November 30. ✩✩✩✩✩ **BH&HPA. 80T. MC. 10S. 2H.** ⌂ ⌕ & ⌿

(7m). Millpond, Little Tarrington, Hereford, Herefordshire HR1 4JA. *01432 890243.* enquiries@millpond.co.uk. www.millpond.co.uk. Owners: Philip & Angela Stock. M50, J2, Ledbury A438 SP Tarrington (about 7m). Second turning R. Site 200yd on R. Coarse fishing on site. Golf nearby. Basics shopping (bread, milk, fruit, veg) 2.5m. PO 4m. Doctor 10 mins by car. Rural setting, peaceful and quiet. 2004 David Bellamy Gold Conversation Award. Open March 1-October 31. ✩✩✩ **BH&HPA. 40T. MC.** ⌂ ⌕ &

(11m). Poston Mill Park, Peterchurch, Golden Valley, Hereford, Herefordshire HR2 0SF. *01981 550225.* enquiries@poston-mill.co.uk. www.bestparks.co.uk. Owner: Wayne & Sarah Jones. On B4348 mid-way Hereford and Hay-on-Wye. Suitable base for touring, walking and fishing. Licensed restaurant on site. 1m to shops, PO, doctor. Open March 15-January 5. ✩✩✩✩✩ **BH&HPA. NCC. 60T. MC. 115S. 1H.** ✿ ⌂ ⌕ & ⌿

(15m). Upper Gilvach Farm, St Margarets, Vowchurch, Hereford, Herefordshire HR2 0QY. *01981 510618.* Owner: A Watkins. Very peaceful farm site with ample space and many walks. Close to many churches and castles. Dogs allowed on leads. Telephone. Suitable for children.Open April-September. **10T. MC. 1H.** 🐕

Leominster

(5m). Arrow Bank Holiday Park, Nun House Farm, Eardisland, Leominster, Herefordshire HR6 9BG. *01544 388312.* enquiries@arrowbankholidaypark.co.uk. www. arrowbankholidaypark.co.uk. Owners: West Country Park Homes. Edithmead, Somerset TA9 4HE. Off A44 Leominster to Rhayader, R fork at Barons Cross garage continue for about 4m, 100yd after Eardisland sign turn R along private drive to junction, park opposite. River fishing on site. Quiet, landscaped park, 4mins walk to Tudor-style village. Supermarket, golf courses, swimming pool 4-5m. Cinema 15m. Open March-October. ☆☆☆ **BH&HPA. 34T. 105S. 5H.** 🐕 🟥

(7m). Fairview Holiday Park, Hatfield, Leominster, Herefordshire HR6 0SD. *01568 760428.* info@fairviewholi daypark.co.uk. www.fairviewholiday.co.uk. Owners: Mr & Mrs S Morgan. The Willows, Hatfield, Leominster, Herefordshire HR6 0SF. From Leominster take A44 to Worcester. After 2.3m turn left, SP Hatfield, continue for 1.7m, turn right. After 1m, turn left into drive. Private fishing within the park, horse-riding (1.5m) and golf (5.5m) nearby. PH 2.5m situated in the heart of countryside. Open March 1-November 30. ☆☆☆ **BH&HPA. 63S. 2H.** 🐕

(6m). Pearl Lake Leisure Park, Shobdon, Leominster, Herefordshire HR6 9NQ. *01568 708326.* info@pearlake.co.uk. www.bestparks.co.uk. Owners: Glenn & Hannah Jones. On the B4362, on the Presteigne edge of the village of Shobdon, NW of Leominster. Family-run park set in 80 acres of parkland and surrounded by countryside. Exclusive 9-hole golf course, 15- acre fishing lake, woodland walks, children's play area, bar and restaurant. Village shop, PO 5mins walk away. Open March 1-November 30. ☆☆☆☆☆ **BH&HPA. 15T. 5MC. 200S.** 🐕 🟥 ♿ ⌀

Townsend Touring Park, Townsend Farm, Pembridge, Leominster, Herefordshire HR6 9HB. *01544 388527.* info@townsendfarm.co.uk. www.townsendfarm.co.uk. Owners: Richard & Geoff Smith. Spacious, 12-acre park. Showers, wash cubicles, toilets, bathroom for disabled people, family bathroom, laundry room. All fully serviced pitches. Lake, amenity and picnic area. On-site farm shop and butchery. Open March 1-mid January. ☆☆☆☆☆ **NCC. 60T. 60MC.** 🐕 🟥 ♿ 🟩

Moorhampton

(10m). Moorhampton Caravan Club Site, The Old Station, Moorhampton, Herefordshire HR4 7BE. *01544 318594.* www.caravanclub.co.uk. Owner: The Caravan Club. East Grinstead House, East Grinstead, West Sussex RH19 1UA. See website for standard directions to site. 10m from Hereford. Caravan Club members only. Hereford 10m. Quiet little site in heart of countryside. Dog walk on site. Toilet blocks. Privacy cubicles. Laundry facilities. Veg prep. Motorhome service point. Golf nearby. Open March-October. **NCC. 47T. MC.** 🐕 🟥 ♿

Ross-on-Wye

(0.25m). Broadmeadow Caravan Park, Broadmeadows, Ross-on-Wye, Herefordshire HR9 7BW. *01989 768076.* broadm4811@aol.com. www.broadmeadow.info. Owner: Brian & Elizabeth Edwards. Broadmeadow is adjacent to the A40 relief road. Access is obtained from the Pancake roundabout off the relief road turning into Ross and taking 1st R into Ashburton Estate Road, following road and turning R just before the round-about. Coarse fishing available on site. Supermarket within 4mins walk from site. Town about 10 mins from site, where pubs and refreshments are open. PO in town centre. Local hospital and doctors are nearby. Open April 1-September 30. ☆☆☆☆☆ **BH&HPA. 150T. MC.** 🐕 🟥 ♿

(6m). Sterrett's Caravan Park, Symonds Yat (West), Ross-on-Wye, Herefordshire HR9 6BY. *01600 890606.* www.ukparks.co.uk/sterretts. Owner: K Rollinson & J & L Sterrett. A40 midway Monmouth to Ross-on-Wye turn Symonds Yat (W). Rural location. Boat trips. Traditional country pub. Recreation area. Fishing. Laundrette. For brochure call 01594 832888. Open February 1-November 30. ☆☆☆ **BH&HPA. 8T. 82S. 3H.** 🐕 🟥

(2m). Yew Tree Inn Caravan Site, Peterstow, Ross-on-Wye, Herefordshire HR9 6JZ. *01625 599545/0790 1816064.* Owner: Barrs Residential & Leisure Ltd. Wizard Country Park, Bollard Lane, Nether Alderley, Macclesfield, Cheshire SK10 4UE. From Ross-On-Wye, A49 to Hereford. Follow for 2m to Peterstow. Turn right before Yew Tree PH. Country park set in the Wye Valley. Apple orchards and miles of walks to rear of park. Local shop and PO 25yd. Bus stop 100yd. Open March 1-October 31. **16T. MC. 27S. 1H.** 🐕 🟥

Symonds Yat West

(0.25m). Symonds Yat Caravan Park Ltd, Symonds Yat West, Herefordshire HR9 6BY. *01600 890883.* enquiries@ campingandcaravan.com. www.campingandcaravan.com. Owner: Mr & Mrs G Simons. A40 to Whitchurch, Symonds Yat West.Ross-on-Wye 7m. Monmouth 4m. Showers. Canoe launch. Fishing. Wye Valley walk. Canoe hire. PHs, restaurants, shops within walking distance. Open March-end October. ☆☆☆ **35T. MC.** 🐕 🟥

SHROPSHIRE

Bishop's Castle

(2.5m). Bow House Caravan Park, Bow House, Bishop's Castle, Shropshire SY9 5HY. *01588 638179.* Owner: D B Meddins. The park is attractively landscaped and gently sloping with panoramic views. Privately-owned holiday homes are set well apart and have individual car parking spaces. Open March 1-January 31. **BH&HPA. 51S.** 🐕 ⌀

(5m). The Green Caravan Park, Wentnor, Bishop's Castle, Shropshire SY9 5EF. *01588 650605.* info@greencaravanpark. co.uk. www.greencaravanpark.co.uk. Owner: Mr & Mrs N Turley & Family. Follow brown tourist signs from A488 and A489. Peaceful riverside park set in Shropshire hills, an Area of Outstanding Natural Beauty. Walks and birdlife. PH at site entrance. David Bellamy Gold Conservation Award. Open Easter-October. **BH&HPA. 140T. MC. 21S.** 🐕 🟥 🟩 ⌀

Bridgnorth

(7m). Bromdon Caravan Park, Wheathill, Burwarton, Bridgnorth, Shropshire WV16 6QT. *01584 823433.* Owner: Mr & Mrs K Partridge. Off the B4364 which runs between Bridgnorth and Ludlow. Clubhouse. Putting, petanque courts,

Please mention Caravan Sites 2006 when replying to advertisers

swings, private dog run, 5-acre play area, goal posts. All tarmac roads and full street lighting. Security barrier, full services. Crown bowls green. Open February 1-December 31. **BH&HPA. 85S.** 🛞 &

(7m). Butts Holding, Alveley, Bridgnorth, Shropshire. *01746 780393*. Owner: R & A Newton. Open March-October. **99S.** 🛞

(6.5m). Chorley Caravan Park, High Green, Chorley, Bridgnorth, Shropshire WV16 6PP. *01746 718476*. Owner: Mr B C Home. Take the B4363 from Bridgnorth. At Billingsley turn off to Chorley. Park is in village by the chapel. Located in countryside. Fishing available. Open March-October. **BH&HPA. 100S.** 🛞 &

(1.5m). Severn Valley Caravan Park, Kidderminster Road, Quattford, Bridgnorth, Shropshire WV15 6QJ. *01746 769257/07976 616326 (m)*. Owner: Mr & Mrs Nedic. New House, Duke Street, Broseley, Shropshire TF12 5LX. Kidderminster 8m, Stourport-on-Severn 10m, Wolverhampton 10m. Open February 1-December 31. **75S. 22H.** 🛞 ☎ &

(1.5m). Stanmore Hall Touring Park, Stourbridge Road, Bridgnorth, Shropshire WV15 6DT. *01746 761761*. stanmore @morris-leisure.co.uk. www.morris-leisure.co.uk. Owners: Morris Leisure. Castle Foregate, Shrewsbury, Shropshire SY1 2EL. 2m from Bridgnorth on A458 to Stourbridge. Caravan Club affiliated site. Set in beautiful grounds, the park has mature trees, a two-acre lake with water lilies, and resident peacocks. Toilet blocks, laundry facilities and motorhome service point. Play area, shop and dog walk on site. Fishing and golf nearby. Facilities for disabled. Suitable for families. Peaceful off-peak. ✰✰✰✰✰ **NCC. 131T. MC.** ✿ 🛞 ☎ & 🛒

(2m). Summerhill Caravan Site, Kidderminster Road, Quatford, Bridgnorth, Shropshire. *01746 765025*. Owner: K K J Properties Ltd. Kidderminster Road, Quatford, Bridgenorth, Shropshire. 2m outside Bridgnorth on the A442 travelling towards Kidderminster. Showers. Club on site. Laundrette. Play park. Open March-November. **40T. 5MC. 220S.** 🛞 ☎ & 🛒

(1m). The Riverside Caravan Park, Kidderminster Road, Bridgnorth, Shropshire WV15 6BY. *01746 765858/762393*. bren@furness4545.freeserve.co.uk. Owner: B Furness. On the A442 Kidderminster to Bridgnorth road. Fishing on the park. Golf, steam trains Severn Valley Railway, shops, PHs, PO, doctor all within 1m. Bridgnorth Market Town. Open 11 months (closed February). **NCC. 8T. MC. 218S.** 🛞 ☎ 🛒

(11m). Three Horse Shoes Caravan Park, Wheathill, Burwarton, Bridgnorth, Shropshire WV16 6QT. *01584 823206*. Owner: Mr C J Pritchard. Brown Clee View, Wheathill, Burwarton, Bridgnorth WV16 6QT. 7m from Ludlow. On the B4364 road. 11m Bridgnorth. Adjoining the country inn. Bar snacks available during inn's opening hours. Good views and suitable base for touring and walking. Showers. Fishing. Many places of interest nearby. Open April-October. **50T. 50MC. 2H.** 🛞

Church Stretton

(2m). Small Batch, Little Stretton, Church Stretton, Shropshire SY6 6PW. *01694 723358*. Owner: Mrs P R Prince. North to south turn R of A49 for Little Stretton A49-B5477 second L. Then right through stream to site. Showers. 2 PHs nearby. Shop, PO, doctor 2m. Open Easter-end September. **BH&HPA. 12T.** 🛞 ☎

Cleobury Mortimer

(2m). Ditton Mill Caravan Park, Cleobury Mortimer, Shropshire DY14 0DJ. *01299 266312*. Owner: Mr & Mrs J W Lunnon. Rousebine Caravan Park, Callow Hill, Rock, Worcs DY14 9DD. On A4117 Ludlow to Kidderminster. 1.5m W of Cleobury Mortimer turn left and follow signposts. Fishing and golf nearby. Open March 1-January 31. **75S.** 🛞 ✍

(8m). The Glen, Catherton Road, Cleobury Mortimer, Shropshire DA14 0LA. *01299 270423/0800 3893565*. www. hillandale.co.uk. On A4117 E off A456 Birmingham, Kidderminster, Tenbury, W off A49 Shrewsbury, Ludlow and Leominster. Park is not suitable for young children. Open March 1-October 31. **25T. MC.** 🛞 ☎

Craven Arms

(7m). Bush Farm, Clunton, Craven Arms, Shropshire SY7 0HU. *01588 660330*. Owner: Mr & Mrs M Adams. From A49 at Craven Arms, 7m W on B4368. SP from Crown Inn at Clunton. Shops at Clun. Forest walks. Stables and cottage for hire. Seasonal touring pitches sometimes available. Fishing nearby. Open March-January. **20T. MC. 5S.** 🛞 ☎ &

(3m). Engine & Tender Inn, Broome, Craven Arms, Shropshire SY7 0NT. *01588 7275*. Owner: Mr W & M C Rossler. B4368 W from Craven Arms for 2m then S on B4367 for 1m. Pub food and children's room. Shower. **9T. 3MC.** ✿ 🛞

(3m). Glenburrell Caravan Site, Horderley, Craven Arms, Shropshire SY7 8HP. *01588 672318*. Owner: Mr R Jones. On the A489. Level site by river. Good touring and walking area. Near Ludlow, Shrewsbury and the Iron Bridge, also the Welsh coast. Open May-October. **T. MC.** 🛞

Ellesmere

(4m). Fernwood Caravan Park, Lyneal, Ellesmere, Shropshire SY12 0QF. *01948 710221*. fernwood@caravan park37.fsnet.co.uk. www.ranch.co.uk. Owner: Ranch Caravan Parks Ltd. Off B5063. Site 22 acres with 40 acres of woodland adjacent, open to caravanners. Own lake with wildfowl and fishing. AA 4 pennants. RAC. Open March 1-November 30. ✰✰✰✰✰ **BH&HPA. NCC. 60T. MC. 165S. 1H.** 🛞 ☎ & 🛒

Talbot Caravan Park, Talbot Street, Sparbridge, Ellesmere, Shropshire SY12 0AG. *01691 623594/622285*. Owner: Mr F E Horton. Hardwick Lodge, Ellesmere, Shropshire. On A495 (A528). Situated in the town of Ellesmere and within a 100yd of shops and lake. Open mid March-mid November. **25T. MC. 4S.** 🛞 ☎

Ludlow

(5m). Orleton Rise Holiday Home Park, Green Lane, Orleton, Ludlow, Shropshire SY8 4JE. *01584 831617*. www. ukparks.co.uk/orleton. Owner: Orleton Rise Park Ltd. Take B4361 Ludlow to Leominster road to Orleton. Turn right at Maidenhead Inn. Site on left. Full facilities. Quiet, spacious, picturesque park. Open March 1-January 31. ✰✰✰✰✰ **BH&HPA. 16T. MC. 82S.** 🛞 ☎ &

(6m). Park House, Brimfield, Ludlow, Shropshire SY8 4NY. *01584 711558*. Owner: Mr C Forbes. On A49 Leominster to Ludlow. Two white milk churns at site entrance. 6m to Leominster. 2m from Herefordshire. 1m north of village of Aston. **6T. 6MC.** ✿ 🛞 ☎

Westbrook Park, Little Hereford, Ludlow, Shropshire SY8 4AU. *01584 711280*. info@bestparks.co.uk. www.bestparks. co.uk. Owner: Alwyn Jones. Just off A456 first on L up lane between Little Hereford Bridge and large house. A beautiful kept traditional quiet touring camp site in a cider orchard on the banks of the river Teme, with 0.5m fishing, local PH within walking distance. Lovely walks off park. Every pitch has its own full services. Open March 1-November 30. **BH&HPA. 54T. 54MC.** 🏕 🕿 ♿

Much Wenlock

> **(2.5m). Presthope Caravan Club Site, Stretton Road, Much Wenlock, Shropshire TF13 6DQ.** *01746 785234.* www.caravanclub.co.uk. Owner: The Caravan Club. East Grinstead House, East Grinstead, West Sussex RH19 1UA. See website for standard directions to site. Set in beautiful countryside suitable for naturalists; wildlife on site. Own sanitation required. Chemical toilet emptying point. Advance booking essential bank holidays. Non-members welcome. Hard-standings. Steel awning pegs required. Calor Gas and Campingaz. Fishing nearby. Walking. Open March-October. **NCC. 73T. MC.** 🏕 🕿 🕿

Newport

King's Head Park Homes, Green Lane, Newport, Shropshire TF10 7LG. *01952 812661.* Owner: S & J Smith. Located in Newport. 12m to Stafford and 10m to Telford. Fishing and golf 10 mins drive. The park is 5 mins walk to centre of Newport and its sports centre. Garage near entrance to park, PH nearby. **BH&HPA. 9T.** ✪ 🏕 🕿 ⌀

Oswestry

(10m). Royal Hill Inn, Kinnerley, Oswestry, Shropshire SO10 8ES. *01743 741242.* Owner: Mrs A & R Pugh. Off A5. Public telephone. Shower. Features within easy reach. Rivers Severn and Vyrnwy, Llangollen and Welsh Hills, Offa's Dyke, Towns of Shrewsbury, Oswestry and Welshpool. Open April 1-October 31. **20T. 5MC. 1S. 4H.** 🏕 ♿

(3.5m). Royal Oak Inn, Trefalch, Oswestry, Shropshire SY10 9HE. *01691 652455.* Owner: Mr & Mrs M Woodcock. Situated near Offa's Dyke path. Many local crafts. Shop 0.25m. Open April-October. **15T.** 🕿

Shrewsbury

(1.5m). Beaconsfield Farm, Upper Battlefield, Shrewsbury, Shropshire SY4 4AA. *01939 210370/01939 210399.* www. beaconsfield-farm.co.uk. Owners: PW & J Poole. 0.5m N of Shrewsbury on A49. Adults only. Traditional restaurant. Indoor swimming pool, fly and coarse fishing pool. Bowling green. AA 5 pennants Best of British member. Golf 3m. ✩✩✩✩✩ **BH&HPA. NCC. 60T. 60MC. 60S. 2H.** ✪ 🏕 🕿 ♿ ⌀

(5m). Bridge Inn Campsite, Bridge Inn, Dorrington (A49), Shrewsbury, Shropshire SY5 7ED. *01743 718209.* Owner: Martin & Audrey Brown. 5M S of Shrewsbury on A49. Set in 1.5 acres at rear of pub. Showers and toilets. PH with catering. **18T. MC.** ✪ 🏕 🕿 ♿

Brow Farm, Ratlinghope, Shrewsbury, Shropshire SY5 0SR. *01588 650641.* Owner: John Sankey, 4m W of Church Stretton. 12m S of Shrewsbury. Next to Ratlinghope Church. Quiet farm site. **20T. 20MC.** ✪ 🏕 ♿

(6m). Cartref, Fords Heath, Shrewsbury, Shropshire SY5 9GD. *01743 821688.* www.caravancampingsites.co.uk/shrop shire/cartref. Owner: Mr T T Edwards & Mrs M Edwards. From Shrewsbury bypass A5, take A458 Welshpool for 2m. SP from Ford village or take B4386 Montgomery road for 2 miles to Cruckton crossroads (site signposted). Now SP from A5

Shrewsbury bypass on Montgomery, at junction with B4386. Small, level site. Peaceful countryside. Toilets, showers, laundry room. Dishwashing area. Free showers. Hot water in basins. AA 2 pennants. Open May-October. **15T. MC.** 🏕 🕿 ♿

(10m). Mill Farm Caravan Park, Hughley, Shrewsbury, Shropshire SY5 6NT. *01746 785208/785255.* mail@millfarm-caravanpark.co.uk. www.millfarmcaravanpark.co.uk. Owner: Mr D M & P Bosworth & M Roberts. On A458 Bridgnorth to Shrewsbury. SP from Harley. 5m Much Wenlock. Farm shop 1m, shopping 5m, golf course 7m. Fishing on park. Open March 1-January 31. ✩✩✩ **BH&HPA. NCC. 28T. 28MC. 90S. 1H.** 🏕 🕿

(1m). Oxon Hall Touring Park, Welshpool Road, Shrewsbury, Shropshire SY3 5FB. *01743 340868.* oxon@ morris-leisure.co.uk. www.morris-leisure.co.uk. Owners: Morris Leisure. Castle Foregate, Shrewsbury, Shropshire SY1 2EL. 2m from Shrewsbury Town Centre on A458 Welshpool Road. 1m from A5. Access to Park and Ride. Children welcome. PHs within walking distance. Close to hospital and doctors. Golf, fishing within 3m. Adjacent to park-and-ride bus service. ✩✩✩✩✩ **BH&HPA. 120T. 30MC. 45S.** ✪ 🏕 🕿 ♿ 🌡 ⌀

(7m). Seven Oaks Caravan Holiday Home Park, Crew Green, Shrewsbury, Shropshire SY5 9BU. *01743 885080.* manager @sevenoaksholidayhomepark.co.uk. Owner: Salop Caravans Sites Ltd. Salop Caravans Ltd, Meole Brace, Shrewsbury, Shropshire. A458 Shrewsbury to Welshpool, turn R on B4393, SP Lake Vyrnwx, about 6m to Seven Oaks. Park developed to high standard, with elevated views of river Severn. Fishing in river and pool. Golf course and health club nearby. Suitable holiday retreat for retired people. Open March 1 - January 14. ✩✩✩✩ **75S.** 🏕 ⌀

Telford

> **(4m). Camping & Caravanning Club Site - Ebury Hill, Ebury Hill, Ring Bank, Haughton, Telford, Shropshire TF6 6BU.** *01743 709334/0870 243 3331.* www.camping andcaravanningclub.co.uk. Owner: Camping & Caravanning Club. Greenfields House, Westwood Way, Coventry CV4 8JH. 2.5m through Shrewsbury on A53. Turn R signed Haughton and Upton Magna. Continue 1.5m site on R. Non-members welcome and may join at site. All units accepted. Own sanitation required. Some all-weather pitches available. A David Bellamy Gold Conservation Award. Fishing is available from site, which is close to Telford Park. Site is 6m from Shrewsbury and well situated for the Severn Valley and Welsh Borders. Nearby is the Shrewsbury Way Footpath. Special deals available for families and backpackers. Open March-October. ✩✩✩✩ **100T. 100MC.** 🏕 🕿

(6m). Pool View Park, 3 Pool View, Buildwas, Ironbridge, Telford, Shropshire TF8 7BS. *01952 433946.* Owner: Cosford Park Homes. Newport Road, Albrighton, Nr Wolverhampton WV7 3NA. Through Ironbridge, with old bridge on left, over small roundabout to T-junction, private road on left after 100yd, follow to site. Fishing, 5 mins drive to shops, PO, doctor. PO on site; pick up 9am and 5pm. Open March 1-October 31. **50T. 50M. 10S. 10H.** 🏕 🕿

(3m). Severn Gorge Park, Bridgnorth Road, Tweedale, Telford, Shropshire TF7 4JB. *01952 684789.* info@severn gorgepark.co.uk. www.severngorgepark.co.uk. Owner: Webb Park Home Estates Ltd. From M54 J4, take A442 for 1m, then A442 SP Kidderminster for 1.6m. Follow SP for Madeley then Tweedale. Level, sheltered site set among woodland. Modern facilities. Suitable base for exploring Ironbridge and Shropshire. ✩✩✩✩ **BH&HPA. NCC. 50T. 50MC.** ✪ 🏕 🕿 ♿ 🌡 ⌀

Wem

(1m). Lower Lacon Caravan Park, Wem, Shropshire SY4 5RP. *01939 232376.* info@llcp.co.uk. www.lowerlaconcaravan park.co.uk. Owner: Mr C H Shingler. Off A49. On to B5065. Heated outdoor swimming pool. Licensed lounge. Food. Golf course 3m. Cinema, shopping centre 10m. **BH&HPA. 270T. 20MC. 50S. 5H.** ✿ ⓜ ⊞ & ⌼

Whitchurch

(1m). Brook House Farm, Grindley Brook, Whitchurch, Shropshire SY13 4QJ. *01948 664557.* Owner: Mrs S Weston. On the A41, N of Whitchurch. Children allowed. Swing and see-saw on field. **5T. 5MC. 5S.** ✿ ⓜ ⌼

(4m). Green Lane Farm, Green Lane, Prees, Whitchurch, Shropshire SY13 2AH. *01948 840460.* greenlanefarm@ tiscali.co.uk. www.greenlanefarm.northshropshire.biz. Owners: Gerry & Pauline Quinn. Off Whitchurch-Newport A41 turn right on to Telford A442 after 150yd turn right for Prees. Site is first farmhouse on right-hand side. Three spacious acres full of flowers. Games green. Children's play area. 1m to local PO, shop and doctor. 4m to swimming pool, 2m to fishing. Golf and horse riding nearby. Site centrally located for local attractions. Open March-October 31. **22T. 20MC.** ⓜ ⊞ & ⌼

STAFFORDSHIRE

Brewood

(0.75m). Homestead Caravan Park, Shutt Green, Shutt Green Lane, Brewood, Staffordshire ST19 9LX. *01902 851302.* david@caravanpark.fsbusiness.co.uk. www.caravan parkstaffordshire.com. Owner: D Breakspeare & J Breakspeare. From J12, M6 head W along A5 towards Telford to Gailey island the A5 intersection of the A449 Wolverhampton - Stafford road. continue along A5 with Spread Eagle PH on your R. Take third L Horsebrook Lane and then second R Shutt Green Lane. Follow along over canal bridge to park. 3 chalets to hire also available. Leisure club with heated indoor pool. All-weather bowling green and croquet. Bar meals. Play area. Fishing, golf, horse riding, country rambles close by. Open March 1-January 7. ✰✰✰✰ **BH&HPA. 150S.** ⓜ

Burton-on-Trent

Beehive Farm, Woodland Lakes, Rosliston, Burton-on-Trent, Staffordshire DE12 8HZ. *01283 763981/0797 338 7315.* info@beehivefarm-woodlandslakes.co.uk. www.beehive farm-woodlandslakes.co.uk. Sitated in 66 acres of woodland. Modern amenity block. Offers: fishing, walks, conservation areas, animal farm, playgroup/play area and tea room. Local services within 0.5m: PO, village PHs, grocery store, newsagent. Local attractions: Alton Towers, Uttoxeter Racecourse, Donnington park. ✰✰ **25T. MC.** ⓜ ⊞ ⌼

Kingfisher Holiday Park, Fradley Junction, Alrewas, Burton-on-Trent, Staffordshire DE13 7DN. *01283 790407.* mail@king fisherholidaypark.com. www.kingfisherholidaypark.com. From A38 dual carriageway take A513 for Kings Bromley. After 2m turn left. Just before canal bridge, turn right along canal bank (tarmac road). Park is past Swan Inn on right. 3m from Lichfield. Picturesque setting at junction of two busy canals. Plenty of narrowboat activity. Own cafe and shop on site. Holiday homes for hire and sale. Alton Towers and Drayton Manor Park nearby. Free fishing on canal. Local village 2m (PHs, takeaway etc). Golf club 2.5m. Shopping centre 3m. Open March-October. ✰✰✰✰✰ **BH&HPA. 97S. 6H.** ⓜ ⌼ ⌖

Cheadle

(0.5m). Hales Hall Caravan & Camping Park, Oakamoor Road, Cheadle, Staffordshire ST10 4BQ. *01538 753305.* Owner: Mr & Mrs R Clare. From Cheadle B5417 to Alton Towers & Oakamoor. Site on L about 0.5m. Swimming pool. Games room. Bar and bar meals. Limited facilites off peak. Rally field. Open March-November. **50T. 30MC. 30S.** ⓜ ⊞ ⌼

Leek

(2.75m). Blackshaw Moor Caravan Club Site, Leek, Staffordshire ST13 8TW. *01538 300203.* www.caravan club.co.uk. Owner: The Caravan Club. East Grinstead House, East Grinstead, West Sussex RH19 1UA. See website for directions to site. Suitable for families. All hard-standings. Play equipment. Dog walk. Toilet blocks. Privacy cubicles. Laundry facilities. Baby toddler washroom. Veg prep. Motorhome service point. Calor Gas and Campingaz. Golf, fishing, watersports nearby. Advance booking bank holidays and weekends. Non-members welcome. No late night arrivals. Open March-October. **NCC. 89T. MC.** ⓜ ⊞ & ⌼

(2m). Camping & Caravanning Club Site - Leek, Blackshaw Grange, Blackshaw Moor, Leek, Staffordshire ST13 8TL. *01538 300285/0870 2433331.* www.campingandcaravanningclub.co.uk. Owner: Camping & Caravanning Club. Greenfields House, Westwood Way, Coventry CV4 8JH. On main A53 Leek to Buxton. 200yd past sign for 'Blackshaw Moor' on left. Suitable base for touring Peak District, Alton Towers. Leek town centre full of interesting shops and markets. Potteries of Staffordshire close to site. Fly and coarse fishing locally. Tissington Trail within easy reach for walkers and cyclists. Caravans, motor caravans and tents accepted. Non-members welcome. Special deals for families and backpackers. ✰✰✰ **70T. 70MC.** ✿ ⓜ ⊞ &

(3.5m). Glencote Caravan Park, Churnet Valley, Station Road, Leek, Staffordshire ST13 7EE. *01538 360745.* canistay @glencote.co.uk. www.glencote.co.uk. Owner: Syd & Hilda Birch. On A520 Leek to Stone. Small, family-run park, flat, firm and well lit. Showers. Laundry. Fishing, golf and swimming nearby. Open March-October. ✰✰✰✰ **BH&HPA. 40T. MC. 15S.** ⓜ ⊞

Rugeley

(3m). Camping & Caravanning Club Site - Cannock Chase, Old Youth Hostel, Wandon, Rugeley, Staffordshire WS15 1QW. *01889 582166/0870 2433331.* www.campingandcaravanningclub.co.uk. Owner: Camping & Caravanning Club. Greenfields House, Westwood Way, Coventry CV4 8JH. From Rugeley take A460, turn L at 'Hazelslade' SP and R in 1m for site. Non-members welcome. All units welcome. Quiet site set in heathland and forest. Suitable for walkers. Cannock for shops, leisure centre and market place. Special deals for families and backpackers. Open March-October. ✰✰✰✰ **60T. 60MC.** ⓜ ⊞ &

Love Lane Caravan Site, Love Lane, Rugeley, Staffordshire WS15 2HJ. *01889 583439.* Owner: Mrs P Jones. The Bungalow, Love Lane, Rugeley. 9m from Stafford A51, 7m from Lichfield A51. 5 mins walk to town and shops. 10 mins walk to PO and doctor. Touring pitches sometimes available. No children or animals. **BH&HPA. 6T.** ⌖

(2m). Silver Trees Caravan Park, Stafford Brook Road, Penkridge Bank, Rugeley, Staffordshire WS15 2TX. *01889 582185.* enquiries@silvertreescaravanpark.co.uk. www.silvertreescaravanpark.co.uk. Owner: TO & GE Barber & RL & N Seed. 2m W of Rugeley off A51 on to unclassified road towards Penkridge turn R by white fence. No tourers. Indoor swimming pool. Tennis. Laundry. RAC appointed. Rose Award. Open April-October for hire caravans; open March-January for owner-occupiers. ☆☆☆☆ BH&HPA. 100S. 8H. ⚓

Stafford

(7.75m). High Onn Caravan Club Site, Church Eaton, Stafford, Staffordshire ST20 0AX. *01785 840141.* www.caravanclub.co.uk. Owner: The Caravan Club. East Grinstead House, East Grinstead, West Sussex RH19 1UA. See website for standard directions to site. Caravan Club members only. Peaceful, rural site with views into Shropshire and towards Wales. Own sanitation required. Chemical toilet emptying points. Dog walk adjacent. Part hard-standing. Steel awning pegs required. Gas. Motorhome service point. Local attractions include Ironbridge. Open March-October. **NCC. 70T. MC.** ⚓ 🔌

Stoke-on-Trent

(10m). The Cross Inn Caravan Park, Cauldon Low, Stoke-on-Trent, Staffordshire ST10 3EX. *01538 308338.* adrian_weaver@hotmail.com. www.crossinn.co.uk. Owner: A B Weaver & P Wilkinson. On A52 Stoke-Ashbourne road. Alton Towers 3m, Peak Park 5 mins. PH/restaurant on site. Carvery all day Sunday. Families welcome. Family room with pool and football tables. Alton Towers 3m. Open March-November. ☆☆☆☆☆ **20T. MC. 6H.** ⚓ 🔌 ♿

(15m). The Star Caravan and Camping Park, Cotton, Nr Alton Towers, Stoke-on-Trent, Staffordshire ST10 3DW. *01538 702219.* www.starcaravanpark.co.uk. Owner: Mark & Margaret Mellor. 1.25m from Alton Towers (closest site) within easy reach of Peak Park and Matlock Bath. 15m from Potteries, about 9m from market town of Ashbourne, Leek and Uttoxeter. 200yd from Old Star Inn. 3.5m Cheadle. Site is on Star Road, B5417. Calor Gas. Facilities for disabled visitors. Fishing 2m, golf course 1m. Extra shops, PO, doctor all 2-3m. Central location for Alton Towers, Cheadle, Leek, Uttoxeter, Ashbourne; Potteries and Peak District. AA 3 pennants. Rose Award. Open March 11-November 5. ☆☆☆☆ **BH&HPA. 60T. 30MC. 65S. 9H.** ⚓ 🔌 ♿

Stone

(1m). The Brooms Park, Walton, Stone, Staffordshire ST15 0BQ. *01785 819190.* Owner: Mr D E & J E Bourne. On A34, behind Stonehouse hotel. No children. **23H.** ✿ ✐

Tamworth

(3m). Drayton Manor Park, Fazeley, Tamworth, Staffordshire B78 3TW. *01827 287979.* info@draytonmanor.co.uk. www.draytonmanor.co.uk. On A4091, near J9 and J10, M42, exit T2, M6 toll. Theme park with camping and caravan site, for families only. Over 100 rides and attractions plus shops and food. Open Easter-October. **75T. MC.** ⚓ ♿ 🐾

Uttoxeter

(0.5m). Uttoxeter Racecourse Caravan Club Site, Wood Lane, Uttoxeter, Staffordshire ST14 8BD. *01889 564172.* www.caravanclub.co.uk. Owner: The Caravan Club. East Grinstead Club, East Grinstead House, East Grinstead, West Sussex RH19 1UA. See website for standard directions to site. On National Hunt Racecourse, with beautiful views over open countryside and golf course adjacent. Racing free to site users. Dog exercise area. Advance booking advised bank holidays, weekends and race days. Non-members and tent campers welcome. Toilet blocks. Privacy cubicles. Laundry facilities. Baby/toddler washroom. Veg prep. MV service point. Gas. Play area. Suitable for families. Alton Towers nearby. Open March-November. **NCC. 76T. MC.** ⚓ 🔌

WARWICKSHIRE

Alcester

(3m). Fish Inn, Wixford, Alcester, Warwickshire. *01789 778593.* Owner: Mr S R Coombs. Open April 1-September 30. **14S.** ⚓

Bidford-on-Avon

(3m). Dovecote Riverside Caravan Park, Welford Road, Barton, Bidford-on-Avon, Warwickshire B50 4NP. Owner: Mrs E M Gill. The Lodge, 276a Alcester Road, Stratford-on-Avon, Warwickshire CV37 9QX. Off A439. Open March 1-December 31. **40S.**

(5m). The Golden Cross Leisure Park, Wixford Road, Ardens Grapton, Bidford-on-Avon, Warwickshire B50 4LG. *01789 772420.* Owner: Mrs P S Vardy-Smith. Showers and laundry room. Open March 1-October 31. **2T. 2MC. 16S.**

Henley-in-Arden

Island Meadow Caravan Park, The Mill House, Aston Cantlow, Henley-in-Arden, Warwickshire B95 6JP. *01789 488273.* holiday@islandmeadowcaravanpark.co.uk. www.island meadowcaravanpark.co.uk. Owner: PH & CA Lewis-Jones, KE Hudson. Off A3400 and A46 NW of Stratford (6m) in the village of Aston Cantlow. 3m from Alcester. Quiet, rural park on the river Alne in historic and picturesque village close to Stratford. Fishing free to guests. David Bellamy Gold Conservation Award. Booking essential at peak periods. Open March 1-October 31. ✩✩✩ **BH&HPA. 24T. MC. 51S. 5H.** ⌂ ⊕ ⅙ ⏇

Market Bosworth

Bosworth Water Trust, Far Coton Lane, Market Bosworth, Warwickshire CV13 6PD. *01455 291876.* Owners: Nigel & Jo Ryley. Friezeland Farm, Wellsborough Road, Market Bosworth, Warwickshire CV13 6PD. Windsurfing, sailing, canoeing, crazy golf, fishing. ✩✩✩ **BH&HPA. 56T.** ✿ ⌂ ⊕ ⅙ ⏇

Marston

(1m). Marston Caravan, Touring & Camping Park, Old Kingsbury Road, Marston, Warwickshire B76 0DP. *01675 470902.* Owner: A I Loveridge. 1 Doverdale Park Homes, Kidderminster Road, Droitwich, Worcs WR9 0NU. J9 Off M42, take A4097 towards Kingsbury. Marston Caravan Park is 0.75m on left-hand side. Park is 5m from Sutton Coldfield. New toilet/ shower block. **60T. MC.** ✿ ⌂ ⊕ ⅙

Meriden

Somers Wood Caravan & Camping Park, Somers Road, Meriden, Warwickshire, CV7 7PL. *01676 522978.* enquiries@somerswood.co.uk. www.somerswood.co.uk. Owners: Marc & Angela Fowler. From A45 take 452, SP Meriden/Leamington. 1m at next roundabout turn L on to B4102 (Hampton Lane) site 0.5m on left-hand side. 4m from Solihull. Exclusively adults only. Adjacent to golf course with clubhouse and coarse fishery. Shops 0.5m, 3m from the National Exhibition Centre. 7 nights for the price of 5 on selected weeks. Open February 1- December 15. ✩✩✩✩✩ **BH&HPA. 48T. 48MC.** ⌂ ⊕

Nuneaton

Castle View Caravan Site, 34 Castle Road, Hartshill, Nuneaton, Warwickshire. *024 76392185.* Owner: Mr R Ingleston. Brynffynon, Forge, Machynlleth, Powys SY20 8RN. Children allowed. **4T.**

Rugby

(7m). Lairhillock Park, Sandy Lane, Marton, Rugby, Warwickshire CU23 2UR. *01926 632119.* Owner: Jean K Elgar. On A423 1m S of Marton. 6m from Leamington Spa, 7m from Rugby and Coventry.15m from Banbury. **BH&HPA. T.** ✿ ⌂ ⊕ ⌀

Shipston-on-Stour

(4m). Parkhill Farm, Halford, Shipston-on-Stour, Warwickshire CV36 5DQ. *01608 662492.* Owner: Long. Open Easter-October. **20T. 10MC.** ⌂

Southam

(3m). Holt Farm, Southam, Warwickshire CV47 1NJ. *01926 812225/07790 959638.* neil@holtfarm.fslife.co.uk. www.holt farm.fslife.co.uk. Owner: N G & A C Adkins. From Southam bypass follow camping and caravan signs. Site 3m from Southam off Priors Marston Road. Quiet site on family farm, ideal for exploring Warwickshire. Dogs allowed on leads. Calor Gas. Free fishing. Open March 1-October 31. **45T. MC.** ⌂ ⊕

Stratford-upon-Avon

(1m). Avon Caravan Park, Warwick Road, Stratford-upon-Avon, Warwickshire CV37 0NS. *01789 299492.* info@strat fordcaravans.co.uk. www.stratfordcaravans.co.uk. Owner: Avon Estates Ltd. On A439 Warwick to Stratford, 1m to Stratford centre. Riverside location with river taxi to Stratford town centre. 1.5m of free fishing. Our Millenium bridge opens up numerous amenities. Golf course, cinema, leisure centre nearby. Open March 7-January 7. **BH&HPA. NCC. 250S.** ⌂ ⅙

(4m). Binton Bridges Caravan Park, Binton Road, Welford-on-Avon, Stratford-upon-Avon, Warwickshire CV37 8PN. *01789 751751.* joe.sugden@virgin.net. www.bintonbridges park.co.uk. Owners: Joe & Linda Sugden. Off B439 toward Welford, on left hand side next to river Avon. Pretty riverside site with moorings and fishing. Village facilities within easy walking distance. Open March 1-October 31. **BH&HPA. 39S.** ⌂

(2m). Dodwell Park, Evesham Road, B439, Stratford-upon-Avon, Warwickshire CV37 9SR. *01789 204957.* enquiries@ dodwellpark.co.uk. www.dodwellpark.co.uk. Owner: Mr M J R & Mrs S B Bennett. From Stratford-upon-Avon take the B439 towards Bidford-on-Avon for 2m. Park is on the L and is SP. Country walks to Luddington village and river Avon. Suitable base for touring the Cotswolds and Warwick Castle. ✩✩✩ **BH&HPA. 50T. 50MC.** ✿ ⌂ ⊕ ⏇ ⌀

(4m). Newlands Caravan Park, Loxley Lane, Wellesbourne, Stratford-upon-Avon, Warwickshire CV35 9EN. *01789 841096/0776 1747282.* www.newlands-caravan-park.co.uk. Owners: Mr & Mrs C Warr. From M40/A46 Junction take A429 through Barford. Turn R go through Charlcote to crossroads. Straight over past all flying schools. Newlands is 2nd bungalow on right, opposite helicopter school. Site has hard standings and shower and toilet block. 5mins walk to licensed cafe. Well situated to explore the Cotswolds, Warwick Castle, and the many National Trust properties in the area. Theatres, restaurants, shopping and Shakespeare properties can be enjoyed at nearby Stratford-upon-Avon. **23T. 10MC.** ✿ ⌂ ⊕

(1m). Riverside Caravan Park, Tiddington Road, Stratford-upon-Avon, Warwickshire CV37 7AB. *01789 292312.* info@stratfordcaravans.co.uk. www.stratfordcaravans.co.uk. Owner: Avon Estates Ltd. Take B4086 Tiddington Road from the bridge in Stratford. As you enter the village of Tiddington the park entrance is on the left hand side opposite the NFC. Riverside location with river taxi service to Stratford town centre. Bar, clubhouse and restaurant offers many nights of entertainment. 1.5m of free fishing. Golf course, cinema, leisure centre, restaurants all nearby. Open March 7-January 7. **BH&HPA. NCC. 150T. MC. 60S. 25H.** ⌂ ⊕ ⅙ ⏇ ⌀

(1m). Riverside Caravan Park, Tiddington Road, Stratford-upon-Avon, Warwickshire CV37 7AB. *01789 292312.* info@stratfordcaravans.co.uk. www.stratfordcaravans.co.uk. Owner: Avon Estates Ltd. Travelling from the A422 in Stratford turn north E on to the B4086 for about 1m. Site is on left on entering Tiddington. A riverside location with river taxi to Stratford. Well laid-out touring park with new facilities. New bridge has opened the park up for more activities. Golf, bar and restaurants nearby. Free fishing. Pets are welcome. No tents allowed. Open April 1-October 31. **BH&HPA. NCC. 150T. MC. 60S. 20H.** ⚲ 🏕 ⚹ ☎

(1m). Stratford-on-Avon Racecourse Touring Park, Luddington Road, Stratford-on-Avon, Warwickshire, CV37 9SE. *01789 201063/01789 267949.* info@stratford racecourse.net. www.stratford-dracecourse.net. From the M40, J15, S on to the A46, follow signs to Racecourse. From SW leave the M5 for Evesham, N on the A46. Combine horse racing with a visit to this touring park close to the heart of Shakespeare's country. Facilities for over 100 caravans and tents. Level grass with tarmac access road, shower block, launderette, limited disabled facilities, Premium pitches with electricity, chemical toilet emptying and water points, and small permanent play area. 400yd to shop, 1m walk into town. Open March-September. **100T. MC.** ⚲ 🏕 ⚹

(6m). The Cottage of Content, 15 Welford Road, Barton, Stratford-upon-Avon, Warwickshire B50 4NP. *01789 772279.* Owner: Mr J F Gash. Site is situated on the river Avon, fishing is available. Golf course2m away, shops and a health centre 1m away. Open March 1-November 1. **25T. MC.** 🏕

West View Caravan Park, Barton Road, Welford-on-Avon, Stratford-upon-Avon, Warwickshire. Owner: Mr & Mrs N Smith. Park is situated off the A439. Open March-October. **30S.**

Studley

(3m). Outhill Caravan Park, Hardwick Lane, Outhill, Studley, Warwickshire B80 7DY. *01527 852160.* Owner: Mrs D Wofford. Off A4189, Outhill Farm is first house on left after turning off A4189 on to lane towards Studley. Turning is at top of hill 3.5m from Henley-in-Arden and 1.5m from Mappleborough Green, SP, Morton Bagot 1.5m. Undeveloped quiet country park. Please book in advance. Open April-November. **BH&HPA. 14T. 4MC.** 🏕

Warwick

Warwick Racecourse Caravan Club Site, Hampton Street, Warwick, Warwickshire CV34 6HN. *01926 495448.* www.caravanclub.co.uk. Owner: The Caravan Club. East Grinstead House, East Grinstead, West Sussex RH19 1UA. See website for standard directions to site. Set on grass and tarmac in racecourse enclosure, 6 mins walk from Warwick centre. Free access to racing. Non-members welcome. Toilet blocks. Privacy cubicles. Laundry facilities. Veg Prep. Motorhome service point. Gas. No late-night arrivals. Open March-January. **NCC. 55T. MC.** 🏕 ⚹ ⚲

WEST MIDLANDS

Birmingham

(1m). Chapel Lane Caravan Club Site, Chapel Lane, Wythall, Birmingham West Midlands B47 6JX. *01564 826483.* www.caravanclub.co.uk. Owner: The Caravan Club. East Grinstead House, East Grinstead, West Sussex RH19 1UA. See website for standard directions to site. Non-members welcome. Convenient for NEC. All hardstandings. Toilet blocks. Privacy cubicles. Laundry facilities. Veg prep. Motorhome service point. Gas supplies. Playframe. Storage pitches. Fishing, golf and NCN cycle path 5m. Peaceful off-peak. ☆☆☆☆☆ **NCC. 99T. MC.** ⚹ 🏕 ⚲ ⚹

Halesowen

(1m). Camping & Caravanning Club Site - Clent Hills, Fieldhouse Lane, Romsley, Halesowen, West Midlands B62 0NH. *01562 710015/0870 243 3331.* www.campingandcaravanningclub.co.uk. Owner: Camping & Caravanning Club. Greenfields House, Westwood Way, Coventry CV4 8JH. M5, J3, take A456 then L on B4551 to Romsley, turn R past Sun Hotel take 5th L, SP Bell End and Broughton. Site 330yd on L. Hidden away, peaceful, tranquil atmosphere with 7.5 acres suitable for all units. In heart of country. Close to Welsh Borders. Play area. Birmingham and attractions such as National Sealife Centre, Millenium Point and Botanical Gardens only 15m. Close to Black Country Museum in Dudley. Nearby Seven Valley Railway. Non-members welcome. Special deals for families and backpackers. Open March-October. ☆☆☆☆☆ **95T. 95MC.** 🏕 ⚲ ⚹

Please mention Caravan Sites 2006 when replying to advertisers

Kingswinford

(4m). Ashwood Marina, Greensforge, Kingswinford, West Midlands DY6 0AQ. *01384 295535.* Owner: Ashwood Contracting and Development Co Ltd. Storage facility for 12 touring vans. Open April-October. **7S.** ♈

Sutton Coldfield

Camping & Caravanning Club Site - Kingsbury Water Park, Kingsbury Water Park, Bodymoor Heath Lane, Sutton Coldfield, West Midlands B76 0DY. *01827 874101/0870 243 3331.* www.campingandcaravanning club.co.uk. Owner: Camping & Caravanning Club. Greenfields House, Westwood Way, Coventry CV4 8JH. Leave M6 at J4 and follow A446 N, turn R at junction with A4097. After 1.5m turn L at Water Park sign, continue for 0.5m then turn R at C&CC sign. Surrounding the site are 600 acres of Kingsbury Water Park with lakes and countryside to explore. The park is ideal for walking, cycling, birdwatching and fishing. Gold award for excellence in tourism by the Heart of England Tourist Board. All units accepted. Non-members welcome. Water sports available at the Water Park complex. Nearby attractions include Drayton Manor Family Theme Park, Twycross Zoo, National Sea Life Centre, Cadbury World and the city museum art gallery. Try skiing and snowboarding on real snow at Snowdrome at nearby Tamworth. Special deals available for families and backpackers. ✰✰✰✰✰ **150T. 150MC.** ✿ ♈ ◕ ㋙

WORCESTERSHIRE

Bewdley

Butt Town Meadow, Northwood Lane, Wribbenhall, Bewdley, Worcestershire CY12 1AH. *01299 403692.* Owner: Mr J E Hurst. Open March 1-December 31. **91S.** ♈

(0.3m). Riverside Caravan Park, Dowles Road, Bewdley, Worcestershire DY12 2RE. *01299 400787.* Owner: A & I & M Loveridge. 1 Doverdale Park Homes, Kidderminster Road, Droitwich, Worcestershire WR9 0NU. On the B4194, adjacent to Bewdley town and river Severn. Looking on to Severn Valley railway. Walks nearby. Beside the river Severn. Golf course 1m. Bewdley town PHs/restaurants, shops etc within walking distance. **213S.** ✿ ♈ ◕ ㋙

(3m). Rousbine Park, Calow Hill, Rock, Bewdley, Worcestershire DY14 9DD. *01299 266312.* Owner: Mr & Mrs Lunnon. On A456 Bewdley to Tenbury. Picturesque park, 3m local towns, 20m Birmingham. On bus route. Showers, laundry room. Play area. Wyre Forest walks. Golf course within 1.5m. Open March 1-January 31. **84S.** ♈

(1.5m). The Woodlands Holiday Home Park, Dowles Road, Bewdley, Worcestershire DY12 3AE. *01299 403208/266415.* www.woodlands-bewdley.co.uk. Easy access from M5, M6 and M42. Quiet park situated in 40 acres of countryside on edge of Wyre Forest. Open March 1-February 28. **BH&HPA. 8T. MC. 150S.** ♈ ◕

(4m). Wyre Forest Caravan Park, Sugars Lane, Far Forest, Bewdley, Worcestershire DY14 9UN. *01299 266460.* Owner: Mr & Mrs M&J Knapper. Off the A4117. Licensed club. Children's room. Swimming pool. Laundrette. Caravan sales. Fishing, golf, children's farm. Country walks all nearby. 0.5m to shops and PO. Open March 1-October 31. **BH&HPA. 166S. 5H.** ♈ ㋙

Bringsty

Boyce Caravan Park, Boyce Farm, Stanford Bishop, Bringsty, Worcestershire WR6 5UB. *01886 884248.* enquiries@boyce holidaypark.co.uk. www.boyceholidaypark.co.uk. Owners: Richards & Bateson. Turn R off A44 Bromyard to Worcester on to B4220 SP Malvern. After 1.75m turn sharp L SP Linley Green. Then first R or follow caravan signs, about 3.5m from Bromyard. 14m from Worcester. Peaceful park with showers, laundry etc. Farm walks and fishing on premises. No flooding. Shopping 3m, golf 7m, cinema and swimming pool 12m. Open March-October for tourers (weather permitting); open February-December for holiday homes. **BH&HPA. 25T. MC. 100S.** ♈ ◕ ㋙

Broadway

Broadway Caravan Club Site, Station Road, Broadway, Worcestershire WR12 7DH. *01386 858786.* www.caravanclub.co.uk. Owner: The Caravan Club. East Grinstead House, East Grinstead, West Sussex RH19 1UA. See website for standard directions to site. Club members only. Landscaped on two levels, the site is on the edge of one of the loveliest of the golden-stoned villages of the Cotswolds. Toilet blocks, laundry facilities, baby and toddler washroom and Motorhome service point. Good area for walking, dog walk on site and golf nearby. Suitable for families. Open March-October. **BH&HPA. 115T. MC.** ♈ ㋙ ㋛ ∅

(1m). Leedons Park, Childswickham Road, Broadway, Worcestershire WR12 7HB. *01386 852423.* www.allenscara vans.com. Owners: Allens Caravans. Wootton Hall, Wootton Wawen, Henley in Arden B95 6EE. From Evesham take the A44 to Oxford. After 5m, at main island take third exit (Broadway Village). After 150yd, turn right down Pennylands Bank. At T-junction turn left. Entrance to Leedons Park is 250yd on the right. Shop, cafeteria, laundrette, heated outdoor swimming pool, play area, tennis court and pets corner. Shops, restaurants etc in nearby Broadway. Open all year for tourers; open March-December for owner-occupied holiday caravans. **BH&HPA. NCC. 350T. MC. 85S. 11H.** ✿ ♈ ◕ ㋙ ㋛

Droitwich

Fruiterer's Arms, Uphampton, Ombersley, Droitwich, Worcestershire WR9 0JW. *01905 620305/620527.* Owner: T & E May. On the A449. Children allowed. Open April 1-October. **BH&HPA. 15S.** ♈ ㋛ ∅

Evesham

(4m). Abbot's Salford Caravan Park, Abbot's Salford, Evesham, Worcestershire WR11 8UN. *01386 870244.* www.allenscaravans.com. Owners: Allens Caravans. Wootton Hall, Wootton Wawen, Henley in Arden B95 6EE. On the A46 take turning to Abbot's Salford. The lane to park is opposite PH in village. Laundrette, shop and cafe. Outdoor swimming pool, private club, fishing, boating. Playground. Private boat moorings. Shops, restaurants, etc. in nearby towns of Evesham and Stratford. Open March 7-January 7. **BH&HPA. NCC. 350S.** ♈ ㋙

(2m). Evesham Vale Caravan Park, Yessell Farm, Boston Lane, Charlton, Evesham, Worcestershire WR11 2RD. *01386 860377.* Owner: E P Edwards. Off A44 Pershore to Evesham SP Charlton. Farm 0.75m on double bend. Open April 1-October. **40T. MC. 100S.** ♈ ◕ ㋙

(0.5m). Hampton Ferry Caravan Park, Boat Lane, Evesham, Worcestershire. *01386 442458.* www.hamptonferry.com. Owners: S M & D R Raphael. Quiet, secluded site. Permanent sites full. Fishing. Rallies welcome. Occasionally caravans for sale. Town centre, cinema, bingo hall, shopping centre all within few minutes walk. Open March 1-December 31. **70S.** 🐾 🛇

(5m). Long Carrant Park, Cheltenham Road, Ashton under Hill, Evesham, Worcestershire WR11 7QP. *01386 881724.* malcolmportman@aol.com. Owners: Mr & Mrs Eleanor & Stephen Portman. Located south of Evesham on the A46, opposite the Vale services. Nestled at the base of Bredon Hill and only 7m from Tewkesbury, 11m from Cheltenham. 24hr restaurant/shop opposite park. **BH&HPA. 45T.** ❖ 🐾 🛇

(4m). Offenham Park, Fish & Anchor Crossing, Offenham, Evesham, Worcestershire WR11 8QT. *01386 442011.* offenhampark@freenetname.co.uk. www.offenhampark.co.uk. Owner: C&K Pilling. Situated on B4510 between Evesham and Cleeve Prior, on Offenham Road, opposite Fish & Anchor Inn. Village Inn opposite. Winner of David Bellamy Silver Conversation Award. Between Nature reserve and river. 0.5m to exclusive private fishing. A retreat of total peace quiet and tranquility, nature. Shopping 1m. Tennis, bowling 1.5m. Evesham and cinema 4m. Golf 5m. Theatre 12m. Open March 1-January 31. **BH&HPA. 75S.** 🐾 ♿

Pippens Green Parks Ltd, Waterside, Evesham, Worcestershire WR11 6BU. *01386 860063.* Owner: Mr & Mrs C L Crowe. Off A44. Open March 1-January 31. **BH&HPA. 4T. MC. 10S. 6H.** 🐾 🛇

(6m). Ranch Caravan Park, Honeybourne, Evesham, Worcestershire WR11 7PR. *01386 830744.* enquiries@ranch.co.uk. www.ranch.co.uk. Owner: Ranch Caravan Parks Ltd. From Evesham take B4035 to Badsey and Bretforton, turn L to Honeybourne. Site SP. Licensed club. Heated outdoor swimming pool. Golf 4m, shopping 6m. Contact: Mr Andy Attridge. Open March 1-November 30 for tourers; open Easter-October for hire holiday caravans. ☆☆☆☆☆ **BH&HPA. NCC. 120T. MC. 197S. 4H.** 🐾 🛇 ♿ 🛇

(2.5m). Small Moors Holiday Park, Anchor Lane, Harvington, Evesham, Worcestershire WR11 5NR. *01386 870446.* www.ukparks.co.uk/smallmoors. Owner: BA & JV Saunders. Off the B439. Shop and PO in 0.5m. Fishing, golf walking distance. Open March 15-October 31. **BH&HPA. 100S.** 🐾

Weir Meadow Holiday & Touring Park, Lower Leys, Evesham, Worcestershire WR11 3AA. *01386 442417.* www.allenscaravans.com. Owners: Allen Caravans. Wootton Hall, Wootton Wawen, Henley in Arden B95 6EE. Turn off the A44 by Workman Bridge into Port Street, then left into Burford Road, Evesham. Park is at the bottom of the road on the right hand side. Tourer section on river bank. Seasonal moorings. One caravan is adapted for disabled people. Free fishing for patrons. Shops, restaurants, cinema etc in Evesham. Open March 1-December 31. **BH&HPA. NCC. 63T. MC. 130S. 12H.** 🐾 🛇 ♿

(5m). Wharfavon Park, Westside, North Littleton, Evesham, Worcestershire WR11 8QP. *01386 832482.* wharfavon@aol.com. Owner: S & J Arnold. Off B4085.

Indoor spa pool, laundry, table tennis, play area, solarium. Tourist information room. Pub nearby. Caravan and lodges for sale, lodges for hire. Open March-October (open 12 months for some lodges). **24S.**

Hanley Swan

(1m). Camping & Caravanning Club Site - Blackmore, Blackmore Camp Site No 2, Hanley Swan, Worcestershire WR8 0EE. *01684 310280/0870 2433331.* www.campingandcaravanningclub.co.uk. Owner: Camping & Caravanning Club. Greenfields House, Westwood Way, Coventry CV4 8JH. From J7 of the M5. Watch for Blackmore Camp, sign at junction of the B4211. All approaches to site are well signposted. Located 4m from Malvern. Splendid centre for touring countryside of the Malvern Hills and Severn Valley. All units are accepted. Non-members welcome. Ball games area available. The site is conveniently situated for Tewkesbury and Great Malvern. Special deals available for families and backpackers. ☆☆☆☆ **200T. 200MC.** ❖ 🐾 🛇 ♿

(1m). Oakmere Park, Hanley Swan, Worcestershire WR8 0DZ. *01684 310375.* Owner: Mr & Mrs B Piercy. Park is located on the B4209 1.5m E of Great Malvern. Open March-October for holiday vans. **BH&HPA. 20T. 4MC. 70S.** 🐾 🛇 🛇 ⌀

Hawford

Mill House Caravan & Camping Site, Mill House, Hawford, Worcestershire WR3 7SE. *01905 451283.* millhousecaravan site@yahoo.co.uk. Owner: Mrs J G Ellaway. On the A449, N 3m from centre of Worcester. Quiet, level, grassy site. Dogs to be exercised off site, kept on leads. Coarse fishing (small river). Open April-October. **100T. MC.** 🐾 🛇 🛇

Holt Heath

Holt Fleet Farm, Holt Fleet, Holt Heath, Worcestershire. *01905 620512.* Owner: Mr G T Barnett. On the A4133. Three miles from Droitwich. Doctor and PO in village 1.5m, local shops 100yd. Club on site. Open April-October. **75T. MC. 99S.** 🐾 🛇

Kidderminster

(3m). Austcliffe Leisure Homes Park, Cookley, Kidderminster, Worcestershire DY10 3UR. *01562 851277.* Owner: N & R Marshall. Located off A449 Wolverhampton to Kidderminster road. Garden plots with all mains services. Canal side mooring, fishing. Peace and tranquility assured. Over-50s only. Open February 7-January 7. **BH&HPA. 98S.** 🐾 ⌀

(9m). Bank Farm Caravan Park, Arley, Bewdley, Kidderminster, Worcestershire DY12 3ND. *01299 401277.* bankfarm@tinyworld.co.uk. www.bankfarmholidaypark.co.uk. Owner: O T Davies. Take B4194 out of Bewdley. After 3.5mturn for Arley. At New Inn PH bear left and follow for 1m to park. Open March-January. **BH&HPA. 9T. 9MC. 99S. 9H.** 🐾 🛇

(2m). Camping & Caravanning Club Site - Wolverley, Brown Westhead Park, Wolverley, Kidderminster, Worcestershire DY10 3PX. 01562 850909/0870 2433331. www.campingandcaravanningclub.co.uk. Owner: Camping & Caravanning Club. Greenfields House, Westwood Way, Coventry CV4 8JH. From Kidderminster A449 to Wolverhampton, turn left at lights onto B4189 signed Wolverley. Follow brown camping signs, turn right. Site on left. Quiet, secluded site with peaceful ambience. Children's play area. Close to Severn Valley Railway. All units accepted. Non-members welcome. Adjacent to Staffordshire and Worcestershire Canal, ideal for walking or cycling. Golf and horse riding locally. Birmingham and its attractions just a short drive away. Special deals available for families and backpackers. Open March-October. ☆☆☆ **115T. 115MC.** ♒ ♨ ♿

Malvern

(3.5m). Riverside Caravan Park, Little Clevelode, Malvern, Worcestershire WR13 6PE. 01684 310475. www.ukparks.co.uk/riversidecp8. Owner: Mr & Mrs Nock. Halfway between Worcester and Upton-on-Severn on the B4424. Club. Fishing. Tennis. Play area. Laundrette. AA 3 pennants. Open March-December for holiday homes; open April-October for tourers. ☆☆☆ **BH&HPA. 70T. MC. 130S. 5H.** ♨ ♒

(6m.). Three Counties Park, Sledge Green, Berrow, Malvern, Worcestershire WR13 6JW. 01684 833439. Owner: J & E Fury Park Homes. On A438 Tewkesbury to Ledbury Road. Separate touring park with showers and chemical toilet disposal. David Bellamy Conservation Award. Open Easter-October 31. **BH&HPA. 30T. 20MC.** ♒ ♨ ♿ ⌀

Pershore

(3m). Eckington Riverside Park, Eckington, Pershore, Worcestershire WR10 3DD. 01386 750985. Off the A440. Open March 1-October 31. **10T. 10MC. 50S.** ♒ ♨

(3m). The Springs Lakeside Holiday Home Park, Salters Lane, Lower Moor, Pershore, Worcestershire WR10 2PD. 01386 861851. www.allenscaravans.com. Owners: Allens Caravans. Wootton Hall, Wootton Wawen, Henley-in-Arden B95 6EE. Turn off A44 (Evesham to Worcester) at Lower Moor into Salters Lane. The Springs is 1m on right. Indoor heated swimming pool, club. Landscaped grounds. Private fishing, nature reserves, water sports. Open March 7-January 7. **BH&HPA. NCC. 150S.** ♒ ♿ ⌀

Shrawley

Brant Farm Caravan Park, Shrawley, Worcestershire WR6 6TD. 01905 620470. Owner: Mr N T O'Hara. Brant Farmhouse. On B4196 Worcester to Stourport on left in centre of Shrawley between Rose and Crown and New Inn PHs. 3m from Stourport. Shrawley Woods within 5 mins walking distance. Fishing nearby. Open March 7-January 7. **14T. 4MC. 21S.** ♒ ♨

Stanford Bridge

The Bridge, Riverside Leisure Caravan Park, Stanford Bridge, Worcestershire WR6 6RU. 01886 812771. Owner: Mr C Powell. Hot and cold showers. Toilets. River fishing on site. Golf, PO, doctor 2.5m. Open Easter-September 30. **15T. 6MC.** ♒ ♨

Stourport-on-Severn

(1m). Greenlawns Caravan Park, Worcester Road, Stourport-on-Severn, Worcestershire DY13 9PB. 01299 822316. Owner: Mr D M Brookes. A4025 Stourport to Worcester. Rear of Cooks Garden Centre. Open March 1-December 31. **BH&HPA. 30S.** ♒ ♨

(1m). Lickhill Manor Caravan Park, Stourport-on-Severn, Worcestershire DY13 8RL. 01299 871041. excellent@lickhillmanor.co.uk. www.lickhillmanor.co.uk. Owners: Denis Lloyd Jones. SP at crossroads with traffic lights on B4195 Bewdley to Stourport. Riverside position, level ground, superb washrooms. Online booking for tourers and tents. Fishing, many attractions in the area to suit all ages. Town centre, leisure centre 1m. Golf 2m. ☆☆☆☆☆ **BH&HPA. 120T. 15MC. 124S.** ♿ ♒ ♨ ♿

(0.75m). Lincomb Lock Caravan Park, Titton, Stourport-on-Severn, Worcestershire DY13 9QR. 01299 823836. info@hillandale.co.uk. www.hillandale.co.uk. Owners: D & D Lloyd Jones Securities Ltd. Take A4025 out of Stourport. After 0.75m R on left-hand bend just after house with two stone dogs on wall. Alongside the river Severn with fishing. Golf 0.5m. Town and leisure centre 1m. Open March-January. ☆☆☆ **BH&HPA. 14T. 6MC. 118S.** ♒ ♨ ⌀

(0.25m). Redstone Caravan Park, The Rough, Stourport-on-Severn, Worcestershire DY13 0LD. 01299 823872. redstonecaravans@btconnect.com. Owner: Mrs S Franks. A451 from Kidderminster to Stourport, through town centre, over bridge, 2nd L into The Rough. Alongside river Severn. Fully licensed club with music. Laundrette. Play area. Takeaway. Club open at weekends. Open February 1-December 31. **BH&HPA. 30T. 6MC. 290S.** ♒ ♨ ♿ ♒

(1.50m). Severnside Caravan Park, Sandy Lane, Titton, Stourport-on-Severn, Worcestershire DY13 9PY. 01299 824976. www.allenscaravans.com. Owners: Allen Caravans. Wootton Hall, Wootton Wawen, Henley in Arden B95 6EE. On A4025 (Worcester road) turn R into Sandy Lane. Own river frontage, private fishing. Clubhouse. Play area. Heated outdoor swimming pool. Fishing. Laundry. Shop. Golf course about 2m, shopping centre about 1.5m. Open March 1-December 31. **BH&HPA. NCC. 179S.** ♒ ♒

Walshes Farm Caravan and Camping Site, Off Dunley Road, Stourport-on-Severn, Worcestershire DY13 0AA. 01299 877577. Owner: C Robson. Off A451. 500yd from town. Bottled gas. Open February 1-December 31. **BH&HPA. 250S. 12H.** ♿ ♒

Tenbury Wells

(3m). Knighton-on-Teme Caravan Park, Knighton-on-Teme, Tenbury Wells, Worcestershire WR15 8NA. 01584 781246. kotcaravans@btinternet.com. www.kotcaravans.com. Owner: Mr J R Powell. Off A456 at Newnham Bridge SP Knighton-on-Teme. PH opposite park. Please ring for detailed directions. David Bellamy Silver Conservation Award. Shower block, children's play area. Cinema in Tenbury Wells. Golf, fishing available nearby. Open March-January 2. **BH&HPA. 4T. MC. 90S. 1H.** ♒ ♨

(2m). Orchard Holiday Park, New House Farm, St Michaels, Tenbury Wells, Worcestershire WR15 8TW. 01568 750 /618/245/460. enquiries@orchardholidaypark.co.uk. www.orchard holidaypark.co.uk. Owners: Bill & Margaret Jones. On A4112 between Leominster and Tenbury Wells. Caravan Club site. Countryside location. Pools. Suitable sitel for fishing and walking. 9 and 18-hole golf courses nearby. Village PHs and restaurants. Severn Valley steam railway, Bewdley Safari Park. Open March 1-December 31. **5T. MC. 33S.** ♿ ♒ ♨

(6m). Wigley Orchard Caravan Park, Stoke Bliss, Tenbury Wells, Worcestershire WR15 8QH. 01885 410331. enquiries@wigleyorchard.co.uk. www.wigleyorchard.co.uk. Owner: Mr & Mrs W B Griffiths. W off B4203 Bromyard to Witley, near Upper Sapey golf club. Good fishing. Peaceful site Lovely views. Holidays booked through Hoseasons. Golf, pub 2m. Fish and chips 6m. Beach 96m. Open March-December. **BH&HPA. 70S. 20H.** ♒

Worcester

> **Blackmore Caravan Club Site, Blackmore End, Hanley Swan, Worcester, Worcestershire WR8 0EE.** *01684 310505.* www.caravanclub.co.uk. Owner: The Caravan Club. East Grinstead House, East Grinstead, West Sussex RH19 1UA. See website for standard directions to site. 2.5m from Great Malvern. Club members only. The Malvern Hills overlook the site which is level, open, blissfully quiet and recommended for a peaceful holiday. Toilet blocks. Privacy cubicles. Laundry facilities. Veg prep. Motorhome Service point. Calor Gas and Campingaz. Play equipment. Dog walk. Walking. Family site. Mums' and toddlers' room, small football pitch. Open March-October. **NCC. 243T. MC. 🐕 🅰 ♿ 🛒**

> **Bromyard Downs Caravan Club Site, Brockhampton, Bringsty, Worcester, Worcestershire WR6 5TE.** *01885 482607.* www.caravanclub.co.uk. Owner: The Caravan Club. East Grinstead House, East Grinstead, West Sussex RH19 1UA. See website for standard directions to site. Woodland site is well situated in countryside between the cathedral cities of Worcester and Hereford. The site is arranged in two linked areas and is suitable for those seeking a rural holiday. Walking is a pleasure from the site, over Bromyard Downs, Bringsty Common or in the National Trust estate at Brockhampton with its lovely timbered moated manor house. Some hard-standings and dog walk nearby. No toilet block. Open March-October. **NCC. 40T. MC. 🐕 🅰**

(5m). Coppice Leisure Park, Ockeridge Wood, Worcester, Worcestershire WR6 6YP. *01886 888305.* info@hillandale.co.uk. www.hillandale.co.uk. A443 N from Worcester, through Holt Heath, 0.5m L at caravan sign,1m on L. Set in 200 acres of woodland. Club. Heated swimming pool. Open March-January. **BH&HPA. 15T. 15MC. 130S. 🐕 🅰**

(3m). Gunburn Farm, Sinton Green, Grimley, Worcester, Worcestershire. *01905 640280.* Owner: Messr H J Humphries. Fishing pool. **100T. MC. ❀ 🐕**

(1.5m). Ketch Caravan Park, Bath Road, Worcester, Worcestershire WR5 3HW. *01905 820430.* Owner: E P Edwards. 1.5m from Worcester city centre (Bath road A38) on route to Tewkesbury. Fishing. Open April 1-October 31. **30T. MC. 70S. 🐕 🅰**

(7m). Lenchford Meadow Park, Shrawley, Worcester, Worcestershire WR6 6TB. *01905 620246.* info@lenchford.co.uk. www.lenchford.co.uk. Owner: Mrs M Bendall. On A443, B4196 Worcester-Holt Heath-Stourport, 1m from Holt Heath (Red Lion) on right-hand side. No tourers. Boat slipway. Fishing. Shops & PO 5mins; doctor, golf course 10mins. Country walks nearby. Open February 7-January 6. **BH&HPA. 66S. 🐕 🅰**

(10m). Pool House Caravan Park, Upton-on-Severn, Worcester, Worcestershire WR8 0PA. *01684 594799.* Owner: C B Webb. On B2411. All caravans must be removed during winter months. Open April-October 31. **24T. 🐕 🅰**

(3m). Seaborne Leisure Caravan Park, Court Meadow, Kempsey, Worcester, Worcestershire WR5 3JL. *01905 820295/07977280466.* Owners: Mr P Alden & Mr & Mrs G Chambers. Off A38 Worcester to Tewksbury, 3m S of Worcester in Kempsey village. Turn opposite Crown Inn, SP St Mary's Church, follow road round until church is behind you then L into Court Meadow. On bank of river Severn. Set within 12 acres.PH with restaurant within grounds, offering occasional entertainment. On-site laundry room, showers. 4 other PHs, PO and convenience store within walking distance. Not suitable for children under 14 years old. Dogs at park owner's discretion only. Open March 1-December 31. **BH&HPA. 20T. 10MC. 105S. 🅰**

DERBYSHIRE

Ambergate

(1m). The Firs Farm Caravan & Camping Park, Crich Lane, Nether Heage, Ambergate, Derbyshire DE56 2JH. *01773 852913.* Owner: Stella Ragsdale. S of Ambergate, turn left off A6 and follow signs for 1m. Exclusively for adults. Friendly, quiet, well-maintained, landscaped park with panoramic views. Heated facilities. Many local attractions to visit. Friendly local PHs and restaurants. ☆☆☆☆ **60T. 60MC. ❀ 🐕 🅰**

Ashbourne

(2m). Bank Top Farm, Fenny Bentley, Ashbourne, Derbyshire DE6 1LF. *01335 350250.* Owner: Mr & Mrs Cotterell. Leave Ashbourne on A515, Buxton in 2m take right-hand fork on to B5056, Bakewell road, site is 200yd along on R opposite to Bentley Brook Hotel. Working farm. Showers. AA 3 pennants. Open Easter-September 30. **45T. 5MC. 🐕 🅰 🛒**

> **(6m). Blackwall Plantation Caravan Club Site, Kirk Ireton, Ashbourne, Derbyshire DE6 3JL.** *01335 370903.* www.caravanclub.co.uk. Owner: The Caravan Club. East Grinstead House, East Grinstead, West Sussex RH19 1UA. See website for standard directions to site. Set in a pine plantation, convenient base for walkers, with scenery of Dovedale and surrounding countryside. Carsington water 15mins walk away. Advance booking essential. Dog walk. Non-members welcome. Toilet block with privacy cubicles, laundry facilities and baby/toddler washroom. Motorhome service point. Play equipment. Suitable for families. Open March-October. ☆☆☆☆ **NCC. 128T. MC. 🐕 🅰 ♿**

(0.5m). Callow Top Holiday Park, Buxton Road, Ashbourne, Derbyshire DE6 2AQ. *01335 344020.* enquiries@callowtop. co.uk. www.callowtop.co.uk. Owner: Mr & Mrs Palmer. On A515 Buxton road. Full facilities including heated pool, games room, restaurant and PH etc. Flat pitches. Adjacent to Tissington Trail cycle path. Family site in countryside. Alton Towers 20 mins. Fishing on site. Open weekend before Easter-November. ☆☆☆☆ **BH&HPA. 160T. MC. 40S. 2H. 🐕 🅰 ♿ 🛒**

Carsington Fields Caravan Park, Millfields Lane, Nr Carsington Water, Ashbourne, Derbyshire DE6 3JS. *01335 372872.* www.carstingtoncaravanning.co.uk. Owners: Judy & Peter Booth. Aysgarth, Charnwood Avenue, Belper, Derbyshire. Turn R off A517 Belper to Ashbourne within 0.25m past Hulland Ward into Dog Lane in 0.75m turn R SP Carsington. The site is on the R within 0.75m. 400yd from Carsington water. 1.5m from nearest shop/PO. Open Easter-end of October. **10T. 10MC. 🐕 🅰**

(2.5m). Closes Caravan Park, Kniveton, Ashbourne, Derbyshire DE6 1JL. *01335 343191.* Owner: Mr W R & E M Wildgoose. Signposted off B5035 Ashbourne to Wirksworth road 400yd opposite church. Edge of Peak Park and Dovedale. Central touring area for places of interest and Alton Towers. AA 3 pennants. Open Easter-October 1. **35T. MC. 🐕 🅰**

(1m). Gateway Caravan Park, Osmaston, Ashbourne, Derbyshire DE6 1NA. *01335 344643.* karen@gatewaypark. fsnet.co.uk. www.ashbourne-accommodation.co.uk. Owner: Mr P Cranstone & Miss K H Peach. 1m S of Ashbourne off A52. Set amid countryside. Flat site. Licensed bar open weekends, March-November, daily during school holidays. Entertainment Saturday nights during school holidays. Games room, laundry. Nearby fishing, golf, tennis, swimming, climbing. Close to Alton Towers. Suitable base for touring Peak District. AA pennants. **200T. MC.** ✿ 🛇 🗶 🐾

Highfield Farm Caravan Park, Fenny Bentley, Ashbourne, Derbyshire DE6 1LE. *0870 741 8000.* www.highfieldsfarmcaravanpark.co.uk. Owner: Mr & Mrs G & I Redfern. 3m N of Ashbourne. On A515 Ashbourne to Buxton Road. Tissington Trail runs along the side of the park. Well stocked shop, heated indoor swimming pool. Large play area. Laundry room. Cycle hire on site. Playground. Rally fields. Booking advisable at peak periods. Open March 1-October 31. **BH&HPA. 55T. 4MC. 50S. 1H.** 🛇 🗶 🐾

(4m). Ilam Park Caravan Club Site, Ilam Hall, Ashbourne, Derbyshire DE6 2AZ. *01335 350310.* www.caravanclub.co.uk. Owner: The Caravan Club. East Grinstead House, East Grinstead, West Sussex RH19 1UA. See website for standard directions to site. Club members only. Country site is located in the grounds of the National Trust's Ilam parkland surrounded by trees. Own sanitation required. Good area for walking. NCN route nearby. Peaceful off-peak. Open March-October. **NCC. 20T. MC.** 🛇 🗶

(6m). Rivendale Caravan & Leisure Park, Buxton Road, Alsop-en-le-Dale, Ashbourne, Derbyshire DE6 1QU. *01335 310311.* caravan@rivendalecaravanpark.co.uk. www.rivendale caravanpark.co.uk. Owner: Alsop Rivendale Ltd. 30a Town Street, Duffield, Belper, Derbyshire DE56 4EH. Heading N from Ashbourne, take the A515 towards Buxton. Find Rivendale after 6m on the right-hand side. 25 acres of pasture and woodland. Close Tissington Trail. Hard standings with 16amp supplies. New underfloor heated toilet and shower block. Warden: Susan Bailey. Cafe and bar. David Bellamy Gold Conservation Award. Open mid Feb-year end including Christmas and New Year. ✿✿✿✿ **BH&HPA. 105T. 35M. 30S.** 🗶 🛇 🗶 🐾

Bakewell

(3m). Broadmeadow Caravan Site, Alport, Bakewell, Derbyshire DE4 1LH. *01629 636545.* Owner: Mr R A Walker. Old Forge Farm, Broadmeadow, Alport, Bakewell, Derbyshire. Off A6. Open March 1-October 31. **5T. 30S.**

(3m). Camping & Caravanning Club Site - Bakewell, c/o Hopping Farm, Youlgreave, Bakewell, Derbyshire DE45 1NA. *01629 636555/0870 2433331.* www.camping andcaravanningclub.co.uk. Owner: Camping & Caravanning Club. Greenfields House, Westwood Way, Coventry CV4 8JH. A6/B5056 after 0.5m turn R to Youlgreave, turn sharp L after church down Bradford lane, opposite George Hotel. 0.5m to sign turn R. In the heart of the Peak District National Park. 14-acre site. Local attractions include Speedwell Cavern in Castleton and Chatsworth House. Accepts all units. Non-members welcome. Own sanitation essential. Special deals available for families and backpackers. Open March-October. ✿✿✿ **100T. 100MC.** 🗶 🛇

(4m). Chatsworth Park Caravan Club Site, Baslow, Bakewell, Derbyshire DE45 1PN. *01246 582226.* www.caravanclub.co.uk. Owner: The Caravan Club. East Grinstead House, East Grinstead, West Sussex RH19 1UA. See website for standard directions to site. Set in an old walled garden on 1000-acre Chatsworth Estate with views of surrounding countryside. No entrance through Chatsworth Estate. Please arrive after 1pm due to congestion and bottleneck in area. Playground. Advance booking essential. Dog walk. Non-members welcome. Toilet block with privacy cubicles and laundry facilities. Bab/toddler washroom. Motorhome service point. Open March-January. ✿✿✿✿✿ **NCC. 120T. MC.** 🗶 🛇 🗶

(1m). Greenhills Holiday Park, Crowhill Lane, Bakewell, Derbyshire DE45 1PX. *01629 813052.* info@greenhills leisure.com. www.greenhillsleisure.com. Owner: Mr J A Green. From A6 (Buxton-Matlock), 0.25m E at Ashfour-in-the-Water, turn S into Crowhill Lane, SP. Calor Gas sales. Licensed bar. Laundry. Showers. Shop open April to end of October. Suitable for an overnight stop or longer stays. Open March 1-October 31. **BH&HPA. 70T. 70MC. 65S.** 🗶 🛇 🗶 🐾

(4.5m). Hopping Farm, Bakewell, Derbyshire. *01629 636302.* Owner: Mr B Frost. Showers. Open April 1-September 30. **15T. MC. 19S. 1H.** 🛇

Buxton

(0.75m). Cold Springs Farm, Manchester Road, Buxton, Derbyshire SK17 6ST. *01298 22762.* Owner: Mr S Booth Millward. Take the A5004 from town centre. **20T. MC.** ✿ 🗶 🛇

(6m). Cottage Farm Caravan Park, Beech Croft, Blackwell, Taddington, Buxton, Derbyshire SK17 9TQ. *01298 85330.* mail@cottagefarmsite.co.uk. www.cottagefarmsite.co.uk. Owner: Ms Julie Gregory. Off A6 midway between Buxton and Bakewell. SP. Level hard-standings. Winter opening with minimum facilities; open November-February with water tap hook-up and chemical toilet emptyng pointl. ✿✿✿ **BH&HPA. 30T. 5MC.** ✿ 🗶 🛇 🐾

(10m). Endon Cottage, Hulme End, Sheen, Buxton, Derbyshire SK17 0HG. *01298 84617.* Owner: Mrs J Naylor. In Beresford Lane off Beresford Dale. Mains water. Eggs available. **10T. 6MC. S. H.** ✿ 🗶

(2m). Grin Low Caravan Club Site, Grin Low Road, Ladmanlow, Buxton, Derbyshire SK17 6UJ. *01298 77735.* www.caravanclub.co.uk. Owner: The Caravan Club. East Grinstead House, East Grinstead, West Sussex RH19 1UA. See website for standard directions to site. Landscaped site set in heart of Peak District National Park. Advance booking advised. Play area and playframe. Tents accepted. Most pitches are hard-standings. Dog walk nearby. Non-members welcome. Toilet block, laundry facilities, baby/toddler washroom. Motorhome service point. Golf nearby. Open March-October. ✿✿✿✿✿ **NCC. 117T. MC.** 🗶 🛇 🗶

(0.5m). Lime Tree Park, Dukes Drive, Buxton, Derbyshire SK17 9RP. *01298 22988.* www.ukparks.co.uk/limetree. Owner: Mr R & A Hidderley. off A515, 1m S of Buxton. Duke's Drive links A515 to A6. In a rural valley setting, though within 20mins walk of Buxton. Suitable base for walking and cycling in Peak District. Open March 1-October 31. ✿✿✿✿ **BH&HPA64T. MC. 36S. 10H.** 🗶 🛇 🗶 🐾

(7m). Longnor Wood 'Just for Adults' Caravan & Camping Park, Longnor, Buxton, Derbyshire SK17 0NG. *01298 83648.* enquiries@longnorwood.co.uk. www.longnorwood.co.uk. Owner: Paul and Lindsey Hedges. On reaching Longnor crossroads follow site signs for 1.25m to site. Peaceful site in the heart of the country and central for many Peak District attractions, including Chatsworth House, Hartington, Bakewell and the beautiful dales. Putting green, boules court and croquet. Adults only. AA 4 pennants. Open March 1-October 31. ✩✩✩✩ **BH&HPA. 33T. 33MC. 14S. 3H.** ↝ 🖵 🛴

(9m). Newhaven Caravan & Camping Park, Newhaven, Buxton, Derbyshire SK17 0DT. *01298 84300.* www.newhavencaravanpark.co.uk. Owner: R & K Macara. At junction A5012 and A515 halfway between Ashbourne and Buxton. Modern, 30-acre site in the heart of the Peak National Park. Restaurant adjacent. Phone on site. Playroom. Laundrette. AA 3 pennants. Open March 1-October 31. ✩✩✩ **BH&HPA. NCC. 95T. 10MC. 73S.** ↝ 🖵 🛴

(5m). The Pomeroy Caravan and Camping Park, Street House Farm, Pomeroy, Flagg, Buxton, Derbyshire SK17 9QG. *01298 83259.* Owner: Mr & Mrs J Melland. On A515 adjoining High Peak Trail central site for Peak National Park. Ashbourne 16m. Showers. Hand and hair-dryers and shaver points. Laundrette. Gas supplies. Site fully lit. Open Easter/April 1-October 31. ✩✩ **30T. MC.** ↝ 🖵

Castleton

(2.5m). Rowter Farm, Hope Valley, Castleton, Derbyshire S33 8WA. *01433 620271.* Owner: Mrs B Hall. 2.5m W of Castleton off B6061. Flat field, partly sheltered overlooking Man Tor. Excellent for walkers and touring Peak District. Castleton has 6 hotels, good range of shops and tearooms. Parking alongside units, reasonable rates. Open Easter-October. **5T. 5MC.** ↝

Chesterfield

(5m). Millfield Touring & Camping Park, Old Tupton, Chesterfield, Derbyshire S42 6AE. *01246 861082.* Owner: Mr & Mrs A Bateman. Woodthorpe Mill Farm, Old Tupton, Chesterfield, Derbyshire S42 6AE. Off A61Alfreton to Chesterfield. We are within walking distance of a Spar shop. There is pitch and put course nearby. GS. **20T. MC.** ↝ 🖵

Derby

(8m). Donington Park Farmhouse Hotel, Melbourne Road, Isley Walton, Derby, Derbyshire DE74 2RN. *01332 862409.* info@parkfarmhouse.co.uk. parkfarmhouse.co.uk. Owner: J Shields. At exit 23A & 24 of M1, take A453 past East Midlands airport. Turn right at Isley Walton, site is 0.5 mile on right. Golf course and Donington Park Grand Prix Collection half mile. Open all year except Christmas. ✩✩✩ **50T. 20MC.** ✿ ↝ 🖵 ♿

(4m). Elvaston Castle Country Park Caravan Club Site, Borrowash Road, Elvaston, Derby, Derbyshire DE72 3EP. *01332 573735.* www.caravanclub.co.uk. Owner: The Caravan Club. East Grinstead House, East Grinstead, West Sussex RH19 1UA. See website for standard directions to site. Very attractive site in well-kept 200-acre country park. Families will enjoy castle, lake and large play area in castle grounds. Advance booking essential. Non-members welcome. Toilet block. Tent campers welcome. Fishing and golf nearby. Ideal for walkers. Local attractions include Alton Towers, American Adventure, Tales of Robin Hood and Denby Pottery. Battery charging, gas, dog walk nearby. Suitable for families. Open March-October. **NCC. 47T. MC.** ↝ 🖵

Doveridge

Cavendish Caravan & Camping Site, Derby Road, Doveridge, Derbyshire DE6 5JR. *01889 562092.* Owner: Mr G Wood. Take the Doveridge sign off the A50. Shop, PO, PH within 300yd or less. Doctors, garages, golf course within 2-3m. **15T. MC.** ✿ ↝ 🖵

Edale

Coopers Camp & Caravan Site, New Fold Farm, Edale, Derbyshire S30 2ZD. *01433 670372.* Owner: Mr R M Cooper. Turn R at Hope Church, off A625, 5m to centre of Edale village. **15T. 120MC. 11S.** ✿ ↝ 🖵 🛴

(25m). Waterside Farm, Barker Booth Road, Edale, Derbyshire S30 2ZL. *01433 670215.* Owner: Mrs J M Cooper. Dogs allowed on leads. Open April 1-September 30. **10T. 20S.**

Glossop

(3m). Woodseats Holiday Home Park, Woodseats Lane, Charlesworth, Glossop, Derbyshire SK13 5DR. *01457 863415.* woodseatspark@btinternet.com. www.btinternet.com/~woodseatspark. Owner: D Lyon & J Dorman. Off A626. Small, peaceful site with views over open farmland. Village 0.75m. Personal service from owner on site. Colour brochure available. Open February 1-December 31. **BH&HPA. 25S.**

Hayfield

(1m). Camping & Caravanning Club Site - Hayfield, Kinder Road, Hayfield, Derbyshire SK22 2LE. *01663 745394/0870 2433331.* www.campingandcaravanning club.co.uk. Owners: Camping & Caravanning Club. Greenfields House, Westwood Way, Coventry CV4 8JH. A624 - Glossop to Chapel en le Frith. Hayfield by-pass, follow wooden carved signs to site. 4m N of Chapel en Le Frith. 5m from Glossop. Site set on the banks of the River Sett, suitable for fell and moorland walkers. National Trust Kinder Roundwalk is good for the bird-watchers and botanists.No towed caravans permitted. Non-members welcome. Special deals available for families and backpackers. Open March-October. ✩✩✩ **90MC.** ↝

High Peak

Ringstones Caravan Park, Yeardsley Lane, Furness Vale, High Peak, Derbyshire SK23 7EB. *01663 747042.* mo@ring-stones.demon.co.uk. Owner: Mrs M A Hallworth. 1 Charlesworth Road, Furness Vale, High Peak, Derbyshire SK23 7PP. From Whaley Bridge, A6 to Furness Vale. Turn off A6 at Cantonese restaurant by pelican crossing then 0.75m up Yeardsley Lane. 10m from Buxton. Quiet site on working farm, with views of the Peak District. Small shop, PO, train station and bus stop all within 0.75m. Tennis, bowling, football pitch, 3 PHs within walking distance. 3m to supermarket, swimming pool, leisure centre. Golf, rock climbing nearby. Open March 1-October 31. **10T. 10MC. 44S.** ↝

Hope Valley

Eden Tree Caravan Park, Eccles Lane, Bradwell, Hope Valley, Derbyshire S33 9JT. *01433 623444.* Owner: Mr M Allcroft. Off B6049 at New Bath Inn in Bradwell. 9m from Bakewell and 8m Buxton. Electric hook-ups. Showers. All grass site. Within easy walking distance of shops. Booking advisable. Dogs on leads allowed on touring field only. Shops and PO 0.5m. Doctors 2m. Fishing, golf course 3m. Open March-October. **BH&HPA. 15T. 5MC. 60S.** ↝ 🖵

Laneside Caravan Site, Laneside, Hope, Hope Valley, Derbyshire S33 6RR. *01433 620215.* laneside@lineone.net. www.lanesidecaravanpark.co.uk. Owner: Mrs D Neary. On A6187 Hathersage to Castleton. On Eastern border of Hope Village (200yd), opposite Hope train station. 11m from Buxton. Level, riverside, site surrounded by hills bordering Hope village with late shopping and 3 PHs. Laundry room. Chemical toilet disposal point. Calor Gas. Centrally heated shower block. Golf courses, horse riding and rock climbing all close by. Open March-November. **100T. 10MC. 28S.** ♙ ⊕ ⅙ ⚐

Peakland Caravans, High Street, Stoney Middleton, Hope Valley, Derbyshire S32 4TL. *01433 631414.* peakland2000@aol.com. Owner: A F Clarke. On A623 turn by the Moon Inn up the hill for about 0.3m. Site on right. Quiet, rural park with good views. Open April-end October. ☆☆☆ **BH&HPA. 2S. 14H.** ♙

(0.5m). Swallowholme Caravan Park, Station Road, Bamford, Hope Valley, Derbyshire S33 0BN. *01433 650981.* Owner: Mr John Frogatt. On A6013. 2m S of Ladybower Reservoir. Fishing and golf nearby. Shop 0.25m. Site unsuitable for children. Open April 1-October 31. **45T. 25MC.** ⚐

Matlock

(5m). Barn Farm, Birchover, Matlock, Derbyshire DE4 2BL. *01629 650245.* Owner: Mr Gilbert Heathcote. Off B524 and A6. Matlock 5m. Bakewell 5m. Shop, restaurant and PH in village of Birchover, 250yd from site. Working farm site. **T. MC. 15S.** ♙ ⚐

(4m). Birchwood Farm, Wirksworth Road, Whatstandwell, Matlock, Derbyshire DE4 5HS. *01629 822280.* Owner: Mr F & N Smith. Leave A6 at Whatstandwell, take B5035 Wirksworth Road; site in 1.25m. Showers, shaver point. Hairdryer point. Launderette. Calor Gas sales. Milk, eggs and confectionery for sale. Open March 25-31 October. ☆☆ **40T. 6MC. 24S. 2H.** ♙ ⚐ ⅐

(6m). Haytop Country Park, Whatstandwell, Matlock, Derbyshire DE4 5HP. *01773 852063.* Owner: Mrs E George and Mr H George. Entrance at Whatstandwell Bridge off A6. 65-acre country park with river and woodland. Fishing, boating and canoeing. Long-stay pitches available. Near railway station. **BH&HPA. 30T. 10MC. 60S.** ⚙ ♙ ⚐

Lickpenny Touring Park, Lickpenny Lane, Tansley, Matlock, Derbyshire DE4 5GF. *01629 583040.* lickpenny@btinternet. com. www.lickpennycaravanpark.co.uk. Owners: A & J Reynolds. M1, J28. A38 SP Derby, take Alfreton exit and immediately L turn to A615 for 8m, turn R on to Lickpenny Lane, SP

EDEN TREE HOUSE CARAVAN PARK BRADWELL HOPE VALLEY S33 9JT

Situated on the outskirts of the village. This small friendly, well sheltered site is central for touring the Peak District National Park. Travelling on the B6049 turn at the 'New Bath Inn'. Electric hook ups. Free hot showers. For brochure phone 01433 623444

on R. Fishing nearby. Local shops, doctor, PO 3m. Bus service at end of lane. Rail station in Matlock. ☆☆☆☆ **BH&HPA. 80T. MC.** ⚙ ♙ ⊕ ⅙ ⚐

(2m). Sycamore Country & Camping Park, Lant Lane, Tansley, Matlock, Derbyshire DE4 5LF. *01629 55760.* info@sycamore-park.co.uk. www.sycamore-park.co.uk. Owner: Sycamore Caravans (Mr & Mrs C J Boffey). 2.5m out of Matlock on A632, turn right for Tansley; site 0.5m on right. Rural site with fine views. Showers. Playground. Telephone. Fishing and golf nearby. Open March 15 -October 31. **BH&HPA. 27T. MC. 52S.** ♙ ⚐

Shardlow

Shardlow Marina Caravan Park, London Road, Shardlow, Derbyshire DE72 2GL. *01332 792832.* Owner: Ron Grundy (Melbourne) Ltd. Leave M1 on exit 24 on to A50, exit J1, at roundabout take exit to Shardlow. 5m from Derby. Bar, restaurant and shower block. Fishing. Doctor, hospital within 5m. PO/shop in village. AA 3 pennants. Open March 1-January 31. **BH&HPA. 35T.** ♙ ⚐ ⅖

Sheffield

(12m). Stocking Farm Caravan Site, Calver, Hope Valley, Sheffield Derbyshire S32 3XA. *01433 630516.* Owner: Harvey & Newton. 5m from Bakewell. On A623. Follow the first two signs to Calver Mill then straight ahead. Shop, PO: 0.5m. Doctors: 2m. Dogs on leads. Golf courses, Co-op at Bakewell 5m. Morrison's Chesterfield 10m. Open April 1-October 31. **8T. 2MC. 10S.** ♙

Thulston

Beechwood Park, Main Road, Elvaston, Thulston, Derbyshire DE72 3EQ. *07973 562689.* colinbeech@btconnect. com. www.beechwoodparkleisure.co.uk. Owner: Mr C Beech. Follow signs for Elvaston Castle, park 300yd. Situated in 14 acres of Green Belt. 3 coarse fishing lakes. Children's go-kart track. Shop on site and just 1m to village shops. Adjacent to 300-acre Elvaston Country Park. **45T. MC.** ⚙ ♙ ⊕ ⅙ ⚐

Whatstandwell

Merebrook Caravan Park, Derby Road, Whatstandwell, Derbyshire DE4 5HH. *01773 857010.* Owner: Mrs O N Munslow. On A6, 5m S of Matlock. Situated in the Derwent Valley, entrance well signed in both directions. Open March-October for holiday homes; open all year for tourers. ☆☆☆ **BH&HPA. 75T. MC. 114S.** ⚙ ♙ ⊕ ⅙

LEICESTERSHIRE

Hinckley

(5m). Villa Farm Caravan Park, Wolvey, Hinckley, Leicestershire LE10 3HF. *01455 220493/220630.* www.wolvey caravanpark.itgo.com. Owner: Mr H & PM Rusted. A46 Coventry to Leicester then B4065 (old A46). 0.5m W of Wolvey, M6 exit 2, M69 exit 1. AA 3 pennants. Fishing on site, putting green, games room. **120T. MC.** ⚙ ♙ ⊕ ⅙ ⚐

Loughborough

(4m). Meadow Farm Marina & Touring Caravan Park Ltd, Huston Close, Barrow on Soar, Loughborough, Leicestershire. *01509 816035/812215.* Owner: L B Hinsley. Take A6 from Loughborough or Leicester, then four left turns off the dual carriageway for Mountsorrel, Sileby and Barrow, turn-off brings you to gates 1.5m from A6. Set in 32 acres by the river Soar. Club. Hot showers. Centrally heated toilet and shower block. Free fishing on site. Supermarket close by. **50T. MC.** ⚙ ♙ ⊕ ⅙

Lutterworth

(4.5m). Stanford Park Caravan Site, Lutterworth, Leicestershire LE17 6DH. *01788 860387/860250.* enquiries@ stanfordhall.co.uk. www.stanfordhall.co.uk. Owner: Stanford Hall Estate. Leave M1 J20 on to A427. At traffic lights turn L on to A426, in 0.15m turn L SP Swinford, in 3.2m at B5414 junction, turn R, then L into Stanford Road. OS map ref - 140:SP582790. No sanitation. Motorhome service point. Fishing and golf nearby. Designated dog walk through estate woodland. Visitors staying on site have free admission to Stanford Hall grounds during normal opening times, except on some event days. Open Easter-mid October. **124T.** 🍴 🔌 🛒

Whetstone

Whetstone Gorse Farm, Whetstone Gorse East, Whetstone, Leicestershire LE8 6LX. *0116 2773796.* www.whetstone gorse.co.uk. Owners: Mr & Mrs M H Kind. 6m from Leicester, on A426 to Blaby then L for Countesthorpe, take Willoughby Road out of Countesthorpe in about 2m turn R down Farm Track. Fishing on site (coarse fishing), 4 pools, 5 acres of water. Golf, shops inc PO 2m. Riding stables 3m. Swimming 4m. PHs close by. Rally field with entertainment, barn for hire. **15T. MC.** ✿ 🍴 🔌

LINCOLNSHIRE

Alford

(3m). Woodthorpe Hall Leisure Park, Woodthorpe, Alford, Lincolnshire LN13 0DD. *01507 450294.* enquiries@wood thorpehallleisure.co.uk. www.woodthorpehallleisure.co.uk. Access via Louth to Mablethorpe A157 or Alford, A1104 then B1373. Affiliated18-hole golf course and fishing lake, garden centre and aquatic centre within the grounds. Country inn with family room serves food. Snooker and pool tables. **BH&HPA. 50T. 10MC. 85S. 20H.** ✿ 🍴 🔌 ♿ 🛒

Barton-on-Humber

(0.5m). Silver Birches Tourist Park, Waterside Road, Barton-on-Humber, Lincolnshire DN18 5BA. *01652 632509.* Owner: Mr & Mrs R Shelton. On A15 or 1077. Follow signs for Humber Bridge Viewing Area. Site just past the Sloop PH. Follow viewing area signs to Waterside Road. Site situated next to Humber Bridge only 250yd from viewing area and nature reserves. AA 4 pennants. Open April 1-October 31. **BH&HPA. 24T. 24MC.** 🍴 🔌 ♿

Boston

(10m). Midville Caravan Park, Midville, Skickney, Boston, Lincolnshire PE22 8HW. *01205 270316.* Owner: Steven Vaughan. Off A16 Boston to Grimsby. At Stickney (7.5m from Boston) follow brown and white road signs. Fishing outside park in river. Shops, PO, doctor, etc all within 0.5m. Open March 1-November 30. **BH&HPA. 24T. MC. 45S.** 🍴 🔌

(4m). Orchard Park, Frampton Lane, Hubberts Bridge, Boston, Lincolnshire PE20 3QU. *01205 290328.* www.orchardpark.co.uk. Owner: Mr E & C B May. Off A52 Boston-Grantham. On B1192 Hubberts Bridge. Licensed bar. Fishing lake, restaurant on site. 18-hole golf course with driving range 0.5m. 9-hole golf course 2m. Open March 1-January 31. ✰✰✰ **BH&HPA. 60T. MC. 128S. 3H.** 🍴 🔌 🛒

(1.5m). Pilgrim's Way Camping & Caravan Park, Church Green Road, Fishtoft, Boston, Lincolnshire PE21 0QY. *01205 366646.* pilgrimswaylincs@yahoo.com. www.pilgrims-way. co.uk. Owner: Tony & Maria Potts. Take A52 out of Boston towards Skegness; there are two signs, first on Bargate Bridge,

second on Wainfleet Road, or take any road to Fishtoft. Adults' park. Pilgrims Way is only 1.5m from Boston Centre, 20mins drive to Skegness and Spalding. Quiet park with PHs just up the road. AA 4 pennants. Open Easter-end September. ✰✰✰✰ **22T. MC.** 🍴 🔌 ♿

(8m). White Cat Caravan Park, Shaw Lane, Old Leake, Boston, Lincolnshire PE22 9LQ. *01205 870121.* kevin@klan nen.freeserve.co.uk. www.whitecatpark.com. Owner: Mr & Mrs Lannen. On A52 Boston to Skegness Road. Turn R opposite B1184 Sibsey road. Swings. PO and PH nearby. Restaurant. Suitable base for Skegness and touring the Fens. Seasonal pitches for tourers. Limited facilities for disabled visitors. AA 3 pennants. Equestrian centre 2m. Golf, cinema, shopping 6m. Open April-October. **BH&HPA. 40T. 40MC. 6S. 3H.** 🍴 🔌 ♿ 🛒

Caistor

(1m). Nettleton Caravan Park, Nettleton, Caistor, Lincolnshire LN7 6JQ. *01472 851501.* Owner: Don Amott Caravans Ltd. Off A46 and B1205. Set in 60 acres of pine forest and beautiful parkland. Rustic adventure play area, 9-hole golf course, 3 well-stocked fishing lakes, all-weather tennis, professional sized bowling green, shop and shower block. Open March-November. **30T. MC. 270S.** 🍴 🔌 🛒

Chapel St Leonards

(1m). Eastfields Park, Chapel Point Pleasure Ltd, Eastfields Park, Chapel Point, Chapel St Leonards, Lincolnshire PE24 5UX. *01754 874499.* Owners: Messrs Kirk. Fishing on site, on coast next to beach. Doctor, PO, shop within 1m. Open Easter-mid October. **66T. MC.** 🍴 🔌 ♿

Cleethorpes

(2m). Eperstone Residential Caravan Park, North Sea Lane, Humberston, Cleethorpes, Lincolnshire. *01472 813996.* Off A1031. Open April-October. **28S.** 🛒 ✎

(2m). Thorpe Park Holiday Centre, Humberston, Cleethorpes, Lincolnshire DN35 0PW. *01472 210083.* oewebmaster@bourne-leisure.co.uk. www.thorpeparkholidaycentre.com. Owner: Bourne Leisure Ltd. One Park Lane, Hemel Hempstead, Herts HP2 4YL. From M180 take A180 and follow signs for Grimsby and Cleethorpes town centre. Follow signs for holiday parks and Pleasure Island. Heated indoor pool, licensed club family entertainment, children's club, multi sports court, fishing and golf. Two mini markets, bakery, laundrette. David Bellamy Gold Conservation Award. Open March-November. ✰✰✰ **BH&HPA. NCC. 60T. MC. 211S. 350H.** 🍴 🔌 ♿ 🛒

Grantham

(0.5m). 'Lazyacres', Gorse Lane, Grantham, Lincolnshire. *01476 79354/579354.* Owner: Charles Bennett. Off A1. Hot showers. Electric meters. Hard and soft standings. **40T. 20MC.** ✿ 🍴 🔌

(8m). Woodland Waters, Willoughby Road, Ancaster, Grantham, Lincolnshire NG32 2RT. *01400 230888.* info@woodlandwaters.co.uk. www.woodlandwaters.co.uk. Owners: Mr & Mrs M Corradine. Malden Lodge, Willoughby Road, Ancaster, Grantham, Lincolnshire NE32 3RT. On A153 between Grantham and Sleaford, from S leave A1 at Colsterworth to B6403 to Ancaster. From N leave A1 at Newark to A17 to Sleaford, leave just before RAF Cranwell R to B6403 to Ancaster. 72 acre picturesque park in a beautiful wooded valley with 4 fishing lakes on site. AA 3 pennants. 4 golf courses nearby. Historic city of Lincoln close by and local market towns of Grantham, Newark and Sleaford a short drive. Go-karting, golf, paint balling and horse riding close by. Bar/restaurant, garage with shop at park entrance. ✰✰✰ **60T. 60MC. 12S.** ✿ 🍴 🔌 ♿ 🛒

Horncastle

(1.5m). Ashby Park, West Ashby, Horncastle, Lincolnshire LN9 5PP. *01507 527966.* ashbyparklakes@ad.com. www.ukparks.co.uk/ashby. Owners: Margaret & Robin Francis. 1.5m N of Horncastle between the A153 and A158. Touring site of 70 acres with 7 fishing lakes. David Bellamy Gold Conservation Award. Lincolnshire environmental trophy. Golf 1m, shops 1.5m. Open March 1-January 6. ✫✫✫✫ **BH&HPA. 100T. 10MC. 67S.** ⌂ ⊠ &

Immingham

(5m). Killingholme Caravan Site, Church End, East Halton, Immingham, Lincolnshire DN40 3NX. *01469 540594.* Owner: Mrs T J Chapman. From A180 take A160 towards Killingholme. Turn left at roundabout, site 1.5m on right, opposite church. Semi-rural location. Short drive to beaches/holiday resort. 1m to shop, PO, PH. **20T. 20MC.** ✿ ⌂ ⊠

Lincoln

(3m). Hartsholme Country Park, Skellingthorpe Road, Lincoln, Lincolnshire LN6 0EY. *01522 873578.* SP from A46, 3m S of Lincoln. Sheltered, level site situated in a country park with woods, meadows and lakes. Suitable base for exploring the historic city of Lincoln. Open March 1-October 31; open for Lincoln's Christmas market. ✫✫✫ **50T.** ⌂ ⊠ &

(9m). Lowfields Country Holiday Fishing Retreat, Eagle Road, North Scarle, Lincoln, Lincolnshire LN6 9EN. *01522 778717.* info@lowfields.co.uk. www.lowfields.co.uk. Owner: Lowfields Leisure Ltd. Turn off A1 and take A46 to Lincoln. Turn on to the A1133 to Gainsborough. Stay on road until turn SP North Scarle. Follow road, take R turn over hump backed bridge, turn again then first L. Follow road for 1m. Site is on right-hand side after log cabin. 8 exclusive fishing lakes, laundrette, satellite TV, small children's play area. Golf course, horse riding, swimming, PHs, shops nearby. Open 14 February-14 January. **BH&HPA. 100S. 4H.** ⌂ ∅

(6m). Shortferry Caravan Park, Fiskerton, Lincoln, Lincolnshire LN3 4HU. *01526 398021.* kay@shortferry.co.uk. www.shortferry.co.uk. Owner: Mr R T & P R Hardman & Partners. Off A158 Lincoln to Skegness about 5m. Fishing and tackle shop. Laundry. Outdoor heated (seasonal) swimming pool. PH and restaurant on site. Entertainment most weekends. Coarse and carp lakes. 9-hole pitch and putt. Bowling green. **40T. MC. 250S.** ✿ ⌂ ⊠ & ▙ ∅

(18m). Tattershall Park Country Club, Tattershall, Lincoln, Lincolnshire LN4 4LR. *01526 343193.* www.tattershallpark. co.uk. On the A153 Sleaford to Skegness. 365-acre leisure park with bars. Horse riding, jet skiing, water skiing, canoeing, fishing and boating. Restaurants. Gymnasium, saunas, squash and snooker. Limited facilities for disabled visitors. RAC recommended. Open March-October. ✫✫✫✫✫ **200T. MC. 100S. 10H.** ⌂ ⊠ &

(18m). The Royal Oak Caravan Site, Tattershall Bridge, Lincoln, Lincolnshire LN4 4JL. *01526 342413.* On A153. All enquiries to Manager at No1. Open March-October. **11S.** ⌂

(12m). White Horse Inn Holiday Park, Dunston Fen, Metheringham, Lincoln, Lincolnshire LN4 3AP. *01526 399919.* carol.whitmore2@btinternet.com. whitehorse@dunstonfen.co.uk. Owner: Mr & Mrs Whitmore. Out of Lincoln on B1188 towards Sleaford and Woodhall Spa. About 7m turn R into Dunston village follow tourist signs on to Fen Lane for

5m. On river Witham. Fishing. Moorings. Traditional timbered inn serving meals everyday. Tranquil setting in wide open fen farmland with an abundance of wildlife. Walks, cycle tracks. Open February 1-December 31. ✫✫✫ **BH&HPA. 8T. 6MC. 30S.** ⌂ ⊠

Louth

(10m). Lakeside Park, North Somercotes, Louth, Lincolnshire LN11 7RB. *01507 358315.* Owner: Don Amott Caravans Ltd. A1031 Cleethorpes to Skegness road. Heated indoor pool. Takeaway. Amusements. Indoor leisure complex. Sauna. Laundrette. Water front club. Tennis courts, golf course, bowling green, fitness suite, steam room. Open March 1-November 31. **BH&HPA. NCC. 150T. 100MC. 400S.** ⌂ ⊠ & ∅

(5.5m). Manby Caravan Park, Manby Middlegate, Louth, Lincolnshire LN11 8SX. *01507 327293.* Take B1200 of Louth ring road, 3.5m on left. Entrance to site behind Rix petrol station. Quiet, sheltered, level, 5-acre site with indoor pool. Steam, sauna, jacuzzi, toning tables. 20mins from beach. 5mins from Wolds. Easy access Skegness. Open March 1-October 31. **80T. MC. 7S.** ⌂ ⊠ &

(7m). Saltfleetby Fisheries, Main Road Saltfleetby, Louth, Lincolnshire LN11 7SS. *01507 338272.* saltfleetbyfish@ aol.com. www.saltfleetbyfisheries.co.uk. Owners: Mr & Mrs Musgrave. B1200. Quiet, peaceful, adult-only site. Fishing lakes, well stocked. Shop at entrance to site. Close to Mablethorpe and Skegness. Open March 1-October 31. ✫✫✫ **18T. 1S. 2H.** ⌂ ⊠ & ▙

(10m). Sunnydale Holiday Park, Sea Lane, Saltfleet, Louth, Lincolnshire LN11 7RP. *0871 664 9776.* sunnydale.holiday park@park-resorts.com. www.park-resorts.com. Owner: Park Resorts Ltd. 3rd Floor, Swan Court, Waterhouse Street, Hemel Hempstead, Herts HP1 1FN. Head towards Louth on the B1200 through Manby and Saltfleet. Sea Lane is on R in Saltfleet. The park is about 400yd on the left-hand side. Indoor heated pool, store, bar, cabaret bar, play zone for kids. Outdoor play area, free children's clubs, free family evening entertainment. Sandy beach 2m, 18-hole golf course 9m. Open April-October. ✫✫✫ **BH&HPA. NCC. 320S. 28H.** ⌂ ▙

Mablethorpe

(1m). Camping & Caravanning Club Site - Mablethorpe, Highfield, 120 Church Lane, Mablethorpe, Lincolnshire LN12 2NU. *01507 472374/0870 2433331.* www.campingandcaravanning club.co.uk. Owner: Camping & Caravanning Club. Greenfields House, Westwood Way, Coventry CV4 8JH. Take A157 from Louth to Mablethorpe, then A1104 N and follow the sign to site, which is on the right 1m from the beach. All types of units accepted. Non-members welcome. Located in a flat surrounding area, suitable for cyclists. Site conveniently situated 10-15 mins walk from both town and shore. Lincolnshire Wolds are a haven for birds and animals. Special deals available for families and backpackers. Open March-October. ✫✫✫ **105T. 105MC.** ⌂ ⊠ &

(1m). Denehurst Touring Site, Alford Road, Mablethorpe, Lincolnshire LN12 1PX. *01507 472951.* Owner: Chris Lewin. On A1104 Alford-Louth-Mablethorpe road. Small, family-run site in a country setting close to town centre of Mablethorpe and 1m to beach. Fishing and golf nearby. Open March 1-November 30. **20T. 2H.** ⌂ ⊠

(1m). Golden Sands Holiday Park, Quebec Road, Mablethorpe, Lincolnshire LN12 1QJ. *01507 477060.* oewebmaster@bourne-leisure.co.uk. www.goldensandsholi daypark.com. Owner: Bourne Leisure Ltd. 1 Park Lane, Hemel Hempstead, Hertfordshire HP2 4YL. Head towards Mablethorpe located between Cleethorpes and Skegness on Lincolnshire coast. From Mablethorpe town centre, turn L on to seafront road towards North End. Golden Sands is along this road on the L. Indoor and outdoor pools, go karts, crazy golf, playground. Supermarket. Bakery. Laundrette. Coffee shop. Fish and chip shop. Children's Fun Palace. Free children's club. Daytime and evening entertainment. Multi sports court, adventure playground, go-karts, fishing lake, amusements. Open April-October. ☆☆☆ **BH&HPA. NCC. 355T. MC. 1106S. 418H.** ⛺ 🔌 ♿ 🛒

(1.5m). Grange Farm Leisure Ltd, Alford Road, Mablethorpe, Lincolnshire LN12 1NE. *01507 472814.* www.ukparks.co.uk/grangefarm. Owner: J L & J M Evans. Situated on A1104 twixt Mablethorpe and Maltby-le-Marsh. Fishing open all year, 6 lakes available. Tackle shop. Bar and food. Milk, papers to order. Payphone and laundry facilities next to tackle shop. Open March 1-November 30. **BH&HPA. 35T. 5MC. 174S.** ⛺ 🔌 ♿

(1m). Greenfield Caravan Park, Sutton Road, Trusthorpe, Mablethorpe, Lincolnshire LN12 2PU. *01507 441203.* john@jhgc.freeserve.co.uk. Owner: Mr & Mrs J Conyers. On A52 Mablethorpe to Sutton-on-Sea. Park is a privately-owned caravan park situated on the main A52 coastal road, between Mablethorpe and Sutton-On-Sea with its own access to the beaches of Trusthorpe. Open March-November. **BH&HPA. 105S. 6H.** ⛺ 🛒

Hawthorn Farm Caravan Club Site, Crabtree Lane, Sutton-On-Sea, Mablethorpe, Lincolnshire LN12 2RS. *01507 441503.* www.caravanclub.co.uk. Owner: The Caravan Club. East Grinstead House, East Grinstead, West Sussex RH19 1UA. See website for standard directions to site. 1.25 miles from Sutton-On-Sea. Caravan Club members only. Suitable site for family holidays with excellent facilities, only 0.75m from safe bathing beach. Dog walk. Advance booking advised bank holidays, July and August. Toilet blocks. Privacy cubicles. Laundry facilities. Veg prep. Motorhome service point. Golf, fishing and water sports nearby. Open March-October. **NCC. 115T. MC.** ⛺ 🔌 ♿

(0.8m). Holivans Ltd, Quebec Road, Mablethorpe, Lincolnshire LN12 1QH. *01507 473327.* holivans@enterprise. net. www.holivans.co.uk. Owner: Holivans Ltd. Take A1031 into Mablethorpe, 0.75m along Quebec Road. Adjacent to sand dunes. Open Easter-October 1. ☆☆☆ **BH&HPA. 15T. 6MC. 165S.** ⛺ 🔌 ⌀

Nursery Caravan Park, Seaholme Road, Mablethorpe, Lincolnshire LN12 2NX. *01507 472267.* Owner: Don Amott Caravans. Off A52 Mablethorpe to Sutton-on-Sea. Licensed premises. Calor Gas sales. Open March 15-October 31. **BH&HPA. 95S.** ⛺

(1m). Seacroft Holiday Estate (Trusthorpe) Ltd, Main Bridge, Trusthorpe, Mablethorpe, Lincolnshire LN12 2PN. *01507 472421.* info@seacroftcaravanpark.com. www.seacroft caravan.park.com. Between Mablethorpe and Sutton-on-Sea on A52. Open early March-end October. **BH&HPA. 16T. 240S. 15H.** ⛺ 🔌 ♿ 🛒

St Vincent's Caravan & Camping Park, Seaholme Road, Mablethorpe, Lincolnshire LN12 2NX. *01507 473872.* Owner: Mrs Monica Mitchell. 132 Saffron Road, Wigston, Leicester

LE18 4UP. Site within the town on the south side. Off Seaholme Road. Small (1.4-acre) family park 800yd from beach. Showers and electric shaver points. Open mid March-mid October. **20T. 20MC.** ⛺ ♿

(1m). Sutton Springs Holiday Estate, Sutton Road, Trusthorpe, Mablethorpe, Lincolnshire. *01507 441333.* Owner: Springs Estates (Lincs) Ltd. On A52 between Mablethorpe and Sutton-on-Sea. Open March 1-November 30. **BH&HPA. 430S.** ⛺ 🛒

(2m). Trusthorpe Springs Leisure Park, Trusthorpe Hall, Mablethorpe, Lincolnshire LN12 2QQ. *01507 441384.* Owner: Springs Estates (Lincs) Ltd. Turn off A1104 Alford to Mablethorpe road into Mile Lane, site on left on corner about 2m from Cross Inn. Clubhouse on site with entertainment every Saturday night and most nights in peak season. Laundry room. Children's arcade. Open March 1-November 30. ☆☆ **BH&HPA. 15T. MC. 130S. 12H.** ⛺ 🔌 ♿ 🛒

(1m). Willow Caravan Park, Maltby-le-Marsh, Mablethorpe, Lincolnshire. *01507 450244.* Owner: Don Amott Caravan Kingdom. On A1104. Open March 15-October 31. **T. MC. 150S.** ⛺ 🔌 ♿

Market Deeping

(2.5m). Deepings Caravan Park, Outgang Road, Towngate East, Market Deeping, Lincolnshire PE6 8LQ. *01778 344335.* Owner: B M D & L Bills. From Market Deeping take B1525, SP Spalding. After 2.5m turn left on to unclassified road, site 400yd on right. Calor Gas sales. Fishing on site. Open February 1-December 31. **BH&HPA. 90T. MC. 10S. 2H.** ⛺ 🔌

Market Rasen

(10m). Lincolnshire Lanes Camp Site, Manor Farm, East Firsby, Market Rasen, Lincolnshire LN8 2DB. *01673 878258.* info@lincolnshire-lanes.com. www.lincolnshire-lanes.com. Owner: Mr R Cox. N from Lincoln on A15. 2.5m after RAF Scampton turn right on to minor road, SP Spridlington. At Spridlington church turn L, SP Normanby. Site is 0.75m on left. Follow brown signs from A15. Quiet site 10m N of Lincoln. Neighbouring Saxon reconstruction. Pet exercise area. 2 golf courses within 2m. Good cycling. Cycles, tandem hire. One field for families, one field more tranquil. 3 log cabins for hire. Small shop on site. Some facilities for disabled visitors. ☆☆☆ **15T. 15MC.** ⚘ ⛺ 🔌

(1m). Market Rasen Racecourse Caravan Club Site, Legsby Road, Market Rasen, Lincolnshire LN8 3EA. *01673 842307.* Owner: The Caravan Club. East Grinstead House, East Grinstead, West Sussex RH19 1UA. See website for standard directions to site. Set on edge of the lovely, rolling Lincolnshire Wolds. There's a pay and play golf course adjacent to the site, and within a short distance another golf course and coarse fishing. Non-members and tent campers welcome. Toilet blocks, privacy cubicles and laundry facilities. Motorhome service point. TV room and play area. Good area for walking. Open March-October. **NCC. 55T. MC.** ⛺ 🔌 ♿

Norton Disney

Oakhill Leisure, Oakhill Farm, Butt Lane, Thurlby Moor, Norton Disney, Lincolnshire LN6 9QG. *01522 868771/07773 814057.* ron@oakhill-leisure.co.uk. www.oakhill-leisure.co.uk. Owner: Mr Ron De Raad. A46 Newark to Lincoln, SPThurlby, at roundabout, right at T-junction, round S-bend, straight in front sign for Oakhill Leisure. Turn right then left into park. 6m from

Newark. Children's play area, fishing lake, woodland, country walks. Washing machine, toilet/shower block. PH 1m, shops 4m. **60T. MC. 1S.** ❁ 🐾 🔌 ⚫

Peterborough

(8m). Lakeside Caravan Park, Station Road, Deeping St James, Peterborough, Lincolnshire PE6 8RQ. *01778 343785.* Owner: Bob & June Charlesworth. Take the B1166 from Market Deeping to Crowland, site SP from level crossing. On-site fishing for caravanners and guests only. Not suitable for children aged under 12. Toilets, wash facilities and showers. 0.25m to The Deepings Lakes nature reserve. 240 acres of walks and wildlife. Open February 1-December 31. **10T. 10MC.** 🐾 🔌

Scunthorpe

(2m). Ashfield Park Homes, Burringham Road, Ashby, Scunthorpe, Lincolnshire DN17 2AL. *01724 844781.* Owner: Mr T Peatfield. Scunthorpe Caravan Co, Ashfield, Burringham Road, Scunthorpe DN17 2AL. From Ashby on B1420 to Burringham crossroads, site 300yd west on right-hand side. Adjacent to Superstore. Own sanitation required for tourers. Children allowed. **NCC. T.** ❁ 🐾 🔌 ⚫

(4m). Brookside Caravan & Camping Park, Stather Road, Burton-upon-Stather, Scunthorpe, Lincolnshire DN15 9DH. *01724 721369.* brooksidecp@aol.com. Owner: Linda & Richard Murgatroyd. From Scunthorpe take B1430 to Burton Stather 4m. Turn L in front of Sheffield Arms PH. Down the hill, past the Ferry House Inn. Entrance to park 100yd further on the R. Small, friendly site with modern facilities. 150yd from local PH and river Trent. Situated in an Area of Outstanding Natural Beauty. Suitable for walkers and mountain bikers, and quiet weekends. ☆☆☆☆**35T. 35MC.** ❁ 🐾 🔌 ⚫

Skegness

(3m). Barham Caravan Co Ltd, Skegness Sands, Roman Bank, Skegness, Lincolnshire PE25 1QZ. *01754 762231.* Owner: Barham Caravan Co Ltd. On A152. Swimming pool, Laundrette. Dogs on leads. Open March1-January 5. **BH&HPA. 80T. MC. 209S.** ❁ 🐾 🔌 ⚫ ⚫

(1m). Baythorpe Private Caravan & Chalet Park, Burgh Road, Skegness, Lincolnshire. *01754 898905.* baythorpepark@zen.co.uk. Owner: Reg & Cynthia Wilson-Leary. On the A158 near to the A52 junction. This private non-letting family owned and run park is central for town and beach. Open March 1-November 30. **BH&HPA. 120S.** 🐾 🦾

(0.75m). Beacon Park Home & Holiday Village, Beacon Way, Skegness, Lincolnshire PE25 1HL. *01754 610842/767950.* Set in over 34 acres of lovely, landscaped grounds with two large lakes. Open March 1-May 1. **BH&HPA. 200S** 🐾 ⚫ 🦾 ⚫

(1m). Blenheim Caravan Camp, Church Lane, Skegness, Lincolnshire PE2 1EW. *01754 762602.* Owner: Mr A P Epton & Mrs R E Epton. Open March 15-October 31. **32S.** 🐾 🦾

(4m). Bridge End Touring Site, Bolton's Lane, Ingoldmells, Skegness, Lincolnshire PE25 1JJ. *01754 872456.* Owner: Mrs S Taylor. A small, quiet site with most facilities. Mainly catering for retired people. Walking distance to all amenities. Plenty of fishing in area. Good food. Open Easter to mid-October. **35T. MC.** 🐾 🔌

(2m). Butlins Family Entertainment Centre, Touring Site, Skegness, Lincolnshire PE25 1NJ. *01754 762311.* Owners: Butlins Skyline Ltd. Just outside Skegness on Mablethorpe Road (A52). Open March-October. **170T. 260S.** 🐾 🔌 ⚫ 🦾

(5m). Coastfield Holiday Park, Vickers Point, Ingoldmells, Skegness, Lincolnshire PE251LU. *01754 872437.* N of Skegness on A52. Indoor pool. Adventure playground. Laundrette. On site store. Takeaways. Free children's club. Family entertainment club and bar. Open at Easter. ☆☆☆ **BH&HPA. NCC. 400S. 70H.** 🐾 🦾 ⚫

(3m). Conifer Park Touring Site, Walls Lane, Ingoldmells, Skegness, Lincolnshire PE25 1JH. *01754 762494.* Owner: Chris &Marian Brookes. Take A52 from Skegness towards Ingoldmells, upon reaching Butlins, turn L down Walls Lane, Conifer Park Site is about 0.5m on right. Conifer park site is appreciated by more mature campers who like a clean peaceful site with a country environment. At the same time being only 0.75m from the sea front. Garage, fishing, golf, PO, doctor, vet, shops, swimming, bingo, theatre, Butlins, water-skiing, cafe all nearby. Large market. Open March 1-October 31. **30T.** 🐾 🔌 ⚫

(4m). Countrymeadows Holiday Park, Anchor Lane, Ingoldmells, Skegness, Lincolnshire PE25 1LZ. *01754 874455.* mail@countrymeadows.co.uk. www.countrymead ows. co.uk. Owner: J G & G D Hardy. Hawthorn House, Boltons Lane, Ingoldmells, Skegness PE25 1JJ. 4m N of Skegness on A52 to Ingoldmells, follow A52 through Ingoldmells and take first R on leaving village down Anchor Lane. Park 0.5m on L follow signs to Animal Farm. Showers. Laundrette. Play area. Fishing available. Families only. Close to beach, Hordys Animal farm and 10 mins to Fantasy Island. Open mid March-end October. ☆☆☆ **BH&HPA. 150T. 50MC. 100S.** 🐾 🔌 ⚫ ⚫

(1.5m). Croft Bank Holiday Park, Croft Bank, Skegness, Lincolnshire PE24 4RE. *01754 763887.* Owner: John Aisthorpe. Out of Skegness on A52 towards Boston, park is on the R 1.5m from Skegness. Quiet, peaceful non-letting park under personal supervision of proprietors. Laundrette. Play area. Gas sales. Fishing and golf nearby. Open March 4-November 5. Lodges: March 1-January. **BH&HPA. 112S.** 🐾

(1m). Dainville Caravan Park, Church Lane, Skegness, Lincolnshire PE25 1EW. *01754 764270.* dainville@seymours-caravans.co.uk. www.seymours-caravans.co.uk. Owner: Mr & Mrs G Seymour. Royal Oak Caravan Park, Roman Bank, Skegness PE25 1QP. Off A52 between Skegness and Ingoldmells. Turn L SP Church Lane. Park is 400yd on R. Quiet, park. Golf course nearby. Open March 1st-January 5. **BH&HPA. NCC. 100S. 4H.** 🐾 ⚫

(4m). Duncannon Private Caravan Park, Skegness Road, Ingoldmells, Skegness, Lincolnshire. *01754 873019.* Owner: Mrs K P Slocombe. On A52. Open March 1-October 31. **28S.** 🐾

(1.5m). Garden Bungalow Park, Roman Bank, Skegness, Lincolnshire PE25 1QR. *01754 767201.* gardencity@stateebt-connect.com. Owner: T & K Brown. 1.5m N of Skegness. A52 Roman Bank. Private site and part commercial letting. No pets. Children allowed but the majority of homes are for retirement. Open March 1-October 25. **134S.** ❁

(6m). Greenacres Site, South Road, Chapel St Leonards, Skegness, Lincolnshire. *01754 872467.* Owner: Mr S T Edge. 18 Norwood Road, Skegness, Lincs. First right off South Road at Greenacres Social Club. Open March 16-October 10. **20S.** 🐾

(0.5m). Greenfield Park, Burgh Road, Skegness, Lincolnshire PE25 2RA. *01754 769300.* Owner: Mr R J Turner. 32 Roman Bank, Skegness, Lincs PE25 2SL. On A158. Close to traffic lights in town centre. 10 mins walk from town, near traffic lights, garages, shops, beach, PO, doctor and holiday attractions. All amenities in Skegness. Open March 15-October 31. **BH&HPA. 78S.** 🐾 ⚫ ⚫

(7m). Happy Days Carapark, Trunch Lane, Chapel-St-Leonards, Skegness, Lincolnshire PE24 5TU. *01754 872341.* Owner: Mr & Mrs P A Stewart. Off A52 Skegness to Mablethorpe. Family club with entertainment. PH. Arcade. Supermarket. Outdoor swimming pool. Private access to beach. Open March 1-October 31. **468S.** 🐕 🚿

(4m). Hardy's Tourer Site, Sea Lane, Ingoldmells, Skegness, Lincolnshire PE25 1PG. *01754 874071.* Owner: Mr G D Hardy. A52 N from Skegness to Ingoldmells. Turn R at Ship PH in Ingoldmells, into Sea Lane, 0.5m on R next to Fantasy Island. 5mins from the village centre and the sea. 0.5m down Sea Lane on right. All facilities including laundrette. Close to all the holiday entertainment. Open Easter-end October. **BH&HPA. 150T. 20MC. 58S.** 🐕 🚿 ♿ 🚿

(6m). Hill View Touring Caravan Site, Skegness Road, Hogsthorpe, Skegness, Lincolnshire PE24 5NR. *01754 872979.* Owner: Mrs P A Froggatt. On A52 6m from Skegness on left after the second turning to Chapel St Leonards, site 0.5m from village of Hogsthorpe. 2m from sea. Laundry room. Showers. Chemical toilet emptying point. Site has two fishing lakes. Open March 15-October 31. **60T. MC. 1H.** 🐕 🚿 ♿

(10m). Homelands, Sea Road, Anderby, Skegness, Lincolnshire PE24 5YB. *01507 490511.* www.caravancamp-ingsites.co.uk. Owner: Barry & Ann Brenchley. Through Skegness on A52 coast road. When reaching Mumby, take right turn for Anderby (Colar gas building on left-hand side of turning). Straight through village Homelands on left-hand side. Quiet site mainly used by retired folks. A large driveway is used to keep cars parked if ground is wet. Fishing nearby, golf course a few miles away. Shop, PO, doctors within 2.5m away at Chapel St Leonards. Open March 1-November 30. **10T. 1H.** 🚿

Jackson's Caravan Site, 92 Burgh Road, Skegness, Lincolnshire. *01754 763910.* Owner: Mr D S Jackson. On A52. Open March 15-October 4. **BH&HPA. 215S.** 🐕

(1.5m). Kings Chalet & Caravan Park, Trunch Lane, Chapel St Leonards, Skegness, Lincolnshire. *01754 872540.* Owner: Mrs R Boxall. A52 from Skegness. Licensed club, hairdressing salon. Fish and Chip restaurant and takeaway. Bingo and amusement arcade. Bottled gas. Open March-November. **200S.** 🐕 ♿ 🚿

Lorna Doone Beach Estate, St John's Drive, Ingoldmells, Skegness, Lincolnshire PE25 1LL. *01754 872560.* Owner: Mrs P Laidler. Amusements. Fish shop. Club and Sandancer PH. Open March-October. **15S.** 🐕 🚿

Manor Farm Caravan Park, Sea Road, Anderby, Skegness, Lincolnshire PE24 5YB. *01507 490372.* New site. Family bathroom. Open March 1-November 30. ☆☆ **BH&HPA. 15T. MC.** 🐕 🚿 ♿

(3m). Mayville Caravan Site, Roman Bank, Ingoldmells, Skegness, Lincolnshire PE25 1LF. *01754 872582/871477.* Owner: Mrs J M Sharp. Next door to Fantasy Island. Next door to Fantasy Island and McDonalds. Open March 15-October 31. **BH&HPA. 68S. 2H.** 🐕

(5m). Mill Hill Caravan Park, Chapel Road, Ingoldmells, Skegness, Lincolnshire. *01754 872470.* Owner: Mr Hill. On A52 Skegness to Mablethorpe. Open March 15-October 10. **BH&HPA. 75S.** 🐕

(8m). Nelson Villa Caravan Park, Wiggs Lane, Chapel Point, Chapel St Leonards, Skegness, Lincolnshire PE24 5RL. *01754 872658.* Owner: G & M Kaye. N of Skegness off the A52, Mablethorpe road. Open March 17-October 17. **6T. 2MC. 24S.** 🐕 🚿

(0.5m). North Shore Holiday Centre, Elmhirst Avenue, Rowan Bank, Skegness, Lincolnshire PE25 1SL. *01754 762051.* reception@northshore-skegness.co.uk. www.northshore-skegness.co.uk. Owner: Vincent Bros Ltd. Off A52 road between Skegness and Ingoldmells. Family holidays catered for. Close to seaside and all amenities of Skegness, but set back from the main road. No tents. **BH&HPA. 250T. 340S. 15H.** ♣ ♿ 🐕 🚿 ♿ 🚿

(2m). Rainwater Lake Tourer Park, Low Road, Croft Bank, Skegness, Lincolnshire PE24 3RQ. *01754 765783.* Owner: Mr S J Dennis. S of Skegness on A52, on the right. Coarse fishing on private lake. Open March-October. **10T. MC. 33S. 6H.** 🐕 🚿

(1.5m). Retreat Farm, Croft, Skegness, Lincolnshire PE24 4RE. *01754 762092.* Owner: Mr D Smith. 1.5m S of Skegness on the A52 Boston Road. Open April-October. **20T. 5MC.** 🚿

(0.5m). Richmond Holiday Centre, Richmond Drive, Skegness, Lincolnshire PE25 3TQ. *01754 762097.* sales@richmondholidays.com. www.richmondholidays.com. Owner: Mr Mark Williams & Mrs J G Williams. Payment required for dogs. Supermarket. Post office. Laundrette. Fish and chip shop. Amusement arcade. Nightly entertainment during June-August. Mini-assault course. Heated indoor swimming pool. Whirlpool spa. Sauna, sunbeds and gymnasium. Hairdressing salon, large club with family room. Bottle gas available. PO on site during June-August. Open March 1-November 30. **BH&HPA. 163T. 163MC. 600S. 120H.** 🐕 🚿 ♿ 🚿

(6m). Riverside Caravan Park, Wainfleet Bank, Wainfleet, Skegness, Lincolnshire PE24 4ND. *01754 880205.* Owner: Mr J W & Mrs J Bingham. Leave bypass on to B1195, follow signs. A52 Boston to skegness. Showers. Laundry facilities. Fishing nearby. Shops, PO, doctor, rail, bus all within 1m. Golf 1m. Open March-October. **BH&HPA. NCC. 32T. 2MC.** 🚿

(3m). Rob-Roy, Walls Lane, Ingoldmells, Skegness, Lincolnshire PE25 1JE. *01754 766428.* Owner: Mr G L Cox. Along Roman Bank towards Butlins, turn left facing Butlins Theatre, park is 200yd on left-hand side. Open Easter-October. **22S.**

(7m). Robin Hood Park, South Road, Chapel St Leonards, Skegness, Lincolnshire PE24 5TR. *01754 874444.* Owners: Blue Anchor Leisure Ltd. Off A52 Skegness to Mablethorpe. Restaurant. Indoor heated swimming pools. Miniature golf. Laundry. Playgrounds and soft play and ball pool. Club Tropicana. Shops, various eating places, children's fairground. Open March 1-November 2. ☆☆☆☆ **MC. 750S. 90H.** 🐕 🚿 ♿ 🚿

(0.5m). Rose Villa, 18 Burgh Road, Skegness, Lincolnshire. *01754 763820.* Owner: Mrs F A Dales. Open March 15-September 30. **8T. 8MC. 44S.** 🚿

(7m). Rose's Caravan Park, Anderby Creek, Skegness, Lincolnshire PE24 5XW. *01754 872301.* Owner: Mr D J Rose. Off A52 towards Anderby, then towards Anderby Creek. Club next door. Open March 15-October 31. **74S.** 🐕

(2m). Royal Oak Caravan Park, Roman Bank, Skegness, Lincolnshire PE25 1QP. *01754 764270.* royaloak@seymours-caravans.co.uk. www.seymourscaravans.co.uk. Owner: Mr & Mrs G M Seymour. On A52 Ingoldmells to Skegness. Situated behind Royal Oak PH. Quiet, family-run park. Golf, cinema, shopping within 1-2m. Open March 1-January 5. **BH&HPA. NCC. 200S.** 🐕

Sandfield Holiday Centre, South Road, Chapel St Leonards, Skegness, Lincolnshire. 01754 872286. Owner: Lincolnshire Caravans Ltd. Off A52. Adjacent to safe beach. Club. **BH&HPA. 200S.** 🔥 🛒

(1.75m). Skegness Sands, Winthorpe Avenue, Skegness, Lincolnshire PE25 1QZ. 01754 761484. info@skegness-sands. com. www.skegness-sands.com. Caravan Club affiliated site with its own private access to the promenade and not far from the centre of Skegness. Toilet blocks and laundry facilities. Playground and swimming pool on site. Fishing, golf and watersports nearby. Suitable for families. **NCC. 80T. MC** ⚡ 🔥 🛒 🔥 ⚘ 🛒

(2m). Skegness Water Leisure Park, Walls Lane, Skegness, Lincolnshire. PE25 1JF. 01754 899400. enquiries@skegness waterleisurepark.co.ukwww.skegnesswaterleisurepark.co.uk. A52, turn L on to Walls Lane, opposite Butlins. On-site facilities: fishing, cable tow water skiing, coffee shop, The Barn Inn. Children's play area. Open first Saturday March-last Saturday October. ⭐⭐⭐ **BH&HPA. 280T. 550S.** 🔥 🛒 🔥 ⚘ 🛒

South View Leisure Park, Burgh Road, Skegness, Lincolnshire PE24 2LA. 01754 764893. Owner: Mr Vernon. Situated on A158, Skegness to Lincoln road. **BH&HPA. 100T. 600S.** ⚡ 🔥 🛒 🔥 ⚘ 🛒

(2m). Springfield Camp Site, Wall's Lane, Ingoldmells, Skegness, Lincolnshire PE25 1JE. 01754 763441. info@skeg ness-caravans.co.uk. www.skegness-caravans.co.uk. Owner: Leisure Industry Ltd. Off A158, then A52 Roman Bank. Private non-letting park, close to all amenities. Tarmac roads and hard-standings for cars next to all caravans. Open March-November. **BH&HPA. 22S.** 🔥

(4m). Stevenson Golden Sands Estate, Anchor Lane, Ingoldmells, Skegness, Lincolnshire PE25 1LX. 01754 872483. stevenson@goldensands.gb.com. www.goldend sands.gb.com. Owner: Mr D R & D K Stevenson. S A Stevenson & N Stevenson Clark. 4m N of Skegness, near Fantasy Island. Family- owned park situated next to beach at quieter end of Ingoldmells. Licensed clubhouse with family room, amusement arcade and laundrette. Shop. David Bellamy Silver Conservation Award. Open March 1-November 30. **BH&HPA. 380S.** 🔥 ⚘ 🛒

(2m). Stow's Manor Farm Caravan Site, Winthorpe, Skegness, Lincolnshire PE25 1HY. 01754 762555. Owner: W E C Stow & Son. On A52. Near Butlins Funcoast World, mid-way between Skegness and Ingoldmells. Open April-October. **550S.** 🔥 🛒

(7m). Sunkist, Sea Road, Anderby Creek, Skegness, Lincolnshire PE24 5XW. 01754 872374. jker3003@aol.com. www.sunkistcaravanpark.co.uk. Owner: S & A Kershaw. Turn off A52 between Mumby and Huttuft to Anderby Creek. 300yd from a quiet beach. Good fishing locally. Local golf course open to visitors. Shop adjacent to park. PH with family room nearby. Open March 15-October 31. **BH&HPA. 101S. 4H.** 🔥 ⚘

Sunnycroft Camp, Wall's Lane, Ingoldmells, Skegness, Lincolnshire. 01754 763441. sales@skegness-caravans.co.uk. www.skegness-caravans.co.uk. Owner: Leisure Industry Ltd. On A158. Open March-November. **19S.**

(3m). Sycamore Farm, Chalk Lane, Burgh-Le-Marsh, Skegness, Lincolnshire PE24 5HN. 01754 810833. marilyn@sycamorefarm.fs.net.co.uk. www.sycamorefarm.net. Owner: Mrs M B Bulcok. Travelling on A158 towards the coast, proceed through the village of Burgh-Le-Marsh. Before leaving village, turn left, SP to Addlethorpe and Ingoldmells. Continue for about 1.5m, then turn left into Chalk Lane. Site is about 300yd on right. Site is situated 1m from the village of Burgh-le-Marsh which offers all local amenities, shops, PO etc. There are a number of golf courses nearby and the seafront only 3m away. Site has a private fishing lake on site (small charge). No children. 2 cottages available for hire. **NCC. 28T. 28MC. 2H.** ⚘ 🔥 ⚘

Tagg's Caravan Site, 178 Wainfleet Road, Skegness, Lincolnshire PE25 2ER. 01754 764280. Owner: Mr & Mrs R D Tagg & Sons. A52. About 10 mins walk to town centre. Open March 15-October 31. **40T. MC. 312S.** 🔥 ⚘ ⚘ 🛒

(3m). The Elms, Orby Road, Addlethorpe, Skegness, Lincolnshire PE24 4TR. 01754 872266. Owner: Mrs M M Cragg. Fishing on site. Golf course next door. Shops, PO, doctor within 1m. Open March-October. **T. MC.** 🔥 ⚘ ⚘

(1m). The Paddock Caravan Park, Roman Bank, Skegness, Lincolnshire PE25 1QP. 01754 764270. royaloak@seymours-caravans.co.uk. www.seymourscaravans.co.uk. Owner: Mr G M Seymour. On A52 halfway between Skegness and Ingoldmells. Family-run park close to the sea with well-kept gardens and a quiet ambience. Golf course nearby. Open March 1- January 5. **BH&HPA. NCC. 25S.** 🔥

(6m). The Willows Site, South Road, Chapel St Leonards, Skegness, Lincolnshire. 01754 872467. Owner: Mr S T Edge. 18 Norwood Road, Skegness, Lincs. First right off South Road at White House PH. Site is next to beach. Open March 15-October 15. **20S.** 🛒

(6m). Tomlinson's Leisure Park, South Road, Chapel St Leonards, Skegness, Lincolnshire PE24 5TL. 01754 872241. sales@tomlinsons-leisure.co.uk. www.tomlinsons-leisure. co.uk. Owner: Mrs M B Paterson. Off A52. Turn down private road by The White House Inn, off south road right under sand-hills. Club, indoor heated pool. Shops, cafe, takeaways, beach all nearby. Open March 1-November 30. ⭐⭐⭐⭐ **BH&HPA. 200S. 12H.** 🔥 ⚘ ⚘ 🖋

Sleaford

(9m). Low Farm Touring Park, Spring Lane, Folkingham, Sleaford, Lincolnshire NG34 0SJ. 01529 497322. Owner: Mr & Mrs N R Stevens. Situated just off A15, midway between Bourne and Sleaford. Quiet, family-run park situated within walking distance of conservation village with all amenities, ie shop, PO and PH. Open Easter-end September. ⭐⭐⭐ **BH&HPA. 36T. MC.** 🔥 ⚘

Spalding

(9m). Delph Bank Touring Caravan & Camping Park, Old Main Road, Fleet Hargate, Spalding, Lincolnshire PE12 8LL. 01406 422910. enquiries@delphbank.co.uk. www.delphbank. co.uk. Owner: Mr M Watts & Miss J Lawton. 250yd off A17 between Kings Lynn and Sleaford. Quiet site in centre of village, exclusively for adults. PHs, shop and eating places all within easy walking distance. Open March-November. ⭐⭐⭐⭐ **BH&HPA. 45T. MC.** 🔥 ⚘

(12m). Foremans Bridge Caravan Park, Sutton St James, Spalding, Lincolnshire PE12 0HU. 01945 440346. ann@ anegus.wanadoo.co.uk. www.foremans-bridge.co.uk. Owner: Mrs A Negus. From A17 take B1390 to Sutton St James Park on L after 2m. Rural location adjacent to tranquil Fen waterway. 2 holiday cottages for hire all year. Fishing on site and cycle hire. Open March-November. ⭐⭐⭐⭐ **BH&HPA. 40T. 40MC. 7H.** 🔥 ⚘ ⚘ 🛒

(3m). **Lake Ross Caravan Park, Dozens Bank, West Pinchbeck, Spalding, Lincolnshire PE11 3NA.** 01775 761690. Owner: Mr Martyn Frey. A151 Spalding to Bourne road, just over Pode Hole bridge on left. Friendly atmosphere with club and all amenities. Fishing lake. Open February-December. **17T. 6MC.** ⛺ 🅿 🛠

(15m). **Orchard View Caravan and Camping Park, Broadgate, Sutton St Edmund, Spalding, Lincolnshire PE12 0LT.** 01945 700482. raymariaorchardview@btinternet.com. Owner: Ray & Ria Oddy. A47 Peterborough to Wisbech. At Guyhirn take B1187 to Murrow pass through Parson Drove. Over double bridge, 2nd right then 0.5m on the right. 9mfrom Crowland/Wisbech/Holbeach. Rural site close to fishing, horse riding, golf and Hull to Harwich cycle route. Licensed clubhouse. Peaceful location. Plenty of wildlife. Open March-November. ☆☆☆ **BH&HPA. NCC. 35T. 35MC. 2S. 2H.** ⛺ 🅿 🛠

Spilsby

(3m). **Meadowlands, Monksthorpe Road, Great Steeping, Spilsby, Lincolnshire PE23 5PP.** 01754 830794. www.spilsby. info. Owner: Mr Henry Smith. From A16 to Spilsby town centre, follow Wainfleet road, passing the Bell PH at Halton Holegate, then about 1m turn L. Park is then 0.5m on R. Very quiet country site suitable semi-retired. Aviation heritage, National Trust properties nearby. David Bellamy Gold Conservation Award. Handy for Skegness and the Wolds, local fishing, cycleways, walking or just relaxing. Golf, cinema, seaside nature reserves, all within 10m. Wide range of local shopping, garden centres, etc. **BH&HPA. NCC. 6T. 5MC. 10S. 5H.** ✿ ⛺ 🅿

Stamford

(4m). **Tallington Lakes, Barholm Road, Tallington, Stamford, Lincolnshire PE9 4RJ.** 01778 347000. info@tallington.com. www.tallington.com. Owner: Tallington Lakes Ltd. On the Barholm road, off A16 between Stamford and Market Deeping. 260-acres water sports park. Dry ski slope. Licensed bar and restaurant. Cinema, shopping 4m. Golf course 6m. Open March-January. **100T. MC. 385S. 12H.** ⛺ 🅿 &

Sutton-on-Sea

(1.5m). **Cherry Tree Site, Huttoft Road, Sutton-on-Sea, Lincolnshire LN12 2RU.** 01507 441626. murray.cherrytree@virgin.net. www.cherrytreesite.co.uk. Owner: Geoff & Margaret Murray. 1.5m S of Sutton-on-Sea on left-hand side of road (A52). Entrance via lay-by. Now exclusively for adults. Family-run site close to safe, sandy beaches and delightful Wolds villages. Perfect for touring Lincolnshire. Golf and horse riding nearby. Hardstanding available. Open March-end October. ☆☆☆☆ **BH&HPA. 60T. MC.** ⛺ 🅿 &

(1m). **Kirkstead Holiday Park, North Road, Trusthorpe, Sutton-on-Sea, Lincolnshire LN12 2QD.** 01507 441483. mark@kirkstead.co.uk. www.kirkstead.co.uk. Take A52 coast road to Trusthorpe, turn sharp from Mablethorpe R at 1 BT telephone kiosks, go 300yd along north road. Clubhouse with bar food, children's room and snooker room. Laundry room. Shower block, children's adventure playground. 10mins walk to beach, fishing watercourse at rear of site, rod licence required. Shopping 2m. Golf, cinema 3m. Open March 1-December 1. **40T. MC. 75S. 6H.** ⛺ 🅿 & 🛠

Tattershall

(1.5m). **Willow Holt Caravan and Camping Park, Lodge Road, Tattershall, Lincolnshire LN4 4JS.** 01526 343111. enquiries@willowholt.co.uk. www.willowholt.co.uk. Owner: B & R Stevenson. Leave A153 road at Tattershall market place SP Woodhall Spa. Site on L in 1.5m. Well-drained, family-run

parkland with woods, lakes and abundant wildlife. New facilities block. Fishing on site. Golf, Swimming, horse-riding, tennis, bowls and water-skiing nearby. Dogs on leads allowed. Open March 15-October 31 for tourers; open March 1-January 5 for holiday homes. **90T. MC. 8S.** ⛺ 🅿

Woodhall Spa

(1.5m). **Bainland Country Park, Horncastle Road, Woodhall Spa, Lincolnshire LN10 6UX.** 01526 352903. bookings@bainland.co.uk. www.bainland.co.uk. Owner: Mr & Mrs Craddock. From Woodhall Spa travel E towards Horncastle on the B1191, 1.5m on R next to petrol station. The park of over 40 acres is classified as one of the top parks in Lincolnshire. 18-hole, par-3 golf course. All-weather bowling green, indoor/outdoor tennis, heated indoor swimming pool, sauna, jacuzzi, children's adventure playground, trampoline and many more facilities on site, including bar and restaurant. Open March 21-November 6; bungalow for hire all year. ☆☆☆☆☆ **BH&HPA. NCC. 150T. 150MC. 10S. 10H.** ✿ ⛺ 🅿 & 🛠 🖉

(3m). **Camping & Caravanning Club Site - Woodhall Spa, Wellsyke Lane, Kirkby-on-Bain, Woodhall Spa, Lincolnshire LN10 6YU.** 01526 352911/0870 2433331. wwww.campingandcaravanningclub.co.uk. Owner: Camping & Caravanning Club. Greenfields House, Westwood Way, Coventry CV4 8JH. From Sleaford or Horncastle take A153 to Hailsham. At garage turn on to side road, over bridge, L towards Kirkby on Bain. First turn R signed. Non-members welcome. All units accepted. Parent and baby room. Woodpeckers, kestrels and kingfishers often seen from the site. The lake on site is not for fishing. The town of Woodhall Spa set in a magnificent pine and birch wood is just 3m away. Site is peaceful and relaxing, with a friendly atmosphere. Lincoln is not far away and is well worth a visit. Special deals available for families and backpackers. David Bellamy Gold Conservation Award. Open March-October. ☆☆☆☆ **90T. 90MC.** ⛺ 🅿 &

(0.6m). **Jubilee Park, Stixwould Road, Woodhall Spa, Lincolnshire LN10 6QH.** 01526 352448. Owners|: East Lindsey District Council. On-site facilities include a heated outdoor swimming pool (May-September), bowls, putting, tennis and cycle hire. Open April 1-October 31. ☆☆☆ **88T. MC.** ⛺ 🅿 &

NORTHAMPTONSHIRE

Corby

Top Lodge Caravan Club Site, Fineshade, Corby, Northamptonshire NN17 3BB. 01780 444617. wwww.caravanclub.co.uk. Owner: The Caravan Club. East Grinstead House, East Grinstead, West Sussex RH19 1UA. See website for standard directions to site. Tranquil, open meadowland site surrounded by woodland. Good walks, suitable for wildlife enthusiasts. Dog walk adjacent. Advance booking essential bank holidays and weekends. No toilet block. Motorhome waste point. Non-members welcome. Fishing and golf nearby. Open March-October. **NCC. 80T.** ⛺ 🅿

Kettering

(4m). **Acorn Caravan Site, Cranford Road, Burton Latimer, Kettering, Northamptonshire.** 01536 723777. Owner: T Squires. 0.5m off A6. 11m Northampton, 22m Bedford, 23m Huntingdon. **6T.**

(3m). Kestrel Caravan Park, Windy Ridge, Warkton Lane, Kettering, Northamptonshire NN16 9XG. *01536 514301.* Owner: Mr Butler. A14 J10 over first set of traffic lights and take next turn R. Warkton Lane 1m on right-hand side. Quiet site. Fishing, golf course, shops, PO, doctors all within 1m. **25T. 5MC.** ✿ ▣

Wicksteed Park, Barton Road, Kettering, Northants NN15 6NJ. *01536 512475/08700 621194.* information@wicksteed park.co.uk. From N: leave M1, J9 and join the A14. Exit at J10 and follow brown signs. From S: leave M1, J15 and join A43 then take A14 (J8) E to J10. Set in 147 acres of lakes and parklands, with facilities that include 45 rides and attractions including fishing, pitch-and-putt, year-round events programme, narrow-gauge railway, daytime entertainment shows. Open March-October. **BH&HPA. 60T. 60MC.** ⋔ &

Northampton

(3m). Billing Aquadrome, Crow Lane, Great Billing, Northampton, Northamptonshire NN3 9DA. *01604 408181.* brochures@aquadrome.co.uk. www.billingaquadrome.com. Owner: Billing Aquadrome Ltd. Off A45, 3m from Northampton, 7m from M1 exit 15. Set in 235 acres of beautiful parkland with nine lakes. Excellent facilities. Play areas for children. Snack bars and restaurant. Adventure golf and jet-skiing. Open March-November. ✰✰✰ **BH&HPA. 755T. 755MC. 1000S.** ⋔ ▣ & &

(8m). Overstone Lakes Caravan Park, Ecton Lane, Sywell, Northampton, Northamptonshire NN6 OBD. *01604 645255.* www.allenscaravans.com. Owners: Allens Caravans. Wootton Hall, Wootton Wawen, Henley-in-Arden B95 6EE. Turn L in village of Ecton at the crossroads by The World's End PH into Ecton Lane. Lakeside club. Outdoor heated swimming pool, fishing. Mini-supermarket. Play area, tennis courts. Open March 15-January 15. **BH&HPA. NCC. 650S.** ⋔ & & ∅

NOTTINGHAMSHIRE

Bleasby

Hazelford Caravan Park, Boat Lane, Bleasby, Nottinghamshire NG14 7FT. Owner: I H Moore & Company (Holdings) Ltd. Arkwright House, Moore Park, Crocus Street, Nottingham NG2 3DZ. 4m from Southwell. Open April-October. **50S.** ⋔

Calverton

(1m). New Moor Farm Holiday & Home Park, Moor Lane, Calverton, Nottinghamshire NG14 6FZ. *01159 652426/655351.* Owner: Mr G Kellam. M1 J26, take 610 then A60 Mansfield Road over to 614, take road to follow sign to Calverton, continue through village and we are on the left after Spring Water Golf Course. Fishing. Adjacent golf course. Shops 0.5m away. Cinema about 6m away. **BH&HPA. 40T. 40MC. 84S. 200H.** ✿ ⋔ ▣ &

Gunthorpe

Riverdale Park, Gunthorpe Bridge, Gunthorpe, Nottinghamshire NG14 7EY. *01332 810818.* Owner: Ron Grundy (Melbourne) Ltd. 69 Ryecroft Road, Hemington, Derby DE74 2RE. From Nottingham take A612 to Lowdham, turn R onto A6097 to village of Gunthorpe, by river Trent. Nottingham 6m. GS. Open March 1-January 6. **BH&HPA. 5T. 14S.** ⋔ ▣

Mansfield Woodhouse

(1.5m). Redbrick House Hotel, Peafield Lane, Mansfield Woodhouse, Nottinghamshire NG20 0EW. *01623 846499.* Owner: A Ripley. Set in the heart of Sherwood Forest on the A6075, four miles from Edwinstowe visitors centre. Adult-only site. Secluded site at the rear of the hotel with its public bars and restaurant. Open April-October. **50T. 10MC.** ⋔ ▣ &

Mansfield

(5m). Sherwood Forest Caravan Park, Nr Edwinstowe, Mansfield, Nottinghamshire NG21 9HW. *01623 823132.* Owner: Torksey Caravans Ltd. Quiet retreat in heart of Robin Hood country. Good facilities. Special area for dog exercising on leads. Close to many places of interest. Privately owned and managed by resident warden. **BH&HPA. 150T. 30MC.** ✿ ⋔ ▣ & &

(1m). Tall Trees Park Homes, Old Mill Lane, Forest Town, Mansfield, Nottinghamshire NG19 0JN. *01623 626503/07951 637297.* Owner: James Park Homes. From Mansfield, take A60 Worksop road for about 0.5m then turn R at traffic lights into Old Mill Lane. Mains services. **BH&HPA. 5T. MC.** ✿ ⋔ ▣ ∅

Newark

(6m). Carlton Manor Caravan Park, Ossington Road, Carlton on Trent, Newark, Nottinghamshire NG23 6NU. *01530 835662/07870 139256 (mobile).* Owner: Mr & Mrs A S Goodman. 28 Station Road, Hugglescote, Coalville, Leics LE6 2TLB. Signed site Carlton-on-Trent. A1 London Yorkshire. 12m Lincoln. 15m Nottingham. Fly and coarse fishing nearby. Clean, quiet park. Showers. Level grass. Hotel restaurant opposite park. Shops and doctors in village. Dogs on leads. Tents on touring park. In heart of Robin Hood country. Open April-November. **22T. 5MC.** ⋔

Greenacres Caravan & Touring Park, Lincoln Road, Tuxford, Newark, Nottinghamshire NG22 0JN. *01777 870264.* bailey-security@freezone.co.uk. www.members.freezone.co.uk/bailey-security. Owner: S & M Bailey. A1(N) leave at Tuxford sign. At village centre turn R (church opposite). After Fountain PH, site on L in 50yd. (A6075). A1(S) leave at Tuxford local services sign follow slip road to 'T' junction, turn R, SP Lincoln (A57). After Fountain PH site on L in 50yd (A6075). Ideal for night halts and touring Robin Hood country. Laundry, tourist info, playground, separate recreational field. Euro payments accepted. Local shops, PHs etc (nearest PH 100yd). Open mid March-end October for owner-occupiers; open April-September for hire caravans. ✰✰✰ **BH&HPA. 40T. MC. 39S. 6H.** ⋔ ▣ & &

(5m). Milestone Caravan Park, Great North Road, Cromwell, Newark, Nottinghamshire NG23 6JE. *01636 821244.* Caravan Club affiliated site. Small, pretty and level site with a coarse fishing lake and picnic area. Suitable site for walkers and anglers. Toilet blocks, laundry facilities and MV service point. Golf and NCN cycle route nearby. ✰✰✰✰ **NCC. 120T. MC.** ✿ ⋔ ▣ &

(12m). Orchard Park Touring Caravan & Camping Park, Marnham Road, Tuxford, Newark, Nottinghamshire NG22 0PY. *01777 870228.* info@orchardcaravanpark.co.uk. www. orchardcaravanpark.co.uk. Owner: John & Dorothy Anderson. 1.25m SE of A1, off A6075 Lincoln road. Turn R in 0.75m on to Marnham Road. Site on R in 0.75m. Quiet, sheltered, level site. Suitable base for Sherwood Forest. Modern amenities block. Open March-November. **BH&HPA. 50T. 10MC.** ⋔ ▣ & &

(13m.). The Shannon Caravan & Camping, Wellow Road, Ollerton, Newark, Nottinghamshire NG22 9AP. *01623 869002/07979 018565.* www.caravan-sitefinder.co.uk. Owner: Mrs Buxton. Leave A1 on to A614 SP Nottingham. In 6.5m at roundabout, take A616 SP Ollerton. At next roundabout turn right on A616 SP Newark. Park in 1m on left. Fishing, golf, horse riding, small town, village PH, shop all within 1m. AA 3 pennants. ✰✰✰ **38T. MC.** ✿ ⋔ ▣ &

Please visit the Caravan Club website: www.caravanclub.co.uk

Nottingham

(3.5m). Holme Pierrepont Caravan & Camping Park, National Water Sports Centre, Adbolton Lane, Holme Pierrepont, Nottingham, Nottinghamshire NG12 2LU. *0115 9824721.* holme.pierrpont@leisureconnection.co.uk.www.nationalsports centres.co.uk. Owner: The Sports Council. Leisure Connection PLC. National Water Sports Centre, Nottingham NG12 2LU. 3.5m SEof Nottingham via A52 Grantham road. Site SP National Water Sports Centre. 270 acres country park, water sports available if pre-booked; site is 28 acres of flat grass. Rallies welcome. Close to river, fishing in river and ponds. Open April-October. **360T. MC. ☎ 🏕 ⚃ ⚒**

(7m). Manor Farm Camping & Caravan Site, Thrumpton, Nottingham, Notts NG11 0AX. *0115 9830341.* J24, M1, take A453 Nottingham South in 2m turn L for Thrumpton (after power station). Level field with room on three sides, toilets, showers, electric hook-ups. Close to Derby, Castle Donnington Car Museum and race course, Loughborough and all Nottingham's leisure pursuits. **12T. ❖ 🏕 ⚃**

(5m). Thornton's Holt Camping Park, Stragglethorpe, Radcliffe-on-Trent, Nottingham, Nottinghamshire NG12 2JZ. *01159 332125.* camping@thorntons-holt.co.uk. www. thorntons-holt.co.uk. Owner: Mr P G Taylor. SP from A46 and A52. Showers. Washing-up room. Laundry room. Information room. Indoor heated swimming pool. Play area. 18 hard-standings.100yd to PH and restaurant. 0.5m to golf driving range and course. **CaSSOA. 155T. MC. ❖ 🏕 ⚃ ⚒ ⚒**

(6m). Thrumpton Caravan Site, Manor Farm, Thrumpton, Nottingham, Nottinghamshire NG11 0AX. *01159 830341.* Owner: Mr J Towers. J24 on M1 take Nottingham S, sign in 2m turn L (after power station) , A453. Flat, sheltered, grassy field in lovely village. Toilets and showers. Fishing nearby and walks. Near Derby, Leicester, Loughborough, Castle Donnington race course, museum and Nottingham. **12T. MC. ❖ 🏕 ⚃**

Ratcliffe-on-Soar

(1m). Redhill Marina, Red Hill Marine Ltd, Ratcliffe-on-Soar, Nottinghamshire NG11 0EB. *01509 672770.* Owner: Red Hill Marine Ltd. 1.5m from J24, M1, off A453 at Ratcliffe-on-Soar. 3m Kesworth. Adjoining marina. Fishing. **BH&HPA. 5T. 1MC. ❖ ⚃**

Retford

(5.5m). Manor House Caravan Site, Laneham, Retford, Nottinghamshire DN22 0NJ. *01777 228428.* Owner: A Holloway. Manor House, Laneham, Retford, Nottinghamshire. Off A57 at Dunham-on-Trent. Adults only with tourers. Open March-October. **BH&HPA. 20T. MC. 170S. 🏕 ⚃**

Sutton-In-Ashfield

(3m). Shardaroba Caravan Park, Silverhill Lane, Teversal, Sutton-In-Ashfield, Nottinghamshire NG17 3JJ. *01623 551838.* stay@shardaroba.co.uk.www.shardaroba.co.uk. Owner: Mr J G Bennett. From J28 M1 take A38 to Mansfield, first set of traffic lights turn L on to B6027. At top of hill 1.2m, crossroads straight over, 200yd turn left Peacock Hotel. T junction 1.4m turn R on to B6014 for Stanton Hill, turn L 1.2m at Carnarvon Arms on to Silverhill Lane. Site 300yd on left-hand side. Golf, coarse nearby. 300yd PH. 0.25m restaurant. Opposite walking, bicycle rides. Horse riding country park, Teversal trails. Shops, doctors, etc 1m. Fishing Hardwick Lakes. Loo of the Year award 2005. East Midlands Tourism award. England for Excellence award. ☆☆☆☆☆ **BH&HPA. 100T. 70MC. ❖ 🏕 ⚃ ⚒ ⚒**

Worksop

(4.5m). Clumber Park Caravan Club Site, Lime Tree Avenue, Clumber Park, Worksop, Nottinghamshire S80 3AE. *01909 484758.* www.caravanclub.co.uk. Owner: The Caravan Club. East Grinstead House, East Grinstead, West Sussex RH19 1UA. See website for directions to site. 20-acre site in 4000 acres of parkland where you can walk, cycle or ride. Barbecues with permission. Dog walk. Advance booking essential bank holidays and weekends. Motorhome waste point. Play equipment. Non-members welcome. Toilet blocks. Laundry. Baby/ toddler washroom. Veg prep. Peaceful off-peak. Golf, fishing and NCN cycle path 5m. ☆☆☆☆☆ **NCC. 183T. MC. ❖ 🏕 ⚃ ⚒**

(0.25m). Riverside Caravan Park, Central Avenue, Worksop, Nottinghamshire S80 1ER. *01909 474118.* Owner: Mr S Price. At roundabout JA57/A60 Mansfield, follow international site signs to town centre. Level site with waterside walks. Secluded yet adjacent to town centre. ☆☆☆☆ **BH&HPA. 60T MC. ❖ 🏕 ⚃**

RUTLAND

Oakham

(2m). Ranksborough Hall, Langham, Oakham, Rutland LE15 7ER. *01572 722984.* ranksborough@lineone.net. www.ranksboroughhall.com. Owner: Mr & Mrs Barney. Ranksborough Ltd. A606 Melton to Oakham. In village of Langham. PO, picnic area on site. Free bus to local supermarket. Medical practice/hospital/pharmacy 2m. Bowling green 2m. 3 golf courses nearby. Fishing, birdwatching, sailing, cycling 4m. **BH&HPA. 40T. MC. ❖ 🏕 ⚃ ⚒**

(5m). Rutland Caravan & Camping, Greetham, Oakham, Rutland LE15 7NX. *01572 813 520.* info@rutlandcaravanandcamping.co.uk. www.rutlandcaravanandcamping.co.uk. Owner: Mr Hinch. 3 Shepherds Lane, Greetham, Oakham, Rutland LE15 7NX. From A1 N or S bound on to B668 towards Greetham. R at crossroads before village and 2nd L to site. Next to Greetham village with 3 pubs serving food, shop, garage, garden centre, walk to/from site and Viking Way footpath. Golf course, fishing, horse riding 1m; Rutland water 4m with fishing, cycling, rock climbing, butterflies. AA graded 3 pennants. **30T. 30MC. ❖ 🏕 ⚃ ⚒ ⚒**

CHESHIRE

Chester

(3m). Birch Bank Farm, Stamford Lane, Christleton, Chester, Cheshire CH3 7QD. *01244 335233.* Owner: Mr A W Mitchell. R off A51 Chester to Nantwich, opposite Vicars Cross Golf Club, Christleton-Waverton. Small site on working farm in countryside. Open May 1-October 31. **10T. MC. 🏕 ⚃**

(4m). Chester Fairoaks Caravan Club Site, Rake Lane, Little Stanney, Chester, Cheshire CH2 4HS. *01513 551600.* www.caravanclub.co.uk. Owner: The Caravan Club. East Grinstead House, East Grinstead, West Sussex RH19 1UA. See website for directions to site. Pleasant, open level site with oak trees on boundary, located just off M53. Some hard-standings, toilet block, laundry facilities, baby/toddler washroom, Motorhome service point, play equipment and dog walk on site. Golf, fishing and NCN cycle route 5m. Non-members and tent campers admitted. ☆☆☆☆☆ **NCC. 100T. ❖ 🏕 ⚃ ⚃**

(3m). Chester Southerly Caravan Park, Balderton Lane, Marlston-cum-Lache, Chester, Cheshire CH4 9LF. *01244 671308.* Owner: Tony & Ann McArdle. Off A55 and A483. All pitches are level and attractively situated. Sports and shopping facilties etc. in Chester. Showers, laundry room, play area, public telephone. Calor Gas. Suitable touring base. Rallies by arrangement. **70T. MC. ✿ ⍾ ⌖ ⬛ & ﮞ**

(1.5m). Fir Trees Holiday Park, Ferry Lane, Chester, Cheshire CH1 6QF. *01244 398365.* Owner: Interleisure Parks Ltd. Off A548. By park and ride. Quiet, rural location and very convenient for Chester. Visit the zoo, boat on the Dee, cinemas and restaurants. Playground. Laundry. 20 acre park. David Bellamy Gold Conservation Award. Open March-January. ✰✰✰✰ **BH&HPA. 160S. ⍾ ⌀**

(2.5m). Netherwood Touring Site, Whitchurch Road, Chester, Cheshire CH3 6AF. *01244 335583.* netherwood. chester@btinternet.com. www.netherwoodtouringsite.co.uk. Owner: A Broad-Davies. OS map ref: 117447648. On the A41. Showers, shaver points, hand and hair-dryers. Chemical toilet emptying point. No children. Open March 1-October 31. **15T. 15MC. ⍾ ⬛**

(7m). Northwood Hall Country Touring Park, Dog Lane, Kelsall, Chester, Cheshire CW6 0RP. *01829 752569.* enquiries@northwood-hall.co.uk. www.northwood-hall.co.uk. Owner: Mr & Mrs Nock. Northwood Hall, Dog Lane, Kelsall, Chester, Cheshire CW6 0RP. Off the A556, 7m E of Chester. Family-run park is set among oak and chestnut trees. Adjacent Delemare Forest. Seasonal pitches available. Fishing, tennis 1m. Golf courses 3-5m. Cinema/shopping 7m. Open March 1-November 30. **30T. 30MC. 2H. ⍾ ⬛**

Congleton

(2m). Daneside Country Park, Holmes Chapel Road, Somerford, Congleton, Cheshire CW12 4SL. *01260 291486.* danesidepark@aol.com. www.danesidecountrypark.co.uk. Owner: Peter & Dawn Lead. On the A54 between Congleton and Holmes Chapel. Please telephone for detailed directions. Quiet country park. David Bellamy Gold Conservation Award. Fishing on lake and river. Open March 1-January 16. **BH&HPA. 108S. ⍾**

Frodsham

(2.5m). The Ridgeway Country Holiday Park, The Ridgeway, Alvanley, Frodsham, Cheshire WA6 6XQ. *01928 734981.* enquiries@ridgewaypark.com. www.ridgewaypark.com. Owners: David & Sue Meeks. J12, M56, follow A56 towards Frodsham. Shortly after passing through the market town, turn left on to B5393. Keep on road until you pass Foxhill Arboretum, then immediately turn left into The Ridgeway, travel for 0.5m to the park on the left. Wood-clad lodges for hire. Shopping andcinema 15 mins, swimming pool 25mins into Chester. Open March 1-January 2. ✰✰✰✰ **BH&HPA. 14S21H. ⍾**

Knutsford

(5m). Pickmere Lake Caravan Park, Mere View Farm, Pickmere, Knutsford, Cheshire WA16 0LG. *01565 733221.* Owner: Mr D Platt. J19, M6 to B5391, right at Red Lion, follow Pickmere lake signs (2.5m). Dogs allowed on leads, except Alsatians, Dobermanns and Rottweilers. Restaurant and inn on perimeter. Boating. Windsurfing. Fishing. Night halt. Children welcome. Shop nearby. Open March 1-mid-January. **BH&HPA. 25T. MC. 100S. ⍾ ⬛ ﮞ ⌀**

(5m). Woodlands Caravan Park, Wash Lane, Allostock, Knutsford, Cheshire WA16 9LG. *01565 723429/01332 810818.* www.ukparks.co.uk/woodlandspark3. Owner: Ron Grundy (Melbourne) Ltd. 69 Ryecroft Road, Hemington, Derby DE74 2RE. J19, M6, go to Knutsford, park is S of Knutsford on A50. Dogs allowed with permission. Fishing on site, golf course nearby. 3m to shops. Open March 1-January 6. **BH&HPA. 30T. MC. 169S. ⍾ ⬛ & ⌀**

Macclesfield

(5m). Capesthorne Hall, Siddington, Macclesfield, Cheshire SK11 9JY. *01625 861779.* info@capesthorne.com. www.capes horne.com. Owner: Mr & Mrs William Bromley-Davenport. Midway between Wilmslow and Congleton. Close to M6 J17,18 & 19. Direct access from A34. Situated in grounds of stately home. Gardens, park, chapel. Woodland walks. Showers. Laundry. 9-hole golf course 3m nearest shop 1.5m, garage 1m. Open April 1-October 31. **30T. MC. ⍾ ⬛**

(4m). Stonyfold Caravan Park, off Leek Road, Bosley, Macclesfield, Cheshire SK11 0PR. *01260 252195.* angus_ash ton@hotmail.com. www.ukparks.co.uk/stonyfold. Owner: Latevalle Ltd. 36 Hall Lane, Sutton, Macclesfield, Cheshire SK11 0EP. About 4m from Macclesfield on Leek road, nearside, 0.5m short of A523/A54 crossroads, up lane near Tilcon sign. Very quiet, woodland site with views and wildlife. Open March 1-January 15. **BH&HPA. 4T. 2MC. 28S. 2H. ✿ ⍾ ⬛**

(6m). Strawberry Wood, Lower Withington, Macclesfield, Cheshire SK11 9DU. *01477 571407.* Owner: Mr P Jenkinson. From J18, M6 take A535 to Macclesfield after 4m take B5392, site entrance 700yd on right-hand side. Small, quiet site set in mature woodland. Hard-standings, showers, toilets. Close to Jodrell Bank radio telescope. Fishing available on site. Open March 1-October 31. ✰✰✰ **BH&HPA. 25T. MC. ⍾ ⬛**

(4m). Wizard Country Park, Bradford Lane, Nether Alderley, Macclesfield, Cheshire SK10 4UE. *01625 585343/0790 1816064*Owner: Barrs Park Ltd. Wizard Country Park, Bradford Lane, Nether Alderley, Macclesfield, Cheshire SK10 4UE. From Alderley edge take B5087 towards Macclesfield. Just past the Wizard restaurant turn right into Bradford Lane. Follow signs to park, which is 1.5m from Alderley Edge. The park is set in the countryside with beautiful views. Close to most amenities. Miles of walks. Open March 1-February 14. **48S. ⍾**

Nantwich

Brookfield Caravan Park, Shrewbridge Road, Nantwich, Cheshire. *0800 387491.* Owner: Crewe & Nantwich Borough Council. Direct Services, Pyms Lane Depot, Pyms Lane, Crewe, Cheshire. Situated on public park close to river Weaver. 5 minutes walk from town. Play area. Open Easter-end September. **25T. MC. ⍾ ⬛**

Northwich

(5m). Daleford Manor Caravan Park, Daleford Lane, Sandiway, Northwich, Cheshire CW8 2BT. *01606 883391.* Owner: Mr Plant. Off A556. Golf, fishing, country walks. Open March 1-October 31. **BH&HPA. 10T. 10MC. 42S. ⍾**

(4m). Lamb Cottage Caravan Park, Dalefords Lane, Whitegate, Northwich, Cheshire CW8 2BN. *01606 882302/888491.* lynne@lccp.fsworld.co.uk. Owner: Mr & Mrs M J Howard. A556 to Sandiway PO/off licence, take road to Winsford, 1.5m on right, white cottage, sign on front. Showers, shaver points, hair-dryers, chemical toilet emptying point, washbasins. Member of Camping & Caravanning Club. Open March 1-October 31. **BH&HPA. 60T. 24MC. 12S. ⍾ ⬛ &**

(4.5m). Woodbine Cottage, Warrington Road, Acton Bridge, Northwich, Cheshire CW8 3QB. *01606 852319.* Owner: Mr Done. 9m SE of Warrington and W of Northwich on A49. Country site on the banks of the river Weaver in the heart of Cheshire. Convenient for many places of interest around Cheshire. Open March-October. **22T. 15MC. 25S. 4H.** ⚑ 🕿 🛒

Warrington

(5m). Holly Bank Caravan Park, Warburton Bridge Road, Rixton, Warrington, Cheshire WA3 6HL. *01617 752842.* Owner: Mr James O Walsh. 2m E of M6 J21. On A57 (Irlam). Turn right at lights into Warburton Bridge Road. Entry on left. Chemical toilet emptying point. Shaver points. Gas. Laundry facilities. Games room. Free showers. Public telephone. AA 3 pennants. 440yd to village with 3 PHs and shop. ✰✰✰✰ **BH&HPA. 60T. 10MC.** ✿ ⚑ 🕿 🛒

Winsford

(1m). Cheshire Broads Caravan Site, Stockhill, Winsford, Cheshire CW7 4EF. *01606 861043.* Owner: Thornley Leisure Parks. Off A54 & M6. Open March 1-January 16. **BH&HPA. NCC. 5T. 210S. 5H.** ⚑ 🕿

Lakeside Caravan Park, Stockshill, Winsford, Cheshire CW7 4EF. *01606 861043.* enq@thornleyleisure.co.uk. www.thorn leyleisure.co.uk. Owner: Thornley Leisure Ltd. Boating and fishing lake. Open March-November. ✰✰✰✰ **BH&HPA. 210S. 4H.** ⚑

(3m). Vale Royal River Park, Bradford Road, Newbridge, Winsford, Cheshire CW7 2PF. *01606 593567.* www.ukparks.co.uk/valeroyal. Owners: R Milner & Sons Ltd. Along Bradford Road from lower roundabout at Winsford. Calor Gas. Fishing. Open March 1-January 14. **BH&HPA. 100S.** ⚑

GREATER MANCHESTER

Oldham

(4m). Moorlands Caravan Site, Ripponden Road, Denshaw, Oldham, Greater Manchester OL3 5UN. *01457 874348.* moorlandscp@aol.com. Owner: Mr & Mrs S M Ashurst. The Moorlands, Rough Hey, Rippenden Road, Denshaw, Saddleworth, Lancashire. J22, M62. Turn right on to A672, SP Denshaw/Oldham. Site about 2m on left-hand side. Shower block. Laundry. **BH&HPA. 20T. 4MC. 29S. 6H.** ✿ ⚑ 🕿

Rochdale

(4m). Hollingworth Lake Caravan Park, Rakewood, Littleborough, Rochdale, Greater Manchester OL15 0AT. *01706 378661.* Owner: F Mills. Round House Farm, Rakewood, Littleborough, Rochdale, Greater Manchester. J21, M62. Follow Hollingworth Lake Country Park sign to Fisherman's Inn. Take Rakewood road then second R. Showers. Laundry. Dryer. Golf, shops, PO, doctors within 1.5m. Pony trekking. Large fishing and boating lake nearby. ✰✰✰ **BH&HPA. 40T. 15MC. 13S. 2H.** ✿ ⚑ 🕿 ♿ 🛒 ✏

Stockport

(7.5m). Elm Beds Farm, Higher Poynton, Stockport, Greater Manchester SK12 1TG. *01625 872370.* Owner: Mr V R Whittaker. At Poynton 2m E off A523. Showers. Shaver points. Gas supplies. Open March 1-October 31. **BH&HPA. 10T. 5MC. 55S.** ⚑ 🕿

LANCASHIRE

Accrington

(.5m). Harwood Bar Caravan Park, Mill Lane, Great Harwood, Accrington, Lancashire BB6 7UQ. *01254 884853.* A59 towards Clitheroe, then the A680 to Great Harwood, 0.5m before Great Harwood on left, first road on left past Nightingale garage. Open February-January. **BH&HPA. 30T. 107S.** ⚑ 🕿

Blackpool

> (3m). Blackpool South Caravan Club Site, Cropper Road, Marton, Blackpool, Lancashire FY4 5LB. *01253 762051.* www.caravanclub.co.uk. Owner: The Caravan Club. East Grinstead House, East Grinstead, West Sussex RH19 1UA. See website for standard directions to site. Caravan Club members only. Probably the nearest site to Blackpool. Suitable location for family holiday. Toilet blocks. Laundry facilities. Baby/toddler washroom. Veg prep. Motorhome service point. Information room. Golf, fishing and water sports nearby. Good area for walking. Open March-January. **NCC. 95T. MC.** ⚑ 🕿 ♿

Flints Caravan Park, River Road, Thornton, Blackpool, Lancashire. *01253 826129.* Owner: Mr D Edwards. 13 Garstang Road East, Poulton-le-Fylde, Blackpool, Lancs. Situated in town. Open March 1-January 10. **19T. 170S.** ⚑

(3m). Gillett Farm Caravan & Camping Park, Peel Road, Peel, Blackpool, Lancashire FY4 5JU. *01253 761676.* Owner: Gillett Farm Caravan & Camping Park Ltd. Travelling on M55 take exit 4 turn L on to A583 to Kirkham. At roundabout go straight across to traffic lights. At lights turn R and immediately L on to Peel Road, 2nd caravan park on R. Showers. Washhouse. Laundrette and ironing room. Telephone. TV and games room. Action Time play centre. Hard-standings for tourers and motor caravans. Chemical toilet emptying point. Calor Gas exchange. Golf course, cinema, shopping centre available within 3m. Open March-October. **BH&HPA. 46T. 6MC. 94S.** ⚑ 🕿 🛒 ✏

Hill View Caravan Park, Cartford Lane, Little Eccleston, Blackpool, Lancashire. *01253 890003.* Owner: Mr Ian Brooks. 210 Breck Road, Poulton FY6 7JZ. Newly developed park. Hard standings. Rural setting within easy reach of coast and lakes. Local shops, PO and weekly market 10 minutes' walk. Payphone. Open March-October. **20S.**

(5m). Kneps Farm Holiday Park, River Road, Thornton-Cleveleys, Blackpool, Lancashire FY5 5LR. *01253 823632.* enquiries@knepsfarm.co.uk. www.knepsfarm.co.uk. Owner: Mr Jonathan Porter. From A585 Kirkham to Fleetwood take B5412 at roundabout, SP Little Thornton. Turn R at mini roundabout after school on to Stanah Road, straight over second mini roundabout leading to River Road. Quiet, family-run park with family bathrooms. Rural retreat close to Blackpool and Wyre countryside. Open March 1-November 15. **BH&HPA. 60T. 10MC. 68S. 2H.** ⚑ 🕿 ♿ 🛒

(4m). Mariclough-Hampsfield Touring SIte, Preston New Road, Peel, Blackpool, Lancashire FY4 5JR. *01253 761034.* tony@mariclough.fsnet.co.uk. www.maricloughhampsfield camping.com. Owner: R A & J Cookson. Off the M55 J4, left on to the A583 straight through lights, 300yd on L. Adults only. Mid-week offers and seasonal pitches. Booking form available. Sheltered, level site. Open Easter-October. **50T. 10MC.** ⚑ 🕿

(3m). Marton Mere Holiday Village, Mythop Road, Blackpool, Lancashire FY4 4XN. *01253 792277.* oewebmaster @bourne-leisure.co.uk. www.martonmereholidayvillage.com. Owner: Bourne Leisure Ltd. One Park Lane, Hemel Hempstead, Herts HP2 4YL. M55, J4. Turn R at the roundabout and take the A583 towards Blackpool. Pass the Windmill and turn R at the Clifton Arms traffic lights, on to Mythop Road. The park is 150yd on the L. Laundrette. Bowling green, tennis courts. Indoor heated pool with water chute. New bowlingo bowling. Outdoor splash zone and multi-sports court. Crazy golf. Cafe. Showbar. Bowling green, trampolines, mini go-karts, tennis courts. Open March-November. ☆☆☆☆ **BH&HPA. NCC. 360T. MC. 922S. 141H.** ➤ ⌂ ⌖ ⌗

(6m). Meadowcroft & Queensgate Caravan Parks, Garstang Road, Great Eccleston, Blackpool, Lancashire PR3 0ZQ. *01995 670266.* Owner: V J Johnson. On A586 Garstang to Blackpool. Gas. Showers. Shaver points. Laundry. Fishing and cafe nearby. Hard-standings. Phone on site. Open March 1-October 31. **BH&HPA. 6T. 2MC. 40S.** ➤ ⌂

(7.5m). Merlewood Country Park, Cartford Lane, Little Eccleston, Blackpool, Lancashire PR3 0YP. *01995 604975/670317.* info@merlewoodcountrypark.co.uk. www. merlewoodcountrypark.co.uk. Owner: Michael Ward. The Office, Wyre Vale Park, A6 Cabus, Garstang, Lancs PR3 1PH. In the village of Little Eccleston off the A586 Blackpool to Garstang road. Family-run park in picturesque setting on hillside overlooking the River Wyre. Children's play area. 2mins from PH. Golf course and leisure centre within 4m. David Bellamy Gold Conservation Award. Open March 1-January 6. **BH&HPA. NCC. 143S.** ➤ ⌂

(3.5m). Newholme Park, 211A Preston New Road, Marton, Blackpool, Lancashire FY3 9TU. *01253 763742.* Owner: Falkus Property Co Ltd. Leave M55 at J4, then follow A583 towards Blackpool. Park located on right-hand side of A583, about 1m from M55 junction. **7T.** ➤ ⌂

(3m). Newton Hall Holiday Centre, Staining Road, Staining, Blackpool, Lancashire FY3 0AX. *01253 882512.* reception@ newtonhall.net. www.newtonhall.net. Owner: Partington's Holiday Centres. On B5266. Flat green bowling complex. Heated indoor pool. Amusement arcade. Cafe. Laundrette. Children's play area. Fishing pond. Open March 1-November 15. **40T. 450S. 40H.** ⌂ ⌖ ⌗

(2m). Normoss Farm Caravan Site, Normoss Road, Poulton-le-Fylde, Blackpool, Lancashire FY3 0AL. *01253 890584.* Owner: Mrs T Walker for Trustees R W Smith. 42 Normoss Road, Hardhorn, Blackpool, Lancashire. Open March-October. **23S.** ⌂ ⌗

(3m). Pipers Height Caravan & Camping Park, Peel Road, Peel, Blackpool, Lancashire FY4 5JT. *01253 763767.* Owner: Mr J Rawcliffe. Exit M55 J4. Turn 1st L on A583 to 1st lights, turn R and sharpL. Site 50yd. Licensed bar and family room. Families only. Laundry. Restaurant. Open March 1-November 30. **80T. MC. 50S.** ➤ ⌂ ⌗

(5m). Pool Brow Caravan Park, Pool Foot Lane, Little Singleton, Blackpool, Lancashire FY6 8LY. *01253 886462.* Owner: Mr J A Gregson. Toilets, showers facilities on site. Open March 1-October 31. **BH&HPA. 37S.**

(2m). Richmond Hill Caravan Park, 352 St Annes Road, Blackpool, Lancashire FY4 2QN. *01253 344266.* bookings@ richmond-hill.freeserve.co.uk. www.richmond-hill.freeserve. co.uk. Owner: Mrs M Armstrong. From M55 follow airport sign, turn right at Halfway House Hotel. Site about 200yd on right. Access from Ivy Avenue. Showers. Calor Gas. Close to beach

1m and town centre 2m. Pleasure beach. Frequent bus service. Supermarket, shops, PH etc within walking distance. Open March 1-end of October. ☆☆☆ **15T. MC. 1H.** ➤ ⌗

(10m). Sandy Bay Caravan Park, Pilling Lane, Preesall, Blackpool, Lancashire FY6 OHG. *01253 810883.* dh@sbay.fsnet.co.uk. Owner: Mr J D Hulme. Off M55, J3 andA585 for Fleetwood. 3rd traffic lights right on to A588. Follow Knott End (B5377) to T-junction, left then 1st right into Pilling Lane. Adjacent to beach. 10mins from all amenities. Open March 1-January 4. **54S.** ⌖

(7m). Sportsmans Caravan Park, Sportsmans Lodge, The Heads, Browns Lane, Stalmine, Blackpool, Lancashire FY6 0JG. *01253 810473.* Owner: Mr W & R McCann. Down M6 exit Kirkham, follow signs to Cleveleys and Fleetwood. 3rd set lights turn R over Shard bridge to Hamble to Stalmine, 2nd turn on L Staynall Lane, 1st R Highgate Lane, 1st L leading to Browns Lane, site is first on the L. Situated on the banks of the river Wyre estuary. 2m to nearest bus stop and PO, PH. No sub letting. Golf 3m; cinema, shopping centre Blackpool 7m. Open March 1-October 31. **BH&HPA. 45S.** ➤

(5m). Stanah House Caravan Park, River Road, Thornton, Blackpool, Lancashire FY5 5LR. *01253 824000.* stanah house@talk21.com. Owner: Mr Stuart Adams. 80 Church Road, Thornton, Cleveleys, Lancs FY5 2TX. Exit 3 M55, A585 Fleetwood right at roundabout, sign to river turn right. Small, touring site overlooking the river Wyre, with views of the Fells and Lake District mountains. Modern toilet block with shower rooms and all amenities, including laundry room. Adventure play area. Open March-October. ☆☆☆ **50T. MC.** ➤ ⌂ ⌖ ⌗

Pipers Height
Caravan Park
Peel Road, Blackpool, Lancashire FY4 5JT
Telephone: 01253 763767
Web: www.pipersheight.co.uk

- This well established family-run park is situated in the rural Fylde area. Approx. 1/2 a mile from junction 4 off the M55
- The park is ideally located within the Fylde area and only 4 miles from the lively and spirited Blackpool and 3 miles from the quiet and tranquil Lytham St Annes
- The park has now opened the new development of 18 luxury Holiday Home plots, each offering individual garden, patio and parking facilities
- We have also extended our seasonal touring pitches for 2006, allowing us to invite a further 50 touring units

NORTH-WEST ENGLAND

(3m). Thornfield Holiday Camp, Staining Road, Blackpool, Lancashire FY3 0BW. *01253 882117.* Manager: S Swinton. Open March 21-October 24. **BH&HPA. 70S.** ♈

(3.5m). Underhill Caravan & Camping Site, Preston New Road, Peel, Blackpool, Lancashire FY4 5JS. *01253 763107.* lesleys@ilph.org. www.underhill.biz. Site is east of Blackpool on the A583 road and only 0.5m from M55 off J4, M55, first left on to A583, site on right through traffic lights. Wardens: Brian & Jacqui Buddle. Open Easter-November 1. ✫✫ **50T. MC.** ♈ ♿ ☎

Whalley Villa Caravan Park, Whalley Lane, Marton, Blackpool, Lancashire FY4 4PL. *01253 761947.* Owner: Clarksons Caravans. Off A583. Open March 1-October 31. **BH&HPA. 56S.** ♈

(4m). Whitmore Farm Caravan Park & Fishery, Bradshaw Lane, Greenhalgh, Kirkham, Blackpool, Lancashire. *01253 836224.* Owner: Mrs S I Moore. J3 on M55. Take A585 to Fleetwood. Turn 2nd left down Back Lane and 2nd left again, Bradshaw Lane. Stocked coarse fishing waters. Open March 1-October 31. **25T. MC.** ♈ ☎

(8m). Willowgrove Park Homes, Sandy Lane, Preesall, Blackpool, Lancashire FY6 0EJ. *01253 811306.* chbarton@bartonparkhomes.freeserve.co.ukwww.barton-parkhomes.co.uk. Owner: Barton Park Homes. Westgate, Morecambe LA3 3BA. Off A588 to Knott End. Park in lakeside setting. Private fishing, birdwatching and children's playground. Level site suitable for wheelchairs. Open March 1-October 31 for tourers. ✫✫✫ **BH&HPA. NCC. 80T. 20MC. 112S.** ♈ ☎ ♿ ⌀

(6m). Windy Harbour Holiday Centre, Little Singleton, Blackpool, Lancashire FY6 8NB. *01253 883064.* info@windyharbour.net. www.windyharbour.net. Owner: Partington's Holiday Centre Ltd. Junction 3, M55. Take third exit off roundabout, signposted A585 Fleetwood, and follow road for about 3m until set of traffic lights. Go straight on, park entrance is about 300yd straight ahead. Fully serviced pitches. Hard-standings for vehicles. Toilet/shower block, washing-up facilities. Rally rates for group bookings on request. Indoor heated swimming pool, junior and teen club, children's play area. Course fishing ponds, amusement arcade. Fish and chip shop, snack bar cafe. Open March 1-November 15. ✫✫✫ **200T. 25MC. 700S. 200H.** ♈ ☎ ♿ ☎

Burnley

(6m). Bridge Heywood Caravan Park, Read, Burnley, Lancashire BB12 7RR. *01254 886103.* Owner: Mr Hanson. Off A671 Whalley to Read road. Park not suitable for children. Bottled gas. Fishing allowed in river and coarse fishing pond. Small dogs only. Open March 1-October 31. **BH&HPA. 6T. 6MC. 86S.** ♈ ☎

Carnforth

(2m). Bolton Holmes Farm, Off Mill Lane, Bolton-le-Sands, Carnforth, Lancashire LA5 8ES. *01524 732854.* Owner: T Mason & Sons. Situated on west side of the A6. S of Carnforth. 7m N of Lancaster. Down Mill Lane. On shore front. Extensive views over Morecambe Bay. 0.75m to nearest shops, PO and doctors, etc. Open April 1-September 30. **25T. 25MC. 40S.** ♈ ☎

Broadwood Caravans, Ingleton, Carnforth, Lancashire LA6 3ET. *01524 241253.* Owner: T S Greenwood & S Longden. On B6255 opposite Waterfalls walk. 0.5m from Ingleton. **BH&HPA. 18S.** ✿ ♈ ☎

(5m). Capernwray House Caravan Park, Capernwray House, Capernwray, Carnforth, Lancashire LA6 1AE. *01524 732363.* thesmiths@capernwrayhouse.com. www.capernwrayhouse.com. Owner: Mr Roy & Mrs M Smith. Leave M6 at J35, follow sign M601 (Over Kellet Quarries) to B6254, at T-junction turn left into Over Kellett. At crossroads in village turn left, proceed for 2m to second site on right. Lovely touring area. Play area. Dog walk area. Heated facilities block. Seasonal tourers. Bed and breakfast. Open March 1-October 31. ✫✫✫ **60T. 5MC.** ♈ ☎ ☎

(1m). Detron Gate Farm, Bolton-le-Sands, Carnforth, Lancashire LA5 9TN. *01524 732842/733617.* Owner: Mr E Makinson. Exit 35 from M6, site is 2m S on A6. Electric shower point, bottled gas supply, hot water supply, laundry facilities, recreation room, children's play area, showers, bus service nearby. Boating, fishing, golf and railway station all nearby. Open Easter-October 1. **BH&HPA. 92T. 10MC. 45S.** ♈ ☎ ☎

(5m). Gibraltar Farm, Silverdale, Carnforth, Lancashire. *01524 701736.* Owner: Mr F W Burrow. Off A6. Open March 1-November 30. **15T. MC.** ♈ ☎

(8m). Holgates Caravan Parks Ltd, Cove Road, Silverdale, Carnforth, Lancashire LA5 0SH. *01524 701508.* caravan@holgates.co.uk. www.holgates.co.uk. 5m NW of Carnforth, J35, M6. Set in an Area of Outstanding Natural Beauty with views of sea and country. Indoor heated swimming pool. Spa bath, sauna, steam room. Games room. Cafe, bar, shop, gym. RSPB reserve at Leighton Moss, 18-hole golf course 2m, cinema 12m, Lake District 20m. Open mid December-mid November. ✫✫✫✫ **BH&HPA. 70T. MC. 350S. 11H.** ♈ ☎ ♿ ☎

(4.5m). Hollins Farm, Far Arnside, Silverdale, Carnforth, Lancashire LA5 0SL. *01524 701767.* Owner: V & C Ribbons. From M6 join A6 at J35. 1m towards Carnforth turn R at traffic lights on to minor road Warton and Silverdale sign. In Warton turn sharp L by gardens. R after level crossing. Fork L past phone box, R into Cove Road second L after children's home into farmyard. In Area of Outstanding Natural Beauty, 5mins walk to shore of Morecambe Bay. Open Easter-October. **T. MC.** ♈

(3m). Intack Caravans, Nether Kellett, Carnforth, Lancashire. *01524 732884.* Owner: Mr E J Ward. Off A6 and M6 Lancaster to Carnforth. Morecambe 6m. Open March 1-January 15. **27S.** ♈

(2m). Morecambe Lodge Caravan Park, Bolton-le-Sands, Shore Lane, Carnforth, Lancashire LA5 8JP. *01524 823260/824361.* andrewtower@f2s.com. morecambe-lodge.co.uk. Owner: Mrs B E Halhead, JK Towers, AJ Towers. S on A6 from Carnforth, or N from Lancaster, follow brown holiday signs at lights on A6 on to coastal road, turn R by first house, follow road to site by shore. Direct access to beach from park, overlooking lake hills. Open March 1-October 31. **BH&HPA. 25T. MC. 181S.** ♈ ☎ ♿

(1m). Netherbeck Holiday Home Park, North Road, Carnforth, Lancashire LA5 9NG. *01524 735101.* info@netherbeck.co.uk. www.netherbeck.co.uk. Owner: Mr F W Holgate. c/o Holgates Caravan Parks Ltd, Middlebarrow Plain, Cove Road, Silverdale, Carnforth, Lancs LA5 0SH. Off M6 exit 35, on to A6 Carnforth. L at traffic lights. L in 300yd at Shovel Inn. Site on R in 0.5m. Laundry. Public phone. Supermarket/PO/railway etc at Carnforth. Open March 1-January 10. ✫✫✫✫✫ **BH&HPA. 45S.** ♈ ♿

(3m). Old Hall Caravan Park, Capernway, Carnforth, Lancashire LA6 1AD. *01524 733276.* info@oldhallcaravan park.co.uk. www.oldhallcaravanpark.co.uk. Owner: Mr D J Wightman. Off the A6 and M6 at J35 to Over Kellet, turn left to Capernwray. Park is 1.5m on the right-hand side. Over 80 acres of private woodland ajoining the park. Public telephone, laundry. Mobile shop daily. Open March 1-January 10. ☆☆☆☆☆ BH&HPA. 38T. 3MC. 220S. ♦ ⚏ ⚹

(3m.). Red Bank Farm, Bolton-le-Sands, Carnforth, Lancashire LA5 8JR. *01524 823196.* archer_mark@ lycos.co.uk. www.redbankfarm.co.uk. Owner: Mr M Archer. Traveling from the A6 at Bolton-le-Sands take the A5015 towards Morecambe, after 500yd turn sharp right, SP shore, right again over railway bridge, turn left along the shore. A working farm. Pets corner. Set on the shore. PHs, restaurants, shop and PO are 1m away. Golf course 3m. Open Easter-October 1. **MC. 40S.** ♦

(2m). Sandside Caravan & Camping Park, The Shore, Bolton-le-Sands, Carnforth, Lancashire LA5 8JS. *01524 822311.* From J35, M6 follow signs for Morecambe about 3m, turn R after Far Pavillion Indian restaurant. Small, quiet site close to beach. Modern facilities block. Laundry Room. AA 3 pennants. Open March 1-4 January. **BH&HPA. 60T. 10MC. 35S.** ♦ ⚏ ⚹

(3m). Scout Crag Holiday Park, Warton, Carnforth, Lancashire LA5 9RY. *01524 734579.* Owner: Mr & Mrs H Daly. J35 off the M6, and follow signs for Lancaster. In Carnforth turn right at traffic lights, follow Warton sign, turn left for Silverdale about 1m along road. Bottled gas. Shops, doctor, dentist, garages, golf, fishing and PHs all within 2m. Open March-January. **BH&HPA. 103S.** ♦ ⚏ ⚹

(2m). South Lakeland Leisure Village, Borwick, Carnforth, Lancashire LA6 1BH. *01524 730823.* enquiries@southlakeland-caravans.co.uk. www.southlake land-caravans.co.uk. Owners: South Lakeland Caravans. South Lakeland House, Main A6, Yealand Redmayne, Carnforth, Lancashire LA5 9RN. Leave the M6 at J35 and follow the A6 north towards Milnthorpe. After 0.5m turn right into Borwick Lane. Village is immediately on your right-hand side. Bar and restaurant. An exclusive development of pine lodge holiday homes around a lakeside setting. Leisure club including indoor swimming pool, gym, sauna, beauty therapy, tapas bar, cofee lounge. Golf three miles, Cinema and shopping centre within 7m. Open February 7-January 7. **BH&HPA. 205S. 33**♦ ⚹

Woodclose Caravan Park, Casterton, Kirkby Lonsdale, Carnforth, Lancashire LA6 2SE. *01524 271597.* michael hodgkins@woodclosecaravanpark.fsnet.co.uk. www.wood closepark.com. Owner: Mr F Hodgkins. Located 0.5m SE of Kirkby Lonsdale off the A65. Small, quiet, family site with the Lake District and Yorkshire Dales a short drive away. Bottled gas. AA 4 pennants. Open March 1-November 1. ☆☆☆☆ **BH&HPA. 21T. 55S.** ♦ ⚏ ⚹ ⚹

Clitheroe

(1.5m). Camping & Caravanning Club Site - Clitheroe, Edisford Road, Clitheroe, Lancashire BB7 3LA. *01200 425294.* www.campingandcaravanningclub.co.uk. Owner: Camping & Caravanning Club. Greenfields House, Westwood Way, Coventry CV4 8JH. A671 to Clitheroe. SP a sports centre. Turn into Greenacre Road L at Edisford Road T-junction. Sports Centre on R, site 50yd on L. 6 acre site accepting all units types. On banks of river Ribble in Ribble Valley, in sheltered wooded setting. Adjacent to site are pitch-and-putt and miniature steam railway. Suitable base for touring Yorkshire Dales. Two ancient hunting forests encompass Clitheroe, those of Pendle and Bowland. Charming ancient market town of Clitheroe is 20mins walk from site. Non members welcome. Special deals for families and backpackers. Open March-October. ☆☆☆☆ **80T. 80MC.** ♦ ⚏ ⚹

(6m). Rimington Caravan Park, Hardacre Lane, Gisburn, Clitheroe, Lancashire BB7 4EE. *01200 445355.* lisa@rimington 2004. freeserve.co.uk. Owners: D, M & S Leeming. Off A682. 1m E of Gisburn Village, SP for Nelson etc. 1st R again. Licensed bar. Luxury bathroom. Laundry. Public phone. Hairdryers. Quiet countryside park. Shopping in village 1m. Town 5m. Golf courses 5 and 8m. Open March 1-October 31. ☆☆☆☆☆ **BH&HPA. 4T. 140S.** ♦ ⚏ ⚹ ⚹

(1m). Shireburn Caravan Park, Waddington Road, Clitheroe, Lancashire BB7 3LB. *01200 423422/423523.* Owner: Shireburn Caravan Park Ltd. Off B6246. Woodland park in Forest of Bowland adjacent to the river Ribble. Licensed clubhouse on site. Laundrette. Fishing nearby. Luxury caravans for hire. Victorian country house with self-catering apartments for hire. Open March 1-October 31; open all year for apartments. **BH&HPA. 10T. 4MC. 140S. 3H.** ♦ ⚏ ⚹

(5m). Stubbins Vale Caravan Site, Stubbins Lane, Sabden, Clitheroe, Lancashire BB7 9EP. *01200 445355.* remingtoncara vanpark@btinternet.com. Owners: David Malcolm & Stephen Leeming. Off A59 & A671. **BH&HPA. T. MC. 38S.** ✿ ♦ ⚏ ⚹

(2m). Three Rivers Mobile Park, Eaves Hall Lane, West Bradford, Clitheroe, Lancashire BB7 3JG. *01200 423523.* enquiries@threeriverspark.co.uk. www.threeriverspark.co.uk. Owner: Ribble Motels Ltd. Turn off A59 at Clitheroe North sign. Continue into West Bradford village. Turn L at T-junction. Take next R, Eaves Hall Lane. Indoor heated swimming pool. Club open all year. Weekend entertainment. Woodland nature trails. New luxury amenities block open. Laundrette. Play area. Open March 1-November 1. ☆☆☆☆ **BH&HPA. 80T. 10MC. 120S. 8H.** ♦ ⚏ ⚹ ⚹

Todber Caravan Park, Gisburn, Clitheroe, Lancashire BB7 4JJ. *01200 445322.* Owner: South Lakeland Caravans. South Lakeland House, Main A6, Yealand Redmayne, Nr Carnforth LA5 9RN. Off A59 on A682 towards Burnley, also J13 from M65, 6m towards Gisburn and Kendal. Bar, shop, laundry, children's play area, entertainment. Volley ball, football. Fishing 1m, shops 2m, golf 5m, cinema 10m. Open March-January. **BH&HPA. 295S.** ♦ ⚹

Fleetwood

(1m). Broadwater Holiday Centre, Fleetwood Road, Fleetwood, Lancashire FY7 8JX. 01253 872796. reception@broad-water.co.uk. www.partingtons.com. Owner: Partington's Holiday Centres Ltd. Newton Hall, Staining, Blackpool, Lancashire. On A585 Thornton to Fleetwood. New outdoor crown bowling green. Shop, PO 5mins walk, Supermarket 5mins drive. Sauna and jacuzzi for over-16s. Open March 1-mid November. **4T. MC. 350S. 8H.** 🖳 ♿

(1.5m). Cala Gran Holiday Park, Fleetwood Road, Fleetwood, Lancashire FY7 8JY 01253 875737. oewebmaster @bourne-leisure.co.uk. www.calagranholidaypark.com. Owner: Bourne Leisure Ltd. One Park Lane, Hemel Hempstead, Herts HP2 4YL. M6 then M55. J3 take A585 to Fleetwood, SP to Fleetwood/Thornton. At the 4th roundabout with the Nautical College on the L, take 3rd exit and the park is along this road on the L. Indoor pool, outdoor splash zones sports and leisure facilities. Children's Club. Licensed club with family entertainment. Mini market, laundrette. Sauna, owners lounge. Cabaret room, sports bar, amusements, bouncy castle, play area. Blackpool's Golden Mile and Pleasure beach. Open March-January for owner-occupiers. ☆☆☆☆ **BH&HPA. NCC. 753S. 248H.** 🏕 ♿ ⚓

Garstang

Foxhouses Park, Long Lane, Scorton, Garstang, Lancashire PR3 1DB. 01995 603271/01524 793282. www.foxhouses park.co.uk. Owners: Wharf Cottage Holiday Parks Ltd, Cabus Nook Lane, Winmarleigh, Garstang LA18 PR3 1AA. M6, J33 take S A6 exit at roundabout. About 30 yd turn L into Hampson Lane, at T junction, turn R, follow road for about 3m then R, into Long Lane. Park is 500yd on R. Small select park. Laundry. Fishing. Shopping centre: 1.5m. Golf, leisure centre 3.5m. cinema 6m. Open March 1-January 31. **BH& HPA. 30S.** 🏕 ♿

(2m). Wharf Cottage Holiday Park, Cabus Nook Lane, Winmarleigh, Garstang, Lancashire PR3 1AA. 01995 603271. www.wharfcottage.co.uk. Owner: Mr & Mrs D E Crabtree. Between Lancaster and Preston (A6), going N L at Burlingham Caravans, 2m R at garage over bridge on the L. Small park. Fishing. Golf, leisure centre, shopping 2m; cinema 6m. Open March 1-January 31. **BH&HPA. 22S. 1H.** 🏕 ♿

Heywood

(1m). Gelder Clough Park, Ashworth Road, Heywood, Lancashire OL10 4BD. 01706 364858. Owner: P & J Chadwick. Oakleigh Cottage, Gelder Wood Country Park, Ashworth Road, Rochdale, Lancashire OL11 5UP. J18, M62 to M66 (signposted Bury) at second exit left, J2 leave M66 turn right on to A58, SP Heywood, at Morrison's supermarket turn left into Bamford Road B6222 to T-junction. Turn left, after 100yd turn right into Ashworth Road, park on right. Open March-October. ☆☆☆☆☆ **BH&HPA. T. MC.** 🏕 🖳 ♿ ⌀

Kirkham

(0.5m). Canada Lodge Caravan Park, Blackpool Road, Kirkham, Lancashire. 01772 687749. Owner: Mr & Mrs A Crawford. 3m from Blackpool. Open March 1 to end-November. **20T.** 🏕 🖳

(1.5m). Mowbreck Park, Mowbreck Lane, Wesham, Kirkham, Lancashire PR4 3HA. 01772 682494. www.mow breckpark.co.uk. Owner: S Carroll. Turn left to Kirkham, left at roundabout to Wesham. Left by St Joseph Church on to Mowbreck Lane. Good local transport. Fishing nearby. Peaceful park set in picturesque countryside, yet close to local amenities. Open March 1-January 16. ☆☆☆☆☆ **BH&HPA. NCC. 176S. 4H.** 🏕 ⚓ ⌀

Lancaster

(6m). Bank End Caravan Site, Cockerham, Lancaster, Lancashire LA2 0DY. 01524 751331. Owner: Mr R B Lawson. On A588. The site is situated on the Lune estuary with the coastal way passing the site entrance. There is a shop 5mins walk away. High tides provide excellent opportunities for many water sports. Rural location. Open March 1-October 31. **52S.** 🏕

(20m). Caravan & Camping Site, Flying Horse Shoe Caravan Site, Clapham, Lancaster, Lancashire LA2 8ES. 01524 251532. alan@laughing-gravy.co.uk. www.laughing-gravy.co.uk. Owner: Laughing Gravy Leisure Ltd. Off A65. Immediately after large sign saying 'Clapham, next right', take next left and follow for 0.5m. Between Settle and Ingleton. Clapham Station. Bottled gas supplies. 24hr warden. Open April-October. **NCC. 45T. 45MC.** 🏕 🖳

(6m). Cockerham Sands Country Club & Caravan Park, Cockerham, Lancaster, Lancashire LA2 0BB. 01524 751387. Owner: Bateson's Hotels (1958) Ltd. Leave M6 at J33. Take A6 Garstang to Glasson Dock for 1.25 miles. Turn right on to Cockerham Road for 2m. Turn right Glasson Dock to Thurnham Hall for 2.25m. Turn left opposite Thurnham Hall at SP 'Park 3 miles'. Outdoor heated pool, licensed club with entertainment, children's play area. Open March-October. ☆☆☆☆ **9T. 9MC. 272S. 38H.** 🏕 🖳 ♿ ⚓ ⌀

Crook O' Lune Caravan Park, Caton Road, Crook O Lune, Lancaster, Lancashire LA2 9HP. 01524 770216. crookolune car avanpark@hotmail.com. www.crookolunecaravanpark.com. 0.5m from M6, J34 on A683 Kirby Lonsdale Road heading East. Family-owned and family-run site. Fishing, walking and rambling nearby. Kirby Lonsdale and historical city of Lancaster only 10mins away with Morecambe Lights and fun parks 15mins. Closed January 3-February 14. **BH&HPA. 170S.** 🏕 ♿

(2.5m). Hawthorns Caravan & Camping Park, Nether Kellet, Lancaster, Lancashire LA6 1EA. 01524 732079. Owner: Mr & Mrs D Wright. M6 J35, cross motor way to B6254 right. Left 1m to junction, left, 300yd on left. 9-hole putting green, library, tropical bird aviary. Wildlife pond. Children welcome. Holiday homes are privately owned; no tourers or tents. Open March 1-November 21. ☆☆☆☆ **BH&HPA. 80S.** 🏕 🖳 ♿

(6m). Mosswood Caravan Park, Crimbles Lane, Cockerham, Lancaster, Lancashire LA2 0ES. 01524 791041. info@moss wood.co.uk. www.mosswood.co.uk. Owner: S Wild. M6, J33 turn left on to A6, afterabout 1m turn right at front of white house on to Cockerham Road, continue to T-junction. Turn right. At next T-junction (Manor PH) turn left. After 1m turn left into Crimbles Lane. Park is 1m on right. Bewarre of horseson

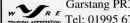
Please mention Caravan Sites 2006 when replying to advertisers

Crimbles Lane. Fishing 400yd. Parachuting, microlights 2m. Golf, horse riding 3m. David Bellamy Gold Conseervatopn Award. Open March 1-October 31. ✫✫✫✫✫ **BH&HPA. NCC. 20T. 20MC. 130S.** 🛏 🔌 ♿ 🎣

(5m). Wyreside Lakes Fishery, Sunnyside Farmhouse, Bay Horse, Lancaster, Lancashire LA2 9DG. *01524 792093.* wyre side2003@yahoo.co.uk. www.wyresidelakes.co.uk. Owner: Mr R E A Birkin. M6, J33, turn left and follow the brown signs. Small site. 1m from PO, Fisherman's Rest licensed bar/restaurant. Toilet/shower block, washroom. Outside washing- up area. Carp, pike, mixed coarse and trout fishing on 13-lake complex. ✫✫✫ **NCC. 26T. MC.** ✿ 🛏 🔌 ♿

Lytham St Annes

(3m). Bank Lane Caravan Park, Bank Lane, Warton, Lytham St Annes, Lancashire PR4 1TB. *01772 633513.* bank lanecp@btconnect.com. Owner: Batesons Hotels Ltd. From Preston exit 31, A584 to Warton.Site hasa play area and laundrette. Open March 1-December 20. **NCC. 40T. 10MC. 180S.** 🛏 🔌

(1m). Eastham Hall Caravan Park, Saltcoats Road, Lytham, Lytham St Annes, Lancashire FY8 4LS. *01253 737907.* Owner: J W Kirkham & Sons Ltd. On B5259. Leave A584 turning right at 1st mini roundabout. Go over railway and right at 2nd mini roundabout, or turn left off M55 on to A585 and straight ahead at 3 roundabouts to B5259. Site in 4m. Secluded park. Open March 1-October 31. ✫✫ **BH&HPA. 130T. 20MC. 281S.** 🛏 🔌 🎣

(2m). Lawnsdale Caravan Park, Lytham Road, Moss Side, Lytham St Annes, Lancashire FY8 4NA. *01253 735246.* Owner: Mr H Burnett. On B5259 between Lytham and Wrea Green. Railway halt adjacent to park. Open February 1-December 14. **BH&HPA. 100S.** 🛏

(1.5m). Oaklands Caravan Park Ltd, Lytham Road, Warton, Lytham St Annes, Lancashire PR4 1AH. *01772 634459.* Owner: John Bamber. J31 Preston A583 towards Blackpool, A584 to Warton. Blackpool 7m. Shops and PH 5mins walk. 2m to beach. Bus service. Dog run. Laundrette. Open 21 December-8 November. **60T. MC. 30S.** 🛏 ♿ 🎣

(1.5m). Sea View Caravan Park, Bank Lane, Warton, Lytham St Annes, Lancashire PR4 1TD. *01772 679336.* Owner: Mr & Mrs Flint. Off A584 Preston to Lytham left on Bank Lane at Ribblefort Art Gallery. Second park on right. Flat, level, quiet, family site with estuary views. Open March 1-end October. **BH&HPA. 16T. MC. 78S. 6H.** 🛏 🔌 ♿ ✐

Morecambe

Glen Caravan Site, Westgate, Morecambe, Lancashire LA3 3NR. *01524 423896.* Owner: Mr C R Hadwen. Site located within Morecambe on Westgate Road. 10-15 minutes walk to the promenade west end. Golf, cinema, shopping centre all within 2m. Open March-January 4. **20T. 5MC. 36S.** 🛏 🔌 ♿

Meadowfield Caravan Park, Middleton Road, Morecambe, Lancashire. Owner: Mr J Collins. **10S. 10H.** 🛏

(3m). Melbreak Caravan Site, Carr Lane, Middleton, Morecambe, Lancashire LA3 3LH. *01524 852430.* Owner: Mr A E & G A Syson. A589 out of Morecambe, SP to Middleton. 1m from sandy beach. Showers. Laundry. Open March 1-October 31. ✫✫✫ **BH&HPA. 10T. 10MC. 32S.** 🛏 🔌 🎣

(3m). Ocean Edge Caravan Park, Moneyclose Lane, Heysham, Morecambe, Lancashire LA3 2XA. *01524 855657.* enquiries@southlakeland-caravans.co.uk. www. oceanedgeleisurepark.co.uk. Owner: South Lakeland Caravans Ltd. South Lakeland House, A6, Yealand Redmayne, Nr Carnforth, Lancs LA5 9RN. Follow M6, A589, B5273 to Lancaster, Morecambe and Port of Heysham at traffic lights at Moneyclose Inn, turn left access road to the park. Indoor heated pool and sauna, boat launch, bowling green. Children's indoor play are, cabaret lounge, 10mins drive from Morecambe. Golf 2m, shops 3m, cinema 5m. Open February-January for holiday caravans; open March-November for tourers. ✫✫✫ **BH&HPA108T. 600S. 40H.** 🛏 🔌 🎣

(0.5m). Regent Leisure Park, Westgate, Morecambe, Lancashire LA3 3DF. *01524 413940.* enquiries@southlakeland-caravans.co.uk. www.southlakeland-caravans.co.uk. Owner: South Lakeland Caravans Ltd. South Lakeland House, A6, Yealand Redmayne, Nr Carnforth, Lancs LA5 9RN. M6, J34 and follow A589 to Morecambe for 2.5m. First left at 3rd roundabout on left 1.5m. Play area. Laundrette. 2 heated outdoor pools. Nightclub complex. Children's indoor play centre. Laundrette. Fast food bar. Entertainment. Cinema, shops 1m, golf 3m. Open March-January. ✫✫✫✫ **BH&HPA. 285S. 55H.** 🛏 ♿ 🎣

(3m). Riverside Caravan Park, Snatchems, Morecambe, Lancashire LA3 3ER. *01524 844193.* info@riverside-more cambe.co.uk. www.riverside-morecambe.co.uk. Owner: Mr A Proctor. Exit 34 off M6 follow signs for Morecambe. Cross river and L at roundabout on Morecambe road. Straight on at roundabout for 0.5m, next door to Golden Ball Hotel. Open March 1-October 31. **50T. 35S. 7H.** 🛏 🔌 ♿

(5m). Shorefields, Middleton Sands, Morecambe, Lancashire LA3 3LL. *01524 852454/07885 835362 (m).* stella @hargreavesho30.fslife.co.uk. Owner: C J & S M Hargreaves. Manor Bungalow, Middleton Sands, Heysham, Lancashire LA3 3LL. Take A589. From J34 of M6, then A683 to Middleton, right into Carr Lane. Beach frontage. Showers. Calor Gas dealers. General store with off-licence sales. Main walkways lit at night. Open March-October. **BH&HPA. 30T. 5MC. 178S.** 🅿 🐕 🛇 🛁

(0.75m). Venture Caravan Park, Langridge Way, Westgate, Morecambe, Lancashire LA4 4TQ. *01524 412986.* mark@ venturecaravanpark.co.uk. www.venturecaravanpark.co.uk. Owner: Mahdeen Leisure Ltd. 1m from seafront, off A589, 6m from J34, M6. Laundrette. Play area. Public phone. Off-licence. Specially adapted holiday caravans for disabled people. Indoor heated swimming pool. Bar with entertainment and bar meals eat in or take away. Cinema, shopping centre 1.25m; golf course, leisure centre 1.5m. Open February 22-January 6. ✩✩✩✩ **BH&HPA. NCC. 56T. MC. 220S. 20H.** ✿ 🐕 🅿 ⚅ 🛁

(0.25m). Westgate Caravan Park, Westgate, Morecambe, Lancashire LA3 3DE. *01524 411448.* Owner: Mr Iain Makinson. Off A589. Open March 1-October 31. ✩✩✩ **BH&HPA. 16T. 16MC. 180S. 6H.** 🐕 🅿 ⚅ 🛁

Nelson

(1.5m). Pendle Valley Caravan Park, Pendlevale, Barrowford, Nelson, Lancashire BB9 6NT. *01282 614755.* Owner: The Hartley family. Open March 1-October 31. **BH&HPA. 206S.** 🐕

High Compley Park

Relax in 17 acres of secluded coastal park one mile from Blackpool. Within walking distance of the ancient market town of Poulton-le-Fylde with its fine restaurants, and shopping malls. Private fishing. Golf nearby. Open for 10½ months. Lodges for sale on new exclusive development, also luxury holiday homes for sale & hire with central heating.

Tel: 01253 888930
Fax: 01253 888931
www.highcompley.co.uk

Garstang Road West, Poulton-le-Fylde, (A586) Near Blackpool FY6 8AR

Ormskirk

(1.5m). Abbey Farm Caravan Park, Dark Lane, Ormskirk, Lancashire L40 5TX. *01695 572686.* abbeyfarm@ yahoo.com. www.abbeyfarmcaravanpark.co.uk. Owner: Joan & Alan Bridge. M6 J27 on to A2509, SP Parbold Island, left B5240 immediate right. Quiet park 1.5m on right, entrance alongside white cottage. Laundry. Gas. Playground. Library. Off-licence shop. David Bellamy Silver Conservation Award. ✩✩✩✩✩ **BH&HPA. 50T. 10MC. 44S.** ✿ 🐕 🅿 ⚅ 🛁

(3.5m). Mount Farm Caravan Site, Bescar Brow, Scarisbrick, Ormskirk, Lancashire. *01704 880249.* Owner: M Lavelle. 0.25m from junction of B5242 with A570, SP Burscough and motorway. Open March-October. **T. MC. 8S.** ✿ 🐕 🅿

(5m). Shaw Hall Caravan Park, Smithy Lane, Scarisbrick, Ormskirk, Lancashire L40 8HJ. *01704 840298.* shawhall@btconnect.com. www.shawhall.com. Owner: Barley Mow Ltd. Situated on Leeds/Liverpool canal 6m from Southport. Clubhouse with entertainment. Open March 1-January 7. **BH&PHA. NCC. 43T. 300S.** 🐕 🅿 ⚅ 🛁

Pilling

Glenfield Caravan Park, Smallwood Hey Road, Pilling, Lancashire PR3 6HE. *01253 790782.* petercottam@tiscali. co.uk. www.ukparks.co.uk/glenfield. Owner: Peter Cottam. Off A588 Blackpool to Lancaster, 3m from Knott-End-on-Sea. Close to village centre. Quiet, family-run park in a rural setting. Full facilities, including laundry room. Shops in village. Fishing, boating, golf within 4m. Open March 1-October 31. **BH&HPA. 8T. 162S.** 🐕 🅿

Poulton-le-Fylde

Breck Caravan Park, 210 Breck Road, Poulton-le-Fylde, Lancashire FY6 7JZ. *01253 890003.* Owner: Mr Ian Bentley Brooks. M55 turn off J3, follow A585 to Poulton village. Site located in village. Open March 1-October 31. **31S.** 🐕 🛁

(1m.). High Compley Caravan Park, Garstang Road West, Poulton-le-Fylde, Lancashire FY6 8AR. *01253 888930.*info@highcompley.co.uk. www.highcompley.co.uk. Owner: High Compley Caravan Park Ltd. From Exit 3 on M55 towards Fleetwood on A585. Turn left on to A586 towards Blackpool. 6.5m from the M55. Fishing on park. Golf, swimming pool, PO, doctor nearby. Shop. Open March 1-January 4 for owner-occupiers; open March 1-November 11 for hire caravans. **BH&HPA. 50T. MC. 175S. 8H.** 🐕 🅿 ⚅ 🛁

(7m). Maaruig Caravan Park, 71 Pilling Lane, Preesall, Poulton-le-Fylde, Lancashire FY6 0HB. *01253 810404.* Owner: Mr P R & Mrs A Woods. Take M6 to M55. Leave M55 at junction with A585 to Fleetwood. Leave A585 at traffic lights for Lancaster and Knott End on A588. Leave A5377 for Knott End on B377 to Pilling Lane (2m). Grassy, level site. Close to beach. Blackpool, Preston, Lancaster, Lake District. Open March 1-January 4. **31T.** 🐕 🅿

(8m). Robins Bank, Danson's Farm, Staynall, Poulton-le-Fylde, Lancashire FY6 9DT. *01253 700042.* Owner: Mr D. Sherdley. Located off the A588. Open March 1-October 31. **30S.** 🐕

(4m). The Heads Holiday Home Park, The Heads, Stalmine, Poulton-le-Fylde, Lancashire FY6 0JG. *01253 812447.* Owner: A Bashall (Stalmine). Off A588. Open March 1-October 31. **BH&HPA. 69S.** 🐕

NORTH-WEST ENGLAND

(3m). **Wardleys Holiday Home Park, Wardleys Lane, Hambleton, Poulton-le-Fylde, Lancashire**. *01253 702230*. Owner: S J & P A Salt. Park lies on bank of river Wyre at Wardley's Creek in Hambleton which can be reached on the A5888 between Poulton-le-Fylde and Lancaster. Full services all pitches. Open March 1-January 4. **BH&HPA. 25S. ⊬**

Preesall

Rosegrove Caravan Park, 81 Pilling Lane, Preesall, Lancashire FY6 0HB. *01253 810866*. Owner: Thompson & Oaks Ltd. Leave M55 at Fleetwood turn off, turn right at toll bridge, follow road for about 7m turn, left then first right, site on left 0.25m adjacent to beach. Laundry facilities, iron. Showers. Hair-dryer. Adventure playground. Open March-January. **50T. MC. ⊬ ⚑ ⚓**

Preston

(15m). **Beacon Fell View Holiday Park, Higher Road, Longridge, Preston, Lancashire PR3 2TY**. *01772 785434/783233*. beaconfell@hagansleisure.co.uk. www.hagans leisure.co.uk. Owner: Hagans Leisure Group. 184 Templepatrick Road, Ballyclare, Co Antrim, N Ireland BT39 0RA. Leave the M6 J32 to Garstang A6. Follow sign to Longridge (not Beacon Fell). At Longridge, straight across roundabout then left at White Bull. Park 1m on right. Commanding views over the Ribble Valley, Park is set in 30 acres of landscaped parkland. Facilities include an indoor heated pool, a family clubhouse with live entertainment, indoor and outdoor play areas and children's club. Open March-November. ✿✿✿ **BH&HPA. NCC. 70T. MC. 397S. 38H. ⊬ ⚑ ⚓**

(9m). **Bridge House Marina & Caravan Park, Nateby, Garstang, Preston, Lancashire PR3 0JJ**. *01995 603207*. Owner: Mr T & E Dodd. Off A6. Open March 1-January 4. ✿✿✿ **BH&HPA. 50T. MC. 20H. ⊬ ⚑ ⚓**

(10m). **Claylands Caravan Park, Cabus, Garstang, Preston, Lancashire PR3 1AJ**. *01524 791242*. alan@clay lands.com. www.claylands.com. Owner: Mr F Robinson. Off the A6 0.25m S of Little Chef. 14 acres of woodland alongside the river Wyre with coarse fishing available on site, also bar and restaurant. Telephone for a free brochure. Open March 1-January 4. ✿✿✿✿ **BH&HPA. 40T. MC. 69S. ⊬ ⚑ ⚓**

Fold House Caravan Park Ltd, Head Dyke Lane, Pilling, Nr Knott End-On-Sea, Preston, Lancashire PR3 6SJ. *01253 790267*. info@foldhouse.co.uk. www.foldhouse. co.uk. Owner: W T Carter. M6, J32 (M55) , go N on A6 towards Garstang for 8m until Flag Hotel. Turn L on to Longmoor Lane, after 1m turn right at T-junction on to Kilcrash Lane. In Stakepool/Pilling village, facing the Elletson Arms hotel, turn L on to A588 Blackpool-Lancaster road. Park is 500yd round the corner on R. 10m from Lancaster. Quiet, family-owned and family-run park. Fully landscaped, bowling green, heated outdoor pools, children's play area, waterfalls, Koi carp pools. Village within 500yd. All shopping 5m. Lakes District 35mins. Open March-November. ✿✿✿✿ **BH&HPA. NCC. 313S. ⚓**

(8m). **Hurst Lea, Cartford Lane, Little Eccleston, Preston, Lancashire PR3 0YP**. *01995 670459*. Owner: Mrs V Chapman. Turn off A586 into Blackpool Old road on left and turn left into Cartford Lane. Carry on to just before Cartford Hotel on right and Hurst Lea is on left. Go into drive to back of bungalow. Fishing nearby, shops, PO, doctor all in the village. Open March 1-October 31. **BH&HPA. 30S. ⊬**

Larbreck Gardens Caravan Park, Larbreck, Great Eccleston, Preston, Lancashire PR3 0XS. *01995 670662/670341*. Owner: J & F M Kirkham. On A586. Blackpool 6.5m. Licensed club. Open March 1-October 31. **BH&HPA. 56S. ⚑**

(11m). **Leisure Lakes Caravan Park, Mere Brow, Nr Tarleton, Preston, Lancashire PR4 6JX**. *01772 813446/814502*. gab@leisurelakes.co.uk. www.visitbritain.co.uk. Owner: Leisure Lakes Ltd. On A565, Southport to Preston road. 6m Southport. Set in 90 acres with pleasant walks and open spaces for children. Full Tourist Board facilities. AA 2 pennants and RAC approved. Coarse fishing. Golf range, 9-hole golf course. Jet-skis and windsurfing. PH on site. Village shop and PO. ✿✿ **110T. MC. ✿ ⊬ ⚑ ⚓ ⚓**

Meadfoot, Cartford Lane, Little Eccleston, Preston, Lancashire PR3 0YP. *01995 670241*. Owner: Mrs M Garner. Blackpool 8m. Open March 1-October 31. **36S. ⊬**

Primrose Bank Caravan Park, Singleton Road, Weeton, Preston, Lancashire PR4 3JJ. *01253 836273*. info@primrose caravanpark.co.uk. Owners: Primrose Bank Caravan Park Ltd (contact: Michael Greaves). 1.5m S of Singleton on B5260 and 5m E of Blackpool. Leave M55 towards Fleetwood on A585 then B5260 is third on L. L at T-junction the park is 1m on L. Hard-standings, easy access. AA listed. Fishing, golf, shops, PO all nearby. Open March 1-January 14. **BH&HPA. 30T. 35S. ⊬**

Queensgate Caravan Park, Little Eccleston, Garstang, Preston, Lancashire PR3 0ZQ. *01995 670223*. david@queens gate-park.fsnet.co.uk. Owner: Dr & DM Thirtlethwaite. Grange Farm, Elswick, Preston PR4 3UA. M6 motorway M55, 3rd junction, follow Fleetwood sign to first set of traffic lights, turn right on A586 for 1m, park is on left. Blackpool 6.5m. Open March 1-January 4. **BH&HPA. 50S. ⊬**

(9m). **Rawcliffe Hall Caravan Park & Country Club, Out Rawcliffe, Wyreside, Preston, Lancashire PR3 6TQ**. *01995 670491*. Owner: The Bagot Family. Off A586. Family site in quiet, wooded location. Club. Open March 1-January 4. **BH&HPA. 233S. ⊬ ⚓**

Ribby Hall Village, Ribby Road, Wrea Green, Kirkham, Preston, Lancashire PR4 2PA. *01772 672222*. Owner: Mr Harrison. M55, J3. Follow signs to Kirkham. Site is about 2m from J3, just outside Wrea Green Village. 5m from Blackpool. Open March 1-January 16. **NCC. 300S. ⊬**

(7m). **Royal Umpire Caravan Park, Southport Road (A581), Croston, Preston, Lancashire PR5 7JB**. *01772 600257*. Owner: F Rowe & Sons. On A581 midway between A59 and A49. Many tourist attractions within an hour's drive. 10m E of Southport, 5m W of Chorley, 1m E of Croston village. ✿✿✿✿ **BH&HPA. 200T. MC. ✿ ⊬ ⚑ ⚓ ⚓**

(10m). **Smithy Caravan Park, Cabus Nook Lane, Winmarleigh, Garstang, Preston, Lancashire PR3 1AA**. *01995 606200*. Owner: Mr J Wilding. M6, J32, join A6 north, after 8m turn right at traffic lights on to B5272 Cockerham Road. After 1.5m turn right at Smith Garage, park on right over canal bridge. Showers. Laundrette. On the Preston-Lancaster Canal. Peaceful and relaxing park. Suitable base for the lakes, Morecambe and Blackpool. Open March 1-January for tourers. **BH&HPA. 20T. 5MC. 87S. ⊬ ⚑**

(7m.). **Sunnyside Caravan Park, Myerscough Hall Drive, Bilsborrow, Preston, Lancashire PR3 0RE**. *01995 640590*. Owner: Mr & Mrs W B Armistead. On A6 Preston to Lancaster. Garstang 4m. Quiet site catering for mature clientele. Open March 1-January 4. **BH&HPA. 68S.**

(12m). The Garden Site, Rawcliffe Hall, Out Rawcliffe, Preston, Lancashire PR3 6TP. *01995 670277.* Owner: Mrs Kay Parkinson. Off A586 to Great Eccleston over Cartford Bridge turn left down first drive on right. Blackpool 8m. Open March 1-January 4. **37S.** ⚓

(8m). Willow Grove Caravan Park, Great Eccleston, Preston, Lancashire PR3 0ZL. *01995 670837.* Owner: Mr D Halsall. On A586. Blackpool 9m. Calor Gas. Open March 1-November 15. **BH&HPA. 8T. MC. 67S.** ⊖

Wyreside Farm Park, Allotment Lane, St Michael's-on-Wyre, Garstang, Preston, Lancashire PR3 0TZ. *01995 679797.* penny.wyresidefarm@freenet.co.uk. riverparks.co.uk. Owner: P J Fletcher. M6, J32 take A6 North Garstang. 3.5m Bilsborrow, turn left into St Michael's road. 3.5m St Michael roundabout, turn right past church, over bridge, past Grapes PH. Garage LHS. round bend withCompton House on left. Allotment Lane opposite. Fishing river (adjacent to park), ponds 500yd. Shop/PO, PH, restaurant, garage/filling station, bowls, tennis all within 0.5m. Golf pay and play 2m. Open March 1-October 31. **BH&HPA. 10T. 10MC. 16S.** ⚓ ⊖

Southport

(1m). Brooklyn Park & Country Club, Gravel Lane, Banks, Southport, Lancashire PR9 8BU. *01704 228534.* Owner: Mr G Harrison. Off A565 at Banks roundabout to Gravel Lane. Licensed club with live entertainment and bar meals most weekends. Launderette. Play area. Public phone. Well-stocked shop. Gas sales. Children allowed in park homes. Open March 1-January 7. **BH&HPA. 100T. MC. 120S. 15H.** ⊖ ⚓ ⚓ ⚓

(6m). Hurlston Hall Country Caravan Park, Southport Road, Scarisbrick, Southport, Lancashire L40 8HB. *01704 841064.* Owner: Mr J & Mrs P A Hayhurst. Open March 1-January 6 for holiday homes; open April 1-October 31 for tourers. ✩✩✩✩ **BH&HPA. 60T. 60MC. 51S.** ⊖ ⚓

(5m). Plex Moss Lane Caravan Site, Off Moor Lane, Woodvale, Southport, Lancashire PR8 3NZ. *01704 573259.* Owner: Mr W Greenwood. Headbolt Farm, Woodvale Road, Ainsdale, Southport PR8 3SY. On A565 along dual carriageway passing RAF Woodvale. At second set of traffic lights turn right into Moor Lane which becomes Plex Moss Lane, park is at the foot of the hill on the left-hand side. Open April 1-October 31. **BH&HPA. 5T. MC. 60S.** ⚓ ⊖

(5m). Riverside Leisure Centre Ltd, Southport New Road, Banks, Southport, Lancashire PR9 8DF. *01704 228886.* Owner: G & E Harrison. On A565. Set in acres of pleasant meadow. Fishing on site. Play area, disco, laundrette, showers. Calor Gas and Campingaz stockist. Evening entertainment. Indoor heated swimming pool. Open March 1-January 7. **BH&HPA. NCC. 178T. MC. 270S.** ⚓ ⊖ ⚓ ⚓

(4m). Willowbank Holiday Home & Touring Park, Coastal Road, Ainsdale, Southport, Lancashire PR8 3ST. *01704 571566.* info@willowbankcp.co.uk. www.willowbankcp.co.uk. From Liverpool take A565 Southport past Formby. RAF Woodvale on L, turn L into coastal road, SP Ainsdale Beach, park 150yd on L. 4 golf courses nearby. David Bellamy Silver Conservation Award. North West Tourist Board Silver Award. Motorhome service point, laundry. Children's play area. Cinema, swimming pool 4m. Southport resort attractions. Good public transport system. Cycle paths. Open March 1-January 10. ✩✩✩✩✩ **BH&HPA. 54T. MC. 225S.** ⚓ ⊖ ⚓

Tarleton

Woodlands Caravan Park, The Marshes Lane, Mere Brow, Tarleton, Lancashire PR4 6JS. *0845 0091493.* chrysler leisure@aol.com. www.secretgardencaravans.co.uk. Owner: Chrysler Leisure Ltd. On B5246. Between Leisure Lakes complex and Martin Mere Wildfowl Trust. 5m from Southport. Peaceful, secluded, owners-only park. Laundrette, internet cafe, putting green, sauna and exercise room. Pets welcome. No children. Close to village shops, 2 PHs and 9-hole golf course within 1m. Open March 1-January 6. **BH&HPA. 43S.** ⚓ ⚓ ⚓

MERSEYSIDE

Formby

(1m). Formby Point Caravan Park, Lifeboat Road, Formby, Merseyside L37 2EB. *01704 874367.* Owner: Mrs M Hinton. W of Formby railway station. Grassy and well-drained park. Near sea, beach and pinewoods. In conservation area. Open April-October. **BH&HPA. 20T. MC. 280S.** ⚓ ⊖

Wirral

(7m). Deeside Caravan Site, Sandymount, Broad Lane, Heswall, Wirral, Merseyside. *01513 426597.* Owner: Mrs L Matthias. Off A540. Showers. Open October 1-October 31. **T. 32S.** ⚓

Wirral Country Park Caravan Club Site, Station Road, Thurstaston, Wirral, Merseyside CH61 0HN. *01516 485228.* www.caravanclub.co.uk. Owner: The Caravan Club. East Grinstead House, East Grinstead, West Sussex RH19 1UA. See website for standard directions to site. The site has several flat grassy pitching areas separated by trees and shrubs, some overlooking the Dee estuary which is easily accessible. Toilet blocks, laundry facilities and motorhome service point. Play equipment. Golf, fishing and NCN cycle route nearby. Good area for walking. Suitable for families. Peaceful off-peak. Open March-October. ✩✩✩✩✩ **NCC. 92T. MC.** ⚓ ⊖ ⚓

Southport Caravan Club Site, The Esplanade, Southport, Lancashire PR8 1RX. *01704 565214.* www.caravanclub.co.uk. Owner: The Caravan Club. East Grinstead House, East Grinstead, West Sussex RH19 1UA. See website for standard directions to site. Caravan Club members only. Situated on the Esplanade of traditional seaside resort, close to famous sands. Dog walk, off site. Gas. Toilet blocks. Privacy cubicles. Laundry facilities. Baby washroom. Veg prep. Motorhome service point. Information room. Play area. Golf, fishing and water sports nearby. Suitable for families. Open March-January. **NCC. 99T. MC.** ⚓ ⊖ ⚓

NORTHUMBRIA

DURHAM
Barnard Castle

(2m). Camping & Caravanning Club Site - Barnard Castle, Dockenflatts Lane, Lartington, Barnard Castle, Co Durham DL12 9DG. *01833 630228/0870 2433331.* www.campingandcaravanningclub.co.uk. Owner: Camping & Caravanning Club. Greenfields House, Westwood Way, Coventry CV4 8JH. From Barnard Castle take B6277 towards Middleton, after 1m at Club sign turn L, site 500yd on L. Well placed for exploring the Pennines and city of Durham. Easy walking distance of Barnard Castle. 10-acre site. Non-members welcome. Caravans, motor caravans and tents accepted. Fishing, golf, horse riding, swimming pool and tennis nearby. Special deals for families and backpackers. Open March-October. ☆☆☆☆ **90T. 90MC.** 🐕 🖃 ♿

(8m). Cote House Caravan Park, Mickleton, Middleton-in-Teesdale, Barnard Castle, Durham DL12 0PN. *01833 640515.* Owner: Mr T P Mitcalfe. By Grassholme Reservoir, 1m out of Mickleton village up Kelton road. Fishing, sailing, shops etc within 2m. Golf 8m. Open March 1-October 31, subject to weather conditions. **10T. 10MC. 50S.** 🐕 🖃

Doe Caravan Site Park, Cotherstone, Barnard Castle, Co Durham DL12 9UQ. *01833 650302.* Owner: WK & MM Lamb. Park is situated in Dales countryside on the edge of the village of Cotherstone. River fishing available near site. Golf course 4m, garage 2m, nearest shop, including PO, 0.5m. Doctors 4m. Bar meals, restaurants etc 0.5-2m. Nature reserve on farm. Open March 1-October 31. ☆☆☆☆ **50T. 20MC.** 🐕 🖃 ♿

(0.5m). East Lendings Caravan Park, Abbey Lane, Startforth, Barnard Castle, Durham DL12 9TJ. *01833 637271.* Owner: Lakeland Leisure Estates Ltd. PO Box 22, Windermere, Cumbria LA23 1GE. Go through Barnard Castle to traffic lights on bridge. Turn left, take second left in Abbey Lane for 0.5m. Laundrette. Showers. Lounge bar. Games room. Play area. Fishing. Open March-October. **BH&HPA. 207S.** 🐕 🖃 🖥

(3m). Hetherick Caravan Park, Kinninvie, Barnard Castle, Durham DL12 8QX. *01833 631173/01388 488384.* info@hetherickcaravanpark.co.uk. www.hetherickcaravanpark.co.uk. Owner: Janet Embleton, Christopher & Ernest Holmes. Located just off B6279 from Staindrop and B6278 from Barnard Castle. Pleasant park located on a working farm in the heart of Teesdale. Conveniently situated for all local attractions. Golf course and sports centre (including swimming pool) within 2m. Open March 1-October 31. **BH&HPA. 30T. 11MC. 86S.** 🐕 🖃 ♿

(8m). Mickleton Mill Caravan Park, The Mill, Mickleton, Barnard Castle, Durham DL12 0LS. *01833 640317.* mickle tonmill@aol.com. Owner: Mr Keith & Carole Atkinson. On the B6277 Alston to Barnard Castle road. Follow road to Mickleton, turn right just past Blacksmith's Arms, at bottom of road bear to the left. On-site fishing on the river Lune is available to caravanners. Open April-October. **BH&HPA. 4T. 4MC. 75S. 1H.** 🐕 🖥

(1.5m). Pecknell Farm Caravan Site, Pecknell Farm, Lartington Road, Barnard Castle, Co Durham DL12 9DF. *01833 638357.* Owner: Mrs A Dent. On B6277. Nearest shops, golf, swimming, PO, doctors are in Barnard Castle. Many walks nearby. 1hr away from lakes. Open April-October. **15T. MC.** 🐕 🖃

(3m). West Roods Working Farm, West Roods, Boldron, Barnard Castle, County Durham DL12 9SW. *01833 690 116.* Owner: Mrs Margaret Lowson. 13.5m W Scotch corner (A1-M), 31.5m Tebay, 36.5m Penrith (M6). SP Lambhill, West Roods, Roods House on north side of A66. Some limited facilities for disabled visitors. Sandpit for children. The farm has Anglo-Saxon fields and a Roman well. From the farm on a clear day you can see the North East Sea (56m). See the outskirts of Durham and the North Yorkshire moors. Shops, chemists, dentists, doctors, in Barnard Castle. Bowes Museum and castles in the area. Fishing/golf/tennis/bowls. No caravan or motorhomes over 22ft long. Open May-mid October. **5T. MC.** 🖃 ♿

Bishop Auckland

(6m). Britton Hall, Westgate-in-Weardale, Stanhope, Bishop Auckland, Durham. *01388 517309.* Owner: Mr M G Pears. On A689 Alston to Stanhope. Open March-October. **10T. 10MC. 30S.** 🐕 🖥

(25m). Brotherlee Holiday Home Park, Westgate-in-Weardale, Bishop Auckland, Durham DL13 1SR. *01388 517276/526457.* Owners: Mr R P Shaw, Mr J S Crow and Mrs J G Crow-Robson. Low Brotherlee, Westgate-in-Weardale, Bishop Auckland, Durham DL13 1SR. Turn off A689 at Westgate beside PH. Travel E for about 1m, park is on L. Park has full mains facilties and LPG. Laundry and 3 acre playing field including golf, putting, football etc. Walking distance from river Wear. Fishing, swimming pool, near shops/PHs etc. Open March 1-October 31. **BH&HPA. 47S.** 🐕 ♿

Country Style Holiday Home Park, Hood Street, St Johns Chapel, Weardale, Bishop Auckland, Durham DL13 1QL. *01388 517333.* Owners: A T Robson and P L Robson. Fairfield House, Westgate-in-Weardale, Bishop Auckland, Co Durham DL13 1LJ. On A689 Alston to Stanhope road, 7m W of Stanhope. Turn L 70yd after market place. Bottled gas sales. Full mains services. Fishing rights, park is situated in village with easy access to its shops, PH. Golf, fishing, swimming pool, also nearby cinema and gym. Open March-October. **30S.** 🐕 ♿ ∅

(14m). Fineburn Caravan Park, Low Bollihope, Frosterley, Bishop Auckland, Durham DL13 2SY. *01388 526658.* Owners: Barry & Angela Wallace. From Wolsingham travelling towards Stanhope go through Frosterley and take L turn to Middleton-in-Teesdale and Hill End. Once through Hill End go over cattle grid. Park is first on L. Also 8 chalets for hire. Fishing and golf courses nearby, set in Area of Outstanding Natural Beauty. Tranquil environment. Swimming pool and leisure complexes nearby. Open April-October; open 11 months for winterised homes. **BH&HPA. 26S.** 🐕

(6m). Greenacres Caravan Park, Hamsterley, Bishop Auckland, Durham DL13 3PY. *01388 488384.* Owner: Raymond & Janet Embleton. 2m from A68 to the centre of Hamsterley, then turn right and travel 200yd along Bedburn Road. Park situated beside road on the right. Tranquil location with views. 200yd from pretty village of Hamsterley with shop/PO and PH. Suitable base for walking and cycling. Hamsterley Forest nearby. Open March-October. **T. 37S.** 🐕

(0.25m). Greenfoot Holiday Home Park, Greenfoot, Stanhope, Bishop Auckland, Durham DL13 2JT. *01388 517473.* info@greenfoot.co.uk. www.greenfoot.co.uk. Owner: Mrs J M Crow, Mr J S Crow & Mrs J G Crown-Robson. c/o Lea View, Brotherlee, Westgate in Weardale, Nr BP Auckland, Durham DL13 1SR. On A689. W of Stanhope on Stanhope to Alston road, 500yd out of village turn R. Bottled gas delivered, full mains services, payphone, laundry, games room, snooker room, large woodland play area. Scenic walks. Golf, fishing, open air swimming pool, nearby shops/PHs etc. Open March-October 31. **BH&HPA. 90S.** ♿

Please visit the Caravan Club website: www.caravanclub.co.uk

Caravan Sites 2006 **77**

(5m). Linburn Caravan Park, Linburn Beck, Hamsterley, Bishop Auckland, Durham DL13 3QL. *01388 488488.* Owner: Terry Kirby. 0.5m from Hamsterley village. Leave A68 at northern end of Toft Hill signposted Hamsterley. Straight on for 2m, turn R at T-junction, park on R after 0.5m. Quiet caravan park. 0.5m from village (shop, PO, pub with restaurant). 1.5m from Hamsterley Forest, pony trekking, mountain biking, walking. Open Easter-end October. **T. 48S. ⚲ 🖭**

(1m). Swinhopeburn Caravan Site, Westgate, Bishop Auckland, Durham. *01388 517326.* Owner: Mr D De Muschamp. Muschamp House, Brotherlee, Westgate-in-Weardale, Bishop Auckland, Durham DL13 1SR. On A689 to Alston, turn left at Hare and Hounds in Westgate where road joins from right, site up bridle path about 300yd. Open March 1-October 31. **36S. ⚲**

The Forge Holiday Home Park, East End, Wolsingham-in-Weardale, Bishop Auckland, Durham DL13 3JU. *01388 517333.* Owners: A T Robson and J A Robson. Fairfield House, Westgate-in-Weardale, Bishop Auckland, Co Durham DL13 1LJ. Heading W on A689 Alston to Wolsingham road. Turn L 50yd before Black Bull PH. Travel 50yd down lane between houses. Full mains services, bottled gas sales, fishing rights on river Wear. Scenic walks located in village with easy access to its shops, PO, PH and restaurant and cafe. Golf, fishing, swimming pool, also nearby 4x4 off-road centre, horse riding. **29S. ⚲ ⚅ ⚏**

(22m). Weardale Holiday Home Park, Westgate-in-Weardale, Bishop Auckland, Durham DL13 1LJ. *01388 517333/526457.* Owner: Mr J S Crow & Mrs J G Crow-Robson. On A689 Alston to Stanhope road, situated in centre of village on R after Coop. Bottled gas sales. Fishing rights, scenic walks, situated near river Wear in Westgate Village with easy access to phone box, shop/PO and PH. Golf, fishing, swimming pool. Open March-October. **BHHPA. 43S. ⚲ ⚅**

(4m). Witton Castle, Witton-le-Wear, Bishop Auckland, Durham DL14 0DE. *01388 488230.* www.wittoncastle.com. Owner: The Lambton Estates. Off A68 and between Toft Hill and Witton-le-Wear. Caravan storage. Bars. Takeaway meals. Fly fishing. Swimming pool. Padling pool, children's playground, games rooms. Laundrette. Bar meals. Special facilities for rallies. Periodic special events. Shopping 2m. Golf 4m. Cinema 10m. Open March 1-January10. **BH&HPA. 180T. MC. 313S. ⚲ 🖭 ⚅ ⚏**

Blackhall Rocks

(4m). Dene Mouth Caravan Park, Coast Road, Blackhall Rocks, Durham TS27 4BL. *01915 860963.* Owner: Mr N P Watson. On A1086. Swimming pool. Bar. Food. Wildlife pond. Open April 1-October 31 for holiday vans and tourers. **BH&HPA. 20T. 10MC. 90S. 4H. ⚲ 🖭**

Consett

(3m). Allensford Caravan & Country Park, Castleside Consett, Durham DH8 9BA. *01207 505572.* info@snootyfox resorts.co.uk. www.snootyfoxresorts.co.uk. Owner: Snooty Fox Resorts Ltd. Tivoli House, Boulevard, Weston-super-Mare, BS23 1PD. The park is easily found from the A1 motorway by taking the A68 heading towards Castleside. Keep on the A68 for Allensford and the park can be found alongside the river Derwent. Large children's adventure park, picnic areas and open recreation areas. Fishing and woodland walks from park. Horse riding (2m), Golf (4m). Open March 1-October 31. **BH&HPA. 30T. MC. 55S. ⚲ 🖭 ⚏**

(3m). Manor Park, Broadmeadows, Castleside, Consett, Durham DH8 9HD. *01207 501000.* Owner: Manor Park Ltd. 2.5m S of Castleside (A68). Quiet, family-run and family-owned country park centrally situated for touring Durham and Northumberland. Supermarkets within 5m radius. Golf range and fishing 2.5m. Open May 1-September 30. ☆☆☆ **BH&HPA. 25T. 5MC. 10S. ⚲ 🖭 ⚅**

(6m). Struthers Farm, Edmundbyers, Consett, Durham DH8 9NL. *01207 255236.* Owner: Mrs J Anderson. On B6278 on the edge of Edmundbyers village near YHA. Near Derwent Reservoir and amid the northern Pennines Area of Outstanding Natural Beauty. Fishing, sailing and golf at Staley Hall. Open April 1-October 31. **5T. 5MC. 15S. ⚲ ⚏**

Darlington

(4m). Newbus Grange Caravan Park, Neasham, Darlington, Durham DL2 1PE. *01325 720973.* Owner: Mr Billy Maguire. Below Darlington, midway between Hurworth and Neasham. 10 mins drive to A1. Quiet, country park.Heated open-air pool June to September. River fishing. Riverside walk, nearby golf course. Village shop 1.5m. Retail park, cinema etc 5m and 15m. Open March 1-January 3. **BH&HPA. 6T. 2MC. 140S. ⚲ 🖭**

(10m). Winston Caravan Park, The Old Forge, Winston, Darlington, Durham DL2 3RH. *01325 730228.* m.willetts@ ic24.net. www.touristnetuk.com/ne/winston. Owner: Mrs M J Willetts. The Old Forge, Winston, Darlington, Durham DL2 3RH. On A67,10m W of Darlington, turn L into Winston Village follow road for 400yd then turn R into site. 5.5m from Barnard Castle. Disabled person's holiday home for hire. Golf course 5.5m. Shops and doctor 2m. PO 200yd. PH 400yd. Open March 1-October 31. ☆☆☆ **10T. 10MC. 11S. 4H. ⚲ 🖭 ⚅**

Durham

(1m). Arbour House Caravan Park, Arbour House Farm, Crossgate Moor, Durham, Durham DH1 4TQ. *01913 842418.* enquiries@arbourhouse.co.uk. www.arbourhouse.co.uk. Owner: John & Rena Hunter. On A167, close to Durham city. Quiet, family farm. Showers, toilets and clothes washing facilities. Cycle tracks, golf courses, PH/restaurant nearby. Walking distance of Durham City. **5T. 5MC. 1S. ⚙ ⚲ 🖭**

(4.5m). Finchale Abbey Farm, Finchale, Durham, Durham DH1 5SH. *01913 866528.* godricawatson@hotmail.com. www.finchaleabbey.co.uk. Owner: Mr E Welsh & Mrs A Watson. Off A1 M at Chester-Le-Street, on A167 (S) follow signs for Arnison Centre. Then signs for Finchale Priory. Countryside setting. Cafe on site, bar at golf range. 24hr security river walks. Hard-standings. Play area for children on holiday park. Shops 1.5m, fishing, golf course 15mins walk. ☆☆☆ **BH&HPA. NCC. 40T. 40MC. 90S. ⚙ ⚲ 🖭 ⚅ ⚏**

(2.5m). Grange Caravan Club Site, Meadow Lane, Durham, Durham DH1 1TL. *01913 844778.* www.cara vanclub.co.uk. Owner: The Caravan Club. East Grinstead House, East Grinstead, West Sussex RH19 1UA. See website for standard directions to site. Open and level site within easy reach of the historic city of Durham. Advance bookings essential. Non-members and tent campers welcome. Hard-standings. Dog walk. Toilet blocks with privacy cubicles and laundry facilities. Fishing and golf nearby. Suitable for families. ☆☆☆☆ **NCC. 75T. MC. ⚙ ⚲ 🖭**

Edmundbyers

Village Green Caravan Park, The Village Green, Edmundbyers, Durham DH8 9NN. *01434 604720.* Owner: Mr C D Knott. Turn off A68, 2m to Edmundbyers Village. Turn R at village green. 5m from Consett. A landscaped, traditional country park set in many acres of woodland and gardens with views of Derwent. Designated Area of Outstanding Natural Beauty. Durham 19m. Golf 3m. Cinema, shopping centre 5m. Grass tennis court cover on park. Pool and table tennis, snooker on park. Football pitch, large adventure play area. Leisure centre with ballroom on site. Open March 1-October 31. **120S.** 🛏 🗟

Frosterley
Eilands Caravan Park, Landieu, Frosterley, Durham. *01388 527230*. Owner: Lakeland Leisure Estates Ltd. Showers. Fishing. Open March 1-October 31. **10T. MC. 80S.** 🛏 🗟 🗟

Middlestone-in-Teesdale
Daleview Caravan Park, Station Bank, Middlestone-in-Teesdale, Durham. *01833 640233*. daleview@caravanpark. onyxnet.co.uk. Owner: Mr & Mrs R E Dunn. Club. Licensed bar with meals for residents and visitors. Open March 1-October 31. **24T. 24MC. 64S.** 🛏 🗟 🗟

Stanley
(1m). Bobby Shafto Caravan Park, Beamish, Stanley, Durham DH9 0RY. *01913 701776*. andrewpeel@harlepeel.freeserve.co.uk. www.ukparks.co.uk/bobbyshafto. Owner: Mr J H Peel. Harle Peel Caravans, Hudson Street, South Shields NE34 0HD. Take A693 for 5m from Chester-le-Street to Beamish. Licensed club. Children's play area. Open March 1-October 31. ✩✩✩ **BH&HPA. 75T. MC. 53S. 3**🛏 🗟 🗟 🗟

Stockton-on-Tees

(1.25m). White Water Park Caravan Club Site, Tees Barrage, Stockton-on-Tees, Durham TS18 2QW, *01642 634880*. www.caravanclub.co.uk. Owner: The Caravan Club. East Grinstead House, East Grinstead, West Sussex RH19 1UA. See website for standard directions to site. Landscaped site adjacent to the largest white water canoeing and rafting course built to international standards in Britain. Toilet blocks, baby and toddler washroom and laundry facilities. Motorhome service point. TV, games and information rooms and play equipment. Fishing, golf and NCN cycle route nearby. Good area for walking. Suitable for families. Non-members and tent campers welcome. ✩✩✩✩✩ **NCC. 115T. MC. ✿** 🛏 🗟 🗟

Tow Law
(2m). Viewly Hill Farm, Viewly Hill, Tow Law, Durham. *01388 730308*. Owner: Mrs Hodgson. Turn off opposite Brown Horse Inn on to B6296, SP Wolsingham, site 0.25m on right. Open April-September. **5T. 3MC.** 🛏

Weardale
Heather View Caravan Park, Stanhope, Weardale, Durham DL13 2PS. *01388 528728*. Owner: Park Leisure 2000. 26-28 Falscrave Road, Scarborough. Shop, set by the river Wear 5 mins walk from picturesque Stanhope, fishing and views. Open March 1-October 31. **BH&HPA. 250S.** 🛏 🗟 🗟

HARTLEPOOL

Hartlepool
Crimdon Dene Holiday Park, Blackhall Rocks, Hartlepool, TS27 4BN. *0871 664 9737*. crimdon.dene@park-resorts.com. www.park-resorts.com. Owner: Park Resorts Ltd. 3rd Floor, Swan Court, Waterhouse Street, Hemel Hempstead, Herts, HP1 1FN. From A19, take B1281 turn SP to Blackhall and drive

through Castle Eden, turn L after about 0.5m SP Blackhall. After 3m, turn R at T junction on to A1086, towards Crimdon. After 1m park is SP. Amusements, free children's club, laundrette, restaurant, family bar. Open April-October. **BH&HPA . NCC. 540S. 2H.** 🛏 🗟 🗟

(3m). Sea View Park, Easington Road, Hartlepool TS24 9RF. *01429 862111*. bev@ashvalelll.fsnet.co.uk. Owner: Hills Brothers Park Homes. On A1086 to Blackhall. Quiet, landscaped park with sea views. Expansive sandy beach 0.75m. Playground. Showers. Shaver and hair-dryer points. Chemical toilet emptying point. Laundrette. Telephone. Calor Gas stockist. Children and pets allowed. ✩✩ **BH&HPA. CaSSOA. 25T. 5MC. 30S. 20H.** 🛏 🗟 🗟

(4m). Wynneholme, Saw Mills Avenue, Blackhall Rocks, Hartlepool TS27 4BL. *0191 5863666*. Owner: Mr G Chapman. On A1086. From Hartlepool, site on main coastal road. entrance gates between phone kiosk and bus shelter at Crimdon Dene. Open April 1-October 31. **1T. 15S.** 🛏 🗟

MIDDLESBROUGH

Middlesbrough
(3m). Middlesbrough Caravan Park, Prissick Sports Centre, Marton Road, Middlesbrough, Middlesbrough TS4 3SA. *01642 300202*. Owner: Middlesbrough Borough Council. Leisure Services, PO Box 69, Vancouver House. On A172. Amenities on site or within 1m, bowls, tennis, 18-hole golf course and driving range. Miniature golf. Leisure farm. Captain Cook birthplace museum. Near beautiful Stewart Park. **20T. MC. ✿** 🗟

(3m). Prissick Sports Centre, Marton Road, Marton, Middlesbrough, Middlesbrough TS4 3SA. *01642 300202*. Owner: Middlesbrough Borough Council. From N and S, A19, A174, A172. Lakes, pets corner and mature parkland 10mins walk. On site tennis. Pitch and putt, croquet green. Captain Cook birthplace museum and conservatory over road in Stewart Park. Mini soccer/cricket. Skate park due to open autumn 2005. Open April-September. ✩✩ **20T. MC.** 🛏 🗟 🗟

NORTHUMBERLAND

Alnwick
(0.5m). Alnwick Rugby Club, Greensfield, Alnwick, Northumberland NE66 1PP. *01665 540109/01665 602342*. Owner: ARFC. On outskirts of Alnwick (S) within sight of A1, from A1 S Alnwick SP take slip road, left at bottom then 2nd left. Tourers only use of club rooms when open. For bookings write to Mr D R Bell, 4 Bondgate Without, Alnwick NE66 1PP. Golf, shops, PO within 0.6m. Open May 1-August 31. ✩ **T. MC.** 🛏 🗟

(1m). Camping & Caravanning Club Site - Dunstan Hill, Dunstan Hill, Dunstan, Alnwick, Northumberland NE66 3TQ. *01665 576310/0870 243 3331*. www.camping andcaravanningclub.co.uk. Owner: Camping & Caravanning Club. Greenfields House, Westwood Way, Coventry CV4 8JH. From A1 take B1340, SP Seahouses. R at T-junction at Christon Bank. 2nd R SP Embleton, 3rd L on to B1339 coastal route, site 2m on L. Set in 14 acres in shadow of Dunstan Borough Castle. 1m from coast with footpath to beach. Non-members welcome and may join at the site. All units accepted. Kielder Water, Europe's largest man-made lake, is nearby. Special deals available for families and backpackers. Open March-October. ✩✩✩✩ **150T. 150MC.** 🛏 🗟 🗟

(10m). New Park Caravan Site, Amble, Alnwick, Northumberland. 01665 710530. Owner: Alnwick District Council. On A1068 between Ashington and Alnwick. PH. Fish and chip shop. Open February-November. **40T. MC. 205S. ♒ ⊕ ⅃**

(9m). Newton Hall Caravan Park, Newton Hall, Newton by the Sea, Alnwick, Northumberland NE66 3DZ. 01665 576 239. patterson@newtonholidays.co.uk. www.newtonholidays. co.uk. Close to Sandy Bay (0.75m approx). 1m from local shops, 9m Alnwick Castle and Bamurgh Castle. Open March 1-November 30. ☆☆☆☆ **BH&HPA. 16T. 16MC. 3S. ♒ ⊕**

> **River Breamish Caravan Club Site, Powburn, Alnwick, Northumberland NE66 4HY.** 01665 578320. www.caravanclub.co.uk. Owner: The Caravan Club. East Grinsted House, East Grinstead, West Sussex RH19 1UA. See website for standard directions to site. Set amid the Cheviot Hills, with walking and cycling in the immediate area. Toilet blocks with privacy cubicles and laundry facilities. Baby and dog walk on site. Non-members and tent campers welcome. Open March-October. **NCC. 86T. MC. ♒ ⊕ ⅃**

(7m). Silver Carrs Caravan Park, Hauxley, Amble, Morpeth, Alnwick, Northumberland NE65 0UD. 01665 713189. www.silvercarrscaravanpark.co.uk. Owner: C J & R Phillips. 25m N of Newcastle, 1m S of Amble, 2m N of Drunidge Bay. Adjacent to beach and nature reserve. Playground and clubhouse on site. Open January 2-November 30. **BH&HPA. NCC. 165S. ♒ ⅃**

Alwinton

(0.25m). Clennell Hall Caravan Park, Clennell Hall, Alwinton, Northumberland NE65 7BG. 01669 650341. Owner: Mr & Mrs J C Pulman. Via Rothbury, B6341 after 4m turn right, SP Alwinton. Over 2nd bridge turn right signed Clennell Hall. Quiet, family-run site at the foot of the Cheviot Hills. AA 3 pennants. Open March-January. **BH&HPA. 50T. MC. 14S. ♒ ⊕ ⅃**

Ashington

Sandy Bay Holiday Park, North Seaton, Ashington, Northumberland NE63 9YD. 0871 664 9764. sandy.bay@park-resorts.com. www.park-resorts.com. Owner: Park Resorts Ltd. 3rd floor, Swan Court, Waterhouse Street, Hemel Hempstead, Herts HP1 1FN. From A1 at Seaton Burn, go on A19, at round-about go on to A189 to Ashington, head N. At 1st roundabout on A189 turn R on to B1334 towards Newbiggin by Sea. Park is on right. Indoor pool, water resorts programme, adventure play-ground, sports court, shop, laundrette, amusements, takeway, children's clubs, family evening entertainment. Alnwick Castle. Open April-October. ☆☆ **BH&HPA. NCC. 474S. 45H. ♒**

Bamburgh

(2m). Bradford Kalms Caravan Park, Bamburgh, Northumberland NE70 7JT. 01668 213432/213595. lwrob@ tiscali.co.uk. www.bradford-leisure.co.uk. Owner: L W Robson. Turn off A1 on to B1341. After crossing railway line, turn R at second R, follow signs, distance from A1 about 3m. Playground. Sunbed, TV room. Laundry, toilets and showers. Open March 16-November 15. ☆☆ **80T. MC. 270S. ♒ ⊕ ⅃**

(1m). Glororum Caravan Park, Glororum, Bamburgh, Northumberland NE69 7AW. 01668 214457. info@glororum-caravanpark.co.uk. www.glororum-caravanpark.co.uk. Owner: E A Dryden and Sons. 1m from Bamburgh on Adderston (B1341) or from A1 take B1341 at Adderstone garage for 4m. Peaceful surroundings within easy reach of Holy Island, Farne Islands, Cheviots and many historic castles. Nearby facilities for horse riding, swimming, golf, tennis and boat trips. Open April 1-October 31. ☆☆☆ **NCC. 80T. 15MC. 150S. ♒ ⊕ ⅃**

(3m). Waren Caravan & Camping Park, Waren Mill, Bamburgh, Northumberland NE70 7EE. 01668 214366. waren@meadowhead.co.uk. www.meadowhead.co.uk. Owner: Meadowhead Ltd. Charterhall, Duns, Berwickshire TD11 3RE. Follow B1342 from A1 to Waren Mill towards Bamburgh. By Budle Bay turn R and follow signs to park. Restaurant with chil-dren's licence. Shop, games room, laundry. Children's play area. Internet access on park. Heated outdoor splash pool (May-September). Golf 2m, cinema 17m. David Bellamy Gold Conservation Award. Open March-January. ☆☆☆☆ **BH&HPA. 180T. 180MC. 300S. 27H. ♒ ⊕ ⅃**

Beadnell

(0.5m). Beadnell Links, Beadnell Harbour, Beadnell, Northumberland NE67 5BN. 01665 720526. b.links@ talk21.com. www.caravanningnorthumberland.com. Owner: Beadnell Links Ltd. Thackwood Nook, Raughton Head, Carlisle, Cumbria CA5 7DT. On B1340. Quiet, family site. Calor Gas. Laundry facilities. Beach 100yd. Open April 1-October 31. ☆☆☆☆ **BH&HPA. 17T. 17MC. 150S. ♒ ⊕**

Swinhoe Links, Beadnell Bay, Beadnell, Northumberland NE67 5BW. 01665 720589. Off A1 for 4m, on beach next to Beadnell village, NE of Alnwick. Open April 1-November 1. **BH&HPA25T. MC. 141S. 3H. ♒ ⊕**

Bellingham

(0.5m). Brown Rigg Caravan & Camping Park, Bellingham, Northumberland NE48 2JY. 01434 220175. enquiries@ northumberlandcaravanparks.comwww.northum berlandcara vanparks.com. Owners: Mr & Mrs Ross. Shops, banks, doctor in Bellingham. Golf course 5mins drive. Fishing permits available on site. 11m to Hadrian's Wall. 9m to Kielder Water. Open: Easter-October 31. ☆☆☆☆ **BH&HPA. 80T. ♒ ⊕ ⅃**

Berwick-upon-Tweed

Berwick Holiday Centre, Magdalene Fields, Berwick-upon-Tweed, Northumberland TD15 1NE. 01289 330294. oewebmaster@bourne-leisure.co.uk. www.berwickholiday centre.com. Owner: Bourne Leisure Ltd. One Park Lane, Hemel Hempstead, Herts HP2 4YL. Park SP on A1 from north and south and you will find signs directing you to Berwick Holiday Centre in the town. Heated indoor and out-door pools, outdoor bowling, amusements, children's clubs. 50-seater restaurant. Laundrette. Aqua bar. Live entertain-ment daily. Supermarket complex. Outdoor multisports court/indoor soft play area. 2 sandy beaches with access. Rose Award. Open March-November. ☆☆☆☆ **BH&HPA. NCC. 782S. 300H. ♒ ⊕ ⅃ ⌂**

(1m). Elmbank Seaview Caravan Park, Spittal, Berwick-upon-Tweed, Northumberland. 01289 306629. Owner: Seaview Caravan Park (Spittal) Ltd. The Old Brickworks, Stobswood, Morpeth, Northumberland NE16 5PZ. Off A1. Touring section in planning stage. Open March 1-October 31. **BH&HPA. 360S. ♒**

(7m). Haggerston Castle Holiday Park, Beal, Berwick-upon-Tweed, Northumberland TD15 2PA. 01289 381414. oeweb master@bourne-leisure.co.uk. www.haggerstoncastleholiday park.com. Owner: Bourne Leisure Ltd. One Park Lane, Hemel Hempstead, Herts HP2 4YL. Park SP from A1. Heated indoor and outdoor swimming pools. Club. Bars. Entertainment. Horse rid-ing. Boating lake. Chinese restaurant. Burger King. Tennis courts. 9-hole golf course. Laundrette. Mini market. Bike hire. Crazy golf. Rose award. David Bellamy Gold Conservation Award. Golf

courses nearby. Beach 5m. Open March-November. ☆☆☆☆☆
BH&HPA. NCC. 159T. MC. 968S. 500H. ⚡🚻♿🅿🛒

(3m). Marshall Meadows Farm, Berwick-upon-Tweed, Northumberland TD15 1UT. *01289 307375.* Owner: Mr & Mrs J Fairbairn. Off A1. Amenities available in Berwick-upon-Tweed, 2m. Open Easter-October. ☆☆☆ **BH&HPA. 90S.** 🚻♿

(1.5m). Ord House Country Park, East Ord, Berwick-upon-Tweed, Northumberland TD15 2NS. *01289 305288.* enquiries@ordhouse.co.uk. www.ordhouse.co.uk. Owner: W Maguire. Off Berwick bypass (A1) at East Ord. Licensed club. AA 5 pennants. Award winner Toilet and Amenity Building & Disabled Suite. David Bellamy Gold Conservation Award. Members of the Best of British sites' groups. Licensed club within the 18th-century manor house. Mini golf and children's play area. Golf and sports centre within 1.5m. ☆☆☆☆☆ **BH&HPA. 75T. 25MC. 244S. 8**🚻♿🚻♿🛒

(0.5m). Seaview Caravan Club Site, Billendean Road, Spittal, Berwick-upon-Tweed, Northumberland TD15 1QU. *01289 305198.* www.caravanclub.co.uk. Owner: The Caravan Club. East Grinstead House, East Grinstead, West Sussex RH19 1UA. See website for standard directions to site. Views of Tweed and old town. Good site for children with safe bathing and play facilities at Spittal beach. Tent campers and non-members welcome. Hard-standings available. Advance booking advised bank holidays, July and August. Toilet blocks. Privacy cubicles. Laundry facilities. Baby/toddler washroom. Veg prep. Motorhome service point. Golf, fishing, cycling and watersports nearby. Open March-October. ☆☆☆☆ **NCC. 100T. MC.** 🚻♿♿

Chathill

Camping & Caravanning Club Site - Beadnell Bay, Beadnell, Chathill, Northumberland NE67 5BX. *01665 720586/0870 2433331.* www.campingandcaravanningclub.co.uk. Owner: Camping & Caravanning Club. Greenfields House, Westwood Way, Coventry CV4 8JH. Site is on L after Beadnell Village, just beyond left-hand bend. 10m from Alnwick. Follow Seahouses SP. 6-acre site with 150 pitches with full facilities next to the beach. Suitable for exploring Northumberland coastline and within easy reach of A1. No towed caravans permitted. Non-members accepted. Motorhomes and tents welcome. Suitable for walkers and cyclists. Special deals available for families and backpackers. Open April-October. ☆☆☆ **150MC.** 🚻

Haltwhistle

(1.5m). Camping & Caravanning Club Site - Haltwhistle, Burnfoot Park Village , Haltwhistle, Northumberland NE49 0JP. *01434 320106/0870 243 3331.* www.campingandcaravanningclub.co.uk. Owner: Camping & Caravanning Club. Greenfields House, Westwood Way, Coventry CV4 8JH. From A69, turn S at sign Alston, Coanwood and Halton Lea Gate. Follow site signs. Site is in the National Trust Bellister Castle Estate on south bank of South Tyne river and 4m from Hadrian's Wall. Close to the Pennine Way on the banks of river South Tyne. All units accepted. Non-members welcome. Fishing available on site. Special deals available for families and backpackers. Open March-October. ☆☆☆☆ **50T. 50MC.** 🚻♿

(3m). Hadrian's Wall Camping and Caravan Site, Melkridge Tilery, Haltwhistle, Northumberland NE49 9PG. *01434 320495.* info@romanwallcamping.co.uk. www.romanwallcamping.co.uk. 300yd S of B6318, 1m W of Once Brewed. 2m due N of Melkridge (A69). 0.5m from Hadrian's Wall world heritage site. ☆☆☆ **30T. MC.** ♿🚻♿🅿♿

(1m). Seldom Seen Caravan Park, Seldom Seen, Haltwhistle, Northumberland NE49 0NE. *01434 320571.* Owner: Mr W & Mrs J E Dale. Off A69. SP Haltwhistle. Quiet, riverside park. David Bellamy Gold Conservation Award. Birdwatching, walks. 2m Hadrian's Wall World Heritage site. Near Northumberland National Park, High Pennines. Golf 5m. Open March-January. **BH&HPA. 20T. MC. 50S.** 🚻♿

(5m). Yont the Cleugh Caravan Park, Coanwood, Haltwhistle, Northumberland NE49 0QN. *01434 320274.* yontthecleugh@yahoo.co.uk. www.yontthecleugh.co.uk. Owner: Ian & Desley Whitaker. SP 4.5m off A69 and 3.5m off A689. Quiet park in unspoilt location. Near Roman wall sites. Bar. Laundry. Play area. Open March 1-January 31. **BH&HPA. 20T. 12MC. 60S.** 🚻♿

Hexham

(10m). Barrasford Park, 1 Front Drive, Hexham, Northumberland NE48 4BE. *01434 681210.* Owner: Mr T & M Smith. 8m north of Corbridge off A68. 60 acres of woodland. Laundry. Licensed clubhouse. Salmon fishing within 2m. Open April 1-October 31. ☆☆ **21T. MC. 120S.** 🚻♿🛒

(1.5m). Causey Hill Caravan Park, Causey Hill, Hexham, Northumberland NE46 2JN. *01434 602834.* causeyhillcp@aol.com. www.causeyhill.co.uk. Owners: Mary Scott and Linda Ogle. 1.5m SW Hexham. Follow B6306 or signs for Hexham racecourse and then Causey Hill. Quiet, woodland walks, wildlife pond. Fishing, golf nearby. Many hard-standings. Views. Open March 1-October 31. ☆☆☆ **BH&HPA. NCC. 25T. 10MC. 65S.** 🚻♿🛒

(2m). Fallowfield Dene, Acomb, Hexham, Northumberland NE46 4RP. *01434 603553.* den@fallowfielddene.co.uk. www.fallowfielddene.co.uk. Owner: Mr P Straker. 2m N of Hexham via A69 bypass (N of river Tyne) for 0.5m W. Turn N on to A6079. Site is 1m beyond village of Acomb. Roman wall nearby. Manager: Dennis & Jen Burnell. Open March-October. ☆☆☆☆ **BH&HPA. 150T. MC.** 🚻♿♿

(2m). Hexham Racecourse, High Yarridge, Hexham, Northumberland NE46 3NN. *01434 606847.* hexrace@aol.com. www.hexham-racecourse.co.uk. Owner: Hexham Steeplechase Co Ltd. The Riding, Hexham, Northumberland NE46 4PF. Off A69 on B6306. On second highest racecourse in Britain, dramatic views across Northumberland. Dog walk. Shops, doctor, dentist, golf course all within 2m. Open May 1-October 1. ☆☆☆ **40T. MC.** 🚻♿

Kielder Water Caravan Club Site, Falstone, Hexham, Northumberland NE48 1AX. *01434 250278.* www.caravanclub.co.uk. Owner: The Caravan Club. East Grinstead House, East Grinstead, West Sussex RH19 1UA. See website for standard directions to site. 4m from Kielder. Fabulous site for an active holiday. Some pitches overlooking Kielder Water, largest man-made lake in Western Europe. Suitable family site with water sports, ponytrekking, horse riding, orienteering, birdwatching, cycling and crazy golf. All pitches on hard-standings but awnings can be erected. Dog walk. Non members and tent campers welcome. Toilet blocks. Laundry facilities. Motorhome service point. Open March-October. ☆☆☆☆ **80T. MC.** 🚻♿♿

(8m). Lilswood Caravan Park, Steel, Hexham, Northumberland NE47 0HX. 01434 604720. Owner: Mr C D Knott. Due south of Hexham Whitley Chapel 5m. Lilswood further 3m crossroads, past St Helen's church. Landscaped, traditional country park sited S of Hexham among rolling hills. Adventure play area, summer house recreation. Golf course 3m, Hexham town shopping centre, cinema and theatre. Open March 1-October 31. **15S.** ⛺

(6m). Poplars Riverside Caravan Park, East Lands End, Haydon Bridge, Hexham, Northumberland NE47 6BY. 01434 684427. Owner: Mrs N Pattison. Near the A69 Newcastle-upon-Tyne to Carlisle road. Secluded riverside site at Haydon Bridge. Fishing on site. Near village and convenient for Hadrian's Wall. Railway station in village. Open March 1-October 31. ✰✰✰✰ **BH&HPA. 11T. MC. 31S.** ⛺ 🚬

(7m). Springhouse Caravan Park, Slaley, Hexham, Northumberland NE47 0AW. 01434 673241. enquiries@springhousecaravanpark.co.uk. www.ukparks.co.uk/springhouse. Owner: Mr C Phillips. SP from A68 at Kiln Pit Hill. Quiet park surrounded by forest and magnificent views. Slaley golf complex nearby. David Bellamy Silver Conservation Award. Open March-October. **BH&HPA. 20T. 20MC. 79S.** ⛺ 🚬 ♿ 🎣

Morpeth

Cresswell Towers Holiday Park, Cresswell, Morpeth, Northumberland NE61 5JT. 0871 664 9734. www.park-resorts.com. Owner: Park Resorts Ltd. 3rd Floor, Swan Court, Waterhouse Street, Hemel Hempstead, Herts HP1 1FN. Follow A19, then A189 to Askington. At Ellington, stay on road and pick up signs for park. Outdoor heated pool, children's clubs, outdoor play area, multi sports court, amusements, laundrette, on site shop, takeway, cafe, clubhouse, family evening entertainment. 18 hole golf course 4m, sandy beach 200yd. Open April-October. ✰✰ **BH&HPA. NCC. 482S. 30H.** ⛺

(6m). Ellington Caravan Park, Ellington, Morpeth, Northumberland NE61 5JR. 01670 861807. Owner: Mr Adrian Fairclough. A1068 0.5m N of Ellington. Five-a-side soccer. Sand pit. Games room. New adventure play area. Licensed club incorporating family room, and adults' bar only and full-size snooker room. Open March 1-December 1. **23T. MC. 189S.** ⛺ 🚬 🎣

Nunnykirk Caravan Club Site, Nunnykirk, Morpeth, Northumberland NE61 4PZ. 01669 620762. www.cara vanclub.co.uk. Owner: The Caravan Club. East Grinstead House, East Grinstead, West Sussex RH19 1UA. See website for standard directions to site. 5.5m from Rothbury. Peaceful site, a haven for wildlife and a birdwatching. Own sanitation required. Good area for walking, dog walk nearby. Fishing within 5m. Non-members welcome. Open March-October. **NCC. 84T. MC.** ⛺ 🚬

Riverside Caravan Site, Rothbury, Morpeth, Northumberland. Owner: Alnwick District Council. Allerburn House, Alnwick, Northumberland NE66 1YY. On B6342. Open April-October. **70S.** ⛺

Newbiggin-by-Sea

(0.25m). Church Point Caravan Park, Newbiggin-by-Sea, Northumberland NE64 6BP. 01670 817443. www.gbholiday parks.co.uk. Owner: G B Holiday Parks Ltd. 6 Leylands Park, Nobs Crook, Colden Common, Winchester SO21 1TH. 2 mins walk from all village amenities. Laundrette. Telephone. Fishing and golf locally. Open March I-November 30. **BH&HPA. NCC. 25T. 5MC. 105S.** ⛺ 🚬

Otterburn

(8m). Border Forest Caravan Park, Cottonshopeburnfoot, Otterburn, Northumberland NE19 1TF. 01830 520259. border forest@btinternet.com. www.borderforestcaravanpark.co.uk. Owner: Mrs A Flanagan. Adjacent A68. 6m S of Scottish border (Carter bar). 8m N of Otterburn. Family-run park situated in beautiful Northumberland Border country. Close to Pennine Way and Kielder Forest. Showers. Timber lodges for hire. Bed and breakfast. Ensuite rooms. Restaurant nearby. Open March 1-October 31. ✰✰✰✰ **BH&HPA. 30T. MC. 18S. 1H.** ⛺ 🚬 ♿

Prudhoe

(1.4m). The High Hermitage Caravan Park, Ovingham, Prudhoe, Northumberland NE42 6HH. 01661 832250. high hermitage@onetel.com. Owner: Mr & Mrs W S Lee. Off A69. SP 'Wylam' and follow main road to apparent T-junction, SP R to Ovingham, continue on main road 1.5m towards Ovingham along riverside. Just after paved and railed-in water extraction point, turn R into concealed entrance. Can also accommodate up to 10 tents. Communal barbecue, giant draught/chess board. Shops, PO, doctor 1m. Within 1.5m: chemists, garage, playgrounds, rail station, restaurants, PHs. Fishing rights on boundary river bank. Cinema, theatre, museum, Newcastle and Hexham 12m. Metro shopping centre 10m. Golf course 4m. Open April 1-October 31. ✰✰✰ **BH&HPA. 5T. 5MC. 30S.** 🚬 ♿

Rothbury

(0.5m). Coquetdale Caravan Park, Whitton, Rothbury, Northumberland NE65 7RU. 01669 620549. enquiries@ coquetdalecaravanpark.co.uk. www.coquetdalecaravanpark. co.uk. Owner: Coquetdale Holidays Ltd. 0.5m S W of Rothbury on road to Newtown. Public telephone. Calor Gas and Campingaz sales. Playground. Shops, PHs and restaurants nearby. Families and couples only. Dogs on leads at all times. Dog walk area. AA 3 pennants. Open Easter-October 31. ✰✰✰ **BH&HPA. 40T. 40MC. 160S.** ⛺ 🚬

Seahouses

Seafield Caravan Park, Seafield Road, Seahouses, Northumberland NE68 7SP. 01665 720628. info@seafield park.co.uk. www.seafieldpark.co.uk. Owner: Mr K Britton. Travelling S leave A1 at Alnwick and follow B1340 direct to Seahouses. If travelling from N leave A1 at Belford and follow B1342 through Bamburgh to Seahouses. Situated central for Seahouses giving access to shops and all local amenities, overlooking Farne Island. Short walk to village. Shower and bath facilities. Laundry. Play park. Open February 9-January 9. ✰✰✰✰✰ **BH&HPA. 18T. MC. 400S. 37H.** ⛺ 🚬 ♿

Stocksfield

Wellhouse Caravan & Camping Park, Wellhouse Farm, Newton, Stocksfield, Northumberland NE43 7UY. 01661 842193. www.wellhousefarm.co.uk. Owners: K J Richardson & Sons. 1m from A69 on B6309 to Matfen & Stamfordham. 7m from Hexham. 1m from Hadrian's Wall trail. 2m from Corbridge fishing and golf. Quiet, family site. Open April-October. ✰✰✰ **40T. 10MC.** ⛺ 🚬 ♿ 🎣

Wooler

Highburn House Caravan and Camping Park, Wooler, Northumberland NE71 6EE. 01668 281344. relax@highburn-house.co.uk. www.highburn-house.co.uk. Owner: Mr R DTait. From A1 take A697 to Wooler, turn L to High Street at the top turn L into Burnhouse road, park is on L. Farm park with good views over Cheviot Hills. Shops, PHs, doctors, dentist etc. 0.25m. Castles, light railway, wild cattle. Scottish border all within 7m. Golf course 2m. Open March 1-December 20. ✰✰✰✰ **BH&HPA. 35T. 65MC. 43S.** ⛺ 🚬 ♿ 🎣 ✏

(0.5m). **Riverside Holiday Park, Wooler, Northumberland NE71 6QG.** *01668 281447.* Owner: lakeland Leisure Estates Ltd. PO Box 22, Windermere, Cumbria LA23 1GE. On A697 on the southern outskirts of Wooler. On edge of Northumbria National Park. Indoor pool. Free river fishing. Takeaway. Laundrette. Site shop. Family lounge bar and clubroom. Open March-January. **BH&HPA. 55T. MC. 443S. 10H.** 🛏 ⌷ ♿ 🛢 ⟁

TYNE & WEAR

Rowlands Gill

Derwent Park Caravan & Camping Park, Mr & Mrs I Jeavons, The Bungalow, Derwent Park, Rowlands Gill, Tyne & Wear NE39 1LG. *01207 543383.* Owner: Gateshead Metropolitan District Council. Dept of Leisure Services, Civic Centre, Regent St, Gateshead, Tyne & Wear NE8 1HH. At junction of A694 and B6314 in Rowlands Gill, 7m SW of Newcastle-upon-Tyne. Flat, sheltered site by river. Hot showers, laundry, playground, tennis, bowls, crazy golf and trout fishing. Near Beamish and Gateshead Metro Centre. 2m from shops, clubs, restaurants. Open March 1-October 31. ✩✩✩✩ **35T. MC. 24S.** 🛏 ⌷ ♿ 🛢

Whitley Bay

(2m). **Old Hartley Caravan Club Site, Whitley Bay, Tyne & Wear NE26 4RL.** *01912 370256.* www.caravan club.co.uk. Owner: The Caravan Club. East Grinstead House, East Grinstead, West Sussex RH19 1UA. See website for standard directions to site. Club members only. Slightly sloping site with views overlooking the sea. Beach 1m. Hard-standings. Toilet blocks. Privacy cubicles. Laundry facilities. Veg Prep. Calor Gas and Campingaz. Motorhome service point. Late night arrivals area. Open March-November. **NCC. 64T. MC.** 🛏 ⌷ ♿

Whitley Bay Holiday Park, The Links, Whitley Bay, Tyne & Wear NE26 4BR. *0871 664 9800.* whitley.bay@park-resorts.com. www.park-resorts.com. Owner: Park Resorts Ltd. 3rd floor, Swan Court, Waterhouse Street, Hemel Hempstead, Herts HP1 1FN. From S: A1 N to Washington, then A19 through the Tyne tunnel (toll payable). Take the signed coast road. Follow the A1058 to Tynemouth seafront, turn L. From N: A1 S to A19 SP to the Tyne tunnel. Take slip road to Whitley Bay, follow signs to park. Indoor pool, water resorts programme, free children's clubs, amily evening entertainment, takeaway, amusements, village shop, laundrette. Metro centre, Millennium Bridge. Open April-October. ✩✩✩ **BH&HPA. NCC. 550S. 70H.** 🛏

KENT

Ashford

(3m). **Broadhembury Camping & Caravan Park, Steeds Lane, Kingsnorth, Ashford, Kent TN26 1N.** *01233 620859.* holiday@broadhembury.co.uk. www. broadhembury.co.uk. Owner: Mr Keith & Jenny Taylor. From M20, exit 10 take A2070 to 2nd roundabout, following signs for Kingsnorth L at second crossroad in village. Channel Ports and Eurotunnel. Suitable base for walking and cycling. Good fishing and golf course with driving range only 5mins away. ✩✩✩✩✩ **BH&HPA. 65T. MC. 25S. 5H.** ⌷ 🛏 ⌷ ♿ 🛢

(4m). **Dean Court Farm, Challock Lane, Westwell, Ashford, Kent TN25 4NH.** *01233 712924.* Owner: Mrs Susan Lister. From the A20 Charing take the A252 for 3m, at Challock turn right signposted for Westwell, site is in 1m. Suitable centre for touring Kent and convenient for the Channel ports. **8T. MC.** ⌷ 🛏

Spill Land Farm Holiday Caravan Park, Benenden Road, Biddenden, Ashford, Kent TN27 8BX. *01580 291379.* www.ukparks.co.uk. Owner: Mr DS Waite & Mr AK Waite. Turn off A262 Biddenden to Tenterden road at Vineyard and Hospital sign, after 0.25m right behind white farm house. 5m from Tenterden. 1.25m from Biddenden. Park is central to the Kent and Sussex Weald with many local attractions. Well suited to over-50s age group looking for a peaceful and more relaxed atmosphere with no clubs or swimming pools. Pitch and putt 1m. Golf course, food shops 5m. Cinema, shopping centre 12m. No motor caravans. No persons under 18 years old permitted in any touring caravan or tent. Open March 1-October 31 weather permitting. **BH&HPA. 65T. 65S.** 🛏 ⌷

Biddenden

(3m). **Woodlands Park, Tenterden Road, Biddenden, Kent TN27 8BT.** *01580 291216.* woodlandsp@aol.com. www. campingsite.co.uk. Owner: Mr R Jessop. Travel along the A28 from Ashford to Tenterden. About 3m before Tenterden take the right-hand turn on to the A262. Site is about 0.5m on right-hand side. Laundrette. New toilet/shower block. Gas and accessories. Central to Kent and East. Sussex attractions. Dogs allowed if under control in touring park. Level park with bus stop at entrance. Open March-October for tourists, weather permitting. ✩✩✩✩ **BH&HPA. 200T. MC. 6S.** 🛏 ⌷ ♿ 🛢

Birchington

(1m). **Quex Caravan Park, Park Road, Birchington, Kent CT7 0BL.** *01843 841273.* info@keatfarm.co.uk. www.keatfarm.co.uk. Owner: Keat Farm Caravans Ltd. Reculver Road, Herne Bay, Kent CT6 6SR. Travelling off the A28 and B2049 follow road signs to Margate, when you reach Birchington turn right at mini roundabout and after 100yd take first turning on right and right again, following tourist board signs. Open March 7-November 7. ✩✩✩✩✩ **BH&HPA. NCC. 88T. MC. 237S.** 🛏 ⌷ 🛢

(3m). **St Nicholas Camping Site, Court Road, St Nicholas-at-Wade, Birchington, Kent CT7 0NH.** *01843 847245.* Owner: E B Broadley. From M2 follow onto A299. At the sign to St Nicholas turn left over bridge into village. Off the A28 at St Nicholas signpost. Level site within reach of five major towns. Gas sales only. Open March 1-October 31. ✩✩✩ **10T. 5MC.** 🛏 ⌷

(1.5m). **Two Chimneys Caravan Park, Shottendane Road, Birchington, Kent CT7 0HD.** *01843 841068/843157.* info@twochimneys.co.uk. www.twochimneys.co.uk. Owner: Mrs L Sullivan. From the A299, turn right into Park Lane (B2048) at Birchington Church. Left fork B2050 'RAF Manston'. first left on to B2049. Site is within 0.5m on right-hand side. Licensed bar. Take away fast food. Heated enclosed pool. Tennis court. Shop, laundry, children's play area, amusement arcade. Golf, cinema, beaches, sea, horse riding, sports centre, watersports, fishing, theme park all within 3m. Open Easter-October 31 for tourers; open March 1-January 17 for owner-occupied holiday caravans. ✩✩✩✩✩ **BH&HPA. NCC. 200T. 20MC. 200S.** 🛏 ⌷ ♿ 🛢

Canterbury

(7m). Ashfield Farm, Waddenhall, Petham, Canterbury, Kent CT4 5PX. *01227 700624.* mpatterson@ashfieldfarm. freeserve.co.uk. Owner: M C Patterson. Situated on B2068 about 6m from Canterbury. Level, well-screened site with modern facilities. 9-hole putting course on site. Kennelling available. Open April 1-October 31. **30T. MC. 1S. 1H.** ♒ ⌂ &

> **(1m). Camping & Caravanning Club Site - Canterbury, Bekesbourne Lane, Canterbury, Kent CT3 4AB.** *01227 463216/0870 2433331.* www.campingandcaravanning club.co.uk. Owner: Camping & Caravanning Club. Greenfields House, Westwood Way, Coventry, CV4 8JH. On A257, turn off opposite golf course. Canterbury Cathedral and many other places of interest within easy reach from site. Suitable location for day trips to France or as a stopover for the Continent. All units accepted. Non-members welcome. Herne Bay nearby. David Bellamy Gold Conservation Award. Special deals available for families and backpackers. ✰✰✰✰ **200T. 200MC.** ✿ ♒ ⌂ &

(10m). Dog & Duck Leisure Parks, Pluck's Gutter, Canterbury, Kent CT3 1JB. *01843 821542/01843 821264.* www.doganddduck.co.uk. Owner: Ms Elizabeth Cash & Ms Susan Fagg. On former B2046 off A253 Sarre to Ramsgate. Pretty country park. David Bellamy Silver Conservation Award. Open mid February-end November; open March 1-January 30 for log cabns. **BH&HPA. NCC. 158S.** ♒

(6m). Rose & Crown, Stelling Minnis, Canterbury, Kent CT4 6AS. *01227 709265.* Owner: Stewart Jackson & Jackie Pinkney. Open March-November. **30T. MC. 6S.** ♒ ⌂

(5m). South View, Maypole Lane, Hoath, Canterbury, Kent CT3 4LL. *01227 860280.* southviewcamping@aol.com. Owner: Mr K R Underdown & Mrs U J Underdown. Off A28. Off A299. Quiet, rural, flat situation. PH 100yd. Laundry facilities. Shop 1m. Thanet beaches 3m. Open April-October. **45T. MC. 20S.** ⌂ &

(4m). Yew Tree Park, Stone Street, Petham, Canterbury, Kent CT4 5PL. *01227 700306.* info@yewtreepark.com. www. yewtreepark.com. Owner: Mr & Mrs D Zanders. On B2068 4m from Canterbury and 9m from J11 of M20. Small, picturesque country park overlooking beautiful Chartham Downs. Well situated for exploring local heritage and Kent. Large open-air swimming pool. Canterbury 4m. Open March-October. ✰✰✰✰ **BH&HPA. 15T. 5MC. 13S. 7H.** ⌂ &

Chatham

(3m). Woolmans Wood, Bridgewood, Rochester Road, Chatham, Kent ME5 9SB. *01634 867685.* woolmans.wood@ currantbun.com. www.woolmans-wood.co.uk Owner: John Western. Woolmans Wood, Rochester Road, Chatham, Kent ME5 9SB. M2, J3, take A229 to Bridgewood roundabout then B2097. Park 0.25m rhs. M20, J6 same as above. Adults only. Shops (Asda), PO within 10 mins walk. Doctor 2m, Golf course 2m. Garage 4m. ✰✰✰✰ **BH&HPA. NCC. 60T. MC.** ✿ ♒ ⌂ &

Deal

(1m). Clifford Park Caravan Site, Thompson Close, Dover Road, Walmer, Deal, Kent CT14 7PB. *01304 373373.* Owner: H B Clifford. A2 to Dover. Last roundabout before docks. A258 to Deal, after about 4.5m turn left, 0.5m past secondhand car

sales and car wash. Calor Gas supplies. Shop 3mins walk. Country walks. Sea 1m. Channel ports 4.5m. Leisure centre 4m. Swimming pool 1m. Open March 1-October 30. **BH&HPA. 15T. 15MC. 160S.** ⌂ &

Dover

> **(3m). Hawthorn Farm, Martin Mill, Dover, Kent CT15 5LA.** *01304 852 658.* info@keatfarm.co.uk. www.keat farm.co.uk. Owners: Keat Farm (Caravans) Ltd. Situated off the main road between Deal and Dover A258. Well signposted. Fishing and golf nearby. Open March 1-November 30. ✰✰✰✰ **BH&HPA. NCC. 147T. MC. 176S.** ♒ ⌂ & &

(3m). St Margaret's Country Club, Reach Road, St Margaret's-at-Cliffe, Dover, Kent CT15 6AG. *0870 4429286.* holidays@gbholidayparks.co.uk. www.gbholiday parks.co.uk. Owners: Park Resorts Ltd. 3rd Floor, Swan Court, Waterhouse Street, Hemel Hempstead, Herts HP1 1FN. From London take M20 or A2 to Dover. Take the A258 and follow signs for St Margarets Cliffe. Turn R on Reach Road. The park is then on R. Indoor pool, restaurant, bar, outdoor play area, children's club, family entertainment, amusements, on site store. Open April-October. ✰✰✰✰ **BH&HPA. NCC. 140S. 25H.** ♒ &

Dymchurch

> **(1m). New Beach Holiday Village, Hythe Road, Dymchurch, Kent TN29 0JX.** *01303 872234.* info@cinqueportsleisure.com. www.cinqueports leisure.com. Owners: Cinque Ports Leisure Ltd. Coghurst Hall Holiday Village, Ivyhouse Lane, Ore, Hastings, East Sussex TN35 4NP. On the coastal road A259 between Hythe and Dymchurch. Indoor pool, children's facilities, restaurant, shops, entertainment. Visit Britain holiday park. Open January-November. ✰✰✰✰**BH&HPA. NCC. 200T. MC. 720S. 27H.** ♒ ⌂ & &

Faversham

(3m). Country View Park, Graveney, Faversham, Kent. *01795 530036.* info@coastandcountryleisure.com. www.coast andcountryleisure.com. Owner: Coast & Country Caravans. Cleve Hill, Graveney, Faversham, Kent ME13 9EF. Follow Graveney signs from A299, through village, past Graveney church, 0.25m on left-hand side. Small, quiet, country park. 1m to beach, 7m to Canterbury. Open March-January 2nd. ✰✰✰✰ **BH&HPA. 5S. 2H.** ♒

Folkestone

> **(4m). Black Horse Farm Caravan Club Site, 385 Canterbury Road, Densole, Folkestone, Kent CT18 7BG.** *01303 892665.* www.caravanclub.co.uk. Owner: The Caravan Club. East Grinstead House, East Grinstead, West Sussex RH19 1UA. See website for standard directions to site. Set in the heart of farming country in the Kentish village of Densole on the Downs. Quiet and relaxed country site, suitable for families. Non-members and tent campers welcome. Toilet blocks. Hard-standings. Privacy cubicles. Laundry facilities. Veg prep. MV service point. Playground. Golf, fishing nearby. Good area for walking. Baby/toddler washroom. Dog walk. ✰✰✰✰ **NCC. 140T. MC.** ✿ ♒ ⌂ &

(4m). Camping & Caravanning Club Site - Folkestone, The Warren, Folkestone, Kent CT19 6PT. *01303 255093/0870 243 3331.* www.campingandcaravanning club.co.uk. Owner: The Camping & Caravanning Club. Greenfields House, Westwood Way, Coventry CV4 8JH. From M2 and Canterbury on A260 take L at island into Folkestone, Hill Road, straight on over crossroads into Wear Bay Road and 2nd L before Martello Tower, site 0.5m on R. This cliff site is situated in an Area of Outstanding Natural Beauty, adjacent to a pebble beach. Non-members welcome. No towed caravans permitted. Folkestone harbour is very picturesque with its own clifftop promenade. Sea fishing is available from the beach. Special deals available for families and back-packers. Open March-October. ✩✩✩✩ **BH&HPA. NCC. 85MC.** 🛏 🔌 ♿

(2.5m). Capel Court Park, Winehouse Lane, Capel-le-Ferne, Folkestone, Kent CT18 7HZ. *01303 253462.* capel@onetel. comwww.capelcourtpark.co.uk. Owner: Capel Investments Ltd. Situated on top of White Cliffs. On Winehouse Lane off New Dover Road, Capel-le-Ferne between Folkestone and Dover on B2011, off A20. Quiet, sheltered, attractive park. Petanque. Bottled gas. Fishing/golf nearby, PO and doctor surgery in village. Panoramic Channel views from adjacent cliffs. Wwalks along the cliffs and across the downs. Open March 1-December 31. **BH&HPA. 75S.** 🛏 ♿ ✍

(2.5m). Little Satmar Holiday Park, Winehouse Lane, Capel-le-Ferne, Folkestone, Kent CT18 7JF. *01303 251188.* info@keatfarm.co.uk. www.keatfarm.co.uk. Owner: Keat Farm Caravans Ltd. Reculver Road, Herne Bay. Inland off B2011 Folkestone to Dover. Quiet park convenient for ferries and Channel Tunnel. Open March-November 30. ✩✩✩✩ **BH&HPA. NCC. 40T. MC. 75S.** 🛏 🔌 🅕

(1.5m). Little Switzerland Caravan and Camping Park, Wear Bay Road, Folkestone, Kent CT19 6PS. *01303 252168.* littleswitzerland@lineone.net. www.caravancampingsites. co.uk. Owner: D Gasson. Off A20. Follow signs Country Park. Hot showers. Shop 0.25m. Laundry room. Licensed restaurant. Open March 1-October 31. **16T. MC. 14S.** 🛏 🔌

(4m). Varne Ridge Caravan Park, 145 Old Dover Road, Capel-le-Ferne, Folkestone, Kent CT18 7HX. *01303 251765.* vrcp@varne-ridge.freeserve.co.uk. ww.varne-ridge. freeserve.co.uk. Owner: David & Evelyn Frantzeskou. Midway between Folkestone and Dover. Clifftop location overlooking the English Channel. Road marked 'Old Dover Road' runs off the B2011 at Capel-le-Ferne. Small, secluded, family-run holiday park, with panoramic views over the Channel to the coastline of France. Suitable touring base. Open March 1-October 31. ✩✩✩✩✩ **BH&HPA. 6T. 6MC. 3S. 8H.** 🛏 🔌

Harrietsham

(1.5m). Hogbarn Village, Hogbarn Lane, Harrietsham, Kent ME17 1NZ. *01622 859648.* info@kingsmead.co.uk. www. kingsmead.co.uk. Owner: Kingsmead Parks Ltd. Kingsmead House, Mytchett Road, Camberley, Surrey GU16 6AE. M20 J8, A20 to Harrietsham and Lenham. Just after Harrietsham village, left into Church Road, carry on along Stede Hill to Hogbarn Lane. Entrance 300yd on right. Set in 20 acres of woodland. Facilities for tourers, motor caravans and holiday homes. Open March 29-October 31. ✩✩✩✩ **NCC. 180S.** 🛏 🔌 ♿ 🅕 ✍

Herne Bay

(4m). Blue Dolphin Park, Reculver Lane, Reculver, Herne Bay, Kent CT6 6SS. *01227 375406.* Owner: S Holloway & L Watson. Off A299. Club. Heated indoor swimming pool. Fishing (beach), shop, PO nearby. Golf, doctor within 4m. Open March 1-January 31. ✩✩✩✩ **BH&HPA. 123S.** ♿

(1m). Hillborough Caravan Park, Reculver Road, Herne Bay, Kent CT6 6SR. *01227 374618.* Owner: Hillborough Properties Ltd. Off A299. Club. Indoor swimming pool. Cafe. Children's recreation room. Open March 13-November 5. **NCC. 30T. MC. 395S. 10H.** 🔌 ♿ 🅕

(2m). The Orchard, Keat Farm, Reculver Road, Herne Bay, Kent CT6 6SR. *01227 374381.* info@keatfarm.co.uk. www. keatfarm.co.uk. Owner: Keat Farm (Caravans) Ltd. Located off the A299. Open March 1-November 30. **BH&HPA. NCC. 24S.** 🛏

(3m). Waterways Caravan Park, Reculver, Herne Bay, Kent. *01227 372620.* info@waterwayscaravanpark.co.uk. www.waterwayscaravanpark.co.uk. Owner: Waterways Caravan & Amusement Park Ltd. 9m from the cathedral city of Canterbury and 45 mins to Dover ferries. Children's play area, clubhouse, amusement arcade, laundry room. 100yd from the Stone beach. Open March 1-January 31. **191S. 10H.** 🅕

Hythe

(2m). Beach Bank Caravan Site, Dymchurch Road, Hythe, Kent. *01303 269484.* Owner: A H & E Farmer. On A259. Licensed club. Open March 1-October 31. **13S. 8H.**

(1.5m). Bluewater Caravan Park, Dymchurch Road, Hythe, Kent CT21 6ND. *01374 267132.* gcaldow@hotmail.com. Owner: Mrs L M Mitchell & Mr G P Caldon. The Mount, Canterbury Road, Lyminge CT18 4HU. Closest caravan park to Hythe. No tourers. Open March 1-October 31. **68S.** ✿

(4m). Daleacres Caravan Club Site, Lower Wall Road, West Hythe, Hythe, Kent CT21 4NW. *01303 267679.* www.caravanclub.co.uk. Owner: The Caravan Club. East Grinstead House, East Grinstead, West Sussex RH19 1UA. See website for standard directions to site. Caravan Club members only. Attractive, level site. Play area. Dog walk. Toilet blocks. Privacy cubicles. Laundry facilities. Veg prep. Motorhome service point. Play equipment. Golf, fishing and water sports nearby. Good for walking. Suitable for families. Open March-October. **NCC. 140T.** ✿ 🕿 ⚒ ♿ 🛱

Folkestone Racecourse Caravan Club Site, Folkestone Racecourse, Westenhanger, Hythe, Kent CT21 4HX. *01303 261761.* www.caravanclub.co.uk. Owner: The Caravan Club. East Grinstead House, East Grinstead, West Sussex RH19 1UA. See website for standard directions to site. 6.5m from Folkestone. Handily located within a couple of miles of the M20 en route to or from the ferries and Channel Tunnel, with easy rail access to London. Toilet blocks with privacy cubicles, laundry facilities, vegetable preparation area and LP gas supplies. Fishing and golf within 5m, water sports, dog walk on site. Good area for walking. Open March-September. **NCC. 52T. 52MC.** ✿ 🕿

Isle of Sheppey

(7m). Harts Holiday Village, Leysdown Road, Leysdown-on-Sea, Isle of Sheppey, Kent ME12 4RG. *01795 510225.* info@cinqueportsleisure.com. www.cinqueportsleisure.com. Owner: Cinque Ports Leisure Ltd. Coghurst Hall Holiday Village, Ivyhouse Lane, Ore, Hastings, East Sussex TN35 4NP. M2, J5 to A249 then pick up B2231 to Leysdown. 9m from Sheerness. Leisure complex with heated swimming pool, paddling pool and slide. Jacuzzi. Play areas and amusement arcade. Clubhouse with free entertainment. 5mins from beach. Hire fleet on site. Bistro. Suitable base for travelling to London. Open March-October. **BH&HPA. NCC. 242S. 25H.** ✿ ♿ 🖉

Leysdown-on-Sea

(0.5m). Priory Hill Holiday Park, Wing Road, Leysdown-on-Sea, Kent ME12 4QT. *01795 510267.* info@prioryhill.co.uk. www.prioryhill.co.uk. M2/M20-A249 to Isle of Sheppey, B2231 to Leysdown follow brown signs to Priory Hill. Clubhouse entertainment, swimming pool (indoor heated) and lots more. Open March-October. **BH&HPA. 55T. MC. 55S.** ✿ 🕿 ♿ 🛱

Maidstone

Little Venice Country Park & Marina, Hampstead Lane, Yalding, Maidstone, Kent ME18 6HH. *01622 814158.* andrew.evans@little-venice.co.uk. www.little-venice.co.uk. Owners: Mr & Mrs A J Evans. M26 for M20, exit J4 on A228 for Maidstone. Over 1st and 2nd roundabouts and at 3rd roundabout turn L on to A2015 SP Yalding. Continue 300yd until signs for Yalding taking right turn onto B2162 along Hampstead Lane. Continue over hump-backed bridge and we are 2nd turning on L. No hire units. Onsite clubhouse/restaurants, sports/recre-ation field. Private river moorings and slipway. Private fishing rights, centrally heated showers, launderette, toilets. Horse trekking, train station, canoe club walking distance. Kent County Hop Farm, golf course 2m. Town 6m. **BH&HPA. 120S.**

(6m). Medway Wharf Marina, Bow Bridge, Wateringbury, Maidstone, Kent ME18 5ED. *01622 813927.* Owner: Miss S J Dozin. A26 from Maidstone to lights at Wateringbury turn left, 0.5m to railway crossing, over Bow Bridge, first right. Showers. Restaurant. Near boats, PH, shop and railway station. Open April 1-October 31. **4T. 4MC. 11S.** ✿

(3m). Pine Lodge Touring Park, A20 Ashford Road, Bearsted, Maidstone, Kent ME17 1XH. *01622 730018.* booking@pinelodgetouringpark.co.uk. www.pinelodgetouringpark.co.uk. Owner: Janet & Stan Hollingsworth. From J8, M20 (Leeds Castle exit), park 1m towards Bearsted and Maidstone. Sheltered site, rural views. Suitable base for Continental ports and touring Kent. Centrally heated facilities block. Easy access. Play area. Shop. Gas. Laundry. Dishwashing room. No dogs. ✰✰✰✰✰ **BH&HPA. 80T. 20MC.** ❁ 🕿 ♿ 🛱

(4m). Scragged Oak Caravan Club Site, Scragged Oak Road, Detling, Maidstone, Kent ME14 3EZ. *01622 739937.* www.caravanclub.co.uk. Owner: The Caravan Club. East Grinstead House, East Grinstead, West Sussex RH19 1UA. See website for directions to site. Caravan Club members only. On North Downs, this site is flat and well screened with trees. Enclosed dog walk. No sanitation. Fishing and golf nearby. Good area for walking. Open March-September. **NCC. 80T. MC.** ✿ 🕿

(1m). Yewtree Mobile Home Park, Maidstone Road, Charing, Maidstone, Kent TN27 0DD. *01233 713551.* Owner: Mr E James. A20 main trunk road to Folkestone. Showers. Washroom. **BH&HPA. 50T. 20MC.** ❁

Margate

(2m). Bradgate Caravan Park, Manston Court Road, Margate, Kent CT9 4LG. *01843 823207.* Owner: Mrs R Vanderweele. Off A256. Licensed club. Swimming pool. Small leisure centre, adults' spa bath, sunbed and sauna. Open March 1-January 17. **BH&HPA. 102S.** 🖉

Minster-on-Sea

(1m). Ashcroft Coast Holiday Park, Plough Road, Minster-on-Sea, Kent, ME12 4JH. *0871 664 9701.* ashcroft.coast@park-resorts.com. www.park-resorts.com. Owners: Park Resorts Ltd. 3rd Floor, Swan Court, Waterhouse Street, Hemel Hempstead, Herts HP1 1FN. Take the A249 towards Sheerness Once on the Island turn right onto B223 into Eastchuch (about 4m). Turn left at the Church and follow road into Plough Lane. Ashcroft is on right-hand side. Heated indoor and outdoor pool. Children's club, adventure playground. Water and sports resorts programmes. Takeaway. Entertainment. Amusements. Open March-October. ✰✰✰✰ **BH&HPA. NCC. 365S19H.** ✿ 🛱

Lazy Days Holiday Park, Bell Farm Lane, Minster-on-Sea, Kent ME12 4JB. *01795 876762.* info@lazyholidays.co.uk. www.lazyholidays.co.uk. Owner: Lazy Days Holiday Parks Ltd. M20, J7 take A249 N towards Sittingbourne and Sheerness. B2231 towards Minster. Straight after traffic lights and next roundabout. Take second L, then R (by phone box) after mini roundabout: Plough Road. Immediately on L is Bell Farm Lane, follow road till entrance of park. Please ring. Adults only, no clubs nor bingo. All pitches have sea views across the Thames estuary. Open March 1-October 31 and December 23-January 2. **BH&HPA. 3T. MC. 31S.** ✿ 🕿

Please mention Caravan Sites 2006 when replying to advertisers

(0.5m). **Willow Tree Caravan Park, Minster-on-Sea, Kent**. *01795 875833*. Owners: D Kiley, P Rock, D Thurlow. Palm Tree Management, Fourth avenue, Warden Road, Eastchurch, Kent ME12 4EW. Children welcome. Open March 1-October 31. **BH&HPA. 80S.** 🐾 🛁

New Romney

(0.25m). **Marlie Farm Holiday Village, Dymchurch Road (A259), New Romney, Kent TN28 8UE**. *01797 363060*. info@cinqueportsleisure.com. www.cinque portsleisure.com. Owner: Cinque Ports Leisure Ltd. Coghurst Hall Holiday Village, Ivyhouse Lane, Ore, Hastings, East Sussex TN35 4NP. Situated on the A259 coast road. Village is close to the beach. Clubhouse, indoor leisure complex with pool. Jacuzzi/play area and cafe. Farm has horses, donkeys, ducks and rabbits. Open March-January. **BH&HPA. NCC. 350T. MC. 222S.** 🐾🐶🚻

(1m). **New Romney Caravan Park, Clark Road, Greatstone, New Romney, Kent TN28 8PE**. *01797 362247*. www.ukparks.co.uk/newromney. caravans@newromney park.fsnet.co.uk. Owner: Hillborough Properties Ltd. Park is located off the A259. Direct routes from London via A/M20 or A/M2. Club. Open April 1-October 31. **BH&HPA. 50T. MC. 170S.** 🐾 📶

Romney Sands Holiday Park, The Parade, Greatstone-on-Sea, New Romney, Kent TN28 8RN. *0871 664 9761*. rom ney.sands@park-resorts.com. www.park-resorts.com. Owner: Park Resorts. 3rd Floor, Swan Court, Waterhouse Street, Hemel Hempstead, Herts HP1 1FN. From London, take the M20 to Ashford. Exit at J10, and follow signposts to Brenzett. Follow signs to New Romney taking first right past Shell garage to the seafront. Turn right onto coast road. Indoor heated pool, children's club, family entertainment, adventure playground, amusements, laundrette, diner, take-away, tennis courts. Open April-October. **BH&HPA. NCC. 581S. 78H.** 🐾

Ramsgate

(2.5m). **Manston Caravan & Camping Park, Manston Court Road, Manston, Ramsgate, Kent CT12 5AU**. *01843 823442*. enquiries@manston-park.co.uk. www.manston-park.co.uk. Owner: Mrs M Neale & Mr B Austen. M2 motorway follow A299 to Monkton roundabout, follow Kent International Airport signs to join B2050. First left after airport, first left opposite Manston Motor Centre, park 400yd on right. Play area. Golf 1m; supermarket, PO 2m. Ramsgate, Margate and Broadstairs 3m. Open April 1-October 31. ☆☆☆☆ **BH&HPA. 80T. 20MC. 40S.** 🐾🐶🛁

(1m). **Pegwell Bay Caravan Park, Pegwell Road, Ramsgate, Kent CT11 0NJ**. *01843 592222*. Owner: Mrs A C Beatty. Take the A299 Thanet Way to the A253. Turn left at double round-about and right immediately at second roundabout into Chilton Lane. (By Vee Wise car sales). Open March 1-January 17. **BH&HPA. 45S. 25H.** ♿

(2.5m). **Preston Parks, Preston Road, Manston, Ramsgate, Kent CT12 5AR**. *01843 823346*. info@preston-parks.com. www.prestonparks.com. Owner: Mr B & Mrs S Austen. Situated off the B2050. In a quiet village location close to all amenities. Laundrette, picnic area, children's play area and woodland walk. 3m to towns of Ramsgate, Broadstairs and Margate. Coastal beaches. Open March 5-January 17. **BH&HPA. 155S.** 🐾 ✎

(5.5m). **The Foxhunter Park, Monkton, Ramsgate, Kent CT12 4JG**. *01843 821311*. foxhunterpark@aol.com. www. saunders parkhomes.co.uk. Owner: Saunders Park Homes Ltd. Off A299. Club. Swimming pool. Beauty Spa. Restaurant. Putting Green, bowls, children's adventure land. Golf courses, fishing, shopping centre etc close by, beaches. Open March 1-October 31. ☆☆☆☆☆ **BH&HPA. NCC. 341S. 40H.** 🐾 ♿ 🛁

(3.5m). **Wayside Caravan Park, Way Hill, Minster-in-Thanet, Ramsgate, Kent CT12 4HW**. *01843 821272*. Owner: Mr & Mrs D Scott. On B2048, 0.5m E of Minster village. Laundrette. Telephone. Play area. Open March 1-October 31. ☆☆☆☆ **BH&HPA. 54S. 15H.**

Rochester

(9m). **Allhallows Leisure Park, Allhallows-on-Sea, Rochester, Kent ME3 9QD**. *01634 270266*. oewebmaster@bourne-leisure.co.uk. www.allhallowsleisurepark.com. Owner: Bourne Leisure Ltd. One Park Lane, Hemel Hempstead, Herts HP2 4YL. M25 J2 SP Canterbury. Take A2 until signs for Gillingham A289/(Grain A228). Follow A289 until roundabout then first exit for A228 Grain. SP from A228. Bars. Indoor and outdoor heated pools. Multi sports court. Nightly entertainment. Playground. Amusement arcade. Fishing lake, stables and bowling green. Laundrette. Tennis court, oasis diner, 9-hole golf course. Open April-November. ☆☆☆☆ **BH&HPA. NCC. 898S. 80H.** 🐾 ♿ 🛁

Romney Marsh

Jesson Court Holiday Village, 69 Jefferstone Lane, St Marys Bay, Romney Marsh, Kent TN29 0SG. *01797 363063*. info@cinqueportsleisure.com. www.cinqueports leisure.com. Owners: Cinque Ports Leisure Ltd. Coghurst Hall Holiday Village, Ivyhouse Lane, Ore, Hastings, East Sussex TN35 4NP. 0.25m E of New Romney on the A259 coast road. Golf, shops and take-away nearby. Open March-February. **BH&HPA. NCC. 37S.** 🐾 ♿

Sandwich

(0.2m). **Sandwich Leisure Park, Woodnesborough Road, Sandwich, Kent CT13 0AA**. *01304 612681*. info@coastand countryleisure.com. www.coastandcountryleisure.com. Owner: Coast & Country Caravans. Cleve Hill, Graveney, Faversham, Kent ME13 9EF. Follow A257 to Sandwich then follow caravan park brown signs. Relaxed park with showers. Town 5 mins on foot. Laundry, phone, playground. Open March-October and weekends in November, December and at Christmas. ☆☆☆☆☆ **BH&HPA. 150T. MC. 100S. 3H.** 🐾 📶 ♿

Seasalter

Blue Anchor Caravan Park, Faversham Road, Seasalter, Kent CT5 4BJ. *01227 263389*. yvetteseparks@btconnect.com. www.southeastparks.co.uk. Owner: South East Parks Ltd. 185 Faversham Road, Seasalter, Whitstable, Kent CT5 4BJ. Outskirts of Whitstable on A299. Private beach. Open March 1-October 31. **BH&HPA. 80S.**

Sevenoaks

(0.5m). **'To The Woods' Caravan & Camping Park, Botsom Lane, West Kingsdown, Sevenoaks, Kent TN15 6BN**. *01322 863751*. Owner: Mrs E Helsdon. White Farm House, Sundridge Hill, Luxton, Kent ME2 1LH. Off the A20. 5m from Swanley. Small, quiet park with limited facilities. Close to mainline railway to London (19m from Central London). **15T.** ✿ 🐾 📶

(4m). Camping & Caravanning Club Site - Oldbury Hill, Styants Bottom, Seal, Sevenoaks, Kent TN15 0ET. 01732 762728/0870 243 3331. www.campingand caravanningclub.co.uk. Owner: Camping & Caravanning Club. Greenfields House, Westwood Way, Coventry CV4 8JH. 0.5m off the A25 between Sevenoaks and Borough Green. Turn L just after Crown Point Inn. Down narrow lane to Styants Bottom, site on L. A 4-acre site. Levelling ramps required. Suitable site for exploring the delights of the Garden of England. All types of units accepted. Non-members welcome. Site is located in National Trust land surrounded by woodland walks. Convenient for Channel ports at Dover and Folkestone. Special deals available for families and backpackers. Open March-October. ☆☆☆☆ 60T. 60MC. ↟ ▣ ♿

Gate House Wood Touring Park, Ford Lane, Wrotham Heath, Sevenoaks, Kent TN15 7SD. 01732 843062. gatehouse wood@btinternet.com. www.gatehousewoodtouring.co.uk. Owners: Mr & Mrs Allen & Mr & Mrs Long. M26, J2A take A20 south towards Maidstone, through traffic lights at Wrotham Heath take first left, SP Trottiscliffe, left at next junction. Gate House Wood is 100yd on left. American RVs welcome. Open March 1-end November (all year by arrangement only); open all year for rallies. ☆☆☆☆☆ BH&HPA. 56T. MC. ▣ ♿ ▤

Sheerness

(7m). Bramley Park, Second Avenue, Warden Road, Eastchurch, Sheerness, Kent ME12 4EP. 01795 880338. Owner: Bramley Park Ltd. Off the A249. Dogs allowed under control. Open March 1-October 31. ☆☆☆ BH&HPA. NCC. 156S. ↟

(2m). Eden Park, Warden Road, Eastchurch, Sheerness, Kent HE12 4ES. 01795 880232. Owner: Mr & Mrs B Garrett. Open March 1-October 31. 62S. ↟

(2m). Fletcher Battery Caravan Park, Warden Road, Eastchurch, Sheerness, Kent ME12 4ET. 01795 880749. Owner: Mr & Mrs B Garrett. Open March 1-October 31. 86S. ↟ ♿ ▤

(2m). Minster Park, The Broadway, Minster, Sheerness, Kent ME12 2DF. 01795 875211. developments@tingdene.net. www.tingdene.net. Owner: Tingdene Developments Ltd. Bradfield Road, Finedon Road, Industrial Estate, Wellingborough, Northants NN8 4HB. Dogs allowed on leads. Open March 1-October 31. BH&HPA. 20H. ↟ ▣

(1m). Sea Breeze Caravan Park, Barton's Point Road, Sheerness, Kent ME12 2BX. 01795 665571/875250. Owner: Mrs D Jackson. 353 Minster Road, Minster, Isle of Sheppey, Kent. On A249. 2 mins from Sheerness town centre. Close to windsurfing beach. Open March 1-October 31. 25S. ↟

(3m). Sea Cliff Caravan Park, Oak Lane, Minster, Sheerness, Kent ME12 3QS. 01795 872262. Owner: Seacliff Holiday Estate Ltd. Off A249, through Minster village, tourist sign on left. On site: club, restaurant, bingo, entertainment, playground, playing field. Within 3-4m: golf, shops, Leysdown amusements. Open March 1-October 31. ☆☆☆ BH&HPA. 40T. MC. 185S. ↟ ▣

(9m). Seaview Holiday Park, Leysdown, Sheerness, Kent ME12 4NB. 01795 510275. Owner: Wickland (Holdings) Ltd. Lyon House, Lyon Road, Romford, Essex RM1 2BG. Heated swimming pool. Open March 7-October 31. BH&HPA. 120S. ↟

(1.5m). Sheerness Holiday Village, Halfway Road, Minster-on-Sea, Sheerness, Kent ME12 3AA. 01795 662638. info@cinqueportsleisure.com. www.cinqueports leisure.com. Owner: Cinque Ports Leisure Ltd. Coghurst Hall Holiday Village, Ivyhouse Lane, Ore, Hastings, East Sussex TN35 4NP. Off M2 and A2 following signs to Sheerness, 0.5m from town on R. Club. Indoor pool. Children's club. Amusements, sports and leisure facilities, playground, on site shop, takeaway and cafe. Open March-October. ☆☆☆ BH&HPA. NCC. 50T. 320S. ↟ ▣ ▤

(0.25m). Shurland Leisure Park, Warden Road, Eastchurch, Sheerness, Kent ME12 4EN. 0871 664 9770. shurland. dale@park-resorts.com. www.park-resorts.com. Owner: Park Resorts Ltd. 3rd floor, Swan Court, Waterhouse Street, Hemel Hempstead, Herts, HP1 1FN. M20 or M2 to A249 to Sheerness. Turn R at the roundabout on the B2231 towards Leysdown. Follow road into Eastchurch and turn L at the church into Warden Road, then first R, second L. Indoor pool, adventure playground, children's club, sports field, amusements, laundrette, cafe and takeaway. Family evening entertainment. Howletts Wild Animal Park nearby. Open April-October. BH&HPA. NCC. 410S. 15H. ↟

(2m). Sunnymead Caravan Park, Warden Road, Eastchurch, Sheerness, Kent. 01795 880235. Owner: L Lewis. Off M2. Club. Laundry. Play area, children's room and play area. Amusements. Open March 1-October 31. 146S. ↟ ▤

(2m). The Wold Caravan Park, Warden Road, Eastchurch, Sheerness, Kent. 01795 880392. Owner: R A & B C Barnes. Open March 1-October 31. BH&HPA. 88S. ↟

Please mention Caravan Sites 2006 when replying to advertisers

(6m). Warden Springs Caravan Park, Warden Springs, East Church, Sheerness, Kent ME12 4HF. 0871 664 9791. warden.springs@park-resorts.com. www.park-resorts.com. Owners: Park Resorts Ltd. 3rd Floor, Swan Court, Waterhouse Street, Hemel Hempstead, Herts HP1 1FN. From M25 take A2, J2. Then take M2, till J5. Follow A249 for 8m then right, on to B2231 to Eastchurch. Turn left following signs for park. Outdoor, heated swimming pool, clubhouse, on site store, takeaway, children's clubs, family evening entertainment. Open April-October. ☆☆☆ BH&HPA. NCC. 48T. MC. 220S. 19H. ⊕ ⊞

Sutton-by-Dover

Sutton Vale Country Club and Caravan Park, Vale Road, Sutton-by-Dover, Kent CT15 5DH. 01304 374155. office@sutton-vale.co.uk. www.sutton-vale.co.uk. Owner: Sutton Vale Caravan Park Ltd. A2, 4m from Dover Whitfield roundabout turn right, 20yd opposite McDonalds into Archers Court Road, 4m on left. Licensed club. Pool. Restaurant. Play area. Sports field. Horse riding next door. Sea fishing 4m. Lake fishing 2m. 4 golf courses within 3m radius. PH 5mins walk. Car ride 2mins. Open March 1-January 31. ☆☆☆☆ BH&HPA. NCC. 14T. 10MC. 70S. 20H. ⊕ ⊞ & ⊞

Thanet

Acol Caravan Park, Acol, Birchington, Thanet, Kent CT7 0JE. 01843 841291. lsgp@acol-caravanpark.co.uk. www.acol-caravanpark.co.uk. Owner: Les & Gina Phillips. Off A28 on B2048. 1m from Birchington. Non-letting leisure retreat. Open Easter-end October. BH&HPA. 40S. ⌀

Tonbridge

(10m). Tanner Farm Touring Caravan & Camping Park, Goudhurst Road, Marden, Tonbridge, Kent TN12 9ND. 01622 832399. enquiries@tannerfarmpark.co.uk. www.tannerfarmpark.co.uk. Owner: S Mannington & Son Ltd. Three miles from Marden, 10m Maidstone from either A229 or A262 on to B2079, midway between Goudhurst & Marden. Caravan Club affiliated site. Peaceful setting in centre of attractive family farm. Mainly flat and grass. Shire horses bred and kept on farm. Bed and breakfast in Tudor farmhouse. David Bellamy Gold Conservation Award. Green Business Tourism Scheme Silver Award. ☆☆☆☆☆ BH&HPA. NCC. 100T. MC. ✿ ⊕ ⊞ & ⊞

(5m). The Hop Farm Country Park, Beltring, Paddock Wood, Tonbridge, Kent TN12 6PY. 01622 872068. Owner: The Hop Farm Ltd. On A228 Paddock Wood, 30mins from J5, M25, 10mins from J4, M20. Secluded site in grounds of largest collection of oast houses in world. Open March-October. 300T. MC. ⊕ & ⊞

Whitstable

(2m). Alberta Holiday Village, Faversham Road, Seasalter, Whitstable, Kent CT5 4BJ. 01227 274485. info@cinqueportsleisure.com. www.cinqueportsleisure.com. Owner: Cinque Ports Leisure Ltd. Coghurst Hall Holiday Village, Ivy House Lane, Ore, Hastings, East Sussex TN35 4NP. Off M2 on A299, L after 2m to Seasalter. Site 1m. Near beach. Suitable base for touring Kent. Laundry, cafe, phone, licensed club, takeaway, food shop. Heated outdoor pool. Play area. Sporting activities. Open March-November. ☆☆☆ BH&HPA. NCC. 300S. ⊕ & ⊞

(2m). Homing Leisure Park, Church Lane, Seasalter, Whitstable, Kent CT5 4BU. 01227 771777. info@coastandcountryleisure.com. www.coastandcountryleisure.com. Owner: Coast & Country Caravans. Cleve Hill, Graveney, Faversham, Kent ME13 9EF. A299, 4m, left into Church Lane towards Seasalter. Park 300yd on L. Licensed club. Laundry, playground, phone, pool, tennis. Open March-October, weekend November and December, and two weeks at Christmas and New Year. ☆☆☆☆☆ BH&HPA. 43T. MC. 195S. 3H. ⊕ ⊞ & ⊞

(1.5m). Meadow Farm Caravan Park, 64 Herne Bay Road, Swalecliffe, Whitstable, Kent. 01227 792534. Owner: Mrs M R Larner. Off A299. Open March 1-October 31. 5T. 76S. 6H. ⊕

(1m). Primrose Cottage Caravan Park, Golden Hill, Whitstable, Kent CT5 3AR. 01227 273694. brian@primrosepark.wanadoo.co.uk. Owner: Mr Brian Campbell. 1m E of Whitstable roundabout on A2990 (Thanet Way), next to Tesco supermarket. Quiet park with no clubhouse. Canterbury 7m. Open March 1-October 31. BH&HPA. 6T. 6MC. 48S. 6H. ⊕ ⊞ & ⊞

(1.5m). Sea View Holiday Village, St John's Road, Swalecliffe, Whitstable, Kent CT5 2RY. 01227 792246. www.cinqueportsleisure.com. info@cinqueportsleisure.com. Owner: Cinque Ports Leisure Ltd. Coghurst Hall Holiday Village, Ivyhouse Lane, Ore, Hastings, East Sussex TN35 4NP. Off A299, at double roundabout L under railway bridge, mini roundabout turn R 600yd on L, lane to park (SP). AA 3 pennants. Open March 1-October 31. BH&HPA. NCC. 171T. MC. 452S. 1H. ⊕ ⊞ & ⊞

TANNER FARM
TOURING CARAVAN & CAMPING
PARK
Goudhurst Road, Marden, Kent TN12 9ND
Tel: 01622 832399 Fax: 01622 832472
e-mail: enquiries@tannerfarmpark.co.uk www.tannerfarmpark.co.uk
Attractively landscaped, peaceful Touring Park set in the centre of 150 acre idyllic Weald family farm. Spotless facilities. Central for a wealth of attractions, including our own Shire Horses.
★ Open All Year ★ 100 Electric Touring Pitches ★ Centrally Heated Toilet Blocks ★ Free showers
★ Dogs Welcome on Leads ★ Children's Play Area ★ Shop/Gas Supplies
★ Launderette ★ Hard Standings ★ Disabled Facilities

Wrotham

Thriftwood Caravan & Camping Park, Plaxdale Green Road, Stansted, Wrotham, Kent TN15 7PB. *01732 822261.* booking @thriftwoodleisure.co.uk. www.thriftwoodleisure.co.uk. Owner: Mr & Mrs K Hollingsworth. From M25, take M20 towards Dover, J2. Follow A2 Northbound and Thriftwood signs. M26 J2A follow A20 Northbound towards West Kingsdown. Gas supplies and refills. Bar. Showers. Shaver points. Chemical toilet emptying point. Tennis nearby. Laundrette. Play area. Outdoor swimming pool. Licensed club house. Open March 1-January 31. ☆☆☆☆☆ **BH&HPA. 150T. MC. 30S5H.** 🛉 📵 🕭 🎗

LONDON

Abbey Wood

Abbey Wood Caravan Club Site, Federation Road, Abbey Wood, London SE2 0LS. *020 83117708.* www.caravanclub.co.uk. Owner: The Caravan Club. East Grinstead House, East Grinstead, West Sussex RH19 1UA. See website for standard directions to site. Only 35mins by train to central London. Rural setting. Playframe. Advance booking essential bank holidays, July and August. Tent campers admitted. Hard- standings. Heated toilet blocks. Privacy cubicles. Laundry facilities. Baby changing facilities. Veg prep. Motorhome service point. Non-members welcome. Golf, water sports and cycling within 5m. ☆☆☆☆☆ **NCC. 220T. MC.** ✿ 🛉 📵 🕭

Chingford

(2m). Lee Valley Campsite, Sewardstone Road, Chingford, London E4 7RA. *020 8529 5689.* scs@leevalleypark.org.uk. www.leevalleypark.org.uk. Owner: Lee Valley Regional Park. Bulls Cross, Enfield, Middlesex EN2 9HG. Site is on A112 between Chingford and Waltham Abbey to the S of M25, leave M25 at J26. Close to M25 and Epping Forest. Play area. Bus stops on site for connection to London. Open April-October. ☆☆☆☆ **200T. MC.** 🛉 📵 🕭 🎗

Crystal Palace

Crystal Palace Caravan Club Site, Crystal Palace Parade, Crystal Palace, London SE19 1UF. *020 87787155.* www.caravanclub.co.uk. Owner: The Caravan Club. East Grinstead House, East Grinstead, West Sussex RH19 1UA. See website for standard directions to site. Adjacent to pleasant park with many attractions for children. Next to National Sports Centre. Excellent facilities. Mainline railway stations to central London within walking distance. Non-members and tent campers welcome (66 tent pitches). Hard-standings. Advance booking necessary. Toilet blocks. Privacy cubicles. Laundry facilities. Veg prep. Motorhome service point. ☆☆☆☆ **NCC. 150T. MC.** ✿ 🛉 📵 🕭

Edmonton

(1m). Lee Valley Camping & Caravan Park, Meridian Way, Edmonton, London N9 0AS. *020 8803 6900/0208 345 6666.* leisurecentre@leevalleypark.org.uk. www.leevalleypark.org.uk.

Owner: Lee Valley Regional Park. Bulls Cross, Enfield, Middlesex EN2 9HG. M25 J25 then turn down A10 towards London and immediately left down A1055. Keep going along this road for 6m; at UCI cinema turn left into leisure centre complex, site is SP. Golf and driving range on site. 0.5m to nearest shops. Open all year except Christmas, Boxing and New Year's Day. ☆☆☆☆ **100T. MC.** ✿ 🛉 📵 🕭 🎗

West Drayton

(1m). Riverside Mobile Home and Touring Park, Thorney Mill Road, West Drayton, London UB7 7ET. *01895 446520.* Owner: K V R Francis. Close to London Airport Heathrow. Cash on entry. No cheques. Stays of not less than two nights. Please telephone for booking. Near West Drayton Post Office. Calor Gas and Camping Gaz. Games room. Time on before 6pm, time off 11.30am. **33T. MC.** ✿ 🛉 📵 🎗

SURREY

Chertsey

(1m). Camping & Caravanning Club Site - Chertsey, Bridge Road, Chertsey, Surrey KT16 8JX. *01932 562405/0870 2433331.* www.campingandcaravanningclub.co.uk. Owner: Camping & Caravanning Club. Greenfields House, Westwood Way, Coventry CV4 8JH. Leave M25 exit 11. Follow signs to Chertsey. At roundabout take first exit to lights. Straight over at next lights. Turn right 400yd turn left into site. Picturesque site on banks of the Thames. Good access to London and surrounding areas. Fishing is permitted from the river bank with the holiday site managers' permission. (Local attractions include Thorpe Park, Windsor Castle and Legoland). Non-members welcome. All units accepted. Special deals available for families and back-packers. ☆☆☆ **200T. 200MC.** ✿ 🛉 📵 🕭

East Horsley

(2m). Camping & Caravanning Club Site - Horsley, Ockham Road North, East Horsley, Surrey KT24 6PE. *01483 283273.* www.campingandcaravanningclub.co.uk. Owner: Camping & Caravanning Club. Greenfields House, Westwood Way, Coventry CV4 8JH. Take the B2039 from the A3, exit marked Ockham, East Horsley, look for postbox on right at Green Lane, access road to site SP on right-hand side. Recreation hall and play area. Next to Horsley Lake, suitable for fishing. Non-members welcome. Site has an abundance of wildlife, including foxes, deer, rabbits and ducks often spotted. Special deals available for families and backpackers. All units accepted. Open March-October. ☆☆☆ **130T. 130MC.** 🛉 📵 🕭

Godalming

(3m). The Merry Harriers, Hambledon, Godalming, Surrey GU8 4DR. *01428 682883.* merry.harriers@virgin.net. Owner: Mr Colin Beasley. Off the A3 on to the A283, turn left to Hambledon after Wormley. 2m S of Milford. Milford or Whitley station 1.5m. Shower and shaver point. **20T. 20MC.** ✿ 🛉

Guildford

Cherryman's Brook, Ponds Lane, Farley Green, AlburyGuildford, Surrey. *01483 202289.* Owner: Mr K Livingston. **12S.** 🛉

(5m). **Edgeley Caravan Park, Farley Green, Albury, Guildford, Surrey GU5 9DW.** 01483 202129. www.haulfryn.co.uk. Owner: Haulfryn Group Ltd. The Warren, Abersoch, Pwllheli, Gwynedd LL53 7AA. M25 J10, take the A3 towards Guildford. Take first J to Send/Ripley. Carry on this road passing through West Clando, on to the A25 to Dorking. Turn right on to the A248 to Albury, and after about 0.5m turn left into New Road, SP for Farley Green. Carry on for 2m, park is situated on the left-hand side. New indoor swimming pool. Horse riding 0.5m, fishing 2m, Spectrum Leisure Centre, cinema, theatre, shopping, golf all 5m. Open from April 1-March 31. **BH&HPA. 285S.** &

Leatherhead

(6m). **Pebble Hill Farm Caravan Site, Shere Road, West Horsley, Leatherhead, Surrey KT24 6ER.** 01483 282098. Owner: Mr R P Hancock. Off the A246 1.5m up Shere Road. Storage only November-February. Open March-October. **20T.**

Lingfield

(1.5m). **Long Acres Caravan & Camping, Newchapel Road, Lingfield, Surrey RH7 6LE.** 01342 833205. Owner: Mr Jeffrey Pilkington. Off J6, M25 S on A22 towards East Grinstead turn L on B2028 towards Lingfield. Clean site, ideal for visiting London, Surrey, Kent and Sussex. Set in 40 acres. Plenty to see and do. 1hr from London by train, 1hr from South Coast. Many local attractions, Hever, Chartwell, Chessington, various gardens. Local fishing and golf. ☆☆☆ **BH&HPA. 60T. 60MC.** ✿ ☛ ▣

Mytchett

Canal Visitor Centre, Mytchett Place Road, Mytchett, Surrey GU16 6DD. 01252 370073. info@basingstoke-canal.co.uk. www.basingstoke-canal.co.uk. Owner: Basingstoke Canal Authority. M3, J4, follow A331 south and turn L to Mytchett. 2.5m from Farnborough. 3m from Camberley. Beautiful canalside setting. Showers and water point on site. 45mins away from London. **15T. 15MC. 15S.** ✿ ☛ & �

Redhill

(4m). **Alderstead Heath Caravan Club Site, Dean Lane, Redhill, Surrey RH1 3AH.** 01737 644629. www.caravanclub.co.uk. Owner: The Caravan Club. East Grinstead House, East Grinstead, West Sussex RH19 1UA. See website for standard directions to site. Non-members admitted. Quiet site surrounded by rolling, wooded countryside, with views. Dog walk on site. Shops 2m away. Toilet blocks. Privacy cubicles. Laundry facilities. Veg preparation. Motorhome service point. Calor Gas and Campingaz. Playframe. Fishing and golf available nearby. Suitable site for families. Local attractions include Chessington World of Adventure. Thorpe Park and Bluebell Line Steam Railway. Some hard-standings. Baby and toddler washroom. Peaceful site off-peak. Good area for walking, NCN cycle path within 5m. ☆☆☆☆☆ **NCC. 85T. MC.** ✿ ☛ ▣ &

Shepperton

Mannygate Park, Mitre Close, Shepperton, Surrey. Owner: Mr & Mrs Sulman. 59 Station Road North, Belvedere, Kent DA17 6JL. Small, private park on the river Thames and within easy reach of central London. M25 5 mins away. **BH&HPA.** ✿

Walton-on-Thames

Camping & Caravanning Club Site - Walton-on-Thames, Fieldcommon Lane, Walton-on-Thames, Surrey KT12 3QG. 01932 220392/0870 243 3331. www.campingandcaravanningclub.co.uk. Owner: Camping & Caravanning Club. Greenfields House, Westwood Way, Coventry CV4 8JH. From M25 J13 to Staines and then to Walton, turn L at traffic lights, SP Molesey at end of Rydens Road, turn L and turn sharp right into Fieldcommon Lane. Site beside river Mole, 15m from London. Club members only. Own sanitation essential. Fishing available from site. Caravans, motor caravans and tents accepted. Golf, horseriding and swimming close by, also Kempton Park Racecourse and Hampton Court. Special deals for families and backpackers. Open March-October. ☆☆ **115T. 115MC.** ☛ ▣

SUSSEX (EAST)

Battle

(2.5m). **Crazy Lane Tourist Park, Whydown Farm, Sedlescombe, Battle, East Sussex TN33 0QT.** 01424 870147. info@crazylane.co.uk. www.crazylane.co.uk. Owner: G C & R J Morgan. South on A21 turn left, 100yd past junction with B2244 opposite Blackbrooks Garden Centre. Small, secluded park situated in a valley in the heart of 1066 country. Within easy reach of beaches and historical sites. Open March 1-November 1. ☆☆☆ **BH&HPA. 36T. 20MC.** ☛ ▣ & ▣

(2m). **Crowhurst Park, Telham Lane, Battle, East Sussex TN33 0SL.** 01424 773344. enquiries@crowhurstpark.co.uk. www.crowhurstpark.co.uk. Owner: Mr C & Mrs E J Simmons. 2m S of Battle on A2100 to Hastings at junction of road to Crowhurst. Licensed club. Gas. Playground. Fishing. Tennis. Restaurant. Large, 17th-century mansion house. Indoor swimming pool, sauna and solarium, beauty treatments, dance studio, gym and shop. Golf 2m. Shopping centre 5m. Cinema 7m. David Bellamy Gold Conservation Award. Open March 1-January 5. ☆☆☆☆☆ **BH&HPA. NCC. 130S. 54H.** & ▣ ◢

(3m). **Normanhurst Court Caravan Club Site, Stevens Crouch, Battle, East Sussex TN33 9LR.** 01424 773808. www.caravanclub.co.uk. Owner: The Caravan Club. East Grinstead House, East Grinstead, West Sussex RH19 1UA. See website for standard directions to site. Located in a former garden with specimen trees and shrubs. Views of distant downs. Dog walk. Advance booking essential bank holidays, July, August and weekends. Toilet blocks with privacy cubicles and laundry facilities. Motorhome service point. Hard-standings. Playground. Fishing and golf nearby. Suitable for families. Shops within 3m away. Non-members welcome. Open March-October. ☆☆☆☆☆ **NCC. 152T. MC.** ☛ ▣ &

(2m). **Senlac Park Caravan Site, Main Road, Catsfield, Battle, East Sussex TN33 9DU.** 01424 773969. www.senlacpark.co.uk. Owner: Mr Wray, Mr Gibbs and Miss Harris. On the B2204 (formerly the A269). 5mins drive from Battle, 15 mins from Hastings. Quiet site set in 20 acres of woodland walks. Riding, golf and fishing available nearby. Open March 1-October 31. **32T. MC.** ☛ ▣ ▣

Bexhill-on-Sea

(1m). **Cobbs Hill Farm Caravan & Camping Park, Watermill Lane, Bexhill-on-Sea, East Sussex TN39 5JA.** *01424 213460/221358.* cobbshillfarmuk@hotmail.com. www.cobbshillfarm.co.uk. Owner: Mr B & L Claxton. From Bexhill take A269, turn right into Watermill Lane. Site is after 1m on left-hand side and is SP. Quiet, farm site with level, sheltered pitches and within easy reach of Battle, Hastings and Eastbourne. Rally field and tent field available. Open April-October. ✩✩✩✩ **BH&HPA. NCC. 45T. 45MC. 13S. 2H.** 🌡 🐕 🏪 🛍

(4m). **Kloofs Caravan Park, Sandhurst Lane, Whydown, Bexhill-on-Sea, East Sussex TN39 4RG.** *01424 842839.* camping@kloofs.com. www.kloofs.com. Owner: Helen & Terry Griggs. From Bexhill take A259 west to Little Common roundabout, turn right into Peartree Lane, 1m turn left to Whydown, signs to site. Quiet, country site about 2m from sea. Modern facilities, play park. ✩✩✩✩✩ **BH&HPA. 50T. MC. 75S.** ✿ 🐕 🏪 ♿ 🛍

Bodiam

(2m). **Bodiam Caravan & Camping, Park Farm, Bodiam, East Sussex TN32 5XA.** *01580 830514.* Owner: Mr Richard Bailey. 3m S of Hawkhurst on right-hand side off the B2244, SP. 10m N of Hastings. Beautiful rural site. Covered play area. Free fishing in river Rother. Walk to Bodiam Castle. Camp fires allowed. Open April 1-October 30. **50T. 10MC.** 🐕 🏪

KLOOFS CARAVAN PARK
Bexhill on Sea, East Sussex

Hooray! All Weather, All Year, Fully Serviced, hard standings for RV/Motor Homes. Ultra modern facilities, Private Washing Wells, central heated, Cat 1 Disabled facilities. Kloof's has a quiet, rural and tranquil setting, 2km from sea. Family run, living on site.
Sandhurst Lane, Whydown
Bexhill on Sea, East Sussex TN39 4RG
Tel: 01424 842839 Fax: 01424 845669
E-mail: camping@kloofs.com
www.kloofs.com

Brighton

Sheepcote Valley Caravan Club Site, East Brighton Park, Brighton, East Sussex BN2 5TS. *01273 626546.* www.caravanclub.co.uk. Owner: The Caravan Club. East Grinstead House, East Grinstead, West Sussex RH19 1UA. See website for standard directions to site. Well located 2m E of Brighton, snuggled into a fold in the South Downs, a short distance inland from the marina and adjacent to extensive recreation grounds. Toilet blocks, laundry facilities and baby/toddler washroom. Motorhome service point, LP gas supplies and veg prep area. Golf, water sports and NCN cycle route nearby. Playground. Suitable site for families. Non-members and tent campers welcome. ✩✩✩✩✩ **NCC. 170T. MC.** ✿ 🐕 🏪 ♿

Crowborough

(0.5m). **Camping & Caravanning Club Site - Crowborough, Goldsmith Recreation Ground, Crowborough, East Sussex TN6 2TN.** *01892 664827/0870 2433331.* www.campingandcaravanning club.co.uk. Owner: Camping & Caravanning Club. Greenfields House, Westwood Way, Coventry CV4 8JH. Leave M25 at exit 5 take A21 to Tonbridge, then A26 through Tunbridge Wells to the northern outskirts of Crowborough. Turn left off A26 into entrance to Goldsmiths Grand, SP Leisure Centre. At top of road turn right into site lane. Views from the site across the Weald to the North Downs. Indoor swimming pool nearby with concession rates for campers. Peaceful, relaxing atmosphere. Non-members welcome. All types of units accepted. Special deals available for families and backpackers. Open March-December. ✩✩✩✩ **90T. 90MC.** 🐕 🏪 ♿

Crowhurst

(0.5m). **Brakes Coppice Park, Forewood Lane, Crowhurst, East Sussex TN33 9AB.** *01424 830322.* brakesco@btinter net.com. www.brakescoppicepark.co.uk. Owner: Mr P & Mrs J C Dudley. Situated off the A2100. 2m from Battle. A small, quiet, secluded park in a beautiful, sheltered position. Close to the beaches of Bexhill and Hastings. Showers. Washing-up and laundry facilities. Coarse fishing available on site. AA 3 pennants. Open March 1-October 31. **BH&HPA. 30T. MC.** 🐕 🏪 🛍

Eastbourne

(2m). **Martello Beach Caravan Park, Pevensey Bay, Eastbourne, East Sussex BN24 6DH.** *01323 761424.* www.haulfryn.co.uk. Owner: Haulfryn Group. Willows Riverside Park, Maidenhead Road, Windsor, Berks SL4 5TR. On the A259, E of Eastbourne. Private beach. Club. Open March 1-October 31. ✩✩✩✩✩ **BH&HPA. NCC. 22T. MC. 350S.** 🐕 🏪 ♿

Hailsham

(4m). **Old Mill Holiday Park, Chalvington Road, Golden Cross, Hailsham, East Sussex BN27 3SS.** *01825 872532.* lucy@jasminewindmill.com. www.jasminewindmill.com. Owners: James Clow & Lucy Howgego. From London turn right off the A22 just past Golden Cross Inn. 100yd on right on Chalvington road. Golf courses within 3m; Spar shop, cash point, PH and PO 150yd. Converted windmill holiday home also in grounds of park. Open April 1-October 31. **BH&HPA. 8T. MC. 18S.** 🐕 🏪

Hartfield

(2m). St Ives Caravan Park, St Ives Farm, Butcherfield Lane, Hartfield, East Sussex TN7 4JX. *01892 770213.* dchapman 05@aol.com. Owner: D J Chapman. From A264 East Grinstead to Tunbridge Wells road, take B2026 to Hartfield, first on R, Butcherfield Lane third on L. Fishing lake adjacent to site, day tickets. Rural location on edge of Ashdown Forest, adjacent to network of footpaths. Open April 1-October 31. **15T. MC.** ☞

Hassocks

(5m). Sandown Caravan Park, Streat Lane, Streat, Hassocks, East Sussex BN6 8RS. *01273 890035.* Owner: Mr J Johnson & Ms E Olsson. Off B2116, 0.5m W of Plumpton. No tourers. Dogs must be under control. Peaceful, rural site at the foot of the South Downs. 20 pitches for tents. Open April 1-September 30. **MC. 9S. 3H.** ☞

Hastings

(5m). Coghurst Hall Holiday Village, Ivyhouse Lane, Ore, Hastings, East Sussex TN35 4NP. *01424 751185.* info@cinqueportsleisure.com. www.cinqueportsleisure.com. Owners: Cinque Ports Leisure Ltd. Goghurst Hall, Ivyhouse Lane, Ore, Hastings, East Sussex TN35 4NP. 3m NE of Hastings located midway between Ore and Three Oaks. Indoor leisure pool, children's club, cafe/restaurant, shop. Golf, horse riding, fishing, bird-watching, walking trails all available nearby. Open first weekend March-first weekend January. **BH&HPA. NCC. 559S.** ☞ & ⚓

(3m). Combe Haven Holiday Park, Harley Shute Road, St Leonards-on-Sea, Hastings, East Sussex TN38 8BZ. *01424 427891.* oewebmaster@bourne-leisure.co.uk. www.coombe havenholidaypark.co.uk. Owner: Bourne Leisure Ltd. 1 Park Lane, Hemel Hempstead, Hertfordshire HP2 4YL. A21 from London and in Hastings take A259 towards Bexhill. Combe Haven SP between Hastings and Bexhill, on right. Indoor and outdoor fun pool. Sports and leisure facilities. Restaurant. Laundrette. Children's club. Daytime and evening entertainment. Burger King. Roller disco, sports drome, playground, 9- hole pitch-and-putt, bowling green, amusements. Open March-January (owners). ✮✮✮✮✮ **BH&HPA. NCC. 948S. 346H.** ☞ & ⚓ ⊘

(6m). Fairlight Wood Caravan Club Site, Watermill Lane, Pett, Hastings, East Sussex TN35 4HY. *01424 812333.* www.caravanclub.co.uk. Owner: The Caravan Club. East Grinstead House, East Grinstead, West Sussex RH19 1UA. See website for standard directions to site. Caravan Club members only. Small, intimate site in flower-rich woodland. Dog walk. Shop 0.5m. Toilet blocks with privacy cubicles and laundry facilities. Motorhome service point. Suitable for families. Open: March-October. **NCC. 40T. MC.** ☞ ⊠ &

(0.5m). Rocklands Holiday Park, Rocklands Lane, East Hill, Hastings, East Sussex TN35 5DY. *01424 423097.* rock landspark@aol.com. Owner: L, J & S Guilliard. From seafront, Old Town end, proceed up The Bourne. Turn R, opposite Stables Theatre, up Harold Road. After Belmont pub turn R up Gurth Road, L into Barley Lane. R into Rocklands Lane. Drive to end. No subletting. Very quiet, no bar or club. 0.5m from

Hastings old town and seafront on East Hill with spectacular views of sea and Heritage coastline. Set in Hastings Country Park designated Area of Outstanding Natural Beauty. Fishing, PO, doctor 1-2m. Open March 1-December 15. ✮✮✮✮ **BH&HPA. 82S.**

(1m). Shearbarn Holiday Park, Barley Lane, Hastings, East Sussex TN35 5DX. *01424 423583,* www.haulfryn.co.uk. Owners: Haulfryn Group Ltd. The Warren, Abersoch, Pwllheli, Gwynedd LL53 7AA. M25, J5 and follow A21 to Hastings. Follow signs to the seafront and turn L. Follow road round to the Stables Theatre and turn R on to Harold Road. Turn R on to Gurth Road, carry on up the hill on to Barley Lane, the park reception if on the R. Bar and club-house, cafe, games room, laundrette, shop, children's play area, local golf and fishing, within easy reach of London. Open March 1-January 15. ✮✮✮ **BH&HPA. NCC. 150T. MC. 180S. 25H.** ☞ ⊠ & ⚓

(1.5m). Spindlewood Country Park, Bricklands Farm, Rock Lane, Ore, Hastings, East Sussex TN35 4JN. *01424 720825.* sales@spindlewood.co.uk. www.spindlewood. co.uk. Owner: The Fleet Family. M25 J5 towards Hastings on A21. Turn R into Junction Road, then R on to B2093 to Ore. Turn L at traffic light on to A259. Turn L after B&Q store, straight on for 200yd into Rock Lane. Park on L. Fully-licensed clubhouse. Laundry facilities. Lake fishing. Golf course 3m. Open March-December. **BH&HPA. 95S. 2H.** ☞ & ⊘

(2.5m). Stalkhurst Camping & Caravan Park, Ivyhouse Lane, Hastings, East Sussex TN35 4NN. *01424 439015.* stalkhurst park@btinternet.com. Owner: Mr & Mrs D Young. A259 from seafront towards Rye. Turn L on to B2093. After about 0.5m Ivyhouse Lane is on R. From A21 at the boundary take road SP A259 Folkestone. After 2.5m turn L into Ivyhouse Lane. Good access. Gently sloping, well sheltered. Games room. Indoor swimming pool. Golf and fishing nearby. 1m to nearest shops and PO. Open March 1-January 15. ✮✮✮ **BH&HPA. 11T. MC. 22S.** ☞ ⊠ ⚓

Heathfield

(1m). Greenviews Caravan Fields, Broad Oak, Heathfield, East Sussex TN21 8RT. *01435 863531.* Owner: Co-Partnership Caravan Association Ltd. On A265 between Board Oak and Heathfield. Licensed club on site (weekends). Spar shop and post office 0.5m away, P:H and restaurant 500yd. Open April 1-October 31. **BH&HPA. 10T. MC. 51S.** ⊠

(4m). Woodland View Touring Park, Horebeech Lane, Horam, Heathfield, East Sussex TN21 0HR. *01435 813597.* Owner: Mr R Harvey. Just off A267, almost opposite Merrydown Cider Co. 12m Eastbourne, 20m Brighton. Quiet site. Showers. Calor Gas sales. Play area. Golf, riding stables and leisure facilities all within a reasonable distance. Open Easter-October 31. **25T. MC.** ⊠

Horam

(0.25m). Horam Manor Touring Park, Horam, East Sussex TN21 0YD. *01435 813662.* camp@horam-manor.co.uk. www.horam-manor.co.uk. On A267 3m S of Heathfield and 10m N of Eastbourne. Tranquil, rural setting in an Area of Outstanding Natural Beauty. Mother and toddler room. Nature trails, farm museum, craft workshops and fishing on estate. Golf course within 0.5m. Shops, PO, doctor within 0.25m. Open March-October. ✮✮✮✮ **BH&HPA. 90T. 10MC.** ☞ ⊠ ⚓

Lewes

(6m). Bluebell Holiday Park, The Broyle, Shortgate, nr Ringmer, Lewes, East Sussex BN8 6PJ. *01825 840407.* bluebellholidaypark.co.uk. Owner: Mr Gene Robinson. M25 take A22 to Halland, turn right on B2192. 1.25m behind Bluebell PH. From A27 take A26 past Lewes, then right on B2192 thro Ringmer 2.5m. Shopping centre 6m. Golf course 5m. Shops 2.5m, PHs 1m. No children. Rural. Open April 1-October 31. **BH&HPA. 40S. 5H.** ♙

(7m). Broomfield Farm Caravan Club Site, Stalkers Lane, East Hoathly, Lewes, East Sussex BN8 6QS. *01825 872242.* www.caravanclub.co.uk. Owner: The Caravan Club. East Grinstead House, East Grinstead, West Sussex RH19 1UA. See website for standard directions to site. 1.5m from East Hoathly. Caravan Club members only. Peaceful, rural site. Own sanitation required. Dog walk. Motorhome service point. Boules pitch. Golf and fishing available nearby. Open: March-October. **NCC. 78T. MC.** ♙ ⊕

Peacehaven

Rushey Hill Caravan Park, The Highway, Peacehaven, East Sussex BN10 8XH. *01273 582344.* islandmeadowparks@fsmail.net. www.islandmeadow.co.uk. Owner: Pratt Developements Unlimited. Holdens Caravan Park, Bracklesham Lane, Bracklesham, Chichester, West Sussex PO20 8JG. Follow A259 from Brighton to Peacehaven. In Peacehaven do not bear left but follow road running parallel to sea along rough road to park. Magnificent views over South Downs and English Channel. Horse racing, fishing and museums are all within easy reach. Golf, sea fishing, Brighton with all entertainments, Newhaven and Lewes. Telephone for free brochure 01243 670207. Demonstration caravan available for inspection at the park. Open January 15-December 31. **200S.** ♙

Pevensey

Bay View Caravan & Camping Park, Old Martello Road, Pevensey, East Sussex BN24 6DX. *01323 768688.* holidays@bay-view.co.uk. www.bay-view.co.uk. Owner: Michael & Diana Adams. On the A259 Eastbourne to Pevensey Bay road. 1m to Pevensey Bay Village. Award-winning park next to beach. Rose Award. Open April 1-October 6. ✰✰✰✰✰ **BH&HPA. 49T. 49MC. 5H.** ♙ ⊕ 🛒

(0.5m). Camping & Caravanning Club Site - Normans Bay, Norman's Bay, Pevensey, East Sussex BN24 6PR. *01323 761190/0870 243 3331.* www.campingandcaravanningclub.co.uk. Owner: Camping & Caravanning Club. Greenfields House, Westwood Way, Coventry CV4 8JH. Head E on A259 from Eastbourne to Pevensey, site SP. From roundabout at junction of A27/A259 follow A259, SP Eastbourne. In Pevensey Bay village take 1st L, SP Beachlands only. After 1.25m site is on L. Well placed for visiting Eastbourne and adjacent to its own private beach. All units accepted. Non-members welcome. Fishing is available from the beach. 80m of walks on the South Downs way. Special deals available for families and backpackers. Open March-October. ✰✰✰✰ **200T. 200MC.** ♙ ⊕ & 🛒

Cannon Caravan Park, Eastbourne Road, Pevensey, East Sussex BN24 6DT. *01323 764634.* Owner: Mr P & Mrs B Barsley. 0.5m from Pevensey Bay, near Eastbourne on A259 between Eastbourne and Pevensey Bay. Close to sea. River fishing. Country footpath to old Pevensey village with Roman and Norman castle. Open Easter-October 31. **70T. MC.** ♙ ⊕ & 🛒

Castle View Caravan & Camping Site, Eastbourne Road, Pevensey, East Sussex BN24 6DT. *01323 763038.* On A259. Licensed shop. Fast food. Laundry. Beach 10 mins. Eastbourne 3m. Baths and showers. Calor Gas. TV Room. Open March-October. **75T. MC. 62H.** ♙ ⊕ 🛒

Fairfields Farm Caravan & Camping Park, Eastbourne Road, Westham, Pevensey, East Sussex BN24 5NG. *01323 763165.* enquiries@fairfieldsfarm.com. www.fairfieldsfarm.com. Owner: Mrs H Reeves. Situated on B2191 in Westham. 3m from Eastbourne. Touring park on a family-run working farm. Close to Eastbourne and a suitable base for exploring the many attractions of the region. Peaceful location with free fishing. Year-round storage available. Open April 1-October 31. ✰✰✰✰ **60T. MC.** ♙ ⊕ 🛒

(1m). Grey Tower Caravan Site, Grey Tower Road, Pevensey, East Sussex BN24 6DP. *01323 762402.* info@greytowerpark.co.uk. www.greytowerpark.co.uk. Owner: Mr A & Mr M Grant. On A259 Eastbourne to Pevensey. Site 3m from Eastbourne town centre. The site benefits from its own beach, ideal for bathing and windsurfing. Sovereign Harbour 0.5m. Situated in the heart of historic countryside dating back to the Battle of Hastings in 1066. Open April-October. **BH&HPA. 85S.** ♙ ⊕ 🛒

(3m). Normans Bay Caravan Park, The Anchorage, Normans Bay, Pevensey, East Sussex BN24 6PS. *01323 761842/767323.* Owner: Mr R J Smith. S of A259 roundabout at Pevensey, situated in village. Quiet, family-run site with laundry facilities. Private beach, free boat park. Open March 1-October 31. ✰✰✰✰ **BH&HPA. 175S.** ♙ & 🛒

Polegate

Peel House Farm Caravan Park, Sayerlands Lane (B2104), Polegate, East Sussex BN26 6QX. *01323 845629.* peelhocp@tesco.net. Owner: Mr & Mrs Webb. Hailsham to Stonecross 1.5m on B2104. Quiet, country site with views to downs; many places of interest within 20m. Walks. Heated toilet block with showers. Games room with TV, pool table tennis and darts. Fishing, riding nearby. Footpath to Cuckoo Trail. Open April 1-October 31. ✰✰✰✰ **BH&HPA. 20T. MC. 11S. 3H.** ♙ ⊕ 🛒

Please mention Caravan Sites 2006 when replying to advertisers

Robertsbridge

(5m). Lordine Court Caravan Park, Staplecross, Ewhurst, Robertsbridge, East Sussex TN32 5TS. *01580 830209.* enq@lordine-court.co.uk. www.lordine-court.co.uk. Owner: Miss C Horvath. Take the A21 towards Hawkhurst take B2244 to Cripps corner. B2165 to Northiam, site on left-hand side. Facilities include laundry room, showers, two bars. Playground. Amusement room. Swimming pool. Restaurant and takeaway. Payphones. Separate pets enclosure. Fishing lake off site under the park's control. Woodland walks. Situated in the countryside but only 10m N of the coastal resorts. Open March-October. **BH&HPA. NCC. 60T. 60MC. 150S. 10H.** 🛏 🏢 🐾

Rye

(4m). Camber Sands Holiday Park, New Lydd Road, Camber, Rye, East Sussex TN31 7RT. *0871 664 9719.* camber.sands@park-resorts.com. www. park-resorts.com. Owners: Park Resorts Ltd. 3rd floor, Swan Court, Waterhouse Street, Hemel Heapstead HP1 1FN. From M25 take the M20 and come off at J10. Come on to A2070, follow signs to Hastings and Rye, staying on A259, take a left turn before Rye, SP for Camber. The park is located 3m along on this road. Four indoor pools, spa bath, adventure playground, multi-sports court, amusements, laundrette, children's clubs, family evening entertainment. Open April-October. ☆☆☆☆ **BH&HPA. NCC. 45T. MC. 741S. 90H.** 🛏 🟦

(2m). Ferryfields, Station Road, Winchelsea, Rye, East Sussex TN36 4JU. *01797 226344.* Owner: Mrs M P Giddings. Site is located off the A259. Park is screened and flat. All mains services to holiday homes. Fishing river alongside. Open March 1-October 31. **BH&HPA. 68S. 2H.** 🛏

(2m). Frenchmans Beach Holiday Village, Rye Harbour, Rye, East Sussex TN31 7TX. *01797 223011.* info@ cinque portsleisure.com. www.cinqueportsleisure.com. Owner: Cinque Ports Leisure Ltd. Coghurst Hall Holiday Village, Ivyhouse Lane, Ore, Hastings, East Sussex TN35 4NP. 0.25m W of Rye on A259, SP Rye Harbour. Family site. Indoor leisure complex, pool. Jacuzzi, clubhouse, summer paddling pool and cafe. Close to beaches. Open March 4-January 4. **BH&HPA. NCC. 230S. 40H.** 🛏 🐾

(7m). Rother Valley Caravan Park, Station Road, Northiam, Rye, East Sussex TN31 6QT. *01797 252116.* info@rothervalley. com. www.rothervalleycamping.co.uk. Owner: Mr F J Holt. A28 Hastings-Tenterden, 50yd to Kent and East Sussex Steam Railway. Fishing 0.5m. Near garage, shops, PO, doctor. Golf 7m. Open March 1-Oct 31. **BH&HPA. CaSSOA. 50T. 10MC. 12S.** 🟦

(2.5m). Stanhope Caravan Site, Windsor Way, Winchelsea Beach, Rye, East Sussex TN36 4HF. *01797 226526.* Owner: Mr M F & C Simpson. Sunset View, Pett Level Rd, Winchelsea Beach, East Sussex. Open March 1-October 31. **BH&HPA. 20S.** 🛏

(3m). The Cock Horse Inn, Peasmarsh, Rye, East Sussex TN31 6YD. *01797 230281.* Owner: Mr & Mrs Joyce. On A268 London to Rye. Quiet site behind Cock Horse Inn. Shower block. Near Rye, Winchelsea, and Romney Marsh. 10m Camber Sands and Hastings. Darts, pool and boules pitch. Open March 1-October 31. **5T. MC. 20S.** 🛏 🟦

(3.5m). Winchelsea Sands Holiday Park, Pett Level Rd, Winchelsea Beach, Rye, East Sussex TN36 4NB. *01797 226442.* info@cinqueportsleisure.com. www.cinqueports leisure.com. Owner: Cinque Ports Leisure Ltd. Coghurst Hall Holiday Village, Ivyhouse Lane, Ore, Hastings, East Sussex TN35 4NP. A259 Rye to Hastings turn L into sea road. Follow for 1m, R opposite church in Winchelsea Beach. Outdoor pool. Laundrette. Playground. Takeaway. Lounge bar, family entertainment club. Children's club. Open March-January. **BH&HPA. NCC. 300S. 30H.** 🛏 ♿

Please visit the Caravan Club website: www.caravanclub.co.uk

(2.5m). **Windmill Caravan Park, Willow Lane, Winchelsea Beach, Rye, East Sussex TN36 4LN.** *01273 595585.* windmill park1@aol.com. www.ukparks.com. Owner: Mr & Mrs G Trevor. 28 Church Lane, Southwick, West Sussex BN42 4GB. Off A259. Open March-October. **BH&HPA. 45S.** 🛦

Seaford

(1m). **Buckle Caravan & Camping Park, Marine Parade, Seaford, East Sussex BN25 2QR.** *01323 897801.* holiday@ buckle-park.freeserve.co.uk. www.buckle-camping.ukti.co.uk. Owner: Mr & Mrs Perry. A259 between Newhaven and Seaford. Quiet, family-run park adjacent to beach. Cross-Channel ferry 5 mins by car. Seasonal and storage pitches available. Bottled gas. Adult-only field available. AA 3 stars. Open March 1-January 2. **BH&HPA. 150T. 150MC.** 🛦 🕿 ◉ ♿

South Heighton

Three Ponds Holiday Park, South Heighton, East Sussex BN9 0TP. *01273 513530.* info@threepondspark.co.uk. www. threepondspark.co.uk. Owner: Barlow Leisure Management Ltd. Located on A26. 2m N of Newhaven. Quiet, family-run park on the edge of South Downs. Close to Newhaven port. Children's play area and laundry. Three private lakes giving excellent fishing and nature conservation areas. 1m away from shops. Brighton/Eastbourne 12m. Open March 1-October 31. **BH&HPA. 155S.** 🛦 ♿ 🎣

St Leonards-on-Sea

(3m).**Beauport Park Holiday Village, Ridge West, St Leonards-on-Sea, East Sussex TN37 7PP.** *01424 851246.* info@cinqueportsleisure.com. www.cinqueports leisure.com. Owners: Cinque Ports Leisure Ltd. Coghurst Hall Holiday Village, Ivyhouse Lane, Ore, Hastings, East Sussex TN35 4NP. 3.5m S of Battle on A2100. 1m from Hastings. Fishing, golf, horse riding, sailing. Open March-December. **BH&HPA. NCC. 650S.** 🛦 ♿

Uckfield

(4m). **Cider House Farm, Blackboys, Uckfield, East Sussex TN22 5JD.** *01825 890303.* Owner: Mr & Mrs R N Pilgrim. Take Uckfield bypass A22 to Halland roundabout. Turn left to Blackboys and Heathfield B2192. Cider House Farm entrance 2m on right. Set in 75 acres of lovely countryside. Small site run by owners to high standard. Open March 1-December 31. **28T. MC.** 🛦 ◉

(8m). **Heaven Farm, Furners Green, Uckfield, East Sussex TN22 3RG.** *01825 790226.* butlerenterprises@farmline.com. www.heavenfarm.co.uk. Owners: John & Margaret Butler. On A275 1m Sof Danehill. 1m N of Sheffield park, Bluebell Railway. Fishing on site. Shop, PO 1m. Golf courses nearby. Doctor 5m. Hospital 8m. AA 2 pennants. **25T. 25T.** ✿ 🛦 🐕 ♿ 🎣

(4m). **Honeys Green Caravan Park, Easons Green, Framfield, Uckfield, East Sussex TN22 5GJ.** *01732 860205.* honeysgreenpark@tiscali.co.uk. Owner: Mrs S Lavender. At Halland roundabout (A22) turn on to B2192 Heathfield road. Site in 0.25m on L. Modern facilities block. Chemical toilet emptying point. Telephone. Walks. Own coarse fishing. Open Easter or April 1-October 31. ✰✰✰ **BH&HPA. 18T. 4MC. 2S. 6H.** 🛦 ◉

Winchelsea Beach

Rye Bay Caravan Park, Pett Level Road, Winchelsea Beach, East Sussex TN36 4NE. *01797 226340.* Owner: Rye Bay Caravan Park Ltd. Off A259 Hastings to Winchelsea. 3.5m from Rye. Club. Open March 1-October 31 for holiday homes; open May-September for tourers. **36T. MC. 260S.** 🛦

Arundel

(6m). **Camping & Caravanning Club Site - Slindon, Slindon Park, Arundel, Sussex BN18 0RG.** *01243 814387/0870 2433331.* www.campingandcaravanning club.co.uk. Owner: Camping & Caravanning Club. Greenfields House, Westwood Way, Coventry CV4 6JH. From A27 Fontwell to Chichester turn R at SP Brittons Lane and 2nd R to Slindon, site is on this road. Within National Trust property of Slindon Park. Own sanitation essential. Non-members welcome. Caravans, motor caravans and tents accepted. Set in an orchard with 40 pitches. Nearby Goodwood Racecourse. Fishing, swimming and golf at Chichester. Walkers' paradise with footpaths and bridleways. Special deals for families and backpackers. Open March-October. ✰✰ **20T. 40MC.** 🛦 ◉

(4m). **Houghton Bridge Tea Gardens & Caravan Park, Amberley, Arundel, West Sussex BN18 9LP.** *01798 831558.* Owner: Mr B E & H M Mead. On B2139 between Arundel and Storrington alongside the river Arun in the heart of the South Downs. Fishing allowed from park also boat hire and trips. PH and restaurant opposite. 3 mins to mainline station for trains to Victoria. Open April 1-November 1. **BH&HPA. 11S. 9H.**

(0.75m). **Maynards Caravan and Camping Park, Crossbush, Arundel, West Sussex BN18 9PQ.** *01903 882075.* Owner: Mr R Hewitt. A27 Arundel to Worthing after 0.75m turn L into Out & Out PH and restaurant. Visit Arundel Castle, bird sanctuary and large Sunday market. Also scenic walks on downs at Burpham, Warnicamp and Wepham. **BH&HPA. 70T. MC.** ✿ 🛦 ◉ ♿ 🎣

(2m). **Ship & Anchor Marina, Ford, Arundel, West Sussex BN18 0BJ.** *01243 551262.* ysm36@dial.pipex.com. Owner: Heywood & Bryett Ltd. Take Ford road from Arundel. On left after level-crossing at Ford. Beside river Arun. PH and restaurant. Shaver points. Bottled gas. Showers and bath. Boating. Fishing. Open March 1-October 31. ✰✰✰ **BH&HPA. 160T. MC.** 🛦 ◉ ♿ 🎣

Billingshurst

(1.5m). **Limeburners Camping Ltd, Newbridge, Billingshurst, West Sussex RH14 9JA.** *01403 782311.* chippy. sawyer@virgin.net. Owner: Mr R C Sawyer. 1.5m W of Billingshurst on A272, turn L on B2133, site 300yd on L. Showers. Chemical toilet emptying point. Licensed bar. Toilets. Gas bottle exchanges. Open April-October. **40T. MC.** 🛦 ◉

Bognor Regis

(4m). **Church Farm Holiday Village, Pagham, Bognor Regis, West Sussex PO21 4NR.** *01243 262635.* oewebmaster@ bourne-leisure.co.uk. www.churchfarmholidayvillage.com. Owner: Bourne Leisure Ltd. One Park Lane, Hemel Hempstead, Herts HP2 4YL. Where A27 roundabout crosses A259 on E outskirts of Chichester, take Pagham exit and continue to roundabout (1m). Turn L and follow road for 3-4m to end. Entrance directly in front of you. Indoor and outdoor pool with sun terrace and patio. Sports and leisure activities, children's club. Rose Award. Welcome Host and David Bellamy Gold Conservation Award. Daytime and evening entertainment. Holiday home owners' lounge. Mini market. Bakery, laundrette. 9-hole golf course. Open March-October. ✰✰✰✰ **BH&HPA. NCC. 939S. 30H.** 🛦 ♿ 🎣

(2m). **Copthorne Caravans, Rose Green Road, Bognor Regis, West Sussex PO21 3ER.** *01243 262408.* copthornecara van@aol.com. Owner: Mr Tony & Mrs Lindsay Leney. A29 turn R just before dual carriageway, after 2m and 2 crossroads

Copthorne on R opposite Texaco station. Small, family park, all mains services. Games room. Ideal for many attractions. Shops and laundrette 50yd. Rose Award. Bognor Regis centre 2m, cinemas, shops etc. Chichester 6m, multiplex cinema, bowling. Open April 1-October 31. ☆☆☆☆ **78S. 10H.** ⅍

(1.5m). Riverside Caravan Centre, Shripney Road, Bognor Regis, West Sussex PO22 9NE. *01243 865823.* info@rivcentre.co.uk. www.rivcentre.co.uk. Owner: Riverside Caravan Centre (Bognor) Ltd. On A29 Pulborough to Bognor. No tourers. Club. Indoor swimming pool. Open Easter or April 1-October 31. ☆☆☆☆☆ **BH&HPA. NCC. 521S. 30H.** ⍩ ⅃

(1.25m). Rowan Park Caravan Club Site, Rowan Way, Bognor Regis, West Sussex PO22 9RP. *01243 828515.* www.caravanclub.co.uk. Owner: The Caravan Club. East Grinstead House, East Grinstead, West Sussex RH19 1UA. See website for standard directions to site. Site screened by trees and with views of downs. 1m from beach. Shops 0.5m. Advance booking advised bank holidays, July and August. Non-members and tent campers welcome. Toilet blocks. Privacy cubicles. Laundry facilities. Veg Prep. Motorhome service point. Gas supplies. Playframe. Dog walk, some hard-standings, shop 50yd, fishing, golf, and NCN cycle path within 5m. Water sports nearby. Open: March-October. ☆☆☆☆☆ **NCC. 100T. MC.** ⍩ ⅁ ⅍

(4m). The Lillies Caravan Park, Yapton Road, Barnham, Bognor Regis, West Sussex PO22 0AY. *01243 552081.* thelillies@hotmail.com. www.lilliescaravanpark.co.uk. Owner: Mr & Mrs P Kennett. A29 Bognor Regis to Eastergate then B2233 to park. Or A29 off A27 towards Fontwell then B2233. Showers, shaver point, chemical toilet emptying point and phone. Gas sales. Close to shops and railway station. Laundrette. In 3 acres of countryside, easy reach of Goodwood, car and horse racing, beaches and leisure amenities. Park has a 'no casual visitors' policy to ensure peaceful holiday. ☆☆☆ **24T. 24MC. 8H.** ✿⍩⅁⅍⅃

Chichester

(5m). Bell Caravan Park, Bell Lane, Birdham, Chichester, West Sussex PO20 7HY. *01243 512264.* Owner: Mr & Mrs F A Brown. Cambridge House, Bell Lane, Birdham, Chichester, West Sussex. From Chichester take A286 SP Wittering to Birdham, opposite garage turn L into Bell Lane, park on L. Open March-October. ☆☆ **BH&HPA. 15T. 15MC. 55S.** ⍩⅁

(7m). Black Horse Caravan Site, Mill Lane, Selsey, Chichester, West Sussex. *01243 604352.* Owner: Mrs M A Luck. On B2145. Open March 1-October 31. **16S.** ⍩

(6m). Briar Cottage Caravan Park, Church Road, East Wittering, Chichester, West Sussex PO20 8PU. *01243 673216.* Owner: Mr C J Wren. Off A286 West Wittering to Chichester. Open March 1-October 31. **65S.**

(4m). Ellscott Park, Sidlesham Lane, Birdham, Chichester, West Sussex PO20 7QL. *01243 512003.* camping@ellscottpark.co.uk. www.ellscottpark.co.uk. Owner: M S Parks. From Chichester A286 to Bracklesham and Wittering, turn L just past Tamplins on R, SP to Butterfly Gardens. Quiet country site. Own produce. Cafe and bus service nearby. Booking essential July and August. AA 3 pennants. Open March 1-October 31. **50T. MC.** ⍩⅁⅍⍿

(5m). Hambrook Holiday Park, Hambrook, Broad Road, Chichester, West Sussex PO18 8RF. *01243 572658.* Owner: Mr & Mrs Sprackling & Mr Dunbar. 1.5m N of A259 at Nutbourne. Local shop and PO 500yd. Open March 1-October 31. **26T. MC. 53S. 2H.** ⍩⅁

(7m). Holdens Caravan Park, Bracklesham Lane, Bracklesham Bay, Chichester, West Sussex PO20 8JG. *01243 670207.* island meadowparks@fsmail.net. www.islandmeadow.co.uk. Owner: Pratt Development Unlimited. Follow signs to Chichester bypass on A27 at Stockbridge roundabout follow A286 to Birdham. At Birdham bear L on B2198 entrance on L, 1m before sea. Park close to Bracklesham Bay with own private club. Phone for free brochure 01243 670207. Golf, horse racing (Goodwood/Fontwell), swimming, walking, horse riding, restaurants, cinemas nearby. Roman palace. Arundel Castle, Portsmouth. Open January 15-December 31. **525S. 5H.** ⍩⅃

(7m). Itchenor Caravan Park, Shipton Green Lane, Itchenor, Chichester, West Sussex PO20 7BZ. *01243 514433.* green wood.parks@virgin.net. www.greenwoodparks.com. Owner: Pratt family. On A286 to Birdham, at Birdham bear R on B2179, next turning on R 400yd. Park entrance on R. Secluded park, with gardens, overlooking farmland and close to Chichester Harbour. Bottled gas. Good shops, doctor and great beach within 2m. Golf course 5m. For free brochure telephone 01243 514433. Open March 1-October 31. **180S. 1H.** ⍩

(3m). Lakeside Holiday Village, Vinnetrow Road, Chichester, West Sussex PO20 1QH. *01243 787715.* info@cinqueportsleisure.com. www.cinqueports.leisure.com. Owner: Cinque Ports Leisure Ltd. Coghurst Hall Holiday Village, Ivyhouse Lane, Ore, Hastings, East Sussex TN35 4NP. Take A27 to Chichester until Bognor road roundabout take Pagham exit, which leads to Lakeside. Set in 220 acres of scenic parkland and a nature reserve with over 150 acres of water covering 12 lakes. **BH&HPA. NCC. 190T. 24MC. 375S.** ✿⍩⅁⅍⅃⍿

(5m). Littlecroft Caravan Park, Somerley Lane, Earnley, Chichester, West Sussex PO20 7HY. *01243 512264.* Owner: Mr F A Brown. Cambridge House, Bell Lane, Birdham, Nr Chichester West Sussex PO20 7HY. Off A286. Small dogs only. Open March 1-October 31. **BH&HPA. 27S.** ⍩

(7m). Red House Farm, Bookers Lane, Earnley, Chichester, West Sussex PO20 7JG. *01243 512959.* clayredhouse@hotmail.com. Owner: Clay & Son. Take road to Witterings from Chichester, 5m fork left at Total garage, 0.5m at sharp bend turn L into Bookers Lane, site 500yd on left. Flat, level. Site 1m from sea and village, car recommended. Suitable for for marina, 8m to Goodwood. Booking advised at peak periods. No single-sex groups. Open Easter-October. **50T. 25MC.** ⍩⅁⍿

(7m). The Nook Caravan Park, Warners Lane, Selsey, Chichester, West Sussex PO20 9EL. *01243 602683.* Owner: Mrs Edgerton & Mr & Mrs Norwood. On B2145 to Selsey turn right at School Lane, right at Padock Lane, left at Warners Lane, site is 200yd on right. Fishing, golf course, swimming pool nearby. 0.5m to high street, PO, medical centre, churches. Open March 1-October 31. **BH&HPA. 40S.** ⍩

(8m). Walnut Tree Caravan Park, West Wittering, Chichester, West Sussex PO20 8NB. *01243 513084.* islandmeadow parks@fsmail.net. www.islandmeadw.co.uk. Owner: Mr P L Pratt. Island Meadow Parks, Holdens Caravan Park, Bracklesham Lane, Bracklesham, Chichester, W Sussex PO20 8JG. Follow signs to Chichester on A27 at Stockbridge r'about A286 to Birdham. Then R, follow signs to West Wittering. Park entrance on R before West Wittering. Close to beach at West Wittering and overlooking Chichester Harbour. Calor Gas. Phone 01243 670207 for free brochure. Demonstration caravans. Golf, horse racing (Goodwood/Fontwell). Roman palace at Fishbourne, Chichester shops. Cathedral, theatre, golf driving range at Hunstow. Open January 15 - December 31. **184S. 1H.** ⍩

(8m). Wandleys Caravan Park, Wandleys Lane, Eastergate, Chichester, West Sussex PO20 6SE. *01243 543235/543384.* Owner: Mrs A Gent. A27 to Fontwell Park then A29 towards Bognor 500yd. Small, quiet, country park. Shop is 0.75m away. Full services to all caravans. Open March 1-October 31. **BH&HPA. 35S. 2H.** 🐕

(6m). Wicks Farm Holiday Park, Redlands Lane, West Wittering, Chichester, West Sussex PO20 8QD. *01243 513116.* www.wicksfarm.co.uk. Owner: Mr R C Shrubb. Off A27 at Chichester, A286/B2179 from Chichester for 6m towards West Wittering, turn R into Redlands Lane. 1m before West Wittering beach. Close to golf, sea and Harbour. Children's play areas. Tennis court. David Bellamy Gold Conservation Award. Open March-October. ✰✰✰✰✰ **BH&HPA. 40MC. 73S.** 🐕 🛢

(3m). Willows Caravan Park, Lidsey Road, Woodgate, Chichester, West Sussex PO20 6SU. *01243 670207.* island meadowparks@fsmail.net. www.islandmeadow.co.uk. Owner: P L Pratt. Island Meadow Parks, Holdens Caravan Park, Bracklesham Lane, Bracklesham, Chichester, W Sussex PO20 8JG. Follow signs to Bognor on A29. Follow signs to Westler Gate, over level crossing. Park entrance on last side of road. Quiet holiday park. Attractive beaches and sea fishing. Golf at Bognor, Goodwood, Hunston and Littlehampton. Horse racing at Fontwell and Goodwood. Chichester, an ancient cathedral town, with good shopping facilities and cinemas. Roman Palace at Fishbourne nearby. Country retreat close to the coast. Open March 1-December 31. **BH&HPA. 187S.** 🐕

Crawley

(2m). Amberley Fields Caravan Club Site, Charlwood Road, Lowfield Heath, Crawley, West Sussex RH11 0QA. *01293 524834.* www.caravanclub.co.uk. Owner: The Caravan Club. East Grinstead House, East Grinstead, West Sussex RH19 1UA. See website for standard directions to site. Caravan Club members only. Suitable for plane spotters. Caravan storage provided. Toilet blocks. Privacy cubicles. Laundry facilities. Motorhome service point. Gas. Dog walk. Local attractions include Thorpe Park. **NCC. 25T. MC.** ✿ 🐕 🛢 ♿

Haywards Heath

(4m). Brighton Sun Club (Naturist Club), Hamshaw, Sloop Lane, Scayneshill, Haywards Heath, West Sussex RH17 7NP. *01444 831675.* www.endornat.demon.co.uk/bsc. Owner: Mr H Bentley. Directions given on receipt of reservation. Golf course, shops, PO, doctor all nearby. Fishing at Hayward Heath 4m away. **2T. 2MC. 6S. 2H.** ✿ 🖭 ♿

Henfield

(2.5m). Downsview Caravan Park, Bramlands Lane, Woodmancote, Henfield, West Sussex BN5 9TG. *01273 492801.* phr.peter@lineone.net. Owner: Mr & Mrs P Harries-Rees. Signed on the A281 in the village of Woodmancote, 2.5m E of Henfield, 9m NW of Brighton Seafront. Small, secluded site in peaceful countryside, close to the South Downs yet within 9m of Brighton. Good walking and cycling routes. Hard-standing pitches, some waste hook-ups. No facilities for children. Doctor 3m. PH 1m, golf 1.5m, shops 2.5m, horse riding 3m, fishing 5m. Open April 1-October 31. ✰✰✰✰ **BH&HPA. 12T. 12MC. 27S.** 🐕 🖭 🛢

(2m). Farmhouse Caravan & Camping, Tottington Drive, Small Dole, Henfield, West Sussex BN5 9XZ. *01273 493157.* Owner: Mrs R Griffiths. Turn off the A2037 in Small Dole. Site is SP in village. Small, quiet, farm site near South Downs and 10m from Brighton. Panoramic views and well away from the main roads. Suitable for families and walkers. Shop and PH nearby. Open March-November. **30T. MC.** 🐕 🖭

(7m). The Royal Oak Caravan Park, Wineham, Henfield, West Sussex BN5 9AY. *01444 881252.* Owner: Mr T D Peacock. Open March 1-October 31. **80S.**

Horsham

(5m). Brooks Green Park, Emms Lane, Brooks Green, Horsham, West Sussex RH13 8QR. *01403 741478.* Owner: Mrs N Doe. On Barns Green to Coolham Road. Worthing 17m Arundel 12m. Bus stops outside gate. Walking distance to PO, shops, PH, club, fishing. Open March-October. **BH&HPA. 30S.**

(10m). Honeybridge Park, Honeybridge Lane, Dial Post, Horsham, West Sussex RH13 8NX. *01403 710923.* enquiries@honeybridgepark.co.uk. www.honeybridgepark.co.uk. Owner: Jeff & Val Burrows. 10m S of Horsham on A24. Turn at the 'Old Barn Nurseries'. Park 300yd on R. Spacious park set on the outskirts of woodlands and beautiful countryside. On the edge of the South Downs and within an Area of Outstanding Natural Beauty. Suitable touring base convenient to Brighton, Chichester and ports. 1hr from theme parks and London by train. Hard-standings and grass pitches, heated amenity blocks, facilities for disabled visitors, licensed shop, takeaway. David Bellamy Gold Conservation Award. ✰✰✰✰ **BH&HPA. NCC. 200T. 40MC.** ✿ 🐕 🖭 ♿ 🛢

(4.5m). Slinfold Caravan Club Site, Spring Lane, Slinfold, Horsham, West Sussex RH13 0RT. *01403 790269.* www.caravanclub.co.uk. Owner: The Caravan Club. East Grinstead House, East Grinstead, West Sussex RH19 1UA. See website for standard directions to site. Caravan Club members only. Imaginatively landscaped site with silver birch, rowan and flowering cherry at the end of a country lane, close to pretty village. No sanitation. Dog walk. Shop 0.5m. Hard-standings. Steel awning pegs advised. MV Service point. Calor Gas and Campingaz. Open March-September. **40T. MC. ⭐ 🖭**

Littlehampton

(1.5m). Brookside, Lyminster, Littlehampton, West Sussex BN17 7QE. *01903 713292.* mark@brooksideuk.com. www. brooksideuk.com. Owner: Brookside Holiday Camp Ltd. On A284 between Littlehampton and Arundel. Swings, play area, sand pit, rocking horse and springers for children. Small games room with table tennis, bar football and pool table. Shops 0.5m. Open March 1-January 6 for owner-occupiers; open April 1-October 31 for hire caravans. ✰✰✰ **BH&HPA. 120S. 10H.**

(1.5m). Daisyfields Touring Park, Cornfield Close, Worthing Road, Littlehampton, West Sussex BN17 6LD. *01903 714240.* daisyfields@f25.com. www.camping&caravanning. co.uk. Owner: L S Rutherford. On A259 Worthing to Bognor Regis. Showers and hair-dryers. Gas. Ball game area and badminton courts. Nature areas. Level, well-drained site. Fishing, golf, horse riding, boating nearby. **80T. 40MC. ✿ ⭐ 🖭 🛒**

(3m). Roundstone House Caravan Park, Old Worthing Road, Angmering, Littlehampton, West Sussex BN16 1DH. *01903 784444.* Owner: Mrs D A Newman. Off A259 Worthing to Littlehampton. Fishing and golf nearby. PO, doctors, shop and Sainsbury's about 0.5m. Beach, sea about 0.75m. South Downs narby. Open March 1-January 3. **20S. ⭐**

(1m). White Rose Touring Park, Mill Lane, Wick, Littlehampton, West Sussex BN17 7PH. *01903 716176.* snowdondavid@hotmail.com. www.whiterosetouringpark.co.uk. Owner: Mr & Mrs D Snowdon. Between Arundel and Littlehampton on A284. L after Six Bells PH. Quiet, family site close to sandy beaches and South Downs. Hedged and open pitches, heated shower block, play area, dog area. Concrete roads. Shops, PO 0.5m. Fishing and golf nearby. Open March 15-December 15. ✰✰✰ **BH&HPA. 135T. MC. 13S. ⭐ 🖭 ♿ 🛒**

Midhurst

(0.25m). Holmbush Caravan Park, The Fairway, Midhurst, West Sussex GU29 9JD. *07836 776704.* greenwood parks@btconnect.com. www.greenwoodparks.com. Owner: Pratt family. Green Wood Parks, Itchenor Caravan Park, Shipton Green Lane, Itchenor, Chichester, W. Sussex PO20 7BZ. A3 to Haslemere, R at Haslemere on A286 to Midhurst. Through town, around circulatory road to New Road, R into Bourne Way, L at T-junction into Fairway. Entrance on R. Fishing lake. Shopping centre 0.5m, golf 3m. Phone for brochure 01243 514433. Open March 1-October 31 and winter weekends. **120S. ⭐**

Petworth

(2m). Camping & Caravanning Club Site - Graffham, Great Bury, Graffham, Petworth, West Sussex GU28 0QJ. *01798 867476/0870 243 3331.* www.camping andcaravanningclub.co.uk. Owner: Camping & Caravanning Club. Greenfields House, Westwood Way, Coventry CV4 8JH. Off the A285. Left turn at sign for Selham Graffham. After 1m turn left, SP for Graffham. 400yd, site entrance on left-hand side, just past house. Set in 20 acres with secluded pitches dispersed in trees and rhododendrons. In heart of South Downs. Non-members welcome. Caravans, motor caravans and tents accepted. Special deals available for families and backpackers. Open March-October. ✰✰✰✰ **90T. 90MC. ⭐ 🖭 ♿**

Selsey

(1m). Warner Farm Touring Park, Warner Lane, Selsey, West Sussex PO20 9EL. *01243 604499.* touring @bunnleisure.co.uk. www.bunnleisure.co.uk. Owner: White Horse Caravan Co Ltd. Paddock Lane, Selsey, West Sussex PO20 9EJ. From the A27 to Chichester, then take the B2145 to Selsey, site is SP from Chichester. Use of three clubhouses, heated swimming pools included with your booking when staying on the touring park. Open March-October. ✰✰✰✰✰ **NCC. 200T. MC. 400S. 150H. ⭐ 🖭 ♿ 🛒**

Steyning

(2m). South Down Caravan Park, Henfield Road, Small Dole, Henfield, Steyning, West Sussex BN5 9XH. *01903 814323.* Owner: Edburton Contractors Ltd. Truleigh Manor Farm, Edburton, Henfield, West Sussex. 3m S of Henfield on A2037, 4m N of Shoreham-by-Sea adjacent to Golding Barn garage and shop. Views of the South Downs. Open April 1-October 31. ✰✰✰✰ **NCC. 8T. 38S. ⭐ 🖭 🛒**

Washington

Washington Caravan & Camping Park, London Road, Washington, West Sussex RH20 4AT. *01903 892869.* washcamp@amserve.com. www.washcamp.com. Owner: Mr M F Edlin. N of Washington on the A283, E of roundabout with A24, SP. 60 tent pitches also available. Halfway stop on South Downs Way below Chanctonbury Ring. Walking, cycling. Close to many places of interest. ✰✰✰✰ **21T. MC. ✿ ⭐ 🖭 ♿ 🛒**

West Wittering

Nunnington Camping Site, Rookwood Road, West Wittering, West Sussex PO20 8LZ. *01243 514013.* nunning tonfarm@hotmail.com. www.camping-in-sussex.com. Owner: Mr & Mrs G Jacobs. Travelling from Chichester A286 on to the B2179. A flat site situated 1m from the sea and 1.5m from

Itchenor for sailing. Shop in village 300yd. Friendly, family site. Small animal park free for our customers. Open Easter-second week October. **125T. MC.** 🐕 🖱 🚐

Wisborough Green

(1m). Bat & Ball, New Pound, Wisborough Green, West Sussex RH14 0EH. *01403 700313.* Owner: Mr K W Turrill. Off the A272 on to the B2133. Calor Gas. **20T. MC.** ✿ 🐕

Worthing

(3.5m). Brook Lane Caravan Park, Brook Lane, Ferring-by-Sea, Worthing, West Sussex BN12 5JD. *01903 242802.* www.ukpark.co.uk/brooklane. Owner: Mr & Mrs Kirby. Off the A259 Littlehampton to Worthing road, on entering Ferring village follow signs to South Ferring, Brook Lane is on the right-hand side opposite the church. Telephone, laundry, gas sales. No awnings or tents. 0.5m to beach and shops. Fishing, golf course nearby. Open March 1-October 31. **BH&HPA. NCC. 5T. 76S.** 🐕 🖱

(2.5m). Northbrook Farm Caravan Club Site, Titnore Way, Worthing, West Sussex BN13 3RT. *01903 502962.* www.caravanclub.co.uk. Owner: The Caravan Club. East Grinstead House, East Grinstead, West Sussex RH19 1UA. See website for standard directions to site. Grassy site set in open countryside with good trees and only 2m from the coast. Non-members are welcome. Storage pitches and hardstandings available. Shops 0.25m away. Toilet blocks. Privacy cubicles. Laundry facilities. Veg preparation area. Motorhome service point. Calor Gas and Campingaz. Playground. Dog walk. Water sports and golf nearby. Suitable site for families. Peaceful off peak. In a good area for walking. Open March-October. ✩✩✩✩ **NCC. 132T. MC.** 🐕 🖱 🖱

(4m). Onslow Caravan Park, Onslow Drive, Ferring by Sea, Worthing, West Sussex BN12 5RX. *01903 243170.* islandmeadowparks@fsmail.net. www.islandmeadow.co.uk. Owner: Pratt Developments Unlimited. Holdens Caravan Park, Bracklesham Lane, Bracklesham, Chichester, West Sussex PO20 8JG. Follow A27, signposted for Ferring, turn into Onslow Drive, drive along to park entrance. Fishing, golf, horse racing, bowls, walking all nearby. Theatres, cinemas, shops, doctor, all within easy reach. Quiet park. Demonstration caravans available for inspection at the park. Open March 1-October 31. **4T. 133S. 1H.** 🐕 🖱

BERKSHIRE

Hurley

Hurleyford Farm Holiday Home Park, Park Office, Mill Lane, Hurley, Berkshire SL6 5ND. *01628 829009.* hurleyfordfarm@btclick.com. www.ukparks.com/hurleyford. From M4, J8/9 take A404 N then A4130 towards Henley on Thames. 1.5m R into Hurley High Street. Right fork by village green into Mill Lane. From M40 J5 A404 S, 3rd exit A4130 towards Henley-on-Thames, then as above. 4m Maidenhead. No permanent children (children may visit occasionally). South bank of R. Thames. Fishing on park. David Bellamy Gold Conservation Award. Mains facilities. Private gardens, working farm. Shop 200yd, PO, PHs and restaurants in village. 0.5m of river frontage. Open March 1-January 31; 8-month licence also available. ✩✩✩ **BH&HPA. 109S.** 🐕 🖱

Maidenhead

Hurley Riverside Park, Park Office, Hurley, Maidenhead, Berkshire SL6 5NE. *01628 823501/824493.* info@hurleyriversidepark.co.uk. www.hurleyriversidepark.co.uk. Owner: Hurley Riverside Park Ltd. A4130 midway between Henley-on-Thames and Maidenhead. Entrance via Shepherds Lane. 1m W of Hurley. Follow signs. 3m from Marlow. Family-run park on bank of Thames. Slipway. Fishing in season. Holiday homes with mains facilities. Gardens. No sub-letting. Laundrette. Shopping, cinema 4m. Golf 3m. Open March 1-October 31. ✩✩✩✩ **BH&HPA. 138T. 30MC. 300S. 10H.** 🐕 🖱 🖱 🚐

Newbury

(2m). Oakley Farm Caravan Park, Wash Water, Newbury, Berkshire RG20 0LP. *01635 36581.* info@oakleyfarm.co.uk. www.oakleyfarm.co.uk. Owner: Mr W Hall. S of Newbury, off A343. From A34 Newbury bypass, take exit Highclere/Wash Common. Left towards Newbury on A343. After 400yd R into Penwood Road. Not suitable for caravans over 22ft long or motor caravans over 24ft. Open March 1-October 31. **30T. MC.** 🐕 🖱

Reading

(2m). Loddon Court Farm, Beech Hill Road, Spencers Wood, Reading, Berkshire RG7 1HT. *01189 883153.* Owner: Executor of D M Morgan. c/o Wellers, Moorfield Road, Slynfield Green, Guildford GU1 1SG. SP J11, M4. Take A33 Basingstoke road south via Spencers Wood. Dogs with tourers only. **30T.** ✿ 🐕

(3m). Sunnylands, Rose Lawn, Burghfield, Reading, Berkshire RG3 3RU. Owner: Bradfield Property Holdings Ltd. Rose Lawn Hotel, Burghfield, Reading, Berkshire RG3 3RU. Off at J12 of the M4. Take the A4 towards Reading and turn right at traffic lights to Burghfield, 4m off the M4. Quiet site located in a country situation. Convenient for Oxford, Windsor and Thames Valley area. No children. **10T. 10MC.** ✿ ⊟

(6m). Wellington Country Park, Riseley, Reading, Berkshire RG7 1BU. *01189 326444*. info@wellington-country-park.co.uk. www.wellington-country-park.co.uk. Off A33 between Reading and Basingstoke, 4m S of the M4, J11. Site set in woodland glades located within country park. Park attractions include animal farm, miniature railway, crazy golf, boating, sandpit and three brand new play areas. Cafe and gift/toy shop. Most amenities within 3m. Open March 13-November 4. ✩✩✩✩ **BH&HPA. 57T. 57MC.** ⊁ ⊟ ⚏

BUCKINGHAMSHIRE

Beaconsfield

(3m). Highclere Farm Country Touring Park, Newbarn Lane, Seer Green, Beaconsfield, Buckinghamshire HP9 2QZ. *01494 874505*. highclerepark@aol.com. www.high clerepark.co.uk. Owner: M F Penfold Ltd. off the A355 Beaconsfield to Amersham road, turn right to Seer Green follow tourist signs. Situated 20m from London. Local rail service to Marylebone 35mins; rail station 1m. Windsor 10m. Peaceful site, suitable base for touring Buckinghamshire. Showers. Laundry. Open March-January. ✩✩✩✩ **BH&HPA. 45T. 45MC.** ⊁ ⊟ ⚬ ⚏

Marlow

(2m). Harleyford Estate, Henley Road, Marlow, Buckinghamshire SL7 2DX. *01628 471361*. info@harley ford.co.uk. www.harleyford.co.uk. Owner: The Harleyford Estate. Situated on the A4155, Henley to Marlow road. Holiday home and lodge park on private historic estate by the Thames. Golf course on site. Open March-November. **120S.** ⊁ ⚬ ⚏

Milton Keynes

Cosgrove Leisure Park, CosgroveMilton Keynes, Buckinghamshire MK19 7JP. *01908 563360*. enquiries@cos grovepark.co.uk. www.cosgrovepark.co.uk. Owner: Whilton Marina Ltd. Whilton Locks, Nr Daventry, Northants NN11 5NH. 2.5m from Stony Stratford. Swimming pool, grocery shop, fishing, tackle and bait, water-skiing, children's play area, mini golf, tennis, amusement park, cafe, takeaway food, fishing. Golf course 4m, central Milton Keynes shopping centre 7m. Open April 1-October 31. **391S.** ⊁ ⚬ ⚏

Newport Pagnell

(0.5m). Lovat Meadow Caravan Park, London Road, Newport Pagnell, Buckinghamshire MK16 9BQ. *01908 610858*. Owner: Newport Pagnell Town Council. Off the M1 J4 (1.5m) take the A509-B526 Newport Pagnell bypass for 0.25m. Secluded riverside site close to Milton Keynes, Silverstone, Woburn Abbey and Safari Park. Heated swimming pool adjacent. Limited facilities. Resident warden. Open mid March-January 7. **40T. MC.** ⊁ ⊟

Olney

(0.5m). Emberton Country Park, Emberton, Olney, Buckinghamshire MK46 5DB. *01234 711575*. emberton park@milton-keynes.gov.uk. www.mkweb.co.uk/emberton park. Owner: Milton Keynes Council. On the A509 Newport Pagnell to Olney road. 200 acres of beautiful parkland. 5 all-year fishing lakes and river Ouse (closed season on river). Visitors' information centre. Rallies welcome, special rates. Open April 1-October 31; open all year for day visitors. ✩✩✩ **130T. MC.** ⊁ ⊟ ⚬ ⚏

Taplow

Amerden Caravan and Camp Site, Old Marsh Lane, Taplow, Buckinghamshire SL6 0EE. *01628 627461*. Owner: Mrs B Hakesley. Leave M4 J7 (Slough West) turn L along A4 towards Maidenhead, 3rd turn L Marsh Lane,1st turn R Old Marsh Lane. Small riverside site. Open April 1-October 31. ✩✩✩✩ **30T. 10MC. 2H.** ⊁ ⊟ ⚬

Uxbridge

Wyatts Covert Caravan Club Site, Tilehouse Lane, Denham, Uxbridge, Buckinghamshire UB9 5DH. *01895 832729*. www.caravanclub.co.uk. Owner: The Caravan Club. East Grinstead House, East Grinstead, West Sussex RH19 1UA. See website for standard directions to site. Situated 1m from Denham. Caravan Club members only. Conveniently placed not far from the M25 and M40, screened by good trees. Toilet blocks, laundry facilities and motorhome service point. Fishing, golf and NCN cycle route nearby. **NCC. 50T. MC.** ✿ ⊁ ⊟ ⚬

EAST DORSET

Bere Regis

(0.75m). **Rowlands Wait Touring Park, Rye Hill, Bere Regis, Dorset BH20 7LP.** *01929 472727.* info@rowlands wait.co.uk. www.rowlandswait.co.uk. Owner: Mr Cargill. From Bere Regis take Wool-Bovington road. Site 0.75m up Rye Hill on right. Private, quiet in Area of Outstanding Natural Beauty. Suitable for nature lovers, birdwatchers and quiet family holidays. Modern facilities. AA Award. David Bellamy Gold Conservation Award. Telephone for free brochure. Open March-October and winter by arrangement. ✰✰✰ **BH&HPA. 71T. MC.** 🛉 ⊟ ⅃

Blandford Forum

(5m). **Lady Bailey Residential Park, Winterborne Whitechurch, Blandford Forum, Dorset DT11 0HS.** *01458 272266.* Owner: J & K Penfold. On A354 Dorchester to Blandford. In heart of countryside. Suitable touring centre for exploring. 6 beaches nearby. Award-winning local PH/restaurant. Children welcome. Open March 16-October 31. **50T. 5MC. 40S.** 🛉 ⊟ ⅃

(2m). **The Inside Park, Blandford Forum, Dorset DT11 9AD.** *01258 453719.* Owner: Mr & Mrs J Cooper. members.aol. com/inspark/inspark. inspark@aol.com. 2m SW of Blandford on Winterborne Stickland road, SP from bypass. Parkland site. Play area. AA 3 pennants. RAC appointed. Open April 1-October 31. ✰✰✰✰ **BH&HPA. 125T. MC.** 🛉 ⊟ ﹠ ⅃

Bournemouth

Mount Pleasant Touring Park, Matchams Lane, Hurn, Bournemouth, Dorset BH23 6AW. *01202 475474.* enq@ mount-pleasant-cc.co.uk. www.mount-pleasant-cc.co.uk. Owner: Peter Dunn. A338 from Bournemouth or Ringwood, turn off at Christchurch-Hurn exit and turn R towards Hurn, at 1st roundabout take 2nd exit on immediate L into Matchams Lane, park 1m on right. Manager: Peter Dunn. AA 4 pennants. Fishing, golf, swimming. Pony trekking, stock car racing, dry ski slope, New Forest nearby, closest park to Bournemouth. PO 1m. Playground. Shop, cafe. Open March 1-October 31; open winter by arrangement. ✰✰✰✰✰ **BH&HPA. 175T. 50MC.** 🛉 ⊟ ﹠ ⅃

Christchurch

(0.5m). **Beaulieu Gardens Holiday Park, Beaulieu Avenue, Christchurch, Dorset BH23 2EB.** *01202 486215.* On A35 Bournemouth to Christchurch. Rose Award park in peaceful surroundings, close to Bournemouth. Open March 1-October 31. ✰✰✰✰✰ **BH&HPA. 60H.**

(3.5m). **Cobbs Holiday Park, 32 Gordon Road, Highcliffe-on-Sea, Christchurch, Dorset BH23 5HN.** *01425 273301/275313.* Owner: Mr J Cobb. Leave A35 Lyndhurst to Christchurch at Somerford roundabout, take A337 to Highcliffe. Look for brown tourist sign to Cobb's Holiday Park, turn left into Gordon road at traffic lights in the village centre. Pleasant, family-run park with enviable loaction near New Forest and beaches. Laundrette, play area, licensed club with free entertainment. Open Easter-October. ✰✰✰✰ **BH&HPA. 45S. 45H.** 🛉 ﹠ ⅃ ⌀

(4m.). **Harrow Wood Farm Caravan Park, Poplar Lane, Bransgore, Christchurch, Dorset BH23 8JE.** *01425 672487.* harrowwood@caravan-sites.co.uk. www.caravan-sites.co.uk. Owner: Mr R L & M L Frampton. A35, 10m W of Lyndhurst. Turn right at Cat & Fiddle. SP from Bransgore. Coarse fishing on site. Open March 1-January 6. ✰✰✰ **BH&HPA. 60T. MC.** ⊟

(6m). **Heathfield Caravan and Camping Park, Heathfield, Bransgore, Christchurch, Dorset BH23 8LA.** *01425 672397.* office@heathfieldcaravanpark.co.uk. Owner: Liz & Jo House. Heathfield Farm, Bransgore, Dorset BH23 8LA. Off A35 from Lyndhurst first right, SP Bransgore, Sopley, Godswincroft, right again. Site on left before cattle grid. From Christchurch first left after East Close Hotel, first right on left before cattle grid.100 extra tourers allowed at peak periods. Children's play area. Golf, fishing, horse riding nearby. Pets welcome on leads. Open March-October. **200T. MC.** 🛉 ⊟ ﹠ ⅃

(2m). **Hoburne Park, Hoburne Lane, Christchurch, Dorset BH23 4HT.** *01425 273379.* www.hoburne.com. Owner: Hoburne Ltd. 261 Lymington Road, Highcliffe-on-Sea, Christchurch, Dorset BH2 3 5EE. From A35 L on to A337. 1st exit off next roundabout. Park on R. Licensed club. Seasonal entertainment. Indoor leisure pool. Outdoor pool. Restaurant. Playground. Hard-court tennis. Mini bowling. Snooker. Laundrette. Open March 1-October 31. ✰✰✰✰✰ **BH&HPA. NCC. 229S.** ﹠

(8m). **Holmsley Caravan & Camping Site, (Forestry Commission), Forest Road, Holmsley, Christchurch, Dorset BH23 7EQ.** *01313 146505.* fe.holidays@forestry.gsi.gov.uk. www.forestholidays.co.uk. Owner: Forestry Commission (Forest Holidays). 231 Corstorphine Road, Edinburgh EH12 7AT. Located off A35 Lyndhurst-Christchurch road, 8m SW of Lyndhurst. Showers, laundry and dishwashing facilities. Booking essential. Brochure request line: 0131 334 0066. Open March-October. ✰✰✰ **BH&HPA. 700T. 300MC.** 🛉 ⊟ ﹠ ⅃

Iford Bridge Home Park, Old Bridge Road, Iford, Christchurch, Dorset BH6 5RQ. *01202 482121.* chbarton@ bartonparkhomes.freeserve.co.uk. www.barton-parkhomes. co.uk. Owner: Bartons Park Homes Ltd. Westgate, Morecambe, Lancs LA3 3BA. On A35, Christchurch to Bournemouth. **BH&HPA. 36T. 36MC.** ✿ ⊟ ⅃ ⌀

(3m). **Longfield, Matchams Lane, Hurn, Christchurch, Dorset BH23 6AW.** *01202 485214.* Owner: Mrs G R Day. From A338 follow signs for Bournemouth Airport, at Hurn roundabout turn right and turn left into Matchams Lane, drive 2m, Longfield on left. Showers. Swimming pool. Laundry. Gas. Battery charging points. Electric hook-ups on all pitches. PO 1m, doctors 3m, main town 4m. Golf and fishing nearby. ✰✰ **15T. MC.** ✿ 🛉 ⊟

(1m). **Meadowbank Holidays Park, Stour Way, Christchurch, Dorset BH23 2PQ.** *01202 483597.* enquiries@meadowbank-holidays.co.uk. www.meadowbank-holidays.co.uk. Take Christchurch exit off A338 follow SP. Advance booking necessary in peak season. Adjacent to public golf course and private fishing on river Stour. Swimming pool, beach 2m. Pub, restaurants 1m. Rose Award. Open March 1-October 31. ✰✰✰✰✰ **BH&HPA. 48T. MC. 200S. 75H.** ⊟ ﹠ ⅃ ⌀

Please mention Caravan Sites 2006 when replying to advertisers

(3m). Mount Pleasant Touring Park, Matchams Lane, Hurn, Christchurch, Dorset BH23 6AW. *01202 475474.* enq@mount-pleasant-cc.co.uk. www.mount-pleasant-cc.co.uk. Owner: Peter Dunn. Take A338 from Bournemouth or Ringwood, turn off at Christchurch-Hurn exit and turn R towards Hurn, at first roundabout 2nd exit on immediate L into Matchams Lane, park 1m on right. Manager: Peter Dunn. 4 AA pennants. Fishing, golf, swimming. Pony trekking, stock car racing, dry ski slope, New Forest nearby. Closest park to Bournemouth PO 1m. Playground area. Shop, cafe. Open March 1-October 31; open winter by arrangement. ☆☆☆☆☆ **BH&HPA. 175T. 50MC.** 🏕 🔌 ♿ 🐾

(3m). Sandhills Holiday Village, Avon Beach, Mudeford, Christchurch, Dorset BH23 4AL. *01425 274584.* info@cinqueportsleisure.com. www.cinqueports leisure.com. Owner: Cinque Ports Leisure Group Ltd. Coghurst Hall Holiday Village, Ivyhouse Lane, Ore, Hastings, East Sussex TN35 4NP. Off A337 Christchurch to Lymington road. Playground. Heated outdoor pool. Family club. Takeaway. Bar. Amusements. Laundrette. Free children's club and evening entertainment. Situated on the seafront. Open March 1-October 31 for owner-occupiers; open Easter-October 31 for hire caravans. ☆☆ **BH&HPA. NCC. 131S. 80H.** ♿ 🐾 ✐

(3m). Tall Trees Holiday Caravan Park, Matchams Lane, Hurn, Christchurch, Dorset BH23 6AW. *01202 477144.* tall trees.park@talk21.com. www.tall-trees.co.uk. Owner: Mr T Miles. About 15m from M27. Heated swimming pool. Quiet, privately owned and run. 6m to Bournemouth and on edge of New Forest. Play area. Open March 1-October 31. **BH&HPA. 80S.**

Corfe Castle

Knitson Farm Tourers Site, Knitson Farm, Corfe Castle, Dorset BH20 5JB. *01929 425121.* tourers@knitson.co.uk. www.knitsonfarm.co.uk. Owner: Mrs J Helfer. Knitson Farm, Corfe Castle, Dorset. L off A351 just after entering Swanage, Washpond Lane, then L at T-junction. Proceed for 0.5m, site on L. Quiet family site on working farm for s/c units. Own sanitation necessary. 1.5m to Swanage Beach, 3m Studland beach, excellent walking area. Near to World Heritage coast. Golf course, tennis, horseriding all nearby. Great mountain biking area. Open Easter-October. **60T. MC.** 🏕

Ferndown

(1m). St Leonards Farm Caravan and Camping Park, Ringwood Road, A31, West Moors, Ferndown, Dorset BH22 0AQ. *01202 872637.* james@love5.fsnet.co.uk. www.stleonards farm.biz. Owner: W E Love & Son. On A31 Ringwood to Ferndown, 5m W of Ringwood opposite Texaco Garage. Suitable base for Bournemouth and Poole. Laundrette. Play area. Open April-October. ☆☆ **BH&HPA. 101T. 101MC. 5S.** 🏕 🔌 ♿ ✐

Poole

(3m). Beacon Hill Touring Park, Blandford Road North, Poole, Dorset BH16 6AB. *01202 631631.* www.beaconhill touringpark.co.uk. Owner: Mrs Rosemary Bond. 0.25m N from J of A35 on to A350 towards Blandford, N of Poole. Cherbourg and Poole for St Malo and Channel Island Ferries. Heated swimming pool. Fully licensed bar with entertainment and takeaway in high season. All-weather tennis court. Coarse fishing lake on site. Children's play area. Open Easter-end September. ☆☆☆ **BH&HPA. 120T. 50MC.** 🏕 🔌 ♿ 🐾

(4m). Huntick Farm, Lytchett Matravers, Poole, Dorset BH16 6BB. *01202 622222.* caravan@huntick622222.fsnet.co. Owner: Mr & Mrs Scrimgeour. Just off the A350 on Poole-Blandford road, take sign to Lytchett Matravers. First left and left at Rose & Crown PH. Site 1m on right. Small, level grass site in wooded surroundings. 10% discount for OAPs. Rallies welcome. Convenient for ferry crossings from Poole. Storage for caravans and boats available. Open April 1-October 31. **30T. MC.** 🏕 🔌

(5m). Merley Court Touring Park, Merley, Wimborne, Poole, Dorset BH21 3AA. *01202 881488.* holidays@merley-court.co.uk. www.merley-court.co.uk. Owner: Mr K J Wright. SP off A31 Wimborne bypass. Family park with superb facilities including leisure garden set in landscaped, walled garden. Open March 1-January 7. ☆☆☆☆☆ **BH&HPA. 160T. MC.** 🏕 🔌 ♿ 🐾

(4m). Organford Manor Caravan Park, Organford, Poole, Dorset BH16 6ES. *01202 622202.* organford@lds.co.uk. Owner: Mrs A M Harrison. First left off A35, after roundabout at

ONLY 3 MILES FROM POOLE FERRY TERMINAL

Partly wooded site, lovely peaceful setting. Excellent facilities with Free Hot Water, including Disabled Shower Room, Heated Swimming Pool, Children's Play Areas, Bar, Shop, Fishing, Tennis, Games Rooms, (Entertainment, coffee shop & Take Away in high season), some Hard Standings, Laundrette, Calor Gas, Public Telephones, etc. *Brochure on application*

TELEPHONE: 01202 631 631
www.beaconhilltouringpark.co.uk

LOCATED ON A350 1/4 MILE NORTH OF JUNCTION WITH A35, 4 MILES NORTH OF POOLE TOWN CENTRE TOWARDS BLANDFORD

Please visit the Caravan Club website: www.caravanclub.co.uk

J of A351 and A35. Site entrance on right in about 0.25m. 30 tent pitches. Shop on site in high season. Open March 16-October 31. ☆☆☆ **BH&HPA. 40T. 10MC. 40S. 5H.** ♒ ⊕ & ⚓

(3m). Pear Tree Touring Park, Organford Road, Holton Heath, Poole, Dorset BH16 6LA. *01202 622434.* info@visit peartree.co.uk. www.visitpeartree.co.uk. From A35 take A351 Wareham, 1st right to Organford. Central for Poole, Bournemouth, Swange, Wareham and New Forest. 24hr supervision. Open April-October. ☆☆☆☆☆ **BH&HPA. 125T. MC.** ♒ ⊕ & ⚓

(3m). Rockley Park Holiday Park, Hamworthy, Poole, Dorset BH15 4LZ. *01202 679393.* oewebmaster@bourne-leisure.co.uk. www.rockleypark.co.uk. Owner: Bourne Leisure Ltd. One Park Lane, Hemel Hempstead, Herts HP2 4YL. Leave M27 and join A31. Follow signs for Poole. In town centre SP for Rockley Park. Alternatively Dorchester bypass to Poole and follow signs for Rockley Park. Heated outdoor and indoor pools. Restaurants and takeaway. Club, bar and family entertainment. Sailing. Windsurfing. Diving. Laundrette. Nature reserve, bowling green, tennis courts. No dogs at bank holidays or school holidays (touring). Welcome host and David Bellamy Gold Conservation Award. Open April-November. ☆☆☆☆☆ **BH&HPA. NCC. 74T. 40MC. 1080S. 320H.** ♒ ⊕ & ⚓

(3m). Sandford Holiday Park, Holton Heath, Poole, Dorset BH16 6JZ. *0870 4440080/0870 0667793.* bookings@west starholidays.com. www.weststarholidays.co.uk. Owner: Weststar Holidays Ltd. 8 Abbey Court, Eagle Way, Sowton, Exeter EX2 7HY. On A351 to Wareham which branches off A35 5m W of Pool. Turn off at Holton Heath traffic lights. Idyllic setting in 64 acres of woodland. Free all-weather facilities, indoor swimming pool, live entertainment and children's clubs. Tent camping facilities. Open March-January. ☆☆☆☆ **BH&HPA. 500T. MC. 299S. 297H.** ♒ ⊕ & ⚓

(3m). South Lytchett Manor Caravan & Camping Park, Lytchett Minster, Poole, Dorset BH16 6JB. *01202 622577.* slmcp@talk21.com. www.eluk.co.uk/camping/dorset/slytchett. Owner: The Hull Family. On B3067 off A35 follow A350 S from J with A31 turn right, first sign to L. Minster, follow road down hill for 1m, park on right at T-junction with B3067. Popular, quiet, family site. TV. Free showers. Laundry. Games room. Takeaway. Open Mid March-Mid October. **BH&HPA. 50T. MC.** ♒ ⊕ & ⚓

Swanage

(0.5m). Cauldron Barn Farm Caravan Park, Cauldron Barn Road, Swanage, Dorset BH19 1QQ. *01929 422080.* cauldron barn@fsbdial.co.uk. Owner: Landopen. From Victoria Avenue into Northbrook Rd, 3rd L into Cauldron Barn Rd. Rural site 800yd from beach. Open mid March-mid November. ☆☆☆☆ **BH&HPA. 12T. 4MC. 169S. 15H.** ⊕ ⌀

(2.5m). Downshay Farm, Haycrafts Lane, Swanage, Dorset BH19 3EB. *01929 480316.* downshayfarm@tiscali.co.uk. www.downshayfarm.co.uk. Owner: Mr M Pike. A351 Swanage then R at Harmans Cross. 0.5m up Haycrafts Lane. Small, family-run site on working dairy farm. Views of Corfe Castle. Open April 1-November 1. **12T. MC.** ♒ ⊕

(3m). Flower Meadow Caravan Site, Flower Meadow, Haycrafts Lane, Harmans Cross, Swanage, Dorset BH19 3EB. *01929 480035.* Owner: Mrs N A Mitchell & Mrs B Hobbs. Midway between Corfe Castle and Swanage. S off the A351 in Harmans Cross towards steam railway. Site 200yd on left. Small, quiet site in Purbeck Hills. Good walking and touring. Sea 3.5m. No dogs in July and August. Open April 1-October 31. **10T. MC.** ⊕

(3m). Haycraft Caravan Club Site, Haycrafts Lane, Swanage, Dorset BH19 3EB. *01929 480572.* www.cara vanclub.co.uk. Owner: The Caravan Club. East Grinstead House, East Grinstead, West Sussex RH19 1UA. See website for standard directions to site. Located in heart of Purbeck countryside and within easy reach of Dorset's coastline. Toilet blocks with privacy cubicles and laundry facilities. Baby and toddler washroom. Fishing and golf 5m, dog walk on site. Suitable for families. Good area for walking. Open March-October. ☆☆☆☆☆ **NCC. 53T. MC.** ♒ ⊕ &

(1.5m). Herston Yards Farm, Washpond Lane, Swanage, Dorset BH19 3DJ. *01929 422932.* Owner: Mr & Mrs Tadgel. Eggs and milk at farm house, mobile shop calls. Open April-October. **80T. 6S.** ♒

Hoburne Residential Park, Hoburne Lane, Swanage, Dorset BH23 4HU. 70MC. 70H.

(1m). Swanage Caravan Park, Panorama Road, Swanage, Dorset BH19 2QS. *01929 422130.* holidaypark@swanage.gov.uk. www.swanagebayviewholidaypark.co.uk. Owner: Swanage Town Council. Dogs allowed in some holiday caravans only. Indoor heated pool. Open March-November. ☆☆☆ **290S. 120H.** ♒ ⚓

(1m). Swanage Coastal Park (Formerly Priestway Holiday Park), Priestway, Swanage, Dorset BH19 2RS. *01590 648331.* holidays@shorefield.co.uk. www.shore field.co.uk. Owner: Shorefield Holidays Ltd. Shorefield Road, Milford on Sea, Hants SO41 0LH. A351 through Wareham and Corfe Castle, past 'Welcome to Swanage' sign into Herston. Turn R into Bell Street. First L into Priests Rd, first R into Park. Site under new ownership – part of the Shorefield Group. Park offers views of sea and Purbeck Hills. 1m to beach and town with shops and cinema. Bottled gas. Open March 24-October 31. ☆☆☆ **BH&HPA. 10T. MC. 108S. 52H.** ♒ ⊕

(1.5m). Ulwell Cottage Caravan Park, Ulwell, Swanage, Dorset BH19 3DG. *01929 422823.* enq@ulwellcottage park.co.uk. www.ulwellcottagepark.co.uk. Owners: Mr J Orchard & Mrs J Scadden. In lovely Isle of Purbeck, 2m from Studland beach, on Swanage road. Family-run park located near sandy beaches, coastal walks and golf. 'Village Inn', heated indoor pool. General shop. Open March 1-January 7. ☆☆☆☆ **BH&HPA. 77T. 140S. 100H.** ♒ ⊕ & ⚓

(1.5m). Ulwell Farm Caravan Park, Ulwell, Swanage, Dorset BH19 3DG. *01929 422825.* ulwell.farm@virgin.net. www.ukparks. co.uk/ulwellfarm. Owner: Mr R J Verge & Mrs C P Knowles. On Swanage to Studland and Sandbanks ferry, entrance 150yd beyond end of 30mph limit on right. Fishing, riding, golf and watersports nearby. Good country and coastal walks. Open April-September 30. ☆☆☆☆ **BH&HPA. 44S. 6H.** ♒ ⊕ ⌀

Wareham

(3m). Birchwood Tourist Park, Bere Road, North Trigon, Wareham, Dorset BH20 7PA. *01929 554763.* www.birchwoodtouristpark.co.uk. Owner: John & Linda Orford. West on A351 at Wareham Railway Station Roundabout, turn R into Bere Rd (unclassified) in a NW. direction towards Bere Regis, through Wareham Forest. Site on R about 0.25m. Hard-standing barrier system. Open March-October. ☆☆☆ **BH&HPA. 175T. MC.** ♒ ⊕ ⚓

Wareham Forest Tourist Park

THE Best of British
TOURING AND HOLIDAY PARKS

Family run landscaped park set in 40 acres of delightful woodlands with open grassy spaces and direct access to Forest walks. Central location for lovely Dorset World Heritage Coastlines and developed to a high standard.

- ☆ Heated Swimming Pool
- ☆ Children's Paddling Pool
- ☆ Table Tennis
- ☆ Children's Adventure Playground
- ☆ Long or Short Term Storage
- ☆ Individual Cubicles in the toilet block for ladies
- ☆ Toilet block heated during winter period

- ☆ Fully Serviced Luxury Pitches
- ☆ Launderette
- ☆ Shop/Off Licence
- ☆ Disabled Facilities & Family bathrooms
- ☆ Owners Tony & Sarah Birch previously from Carnon Downs
- ☆ Woodland Dog Walks

BH&HPA

DAVID BELLAMY CONSERVATION AWARD
SILVER

OPEN ALL YEAR

For further details and free colour brochure
write or phone:
Wareham Forest Tourist Park
North Trigon Wareham Dorset BH20 7NZ
Tel/Fax: 01929 551393
e-mail address: holiday@wareham-forest.co.uk
Please visit our website: www.wareham-forest.co.uk

AA ►◄►

(8m). Durdle Door Holiday Park, Lulworth Cove, Wareham, Dorset BH20 5PU. *01929 400200.* durdle.door@lulworth.com. www.lulworth.com. Owner: Weld Enterprises Ltd. Estate Office, Lulworth Castle, Wareham, Dorset BH20 5QS. SP from West Lulworth village. Open March 1-October 31. ✫✫✫✫ **BH&HPA. 25T. MC. 380S. 30H.** ↿ ⚎ ⌂ ⌇ ⌀

(3m). East Creech Farm, Wareham, Dorset BH20 5AP. *01929 480519.* east.creech@virgin.net. www.eastcreechfarm.co.uk. Owner: Mr P F Best. Take bypass at Wareham, on third roundabout take Furzebrook-Blue Pool road, site 2m on R. Fishing. 3m to shop, doctor and PO. AA 3 pennants. Open April 1-October 31. **55T. MC.** ↿ ⚎

Hunter's Moon Caravan Club Site, Cold Harbour, Wareham, Dorset BH20 7PA. *01929 556605.* www.car avanclub.co.uk. Owner: The Caravan Club. East Grinstead House, East Grinstead, West Sussex RH19 1UA. See website for standard directions to site. Caravan Club members only. Site provides a suitable base for touring Dorset. Toilet blocks, laundry facilities and motorhome service point. Fishing, golf and water sports nearby. Play equipment and dog walk on site. Suitable for families. Peaceful off-peak. **NCC.** ✿ ↿ ⚎ ⚍

Luckford Wood Caravan & Camping Park, Holme Lane, East Stoke, Wareham, Dorset BH20 6AW. *01929 463098.* info@luck fordleisure.co.uk. www.luckfordleisure.co.uk. Owner: J Barnes. From Wareham take A352 towards Wool for 1m, then B3070 to Lulworth for 1m, at West Holme crossroads turn right along Holme Lane, site entrance 1m on R. Storage facilities for caravans, boats and motorhomes. Camp fires and hog roast by arrangement. On site Heli-pad. Open, wooded and shaded areas. Close to Heritage Coast Tank Museum Monkey World. Lodges for hire. Pets welcome Dog walking lane. Bike hire. Rally site. **MC.** ↿ ⚎

(3m). Manor Farm Caravan Park, East Stoke, Wareham, Dorset BH20 6AW. *01929 462870.* info@manorfarmcp.co.uk. www.manorfarmcp.co.uk. Owner: David & Gillian Topp. From Wareham A352 L at Eaststoke redundant church, park 0.75m on R. Or A352, on to B3070, turn right at first crossroad, turn right at SP for site. Family-run, flat, grass touring park on a working farm in 2.5 acres, long and short stay plus winter/summer storage. Bed and breakfast. Small, clean and secluded with showers, toilets and play area. Phone on site. Resident proprietors. Golf nearby Seasonal pitches. RAC appointed. SAE for brochure. Close to Jurassic coast, Monkey world and beaches. Open Easter-September 30. **60T.** ↿ ⚎ ⌂ ⌇

(1.2m). Ridge Farm Camping & Caravan Park, Barnhill Road, Wareham, Dorset BH20 5BG. *01929 556444.* info@ridge farm.co.uk. www.ridgefarm.co.uk. Owner: Mrs J L Pollock. B3075 from Wareham turn L in Stoborough, along New Road to village of Ridge. Site at end of Barnhill Road on L. Quiet, secluded, family-run site on working farm. Level pitches. Hot showers and laundrette. Birdwatching, walking, cycling and boating (slipway nearby). Dogs welcome except in July and August. AA 3 pennants. Open April-September. **60T. MC.** ↿ ⚎ ⌇

Smedmore House Caravan Site, Kimmeridge, Wareham, Dorset BH20 5PG. *01929 480702.* office@smedmore-cara vansite.co.uk. www.smedmore-caravansite.co.uk. Off A351. 1m from Kimmeridge. Caravan Club affiliated site. Members only. Prior booking essential. Open, sloping field surrounded by farmland. Views to the sea, Clavell Tower and the Purbeck Hills. Own sanitation required. Dog walk nearby. Fishing and water sports nearby. Good area for walking. Peaceful off-peak. Managers: B & S Belsten. Open May-October. **42T. MC.** ↿ ⚎

(1.3m). The Lookout Holiday Park, Corfe Road, Stoborough, Wareham, Dorset BH20 5AZ. *01929 552546.* enquiries@cara van-sites.co.uk. Owner: Frampton Leisure. From Wareham A351 to Corfe Castle. Park on left. Games room. Playground. Laundry. Showers. Crazy golf. Rose Award. Open March-end December. ✫✫✫✫ **BH&HPA. NCC. 150T. 150MC. 25S. 35H.** ⚎ ⚍ ⌂ ⌀

(4m). The Woodland Caravan & Camping Park, Glebe Farm, Bucknowle, Wareham, Dorset BH20 5NS. *01929 480280.* Owner: Mr & Mrs R H Parker. Bucknowle Farm, Wareham, Dorset BH20 5PQ. Off A351, right at Corfe Castle, about 0.75m on Church Knowle Rd. No advance bookings. About 4m from beaches. Direct access by public footpath to Purbeck Hills and 0.75m from Corfe Castle. Family site with most essential facilities. AA Award. Open Easter-October 31. **25T. MC.** ↿ ⚎ ⌇

(3m). Wareham Forest Tourist Park, Bere Road, North Trigon, Wareham, Dorset BH20 7NZ. *01929 551393.* holiday@wareham-forest.co.uk. www.wareham-forest. co.uk. Owner: Tony & Sarah Birch. Off A35 midway between Wareham and Bere Regis. Swimming pool. Spacious, level pitches in secluded woodland setting, with direct access into Wareham Forest. Friendly, relaxing, family atmosphere. Shop and pool (high season) play area, seasonal pitches and storage. Central location. ✫✫✫✫✫ **BH&HPA. NCC. 200T. MC.** ✿ ↿ ⚎ ⚍ ⌇

BIRCHWOOD TOURIST PARK

Family-run park, ideally situated for exploring Dorset. Well stocked shop. Off licence. Free hot showers. Children's paddling pool. Bike hire. Fully serviced pitches. Hard standings. Tents welcome.

We accept:

BIRCHWOOD TOURIST PARK
North Trigon, Wareham, Dorset BH20 7PA
Tel: 01929 554763 Fax: 01929 556635
Web: www.birchwoodtouristpark.co.uk

(5m). Whitemead Caravan Park, East Burton Road, Wool, Wareham, Dorset BH20 6HG. *01929 462241.* whitemead@aol.com. whitemeadcaravanpark.co.uk. Owner: Mr & Mrs C Church. Frome Cottage, East Burton Road, Wool, Wareham, Dorset BH20 6HG. Off the A352 Wareham to Dorchester road, north of level crossing in Wool, 200yd on right. 4.5m west of Wareham, 300 yards off the A352 before Wool level crossing. Play area. Lake fishing 4m. Takeaways on site. Breakfast available at weekends. Shop and games room with pool table and darts. New toilet/shower block opened in 2005. Open mid March-October 31. ☆☆☆☆ **BH&HPA. 95T. 95MC.** 🏕 🔌 ♿ 🐾

Wimborne

(1m). Charris Camping & Caravan Park, Candy's Lane, Corfe Mullen, Wimborne, Dorset BH21 3EF. *01202 885970.* enquiries@charris.co.uk. www.charris.co.uk. Owner: Jane Watson & Judith Chapman. 2 Carters Cottages, Candys Lane, Corfe Mullen, Wimborne, Dorset BH21 3EF. Located on the A31, W of Wimborne. Facilities block. Calor Gas supplied. Camping and Caravanning Club listed. Personal service. Open March-January. ☆☆☆☆ **BH&HPA. 45T. 22MC.** 🏕 🔌 🐾

(1.5m). Merley House Holiday Park Ltd, Merley House Lane, Wimborne, Dorset BH21 3AA. *01202 883823.* merley house@supanet.com. www.merleyhouse.co.uk. Owner: P Hammick. Off A31 Wimborne bypass at the A349 Poole round-about. Select, peaceful park set in Dorset countryside. Laundrette. Cafe. Swimming pool. Play area. 9-hole pitch and putt course. Poole and Bournemouth nearby. Cinema/shopping centre 1.5m, golf 3m. Open March 16-January 15. **BH&HPA. 167S.** 🏕 🐾

(1.5m). Springfield Touring Park, Candys Lane, Corfe Mullen, Wimborne, Dorset BH21 3EF. *01202 881719.* Owner: Sheila & John Clark. Turn left off A31, Ringwood to Dorchester, at roundabout at western end of Wimborne bypass; after 400yd turn right into Candys Lane. Family-run park. Convenient for New Forest and coastal resorts. Showers. No charge for awnings. Special offers low season. Within easy distance of fishing, golf, horse riding, swimming, leisure activities, boating on the river Stour. Open mid-March-October. ☆☆☆☆☆ **BH&HPA. 45T. MC.** 🏕 🔌 ♿ 🐾

(1m). Wilksworth Farm Caravan Park, Cranborne Road, Furzehill, Wimborne, Dorset BH21 4HW. *01202 885467.* rayandwendy@wilksworthfarmcaravanpark.cowww.wilks worthfarmcaravanpark.co.uk. Owners: Mr & Mrs R Lovell. N of Wimborne on B3078. Showers. Laundry room. Heated swimming pool. Games room. Tennis court. Large play area. Open March-October. ☆☆☆☆☆ **BH&HPA. 60T. MC. 77S.** 🏕 🔌 ♿ 🐾

HAMPSHIRE

Andover

(3m). Wyke Down Touring Caravan and Camping Park, Picket Piece, Andover, Hampshire SP11 6LX. *01264 352048.* wykedown@wykedown.co.uk. www.wykedown.co.uk. Owner: Mr W Read. International Camping Park signs from A303 trunk road, follow signs to Wyke Down. Swimming pool. PHand restaurant. Golf driving range. Supermarket 2.5m, Town 3m. ☆☆☆ **200T. MC.** ✿ ⍓ 🖾

Ashurst

(5m). Ashurst Caravan & Camping Site, Forestry Commission (Forest Holidays), Lyndhurst Road, Ashurst, Hampshire SO40 7RA. *01313 146505.* fe.holidays@ forestry.gsi.gov.uk. www.forestholidays.co.uk. Owner: Forestry Commission (Forest Holidays). 231 Corstorphine Road, Edinburgh EH12 7AT. SW of Southampton on A35, SP. 2m from Ashurst. Attractive site set in woodland glade. Showers, laundry and dishwashing facilities. Bookings essential. Brochure request line: 01313 340066. Open March-September. ☆☆☆☆ **BH&HPA. 280T. 100MC.** ⍓

Brockenhurst

(1m). Aldridge Hill Caravan & Camping Site, Forestry Commission (Forest Holidays), Brockenhurst, Hampshire S042 7QD. *0131 3146505.* fe.holidays@forestry.gsi.gov.uk. www.forestholidays.co.uk. Owner: Forestry Commission (Forest Holidays). 231 Corstorphine Road, Edinburgh EH12 7AT. Off A337,1m NW of Brockenhurst village. Level site on the edge of Blackwater stream, close to Brockenhurst village. No toilet facilities. Brochure request line: 01313 340066. Open one week of spring bank holiday and July and August. **BH&HPA. 200T. 50MC.** ⍓

(1m). Black Knowl Caravan Club Site, Aldridge Hill, Brockenhurst, Hampshire SO42 7QD. *01590 623600.* www.caravanclub.co.uk. Owner: The Caravan Club. East Grinstead House, East Grinstead, West Sussex RH19 1UA. See website for standard directions to site. Caravan Club members only. Located in ancient royal hunting forest of William the Conqueror and within walking distance of Brockenhurst. Toilet blocks, laundry facilities and motorhome service point. Good walking, golf and NCN cycle route nearby. Suitable for families. Open March-November. **NCC. 120T. MC.** ⍓ 🖾 ⍓

(0.5m). Hollands Wood Caravan & Camping Site, Lyndhurst Road, Brockenhurst, Hampshire SO42 7QH. *01313 146505.* www.forrestholidays.co.uk. Owner: Forest Enterprise Holidays. 231 Corstorphine Road, Edinburgh EH12 7AT. 0.5m N of Brockenhurst on A337, SP. Showers, laundry and dishwashing facilities. Bread and milk sold at office. Brochure request line: 0131 3340066. Open March 18-September 26. ☆☆☆☆ **BH&HPA. 600T. MC.** ⍓ ⍓

(2m). Roundhill Caravan & Camping Site, Forestry Commission (Forest Holidays), Beaulieu Road, Brockenhurst, Hampshire SO42 7QL. *01313 146505.* fe.holidays@forestry.gsi.gov.uk. www.forestholidays.co.uk. Owner: Forestry Commission (Forest Holidays). 231 Corstorphine Road, Edinburgh EH12 7AT. B3055, 2m SE of Brockenhurst, off A337 SP. Toilet facilities include washing cubicles. Dishwashing. Booking advisable. Brochure request line: 0131 3340066. Open March-September. ☆☆☆ **BH&HPA. 500T. MC.** ⍓ ⍓

Fareham

(5m). Dibles Park, Dibles Road, Warsash, Fareham, Hampshire SO31 9SA. *01489 575232.* Owner: Dibles Park Co Ltd. J8, M27 L on to A27 turn right at Sarisbury Green R at T junction left at mini roundabout. Warsash village about 1.5m turn R into Fleet End Road, 2nd turning on R. Showers. Laundry facilities. Shops, PO, doctor available within 0.5m. ☆☆☆☆ **BH&HPA. 14T. MC.** ✿ ⍓ 🖾 ⌀

(2m). Ellerslie Touring Caravan & Camping Park, Down End Road, Fareham, Hampshire PO16 8TS. *01329 822248.* Owner: Mr Symonds. Off A27 (J11 of M27) N at Cams Hall traffic lights, site SP. Bar, squash, hairdresser, sauna, steam room and gymnasium at extra cost. Open March-October. ☆☆ **BH&HPA. 20T. 10MC.** ⍓ 🖾

(4m). Rookesbury Park Caravan Club Site, Hundred Acres Road, Wickham, Fareham, Hampshire PO17 6JR. *01329 834085.* www.caravanclub.co.uk. Owner: The Caravan Club. East Grinstead House, East Grinstead, West Sussex RH19 1UA. See website for standard directions to site. Caravan Club members only. Site located in parkland on edge of Forest of Bere. Good walking from site and convenient for Portsmouth and Isle of Wight. Toilet blocks. Privacy cubicles. Laundry facilities. Baby washroom. Veg prep. Motorhome service point. Play equipment. Good area for walking. Suitable for families. Open March-October. **NCC. 170T. MC.** ⍓ 🖾 ⍓

Fordingbridge

(1.5m). Sandy Balls Holiday Centre, Sandy Balls Estate, Godshill, Fordingbridge, Hampshire SP6 2JZ. *01425 653042.* post@sandy-balls.co.uk. www.sandy-balls.co.uk. Owner: Sandy Balls Estate Ltd. From Salisbury A338 to Fordingbridge, turn off on to B3078, SP Godshill. Fishing on site and nearby, own stables, full leisure centre with pools, gyms etc. 120-acre site with wood and meadowland to explore and enjoy. ☆☆☆☆☆ **BH&HPA. 233T. 233MC. 131S. 120H.** ✿ ⍓ 🖾 ⍓ ⌀

Gosport

(3m). Kingfisher Park, Browndown Road, Gosport, Hampshire PO13 9BE. *023 9250 2611.* info@kingfisher-caravan-park.co.uk. Owner: Mr Sargeant. M27 motorway J9 or J11 to Gosport. Open all year for tourers; March-January for holiday homes. ☆☆☆ **BH&HPA. NCC. 130T. MC. 100S. 30H.** ✿ ⍓ 🖾 🖭

Please mention Caravan Sites 2006 when replying to advertisers

Best of both worlds
South Coast and New Forest

All four of our touring parks are set in peaceful, unspoilt parkland in the beautiful South Coast area.

There are comprehensive leisure facilities available and great entertainment for the whole family.

Pamper yourself in our new 'Reflections' Day Spa at Shorefield Country Park or explore Britain's latest National Park - the New Forest.

For full details, ask for our brochure or browse on-line.

For a really memorable family holiday

01590 648331

e-mail: holidays@shorefield.co.uk

Oakdene Forest Park
St. Leonards, Ringwood, Hampshire

Lytton Lawn Touring Park
Milford on Sea, Hampshire

Forest Edge Touring Park
St. Leonards, Ringwood, Hampshire

Swanage Coastal Park
Swanage, Dorset (formerly Priestway)

Ref: CS

SHOREFIELD
HOLIDAYS LIMITED

www.shorefield.co.uk

Hamble

(1m). Riverside Holidays, Satchell Lane, Hamble, Hampshire SO31 4HR. *02380 453220.* enquiries@riversideholidays.co.uk. www.riversideholidays.co.uk. Owner: Davidson Leisure Resorts Ltd. 21 Compass Point, Ensign Way, Hamble, Hants SO31 4RA. J8, M27 (Southampton East) then B3397 to Hamble, turn L into Satchell Lane. Site is adjacent to marina with restaurant and bar and overlooks the river. Set in the countryside, walking, cycling and sailing. Close to New Forest, Portsmouth and Winchester. 8 Lodges available for hire. Rose Award. AA 3 pennants. David Bellamy Bronze Conservation Award. Open March-October for tourers and holiday caravans; open all year for lodges. ✰✰✰✰ **BH&HPA. NCC. 77T. MC. 38S. 10H.** ⛺ 🐕 ⚿ ◿

Hayling Island

(2m). Camaron Caravan Park, 1/3 Fisherman's Walk, Hayling Island, Hampshire PO11 9QU. *023 9246 4276.* Owner: St Hermans Estate Co Ltd. Lower Tye Farm, Copse Lane, Hayling Island, Hampshire PO11 0RQ. Quiet park in SE corner of island, within walking distance of beach, convenience store and tourist area. Open March 1-October 31. **8S.** ⛺

Relax & explore

the **beautiful south**

RIVERSIDE holidays

Beautiful views over the Marina and River Hamble
● Excellent sailing, walking, fishing and horse riding nearby
● Serviced touring pitches ● Luxurious self-catering accommodation ● Superior pine lodges and static caravans available to hire all year.

You won't regret your stay at Riverside!

Riverside Holidays

Satchell Lane, Hamble, Hampshire SO31 4HR

Please call: 02380 453220

for your free colour brochure or visit our website:
www.riversideholidays.co.uk

(1m). Campion Caravan Park, 8 Fisherman's Walk, Hayling Island, Hampshire PO11 9QU. *023 9246 4276.* Owner: St Hermans Estate Co Ltd. Lower Tye Farm, Copse Lane, Hayling Island, Hampshire PO11 0RQ. Small, family site close to Chichester Harbour and within walking distance of beach and amusements. Tiny park hidden away in SE corner of the island. Easy access to shops, beach and tourist area. Open March 1-October 31. **4S.** ⛺

(1m). Caravelle Caravan Park, 6 Haven Road, Hayling Island, Hampshire PO11 9QX. *023 9246 4276.* Owner: St Hermans Estate Co Ltd. Lower Tye Farm, Copse Lane, Hayling Island, Hampshire PO11 0RQ. Neat park equidistant from beach and Chichester Harbour. Easy access to public transport for town centre shopping. Open March 1-December 31. **12S.** ⛺

(1m). Cummock Caravan Park, 15 Haven Road, Hayling Island, Hampshire PO11 9QX. *023 9246 4276.* Owner: St Hermans Estate Co Ltd. Lower Tye Farm, Copse Lane, Hayling Island, Hampshire PO11 0RQ. Very open park with substantial grass frontage. Close to convenience store, beach and access to public transport. Open March 1-December 31. **7S.** ⛺

(1m). Eastoke Farm Caravan Park, 31 Sandy Point Road, Hayling Island, Hampshire PO11 9RP. *023 9246 4276.* Owner: St Hermans Estate Co Ltd. Lower Tye Farm, Copse Lane, Hayling Island, Hampshire PO11 0RQ. Family park within walking distance of beach, shops, tourist area and access to public transport. Open March 1-December 31. **17S.** ⛺

Elliott's Caravan Estate, 23 Haven Road, Eastoke, Hayling Island, Hampshire PO11 9RX. *02392 466991.* Owner: Elliott's Caravan Estate Co Ltd. A3023 to sea front, R into Southwood Road, L into Nutbourne Road. 4mins walk from beach in a quiet location. 3mins walk from Chichester Harbour. Golf 3m, general store 150yd, village shops 2m. Open March 1-October 31. **BH&HPA. 208S. 2H.** ⛺

(0.25m). Fishery Creek Park, 100 Fishery Lane, Hayling Island, Hampshire PO11 9NR. *02392 462164.* camping @fisherycreek.fsnet.co.uk. www.keyparks.co.uk. Owner: Mr D Emersic. From the A27 cross bridge to Hayling Island and follow SPs. Peaceful park on flat grassland adjoining a tidal creek (own slipway) fishing from bank. 5 mins walk to beach. Showers. Open March 1-October 31. ✰✰✰ **160T. MC.** ⛺ 🐕 ⚿ 🔌

(2m). Fleet Farm Camping, Yew Tree Road, Hayling Island, Hampshire PO11 0QF. *023 9246 3684/07971 235942 (M).* www.haylingcampsites.co.uk. Owner: Colin Good. Yachhaven House, Copse Lane, Hayling Island PO11 0RH. Exit A3M or M27 at Havant. Follow A3023 over road bridge on to island. About 1.5m on island then turn L into Copse Lane, then R into Yew Tree Road, site on L. Storage and rallies catered for. Long- term parking on site. Site on creak. Handy touring area for Portsmouth, New Forest. Golf, fishing, tennis. Family PH and beach nearby. Open March 1-November 1. **75T. MC.** ⛺ 🔌 🔌

Please mention Caravan Sites 2006 when replying to advertisers

(2m). Fleet Farm Caravan Park, Yew Tree Road, Hayling Island, Hampshire PO11 0QE. *023 9246 4276.* Owner: St Hermans Estate Co Ltd. Lower Tye Farm, Copse Lane, Hayling Island, Hampshire PO11 0RQ. Large, family-orientated park in rural north Hayling, close to convenience store and access to public transport. Adjacent creek with slipway access for boating enthusiasts. Open March 1-October 31. **161S.** 🎯 🛒

(2m). Goose Green Caravan Park, 7 Birdham Road, Hayling Island, Hampshire PO11 9QY. *023 9246 4276.* Owner: St Hermans Estate Co Ltd. Lower Tye Farm, Copse Lane, Hayling Island, Hampshire PO11 0RQ. Quiet park in SE Hayling. Close to beach, convenience store and public transport. Open March 1-December 31. **8S.** 🎯

(1m). Greenhaven Caravan Park, 12-20 Haven Road, Hayling Island, Hampshire PO11 9QX. *023 9246 4276.* Owner: St Hermans Estate Co Ltd. Lower Tye Farm, Copse Lane, Hayling Island, Hampshire PO11 0RQ. Recently developed park suitable for families and within walking distance of seafront and tourist area. Open March 1-October 31. **24S.** 🎯

(3m). Lower Tye Campsite, Copse Lane, Hayling Island, Hampshire PO11 0QB. *023 9246 2479.* lowertye@aol.com. www.raylingcampsites.co.uk. Owner: Zita Good. After leaving A3 or A27 for Havant follow A3023 on to Hayling Island, after crossing bridge, turn L site about 1.5m. Family site. Sailing and water-skiing etc. Fishing. Boardsailing. Horse riding. Tennis. Golf nearby. Showers. Laundrette. Swimming pool on site. Long-term parking on site available. Convenient for Chichester, New Forest, Channel ferry crossing from Portsmouth. Open March 1-November 1. **150T. MC.** 🎯 🔌

(2m). Lower Tye Farm Caravan Park, Copse Lane, Hayling Island, Hampshire PO11 0RQ. *023 9246 4276.* Owner: St Hermans Estate Co Ltd. Lower Tye Farm, Copse Lane, Hayling Island, Hampshire PO11 0RQ. Quiet park surrounded by fields and farmland in north Hayling. Convenience store located nearby. Access to public transport within walking distance. Open March 1-October 31. **75S.**

(1m). Seagulls Caravan Park, 3 Sandy Point Road, Hayling Island, Hampshire PO11 9RP. *023 9246 4276.* Owner: St Hermans Estate Co Ltd. Lower Tye Farm, Copse Lane, Hayling Island, Hampshire PO11 0RQ. Quiet, secluded park within walking distance of tourist area, seafront and close to public transport. Open March 1-December 31. **14S.** 🎯

St Hermans Park, St Hermans Road, Hayling Island, Hampshire PO11 9NB. *023 9246 4276.* info@sthermans.co.uk. Owner: St Hermans Estate Co Ltd. Lower Tye Farm, Copse Lane, Hayling Island, Hampshire PO11 0RQ. A3023 From Havant. Follow signs to Mengham. Take Selsmore Road towards Eastoke, Selsmore Road becomes Rails Lane.Turn left into St Hermans Road off Rails Lane. Well-established holiday park close to shops and beach; being developed as a retirement park. Open March 1-October 31. **NCC. 86S.** 🎯

(1m). Sunnymead Too Caravan Park, 9 Haven Road, Hayling Island, Hampshire PO11 9QX. *023 9246 4276.* Owner: St Herman's Estate Co Ltd. Lower Tye Farm, Copse Lane, Hayling Island, Hampshire PO11 0RQ. Small, family park within walking distance of seafront, tourist area and convenience store. Open March 1-October 31. **5S.**

(2m). The Binnacle Caravan Park, 105/107 Eastoke Avenue, Hayling Island, Hampshire PO11 9QR. *023 9246 4276.* Owner: St Hermans Estate Co Ltd. Lower Tye Farm, Copse Lane, Hayling Island, Hampshire PO11 0RQ. Small quiet waterside park with slipway access into Chichester Harbour. Close to convenience store, beach and tourist area. Open March 1-October 31. **6S.** 🎯

(0.5m). The Oven, Manor Road, Hayling Island, Hampshire PO11 0QX. *023 9246 4695.* Owner: Mrs Z Good. Finchwood Farm, Copse Lane, Hayling Island, Hampshire PO11 0QB. On A3023 approx. 3m from bridge, turn right at Mill by roundabout, site is 450yd on left. Blue Flag beach. Heated pool on site. Long-term caravan parking. Rallies welcome. Manager: Mr J Dent & J Macallum. Open March 1-November 1. **300T. MC.** 🎯 🔌 ♿ 🛒

(2m). Triangle Caravan Park, 131 Eastoke Avenue, Hayling Island, Hampshire PO11 9QR. *023 9246 4276.* Owner: St Hermans Estate Co Ltd. Lower Tye Farm, Copse Lane, Hayling Island, Hampshire PO11 0RQ. Well-established waterside park with slipway. Access to Chichester Harbour. Close to beach, tourist area and access to public transport. Open March 1-October 31. **13S.** 🎯

(2m). Two Acres Caravan Park, 113 Eastoke Avenue, Hayling Island, Hampshire PO11 9QR. *023 9246 4276.* Owner: St Hermans Estate Co Ltd. Lower Tye Farm, Copse Lane, Hayling Island, Hampshire PO11 0RQ. Medium-sized park bordering Chichester Harbour. Slipway available for boat enthusiasts. Close to beach and convenience store. Open March 1-October 31. **42S.** 🎯

(2m). Water's Edge Caravan Park, 129 Eastoke Avenue, Hayling Island, Hampshire PO11 9QR. *023 9246 4276.* Owner: St Hermans Estate Co Ltd. Lower Tye Farm, Copse Lane, Hayling Island, Hampshire PO11 0RQ. Waterside park with boat access to Chichester Harbour. Within walking distance of beach, convenience store and tourist area. Close to public transport for town centre shopping. Open March 1-October 31. **15S.** 🎯

Lymington

(5m). Carrington Park, New Lane, Milford-On-Sea, Lymington, Hampshire SO41 0UQ. *01590 642654.* Owner: Mr Milnes. A337 from Lymington, then B3058 to Milford-on-Sea. Coastal park. 5 mins walk to town. No sub-letting. David Bellamy Gold Conservation Award. Open March 1-November 30 and winter weekends. ☆☆☆☆☆ **BH&HPA. 131S.** 🎯 ♿ 📷

(5m). Kelston Caravan Site, 81 Downton Lane, Milford-On-Sea, Lymington, Hampshire SO4 0LG. *01590 641114.* Owner: Mrs A Gorbell. Over-40s only. No tourers. 2m New Milton, 0.25m to sea. Owner-occupants only; no subletting. Open March 1-October 31. **BH&HPA. 17S.**

(2m). Shorefield Country Park, Shorefield Road, Milford-on-Sea, Lymington, Hampshire SO41 0LH. *01590 648331.* holidays@shorefield.co.uk. www.shorefield.co.uk. Owner: Shorefield Holidays Ltd. From M27 take Lyndhurst exit 1on to A337 to Downton. Turn L at Royal Oak PH. 3m from Lymington, 12m from Bournemouth. Rose award. David Bellamy Gold Conservation Award. Club. Heated swimming pool. Beach 800yd. Golf 2m. New Forest 3m. ☆☆☆☆☆ **BH&HPA. 700S. 123H.** ✿ ⊁ ⌖ ⌦ ⌀

Lyndhurst

Denny Wood Caravan & Camping Site, Beaulieu Road, Lyndhurst, Hampshire SO43 7FZ. *01313 146505.* Owner: Forest Enterprise Holidays. 231 Corstorphine Road, Edinburgh EH12 7AT. From Lyndhurst take B3056 for 2.5m. Site on right. No toilet facilities. Booking available all year. Brochure request line: 01313 140066. Open March 24-October 2. **BH&HPA. 170T. 20MC.** ⌖

(2m). Matley Wood Caravan & Camping Site, Forestry Commission (Forest Holidays), Beaulieu Road, Lyndhurst, Hampshire SO43 7FZ. *01313 146505.* fe.holidays@forestry.gsi.gov.uk. www.forestholidays.co.uk. Owner: Forestry Commission (Forest Holidays). 231 Corstorphine Road,

Edinburgh, EH12 7AT. On B3056, 2m SE of Lyndhurst. Quiet grassland site among scattered oaks. No toilet facilities. Permits from Denny Wood Campsite nearby. Booking available all year. Brochure request line: 0131 334 0066. Open March-September. **BH&HPA. 70T. MC.** ⊁

Ocknell/Longbeech Caravan & Camping Site, Fritham, Lyndhurst, Hampshire SO43 7HH. *01313 146505.* Owner: Forest Enterprise Holidays. 231 Corstophine Road, Edinburgh EH12 7AT. B3079 off A31 at Cadnam, then B3078 via Brook and Fritham. Hot and cold washing facilities at Ocknell site. Toilets at Longbeech only for spring and August bank holidays. Booking all year. Brochure request line: 01313 340066. Open March 21-September 29. ☆☆☆ **BH&HPA. 480T. 110MC.** ⊁ ⌖ ⌦

New Milton

(1.25m). Glen Orchard Holiday Park, Walkford Lane, New Milton, Hampshire BH25 5NH. *01425 616463.* enquiries@glenorchard.co.uk. www.glenorchard.co.uk. Owner: B W Arnold & G M Rowland. Off A35 Christchurch to Lyndhurst, at Hinton turn to Walkford after 0.75m turn to New Milton, further 0.75m turn L for park. Recreational facilities, fishing, golf, riding nearby. Close to forest and beaches. Lymington 5m with ferry to Isle of Wight. Recreation centre and fishing 0.75m. Shopping 1.25m. Open March-October. ☆☆☆ **BH&HPA. 19H.** ⌀

(1m). Hoburne Bashley, Sway Road, New Milton, Hampshire BH25 5QR. *01425 612340.* enquiries@hoburne.com. www.hoburne.com. Owner: Hoburne Ltd. 261 Lymington Road, Highcliffe, Christchurch, Dorset BH23 5EE. On B3058 N of New Milton. Showers. Laundrette. Licensed club. Seasonal entertainment. Indoor leisure pool. Two 18m circular outdoor pools. 9-hole, par-3 golf course. Hard-court tennis. Playground. Football field. Snooker. Pool. Rose Award. Open February 24-October 28. ☆☆☆ **BH&HPA. NCC. 307T. 307MC. 426S.** ⊁ ⊟ ⌖ ⌦

(1m). Hoburne Naish, Christchurch Road, New Milton, Hampshire BH25 7RE. *01425 273586.* enquries@hoburne.com. www.hoburne.com. Owner: Hoburne Ltd. 261 Lymington Road, Highcliffe, Christchurch, Dorset BH23 5EE. On A337 between New Milton & Highcliffe. There are 68 lodges and 299 chalets. Indoor and outdoor pools. Tennis courts, children's adventure playground. Restaurant. Seasonal entertainment. Licensed club. Laundrette. Clifftop position. Rose Award. One pet per owner allowed. Themed bar and restaurant with mini ten-pin bowling. Open mid February-mid November and at Christmas and New Year. ☆☆☆☆☆ **BH&HPA. NCC. 462S. 34H.** ⌖ ⌦

(6m). Setthorns Caravan & Camping Site, Forestry Commission (Forest Holidays), Wootton, New Milton, Hampshire BH25 5WA. *01313 146505.* fe.holidays@forestry.gsi.gov.uk. www.forestholidays.co.uk. Owner: Forestry Commission (Forest Holidays). 231 Corstorphine Road, Edinburgh EH12 7AT. SP from A35, Lyndhurst to Christchurch road, 7m SW of Lyndhurst. Woodland site with individual pitches among pine oak trees. No toilet facilities. Booking essential, brochure request line: 0131 3340066. ☆☆☆ **BH&HPA. 250T. MC.** ✿ ⊁ ⊟

(2m). Stanley Caravan Park, Brockhills Lane, New Milton, Hampshire BH25 5QW. *01425 610771.* islandmeadowparks@fsmail.net. www.islandmeadow.co.uk. Owner: P L Pratt. Holdens Caravan Park, Bracklesham Lane, Bracklesham, Chichester, West Sussex PO20 8JG. Follow A337 to New Milton, look for Station Road, over railway line, right into Manor Road, left into Oakwood Avenue over crossroads into Brockhills Lane. Park entrance. Peaceful park built within the grounds of

Stanley's, surrounded by trees. Telephone for free brochure: 01243 670207. Demonstraction caravan available for inspection at the park. Horse riding, golf, beaches all nearby. Beaulieu Motor Museum and ancestral home. Open March 1-October 31. **207S.** 🖾

Ringwood

Ashley Heath Caravan Park, Horton Road, Ringwood, Hampshire BH24 2EH. *01243 670207.* Owner: Pratt Developments Unlimited. Holdens Caravan Park, Bracklesham Lane, Bracklesham, Chichester, West Sussex PO20 8JG. Follow A31 to underpass. Follow signs to Ashley Heath, above underpass, along Horton Road, follow signs to Moors Valley Country Park. Entrance is on R after 1m. Park set in forest and close to country park. For free brochure telephone 01243 670207. Demonstration caravans available for inspection at the park. Golf, horse riding nearby. Ancient market town of Ringwood and Bournemouth within easy reach. Open March 1-October 31. **130S.** 🖾

(3.5m). Back of Beyond Touring Park, 234 Ringwood Road, St Leonards, Ringwood, Hampshire BH24 2SB. *01202 876968.* melandsuepike@aol.com. www.backofbeyondtouring park.co.uk. Owner: M J B & S Pike. W of Ringwood, 2m E of Ferndown, on A31. Adults only. 28 acres of peaceful, unspoilt countryside, off the beaten track. Easy access to local amenities, coast and New Forest. Fishing on site. Open March-October. ☆☆☆ **80T. 80MC.** 🖾 👶 🚻

(2.4m). Camping International, 229 Ringwood Road, St Leonards, Ringwood, Hampshire BH24 2SD. *01202 872817/872742.* campint@globalnet.co.uk. www.users. globalnet.co.uk/~campint. Owner: Pegville Ltd. Athol Lodge, 229 Ringwood Road, St Leonards, Ringwood, Hants. On southern side of A31, W of Ringwood. Family touring park for Bournemouth, New Forest, country and sea. AA 4 pennants. Open March-October. ☆☆☆☆ **BH&HPA. 206T. MC.** 🖾 🚻

(4m). Deer's Leap (New Forest Holiday Homes Park), Linwood, Ringwood, Hampshire BH24 3QX. *01425 473217.* Owner: Cramcrest Ltd. Off A338. In New Forest, next door to well-known local inn. Open March 1-October 31. **BH&HPA. 35S.** 🖾 ✎

(3m). Oakdene Forest Park, St Leonards, Ringwood, Hampshire BH24 2RZ. *01590 648331.* holidays@shore field.co.uk. www.shorefield.co.uk. Owner: Shorefield Holidays Ltd. Shorefield Road, Milford-on-Sea, Hampshire SO41 0LH. Off A31, W of Ringwood. Bournemouth 9m. Licensed club. Entertainment. Cafeteria. Takeaway. Adventure playground. Bordering Avon Forest. Indoor and outdoor pools, gym, sauna, steam room, flume. Open February-December. ☆☆☆ **BH&HPA. 135T. 135MC. 300S. 207H.** 🖾 🚻 👶 🚻 ✎

(4m). Red Shoot Camping Site, Linwood, Ringwood, Hampshire BH24 3QT. *01425 473789.* enquiries@redshoot-campingpark.com. www.red shoot-campingpark.com. Owner: Mrs S J Foulds. Off A31 (M27) at exit 1. Follow signs for New Forest and Linwood, or minor road off A338, 2m N of Ringwood, SP Linwood. Site supervised by owner. Open March 1-October 31. ☆☆☆☆ **30T. 75MC.** 🖾 🚻 👶 🚻

(4.5m). Redcote Holiday Park, 3 Boundary Lane, St Leonards, Ringwood, Hampshire BH24 2SE. *01202 872817/872742.* Owner: Pegville Ltd. Athol Lodge, 229 Ringwood Road, St Leonards, Ringwood, Hants. On the A3 between Ringwood and Ferndown. Table tennis and pool rooms. Heated pool. PH. Laundrette. Battery charging. TV room. Adventure playground. Showers, baby room. Restaurant, takeaway. Children's venue. 5-a-side football and basketball. 70 pitches for tents availabe. Open March-October. **BH&HPA. 75T. MC.** 🖾 🚻

(2m). Shamba Holidays, 230 Ringwood Road, St Leonards, Ringwood, Hampshire BH24 2SB. *01202 873302.* enquiries@shambaholidays.co.uk. www.shamba holidays.co.uk. Owner: Shamba Holidays Ltd. 21 Compass Point, Ensign Way, Hamble, Hampshire SO31 4RA. W of Ringwood on the A31, site SP. Family-run park set in pleasant countryside, with entrance on a private lane. New clubhouse (bar, takeaway, shop, games room and a large-screen TV), play area, free showers. Heated, indoor swimming pool. Winter storage. Seasonal pitches. Open March 1-October 31. ☆☆☆ **BH&HPA. 150T. MC.** 🖾 🚻

(2m). Tree Tops Caravan Park, Hurn Road, Avon Castle, Matchams, Ringwood, Hampshire BH24 2BP. *01425 475848.* Owner: Mr & Mrs S Mullins. A31 to Ringwood, in 0.25m filter left for Matchams, site 1.5m on L. Very quiet site, adults only. No dogs. Fishing, golf, shops, doctor all within 2m. Direct walking access to Avon Heath Country Park. Open March-October. **15T. MC.** 🖾

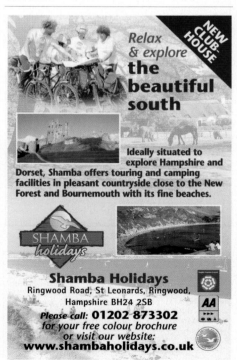

Romsey

(4m). Green Pastures Farm, Ower, Romsey, Hampshire SO51 6AJ. *023 8081 4444.* enquiries@greenpasturesfarm.com. www.greenpasturesfarm.com. Owner: Mr & Mrs A Pitt. SP from J2 M27 (Salisbury direction) and A36 and A3090 at Ower. Family-run site on working farm near New Forest. Convenient ferries for Europe and Isle of Wight. Space for children to play. Local PH with food and real ales. Fishing, golf and swimming nearby. Open March 15-October 31. ☆☆☆ BH&HPA. 45T. MC. ♒ 🖭 ㋡ 🗲.

(3.5m). Hill Farm Caravan Park, Branches Lane, Sherfield English, Romsey, Hampshire SO51 6FH. *01794 340402.* gjb@hillfarmpark.com. www.hillfarmpark.com. Owner: Geoff & Suzy Billett. 4m W Romsey on A27 towards Salisbury. N at 2nd crossroads marked Branches Lane. Site 0.5m on R. 9-hole, par-3 pitch and putt golf course on site. Licensed shop for bread, croissants and pasties daily, and snack meals. Open March-October for tourers; open February-December for holiday homes. ☆☆☆☆ BH&HPA. 120T. 120MC. 6S. 4H. ♒ 🖭 ㋡ 🗲 ∅

Southampton

(10m). Solent Breezes Holiday Village, Hook Lane, Warsash, Southampton, Hampshire SO31 9HG. *01489 572084/559739.* info@cinqueportsleisure.com. www.cinqueportsleisure.com. Owner: Cinque Ports Leisure Ltd. Coghurst Hall Holiday Village, Ivyhouse Lane, Ore, Hastings, East Sussex TN35 4NP. Exit 9 from M27 take last exit at large roundabout, proceed to 2nd roundabout and turn sharp L into Hunts Pond Road. Turn R at junction with Warsash Road, first L into Hook Lane and L into Chilling Lane. Facilities include outdoor heated pool. Private slipway. Tennis court. Village store. Laundrette. Cafe. sun terrace and lounge bar. Free children's club. Rose Award. Open March-October; open weekends November-February. ☆☆☆☆ BH&HPA. NCC. 238S. ♒ 🗲

Southbourne

(0.5m). Camping & Caravanning Club Site - Chichester, Main Road, Southbourne, Hampshire PO10 8JH. *01243 373202/0870 2433331.* www.campingandcaravanningclub.co.uk. Owner: Camping & Caravanning Club. Greenfields House, Westwood Way, Coventry CV4 8JH. 5m W of Chichester, 3m E of Havant, site well marked on N side of A259, off A27. Follow signs Nutbourne or Southbourne. Site on R past Inlands Road. Suitable base for Chichester, South Downs, Bosham and Portsmouth. Close to sea and shops. Set in ancient orchard. Area full of history, with Iron Age hillforts, Roman remains and Norman castles. Non members welcome. All units accepted. Special deals for families and backpackers. Open February-November. ☆☆☆☆ 58T. 58MC. ♒ 🖭 ㋡

Southsea

(5m). Southsea Leisure Park, Melville Road, Southsea, Hampshire PO4 9TB. *023 9273 5070.* info@southsealeisurepark.com. www.southsealeisurepark.com. Owner: Southsea Caravans Ltd. From M27, A27 and A3M, take Southsea exit (A2030 south) and follow signs along Eastern Road. Playground and room, organised activities in season. Heated outdoor pool, showers, laundry room. Restaurant and bar. Direct access to beach. 10mins from cross-Channel ferries. ☆☆☆ BH&HPA. 188T. MC. 51H. ✲ ♒ 🖭 ㋡ 🗲

Winchester

(3m). Balldown Touring Caravan Park, Stockbridge Road, Sparshott, Winchester, Hampshire SO21 2NA. *01962 776619.* Owner: Brian Cooper. N of Winchester on the B3049 (formerly A272) and N of J11 of M3. Open March 1-October 31. 16T. MC. ♒ 🖭

(3m). Morn Hill Caravan Club Site, Morn Hill, Winchester, Hampshire SO211HL. *01962 869877.* www.caravanclub.co.uk. Owner: The Caravan Club. East Grinstead House, East Grinstead, West Sussex RH19 1UA. See website for standard directions to site. Set on outskirts of Winchester, convenient for ferries and exploring New Forest. Advance booking essential bank holidays and July/August. Non-members and tent campers welcome. Motorhome service point, playframe, laundry facilities. Toilet/shower block with privacy cubicles. Veg prep area. Shop 3m. Fishing, golf and cycling routes 5m. Open March-October. ☆☆☆☆ NCC. 150T. MC. ♒ 🖭 ㋡

ISLE OF WIGHT

Adgestone

(1.5m). Camping & Caravanning Club site - Adgestone, Lower Adgestone Road, Adgestone, Isle of Wight PO36 0HL. *01983 403432/0870 2433331.* www.campingandcaravanningclub.co.uk. Owner: Camping & Caravanning Club. Greenfields House, Westwood Way, Coventry CV4 8JH. Turn off A3055 at The Fairway by Manor House PH in Lake, which is between Sandown and Shanklin, past golf course on L, turn R at T-junction, park 200yd on R. 22-acre site adjacent to river Yar, beneath Brading Downs in Area of Outstanding Natural Beauty. Non-members welcome. Caravans, motor caravans and tents accepted. Fishing on site at river and lake. Adventure playground. Outdoor heated swimming pool and takeaway on site. Golf course, Blackgang Chine theme park nearby and marine heritage museum. Special deals for families and backpackers. Open March-October. ☆☆☆☆ 270T. 270MC. 1S. 1H. ♒ 🖭 ㋡ 🗲

Bembridge

(1.5m). Whitecliff Bay Holiday Park, Hillway, Bembridge, Isle of Wight PO35 5PL. *01983 872671.* holiday@whitecliff-bay.com. www.whitecliff-bay.com. Owner: Whitecliff Bay Holiday Park Ltd. Off A3055 Ryde to Sandown on to B3395 to Bembridge and Whitecliff Bay. Heated swimming pools. Licensed clubs. Entertainment. Restaurant. Leisure centre. Snack bar with takeaway, Humphrays play zone, coffee shop, fitness studio. Open Easter-October 31. ☆☆☆☆ BH&HPA. NCC. 400T. MC. 260S. 230H. ♒ 🖭 ㋡ 🗲

Brighstone Bay

(0.75m). Grange Farm Caravan & Camping Site, Military Road, Brighstone Bay, Isle of Wight PO30 4DA. *01983 740296.* grangefarm@brighstonebay.fsnet.co.uk. www.brighstonebay.fsnet.co.uk. Owner: James & Chris Dungey. A3055 coast road midway between Freshwater Bay and Chale. 2-acre level site on small, family-run farm: llamas, pigs, goats, pony, horse, water buffalos etc. Suitable for children. Easy access to sandy beach. 1min. Safe swimming. Walkers paradise, fossil hunting. Camping or self-catering stays in holiday caravans or converted barns. Open March-October 31. ☆☆☆ BH&HPA.NCC. 30T. 30MC. 10H. ♒ 🖭 🗲

Brook

(2m). Compton Farm, Brook, Isle of Wight PO30 4HF. *01983 740215.* Owner: Mr D T Phillips. Just off A3055. 10m from Newport. Working farm. 10mins to clean sandy beach. Golf nearby, riding 3m, shops 2m. National Trust Area of Outstanding Natural Beauty. Open mid May-mid September. ✫✫ **BH&HPA. MC. 12H.** ⊷

Chale

(7m). Chine Farm Camping Site, Military Road, Atherfield Bay, Chale, Isle of Wight PO38 2JH. *01983 740228.* www.chine-farm.co.uk. Owner: Mrs H M Goody. Situated on the south side of the Isle of Wight at Cowleaze Chine, which is midway between the villages of Chale (3m) and Brighstone (2.5m) on the A3055 crossroad. Open May-September. ✫✫ **80T. 20MC.** ⊷

Cowes

(1.5m). Comforts Farm Camping Park, Comforts Farm, Pallance Road, Northwood, Cowes, Isle of Wight PO31 8LS. *01983 293888.* www.comfortsfarm.co.uk. Owner: Mrs V Annett. Off A3020. Open May-October 31. **50T. MC.** ⊷ ⊕ ♿ ⅃

(2m). Gurnard Pines Holiday Village, Cockleton Lane, Cowes, Isle of Wight PO31 8QE. *01983 292395-ext 102.* Off Cowes to Newport road. Open March-October. ✫✫✫✫✫ **BH&HPA. 20T. MC. 78H.** ⊷ ⊕ ♿

(4m). Thorness Bay Holiday Park, Thorness Bay, Thorness, Cowes, Isle of Wight PO31 8NJ. *0871 664 9779.* thorness.bay@park-resorts.com. www.park-resorts.com. Owner: Park Resorts Ltd. 4th Floor, Swan Court, Waterhouse Street, Hemel Hempstead, Herts HP1 1FN. From East Cowes and Fishbourne, follow signs to Newport and take A3054 towards Yarmouth. After 1m take first turn on R and follow signs to Thorness Bay. From Yarmouth, take A3054 towards Newport. After Shalfleet take first L and follow signs to Cowes. After about 5m Thorness Bay will be on L. Showbars. Laundrette. Food court/takeaway. Indoor and outdoor pool. Entertainment. Free children's club. Open March-January for owner-occupiers; open March-October for hire caravans. ✫✫✫✫ **BH&HPA. NCC. 130T. MC. 490S. 140H.** ⊷ ⊕ ⅃ ⌀

Newport

(4m). Island View Holidays, Main Road, Rookley, Newport, Isle of Wight PO38 3LU. *01983 721606.* Off A3020 Newport to Shanklin. PH, restaurant, cafe, games room, play areas, fishing. Set in 22 acres. Open March 1-November 1. ✫✫✫✫ **BH&HPA. 86S. 86H.** ⊷ ♿

Ryde

(3m). Carpenters Farm, St Helens, Ryde, Isle of Wight PO33 1YL. *01983 872450.* Owner: Mrs M Lovegrove. Located off the B3330. Milk and eggs available. Open June-October. ✫✫ **70T. MC.** ⊷ ⊕ ♿

(4m). Field Lane Holiday Park, St Helens, Ryde, Isle of Wight PO33 1UX. *01983 872779.* fieldlane@freeuk.com. www.field lane.cjb.net. Owner: D M & A Stirzaker. Quiet, family park. Rose Award. Open March-October. ✫✫✫✫ **BH&HPA. 33H.**

(4.5m). Hillgrove Caravan Park, Field Lane, St Helens, Ryde, Isle of Wight PO33 1UT. *01983 872802.* holidays@hill grove.co.uk. www.hillgrove.co.uk. Owner: Mr C R & Mrs J Thie. Take the A3055 from Ryde. After 2m, turn left on to the B3330, and on entering St Helens take the first turning on left, Field Lane. Park is at the end of lane. Friendly, family-run park only minutes away from safe, sandy beaches, countryside and many places of interest to explore. Heated outdoor pool, games room, play area and laundrette. Open March-January. ✫✫✫✫ **BH&HPA. 50H.** ⊷ ♿

(3.25m). Kite Hill Farm Caravan & Camping Park, Kite Hill Farm, Wootton Bridge, Ryde, Isle of Wight PO33 4LE. *01983 882543/01983 883261.* barry@kitehillfarm.freeserve. co.uk. www.campingparkisleofwight.com. Owner: J M Abraham. Village shops and doctor 10 mins walk away. **60T. 60MC.** ✿ ⊷ ⊕ ♿

(3m). Nodes Point Holiday Park, St Helens, Ryde, Isle of Wight PO33 1YA. *0871 664 9758.* nodes.point@park-resorts.com. www.park-resorts.com. Owner: Park Resorts Ltd. 3rd Floor, Swan Court, Waterhouse Street, Hemel Hempstead, Herts HP1 1FN. From Fishbourne on the A3054 east towards Ryde. At J with A3055, then left on to B3330 to St Helens. Nodes Point is on the left-hand side. From Cowes on A3021, then as above. Indoor fun-pool with waterslide. Freek children's clubs. Sports resorts programme. Laundrette. Family evening entertainment. Amusements. Horse riding nearby. Open April-October. ✫✫✫✫ **BH&HPA. 240T. MC. 158S. 84H.** ⊕ ⅃

(2m). Pondwell Camping Site, Pondwell Hill, Ryde, Isle of Wight PO34 5AQ. *01983 612330.* info@isleofwightself catering.com. www.isleofwightselfcatering.co.uk. Owner: I.W. Self Catering. Salterns, Seaview, Isle of Wight PO34 5AQ. On the B3340. Shop on site. Laundrette. TV lounge. Within walking distance to the sea. Open April-October 31. ✫✫✫ **BH&HPA. 60T. MC.** ⊕ ⅃

(5m). Woodside Beach Caravan Site, Woodside, Wootton Creek, Ryde, Isle of Wight PO33 4JT. 01983 882386. Owner: Rotch Property Group. 7th Floor, Leconfield House, Curzon Street, London W1Y 7FBB. Off A3054 Ryde to Newport. Both about 5m away. Own beach and moorings. Licensed cafe and bar. Shops, PO, doctors etc on Wootton High Street, about 2m. Open March 1-October 31. **3T. 3MC. 47S. 8H. ⚡ 🅱**

Sandown

(2m). Cheverton Copse Holiday Park, Scotchells Brook Lane, Sandown, Isle of Wight PO36 0JP. 01983 403161. holidays@cheverton-copse.co.uk. www.cheverton-copse.co.uk. Owner: Mr & Mrs M Berry. Cheverton House, Cheverton Copse Park. 1.5m west of town on A3056. Family park in delightful, wooded parkland. Licensed club and games room, entertainment in high season. Modern amenities. Laundry. Play area. Bus 300yds. Supermarket near. Lovely walking area 1.5m to beach. Open April-September. ✰✰✰✰ **BH&HPA. 14T. 12MC. 57H. 🅱**

(1m). Fairway Holiday Park, The Fairway, Sandown, Isle of Wight PO36 9PS. 01983 403462. www.fairwayholidaypark. co.uk. Off A3055. Picturesque camping and caravanning area. Modern caravans with showers. Snack Bar. Licensed club. Laundrette. Arcade. Play area. Open March-October. ✰✰ **BH&HPA. 100T. 30MC. 117H. 🅱 ⚡ ⌀**

(0.25m). Fort Holiday Park, Avenue Road, Sandown, Isle of Wight PO36 8BD. 01983 402858. bookings@fortholiday park.co.uk. www.fortholidaypark.co.uk. Owner: Mr David Sunnucks. On A3055 and B3329 just 2mins from beach and town. Secluded, family park with countryside views. Site is within easy level walking distance of all Sandown's beach. Open March-October. ✰✰✰ **BH&HPA. 45H. 🅱 ⌀**

(1.5m). Old Barn Touring Park, Cheverton Farm, Newport Road, Apse Heath, Sandown, Isle of Wight PO36 9PJ. 01983 866414. oldbarn@weltinet.com. www.oldbarntouring.co.uk. Owner: Mr & Mrs A F Welti. 500yd S of Apse Heath on A3056 Newport to Sandown. 2m to sandy beaches of Shanklin and Sandown. Downland views. Games room. Laundry. Superpitches available. Open May-September. ✰✰✰✰ **BH&HPA. 60T. 60MC. ⚡ 🅱 ⌀**

(3m). Queen Bower Dairy Caravan Park, Alverstone Road, Queen Bower, Sandown, Isle of Wight PO36 0NZ. 01983 403840. queenbowerdairy@aol.com. www.queenbower dairy.co.uk. Owner: Mr M J Reed. Off A3056 Sandown to Newport turn in to Alverstone Road at Apse Heath, entrance 1m on L. 60-acre National Trust copse nearby. Dogs must be exercised off site. PO 1m, Superstore 2m. Open May 1-October 31. **20T. MC. ⚡ 🅱**

Riverside Caravan Park, Avenue Road, Sandown, Isle of Wight PO36 9AL. 01983 402927. Owner: Riverside Caravans Ltd. On A3055 Ryde to Sandown. 10 mins from town. Open April-October. **BH&HPA. 50H.**

(3m). Southland Camping Park, Newchurch, Sandown, Isle of Wight PO36 0LZ. 01983 865385. info@southland.co.uk. www.southland.co.uk. Owner: Viv & Vanessa McGuinness. 3m W of Sandown off A3055/6 on outskirts Newchurch

village. SP from A3056 Newport to Sandown Road. Quiet, rural setting. Flat, generous pitches. Easy access. Suitable touring base. Ferry bookings service available. Open Easter-end September. ✰✰✰✰✰ **BH&HPA. 120T. MC. ⚡ 🅱 ⌀ 🅻**

(1.5m). Village Way, Newport Road, Apse Heath, Sandown, Isle of Wight PO36 9PJ. 01983 863279. Owner: Norma & Dennis. On A3056, follow Sandown sign from Newport. Showers. Laundry. Calor Gas sales. Power points in toilet block. Public telephone. Free carp fishing on site. ✰✰✰ **BH&HPA. 14T. 5MC. 2S. 12H. ⚘ ⚡ 🅱**

Shanklin

(0.5m). Landguard Camping Park, Landguard Manor Road, Shanklin, Isle of Wight PO37 7PH. 01983 867028. land guard@weltinet.com. www.landguard-camping.co.uk. Owner: Mr & Mrs A F J Welti. From Sandown take A3055 towards Lake, turn R on to A3056, turn L at factory into Whitecross Lane. Site 0.25m. Families only. Swimming pool. Within walking distance of town and beach. Open Easter-September. ✰✰✰✰ **BH&HPA. 100T. 50MC. 🅱 ⚡ 🅻**

(0.3m). Lower Hyde Holiday Park, Landguard Road, Shanklin, Isle of Wight PO37 7LL. 0871 664 9752. lower.hyde@park-resorts.com.www.park-resorts.com. Owner: Park Resorts Ltd. 3rd Floor, Swan Court, Waterhouse Street, Hemel Hempstead, Herts HP1 1FN. From Ryde follow A3055 to Shanklin via Sandown and Lake. At Lake turn right at the traffic lights towards Newport (A3056). After about 1m turn left into Whitecross Lane. Lower Hyde is 1m along on the right-hand side. Within walking distance of Shanklin. Outdoor fun pool. Adventure playground. Multi-sports court. Laundrette. Amusements. Takeaway and restaurant. Free children's clubs. Free family entertainment. Advance booking advisable. Open April-October. ✰✰✰✰ **BH&HPA. NCC. 128T. MC. 298S. 153H. 🅱 ⚘ 🅻 ⌀**

(1m). Ninham Country Holidays, Ninham, Shanklin, Isle of Wight PO37 7PL. 01983 864243/866040. info@ninham. fsnet.co.uk. www.ninham-holidays.co.uk. Owner: D H Harvey & Mrs V J Harvey. Off the A3056, west of Lake. In a country park setting overlooking wooded valley with small lakes. Coarse fishing. Play areas. Laundrette. Leisure centre 1m. Water sports school 1m. Advance booking advisable. Outdoor heated swimming pool. Games room. Suitable base for cycling. Open April-September. ✰✰✰✰ **50T. 30MC. 6H. 🅱 ⌀**

St Helens

Old Mill Holiday Park Ltd, Mill Road, St Helens, Isle of Wight PO33 1UE. 01983 872507. inf@oldmill.co.uk. www.oldmill. co.uk. Owner: M A & P M Stephens. From Ryde A3055 to Sandown. Turn off to St Helens the B3330, Mill Road is off Lower Green Road. Sheltered, peaceful locationsuitable for birdwatchers. Solent shipping can be watched from the park. Dogs and new pets not allowed in peak season. Accommodation includes pine cabins and apartments. No tourers. Rose Award. Golf 3m. Tesco 3.5m. Shops 0.5m. Fishing 100yd. ✰✰✰✰✰ **BH&HPA. 36H. ⚘ ⚡ 🅱 & ⌀**

Totland

Ivylands Holiday Park, Totland Bay, The Broadway, Totland, Isle of Wight PO39 0AN. *01983 752480.* web@ivylandsholi daypark.co.uk. www.ivylandsholidaypark.co.uk. Owner: Mr & Mrs G Osman. Located at junction of A3054 and A3055. No pets. Rose Award. Within minutes' walk of sandy beaches. Downland and coastal walks. Shopping 0.5m, Leisure centre 1m, golf course 2m. Open February 1-December 31. ☆☆☆ **BH&HPA. 11H.**

Ventnor

(2m). Appuldurcombe Gardens Holiday Park, Appuldurcombe Road, Wroxall, Ventnor, Isle of Wight PO38 3EP. *01983 852597.* info@appuldurcombegardens. co.uk. www.appuldurcombegardens.co.uk. Owner: Mr P Saunders. Situated just slightly inland between Shanklin and Ventnor, in the village of Wroxhall. Pretty, family holiday site in quiet, unspoilt countryside. Just a few minutes by car from the beaches of Shanklin, Sandown and Ventnor. Open March-October. ☆☆☆☆ **BH&HPA. 100T. 40H.** � 🅿 🛆 🖙 ⌀

(5m). Castlehaven Caravan Site, Castlehaven Lane, Niton Undercliff, Ventnor, Isle of Wight PO38 2ND. *01983 730461/855556.* caravans@castlehaven.co.uk. www.castle haven.co.uk. Owner: Mr L F Wayman-Hales. Mews Cottage, 93 High Street, Ventnor, Isle of Wight PO38 1LU. Off A3055. Below Buddle Inn. On shore. Small secluded site. Refreshment kiosk. Paragliding, surfing, fishing, rambling, birdwatching, fossil hunting, walking distance to PH. Open Easter-October 31. **BH&HPA. 9**🚶 🛆 ⌀

(5m). Meadow View Caravan Site, Hoyes Farm, Newport Road, Niton, Ventnor, Isle of Wight. *01983 730024.* Owner: Mr & Mrs T & S Willis. Ladyacre Farm, Pan Lane, Niton, Isle of Wight. Open from March 1-October 31. **7H.** 🚶

Yarmouth

(4m). Orchards Holiday Caravan & Camping Park, Newbridge, Yarmouth, Isle of Wight PO41 0TS. *01983 531331.* info@orchards-holiday-park.co.uk. www.orchards-holiday-park.co.uk. Owner: Mr T Gray. Park is located on the B3401, E of Yarmouth and 6m W of Newport. Situated opposite Newbridge PO. Caravan Club affiliated site. Package holidays available include return ferry fares for cars, caravans and passengers. Indoor and outdoor heated swimming pools. Bottled gas. Rose Award. David Bellamy Gold Conservation Award. Open mid February-January. ☆☆☆☆ **BH&HPA. 100T. 75MC. 5S. 58H.** ✿ 🚶 🅿 🛆 🛒

(3m). Silver Glades, Solent Road, Cranmore, Yarmouth, Isle of Wight PO41 0XZ. *01983 760172.* holiday@silver-gladesiow.co.uk. www.silvergladesiow.co.uk. Owner: Mr & Mrs R Thorne. Take the A3054 Newport to Yarmouth road. Take the first turning right after the Horse and Groom public house. Silver Glades is a small quiet family-run caravan park situated in country surroundings and bordered by beautiful woodland. Pets are welcome. Open March-end October. ☆☆☆☆ **10H.** 🚶

Please visit the Caravan Club website: www.caravanclub.co.uk

OXFORDSHIRE

Abingdon

(4m). Bridges House Caravan Site, Clifton Hampden, Abingdon, Oxfordshire OX14 3EH. *01865 407725.* Owner: Elizabeth Gower. Fishing on site. Shops, PO, doctor within 0.25m. Open April 1-October 30. **BH&HPA. 12T. 4MC. 40S. 4H.** 🐕 🏠

Banbury

(4m). Anitas Touring Caravan Park (formerly 'Mollington'), Church Farm, The Yews, Mollington, Banbury, Oxfordshire OX17 1AZ. *01295 750731.* Owner: Darrel & Gail Jeffries. Leave M40, J11 onto A422 then A423 Southam road, park 4m on left, just past Mollington village turn. Family-run site on a working farm. All pitches with electric hook-ups. New toilet and shower facilities. Central to many places of interest: Warwick, Stratford, Cotswolds, Blenheim etc. Good fishing nearby and walks to village PH. Large play area for ball games etc. Large area for rallies. ✫✫✫✫ **BH&HPA. 36T. MC.** ✿ 🐕 🏠 &

(3m). Barnstones Caravan Site, Barnstones, Great Bourton, Banbury, Oxfordshire OX17 1QU. *01295 750289.* Owner: Mr D J Boddington. Leave Banbury on A423 SP Southam. After 3m turn R, SP Great Borton. Site on R in 100yd. If using M40 leave J11 Banbury and follow sign to Chipping Norton, over 2 roundabouts. At 3rd roundabout turn R, SP Southam on to A423. Golf course 2.5m. Fishing, doctor, PO, shop 1m. PH serving food 150yd. Garage 0.5m. ✫✫✫✫ **55T. MC.** ✿ 🐕 🏠

(3.5m). Bo Peep Farm Caravan Park, Aynho Road, Adderbury, Banbury, Oxfordshire OX17 3NP. *01295 810605.* warden@bo.peep.co.uk. www.bo.peep.co.uk. Owner: Mr A J Hodge. Situated on B4100 0.5m E of Adderbury and 3m S of Banbury. Access via M40, J10. Caravan Club affiliated site. Tranquil 13-acre touring site set in 85 acres of farmland. River frontage and woodland walks. Central for Oxford, Blenheim, Stratford-on-Avon and Warwick Castle. Year-round caravan storage available. Open April-October. ✫✫✫✫ **BH&HPA. 112T. MC.** 🐕 🏠 🦮

Bicester

(5m). Godwin's (Oxford) Ice Cream Farm Caravan Park, Northampton Road, Weston-on-the-Green, Bicester, Oxfordshire, OX25 3QL. *01869 351647.* neil@westononthe green.freeserve.co.uk. Owner: Neil & Lorna Godwin. Situated two minutes from J9 of the M40, midway between Oxford and Bicester. Home-made ice cream made on the farm using own herd's milk. Cafe, bar/restaurant and shop. Golf course nearby. Nationwide cycle track linking Oxford to Milton Keynes (route 51). Oxfordshire way footpath. PO, shops, PH/restaurants 10 mins walk away. Open March-October. **60T.** 🐕 🏠 🦮 &

(4m). Heyford Leys Caravan Site, Upper Heyford, Bicester, Oxfordshire OX6 3LU. *01869 232048.* Owner: D J & B J Buxey & Son. Off B4030 Chipping Norton to Bicester. 2m from M40. Washing facilities. Play area. GS. ✫ **BH&HPA. 20T. 10MC. 16S.** 🏠 🦮

Bletchingdon

Greenhill Leisure Park, Greenhill Farm, Station Road, Bletchingdon, Oxfordshire OX5 3BQ. *01869 351600.* info@greenhill-leisure-park.co.uk. www.greenhill-leisure-park. co.uk. Owners: Mr & Mrs P Bagnall. From Oxford on to A34 N, turn on to B4027. Bletchingdon site 0.5m after village. 3m from Woodstock. Quiet and spacious farm site scheduled to open

Easter 2006. Pets' corner, farm animals. Riverside walks, fishing on site. Rally field. Heated toilet block. Suitable base for touring the Cotswolds, 3m from Bleinheim Place. **40T. 40MC.** ✿ 🐕 🏠 & 🦮

Burford

Burford Caravan Club Site, Bradwell Grove, Burford, Oxfordshire OX18 4JJ. *01993 823080.* www.caravan club.co.uk. Owner: The Caravan Club. East Grinstead House, East Grinstead, West Sussex RH19 1UA. See website for standard directions to site. Spacious site opposite Cotswold Wildlife Park. Some hard-standing pitches, toilet block with privacy cubicles and laundry facilities. Motorhome service point, playground, shops within 2m and dog walk on site. Open March-October. ✫✫✫✫✫ **NCC. 120T. MC.** 🐕 🏠 &

Charlbury

(1m). Cotswold View Caravan & Camping Site, Enstone Road, Charlbury, Oxfordshire OX7 3JH. *01608 810314.* cotswoldview@gfwiddows.f9.co.uk. www.cotswoldview.co.uk. Owner: Mr & Mrs Widdows. 2m off A44 at Enstone on to B4022. Blenheim Palace 5m, Stratford-on-Avon 29m. Family-run site on the eastern edge of the Cotswolds. Suitable centre for touring and walking, overlooking the Evenlode Valley. Also available: bed and breakfast and self-catering cottages. Skittle alley, giant chess, tennis court. Freephone 0800 0853474. Open April 1-October 31. ✫✫✫✫ **125T. MC.** 🐕 🏠 & 🦮

Chipping Norton

(2.5m). Camping & Caravanning Club Site - Chipping Norton, Chipping Norton Road, Chadlngton, Chipping Norton, Oxfordshire OX7 3PE. *01608 641993/0870 2433331.* www.campingandcaravanning club.co.uk. Owner: Camping & Caravanning Club. Greenfields House, Westwood Way, Coventry CV4 8JH. Take Oxford ring road, A3400 to Stratford-upon-Avon, then A44 in Chipping Norton take A361 for Burford. In 1.5m bear L at fork, SP Chadlington. Set in Cotswolds countryside. Site has children's play area and a woodland walk adjacent to the site. Local villages such as Stow-on-the-Wold and Bourton-on-the-Water are worth a visit. Oxford and Stratford are both only 20m away. Non members welcome. Special deals available for families and backpackers. Open March-October. ✫✫✫✫ **105T. 105MC.** 🐕 🏠 &

(10m). The New Inn, Nether Westcote, Chipping Norton, Oxfordshire OX7 6SD. *01993 830827.* Owner: Mr Steve Rix. Left off A424, Stow-on-the-Wold to Burford. ✫ **25T. MC.** ✿ 🐕 🏠

Henley-on-Thames

(0.75m). Four Oaks Caravan Club Site, Marlow Road, Henley-on-Thames, Oxfordshire RG9 2HY. *01491 572312.* www.caravanclub.co.uk. Owner: The Caravan Club. East Grinstead House, East Grinstead, West Sussex RH19 1UA. See website for standard directions to site. Club members only. Shops 0.5m. Pleasant green and level site with mature trees. Within walking distance of Henley. Hard-standings. Toilet blocks. Privacy cubicles. Laundry facilities. Baby/toddler washroom. Veg prep. Motorhome service point. Dog walk on site. Playground. Suitable for families. Open March-October. **NCC. 91T. MC.** 🐕 🏠 &

Kidlington

(4m). Lince Copse Waterside Touring Caravan & Camping Park, Enslow, Nr Bletchingdon, Kidlington, Oxfordshire OX5 3AY. *01869 351321.* sales@kingsground.co.uk. Owner: R Haynes. Kingsground Narrow Boats, Building 103, Upper Heyford Business Park, Bicester, Oxfordshire. On the A4095 near junction with B4027, 6m from M40 J9 and 1m E of A4260. In the heart of the Cherwell Valley alongside Oxford Canal. Canal trips available locally. Fishing and golf nearby. Restaurant and PH 5 mins from park entrance. Close to Blenheim Palace. Open April-November. **25T. MC.** 🛒 🕭 💷 🛢

Oxford

(8m). Benson Waterfront Holiday Park, Benson Cruiser Station, Benson, Oxford, Oxfordshire OX10 6SJ. *01491 838304.* bensonwaterfront@btopenworld.com. www.water frontcafe.co.uk. Owner: B North & Sons (WW) Ltd. On A4074 Oxford to Henley at T-junction B4009. On river Thames. Close to Benson village and its facilities. Restaurant and shop. Children allowed. Boat hire available. Open March 1-January 31. **BH&HPA. 20T. MC. 25S.** 🛒 💷 🕭 & 🛢

> **(1m). Camping & Caravanning Club Site - Oxford, 426 Abingdon Road, Oxford, Oxfordshire OX1 4XN.** *01865 2440880870 243 3331.* www.campingandcaravanning club.co.uk. Owner: Camping & Caravanning Club. Greenfields House, Westwood Way, Coventry CV4 8JH. South side of Oxford, take A4144 to city centre from ring road, SP from A34. Being close to historic city centre, site is a suitable touring base. Good access to M4/M40. Non-members welcome. All types of units accepted. University city offers more than 650 listed buildings. Special deals available for families and backpackers. ✰✰✰ **85T. 85MC.** ✿ 🛒 💷

(7m). Diamond Farm Caravan & Camping Park, Islip Road, Bletchington, Oxford, Oxfordshire OX5 3DR. *01869 350909.* warden@diamondpark.co.uk. www.diamondpark. co.uk. Owner: Mr Roger Hodge. N of Oxford on the B4027 from M40, J9, on to the A34 south for 3m, follow signs for Bletchingdon. Heated swimming pool, clubhouse, games room, snooker table and play field. New toilet block, family bathroom, laundrette, dog walk next to site. AA 4 pennants. Open February-November. ✰✰✰✰ **37T. MC.** 🛒 💷 🛢

(23m). Swiss Farm International Caravan and Camping Park, Marlow Road, Henley-on-Thames, Oxford, Oxfordshire RG9 2HY. *01491 573419.* enquiries@swissfarm camping.co.uk. www.swissfarmcamping.co.uk. Owner: Mr J W Borlase. On A4155 near river. Once in Henley follow signs out towards Marlow. Site is on the left just outside town centre after rugby club. International, family-run site. Facilities include open air swimming pool, fishing lake, licensed bar and games room. Open March 1-October 31. ✰✰ **BH&HPA. 120T. 20MC. 6H.** 🛒 💷 &

Wallingford

(0.25m). Bridge Villa Caravan & Camping Park, Crowmarsh Gifford, Wallingford, Oxfordshire OX10 8HB. *01491 836860.* Owner: Messrs Eltownsend and Son. Off the A4130 in the village of Crowmarsh Gifford, near Wallingford Bridge. Showers . Shaver and hair-dryer points. Gas supplies. Laundrette within 250yd. Ironing room available. Many sporting facilities within 2m of site. Information on request. Open February 1-December 31. **BH&HPA. 111T. MC.** 🛒 💷 & 🛢

(0.25m). Riverside Park, The Street, Wallingford, Oxfordshire OX11 8EB. *01491 835232.* Owner: Soil Leisure. Culham Science Centre, Building C2, Main Avenue, Abingdon OX14 3DB. Approach from E on A4130 as access is difficult at end of Wallingford Bridge. Wallingford is on the A4074, Oxford to Reading road. Lights control a single-file traffic flow. Fishing. 5 mins walk to shops. Outdoor heated swimming pool. Small shop selling ice creams and drinks. Open May-September. **23T.** & 🛢

Witney

(10m). Bablockhythe Riverside Caravan Park, Northmoor, Witney, Oxfordshire OX29 5AT. *01865 882236.* greenwood parks@btconnect.com. www.greenwoodparks.com. Owner: Pratt family. Green Wood Parks, Itchenor Caravan Park, Shipton Green Lane, Itchenor, Chichester, West Sussex PO20 7BZ. A415, Abingdon to Kingston Bagpuize, turn R after two hump-back bridges towards Standlake and then Northmoor. Park located along the banks of the Thames: fishing, boat mooring, available. Shopping centre, golf 10m. Telephone for free brochure: 01243 514433. Open April 1-October 31. **317S. 1H.** 🛒

(4m). Hardwick Parks, Downs Road, Standlake, Witney, Oxfordshire OX29 7PZ. *01865 300501.* info@hardwick parks.co.uk. www.hardwickparks.co.uk. Owner: Hardwick Parks Ltd. Off the A415. Fishing. Windsurfing. Water-skiing. Jet-skiing on 40-acre lake. Licensed clubhouse with food to eat in or take away. Golf course 4m. Horse riding 0.5m. Open April-October. ✰✰✰ **BH&HPA. 164T. 50MC. 153S. 6H.** 🛒 💷 & 🛢

(5.5m). Lincoln Farm Park, High Street, Standlake, Witney, Oxfordshire OX29 7RH. *01865 300239.* info@lincolnfarm. tourist net.uk.com. www.lincolnfarm.touristnet.uk.com. Owner: Mr Keith Fletcher. 5.5m SE on A415 in High Street. 2 indoor swimming pools, Spa pools and saunas on site, children's pool all indoors. Fitness centre. Fishing nearby in private lake. Open February 1-mid November. ✰✰✰✰✰ **BH&HPA. 90T. MC.** 🛒 💷 & 🛢

Woodstock

> **(0.75m). Bladon Chains Caravan Club Site, Bladon Road, Woodstock, Oxfordshire OX7 1PT.** *01993 812390.* www.caravanclub.co.uk. Owner: Caravan Club. East Grinstead House, East Grinstead, West Sussex RH19 1UA. See website for standard directions to site. Caravan Club members only. Level site surrounded by magnificent trees. Toilet blocks, laundry facilities and motorhome service point. Significant areas of interest and NCN cycle route nearby. Open March-October. **NCC. 95T. MC.** 🛒 💷 &

WILTSHIRE

Calne

(1.5m). Blackland Lakes Holiday and Leisure Centre, Blackland Leisure Ltd, Stockley Lane, Calne, Wiltshire SN11 0NQ. *01249 813672.* info@blacklandlakes.co.uk. www.blacklandlakes.co.uk. Owner: Mr & Mrs John Walden. East of Calne off A4, SP. Scenic, sheltered, friendly, site with lakes and coarse fishing. 17 acres. Superpitches. Play areas. Laundry room. Good touring and family holiday centre.RAC appointed. AA 3 pennants. Mother and baby and disabled rooms. No clubhouse. No static holiday homes. 1m trail. 6 paddocks (adult only). Open March-end October. **180T. MC.** 🛒 💷 & 🛢

Chippenham

(4m). Piccadilly Caravan Site, Folly Lane West, Lacock, Chippenham, Wiltshire SN15 2LP. 01249 730260. piccadilly lacock@aol.com. Owner: Peter Williams. Off A350 Chippenham to Melksham road SP to Gastard with caravan symbol. Set in open countryside 0.5m from historic National Trust village of Lacock. Suitable touring centre. Open April-October. ✰✰✰✰✰ **BH&HPA. 40T.** 🛲 ⌷

(3m). Plough Lane Caravan Site, Kington Langley, Chippenham, Wiltshire SN15 5PS. 01249 750146. plough lane@lineone.net. www.ploughlane.co.uk. Owners: Roger and Helen Wilding. Signed from A350 North of Chippenham (J17, M4). Adults only. All pitches hard-standing, half grass. PHs nearby. Bus service from outside site. Suitably located for touring Wiltshire, Cotswolds and Bath. Open mid March-mid October. ✰✰✰✰✰ **BH&HPA. 50T. 50MC.** 🐾 ⌷ ♿

Devizes

(3m). Bell Caravan & Camping Site, Andover Road, Lydeway, Devizes, Wiltshire SNI0 3PS. 01380 840230. Owner: Allan & Lesley Nash. 3m SE of Devizes on the A342 Andover road. Heated swimming pool. Hot takeaway food. Off-licence. Games room. Covered barbecue area. Table tennis. Open April 1-October 1. **BH&HPA. 25T. 10MC.** 🛲 🛒

Malmesbury

(0.25m). Burton Hill Caravan & Camping Park, Arches Lane, Malmesbury, Wiltshire SN16 0EH. 01666 826880. stay@ burtonhill.co.uk. www.burtonhill.co.uk. Owners: W & A Hateley. Office address: Overmeade, Arches Farm, Malmesbury, Wiltshire SN16 0EH. Off the A429 Chippenham to Malmesbury road, Arches Lane, opposite Malmesbury Hospital. 5m N of M4, J7. Burton Hill is a level, grassy site overlooking the town and farmland. 5-10mins walk along part of the town's river walk into Malmesbury, where there are PHs, shops, supermarket, restaurants, swimming pool. Many walks and cycle ways. Shopping at the Outlet Centre, Swindon. Open April 1-October 31. ✰✰ **BH&HPA. 30T. 30MC.** 🛲 ♿

Marlborough

(6m). Hillview Park, Oare, Marlborough, Wiltshire SN8 4JG. 01672 563151. Owner: R A Harriman. S of Marlborough on A345. Level site. Showers. SAE for brochure. Advance booking advisable. Shops and rail station within 2m. Open April-September. ✰✰✰ **BH&HPA. 10T. 10MC.** 🛲 ⌷

(1m). Postern Hill - Savernake Forest, Forestry Commission (Forest Holidays), Postern Hill, Marlborough, Wiltshire SN8 4ND. 01672 515 195. fe.holidays@forestry.gsi.gov.uk. www. forestholidays.co.uk. Owner: Forestry Commission (Forest Holidays). 231 Corstorphine Road, Edinburgh EN12 7AT. 1m S of Marlborough on the A346 towards Tidwerth. Set in a woodland park, a quiet site suitable for exploring historic Wiltshire. No toilet facilities. Brochure request line: 0131 334 0066. Open early March-end September. **BH&HPA. 170T. MC.** 🛲 ⌷

Marston Meysey

Second Chance Touring Park, Marston Meysey, Wiltshire SN6 6SZ. 01285 810675/810939. Owner: B Stroud. Midway between cirencester and Swindon along A419. turn off at Fairford/Latton, SP. Proceed until Castle Eaton SP. Turn R, park 150yd on R. 3.5m from Fairford. Upper Thames riverside location on edge of the Cotswolds. Fishing on site. Explore the Isis with your own canoe. Golf course nearby. 3.5m to shops, doctor, PO. Close to Roman town Cirencester, capital of Cotswolds. Open March 1-November 30. **26T. MC.** ⌷

Melksham

(2m). Camping & Caravanning Club Site - Devizes, Spout Lane, Nr Seend, Melksham, Wiltshire SN12 6RN. 01380 828839/0870 2433331. www.campingand caravanningclub.co.uk. Owner: Camping & Caravanning Club. Greenfields House, Westwood Way, Coventry CV4 8JH. On A361 from Devizes turn R on to A365 over canal and next L down the lane beside Three Magpies PH, site on R. Bordering the Kennett and Avon Canal, 4m from Devizes. 90 pitches. Non-members welcome. Caravans, motor caravans and tents accepted. Fishing available all year round in canal adjacent to site. Special deals available for families and backpackers. David Bellamy Silver Conservation Award. ✰✰✰✰✰ **90T. 90MC.** ✿ 🛲 ♿

Salisbury

(3m). Alderbury Caravan & Camping Park, Old Southampton Road, Whaddon, Salisbury, Wiltshire SP5 3HB. 01722 710125. Owner: N Cambell. A36 to Southampton and follow signs for Alderbury and Whaddon. Clean, pleasant site on edge of village, opposite Three Crowns inn. Showers, utility room and telephone. Suitable location for Stonehenge and New Forest. **39T. MC.** ✿ 🛲 ⌷ ♿

(1.5m). Camping & Caravanning Club Site - Salisbury, Hudson's Field, Castle Road, Salisbury, Wiltshire SPI 3RR. 01722 320713/0870 243 3331. www.campingand caravanningclub.co.uk. Owner: Camping & Caravanning Club. Greenfields House, Westwood Way, Coventry CV4 8JH. 1.5m from Salisbury on A345. Large open field next to Old Sarum. Site is 30mins walk along river Avon from Salisbury. A visit to the city is a must, with its shops and spectacular cathedral. Iron Age Settlement of Old Sarum, preserved by English Heritage is nearby. Gliding, fishing, horse riding and cycling are all within easy reach of the site. Non-members welcome. All types of units accepted. Special deals available for families and backpackers. Open March-October. ✰✰✰✰ **150T. 150MC.** 🛲 ⌷ ♿

Church Farm Caravan & Camping Park, The Bungalow, High Street, Sixpenny Handley, Salisbury, Wiltshire SP5 5ND. 01725 552563. churchfarmcandcpark@yahoo.co.uk. www. churchfarmcandcpark.co.uk. Owner: Mr S Judd. Shops, PH, PO and butcher's 2mins walk in village. Golf course 4m. Bus service through village. Lots of walking. Central for touring. ✰✰✰ **20T. 20MC. 2S.** ✿ 🛲 ⌷ ♿

(4m). Coombe Touring Caravan Park, Race Plain, Netherhampton, Salisbury, Wiltshire SP2 8PN. *01722 328451.* Owner: Brian & Margaret Hayter. Take A36 Salisbury to Warminster, 2m from Salisbury outskirts, turn at traffic lights onto A3094. Next to Salisbury racecourse. Laundrette. Gas supplies. Shop open Easter to September. SAE for brochure. 2.5m to shops, PO. Golf nearby. AA 4 pennants. Open: March-December. **BH&HPA. 45T. 5MC.** 🐕 ⊡ ♿ ⚓

(10m). Green Hill Farm Camping & Caravan Park, New Road, Landford, Salisbury, Wiltshire, SP5 2AZ. *02380 811506/01794 324117.* Owner: Mrs J & Mr P Osman. Storms Farm, Kewlake Lane, Cadnam, Hants SO40 2NT. M27 south bound exit J2. A36 Salisbury road 3m BP garage on left take next left into new road SP Nomansland, site on left 1m along new road. Adults only. Within New Forest Heritage area. Two lakes, fishing on site. Shops, PO 1m, Doctors 2.5m. Suitable base for walking or cycling; direct access to New Forest at rear of site. PHs and eating-houses in easy reach. Dogs must be kept on leads on site and farm areas. Calor Gas and eggs stocked. AA 3 pennants. **100T. 50MC.** ✿ 🐕 ⊡

(9m). Hillside Caravan Club Site, Andover Road, Lopcombe Corner, Salisbury, Wiltshire SP5 1BY. *01980 862527.* www.caravanclub.co.uk. Owner: The Caravan Club. East Grinstead House, East Grinstead, West Sussex RH19 1UA. See website for directions. Caravan Club members only. Set in rolling countryside, most pitches in woodland glades in Area of Outstanding Natural Beauty. Toilet blocks. Veg prep. Gas. Motorhome service point. Shop 3m. Near Salisbury Cathedral and Sherbourne Castle. Open March-October. **NCC. 46T. MC.** 🐕 ⊡

(11m). Stonehenge Park, Orcheston, Salisbury, Wiltshire SP3 4SH. *01980 620304.* admin@stonehenge touringpark. com. www.stonehengetouringpark.com. Owner: Mrs J Young. Off A360, Devizes to Salisbury. Quiet, level, country site. Close to Stonehenge. Booking advisable. Dogs on leads. Children allowed. ✰✰✰ **BH&HPA. 30T. MC.** ✿ 🐕 ⊡ ⚓

Tilshead

Brades Acre Caravan Site, The Bungalow, Tilshead, Wiltshire SP3 4RX. *01980 620402.* Owner: Mr G Brades. A360 Salisbury to Devizes. Salisbury 14m. Devizes 10m. **25T. 25MC.** ✿ 🐕 ⊡ ⚓

Warminster

(5m). Longleat Caravan Club Site, Longleat, Warminster, Wiltshire BA12 7NL. *01985 844663.* www.caravanclub.co.uk. Owner: The Caravan Club. East Grinstead House, East Grinstead, West Sussex RH19 1UA. See website for standard directions to site. Parkland site. Non-members welcome. Advance booking advised bank holidays and July/August. Toilet block. Privacy cubicle. Laundry facilities. Baby/toddler washroom. Veg prep. Motorhome service point. Calor Gas and Campingaz. Play equipment. Childrens' room (music and videos). Water sports. Suitable for families. Some hardstandings, dog walk, good area for walking, fishing and NCN cycle path within 5m. Open March-October. ✰✰✰✰✰ **NCC. 165T. MC.** 🐕 ⊡ ♿

Westbury

(3.5m). Brokerswood Country Park, Brokerswood, Westbury, Wiltshire BA13 4EH. *01373 822238.* woodland.park@virgin.net. www.brokerswood.co.uk. Owner: Mrs S H Capon. Follow brown tourist signs from A36 or A361. 3.5m N of Westbury. 5m from Trowbridge. Set in 80 acres woodlands with lake and Heritage centre. Adventure playground. Narrow-gauge railway. Toddlers' undercover play area. Coarse fishing. David Bellamy Gold Conservation Award. ✰✰✰ **BH&HPA. 50T. 20MC.** ✿ 🐕 ⊡ ♿ ⚓

BATH

Bath

(2m). Bath Marina & Caravan Park, Brassmill Lane, Bath BA1 3JT. *01225 424301.* arthur.currie@britishwaterways.co.uk. www.bathcaravanpark.com. Owner: British Waterways Marina Ltd. M4, J19 on to A4174, to A4 Bath. Pass through Saltford. Cross over the river Avon and pass the park and ride on your L. On your R is Capricorn Motors. Turn R into Brassmill Lane. Park is 100yd on R. Carefully landscaped park to maximise privacy. Centre of Bath and entrance to Kennet and Avon canal 1m upstream from Weston Lock, which lies 1m away. Freezer pack services, laundry, children's play area. Family PH a few minutes' walk from park. AA 4 pennants. ✰✰✰✰ **88T. MC.** ✿ 🐕 ⊡ ♿

Bury View Farm, Corston Fields, Bath BA2 9HD. *01225 873672.* salbowd@btinternet.com. Owner: Mr & Mrs J A Bowden. On A39 Wells to Bath midway between Wheatsheaf Inn and Corston Car Sales. 3m from Keynsham and 2.5m Saltford. Dogs allowed on leads. Fishing, golf nearby. 2m to PO and shop, 3m to doctor. **15T. MC.** ✿ 🐕 ⊡

(2m). Newton Mill Caravan & Camping Park, Newton Road, Bath BA2 9JF. *01225 333909.* newtonmill@hot mail.com. www.campinginbath.co.uk. Owner: Mr & Mrs K W Davies. A4 towards Bristol. At roundabout by Globe PH take exit SP Newton St Loe, park is 1m on L. Located in a secluded valley, the park is a suitable touring centre with a nearby frequent bus service and level, traffic-free cycle path to centre of Bath. Site has Old Mill bar, restaurants and gardens, which lie beside the millstream. Separate tent camping meadows. Heated amenities include bathrooms. Loo of the Year Award 2005. AA 4 pennants. David Bellamy Gold Conservation Award. ✰✰✰✰ **BH&HPA. 90T. MC.** ✿ 🐕 ⊡ ♿ ⚓

BRISTOL

Bristol

(2m). Baltic Wharf Caravan Club Site, Cumberland Road, Bristol BS1 6XG. *01179 268030.* www.caravan club.co.uk. Owner: The Caravan Club. East Grinstead House, East Grinstead, West Sussex RH19 1UA. See website for standard directions to site. A waterside site in the heart of the city's dockland. Non-members welcome. No tents. Advance booking essential bank holidays and weeks either side, also July/August. Motorhome service point. Heated toilet block with laundry facilities. Golf nearby. ✰✰✰✰ **NCC. 58T. MC.** ✿ 🐕 ⊡ ♿

Bath Chew Valley Caravan Park, Ham Lane, Bishop Sutton, Bristol BS39 5TZ. *01275 332127.* enquiries@bathchew valley.co.uk. www.bathchewvalley.co.uk. Owner: Keith Belton. On the A368 Bath to Weston-super-Mare road. At Bishop Sutton turn opposite Red Lion pub. Approach from the A38 or A37. Set among flowers and shrubs. 800yd from Chew Valley lake, famous for rout fishing and birdlife. Adults only. David Bellamy Gold Conservation Award. Suitable base for exploring Bath and Mendip Hills. ✰✰✰✰✰ **BH&HPA. NCC. 31T. 14MC.** ✿ ♀ ⊟

(9m). Brook Lodge Farm Camping & Caravan Park, Cowslip Green, Nr Bristol, Bristol BS40 5RB. *01934 862311.* brooklodgefarm@aol.com. www.brook lodgefarm.com. Owner: Mrs J House. From historic city of Bristol take A38 SW, 9m Sp on L. Modern facilities and centrally located for Bristol, Bath, Cheddar, Wells, Mendip Hills, Clevedon. Small, family-run park. Farm shop within walking distance. Recreational quiet room, under cover with TV and soft drink, confectionery. Children's play areas. Bus service to Bristol from 1m walking distance. AA approved. Green tourism and Welcome to Excellence award. Fishing on Blagdon Lake, 2m. Walking, cycling in nearby country lanes. Cycle hire, caravan hire, outdoor pool (July-September). Open March 1-November 1; restricted use rest of year. ✰✰✰ **29T. MC. 2H.** ⊟

Congresbury

(4m). Oak Farm Touring Park, Weston Road, Congresbury, Bristol BS49 5EB. *01934 833246 / 07989 319686 (m).* Owner: B A Sweet. Mid-way between Bristol and Weston-super-Mare on A370, 4m from J21, M5. Small dogs allowed with permission. Level orchard site, close to all amenities. Booking advised. Golf course nearby. Fishing. Village with shops close by. Next door to Greek restaurant. Open April 1-October 1. ✰ **10T. 5MC. 20S.** ⊟ ℤ

CORNWALL

Bodmin

> **(1m). Camping & Caravanning Club Site - Bodmin, Old Callywith Road, Bodmin, Cornwall PL31 2DZ.** *01208 73834.* www.campingandcaravanningclub.co.uk. Owner: Camping & Caravanning Club. Greenfields House, Westwood Way, Coventry CV4 8JH. On A30 at Bodmin, turn off dual carriageway at A389 and follow signs to site. Site is on L, along Old Callywith Road. Within easy reach of all the attractions of the Cornish Riviera. Take advantage of attractions such as Eden Project, The Lost Gardens of Heligan and the Wheal Martyn China Clay museum near to the site. Non-members welcome. All units accepted. Special deals available for families and backpackers. Open March-October. ✰✰✰✰ **130T. 130MC.** ♀ ⊟ &

Croft Farm Holiday Park, Luxulyan, Bodmin, Cornwall PL30 5EQ. *01726 852463.* roger@whittingham2.freeserve. co.uk. Owner: Dr Roger and Mrs Gudfinna Whittingham. 'Hekla', Bay View Road, Looe, Cornwall PL13 1JP. Follow directions to the Eden Project from Tywardreath Highway, then follow road signs to Luxulyan village. Park is on the left, 0.75m from village. Quiet, sheltered park conveniently located close to St Austell Bay, with spectacular coastline and the Luxulyan Valley nearby. Children allowed. 1.5m from the Eden Project. Open March-January. ✰✰✰✰ **BH&HPA. 52T. MC. 26S. 20H.** ♀ ⊟ ℤ

(5m). Glenmorris Park, Longstone Road, St Mabyn, Bodmin, Cornwall PL30 3BY. *01208 841677.* gmpark@dircon.co.uk. Take B3266 between Camelford and Bodmin, park 0.25m from road. 10 level acres. Quiet and secluded family-run park. Heated pool. Play area. Games room. Dogs allowed in touring fields only. Open Easter-October 31. ✰✰✰ **BH&HPA. 80T. MC. 4S. 6H.** ♀ ⊟ ℤ

Lanarth Inn Caravan Park, St Kew Highway, Bodmin, Cornwall PL30 3EE. *01208 841215.* Owner: Mrs J Buckley. On A39 4m E Wade Bridge. Set in 10 acres of landscaped gardens. Ideal location for touring. PO, doctor, supermarket 2mins away. Modern showers. Licensed bar, outdoor swimming pool, games room. Family camping and barbecue available. AA 2 pennants. Golf 300yd. Open April 1-October 31. **86T. MC. 5H.** ♀ ⊟

(4m). Ruthern Valley Holidays, Ruthern Bridge, Bodmin, Cornwall PL30 5LU. *01208 831395.* ruthern.valley@bt connect.com. www.self-catering-ruthern.co.uk. Owner: Mr & Mrs T J Zair. From Bodmin, leave on A391 (St Austell). Take 2nd right for Nanstallon. By Pressingol Pottery, 2nd L turn to Ruthern Bridge. L at bridge. Site 400yd on L. Quiet site in unspoilt valley. Touring centre or overnight stop. No dogs July/August. Close to Camel trail. Eden Project 10m. David Bellamy Gold Conservation Award. Open April-September. ✰✰✰✰ **BH&HPA. 30T. 16MC. 6H.** ♀ ⊟ ℤ

Boscastle

(2.5m). Lower Pennycrocker Farm, St Juliot, Boscastle, Cornwall PL35 0BY. *01840 250257.* pennycrocker.com. Owner: Mr Brian Heard. 2.5m N of Boscastle on B3263 SP Pennycrocker. Own farm produce available. Open Easter-September 30. **40T. MC.** ♀ ⊟

Bude

(1m). Bude Holiday Park, Maer Lane, Bude, Cornwall EX23 9EE. *01288 355955.* Off A39, through town centre and follow signs to park. Large heated swimming pool. Clubhouse with nightly entertainment. Two bars. Arcade, pool room, TV room. Restaurant and takeaway. Play area. Open April-October. ✰✰✰ **BH&HPA. 250T. MC. 131H.** ♀ ⊟ & ℤ

> **(3m). Budemeadows Touring Holiday Park, Poundstock, Bude, Cornwall EX23 ONA.** *01288 361646.* holiday@budemeadows.com. www.budemeadows.com. Owner: Mrs Wendy Jones. A39 S from Bude for 3m. Site on L after Widemouth turn off. Heated outdoor swimming pool. TV lounge and games room. Licensed bar. Private ladies' suites. Washing-up sinks. Hair-dryers. Showers. Laundrette. Playground. Telephone. Internet access. Bathroom (baby bath and changing room). ✰✰✰✰✰ **145T. MC.** ✿ ♀ ⊟ & ℤ

> **(9m). Camping & Caravanning Club Site - Bude, Gillards Moor, St Gennys, Bude, Cornwall EX23 0BG.** *01840 230650/0870 2433331.* www.campingandcaravan ningclub.co.uk. Owner: Camping & Caravanning Club. Greenfields House, Westwood Way, Coventry CV4 8JH. From Wadebridge heading N on A39 towards Bude. Site on L, SP. 10m from Camelford. Suitable position for touring. Near coastal paths in King Arthur country. Cyclists well catered for, with 42m of traffic-free routes stretching from Bude to Bodmin. All units accepted. Non-members welcome. Site has good surfing beaches nearby. Special deals for families and backpackers. Open April-October. ✰✰✰✰ **100T. 100MC.** ♀ ⊟ &

WEST COUNTRY

(5m). Cornish Coasts Caravan & Camping Park, Middle Penlean, Poundstock, Bude, Cornwall EX23 0EE. *01288 361380.* info.1@cornishcoasts.co.uk. www.cornishcoasts.co.uk. Owner: Mrs J Woods. On the A39, S of Bude. Peaceful, friendly site with views and level terrraced pitches. Close to beaches and south-west coastal path. Suitable touring base. Showers. Laundry. Play area. Telephone. Open Easter-October. **BH&HPA. 45T. 10MC. 4S. 4H.** ⛺ 🔌 ⚓

(5m). East Thorne Touring Park, Kilkhampton, Bude, Cornwall EX23 9RY. *01288 321654.* keith.ovenden@btinternet.com. Owner: Mr & Mrs Ovenden. 5m N of Bude on A39. Take B3254 0.5m to site. Family-run site set in quiet farmland. Games room. Playground. Open March-October 31. **29T. 29MC.** ⛺ 🔌

(9m). Edmore Tourist Park, Wainhouse Corner, Jacobstow, Bude, Cornwall EX23 0BJ. *01840 230467.* edmore@touristpark.freeserve.co.uk. www.cornwallvisited.co.uk. Owner: Yvonne Gibbons. Site off A39 (250yd), SP at Wainhouse Corner. Showers, washing-up sinks. Play area. Dogs allowed on leads. Open Easter-October 31. **28T. MC. 2H.** ⛺ 🔌

(10m). Hentervene Caravan & Camping Park, Crackington Haven, Bude, Cornwall EX23 0LF. *01840 230365.* contact@hentervene.co.uk. www.hentervene.co.uk. Owner: Mr & Mrs D R Turner. Off A39. Bude-Camelford road at Otterham station. Quiet meadow park near sandy beach. Entertainment facilities for children, DIY barbecue. Games room and baby bathroom. Pets welcome. Laundrette. TV lounge. Water sports, fishing, horse riding nearby. Suitable touring base. Winter storage available for tourers. ✰✰✰ **BH&HPA. 44T. 44MC. 32S. 6H.** ✿ ⛺ 🔌

(8m). Hilton Woods Park, Whitstone, Bude, Cornwall EX22 6TW. *01288 341338.* www.hiltonwoodspark.co.uk. Owners: Hilton Woods Park Ltd. The Lodge, Chester Road, Delamere, Nr Northwich, Cheshire CW8 2HB. From M5, exit J31, follow A30 towards Launceston. Exit at Launceston on to B3254. Follow road until Whitstone turn L at SP for Whitstone Head. Follow the lane for 2m until reaching the park. Children's play area. 3m to Widemouth Bay beach. **50S. 6H.** ✿ ⛺ ⚓

(3m). Ivyleaf Camping Sites, Ivyleaf Hill, Bush, Bude, Cornwall EX23 9LD. *01288 321442.* Owner: N A Butcher's. North of Bude on A39, turn right into Ivyleaf Hill, site halfway up hill on the right. Quiet, family-owned site. Sheltered site with views. **10T. 5MC. 2H.** ✿ ⛺ 🔌

(6m). Keywood Caravan Park, Whitstone, Bude, Cornwall EX22 6TW. *01288 341338.* info@keywoodholidays.co.uk. www.keywoodholiays.co.uk. Owner: Mr N Grandison. Follow B3254 from Bude until reaching Whitstone, see SP, turn left and follow country road, site entrance on the right. Licensed club. Laundrette Play area etc. Open March 31-October 31. **BH&HPA. 25T. 25MC. 24S. 14H.** ⛺ 🔌 ⚓

(5m). Penhalt Farm Holiday Park, Widemouth Bay, Bude, Cornwall EX23 0DG. *01288 361210.* denandjennie@penhaltfarm.fsnet.co.uk. www.penhaltfarm.co.uk. Owner: Mr D J Marks. 4m S of Bude on A39, take 2nd R for Widemouth Bay, turn L at bottom by W B Hotel. Family site 0.6m on R. Sea views. Close to coastal path, 1.5m from sandy beach. Laundry. Play area. Telephone. Gas. Widemouth Bay, well-known surfing beach. Garage, PO in Widemouth Bay.Open Easter-October. ✰✰✰ **100T. MC. 1S. 1H.** ⛺ 🔌 ♿ ⚓

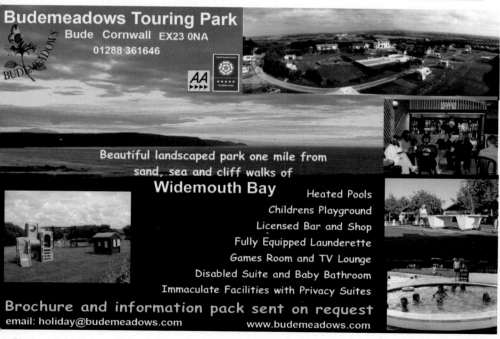

(4m). Penstowe Caravan and Camping Park, Stibb Road, Kilkhampton, Bude, Cornwall EX23 9QY. *01288 321601.* info@penstoweholidays.co.uk. www.penstoweholidays.co.uk. Owners: Mr & Mrs Parker. Family-owned park in a peaceful countryside location with views of sea. Walking distance to Kilkhampton village with shops. PO and PH nearby. Sandymouth beach 2m. Bude about 4m. Six local beaches within 6m. ☆☆☆☆ **BH&HPA. NCC. 120T. MC.**

(3m). Red Post Inn, Launcells, Bude, Cornwall EX23 9NW. *01288 381305.* gsharp@redpostinn1.wanadoo.co.uk. Owner: Mr & Mrs Sharp. E of Bude off A3072. Level, well-sheltered, family site, a suitable base for touring north Devon and Cornwall. Bar and restaurant. Laundrette. Sporting facilities nearby. Showers. Children's playground. **BH&HPA. 40T. 40MC. 3S.**

(3m). Red Post Meadows, Launcells, Bude, Cornwall EX23 9NW. *01288 381306.* Owner: Mr & Mrs Parnell. Off A3072. Good, level, well-sheltered family site. Suitable base for touring north Devon and Cornwall. Showers. Takeaway meals. Bottled gas. Laundry. Sporting facilities nearby. **20T. 20MC.**

(4m). Sandymouth Bay Holiday Park, Sandymouth Bay, Bude, Cornwall EX23 9HW. *01288 352563.* reception@sandymouthbay.co.uk. www.dolphinholidays.co.uk. Owners: M & B Joce. On the Bude to Kilkhampton road (A39), 3m from Bude. Extensive coastal and countryside views. Licensed clubhouse with entertainment. Shower block, play area, Laundrette. Gas sales. Indoor swimming pool. Sauna. Solarium. Crazy golf. Cafe/diner. Coarse fishing. Open March-October. ☆☆☆☆ **BH&HPA. NCC. 53T. MC. 160H.**

(0.5m.). Upper Lynstone Camping & Caravan Park, Bude, Cornwall EX23 0LP. *01288 352017.* reception@upperlynstone.co.uk. www.upperlynstone.co.uk. Owner: Mr & Mrs J Cloke. S of Bude on coastal road to Widemouth Bay. Quiet, family site situated within walking distance of town, sandy beach, bars and restaurants. Coastal footpath from park. Open Easter-October. ☆☆☆☆ **BH&HPA. NCC. 65T. MC. 45S. 19H.**

(3m). Widemouth Bay Caravan Park, Widemouth Bay, Bude, Cornwall EX23 0DF. *01271 866766/01288 361208.* mail@jfhols.co.uk. www.johnfowlerholidays.com. Owner: John Fowler Holidays. Marlborough Road, Ilfracombe, Devon EX34 8PF. Off the A39. Modern, family park a few minutes from a lovely beach. Licensed club with entertainment and children's club. New tropical heated pool, crazy golf, bistro and takeaway. Open March-October. **BH&HPA. 327T. 327MC. 200S. 200H.**

(2m). Willow Valley Holiday Park, Dye House, Bush, Bude, Cornwall EX23 9LB. *01288 353104.* willowvalley@talk21.com. www.caravansitecornwall.co.uk. Owner: John & Janet Holden. Located N of Bude on the A39. 3m S of Kilkhampton. Small, sheltered site in theStrat valley. Friendly atmosphere. Modern facilities block with laundry. Write or telephone for our colour brochure. Open March-January. **BH&HPA. 45T. MC. 4H.**

(2m). Wooda Farm Park, Poughill, Bude, Cornwall EX23 9HJ. *01288 352069.* enquiries@wooda.co.uk. www.wooda.co.uk. Owner: Mrs G Colwill. From the A39 north of Stratton, take the Poughill/Coombe Valley road for one mile. Go through crossroads and Wooda is 200yd on your right-hand side.Family-run park 1.25m from sandy beaches. Adventure playground, woodland walks, well-stocked coarse fishing lake, licensed restaurant, off-licence, takeaway, farmyard friends, fun golf course. Splash indoor pool is nearby. Open: April-October. ☆☆☆☆☆ **BH&HPA. 200T. MC. 55H.**

Callington

(3m). Trehorner Farm Holiday Park, Lower Metherell, Callington, Cornwall PL17 8BJ. *01579 351122.* midgecarter@aol.com. www.trehorner.co.uk. Owners: N & VJ Carter. Off the Tavistock to Callington road. Follow the donkey park sign, then follow the Metherell signs. Peaceful farm park set in the Tamar Valley, off the A390 Tavistock to Callington road. Heated outdoor pool. Village inn nearby. Golf course, shops, doctors are all nearby. Very safe for children. Rose Award. David Bellamy Bronze Conservation Award. Open March-December. ☆☆☆☆ **BH&HPA. 5T. 4S. 11H.**

Camborne

(2m). Magor Farm Caravan Site, Tehidy, Camborne, Cornwall TR14 0JF. *01209 713367.* www.magorfarm.co.uk. Owner: H Williams and Son. Take Camborne (west) exit off A30. Turn right over A30 bridge, in about 0.5m go straight across, blind left-hand corner. Site is 1.5m farther on over hill. Sheltered site with wooded surroundings within easy reach of all Cornwall's famous beauty spots and beaches. SP from Portreath cliff road near Hell's Mouth cafe. Play area. Laundrette, free showers. Electric shaving points. Country park nearby. RAC and Caravan Club. Tehidy golf club 2m, leisure centre, local coarse fishing, Camborne, Redruth, Mining Heritage Centres. Open Easter-October. **40T. MC.**

 Please mention Caravan Sites 2006 when replying to advertisers

Camelford

(1m). Juliot's Well Holiday Park, Camelford, Cornwall PL32 9RF. 01840 213302. juliot.well@holidaysincornwall.net. Owner: Kim & Phil Bolindy. Through Camelford on A39, take 2nd R, then first L. Site 400yd down lane on R. Swimming pool. Tennis court. PH garden, play area. Badminton. Licensed bar. Restaurant. Open March 1-October 31. ☆☆☆ **BH&HPA. 75T. MC. 64H.** 🐕 ⊖ 🛒

(1m). Lakefield Caravan Park & Equestrian Centre, Lower Pendavey Farm, Camelford, Cornwall PL32 9TX. 01840 213279. Owner: Mr & Mrs D E Perring. A30 from Exeter to Launceston, shortly after A395 join the A39 to Camelford. In 2m turn right on to B3314 and the left on to B3266 park is 100yd on the right. Site now runs a riding school next door. Open April 1-October 31. **40T. MC.** 🐕 ⊖ 🛒

> **Valley Truckle Caravan Club Site, Camelford, Cornwall PL32 9RF.** 01840 212206. www.caravanclub.co.uk. Owner: The Caravan Club. East Grinstead House, East Grinstead, West Sussex RH19 1UA. See website for standard directions to site. Caravan Club members only. Small, attractive site, peaceful off-peak. An adjacent tennis course and a championship golf course are within easy walking distance. Toilet blocks, laundry facilities and motorhome service point. Dog walk nearby. Good area for walking, fishing and NCN cycle route nearby. Facilities for disabled. Suitable for families. Open March-October. **NCC. 60T. MC.** 🐕 ⊖ ♿

(7m). West End Farm, Tresparrett, Camelford, Cornwall PL32 9SX. 01840 261612. Owner: Mr D Routly. 2m from Boscastle. Turn left on A39 Camelford to Bude. Open Easter-September. **10T. 10MC.** 🐕

Delabole

(0.2m). Planet Caravan Park, Delabole, Cornwall PL33 9BG. 01840 213361. Owner: Mr & Mrs R W Round. 4m W of Camelford and 6m S of Tintagel. SW end of village on B3314 off A39. Quiet park, good views. Touring centre. Shop 300yd. **BH&HPA. 40T. 40MC. 10H.** ⚓ ⊖

Falmouth

(3.5m). Menallack Farm, Treverva, Falmouth, Cornwall TR10 9BP. 01326 340333. menallack@fsbdial.co.uk. Owner: Mr & Mrs J Minson. Off Falmouth to Gweek road, 0.75m beyond Treverva village on left-hand side. Doctor in Constantine 3m. PO, fishing, golf, sailing, Asda supermarket all nearby within 3m. Peaceful park in attractive surroundings, close to many attractions. Open Easter-October 31. **30T. 30MC.** 🐕 ⊖ 🛒

(2m). Pennance Mill Chalets, Camping & Caravan Park, Pennance Mill Farm, Maenporth, Falmouth, Cornwall TR11 5HY. 01326 312616/317431. Owner: Mr A J Jewell. (A39) from Truro to Falmouth, follow brown international camping and caravan signs to the Hillhead roundabout. Turn right, then straight across at the next crossroads. Continue on for 2m to the Maenporth beach road down hill to Pennance Mill Farm. Farm is on left. Family-run site established 1929. Close to Maenporth beach and Falmouth golf course within 1m. Falmouth town 2m. Open March/Easter-October. ☆☆ **40T. 10MC. 4H.** 🐕 ⊖ ♿ 🛒

(2.5m). Tregedna Farm, Falmouth, Cornwall TR11 5HL. 01326 250529. Owner: Mr F M Harris. From Truro A39 to Falmouth. Half mile from sandy beach. Showers. Laundry sinks. Play area. Electric hook-ups. Telephone, shop. Open April-September. ☆☆ **40T.** 🐕 ⊖ 🛒

(1.5m). Twinbrook Park, Swanpool Road, Falmouth, Cornwall TR11 5BH. 01326 313727. twinbrook@globalnet.co.uk. www.twinbrook.co.uk. Owner: M Cudlipp. A30 to Carland (Wind Farm) roundabout. A39 to Falmouth, turn R at Hillhead roundabout turn L to Falmouth pitch and putt, park on R. Heated indoor swimming pool. Adjacent Falmouth golf club. Open May-September. **BH&HPA. 48H.**

Fowey

(1.5m). Penhale Caravan and Camping Park, Fowey, Cornwall PL23 1JU. 01726 833425. info@penhale-fowey.co.uk. www.penhale-fowey.co.uk. Owner: Mrs M Berryman. On 3082, Par to Fowey. Close to lovely walks and sandy beaches. Splendid views. No overcrowding. David Bellamy Conservation Award. Open April-October. ☆☆☆ **BH&HPA. 45T. 10MC. 10S. 8H.** 🐕 ⊖ 🛒

(1m). Penmarlam Caravan & Camping Park. Bodinnick-by-Fowey, Fowey, Cornwall PL23 1LZ. 01726 870088. info@penmarlampark.co.uk. www.penmarlampark.co.uk. Owner: Marcus Wallace. From Liskeard A38, then A390 turn L on B3359. Follow signs to Bodinnick. Level, grassy site, views. Quay, slipway and storage for small boats. Laundry room. Bottled gas. Modern amenities block, off-licence. Open Easter-October. ☆☆☆☆ **BH&HPA. 65T. 65MC.** 🐕 ⊖ ♿ 🛒

(0.5m). Polruan Holidays Camping & Caravanning, Polruan-by-Fowey, Fowey, Cornwall PL23 1QH. 01726 870263. polholiday@aol.com. Owner: Mr & Mrs R J Hemley. 12m SE of St Austell, off A390 Fowey to Polperro. Select park, surrounded by sea. National Trust farmland, Fowey estuary. Open Easter-September. ☆☆☆☆ **BH&HPA. 7T. 7MC. 11H.** 🐕 ⊖ 🛒

Hayle

(3m). Atlantic Coast Caravan Park, Upton Towans, Hayle, Cornwall TR27 5BL. 01736 752071. enquiries@atlanticcoast-caravanpark.co.uk. www.atlanticcoast-caravanpark.co.uk. Owner: P S & M Smith. 53 Upton Towans, Gwithian, Hayle TR27 5BL. Off B3301. On edge of St Ives Bay, in sand dunes. Small bar. Licensed shop. Charges made for dogs. Open April 1-October 31. **BH&HPA. 17T. MC. 33H.** 🐕 ⊖ 🛒

(0.75m). Beachside Holiday Park, Hayle, Cornwall TR27 5AW. 01736 753080. Owner: Beachside Leisure Holidays Ltd. Leave A30 at Hayle. Beside sea, amidst sand dunes in St Ives Bay. Heated swimming and paddling pool. 100 chalets for hire. Open Easter-October 1. ☆☆☆☆ **BH&HPA. 90T.** ⊖ 🛒

(4m). Calloose Caravan Park, Leedstown, Hayle, Cornwall TR27 5ET. 01736 850431. www.calloose.co.uk. Owner: Mr & Mrs P V Gardner. Off B3302. Sheltered, family park. Swimming pool. Licensed bar. Games room. Laundry. Snacks. Skittle alley. Bar meals and takeaway. Pay phone. Tennis courts. Trout fishing. Crazy golf. Rose Award. AA 4 pennants. Open April 1-October 1. ☆☆☆☆☆ **BH&HPA. 120T. MC. 17H.** 🐕 ⊖ ♿ 🛒

> **(3m). Godrevy Park Caravan Club Site, Upton Towans, Hayle, Cornwall TR27 5BL.** 01736 753100. www.caravanclub.co.uk. Owner: The Caravan Club. East Grinstead House, East Grinstead, West Sussex RH19 1UA. See website for directions. Club members only. Peaceful off-peak. Spacious site surrounded by gorse-covered sand dunes. 1m sandy beach. Dog walk adjacent. Shop 200yd. Advance booking advised June, essential July/August. Toilet block, privacy cubicles, laundry facilities, baby and toddler washroom. Motorhome service point. Boules. Fishing nearby. Veg prep, Calor Gas and Campingaz. NCN cycle route 5m. Open March-October. **NCC. 117T. MC.** 🐕 ⊖ ♿

(3m). Higher Trevaskis Caravan & Camping Park, Gwinear Road, Connor Downs, Hayle, Cornwall TR27 5JQ. *01209 831736.* Owner: Johanna & Duncan Leech. Leave the A30 dual carriageway at Camborne West exit. Follow signs to Connor Downs (A3047), turn left at crossroads entering village. Park is 0.75m on right-hand side. Secluded, family-run countryside park. Well situated for visiting local beaches and attractions of West Cornwall. Touring only. Spacious level pitches in small enclosures. Designated play areas. Open mid April-end September. ☆☆☆☆ **BH&HPA. 82T. MC.** ⚡ 🏕 & 🏊

(3m). Parbola Holiday Park, Wall Gwinear, Hayle, Cornwall TR27 5LE. *01209 831503.* bookings@parbola.co.uk. www.parbola.co.uk. Owner: Mr & Mrs Norman. Off the A30. At Hayle roundabout take the first exit to Connor Downs, at end of village turn right to Carnhell Green. Go over railway crossing and continue to T-Junction, turn right. Park is located 1m farther along on the left-hand side. Large, well-spaced pitches are situated in woodland or parkland. Showers. Swimming pool. Adventure playground. Crazy golf. Games room. Table tennis. TV rooms. Laundrette. Washing up facilities. Mother and baby room. Under-5s' play area. Off-licence. Open Easter-October. **BH&HPA. 110T. 34H.** ⚡ & 🏊

(0.3m). Riviere Sands Holiday Park, Riviere Towans, Phillack, Hayle, Cornwall TR27 5AX. *01736 752132.* www.havenholidays.com. Owner: Bourne Leisure Ltd. 1 Park Lane, Hemel Hempstead, Hertfordshire HP2 4YL. Park is located off the A30, at Hayle, and situated on cliffs overlooking the beach. Indoor and outdoor pool complex. Laundrette. Fast food and takeaways. Sports and leisure facilities. Children's clubs. Daytime and evening entertainment for all the family. Just 20 mins from the Tate Gallery at St Ives, and 30-40 mins from the Eden Project and Minack Theatre. Open April-end September. ☆☆☆ **BH&HPA. NCC. 308H.** & 🏊

(1m). St Ives Bay Holiday Park, 73 Loggans Road, Upton Towans, Hayle, Cornwall TR27 5BH. *01736 752274.* stivesbay@dial.pipex.com. www.stivesbay.co.uk. Take the Hayle exit off the A30, at mini-roundabouts turn right on to the B3301, SP Portreath. 600yd along the B3301. Easy access to beach. Indoor heated swimming pool. Takeaway. Hire shop. Brochure available. Open May-September. ☆☆☆☆ **BH&HPA. 200T. MC. 250H.** ⚡ 🏊

Helston

(6m). Boscrege Caravan Park, Ashton, Helston, Cornwall TR13 9TG. *01736 762231.* enquiries@caravanparkcornwall.com. www.caravanparkcornwall.com. Owner: T Armstrong. Off A394 Penzance to Helston. Flat and sheltered park. Shower. Washing-up room and laundry. Games room, TV, microwave. Open Easter or April 1-October 31. ☆☆☆ **50T. MC. 26H.** 🏕 ⚡

(10m). Chy Carne Chalet Caravan & Camping Park, Kennack Sands, Kuggar,Ruan Minor, Helston, Cornwall TR12 7LX. *01326 290841.* muxlow@ntlworld.com. www.caravancampingsites.co.uk. Owner: R F & B A Muxlow. Turn right off B3293 Helston to St Keverne at Traboe Cross. 12 chalets for hire. Gas supplies. Near coastal path, 10 mins walk to clean, safe beach. AA 3 pennants. Open Easter-October. **14T. MC. 18H.** 🏕 ⚡ 🏊

(10m). Criggan Mill, Mullion Cove, Helston, Cornwall TR12 7EU. *01326 240496.* info@crigganmill.co.uk. www.criggansmill.co.uk. Owner: Mr & Mrs M Bolton. On B3296. 200yd from Mullion Cove. ☆☆☆☆☆ **BH&HPA. 29S.** ✿ 🏕 🏊

(5m). Franchis, Cury Cross Lanes, Mullion, Helston, Cornwall TR12 7AZ. *01326 240301.* enquiries@franchis.co.uk. www.franchis.co.uk. Owner: Mr & Mrs B Thompson. On A3083 Helston to Lizard. Quiet, family-run park in an Area of Outstanding Natural Beauty. Close-mown grass and woodland. Beaches, Helford river and Flambards theme park close by. Local to Glendurgan, Trebar and Trevano gardens. AA 3 pennants. Open Easter-October. **BH&HPA. 70T. MC. 12H.** 🏕 ⚡ 🏊

(10m). Gwendreath Farm Holiday Park, Kennack Sands, Ruan Minor, Helston, Cornwall TR12 7LZ. *01326 290666.* tom.gibson@virgin.net. www.tomandlinda.co.uk. Owner: Mr T Gibson. From Helston take A3083, turn L on B3293, SP St Keverne, continue for 4m to Goonhilly Earth Station, take next R, then next L. At end of lane turn R over cattle grid and drive through Seaview and stop at second reception. AA 3 pennants. Open Easter-October. **BH&HPA. 10T. 10MC. 30H.** 🏕 ⚡

(10m). Henry's Camp Site, Caerthillian Farm, The Lizard, Helston, Cornwall TR12 7NX. *01326 290596.* Owner: Mr R Lyne & Mrs J C Lyne. Take B3083 from Helston. Enter village take first R across village green then second R. Sea views. Beaches closeby. Near amenities in village centre but secluded. **10T. 10MC.** ✿ 🏕 ⚡

(10m). Kennack Sands Caravan Park, Ruan Minor, Helston, Cornwall TR12 7LT. *01326 290533.* holidays@kennack.co.uk. www.kennack.co.uk. Owner: Mr & Mrs Flower. Off B3293. New caravans for sale on park. Outdoor heated pool, games room, laundry, playground on park. Riding, golf course nearby. 5mins walk to clean sandy award winning beach. Parking next to beach, beach cafe. Open March-October. **BH&HPA. 50S.** 🐕

(10m). Little Trevothan Caravan Park, Coverack, Helston, Cornwall TR12 6SD. *01326 280260.* mmita@btopenworld. com. www.littletrevothan.com. Owner: R & M Mita. SP from the B3293 at Zoar garage. Just 0.75m from the picturesque fishing village of Coverack. Spacious, family site with level, grassy pitches. Showers. Children's playground. Walks. No noisy club. AA 3 pennants. Colour brochure available. Open April-October. **BH&HPA. 25T. 25MC. 5S. 14H.** 🐕 ⊠ 🛒

(3m). Lower Polladras Touring Park, Carleen, Helston, Cornwall TR13 9NX. *01736 762220.* polladras@hotmail.com. Owner: R J Bell. Take the B3302 off the A394 Helston to Penzance road. Turn left to Carleen village, after 0.75m from the A30 take the B3303 after the junction with the B3302, take first right to Carleen. Tranquil and beautiful surroundings set in a small hamlet. Quiet, family-run site. AA 3 pennants. Open March 26-October 31. **BH&HPA. NCC. 60T. 60MC.** 🐕 ⊠ 🛒

(1.5m). Mullion Holiday Park, Ruan Minor, Helston, Cornwall TR12 7LJ. *0870 444 0080/0870 444 5344.* bookings@weststarholidays.co.uk. www.weststarholidays. co.uk. Owner: Weststar Holidays Ltd. 8 Abbey Court, Eagle Way, Sowton, Exeter EX2 7HY. Follow the road to The Lizard from Helston, A3083. After about 7m we are on the L. Close to sandy beaches and coves, spectacular cliffs and coastline, and family attractions. Free all-weather facilities, including indoor swimming pool, live entertainment and children's clubs. Golf course and fishing within 3m. Open March-October. ✰✰✰✰ **BH&HPA. 150T. MC. 347H.** 🐕 ⊠ 🛒

(3m). Penmarth Farm, Coverack, St Keverne, Helston, Cornwall TR12 6SB. *01326 280389.* Owner: Mr B Roskilly. Off the B3293. Eggs are sold from the farm. Woodland walk and pond. Picnic area. Just a short walk to picturesque Coverack village: shops, PO and doctor. Open April 1-October 31. **16T. 6MC. 4H.** 🐕

(2.5m). Poldown Caravan Park, Carleen, Helston, Cornwall TR13 9NN. *01326 574560.* poldown@poldown.co.uk. www.poldown.co.uk. Owner: G & N Peyrin. Follow Penzance road from Helston (A394) for about 1m. Turn R at Hilltop garage on to B3302 to Hayle. Take 2nd L, site 0.75m down lane. Secluded site suitable for exploring west Cornwall. Near sandy coves and beaches (3m). Shopping centre, attraction park, fishing trips 2m, golf 2.5m. Open April-September. ✰✰✰✰ **10T. 10MC. 7S.** 🐕 ⊠

(3m). Retanna Holiday Park, Edgcumbe, Helston, Cornwall TR13 0EJ. *01326 340643.* retannaholpark@lineone.net. www.retanna.co.uk. Owner: Mr C & Mrs M Neville. On A394, midway Falmouth-Helston. Peaceful, green holiday park, suitable for couples and families. Shop, reception and takeaway. AA 3 pennants. Open April-October. **BH&HPA. 24T. 24MC. 40S. 29H.** ⊠ 🦽 🛒

(9m). Sea Acres Holiday Park, Ruan Minor, Kennack Sands, Helston, Cornwall TR12 7LT. *01326 290064.* enquiries@parkdeanholidays.co.uk. www.parkdeanholidays.co.uk. Owner: Parkdean Holiday Plc. 2nd floor, One Gosforth Way, Gosforth Business Park, Newcastle-upon-Tyne NE12 8ET. A39 to Truro, through Truro and head for Helston on A394. B3293 to Kennach Sands, head towards beach. Indoor heated pool, family clubhouse, restaurant and takeaway. Mini supermarket, crazy golf, children's club. Open March-October. ✰✰✰✰ **50T. 50MC. 132H.** 🐕 ⊠ 🦽 🛒

(10m). Silver Sands Holiday Park, Gwendreath, Ruan Minor, Helston, Cornwall TR12 7LZ. *01326 290631.* enquiries@silversandsholidaypark.co.uk. www.silversandsholidaypark.co.uk. Owner: Mr & Mrs C W Pullinger. Take A3083 from Helston, then B3293. After Goonhilly turn R. In 1.50m turn L, SP Gwendreath. 20 tents also available. 800yd walk to award-winning sandy beach. On edge of The Lizard National Nature Reserve. Laundrette. Open April-September. ✰✰✰ **BH&HPA. 14T. 14MC. 14S.** 🐕 ⊠ 🦽 ⌀

(10m). Teneriffe Farm, Predannack, Mullion, Helston, Cornwall TR12 7EZ. *01326 240293.* Owner: Mr A B Thomas. Off A3083. Sea view. Laundrette. Public telephone. Calor Gas supplies. SAE for bookings and details. Open Good Friday-October. **20T. MC.** 🐕 ⊠

(7m). The Friendly Camp Caravan Park, Tregullas Farm, Ruan Minor, Helston, Cornwall TR12 7LJ. *01326 240387.* Owner: Mr J Bennetts. On A3083 Lizard to Helston road near junction with B3296 Mullion road. Open April 1-October 31. **12T. 6MC. 12H.** 🐕 🛒

Land's End

(4.5m). Cardinney Caravan and Camping Park, Crows-an-Wra, Land's End, Cornwall TR19 6HX. *01736 810880.* cardinney@btinternet.com. www.cardinney-camping-park. co.uk. Owner: Liz & Kevin Lindley. Situated on the A30 between Penzance and Land's End. 5m from Penzance. Peaceful site. Games room. Laundry room. Showers. Chemical toilet emptying point. Licensed cafe and takeaway. Off licence. Gas. Spacious pitches. Hard-standings. Open February 1-November 30. ✿✿✿ **BH&HPA. NCC. 105T. MC. 4H.** ⌂ ⊖ ⌘

Launceston

(7m). Chapmanswell Caravan Park, Chapmanswell Well, St-Giles-on-the-Heath, Launceston, Cornwall PL15 9SG. *01409 211382.* george@chapmanswellcaravanpark.co.uk. www.chapmanswellcaravanpark.co.uk. Owner: Mr G Avery. Off A388, Launceston to Holsworthy road, at Chapmanswell take left turning to Boyton; site is 200yd along on L. Quiet, country park supervised by the owner. Hard-standings and grass pitches. Laundry facilities. Central for touring Devon and Cornwall. Caravan storage available. Fishing, golf, water sports on reservoir within 7m. **BH&HPA. 35T. 1MC. 40S.** ✿ ⌂ ⊖ ⌘

(7.5m). Tredaule Manor Caravan Park, Altarnun, Launceston, Cornwall PL7 5RW. *01566 86208.* jspragg@tredaulemanor.co.uk. www.ukparks.co.uk/tredaule. Owner: Mr James Spragg. Tredaule Manor House, Tredaule, Launceston, Cornwall. Off A30 at Five Lanes exit, follow Tredaule signs. All mains services. Open Easter-September 30. **BH&HPA. 18S.** ⌂

Liskeard

Colliford Tavern Campsite, St Neot, Liskeard, Cornwall PL14 6PZ. *01208 821335.* info@colliford.com. www.colliford.com. Owner: Kevin, Alyson, Lee and Michelle Cooper. Off the A30, 2m W of Bolventor on Bodmin Moor. 8m from Bodmin. Quiet, family-run, sheltered site near Colliford Lake. Tavern and restaurant. Modern showers. Dishwashing. Laundry and baby care facilities. AA 4 pennants. Telephone for brochure. Open April-October. **30T. 10MC.** ⌂ ⊖ &

(3m). Great Trethew Manor Caravan Park, Horningtops, Liskeard, Cornwall PL14 3PY. *01503 240663.* great. trethew.manor@yahoo.com. www.great.trethew.manor.co.uk. Owner: Mr M J Peacock. Situated E of Liskeard, turn off A38 on to B3251, follow for 0.25m to drive entrance. Small, well-drained site in 30 acres of woodlands and gardens, with use of adjoining park facilities. Play areas, fishing, tennis court. Open March-October. **55T. MC.** ⌂ ⊖ ⌘

(4m). Pine Green Caravan and Camping Park, Doublebois, Liskeard, Cornwall PL14 6LE. *01579 320183.* mary.ruhleman @btinternet.com. www.pinegreenpark.co.uk. Owner: Pine Green Developments. 7 Park Avenue, Barnstaple, Devon EX31 2ET. W of Liskeard via the A38 through Dobwalls towards Bodmin, turn left on to the B3360 at Doublebois. Peaceful, wooded park 150yd on the right-hand side. Warden on site. Golf course nearby. Shop, PO 2m. Doctor 3m. Open January-December. ✿✿✿✿ **BH&HPA. 50T. MC. 1S.** ✿ ⌂ ⊖

(6m). Trenant Chapel House, Trenant Caravan Park, St Neot, Liskeard, Cornwall PL14 6RZ. *01579 320896.* Owner: Mrs Parry. Off the A38 at Dobwalls Theme Park follow signs to St Neot then Trenant Caravan Park signs. A small, quiet country park bounded by a tributary of the river Fowey. Showers. Laundry facilities. Open April 1-October 31. **12T. MC.** ⌂ ⊖

Looe

(2m). Camping Caradon, Trelawne, Looe, Cornwall PL13 2NA. *01503 272388.* information@campingcaradon.fsnet.co.uk. www.campingcaradon.co.uk. Owners: Davey & Boult. W of Looe via A387 to Polperro, park is off B3359. 2.25 acres of level pitches. Sea 2m. Club. Open Easter-October 31. **BH&HPA. 85T. 85MC. 1H.** ⌂ ⊖ ⌘

(4.5m). Great Kellow Caravan & Camping Site, Polperro, Looe, Cornwall PL13 2QL. *01503 272387.* Owner: Mr N J Williams. Situated off the A387. Quiet, level site on dairy farm, with sea views. Open March-January. **30T. MC. 6S. 4H.** ⌂ ⊖

(4m). Killigarth Manor Estate Caravan & Camping Park, Polperro, Looe, Cornwall PL13 2JQ. *01503 272216.* www. killigarth.co.uk. Owner: Killigarth Manor Estate Ltd. Cross Tama bridge A38, turn left at roundabout, SP Looe. Right A387, cross over bridge in Looe. 3.5m out turn left, SP Killigarth. Park run by Stephen family for your family. Situated in an Area of Outstanding Natural Beauty. New indoor pool. Entertainment daily. Adventure playground. Tennis court. Club. Takeaway and restaurant. Dogs allowed with tourers. Fishing, golf course and Eden project nearby. Open April-November. ✿✿✿✿ **BH&HPA. 202T. MC. 143H.** ⊖ & ⌘

(1m). Looe Bay Holiday Park, East Looe, Looe, Cornwall PL13 1NX. *0870 444 0080.* bookings@weststarholidays.co.uk. www.weststarholidays.co.uk. Owner: Weststar Holidays Ltd. 8 Abbey Court, Eagle Way, Sowton, Exeter EX2 7HY. From Plymouth A38 towards Liskeard, L at Trerulefoot on to A374, then R on A377. Park on B3253 1.5m from Looe. Set in countryside where winding lanes lead you to sandy beaches and unspoilt fishing villages. All-weather facilities including multi- sports court, indoor heated swimming pool and free children's clubs. Free nightly entertainment. Lodges available for hire. Open March-October and New Year. ✿✿✿ **BH&HPA. 342H.** ⌂ ⌘

> **(1.5m). Looe Caravan Club Site, St Martin, Looe, Cornwall PL13 1PB.** *01503 264006.* www.caravan club.co.uk. Owner: The Caravan Club. East Grinstead House, East Grinstead, West Sussex RH19 1UA. See website for standard directions to site. Caravan Club members only. Calor Gas sales. Open air heated swimming pool. Mini-golf. Tennis courts. Play area. Public phone. Dog walk. Some hard-standings, part sloping, levelling blocks required. Storage pitches. Motorhome service point. Toilet blocks, laundry facilities. Volleyball area. Golf and water sports nearby. Good area for walking. Suitable for families. NCN cycle route within 5m. **190T. MC.** ✿ ⌂ ⊖ & ⌘

(2m). Oaklands Park, Polperro Road, Looe, Cornwall PL13 2JS. *01503 262640.* info@oaklands-park.co.uk. www.oaklands-park.co.uk. Owner: Acorn Parks Ltd. The Office, Oaktree Park, Locking, Weston Super Mare BS24 8RG. A38 to Plymouth. Cross Tamar bridge and through tunnel at Saltash. Straight across roundabout on the A38. Next roundabout exit left on A374. After 1m turn right on to A387 to Looe. Go through town centre over bridge follow road to Polperro and Pelynt for 2.5m. Park on R. Perfect location between Looe and Polperro. Wonderful views over countryside. Peaceful park. Pets welcome; designated dog walk area. Shop, laundrette. New development for holiday caravans and lodges. Beach, sailing, fishing, horse riding. Open April-September for tourers; open 11 months for holiday homes. **BH&HPA. 180T. 180MC. 170S.** ⌂ ⊖ & ⌘ ⌀

(2.5m). **Polborder House Caravan & Camping Park, Bucklawren Road, St Martins, Looe, Cornwall PL13 1NZ.** *01503 240265.* reception@peaceful-polborder.co.uk. www. peaceful-polborder.co.uk. Owner: Mr Ray & Mrs Josie Frankland. E of Looe off the B3253, follow signs for Polborder and Monkey Sanctuary. Award-winning park in peaceful countryside. Public phone, baby room. Golf and fishing nearby. Beach 1.5m. Open March-October. ✰✰✰✰ **BH&HPA. 31T. MC. 5H.** ⛺ 🔌 🛒

(2m). **Seaview Holiday Village, Polperro, Looe, Cornwall PL13 2JE.** *01503 272335.* Owner: J K Shaw. Off the A387. Situated between Looe and Polperro. Club. Indoor, outdoor pool sauna, steam room and leisure facilities. Golf 4m. Plymouth 24m. Open Easter-November. ✰✰✰✰ **BH&HPA. 53H.** ⛺ 🛒

(2m). **Talland Caravan Park, Looe, Cornwall PL13 2JA.** *01503 272715.* www.tallandcaravanpark.co.uk. Owner: Mr & Mrs R S Haywood. Cross Looe bridge, at top of hill in about 1m turn left for Talland Bay, park is 1m on L. Adjacent to coast path and beaches. AA 3 pennants. Open April 1-October 31. **BH&HPA. 80T. 46S. 24H.** ⛺ 🔌 🛒

(1.25m). **Tencreek Caravan & Camping Park, Polperro Road, Looe, Cornwall PL13 2JR.** *01503 262447.* reception@ tencreek.co.uk. www.dolphinholidays.co.uk. Owners: Dolphin Holidays. On the A387, Looe to Polperro road. Family park overlooking sea. Public telephone. Heated indoor swimming pool with 45-metre water flume. Laundrette. Showers. Play area, amusement arcade. Takeaway meals. Gas sales. Chemical toilet emptying points. Licensed club with entertainment. Rose Award. ✰✰✰✰ **BH&HPA. 250T. 50MC. 43H.** ✿ ⛺ 🔌 ⚓ 🛒 ⌀

(1.5m). **Tregoad Farm Touring Caravan & Camping Park, St Martins, Looe, Cornwall PL13 1PB.** *01503 262718.* tre goadfarmtccp@aol.com. www.cornwall-online.co.uk/tregoad. Owner: Mr F Werkmeister. E of Looe on B3253, Plymouth to Looe. Well-drained site, scenic walks. Easy access to beaches and moors. Showers. Laundrette. Bottled gas. 3 coarse fishing lakes. Bar/bistro. Rallies welcome. Open April-October. ✰✰✰ **BH&HPA. 150T. MC. 3S.** ⛺ 🔌 🛒 ⌀

(2m). **Trelawne Manor Holiday Park, Looe, Cornwall PL13 2NA.** *01503 272151.* Set around stately manor house with family entertainment and children's clubs. Indoor and outdoor pools with flume. Tennis court. Laundrette. Table tennis, games arcade and games room. Open Easter-October. ✰✰✰✰ **BH&HPA. NCC. 163H.** 🔌 ⚓ 🛒

(3m). **Trelay Farmpark, Pelynt, Looe, Cornwall PL13 2JX.** *01503 220900.* stay@trelay.co.uk. www.trelay.co.uk. Owner: Graham & Heather Veale. 0.5m S of Pelynt on B3359. Small, uncommercialised, family-run park surrounded by farmland. Laundry. Toilet block suite for disabled people. Shops/restaurants in Pelynt (10mins walk). Eden Project 12m W. Polperro 3m. Fishing, golf, diving nearby. Open April 1-October 31. ✰✰✰✰ **BH&HPA. 50T. MC. 20S. 4H.** ⛺ 🔌 ♿

Lostwithiel

(1m). **Downend Camp Site, Lostwithiel, Cornwall PL22 0RB.** *01208 872363.* Owner: Mr J Hawke. On A390. Open March 1-October 31. **10T. 4MC. 2H.** ⛺ 🔌 🛒

(1.5m). **Powderham Castle Tourist Park, Lanlivery, Nr Fowey, Lostwithiel, Cornwall PL30 5BU.** *01208 872277.* Owner: J Buckley Evans. Off A390, SW of Lostwithiel, turn right at SP Powderham Castle, site is 400m north. Quiet,

uncommercialised select park. Suitable location for touring all Cornwall and near to the Eden Project. Children's activity centre, indoor badminton, soft tennis. TV room. Laundrette. Seasonal pitches and tourer storage. David Bellamy Silver Conservation Award. Open Easter-October. ✩✩✩✩✩ **BH&HPA. 65T. 10MC. 38S.** 🚐 🔌

Marazion

Mounts Bay Caravan Park, Green Lane, Marazion, Cornwall TR17 0HQ. *01736 710307.* mountsbay@onetel.com. www.mountsbay-caravanpark.co.uk. Owner: Aidan & Elliot Smith. Off A394. 500yd from Marazion. About 50yd from beach, opposite St Michael's Mount. Familes and couples only. Laundry. Heated outdoor pool. Penzance, cinema 3m. Horseriding 7m. Leisure centre/indoor pool 8m. Rose Award. Open March 15-January 15. ✩✩✩✩✩ **17H.**

(0.5m). Wheal Rodney, Gwallon Lane, Marazion, Cornwall TR17 0HL. *01736 710605.* reception@whealrodney.co.uk. www.whealrodney.co.uk. Owner: Mr & Mrs S P Lugg. Off A394. At Crowlas take road SP Rospeath, site is 1.5m on right. Showers, laundry facilities. Sauna. Heated indoor swimming pool. Holiday storage. Fishing, horse riding nearby. 0.5m to St Michaels mount and beaches. AA 3 pennants. **BH&HPA. 35T. MC. 10H.** ✿ 🚐 🔌

Mevagissey

(1m). Heligan Woods Caravan Park, St Ewe, Mevagissey, Cornwall PL26 6EL. *01726 843485.* info@pentewan.co.uk. www.pentewan.co.uk. Owner: Pentewan Sands Ltd. Pentewan, St Austell PL26 6BT. 6m S of St Austell, W off B3273 (Gorran) road. 12 acres, grassy site with mature trees and bushes. Part sloping and sheltered, overlooking Mevagissey Bay. Close by

Lost Garden of Heligan. Facilities of Pentewan Sands, including own private beach freely available to customers of Heligan Woods. No single-sex groups, no jet-skis. On-site warden. Secure caravan and boat storage. Open March 23-November 30. ✩✩✩✩ **BH&HPA. 85T. 85MC. 14S. 16H.** 🚐 🔌 ⚓ 🛒

(4m). Pentewan Sands Holiday Park, Pentewan, Mevagissey, Cornwall PL26 6BT. *01726 843485.* info@pentewan.co.uk. www.pentewan.co.uk. Owner: Pentewan Sands Ltd. On B3273. S of St Austell towards Mevagissey. Look for large site beside beach on your left. Large, safe, sandy private beach, boat launching facilities. Clubhouse, shop, restaurant and takeaway. Showers. Laundrette. Large level pitches. No jet-skis. Traditional family site; no single-sex groups. Caravan and boat storage. Open March 21-November 1. ✩✩✩✩ **BH&HPA. 420T. MC. 121H.** 🔌 ⚓ 🛒

Newquay

(5m). Camping & Caravanning Club Site - Tregurrian, Newquay, Cornwall TR8 4AE. *01637 860448.* www.campingandcaravanningclub.co.uk. Owner: Camping & Caravanning Club. Greenfields House, Westwood Way, Coventry CV4 8JH. From A3059 to Newquay. 1.5m on after service station, R to Newquay airport, continue to J, then L at Tregurrian. Follow Watergate Bay signs. Watergate Bay beach always popular with youngsters and excellent for surfers. Non-members welcome. All units welcome. Fishing, horse riding, golf, PO, shops, cycle routes, doctor, hospital, swimming pool, zoo, Eden Project, all within reach by car or public transport. Special deals for families and backpackers. Open April-October. ✩✩✩✩ **90T. 90MC.** 🚐 🔌 ⚓

(6m). Carworgie Manor Park, Newquay, Cornwall TR8 4LX. *01726 860775*. Family holiday park set in 16-acres of wooded estate around Manor House. Swimming pool, entertainment, bars, restaurant, laundrettte, crazy golf, children's hour and play-ground, games room etc. Open March 1-December 31. **BH&HPA. 151H.** 🛒

(3.5m). Crantock Beach Holiday Park, Crantock, Newquay, Cornwall TR8 5RH. *01637 871111*. enquiries@parkdeanholi days.co.uk. www.parkdeanholidays.co.uk. Owner: Parkdean Holidays Plc. 2nd Floor, One Gosforth Park Way, Gosforth Business Park, Newcastle-upon-Tyne NE12 8ET. W of Newquay, off A3075, SP Crantock. Quiet, peaceful park with views across a sandy, family beach, which is a short walk away. Light evening entertainment, bar, children welcome, play areas, pitch and putt, takeway food. Launderette. Open April-October 30. ☆☆☆☆ **BH&HPA. NCC. 169H.** 🐾 🛒

Crantock Plains Touring Park, Crantock, Newquay, Cornwall TR8 5PH. *01637 831273/830955*. www.crantock-plains.co.uk. Owner: Mr Gibbes. The Orchard, Halwyn Hill, Crantock, Newquay, Cornwall TR8 5RA. 2.5m S of Newquay via A3075, Redruth road. After lake on R, garage on L. Continue over mini roundabout. Site on R 0.5m along second SP lane to Crantock. Beach 1.5m. Families and couples only. Swings. Recreation area. AA 3 pennants. Storage facilities all year. Open Easter-September 30. ☆☆☆ **NCC. 40T. 40MC.** 🐾 🕿 🛒

(2m). Hendra Holiday Park, Newquay, Cornwall TR8 4NY. *01637 875778*. enquiries@hendra-holidays.com. www.hendra-holidays.com. Owner: Mr & Mrs R Hyatt. From M5 at Exeter, take A30 to the Highgate Hill junction, follow sign for A392 to Newquay. At Quintrell Downs go straight across the roundabout

and on for 0.5m. Hendra Holiday Park is on the L. Family-run park for couples and families. Heated outdoor pool and indoor fun pools with waterslide. Food bar. Laundrette. Sauna. Bars. Children's complex and club. Entertainment. Restaurant. Riding, fishing and golf within 2m. Freephone brochure line: 0500 242523. Open March-October. ☆☆☆☆ **BH&HPA. 600T. MC. 280H.** 🐾 🕿 ♿ 🛒 ⌀

(3m). Holywell Bay Holiday Park, Holywell Bay, Newquay, Cornwall TR8 5PR. *01637 871111*. enquiries@parkdeanholi days.co.uk. www.parkdeanholidays.co.uk. Owner: Parkdean Holidays Plc. 2nd Floor, One Gosforth Park Way, Gosforth Business Park, Newcastle-upon-Tyne NE12 8ET. 6m W of Newquay off A3075, SP Cubert and Holywell Bay. Peaceful valley with a sandy, family beach a short walk away. Children's club, free nightly entertainment, heated pool with 300ft slide, amusements, Launderette, takeaway food. Open March-October. ☆☆☆☆ **BH&HPA. NCC. 75T. 75MC. 149H.** ♿ 🛒

(5m). Magic Cove Touring Park, Mawgan Porth, Newquay, Cornwall TR8 4BZ. *01637 860263*. magic@redcove.co.uk. www.redcove.co.uk. Owner: Lesley Campbell. Situated halfway between Newquay and Padstow on the north Cornish coast. Level site 300yd from the beach. Water and drain adjacent to each pitch. Open Easter-October. **26T. MC.** 🐾 ♿

(6m). Mawgan Porth Holiday Park, Mawgan Porth, Newquay, Cornwall TR8 4BD. *01637 860322*. mawgan porthhp@fsbdial.co.uk. www.mawganporth.co.uk. Owner: Mawgan Porth Holiday Park Ltd. Off B3276. Newquay to Padstow coast road, 400yd inland. Sandy beach 400yd. Countryside location. Tennis courts nearby. ☆☆☆☆ **BH&HPA. 27S.** ⌀ ♿ 🛒

(4m). Monkey Tree Holiday Park, Rejerrah, Newquay, Cornwall TR8 5QL. *01872 572032.* enquiries@monkeytreeholidaypark.co.uk. ww.monkeytreeholidaypark.co.uk. Owner: Walker Leisure. 800yd off A3075, between Newquay and Perranporth. Site is only a short distance from Cornwall's popular surfing beaches. Lounge bar. Restaurant. Games room. Cafe. Laundry. Heated swimming pools. Sauna and solarium. Excellent disabled facilities. Clubhouse with entertainment, restaurant, shop. Euro-tents for hire. **450T. MC. 48S.**

(4m). Newperran Holiday Park, Rejerrah, Newquay, Cornwall TR8 5QJ. *0845 1668407.* www.newperran.co.uk. Owner: Keith & Christine Brewer. On A3075. Laundrette. Games TV room. Playgrounds. Heated swimming pool. Crazy golf. Off-licence. Cottage Inn and cafe. Open March-October. ☆☆☆☆ **BH&HPA. 270T. MC. 4S. 6H.**

(2m). Newquay Holiday Park, Newquay, Cornwall TR8 4HS. *01637 871111.* enquiries@parkdeanholidays.co.uk. www.parkdeanholidays.co.uk. Owner: Parkdean Holidays Plc. 2nd Floor, One Gosforth Park Way, Gosforth Business Park, Newcastle-upon-Tyne NE12 8ET. Off A3059, in direction of Newquay, after 4m park is SP at bottom of hill. Children's club, free nightly entertainment, 3 heated swimming pools, 200ft water slide, amusements, pool, snooker, pitch and putt, crazy golf, playground, restaurant, takeaway food, Laundrette. Open March-October. ☆☆☆☆ **BH&HPA. NCC. 259T. 259MC. 197S. 137H.**

(3m). Perran Quay Tourist Park, Hendra Croft, Rejerrah, Newquay, Cornwall TR8 5QP. *01872 572561.* rose@perran-quay.co.uk. www.cornwall-online.co.uk/perran-quay. Owner: R Northfield & R Brown. On A3075 midway between Newquay and Perranporth. Bar and restaurant. Play area. Outdoor heated swimming pool. Showers. Laundrette. Open Easter-October 31. **135T. MC.**

(1.5m). Porth Beach Tourist Park, Porth, Newquay, Cornwall TR7 3NH. *01637 876531.* info@porthbeach.co.uk. www.porthbeach.co.uk. Owner: Mr & Mrs J Kase. Turn R off A30 at Indian Queens on to A392 to Quintrell Downs roundabout. A3058 to Newquay, at Porth, Four Turnings, turn R on to B3276, coast road to Padstow. Close to beach. Playground. Shops near. Laundrette. Riding, fishing and boating 1m. Open April-October. ☆☆☆☆ **BH&HPA. 201T. MC. 18H.**

(4m). Quarryfield Caravan & Camping Park, Crantock, Newquay, Cornwall TR8 5RJ. *01637 872792.* Owner: C H WinnTretherras, Newquay, Cornwall TR7 2RE. Off A3075 Redruth to Newquay road to Crantock village, turn right by telephone booth and right into road opposite. Shop adjoining. Charges made for dogs. Licensed bar, heated swimming pool. 10 mins to beach. Open March-October 31. **BH&HPA. 15T. 15MC. 40H.**

(2.5m). Riverside Holiday Park, Lane, Newquay, Cornwall TR8 4PE. *01637 873617.* info@riversideholidaypark.co.uk. www.riversideholidaypark.co.uk. Owner: U-Tow Caravans Ltd. Off A392 at Quintrell Downs go straight across at roundabout, then take second turning on L, SP Gwills, past Lane Theatre and follow signs. On site: river fishing, games room, bar, cafe/takeway, swimming pool, showers, laundry. Short drive: sandy beaches, horse riding, amusements and other amenities. Open Easter-end October. ☆☆☆ **BH&HPA. 140T. MC. 6S. 30H.**

(1m). Rosecliston Park, Trevemper, Newquay, Cornwall TR8 5JT. *01637 830326.* Owner: K Gregory. Located on the A3075 Newquay to Redruth road. Site offers good recreational facilities in a pleasantly designed park. Open to singles and couples only. Open Whitsun-September. **BH&HPA. 126T. MC.** ⛺🚐🚾

(5m). Summer Lodge Holiday Resort, Whitecross, Newquay, Cornwall TR8 4LW. *01726 860415.* info@snooty foxresorts.co.uk. www.snootyfoxresorts.co.uk. Owners: Snooty Fox Resorts Ltd. Tivoli House, Boulevard, Weston-super-Mare BS23 1PD. From M5 take A30, then turn on to A392 to Newquay, SP at Whitecross. Conveniently situated for touring. Facilities include heated swimming pool, cafe, take-away, club with live entertainment. Golf. Horse riding, full range of water sports. Open March-October 31. **BH&HPA. 100T. 157S.** ⛺🚐🚾∅

(5.5m). Sun Haven Valley Caravan & Camping Park, Mawgan Porth, Newquay, Cornwall TR8 4BQ. *01637 860373.* tracey healey@hotmail.com. www.sunhavenvalley.co.uk. Owner: Tracey & Keith Healey. Turn right off the B3276, Newquay to Padstow coast road, park is on the left-hand side about 0.75m from the coast. Dogs are allowed on touring field. Families and couples only. Fishing and golf available nearby. Open April-October 31. ☆☆☆☆☆ **115T. 3MC. 30H.** ⛺🚐♿🚾∅

(3m). Sunnyside Holiday Park, Quintrel Downs, Newquay, Cornwall TR8 4PD. *01637 873338.* info@sunnyside.co.uk. www.sunnyside.co.uk. Owner: Mr D A Gamble. Situated off A392 Newquay road. 18-30s' type holiday park. Nightclub. Swimming pool. Restaurant etc. Not suitable for families with children. Open March-January. **BH&HPA. 10MC. 155S. 155H.** ⛺🚾

(6m). The Meadow, Holywell Bay, Newquay, Cornwall TR8 5PP. *01872 572752.* www.holywellbeachholidays.co.uk. Owner: Mr D J Humphrey. Turn right off A3075, 3m out of Newquay. Small, family-run site bordered by trees and stream, 500yd walk to large, sandy beach. 300yd to shop and inn. Open Easter-October. **6T. 9H.** ⛺🚐

(5m). Treago Farm Caravan and Camping Site, Crantock, Newquay, Cornwall TR8 5QS. *01637 830277.* tregofarm@ aol.com. www.tregofarm.co.uk. Owner: Mr J A & P A Eastlake. Off A3075, 2m S of Newquay follow signs to Crantock and the Treago, then West Pentire signs. Open March 3-November 11. **BH&HPA. 90T. MC. 10H.** ⛺🚐🚾

(3m). Tregustick Holiday Park, Porth, Newquay, Cornwall TR8 4AR. *01637 872478.* Owner: R Hutchinson & L Watson. Off B3276. Open Easter-October 31. **BH&HPA. 25MC. 26H.** 🚾

(6.5m). Trekenning Tourist Park, Trekenning, Newquay, Cornwall TR8 4JF. *01637 880462.* holidays@trekenning.co.uk. www.trekenning.co.uk. Owner: Brian & Gayle Thomas & Bob & Joy Ashton. Just off A39, 0.5m S of St Columb. 10mins Newquay, 4m Watergate and Mawgan Porth beaches. Swimming pool. Launderette. Licensed bar. Games room. Family bathrooms, showers. Washing-up basins. Dogs by arrangements. ☆☆☆☆ **BH&HPA. NCC. 75T. MC.** ✪⛺🚐🚾

(3m). Treloy Tourist Park, Newquay, Cornwall TR8 4JN. *01637 872063/01637 876279.* holidays@treloy.co.uk. www.treloy.co.uk. Owner: Mr J Paull. Just off A3059 Newquay road. Heated swimming pool, licensed bar, family room, entertainment, cafe/takeaway. Shop. Free showers. TV/games room. Adventure playground. Coarse fishing nearby. Own golf course concessionary green fees. Open April-end September. ☆☆☆ **BH&HPA. 140T. MC.** ⛺🚐♿🚾

Please visit the Caravan Club website: www.caravanclub.co.uk

(0.5m). **Trenance Holiday Park, Edgecumbe Avenue, Newquay, Cornwall TR7 2JY.** *01637 873447.* enquiries@ trenanceholidaypark.co.uk. www.trenanceholidaypark.co.uk. Owner: Mr P A & A W Hoyte. 1, Treninnick Hill, Newquay, Cornwall. On the A3075, Newquay to Truro road. Games room. Restaurant and takeaway. Nearest park to Newquay town centre, 0.5m. Open April 1-October 31. ☆☆☆ **BH&HPA. 50T. 50MC. 134H.** 🌐 🗲 🖉

(1m). **Trencreek Holiday Park, Trencreek, Newquay, Cornwall TR8 4NS.** *01637 874210.* trencreek@btconnect.com. www.trencreekholidaypark.co.uk. Owner: Mr J Hautot. Take the A392 to Quintrell Downs, turn right Newquay, east to Porth, after four turnings, left into Trevenson Rd. Takeaway cafe. TV and games room. Laundrette. Swimming pool. Licensed bar with entertainment. Children's room. Playfield. Coarse fishing. AA 4 pennants. Open April -September. ☆☆☆☆ **194T. MC. 26H.** 🌐 ♿ 🗲

(2m). **Trethiggey Touring Park, Quintrell Downs, Newquay, Cornwall TR8 4QR.** *01637 877672.* enquiries@trethiggey.co.uk. www.trethiggey.co.uk. Situated off the A3058. Family site with countryside views. Level pitches. Takeaway food. Laundrette. Games room. Adventure playground. Caravan storage. Dog walk area. Fishing and local PH a few mins walk away. 15 miles from the Eden Project. David Bellamy Silver Conservation award. Open March 1-January 1, including Christmasmas and New Year. ☆☆☆ **BH&HPA. 157T. MC. 12H.** 🐾 🌐 ♿ 🗲

(4.5m). **Trevarrian Holiday Park, Mawgan Porth, Newquay, Cornwall TR8 4AQ.** *01637 860381.* holidays @trevarrian.co.uk. Owner: Dave & Tish Phillips. Level grassy site. Facilities include: heated pool, games room, bar, tennis court, pitch and putt, and sports field. Open Easter-end September. **BH&HPA. 185T. MC.** 🐾 🌐 🗲

(1.5m). **Trevelgue Caravan Park, Porth, Newquay, Cornwall TR8 4AS.** *01637 851851.* Owner: Mr S Christopher. Located off the B3276 Padstow to Newquay road. Club. Swimming pool. Jaccuzzi. Laundrette. Cafe. Surf shop, board and bike hire. Dogs allowed at the park owner's discretion. **90T. MC. 154H.** ✿ 🌐 ♿ 🗲 🖉

Quarryfield Caravan & Camping Park

Crantock, Near Newquay, Cornwall TR8 5RJ

Caravans/chalets to let. All with W.C.s, elec., fridge, fire. Colour TV. All with showers or bathrooms. 10 mins. beach. Licensed Bar, heated swimming pool, showers, laundry, electric hook ups, children's play area and games room, shop. Also flats in Newquay.

Prices on application.

SAE for Brochure:
C H Winn, Tretherras, Newquay, Cornwall TR7 2RE.
Tel: (01637) 872792.

Carnevas
Farm
Porthcothan.
Beach.

wquay,
lapark@
Caravan
l, crazy
e. Well
October

(6m). White Acres Holiday Park, Whitecross, Newquay, Cornwall TR8 4LW. *01726 862100.* enquiries@parkdeanholidays.co.uk. www.whiteacres.co.uk. Owner: Parkdean Holidays Plc. 2nd Floor, One Gosforth Way, Gosforth Business Park, Newcastle-upon-Tyne NE12 8ET. A392 to Newquay, travel over 1st roundabout, park entrance on right. Heated indoor pool, Fun Factory, bowling and amusements. Bar, restaurant and live family entertainment. 15 fishing lakes. Open March-January. ☆☆☆☆☆ BH&HPA. NCC. 75T. 75MC. 296S. 246H. ⚑ ◨ ♿ ⚖

Otterham

St Tinney Farm Holidays, St Tinney Farm, Otterham, Cornwall PL32 9TA. *01840 261274.* info@st-tinney.co.uk. www.st-tinney.co.uk. Owner: M & E Windley. 10m S of Bude, just off A39. Good touring centre. 4 coarse fishing lakes. Farm animals. Pony rides. Dogs allowed on touring site only. AA 3 pennants. Open Easter-October 31. **BH&HPA. 20T. 6S. 9H.** ◨ ⚖ ∅

Bay,
ookings
A3075
, most
course
ds. Full
abaret.
n Park.
ts for
nire. Open Easter-September. ☆☆☆☆☆ BH&HPA. 250T. 250MC. ⚑ ◨ ♿ ⚖

Padstow

(4m). Carnevas Farm Holiday Park, St Merryn, Padstow, Cornwall PL28 8PN. *01841 520230.* www.carnevasholidaypark.co.uk. Owner: The Brewer Family. From St Merryn take B3276 towards Porthcothan Bay, about 2m, turn R opposite Tredrea Inn. Beach 0.5m. Family-run site. Showers, laundry, children's play area, games room, bar. Rose Award. Beach 0.5m. Fishing, golf course nearby. Open April-October. ☆☆☆☆ **BH&HPA. 195T. MC. 9H.** ⚑ ◨ ♿ ⚖

(4m). Watergate Bay Tourist Park, Trequrrian, Watergate Bay, Newquay, Cornwall TR8 4AD. *01637 860387.* watergatebay@email.com. www.watergatebaytouringpark.co.uk. Owner: Mr B & Mrs C M Jennings. N of Newquay on B3276 coast road to Padstow at Watergate Bay. Heated pool, licensed bar, evening entertainment, cafeteria, adventure playground, sports field, dog exercise area, free minibus to beach and access to coastal footpath. Open March 1-November 30. **BH&HPA. 171T. 171MC. S. H.** ⚑ ◨ ♿ ⚖

(3m). Harlyn Sands Caravan Park, Lighthouse Road, Trevose Head, St Merryn, Padstow, Cornwall PL28 8SQ. *01841 520720.* Owner: Mr Richards. Open April-October. **BH&HPA. 150T. MC. 250S. 40H.** ⚑ ◨ ♿ ⚖

(3m). Higher Harlyn Park, St Merryn, Padstow, Cornwall PL28 8SG. 01841 520022. pbharlyn@aol.com. www.cornwall-online.co.uk. Owner: Mr P H, C A & M H Bennett. Off B3276. Licensed bar. Outdoor heated swimming pool. Laundrette. Diner. St Merryn village is only a 5mins flat walk away. Open Easter-October. **325T. MC. 30H.** 🏕 🚐 🚻 🏊

(3m). Maribou Holiday Park, St Merryn, Padstow, Cornwall PL28 8QA. 01841 520520. Owner: T J Orriss Maribou (Holidays) Ltd. Take B3274 off A30, second road left after roundabout to St Merryn. Open site within easy reach of surfing beaches. Licensed bar. Takeaway. Shaver points. Laundry. Showers. Open Easter-October. **100T. MC. 100S. 100H.** 🏕 🚐 🚻

(4m). Mother Ivey's Bay Caravan Park, Trevose Head, Padstow, Cornwall PL28 8SL. 01841 520990. info@motheriveysbay.com. www.motheriveysbay.com. Owner: Patrick & Caroline Langmaid. 4m from Padstow, SP off the B3276, Padstow to Newquay coast road (Trevose Head). Coastal location. Private beach. Golf, fishing and water sports available nearby. Open April 1-October 31. ☆☆☆☆ **BH&HPA. 100T. MC. 250S. 48H.** 🏕 🚐 🚻 🏊 🚶

(4m). Old MacDonald's Farm, Porthcothan Bay, Padstow, Cornwall PL28 8LW. 01841 540829. oldmacdonalds farm@ tinyworld.co.uk. Owner: John & Karen Nederpel. On the B3276 coast road between Padstow and Newquay, look for signs. Quiet park suitable for families. Free entrance to farm park during stay. Showers. Play area. Pony rides on site. Sporting facilities nearby. 0.5m from beach, which is suitable for surfing and swimming. Advance bookings accepted. Brochure available. **T. MC.** ✿ 🏕 🚐 🚻 🏊

(1.5m). Padstow Holiday Park, Cliff Downe, Padstow, Cornwall PL28 8LB. 01841 532289. alex@cliffdowne. freeserve.co.uk. padstowholidaypark.co.uk. Owner: Mr & Mrs Barnes. On main A389, Padstow road. Near to several sandy beaches. Quiet, family-run park in coutryside setting. Footpath to Padstow. Level, well-maintained. Uncrowded and friendly. Open March 1-December 31. **BH&HPA. 83S. 1H.** 🚐

(4m). Seagull Tourist Park, St Merryn, Padstow, Cornwall PL28 8PT. 01841 520117. Owner: Mrs Wendy Pollard. B3274 via St Columb bypass to Padstow; SPs to St Merryn, past Maribu to Point Curlew. After 100yd turn L to site, follow road through farm. Quiet, family site with easy access. Coastal views and sandy beaches nearby. All-year storage facilities. Booking essential. Quaint fishing port of Padstow with famous seafood restaurant. Golf, surfing, cliff walks, bike trails, activities and interests nearby. Open Easter or April 1-October 31. **50T. 10MC. 36S. 4H.** 🏕 🚐

(2m). Tregavone Touring Park, Tregavone Farm, St Merryn, Padstow, Cornwall PL28 8JZ. Owner: Mr & Mrs J Dennis. SW of Padstow on A389. 4-acre, quiet, family-run site with unspoilt countryside views. Suitable base for sandy beaches and touring Cornwall. 2m to picturesque Padstow, fishing and golf course. AA 2 pennants. Open March-October. **40T. MC.** 🏕 🚐

(1m). Trerethern Touring Park, Padstow, Cornwall PL28 8LE. 01841 532061. camping.trerethern@btinternet.com. www. trerethern.co.uk. Owner: Mr Barnes. On A389 SW of Padstow. Easy access. Panoramic views and public footpath to Padstow. Storage available. New en-suite pitches. Colour brochure available. Motorvan waste disposal point. Open April-early October. ☆☆☆☆ **100T. MC.** 🏕 🚐 🚻 🏊

(4m). Trethias Farm Caravan Site, Treyarnon Bay, St Merryn, Padstow, Cornwall PL28 8PL. 01841 520323. Owner: David & Sandi Chandler. Off B3276 from St Merryn, past Farmers Arms, 3rd turning right, park signed from here. Shop and beach nearby. Golf course 2m, PO, doctor 1.5m. David Bellamy Gold Conservation award. Open April 1-September 30. ☆☆☆ **BH&HPA. 63T. MC. 65S.** 🏕 🚐

(4m). Trevean Caravan and Camping Park, St Merryn, Padstow, Cornwall PL28 8PR. 01841 520772. Owner: Mrs J Raymont. From St Merryn village take the B3276, Newquay road, for 1m, turn left for Rumford, site 0.25m on right. Family site, situated near sandy surfing beaches. Coastal footpaths with spectacular scenery of the north Cornish coast. Open April 1-October 31. ☆☆☆ **BH&HPA. 24T. 12MC. 3H.** 🏕 🚐

(4m). Treyarnon Bay Caravan & Camping Park, Treyarnon Bay, Padstow, Cornwall PL28 8JR. 01841 520681. www. treyarnonbay.co.uk. Owner: Old & Partridge. Off B3276 Newquay to Padstow road, turn off for Treyarnon Bay, follow lane into beach car park. Holiday park adjacent. Family site 200yd from beach overlooking Treyarnon Bay. Coastal walks and surfing. Site wardens: Brian and Yvonne Hinsley. Open April 1-September 30. **55T. MC. 200S. 60H.** 🏕 🚐 🚻

Par

Par Sands Holiday Park, Par Beach, Par, Cornwall PL24 2AS. 01726 812868. holidays@parsands.co.uk. www.parsands.co.uk. 4m from St Austell. Quiet, family holiday park alongside large, safe, sandy beach. Indoor heated pool with aquaslide, bowling green, tennis, badminton, cycle hire and crazy golf. Level, grassy touring pitches. Suitable base for exploring Cornwall. Pets welcome. 3.5m from Eden Project. David Bellamy Gold Conservation Award. Open April 1-October 31. ☆☆☆☆ **BH&HPA. 150T. MC. 210S. 50H.** 🏕 🚐 🚻

Penryn

(2.5m). Calamankey Farm, Longdowns, Penryn, Cornwall TR10 9DL. 01209 860314. calamankey@boltblue.com. www.calamankey.boltblue.net. Owner: Mr C C Davidson. On A394 opposite Gulf filling station in Longdowns village. Site on working farm in open countryside with views to St Mawes and Roseland Peninsula. Centrally situated (Truro 10m, Helston 9m, Redruth 9m, Falmouth 4m), suitable base for exploring Ther Lizard and Helford river. Many family attractions nearby (Flambards theme park, seal sanctuary, Poldark Mine). Local shop/PO and PH 20yd from drive entrance. Large ASDA store 1.5m. Golf, boating, fishing, tennis, scuba diving, riding, sailing and swimming all available nearby. Open Easter-November. **45T. 15MC. 4H.** 🏕 🚐

Please mention Caravan Sites 2006 when replying to advertisers

WEST COUNTRY

Penzance

(5m). Boleigh Farm, Lamorna Cove, Penzance, Cornwall TR19 6BN. *01736 810305.* Owner: Mr D Eddy. 5m from Penzance on B3315, past cove and take first right. Small farm site. Gas. Showers. Open Easter-October. **15T. 15MC. ⌇ ◖**

(1m). Bone Valley Caravan & Camping Park, Heamoor, Penzance, Cornwall TR20 8UJ. *01736 360313.* bonevalley candcpark@fsbdial.co.uk. www.cornwalltouristboard.co.uk/ bonevalley. Owner: Margaret & Bob Maddock. Follow A30 Penzance bypass, turn off at Heamoor roundabout, continue through Heamoor to caravan and camping sign on right. Continue down hill to next sign on left, SP Bone Valley, site 200yd on L. Sheltered, clean and friendly. Supervised 24hr. Limited facilities for disabled people in some holiday caravans. TV room, laundry facilities, kitchen with microwave and electric kettle, shower/toilet block. Baby changing facilities. Bottled gas supplies, battery charging. AA 3 pennants. **15T. MC. 4S. ✿ ⌇ ◖ & ▨**

(7m). Camping & Caravanning Club Site - Sennen Cove, Higher Tregiffian Farm, St Buryan, Penzance, Cornwall TR19 6JB. *01736 871588/0870 243 3331.* www.campingandcaravanningclub.co.uk. Owner: Camping & Caravanning Club. Greenfields House, Westwood Way, Coventry CV4 8JH. Follow A30 towards Land's End. Turn R on to A3306 St Just/Pendeen Road. Site 300yd on L. 4-acre site with 75 pitches accepting all units. Sennen Cove Blue Flag beach within easy reach. Non-members welcome. Ball games' area and playing field available. On a farm in peaceful countryside near coast. Special deals for families and backpackers. Open April-October. ✰✰✰✰ **75T. 75MC. ⌇ ◖ &**

(2.5m). Garris Farm, Gulval, Penzance, Cornwall TR20 8XD. *01736 365806.* Owner: Mr I A Phillips. Leave A30 at Crowlas on B3309 to Ludgvan and Gastlegate. On road to Chysanster, ancient village. Quiet, farm site, established 1920. Open April-October. **20T. 20MC. ⌇**

(7m). Kelynack Caravan and Camping Park, St Just, Penzance, Cornwall TR19 7RE. *01736 787633.* steve@key nackholidays.co.uk. Owner: Mr S J Edwards. On B3306, St Ives to Land's End. 1m S of St Just, alongside stream in secluded valley. Close to the coast. David Bellamy Gold Conservation Award. 1m from shops, PHs, PO, doctors. 2m from golf course. Open April 1-October 31. **6T. 20MC. 11H. ⌇ ◖ & ▨**

(6m). Kenneggy Cove Holiday Park, Higher Kenneggy, Rosudgeon, Penzance, Cornwall TR20 9AU. *01736 763453.* enquiries@kenneggycove.co.uk. www.kenneggy cove.co.uk. Owner: Linda Garthwaite. Off A394, Helston to Penzance, 3m E of Marazion on south coast. Quiet, family site in landscaped garden setting. Rose Award. In Area of Outstanding Natural Beauty. Sea views. 12mins walk to SW coastal path and safe, secluded sandy beach. Clean facilities with free hot water and hair-dryers. Laundrette, payphone, children's play area. Shop and take-away service. Quiet site, operating a policy of no noise after 10pm or before 8am. Open April 1-October 31. ✰✰✰✰ **BH&HPA. 60T. 30MC. 9S. 9H. ⌇ ◖ ▨**

(7m). Levant House, Levant Road, Pendeen, Penzance, Cornwall TR19 7SX. *01736 788795.* Owner: Mr J H A Boyns. On B3306 3m N of St Just-in-Penwith. Fishing, golf, cliff climbing nearby. Shop, PO, doctors 4mins drive. Coastal path 5-7 mins walk. Open April 1-October 31. **44T. MC. ⌇ ◖**

(6m). Lower Treave Caravan Park, Crows-an-Wra, St Buryan, Penzance, Cornwall TR19 6HZ. *01736 810559.* camp ing@lowertreave.co.uk. www.lowertreave.co.uk. Owner: Mr & Mrs N A Bliss. W of Penzance on A30. Quiet, family site at the heart of the Land's End penisula. Panoramic, rural views to the sea. Sheltered grass terraces. Sennen Blue Flag beach 2.5m. Open Easter-October. **BH&HPA. 80T. 5MC. 5H. ⌇ ◖ ▨**

(6m). River Valley Country Park, Relubbus, Penzance, Cornwall TR20 9ER. *01736 763398/0845 6012516.* rivervalley @surfbay.dircon.co.uk. www.rivervalley.co.uk. Owner: J E & M J Taylor. Surf Bay Leisure, The Airfield, Winkleigh, Devon EX19 8DW. 3m NE of Marazion. From Hayle B3302 to Leedstown, turn right on to B3280 to Townsend and straight on to Relubbus. Quiet, rural, family park on banks of clear shallow stream. Short or long stays welcome. Large level pitches. Open March-January for holiday homes; open March-January for tourers. ✰✰✰✰✰ **BH&HPA. NCC. 150T. MC. 38H. ⌇ ◖ ▨**

(4.5). Roseland's Caravan & Camping Park, Dowran, St Just, Penzance, Cornwall TR19 7RS. *01736 788571.* camping@ roseland84freeserve.co.uk. www.roselands.co.uk. Owner: Peter & Jane Hall. From Penzance on A3071 to St Just, 6m, SP on R 800yd. Games room, play area, showers, laundrette. Breakfast and evening meals served in new conservatory. Sea views. Level pitches. Suitable base for walking, water activities and local attractions including golf course. Eden Project 75mins drive, Maritime Museum 30mins drive. Open January 1-October 31. ✰✰✰ **BH&HPA. 7T. 7MC. 15S. ⌇ ◖ ▨ ⊘**

(8m). Seaview Holiday Park, Sennen, Penzance, Cornwall TR19 7AD. *01736 871266.* seaview.landsend@btopenworld.com. www.seaview.org.uk. Owner: Mrs Brownbridge. On A30 Penzance to Land's End. Family park. Outdoor swimming pool, cafe and barbecue area, tennis court on site. Bike hire. Crazy golf, extended play area, playtrain, table tennis. Laundrette. Trampolines, pizza takeaway. Cinema in Penzance. Minack open-air theatre. Golf 3m. ✰✰ **BH&HPA. 60T. 20MC. 95S. 75H. ✿ ◖ ▨**

Threeways Caravan Club Site, St Hilary, Goldsithney, Penzance, Cornwall TR20 9DU. *01736 710723.* www.caravanclub.co.uk. Owner: The Caravan Club. East Grinstead House, London Road, East Grinstead, West Sussex RH19 1UA. See website for standard directions to site. 2m from Marazion. Caravan Club members only. Attractive site in parkland setting, with views. Peaceful off-peak. Levelling blocks required, steel awning pegs required. Gas. No sanitation. Dog walk. Motorhome service point. Fishing, golf and water sports nearby. Suitable for families. NCN cycle route within 5m. Open March-October. **NCC. 60T. MC. ⌇ ◖**

(5m). Tower Park Caravans (FCS), St Buryan, Penzance, Cornwall TR19 6BZ. *01736 810286.* enquiries@towerpark camping.co.uk. www.towerparkcamping.co.uk. Owner: Dave & Joyce Green. From A30, Land's End road, turn L on B3283, SP St Buryan. Site is 300yd from village on St Just road. Level grass with sheltering hedges. Beaches nearby. Trampolines, pizza take-away.Shower. Laundry and shop. Minack Theatre nearby. Open March 7-January 7. ✰✰✰ **BH&HPA. 60T. 42MC. 5H. ⌇ ◖ & ▨**

(6m). Trevair Caravan Park, South Treveneague, St Hilary, Penzance, Cornwall TR20 9BY. *01736 740647.* philandval@ trevair.freeserve.co.uk. www.trevairtouringpark.co.uk. Owner: Mr & Mrs Luxford. 2m NE of Marazion on B3280. Set in 3 secluded acres surrounded by fields and woodland. Well-maintained, family site. AA 3 pennants. Open Easter-October 31. **20T. MC. 3H. ⌇ ◖**

(7m). Trevedra Farm Caravan Club Site, Sennen, Land's End, Penzance, Cornwall TR19 7BE. *01736 871835/01736 871818.* nicholastrevedra@farming.co.uk. www.sennen-cove.com/ trevedra. Owner: Mr & Mrs J M Nicholas. Turn R off A30 just after B3306 junction. 2.5m from Land's End. Caravan Club affiliated site. Non-members and tent campers welcome. Certain areas for members only. Public telephone. Calor Gas and Campingaz. Shower block. Laundrette. Footpath to Gwenver Beach and coastal path. Open April-October 31. **60T. MC.** ⛺ 🔌 ♿ 🧺

(6m). Treverven Touring Caravan & Camping Site, St Buryan, Penzance, Cornwall TR19 6DL. *01736 810200.* Owner: Mrs H M Gwennap. Located on the B3315 coastal road. Quiet, farm site with excellent sea views. Easy access to coves and beaches. Well situated for touring west Cornwall. Showers. Shaver points. Hair-dryers. Laundry facilities. Deep freeze. Children's play area, lovely walks. AA 3 pennant site. Open Easter-October 31. **BH&HPA. 75T. 75MC.** ⛺ 🔌 ♿ 🧺

Wayfarers Caravan & Camping Park, St Hilary, Penzance, Cornwall TR20 9EF. *01736 763326.* wayfarers@eurobell.co.uk. www.wayfarerspark.co.uk. Owner: Steve & Elaine Holding. From Penzance A30 roundabout, left on to A394. First roundabout, left on to B3280, proceed for 1.5m. Wayfarers on left-hand side, 2m from Marazion. Adults only Two village PHs within 1m. Landscaped park with marked, level pitches. Laundrette. Golf, horse riding. Coastal walks, water sports. Fishing 1m. Open March-November. ☆☆☆ **BH&HPA. 40T. 5MC. 6S. 4H.** ⛺ 🔌 🧺 ✎

Perranporth

(0.5m). Atlantic Coast Caravans, 33 Droskyn Way, Perranporth, Cornwall TR6 0DS. *01872 572555.* Owner: Mrs J Byatt. A30 to B3284 to Perranporth. Laundrette on site. No charges for gas or electricity. Every caravan has a beach view. 800yd to beach. Fishing, golf, tennis, gliding, riding all availalbe within 1m. Perranporth beach, patrolled by lifeguards, is renowned for its surf, sand dunes. Open March-October. **BH&HPA. 8H.** 🧺

(2.5m). Perran Springs Holiday Park, Goonhavern, Perranporth, Cornwall TR4 9QG. *01872 540568.* info@perran springs.co.uk. www.perransprings.co.uk. Owner: T Howard & M Thomas. Leave A30, turn right on to the B3285, SP Perranporth. Follow brown tourism signs marked 'Perran Springs' for 1.5m. Entrance to park on right-hand side. Award-winning, quiet, family park, 21 acres. Private, stocked coarse fishing lakes, licensed shop, Eurotents, spacious level pitches, hook-ups, play area, laundrette, panoramic country-side views. Open Easter-October. **BH&HPA. 120T. MC. 6S. 6H.** 🔌 ♿ 🧺

(1m). Perran-Sands Holiday Park, Perranporth, Cornwall TR6 0AQ. *01872 572205.* oewebmaster@bourne-leisure. co.uk. www.perransandsholidaypark.co.uk. Owner: Bourne Leisure Ltd. 1 Park Lane, Hemel Hempstead, Hertfordshire HP2 4YL. From Exeter take A30 through Devon and Cornwall. 1m beyond Wind Farm roundabout (Mitchell) turn right on to the B3285 towards Perranporth. Perran Sands is on the hill before going down hill into Perranporth. Heated indoor pool, daytime and evening entertainment for all the family. All- weather, multi-sports court. Adventure play-ground. Near beach, golf course nearby. Near tEden Project. Open March-October. ☆☆☆ **BH&HPA. NCC. 450T. 487S. 274H.** ⛺ 🔌 ♿ 🧺

(1m). Perranporth Caravan Holidays, Perran Sands, Perranporth, Cornwall TR6 0AE. *01872 572385.* www.cara vanscornwall.co.uk. Owner: Mr R A Abram. 1 Crow Hill, Bolingey, Perranporth, Cornwall TR6 ODG. A30, follow signs to Perranporth; from The New Inn, the park entrance is 1.25m on the R. All facilities of adjacent Perran Sands are available to holiiday makers, including shop, club, heated swimming pool etc. 5mins drive to golf. 10mins drive to shops in village. 20mins drive to cinema. Open April-October. ☆☆☆ **BH&HPA. 16S. 12H.** ⛺ 🧺 ✎

(1.5m). Rosehill Farm Tourist Park, Goonhavern, Perranporth, Cornwall TR4 9LA. *01872 572448.* Owner: Mark & Lyn Hooper. On B3285. Well-stocked shop. Games room. Laundry. New shower block. Free showers/hairdryers. Family room and room for disabled visitors. Heated outdoor pool. Children's play area. Pets welcome. Booking advisable July-August. Resident owners. Open Easter-end-September. **BH&HPA. 95T. MC.** ⛺ 🔌 ♿ 🧺

(1.5m). Roseville Holiday Park, Goonhavern, Perranporth, Cornwall TR4 9LA. *01872 572448.* www.rosevilleholiday park.co.uk. Owner: J & W Inkster. 8m from New Quay, 10m from Truro. On B3285. iSurfing/walking beach. 10m from Eden Project. Suitable base for touring Cornwall. AA 3 pennants. Open April-October. **BH&HPA. NCC. 85T. 20MC. 10S. 10H.** ⛺ 🔌 ♿ 🧺

Polzeath

(0.125m). Tristram Caravan & Camping Park, Polzeath, Cornwall PL27 6UG. *01208 862215.* paul@tristramcampsite.fsnet.co.uk. www.rockinfo.co.uk. Owner: Mr R R & Mrs B Harris. South Winds, Polzeath, Nr Wadesbridge, Cornwall PL27 6QU. 7m N of Wadebridge via B3314, road signs to Polzeath. On clifftop overlooking beach with own private access. Site is fenced off for safety. Showers. Laundry. Takeaway. Bookings advisable in school holidays. Fishing, surfing, boating, skiing, golf, potholing, all nearby. AA 3 pennants. Open March-November. **BH&HPA. 90T. 50MC.** ⛺ 🔌 🧺

Portreath

(1.5m). Tehidy Holiday Park, Harris Mill, Illogan, Portreath, Cornwall TR16 4JQ. *01209 216489/314558.* holiday@ tehidy.co.uk. www.tehidy.co.uk. Owner: Mr & Mrs J & G Williams. Take B3300 out of Redruth, left at fork, left again at Cornish Arms PH. Laundrette. Showers. Games room. Playground. Payphone. Off-licence. Shaver points. Gas sales. Suitable base for exploring coastlines. Dogs welcome by prior agreement. Open April-October. ☆☆☆☆ **BH&HPA. 18T. 20H.** 🔌 ♿ 🧺 ✎

Redruth

(6m). Caddys Corner Farm, Carnmenellis, Redruth, Cornwall TR16 6PH. *01209 860275.* Owner: A J & F Rudge. 6m from Helston. A30 to Redruth then B3297 towards Helston. After 1m turn left towards Stithians. After 4m turn right opposite Carnmenellis PO. Showers. Laundry room. Open Easter-October 31. **5T. 5MC. 5H.** ⛺ 🔌

(2m). Cambrose Touring Park, Portreath Road, Redruth, Cornwall TR16 4HT. *01209 890747.* cambrosetouringpark@ supanet.com. www.cambrosetouringpark.co.uk. Owner: Mr & Mrs R G Fitton. Off B3303, Redruth to Portreathe. Past Gold Centre, first R, SP Porthtowan, site is 100yd on L. Small, family- run park. Heated outdoor pool from May to September. Adventure playground, mini football pitch away from camping area. Wet weather room. Open April-October. ☆☆☆ **60T. 2H.** ⛺ 🔌 ♿ 🧺

Please mention Caravan Sites 2006 when replying to advertisers

STUNNING LOCATIONS CORNWALL
POLZEATH
EXCELLENT FACILITIES

One of the most spectacular, safest and best surfing beaches in Cornwall. Visitors return each year to enjoy the beauty and safety of its golden sands and clear blue sea.

Tristram

South Winds

We have two prime sites at Polzeath. Tristram above right and shown on the aerial picture is on the gently sloping cliff overlooking the beach with direct access to the beach. The site is private and safe for children. It also has its own shop, restaurant and take away on site. South Winds above left is different, families like the peace and quiet with beautiful sea and panoramic rural views yet only half a mile from the beach. Both sites have modern toilets, showers and laundry facilities.

01208 862215 (Tristram)
01208 863267 (South Winds)
Fax: **01208 862080** **www.rockinfo.co.uk**
South Winds, Polzeath, Cornwall PL27 6QU
paul@tristramcampsite.fsnet.co.uk

AA

BRITISH HOLIDAY HOME PARKS ASSOCIATION

APPROVED Cornwall ACCOMMODATION

MasterCard VISA

WEST COUNTRY

(2m). Lanyon Holiday Park, Loscombe Lane, Four Lanes, Redruth, Cornwall TR16 6LP. *01209 313474.* jamierielly@btconnect.com. www.lanyonholidaypark.co.uk. Owner: Mr & Mrs J Rielly. On the B3297, Redruth to Helston road, within the confines of Four Lanes village. Family-run park set in countryside looking out towards the sea. Heated covered pool, games room, bar and restaurant, play park, laundrette, three modern toilet and shower blocks, part time shop, pets welcome, large dog walking paddock. 10 mins walk to village with PHs, shops and bus stop. Within 2m of fishing, water sports, horse riding, walking, cycling path. Cinema, market indoor/outdoor, leisure centre three miles. Beach 5m. No groups of young people. Rose award. Open 11 months. ✰✰✰✰ **BH&HPA. 25T. 25MC. 40S. 20H.** ⌂ ⌯ ⚑

(2m). Tresaddern Holiday Park, St Day, Redruth, Cornwall TR16 5JR. *01209 820459.* Owner: Roy & Gill Roberts. E of Redruth on the B3298, site is SP. A small, quiet site central for touring south Cornwall. Open, close-mown meadow screened by hedging. Four chalets also available for hire. Open April 1-October 31. **BH&HPA. 15T. 15MC. 13H.** ⌂ ⚑

Saltash

(4m). Dolbeare Caravan and Camping Park, St Ive Road, Landrake, Saltash, Cornwall PL12 5AF. *01752 851332.* dolbeare@btopenworld.com. www.dolbeare.co.uk. Owner: John Taylor & Mark Woodason. W of Saltash via A38 to Landrake. Then N to Blunts and Quethiock to site about 1m on R. Flat and gently sloping. Dog exercise field. Hardstandings with drainage. Showers. Rural setting near many places of interest. Only 20mins from centre of Plymouth, Looe and coast. PO 1m, doctor 4m. Eden Project 30mins. Golf course nearby in St Mellion, fishing, walks. ✰✰✰✰ **BH&HPA. 60T. 60MC.** ✿ ⌂ ⚑

(3.5m). Notter Bridge Caravan & Camping Park, Notter Bridge, Saltash, Cornwall PL12 4RW. *01752 842318.* holidays@notterbridge.co.uk. www.notterbridge.co.uk. Owner: David & Beryl Hacking. Situated on the A38. 3.5m W of Tamar Bridge, Plymouth. Sheltered, level site in a picturesque, wooded valley with river frontage. PH/food opposite, good centre for touring Plymouth, Cornwall and Devon. Fishing. Golf, sailing, supermarket, pool available within 3m. Open April-September. **BH&HPA. 23T. 23MC. 17S. 6H.** ⌂ ⚑ ⅊

St Agnes

(2m). Beacon Cottage Farm Touring Park, Beacon Drive, St Agnes, Cornwall TR5 0NU. *01872 552347/553381.* beaconcottagefarm@lineone.net. www.beaconcottagefarmholidays.co.uk. Owner: Mr & Mrs J Sawle. Leave the A30 at roundabout and follow the B3277 to St Agnes, at mini-roundabout take a left turn towards Chapel Porth and follow signs to park. Site is signposted. Showers. Shaver points. Telephone. Showers. Laundry and dishwashing facilities. Gas available. Play area. Dog exercise field. Open April-October. ✰✰✰✰ **BH&HPA. 50T. 50MC.** ⌂ ⚑ ⅊

(1m). Presingoll Farm, St Agnes, Cornwall TR50 0PB. *01872 552333.* pam@presingollfarm.fsbusiness.co.uk. www.presingollfarm.fsbusiness.co.uk. Owner: Mrs P Williams. Located off the main A30. At Chyverton Cross roundabout take the A3277 for St Agnes. Park is about 3m on the right-hand side. Surfing beaches 2m. Village is only a walking distance of about 0.75m. Many leisure facilities are within 2-3m. Dairy produce available. AA 3 pennants. Open April 1-October 31. **90T. MC.** ⌂ ⚑ ⅊ ⚑

(0.75m). St Agnes Beacon Caravan Club Site, Beacon Drive, St Agnes, Cornwall TR5 0NU. *01872 552543.* www.caravanclub.co.uk. Owner: The Caravan Club. East Grinstead House, London Road, East Grinstead, West Sussex RH19 1UA. See website for standard directions to site. Caravan Club members only. Panoramic views of Cornish coastline from this gently sloping site. Peaceful off-peak. Conveniently located for some of best beaches in Cornwall, good area for walking. Dog walk on site. Tradesman calls. Advance booking advised for mid-June to August. No sanitation. Calor Gas and Campingaz, laundry. Recycling facilities. Motorhome service point. Open March-October. **NCC. 112T. MC.** ⌂ ⚑

St Austell

(3m). Carlyon Bay Camping & Caravan Park (Bethesda), Bethesda, Carlyon Bay, St Austell, Cornwall PL25 3RE. *01726 812735.* holidays@carlyonbay.net. www.carlyonbay.net. Owner: Mr & Mrs L Taylor. SP off the A3082 near J with the A390. Path to beach. 1.5m from the Eden Project. Open April-October. ✰✰✰✰✰ **130T. 50MC.** ⌂ ⚑ ⅊

(4m). Carnmoggas Holiday Park, Little Polgooth, St Austell, Cornwall PL26 7DD. *01179 623792.* Owner: C F Gigg. Between A390 and B3273. Small family park. Licensed clubhouse. Heated indoor pool. Snooker, skittles and pool. Pets welcome. Indoor bowling greens. Sandy Pentewan beach 3m and weekly markets at St Austell. Open Easter-November. **BH&HPA. 30H.** ⌂ ⚑ ⅊

(1.5m). Duporth Holiday Village, St Austell, Cornwall PL26 6AJ. *01726 65511.* Owner: Mr Joce. Enter Cornwall on the A30, turn off on to the A391 to St Austell. Turn right on to the A390, at roundabout follow signs to Truro. Take next turning left 0.5m on left. Open March-October. ✰✰✰✰ **BH&HPA. NCC. 36H.** ⅊

(3m). Penhaven Touring Park, Pentewan Road, St Austell, Cornwall PL26 6DL. *01726 843687.* enquiries@penhaventouring.co.uk. www.penhaventouring.co.uk. Owner: Ian & Angela Hackwell. South from St Austell on B3273 towards Mevagissey on left, after village of London Apprentice. Situated between Eden Project and Heligan Gardens, this quiet, family site is located in a sheltered valley. Level pitches, grass and hardstandings. Family shower rooms, laundry, heated swimming pool and play area. Open April 1-October 31. ✰✰✰✰ **BH&HPA. 105T. MC.** ⌂ ⚑ ⅊ ⚑

(3m). Resugga Green Homes Park, Penwithick, St Austell, Cornwall PL26 8YP. *01726 850710.* www.ukparks.co.uk/resugga. Take B3374 towards Bugle and Bodmin, go through vilage of Penwithick, turn right at bus shelter on right. Site SP. Children allowed. **BH&HPA. 4T.** ⌂ ⚑

(1.5m). River Valley Holiday Park, London Apprentice, St Austell, Cornwall PL26 7AP. *01726 73533.* j.clemo@tesco.net. cornwall-holidays.co.uk. Owner: Mr & Mrs John Clemo. Just off B3273, in the small hamlet of London Apprentice. Quiet, family park set in the Pentewan Valley with an off-road cycle trail to the beach. Open April 1-September 30. ✰✰✰✰✰ **BH&HPA. 40T. MC. 40H.** ⌂ ⚑ ⅊ ⚑ ⌀

(10m). Sea View International Caravan Park, Boswinger, Gorran, St Austell, Cornwall PL26 6LL. *01726 843425.* enquiries@seaviewinternational.com. www.seaviewinternational.com. Owner: Mr & Mrs C J Royden. From St Austell take the B3273, signed Mevagissey. Prior to village, turn

Please mention Caravan Sites 2006 when replying to advertisers

right following brown signs (avoids narrow streets). 3.5m from Mevagissey. Large, level pitches for tourers and tents overlooking bay with award-winning beaches. Close to the Eden Project and Heligan.Heated pools. All facilities centrally heated. Extensive play area. Write or phone for free brochure. Offers outside peak season. Open March-October. ☆☆☆☆☆ BH&HPA. 165T. MC. 38S. 38H. ⚓ 🔌 ♿ 🛒 ∅

(2m). Sun Valley Holiday Park, Pentewan Road, St Austell, Cornwall PL26 6DJ. *01726 843266.* reception@sun-valley holidays.co.uk. www.sunvalleyholidays.co.uk. Owner: Mr C Mynard. From St Austell take B3273 to Mevagissey. Park 2.5m on right-hand side. Suitable touring centre situated in wooded valley 1m from the sea. Licensed club and indoor swimming pool. Open Easter-October 31. ☆☆☆☆☆ BH&HPA. 22T. MC. 64H. ⚓ 🔌 🛒 ∅

(7m). Tregarton Park, Gorran, Nr Mevagissey, St Austell, Cornwall PL26 6NF. *0870 744 9971.* reception@tregarton. co.uk. www.tregarton.co.uk. Owner: The Hicks Family. Large hedged pitches, either grass or hard-standings, situated in a sheltered park, with glimpses of the sea through the valley. On site: shop, takeaway, large heated swimming pool. 2mins from beaches and the Lost Gardens of Heligan, 20mins from the Eden Project. Sports facilities nearby, including golf and fishing. Open April 1-October 31. BH&HPA. 125T. MC. ⚓ 🔌 🛒

(10m). Trelispen Caravan & Camping Park, Gorran Haven, St Austell, Cornwall PL26 6HT. *01726 843501.* trelispen@ care4free.net. Owner: Dr James Whetter. The Roseland Institute, Gorran, St Austell, Cornwall. From St Austell take the B3273 to Mevagissey, then the road to Gorran Haven. Level park, near cliffs and sea, with private nature reserve. Laundry. Showers. Open Good Friday or April 1-October 31. 10T. 40MC. ⚓ 🔌

(5m). Trencreek Farm Country Holiday Park, Hewas Water, St Austell, Cornwall PL26 7JG. *01726 882540.* reception@trencreek.co.uk. www.trencreek.co.uk. Owners: Surf Bay Leisure. The Airfield, Winkleigh, Devon EX19 8DW. On the B3287. Also available 13 Rent a Tents and 9 chalets. Many farmyard pets. Perfect park for families with young children. Heated swimming pool. Fishing. Lakes. Playgrounds. Tennis court. Pitch and putt. Takeaway. Supervised children's club. Open March-October. BH&HPA. NCC. 184T. MC. 2S. 37H. ⚓ 🔌 ♿ 🛒

(9m). Treveor Farm Caravan & Camping Park, Gorran, St Austell, Cornwall PL26 6LW. *01726 842387.* info@treveor farm.co.uk. www.treveorfarm.co.uk. Owner: Mrs M Parkhouse. Take B3273 from St Austell, having passed Pentewan Beach, go up hill and turn right to Gorran. After about 4m turn right at sign boards. Coarse fishing.Village shop, PO, coastal path and beaches within 1m. Lost Gardens of Heligan 3m, Mevagissey 5m, Eden project is 12m. Open April-October. 50T. MC. ⚓ 🔌

(1.5m). Trewhiddle Holiday Estate, Pentewan Road, St Austell, Cornwall PL26 7AD. *01726 879420.* dmcclelland @btconnect.com. www.trewhiddle.co.uk. Owner: Mr D McClelland. Take the B3273 Mevagissey road from St Austell. Estate is 0.75m on right. Gently-sloping park extending to 16.5acres. Well situated for touring Cornwall. Site open all year for tourers, closed in February for holiday homes. 15mins from the Eden Project. Open March 1-January 31. ☆☆☆☆ BH&HPA. NCC. 104T. MC. 68S. 35H. ✿ ⚓ 🔌

St Columb

(1m). Camping & Caravanning Club Site - Trewan Hall, Trewan Hall, St Columb, Cornwall TR9 6DB. *01637 880261.* www.trewan-hall.co.uk. Owner: Camping & Caravanning Club, Greenfields House, Westwood Way, Coventry CV4 8JH. From the intersection of the A3059 and A39 go north on the A39 for 1.5m, turn left, site 0.5m on left-hand side. Club members only. All types of units accepted. Showers, hot snacks, telephone, chemical toilet emptying points, swimming pool. Site is set in the midst of 36 acres of woodland and is a David Bellamy Gold Conservation Park. The Eden Project is just 13m away. Open May-September. 200T. 200MC. ⚓ 🔌 ♿ 🛒

Gnome World Touring Park, Indian Queens, St Columb, Cornwall TR9 6HN. *01726 860812.* Owner: Mr H W J Pring. Situated off the new bypass at Indian Queens. CS98. A 4.5-acre quiet, level, relaxing park with views over Goss Moor and beyond. Central for touring Cornwall. No bars or amusements. Pay phone. Open March-December. 50T. MC. 25H. ⚓ 🔌 🛒 ∅

St Columb Major

(1m). Southleigh Manor Tourist Park, St Columb Major, Cornwall TR9 6HY. *01637 880938.* enquiries@southleigh-manor.com. www.southleigh-manor.com. Owners: Bob & Kathy Prescott. E of St Columb Major. A3059, SP Springfield park centre. Licensed bar and dining area. Heated swimming pool, sauna and spa bath. Play area. Very family orientated. Open only to naturist couples and families. Open Easter-end October. 50T. 50MC. 8H. ⚓ 🔌 🛒

(1.25m). Tregatillian Park, St Columb Major, Cornwall TR9 6JH. *01637 880482.* reception@tregatillian.co.uk. www.tre gatillian.co.uk. Owner: Mr Turner. From St Columb major roundabout, take road SP to Tregatillian and Castle An Dinas. Take first L, SP Tregatillian. Follow lane 0.75m to park. 7m from Newquay. Rose Award. Fishing 3m, golf 5m. Shops, doctor, PO 1.25m. Open May to September 30. ☆☆☆☆ BH&HPA. 33H. ⚓

St Ives

(0.50m). Ayr Holiday Park, Higher Ayr, St Ives, Cornwall TR26 1EJ. *01736 795855.* recept@ayrholidaypark.co.uk. www.ayrholidaypark.co.uk. Owner: Mr R D Baragwanath. 0.5m from town centre turn off B3306 into Bullans Lane or Carnellis Road, and then to Ayr Terrace. Dogs allowed with permission. ☆☆☆☆ BH&HPA. 35T. 15MC. 43H. ✿ ⚓ 🔌

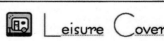

(2.5m). Balnoon Camping Site, Halsetown, St Ives, Cornwall TR26 3JA. 01736 795431. nat@balnoon.fsnet.co.uk. Owner: Mrs J M Long. From A30 take A3074 to St Ives, first L at second roundabout and second R, SP Balnoon, site is about 3m from A30. Sheltered site 2m from sea. Facilities nearby, PH, horse riding, golf course, fishing, coastal footpath. AA 2 pennants. Open Easter-October. **BH&HPA. 15T. 8MC.** ♒ ⚑ ⚒

(1m). Hellesveor Carvan & Camping Site, St Ives, Cornwall. 01736 795738. Owner: G & H Rogers. On B3306 Land's End to St Ives. 1m town, beaches. 0.5m shop and PO. Riding, fishing and golf nearby. Doctor 1m. Open Easter-October. **8T. MC. 14H.** ♒ ⚑

(2m). Little Trevarrack Tourist Park, Laity Lane, Carbis Bay, St Ives, Cornwall TR26 3HW. 01736 797580. littletrevarrack @hotmail.com. www.littletrevarrack.co.uk. Owner: Neil Osborne. From A30, A3074 towards St Ives through village of Lelant. On approaching Carbis Bay turn L at crossroads, opposite turning for beach. Continue across next junction, site entrance 150yd on R. Showers. Laundry. AA 3 pennants. Bus service to St Ives high season. Walking distance to beach. Open Easter-end of October. ✰✰✰✰ **BH&HPA. 235T. 235MC.** ♒ ⚑ ⚑

(2.5m). Penderleath Caravan & Camping Park, Towednack, St Ives, Cornwall TR26 3AF. 01736 798403. www.pender leath.co.uk. Owner: Scott & Denise Stevens. Off B3311 from St Ives take 1st right turn after Halsetown. After 0.25m take left fork. Located in Area of Outstanding Natural Beauty with good views. Peaceful, family-run and supervised park. Quiet olde Worlde licensed bar on site. Open spring bank holiday-September. ✰✰✰✰ **BH&HPA. 75T. 75MC.** ♒ ⚑ ⚑ ⚒

(2m). Polmanter Tourist Park, Halsetown, St Ives, Cornwall TR26 3LX. 01736 795640. reception@polmanter.com. www.polmanter.com. Owner: Mr P J Osborne. Off B3311, take HR route off the A30 to St Ives. Swimming pool. Tennis courts. Family lounge. Games room. Lounge bar. TV. Golf nearby. Open April-October. ✰✰✰✰✰ **BH&HPA. 240T. MC.** ♒ ⚑ ⚒

(4.5m). Sunny Meadow Holiday Park, Lelant Downs, Hayle, St Ives, Cornwall TR27 6LL. 01736 752243. sunnymeadocorn wall@hotmail.com. Owner: Miss A Carter. Off A30 bypass, take B3311, SP St Ives . Coach route. **BH&HPA. 3T. 3MC. 7H.** ✿ ♒ ⚑

(1.5m). Trevalgan Holiday Farm, Trevalgan Farm, St Ives, Cornwall TR26 3BJ. 01736 796433. enquiries@trevalganholi dayfarm.co.uk. www.trevalganholidayfarm.co.uk. Owner: Mr M Osborne. Follow B3311 (day visitors) route from A30 towards St Ives, turn left on to B3306, St Ives to Lands End, follow brown tourist signs. Quiet, family park with views and walks to coast path. Clifftop picnic tables. Hot showers. Laundry. Games and TV room. Food, takeaway. Sports field. Farm trail, pets corner. Shop. Close to St Ives and beaches. Open Easter-September 30. ✰✰✰✰ **BH&HPA. 120T.** ♒ ⚑ ⚒

St Just

(0.5m). Trevaylor Caravan and Camping Park, Botallack, St Just, Cornwall TR19 7PU. 01736 787016. bookings@trevay lor.com. www.trevaylor.com. Owner: Mr & Mrs W Sanderson. On B3306, St Just to St Ives. Laundry, games room, takeaway. Bar and food. Open April-November. **55T. MC.** ♒ ⚑ ⚒

Taunton

(2m). Cornish Farm Touring Park, Shoreditch, Taunton, Somerset TA3 7BS. 01823 327746. info@cornishfarm.com. www.cornishfarm.com. Owners: Mr & Mrs E Jones. Level, well-drained site. Fully-tiled and heated toilets and showers. Family room and laundry. Well-lit park.. AA 3 pennants. **T. MC.** ✿ ♒ ⚑ ⚑

Tintagel

(0.75m). Bossiney Farm Caravan Site, Bossiney Farm, Tintagel, Cornwall PL34 0AY. 01840 770481. www.bossiney farm.co.uk. Owner: Mr R L Wickett. On B3263, from Tintagel to Boscastle. Near cliffs and beach. Sheltered and flat walking and touring centre. Pets welcome. Free colour brochure. Children allowed. Open April-October. ✰✰✰✰ **20T. 10MC. 20H.** ♒ ⚑ ⚑ ⚒

The Headland Caravan & Camping Site, Atlantic Road, Tintagel, Cornwall PL34 0DE. 01840 770239. headland.cara vanp@btconnect.com. www.headlandcaravanpark.co.uk. Owner: Mr & Mrs M H Francis. From B3263 through village to site. 3mins walk to centre of Tintagel. 2mins walk from coastal paths and 15mins walk to swimming beach. Essential needs sold on site. Calor Gas and Camping Gaz supplies. Laundrette. Public telephone. Open Easter-October. **BH&HPA. 20T. 20MC. 3S. 27H.** ♒ ⚑ ⚒

(1.5m). Trewethett Farm Caravan Club Site, Trethevy, Tintagel, Cornwall PL34 0BQ. 01840 770222. www.car avanclub.co.uk. Owner: The Caravan Club. East Grinstead House, East Grinstead, West Sussex RH19 1UA. See website for standard directions to site. Clifftop setting, overlooking Bossiney Cove with its safe sandy. Fishing, golf and NCN cycle route nearby, good area for walking. Non-members and tent campers admitted. Open March-October. ✰✰✰✰✰ **NCC. 124T. MC.** ♒ ⚑ ⚑

Torpoint

(10m). Carbeil Caravan & Camping Park, Treliddon Lane, Downderry, Torpoint, Cornwall PL11 3LS. 01503 250636. Owner: Mrs J Stocker & Ms L Stocker. Sheltered, flat, family park, easily accessible and under new ownership. 500yd from shingle and rocky beach. Swimming pool and table tennis. Suitable base for coastal walks along National Trust footpaths. Open March-October. **BH&HPA. 10T. MC. 8S. 8H.** ⚑ ⚒

(6m). Whitsand Bay Holiday Park Ltd, Millbrook, Torpoint, Cornwall PL10 1JE. 01752 822597. Owner: Mr R Wintle. Off B3247. 8m from Plymouth with panoramic views. South-east Cornwall's award-winning park. Full range of facilities including heated pool. Club with entertainment. Free colour brochure. Open March 1-December 31. **BH&HPA. 21T. 21MC. 44S. 55H.** ⚑ ⚑ ⚒

Truro

Camping & Caravanning Club Site - Veryan, Tretheake Manor, Veryan,Truro, Cornwall TR2 5PP. 01872 501658/0870 243 3331. www.campingandcara vanningclub.co.uk. Owner: The Camping & Caravanning Club. Greenfields House, Westwood Way, Coventry CV4 8JH. 2m S of Tregony on the A3078, turn left for Veryan after petrol station and follow international signs. Site on left-hand side. Set in 9 acres of Roseland Peninsula. On-site facilities include laundrette, coarse fishing, playground, games room, TV room, beach and coastal path 1.5m. Holiday lodge for hire. Close by is the Eden Project. Nearby coastline dotted with unspoilt beaches and tiny fishing villages. All types of units accepted. Non-members welcome. Special deals available for families and backpackers. Open March-October. ✰✰✰✰ **150T. 150MC.** ♒ ⚑ ⚑

(2.5m). Carnon Downs Caravan & Camping Park, Carnon Downs, Truro, Cornwall TR3 6JJ. *01872 862283.* www.carnon-downs-caravanpark.co.uk. Owner: Markrun Ltd. Between Truro and Falmouth off A39 at Carnon Downs roundabout. Easy access. David Bellamy Gold Conservation Award. ☆☆☆☆☆ **BH&HPA. 120T. 1H.** ❀ ┭ ◙ ᕒ

(6m). Chacewater Park, Cox Hill, Chacewater, Truro, Cornwall TR4 8LY. *01209 820762.* chacewaterpark@aol.com. www.chacewaterpark.co.uk. Owner: R A & D Peterken. From A30 take A3047 to Scorrier, left at Crossroads Hotel take B3298 1.25m, left to Chacewater 0.75m, sign directs you to park. Flat, grassy, quiet park central for touring west Cornwall. Exclusively for adults over 30. Dogs allowed on touring pitches by prior agreement only. Open May-September. ☆☆☆☆ **BH&HPA. 100T.** ┭ ◙ ᕒ

(5m). Chiverton Caravan & Touring Park, Blackwater, Truro, Cornwall TR4 8HS. *01872 560667.* chivertonpark@btopenworld.com. www.chivertonpark.co.uk. Owner: Mr & Mrs Ford-Dunn. From A30 Chiverton roundabout take B3277 to St Agnes, 0.5m turn L. Park 200yd on L. Limited facilities for disabled people. Dogs allowed. Quiet, family-run park. Shop/off-licence, laundry room, children's Play area. PO and shop in Blackwater, doctors in St Agnes/Chacewater. Swimming, surfin, golf, fishing, horse riding within 5m. Sauna, steam room, gym. Fully- heated toilet and shower block. Open February 7-January 7. **BH&HPA. 30T. MC. 50S. 47H.** ┭ ◙ ᕒ ᕒ ∅

(4m). Cosawes Caravan Park Ltd, Perran-ar-Worthal, Truro, Cornwall TR3 7QS. *01872 863724.* info@cosawes.com. www.cosawes.com. Owner: Mr AR Fraser. On the A39, Truro to Falmouth road. Set in 100 acres of wooded valley between Truro and Falmouth. **BH&HPA. 20T. 20MC.** ❀ ┭ ◙

(6m). Killiwerris Touring Park, Penstraze, Truro, Cornwall TR4 8PF. *01872 561 356.* killiwerris@tiscali.co.uk. www.killiwerris.co.uk. Owner: Mike & Lin Hills. Travel along A30 towards Penzance, about 28m W of Bodmin, at Chiverton Cross roundabout, take 3rd exit, SP Blackwater. After 500yd turn L, park within 1m. Adults only. Laundrette. Central for sightseeing. Horse riding, golf course, fishing, local shops all within 1m. Open April 1- end October. ☆☆☆☆ **BH&HPA. 20T. 10MC.** ┭ ◙

(3m). Liskey Holiday Park, Greenbottom, Chacelwater, Truro, Cornwall TR4 8QN. *01872 560274.* info@liskey.co.uk. www.liskey.co.uk. Owner: Jason Masters. Off A390 between Chacewater and Threemilestone. Situated W of Truro, Liskey is is a suitable base for exploring most of Cornwall. Shops, golf courses, fishing lakes are only 3m away. Special offers are available for the over-50s. Internet access available. ☆☆☆☆ **BH&HPA. 70T. 70MC. 23S. 23H.** ❀ ┭ ◙ ᕒ ᕒ ∅

(9m). Penrose Farm Touring Park, Goonhavern, Truro, Cornwall TR4 9QF. *01872 573185.* www.penrosefarm.co.uk. Owner: Mr & Mrs C Southey. From the A30 turn right on to the B3285 Perranporth. Site 1.5m on left. 2.5m from Perranporth beach. Quiet, level, sheltered park with animal centre and adventure playground. No club or bar. Families and couples only. Open April 1-October 31. ☆☆☆ **BH&HPA. 105T. MC.** ┭ ◙ ᕒ

(8m). Porthtowan Tourist Park, Mile Hill, Porthtowan, Truro, Cornwall TR4 8TY. *01209 890256.* admin@porthtowantouristpark.co.uk. www.porthtowantouristpark.co.uk. Owner: Mr & Mrs Jonas. Drive along A30 until you reach the exit for 'Redruth to Porthtowan'. Cross the A30, and continue through North Country to T-junction, turn right up the hill. Park entrance is about 0.5m on left. Level, grassy site. 1m from beach. Ideal for touring Cornwall and Coastal Path. Open Easter-October. **BH&HPA. 50T. MC.** ┭ ◙ ᕒ ᕒ

Ringwell Valley Holiday Park, Bissoe Road, Carnon Downs, Truro, Cornwall TR3 6LQ. *01872 862194.* keith@ringwell.co.uk. www.ringwell.co.uk. Owner: Keith & Julie Horsfall. SP from main A39, Truro to Falmouth road. Well positioned for exploring north and south coasts. 12-acre, pretty, peaceful Rose Award park. Restaurant, bar, takeaway and swimming pool. Open April-September. ☆☆☆☆ **BH&HPA. 30T. MC. 44H.** ┭ ◙ ᕒ

Rose Hill Touring Park, Rosehill, Porthtowan, Truro, Cornwall TR4 8AR. *01209 890802.* reception@rosehillcamping.co.uk. www.rosehillcamping.co.uk. Owner: Mr & Mrs J E Barrow. From A30 follow B3277 SP Porthtowan, brown tourism signs to Rosehill. Site is 50yd past Beach Road. 3m from Redruth. Sheltered woodland site 4mins level walk to beach, PHs, restaurants. Fresh bread baked daily on premises. Fully-equipped laundrette. Open April-October. ☆☆☆☆ **NCC. 50T. 20MC.** ◙ ᕒ ᕒ

(2.5m). Silverbow Park, Goonhaven, Truro, Cornwall TR4 9NY. *01872 572347.* Owner: Mr & Mrs G A Taylor. 0.5m S of Goonhavern Village. On A3075, Newquay to Redruth. No noisy clubs or bars. All-weather and grass tennis courts, badminton courts, short mat bowls. Heated swimming pool. Games room. Playground. Laundry. Bath. Showers. Open May-October 14. ☆☆☆☆☆ **BH&HPA. 90T. MC. 14H.** ┭ ◙ ᕒ ᕒ

(2m). Summer Valley Touring Park, Shortlanesend, Truro, Cornwall TR4 9DW. *01872 277878.* res@summervalley.co.uk. www.summervalley.co.uk. Owner: Mr & Mrs C R Simpkins. Site SP on B3284 2.5m from Truro, 1.5m from A30. Quiet, family-run site with new facilities. Laundrette. AA approved. David Bellamy Conservation Award. Open April 1-October 31. ☆☆☆☆ **BH&HPA. 60T. MC.** ┭ ◙ ᕒ

Merrose Farm Caravan Club Site, Portscatho, Truro, Cornwall TR2 5EL. *01872 580380.* www.caravanclub.co.uk. Owner: The Caravan Club. East Grinstead House, East Grinstead, West Sussex RH19 1UA. See website for standard directions to site. Caravan Club members only. Well-landscaped parkland on Roseland Peninsula with good views of surrounding countryside. Some hard-standings, toilet block, privacy cubicles, laundry facilities, baby and toddler washroom. Gas, boules pitch. Peaceful off-peak. Dog walk on site. Advance booking essential June to August. Motorhome service point. Playfield and equipment. Water sports. Suitable for families. Beach and NCN cycle route 5m. Open March-October. **NCC. 178T. MC.** ┭ ◙ ᕒ

Treamble Valley Caravan Club Site, Rose, Truro, Cornwall TR4 9PR. *01872 573675.* www.caravanclub.co.uk. Owner: The Caravan Club. East Grinstead House, London Road, East Grinstead, West Sussex RH19 1UA. See website for standard directions to site. 1.5m from Perranporth. Caravan Club members only. Motorhome service point. Fishing, golf and water sports nearby. Facilities for walking disabled people. Suitable for families. Some hardstanding, toilet block, privacy cubicles, laundry, Calor Gas and Campingaz, dog walk on site, storage pitches. Peaceful off-peak, good area for walking, beach and NCN cycle route within 5m. Open March-October. **NCC. 120T. MC.** ┭ ◙ ᕒ

WEST COUNTRY

(14m). Treloan Coastal Farm, Treloan Lane, Portscatho, Truro, Cornwall TR2 5EF. 01872 580899. holidays@ treloan.freeserve.co.uk. www.coastalfarmholidays.co.uk. Owner: Mr V Barry. A30 take A3076 to Truro then A390 to St Austell. A3078 to St Mawes. At Trewithian turn to Gerrans/Portscatho until church where Treloan Lane runs alongside Royal Standard PH. Small, traditional organic farm overlooking spectacular south coast, Peaceful surroundings. 3 secluded coves, coastal footpath and villages with shops within few mins walk. Shire horses, Jersey cows. Mooring facilities, seasonal pitches, winter storage. **45T. 6MC. 8S. 5H.** ✿ 🐾 ⊡ ⅙ ⌀

(6m). Trethem Mill Touring Park, St Just-in-Roseland, St Mawes, Truro, Cornwall TR2 5JF. 01872 580504. reception @trethem.com. www.trethem.com. Owner: D & I Akeroyd. Follow brown signs on A3078 for Trethem Mill. 3m N of St Mawes. Small, clean, family park. Suitable location for beaches, water sports, country walks and exploring Cornwall. Open April 1-mid October. ✰✰✰✰✰ **BH&HPA. 84T. 84MC.** 🐾 ⊡ ⅙ ⅃

(5m). Trevarth Holiday Park, Blackwater, Truro, Cornwall TR4 8HR. 01872 560266. trevarth@lineone.net. Owner: Mr John Goldring. 300yd from Blackwater exit off Chiverton roundabout on A30. 4.5m NE of Redruth. Small, family-run park in convenient location for north and south coastal resorts. Golf, cinema, leisure centre 5m. Open April-October. ✰✰✰✰ **BH&HPA. 35T. MC. 20S. 20H.** 🐾 ⊡

(15m). Trewince Manor, Portscatho, Roseland Peninsula, Truro, Cornwall TR2 5ET. 01872 580289. enquiries@trewince.co.uk. www.trewince.co.uk. Owner: Mr Peter Heywood. From St Austell A390 to Truro. Bear left on B3287 to Tregony. Follow signs St Mawes then at Trewithion (7m from Tregony) turn left to St Anthony, site SP. In Area of Outstanding Natural Beauty on Heritage Coast. Laundrette. Games room. TV room. Restaurant, lounge, bar. Takeaway. Own quay and moorings. Indoor heated pool, sauna, spa bath. AA 3 pennants. Open May-September. **25T. 7MC.** 🐾 ⊡

Wadebridge

(3m). Dinham Farm Caravan & Camping Park, St Minver, Wadebridge, Cornwall PL27 6RH. 01208 812878. info@din hamfarm.co.uk. www.dinhamfarm.co.uk. Owner: Mr & Mrs Mably. Off B3314. Secluded, family park overlooking river Camel. Near Rock, Polzearth and Daymer bays. Heated pool. Open April 1-October 30. **40T. 40MC. 20S. 7H.** 🐾 ⊡

(4m). Gunvenna Touring Caravan & Camping Park, St Minver, Polzeath, Wadebridge, Cornwall PL27 6QN. 01208 862405. Owner: Mr & Mrs P Diamond. On the B3314. Easy access. Within easy reach of safe, sandy beaches. Play area. Laundry facilities. Shower blocks. Shaver points. Hair-dryers. Restaurant and garden with private indoor heated swimming pool. Cottage for hire. Golf, cinema and shops in Wadebridge 4m. AA 4 pennants. Open Easter-October 31. ✰✰✰✰ **BH&HPA. 75T. MC. 20S. 2H.** 🐾 ⊡ ⅃

(0.5m). Little Bodieve Holiday Park, Bodieve Road, Wadebridge, Cornwall PL27 6EG. 01208 812323. berry@little bodieveholidaypark.fsnet.co.uk. www.littlebodieve.co.uk. Owner: Karen & Christopher Berry, Barbara Hills. N of Wadebridge. A39, at Camelford turn N at 2nd roundabout in Wadebridge, on to B3314. Site SP and is 600yd R. 4m from beach. Heated outdoor swimming pool, waterslide. Clubhouse with live entertainment in high season. Bar meals. Near to Camel Trail. 25mins drive to Eden Project. Club rallies welcome. Open April-October. ✰✰✰✰ **195T. MC. 75S. 17H.** 🐾 ⊡ ⅙ ⅃

(3m). Little Dinham Woodland Caravan Park, St Minver, Rock, Wadebridge, Cornwall PL27 6RH. 01208 812538. little dinham@hotmail.com. www.littledinham.co.uk. Owners: Martin & Claire Chaplin. Take A30 to Cornwall, exit at Bodmin junction. Proceed through Bodmin to Wadebridge. At Wadebridge, take B3314 to Rock/Polzeath, follow road and after 3m SP Little Dinham Caravan, park is on L. Licensed clubhouse. Laundrette. Children's play area. Heated indoor swimming pool. The site looks on to Dinham Creek and is a good base for bird watchers and nature lovers. 3m from Rock. Open April 1-October 31. ✰✰✰ **BH&HPA. 53S. 6H.** 🐾 ⌀

(7m). Lundynant Caravan Site, St Minver, Polzeath, Wadebridge, Cornwall PL27 6QX. 01208 862268. Owner: Miss R H Love. Off B3314 to New Polzeath. Open April-October. **20T. MC. 41S. 7H.** 🐾 ⊡

(4m). Music Water Caravan Site, Rumford, Wadebridge, Cornwall PL27 7SJ. 01841 540257. Owner: The Mabbley Family. S of Padstow, from A39 Wadebridge to St Columb road, turn N on B3274 for 2m then W for 500yd to site. 3m from sea. Open April-October. **140T. MC. 7S. H.** 🐾 ⊡

(7m). Polzeath Beach Holiday Park, Trenant Nook, Polzeath, Wadebridge, Cornwall PL27 6ST. 01208 863320. Owner: Mrs L C Moriarty. From roundabout at Wadebridge boundary take B3314 to Polzeath. In Polzeath turn R, opposite Spar shop and carry on through car park and over Ford into park. Swimming, fitness centre, clubhouse open to non-members. Shops and PO 500-600yd. 18-hole golf course 1.5m. Open April 1-October 31. ✰✰✰✰ **BH&HPA. 44S. 22H.** 🐾

Rose Award Park overlooking a wooded valley only 4 miles from picturesque Padstow, The Camel Trail and many superb sandy beaches.
Luxury 6 berth Caravans, fully equipped to a high standard.
Excellent amenities on site: Heated Outdoor Pool, Children's Play Area, Games Room, Crazy Golf, Launderette, Shop.
Superb facilities for Tents and Tourers, inc luxury Hook-ups, Showers/Toilets.

BOOKING LINE 01208 812830
Fax: 01208 812835

St. Issey, Wadebridge
Cornwall PL27 7RL

www.trewincefarmholidaypark.co.uk
E-mail: holidaysetrewincefarm.fsnet.co.uk

144 Caravan Sites 2006   *Please mention Caravan Sites 2006 when replying to advertisers*

(3.5m). **Ponderosa Caravan Park, St Issey, Wadebridge, Cornwall PL27 7QA.** *01841 540359.* Owner: G Henwood. Park is open from April 1-October 31. **40T. 20MC. 6S. 1H.** ♙♿♨

(7m). **South Winds Touring Caravan & Camping Park, Polzeath, Wadebridge, Cornwall PL27 6QU.** *01208 863267.* gill@anns-cottage.fsnet.co.uk. www.rockinfo.co.uk. Owner: Mrs B Harris. Seven miles north of Wadebridge via the B3314 road signs to Polzeath. Quiet site with views of the sea and countryside; only 0.5m from beach. Flat and well-drained with showers and laundry. Booking advisable in school holidays. AA 3 pennants. Open Easter-October. **BH&HPA. 100T. 50MC.** ♙♿♨

(3m). **St Minver Holiday Park, St Minver, Wadebridge, Cornwall PL27 6RR.** *01208 862305.* enquiries@parkdeanholidays.co.uk. www.parkdeanholidays.co.uk. Owner: Parkdean Holidays Plc. 2nd Floor, One Gosforth Way, Gosforth Business Park, Newcastle-upon-Tyne NE12 8ET. Take the A389, then the A39, and follow SPs for Port Isaac. Indoor pool with waterslide, children's club and amusements. Bar, takeaway and live family entertainment. Golf 1m. Wadebridge for shops and cinema. Open March-November. ✰✰✰✰ **BH&HPA. NCC. 120T. 282S.** ♙♿♨

(2m). **The Laurels Holiday Park, Padstow Road, Whitecross, Wadebridge, Cornwall PL27 7JQ.** *01208 813341.* anicholson@thelaurelsholidaypark.co.uk. www.thelaurelsholidaypark.co.uk. Owner: Mr & Mrs A Nicholson. Near the junction of the A39 and A389 Padstow (five miles). West of Wadebridge. An ideal touring centre. In an area of outstanding natural beauty. A small, relaxing park in family run friendly atmosphere. Individual shrub lined pitches. Excellent facilities. Supermarket one mile away. Numerous pubs/restaurants. Camel trail, Eden Project and sandy beaches nearby. Open April-October. ✰✰✰✰ **BH&HPA. NCC. 30T. MC.** ♙♿

(5m). **Trenant Steading Touring Park, New Polzeath, St Minver, Wadebridge, Cornwall PL27 6SA.** *01208 869091.* Owner: Robert Love. Park is located off the B3314 and is NW of Wadebridge. Situated close to safe, sandy beaches, surfing, water skiing and boating. Golf course nearby; also shops, PO, eating places. Open Easter-October. **30T. MC.** ♙♿

(3.5m). **Trewince Farm Holiday Park, St Issey, Wadebridge, Cornwall PL27 7RL.** *01208 812830.* holidays@trewincefarm.fsnet.com. www.trewincefarmholiday park.co.uk. Owner: M John & Betty Brewer. Park is situated off the main A389, Wadebridge to Padstow road. Open Easter-October. ✰✰✰✰ **BH&HPA. 35T. 35MC. 20S. 20H.** ♙♿♨

(7m). **Valley Caravan Park, Polzeath, Wadebridge, Cornwall PL27 6SS.** *01208 862391.* Owner: Mr M Taylor. From Wadebridge take the B3314, and follow signs to Polzeath, upon descending into village take turning opposite beach between the shops. Open February-December. **60T. 5MC. 60S. 40H.** ♿

DEVON

Ashburton

(1.25m). **Ashburton Caravan Park, Waterleat, Ashburton, Devon TQ13 7HU.** *01364 652552.* info@ashburtoncaravan park.co.uk. www.ashburtoncaravanpark.co.uk. Owner: Mr R Pummell & Mrs P Pummell. Off A38 to centre of Ashburton, turn into North St, bear right before bridge, SP Waterleat. AA 4 pennants. Rose Award. Open Easter-September. ✰✰✰✰ **BH&HPA. 35MC. 15S. 10H.** ♙♿

(2m). **Parkers Farm Holiday Park, Higher Mead Farm, Ashburton, Devon TQ13 7LJ.** *01364 652598.* parkers farm@btconnect.com. www.parkersfarm.co.uk. Owner: Roger & Rhona Parker. From Exeter, A38 to Plymouth. When you see the sign Plymouth 26, take 2nd left at Alston Cross SP to Woodland and Denbury. Children and pets welcome. Family-run, genuine farm site in Dartmoor National Park. RAC approved, AA 4 pennants. Open Easter-end October. ✰✰✰ **BH&HPA. 40T. 20MC. 2S. 25H.** ♙♿♨

(1m). **River Dart Country Adventures, Holne Park, Ashburton, Devon TQ13 7NP.** *01364 652511.* enquiries@river dart.co.uk. www.riverdart.co.uk. Owner: Mr Mark Simpson. From Exeter, Plymouth take A38 to Ashburton then follow signs to Two Bridges, entrance 1.25m on L. From Tavistock and Dartmoor take Two Bridges road towards Ashburton, turn R 1m after Holne Bridge. Fly fishing on river Dart. Extensive adventure playgrounds. Open April-September. ✰✰✰✰ **170T. MC.** ♙♿♨

Axminster

(3m). **Andrewshayes Caravan Park, Dalwood, Axminster, Devon EX13 7DY.** *01404 831225.* info@andrewshayes.co.uk. www.andrewshayes.co.uk. Owners: Mr H K & Mrs S D Lawrence. Off A35, 6m Honiton. Turn N at Taunton Cross (by garage/Little Chef), SP Stockland and Dalwood. 150yd to park. Bar and restaurant. Heated outdoor swimming pool. Playpark. Games room. Laundrette. Take away open July and August. Rose Award. Fishing 3m. Golf course, cinema about 6.5m. Beach 6m. Open March-December. ✰✰✰✰ **BH&HPA. 145T. 5MC. 80S. 20H.** ♙♿♨

Barnstaple

(2m). **Brightlycott Barton Caravan & Camping Site, Barnstaple, Devon EX31 4JJ.** *01271 850330.* friend.brightly cott@virgin.net. Owner: Charles & Julia Friend. 2m NE of Barnstaple off A39. Road to farm site is SP Brightlycott and Roborough. Central touring site with panoramic views of moor and estuary. Leisure centre in Barnstaple. Fishing, golf, horse riding, swimming and tennis all available nearby. Games room, play area. Chemical toilet emptying point. Open mid March-mid November. **20T. MC.** ♙♿

(3.5m). Chivenor Caravan Park, Chivenor Cross, Barnstaple, Devon EX31 4BN. *01272 812217*. chivernorcp@lineone.net. www.chivernorcaravanpark.co.uk. Owners: Rob & Su Massey. Easy access off the A361 Barnstaple to Ilfracombe road. Small family-run site. 100yd from the famous Tarka Trail. All amenities either on site or within close proximity. Centrally located for touring. Open March 15-January15. **BH&HPA. 25T. 5MC. 8S. 7H.** ⛺ 🔌 ⚡

(3.5m). Crossway Country Park Caravan & Camping Site, Landkey, Barnstaple, Devon EX32 0MM. *01271 830352*. Owner: Mrs A E Balment. On C783. Open March-November. **60T. MC.** ⛺ ⚡

(10m). Greenacres Touring Caravan Park, Greenacres Farm, Bratton Fleming, Barnstaple, Devon EX31 4SG. *01598 763334*. Owner: A J Ridd-Jones. Easy access from A399, M5, J27, take A361 at Little Chef (North Aller roundabout) turn R (A399) to Blackmoor Gate about 10m. Family-run park, separate part of working farm on edge of Exmoor National Park. Coast only 5m away. AA 3 pennants. Open April-October. ☆☆☆☆ **30T. MC.** ⛺ 🔌 ⚡

(2m). Tarka Holiday Park (previously known as Midland Caravan Park), Ashford, Barnstaple, Devon EX31 4AU. *01271 343691*. info@tarkaholidaypark.co.uk. www.tarkaholiday park.co.uk. Owner: Mr & Mrs Fry. Take A361 Barnstaple to Ilfracombe road. Site is on R 2m from Barnstaple. Sheltered grass parkland site on A361. AA 3 pennants. David Bellamy Silver Conservation Award. Open Easter-mid November. **BH&HPA. 35T. MC. 61S.** ⛺ 🔌 ⚡

Bideford

(8m). Bideford Bay Holiday Park, Bucks Cross, Bideford, Devon EX39 5DU. *0871 664 9707*. bideford.bay@park-r esorts.com. www.park-resorts.com. Owner: Park Resorts Ltd. 3rd Floor, Swan Court, Waterhouse Street, Hemel Hempstead, Herts HP1 1FN. Leave M5 at J27 (Tiverton) and follow signs marked A361 Barnstaple. At Barnstaple take A39, SP Bude, continue on this road bypassing Bideford. Park is on the right-hand side in the village of Buck's Cross, W of Bideford. Bar. Club. Heated outdoor and indoor pools. Laundrette. Entertainment. Crazy golf. Playground. Open April-October. ☆☆☆☆ **BH&HPA. NCC. 202S. 44H.** ⛺ ⚡

(9m). Dyke Green Farm Camp Site, Clovelly, Bideford, Devon EX39 5RU. *01237 431279*. Owner: Mrs J Johns. Sheltered, level site just off roundabout at Clovelly Cross. Breakfast available at farm also bed and breakfast. Open Easter-October. **40T. 40MC.** ⛺ 🔌 ⚡

(13m). Hartland Caravan & Camping Park, Southlane, Hartland, Bideford, North Devon EX39 6DG. *01237 441876/441242*. Owners: L Allin. Alsa Cottage, Hartland, Bideford, Devon EX39 6DG. From A39 through Clovelly, straight on at roundabout, take first R. SP Hartland B3248. On entering village, site is on L. Quiet, family-run site set in 6 acres of well-maintained meadows, 4mins walk to shops/PH. New toilet/shower block. Baby changing/family/disabled people's room. Laundry facilities. Small fishing lake. Convenient for coastal footpath, beaches and woodland walks. Caravan storage. **20T. 20MC. 2H.** ✿ ⛺ 🔌 ⚡

(7m). Steart Farm Touring Park, Horn's Cross, Bideford, Devon EX39 5DW. *01237 431836*. steart@tiscali.co.uk. Owner: R C & L F Croslegh. From Bideford follow A39 W (signed Bude). 2m after Horns Cross, site entrance on R. Set in 17 acres overlooking Bideford Bay. 1m from sea. Dog exercise field. Children's playing field. Open Easter-September. ☆☆☆ **75T. MC.** ⛺ 🔌 ⚡

Braunton

(5m). Bayview Farm Holidays, Croyde Bay, Braunton, Devon EX33 1PN. *01271 890501*. www.bayviewfarm.co.uk. Owner: George & Janet Hakin. M5, J27, take A361 then on to B3231 at Braunton. Site is on R approaching Croyde Village. Few minutes' walk to sandy beach and olde worlde village. Dogs by arrangement. Open March-October. **BH&HPA. 70T. MC. 3H.** ⛺ 🔌 ⚡

(1m). Lobb Fields Caravan & Camping Park, Saunton Road, Braunton, Devon EX33 1EB. *01271 812090*. info@ lobb-fields.com. www.lobbfields.com. Owner: Mrs E Dodge, Mrs J Bury, Mrs J Smith-Bingham. 8 Willoway Lane, Braunton, Devon EX33 1AS. From Barnstaple W on A361, 6m to Braunton. In Braunton take B3231 towards Croyde, park on R. Large grassy park 1.5m from Saunton beach faces S with panoramic views. Golf, all shops, doctor, garages, Tarka Trail for cycling and walking 1m. Fishing 3m. All water sports nearby. Open March-October. ☆☆☆☆ **BH&HPA. 100T. 80MC.** ⛺ ⚡ &

Brixham

(0.5m). Centry Touring Caravan & Tent Site, Centry Road, Brixham, Devon TQ5 9EY. *01803 853215*. jlacentry.touring @talk21.com. www.english-riviera.co.uk. Owner: Mrs J Allen. Mudberry House, Centry Road, Brixham, Devon TQ5 9EY. Approaching Brixham on 3022 follow signs for Berry Head Country Park. Small site close to town and beaches. Showers. Milk and newspapers available. Shop nearby. Advance booking for July and August. SAE for brochure. Open Easter-October. ☆☆ **BH&HPA. 30T. MC.** ⛺ 🔌

(3m). Galmpton Touring Park, Greenway Road, Galmpton, Brixham, Devon TQ5 0EP. *01803 842066*. galmptontouring park@hotmail.com. www.galmptontouringpark.co.uk. Owner: Chris & Pam Collins. A380 Torbay ring road then A379 towards Brixham, park SP on the right through Galmpton village. Family park with views of river Dart and close to beaches and all Torbay attractions. Good access. No dogs in peak period. Two self-catering cottages and two studios available for hire. Open Easter-September. ☆☆☆ **BH&HPA. 120T. MC.** ⛺ 🔌 & ⚡

(2m). Hillhead Holiday Park, Hillhead, Brixham, Devon TQ5 0HH. *01803 853204*. www.caravanclub.co.uk. Owner: The Caravan Club. East Grinstead House, London Road, East Grinstead, West Sussex RH19 1UA. See website for standard directions to site. Set in 22 acres of countryside. Non-members and tent campers welcome, part sloping, toilet blocks, privacy cubicles, baby and toddler washroom, baby changing facilities, laundry, motorhome service point, veg prep area, battery charging, Calor Gas and Campingaz, games room. Information room, club, bar, restaurant, takeaway, playground, play area, play equipment, dog walk on site, swimming pool, fishing, golf and watersports nearby. Suitable for families, good area for walking. Open March-October. ☆☆☆☆☆ **NCC. 200T. MC.** ⛺ 🔌 & ⚡

(1m). South Bay Holiday Park, St Mary's Road, Brixham, Devon TQ5 9QW. *01803 853004/854347*. www.johnfowlerholi days.com. Owner: John Fowler Holidays. Marlborough Road, Ilfracombe EX34 8PF. From Exeter take A38/A380/A3022 to Brixham. Just after 'Welcome to Brixham' sign follow brown sign to Upton Manor Farm (annexe to South Bay HP) bringing you to the gates. Laundrette. Indoor and outdoor pool complex. Takeaway. Convenience store. free children's club. Sports and leisure facilities. Family club and bar. Rose Award. Open March 2 - November 2. ☆☆☆☆ **BH&HPA. NCC. 314S. 105H.** ⛺ ⚡

Please mention Caravan Sites 2006 when replying to advertisers

Buckfast

Churchill Farm Camp Site, Churchill Farm, Buckfast, Devon TQ11 0EZ. *01364 642844.* apedrick@farmersweekly.net. Owner: A Pedrick. From A38, follow signs for Buckfast Abbey, proceed up hill then L at crossroads, farm entrance opposite church. Panoramic views of Dartmoor overlooking Buckfast Abbey. Suitable base for exploring Dartmoor and south Devon. Open Easter-October. **5T. 10MC. ⚓ 🗲 ♿**

Buckfastleigh

(1.5m). Beara Farm Caravan & Camping Site, Beara Farm, Colston Road, Buckfastleigh, Devon TQ11 0LW. *01364 642234.* Owner: Mr W J Thorn. From Exeter leave A38 at Dart Bridge. Follow signs to South Devon Steam Railway and Butterfly Farm. Take first L after passing entrance. SP Old Totnes road. After 0.5m turn right, site 1m. Also SP. Site is close to river Dart. Within easy reach of sea and Dartmoor. Fishing nearby. Steam railway, butterfly and otter park, Buckfast Abbey, Pennywell Farm all within short distance. **10T. MC. ❄ ⚓**

(3m). Bowden Farm, Buckfastleigh, Devon TQ11 0JG. *01364 643219.* Owner: Mrs R C Ashford. Take Wallaford road out of Buckfastleigh then after 3m take 2nd turning on right. Bowden is first farm on right. Quiet site with panoramic views over Dartmoor and within 10 mins walking distance of the famous Abbotts Way. **20T. 20MC. 20S. 1H. ❄ ⚓**

Budleigh Salterton

(3m). Ladram Bay Holiday Centre, Budleigh Salterton, Devon EX9 7BX. *01395 568398.* Owner: Mr F W S Carter. Off A3052 follow signs to Ladram Bay. Limited facilities for disabled visitors. Private beach. Indoor heated pool. Laundrette. Cafeteria. Takeaway. Doctors surgery. PH with free entertainment during peak season. Open April 1-September 30. **54T. 200MC. 370S. 104H. ⚓ 🗲 ♿ 🍴 ⌀**

Chudleigh

(4m). Finlake Holiday Park, Chudleigh, Devon TQ13 0EJ. *01626 853833.* www.haulfryn.co.uk. Owner: Haulfryn Group. The Warren, Abersoch, Pwllheli, Gwynedd LL53 7AA. A38 Exeter to Plymouth, Chudleigh Knighton turn-off. Follow signs for Chudleigh Knighton, Finlake on the right. Free awning area. Bars. Children's games room and play area. Entertainment. Indoor heated pool. Outdoor pool and giant waterslide. Tennis. Pitch and putt. Fishing and nature trails. Horse riding stables, gym, beauty salon. Open December-October for owner-occupiers; open all year for hire caravans. **BH&HPA. NCC. 287T. MC. 165S. 9H. ❄ ⚓ 🗲 ♿ 🍴**

(1m). Holmans Wood Holiday Park, Chudleigh, Devon TQ13 0DZ. *01626 853785.* enquiries@holmanswood. co.uk. www.holmanswood.co.uk. Owner: Mr & Mrs A Barzilay. Follow M5 to Exeter. A38 towards Plymouth. From top of Haldon Hill, past racecourse. Park is 100yd on L. Well situated for Dartmoor, Exeter and Torquay. Seasonal pitches and storage available. Tents welcome. Neat and level park in countryside setting. Showers. Open March 15-October 31. ☆☆☆☆ **BH&HPA. 100T. MC. 25S. 🗲 ♿**

Colyton

(2m). Ashdown Caravan Park, Colyton, Devon EX13 6HY. *01297 21587.* Owner: G T & I M Salter & A C Arbourne. Off A3052 Lyme Regis Exeter road 3m W of Seaton, at Stafford Cross turn north towards Colyton, site 0.5m on the left. Family-run park in a spacious, quiet position, no bars or clubs. Several coastal resorts within easy reach. Level pitches. Open April 1-November 1. **90T. MC. 2S. ⚓ 🗲 🍴**

(2m). Leacroft Touring Park, Colyton Hill, Colyton, Devon EX24 6HY. *01297 552823.* Owner: Anne & John Robinson. SP from A3052 Sidmouth to Lyme Regis, at Stafford Cross, do not go into Colyton. Peaceful site in open countryside with views to Lyme Bay. Picturesque villages and woodland walks nearby. Suitable touring base. Hard-standings. Storage facilities. Open Easter-October. ☆☆☆☆ **BH&HPA. 118T. 8MC. ⚓ 🗲 ♿ 🍴**

Combe Martin

(1m). Manleigh Holiday Park, Rectory Road, Combe Martin, Devon EX34 0NS. *01271 883353.* info@manleighpark.co.uk. www.manleighpark.co.uk. Owner: Ms Linda Whitney. On A399. 6m from Ilfracombe. Children's play area. Pool. Laundry. Dog exercise area. Chalet and caravans for hire. Sea 1m. Golf, cinema, indoor swimming pool within 5-6m. Open March 17-January 17. ☆☆☆☆ **BH&HPA. 2414H. ⚓ ♿ ⌀**

Newberry Farm Touring & Camping Park, Newberry Farm, Woodlands, Combe Martin, Devon EX34 0AT. *01271 882334.* enq@newberrycampsite.co.uk. www. newberrycampsite.co.uk. Owner: Mr T Greenaway. On the A399. NW edge of Combe Martin. Peaceful countryside location on N Devon Coast. Combe Martin village with beach, shops, cafes, PHs in 5mins walk. Coarse fishing lake. No dogs. Open Easter-October. ☆☆☆☆ **BH&HPA. 25T. 25MC. 🗲 ♿**

Croyde Bay

Croyde Burrows, Croyde Bay, Devon EX33 1NY. *01271 890477.* enquiries@ruda.co.uk. www.ruda.co.uk. Owner: Parkdean Holidays Plc. 2nd floor, One Gosforth Way, Gosforth

Business Park, Newcastle-upon-Tyne NE12 8ET. Park is located off the B3231 road. England for Excellence Silver award winner. Open March 15-October 31. ☆☆☆☆ **BH&HPA. NCC. 93T. 93MC. 261S.** 🗮 ⅙ 🗮

Ruda Holiday Park, Croyde Bay, Devon EX33 1NY. *01271 89671.* enquiries@parkdeanholidays.co.uk. www.ruda.co.uk. Owner: Parkdean Holidays Plc. 2nd Floor, One Gosforth Way, Gosforth Business Park, Newcastle-upon-Tyne NE12 8ET. Leave M5 at J27 for A361 to Barnstaple and Braunton then B3231 to Croyde. 4m from Braunton. Park is 100yd from own beach. Fishing. Club with entertainment. Heated indoor fun pool. Organised children's activities. Phone for brochure. Rose Award. England for Excellence 'Holiday Park of the Year' Silver award. Open March-November; open all years for lodges and apartments. ☆☆☆☆ **BH&HPA. NCC. 91T. 91MC. 280S. 237H.** 🗮 ⅙ 🗮

Cullompton

(5m). Forest Glade Holiday Park, Cullompton, Devon EX15 2DT. *01404 841381.* enquiries@forest-glade.co.uk. www.forest-glade.co.uk. Owner: Mr N P Wellard. Please contact park for details. Flat, sheltered, secluded park in forest situated on the Blackdown Hills, an Area of Outstanding Natural Beauty.

Heated indoor pool. Adventure play area. All-weather tennis court. Snacks and takeaway food. Games room. Free colour brochure on request. Touring caravans must phone for access route. Golf 6m, cinema 11m, shopping centre 20m. Open March-end October. ☆☆☆☆ **BH&HPA. 80T. MC. 55S. 25H.** 🗮 ⅙ 🗮 ⌀

(4m). Waterloo Inn Camping & Caravan Park, Uffculme, Cullompton, Devon EX15 3ES. *01884 841342.* Owner: Mr & Mrs Fry. About 0.25m from the M5 J27. Located on the Wellington to Willand road at Waterloo Cross. Inn and food. **50T. 50MC. 5H.** ⚙ 🗮 🗮

Dartmouth

(2m). Deer Park Caravan & Camping, Dartmouth Road, Stoke Fleming, Dartmouth, Devon TQ6 0RF. *01803 770253.* info@deerparkinn.co.uk. www.deerparkinn.co.uk. Owner: Peter & Sarah Keane. Located on the A379, Kingsbridge to Dartmouth road. At the eastern end of Stoke Fleming. Free house inn and restaurant. Swimming pool. Adventure playground. Takeaway food. Flats also available for hire. 1m from Blackpool Sands. Open March 15-November 15. **BH&HPA. 160T. MC.** 🗮 🗮 ⅙

Please mention Caravan Sites 2006 when replying to advertisers

(2.5m). **Leonards Cove, Stoke Fleming, Dartmouth, Devon TQ6 0NR.** *01803 770206.* enquiry@leonards cove.co.uk. www.leonardscove.co.uk. On A379, Dartmouth to Kingsbridge. Within village of Stoke Fleming, walking distance Blackpool Sands. Sea views from the camping/touring field. Village PO/stores. Golf and country club 3m. Open March-October. **10T. 10MC. 50S. 3H.** 🖳🛇

(2m). **Little Cotton Caravan Park, Dartmouth, Devon TQ6 0LB.** *01803 832558.* enquiries@littlecotton.co.uk. www.little cotton. co.uk. Owner: Paul & Dorothy White. Off B3207. Leave A38 at Buckfastleigh, A384 to Totnes, from Totnes to Halwell on A381, at Halwell take A3122 Dartmouth Road. Park on R of entrance to town. Seven acres, level and gently sloping, some sheltered with scenic outlook. Park-and-ride service adjacent. Suitable touring base. Showers. Golf course nearby. Open mid March-October. **BH&HPA. 95T. 10MC.** 🛇 🖳 ⚲ 🛒

(5m). **Woodlands Leisure Park, Blackawton, Dartmouth, Devon TQ9 7DQ.** *01803 712598.* fun@woodlandspark.com. www.woodlandspark.com. Owners: Bendalls Leisure Ltd. SP from A38 and Totnes. Spacious pitches in countryside setting. Bathrooms, laundry, showers. Two nights stay gives free entrance to 60-acre leisure park. 3 watercoasters, 500m toboggan run and arctic gliders, commando course, action tracks and Master Blaster. Live entertainment days, indoor falconry centre with flying displays. Undercover play areas. Open Easter-November. **BH&HPA. 175T. 50MC.** 🛇 🖳 ⚲ 🛒

Dawlish

(2m). **Cofton Country Holidays, Starcross, Dawlish, Devon EX6 8RP.** *01626 890111.* info@coftonholi days.co.uk. www.coftonholidays.co.uk. Owner: Mr & Mrs W G Jeffrey. On the A379 to Dawlish road after Cockwood village. Heated swimming pool. Adventure playground and woodland trails. Takeaway. Swan PH (two bars), family rooms. Coarse fishing. Woodland walks. Free showers. Laundrette. Short drive to Dawlish Warren beach. Open March-October. ☆☆☆☆ **BH&HPA. 450T. MC. 62H.** 🛒 🖳 ⚲ 🛒

(1m). **Golden Sands Holiday Park, Week Lane, Dawlish, Devon EX7 0LZ.** *01626 863099.* info@goldensands.co.uk. www.goldensands.co.uk. Owner: Mr M Evans. From M5 Exeter take A379 to Dawlish. 2m after Starcross the park is SP on the left. Week Lane is second left past garage on R. Heated indoor and outdoor pool. Licensed club and free entertainment. Small, select touring park. 0.5m to safe, sandy beach. Family run for families. Suitably located for touring South Devon. Open Easter-October 31. ☆☆☆☆ **BH&HPA. 55T. MC. 113H.** 🖳 ⚲ 🛒 ⬚

(1m). **Lady's Mile Touring Park, Exeter Road, Dawlish, Devon EX7 0LX.** *01626 863411.* www.ladysmile.com. Owner: Mr A J Jeffery. On A379 Exeter to Dawlish road. Easy access from J30 of the M5. Indoor and outdoor heated swimming pools with 100ft water chutes. Play area and games room. Takeaway food. Bar. Launderette. Showers. Short distance Dawlish Warren beach and town. Open mid March-October 31. ☆☆☆☆ **BH&HPA. 486T. 486MC. 65S. 65H.** 🛒 🖳 ⚲ 🛒 ⬚

Leadstone Camping, Warren Road, Dawlish, Devon EX7 0NG. *01626 864411.* info@leadstonecamping.co.uk. www.leadstonecamping.co.uk. Owner: Mr A C I Bulpin. Walnut Cottage, Ham Lane, Shaldon, Devon TQ14 0HW. M5, J30. Take A379 to Dawlish. On approachng Dawlish turn L on brow of hill signed Dawlish Warren. Site 0.5m on R. Rolling grassland in natural secluded bowl 0.5m from Dawlish Warren beach and nature reserve. One night stop-overs welcome. Suitable touring base. Open June 17-September 3. ✩✩✩ **28T. 28MC.** ⁕ ⊟ ⍛

(1m). Seaway Holiday Park, Littleweek Lane, Dawlish, Devon EX7 0LS. *01626 865648.* Owner: Mr & Mrs V Came. Level site with parking beside each caravan. All carvans fitted with showers and colour TV. Open March 15-January 15. **BH&HPA. 18H.** ⁕ ⅋ ⍛

(1m). Smuggler's Caravan Park, Holcombe, Dawlish, Devon EX7 0JF. *01626 863056.* Owner: Mr Fairweather. On A379 Dawlish to Teignmouth.Quiet. Levelling devices available for motor caravans. Shop nearby. Open March-October. **4T. MC. 20S. 7H.** ⁕ ⊟

Dawlish Warren

(0.25m). Dawlish Sands Holiday Park, Warren Road, Dawlish Warren, Devon EX7 0PG. *01626 862038.* Leave M5 Exeter, take A379 Dawlish, at Cockwood harbour left over bridge signed Dawlish Warren, park on left after 1m. Swimming pool, play park, laundrette, live entertainment for families, childrens club. General manager: Chris Weeks. Open March 27-October 31. ✩✩✩✩ **BH&HPA. 202H.** ⅋ ⍛

(1.5m). Hazelwood Park, Warren Road, Dawlish Warren, Devon EX7 0PF. *01626 866273.* homes@hazelwood.co.uk. www.hazelwood.co.uk. Owner: Hazelwood Caravans and Chalets Ltd. Off A379 Exeter to Dawlish. Holiday homes for sale. Licensed club. Heated swimming pool. Playground. Laundrette. Fishing. Cot and linen hire. Beach 750yd. Children welcome. Golf course, riding stables, tennis courts. Open February 1-January 14 for owner-occupiers; open Easter-end September for hire. **BH&HPA. 120S.** ⁕ ⅋ ⍛ ⌀

(1.5m). Lee Cliff Park, Dawlish Warren, Devon EX7 0NE. *01626 862269.* Owner: Mr & Mrs Carr. Take A379 from Exeter towards Dawlish. At Cockwood turn left, over bridge and follow road into Dawlish Warren. Sbout 9m from Exeter. Small, select family-run site. 250yd from the beach. 3 mins walk to Dawlish Warren rail station. Bus stop adjacent to site. Caravans, apartments and chalets for rent/hire. Shops, PO, doctor and golf club all within a very short level walk. Open March-October 31. **12H.** ⁕

Peppermint Park, Warren Road, Dawlish Warren, Devon EX7 0PQ. *01626 863436.* info@peppermintpark.co.uk. www.peppermintpark.co.uk. Owner: Mr G Hawkins. Leave M5 at Exeter. Take A379 SP to Dawlish, take left turn to Dawlish Warren just before entering Dawlish. Showers. Laundrette. Dog exercise enclosure. Heated pool with water slide. Play area. Games room. Licensed club. Coarse fishing lake. Golf course 0.25m. David Bellamy Gold Conservation Award. Open April-October. ✩✩✩✩ **BH&HPA. 250T. MC. 34H.** ⁕ ⊟ ⍛

(2m). Welcome Family Holiday Park, Warren Road, Dawlish Warren, Devon EX7 0PH. *01626 862070.* fun@welcomefamily.co.uk. www.welcomefamily.co.uk. Owner: Swan Holidays (Westward) Ltd. Off A379 Exeter to Teignmouth. 2m from Dawlish. Extensive facilities, including four indoor pools and entertainment. Lots for children to do. Level walk to sandy beach. Pets welcome. Gold courses, fishing 0.5m. Beach 600yd. Open March-October. ✩✩✩✩ **410S. 281H.** ⁕ ⅋ ⍛

Exeter

(11m). Barley Meadow Caravan & Camping Park, Crockernwell, Exeter, Devon EX6 6NR. *01647 281629.* angela.waldron@btopenworld.com. www.barleymeadow.co.uk. Owner: Angela & Terry Waldron. Crockernwell turning off A30 Exeter to Okehampton road. Passing through Cheriton Bishop, site on left in Crockernwell. AA 3 pennants. Grassy site with good access. Heated shower block. Seasonal pitches available. Hard-standing pitches. Garage, shop, PO, doctors all 1m away.

Please mention Caravan Sites 2006 when replying to advertisers

Okehampton 7m. Fishing, golf course nearby. Overnight stops welcome to and from Cornwall (within Dartmoor National Park). Walkers welcome. Packed lunches available. Children's play area. Open March 15-November 15. **BH&HPA. 40T. 10MC.** ⛺ ⌂ & ⛵

Castle Brake, Castle Lane, Woodbury, Exeter, Devon EX5 1HA. 01395 232431. reception@castlebrake.co.uk. www.castle brake.co.uk. Owner: T Walker. M5, J30. Take A3052 to Halfway Inn. Turn R B3180 to Exmouth. Turn R after 2m to Woodbury. 4m from Exmouth. Grassy, level park between Exeter and Exmouth. Medium-size park with lovely facilities. Holiday caravans for hire. Shower blocks, sauna, steam, bar and restaurant. Adventure playground. Extensive heathland 500yd. Sandy beach 6m. Caravan storage and seasonal pitches available. David Bellamy Gold Conservation Award. Rose Award. Good area for walking. Open March-October. ✰✰✰✰ **BH&HPA. 70T. 10MC. 35S. 14H.** ⛺ ⛵ &

(6m). Exeter Racecourse Caravan Club Site, Kennford, Exeter, Devon EX6 7XS. 01392 832107. www.caravan club.co.uk. Owner: The Caravan Club. East Grinstead House, East Grinstead, West Sussex RH19 1UA. From Plymouth on A38 turn left immediately past Little Chef at top of Haldon Hill into underpass, SP Exeter racecourse. Follow racecourse signs then club signs. Located at top of Haldon Hill with superb views. Good base for exploring Exeter and Dartmoor. Advance booking essential bank holidays and advised June-August. Non-members and tent campers welcome. Free access to racing. Toilet block and laundry facilities. Motorhome service point. Veg prep area, Calor Gas and Campingaz, fishing nearby. Peaceful off-peak, good area for walking. Open March-October. **NCC. 100T. MC.** ⛺ ⛵

(5m). Haldon Lodge Farm Caravan & Camping Site, Clapham, Nr Kennford, Exeter, Devon EX6 7YG. 01392 832312. Owner: Mr D L Salter. S of Exeter, off A38, Kennford Services. Turn left through Kennford village past PO. Proceed to motor bridge turn left Dunchideock. 1m to caravan park. Peaceful, family site; suitable touring base. 15 mins from sea and Exeter. Forest nature trails, riding and trekking. Fishing, shop on site. PO, doctor's surgery, all a short distance from site. **45T. 45MC. 4H.** ✿ ⛺ ⛵ ⛵

(4m). Kennford International Caravan Park, Exeter, Devon EX6 7YN. 01392 833046. ian@kennfordint.fsbusiness.co.uk. www.kennfordint.co.uk. Owner: Mr & Mrs Hopkins. 1m from end of M5 alongside A38. Family-run park. Individually hedged pitches. 10% discount on holiday bookings for over-50s and

Tamba members. Suitable touring centre for Dartmoor, Torquay and the whole of south Devon. Full facility park near country walks. ✰✰✰✰ **BH&HPA. 120T. MC. 21S.** ✿ ⛺ ⛵ &

(8m). Springfield Holiday Park, Tedburn St Mary, Exeter, Devon EX6 6EW. 01647 24242. springhol@aol.com. www. springfieldholidaypark.co.uk. Owner: Martin & Eileen Johnson. From J31 of M5 travel W on A30. 3rd exit (Woodleigh Junction) follow signs. Suitable base for touring Dartmoor. Good views. Open March-November. ✰✰✰✰ **BH&HPA. 88T. 20MC. 19S. 5H.** ⛺ ⛵

Torquay Holiday Park, Kingskerswell Road, Torquay, Exeter, Devon TQ2 8JU. 01803 323077. Off A380 Exeter to Torquay road. 3m from Torquay. Indoor fun pool. Crazy golf. Tennis. Adventure playground. Ten-pin bowling. Laundrette. Restaurant and takeaway. Free childrens clubs. Free daytime and evening entertainment. Rose Award. Open March to October. ✰✰✰ **BH&HPA. NCC. 180S.** ⛵

Webbers Farm Caravan & Camping Park, Castle Lane, Woodbury, Exeter, Devon EX5 1EA. 01395 232276. www.webberspark.co.uk. From M5 J30 take A376 then B3179 to Woodbury, then follow brown and white signs. A friendly, family farm close to Woodbury village. Countryside views. Lots of space to relax. Convenient for beaches, golf, fishing, walking, cycling and exploring east Devon. All-year tourer storage. Brochure available. Open Easter-September. ✰✰✰✰✰ **BH&HPA. 115T. MC.** ⛺ ⛵ & ⛵

Woodland Springs Touring Park, Venton, Drewsteighton, Exeter, Devon EX6 6PG. 01647 231695. enquiries@woodland springs.co.uk. www.woodlandsprings.co.uk. Owners: Chris & Jan Patrick. From A30 Merrymeet roundabout follow A382 Moreton Hampstead. Then brown tourist signs. 8m from Okehampton. Adults only. Peaceful, natural park within Dartmoor National Park. Suitable base for touring Devon, Cornwall, South-West. Special offers available. ✰✰✰ **BH&HPA. 85T. 85MC.** ✿ ⛺ ⛵

Exmouth   22 6 22 6

(3m). Devon Cliffs Holiday Park, Sandy Bay, Exmouth, Devon EX8 5BT. 01395 ~~226260~~. oewebmaster@bourne-leisure. co.uk. www.devoncliffsholidaypark.co.uk. Owner: Bourne Leisure Ltd. 1 Park Lane, Hemel Hempstead, Hertfordshire HP2 4YL. M5 exit 30 after Exeter and take A376 for Exmouth. At Exmouth follow the brown tourism signs to Sandy Bay and this will bring you directly on to the park. Indoor and outdoor fun

pools. Free children's clubs. Adventure playground. All-weather, multi-sports court. Daytime and evening entertainment. Spa complex. 3 family bars, bungee play area, shopping arcade. Direct access to beach. Town 3m, golf courses 5m. Exeter 12m. Open April-October. ✰✰✰✰ **BH&HPA. NCC. 82T. MC. 1770S. 750H.** ⛺🔌👤🅿🛁⊘

Great Torrington

(1m). Greenways Valley, Caddywell Lane, Great Torrington, Devon EX38 7EW. 01805 622153. enquiries@greenwaysvalley. co.uk. www.greenwaysvalley.co.uk. Owner: Mr & Mrs Barnes. Off B3227 Torrington to South Molton. Small peaceful park, south facing, above a wooded valley. Walking distance to town. Fishing, walking, cycling. Beach 20mins. Heated outdoor pool. Short tennis court, games room, play area. Holiday lodges for sale. Open March-October for hire caravans; open 11 months for owner-occupied lodges. ✰✰✰✰ **BH&HPA. 8T. MC. 13S. 5H.** 🔌

(2m). Smytham Manor Leisure, Smytham Manor, Little Torrington, Great Torrington, Devon EX38 8PU. 01805 622110. info@smytham.co.uk. www.smytham.co.uk. Owner: Great Leisure Ltd. S of Torrington towards Okehampton on A386. 25 acres of gently undulating grounds with ponds. Showers, shaver points. Laundry facilities. Play area, games room. Heated outdoor swimming pool and sun terrace. Licensed bar. Putting green, direct access to Tarka Trail. Caravan Club. Booking advisable. Close to moors and beaches. RHS Rosemoor and Dartington Crystal 1.5m. Open March-October. ✰✰✰✰ **BH&HPA. 30T. 20MC. 94S. 5H.** ⛺🔌👤🛁⊘

Kingsbridge

(5m). Bigbury Bay Caravan Park, Challaborough, Bigbury-on-Sea, Kingsbridge, Devon TQ7 4HT. 01548 810363. Owner: Iford Caravans Ltd. Open March 1-January 10. **BH&HPA. 123S.** ⛺🛒

(8m). Camping & Caravanning Club Site - Slapton Sands, Middle Grounds, Slapton, Kingsbridge, Devon TQ7 2QW. 01548 580538. www.campingandcaravanningclub.co.uk. Owner: Camping & Caravanning Club. Greenfields House, Westwood Way, Coventry CV4 8JH. On A379 from Kingsbridge, site entrance on R 0.25m beyond brow of hill approaching Slapton Village. Motorhome and tents of non-members welcome. Caravan owners must be members. Keen ornithologists will enjoy visiting wild bird sanctuary at Slapton Ley. Blackpool sands, 4m, popular with families. Sea fishing from beach near site. Special deals available for families and backpackers. Open March-October. ✰✰✰✰ **8T. 115MC.** ⛺🔌👤

(9m). Challaborough Bay Holiday Park, Challaborough Beach, Bigbury-on-Sea, Kingsbridge, Devon TQ7 4HU. 01548 810771. enquiries@parkdeanholidays.co.uk. www.parkdeanholidays.co.uk. Owner: Parkdean Holidays Plc. 2nd Floor, One Gosforth Way, Gosforth Business Park, Newcastle-upon-Tyne NE12 8ET. Off A379 Plymouth to Kingsbridge. B3392 towards Challaborough. Laundrette. Play area, free children's clubs. Diving, fishing. Sports and leisure facilities. Takeaway. Family club and bar. Coastal walks, beautiful surroundings and places of interest nearby No local public transport. Open March-November. ✰✰✰✰ **BH&HPA. NCC. 260S. 103H.** ⛺🛒

(5m). Higher Rew Caravan & Camping Park, Malborough, Kingsbridge, Devon TQ7 3DW. 01548 842681. enquiries@higherrew.co.uk. www.higherrew.co.uk. Owner: Mrs V Squire. Follow A381 towards Salcombe. At Malborough turn R following signs for Soar. After 1m turn L towards Combe/South

Sands. Rural situation. Good, clean facilities. Close to beaches, Salcombe Estuary and cliff walks. Level pitches, all with rural views. Tennis court for hire. Open Easter-31 October. ✰✰✰✰ **25T. 50MC.** ⛺🔌🛒

(1m). Island Lodge Caravan & Camping Site, Stumpy Post Cross, Kingsbridge, Devon TQ7 4BL. 01548 852956/07968 222007. Owner: Kay Parker. Travelling S from Totnes on A381. Turn R at Stumpy Post Cross. Next turning L to site entrance. Unspoilt, rural site within easy reach of beaches and moors. Suitable for a quiet holiday for couples and families. Laundry facilities. Good clean modern facilities. Fridge, freezer and microwave facilities on site. Easy access. Sea glimpses. Licensed caravan/boat storage. **25T. 10MC.** 🐕⛺🔌👤

(6m). Karrageen Caravan & Camping Park, Bolberry, Malborough, Kingsbridge, Devon TQ7 3EN. 01548 561230. phil@karrageen.co.uk. www.karrageen.co.uk. Owner: Phil & Nikki Higgin. Take A381 towards Salcombe. At Malborough turn R, after 0.6m turn R (sp Bolberry). After 0.9m park on right. 4m from Salcombe. Terraced, level, tree lined pitches with a view. National Trust clifftop walks. Hot takeaway and shop. Beach 1m. First class facilities. AA 3 pennants. See advertisement under 'Salcombe'. Open March 15-September 30. ✰✰✰✰ **BH&HPA. 20T. 65MC. 25S. 6H.** ⛺🔌👤🛁

(3m). Mounts Farm Touring Park, The Mounts, East Allington, Kingsbridge, Devon TQ9 7QJ. 01548 521591. mounts.farm@lineone.net. www.mountsfarm.co.uk. Owner: Phil & Karen Meacher & Mrs Peggy Wain. 3m N of Kingsbridge on A381. Quiet, family-run site, suitable base for touring South Devon. Showers. No charges for awnings, pets and children. Shop with camping accessories. Many beaches and attractions nearby. Brochure available. Children's play field. Open April-October. **50T. MC.** ⛺🔌🛒

(5m). Old Cotmore Farm Touring Caravan & Camping Park, Old Cotmore Farm, Stokenham, Kingsbridge, Devon TQ7 2LR. 01548 580240. graham.bowsher@btinternet.com. www.oldcotmorefarm.co.uk. Owner: Lyn & Graham Bowsher. From Kingsbridge, A379 towards Dartmouth. At Stokenham village turn at mini roundabout to Beesands. Park 1m on right, SP. Picturesque park, 1m from sea and glorious beaches. Holiday cottages available at farm. AA 3 pennants. Open March 15-October 31. **BH&HPA. 30T. MC.** ⛺🔌👤🛒

(1m). Parkland Caravan & Camping Site, Sorley Green Cross, Kingsbridge, Devon TQ7 4AF. 01548 852723. enquiries@parklandsite.co.uk. www.parklandsite.co.uk. Owner: James K Parker. A38 S turn off at Totnes junc. (A384). At Totnes take A381 for 10m to Stumpy Post Cross junction, follow A381 to R and follow tourist signs. 3-acre site. Free electric hook-ups. Seasonal pitches. Modern facilities, toilet suites for families and disabled visitors. Views of Salcombe; nearest site to Bantham beach. Storage. **45T. 5MC.** 🐕⛺👤

(6m). Start Bay Caravan Club Site, Stokenham, Kingsbridge, Devon, TQ7 2SE. 01548 580430. www.caravanclub.co.uk. Owner: The Caravan Club. East Grinstead House, East Grinstead, West Sussex RH19 1UA. See website for directions to site. Club members only. Family siute. Long, gently sloping meadow site screened with shrubs and trees. Toilet blocks, laundry facilities and motorhome service point. Play equipment and dog walk on site. Fishing and water sports nearby. Good area for walking. Facilities for disabled visitors. Sea only 0.75m. Open March-October. **NCC. 85T. MC.** ⛺🔌👤

Lyme Regis

Hunters Moon Country Estate, Wareham Road, Hawkchurch, Lyme Regis, Devon EX13 5UL. *01297 678402.* www.huntersmooncountryestate.co.uk. Owners: Totemplant (Leisure) Ltd. Cove Park, Pennsylvania Road, Portland, Dorset. Turn off A35 on to B3165 SP Crewkerne follow signs 2.5m turn L. Shop, bar, restaurant and take-away at high season, free showers, play area. 5m from sea at Lyme Regis or Charmouth. Quiet park overlooking Axe Valley. Donkey sanctuary. Many sporting activities, sailing, diving and many tourist attractions. Swimming pool, beach nearby. Open March 15-November 15. ☆☆☆☆ **149T. MC. 30S. 5H.**

Lynton

(2m). Camping & Caravanning Club Site - Lynton, Caffyn's Cross, Lynton, Devon EX35 6JS. *01598 752379/0870 243 3331.* www.campingandcaravanningclub.co.uk. Owner: Camping & Caravanning Club. Greenfields House, Westwood Way, Coventry CV4 8JH. M5, J27 on to A361 to 2nd South Molton roundabout. R on to A399 to Blackmoor gate. R on to A39 towards Lynton, L after 5m, signed Caffyns, immediately R to site in 1m. Set in 5.5 acres, with pitches accepting all types of units, on cliff overlooking Bristol Channel. Non-members welcome. Close to Exmoor National Park. Walks in surrounding, rugged countryside. Quiet site with views over countryside. Special deals available for families and backpackers. Open March-October. ☆☆☆ **105T. 105MC.**

(2m). Channel View Caravan and Camping Park, Manor Farm, Lynton, Devon EX35 6LD. *01598 753349.* channelview@bushinternet.com. www.channel-view.co.uk. Owner: Mr R C Wren. On A39 Barnstaple to Lynmouth. PH and restaurant nearby. Fully serviced pitches available, cafe on site. Open March 15-November 15. ☆☆☆☆ **BH&HPA. 76T. MC. 20S. 5H.**

Modbury

(3m). Moor View Touring Park, California Cross, Modbury, Devon PL21 0SG. *01548 821485.* info@moorviewtouringpark.co.uk. www.moorviewtouringpark.co.uk. Owner: Edward & Liz Corwood. From A38 westbound, leave at Wrangaton Cross (signed Modbury, Ermington) turn left, straight on at crossroads and follow park signs. Rural, family-run park backing on to woodland, with panoramic views towards Dartmoor, close to coastal walks and beaches. All pitches have electric hook-ups. Hard-standings, fully serviced pitches. Seasonal pitches. Centrally heated luxury showers, shop, laundry and play area. TV, games and information room. Open March 15-November 15. ☆☆☆ **BH&HPA. 68T. MC.**

(2m). Pennymoor Camping and Caravan Park, Modbury, Devon PL21 0SB. *01548 830542/830269.* www.pennymoor-camping.co.uk. Owner: R A & M D Blackler. From Exeter leave A38 at Wrangaton Cross turn left for 1m to crossroads, straight across and continue for approx. 4m to petrol garage then take 2nd left and continue for 1m. Peaceful, family site with panoramic views. Open March 15-November 15. ☆☆☆☆ **119T. 35MC. 45S. 25H.**

Newton Abbot

(5m). Cockingford Farm, Widecombe-in-the-Moor, Newton Abbot, Devon TQ13 7TG. *01364 2258.* Owner: Mr H J Lentern. 1.5m S of Widecombe. Open April 1-November 1. **5T. 10MC. 25S.**

(2.5m). Compass Caravans Touring Park, Higher Brocks Plantations, Teigngrace, Newton Abbot, Devon TQ12 6QZ. *01626 832792.* enquiries@compasscaravansdevon.com. www. compasscaravansdevon.com. Owners: John & Karen Lewis. Alongside A38 westbound, SP Teigngrace. Entrance 100yd on L. Accessory shop. Workshop, storage. Seasonal sites. Sales. Local shops and PO 1m. Country park 150yd. **36T. MC.**

(2.5m). Dornafield Touring Park, Two Mile Oak, Newton Abbot, Devon TQ12 6DD. *01803 812732.* enquiries@dornafield.com. www.dornafield.com. Caravan Club affiliated site. Set in a quiet valley close to an ancient farmhouse and surrounded by countryside. Toilet blocks, laundry facilities, baby and toddler washroom and motorhome service point. Games room, play equipment and dog walk on site. Fishing, golf and NCN cycle route nearby. Suitable for families. Open March-October. ☆☆☆☆☆ **NCC. 135T. MC.**

(3m). Lemonford Caravan Park, Bickington, Newton Abbot, Devon TQ12 6JR. *01626 821242/821263.* mark@lemonford.co.uk. www.lemonford.co.uk. Owner: Mark & Debbie Halstead. From Exeter along A38 towards Plymouth take A382 turn off, on roundabout take 3rd exit to Bickington. From Plymouth take A383 turn off to Bickington. Quiet, friendly, family run park, close to the coast and the moor. Golf course, cinema, shopping 3m in Newton Abbot. Horse riding 4m. Open March 25-October 31 for tourers; open March 15-January 14 for holiday homes. ☆☆☆☆☆ **BH&HPA. 70T. 25MC. 40S. 15H.**

(5m). Lower Aish, Poundsgate, Newton Abbot, Devon TQ13 7NY. *01364 3229.* Owner: Mr M Wilkinson. On B3357 Tavistock to Ashburton. Open March-November. **35S.**

(3m). Ross Park, Park Hill Farm, Moor Road, Ipplepen, Newton Abbot, Devon TQ12 5TT. *01803 812983.* enquiries@rossparkcaravanpark.co.uk. www.rossparkcaravanpark.co.uk. Owner: Mark & Helen Lowe. On A381 between Newton Abbot and Totnes, follow brown tourist signs at Park Hill Cross roads and Jet filling station. Site has tropical conservatory and garden-style pitches. Dog walks. Adventure playground. Golf course adjacent, fishing 3m. Open March 1-January 2. ☆☆☆☆☆ **BH&HPA. 110T. 110MC.**

(3m). Stover Caravan Club Site, Stover, Newton Abbot, Devon TQ12 6QG. *01626 361430.* www.caravanclub.co.uk. Owner: The Caravan Club. East Grinstead House, London Road, East Grinstead, West Sussex RH19 1UA. See website for standard directions to site. Caravan club members only. A quiet, open site in country park on edge of Dartmoor. Suitable for mature caravanners looking for peace and interesting walking. No sanitation. Some hard-standings. Calor Gas and Campingaz, dog walk on site. Motorhome service point. Fishing and golf nearby. Open March-October. **NCC. 70T. MC.**

(2m). Twelve Oaks Farm Caravan Park, Twelve Oaks Farm, Teignrace, Newton Abbot, Devon TQ12 6QT. *01626 352769.* info@twelveoaksfarm.co.uk. www.twelveoaksfarm.co.uk. Owner: A W & A R Gale. From Exeter A38 Plymouth bound. Turn L SP Teigngrace (before Drumbridges roundabout), continue for 1.5m through village to Twelve Oaks on your left. Family-run site on a working farm of nearly 250 acres. Bordered by river Teign. Coarse fishing. Heated outdoor swimming pool. Rallies welcome. Caravan storage. Self=catering holiday cottages for hire. ☆☆☆☆ **BH&HPA. 25T. 25MC.**

(2m). Ware Barton, Kingsteignton, Newton Abbot, Devon TQ12 3QQ. *01626 354025.* Owner: Mr W T Batting. On A381 Teignmouth to Newton Abbot.1m E of Kingsteignton, 2.5m W of Teignmouth, NE of Newton Abbot. Secutity gate. Shops, PO, Doctors, Fishing, Golf course all within 3 miles. Open Easter-October 1. **50T. MC. 30S.** ⚲

(3m). Woodville Caravan Park, Totnes Road, Ipplepen, Newton Abbot, Devon TQ12 5TN. *01803 812240.* woodvillepark@lineone.net. Owners: Colin & Jo Litte. 3.5 acre, family-run site. Quiet location for adults only. Spacious, individual, all-weather pitches. Adjacent to the park is Fermoy's Garden Centre, selling groceries and other goods. Golf course opposite. Open March 1-January 1 (10 months). **32T. 12MC.** ⚲ ▣ &

Newton Ferrers

Briar Hill Farm Caravan & Camping Park, Briar Hill Farm, Newton Ferrers, Devon PL8 1AR. *01752 872252.* Owners: Simon & Valerie Lister. 10m from Plymouth. Quiet, picturesque site in the centre of Newton Ferrers within 250yd of local shops (PO, grocery, butcher and chemist) and PH. Set on the opposite side of Newton Creek to Noss Mayo, which is a branch of the Yealm estuary. Showers and laundry facilities. Open March-November. **50T.** ✿ ⚲ ▣

North Tawton

(2m). Nichols Nymett Holiday Park, North Tawton, Devon EX20 2BP. *01837 82484.* Michael & Angela Stupiak. M5 J31. Take A30 towards Okehampton, first left at first roundabout, Whiddon Down, past Little Chef and first right (B3219), SP North Tawnton. 3 to 4m to crossroad, turn R to Bow (A3072). 1.5m to Nichols Nymett. Fishing 200yd. Golf course, shops, PO within 2-3m. Open March 15-October 31. **BH&HPA. 25S. 4H.** ⚲

Holsworthy

(5m). Hedley Wood Caravan & Camping Park, Bridgerule, Holsworthy, Devon EX22 7ED. *01288 381404.* alan@hedley wood.co.uk. www.hedleywood.co.uk. Owner: Mr A Bryant. Take A3072 Holdsworth to Bude, midway turn S on to B3254 to Launceston. 2.5m turn right 500yd on R. Woodland, family-run site with god views and a relaxed atmosphere. Pets welcome, daily kennelling, dog walk and nature trail. Clubroom, bar. Adventure area. Open and sheltered areas. Caravan storage. ✿✿ **BH&HPA. 80T. 40MC. 1S. 15H.** ✿ ⚲ ▣ & ▨

(4m). Lufflands Caravan Park, Bradworthy Road, Holsworthy, Devon EX22 7PJ. *01409 241426.* www.go.to/lufflands. Owner: K & S Bennett. Off the A3072 on Holsworthy to Bradworthy road. Bradworthy 3m. Quiet family run site in rural setting. Licensed bar. Games room. Fishing, watersports, village shop and PH 2m. Golf 4m. Open March 15-October 31. **BH&HPA. 34S. 2H.**

Honiton

(1m). The Cedars at Otter Valley Park, Honiton, Devon EX14 4PA. *01934 823288.* info@oaktreeparks.co.uk. www.ottervalley park.co.uk. Owners: Oaktree Parks Ltd. The Office, Oaktree Park, Locking, Weston-Super-Mare BS24 8RG. From Exeter: take the second exit to Honiton off A30, SP to Dorchester, A35 (green sign) and Luppit/Dunkerswell/Axminster (white sign). Cross bridge over A30 and take first left to Cotleigh/Stockland. Keep right and take left into Northcote Road. Keep left. Shops, bank, PO 1m. **BH&HPA. 37S.** ✿ ⚲ & ⌀

Ilfracombe

(1m). Beachside Holiday Park, Beach Road, Hele Bay, Ilfracombe, Devon EX34 9QZ. *01271 863006.* enquiries@ beachsidepark.co.uk. www.beachsidepark.co.uk. Owner: Steven, Janette, Paul & Teresa Crockett. About 1m from Ilfracombe on A399 to Combe Martin. Quiet park. No clubhouse or bar but good local amenities. Well positioned right next to the beach in a peaceful cove, designated as an Area of Outstanding Natural Beauty. All caravan holiday-homes have sea views. No touring or camping facilities. Cinema 1m. Golf course 5m. Open March-October. ✿✿✿✿✿ **BH&HPA. 27S. 27H.** ⚲ ⌀

(2.5m). Big Meadow Caravan & Camping Park, Watermouth, Ilfracombe, Devon EX34 9SJ. *01271 862282.* www.bigmeadow.co.uk. Owner: Mr D L Wassall. Situated on the coast road A399, between Ilfracombe and Combe Martin. Family site on the coastline between Combe Martin and Ilfracombe. Watermouth Harbour and beach 200yd. Children's play area. The Old Sawmill Inn and restaurant adjoins the site. Open Easter to October. **15T. 110MC.** ⚲ ▣ &

(2.5m). Brook Lea Caravan Club Site, West Down, Ilfracombe, Devon EX34 8NE. *01271 862848.* www.car avanclub.co.uk. Owner: The Caravan Club. East Grinstead House, East Grinstead, West Sussex RH19 1UA. See website for standard directions to site. In an elevated position 3m inland from Ilfracombe with superb views to the north and west coasts and across Dartmoor. Non-members welcome. No sanitation. Advance booking advised for July and August. Motorhome service point. Playfield. Golf, fishing and water sports nearby. Good area for walking. Suitable for families. Calor Gas and Campingaz. Dog walk. Storage pitches. Peaceful off- peak. Recycling facilities. Within 5m of NCN cycle route. Open April-September. **NCC. 77T. MC.** ⚲ ▣

Glenavon Beach Holiday Park, Woodlands, Combe Martin, Ilfracombe, Devon. *01271 866766.* Owner: John Fowler Holidays. Marlborough Road, Ilfracombe, Devon EX34 8PF. Park is situated on the A399. Club. Heated swimming pool, children's pool. Sauna. Open March-October. **7S. 75H.** ⚲ ▨

(1m). Hele Valley Holiday Park, Hele Bay, Ilfracombe, Devon EX34 9RD. *01271 862460.* holidays@helevalley.co.uk. www. helevalley.co.uk.Owner: Mr & Mrs D Dovey. Hele Valley is E of town centre. Follow brown tourist signs on the A399 to take a right turn to Hele Valley. Holiday park within walking distance of beach and town. Modern caravans, lodges, cottages and camping facilities. Laundrette, two children's play areas. Pets welcome. Cinema, theatre, boat trips, fishing and shopping within 0.5m. Golf, indoor heated pool and horse riding and quad bikes 3m. Open April 1-October 31 for tourers and holiday caravans; open all year for cottages. ✿✿✿✿ **BH&HPA. 15MC. 80S. 20H.** ⚲ ▣ &

(5m). Hidden Valley Park, West Down, Ilfracombe, Devon EX34 8NU. *01271 813837.* relax@hiddenvalleypark.com. www.hiddenvalleypark.com. Owner: Martin & Dawn Fletcher. From junction 27 of the M5 take the A361 to Barnstaple, continue on the A361 towards Ilfracombe. Secluded site in wooded valley with numerous birds and wildlife. Only a few mins' drive from coast and Exmoor National Park. Sheltered, level, grass and hard-standing pitches. Showers, laundry and dishwashing facilities. Restaurant and bar, with indoor games rooms. Two outdoor play area. Dog walking. Woodland walks. David Bellamy Gold Conservation Award. AA 5 pennants. ☆☆☆☆ BH&HPA. 135T. 74MC. ✿ ⊶ ◖ ⧖ ⚲

(2.5m). Little Meadow Camping Site, Lydford Farm, Watermouth, Ilfracombe, Devon EX34 9SJ. 01271 866862. info@littlemeadow.co.uk. www.littlemeadow.co.uk. Owner: Nick Barten. E of Ilfracombe on the A399. Small, tranquil, uncommercialised site with views of the Bristol Channel. Shop on site. Golf course, sea fishing, trips to Lundy Island, horse riding available. On the SW coastal footpath. Open Easter-September. **10T. 50MC. 3S. 3H.** ⊶ ◖ ⚲

(3m). Mill Park Touring Site, Berrynarbor, Combe Martin, Ilfracombe, Devon EX34 9SH. 01271 882647. millpark@ globalnet.co.uk. www.millpark.co.uk. Owner: Brian & Mary Malin. Between Ilfracombe and Combe Martin, take turning off the A399, opposite the Sawmills Restaurant for pretty Berrynarbor. Picturesque, level park in a woodland setting with a waterfall and stream-fed coarse fishing lake. Showers. Well-stocked shop. Bar and hot meals. Off-licence. Telephone. Laundry. Children's play area. Dog walking. Open March 15-November 15. **125T. MC.** ⊶ ◖ ⧖ ⚲

(3.5m). Napps Touring Holidays, Old Coast Road, Berrynarbor, Ilfracombe, Devon EX34 9SW. 01271 882557. info@napps.fsnet.co.uk. www.napps.co.uk. Owner: R M Richards. Leave M5 at J27 on to the A391 for about 20m, turn right at Aller Cross roundabout, follow signs to Combe Martin (about 17m), drive through Combe Martin, Napps is 1.5m past Combe Martin beach, SP on the right-hand side. Situated on the edge of Exmoor.Modern amenity block. Tennis court. Heated swimming pool, paddling pool. Takeaway food. Family bar, beer garden. Adventure playground. Laundrette. Beach. Winter and summer storage. Shop, off- licence, games room. Nearest shops, PO, doctors, restaurants 1.5m. Fishing 0.5m; golf 2m; horse riding 3.5m. Open Easter-November 1. **100T. 100MC.** ⊶ ◖ ⧖ ⚲

(5m). Sandaway Beach Holiday Park, Combe Martin, Berrynarbor, Ilfracombe, Devon EX34 8PF. 01271 866766/883155. Owner: John Fowler Holidays. On the A399 Ilfracombe to Combe Martin road. Club. Heated pool. Family site with private beach. Children's club. Licensed club with entertainment. Close Exmoor National Park. AA 4 pennants and Rose Award. Open March-October. ☆☆☆☆ **23T. 23MC. 86H.** ⊶ ◖ ⚲

(4m). Stowford Farm Meadows, Berry Down, Combe Martin, Ilfracombe, Devon EX34 0PW. 01271 882476. enquiries@stowford.co.uk. www.stowford. co.uk. Owner: Mr W D Rice. Situated off the A3123 between Berry Down Cross and Lynton Cross. AA 4 pennants. Caravan sales, service and accessories. Horse riding, mini zoo, crazy golf, indoor pool, and bar. Cycle hire available, shop, take-away, restaurant, awnings and tents. ☆☆☆☆ **BH&HPA. CaSSOA. 671T. 29MC.** ✿ ⊶ ◖ ⧖ ⚲

(2.5m). Watermouth Cove Holiday Park, Berrynarbor, Ilfracombe, Devon EX34 9SJ. 01271 862504. info@water mouthcoveholidays.co.uk. www.watermouthcoveholidays.co.uk. Owner: Mr & Mrs A Parr. Under family management. Swimming pools. Club with entertainment. Bar meals, takeaway, outside play area, table tennis, laundry, free hot water. Headland walks. Situated adjacent to the harbour. Private beach and caves. Shop and arcade. Sea fishing available nearby. Luxury chalets. Open March-October. **BH&HPA. 90T. 90MC.** ⊶ ◖ ⚲

Ivybridge

(4m). Broad Park Caravan Club Site, Higher East Leigh, Modbury, Ivybridge, Devon PL21 0SH. 01548 830714. www.caravanclub.co.uk. Owner: The Caravan Club. East Grinstead House, London Road, East Grinstead, West Sussex RH19 1UA. See website for standard directions to site. Suitable base from which to explore south Devon. Non-members welcome. Toilet blocks with privacy cubicles and laundry facilities. Some hard-standings, veg prep area, gas supplies. Dog walk on site. Peaceful off-peak. Good area for walking. Motorhome service point. Playfield and play equipment. Boules pitch. Suitable for families. Open March-October. **NCC. 112T. MC.** ⊶ ◖ ⧖

(7m). Camping & Caravanning Club Site - California Cross, Modbury, Ivybridge, Devon PL21 0SG. 01548 821297/0870 2433331. www.campingandcaravanning club.co.uk. Owner: Camping & Caravanning Club. Greenfields House, Westwood Way, Coventry CV4 8JH. Leave A38 at Wranton Cross, on to A3121, continue on crossroads. Cross over on to B3196. Turn L before filling station, SP Dartmouth, site on R. Situated 8m from Bigbury-on-Sea with sandy beach and golf course. Salcombe 12m, centre for yachting. All units accepted. Non-members welcome. Indoor and outdoor swimming pools situated 7m away. Special arrangements for early morning site departure for Plymouth Ferry crossings available. Special deals available for families and backpackers. Open April-October. ☆☆☆☆ **80T. 80MC.** ⊶ ◖ ⧖

Okehampton

(6m). Bridestowe Caravan Park, Glebe Park, Bridestowe, Okehampton, Devon EX20 4ER. 01837 861261. Owner: Mrs W A Young, Mr G W Young & Mr M S Young. From Okehampton, turn off A30, SP Bridestowe; in village follow caravan signs to park. Children allowed. Open March 1-December 30. ☆☆☆ **BH&HPA. 13T. 13MC. 30S. 6H.** ⊶ ◖ ⚲

(3m). Bundu Camping & Caravan Park, Sourton Down, Okehampton, Devon EX20 4HT. 01837 861611. francesca@ bundusagent.wanadoo.co.uk. www.bundu.co.uk. Owner: Mr M & Mrs F Sargent. From A30 take slip road A386 to Tavistock, L at T-junction then L again 100yd. Site 0.5m ahead. Access good. Level site in Dartmoor National Park. Direct access onto National Cycle Way. Adjacent Inn. Short walk to garage and shop. Golf, fishing and horse riding within a few miles. **BH&HPA. 28T. 10MC.** ✿ ⊶ ◖

Camping & Caravanning Club Site - Lydford, Lydford, Okehampton, Devon EX20 4BE. 01822 820275/0870 2433331. www.campingandcaravanning club.co.uk. Owner: Camping & Caravanning Club. Greenfields House, Westwood Way, Coventry CV4 8JH. From A30 take A386 to Tavistock, continue to filling station on R. Turn R to Lydford. At War Memorial, turn R. Site signed 200yd. Site located in quiet, rural setting with plenty of space for children's games. Non-members welcome. All units accepted. Walks around the woodlands of Lydford Gorge and along the ravine take you to dramatic 27-metre White Lady waterfall and the Devil's Cauldron whirlpool. Dartmoor is within easy walking distance. Special deals available for families and backpackers. Open March-October. ☆☆☆☆ **70T. 70MC.** ⊶ ◖

(7m). Dartmoor View Holiday Park, Whiddon Down, Okehampton, Devon EX20 2QL. 01647 231545. info@dartmoorview.co.uk. www.dartmoorview.co.uk. Owner: S D Cliff & J Cliff. Located off the old A30 near the junction with the A382. Calor Gas and Camping Gaz. Club. Licensed bar. Heated swimming pool. Play area. Laundrette. Games room with TV. Licensed shop. AA 4 pennants. Cycle hire available. Open March-January. ✩✩✩✩✩ BH&HPA. 75T. MC. 80S. ⚹ ☃ ☙

(0.5m). Moorcroft Leisure Park, Exeter Road, Okehampton, Devon EX20 1QF. 01837 55116/54253. Owner: Alan & Susan Dorrington. Located on main A30 Exeter to Okehampton road. Heated swimming pool. Bar. AA 3 pennants. **25T. MC.** ❋ ⚹ ☙

Paignton

(1.5m). Ashvale Holiday Park, Goodrington Road, Paignton, Devon TQ4 7JD. 01803 843887. info@beverley-holidays.co.uk. www.beverley-holidays.co.uk. Two miles south of Paignton on the A3022, turn left into Goodrington Road. Club, bar, restaurant, playground and swimming pool. Beach, golf course 1m. Cinema 1.5 miles away. Open April 1-October 31. ✩✩✩✩ BH&HPA. **NCC. 159S.** ☙

Please remember to mention *Caravan Sites 2006* when you contact any sites listed in this guide, or when you respond to any advertisements.

(1m). Barton Pines, Blagdon Road, Paignton, Devon TQ3 3YG. 01803 553350. info@bartonpines.com. www.bartonpines.com. Owner: Mr McClarron. Turn right off the A380 (Newton Abbot to Torquay road) on to the A380 (Torbay ring road to Paignton). After 2m turn right at Preston Down roundabout, SP for Berry Pomeroy and Barton Pines, 2m, crossroads, SP Barton Pines. Heated outdoor pool. Tennis. Open March 1-October 31. ✩✩✩ **33T. MC.** ⊕ ⚹

(2m). Beverley Park Holiday Centre, Goodrington Road, Paignton, Devon TQ4 7JE. 01803 843887. info@beverley-holidays.co.uk. www.beverley-holidays.co.uk. Off the A379 Dartmouth to Paignton road. Sea views overlooking Torbay. South West England Tourism Excellence 'Caravan Park of the Year' 2004/2005. David Bellamy Gold Conservation Award. Club. Bar. Restaurant. Heated indoor and outdoor pools. Tennis court. Sauna and fitness suite, playground. Beach, golf course 1m. Cinema 1.5m. ✩✩✩✩✩ BH&HPA. **NCC. 189T. 50MC. 211S. 195H.** ❋ ⊕ ☃ ☙

(2m). Bona Vista Holiday Park, Totnes Road, Paignton, Devon TQ4 7PY. 01803 551971. bonavista@tiscali.co.uk. www.bona-vista.co.uk. Owner: Mr & Mrs G H Hill. On the A385. Small, quiet site, three flats to let. Fishing nearby. Open all year except Christmas. ✩✩✩✩ BH&HPA. **13S. 13H.** ❋ ⚹

(3m). Byslades Camping & Caravan Park, Totnes Road, Paignton, Devon TQ4 7PY. 01803 555072. info@byslades.co.uk. www.byslades.co.uk. Owner: Robert & Kay Wedd. 2m W of Paignton situated on A385. Park set in 23 acres of countryside. Level, terraced pitches. No dogs mid July to end August. Totnes, the South Hams and Dartmoor National Park all nearby. Open mid May-September. ✩✩✩✩ BH&HPA. **170T. 20MC.** ⚹ ⊕ ☃ ☙

(3m). Falcon Park, Totnes Road, Paignton, Devon TQ4 7PZ. 01803 663217. Owner: OMNI Support Services Ltd. On A385, Totnes Road. Indoor swimming pool, sauna, bar and entertainment. Open March 1-January 14. **70S.** ☃ ⌀

Please mention Caravan Sites 2006 when replying to advertisers

WEST COUNTRY

(2.5m). Halfway Caravan Park, Totnes Road, Paignton, Devon TQ4 7PY. *01803 557289.* Owner: Mr & Mrs K Marsden. Small, peaceful park in pretty garden setting with rural views. Between historic town of Totnes and lively resorts of Paignton and Torquay. Brixham amd Dartmoor near. Countryside holiday near sea. Open Easter-November. **BH&HPA. 12H.** 🛉

(1.5m). Hoburne Torbay, Grange Road, Goodrington, Paignton, Devon TQ4 7JP. *01803 558010.* enquiries@hoburne.com. www.hoburne.com. Owner: Hoburne Ltd. 261 Lymington Road, Highcliffe, Christchurch, Dorset BH23 5EE. S on A380 (Paignton Ring Road) for 1m after junction with A385. L into Goodrington Rd for 0.75m then L into Grange Rd. Park is SP. Licensed club and theme restaurant. Outdoor and indoor pool. Seasonal entertainment. Cafeteria. Shop. Adventure playground. Soft play area and mini bowling. Rose Award. David Bellamy Bronze Conservation Award. Open March-October. ✩✩✩✩ **BH&HPA. NCC. 189T. 189MC. 463S. 132H.** 🔌 🛁

(1.5m). Marine Park Holiday Centre, Grange Road, Paignton, Devon TQ4 7JR. *01803 843887.* info@beverley-holidays.co.uk. www.beverley-holidays.co.uk. Off A379 Dartmouth to Paignton. Nestling in the hillside in peaceful surroundings, with views of Torbay. Beach, golf course 1m. Cinema 1.5m. Open mid March-October 31. ✩✩✩✩ **BH&HPA. NCC. 21T. 61H.** 🔌

(1.5m). Paignton Holiday Park, Totnes Road, Paignton, Devon TQ4 7PW. *01803 550504.* www.haulfryn.co.uk. Owner: Haulfryn Group. The Warren, Abersoch, Pwllheli, Gwynedd LL53 7AA. 1.5m due W of Paignton on A385. Swimming pools. Shop. Entertainment. Thatched PH. Bars. Cafe. Laundry. Play area. Torbay and Dartmoor National Park nearby. Open March-October. ✩✩✩ **BH&HPA. 231T. MC. 100S. 92H.** 🔌 🛁

(1.5m). Waterside Holiday Park, Three Beeches, Paignton, Devon TQ4 6NS. *01803 842400.* On A379 Paignton to Brixham. Open March-October. ✩✩✩✩ **BH&HPA. 210H.** 🛉 🛁

(1.5m). Whitehill Country Park, Stoke Road, Paignton, Devon TQ4 7PF. *01803 782338.* info@whitehill-park.co.uk. www.whitehill-park.co.uk. Off A385 Totnes to Paignton. David Bellamy Gold Conservation award. Countryside and woodland walking nearby. Bar, restaurant, takeaway, heated pool, playgrounds, arcade, shop. Golf and cinema 2m. 3m to beach. Open April-September. ✩✩✩✩ **BH&HPA. 269T. 269MC. 60S. 60H.** 🔌 🛁

(3m). Widend Touring Park, Berry Pomeroy Road, Marldon, Paignton, Devon TQ3 1RT. *01803 550116.* Owner: Roger & Heather Cowen & Family. A380 Torbay Ring road. Turn towards Marldon at 2nd roundabout. At next roundabout 2nd left into Five Lanes. Head towards Berry Pomeroy and Totnes through Marldon Village. Park on R 0.5m past Marldon. 4m to Torbay seafront. Spacious, family-run park. Views of sea, countryside. Heated outdoor pool, adventure playground, games room, takeaway, bar and family room. Couples and families only. No dogs mid-July and August. Seasonal touring pitches. Tourer storage. Open Easter-October. ✩✩✩✩ **BH&HPA. 207T. 207MC.** 🛉 🔌 ♿ 🛁

Parracombe

(0.25 m). Lorna Doone Farm, Parracombe, Devon EX31 4RJ. *01598 763576.* Owner: Miss L Hunt. On A39 Barnstaple to Lynton. Open March-October. **25T. MC.** 🛉

Plymouth

(5m). Brixton Camping & Caravan Park, Venn Farm, Brixton, Plymouth, Devon PL8 2AX. *01752 880378.* Owner: Mr B H Cane. On A379 3.5m SE of Laira Bridge 0.5m W of Brixton. Quiet site with showers. Restaurant, PH, fish and chip shop, PO. Beach 2.5m. River Yealm 0.5m. Open March 15-November 15. **43T. MC.** 🛉 🔌

(7m). Churchwood Valley Holiday Cabins, Wembury Bay, Plymouth, Devon PL9 0DZ. *01752 862382.* churchwoodvalley@btinternet.com. www.churchwoodvalley.com. Owner: J C & S A Stansell. A379 to Elburton, follow Langdon Court signs to Staddiscombe village, then 2nd left, follow Churchwood signs. Comfortable cabins in wooded valley. Close to beaches, coastal walks and countryside. Pets welcome. Riding stables and golf nearby. Man-made attractions 20 mins drive in Plymouth. David Bellamy Gold Conservation Award. Open April-December and Christmas and New Year. ✩✩✩✩ **BH&HPA. 69S. 55H.** 🛉 🛁

Plymouth Sound Caravan Club Site, Bovisand Lane, Down Thomas, Plymouth, Devon PL9 0AE. *01752 862325.* www.caravanclub.co.uk. Owner: The Caravan Club. East Grinstead House, East Grinstead, West Sussex RH19 1UA. See website for directions to site. Within easy reach of historic port, set on headland outside Plymouth with broad views over Sound and close to SW Coastal footpath and lovely beaches. Own sanitation required. Good for walking; dog walk on site. Golf, watersports and NCN cycle route nearby. Suitable for families. Open March-October. **NCC. 60T. MC.** 🛉 🔌

ENGLISH RIVIERA
BEVERLEY HOLIDAYS, TORBAY
LUXURY HOLIDAY PARK
Popular family Holiday Park. Luxury Lodges, Holiday Homes & Modern Touring Facilities. Lots of activities and fun for the whole family.
01803 661 968 FOR FREE BROCHURE
www.beverley-holidays.co.uk/cs

(3.5m). Riverside Caravan Park, Liegham Manor Drive, Longbridge Road, Marsh Mills, Plymouth, Devon PL6 8LL. *01752 344122.* office@riversidecaravanpark.com. www.river sidecaravanpark.com. Owners: Ian Gray. Take Plymouth slip road from A38 to large roundabout, around roundabout, take road to Plymouth, 1st traffic lights, turn L. **132T. 132MC. ✿ ⚓ ▣**

(8m). Smithaleigh Caravan & Camping Park, Plympton, Plymouth, Devon PL7 5AX. *01752 893194.* Owner: Mr M W Jones. Off the A38. Motel and restaurant on site. **120T. MC. ✿ ⚓ ▣ ⏚ ⏚**

(5m). Stamford Fort Country Club, Jennycliff, Plymouth, Devon. *01752 402576.* Owner: Mr R C Larson. Open March-October. **T. MC. 47S. 20H.**

Putsborough

Putsborough Sands Caravan Site, Georgham, Braunton, Putsborough, Devon EX33 1LB. *01271 890230/890121.* rob@putsborough.com. www.putsborough.com. Owner: Mr R Tucker. The Anchorage, Putsborough, Georgeham, Braunton, N Devon EX33 1LB. 4m from Braunton, on B3231. Booking essential. Site overlooks and is adjacent to Putsborough Sands. Open April 1-October 10. **BH&HPA. 25T. ⚓ ▣ ⏚ ⏚**

Salcombe

(2m). Alston Farm Camping & Caravan Site, Kingsbridge, Salcombe, Devon TQ7 3BJ. *01548 561260/0780 8030921.* alston.campsite@ukgateway.net. www.welcome.to/alston farm. Owner: Mr P W Shepherd. Off A381. Level, sheltered site. AA 3 pennants. Open mid March-end October. **40T. 15MC. 58S. ⚓ ▣ ⏚ ⏚**

(3m). Bolberry House Farm Caravan & Camping Park, Bolberry, Malborough, Salcombe, Devon TQ7 3DY. *01548 561251/560926.* bolberry.house@virgin.net. www.bolberry parks.co.uk. Owner: Dudley & Jessie Stidson. A381 Kingsbridge to Salcombe. At Malborough follow signs to Bolberry. Quiet, family-run park amid coastal countryside, good access to cliff walks and all boating facilities and safe, sandy beaches 1m. Children's play area and barn. Dogs welcome; separate exercising paddock. Low-season discounts with special rates for over-50s. AA 3 pennants. Open Easter-October. ✰✰✰ **23T. MC. 10S. 5H. ⚓ ▣ ⏚ ⏚**

(3m). Sun Park, Soar Mill Cove, Malborough, Salcombe, Devon TQ7 3DS. *01548 561378.* bj.sweetman@talk21.com.

www.sun-park.co.uk. Owner: Mrs B J Sweetman. On entering village of Malborough (on Kingsbridge to Salcombe road) turn sharp right, SP Soar. Park is 1.5 m along this road on right-hand side. Peaceful site, surrounded by National Trust land. Walking distance to beach. Playground. Indoor games and TV room. Open Easter-September. **15T. 5MC. 34S. 28H. ⚓ ▣**

Seaton

(0.5m). Axe Vale Caravan Park, Colyford Road, Seaton, Devon EX12 2DF. *0800 0688816.* info@axevale.co.uk. www.axevale.co.uk. Owner: Peter & Kathryn Thomas. Quiet park overlooking the Axe valley. A3052 to Colyford, turn off S by General Store, then 1.5m on left. Open March-October. ✰✰✰ **BH&HPA. 68H. ⚓ ⏚ ✎**

(2m). Beer Head Caravan Park, Beer, Seaton, Devon EX12 3AH. *01297 21107/20003.* www.beer-head.com. Owner: Mrs A E Dormor. Off A3052. Quiet, peaceful, family-run park with panoramic views. Steep hillside. Established more than 40 years. Beer village within walking distance. Good centre for boating, fishing and walking. Showers. Laundrette. Calor Gas. Golf course nearby. Open Easter-October 31. **297S. 80H. ⚓ ▣ ⏚**

(5m). Berry Barton, Branscombe, Seaton, Devon EX12 3BD. *01297 680208.* Owner: TM, AE White & Co. Off A3052. Mains water, drainage and electricity. 1m of coastline on 300-acre dairy and beef farm. Shetland ponies. Fishing, riding, golf, shops within five miles. PO, stores in village. Doctor in village once a week. Surgery in Beer 3m, Seaton 5m. Open March 15-November 15. **BH&HPA. 3T. MC. 62S. 9H. ⚓ ▣**

Lyme Bay Holiday Village, 87 Harbour Road, Seaton, Devon EX12 2NE. *01297 21816.* Owner: Renowned Ltd. From the A3052, take the B3172, SP Seaton. Follow road through Axmouth and then alongside the river Axe. After crossing bridge over river you will find village about 200yd on the right-hand side. Open April-December. **BH&HPA. NCC. 150H. ⚓ ⏚**

(0.5m). Manor Farm Caravan Site, Seaton Down Hill, Seaton, Devon EX12 2JA. *01297 21524.* tim.salter@ talk21.com. www.manorfarm.net. Owner: Mr M Salter. Off A3052 at Tower Cross, Seaton clearly signed. Views of Lyme Bay and Axe Valley. Spacious, quiet, farm site with good facilities. Beach 1m. Open March-October. **104T. 20MC. ⚓ ▣ ⚓**

(4.5m). The Sea Shanty, Branscombe, Seaton, Devon EX12 3DP. *01297 680226.* Owner: A J & R E Sellick. Off A3052. Open March 15-October 31. **64S. ⚓ ⏚**

Please mention Caravan Sites 2006 when replying to advertisers

Sidmouth

(2m). Dunscombe Manor Caravan Park, Salcombe Regis, Sidmouth, Devon EX10 0PN. 01395 513654. dunscombe.manor@lineone.net. www.dunscombe-manor-caravan-park.co.uk. Owner: DJ, IG, CM & CC Morgan. A3052 Exeter to Lyme Regis. E of Sidford. Turn R Dunscombe. Weston Brandcombe turning. Follow caravan park signs and continue to the end of lane. Weston Mouth Beach; Heritage Coastline; Coastal footpath. Peace and tranquility. National Trust land. Area of Outstanding Natural Beauty. Open March 15-October 31. **BH&HPA. 68S. ⚲**

(3m). Kingsdown Tail Caravan & Camping Park, Salcombe Regis, Sidmouth, Devon EX10 0PD. 01297 680313. info@kingsdowntail.co.uk. www.kingsdowntail.co.uk. Owner: Mr I J Mckenzie-Edwards. Adjacent to A3052, E of Sidmouth. Family-run, quiet, five-acre park. Level and sheltered just inland from Devon's stunning heritage coastline. A variety of craft, animal and historic attractions close by. Open March 15-November 15. ☆☆☆☆ **BH&HPA. 100T. MC. 2H. ⚲ ⊟ ⚑**

(3m). Oakdown Touring & Holiday Home Park, Weston, Sidmouth, Devon EX10 0PH. 01297 680387. enquiries@oakdown.co.uk. www.oakdown.co.uk. Owner: Mr & Mrs R Franks. On the A3052, E of Sidmouth. Level, closely mown, landscaped park. Play area. Microwave. Deep freeze. Laundry. Free hot water. Family bathrooms and dishwashing facilities all centrally heated. Field trail to world famous Donkey Sanctuary. Serviced superpitches available. Alarmed caravan storage. Adjacent to 9- hole, par-3 golf course. Open March 26-October 31. ☆☆☆☆☆ **BH&HPA. 100T. MC. 46S. 16H. ⚲ ⊟ ⚷**

(5m). Putts Corner Caravan Club Site, Sidbury, Sidmouth, Devon EX10 0QQ. 01404 42875. www.caravanclub.co.uk. Owner: The Caravan Club. East Grinstead House, London Road, East Grinstead, Sussex RH19 1UA. See website for standard directions to site. Open site surrounded by trees, a good base from which to explore south Devon and Dorset. Toilet with privacy cubicles block and laundry facilities. Motorhome service point. Dog walk nearby. Play equipment. Boules pitch. Non-members welcome. Open March-October. ☆☆☆☆☆ **NCC. 113T. MC. ⚲ ⊟ ⚷**

(1.5m). Salcombe Regis Caravan & Camping Park, Salcombe Regis, Sidmouth, Devon EX10 0JH. 01395 514303. info@salcombe-regis.co.uk. www.salcombe-regis.co.uk. Owner: Mr Neil Hook. 0.5m E of Sidmouth, SP off A3052. Exeter to Lyme Regis coast road. Off-licence. Hardstandings for tourers and motor caravans. Nearest park to Sidmouth. Situated in an Area of Outstanding Natural Beauty on the Heritage coast. Suitable base for exploring rural east Devon. 2m from Sidmouth golf club, cinema, shops. Open Easter-November. ☆☆☆☆☆ **BH&HPA. 40T. 40MC. 10S. ⚲ ⊟ ⚷**

South Brent

1.5m). Cheston Caravan Park, Wrangaton Road, South Brent, Devon TQ10 9HF. 01364 72586. enquiries@chestoncaravanpark.co.uk. www.chestoncaravanpark.co.uk. Owner: E Gourley. A38 Exeter, leave at slip road marked Wrangaton Cross turn right at top of slip road and follow signs. From Plymouth take South Brent, Woodpecker slip road go under A38 rejoin A38 then follow directions from Exeter. Level site. Showers. Laundry. Set in Dartmoor National Park. Fishing, golf, shop, PO, doctor, horse riding, leisure centre, all nearby. Open March 15-January 15. **24T. MC. ⚲ ⊟ ⚷ ⚑**

Edeswell Farm, Rattery, South Brent, Devon TQ10 9LN. 01364 72177. welcome@edeswellfarm.co.uk. www.edeswellfarm.co.uk. Owner: Mr & Mrs Ashworth. Take A385 off A38 (Marley Head turn-off), SP to Paignton. Edeswell Farm is situated 0.5m along on the right-hand side. 5m from Totnes. Small, friendly park with spectacular country views and indoor heated pool, set in 23 acres of private land with meadow and woodland walks, children's play area, bar and freshly cooked bar foof. David Bellamy Conservation Award. New holiday lodges for sale. 3 cottages also for hire. Golf course 2m, fishing next door via private path. Open February 5-January 5. ☆☆☆ **BH&HPA. 46T. 18MC. 60S. 22H. ⚲ ⊟ ⚑**

(0.5m). Great Palstone Caravan Park, South Brent, Devon TQ19 9JP. 01364 72227. Owner: Ms Joan R Morgan. Off A38. Free guided walks on the moor. Laundrette. Shower block. Storage and seasonal pitches. Open March 15-November 15. **50T. MC. ⚲ ⊟ ⚷**

South Molton

(4m). Black Cock Inn & Camping Park, Molland, South Molton, Devon EX36 3NW. 01769 550297. Owner: Mr & Mrs A W Bull. Signposted A361. Laundry. PH. Indoor heated swimming pool. Hot showers. **64T. 64MC. 2S. 2H. ⚙ ⚲ ⊟ ⚷**

(4m). Molland Caravan & Camping Park, Blackcock Inn, Molland, South Molton, Devon EX36 3NW. 01769 550297. Owner: Mr Allan Bull. Follow Blackcock Inn sign on the A361 approximately 4m east of South Molton. **65T. 65MC. 2S. 2H. ⚙ ⚲ ⚷**

(4.5m). Romansleigh Holiday Park, Odam Hill, South Molton, Devon EX36 4NB. 01769 550259. romhols@lineone.net. Owner: John & Heather Gazeley. On B3137, South Molton to Witheridge road. SP right, 2m past Alswear. 10m Exmoor, 20m coast. 14-acre secluded, rural site, suitable touring base for Devon. Heated pool. Games room. Licensed club and bar open all year. Snooker and pool, skittle alley. TV. Pet animals. Open March 15-October 31. **BH&HPA. 10T. 3MC. 45S. 10H. ⚲ ⊟**

Tavistock

(2m). Dartmoor Country Holidays, Magpie Leisure Park, Yelverton, Tavistock, Devon PL20 7RY. 01822 852651. Owner: Mr Bidder. On A386, Tavistock to Plymouth road, SE of Tavistock. 10-acre, woodland site on edge of Dartmoor National Park, alongside river Walkham. Pine lodges also available. Manager: Mrs R Berks. Open March-November. **BH&HPA. 30T. MC. 15S. 3H. ⚲ ⊟**

(2m). Harford Bridge Holiday Park, Peter Tavy, Tavistock, Devon PL19 9LS. 01822 810349. enquiry@harfordbridge.co.uk. www.harfordbridge.co.uk. Owner: Mr G Williamson. Off A386 Okehampton to Tavistock Road, take Peter Tavy turn. Level, sheltered park on the river Tavy in Dartmoor National Park. Rose Award. Fly fishing, tennis, walking. Golf, pony trekking, swimming pool all nearby. Cinema, shops, PO, doctor, garage all within 2m. ☆☆☆☆ **BH&HPA. 80T. 40MC. 30S. 17H. ⚙ ⚲ ⊟ ⚷ ⚑**

(2m). Higher Longford Caravan & Camping Park, Moorshop, Tavistock, Devon PL19 9LQ. 01822 613360. stay@higherlongford.co.uk. www.higherlongford.co.uk. Owner: Mr & Mrs Deane & Mrs I Collins. From Tavistock take B3357 towards Princetown. 2m on right-hand side, before hill on to moors. Small, family-run park, nestling on the lower slopes of the national park.Toilet block heated. Bath and children's room. Shop, takeaway, off-licence, laundrette. Camper's lounge with pool tables and TV. Suitable base for touring Dartmoor. Grass or hard-standing pitches on level, sheltered areas, with views. Multi-serviced, electric pitches. Storage available. Swimming, fishing, golf and walking all nearby. Cinema, shopping, supermarket within 2m. ✩✩✩✩ **BH&HPA. 80T. 52MC. 4H. ✿ ⊨ ☎ ♿ ☎ ⌀**

(2.5m). Langstone Manor Camping and Caravan Park, Moortown, Tavistock, Devon PL19 9JZ. *01822 613371.* web@langstone-manor.co.uk. www.langstone-manor.co.uk. Owner: D & J Kellett. Off A386 near Tavistock, take B3357 road to Princetown, after about 1.5m turn R and at crossroads, follow brown signs. Quiet, secluded park with direct access on to Dartmoor National Park. Lounge bar serving evening meals. Games room. National Trust properties, gardens, golf, fishing, horse-riding, climbing nearby. Suitable base for exploring Devon and Cornwall. Swimming pool and slides. Cinema. Open March-November. ✩✩✩✩ **BH&HPA. 20T. 20MC. 25S. 7H. ⊨ ☎**

(4m). Woodovis Park, Gulworthy, Tavistock, Devon PL19 8NY. *01822 832968.* info@woodovis.com. www.woodovis.com. Owner: John & Dorothy Lewis. 3.5m W of Tavistock via A390 Callington and Liskeard road. Turn R at crossroads SP Lamerton, Chipshop. Park sign 1.5m on L. Spacious, peaceful, rural site with views. Showers, heated indoor pool, sauna and jacuzzi, mini golf, games room. Play area. Bread/croissants baked on site daily. Tavistock: theatre, cinema, shops 4m. Golf 4m. Fishing 2m. Plymouth 15m. Eden project about 45 mins drive. Open March 26-October 28. ✩✩✩✩✩ **BH&HPA. 50T. 50MC. 35S. 17H. ⊨ ☎ ♿ ☎**

Teignmouth

(2m). Coast View Holiday Park, Torquay Road, Shaldon, Teignmouth, Devon TQ14 0BG. *01626 872392.* www.coastview.co.uk. On A379. Shop, bar, indoor swimming pool, adventure playground. Holiday chalets and caravans. Open March-November. ✩✩✩✩ **BH&HPA. 7T. MC. 90H. ⊨ ☎ ☎**

(2m). Devon Valley Holiday Village, Ringmore, Shaldon, Teignmouth, Devon TQ14 4EY. *01626 872525.* A380 towards Torbay then B3195 alongside river. Heated, indoor swimming pool. Children's club. Indoor amusements and games. Cafe. Laundrette. Cabaret club, riverside PH and restaurant. Open Easter-October. ✩✩✩✩ **BH&HPA. NCC. 88H. ⊨ ♿ ☎**

(3m). Wear Farm, Newton Road, Bishopsteignton, Teignmouth, Devon TQ14 9PT. *01626 775249/779265.* nigdavey@aol.com. Owner: E S Coaker & Co. On A381 between Teignmouth and Newton Abbot. Pleasant site beside river Teign with views over the estuary. Showers. Laundrette. Play area. Free brochure. Open Easter-October. **100T. 47MC. 92S. 8H. ⊨ ☎ ☎**

Tiverton

(5m). Minnows Caravan Club Site, Sampford Peverell, Tiverton, Devon EX16 7EN. *01884 821770.* www.ukparks. co.uk/minnows. Owner: Zig & Krystyna Grochala. Leave M5, J7. Take A361 Barnstaple. After 0.25m take slip road on left and follow brown signs. Caravan Club affiliated site. Coarse fishing on adjacent Grand Western Canal. Bottled gas supplies. 15mins walk to PH, shops, PO, doctor and tennis courts. Non-members welcome. Golf driving range within 0.5m. Public transport nearby. Off-road cycling route and walking on canal paths. Open March-November. **BH&HPA. 45T. MC. ⊨ ☎ ♿**

(8.5m). West Middlewick Farm, Nomansland, Tiverton, Devon EX16 8NP. *01884 861235.* gibsons.kensfield@virgin.net. http://freespace.virgin.net/gibsons.kensfield. Owner: John & Jo Gibson. From Tiverton take B3137 towards South Molton. Site is 1m beyond Nomansland on north side of road. Small, informal site under same family management for the last 70 years. Hardstandings. Bed and breakfast. Working farm with views and walks. Level, 3-acre field with easy access. Central for touring Devon. Shops, PH and PO 1m. **15T. MC. ✿ ⊨ ☎ ♿**

Yeatheridge Farm Caravan Park, East Worlington, Witheridge, Tiverton, Devon EX17 4TN. *01884 860330.* yeatheridge@talk21.com. www.yeatheridge.co.uk. Owner: Mr A & Mrs A J Hosegood. Off the B3137 (old A373) Witheridge and A377 on B3042. Indoor heated swimming pool. Coarse fishing. Working farm. Horse riding. Panoramic views. About 2.5m of woodland, nature and river bank trails. Open Easter-September 30. ✩✩✩✩ **BH&HPA. NCC. 85T. MC. 6S. ⊨ ☎ ☎**

(7m). Zeacombe House Caravan Park, East Anstey, Tiverton, Devon EX16 9JU. *01398 341279.* enquiries@zeacombeadult retreat.co.uk. www.zeacombeadultretreat.co.uk. Owner: Peter & Lin Keeble. Exit J27 to A361 Tiverton. Turn right next roundabout, A396 Minehead Dulverton 5m, Exeter Inn left to B3227. At SP South Molton, 5m, turn left. Level, lawned site. Hardstandings. Showers, shaver points, hair-dryers and laundry room. Gas supplies. Home-cooked food available daily. Good centre for touring Exmoor, Taunton, Minehead and Exeter. Adults only. AA 4 pennants. Open March-October. ✩✩✩✩ **BH&HPA. NCC. 60T. 10MC. ⊨ ☎ ☎**

Torquay

(2m). Widdicombe Farm Touring Park, Compton, Torquay, Devon TQ3 1ST. *01803 558325.* enq@torquaytouring.co.uk. www.widdicombefarm.co.uk. Owner: Gordon & Thelma Glynn. 2.5m from Torquay and Paignton. On the A380, Torquay to Paignton ring road. Park has good views and is landscaped to provide spacious, level pitches. Easy access, no narrow country lanes. Facilities include ladies' private washrooms, laundrette and bathroom, shop. Hayloft entertainment bar and Poppy Restaurant. Discounts for over-60s. Separate family area and adults-only areas. Fully serviced pitches available in adult-only section. Open March-mid October. ✩✩✩✩ **BH&HPA. 100T. 50MC. 3H. ⊨ ☎ ♿ ☎**

Totnes

Higher Well Farm Holiday Park, Waddeton Road, Stoke Gabriel, Totnes, Devon TQ9 6RN. *01803 782289.* higherwell@talk21.com. www.higherwellfarmholidaypark.co.uk. Owner: Mr & Mrs John & Liz Ball. Follow A380 from Exeter and Newton Abbot towards Torquay and then turn R on to the ring road. Turn R for Totnes on to A385. Turn L at Collaton Carvery pub for Stoke Gabriel and follow direction signs. Park situated 3.5m from Paignton. 1m from village of Stoke Gabriel on river Dart. Golf course, leisure centre 3m. Cinema 4m. Open Easter-October. ✩✩✩✩ **BH&HPA. 80T. 80MC. 18H. ⊨ ☎ ♿ ☎**

Please mention Caravan Sites 2006 when replying to advertisers

Steamer Quay Caravan Club Site, Steamer Quay Road, Totnes, Devon TQ9 5AL. *01803 862738.* www.caravanclub.co.uk. Owner: The Caravan Club. East Grinstead House, London Road, East Grinstead, West Sussex RH19 1UA. See website for standard directions to site. Quiet, green and open site with rural views yet within a short walk of bustling Totnes. Advance booking essential bank holidays. Non-members welcome. Toilet block and laundry facilities. Battery charging available. Veg prep area, Calor Gas and Campingaz. Peaceful off-peak. Beach nearby, good area for walking, recycling facilities, NCN cycle route within 5m. Fishing and golf nearby. Suitable for families. Open March-October. **NCC. 40T. MC. ⊶**

Umberleigh

(0.25m). Camping & Caravanning Club Site - Umberleigh, Over Weir, Umberleigh, Devon EX37 9DU. *01769 560009/0870 2433331.* www.campingand caravanningclub.co.uk. Owner: Camping & Caravanning Club. Greenfields House, Westwood Way, Coventry CV4 8JH. On A377 from Barnstaple turn right, on to B3227 at Umberleigh sign, site on right in 0.25m. Situated in beautiful and sheltered Taw valley. Within easy reach of beaches, surfing and swimming. Fishing, on-site also games room, skittle alley, pool table, table tennis, public phone, ice-pack freezing, launderette, new tennis court with free tennis coaching for children during high season, non-members welcome. All units accepted. Special deals available for families and backpackers. Open March-October. ✩✩✩✩ **60T. 60MC. ⊶ ⊕ ⚲**

Snapdown Farm Caravans, Snapdown, Chittlehamholt, Umberleigh, Devon EX37 9PF. *01769 540708.* mab@fish.co.uk. www.northdevon.co.uk/accommodations/ snapdown.htm. Owner: Mrs M N Bowen. 6m from South Molton. Directions are sent with bookings. Peaceful countryside. Outside seating and picnic tables. Woodland walks. Goats to feed and milk. Pets welcome. Sea and moors within easy reach. reductions for couples. Open May-October. **BH&HPA. 6H. ⊶ ⚲**

Westward Ho!

(0.2m). Beachside Holiday Park, Merley Road, Westward Ho!, Devon EX39 1JX. *01237 421163/0845 6012541.* beach side@surfbay.dircon.co.uk. www.beachsideholidays.co.uk. Owner: Mr J E Taylor. Surf Bay Leisure, The Airfield, Winkleigh, Devon EX19 8DW. M5, J27, take A361 to Barnstaple then A39 for Bude. Over Torridge Bridge, over roundabout, about 1m turn right for Westward Ho!. Down Stanwell Hill and turn left at bottom into Merley Road, park second on right. Rose Award. Views of sandy beach and the sea. Golf course 0.5m. Large shopping centre 1m. Cinema 9m. Open March-October 31. ✩✩✩✩ **BH&HPA. NCC. 52H. ⚲**

(0.25m). Braddicks Holiday Centre, Merley Road, Westward Ho!, Devon EX39 1JS. *01237 473263.* holidays@braddicksholi daycentre.co.uk. www.braddicksholidaycentre.co.uk. Owner: Mr G Braddick & Mr R Braddick. M5, J27 on to the North Devon Link Road (A361). A39 from Barnstaple to Bideford, continue till turning marked Westward Ho! The road will take you down a steep hill called Stanwell Hill. At bottom take immediately L turn into Merley Road. Park located at the end of the road on right-hand side. Selection of self-catering, chalets, apartments and caravans beside blue flag beach. Seasonal entertainment in

function suite. On-site bar and restaurant. Suitable base for walking, golfing, surfing and exploring Devon and Cornwall. **60T. 22H. ✿ ⊶ ⚲**

(0.25m). Sunray Caravan Gardens, Merley Road, Westward Ho!, Devon EX39 1JS. *01237 474800/01237 471663.* super service@roslynandsunray.co.uk. www.roslynandsunray.co.uk. Owner: Mr & Mrs N V Waite. 6 Ferndown Close, Londonderry Farm, Bideford EX39 3QS. Small, site with panoramic views, 200yd from promenade. Pets welcome in some caravans by arrangement. Open Easter-October 31. **15H. ⊶ ⚲**

Surf Bay Holiday Park, Golf Links Road, Westward Ho!, Devon EX39 1HD. *01237 471833/0845 6011132.* surfbayholi daypark@surfbay.dircon.co.uk. www.surfbay.co.uk. Owner: Mr J E Taylor. Surf Bay Leisure, The Airfield, Winkleigh, Devon EX19 8DW. M5 to J27, A361 Barnstaple. At Barnstaple, take A39 Bideford/Bude road. Follow the road over the Torridge Bridge, at roundabout head for Westward Ho! At Westward Ho!, take second turning on right Beach Road. Own access to beach. Entertainment, golf course nearby. Extensive array of shops and facilities in Westward Ho! Cinema in Barnstaple (7m). Golf course 0.6m. Shopping centre about 1m. Open March-end-October. ✩✩✩✩ **BH&HPA. NCC. 62S. 34H. ⚲**

Winkleigh

Dolton Caravan Park, The Square, Dolton, Winkleigh, Devon EX19 8QF. *01805 804536.* Owner: David & Joan Cadman. Site is just off main square of Dolton village about 5m from Winkleigh. At rear of Royal Oak PH. Open mid March-mid November. **25T. MC. ⊶ ⊕ ⚲**

(1m). Four Seasons Village, Winkleigh, Devon EX19 8DP. *01837 83456.* Owners: Mr & Mrs Richard Hearne. On B3220. Swimming pool, club, laundry, takeaway. Children allowed in retirement homes. Open March 15-October 31. **5T. 80S. 12H. ⊶ ⚲ ⚲**

Woolacombe

Damage Barton Caravan Club Site, Mortehoe, Woolacombe, Devon EX34 7EJ. *01271 870502.* info@damagebarton.co.uk. www.damagebarton.co.uk. Members only. This site is set on an historic working beef and sheep farm of 600 acres, run by the Lethbridge family since 1962. Toilet blocks, laundry facilities and motorhome service point. Play area and dog walk on site. Golf, water sports and NCN cycle route nearby. Peaceful off-peak. Suitable for families. Good area for walking. Open March-November. **110T. 110MC. ⊶ ⊕ ⚲**

(1m). Easewell Farm Holiday Parc, Mortehoe, Woolacombe, Devon EX34 7EH. *01271 870343.* goodtimes@woolacombe.com. www.woolacombe.com. Owner: Mr R Lancaster. Woolacombe Bay Holiday Parcs, Woolacombe, Devon EX34 7EW. M5, J27 take A361. Turn left at Mullacott Cross to Mortehoe village. Easewell is SP on the right before the village. Indoor heated pool, bar, restaurant and take-away. Bus to beach. Use of facilities at three other nearby holiday parcs. Fishing nearby. Golf course on site. Doctor, shops 10 mins by car. PO within 10 mins walk. Open March-October. ✩✩✩✩ **BH&HPA. NCC. 133T. 30MC. 1H.** 🛪 🖭 &🗲

(1m.). Golden Coast Holiday Village, Woolacombe, Devon EX34 7HW. *01271 870343.* goodtimes@woolacombe.com. www.woolacombe.com. Owner: Woolacombe Bay Holiday Parcs. Station Road, Woolacombe, Devon EX34 7HW. M5 J27, A361 Barnstaple to Mullacott Cross. First exit to Woolacombe. Follow signs. Tennis, cabaret, children's club. Hair and beauty salon. Ten-pin bowling, fishing, golf course nearby. Bus to beach. 5 heated indoor and outdoor pools, restaurant and take-away, bar, creche (OFSTED approved), shop, cinema, sauna, solarium, amusements. Open February-January. ✩✩✩✩ **BH&HPA. NCC. 91T. MC. 80H.** 🖭 🗲

(1m). Little Roadway Farm Camping Park, Woolacombe, Devon EX34 7HL. *01271 870313.* Owner: Steve & Vanessa Malin. J27 off the M5, on to the A361, Barnstaple road, towards Ilfracombe. Mullacott Cross roundabout left towards Woolacombe B3343, first L B3231 towards Georgeham, 2m on left, turn left then right for camping park. Open March-November. **200T. MC.** 🛪 🖭 🗲

(1m). North Morte Farm Caravan Park, North Morte Road, Mortehoe, Woolacombe, Devon EX34 7EG. *01271 870381.* info@northmortefarm.co.uk. www.northmortefarm.co.uk. Owner: Mr R C Easterbrook. Off B3343. In Mortehoe village turn off at PO on to North Morte Road, park is 500yd on L. Quiet, family park in countryside. Showers. Laundry room. Play area. Payphone. Sea 500yd. Golf course, shop 0.5m. Open April 1-end September. ✩✩✩✩ **BH&HPA. 25T. MC. 73S. 23H.** 🛪 🖭 &🗲

(1m). Twitchen Parc, Mortehoe, Woolacombe, Devon EX34 7ES. *01271 870343.* goodtimes@woolacombe.com. www.woolacombe.com. Owner: Woolacombe Bay Holiday Parcs. Station Road, Woolacombe, Devon EX34 7HW. M5, J27, A361 from Barnstaple left, on B3343 1.75m. Keep R, SP Mortehoe for 1.5m. Park on L. Licensed club. Entertainment. Indoor and outdoor pool. Games room. Shop. Laundrette. Adventure playground. Children's club. Bus to Beach. Sauna, sunshower, bar, restaurant and takeaway, fishing, golf course. Open March-October. ✩✩✩✩ **BH&HPA. NCC. 334T. MC. 232H.** 🛪 🖭 🗲

(1.5m). Warcombe Farm Camping Park, Station Road, Mortehoe, Woolacombe, Devon EX34 7EJ. *01271 870690.* info@warcombefarm.co.uk. www.warcombefarm.co.uk. Owners: Martin & Christine Grafton. Turn right off the B3343 towards Mortehoe, park is on the right-hand side in less than 1m. Sea views from park. Play area. Fishing lake. Restaurant/food takeaway. Open March 15-October 31. ✩✩✩✩ **BH&HPA. 25T. 75MC.** 🛪 🖭 &🗲

(2m). **Willingcott Caravan Club Site, Woolacombe, Devon EX34 7HN.** *01271 870554.* www.caravanclub. co.uk. Owner: The Caravan Club. East Grinstead House, London Road, East Grinstead, West Sussex RH19 1UA. See website for standard directions to site. Caravan Club members only. Spacious site with views over Lundy and only 2m from best sandy beach in the county. Toilet block with privacy cubicles and laundry facilities. Some hardstandings, motorhome service point, veg prep area, Calor Gas and Campingaz, dog walk nearby. Peaceful off-peak. NCN cycle route in 5m. Boules pitch. Play equipment. Fishing, golf and water sports nearby. Suitable for families. Open March-October. **NCC. 165T. MC. ⚓ 🏠 ⚐ ♿**

(0.75m). **Woolacombe Bay Holiday Village, Sandy Lane, Woolacombe, Devon EX34 7AH.** *01271 870343.* good times@woolacombe.com. www.woolacombe.com. Owner: Woolacombe Bay Holiday Parcs. Station Road, Woolacombe, Devon EX34 7HW. M5 J27, A361 from Barnstaple, then first exit at Mullacott Cross, R turn to Mortehoe. Indoor and outdoor pools, Romano health spa, tennis, golf, free cabaret and children'sclub. Bus between sites and beach. Shop, restaurant and take away, bar, solarium. Open March-October. ☆☆☆☆ **BH&HPA. NCC. T. MC. 233H. 🏠 ⚐ 🐾**

Woolacombe Sands Holiday Park, Beach Road, Woolacombe, Devon EX34 7AF. *01271 870569.* lifesabeach@woolacombe.sands.co.uk. www.woola combe-sands.co.uk. Owner: Richards Holidays. Set in countryside overlooking Woolacombe's sandy beach. Facilities include indoor heated pool, club, entertainment. Laundrette. Showers. Indoor heated pool. Children's club May-Sept. Open April-October. ☆☆☆ **BH&HPA. 120T. MC. 73S. 60H. 🏠 ⚐ 🐾 ♿**

Yelverton

Magpie Leisure Park, Dartmoor Country Holidays, Yelverton, Devon PL20 7RY. *01822 852651.* Owner: Mr P G Bidder. A386 from Plymouth to Tavistock. R after Horrabridge. Tranquil small park within easy access of local amenities. Borders Dartmoor National Park. Children's play area. Dogs to be kept on leads. Sailing, fishing, golf, horse riding nearby. **BH&HPA. 135**

SOMERSET

Brean

Golden Sands Caravan Park, South Road, Brean, Somerset TA8 2RF. *01278 751322.* Owner: Mr & Mrs J Rowley. From M5 J22 follow signs for Berrow and Brean. 200yd from Pontins, Leisure centre, shops. Open March-November. **BH&HPA. 22S. 🏠**

(5m). **Warren Farm Holiday Centre (Isis Park), Brean Sands, Brean, Somerset TA8 2RP.** *01278 751227.* enquiries@warren-farm.co.uk. www.warren-farm.co.uk. Owner: HG & J Harris. Leave M5, J22 and follow B3140 through Burnham-on-sea to Berrow and Brean. Site is 1.5m past Brean Leisure Park. Flat, grassy park within 100yd of 5m of sandy beach. Family park. Beachcomber licensed club, indoor play facilities. Dogs not allowed in hire caravans. Riding, swimming, golf nearby. Open April-end October. ☆☆☆☆ **BH&HPA. NCC. 400T. 100MC. 250S. 11H. 🏠 ⚐ ♿ 🐾**

Yellow Sands, Coast Road, Brean, Somerset TA8 2RH. *01278 751349.* icj@breanbeach.co.uk. www.breanbeach.co.uk. Owner: Mr & Mrs I C James. Open March 1-December 31. ☆☆☆☆ **BH&HPA. 36S. 6H. 🏠 ♿**

Bridgwater

(6m). **Mill Farm Caravan & Camping Park, Fiddington, Bridgwater, Somerset TA5 1JQ.** *01278 732286.* www.mill-farm-uk.com. Owner: Mr M J Evans. M5 J23 or 24 to Bridgwater, take A39 (Minehead direction) for 6m. Turn right to Fiddington, follow caravan and camping signs. Sheltered site. Three heated swimming pools, riding centre, canoes and boating on shallow lake. ☆☆☆☆ **BH&HPA. 125T. 25MC. ✿ 🏠 ⚐ ♿ 🐾**

(3m). **The Fairways International Caravan & Camping Park, Bath Road, Bawdrip, Bridgwater, Somerset TA7 8PP.** *01278 685569.* fairwaysint@btinternet.com. www.fairwaysint.btinter net.co.uk. Owner: Mr & Mrs Walker. Situated at the J of A39 with B3141 (from which access is gained); 1.5m off J23 of M5 in Glastonbury direction. Showers and shaver and dryer points, laundrette, chemical toilet emptying point. Sports facilities and sandy beaches nearby. Fishing 0.5m, boating 2 miles. Open March 1-November 16. ☆☆☆☆ **BH&HPA. 200T. MC. 🏠 ⚐ ♿ 🐾**

Burnham-on-Sea

(3.5m). **Beachside Holiday Park, Coast Road, Brean Sands, Burnham-on-Sea, Somerset TA8 2QZ.** *01278 751346/08000 190322.* enquiries@beachsideholidaypark.co.uk. www.beach sideholidaypark.co.uk. Owner: Mr & Mrs Cloe James, Mr Tony James. M5, J22, W to Burnham-on-Sea, then north to Brean. Quiet park with private sand dunes and beach. Shop within 500yd. Open March-November. ☆☆☆☆ **BH&HPA. 115S. 40H. 🏠 ♿ ⊘**

(3m). **Brean Beach Holiday Park, Coast Road, Brean, Burnham-on-Sea, Somerset TA8 2RH.** *01278 751349.* icj@breanbeach.co.uk. www.breanbeach.co.uk. Owner: Mr & Mrs I James. Leave M5 J22, follow signs to Brean (3m). Park on seaside opposite Pontins. Quiet park with children's play area. Parking by homes. Open March/April-October. ☆☆☆ **BH&HPA. 18S. 12H. 🏠 ♿ 🐾**

(5m). **Brean Down Inn, Brean, Burnham-on-Sea, Somerset TA8 2RR.** *01278 751420.* Owner: Clarkes. Open March 1-October 31. **BH&HPA. 45S. 🏠**

(4m). **Brightholme Holiday Park, Coast Road, Brean, Burnham-on-Sea, Somerset TA8 2QY.** *01278 751327.* brightholme@burnham-on-sea.co.uk. www.burnham-on-sea. co.uk/brightholme. Owner: Mr & Mrs M Berryman. Leave M5 at J22. Follow signs to Burnham-on-Sea, Berrow, Brean Down. Park is on L 500yd past Berrow beach entrance. Licensed bar with restaurant. Play area. Laundry. Direct access to sandy beach. Golf course across road. 5-10mins to shops. Doctors in Burnham-on-Sea. Open March 1-mid November. ☆☆☆ **BH&HPA. 78S. 15H. 🏠**

(1m). **Burnham Touring Park, Stoddens Road, Burnham-on-Sea, Somerset TA8 2NZ.** *01278 788355.* bobabelcain@btopen world.com. www.basc.co.uk. Owner: Burnham Association of Sports Clubs. M5, J22, head to Burnham-on-sea. Turn right at Tesco roundabout, travel 0.5m to sharp left bend. Site is 100yd on right, after bend. 30-acre, quiet, sheltered sports ground close to beach and shops. Suitable for self-sufficient caravanners. Facilites include use of clubhouse facilities. Skittles and pool in clubhouse. Booking advisable. Open March 1-December 31. **BH&HPA. NCC. 20T. MC. 🏠 ⚐**

(0.25m). **Burnham-On-Sea Holiday Village, Marine Drive, Burnham-on-Sea, Somerset TA8 1LA.** *01278 795651*. oewebmaster@bourne-leisure.co.uk. www.burhamholidayvillage.com. Owner: Bourne Leisure Ltd. One Park Lane, Hemel Hempstead, Herts HP2 4YL. M5, J22. L at roundabout onto A38 to Highbridge. Continue over mini-roundabout and railway bridge. Next R, B3139 to Burnham. Turn L after Total garage on to Marine Drive, park is 400yd on L. Located on esplanade facing the sea and adjoining town centre. 95 acres of level parkland with indoor and outdoor swimming pools. 2 clubs with live entertainment. Mini market. Bakery. Laundrette. Childrens play area. Rose Award and David Bellamy Gold Conservation Award. Open March-November. ☆☆☆☆ BH&HPA. NCC. 75T. MC. 642S. 268H. ⊕ & ⚑

(4.5m). **Central Caravan Park, Diamond Farm, Brean, Burnham-on-Sea, Somerset**. *01278 751263*. trevor@diamondfarm42.freeserve.co.uk. www.diamondfarm.co.uk. Owner: Mr M R Hicks Ltd. Diamond Farm, Brean, Burnham-on-Sea, Somerset. On coast road Burnham to Brean. Off B3140. Near junction Lympsham/Weston-super-Mare. Close Brean shops. 0.5m golf course. Own access to beach. PH and shops 200yd. Golf course 0.5m. Open February-January. **18S.** ⚑

(4.5m). **Diamond Farm Caravan Park, Weston Road, Brean, Burnham-on-Sea, Somerset TA8 2RL.** *01278 751263*. trevor@diamonfarm42.freeserve.co.uk. www.diamondfarm.co.uk. Owner: Mr M H R Hicks Ltd. Off the A370 Weston-super-Mare to Brean. From Burnham to Brean coast road take junction to Weston and Lympsham, Diamond Farm is 800yd from junction. Working farm. Laundry facilities. 0.5m to golf, beach. Open March-October. ☆☆☆ **108S.** ⚑ ⊕ & ⚑

(3m). **Happy Days Caravan Park, Church Road, Brean, Burnham-on-Sea, Somerset TA8 2SF.** *01278 751392*. Owner: Mr & Mrs P Richman. Leave M5 J22, take B3140 and follow signs at Burnham-on-Sea towards Brean Down, past Plimley garage on left, and park is 200yd on the right. Open March 1-October 31. **BH&HPA. 31S.**

(3m). **Holiday Resort Unity, Coast Road, Brean Sands, Burnham-on-Sea, Somerset TA8 2RB.** *01278 751235*. admin@hru.co.uk. www.hru.co.uk. Off M5 J22. Follow signs for Brean Leisure Park for 4.5m. Choice of bars with entertainment, choice of food venues. Pool with slides, golf, riding, fishing, children's club. Fun park with 50 rides and attractions, cinema, bingo, play area. Weston-super-Mare 8m. Open February-November. ☆☆☆ **BH&HPA. 850T. MC. 580S. 450H.** ⚑ ⚑ & ⚑

(1m). **Home Farm Holiday Park & Country Club, Edithmead, Burnham-on-Sea, Somerset TA9 4HD.** *01278 788888*. office@homefarmholidaypark.com. www.homefarmholidaypark.com. Owner: Mr G Atkinson. M5 J22, to Burnham-on-Sea, Edithmead. Level. Heated showers and bathrooms. Laundrette. Gift shop. Adventure playground. Fishing. Licensed bars, entertainment. Pool. Caravan servicing and sales. Open February-January. ☆☆☆☆☆ **BH&HPA. 650T. 50MC. 180S.** ⚙ ⚑ ⊕ & ⚑ ✎

(3.5m). **Hurn Lane Caravan Club Site, Berrow, Burnham-on-Sea, Somerset TA8 2QT.** *01278 751412*. www.caravanclub.co.uk. Owner: The Caravan Club. East Grinstead House, East Grinstead, West Sussex RH19 1UA. See website for directions. Caravan Club members only. Family holiday location only 15 mins walk from safe, sandy beach. Play area. No arrivals before 12noon. Toilet blocks. Privacy cubicles. Laundry facilities. Veg prep. Motorhome service point. Gas supplies. Play equipment. Late-night arrivals' area. Golf, fishing and water sports nearby. Open March-November. **NCC. 135T. MC.** ⚑ ⊕ &

(5m). Kinnoull & Pinmoor Caravan Site, South Road, Brean, Burnham-on-Sea, Somerset TA8 2RD. *01278 751385.* Owner: Mrs J M Price. Harvee, Church Road, Brean, Somerset TA8 2SF. M5 junction 22 Edithmead, direct to Burnham-on-Sea to Brean. Direct access to beach. Shops, PHs, leisure centre and coach tours within 150yd of site entrance. Open Easter-October. **BH&HPA. 54S. 15H.**

(0.5m). Lakeside Holiday Park, Westfield Road, Burnham-on-Sea, Somerset. *01278 792222.* www.lakesideholidays. co.uk. Owner: Wilson Leisure Ltd. Exit 22 M5. Follow signs for Burnham and at roundabout by Esso garage, for Berrow. Turn R into Westfield Road, opposite swimming pool. Short, level walk to beach and town. 3-acre private fishing lake. Club complex provides live family entertainment, poolside conservatory, bistro/takeaway. Heated swimming pool and walled sun terrace, children's playground, laundrette, bicycle hire. Open Easter-end of October. ✩✩✩✩ **189S. 82H.** ⚅ ⌀

(4m). Lazy Days Holiday Park, Brean Sands, South Road, Burnham-on-Sea, Somerset TA8 2RD. *01278 751283.* Owner: Kear, Winter, Wheadon. Off B3140 Burnham to Brean. Licensed club and bar. Garden with children's play area. Open March-October. **BH&HPA. 15H.** ➤

(4m). Merrybee Caravan Site, Coast Road, Brean, Burnham-on-Sea, Somerset TA8 2RL. *01278 751263.* Owner: Mr R Hicks Ltd. Diamond Farm, Brean, Burnham-on-Sea, Somerset. Into Brean along coast road. Site is set back next to Pontins travelling N. Within walking distance of all amenities in Brean, including beach. 2m from championship golf course. 0.5mto golf course, beach. Open March-October. **100S.** ➤

Newcombe Caravan Park, Westfield Road, Burnham-on-Sea, Somerset TA8 2QX. *01278 782154.* Owner: Davies. Off A38, on B3139. Open March-October. **85S.**

(6m). Northam Farm Caravan Park, South Road, Brean, Burnham-on-Sea, Somerset TA8 2SE. *01278 751244.* enquiries@northamfarm.co.uk. www.northamfarm.co.uk. Owner: Mr M H Scott. Easy access from M5, J22. Follow signs to Brean, site is 0.5m past leisure park on right-hand side. Fishing lake on park. Open March-October. ✩✩✩✩ **BH&HPA. NCC. 350T. 350MC.** ➤ 🔌 ⚅ 🔋

(0.5m). Retreat Caravan Park, Berrow Road, Burnham-on-Sea, Somerset TA8 2ES. *0700 7387328.* whc@retreat.uk.com. www.retreat.uk.com. Owner: Retreat Estates (B.O.S) Ltd. P O Box 8, Glastonbury, Somerset BA6 9YF. J22, M5, take B3140 to Burnham-on-Sea. Follow road towards Berrow for 0.5m. Turn L into the park just after Brightstowe Road. Secluded park just before petrol station, with direct access to beach. Caravan holiday-homes only to purchase for the specific use by owners and their families and friends. No commercial letting. Next door to golf course. Tennis courts, indoor swimming pool, shopping all within 0.5m. Open late February-early January. ✩✩✩✩✩ **BH&HPA. NCC. 200S.** ➤ ⚅

(3m). Sandy Glade Holiday Park, Coast Road, Berrow, Burnham-on-Sea, Somerset TA8 2QX. *01278 751271.* info@sandyglade.co.uk. www.sandyglade.co.uk. Owners: John Fowler Holidays. Off M5 J22. Follow signs for Brean and Berrow. Cabaret, clubhouse, indoor pool. Shop and takeaway. Children's club. Adventure playground. Laundry. Opposite the beach. Chalets and villas for hire. Open March-November. ✩✩✩✩ **BH&HPA. 300S. 100H.** ➤ ⚅ 🔋

(4m). Skoorblands, Brean, Burnham-on-Sea, Somerset TA8 2RF. *01278 751513.* skoorbland@aol.com. Owners: Mr & Mrs W W Godwin. Off M5. Caravans for sale. Private use only, no letting. Open April 1-october 31. **BH&HPA. 43S.** ➤

(4m). Southfield Farm Caravan Park, Brean, Burnham-on-Sea, Somerset TA8 2RL. *01278 751233.* office.southfield@ btinternet.com. Owner: A G Hicks Ltd. Off B3139, J22, M5, 4m N of Burnham. Golf course and entertainments nearby. Own access to beach. Open May-September. **BH&HPA. 200T. MC. 296S.** ➤ 🔌 ⚅ 🔋

(3m). Summerhaze Holidays, South Road, Brean, Burnham-on-Sea, Somerset TA8 2RD. *01453 762074.* Owner: Chris & Jacqueline Grace. Off A38 Brean to Berrow. J22, M5. Small, quiet site with direct access to private beach. Shop and PO 200yd. Open March 1-November 1. **13S.** ➤

(4m). Sunningcrest Caravan Park, Coast Road, Brean, Burnham-on-Sea, Somerset TA8 2RA. *01278 751221/751470.* Owner: Mr & Mrs C Lodge & Mrs & Mrs J Lodge. M5, J22 follow signs to Brean for about 5m, pass Berrow Beach entrance, park about 400yd on seaward side. On site: tennis court, sauna, children's play area, laundrette, reception, 24hr payphone. Private access to sandy beach. Within 2m: choice of PHs, eateries, fun-fair, golf course, fishing lake, horse riding, swimming pool, 10-pin bowling, garden centre and supermarket. Open March-October. **BH&HPA. 132S. 2H.** ➤

The Burrows Holiday Park, Coast Road, Berrow, Burnham-on-Sea, Somerset TA8 2RH. *01278 751349.* icj@brean beach.co.uk. www.breanbeach.co.uk. Owner: Mr & Mrs Ian James. Leave M5, J22, to Brean (3m) and Berrow. The park is

situated at entrance to Brean, one of 3 parks owned by Brean Beach Holiday Parks.Open March 1-October 31. **BH&HPA. 33S. 10H.** 🛲

(4m). The Warren Caravan Park, South Road, Brean, Burnham-on-Sea, Somerset TA8 2RF. *01278 751277/07885 575160 (mobile).* Owner: Mr A E Kerby. On seaward side, coast road Burnham to Brean. Next to 7m beach on natural sand dunes. Some trees etc. Adjoining shop. Fishing, golf nearby. No subletting. Open first Friday April-third Sunday October. **BH&HPA. 77S.** 🛲 &

(4m). Three Acres Caravan Park, Brean, Burnham-on-Sea, Somerset TA8 2RF. *01278 751313.* Owner: R J & J A Cottey. M5, J22, follow sign to Burnham on Sea, then sign to Brean; site is past Pontins on left. Access to beach. Licensed club with entertainment. Laundrette. Dogs by arrangement. Golf, shops nearby. Cinema 2m. Open March 31-October 31. **BH&HPA. 70S. 25H.** 🛲

(5m). Westward Rise Holiday Park, South Road, Brean, Burnham-on-Sea, Somerset TA8 2RD. *01278 751310.* westwardrise@breansands.freeserve.co.uk. www.breansands.freeserve.co.uk. Owner: R S & M I Tropman & R W & D F Tropman. Off A38 Brean to Berrow, J22, M5. Chalets with central heating for hire all year. Open February 10-January 10. **BH&HPA. 14S.** 🛲

Chard

(1.5m). Alpine Grove Touring Park, Alpine Grove, Forton, Chard, Somerset TA20 4HD. *01460 63479.* stay@alpinegrovetouring.com. www.alpinegrovetouring.co.uk. Owner: Jean & John Valentine. 2m from Cricket St Thomas, 10m from coast, follow signs to Forton from A358 on to B3162 and A30 on to B3167. 7.5-acre park of oaks and rhododendrons. Hard-standing area. Showers, laundry, swings, heated pool, trampoline, walking and cycling. Open April 1-October 1. ✰✰✰✰ **BH&HPA. 40T. 40MC.** 🛲 🔌 🛒

(4m). Five Acres Caravan Club Site, Beetham, Chard, Somerset TA20 3QA. *01460 234519.* www.caravanclub.co.uk. Owner: The Caravan Club. East Grinstead House, East Grinstead, West Sussex RH19 1UA. See website for standard directions to site. Rural site, peaceful off-peak site, slightly sloping. Non-members welcome. Advance bookings advised, bank holidays and July/August. Some hard-standings. Toilet blocks. Laundry facilities. Veg prep. Motorhome service point. Calor Gas and Campingaz. Suitable for families. NCN cycle path within 5m. Open March-October. ✰✰✰✰ **NCC. 74T. MC.** ✿ 🛲 🔌 &

(3m). South Somerset Holiday Park, The Turnpike, Chard, Somerset TA20 3EA. *01460 66036.* sshpturnpike@aol.com. Owner: R M Weeks. 3m W of Chard on A30 to Exeter. Facilities' block heated in cold weather. Children's play area. 4-acre dog walk area. All-weather pitches. Many local attractions. Open March 1-January 31. **110T. MC. 42S.** ✿ 🛲 🔌 &

Cheddar

(1m). Broadway House Caravan and Camping Park, Axbridge Road, Cheddar, Somerset BS27 3DB. *01934 742610.* enquiries@broadwayhouse.uk.com. www.broadwayhouse.uk.com. Owner: Mr & Mrs D R Moore. Exit 22 (M5) follow brown signs for Cheddar Gorge. On A371 midway between Cheddar and Axbridge. Heated pool. Licensed bar with family room. TV. Laundrette. Showers, bathrooms, playgrounds, archery, abseiling, caving canoeing etc. Crazy golf and skate board park. Open March-November. ✰✰✰✰ **BH&HPA. 400T. MC. 35H.** 🛲 🔌 & 🛒

(3m). Bucklegrove Caravan Park, Wells Road, Rodney Stoke, Cheddar, Somerset BS27 3UZ. *01749 870261.* info@bucklegrove.co.uk. www.bucklegrove.co.uk. Owner: Mr & Mrs D Clarke. On A371 midway between Wells and Cheddar. Landscaped, family-run park with very clean, modern facilities. Indoor heated pool. Spacious pitches with parking beside caravans. Open March-January. ✰✰✰✰ **BH&HPA. 100T. 5MC. 35S. 7H.** 🔌 & 🛒

Cheddar Bridge Touring Park, Draycott Road, Cheddar, Somerset BS27 3RJ. *01934 743048.* enquiries@cheddarbridge.co.uk. www.cheddarbridge.co.uk. M5, J22. On A371 through Cheddar Village. Next to football club on R. Riverside setting. Adults only. Walking distance to shops, village and gorge. Fishing, PO, doctors, very quiet. Views of Mendips. Open March-November. ✰✰✰✰ **BH&HPA. 45T. 3H.** 🛲 🔌 & 🛒

Cheddar Caravan Club Site, Gas House Lane, Draycott Road, Cheddar, Somerset BS27 3RL. *01934 740207.* www.caravanclub.co.uk. Owner: The Caravan Club. East Grinstead House, East Grinstead, West Sussex RH19 1UA. See website for standard directions to site. Caravan Club members only. This site is situated on the edge of Cheddar village and offers views of the Mendips and surrounding countryside. Toilet blocks and laundry facilities. Fishing, golf and water sports nearby. Good area for walking. Peaceful off-peak. Open March-October. **NCC. T. MC.** 🛲 🔌 &

Froglands Farm Caravan & Camping Park, Cheddar, Somerset BS27 3RH. *01934 742058/743304.* Owner: J Moore. On A371 Weston-super-Mare to Wells. Manager: Mrs J Moore. Situated in Area of Outstanding Natural Beauty, close to shops and Cheddar Gorge. Open Easter-October. **40T. 20MC.** 🛲 🔌 🛒

(3m). Netherdale Caravan & Camping Park, Bridgwater Road (A38), Sidcot, Winscombe, Cheddar, Somerset BS25 1NH. *01934 843007.* camping@netherdale.net. www.netherdale.net. Owner: Mr VJ Mortimer. Easy to find on A38, midway between Bristol and Bridgwater. Showers, washbasins, shaver points. Play area. Sports centre, riding and fishing 3m.

Walking area. Footpath from site. Hale Coombe and Mendip Hills adjoining. Dry ski slope nearby. Golf course 4m, cinema 8m. Restaurant adjacent. Dogs allowed only on leads. Shopping centre 4 mins by car (free parking). Also filling station with shop 500yd from site. Sports centre, activity centre, dry ski slope, golf and fishing within 4m radius. Open March 1-October 31. **30T. MC. 37S.** 🐕 ⊡

(2m). Rodney Stoke Caravan Site, Rodney Stoke Inn, Cheddar, Somerset BS27 3XB. *01749 870209.* Owner: Neil Sinclair. Located on the A371 midway between Cheddar and Wells. Suitable base for sightseeing. Restaurant, Bar snacks. Children welcome. **20T. MC.** ❖ 🐕 ⊡

Clevedon

(3m). Coast Caravan Park, Down Road, Walton Bay, Clevedon, Somerset BS21 7AT. *01275 872818.* coastcaravanpark@tiscali.co.uk. www.ukparks.co.uk/coast. Owners: Mrs S Ross, Maria & Andy Norrie. About 3m from the M5, J20. Situated between Clevedon and Portishead on the coast road. Peaceful and picturesque holiday park surrounded by countryside and overlooking the Bristol Channel. Golf, shopping centre, cinema within 2-3m. Open March-October. **BH&HPA. 78S.** 🐕

(1m). Colehouse Caravan Park, Colehouse Farm, Clevedon, Somerset BS21 6TQ. *01275 872680.* Owner: Colin Alexander. Level site on a working dairy farm, rally field available. Hard- standings for tourers and campervans.Open March 1-January 31. **BH&HPA. 51T. 20MC. 38S. 8H.** 🐕 ⊡

(3m). Two Acres Caravan Park, Walton Bay, Clevedon, Somerset BS21 7AY. *01275 873634.* Owner: Mr P Brown. Open March-October. **3S. 11H.**

(1m). Warren's Holiday Village, Colehouse Lane, Clevedon, Somerset BS21 6TQ. *01275 871666.* www.warrensholidayvillage.co.uk. Owner: Richard Warren. Level ground with private fishing. Also 45 chalets for hire. Licensed clubhouse. **BH&HPA. 150T. MC. 47S. 16H.** ❖ 🐕 ⊡ & ⌀

Dulverton

(5m). Exe Valley Caravan Site, Bridgetown, Dulverton, Somerset TA22 9JR. *01643 851432.* paul@paulmatt.fsnet.co.uk. www.exevalleycamping.co.uk. Owner: Christine & Paul Matthews. The Mill House, Bridgetown, Dulverton, Somerset TA22 9JR. On the A396. From Tiverton to Minehead. Laundry facilities. Showers. Hot water. Shaver points. Gas supplies. Free fly fishing. Adults only. Open March 1-October 31. **30T. 30MC.** 🐕 ⊡ & ⌫

Exmoor House Caravan Club Site, Dulverton, Somerset TA22 9HL. *01398 323268.* www.caravanclub.co.uk. Owner: The Caravan Club. East Grinstead House, East Grinstead, West Sussex RH19 1UA. See website for standard directions to site. Suitable base for exploring Exmoor. Pretty site overlooked by wooded hillsides and a few hundred yards from village. Shops 200yd. Dog walk. Gas and Gaz. MV waste. Non-members welcome. Advance booking necessary. Do not arrive before 1pm. Some hard-standings. Toilet blocks. Privacy cubicles. Laundry facilities. Veg prep. Fishing, NCN cycle path within 5m. Peaceful off-peak. Open March-January. ✰✰✰✰ **64T. MC.** 🐕 ⊡ &

(3m). Lakeside Caravan Club Site, Higher Grants. Exebridge, Dulverton, Somerset TA22 9BE. *01398 324068.* www.caravanclub.co.uk. Owner: The Caravan Club, East Grinstead House, East Grinstead, West Sussex RH19 1UA. See website for standard directions to site. Situated in a quiet village with attractive rural views towards Exmoor. Toilet blocks and laundry facilities, gas supplies. Good area for walking; dog walk on site. Fishing and NCN cycle route within 5m. Peaceful site off-peak. Non-members welcome. Open March-October. ✰✰✰✰ **BH&HPA. 50T. MC.** 🐕 ⊡

Glastonbury

(0.5m). Isle of Avalon Touring Caravan Park, Godney Road, Glastonbury, Somerset BA6 9AF. *01458 833618.* Owner: Mr & Mrs M Webb. A39 west of Glastonbury. B3151, SP Godney. 500yd on the right. Flat, level, landscaped park, located in quiet setting within easy walking distance of Glastonbury. Rallies welcome. ✰✰✰✰✰ **BH&HPA. 70T. MC.** ❖ 🐕 ⊡ & ⌫

(3m). The Old Oaks Touring Park, Wick Farm, Wick, Glastonbury, Somerset BA6 8JS. *01458 831437.* info@theoldoaks.co.uk www.theoldoaks.co.uk. Owner: Mr & Mrs J White. Turn L off A361 Glastonbury to Shepton Mallet road. 2m from Glastonbury at Wick SP. Small, friendly park exclusively for adults. Set in unspoilt countryside with panoramic views, spacious pitches, coarse fishing. Open March 1-October 31. ✰✰✰✰✰ **BH&HPA. 80T. MC.** 🐕 ⊡ & ⌫

Highbridge

(2m). Edithmead Park Homes, Edithmead, Highbridge, Somerset TA9 4HE. *01278 783475.* info@edithmeadleisure.com. www.edithmeadleisure.com. Owner: West Country Parks. Situated 1.5m from Burnham-on-Sea and within easy reach of Wells and Taunton. Landscaped gardens. On site club house. Bus stop at main gate. Open February 10-January 10. **BH&HPA. 150T. 103S.** 🐕 ⊡ & ⌫ ⌀

Ilminster

(3m). Stewley Cross Caravan Site, Stewly Cross Filling Station, Ashill, Ilminster, Somerset TA19 9NP. *01823 480314.* Owner: Mr & Mrs T C Hirons. Off A358 between Taunton and Ilminster. Open April-October. **5T. MC.** 🐕 ⌫ ⌀

(2.5m). Thornleigh Caravan Park, Hanning Road, Horton, Ilminster, Somerset TA19 9QH. *01460 53450.* ken-shirt@supanet.com. www.thornleigh-cp.fsnet.co.uk. Owner: Mr & Mrs K G White. W of Ilminster take A358 SP Chard for 0.25m and turn R at Lamb Inn, site 0.75m on L. Flat, grassy, open field on edge of village with PO and PH nearby. 18m from coast, 6m Cricket St Thomas, Yeovilton Air Museum and National Trust properties nearby. Village location. Sauna. Suitable for rallies. Small village hall nearby. Open March-October. **20T. MC.** 🐕 ⊡ &

Langport

(1.5m). Bowdens Crest Caravan & Camping Park, Bowden's, Langport, Somerset TA10 0DD. *01458 250553.* bowcrest@btconnect.com. www.bowdenscrest.co.uk. Owner: Mrs May. Off A372 Bridgwater to Langport. Tranquil, level site. Licensed bar, laundry, washing-up sinks and showers. Shop and meals available. Children and pets welcome. Near fishing, walking, cycling and many local attractions. Fishing 1m, cycling routes 2m, golf 4m. ✰✰✰ **BH&HPA. 30T. MC. 30S. 12H.** ❖ 🐕 ⊡ & ⌫

PURCHASE A CARAVAN HOLIDAY HOME at Retreat Caravan Park, and you are choosing the ideal holiday setting for you and your family.

your own holiday retreat...

Take advantage of the splendid local amenities and easy access that makes the Retreat Caravan Park so popular - just $2\frac{1}{2}$ miles from the M5, junction 22.

Situated on the quiet Somerset coast, the park enjoys a superb location with direct access to a wide sandy beach; and pleasant beach walks to Burnham-on-Sea and Berrow.

Enjoy riding, swimming, water skiing, sailing, a round of golf or explore the beautiful countryside with its many attractions.

The Park is quiet and well cared for and is open every month of the year (except early January to late February). However caravan holiday homes may not be occupied for permanant residence.

For further information please contact
Roger, Rosemary or Debbie at:
Retreat Estates (Burnham-on-Sea) Ltd,
PO Box 8, Glastonbury, Somerset, BA6 9YF
Telephone: **0700 RETREAT (0700 7387328)**
Fax: **0700 4 FAX RET (0700 4329738)**
Email: **csg@retreat.uk.com**
Website: **www.retreat.uk.com**

Retreat Caravan Parks
Burnham-on-Sea

This could be your first step towards a lifetime of enjoyable holidays and weekend breaks for you and your family!

New & pre-owned caravan holiday homes for sale

(2m). **Thorney Lakes Caravan & Camping Park, Thorney Lakes, Muchelney, Langport, Somerset TA10 0DW.** *01458 250811*. enquiries@thorneylakes.co.uk. www.thorneylakes.co.uk. Owners: R & A England. A303, Podimore r'about, A372 to Langport. At Huish Episcopi church turn L for Muchelmy and then 100yd L again, SP Muchelmy and Crewkerne. 2m to Park. Fishing on site. Golf course nearby. 2m to Langport for shops and doctor. Open Easter-end of October. ☆☆☆ **BH&HPA. 36T. 36MC.** ⅋ 🌣 &

Martock

(1m). **Southfork Caravan Park, Parrett Works, Martock, Somerset TA12 6AE.** *01935 825661*. southforkcaravans@bt connect.com. www.ukparks.co.uk/southfork. Owner: Mr & Mrs M A Broadley. 8m NW of Yeovil. 2m N of A303. Small, peaceful, rural, level site near river Parrett. Heated amenities' block. Play area. AA 4 pennants. Numerous places of interest nearby for all age groups. Approved touring caravan workshop for repairs/servicing; accessories and spares. Fishing. Village 1m. ☆☆☆ **BH&HPA. NCC. 30T. MC. 3S. 3H.** 🌣 ⅋ 🌣 💄 🌣

Minehead

(5m). **Burrowhayes Farm, Caravan & Camping Site, West Luccombe, Porlock, Minehead, Somerset TA24 8HT.** *01643 862463*. info@burrowhayes.co.uk. www.bur rowhayes.co.uk. Owner: Mr & Mrs J C Dascombe. 5m W of Minehead turn L off A39 to West Luccombe site 0.25m on R. Between Minehead and Porlock on National Trust Estate of Holnicote in Exmoor National Park. Riding stables on site, popular with walkers and riders. Phone, laundrette, free showers, well stocked shop. Cinema, golf, swimming pool, supermarket all 5m. Open March-October. ☆☆☆☆ **BH&HPA. 54T. MC. 20H.** ⅋ 🌣 💄

(2m). **Camping & Caravanning Club Site - Minehead, Hill Road, North Hill, Minehead, Somerset TA24 5LB.** *01643 704138/0870 243 3331*. www.campingandcaravan ningclub.co.uk. Owner: Camping & Caravanning Club. Greenfields House, Westwood Way, Coventry CV4 8JH. From A39 towards town centre. At T-junction R on to dual carriageway. L into Blenheim Rd, then L into Martlett Road, L around War Memorial into St Michael's Rd. Past church into Moor Road, then on to Hill Rd, site on R. 3.75-acre site. Non-members welcome. No towed caravans. On top of hill giving spectacular views. Coastal path 0.5m from site. Suitable base for exploring Exmoor. Special deals for families and backpackers. Open May-September. ☆☆☆ **60MC.** ⅋ 🌣

(16m). **Halse Farm Caravan & Camping Park, Winsford, Minehead, Somerset TA24 7JL.** *01643 851259*. brown@halse farm.co.uk. www.halsefarm.co.uk. Owner: Mrs Laetitia Brown. SP from the A396. In Winsford turn left in front of thatched PH. 1m on, entrance on left immediately after cattle grid. 5m from Dulverton. In Exmoor National Park, adjacent to moor on working farm. Peaceful. Spectacular views. Laundrette. Shop, PH, garage within 1m. Open March 21-October 31. ☆☆☆ **BH&HPA. 22T. MC.** ⅋ 🌣 &

(4m). **Hoburne Blue Anchor, Blue Anchor Bay, Minehead, Somerset TA24 6JT.** *01643 821360*. enquiries@hoburne.com. www.hoburne.com. Owner: Hoburne Ltd. 261 Lymington Road, Highcliffe, Christchurch, Dorset BH23 5EE. From A39 take B3191 for 1.75m. Park is on R. Indoor leisure pool. Self-service shop. Laundrette. Adventure playground and crazy golf. Rose Award. Open March-October. ☆☆☆☆ **BH&HPA. NCC. 103T. 103MC. 250S. 40H.** 🌣 💄

(1m). **Minehead & Exmoor Caravan & Camping Park, Porlock Road, Minehead, Somerset TA24 8SN.** *01643 703074*. Owner: Mrs P M Jones. Barberton, Middlecombe, Minehead, Somerset TA24 8SW. Off A39 W of Minehead centre, situated in open country. Area of Outstanding Natural Beauty, on edge of Exmoor. Calor Gas. Telephone. Open March-third week October. **25T. 25MC.** ⅋ 🌣 🌣 &

Minehead Caravan Club Site, Hopcott Road, Minehead, Somerset TA24 6DJ. *01643 704345*. www.caravanclub.co.uk. Owner: The Caravan Club. East Grinstead House, East Grinstead, West Sussex RH19 1UA. See website for standard directions to site. Caravan Club members only. Small, hillside site well screened from the road and with lviews over hills behind nearby Minehead. Beach 0.5m. Bathing off the nearby coast can be dangerous. Some hard-standings. Toilet blocks. Laundry facilities. Veg prep. Motorhome service point. Calor Gas and Campingaz. No late-night arrivals' area. Golf nearby. Good area for walking. Suitable for families. Open February-October. **NCC. 51T. MC.** ⅋ 🌣 &

(6m). **Porlock Caravan Park, Highbank, Porlock, Minehead, Somerset TA24 8ND.** *01643 862269*. info@porlockcaravan park.co.uk. www.porlockcaravanpark.co.uk. Owner: Tony & Denise Hardick. A39 Minehead to Porlock, in Porlock turn right B3225 Weir, park SP. Quiet, family-run park in Vale of Porlock. Excellent for touring, walking, riding centre for Exmoor. 2 mins to village, beach close by. Children allowed. David Bellamy Gold Conservation Award. Open March 20-October 31. ☆☆☆☆ **BH&HPA. 40T. MC. 56S. 9H.** ⅋ 🌣

(5m). **The Beeches Holiday Park, Blue Anchor Bay, Minehead, Somerset TA24 6JW.** *01984 640391.* info@beeches-park.co.uk. www.beeches-park.co.uk. Owner: Mr G Daniel. On the B3191, Minehead to Watchet road. Off the A39. Panoramic views overlooking Blue Anchor Bay. Situated at the gateway to Exmoor, Quantocks and Brendon Hills. Fishing, pony-trekking, walking and golf nearby. Heated swimming pool. Playground. Laundrette, convenience store. Rose Award. Open February 1-December 31. ☆☆☆☆ **BH&HPA. 150S. 20H.** ⚊ ⚊ ⚊

Priddy Wells

(0.5m). **Camping & Caravanning Club Site - Cheddar, Mendip Heights, Townsend, Priddy Wells, Somerset BA5 3BP.** *01749 870241.* www.campingandcaravanning club.co.uk. Owners: The Camping and Caravanning Club. Greenfields House, Westwood Way, Coventry CV4 8JH. A39 N from Wells, turn L B3135 toward Cheddar for 4.5m, turn L for 200yd. Peaceful, rural park in an Area of Outstanding Natural Beauty. Close to Cheddar, Wookey Hole and Wells. Cycling, walking, abseiling and caving. David Bellamy Gold Conservation Award. Tents, caravans and motorhomes accepted. Non-members welcome. Special deals available for families and backpackers. Open March 3-November 15. ☆☆☆☆ **90T. 90MC. 2S. 2H.** ⚊ ⚊ ⚊

Radstock

Old Down Touring Park, Emborough, Radstock, Somerset BA3 4SA. *01761 232355.* olddown@talk21.com. www.old downtouringpark.co.uk. Owner: Mr & Mrs L Bleasdale. From Shepton Mallet 6m N on A37 turn right on B3139, entrance on right opposite the Old Down Inn. 6m NE of Wells via the B3139. Convenient for Bath, Wells and Mendips and Bath and West Showground. Fishing nearby, 2 golf courses and swimming pool close to site. In the village there is a PH, filling station and Co-op supermarket. Open March-November. **BH&HPA. 30T. MC.** ⚊ ⚊ ⚊

Shepton Mallet

(1m). **Manleaze Caravan Park, Cannards Grave, Shepton Mallet, Somerset BA4 4LY.** *01749 342404.* Owner: Mr A A Manly. Hope Cottage, 4 Cannards Grave, Shepton Mallet, Somerset BA4 4LY. Between the A37 and A371, entrance on the A371, S of Shepton Mallet. **25T. 25MC. 3H.** ⚊ ⚊ ⚊

Stoke St Michael

(0.5m). **Phippens Farm, Stoke St Michael, Somerset BA3 5JH.** *01749 840395.* jenniferandstan@hotmail.com. Owner: Mr & Mrs Francis. Stoke St Michael to Oakhill Road. Shepton Mallet 4.5m, Bath 13m. Reasonably level site. Open Easter-October. **10T. MC.** ⚊ ⚊

Street

(2m). **Bramble Hill Caravan & Camping Park, Bramble Hill, Walton, Street, Somerset BA16 9RQ.** *01458 442548.* www.caravancampingsites.co.uk. Owner: Mrs Rogers. On the A39, SP. Quiet and relaxing site situated in the centre of the Polden Hills. Suitable touring base. Views and walks. Swimming, fishing and restaurants within easy reach. Clarks Village, Sainsbury's supermarket 1m. Dogs allowed on leads. Open April-October. **40T. 20MC.** ⚊

Taunton

(4m). **Ashe Farm Caravan Site, Thornfalcon, Taunton, Somerset TA3 5NW.** *01823 442567.* camping@ashefarm. fsnet.co.uk. Owner: Mrs J M Small. Leave M5 at J25, head SE. Take A358 for 2.5m, turn R at Nags Head. Peaceful, family-run farm site with lovely views, central for touring. Showers, wash-room, play area, games room, tennis court and dog walk. Golf course within 3m. Open April 1-October 31. ☆☆☆ **20T. 10MC. 2H.** ⚊ ⚊ ⚊

(6m). **Holly Bush Park, Culmhead, Taunton, Somerset TA3 7EA.** *01823 421515.* info@hollybushpark.com. www.hollybush park.com. Owner: Gary & Rachel Todd. From J25 on M5 follow directions for Taunton. At first traffic lights turn L and follow signs for racecourse and Corfe. 3.5m after Corfe turn R at cross-roads then R again, park on L. Peaceful site in the Blackdown Hills, Area of Outstanding Natural Beauty. Phone, gas and laundrette on site. Fishing, golf, swimming nearby. Surrounded by forestry commission woods, suitable for walking, cycling etc. PH 100yd. No charges made for dogs, children under 3yrs. ☆☆☆☆ **BH&HPA. 40T. MC.** ⚊ ⚊ ⚊

Home Farm Holiday Centre, St Audries Bay, Williton, Taunton, Somerset TA4 4DP. *01984 632487.* mike@home farmholidaycentre.co.uk. www.homefarmholidaycentre.co.uk. Owner: Michael and Patricia Nethercott. A39 Bridgwater towards Minehead for 17m. At West Quantoxhead take B3191, SP Watchet, Blue Anchor, 1st R in 0.5m. Mile-long drive with ramps. 2m from Williton. Family-run site with private beach. Indoor swimming pool. Licensed club. Laundry room. Play area and dog walk. Bungalows and caravans for hire. Shop and bar closed November-March, pool open all year. 3 AA pennants. **BH&HPA. 30T. 10MC. 230S. 5H.** ⚊ ⚊ ⚊ ⚊

(18m). Lowtrow Cross Inn Caravan & Camping Park, Upton, Wiveliscombe, Taunton, Somerset TA4 2DB. *01398 371199.* lowtrowcross@aol.com. www.lowtrowcross.co.uk. Owner: Sue Tanser. From N exit motorway to Taunton, Wiveliscombe, Huish Champflower, Upton. From S exit motorway to Tiverton, Bampton follow B3190 (signs to Wimbleball Lake) site 1m N of Upton, borders Devon and Somerset. 7m from Dulverton. Adults only. Quiet edge of Exmoor. Shower block. Laundry. Use of freezer and microwave. Small shop for essential items only. Inn with restaurant. Open Easter-end of October. ☆☆☆☆ **20T. MC. 3S. 2H.**

(10m). Quantock Orchard Caravan Park, Flaxpool, Crowcombe, Taunton, Somerset TA4 4AW. *01984 618618.* www.flaxpool.freeserve.co.uk. Owner: Mr & Mrs M Barrett. 10m from Taunton off A358, Minehead road. Just outside Crowcombe Village. Small, family-run park at foot of Quantock Hills. New fitness suite. ☆☆☆☆ **BH&HPA. 55T. 15MC.**

(15m). St Audries Bay Holiday Club, St Audries Bay, West Quantoxhead, Taunton, Somerset TA4 4DY. *01984 632515.* mrandle@staudriesbay.co.uk. www.staudriesbay.co.uk. Owner: M Randle. Off the A39. 2m from Williton. Minehead 8m. Level site overlooking sea. Free family entertainment. Sports and leisure facilities. Licensed Bar and Restaurant. All-day servery. Indoor pool. Level site. Open May-October. ☆☆☆☆ **BH&HPA. 20T. 3MC. 80S. 10H.**

(12m). Waterrow Touring Park, Waterrow, Wiveliscombe, Taunton, Somerset TA4 2AZ. *01984 623464.* www.waterrowpark.co.uk. Owner: Mr & Mrs A Taylor. 3m SW of Wiveliscombe via the B3227. 300yd past The Rock PH at Waterrow. Gently sloping site in an attractive river valley. Exclusively for adults. One holiday home for hire. Fly fishing on site. Dog walking field and day kennels. Landscaped hard-standings, spacious pitches all with views. Watercolour painting holidays and fly fishing tuitions. PH nearby. David Bellamy Gold Conservation Award. ☆☆☆☆☆ **BHHPA. 40T. 30MC. 1S.**

Watchet

(1m). Bridge Park, Doniford, Watchet, Somerset TA23 0TH. *01823 433750.* Owner: A B Bennett. Holiday caravans on mainly residential site. Near Exmoor, beaches and interesting places to visit. **BH&HPA. 4H.**

(2m). Doniford Bay Holiday Park, Doniford, Watchet, Somerset TA23 0TJ. *01984 632142.* oewebmaster@bourne-leisure.co.uk. www.donifordbayholidaypark.com. Owner: Bourne Leisure Ltd. 1 Park Lane, Hemel Hempstead, Hertfordshire HP2 4YL. M5, J23, then A38 towards Bridgwater. Then A39 towards Minehead. After about 15m, in West Quantoxhead, fork R after St Audries garage. Doniford Bay is about 1m farther on R. Heated indoor and outdoor pools. Children's clubs. Entertainment for whole family. Convenience store. Bakery. Laundrette. All-weather, multi-sports court. Open April-October. ☆☆☆☆ **BH&HPA. NCC. 46T. MC. 498S. 191H.**

(1m). Helwell Bay Holidays, Helwell Bay, Watchet, Somerset TA23 0UG. *01984 631781.* Helwellbay@yahoo.co.uk. www.helwellbay.co.uk. Owner: Mrs J Howe. On B3191, off A39 Bridgwater to Watchet. Close to town. Situated on level ground, overlooking the Bristol Channel and adjacent to the West Somerset Steam Railway, about 8 mins walk into Watchet. Open March-October. ☆ **BH&HPA. 16H.**

Lorna Doone Holiday Park, Watchet, Somerset TA23 0BJ. *01984 631206.* mail@lornadoone.co.uk. www.lornadoone.co.uk. Owner: Ros & Brodie McIntyre. On B3191. 400yd away from Watchet. Small, peaceful park, 5mins walk from Watchet station on the West Somerset Steam Railway and quaint old harbour town of Watchet. Suitable base for walking the Quantocks, Brendon Hills and Exmoor. Rose Award. Full or part-week bookings are accepted. Open March-October. ☆☆☆☆☆ **BH&HPA. 29S. 12H.**

(1m). Sunny Bank Holiday Caravans, Doniford, Watchet, Somerset TA23 0UD. *01984 632237.* holidays@sunnybankcp.co.uk. www.sunnybankcp.co.uk. Owner: Mr & Mrs P Harrison. A39 from Bridgwater at West Quantoxhead turn right onto B3191. Bottom of steep hill turn right for park. Small, quiet family park overlooking the sea. Heated swimming pool. Short breaks. Pets welcome. Open March 1-October 31. ☆☆☆☆☆ **BH&HPA. 37S. 17H.**

(1m). Warren Bay Caravan Park, Watchet, Somerset TA23 0JR. *01984 631460.* Owner: A P Pring. On B3191, Minehead to Watchet. Bottled gas. Open Easter-October 31. **100T. MC. 155S. 5H.**

(1m). Warren Farm, Watchet, Somerset TA21 0JP. *01984 631220.* Owner: Mr & Mrs Geoffrey Bosley. Showers. Calor Gas. Facilities for clothes washing and dishwashing. Washbasin and toilet for disabled people. Adjacent to beach. 275 acres, working farm established 1928. 20 tents pitches also available. Open Easter-end September. **80T. MC. 18S.**

(0.5m). West Bay Caravan Park, Cleeve Hill, Watchet, Somerset TA23 0BJ. *01984 631261.* alistair@westbay 2000.freeserve.co.uk. www.westbaycaravanpark.co.uk. Owner: Mr & Mrs A Austin. On B3191 off A39. 400yd from Watchet Harbour on Blue Anchor Road on R. Panoramic sea views. Small quiet, family-run site. Open March 1-October 31. ☆☆☆☆ **BH&HPA. 32S. 6H.** ⚓

Wedmore

Splott Farm, Blackford, Wedmore, Somerset BS28 4PD. *01278 641522.* Owner: Mr S B G Duckett. On the B3139, Highbridge to Wells road. 5m from Burnham-on-Sea. Peaceful, undeveloped site of 4.5 acres. Showers. Good centre for touring many places of interest. Good views. Local golf course at Wedmore, local fishing lakes 5 mins away by car. Storage available. Open March-November. **32T. 4MC.** ⚓ ☯

Wellington

(1m). Cadeside Caravan Club Site, Nynehead Road, Wellington, Somerset TA21 9HN. *01823 663103.* www.caravanclub.co.uk. Owner: The Caravan Club. East Grinstead House, East Grinstead, West Sussex RH19 1UA. See website for standard directions to site. This is a well screened rural site with distant views of the surroundings hills and within a 10 mins walk of Wellington. No toilet block. Dog walk on site and recycling facilities within 1m. Open March-January. **NCC. 18T. MC.** ⚓ ☯

Wells

(1.5m). Homestead Park, Wookey Hole, Wells, Somerset BA5 1BW. *01749 673022.* enquiries@homesteadpark.co.uk. www.homesteadpark.co.uk. Owner: Ingledene Ltd. Leave Wells by A371 to Cheddar, turn R for Wookey Hole. Sheltered, picturesque site. Wookey Hole caves 250yd. Full facilities. Adults only; no children under 18. Small caravans and motorhomes only. 1 axle weight limit on bridge, which forms entrance to camping field. Open Easter-September 30. **BH&HPA. 30T. MC.** ⚓ ☯ ⚓

Weston-super-Mare

(2m). Camping & Caravanning Club Site - Weston Super Mare, West End Farm, Locking, Weston-super-Mare, Somerset BS24 8RH. *01934 822548.* www.campingandcaravanningclub.co.uk. Owner: Camping & Caravanning Club. Greenfields House, Westwood Way, Coventry CV4 8JH. M5, exit 21, take A370 to Weston, follow Helicopter Museum signs. Take first turning R after museum entrance, passing park home site on L. At end of road, as you enter West End Farm, turn R into site. Club members only. Traditional seaside holiday resort, Cheddar Gorge and Wooky Hole are nearby. Fishing, golf and horse riding nearby. Bath, Bristol and Glastonbury are also close. Special deals available for families and backpackers. All types of units accepted. Open March-October. ☆☆☆ **90T. 90MC.** ⚓ ☯ ⚓

(2m). Airport View Caravan Site, Moor Lane, Worle, Weston-super-Mare, Somerset BS27 7LA. *01934 622168.* Owner: Mr B J Bartlett. From J21 M5 into Weston-super-Mare second roundabout, take third exit then first left, Airport View is at the end on the right. Family-run park with new facilities block, licensed club, games and laundry room. Open March 1-October 31. **BH&HPA. 135T. 50MC. 3H.** ⚓ ☯ ⚓

(3m). Carefree Holiday Park, 12 Beach Road, Sand Bay, Weston-super-Mare, Somerset BS22 9UZ. *01934 624541.* Owner: Giles & Vicki Moroney. M5, J21, follow signs for Sand Bay, Site is located directly opposite the Sand Bay beach. Peaceful location. PH 200yd, golf course 1m. Laundry on site. Open March-November. ☆☆☆☆ **BH&HPA. 24S.** ⚓

(3m). Country View Caravan & Touring Park, 29 Sand Road, Sand Bay, Weston-super-Mare, Somerset BS22 9UJ. *01934 627595.* Owner: Giles & Vicki Moroney. Come off exit 21on the M5, follow signs to Sand Bay, along Queen's Way, into Norton Lane then Sand Road. 200yd from beach. Outdoor heated swimming pool. Licensed club. Dogs allowed. Shop, children's play area. Golf 1m. Open March-January. ☆☆☆☆ **BH&HPA. 120T. MC. 65S.** ⚓ ☯ ⚓ ⚓

(3m). Gables Caravan Park, Sand Road, Sand Bay, Weston-super-Mare, Somerset. *01934 624859.* Owner: Mrs B Thomas. Off A370. Gas. Open March-January. **22S.**

(1m). Manor Park, Grange Road, Uphill, Weston-super-Mare, Somerset BS23 4TE. *01934 823288.* info@oak treeparks.co.uk. www.oaktreeparks.co.uk. Owners: Oaktree Parks Ltd. The Office, Oaktree Park, Locking, Weston-super-Mare BS24 8RG. M5, J22, A370 SP to Weston-super-Mare, about 10m. At roundabout keep L to Weston-super-Mare. At roundabout (hospital opposite), take 1st exit (L) in Grange Rd, SP Uphill and hospital. Manor Park about 100yd on L. Swimming pool, golf: 0.5m. Shopping centre, bank, PO, cinema: 1m. Open February 15-January 31. **BH&HPA. 38S.** ⚓ ✎

(1.5m). Purn Holiday Park, Bridgwater Road (A370), Bleadon, Weston-super-Mare, Somerset BS24 0AN. *01934 812342.* info@snootyfoxresorts.co.uk. www.snootyfoxresorts.co.uk. Owners: Snooty Fox Resorts Ltd. Tivoli House, Boulevard, Weston-super-Mare BS23 1PD. Leave M5, J21, and take signs for Weston hospital, turn left at hospital roundabout on to A370, park 1m on right. Licensed club with entertainment, dining and dancing, children allowed. Heated swimming pools, games room etc. Open March-January. **BH&HPA. 96T. 115S. 5H.** ⚓ ☯ ⚓ ✎

(2m). Quex Holiday Caravans, 14 Beach Road, Sand Bay, Weston-super-Mare, Somerset BS22 9UZ. *01934 624375.* Owner: Mr B A & Mrs J M Ladds. Off A38. Local PO, shops and two PGHs. Bus stop just a few yards from park. Open April-October. **9H.** ⚓

(2m). Rose Tree Caravan Park, Lower Norton Lane, Norton Kewstoke, Weston-super-Mare, Somerset BS22 9YR. *01934 620351.* Owner: Miss Donna Diamond. A370 Queensway. Kewstoke, Lower Norton Lane. First site off Lower Norton Lane. Open April-October. **20T. MC.** ⚓ ☯

Rugby Football Club W-S-M, The Recreation Ground, Sunnyside Road, Weston-super-Mare, Somerset BS23 3PA. *01934 647906.* Owner: W-S-M R.F.C. From J21 M5 follow Weston-Super-Mare signs through 5 roundabouts. After 5th roundabout take first left and rugby ground is on the left. Close to all amenities, beach, swimming, 500yd to shops, in town centre near railway station. Bristol, Cheddar, Somerset Levels, Bath, Taunton all within one hour's drive. Open March 1-November 3. **21T. MC.** ⚓ ☯ ⚓

West Acres Touring Park, Westacres Farm, West Wick, Weston-super-Mare, Somerset BS24 7TL. *01934 510796.* Owner: R K & J Osmond. From J21, M5, follow signs to West Wick, over mini roundabout, left at T-junction. Park 100yd on left. Quiet, family-run park. Secure caravan storage compound situated next to site. **CaSSOA. 100T. MC.** ✿ ⚓ ☯

(2m). West End Farm Caravan & Camping Park, Locking, Weston-super-Mare, Somerset BS24 8RH. *01934 822529.* Owner: Mr & Mrs R Nation. Leave M5, J21, follow signs for International Helicopter Museum, first right after museum, site signed. Large, level site is 2.5m from M5. Quiet, well-sheltered, family park. ☆☆☆ **BH&HPA. CaSSOA. 70T. 10MC. 20S.** ✿ ⊹ ☺ ⅄ ⅃

(4m). Weston Gateway Tourist Caravan Park, West Wick, Weston-super-Mare, Somerset BS24 7TF. *01934 510344.* Owner: Mr W J E Davies. Off M5, J21 on to A370, SP for Westwick. Supermarket 0.5m. Fishing, golf, horse riding, dry slope skiing all within 3m. No single parties or commercial vehicles allowed on park. Maximum 2 dogs per unit. Open March-October; open weekends only mid March-end April. **BH&HPA. 175T. MC.** ⊹ ☺ ⅃

Wincanton

(0.5m). Wincanton Racecourse Caravan Club Site, Wincanton, Somerset BA9 8BJ. *01963 34276.* www. caravanclub.co.uk. Owner: Caravan Club. East Grinstead House, East Grinstead, West Sussex RH19 1UA. See website for standard directions to site. Attractive location in open countryside with views to Bruton Forest and Downs. TV and information room. 9-hole golf. Dog walk. Shops 1m. Shower for disabled visitors. Non-members and tent campers welcome. Toilet blocks and laundry facilities. Calor Gas. Open March-Oc tober. **50T. MC.** ⊹ ☺ ⅃

Yeovil

(3m). Halfway Caravan Park, Halfway House Inn, Chilthorne Domer, Yeovil, Somerset BA22 8RE. *01935 840350.* halfway@paulspub.freeserve.co.uk. **20T. 20MC.** ✿ ⊹ ☺ ⅃

(8m). Long Hazel International Caravan & Camping Park, High Street, Sparkford, Yeovil, Somerset BA22 7JH. *01963 440002.* longhazelpark@hotmail.com. www.spark ford.f9.co.uk/lhi.htm. Owners: Mr & Mrs A R Walton. Just off A303/A359 junction. At Hazelgrove Services, follow brown and white tourists signs into the village. Level site, 40 hard-standings. Holiday lodges for sale and rent. Near to village inn and McDonalds. Walking distance to shop/garage. Public Telephone. Play area. Bus stop outside. Lots to see and do including Haynes Motor Museum and Fleet Air Arm Museum. Open February 16-January 16. ☆☆☆ **BH&HPA. 75T. 75MC. 3H.** ⊹ ☺ ⅃

WEST DORSET

Bridport

(1.5m). Binghams Farm Touring Caravan Park, Melplash, Bridport, Dorset DT6 3TT. *01308 488234.* enquiries@bing hamsfarm.co.uk. www.binghamsfarm.co.uk. Owner: Lisa & Alistair Herbert. Turn off the A35 in Bridport, at roundabout on to A3066 (SP Beaminster) after 1.5m turn L into farm road. Adult-only, family-run park. Heated facilities. Bar/restaurant. Views over Dorset's Brit Valley, yet site is only 4.5m from the coast. ☆☆☆☆ **BH&HPA. 78T. MC.** ⊹ ☺ ⅃

(3m). Coastal Caravan Park, Annings Lane, Burton Bradstock, Bridport, Dorset DT6 4QP. *01308 897361.* Owner: West Dorset Leisure Holidays. In village of Burton Bradstock turn at Anchor Hotel, second right into Annings Lane; park 1m on right-hand side. Golf nearby. David Bellamy Silver Conservation Award. Open March-November. ☆☆☆ **BH&HPA. 25T. MC. 94S.** ⊹ ☺ ⌀

(1.5m). Eype House Caravan & Camping Site, Eype, Bridport, Dorset DT6 6AL. *01308 424903.* enquiries@eype house.co.uk. www.eypehouse.co.uk. Owner: Sue & Graham Dannan. Off A35 to Honiton take turning to Eype, then the turning to the sea. Follow lane to the bottom, entrance to park on R. 200yd to beach, on the Dorset Coastal Path. Open Easter-October. ✩✩✩ **BH&HPA. 20MC. 35H.** ⊶ ⚠ ⊘

(2m). Freshwater Beach Holiday Park, Burton Bradstock, Bridport, Dorset DT6 4PT. *01308 897317.* info@freshwaterbeach.co.uk. www.freshwaterbeach. co.uk. Owner: R Condliffe. 2m from Bridport on B3157. Bridport to Weymouth coast road. Private beach. Amusements. Club. Entertainment. Takeaway food. Swimming pools. Riding. Laundrette. Dogs allowed except in hire caravans. Golf course adjoining site. Licensed restaurant, 3 bars. Play area. Coastal walks. Open March 15-November 10. ✩✩✩✩
BH&HPA. 250T. 50MC. 289S. 60H. ⊶ ⚑ & ⚠

(3m). Golden Cap Caravan Park, Seatown, Chideock, Bridport, Dorset DT6 6JX. *01308 422139.* holidays@ wdlh.co.uk. www.wdlh.co.uk. Owner: West Dorset Leisure Holidays Ltd. Highlands End Holiday Park, Eype, Bridport, Dorset DT6 6AR. Off A35 Lyme Regis to Bridport. Turn off to Seatown from Chideock, follow this road and park can be found at the end on the left. Overlooked by Golden Cap clifftop and surrounded by National Trust countryside on Heritage coastline. Suitable base for walking the coastal path. David Bellamy Gold Conservation Award. Golf 3m. Open March-November. ✩✩✩✩✩ **BH&HPA. 108T. MC. 220S. 12H.** ⊶ ⚑ ⚠

(1.5m). Highlands End Farm Holiday Park, Eype, Bridport, Dorset DT6 6AR. *01308 422139.* holidays@wdlh.co.uk. www.wdlh.co.uk. Off A35,1m W of Bridport, take SP to Eype, follow road round and follow brown signs to Highlands End. Family park with of Lyme Bay and Heritage coastline. Indoor heated swimming pool and leisure complex, lounge bar with meals. Tennis court. Pitch and putt course. David Bellamy Gold conservation award. Golf 2m. Open March-November. ✩✩✩✩✩ **BH&HPA. 120T. 120MC. 160S. 18H.** ⊶ ⚑ & ⚠ ⊘

(6m). Home Farm, Rectory Lane, Puncknowle, Bridport, Dorset DT2 9BW. *01308 897258.* Owner: Miss R Laver. Home Farm, Puncknowle, Dorchester, Dorset DT2 9BW. On A35 between Dorchester and Bridport, turn off to Litton Cheney and follow road to Puncknowle. On B3157 between Bridport and Weymouth turn off at Bull Inn, Swyre. Scenic views from park. Bottled gas, ice pack freezing. Thatched PH in village. Good centre for touring. Fishing, beach 1.5m. Golf course 5m. Open April 1-October 21. **20T. 5MC. 14S.** ⊶ ⚑

(4m). Larkfield Caravan Park, Bredy Lane, Burton Bradstock, Bridport, Dorset DT6 4QZ. *01308 422139.* holi days@wdlh.co.uk. www.wdlh.co.uk. Owner: West Dorset Leisure Holidays. Highlands End, Eype, Bridport DT6 6AR. On E

side of village of Burton Bradstock, on the road to Long Bredy. 4 mins walk from beach and village facilities. Golf course 1m. Open March-November. **BH&HPA. 59S.** ⊶ ⊘

(6m). Manor Farm Holiday Centre, Charmouth, Bridport, Dorset DT6 6QL. *01297 560226.* enq@manorfarmholidaycen tre.co.uk. www.manorfarmholidaycentre.co.uk. Owner: R C Loosmore & Son. In centre of Charmouth off bypass (A35). Licensed bar. Family room. Bar, entertainment. Pool. Fish and chip takeaway. Play area. Riding. Golf, fishing nearby. 10min level walk to beach. Cinema 3m. Shopping centre 6m. Open all year for holiday caravans; open mid March-October for tourrers. ✩✩✩ **239T. MC. 29S. 14H.** ✿ ⊶ ⚑ & ⚠

(4m). Old Coastguard Holiday Park, Burton Bradstock, Bridport, Dorset DT6 4RL. *01308 897223.* oldcoastguard@hot-mail.com. www.oldcoastguard.co.uk. Owner: Mrs J M Barnikel & L & G Connolly. On B3157 between Burton Bradstock and Swyre. Adjoining beach. Only caravan owners' dogs on park. Open March 16-October 31. **BH&HPA. 124S.** ⊶ ⊘

(1.5m). West Bay Holiday Park, West Bay, Bridport, Dorset DT6 4HB. *01308 422424.* enquiries@parkdeanholidays.co.uk. www.parkdeanholidays.co.uk. Owner: Parkdean Holidays Plc. 2nd Floor, One Gosforth Way, Gosforth Business Park, Newcastle-upon-Tyne NE12 8ET. Off A35, Dorchester to Bridport. Indoor pool. Mini golf. Adventure playground. Laundrette. Takeaway. Coffee shop. Free children's club. Family club and bar. Cabaret, disco, restaurant, arcade, pool tables, darts. Golf course 0.5m. Open March-November. ✩✩✩ **BH&HPA. NCC. 130T. MC. 299S. 262H.** ⊶ ⚑ & ⚠

Charmouth

Camping & Caravanning Club Site - Charmouth, Monkton Wylde Farm, Charmouth, Dorset DT6 6DB. *01297 32965/0870 2433331.* www.campingandcaravan ningclub.co.uk. Owner: Camping & Caravanning Club. Greenfields House, Westwood Way, Coventry CV4 8JH. On A35 from Dorchester, turn R 0.5m past end of dual carriageway, SP 'Marskwood, B3165'. Site on left-hand side. On Dorset/Devon border. 20m coastal path nearby. Non- members welcome. All types of units accepted. David Bellamy Gold Conservation Award. Fossil hunting along Charmouth coast. Undercliffe Nature Reserve and Cobb Harbour nearby. Special deals for families and backpackers. Open March-October. ✩✩✩✩✩ **80T. 80MC.** ⊶ ⚑ &

(1m). Dolphins River Park, Berne Lane, Charmouth, Dorset DT6 6RD. *01308 868180/0800 074 6375.* dolphins@lewesdon. fsworld.co.uk. www.dolphinsriverpark.co.uk. Owner: D Borradaile. 5m W of Bridport on the A35, turn right to Whitchurch Cannonilorum (opposite Charmouth slip road). Park is 300yd on left-hand side. Secluded, quiet 'garden park' on banks of river Char, 1m from the beach. Golf, cinema, shopping within 2-5m. Open April-October. ✩✩✩✩ **BH&HPA. 35S. 10H.** ⊶ ⊘

(2m). Monkton Wyld Farm, Charmouth, Dorset DT6 6DB. *01297 34525*. holidays@monktonwyld.co.uk. www.monkton wyld.co.uk. Owner: Mr S Kewley. From Charmouth A35 west towards Axminster. 0.6m after dual carriageway, right turn, SP for B3165 to Marshwood and Crewkerne. Spacious site. Shop and PH 1m. Shower block with family room. Play area. Low-season discounts. Caravan storage. Sandy beach 3m. Holiday apartment in farmhouse available for hire. Open Easter-October 30. ☆☆☆☆ **BH&HPA. 60T. MC.** ☖ ⚑ ⚲ ⚓

(0.5m). Seadown Holiday Park, Bridge Road, Charmouth, Dorset DT6 6QS. *01297 560154*. www.sead-ownholiday park.co.uk. Loated off the A35, Bridport to Axminster road, SP to Charmouth; in main street turn left into Bridge Road. Open March-October. ☆☆☆☆☆ **50T. 10MC. 110S. 40H.** ⚑ ⚲ ⚓

(1m). Wood Farm Caravan Park, Axminster Road, Charmouth, Dorset DT6 6BT. *01297 560697*. holidays@woodfarm.co.uk. www.woodfarm.co.uk. Owner: MacBennet Ltd. Off the A35, to the west side of Charmouth. Caravan Club affiliated site. Nonmembers and tent campers welcome. Manager: J Bremmer. Member of Best of British Park sites group. World Heritage Coast and spectacular rural scenery. Area is famous for its rugged coastline and is littered with fossils from the Jurassic age. Suitable base for walkng. Open April-October. ☆☆☆☆☆ **BH&HPA. NCC. 116T. MC. 80S. 3H.** ⚑ ⚲ ⚓ ⚒

Dorchester

(7m). Camping & Caravanning Club Site - Moreton, Station Road, Moreton, Dorchester, Dorset DT2 8BB. *01305 853801/0870 243 3331*. www.campin-gandcaravanningclub.co.uk. Owner: Camping & Caravanning Club. Greenfields House, Westwood Way, Coventry CV4 8JH. From Poole on the A35, continue poast Bere Regis, turn left B3390 signposted for Alfpuddle. After about two miles site on left before Moreton Station and next to Frampton Arms Pub. In a popular holiday area, 7m from Weymouth and Dorchester. Two holiday bungalows available to let. Local leisure centre has large indoor pool with wave machine. Other local attractions include dry ski slope and cider museum. Visit Dorchester on Wednesday for market day. Special deals available for families and backpackers. Non members welcome. All units accept-ed. Open March-November. ☆☆☆☆☆ **118T. 118MC. 2H.** ⚑ ⚲ ⚓

(8m). Clay Pigeon Caravan Park, Wardon Hill, Evershot, Dorchester, Dorset DT2 9PW. *01935 83492*. cheryl@clay pigeoncp.wanadoo.co.uk. Owner: Mr G Brook & Mr B Crook. Park is located on the A37 midway between Yeovil and Dorchester. Suitable centre from which to tour 'Hardy' country. Level, gently sloping mature site. Heated toilet block with showers. Fishing, shooting, karting, golf and rid-ing all available nearby. Rally field available. ☆☆☆ **BH&HPA. 60T. MC.** ✿ ⚑ ⚲ ⚓

(7m). Creek Caravan Site, Ringstead, Dorchester, Dorset DT2 8NG. *01305 852251*. www.dorsetcoastcaravans.com. Owner: Ringstead Caravan Co. Take the A352 to Warmwell roundabout. Then the A353 towards Weymouth, through Poxwell, then left right over hill. On coast 5m E of Weymouth. Tranquil surroundings, views. Children welcome. No charge for dogs. Open April 1 or Easter-October 31. **30S. 4H.** ⚑

(5.5m). Crossways Caravan Club Site, Crossways, Dorchester, Dorset DT2 8BE. *01305 852032*. www.cara vanclub.co.uk. Owner: The Caravan Club. East Grinstead House, East Grinstead, West Sussex RH19 1UA. See website for standard directions to site. 8.5m from Weymouth. Landscaped site, suitable base for touring Dorset. Non-members welcome. Dog walk. Advance booking essential bank holidays and July and August. Hard-standings. Shower blocks and laundry facilities, with privacy cubicles. Motorhome service point. Open March-October ☆☆☆☆ **NCC. 122T. MC.** ⚑ ⚲ ⚓

(8m). Giants Head Camping & Caravan Park, Old Sherborne Road, Dorchester, Dorset DT2 7TR. *01300 341242*. holidays @giantshead.co.uk. www.giantshead.co.uk. Owner: Mr R Paul. From Dorchester, into town avoiding bypass, from top of town roundabout, take Sherborne road after about 500yd, fork right at Loders Garage, signposted. From Cerne Abbas take Buckland Newton road. Cottage and chalets available. Shops, PO, doctor, fishing, golf all within 2-3m. Good walking area and views. Open Easter-October. ☆☆ **BH&HPA. 50T. MC.** ⚑ ⚲

Gorselands Caravan Park, West Bexington-on-Sea, Dorchester, Dorset DT2 9DJ. *01308 897232*. gorseland@ ukonline.co.uk. www.ukparks.co.uk/gorselands. 6m E of Bridport on B3157, turn R at Bull Inn in Swyre Village. Park 100yd on R. Peaceful park overlooking Lyme Bay. Suitable base for exploring West Dorset coast and countryside. Open March-November. ☆☆☆☆ **BH&HPA. 120S. 30H.** ⚑ ⚓ ⌗

(3m). Morn Gate Caravan Park, Bridport Road, Dorchester, Dorset DT2 8PS. *01305 889284*. morngate@ukonline.com. www.morngate.co.uk. Owner: Mr A Jackson. On A35 Dorchester to Bridport. No tourers. Calor Gas. Children allowed. Open March-January 12. ☆☆☆ **BH&HPA. 4S. 13H.** ⚑ ⚲ ⌗

(6m). Sandyholme Holiday Park, Moreton Road, Owermoigne, Dorchester, Dorset DT2 8HZ. *01305 852677*. smeatons@sandyholme.co.uk. www.sandyholme.co.uk. Owner: Mike & Libby Smeaton. Off A352. Quiet, family park in Hardy countryside with all amenities. Games room, play park and licensed bar with food (open peak times). Central for Weymouth, Dorchester and Lulworth Cove. David Bellamy Gold Conservation Award. Golf, cinema, shopping centre within 5m. Open Easter or April 1-October 31. ☆☆☆☆ **BH&HPA. 55T. MC. 50S. 26H.** ⚑ ⚲ ⚓ ⌗

(6m). Warmwell Country Touring Park, Warmwell Road, Warmwell, Dorchester, Dorset DT2 8JD. *01305 852313*. stay@warmwell-country-touring-park.co.ukwww.warmwell-country-touring-park.co.uk. Owner: Mundays Caravan Parks Ltd. Easy to find on B3390, which joins A35 between Bere Regis and Tolpuddle, A353 from Weymouth, and A352 Dorchester to Wareham Road. 15-acre site in an Area of Outstanding Natural Beauty. Open or woodland pitches. Resident manager, cctv and electronic barrier access, licensed family bar, laundrette, heated toilet blocks. 3 AA pennants. 6m to Dorchester and Weymouth beaches. Open March-December. ☆☆☆☆ **BH&HPA. 190T. MC.** ⚑ ⚲ ⚓ ⚒

Gillingham

(1m). Thorngrove Camping & Caravan Park, Thorngrove House, Common Mead Lane, Gillingham, Dorset SP8 4RE. *01747 821221*. Owner: Peter Richardson. Located in Blackmore Vale with good views. Quiet site near to PO (0.5m) and super-market (1m). Fishing nearby. ☆☆☆☆ **BH&HPA. T. MC.** ✿ ⚑ ⚲ ⚓ ⚒ ⌗

Lyme Regis

(1m). Hook Farm Caravan and Camping Park, Hook Farm, Gore Lane, Uplyme, Lyme Regis, Dorset DT7 3UU. *01297 442801*. information@hookfarm-uplyme.co.uk. www.hookfarm-uplyme.co.uk. Owner: Adrian and Laraine Morgan. Take B3165 off A35 into Uplyme. Turn R opposite Talbot Arms PH into Gore Lane. Off A3052 take directions to Uplyme (Gore Lane) before entering Lyme Regis. Gas sales. Golf, cinema, shopping and beach: 1m. 400yd to newsagent and village PH. AA 3 pennants. Open March-December. **40MC. 17S. 4H.** ⚑ 🚐 & 🛁

(3m). Newlands Holiday Park, Charmouth, Lyme Regis, Dorset DT6 6RB. *01297 560259*. enq@newlandsholidays.co.uk. www.newlandsholidays.co.uk. Owner: Newlands Ltd. On A35, Bridport to Lyme Regis. Two swimming pools. Good views. Heritage coast village near Lyme Regis. Short stroll to beach. Suitable base for touring and walking. Golf course 2.5m. Cinema 3m. Open all year except Christmas Day and Boxing Day. ✰✰✰✰ **BH&HPA. 200T. MC. 86S. 50H.** ✿ ⚑ 🚐 & 🛁

> **(3m). Shrubbery Touring Park, Rousdon, Lyme Regis, Dorset DT7 3XW.** *01297 442227*. www.ukparks.co.uk/shrubbery. Owner: Mr J Godfrey. W of Lyme Regis on the A3052 coast road. The Shrubbery is a level site situated in an unspoilt and uncommercialised part of the World Heritage coastline of natural beauty. Suitable base for fossil hunters. Open March 1-October 31. ✰✰✰ **BH&HPA. 120T. 10MC.** ⚑ 🚐 & 🛁

(1m). Timber Vale Caravan Park, Charmouth Road, Lyme Regis, Dorset DT7 3HG. *01297 442585*. Owner: Mr J Eaton. 7 Dragons Hill, Lyme Regis, Dorset DT7 3HW. On A3052, Charmouth to Lyme Regis road, after leaving the A35. David Bellamy Silver Conservation Award. For families' use only. Golf 0.5m, shops and cinema 1m. Open end March-end October. **BH&HPA. 153S. 3H.** ⚑ 🛁

(3.5m). Westhayes Caravan Park, Rousdon, Lyme Regis, Dorset DT7 3RD. *01297 23456*. Owner: Mundays Caravan Park Ltd. 3m from Lyme Regis and Seaton on the A3052. Shop, bar, bar food available, laundrette, showers. Outdoor heated swimming pool. Indoor dishwashing area. Facilities limited in winter. Fishing, golf nearby. Open March 1-mid January. ✰✰✰✰ **BH&HPA. NCC. 106T. MC. 62S.** ✿ ⚑ 🚐 & 🛁

Portland

(0.25m). Glen Caravans Holiday & Residential Park, Wakeham, Portland, Dorset DT5 1HP. *01305 823548*. www.glencaravanpark.co.uk. Owner: Mr & Mrs Cade. On A354 Portland to Wakeham. 7m from Weymouth. Electricity supply. Beach about 300yd. 5mins to shops, PO and doctor. **7H.** ✿ ⚑

Shaftesbury

(2m). Blackmore Vale Caravan & Camping Park, Sherborne Causeway, Shaftesbury, Dorset SP7 9PX. *01747 852573/ 851523*. www.caravancampingsites.co.uk/dorset. Owners: Mr & M rs F Farrow. A30, W of Shaftesbury. Scenic views and good touring base. Close to Gold Hill and Saxon abbey ruins. 2 AA pennants. **20T. 10MC.** ✿ ⚑ 🚐

Shaftesbury F.C., 'Cockrams', Coppice Street, Shaftesbury, Dorset SP7 8PF. *01747 853990*. Owner: Shaftesbury F.C. 400 yds from town. Ring between 9am and 10.30am and between 7pm and 11pm. Open May-September. **15T. MC.** ⚑ 🛁

Weymouth

(4m). Bagwell Farm Touring Park, Chickerell, Weymouth, Dorset DT3 4EA. *01305 782575*. enquiries@bagwellfarm.co.uk. www.bagwellfarm.co.uk. Owner: Mrs I E Tupper. 4m W of Weymouth on B3157. Stunning countryside setting with sea views. Licensed restaurant/bar with large sun terrace, fast food grill. Fully stocked mini-market. Suitable base for Dorset and Jurassic Coast. ✰✰✰✰ **BH&HPA. 320T. 150MC.** ✿ ⚑ 🚐 & 🛁

(3m). Chesil Beach Holiday Park, Portland Road, Wyke Regis, Weymouth, Dorset DT4 9AG. *01305 773233*. info@chesiholidays.co.uk. www.chesilholidays.co.uk. Owner: Waterside Holiday Group Ltd. On A354 Weymouth. Heated indoor funpool with flume, clubroom and bars, live entertainment, Children's club, convenience store, snack bar, takeaway, laundrette. Open April-October. ✰✰✰✰ **BH&HPA. NCC. 35T. 175H.** 🚐 & 🛁

(2m). East Fleet Farm Touring Park, Fleet Lane, Chickerell, Weymouth, Dorset DT3 4DW. *01305 785768*. enquiries@eastfleet.co.uk. www.eastfleet.co.uk. Owner: Mr J Whitfield. B3157 from Weymouth, L at Chickerell TA Camp. Peaceful and spacious park on working organic farm overlooking Fleet and Chesil Bank. Open March 16-end October. ✰✰✰✰ **BH&HPA. 150T. 50MC.** ⚑ 🚐 & 🛁

(1.5m). Littlesea Holiday Park, Lynch Lane, Weymouth, Dorset DT4 9DT. *01305 783683*. oewebmaster@bourne-leisure.co.uk. www.littleseaholidaypark.com. Owner: Bourne Leisure Ltd. 1 Park Lane, Hemel Hempstead, Hertfordshire HP2 4YL. A35 to Dorchester then A354 to Weymouth. Turn R at 1st and 2nd roundabouts, direction Portland, 3rd roundabout L, in direction of Chickerell and Portland. Go straight across traffic lights, at end of Benville Road, turn R at traffic lights L into Lynch Lane. Park is at end of road. Indoor and outdoor fun pools, waterslides. Licensed clubs, entertainment centre, amusements. Takeaway. Laundrette. 2 playgrounds. 3 mins drive from PO, doctor. Park is on bus route. Open Easter-end October. ✰✰✰✰ **BH&HPA. NCC. 140T. 700S. 170H.** ⚑ 🚐 🛁 ⌀

(5m). Osmington Mills Holidays Ltd, Ranch House, Osmington Mills, Weymouth, Dorset DT3 6HB. *01305 832311*. holidays@osmingtonmillsfsnet.co.uk. www.osmington-mills-holidays.co.uk. From Weymouth take A353 east for 5m. Turn right to Osmington Mills, SP. Heated swimming pool. Clubhouse. Children's room. Horse riding nearby. Fishing on site. Dogs allowed by arrangement. Open Easter-October 31. **BH&HPA. NCC. 10S. 64H.** 🚐 ⌀

(1.5m). Pebble Bank Holiday Park, Wyke Regis, Weymouth, Dorset DT4 9HF. *01305 774844*. info@pebblebank.co.uk. www.pebblebank.co.uk. From harbour roundabout in Weymouth, follow road for Portland, at mini roundabout turn R on to Wyke road, B3156. Camp Road 1m. Laundry, showers. Play area. Licensed bar. Open April 1-early October. ✰✰✰ **BH&HPA. 40T. MC. 70S. 18H.** ⚑ 🚐

(6m). Portesham Dairy Farm Camp Site, Bramdon Lane, Portesham, Weymouth, Dorset DT3 4HG. *01305 871297*. malcolm.doble@talk21.com. Owners: Mr J M & Mrs S J Doble. B3157 Weymouth to Bridport coast road. Calor Gas and Campingaz from farmhouse. Play area. Laundrette, fishing and horse riding nearby. Abbotsbury 2m with Swannery Thithe barn and sub-tropical gardens. Garage, PO, PH serving food and doctor nearby. Open March 15-October 31. ✰✰✰ **30T. 30MC.** ⚑ 🚐 &

(5m). Ranch House Caravan Park, Osmington Mills, Weymouth, Dorset. *01305 832311*. Owner: Osmington Mills Holidays Ltd. On A353 Warmwell to Weymouth, turn S to Osmington Mills. Clubhouse. Heated pools. Fishing and riding on the park. Dogs allowed by arrangement. Open March-October. **BH&HPA. 20T. 10S. 70H.** 🚐 & 🛁

(1.5m). **Redlands Farm Caravan Park, 369 Dorchester Road, Weymouth, Dorset DT3 5AP.** *01305 812291.* Owner: Mr S Bailey. On A354, Dorchester to Weymouth. Conveniently situated in a semi-rural location backing on to open fields. Safeway supermarket 5 mins walk. Buses run from outside entrance every 15 mins or so. Open March 1-November 30. **99S. 30H.** ⚡

(3m). **Seaview Holiday Park, Preston, Weymouth, Dorset DT3 6DZ.** *01305 833037.* www.havenholidays.com. Owner: Bourne Leisure Ltd. 1 Park Lane, Hemel Hempstead, Hertfordshire HP2 4YL. Take A353 from centre of Weymouth to Preston. Indoor and outdoor pools. Laundrette. Shops. Takeaway. Children's club. Daytime and evening entertainment for all the family. Open March-October. ✰✰✰ **BH&HPA. NCC. 70T. 32MC. 254S. 239H.** ⚡ ☺ ⚲

(7m). **Warmwell Holiday Park, Warmwell, Weymouth, Dorset DT2 8JE.** *01305 852911.* Follow ring road around Dorchester and head towards Poole. Take A352 towards Wareham. At 1st roundabout take 1st exit to Warmwell village. Park is 3m on L. Heated indoor swimming pool. Daytime and evening entertainment for whole family. Children's clubs. All-weather, multi-sports court. Dry ski-slope. Fishing lakes. Convenience store. Bakery. Laundrette. Garden restaurant. Brewers Quay, Portland, Bovington Tan Museum and Dinosaur Land are all close by. Open March-October. ✰✰✰ **BH&HPA. NCC. 208S.** ⚡ ⚲

(1.5m). **Waterside Holiday Park, Bowleaze Cove, Weymouth, Dorset DT3 6PP.** *01305 833103.* info@waterside-holidays.co.uk. www.watersideholidays.co.uk. Owner: Waterside Holiday Group Ltd. Off A353. Park is situated 100yd from beach at Bowleaze Cove. 1.5m from main Weymouth beach.Rose Award. Extensive indoor and outdoor leisure facilities. Open April-October. ✰✰✰✰ **BH&HPA. NCC. 70T. MC. 500S. 200H.** ☺ ⚲

(2.5m). **Weymouth Bay Holiday Park, Preston, Weymouth, Dorset DT3 6BQ.** *01305 835377.* oewebmaster@bourne-leisure.co.uk. www.weymouthbayholidaypark.co.uk. Owner: Bourne Leisure Ltd. 1 Park Lane, Hemel Hempstead, Hertfordshire HP2 4YL. A35 to Dorchester and turn off on A354, SP Weymouth. From Weymouth centre, take A353 to Preston, the park is on the R, 10mins from Weymouth. Heated indoor and outdoor fun pools. Daytime and evening entertainment for all the family. Restaurant. Children's clubs. Open March-November. ✰✰✰✰ **BH&HPA. NCC. 75T. 745S. 35H.** ⚡ ☺ ⚲

(3m). **White Horse Holiday Park, Osmington Hill, Weymouth, Dorset DT3 6ED.** *01305 832164.* whitehorsepark @whitehorsepark.co.uk. www.whitehorsepark.co.uk. Owner: C & E Bratchell. Off A353, between Preston and Osmington. Small holiday park with laundry facilities. Sea and country views. Good walking country. Near coastal path. Village 0.5m. Weekend and short breaks possible outside peak summer season. Single-sex groups, sports clubs etc by special arrangement only. Golf course, shopping, cinemas 2-3m. Open March 1-January 15. ✰✰✰ **BH&HPA. 13S. 9H.** ⚡

EAST YORKSHIRE

Beverley

(1m). **Lakeminster Park Caravan Site, Hull Road, Beverley, East Yorkshire HU17 0PN.** *01482 882655.* Owner: Mr & Mrs B Rushworth. Bleach House, Hull Road, Beverley, East Yorkshire HU17 0TA. Off A1174. Fishing. Drinks licence. Food. **20T. 20MC. 30S.** ✿ ⚡ ☺ ⚲ ☕ ⚲

Bridlington

(6m). **Barmston Beach Holiday Park, Sands Lane, Barmston, Bridlington, Yorkshire YO25 8PJ.** *0871 664 9704.* barm stan.beach@park-resorts.com. www.park-resorts.com. Owner: Park Resorts Ltd. 3rd Floor, Swan Court, Waterhouse Street, Hemel Hempstead, Herts HP1 1FN. Southbound take A165 from Bridlington to Kingston-upon-Hull. Northbound, take A165 from Hull. Barnston Beach is SP about 6m S of Bridlington. Situated on coast. Licensed club. Free children's club. Shop, laundrette, cafe. Amusement. Fish and chips shop. Outdoor play area, heated outdoor pool with splash area. Visiting entertainment cabaret. 4 golf courses within 10m. Yorkshire Moors, steam railway. Historic cities of Beverley and York. Open April-October. ✰✰✰✰ **BH&HPA. NCC. MC. 346S. 15H.** ⚡ ☺ ⚲

(5m). **Black Bull Inn, Barmston, Bridlington, East Yorkshire.** *01262 8468244.* Owner: Ms E Oates. On A165. Open March 1-November 30. **24S. 1H.** ⚡

North Bay Leisure Park, Lime Kiln Lane, Bridlington, East Yorkshire YO16 5TG. *01262 673733/01262 677318.* enquiries@northbayleisure.co.uk. www.northbayleisure.co.uk. Off B1255. Open March 1-November 30. ✰✰✰✰ **BH&HPA. 350S. 33H.** ⚡ ⚲

(2m). **Old Mill Caravan Park, Bempton, Bridlington, East Yorkshire YO15 6XE.** *01262 673565.* Owner: Mr Wood. Take B1255 from Bridlington to Flamborough at Marton, turn left, SP Bempton, after 1m turn right; site is 500yd on right. Village railway station 300yd. Village pub 0.5m. Bempton Cliffs bird sanctuary 1m. Open April 1-October 31. **27T. MC. 28S.** ☺

(4m). **Railings Caravan Park, Jewison Lane, Sewerby, Bridlington, East Yorkshire.** *01262 672733.* Owner: Mr E W S Thompson. 3 North Marine Drive, Bridlington YO15 2JF. Quiet, privately owned site suitable for retired or semi-retired people. Open March 1-October 31. **25S.** ⚡

(3m). **Shirley Caravan Park, Jewison Lane, Bridlington, East Yorkshire YO16 5YG.** *01262 676442.* Owner: Flower of May Holiday Parks Ltd. At roundabout on A165, take B1255 Flamborough; Jewison Lane is on left after 2m, park on left after level crossing. Rural setting 3m from Flamborough Head. Lounge bar. Showers. Laundrette. Playground. New indoor pool/leisure centre. AA 3 pennants. Open March-October. **45T. 400S. 10H.** ⚡ ☺ ⚲

(1m). **South Cliff Caravan Park, South Cliff, Wilsthorpe, Bridlington, East Yorkshire YO15 3QN.** *01262 671051.* south cliff@eastriding.gov.uk. www.southcliff.co.uk. Owner: East Riding of Yorkshire Council. On A165, Hull to Bridlington. All

Please mention Caravan Sites 2006 when replying to advertisers

touring pitches hard-standings. Multi-purpose play area. Club, shop, laundrette, takeaway. Golf course and boat launch nearby. Open March 1-November 30. ☆☆☆☆ **BH&HPA. 184T. MC. 756S. 10H.** 🚐 ᴥ 🛁

(2m). The Poplars Touring Park and Motel, 45 Jewison Lane, Sewerby, Bridlington, East Yorkshire YO15 1DX. *01262 677251.* www.the-poplars.co.uk. From N side of Bridlington take B1255 to Flamborough, take 2nd L off Z-bend. Small touring park with modern toilet and shower facilities. Adjacent to family PH and restaurant (seasonal). Golf course and coastal path within 1m. Open March 1-November 14. ☆☆☆☆ **BH&HPA. 30T. MC.** 🀥 🚐

(1m). The White House Caravan Park, The White House, Wilsthorpe, Bridlington, East Yorkshire YO15 3QN. *01262 673894.* www.whcps.co.uk. Owner: Mr D Worsman. 1m S of Bridlington off the A165, follow road round, entry on R. Level park divided into two areas. Owner and warden in residence. Shop and club near. David Bellamy Gold Conservation Award. Golf course, sailing/windsurfing. Open March 1-November 30. ☆☆☆☆☆ **BH&HPA. 169S.** 🀥 ⌀

(4m). Thornwick and Sea Farm Holiday Centre, North Marine Road, Flamborough, Bridlington, East Yorkshire, YO15 1U. *01262 850369.* enquiries@thornwickbay.co.uk. www.thornwickbay.co.uk. Owner: Mr S H Gibbon. From Bridlington A164, follow B1255 to Flamborough. Go through the village to the 'North Landing'. The park is to your L. Superpitch facilities. Set on the Flamborough headland Heritage Coast. Pool, gym, bars and entertainment on site. Close to 2 golf courses. Open March 1-October 31. ☆☆☆☆ **BH&HPA. 250T. 1200S. 62H.** 🀥 🚐 ᴥ 🛁

Cowden

(4m). Cowden Caravan Park, Cowden, East Yorkshire HU11 4UL. *01964 527393.* Owner: A & A R Larkham. On B1242. Beach 200yd. Private fishing lake. Aviary. Playground. Putting green. Bingo. PH 100yd. Gas sold on site. Open March-December. **25T. MC. 217S.** 🀥 🚐 🛁

Driffield

(3m). Atwick Caravan Site, Atwick, Driffield, East Yorkshire. *01964 534241.* Owner: A S Hornby & Sons. 'Whencliffe', Cliff Road, Atwick, Driffield, East Yorkshire YO25 8DF. Clifftop site 2m north of Hornsea. Open March-October inclusive. **T. MC. 30S.** 🀥 🚐

(6m). Crossways Caravan Site, Mill Lane, Skipsea, Driffield, East Yorkshire. *01262 468501.* Owner: Mr R S Ackroyd. Eastholme Farm, 5 Skipsea Road, Beeford, Driffield, East Yorkshire. Site close to sea, clubs and amusements. Bridlington 6m. Fish shop on site. Open April-October 31. **12S.** 🀥

(10m). Dacre Lakeside Park, Brandesburton, Driffield, East Yorkshire YO25 8RT. *01964 543704.* dacresurf@aol.com. www.dacrepark.co.uk. Owner: Sandsfield Gravel Co Ltd. Catick Lane, Brandesburton, Driffield, East Yorkshire YO25 8SA. From M62 exit 38, take B1230 E to Beverley then follow signs to Bridlington. Site entrance off A165. 14-acre site accepting all types of units. 10-acre lake with windsurfing. 18-hole golf course. Open March-October. ☆☆☆☆ **BH&HPA. 120T. MC.** 🀥 🚐 ᴥ 🛁

(8m). Fosse Hill Caravan & Jet Ski Centre, Catwick Lane, Brandsburton, Driffield, East Yorkshire YO25 8SB. *01964 542608.* janet.fossehill.co.uk. www.fossehill.co.uk. Owner: Mr & Mrs Butterfield. From M62, exit 38. Take B1230 E to Beverley and A165 towards Bridlington at signpost. 4m inland from

Hornsea. Fishing, golf nearby. 1m to restaurants, PO, butcher's etc. Open March 1-October 31. ☆☆ **BH&HPA. 75T. 75MC.** 🀥 🚐 ᴥ 🛁

(8m). Galleon Beach Caravan Park, Southfield Lane, Ulrome, Driffield, East Yorkshire. *01262 468501.* Owner: Mr R Ackroyd. Eastholme Farm, 5 Skipsea Road, Beeford, Driffield, East Yorkshire. Bridlington 7m, Hornsea 6m. Open March 1-October 31. **T. 28S.** 🀥 🚐 🛁

(9m). Skipsea Sands Caravan Park, Mill Lane, Skipsea, Driffield, East Yorkshire YO25 8TZ. *01262 469030.* Follow B1249 from Driffield or A165 from Bridlington. Turn on to B1249 at Beeford. Follow brown tourist signs from Skipsea village. 10m from Bridlington. Close to beach with bars, amusements, laundrette and play area. Indoor swimming pool, ten-pin bowling, fitness suite, sports facilities. Open March 1-November 30. ☆☆☆☆ **NCC. 90T. MC. 650S. 60H.** 🀥 🚐 ᴥ 🛁 ⌀

(3m). Skirlington Leisure Park, Skipsea, Driffield, East Yorkshire YO25 8SY. *01262 468213/468466.* enquiries@ skirlington.com. www.skirlington.com. Situated between the villages of Skipsea and Atwick on B1242. 1.5m from Hornsea. 9-hole putting course. Fishing pond. Animal farm. Indoor swimming pool. Restaurant and bars with full entertainment in season. Open March 1-December 31. ☆☆☆☆ **BH&HPA. 225T. MC. 550S. 16H.** 🀥 🚐 ᴥ 🛁

Thorpe Hall Caravan & Camping Site, Thorpe Hall, Rudston, Driffield, East Yorkshire YO25 4JE. *01262 420393/420574.* caravansite@thorpehall.co.uk. www.thorpehall.co.uk. Owner: Sir Ian Macdonald of Sleat. 4m from Bridlington. 4.5 acres situated in former walled garden at Thorpe Hall. Fishing on site. Play area, games room and laundry. Manager: Mrs Jayne Chatterton. Open March 1-October 31. ☆☆☆ **BH&HPA. 78T. 78MC.** 🀥 🚐 ᴥ 🛁

(7m). Top View Caravan Park, Ulrome, Skipsea, Driffield, East Yorkshire YO25 8TP. *01262 468771.* Owner: B J Woodcock. 15 Pinfold Street, Bridlington, East Yorkshire. Near village. Open March 1-November 30. **BH&HPA. 92S.** 🀥

Hornsea

(0.25m). Longbeach Leisure Park, South Cliff, Hornsea, East Yorkshire HU18 1TL. *01964 532506.* pat@longbeach-leisure.co.uk. www.longbeach-leisure.co.uk. Laundrette, play room and play area. Payphone. 9-hole pitch and putt golf course. Direct access to beach. Leisure centre 250yd. New for Open March 1-December 31. ☆☆☆☆ **BH&HPA. 50T. MC. 420S.** 🀥 🚐 🛁

Promenade Caravan Park, South Promenade, Hornsea, East Yorkshire HU18 1TH. *01964 535827.* Owner: Mr & Mrs R Pyle. Golf course nearby. Sea fishing, local market Wednesday and Sunday. Open March 1-October 31. **70S.** 🀥

(0.75m). Springfield Farm Caravan Park, Atwick Road, Hornsea, East Yorkshire HU18 1EJ. *01964 532253.* Owner: Mr & Mrs A Hammond. N of Hornsea on B1242, SP Bridlington; site at top of hill on left. Milk available. Open Easter-October 31. **30T. MC.** 🚐 ᴥ

Hull

(8m). Burton Constable Caravan Park, Old Lodges, Sproatley, Hull, East Yorkshire HU11 4LN. *01964 562508.* On B1238 Hull to Aldborough. Modern facilities. Shaver points. Laundry room. Licensed club. Chemical toilet emptying points. Telephone. Calor and Campingaz available. Site shop. Open March 1-October 31. ☆☆☆☆ **BH&HPA. 160T. 15MC. 150S.** 🀥 🚐 ᴥ 🛁

(7m). Easington Beach Caravan Park, Easington, Hull, East Yorkshire HU12 OTY. *01964 650293.* Owner: Easington Caravan Sites Ltd. On B1445. Heated indoor swimming pool. Tennis and badminton courts. Bowling and putting greens. Club. Laundrette. Playground. Pets corner includes big Koi carp fish pond and 150 foreign birds. Open March-October. **40T. MC. 250S. 15H.** 🛏 ⚲ ⚲

(4m). Entick House, Ings Lane, Dunswell, Hull, East Yorkshire HU6 0AL. *01482 807393.* Owner: E D Robinson. Down to bottom of lane near river Hull. **8T. 8MC.** ⚲ 🛏 ⌀

(17m). Patrington Haven Leisure Park, Patrington Haven, Hull, East Yorkshire HU12 0PT. *01964 630071.* sales@phlp.co.uk. www.phlp.co.uk. Owner: Mr G H Sparkes. Take the A1033, Hull to Withernsea road. Turn first R in village of Patrington. Full mains service. 3 bars, family room. Heated indoor swimming pool. Sauna. Jacuzzi. Solarium. Bowls, Gymnasium. Well-stocked fishing lake. Rose Award. Open March 7-January 7. ✩✩✩✩✩ **BH&HPA. NCC. 490S.** 🛏 ⚲ ⚲

Pocklington

(1m). Southmoor Park, The Balk, Pocklington, East Yorkshire YO42. *01759 301216.* southmoorpark@tiscali.co.uk. www.southmoorpark.co.uk. Owners: LP, PJ & PG Lemon. Lyncroft, Sutton Lane, Barmby Moor, Pocklington, YO42 4HX. Turn off the A1079 Hull to York road at the B1247 to Pocklington junction 250yd on the right. Adjacent PH/restaurant. Two golf courses, gliding club, cinema, market, shops, swimming pool, sports centre within 2m. **BH&HPA. 8S.** ⚲

Roos

(3m). Sand-le-Mere Caravan & Leisure Park Ltd, Seaside Road, Tunstall, Roos, East Yorkshire HU12 0JQ. *01964 670403.* info@sand-le-mere.co.uk. www.sand-le-mere.co.uk. Owner: Mr A C Ellis. M62 on to A63 Hull-Hedon. Right on to A1033, right on to B1362, left on to local roads, Roos. Right on to B1242. Amenities include PH, club, shop, cafe, restaurant, heated swimming pool, play area and fishing mere. Bowling. Children allowed. Golf 3m. Cinema, shopping centre 20m. No tourers. Open March 1-December 31. ✩✩✩✩ **575S. 30H.**

Skipsea

Far Grange Park, Skipsea, East Yorkshire YO25 8SY. *01262 468010.* enquiries@fargrangepark.co.uk. www.fargrangepark. co.uk. Owner: Mr McCann. Off B1242, Bridlington to Hornsea coast road. Family-owned coastal park. Catering for privately owned holiday homes and hire fleet only. No touring facilities. Wildlife park, adjacent golf course, Hornsea freeport. Open March-December. ✩✩✩✩✩ **BH&HPA. 700S. 43H.** 🛏 ⚲ ⚲

Mill Farm Country Park, Mill Lane, Skipsea, East Yorkshire YO25 8SS. *01262 468211.* Owner: Judy Willmott. A165 Hull to Bridlington. At Beeford take B1249 to Skipsea. At crossroads turn R, then first L up Cross Street, which leads on to Mill Lane. Booking office at Mill Farm on R. Bridlington 8m. Level site surrounded by mature hedges. Shaver points, showers,

dishwashing with free hot water. Farm walk. Sea 0.5m. Shop, PH in the village. Swimming pool, fishing and golf nearby. Open March 10-October 1. **35T. 35MC.** 🛏 ⚲ ⚲

Withernsea

(0.5m). Goodwin Caravan Park, Queen Street South, Withernsea, East Yorkshire. *01964 612233.* Owner: Highfield Caravans Ltd. On A1033, 5mins walk from town. Quiet park suited to retired people or those looking for a peaceful holiday, with the added attraction of Withernsea golf course next door. Tesco next to park. Open mid March-October 31. **120S.** 🛏

(0.5m). Highfield Caravan Park, Queen Street, Withernsea, East Yorkshire. *01964 612233.* www.highfield-caravans.co.uk. Owner: Mr M Kemp & Partners. On A1033. 5mins walk from town. Small, private park suitable relaxing holiday, situated next to beach and seafront with promenade. Well-established fishing lake. Tesco opposite site. Golf course 5mins walk. Open April 1-October 31. **BH&HPA. 113S.** 🛏

(1m). Long Meadows Holiday Park, Waxholme Road, Withernsea, East Yorkshire HU19 2BT. *01964 613319.* Owner: J, P A, R M & D K Stephenson. Children allowed. Open March 7-January 6. **BH&HPA. 225S.** 🛏 ⚲

(1m). Willows Holiday Park, Hollym Road, Withernsea, East Yorkshire HU19 2NP. *01964 612821/612233.* www.highfield-caravans.co.uk. Owner: Mr M Kemp & Mrs J Kemp. On A1033. First on the L on entering Withernsea. Showers, club, play area, coarse fishing lake, mini-golf. Laundry. Electric hook-ups bookable in advance. Located within easy reach of sea and town centre. Luxury caravans to hire. 0.25m to golf course and Tesco supermarket. 0.75m to town centre. Open March 4-January 3. ✩✩✩✩ **40T. 5MC. 168S. 2H.** 🛏 ⚲

(0.5m). Withernsea Holiday Park, North Road, Withernsea, East Yorkshire HU19 2BS. *0871 664 9803.* withernsea.holi daypark@park-resorts.com.www.park-resorts.com. Owners: Park Resorts Ltd. 3rd Floor, Swan Court, Waterhouse Street, Hemel Hempstead, herts HP1 1FN. From J88 on the M62 take the A63 through Hull. At the end of the dual carriageway, turn R on to the A1033, and follow signs for Withernsea. Follow A1033 through the village and turn on to B1242. Park is 0.5m on R. Adventure playground, children's club, outdoor play area, amusements, laundrette, on site shop, free family evening entertainment. Freeuse of local indoor pool (1m). Sandy beach 200yd. Open April-October. **BH&HPA. NCC. 366S. 5H.** 🛏 ⚲

NORTH YORKSHIRE

Acaster Malbis

Poplar Farm Caravan Park, Acaster Malbis, North Yorkshire YO23 2UH. *01904 706548.* Owner: G Taylor. Four miles south of York, turn off the A64 at Copmanthorpe junction (A1237) follow signs. Family-run park on the banks of river Ouse, river-bus service to York through. Bar and restaurant. Open end March- end October. **BH&HPA. 80T. MC. 50S. 4H.** 🛏 ⚲ ⚲

(5m). The Old Post Office Caravan Park, Mill Lane, Acaster Malbis, North Yorkshire YO23 2UJ. *01904 702448/706288.* Owner: Mrs V Baren, Nr S Shoobridge. Willow Garth, Mill Lane, Acaster Malbis, Yorks YO23 2UJ. Leave A64 at Copmanthorpe, SP Acaster Malbis, follow for 2m. 5m from York. Open April 1-End October. **10T. MC. 64S.** 🐾 ▣

Boroughbridge

(1m). Blue Bell Caravan Site, Blue Bell Hotel, Kirby Hill, Boroughbridge, North Yorkshire YO51 9DN. *01432 322380.* Owner: Mrs J Townend. From York-A59 to Boroughbridge. Open April-October. **BH&HPA. 4T. 4MC. 25S.** 🐾

(0.75m). Camping & Caravanning Club Site - Boroughbridge, Bar Lane, Roecliffe, Boroughbridge, North Yorkshire YO51 9LS. *01423 322683/0870 2433331.* www.campingandcaravanningclub.co.uk. Owner: Camping & Caravanning Club. Greenfields House, Westwood Way, Coventry CV4 8JH. Leave A1, SP Bouroughbridge, turn west off the main street, SP Roecliffe, site on right. Near to moors and dales on the banks of river Ure with fishing and boating. All units accepted. Non-members welcome. The site also hasa recreation hall with pool table and colour TV. Special deals available for families and backpackers. ✫✫✫✫✫ **85T. 85MC.** ✿ 🐾 ▣ ☇

Crown Inn, Roecliffe, Boroughbridge, North Yorkshire. *01423 322578.* Owner: Mr P M Barker. Off A1 Boroughbridge, 1.5m into Roecliffe. Rallies allowed for up to 80 tourers. Open March 1-October 31. **8T. MC. 32S.** 🐾 ▣ ☇

The Old Hall, Langthorpe, Boroughbridge, North Yorkshire YO51 9BZ. *01423 322130.* Off A1/A168 in village of Langthorpe off the Ripon Road, B6265, out of Boroughbridge. Open Easter/April-October 31. ✫✫✫ **BH&HPA. 10T. 10MC. 100S.** 🐾 ▣

Cawood

Cawood Holiday Park, Ryther Road, Cawood, North Yorkshire YO8 3TT. *01757 268450.* cawoodpark@aol.com. www.cawoodpark.co.uk. Owner: Andrew & Esther Pringle. On B1222 from A1 or York to Cawood traffic lights, and on B1223, SP Tadcaster, for 1m, park is on left. York 10m. Selby 5m. Laundrette. Pool tables. Coarse fishing. Lakeside bar. Entertainment. AA 4 pennants and RAC awards. 3 homes adapted for disabled visitors. New indoor swimming pool. Seasonal pitches available for touring caravans. ✫✫✫✫✫ **BH&HPA. 60T. 60MC. 10S. 10H.** ✿ 🐾 ▣ ☇ ☇ ✎

Coneysthorpe

(5m). Castle Howard Caravan & Camping Site, Coneysthorpe, North Yorkshire YO60 7DD. *01653 648366/ 648316.* lakeside@castlehoward.co.uk. Owner: Castle Howard Estate Ltd. The Estate Office, Castle Howard, York YO6 7DA. 6m SW of Malton. follow Castle Howard signs. Good touring centre, adjoining 70-acre lake. Well-drained site, good position for woodland and country walks. Dogs allowed under strict control. Open March 1-October 31. ✫✫✫✫ **BH&HPA. 40T. MC. 120S.** 🐾 ▣ ☇

Easingwold

(1.5m). Easingwold Caravan & Camping Park, White House Farm, Easingwold, North Yorkshire YO6 3NF. *01347 821479.* Owner: Mr G & K M Hood. 9m S of Thirsk, N of Easingwold. Quiet site close to York and Herriot country. Suitable stopover to and from Scotland. Open March 1-October 31. **30T. 30MC. 30S. 2H.** 🐾 ▣

Filey

(6m). Blue Dolphin Holiday Park, Gristhorpe Bay, Filey, North Yorkshire YO14 9PU. *01723 515155.* oewebmaster@ bourne-leisure.co.uk. www.bluedolphinholidaypark.com. Owner: Bourne Leisure Ltd. 1 Park Lane, Hemel Hempstead, Hertfordshire HP2 4YL. Park lies directly on A165 between Bridlington and Scarborough and is situated about north of Filey. Amusement arcade. Indoor and outdoor swimming pools. Supermarket. Takeaway. Laundry. Bars. Indoor fun palace. Adventure playgrounds. Mini ten-pin bowling. All-weather sports court. Children's clubs. Family entertainment. Golf 2m. Cinema, Scarborough 5m. York 35m. Open March-November. ✫✫✫✫ **BH&HPA. NCC. 430T. MC. 900S. 240H.** 🐾 ▣ ♿ ☇

(2m). Crows Nest Caravan Park, Gristhorpe, Filey, North Yorkshire YO14 9PS. *01723 582206.* enquiries@crowsnestcar avanpark.com www.crowsnestcaravanpark.com. Owner: Mr Ian Palmer. N of Filey, 5m S of Scarborough, off A165. Privately owned Rose Award park with full facilities. Suitable site for family holidays and weekend breaks. Shop, bar, indoor heated swimming pool, games room, play area, fish and chip shop. Open March 1-November 1. ✫✫✫✫ **50T. 18MC. 217S. 50H.** 🐾 ▣ ☇

Filey Brigg Camping & Caravan Park, North Cliff, Filey, North Yorkshire YO14 9ET. *01723 513852.* Owners: Scarborough Borough Council. Scarborough Sports Centre, Filey Road, Scarborough YO11 2TP. 0.5m from Filey town centre on the A165 road to Scarborough. On cliffs immediately north of Filey. Well-equipped holiday site. Maximum stay 21 days. Path to beach. Laundry. AA 3 pennants. Open Easter-October 31. ✫✫✫ **140T. MC.** 🐾 ▣ ☇

Muston Grange Caravan Park, Muston Road, Filey, North Yorkshire YO14 0HU. *01723 512167.* Central to Filey Town. Quiet, family-run park. 10mins walk to 5m of golden beach. Hard-standing pitches, new shower/laundrette block and small shop/reception. Childrens' play park. Pets welcome on leads. Open March-November. **250T. MC.** 🐾 ▣ ☇

(3m). Orchard Farm Holiday Village, Stonegate, Hunmanby, Filey, North Yorkshire YO14 0PU. *01723 891582.* Owner: Mr & Mrs D Dugdale. Turn right off A165 road to Hunmanby 0.25m on right. Level, secluded site with full amenities. Indoor pool, bar, entertainment, play area, private fishing. Beaches nearby. Historical village. Open end March-October. ✫✫✫✫✫ **BH&HPA. NCC. 85T. MC. 46S.** 🐾 ▣ ♿ ☇ ✎

(3m). Primrose Valley Holiday Park, Primrose Valley, Filey, North Yorkshire YO14 9RF. *01723 516641.* oewebmaster@ bourne-leisure.co.uk. www.primrosevalleyholidaypark.com. Owner: Bourne Leisure Ltd. 1 Park Lane, Hemel Hempstead, Hertfordshire HP2 4YL. Situated directly on A165 between Scarborough and Bridlington, S of Filey. Large, multi-level heated pool complex. Multi-sports court. Adventure playground, mini golf game, climbing wall, boating lake, fun fair, abseiling, go-karts, convenience store, 2 cabaret bars, sports bar, restaurants, family entertainment. Open March-January. ✫✫✫✫ **BH&HPA. NCC. 50T. 1183S. 340H.** 🐾 ▣ ☇

(5m). Reighton Sands Holiday Park, Reighton Gap, Filey, North Yorkshire YO14 9SJ. *01723 892415.* oewebmaster@ bourne-leisure.co.uk. www.reightonsandsholidaypark.com. Owner: Bourne Leisure Ltd. 1 Park Lane, Hemel Hempstead, Hertfordshire HP2 4YL. Situated on A165 between Bridlington and Scarborough, S of Filey. Heated indoor swimming pool. Laundrette. Children's club. Family entertainment. Ten-pin bowling. Adventure playground. Convenience store. Outdoor sports. Access to blue flag beach. Golf course 3m. Open March-November. ✫✫✫ **BH&HPA. NCC. 152T. MC. 760S. 113H.** 🐾 ▣ ♿ ☇ ✎

(0.3m). **Wrights Seadale Caravan Camp Ltd, Seadale Camping Ground, Seadale, Filey, North Yorkshire YO14 0HT.** *01723 513538.* Owner: Wrights Seadale Caravan Camp Ltd. Hillcrest, 10 Scarborough Road, Filey, North Yorkshire YO14 9EF. From Muston road turn into Grange Avenue or into Clarence Drive, proceed along Padbury Avenue to camp entrance. Dogs on leads. 0.5m to fishing, shops, PO, doctor. 0.25m to golf course. Open April 1-September 30. **BH&HPA. 200S.** 🐾

Great Ouseburn

Lower Dunsforth Caravan Park, Great Ouseburn, North Yorkshire YO5 9SA. *01765 677014.* Owner: Mr A & Mrs D Wallace. Whales Close, Ings Lane, Bishop Monkton, North Yorkshire. Park is located off the B6265 York road. Bottled gas. **4S.** 🐾

Guisborough

(1m). **Tocketts Mill Caravan Park, Skelton Road, Guisborough, North Yorkshire TS14 6QA.** *01287 610182.* Owner: David & Susan Wainwright. Located off the A173 road from Guisborough, on the road to Skelton. Laundry facilities. Play area. PH on park. AA 3 pennants. Open March 1-January 4. **50T. 50MC.** 🐾 🔌 ♿

Harrogate

(2m). **Bilton Park, Village Farm, Bilton Lane, Harrogate, North Yorkshire HG1 4DL.** *01423 863121.* biltonpark@tcs mail.net. Owner: Mrs A M Ashton. Travelling from the A59 in Harrogate, between A661 and A61, turn into Bilton Lane at Skipton Inn. Park is situated 1.25m along Bilton Lane. Open March-End October. ✩✩✩ **BH&HPA. 25T. 5MC. 25S.** 🐾 🔌 🛒

(1.5m). **Great Yorkshire Showground Caravan Club Site, Wetherby Road, Harrogate, North Yorkshire HG3 1TZ.** *01423 560470.* www.caravanclub.co.uk. Owner: The Caravan Club. East Grinstead House, East Grinstead, West Sussex RH19 1UA. See website for standard directions to site. Located just off the A661 road, this flat and pleasantly open site could hardly be more conveniently situaed to Harrogate, the floral capital of Yorkshire. Non-members and tent campers welcome. Peaceful off-peak, Some hard-standings, Calor Gas and Campingaz, play equipment, dog walk nearby. Toilet blocks. Laundry facilities. Veg preparation. Suitable for families. Beach and golf within 5m, recycling facilities. Open March-November. ✩✩✩ **NCC. 71T. MC.** 🐾 🔌 ♿

(14m). **Heathfield Caravan Park, Ramsgill Road, Pateley Bridge, Harrogate, North Yorkshire HG3 5PY.** *01423 711652.* Owner: A & J Harker. Turn off the B6265 at Pateley Bridge on to unclassified road SP for Wath and Ramsgill, turn left, park is SP. Pateley Bridge 1m. Set in area with many walking opportunities. Open March-October. **BH&HPA. 10T. 2MC. 170S.** 🐾 🔌 🛒

(4m). **High Moor Farm Park, High Moor Farm, Skipton Road, Harrogate, North Yorkshire HG3 2LZ.** *01423 563637/564955.* Owner: Mr & Mrs P Kershaw. On the A59 Harrogate to Skipton road. Bar. Restaurant. Swimming pool. Club. Golf on site. Fishing. Bowling green. Open April-October. ✩✩✩✩ **BH&HPA. 160T. 6MC. 158S.** 🐾 🔌 ♿ 🛒

(12m). **Low Wood Caravan Park, Pateley Bridge, Harrogate, North Yorkshire HG3 5PZ.** *01423 711433.* Owner: Mrs M E Simpson. Spring House, Heathfield, Pately Bridge, North Yorkshire. Follow Low Wath road out of Pateley Bridge, turn left after Water Mill Inn to Heathfield, 300yd left and follow signs to park. Second park on left. Open April-October. **BH&HPA. T. MC. 48S.** 🐾 🔌

(10m). **Manor House Farm Caravan Site, Summerbridge, Harrogate, North Yorkshire HG3 4JS.** *01423 780322.* Owner: T J Houseman & M J Liddle. Off the B6165 between Harrogate and Pateley Bridge, near the river Nidd. Peaceful site and close to many beauty spots, including Brinhan Rocks and Fountains Abbey. Hard-standings on different levels. No dogs allowed. Good walking area. Adjacent to Nidderdale Way. Ripley 5m, Pateley Bridge 5m. 2 mins to village shops and doctor. Open March 1-October 31. **BH&HPA. 40T. MC. 40S.** 🔌

(3m). **Ripley Caravan Park, Knaresborough Road, Ripley, Harrogate, North Yorkshire HG3 3AU.** *01423 770050.* Owner: Mr P & V House. Whiteoaks, Ripley, Harrogate, North Yorkshire HG3 2AU. Take the A61 N Harrogate to Ripon, at Ripley roundabout take the B6165 to Knaresborough, site is 300yd on left-hand side. Level, country park with indoor heated pool, laundrette, playground, games and nursery play room, sauna and football pitch. Golf course nearby. PO in village. David Bellamy Gold Conservation Award. Open Easter-October 31. ✩✩✩✩ **BH&HPA. 100T. 100MC. 40S.** 🐾 🔌 ♿ 🛒

(14 m). **Riverside Caravan Park, Low Wath Road, Pateley Bridge, Harrogate, North Yorkshire HG3 5HL.** *01423 711383/711320.* Owner: Mr D H & C A Weatherhead. B6265 or B6165 into Pateley Bridge; site situated about 0.25m along Low Wath Road on the right. Open April 1-October 31. **BH&HPA. 47T. 5MC. 110S.** 🐾 🔌

(3m). **Rudding Holiday Park, Follifoot, Harrogate, North Yorkshire HG3 1JH.** *01423 870439.* holiday-park@rudding park.com. www.ruddingpark.com. Owner: Mr Simon Mackaness. S of Harrogate between the A661 and A658. Site set in parkland. Ideal touring centre. Facilities include heated outdoor swimming pool, playground and games room, 18-hole golf course and driving range, shop, Deer House family PH. Cinema, shops in Harrogate. Open March-January. ✩✩✩✩✩ **BH&HPA. NCC. 141T. 141MC. 95S.** 🐾 🔌 ♿ 🛒

(1m). Shaw's Trailer Park, Knaresborough Road, Harrogate, North Yorkshire HG2 7NE. *01423 884432.* www.shawstrailerpark.co.uk. Owner: Mr J Shaw. On the A59 between Harrogate 1m and Knaresborough 2.5m. Entrance is next to Johnson's cleaners. Harrogate side of Starbeck railway station. Shower facilities, telephone, children's play area. Fishing available, golf course, ponies/horses. ✩✩✩ **BH&HPA. NCC. 45T. 10MC. 25S.** ✿ ⛵ 🐴 🖭 🛠

(20m). Studfold Farm, Lofthouse, Harrogate, North Yorkshire HG3 5SG. *01423 755210.* www.studfoldfarm. co.uk. Owner: Mr F Walker. Seven miles from Pateley Bridge at head of Nidderdale. Suitable base for walking and touring other Yorkshire dales. Level site on working farm, near to Howstean Gorge. Village, PO 0.5m. Shopping, golf, fishing 7-10m. Open April 1-October 31. ✩✩✩ **BH&HPA. 24T. 12MC. 60S.** 🐴 🖭 🛠

(1.5m). The Cardale Estate, Cardale Woods, Beckwithshaw, Harrogate, North Yorkshire HG3 1QL. *01423 530760.* Owner: Mr & Mrs M Clarke. Club Hideaway site on estate. Tarmac roads; ramps available if required. Open March 1-January 31. **5T. 5MC. 50S.** 🐴 🖭 ♿

(9m). Warren Forest Caravan Park, Warsill, Ripley, Harrogate, North Yorkshire HG3 3LH. *01765 620683.* enquiries@warren forestpark.co.uk. www.warrenforestpark. co.uk. Owner: R S & L B Stanley. Situated between Ripley and Pateley Bridge and Fountains Abbey. Quiet, secluded park in woodland setting. Putting. Library. No tourers. Open March 15-November 15. ✩✩✩✩✩ **BH&HPA. 100S.** 🐴

(15m). Westfield Farm, Heathfield, Pateley Bridge, Harrogate, North Yorkshire HG3 5BX. *01423 711880.* Owner: E Simpson. Low Wood Farm, Bewerley, Pateley Bridge, Harrogate, N Yorks HG3 5BX. Off B6265, Pateley Bridge to Ripon. NW of Pately Bridge take Ramsgill Road, after 1mturn left towards Heathfield, left again in 100yd, site is the third on the L. Open April 1-October 31. **BH&HPA. 10T. 5MC. 60S.** 🐴 🖭

(7m). Yorkshire Hussar Inn Holiday Caravan Park, Markington, Harrogate, North Yorkshire HG3 3NR. *01765 677327.* yorkshirehussar@yahoo.co.uk. www.ukparks.co.uk/ yorkshirehussar. Owner: J S Brayshaw (Caravans) Ltd. W off the A61 about halfway between Harrogate and Ripon, turn west at Wormald Green. 1m into village of Markington. Secluded, family park behind village inn, close to Fountain Abbey, Brimham Rocks, Herriott and Emmerdale country. PO and shop in village. Play area. Laundrette. Showers. PH. AA 3 pennants. Fishing, golf, racing, tennis, swimming 5m. Cinema 8m. Open March 1-October 31. ✩✩✩✩ **BH&HPA. 20T. 10MC. 75S. 5H.** 🐴 🖭 ♿

Hawes

(0.5m). Bainbridge Ings Caravan Site, Hawes, North Yorkshire DL8 3NU. *01969 667354.* janet@bainbridge-ings.co.uk. www.bainbridge-ings.co.uk. Owner: Mr & Mrs M Facer. Approaching Hawes from Bainbridge on the A684 turn left at SP marked 'Gayle 300 yards'. Fishing nearby. Washing machine and tumble dryer. Good centre for walking and touring the Yorkshire Dales. Shops, bus service within 0.5m. Train station, 7m. Lovely views from site of surrounding hills. Gas sold. Open April 1-October 31. ✩✩ **30T. 10MC. 15S. 2H.** 🐴 🖭

(0.25m). Brown Moor Caravan Club Site, Brunt Acres Road, Hawes, North Yorkshire DL8 3PS. *01969 667338.* www.caravanclub.co.uk. Owner: The Caravan Club. East Grinstead House, East Grinstead, West Sussex RH19 1UA. See website for standard directions to site. Caravan Club members only. Site located in Wensleydale between the river Ure and market town of Hawes. Toilet blocks, laundry facilities, baby and toddler washroom and motorhome service point. Dog walk and games room on site. Good area for walking. Fishing nearby. Suitable for families. Peaceful off-peak. Open March-January. **NCC. 110T. MC. ⊞ ☺ ⅋**

(0.25m). Honeycott Caravan Park, Ingleton Road, Hawes, North Yorkshire DL8 3LH. *01969 667310.* info@honeycott.co.uk. www.honeycott.co.uk. Owner: Kelvin & Anne Hughes. On the B6255 Hawes to Ingleton road. Small, quiet, family park. Suitable base for touring the Yorkshire Dales National Park. Convenient for shops and restaurants. Open March 1-October 31. ✰✰✰✰ **BH&HPA. 18T. MC. 28S. 7H. ⊞ ☺**

(2m). Shaw Ghyll, Simonstone, Hawes, North Yorkshire DL8 3LY. *01969 667359.* rogerstott@aol.com. Owner: Mr & Mrs R Stott. Follow signs from Hawes to Muker, for 2m. Site is 400yd past Simonstone Hall Country Guest House on the L. Secluded site by a small trout stream with a backdrop of hills. New facilities block. Hot showers. Hair and hand dryers. River fishing, fell walking. Open March-October. **30T. ⊞ ☺**

The Greens, Hawes, North Yorkshire. *01969 667297.* Owner: Mrs H A Heseldene. On A684 Leyburn to Kendal. Open Easter-October 31. **15S. ⊞**

Helmsley

(4m). Foxholme Touring Caravan Park, Harome, Helmsley, North Yorkshire YO62 5JG. *01439 770416/771696.* Owner: Mr K J R Binks. Leave Helmsley on the A170 in the direction of Scarborough, take first turn right, SP Harome, in village turn left at church and then follow signs. Laundry. Gas. Washbasins in private cubicles. Send stamp for brochure. Open March 1-October 31. ✰✰✰✰✰ **BH&HPA. 60T. MC. ⊞ ☺ ⅋ ⅃**

(2m). Golden Square Caravan & Camping Park, Golden Square, Oswaldkirk, Helmsley, North Yorkshire YO6 25YQ. *01439 788269.* e-mail: barbara@goldensquarecaravanpark.freeserve.co.uk. www.goldensquarecaravanpark.com. Owner: Mr & Mrs D Armstrong. S of Helmsley, off B1257, Malton to Ampleforth. Ampleforth 1m. Secluded site surrounded by open countryside and woodland. Magnificent views. Heated bathroom. Laundrette. Shop. Outdoor/indoor play areas. Sports centre, fishing and golf nearby. De-luxe all service pitches, seasonal pitches and storage compound. Open March 1-October 31. ✰✰✰✰✰ **BH&HPA. 110T. 110MC. 1H. ⊞ ☺ ⅋ ⅃**

(4m). Wombleton Caravan Park, Moorfield Lane, Wombleton, Helmsley, North Yorkshire YO62 7RY. *01751 431684.* www.europage.co.uk/wombletonpark. E of Helmsley, stay on A170 until you see sign for Wombleton. Go straight through village, turn L for park. Quiet and level with modern facilities. Seasonal pitches available. Under new management. Open Easter-October 31. ✰✰✰✰✰ **BH&HPA. 78T. MC. ⊞ ☺ ⅃**

(3m). Wrens of Ryedale Caravan Camp Site, Gale, Nawton, Helmsley, North Yorkshire YO62 7SD. *01439 771260.* dave@wrensofryedale.fsnet.co.uk. www.wrensofryedale.fsnet.co.uk. Owner: G D & L J Smith. Off A170 in Beadlam. Small, family-run site in the heart of the Ryedale countryside. Suitable base for North York Moors, dales, coast and York. Open April 1-October 31. ✰✰✰✰ **BH&HPA. 30T. 15MC. ⊞ ☺ ⅃**

Ingleton

(1m). Greenwood Leghe Holiday Home Park, Ingleton, North Yorkshire LA6 3DP. *01524 241511.* stocks@greenwoodleghe.co.uk. www.greenwoodleghe.co.uk. Owner: R W & J A Stocks. On A65, Kirkby Lonsdale to Settle. About 1m from centre of Ingleton in direction of Settle, turn L off A65 into tree-lined drive. Suitable base for walking and touring. Footpaths lead directly from park. Centre for Yorkshire Dales and Lake District. **BH&HPA. 143S. ✿ ⅃**

(1m). Inglewood Holiday Home Park, Thornton-in-Lonsdale, Ingleton, North Yorkshire LA6 3PB. *01524 241511.* stocks@greenwoodleghe.co.uk. www.ukparks.co.uk/inglewood. Owner: R W & J A Stocks. 0.5m off A65, Kirkby Lonsdale to Settle, to hamlet of Thornton-in-Lonsdale. Park adjacent to Marton Arms country inn with restaurant. Suitable base for walking and touring. Centre for Dales and Lakes. Famous area for mountains, waterfalls and caves. Within yards of the ancient church. **BH&HPA. 18S. ⅃**

(2m). Parkfoot Holiday & Park Homes, Bentham Road, Ingleton, North Yorkshire LA6 3HR. *015242 61833.* sales@parkfoot.co.uk. www.parkfoot.co.uk. Owner: Parkfoot Holiday Homes Ltd. Parkfoot Caravan Park, Bentham Road, Ingleton, Via Carnforth LA6 3HR. Bentham Road is on the W side of the A65 at Ingleton, S of the Iron Bridge. From S M6 exit 34 take A683, A687, and A65 S. From N, M6 exit 36 take A65 S. Riverside setting in the old West Riding, overlooking dales, on the road to the lakes. Between Ingleton and Bentham. Ask for brochure and sales list. Golf 1m. Horse riding, shops 2m. Fishing nearby. Open February 1-November 30. ✰✰✰✰✰ **BH&HPA. 176S. ⊞ ⅊ ⌀**

(1.5m). Trees Holiday Home Park, Westhouse, Ingleton, North Yorkshire LA6 3NZ. *01524 241511.* stocks@greenwoodleghe.co.uk. www.ukparks.co.uk/trees. Owner: R W & J A Stocks. Along A65 N of Ingleton, to hamlet called Westhouse. Suitable base for walking and touring. Excellent centre for Yorkshire Dales and Lake District. Famous area for mountains, waterfalls and caves. **BH&HPA. 9T. MC. 20S. ⊞ ☺**

Knaresborough

(3m). Allerton Park Caravan Park, Allerton Mauleverer, Knaresborough, North Yorkshire HG5 0SE. *01423 330569.* enquiries@yorkshireholidayparks.co.uk. www.yorkshireholidayparks.co.uk. Owner: Mr & Mrs D Hind. From A1 take A59 1m towards York. Peaceful site well placed for exploring Yorkshire. Amenities block. Play area. Laundrette. Telephone. Calor Gas. 3 lodges for hire. Open February 1-January 3. ✰✰✰✰ **BH&HPA. 50T. MC. 100S. 5H. ⊞ ☺ ⅃**

(2m). Kingfisher Caravan Park, Low Moor Lane, Farnham, Knaresborough, North Yorkshire HG5 9DQ. *01423 869411.* Owner: Richardson. From Knaresborough take A6055, SP Boroughbridge, turn L for Farnham. Turn left. Site 1m from church on the left-hand side. Sheltered area for touring caravans and level hard-standings for motor caravans. Facilities include fwashing up area, showers, laundry, large playground. Most sporting facilities nearby. Fishing available. Open March 1-October 31. ✩✩✩ **BH&HPA. 30T. 10MC. 140S. 10H.** 🐾 🎦 ♿ 🛒

(2m). Knaresborough Caravan Club Site. New Road, Scotton, Knaresborough, North Yorkshire HG5 9HH. *01423 860196.* www.caravanclub.co.uk. Owner: The Caravan Club. East Grinstead House, East Grinstead, West Sussex RH19 1UA. See website for standard directions to site. The site offers a gateway to the Yorkshire Dales and the many attractions of the North of England. Toilet blocks with privacy cubicles, laundry facilities and baby/toddler washroom. Motorhome service point and vegetable preparation area. Bar, restaurant and children's playroom. Fishing, golf and NCN cycle track within 5m. Dog nearby, good area for walking. Ideal for families. Non-members and tent campers admitted. Open March-January. ✩✩✩✩✩ **NCC. 62T. MC.** 🐾 🎦 ♿

(0.5m). Riverside Caravan Park, York Road, Knaresborough, North Yorkshire HG5 0SS. *01302 700050.* Owner: Mr R Smith. c/o 6 Riverside Park, York Road, Knaresborough, North Yorkshire HG5 0SS. On A59, York to Knaresborough. Fishing and canoeing on river Nidd. 3m west of A1. No children. Open March 1-January 7. **BH&HPA. 15S.** 🐾 ♿ 🖉

(2m). Scotton Park Caravans, New Road, Scotton, Knaresborough, North Yorkshire HG5 9HH. *01423 864413.* Owner: Mr J A Smith. Abbot's Knoll, Abbey Road, Knaresborough, North Yorkshire HG5 8HX. On B6165, out of Knaresborough towards Ripley, 1.5m on right. Bus stop at entrance. Easy access, all tarmac roads. Hire caravans all on mains services with hot showers and TV. Rose Award. Golfand horse riding 2m. Open March 1-January 6 for owner-occupiers; open April-October for hire caravans. **BH&HPA. 6S. 4H.** 🐾 ♿ 🖉

Lancaster

(3m). Goodenbergh Country Holiday Park, Low Bentham, Lancaster, North Yorkshire LA2 7EU. *01524 262022.* office@goodenbergh.freeserve.co.uk. www.goodenbergh leisure.co.uk. Owner: George Luscombe Builders Ltd (Goodenbergh Leisure). Off A65 to Low Bentham, motorway J34 to Bentham in Wennington, second left, park SP. Developing a woodland walk around the perimeter of the park. David Bellamy Gold Conservation Award. Laundry on park. Open March 1-January 4. **BH&HPA. 147S.** 🐾 🛒

(11m). Riverside Caravan Park, High Bentham, Lancaster, North Yorkshire LA2 7LW. *01524 261272.* info@riversidecar avanpark.co.uk. www.riversidecaravanpark.co.uk. Owner: J Marshall & Son. M6 J34, turn on to A683 towards Kirkby Lonsdale. Turn right before Hornby on to B6480, SP High Bentham. Right turn by Black Bull Hotel. Park is 0.5m on right. Laundry room, indoor games room, outdoor adventure playground, fishing on private stretch of river. Market town of Bentham with shops, PHs and takeaways, 5mins walk from park and golf course. David Bellamy Gold Conservation Award. Open March 1-January 2. ✩✩✩✩ **BH&HPA. 30T. 30 MC. 205S.** 🐾 🎦 ♿

Leyburn

(5.5m). Akebar Park (Wensleydale), Leyburn, North Yorkshire DL8 5LY. *01677 450201/450591.* Owner: Mr J C P Ellwood. 7 miles west from A1, at Leeming Bar take A684 from Bedale to Leyburn and follow the brown signs. 18 and 9-hole golf course and driving range, Friars Head PH and restaurant

adjacent. Licensed shop. Showers. Fishing. Calor Gas. Laundry. Children's boating. Bowling and croquet green. Dogs allowed on leads on the park but not in hire vans. PGA golf professional now available for lessons, pro shop also available. Hospital at Northallerton, doctors at Bedale and Leyburn. Swimming pools at Richmond and Bedale. Open March 1-January 2. **BH&HPA. 140T. MC. 150S. 5H.** 🐾 🎦 🛒

(3m). Carr End House, Marsett, Nr Bainbridge, Leyburn, North Yorkshire DL8 3DE. *01969 50346/01845 577425.* Owner: Mr P Belward. Off A684 at Bainbridge, overlooking Lake Semer Water. Fishing. Sailing. Windsurfing. Night halt. Open March 1-October 30. **3T. 3MC. 12S.** 🎦

(4.5m). Chantry Caravan Park, West Witton, Leyburn, North Yorkshire DL8 4NA. *01969 622372.* Owner: R H & J A Darling. Near A684. Laundrette. New pitches for 12ft-wide holiday homes. Peaceful site. Open March 1-January 14. **BH&HPA. 5T. 2MC. 150S.** 🐾 🛒

(3m). Constable Burton Hall Caravan Park, Constable Burton, Leyburn, North Yorkshire DL8 5LJ. *01677 450428.* Owner: Mr M C A Wyvill. Leave A1 at A684 between Bedale and Leyburn. Milk, papers and gas sales only. Restaurant and PH opposite site entrance. Wardens: George and Dulcie Stavers. Golf course nearby. Constable Burton Hall Gardens open to the public. Open April 1-October 31. ✩✩✩✩ **BH&HPA. 110T. 10MC.** 🐾 🎦 ♿

(1m). Lower Wensleydale Caravan Club Site, Harmby, Leyburn, North Yorkshire DL8 5NU. *01969 623366.* www.caravanclub.co.uk. Owner: The Caravan Club. East Grinstead House, East Grinstead, West Sussex RH19 1UA. See website for standard directions to site. Set within the hollow of a disused quarry, now overrun with wildflowers and mosses. Non-members welcome. Tent campers welcome in separate area. No late-arrivals' area. Toilet blocks. Privacy cubicles. Laundry facilities. Veg prep. Waste disposal for motor caravans. Information room. Good area for walking. Open March-November. **NCC. 100T. MC.** 🐾 🎦 ♿

(9m). Street Head Caravan Park, Newbiggin, Bishopdale, Leyburn, North Yorkshire DL8 3TE. *01969 663472/663571.* d.coop@btinternet.com. Owner: Mr D J Cooper. High Green Farm, Thoralby, Leyburn, North Yorkshire DL8 3SU. Off A684, Leyburn to Hawes. About 2m from Aysgarth. On B6160 and adjacent to Street Head Inn. Small, quiet park in middle of Yorkshire Dales National Park. Open March 1-October 31. **25T. 10MC. 45S.** 🐾 🎦 🛒

(1.5m). The Orchard Caravan Site, The Busks, Middleham, Leyburn, North Yorkshire DL8 4PR. *01969 623242.* Owner: Mrs L H Lofthouse. Busks Cottage, Middleham, Leyburn, N. Yorkshire. Off A684/A6108 from Ripon. A1 Darlington. Small, quiet site. No children. 18m from Ripon via Washam. Darlington 25m via Richmond and Leyburn. Open March 1-October 31. **25S.** 🐾

(7m). Westholme Caravan & Camping Park, Aysgarth, Leyburn, North Yorkshire DL8 3SP. *01969 663268.* Owner: A & I Woodhouse Ltd. Off A684 Leyburn to Hawes. 1m to E of Aysgarth. Attractive, well maintained park with views within the boundary of the Yorkshire Dales National Park. Laundry. Play area. Dog walk. Fishing. Licensed club. Meals available when club open. TV room. AA 4 pennants. Open March-October. **BH&HPA. 70T. MC. 44S.** 🐾 🎦 🛒

Malton

(6m). Ashfield Country Manor, Kirby Misperton, Malton, North Yorkshire YO17 0UU. *01653 668555.* Owner: Mr & Mrs S Bulmer. Situated between Pickering and Malton turn off A169 to Kirby Misperton. Open March-October. **BH&HPA. 100T. MC.** ⛺ ⚑ ☎

(8m). Flamingo Land Theme Park, Zoo & Holiday Village, Kirby Misperton, Malton, North Yorkshire YO17 6UX. *01653 668585.* info@flamingoland.co.uk. www.flamingoland.co.uk. Owner: Mrs M Gibb. Flamingo Land Ltd. Off A169, Malton to Pickering. Leisure complex, golf course, entertainment within family fun park. More than 100 free attractions, including roller-coaster, family rides, 6 shows and an extensive zoo. Open March-October. **BH&HPA. 1000T. MC. 713S. 101H.** ⛺ ⚑ ☎ ⚒

(10m). The Snooty Fox, East Heslerton, Malton, Yorkshire YO17 8EN. *01944 710 554.* Owners: S & J Butterworth. Ganton golf 10mins away. Wold Way, close to coast and dales. Charge for dogs. **30T. MC.** ✿ ⛺ ⚑ ☎ ♿

Northallerton

(5m). Blacksmiths Arms Caravan Site, Swainby, Northallerton, North Yorkshire. *01642 700303.* Owner: Mr & Mrs G W Simpson. Off A19 on to the A172. Open March 1-October 31. **12T. 12MC.** ⛺

(6m). Cote Ghyll Caravan & Camping Park, Osmotherley, Northallerton, North Yorkshire DL6 3AH. *01609 883425.* hills@coteghyll.com. www.coteghyll.com. Owner: Mr & Mrs J Hills. Exit A19 at A684 Northallerton junction, travel into Osmotherley village. Turn L in village centre and follow road for 0.25m to the park. Family site in peaceful valley of North York Moors National Park. New for 2006: luxury heated shower block with bathroom. Superpitches, seasonal pitches, tourer storage. Rose Award. Play area and stream. Village PHs/shops within 10mins walk. Adjacent to Cleveland Way, coast to coast, Lyke Wake Walk and National Cycleway. Golf, fishing, horse riding, sports centre and market towns all within 6m. Open March 1-October 31. ✰✰✰✰ **BH&HPA. 77T. 77MC. 18S. 3H.** ⛺ ⚑ ☎ ♿

(4m). Hutton Bonville Caravan Park, Hutton Bonville, Northallerton, North Yorkshire DL7 0NR. *01609 881416.* hutton-b@hotmail.com. Owner: Leisure Parks. Fern Bank FM, Crooklands, Nr Milnthorpe, Cumbria LA7 7PB. On A167, 13m from Darlington. Suitable for retired/semi-retired people. Shops, doctors, fishing, golf etc all close by. Open March 1-January 7. **BH&HPA. 75S.** ⛺

(6m). Pembroke Caravan Park, Leeming Bar, North Allerton, North Yorkshire DL7 9BW. *01677 422652/422608.* Owner: G & S Liddell. Pembroke House, 19 Low Street, Leeming Bar, Northallerton, North Yorkshire. 0.5m from A684, 1m from A1. 3m from Bedale. Conveniently situated for touring the Yorkshire Dales, North Yorkshire Moors and historic city of York. PO and PH with bar food in small village. Takeaway on site. Golf course 3m. Fishing 2m. Open March 1-October 31. ✰✰✰ **25T. MC. 2H.** ⛺ ⚑ ☎

(6m). Willowgarth, Gatenby, Bedale, Northallerton, North Yorkshire. *01677 422853.* Owner: Mrs M T Exelby. Off A1. No children. **5S.** ⛺

Pickering

(1m). Black Bull Caravan & Camping Park, Malton Road, Pickering, North Yorkshire YO18 8EA. *01751 472528.* Owner: Mrs Louise Wright. S of Pickering on the A169, behind Black Bull PH. Quiet, family site. Showers. Laundry.

Children's playground, playfield, games room, takeaway and bar meals. Static holiday caravans for hire on separate field. Nearby swimming, fishing, tennis, golf, steam railway, theme park and zoo, shops. Open March 1-31 October. **30T. MC. 30S. 5H.** ⛺ ☎

(2m). Overbrook Caravan Site, Maltongate, Thornton-le-Dale, Pickering, North Yorkshire YO18 7SE. *01751 474417.* enquiry@overbrookcaravanpark.co.uk. www.overbrookcaravanpark.co.uk. Owner: Hilary Scales & Graham Hoyland. Station House, Maltongate, Thornton-le-Dale, Pickering, North Yorkshire YO18 7SE. Off the A170. Turn down Maltongate to village station or turn right off A169 to Thornton-le-Dale, site of old railway station on R. Exclusively for adults. Level, well-drained site, resident owners. 0.5m level walk to shops, PO, PHs, tea rooms and bus route. Centrally located for sightseeing. Open March 1-October 31. ✰✰✰ **BH&HPA. 50T. 10MC.** ⛺ ☎

(9m). Rosedale Caravan Park, Rosedale Abbey, Pickering, North Yorkshire YO18 8SA. *01751 417272.* Owner: Flower of May Holiday Parks Ltd. Batteries charged. Play and equipment area. Showers. Shaver points. Calor Gas and Campingaz. PHand takeaway within 100yd of park. Open April-mid-October. **53T. MC. 35S.** ⛺ ☎

(7m). Spiers House Caravan & Camping Site, Forestry Commission (Forest Holidays), Cropton, Pickering, North Yorkshire YO18 8ES. *01751 417591.* fe.holidays@forestry.gsi.gov.uk. www.forestholidays.co.uk. Owner: Forestry Commission (Forest Holidays). 231 Corstophine Road, Edinburgh EH12 7AT. A170 W from Pickering. 1m N of Cropton on the Rosedale road, turn right to site. Suitable base from which to explore the North Yorkshire Moors National Park. Good walking from the site. Advance booking advised. Brochure request line: 01313 340066. Open March-September. ✰✰✰ **BH&HPA. 150T. MC.** ⛺ ♿ ☎

(1.5m). Upper Carr Touring Park, Upper Carr Lane, Malton Road, Pickering, North Yorkshire YO18 7JP. *01751 473115.* harker@uppercarr.demon.co.uk. www.uppercarr.demon.co.uk. Owner: Martin & Josette Harker. Off the A169, S of Pickering. Level, family park with licensed shop, laundry, pets corner, play area, cycle hire, payphone. Golf, pub, swimming, walking, and fishing nearby. 30 mins to York, Scarborough, Whitby and North Moors National Park. Brochure available. Open March 1-October 31. ✰✰✰✰✰ **BH&HPA. 80T. MC.** ⛺ ☎ ♿

(6m). Vale of Pickering Caravan Park, Carr House Farm, Allerston, Pickering, North Yorkshire YO18 7PQ. *01723 859280.* tony@valeofpickering.co.uk. www.valeofpickering.co.uk. Owner: Tony & Marjorie Stockdale. 4.5m E of Pickering, off the A170 (Scarborough) and B1415 (Malton). Modernised facilities. Showers. Laundrette. Ladies' and gents' bath. Hair-dryer. Gas supplies. Fishing 1m. Forestry walks 2m. Large play area. Microwave oven. Fully-lit. Off-licence. Play and games area. Open March 1-January 10. ✰✰✰✰✰ **BH&HPA. 120T. MC.** ⛺ ☎ ♿ ☎

(2.5m). Wayside Caravan Park, Wrelton, Pickering, North Yorkshire YO18 8PG. *01751 472608.* waysideparks@freenet.co.uk. www.waysideparks.co.uk. Owner: V R Goodson. 2a Clarence Drive, Filey YO14 0AA. Off the A170 from Pickering, 2.5m W at Wrelton. Touring centre for moors. South-facing park with country views and modern facilities. Historic steam railway. Fishing, golf course, service station and shop, PO all nearby. Open April-October. ✰✰✰ **BH&HPA. 62T. 10MC. 80S.** ⛺ ☎ ♿ ☎

Redcar

(1m). Coatham Caravan Park, York Road, Redcar, North Yorkshire. *01642 483422*. Owner: Mr & Mrs A J Barney. 10mins from beach and boating lake. Bus stop close to park. 1m to Redcar racecourse. Dogs allowed under control. Golf nearby, shop, PO few minutes' walk, park nearby. Fishing and bowls, horse riding 5mins walk; doctor Coatham Health Centre 5mins by car. Open March 1-October 31. **BH&HPA. 20T. MC. 90S. 2H.** ✿ ▣

Richmond

(2m). Brompton-on-Swale Caravan Park, Brompton-on-Swale, Richmond, North Yorkshire DL10 7EZ. *01748 824629*. brompton.caravanpark@btinternet.com. www.bromptoncaravanpark.co.uk. Leave A1 at Catterick A6136 exit, take B6271 to Brompton-on-Swale. Park 1m on L after Brompton-on-Swale on Richmond road. Site set on banks of river Swale. Fully serviced pitches. Free heated showers/washing-up water. Baby change facilities. No teenagers (families with children 12 years and under). Semi-retired and retired couples only. Licensed shop. Laundry. Play area. Dawn to dusk lighting. David Bellamy Gold Conservation Award. Fishing. Some special offers, phone for details. On-site takeaway for pizzas, burgers, fish and chips. Open March 20-October 31. ✩✩✩✩✩ **BH&HPA. 177T. MC. 22S.** ✿ ▣ ♿ ▩

(6m). Foxhall Caravan Park, Ravensworth, Richmond, North Yorkshire DL11 7JZ. *01325 718344*. Owner: Mr John D Stoker. From Scotch Corner, take A66, 5m W take first turn left to Ravensworth. Site is 500yd on R. Quiet, friendly, woodland site. All hard-standings. Showers. Chemical toilet emptying pooint. Play area. Calor butane and propane gas available. AA and Caravan Club approved. Open April 1-October 31. **10T. MC. 55S.** ✿ ▣

(3.5m). Hargill House Caravan Club Site, Hargill House, Gilling West, Richmond, North Yorkshire DL10 5LJ. *01748 822734*. www.caravanclub.co.uk. Owner: The Caravan Club. East Grinstead House, East Grinstead, West Sussex RH19 1UA. See website for standard directions to site. Part-sloping site with views over the Yorkshire Dales National Park. Non-members welcome. Hard-standings. Toilet blocks. Privacy cubicles. Laundry facilities. Veg prep. Motorhome service point. Golf, fishing nearby. Good area for walking. Dog walk. Open March-November. ✩✩✩✩ **NCC. 66T. MC.** ✿ ▣ ♿

(11m). Orchard Caravan Park, Mill Holme, Reeth, Richmond, North Yorkshire DL11 6TT. *01748 884475*. Owner: Mr & Mrs M Bell. Off B6270 at the bottom of Back Lane. Shop adjacent to park. Village, PO, doctor within 4mins walk. Open April 1-October 31. **BH&HPA. 26T. MC. 30S. 1H.** ✿ ▣

(1m). Richmond (Yorks) Caravan Park, Reeth Road, Richmond, North Yorkshire DL10 4TH. *01748 822362*. richmondcaravanpark@fsmail.net. www.richmondcaravanpark.com. Owner: Messrs C&P Howley. Off A1/M at Scotch Corner to Richmond on A6108, W out of Richmond. Follow A6108 to Reeth; park, SP, is at end of road. Fishing available. Golf club in area. Open March 1-October 31. **BH&HPA. 42S.** ✿ ▣

(3m). Scotch Corner Caravan Park, Scotch Corner, Richmond, North Yorkshire DL10 6NS. *01748 822530*. mar shallleisure@aol.com. Owner: W & E Marshall. The Bungalow, Hartforth Lane, Gilling West, Richmond DL10 5JP. From Scotch Corner take A6108 Richmond road for 250yd, then across to other carriageway and return 200yd to site entrance. Bar and restaurant adjacent. Fishing, golf available at Richmond. Convenient night halt only 0.25m from A1. Access to nearby leisure centre. Open Easter-October. **96T. MC.** ✿ ▣ ♿ ▩

(2.5m). Swaleview Caravan Park, Reeth Road, Richmond, North Yorkshire DL10 4SF. *01748 823106*. Owner: Mr & Mrs AP, EL Carter. W of Richmond on A6108 Leyburn. Fishing. Laundry. Games room. Play area. Showers. National park. Open March-October. **BH&HPA. NCC. 50T. 10MC. 133S. 2H.** ✿ ▣ ♿ ▩

(6m). Tavern House Caravan Site, Newsham, Richmond, North Yorkshire DL11 7RA. *01833 621223*. Owner: Mr Stephen Thompson. 7m W from Scotch Corner in centre of village. Adults only. Quiet, enclosed site. Showers. Laundry facilities. Dogs on leads allowed. Good walking, bike riding. Open March 1-October 31. **6T. MC. 22S. 1H.** ✿ ▣

(24m). Usha Gap Caravan & Camp Site, Usha Gap, Muker, Richmond, North Yorkshire DL11 6DW. *01748 886214*. ushagap@btinternet.com. www.ushagap.btinternet.co.uk. Owner: Mrs A Metcalfe. B6270. 20m from Richmond, W of Richmond along Swale Dale or over Buttertubs Pass from Hawes. Small, family-run site on farm. Showers. Washing-up facilities. Dryer. 0.25m from village shop and pub. Shop, PO, PH serving meals, fishing all within 0.25m. **12T. 12MC.** ✿ ✿

Ripon

Black Swan Holiday Park, Rear of Black Swan Hotel, Fearby Masham, Ripon, North Yorkshire HG4 4NF. *01765 689477*. info@blackswanholiday.co.uk. www.blackswanholiday.co.uk. Owner: Mr J McCourt. Off A6108, 0.25m NW of Masham, site 2m left at rear of Black Swan. Open March-November. ✩✩✩ **BH&HPA. 50T. 5MC. 4S. 2H.** ✿ ▣ ▩

(9m). Fir Tree Farm Holiday Homes, Fir Tree Farm, Grewelthorpe, Ripon, North Yorkshire HG4 3DL. *01765 658727*. firtreefarmhouse@aol.com. www.firtree-farm-holiday-homes.co.uk. Owner: Eric & Jane Simpson. From Kirkby Malzeard turn R Ringbeck road. Follow road for nearly 4m. Park on right-hand side. Site for 15 timber lodges: at present 1 let, 9 privately owned. Planning for another 5. Children welcome. Golf, horse riding, fishing 3m. Open 51 weeks. ✩✩✩ **15S. 1H.** ✿

Old Station Holiday Park, Old Station, Low Burton, Masham, Ripon, North Yorkshire HG4 4DF. *01765 689569*. oldstation@tiscali.co.uk. oldstation-masham.co.uk. Owners: The Grainger Family. The Bungalow, Station Yard, Low Burton, Masham, Ripon, North Yorkshire HG4 4DF. From A1, Sinderby J on to B6267 to Masham W. From Harrogate A61 to A6108 N, Ripon to Masham. From Leyburn A6108 S. Quiet secluded park, footpaths to town 0.5m. Garage nearby sells gas, shops, PO and doctor. Many walks by river or farther away. Children's play-park nearby. Brewery tours. Many local events. Open March 1-November 30. **BH&HPA. 50T. MC.** ✿ ▣ ♿

(1m). River Laver Holiday Park, Studley Road, Ripon, North Yorkshire HG4 2QR. *01765 690508*. riverlaver@lineone.net. www.riverlaver.co.uk. Owner: Mr & Mrs G Scholey. Off B6265 towards Fountains Abbey. Level, secluded, family-run park with good facilities. Hard-standings available with drain and water point. Suitablel base for touring the Yorkshire Dales and North York Moors. Shop and gas sales on site. Golf 2m, shopping 1m, cinema 10m. Open March 1-January 3. ✩✩✩✩✩ **BH&HPA. 42T. 8MC. 79S.** ✿ ▣ ♿ ▩

(5.5m). Sleningford Watermill Caravan Park, North Stainley, Ripon, North Yorkshire HG4 3HQ. *01765 635201*. www.ukparks.co.uk/sleningford. Follow signs for the Lightwater Valley, taking A6108 out of Ripon, site is clearly SP. Alternatively leave A1 at the B6267, Masham to Thirsk road, and follow Lightwater Valley signs. Quiet, riverside site. Holiday flat also available for hire. On site fly fishing and white water canoeing on river Ure. Suitable base for walking, bird and wild flower spotting. Central for Herriot country and the N Yorks Dales. PO and garage 1-2m away. Doctor's surgery 4m. Golf courses, shops 5m. Site has small shop. Open April-October. ✩✩✩ **BH&HPA. 25T. 30MC. 25S.** 🛏 🔌 ♿ 🛒

(1m). Ure Bank Caravan Park, Ure Bank Top, Ripon, North Yorkshire HG4 1JD. *01765 602964.* Owner: Lookers Burtree Caravans Ltd. Burtree Parks, 19A Front Street, West Auckland. Off A61. Dogs allowed under control. Showers. Laundrette. Lounge bar. Playground. Games room. Open March 1-October 31. **BH&HPA. 175T. MC. 200S.** 🛏 🔌 ♿ 🛒

(5m). Winksley Banks Caravan Park, Galphay, Ripon, North Yorkshire HG4 3NS. *01765 658439.* keith@bronco.co.uk. www.winksleybanks.com. Owner: Mr K Bancroft. Situated 1m N of Winksley Village on the road to Kirkby Malzeard. No tourers. Laundry room. Payphone. Playground. Trout and coarse fishing. Shops, garage, doctor 1.5m. Golf nearby. Area of Outstanding Natural Beauty. On cycle byway in North Yorkshire. Open March 1-January 7. **103S.** 🛏

(5m). Woodhouse Farm Caravan and Camping Park, Winksley, Ripon, North Yorkshire HG4 3PG. *01765 658309.* woodhouse.farm@talk21.com. www.woodhousewinkley.com. Owner: A M Hitchen. SP after 3.5m, off B6265, Ripon to Pateley Bridge, at Winksley, and Grantley right hand turn-off. Licensed shop. TV and games room. Play equipment. Laundrette. Suitable touring base for Yorkshire Dales. Licensed restaurant serving home cooked food and real ale. Open March-October 31. ✩✩✩✩ **BH&HPA. 160T. 5MC. 60S.** 🛏 🔌 ♿ 🛒 ⌀

Saltburn-by-the-Sea

(5m). Grinkle Caravan Park, Grinkle, Easington, Saltburn-by-the-Sea, North Yorkshire TS13 4UB. *01287 640401.* Owner: G M V O'Neill. Travel along the A171 or A174, follow signs to Grinkle Park Hotel. Set in 35 acres of parkland, 2.5 m from sea, moors and Cleveland Way. Riding and sailing nearby. Adults only. Open March 1-October 31. **BH&HPA. 30S. 8H.**

(3m). Margrove Park Caravan Site, Boosbeck, Saltburn-by-the-Sea, North Yorkshire TS12 3BZ. *01287 653616.* keith@margrove.fsnet.co.uk. www.margroveparkholidays.co.uk. Owner: The Skelton Estate. From Guisbrough follow A171, SP Whitby, for about 2m. When you should turn left on to the minor road, SP Margrove park and Lindale in about 0.25m, turn right into the site. Showers. Manager: K & M Crossman. Shops 2m. PO 1m. Fishing, golf course nearby. Plenty of walking, 0.5m to Cleveland Way. Open April 1-October 31. **6T. 4MC.** 🛏

Scarborough

(4m). Arosa Caravan & Camping Park, Ratten Row, Seamer, Scarborough, North Yorkshire YO12 4QB. *01723 862166.* Owner: Messrs. D G & N R Cherry. S of Scarborough on A64, York road. Quiet, family site in countryside. Suitable touring base. Modern facilities. TV and games room. Play area. Laundrette. Public phone. Clubhouse. Entertainment in high season. Open March 1-January 4. ✩✩✩✩ **BH&HPA. 92T. MC.** 🛏 🔌 ♿ 🛒

(4m). Browns Caravan Park, Mill Lane, Cayton Bay, Scarborough, North Yorkshire YO13 3NN. *01723 582303.* info@brownscaravan.co.uk. www.brownscaravan.co.uk. Owner: R J & D Brown. S of Sacarborough, just off A165. Turn right at Cayton Bay traffic lights. Licensed bar serving food with children's room and play area. Games room. Laundrette.Open mid March-end October. ✩✩✩✩✩ **BH&HPA. 35T. 110S.** 🛏 🔌 🛒

(1m). Camping & Caravanning Club Site - Scarborough, Field Lane, Burniston Road, Scarborough, North Yorkshire YO13 0DA. *01723 366 212/0870 243 3331.* www.campingandcaravanning club.o.uk. Owners: Camping & Caravanning Club. Greenfields House, Westwood Way, Coventry CV4 8JH. On west side of A165, 1m N of Scarborough. Site is set in 20 acres, with views over the Yorkshire countryside. Situated high on the hills outside the village of Scalby and just N of the Victorian seaside resort of Scarborough. All units welcome. Some all-weather pitches available. Laundry facilities, children's play area. Swimming, fishing and tennis all available nearby. Non-members welcome. Special deals available for families and backpackers. Open March-October. ✩✩✩ **300T. 300MC.** 🛏 🔌 ♿ 🛒

(3m). Cayton Bay Holiday Park, Mill Lane, Cayton Bay, Scarborough, North Yorkshire YO11 3NJ. *0871 664 9725.* cayton.bay@park-resorts.com. www.park-resorts.com. Owner: Park Resorts Ltd. 3rd floor, Swan Court, Waterhouse Street, Hemel Hempstead, Herts HP1 1FN. Cayton Bay is just off the A165, S of Scarborough. On reaching traffic lights at Cayton Bay, turn into Mill Lane. Park entrance is on left-hand side. Amusements. Adventure playground. Indoor fun pool. Restaurant. Laundrette. Showbar. Free children's club. Free family evening entertainment. Open April-October. ✩✩✩✩ **BH&HPA. NCC. 475S. 149H.** 🛏 ♿ 🛒

(3m). Cayton Village Caravan Park Ltd (Dept 11), Mill Lane, Cayton Bay, Scarborough, North Yorkshire YO11 3NN. *01723 583171.* info@caytontouring.co.uk. www.caytontouring. co.uk. Owner: Mrs C Croft. 4m Filey, 0.5m Cayton Bay. A165 S of Scarborough, turn inland at Cayton Bay. Site on right-hand side in 0.5m. A64 take B1261, SP Filey, in Cayton, take second L after Blacksmiths Arms. Park is 200yd on L. Sheltered park 0.5 m to beach, adventure playground, showers, dishwashing, 3-acre dog walk. Adjoining church. 2 PHs, fish and chip shop, bus service. Seasonal pitches available. Golf nearby. Open March 1-January 4 and Christmas and New Year. ✩✩✩✩ **BH&HPA. 200T. MC.** 🛏 🔌 ♿ 🛒

Coachman Caravan Park, Snainton, Scarborough North Yorkshire. *01751 473189.* www.coachmancaravanpark.co.uk. Owners: GC & JM Senior. Village Farm, Wilton, Pickering, North Yorkshire YO18 7LE. 8m from Pickering. Ideal walking/cycling. Between Pickering and coast. Fishing nearby. Shop/PO in adjacent village. Not suitable for children. Brochure available. Open March 1-October 31. **12T.** 🛏 🔌

Please mention Caravan Sites 2006 when replying to advertisers

(5m). Flower of May Holiday Park, Lebberston Cliff, Scarborough, North Yorkshire YO11 3NU. *01723 584311.* info@flowerofmay.com. www.flowerofmay.com. Owner: Mr J G Atkinson. On A165 Filey to Scarborough. Games room. Family room. Bar. Laundry. Supermarket. Free play area. Indoor heated pool. Dogs allowed early and late season. Rose Award. Golf, basketball, bowling. Open March-October. Hire: Easter-September. ✩✩✩✩✩ **BH&HPA. 276T. MC. 190S. 37H.** ⚑ ⚑ ⚑

(2m). Gristhorpe Cliff Top Camp, Stone Pit Lane, Gristhorpe, Scarborough, North Yorkshire YO14 9HG. *08609 43617.* Owner: G E & J A Williamson. On A165 between Filey and Scarborough. Open April 1-September 30. **BH&HPA. 10T. MC. 145S.** ⚑

(2m). Jacobs Mount Caravan Park and Camping Site, Stepney Road, Scarborough, North Yorkshire YO12 5NL. *01723 361178.* www.jacobsmount.co.uk. Owner: Mr G Dale. Manager: Mr P Benjamin. W of Scarborough, on A170, Thirsk road. Level, all-weather pitches. Tap, drain, electrics etc. Licensed club. Bar meals. 2 play areas. Family room. New centrally heated shower block. Laundry facilities. Street lights. Rose Award. AA 4 pennants. Open March-January. ✩✩✩✩✩ **BH&HPA. 140T. 16MC. 48S. 10H.** ⚑ ⚑ ⚑ ⚑

(9m). Jasmine Park, Cross Lane, Snainton, Scarborough, North Yorkshire YOl3 9BE. *01723 859240.* info@jasmine park.co.uk. www.jasminepark.co.uk. Owner: David and Cynthia Hinchliffe. Turn S off A170 in Snainton (midway between Pickering and Scarborough), SP off A170 in Snainton. Level, well-drained site. Suitable base for coast and country. Bathroom for disabled visitors. David Bellamy Gold Conservation Award. 2005 national finalist of England's Caravan Park of the Year. Open March 1-December 31. ✩✩✩✩✩ **BH&HPA. 70T. MC. 1H.** ⚑ ⚑ ⚑ ⚑

(5m). Lebberston Touring Park, Filey Road, Lebberston, Scarborough, North Yorkshire YO11 3PE. *01723 585723.* info@lebberstontouring.co.uk. www.leb berstontouring.co.uk. Owner: Mark & Jane Bozeat. From A64 or A165 take B1261 to Lebberston. 3m from Filey. Quiet, country location with well-spaced pitches, with extensive south-facing views. Suitable for those seeking a peaceful, relaxing break. Modernised amenity blocks. Dog area. Suitable touring baseOpen March 1-October 31. ✩✩✩✩✩ **BH&HPA. 125T. MC.** ⚑ ⚑ ⚑

Lowfield Camping Park, Downdale Road, Staintondale, Scarborough, North Yorkshire YO13 0EZ. *01723 870574.* www.lowfieldcaravanandcamping.co.uk. Quiet, rural site . Golf course, fishing, shop nearby. Horse riding, llama trekking. Open February-December.**T. MC.** ⚑ ⚑ ⚑

(6m). Merry Lees Caravan Park, Merry Lees, Staxton, Scarborough, North Yorkshire YO12 4NN. *01944 710080.* sales@merrylees.co.uk. www.merrylees.co.uk. Owner: Mr & Mrs Aldred. On the A64, Scarborough to Staxton road. Quiet,

secluded site in a silver birch wood with pitches around a small lake. Convenient for coast and moors. Many wild birds on the park. Open March 1-October 31. **BH&HPA. 32T. MC.** ⚑ ⚑

(2m). Scalby Close Park, Burniston Road, Scarborough, North Yorkshire YO13 0DA. *01723 365908.* info@scalby closepark.co.uk. www.scalbyclosepark.co.uk. Owner: P F & M Bayes. Park signed 400yd on A165 N of Scarborough. Family-owned and family-run site with level, sheltered pitches. Suitable base for touring North York Moors and coast. Just 2m from Scarborough's North Bay attractions: pools, boating, etc. Open March-October. ✩✩✩✩ **BH&HPA. 42T. 5MC. 5H.** ⚑ ⚑ ⚑

(2m). Scalby Manor Touring Caravan and Camping Park, Burniston Road, Scarborough, North Yorkshire YO13 0DA. *01723 366212.* Owner: Scarborough Borough Council. Londesborough Lodge, The Crescent, Scarborough, North Yorkshire YO11 2PW. On A165, N of Scarborough, off main coast road. Supermarket with off-licence. Fish and chip shop. Laundry. Playground. Short walk to sandy beach. AA 4 pennants. Licensed hotel and restaurant next door. Open Easter-October 31. ✩✩✩ **375T. MC.** ⚑ ⚑ ⚑ ⚑

(4m). Spring Willows Touring Caravan & Camping Park, Main Road, Staxton, Scarborough, North Yorkshire YO12 4SB. *01723 891505.* fun4all@springwillows.fsnet.co.uk. www.springwillows.co.uk. A64, Filey to Bridlington road, to Staxton roundabout. Bar. Free hot showers. Swimming pool. Laundry. Sauna. Bistro. Games room. Takeaway. Playground. Children's club. Free entertainment. AA 4 pennants. Open March-January. ✩✩✩✩✩ **BH&HPA. 184T. MC.** ⚑ ⚑ ⚑ ⚑

(6m). St Helens in the Park, Wykeham, Scarborough, North Yorkshire YO13 9QD. *01723 862771.* www.sthelenscaravan park.co.uk. Owner: St Helens in the Park Ltd. Showers, baths, laundry. Takeaway. Playgrounds. In North Yorks Moors National Park. Bike hire. ✩✩✩ **BH&HPA. 250T. MC.** ⚑ ⚑ ⚑ ⚑ ⚑

(4m). West Ayton Caravan Club Site, Cockrah Road, West Ayton, Scarborough, North Yorkshire YO13 9JD. *01723 862989.* www.caravanclub.co.uk. Owner: The Caravan Club. East Grinstead House, East Grinstead, West Sussex RH19 1UA. See website for standard directions to site. Club members only. Family holiday site. Toilet blocks. Privacy cubicles. Laundry facilities. Baby/toddler washroom. Veg prep. Motorhome service point. Games room. Playfied and play equipment. Golf, fishing nearby. Open March-November. **NCC. 162T. MC.** ⚑ ⚑ ⚑

Selby

(6m). Oakmere Caravan Park and Coarse Fishery, Hill Farm, Skipwith, Selby, North Yorkshire YO8 5SN. *01757 288910.* Owners: M G Patrick & Sons. From York take A19 to Escrick, turn L to Skipwith about 3m. Oakmere is just outside village. Peaceful, 300-acre working farm set in the middle of Skipwith Nature Reserve with 9 acres of landscaped fisheries. Pets welcome. York and golf courses nearby. Local shops. Open March 1-October 31. ✩✩✩✩ **30T.** ⚑ ⚑ ⚑

(4m). **The Ranch Caravan Park, Cliffe Common, Selby, North Yorkshire YO8 6EF.** *01757 638984.* ltbrownridge@aol.com. www.ranchcaravanpark.f9.co.uk. M62, J37 (Goole), take A63 towards Selby. At Cliffe turn R and travel for 1m, then turn L at crossroads. Entrance to park 80yd on the R. Set in 6 acres of woodland, family-run site well situated in the heart of Yorkshire. Various leisure activities nearby. Village shop and PH. ☆☆☆☆ **50T. 50MC.** ✿ ⌇ ⊡ ⅙

Settle

(6m). **Crowtrees Park, Tosside, Long Preston, Settle, North Yorkshire BD23 4SD.** *01729 840278.* hol@crowtreespark. co.uk. www.crowtreespark.co.uk. Owner: C M C (Preston) Ltd. Off B6478. No touring facilites. Indoor swimming pool. Adventure playground. 17th-century inn and restaurant. Also 6 lodges for hire. Owner: Mr H Cowburn. Open March 14-January 31. ☆☆☆☆☆**BH&HPA. 240S.** ⌇ ⅃

(2.5m). **Knight Stainforth Hall, Little Stainforth, Settle, North Yorkshire BD24 0DP.** *01729 822200.* info@knightstain forth.co.uk. www.knightstainforth.co.uk. Owner: Mrs S Maudsley. Turn off A65 into Settle, then turn opposite Settle community college on to Stack House lane, site is then 2m. Open March-October. ☆☆☆☆ **BH&HPA. NCC. 50T. 50MC. 60S.** ⌇ ⊡ ⅃

(1m). **Langcliffe Caravan Park, Settle, North Yorkshire BD23 9LX.** *01729 822387.* info@langcliffe.com. www.langcliffe.com. Owner: Mr & Mrs J T Smith. Off A65 on to B6480, continue on B6479 to Horton in Ribblesdale. Go past Watersbed Mill and take next turning L. Park is at end of lane. Children's playground, laundrette, toilets and showers. Golf course, fishing, swimming pool, restaurants and PHs all within 1m. Open March - January. **BH&HPA. 61T. MC. 55S.** ⌇ ⊡ ⅙

Sheriff Hutton

(1.5m). **Camping & Caravanning Club Site - Sheriff Hutton, Bracken Hill, Sheriff Hutton, North Yorkshire YO60 6QG.** *01347 878660/0870 243 3331.* www. campingandcaravanningclub.co.uk. Owner: Camping & Caravanning Club. Greenfields House, Westwood Way, Coventry CV4 8JH. From York follow Earswick/Strensall signs. Keep left at filling station and Ship Inn. Site 2nd on right. 10-acre site. Convenient for visiting York, North York Moors National Park and east coast. All types of units accepted. Non-members welcome. Seaside resorts Bridlington, Scarborough and Filey are within easy reach. Special deals available for families and backpackers. Open March-October. ☆☆☆☆ **90T. 90MC.** ⌇ ⊡ ⅙

Skipton

(4.5m). **Eshton Road Caravan Site, Gargrave, Skipton, North Yorkshire BD23 3AN.** *01756 749229.* Owner: F Green & Son Ltd. Off A65. Fishing on site. Golf course 4m. Shops, PO, doctor 5 mins walk. **BH&HPA. 20T. MC. 14S.** ✿ ⌇ ⊡

(15m). **Hawkswick Cote Caravan Park, Arncliffe, Skipton, North Yorkshire BD23 5PX.** *01756 770226.* Owner: Lakeland Leisure Estates Ltd. PO Box 22, Windermere, Cumbria LA23 1GE. B6265 from Skipton. At Threshfield take B6160, 0.25m past Kilnsey, L into Littondale, park 1.5m on left. 5m from Grassington. AA 4 pennants. Manager: Mr E Carter. Nearest small town is 5m (medical centre, doctors). Climbing available nearby. Fishing, local PH/restaurant 2.5m. Garage, pony treking 3m. Leisure Centre 4m. Cinema 15m. Open March 6-November 14. **BH&HPA. NCC. 50T. MC. 90S.** ⌇ ⊡ ⅙ ⅃

(8m). **Howgill Lodge Caravan Park, Barden, Skipton, North Yorkshire BD23 6DJ.** *01756 720655.* info@howgill-lodge.co.uk. www.howgill-lodge.co.uk. Owner: Mrs Ann Foster. Turn off B6160 at Barden Tower, park 1m on R. Site offers views over Wharfedale. Good walking area. Gas sales. Dogs allowed with tourers only. David Bellamy Gold Conservation Award. Open April 1-October 31. ☆☆☆☆☆ **BH&HPA. 15T. 15MC. 4H.** ⌇ ⊡ ⅃

(9m). **Long Ashes Park, Threshfield, Skipton, North Yorkshire BD23 5PN.** *01756 752261.* info@longashespark.co.uk. www.long ashespark.co.uk. Owner: Warfield Park Homes Ltd. Maclaren House, Bracknell, Berks RG42 3RA. Set in Yorkshire Dales National Park, 3m from Grassington on B6160 towards Kettlewell. Leisure club with heated indoor pool, sauna, gym, beauty spa, clubroom and lounge. Dales Inn serving home cooked food, bed and breakfast, play area. Dogs welcome. Golf, fishing, riding nearby. Open March 1-December 31. ☆☆☆☆ **BH&HPA. NCC. 120S.** ⌇ ⊡ ⅙ ⌀

(0.5m). **Overdale Park, Harrogate Road, Skipton, North Yorkshire BD23 6AA.** *01756 793480.* Owner: Mr & Mrs Corfield. On A59 Harrogate to Skipton road. Calor Gas available. Open February-December 31. **75S.** ⌀

Strid Wood Caravan Club Site, Bolton Abbey, Skipton, North Yorkshire BD23 6AN. *01756 710433.* www.caravanclub.co.uk. Owner: The Caravan Club. East Grinstead House, East Grinstead, West Sussex RH19 1UA. See website for standard directions to site. Set in open glade surrounded by woodland and Yorkshire Dales. Non-members welcome, advance booking essential. All hard-standings, steel awning pegs required, gas supplies, dog walk on site. Toilet blocks. Privacy cubicles. Laundry facilities. Baby changing facilities. Veg prep. Motorhome service point. Information room. Good area for walking. Fishing and water sports nearby. Peaceful off peak. Open March-January. ☆☆☆☆ **NCC. 57T. MC.** ⌇ ⊡ ⅙

(1.2m). **Tarn Caravan Park, Stirton, Skipton, North Yorkshire BD23 3LQ.** *01756 795309.* Owner: Thornrold Developments Ltd. Off B6265. Take the Skipton bypass, on the north roundabout go SW on road signed 'Local traffic only'. After 200yd turn right, SP. Only one dog allowed per van but no Alsatians, Rottweilers or Pit Bulls etc. Open March 21-October 31. **32T. 32MC. 224S.** ⌇ ⊡

(6m). **Threaplands House Farm, Cracoe, Skipton, North Yorkshire BD23 6LD.** *01756 730248.* Owner: Mr J C Wade. Access via Skipton to Grassington B6265. Calor and Campingaz on site. Fishing, shops, Doctor, PO, shopping within 3m. Golf course, cinema 6m. Open March 1-October 31. **BH&HPA. 30T. MC. S. 2H.** ⌇ ⊡ ⅃

Wharfedale Caravan Club Site, Long Ashes, Threshfield, Skipton, North Yorkshire BD23 5PN. *01756 753340.* www.caravanclub.co.uk. Owner: The Caravan Club. East Grinstead House, East Gri nstead, West Sussex RH19 1UA. See website for standard direc-tions to site. Caravan Club members only. Set in heart of Yorkshire Dales, site is screened with mature trees and is in two fields divided by a drystone wall characteristic of the area. Toilet blocks, laundry facilities and baby and tod-dler washroom. Motorhome service point. Play equip-ment and dog walk on site. Good area for walking and fishing nearby. Suitable for families. Open March-January. **NCC. 118T. MC.** ⌇ ⊡

(9m). Wood Nook Caravan Park, Skirethorns, Threshfield, Skipton, North Yorkshire BD23 5NU. *01756 752412.* enquiries@woodnook.net. www.woodnook.net. Owner: Mr Thompson. From Skipton take B6265 to Threshfield, then B6160 for 100yd. Turn left after garage into Skirethorns Lane. Entrance clearly SP at 300 and 600yd. Licensed shop. Children's play area. Open March 1-October 31. ✰✰✰✰ BH&HPA. **20T. 20MC. 10H.** 🐾 🔌 🛃

Slingsby

(0.5m). Camping & Caravanning Club Site - Slingsby, Railway Street, Slingsby, North Yorkshire YO62 4AA. *01653 628335/0870 243 3331.* www.campingand caravanningclub.co.uk. Owner: Camping & Caravanning Club. Greenfields House, Westwood Way, Coventry CV4 8JH. At Slingsby on B1257 turn downhill to site on R at end of village. 3-acre site, accepting all types of units. Site is mainly grass with some hard-standings. Close to the North York Moors and several seaside resorts. Non-members welcome. Nearby Malton is a lively market village. Special deals available for families and backpackers. Open March-October. ✰✰✰✰✰ **60T. 60MC.** 🐾 🔌 ♿

Robin Hood Caravan & Camping Park, Green Dyke Lane, Slingsby, North Yorkshire YO62 4AP. *01653 628391.* info@robinhoodcaravanpark.co.uk. www.robinhoodcaravan park.co.uk. Owner: Rebecca Palmer-Bunting. Situated on B1257, Malton to Helmsley road. In the heart of Ryedale, this privately owned park offers peace and is a suitable centre for York, the moors, Heartbeat country, and the seaside resorts of Scarborough, Whitby and Filey. Open March 1-October 31. ✰✰✰✰✰ **40T. MC. 35S. 25H. 3R.** 🐾 🔌 ♿ 🛃

Stokesley

(3m). Carlton Caravan Park, Carlton-in-Cleveland, Stokesley, North Yorkshire TS9 7DJ. *01642 712287.* Owner: J Burton. S of Stokesley, just off A172. Situated in national park at the foot of the Cleveland Hills, in picturesque village of Carlton. Adventure play area. On-site PH with garden. Open March 1-October 31. **12T. 6MC. 8S. 1H.** 🐾 🔌

Sutton-on-the-Forest

Ponderosa Caravan & Camping, Sutton-on-the-Forest, North Yorkshire YO6 1ET. *01347 810744/810706.* Owner: W I S & J Whatnell. B1363 from York (6.5m), SP on B1363. Site 800yd. Country inn and restaurant. Children's play area. Showers. Washing facilities. Children allowed. Tents also welcome. **30T. MC. 58S.** ✿ 🐾 🔌

Tadcaster

(5m). White Cote Caravan Park, Ryther Road, Ulleskelf, Tadcaster, North Yorkshire LS24 9DY. *01937 835231.* Owner: Ms J A Hunter. Off A162 S of Tadcaster, E on B1223 towards Selby. Showers. Chemical toilet emptying point. Sheltered, well-maintained site. Licensed bar. Family room. Fresh milk and ice cream available. AA 3 pennants. Open March 1-January 31. **25T. MC.** 🐾 🔌

Thirsk

(1.5m). Carlton Miniott Park, Sandhutton Lane, Carlton Miniott, Thirsk, North Yorkshire YO7 4NH. *01845 523106.* Owner: Messrs Jenkins & Lancefield. Take road for 'Sandhutton' off A61, site entrance 400yd on right. 7-acre lake for fishing, canoeing, rowing and sailing. Open March 31-October 31. **40T. MC.** 🔌

(4m). Cleavehill Caravan Park, 'Low Cleaves', Sutton, Thirsk, North Yorkshire YO7 2PY. *01845 597229.* Owner: Mrs P M Hoyle. A170, Thirsk to Scarborough, sign in Sutton Village. Showers. Laundry room. Fridge and freezer available. Small, private farm site. Open April-October. **3T. 5MC. 14H.** 🐾

(5.5m). Nursery Garden Holiday Home Park, Baldersby Park, Rainton, Thirsk, North Yorkshire YO7 3PG. *01845 577277.* nurserygardencp@talk21.com. Owner: Roy & Liz Yates. From J49 A1(M), take A168 to Thirsk/Teeside. Exit at the first J to Asenby. Take first L to Rainton, before the Crab and Lobster, and the park is 0.5m on the R. Level, grassed, quiet site, in walled garden area with laundry. Visiting mobile shop. PHs, restaurants 1m. Nearby fishing and golf 2m. Cinema, shops 5m. Open March 1-January 6. ✰✰✰✰ BH&HPA. **20T. MC. 62S.** 🐾

(2.5m). Scenecliffe Caravan Park, Moor Lane, Bagby, Thirsk, North Yorkshire YO7 2PN. *01845 597368.* lenwalker@ scenecliffe.fsnet.co.uk. Owners: Mrs I & Mr L Walker. Take A170 from Thirsk (ignore caravan ban sign). 2.5m from Thirsk, turn R at sign marked Bagby. The site is then 0.5m on R. Village of Bagby is 0.25m away with one PH but no shops. Adults only. 5 pitches with electrics and 5 without generally available during the season. Fishing sites within 2-3m. Gliding club 3m, golf courses 3m and 10m. Thirsk has most facilities such PO, doctors, cinema, swimming baths, etc. Open April-October. **28T.** 🐾 🔌

(1m). Sowerby Caravan Park, Sowerby, Thirsk, North Yorkshire YO7 3AG. *01845 522753.* Owner: Mr A & S Webster. Off A19 follow council signs. Quiet, rural park with river frontage. Open March-October. BH&HPA. **25T. 80S.** 🐾 🔌 ♿ 🛃

(4m). Swaleside Park, Topcliffe, Thirsk, North Yorkshire YO7 3PB. *01845 577802.* www.swaleside.com. Owner: Mr & Mrs J Fletcher. On A168 take turning to Topcliffe, the park is by the river bridge, laid out on the bank of the river Swale, with private fishing and woodland walks. Village shop and PHs within walking distance. Open March-October and weekends in winter. BH&HPA. **58S.** 🐾

(3m). Thirkleby Hall Caravan Park, Thirkleby Hall, Thirsk, North Yorkshire YO7 3AR. *01845 501360.* greenwood. parks@virgin.net. www.greenwoodparks.com. Owner: Pratt family. Green Wood Parks, Itchenor Caravan Park, Shipton Green Lane, Itchenor, Chichester, West Sussex PO20 7BZ. On A19, York to Thirsk, access road lies E of A19. Park built within grounds of a former stately home, with lake and extensive woods. Bar. Games room. Fishing lake on park. Playground. Golf course 3m, weekly market in Thirsk 3m, York 16m. AA 2 pennants. Telephone for free brochure: 01243 514433. Open March 1-January 5. **50T. 50MC. 195S. 1H.** 🐾 🔌 🛃

(0.25m). Thirsk Racecourse Caravan Club Site, Station Road, Thirsk, North Yorkshire YO7 1QL. *01845 525266.* www.caravanclub.co.uk. Owner: The Caravan Club. East Grinstead House, East Grinstead, West Sussex RH19 1UA. See website for standard directions to site. On this site you are pitched within sight of the main racecourse stand, only a 5mins walk from the market town of Thirsk. Toilet blocks and laundry facilities, vegetable preparation area. Calor Gas and Campingaz. Dog walk on site, golf and NCN cycle route nearby. Non-members and tent campers welcome. Suitable for families. Open March-October. NCC. **60T. MC.** 🐾 🔌

(5m). White Rose Leisure Park, Hutton Sessay, Thirsk, North Yorkshire YO7 3BA. *01845 501215.* Owner: Mr M & J Holden. The Park is situated off the A19 towards York. Outdoor and indoor swimming pools. PH. Laundry. Games room. Play park. Open March 1-October 31. **BH&HPA. 231T. MC.** ⚲🇬🇧♿☎

(4m). York House Caravan Park, Balk, Bagby, Thirsk, North Yorkshire YO7 2AQ. *01845 597495.* phil.brierley@which.net. www.yhcparks.info. Owners: York House Caravans. The Bungalow, Wetherby Road, Boroughbridge, York YO51 9HS. Travelling from Thirsk on the A19 take the left turn, SP for Bagby, Balk, Kilburn. Go through Bagby to T-junction, turn right, go 500yd down hill, park is on the left-hand side. Local PH and meals nearby. Shopping, cinema 4m, golf 6m. Open April 1-October 31. ☆☆☆☆ **BH&HPA. 20T. 20MC. 220S.** ⚲♿☎∅

Welburn

Jamie's Cragg Caravan Park, Castle Howard Station Road, Welburn, North Yorkshire YO6 7EW. Owner: Mr P B & Mrs A Riley. On the A64, York to Scarborough road. Shop within 1m. Open March 1-October 31. **BH&HPA. 120S.** ⚲

Whitby

(9m). Abbots House Farm, Camping & Caravan Site, Goathland, Whitby, North Yorkshire YO22 5NH. *01947 896270/896026.* goathland@enterprise.net. www.abbots house.org.uk. Owners: Mr & Mrs Cox and Mr & Mrs Jenkinson. From Whitby S on to the A169, take Goathland sign. Site 0.5m along lane beside Goathland Hotel. Moorland scenery and North Yorkshire Moors Steam Railway. 'Heartbeat' country. Facilities include showers, toilets, freezer pack exchange. No charges for dogs and awnings. Open Easter-October 31. **90T. 90MC. H.** ⚲

(9m). Brow House Farm, Goathland, Whitby, North Yorkshire YO22 5NP. *01947 896274.* Owner: Mr J T Jackson. Directions York-Pickering-Goathland or Middlesborough-Whitby-Goathland. Showers. Bottled gas on site. Shops, PO within 0.5m. Doctor 4m. Fishing, golf 7-8m. Open March 1-October 31. ☆ **30T. 10MC.** ⚲🇬🇧♿

(7m). Burnt House Holiday Park, Ugthorpe, Whitby, North Yorkshire YO21 2BG. *01947 840448.* www.caravancamping sites.co.uk. Owner: A & S Booth. Off the A171, Whitby to Guisborough road, SP to Ugthorpe village, 275yd on right. Showers. Play area. Calor Gas sales. Laundry. Hard-standings or grass. Well-lit site. Holiday cottage available for hire. Country PHs nearby. Open March-October 31. **BH&HPA. 80T. MC. 50S.** ⚲🇬🇧

(8m). Grouse Hill Caravan Park, Fylingdales, Whitby, North Yorkshire YO22 4GH. *01947 880543.* Owner: Mr W V Butterfield. Off the A171 between Scarborough and Whitby, highway sign north of Flask Inn. Quiet, family site situated in moorland valley with extensive moorland walks. AA 3 pennants. 40 new hard-standings with electrics and water. Open Easter-October 31. **175T. MC.** ⚲🇬🇧♿☎

(5.5m). Ladycross Plantation, Egton, Whitby, North Yorkshire YO21 1UA. *01947 895502.* enquiries@ladycross-plan tation.co.uk. www.ladycrossplantation.co.uk. D.H.& L.Miller. Off A171, Whitby to Guisborough road. Turn at sign-post to Egton. Peaceful, sheltered site in North York Moors National Park. David Bellamy Conservation Award. AA 3 pennants. Open March-October. ☆☆☆☆ **BH&HPA. 100T. 6 MC.** ⚲🇬🇧

(4.5m). Low Moor Caravan Club Site, Redgates, Whitby, North Yorkshire YO22 5JE. *01947 810505.* www.caravanclub.co.uk. Owner: The Caravan Club. East Grinstead House, East Grinstead, West Sussex RH19 1UA. See website for standard directions to site. Tranquil site set in the North York Moors National Park. No sanitation. Pitching areas are pleasantly open and spacious. Non-members welcome. Boules pitch, mini-golf. Information room. Motorhome service point. Open April-October. **NCC. 85T. MC.** ⚲🇬🇧

(5.5m). Middlewood Farm Holiday Park, Middlewood Lane, Fylingthorpe, Robin Hood's Bay, Whitby, North Yorkshire YO22 4UF. *01947 880414.* www.middlewoodfarm.com. Owner: Mr & Mrs P Beeforth. Scarborough/Whitby A171 turn for Robin Hood's Bay and Fylingthorpe. At Fylingthorpe cross-roads and PO turn into Middlewood Lane. Good views and walking country. Adventure playground. Laundrette. Telephone. 10 mins walk to beach. PH and shop 5 mins walk. Calor Gas and Campingaz. Rose Award. David Bellamy Gold Conservation Award. Fishing, golf, sailing, tennis, bowls nearby. Open March 1-October 31 for tourers; open March 1-January 4 for holiday caravans. ☆☆☆☆☆ **BH&HPA. 20T. 50MC. 30H.** ⚲☎

(3m). Northcliffe Holiday Park, Bottoms Lane, High Hawsker, Whitby, North Yorkshire YO22 4LL. *01947 880477.* enquiries@northcliffe-seaview.com. www.north cliffe-seaview. com. Owner: S & S Martin. S Whitby, A171 L on to B1447, site is 0.5m along private road on L. Sea views. Open mid March-end October. ☆☆☆☆ **BH&HPA. 72T. 165S.** 🇬🇧♿☎∅

(4m). Rigg Farm Caravan Park, Stainsacre, Whitby, North Yorkshire YO22 4LP. *01947 880430.* Owner: D A & A E Stuart. Approaching Whitby on A171 take B1416. 1.5m S of Ruswarp, turn into unclassified road, SP Sneatonthorpe, Hawkser. Stainsacre (and Rigg Farm). Site about 2m on L. Small, quiet site in national park with scenic views. Separate site for tourers. Children allowed. Separate tent pitches also available. AA 3 pennants. Open March 1-October 31. **BH&HPA. 14T. MC. 15S. 5H.** ⚲☎

(1m). Sandfield House Farm Caravan Park, Sandsend Road, Whitby, North Yorkshire YO21 3SR. *01947 602660.* info@sand fieldhousefarm.co.uk. www. sandfieldhousefarm.co.uk. Owner: Mr M P & C M Warner. N of Whitby centre on A174 coast road, next to Whitby Golf Club. Quiet, friendly park surrounded by undulating countryside. 0.25m from long, sandy beach. 0.5m from shops and hotel. Adjacent golf course. Open March-October. ☆☆☆☆☆ **BH&HPA. 60T. MC.** ⚲☎

(3m). Seaview Holiday, Bottoms Lane, High Hawsker, Whitby, North Yorkshire YO22 4LL. *01947 880477.* enquiries@seaview-northcliffe.com. www.seaview-northcliffe. com. Owner: Sue & Steve Martin. Off A171, on to B1447. Quiet, family-owned Rose Award park. Panoramic views to Whitby Abbey and the sea. Cycle trail on park boundary. Tennis, bowling 2m. Cinema, theatre 3m. Golf course 5m. Open mid March-October 31. ☆☆☆☆☆ **BH&HPA. 100S.** ♿

(8m). Serenity Touring Caravan & Camping Park, Hinderwell, Whitby, North Yorkshire TS13 5JH. *01947 841112.* patandni@aol.com. Owner: Nigel and Pat Little. Stable Cottage, High Street, Hinderwell, North Yorkshire TS13 5JH. Situated N of Whitby on A174. Cleveland Way 1m. Quiet, sheltered, secure site with lovely country views. Mainly adults. 0.5m from sea. Marvellous coastal, country and moorland walks. Village shops, public telephone and pubs all nearby. Open March 1-October 31. **BH&HPA. 20T. 20MC.** 🚱 🔌

(8m). The Flask Holiday Home Park, Fylingdales, Robin Hoods Bay, Whitby, North Yorkshire YO22 4QH. *01947 880592.* flaskinn@aol.com. www.flaskinn.com. Owner: J & G Allison. Park is located on A171, Scarborough to Whitby road. Open Easter-October. ✰✰✰✰ **BH&HPA. 46S. 10H.** 🚱 🔌

(6m). Top Bay Bank, Robin Hoods Bay, Whitby, North Yorkshire YO22 4RH. *01947 880824.* Owner: Mrs B Fewster. Prospect Fields, Robin Hood's Bay, Whitby, North Yorkshire. 500yd from village, 18m from Scarborough. Open April 1-October 31. **T. 10S.** 🚱

(8m). Ugthorpe Lodge Caravan & Camping Site, Ugthorpe, Whitby, North Yorkshire YO21 2BE. *01947 840518.* Owner: D Stainsby. On A171 Guisborough to Whitby. Quiet, family site with full services. Views. PH and restaurant on site. Separate field for rallies. Barbecue facilities. Play area. Fishing 2m. Golf, beach 5m. Open April 1-October 31. **20T. 20MC. 70S.** 🚱 🔌 🔌

(10m). Warp Mill Caravan Park, Staithes, Saltburn-by-Sea, Whitby, North Yorkshire. *01947 840291.* Owner: Mr T R Puckrin. On A174. Open April-October 31. **T. MC. 46S. 2H.** 🚱

(1.5m). Whitby Holiday Park, Saltwick Bay, Whitby, North Yorkshire YO22 4JX. *01947 602664.* Normanhurst Enterprises Ltd, 9 Burscough Street, Ormskirk, Lancs L39 9EG. S of Whitby, follow signs for Whitby Abbey. R at T-junction. Secluded beach. Club. PH. Takeaway. Playground. Laundrette. Golf nearby. Open April-October. ✰✰✰✰ **BH&HPA. NCC. 200T. 87S. 25H.** 🚱 🔌 🔌

(3.5m). York House Caravan Park, High Hawsker, Whitby, North Yorkshire YO22 4LW. *01947 880354.* Owner: Mr D I Jackson. Off A171 Scarborough to Whitby. Golf, shopping, cinema in 3.5m. Open March-October. ✰✰✰59T. 59MC. 41S. 🚱 🔌 & 🔌

York

Alders Caravan Park, Homefarm, Monk Green, Alne, York, North Yorkshire YO61 1RY. *01347 838722.* enquiries@home farmalne.co.uk. www.alderscaravanpark.co.uk. Owners: Mr J D Whiteley & Mrs R H Price. 3m from Easingwold. Tennis courts, PO, PH with restaurant in village. Golf and fishing in 3m. Open March 1- October 31. ✰✰✰✰✰ **BH&HPA. 40T. MC.** 🚱 🔌 &

(3m). Beechwood Grange Caravan Club Site, Malton Road, York, North Yorkshire YO32 9TH. *01904 424637.* www.caravanclub.co.uk. Owner: The Caravan Club, East Grinstead House, East Grinstead, West Sussex RH19 1UA. See website for standard directions to site. In open countryside outside York, screened with trees and hedges. Suitable touring base for the city and for Yorkshire's varied attractions. Toilet block and baby/toddler washroom, laundry facilities, veg prep, Motorhome service point, play area, dog walk on site. Open March-November. ✰✰✰✰✰ **NCC. 111T. MC.** 🚱 🔌 &

(3.5m). Chestnut Farm Holiday Park, Acaster Malbis, York, North Yorkshire YO23 2UQ. *01904 704676.* enquiries@chest nutfarmholidaypark.co.uk. www.chestnutfarmholidaypark.co.uk. Owner: S G & A J Smith. Family-run park in village by river Ouse 3.5m from York. Suitable base for touring dales, coasts and moors. Rose Award. Open March-end November. ✰✰✰✰✰ **BH&HPA. 25T. MC. 51S. 5H.** 🚱 🔌 🔌

(9m). Fangfoss Old Station Caravan Park, Fangfoss, York, North Yorkshire YO41 5QB. *01759 380491.* fangfoss@ pl2000.co.uk. www.ukparks.com/fangfoss. Owner: Mr & Mrs F L Arundel. 2m from A1079 at Wilberfoss. Small, quiet park at foot of wolds. Laundry facilities. Play area. Campingaz. AA 3 pennants. Open March 1-October 31. **BH&HPA. 75T. MC.** 🚱 🔌 🔌

(8m). Goose Wood Caravan Park, Sutton-on-the-Forest, York, North Yorkshire YO61 1ET. *01347 810829.* enquiries@ goosewood.co.uk. www.goosewood.co.uk. Owner: Sue & Eddie Prince. From A1237 (York outer ring road) take B1363 north, pass the Haxby-Wigginton junction, take next right, and follow signs. When coming from the N, take first L after 2nd Easingwold roundabout (A19) into Huby, then Sutton-on-the-Forest. Peaceful, rural park, convenient for York. All hard-standing pitches with patio and electric hook-ups. Fishing on site. ✰✰✰✰✰ **BH&HPA. 75T. MC. 10S. 30H.** ✿ 🚱 🔌 🔌

Greystones Farm, Towehore, Moor Lane, York, Yorkshire YO32 9ST. *01904 490405.* Owner: Mr Adam Chapman. **T.**

Hollybrook Caravan Park, Penny Carr Lane, Easingwold, York, North Yorkshire YO61 3EU. *01347 821906.* info@holly brookpark.co.uk. Owner: Chris & Alice Cameron. Off A19 York to Thirsk road. Approaching Easingwold take first right, SP Stillington. In 0.5mile turn right into Pennycarr Lane; site is on right after 0.3m. Well-equipped, secluded, level grass site. No children. AA 3 pennants. Fishing, golf nearby. Open March 1-December 31. **30T. 30MC.** 🚱 🔌

(4m). Homelea Caravan & Camp Site, York Road, Elvington, York, North Yorkshire YO4 5AX. *01904 608220.* Owner: Mrs Jean Pollard. Situated on B1228 opposite Elvington Air Museum. Peaceful site. Barbecue area. Close to livestock centre, PH and cafe. **20T. 50MC.** ✿ 🚱 🔌 🔌

(8m). Lake Cottage, Wheldrake Lane, Elvington, York, North Yorkshire YO4 5AZ. *01904 608255.* Owner: Mr Stan Britton. Off A1079 and B1228. Coarse and game fishing on site. Wild fowl and Nature reserves within 3m. Golf club, 2m. Showers. Gas, milk and papers available. Bus service picks up at site for town. Booking and deposit advised. Winner of York in Bloom' annual contest for the past 9 years. Level site suitable for disabled anglers, including wheelchair approach to fishery. Coarse fishing on site. Specimen carp. Wild fowl nature reserve 3m. **13T. MC. 4H.** ✿ 🚱 🔌 &

(8m). Lakeside Adult Touring Park and Coarse Fishery, Lakeside, Bielby, Nr Pocklington, York, Yorkshire YO42 4JP. *01759 318100.* richard@lakesidewebsite.com. www.lakesidewebsite.com. Owners: Mr R Smith. 6-acre fishing lake on site. Tradesmen call each day. **42T. MC.** ✿ 🚱 🔌

(4m). Moor End Farm, Acaster Malbis, York, Yorkshire YO23 2UQ. *01904 706727.* moorendfarm@acaster99.fsnet.co.uk. www.ukparks.co.uk/moorend. Owner: Mr G H Hall. Off A64 York (4m) to Tadcaster, turn off at Copmanthorpe and follow signs to Acaster Malbis. Showers. AA 2 pennants. RAC approved. Open April-October. ✪✪✪✪ **BH&HPA. 10T. MC. 2S. 2H.** 🐕 📵

(6m). Moorside Caravan Park, Lords Moor Lane, Strensall, York, North Yorkshire YO32 5XJ. *01904 491208/491865.* www.moorsidecaravanpark.co.uk. Owner: Mr P Smith. Take Strensall turn off A1237 and head towards Flaxton. Opposite York golf course. Washing-up area and laundry facilities. Showers. Fishing on site. No children. Dogs must be kept on leads at all times. Golf course nearby. Open March-October. ✪✪✪✪✪ **40T. 10MC.** 🐕 📵 ♿

(4m). Naburn Lock Caravan Park, Naburn, York, North Yorkshire YO19 4RU. *01904 728697.* wilks@naburnlock.co.uk. www.naburnlock.co.uk. Owner: PT & CE Wilkinson. S of York. From York take A19. Turn R on B1222, 2.5m. River fishing. Riding. Laundrette. Dogs on leads welcome. Riverboat from park. Service bus from park entrance. PH 10mins walk. Restaurants nearby. Cycle track in village. Open March 1-November 6. **BH&HPA. 100T. MC.** 🐕 📵 ♿ 🛶

(3.5m). Rawcliffe Manor Caravan Park, Manor Lane, Shipton Road, York, North Yorkshire YO3 6TZ. *01904 640845.* www.lysanderarms.co.uk. Owner: Ms C Ellerby. Off A19 at junction with A1237, new bypass. Adults. 13 Superpitches with water, drainage, waste, electric and satellite TV. Club. Gas available on site. Tesco superstore. 12-screen cinema. Bowling alley and shopping complex next to site. New PH with entertainment on site, also a la carte restaurant, which has a Sunday carvery. ✪✪✪✪✪ **BH&HPA. 13T. MC.** ✿ 🐕 📵 ♿

(2m). Riverside Caravan & Camping Park, York Marine Services, Ferry Lane, Bishopthorpe, York, North Yorkshire YO23 2SB. *01904 704442/705812.* Owner: York Marine Services Ltd. A64 York exit to Bishopthorpe A1036 at Bishopthorpe, go down main street then right on to Acaster Lane, then left 2m into Ferry Lane, drive through car park to site, 400yd from Bishop's Palace. Attractive site alongside river Ouse with moorings, slipways and river bus service to York. Showers. 5 tents available for hire. Open April 1-October 31. **5T. 15MC.** 🐕 📵

Rowntree Park Caravan Club Site, Terry Avenue, York, North Yorkshire YO23 1JQ. *01904 658997.* www.caravanclub.co.uk. Owner: The Caravan Club. East Grinstead House, East Grinstead, West Sussex RH19 1UA. See website for standard directions to site. Level site on the banks of the river Ouse. Motorhome waste pooint. Advance booking essential. Non-members and tent campers welcome. Toilet blocks. Privacy cubicles. Laundry facilities. Veg prep. Information room. Suitable for families. Local attractions include Jorvik Viking centre and York Minster. Fishing, golf, watersports all nearby. ✪✪✪✪✪ **NCC. 102T. MC.** ✿ 🐕 📵 ♿

Shouth Lea Caravan Park, The Balk, Poklington, York, Yorkshire YO42 2NX. *01759 303467.* info@south-lea.co.uk. www.south-lea.co.uk. Owners: Paul and Christine Tolworthy. Turn off A1079, York-Hull, at the Yorkway Motel on to B1247. Park is situated 400yd on L. Set in 15 acres of flat grassland. 1m from Poklington. Shower/toilet facilities, large play area, security barrier. Golf and fishing within 5m. Conveniently situated for visiting York, the east coast and Yorkshire moors. Open March-October. ✪✪✪✪ **BH&HPA. 60T. MC.** 🐕 📵

(6m). Swallow Hall Touring Caravan Park, Crockey Hill, York, North Yorkshire YO1 4SG. *01904 448219.* Owner: Mr J Scutt. Situated E off A19 between York and Selby, SP Wheldrake. Secluded 5-acre site. Forest walks. 18-hole, par-3 golf course adjoining. Driving range. New tennis court. Hot showers. AA 2 pennants. Open Easter-October. **25T. 5MC.** 🐕

(7m). The Hollicarrs Riccak Road, Escrick, York, North Yorkshire YO19 6ED. *0800 9808070.* sales@thehollicarrs.com. www.thehollicarrs.com. Owner: Mr Charles Forbes Adam. A64 to York, A19 to Selby. Hollicarrs located on left of A19, 1m from Escrick village. Tennis court, bowling green, fishing lake, nature walks, cycle hire all available on site. Golf course, shopping 4m. Cinema 6m. Open March 1-January 2. ✪✪✪✪✪ **BH&HPA. 140S.** 🐕 📵

(7m). The Old Gate House, Wheldrake Lane, Elvington, York, Yorkshire YO41 4AZ. *01904 608225.* Owner: Mr & Mrs G L Gatenby. By pass York on A64. Turn east on A1079, then on B1228 to Elvington. After about 3m turn right opposite garage to Wheldrake. Site is 1m on left. Wheldrake Ing nature reserve, Yorkshire Air Museum 2m. Fishing, golf nearby. Garage with shop 1m. Open March 1-October 31. **10T. 10MC.** 🐕 📵 ♿

Tollerton Holiday Park, Station Road, Tollerton, York, North Yorkshire YO6 2HD. *01347 838313.* greenwood. parks@btcon nect.com. www.greenwoodparks.com. Owner: Pratt Family. Green Wood Parks, Itchenor Caravan Park, Shipton Green Lane, Itchenor, Chichester, West Sussex PO20 7BZ. Situated off A19 between York and Easingwold, Tollerton and Linton-on-Ouse turn-off. Children's play ground. Washing machine. AA 3 pennants. Shop, PO in Tollerton 0.5m. Golf, fishing within 3m. Good shopping in York. Telephone for free brochure: 01243 514433. Open March 1-November 30. **50T. 10MC. 12S. 11H.** 🐕 📵 ♿

(8m). Weir Caravan Park, Stamford Bridge, York, North Yorkshire YO41 1AN. *01759 371377.* enquiries@yorkshireholi dayparks.co.uk. www.yorkshireholidayparks.co.uk. Owner: Mr & Mrs D Hind. On A166, Bridlington to York. Fishing allowed, boats for hire. 5mins walk to village. Open March 1-October 31. ✪✪✪✪ **BH&HPA. 10T. 10MC. 100S. 8H.** 🐕 📵

Willow House Caravan Park, Wigginton Road, Wigginton, York, North Yorkshire YO32 2RH. *01904 750060.* info@willow houseyork.co.uk. www.willowhouseyork.co.uk. Owner: Mr & Mrs J Pulleyn. From A1237 north side of York outer ring road, take B1363 SP Wigginton; site is 1m on R. Coarse fishing. Shops, PO 1m. **T. MC.** ✿ 🐕 📵 ♿

(2m). **York Lakeside Lodges, Moor Lane, York, North Yorkshire YO24 2QU.** *01904 702346.* neil@yorklakeside lodges.co.uk. www.yorklakesidelodges.co.uk. Owner: Mr Manasir. Self-catering lodges available. ✰✰✰✰✰ **BH&HPA. 16H.** ✿ ⅋

(5m). **York Touring Caravan Park, Greystones Farm, Towthorpe Moor Lane, York, North Yorkshire YO32 9ST.** *01904 499275.* info@yorkcaravansite.co.uk. www.yorkcaravansite.co.uk. Owners: Graham & Mary Chapman. Take Strensall/Haxby, turn off the A64. Park is 1m on the left-hand side. On-site golf range and 9-hole putting course. Fishing available on nearby farm lake. 3 golf courses within 5m. Strensall village 2m (shops, PO, doctor). New park facilities include showers, toilets, laundry room. Children's play area and assault course. ✰✰✰ **BH&HPA. 20T. 20MC.** ✿ ⅋ 🕭 ⅍

SOUTH YORKSHIRE

Barnsley

(3m). **Greensprings Touring Park, Rockley Abbey Farm, Rockley Lane, Worsbrough, Barnsley, South Yorkshire S75 3DS.** *01226 288298.* Owner: J B & M Hodgson. Off the M1, J36, take the A61 towards Barnsley left after 0.25m, park 1m down hill on L. Site nestles in wood and farmland in the Pennine foothills. Suitable for a relaxing break on journeys north and south or for touring the Peak District and Pennine Yorkshire. Open April-October. **BH&HPA. 60T. MC.** ⅋ 🕭

Castleton

(0.5m). **Losehill Hall Caravan Club Site, Hope Valley, Castleton, Derbyshire, S33 8WB.** *01433 620636.* www.caravanclub.co.uk. Owner: The Caravan Club. East Grinstead House, East Grinstead, West Sussex RH19 1UA. See website for standard directions to site. Newly refurbished site, peaceful off-peak, suitable for all kinds of outdoor activities. New facilities block with family and baby wash room. Laundry facilities. Veg prep. Motorohme service point. Calor Gas and Campingaz. Play equipment. Dog walk on site. Non-members and tent campers welcome. Fishing and golf nearby. Good area for walking. Suitable for families. Some hard-standings. Shop 50yd from site. Fishing, golf 5m. ✰✰✰✰✰ **NCC. 78T. MC.** ✿ ⅋ 🕭 ⅍

Doncaster

(8m). **Hatfield Water Park, Old Thorne Road, Hatfield, Doncaster, South Yorkshire DN7 6EQ.** *01302 841572.* hatfield.waterpark@doncaster.gov.uk. Owner: Doncaster Metropolitan Borough Council. Directorate of Leisure Services, Council House, Doncaster. Situated about halfway between Doncaster and Thorne on the A18. Leave M18 at J5, on to M180 then leave at J1, for A18 and follow signs for Hatfield. Site incorporates a lake with water sports facilities. Fishing also available by day ticket. Residential accommodation in bunkhouse-style dormitories available for organised groups. Children's playground. Hot and cold drinks, snacks, ice creams available from visitor centre. Local shops 10 mins walk. Superstores (Tesco/Sainsbury's) 10 mins by car. Open April-October. ✰✰✰ **75T. MC.** ✿ ⅋ 🕭 ⅍

(8m). **Woodcarr Park, Sandtoft Road, Belton, Doncaster, South Yorkshire DN9 1PN.** *01427 873487.* Owners: BJ & JWilliams. Junction 2, M180 for Gainsborough A161. Turn right at mini roundabout. Sandtoft Road. Quiet, secluded site. Over-50s' site. No facilities for children. David Bellamy Gold Conservation Award. Museums, shopping, east coast 30mins. Fishing, golf nearby. Open February 5 -January 6. **BH&HPA. 5T. 20S.** ⅋ 🕭 🛦

(1m). **Yorkshire Caravans of Bawtry Ltd, Great North Road, Bawtry, Doncaster, South Yorkshire DN10 6DG.** *01302 710366.* Contact Mr D J Smith. **CaSSOA. 5T.** ⅋

Sheffield

(4m). **Fox Hagg Farm, Lodge Lane, Rivelin, Sheffield, South Yorkshire S6 5SN.** *01142 305589.* Owner: Mrs M Dyson & Son. W of Sheffield on the A57. Between Sheffield and Peak District. Laundry. Showers. Rivelin PO, shops and doctor nearby. Rock climbing, golf nearby. Space for 50 tents. Open April 1-October 31. **10T. 10MC. 20S.** ⅋ 🕭 ⅍

(25m). **Waterside Farm, Barber Booth Road, Edale, Hope Valley, Sheffield, South Yorkshire S33 7ZL.** *01433 670215.* Owner: Mrs J M Cooper. Off the A625. Milk and eggs sold on site. Hot water and showers on site. Cafe within 0.5m open 7 days a week. PO and shop 1m. Pony trekking 2m. Open April 1-September 30. **10T. MC. 20S.** ⅋

WEST YORKSHIRE

Bingley

(2.5m). **Harden and Bingley Holiday Park, Goit Stock Lane, Harden, Bingley, West Yorkshire BD16 1DF.** *01535 273810.* Owner: Ms J Dunham & Mr P Davis. Off B6429. At Harden village turn left ont o Wilsden road, then R at bridge on to Goit Stock Lane. Peaceful, country site set in private woodlands with waterfalls. Local shops 0.5m. Fishing, horse riding, golf, courses close by. Open April 1-October 31. ✰✰✰✰ **BH&HPA. 6T. 6MC. 77S.** ⅋ 🕭 ⅍

Elland

(0.5m). **Elland Hall Farm Caravan Park, Exley Lane, Elland, West Yorkshire HX5 0SL.** *01422 372325.* Owner: J S Morton and Sons. Open March 1-October 31. **BH&HPA. 10T. MC.** 🕭

Guiseley

(2m). **Moor Valley Park, Mill Lane, Hawksworth, Guiseley, West Yorkshire LS20 8PG.** *01943 876083.* Owner: Moor Valley Leisure Ltd. Situated off the A6038. 10 mins from Harry Ramsden's and the 'Woolpack' of Emmerdale Farm. New motel with bed and breakfast now open. Open March 1-January 31. **BH&HPA. 85S.** ⅋ 🕭

Haworth

(1m). **Upwood Holiday Park, Blackmoor Road, Oxenhope, Haworth, West Yorkshire BD22 9SS.** *01535 644242.* cara vans@upwoodholidaypark.fsnet.co.uk. www.upwoodholiday park.fsnet.co.uk. Owner: F Towers. A629 to B6141, Denholme Oxenhope. Turn into Blackmoor Road. Site 0.5m. Level pitches, panoramic views over surrounding countryside. Gas. Showers. Games room. Laundry. Bar with family room and food. Play area. Open March 1-January 5. ✰✰✰✰ **BH&HPA. 68T. 2MC. 49S. 2H.** ⅋ 🕭 ⅍ ✐

Hebden Bridge

> **(2.5m). Lower Clough Foot Caravan Club Site, Cragg Vale, Hebden Bridge, West Yorkshire HX7 5RU.** *01422 882531.* www.caravanclub.co.uk. Owner: The Caravan Club. East Grinstead House, East Grinstead, West Sussex RH19 1UA. See website for standard directions to site. Site is tucked away off the road, well screened and gently sloping. Motorhome service point and Calor Gas and Campingaz exchanges. Fishing, golf, watersports and NCN cycle route nearby. Good area for walking. Peaceful off-peak. Open March-November. NCC. 45T. MC. ⛟ ⌷

(3m). Pennine Camp & Caravan Site, High Greenwood House, Heptonstall, Hebden Bridge, West Yorkshire HX7 7AZ. *01422 842287.* Owner: Mr G Sunderland. From Hebden Bridge take Heptonstall Road, then follow camping and caravan signs; site is adjacent to club site. Golf course, shops, garages, doctor 3m. PO, fishing and climbing within 1m. Early bookings required. Open April-October. **5T. 5MC. 1H.** ⛟ ⌷

Holmfirth

(1.5m). Holme Valley Camping & Caravan Park, Thongsbridge, Holmfirth, West Yorkshire HD9 7TD. *01484 665819.* enquiries@holmevalleycamping.com. www.holme valleycamping.com. Owners: Mr & Mrs Philip and Hazel Peaker. Halfway between Holmfirth and Honley in valley, at bottom of the A6024 (turn off main road by the bottle banks). Set in the heart of the 'Last of the Summer Wine' country and on the fringe of the Peak District National Park. Laundry room. On-site angling. Enclosed play area. David Bellamy Gold Conservation Award. ☆☆☆☆ **BH&HPA. 62T. 62MC.** ⌷ ⛟ ⌷ ⌷

Huddersfield

(7m). Earths Wood Caravan Park, Bank End Lane, Clayton West, Huddersfield, West Yorkshire HD8 9LJ. *01484 863211/864266.* Owner: S M & J L Auckland. The Hollins, Barnsley Road, Clayton West, Huddersfield, West Yorkshire. Off A636 Barnsley road. On West Yorks and South Yorks border. Open March-October. **45T. 5MC.** ⌷

Ilkley

(3m). Olicana Caravan Park, High Mill, Addingham, Ilkley, West Yorkshire LS29 0RD. *01943 830500.* Owner: Mr & Mrs J K Pape. On B6160. Fishing. Dogs on leads. Bottled gas sales. Open April 1-October 31. **5T. MC. 50S.** ⛟ ⌷

(7m). Yorkshire Clarion Clubhouse, Chevin Road, West Chevin Road, Menston, Ilkley, West Yorkshire LS29 6BL. *01943 878165.* Owner: Yorkshire Clarion Clubhouse Ltd. A660 from Otley towards Guiseley. Turn left at crossroads near Hare and Hounds PH, Buckle Lane, keep left at Chevin Inn. Site 200yd on right. Secretary: H Beardshall,15 Barnsley Road, Wakefield WF1 5JU. Open April-October. **BH&HPA. 10T. 2MC.**

Keighley

(2m). Bronte Caravan Park & Storage, Off Halifax Road, Keighley, West Yorkshire BD25 5QF. *01535 649111/222.* bronte@brontecaravanpark.co.uk. www.brontecaravanpark.co.uk. Owners: Marshall & Gregson Ltd. From Keighley, follow the Halifax and Haworth signs to pick up Halifax Road, A629, Park is 1.5m on R. Peaceful park. Security barriers with access/exit key. On-site fishing. Own deer park and lake with black swans and other wildlife. Open March 1-end January. ☆☆☆☆☆ **BH&HPA. 114T. MC. 48S.** ⛟ ⌷ ⌷ ⌷

(5m). Brown Bank Caravan Park, Brown Bank Lane, Silsden, Keighley, West Yorkshire BD20 0NN. *01535 653241.* timlay cock@btconnect.com. Owner: Mr T J Laycock. Off the A6034 from Silsden, 2m, or from Addingham. Peaceful site on edge of Ilkley Moor. Suitable base for the dales with many local walks. Golf courses 1-2m, pony trekking, cinema, swimming, shopping, all within 2-5m. Open April 1-October 31. **15T. 10MC. 100S.** ⛟ ⌷ ⌷

Cringles Park, Bolton Road, Silsden, Keighley, West Yorkshire BD20 0JY. *01535 655386.* Owner: Ms Tina Gavin. On the A6034 between Keighley, 6m, and Ilkley, 5m. No dogs allowed with tourers. Bus stop immediately outside park. 0.5m from Silsden village, PHs and shops. Open April 1-October 31. **BH&HPA. 12T. MC.** ⛟

(6m). Dales Bank Holiday Park, Low Lane, Silsden, Keighley, West Yorkshire BD20 9JH. *01535 653321/656523.* Owner: Mr R M Preston. Off A65. Licensed bar. Cafe. Games room. Lodge rooms. Bed and breakfast. Open Good Friday or April 1-October 31. ☆☆ **52T. 10MC.** ⛟ ⌷ ⌷ ⌷

Leeds

(7m). Glenfield Caravan Park, Blackmoor Lane, Bardsey, Leeds, West Yorkshire LSl7 9DZ. *01937 574657.* glenfieldcp @aol.com. www.ukparks.com. Owner: Mr & Mrs Lynda and Vic Cross. 102 Blackmoor Lane, Bardsey, Leeds, West Yorkshire LS17 9DZ. Off A58 at Bardsey. From Wetherby A1. Church Lane 1.5m up hill on R. From Leeds A58. L at Shadwell, follow right fork then 1m down hill on L. Quiet, country site, surrounded by golf courses and country inns. AA 3 pennants. Suitable touring base for Wetherby, Harrogate and Knaresbrough. Walking in nearby nature neserve. **BH&HPA. 30T. MC.** ⌷ ⛟ ⌷ ⌷

(7m). Haighfield Caravan Site, Blackmoor Lane, Bardsey, Leeds, West Yorkshire LS17 9DY. *01937 574658.* Owner: Mrs Brownbridge. Haighfield Bungalow, 5 Blackmoor Lane, Bardsey, Wetherby, West Yorkshire LS17 9DY. 4m from Wetherby, off the A58, Leeds to Wetherby road, turn left at Bardsey into Church Lane, go past the Bingley Arms to the top of the hill, park is in 50 yards on the left-hand side. Showers, laundry, public telephone. **BH&HPA. 4MC. 30S. 30H.** ⌷ ⌷

(7m). Moor Lodge Caravan Park, Blackmoor Lane, Bardsey, Leeds, West Yorkshire LSl7 9DZ. *01937 572424.* Owner: Mr R Brown. Off the A58, 7m from Leeds, left at Shadwell sign then follow caravan signs. ☆☆☆☆ **BH&HPA. 12T. 12MC. 60S.** ⌷ ⛟ ⌷

(4m). Roundhay Caravan & Camping Park, Elmete Lane, Leeds, West Yorkshire LS8 2LG. *01132 652354.* Owner: Leeds City Council. City of Leed Promotions & Tourism, Town Hall, The Headrow, Leeds LS1 3AD. Park is situated in Roundhay 700-acre public park with its year-round Tropical World, close to the Royal Armouries, Medical Museum at Jimmy's. Suitable base for touring York, Bronte, Herriot country and the Yorkshire Dales. Showers, laundrette, play area and public telephone. Tourist information. Open March-November. **60T. MC.** ⛟ ⌷ ⌷

(7m). St Helenas Caravan Park, Otley Old Road, Horsforth, Leeds, West Yorkshire LS18 5HZ. *0113 2841142.* www.ukparks.co.uk/sthelenas. 1.5m from the A658, and 2.5m from Leeds/Bradford airport. Well-kept site. Close to local amenities and attractions. Walks, Yorkshire Dales and market towns. Booking necessary. Open April-October. ☆☆☆☆ **BH&HPA. 40T. 10MC.** ⛟ ⌷

Please mention Caravan Sites 2006 when replying to advertisers

Shipley

(1m). Crook Farm Caravan Park, Glen Road, Baildon, Shipley, West Yorkshire BD17 5ED. *01274 584339.* www.dalescaravanparks.co.uk. Owner: Richard Darling. TV. Games room. Licensed club, bar with entertainment, pool room. Children's play area. Launderette and shower block. Dogs on leads welcome. Golf adjacent, shops 0.5m, cinema and public pool 2m. Bronte country. GS.Open March 1-January 14. **BH&HPA. 3T. 180S. 20H.** ⚓ 🔌

(4m). Dobrudden Caravan Park, Baildon Moor, Baildon, Shipley, West Yorkshire BD17 5EE. *01274 581016.* liz@dobrudden.co.uk. www.dobrudden.co.uk. Owner: Mrs E R Lawrence & Mr P A Lawrence. Showers. Laundry. Calor Gas sales. Golf, shops 2m. Horse riding 3m. Open March 1-December 31. **BH&HPA. 10T. 10MC. 90S. 25H.** ⚓ 🔌 ♿

Wakefield

(5m). Nostell Priory Holiday Park, Doncaster Road, Nostell, Wakefield, West Yorkshire WF4 1QD. *01924 863938.* www.nostellprioryholidaypark.co.uk. Owner: National Trust. Off A638 Wakefield to Doncaster. Tranquil, secluded, woodland park within the estate of a stately home. On-site fishing lakes. 5m to shopping centre, golf, swimming and boating. Open April 1-September 30. ✫✫✫✫ **BH&HPA. 60T. MC. 60S.** ⚓ 🔌

Wetherby

(4m). Maustin Caravan Park, Kearby-with-Netherby, Wetherby, West Yorkshire LS22 4DA. *01132 886234.* info@maustin.co.uk. www.maustin.co.uk. Owner: Mr & Mrs W Webb. South-facing, sheltered site in Lower Wharfe Valley between Harrogate (5m) and Wetherby, close to Harewood House. Telephone for directions or see website. Peaceful site. Flat green bowling. Restaurant/bar on the park. Brochure on request. Harewood House nearby. Open March 1-January 28. ✫✫✫✫✫ **BH&HPA. NCC. 20T. 5MC. 73S. 2H.** ⚓ 🔌 ♿ 🏕

ABERDEEN

Bridge of Dee

(1.5m). Craighill Caravan Park, Stonehaven Road, Bridge of Dee, Aberdeen AB1 5XJ. *01224 781973.* Owner: Marywell Park Homes Ltd. Marywell, Stonehaven, Aberdeen. On A90. Showers. Children allowed. Open April-October. **20T. 5MC. 4S. 2H.** ⚓ 🔌

Maryculter

(6m). Lower Deeside Holiday Park, Maryculter, Aberdeen AB12 5FX. *01224 733860.* enquiries@lower deesideholiday park.com. www.lowerdeesideholidaypark. com. Owner: Mrs A K Mitchell. Site conveniently situated at the gateway to Royal Deeside on the B9077, W of Aberdeen. Follow signs for Maryculter. Peaceful site and good touring base for the North- East. ✫✫✫ **45T. MC. 44S. 9H.** ✿ ⚓ 🔌 ♿ 🏕

Nigg

Nigg Park Home Estate, Altens Farm Road, Nigg, Aberdeen AB12 3HX. *01224 696679.* On A956 Stonehaven to Aberdeen. From all directions follow lorry park signs and when reaching lorry park, follow caravan park signs. Dogs allowed on touring pitches only. **BH&HPA. 69T.** ✿ ⚓ 🔌

ABERDEENSHIRE

Aberdeen

(8m). Skene Caravan Park, Mains of Keir, Skene, Aberdeen, Aberdeenshire AB32 6YA. *01224 743282.* Owner: Thomas Mitchell. Shop 0.5m. PO and doctor 2.5m. Open Apri l- October. ✫✫✫ **NCC. 10T. MC. 5S. 5H.** ⚓

Aboyne

(0.5m). Aboyne Loch Caravan Park, Aboyne, Aberdeenshire AB34 5BR. *01339 886244.* Owner: P & A Garioch. Off A93. Dogs allowed, but only one per caravan. Fishing and boats on Loch. Shops, PO etc 0.5m. Dog walk around loch, golf beside park. Open April-October. **BH&HPA. 35T. MC. 84S.** ⚓ 🔌 ♿

(0.5m). Drummie Hill Caravan Park, Tarland, Aboyne, Aberdeenshire AB34 4UP. *01339 881388/881264.* Owner: Mr Albert E Calder. Corrielea, Aboyne, Aberdeenshire AB34 4UP. Enter Tarland on B9119, bear left before bridge, after 600yd site is on left. Nearest village is Tarland. Showers. Laundry. Calor Gas. Public phone. Waste disposal. Games room with pool table and machines. Open April-October. **30T. MC. 57S. 6H.** ⚓ 🔌 🏕

Alford

Haughton House Caravan Park, Montgarrie Road, Alford, Aberdeenshire AB33 8NA. *01975 562107.* www.aberdeen shire.gov.uk. Owner: Aberdeenshire Council. Landscape Services, Harlow Way, Inverurie AB51 4SG. Situated 25m W of Aberdeen. Rural location. Suitable touring base. Fishing and golf on or adjacent to site. Dogs allowed but not in hire holiday caravans. 5 flats and 1 bungalow also for hire. Open late March-September. ✫✫✫ **170T. MC. 50S.** ⚓ 🔌 ♿

Ballater

(300 mtrs)Ballater Caravan Park, Anderson Road, Ballater, Aberdeenshire AB35 5QR. *01339 755727.* www.aberdeen shire.gov.uk. Owners: Aberdeenshire Council. Landscape Services, Harlow Way, Inverurie AB51 4SG. Off A93. Scenic setting and open view of hills. Park is set beside the river Dee. 30mins drive to Queen Victoria's 'Dear Paradise', Royal Deeside and Cairngorm National Park. Open April-October. ✫✫✫ **139T. MC. 93S.** ⚓ 🔌 ♿ 🏕

(0.5m). The Invercauld Caravan Club Site, Glenshee Road, Braemar, Ballater, Aberdeenshire AB35 5YQ. *01339 741373.* www.caravanclub.co.uk. Owner: The Caravan Club. East Grinstead House, East Grinstead, West Sussex RH19 1UA. See website for standard directions to site. Site is on fringe of the village of Braemar, 1100ft above sea level, and the eastern gateway to the Cairngorms. Suitable site for walkers and mountain bikers. Non-members welcome. Tent campers welcome. Some hard-standings. Facilities for skiers, ski rocks, boot store, drying room and community room. Toilet block, privacy cubicles, laundry, motorhome service point, veg prep area, gas, playground, dog walk. Suitable for families. Peaceful off-peak. Fishing and golf within 5m. Advance booking essential at all times. Open December-October. ✫✫✫✫ **NCC. 97T. MC.** ⚓ 🔌 ♿

Banchory

(1m). Banchory Lodge Caravan Park Ltd, Dee Street, Banchory, Aberdeenshire AB31 5HT. *01330 822246.* Owner: Mr P & A Garloch. Open April-October. **BH&HPA. 25T. 5MC. 120S.** ⚓ 🔌

(4m). Campfield Caravan Park, Glassel, Banchory, Aberdeenshire AB31 4DN. *01339 882250.* On A980, Alford to Banchory, N of Banchory. Open April 1-September 30. ☆☆☆☆ **BH&HPA. 8T. 8MC. 25S. 2H.** 🐕 🔌 🔧

(5m). Feughside Caravan Park, Strachan, Banchory, Aberdeenshire AB31 6NT. *01330 850669.* contact-us@feugh sidecaravanpark.co.uk. www.feughsidecaravanpark.co.uk. Owner: Mr G Hay. Mount Battock, Strachan, Banchory, Aberdeenshire AB31 6NT. Take B974 from Banchory W to Strachan, then B976 to Feughside Inn, turn R, site is behind inn. Quiet, family-run park. Level, grassy site, with hotel adjacent. Fishing nearby, forest walks 1.5m, shops 2m. Several golf courses in area. Open April 1-mid October. ☆☆☆☆ **BH&HPA. 22T. MC. 48S.** 🐕 🔌 ♿

(2m). Silver Ladies Caravan Park, Strachan, Banchory, Aberdeenshire AB31 6NL. *01330 822800.* Owner: Normanhurst Enterprises Ltd. S of Banchory on left of B974 Fettercairn Road. Fishing nearby. Castle and whisky trails. David Bellamy Gold Conservation Award. Aberdeen 25m. Open April 1-October 31. ☆☆☆☆ **BH&HPA. 18T. MC. 70S. 15H.** 🐕 🔌 🔧

(1.5m). Silverbank Caravan Club Site, North Deeside Road, Banchory, Aberdeenshire AB31 5PY. *01330 822477.* www.caravanclub.co.uk. Owner: The Caravan Club. East Grinstead House, East Grinstead, West Sussex RH19 1UA. See website for standard directions to site. Caravan Club members only. Close to river Dee. Convenient for walking, pony trekking, golf and fishing. Indoor pool at Banchory. All hard-standings, toilet block (privacy cubicles), laundry facilities, veg prep, motorhome service point, Calor Gas and Campingaz, shops 0.5m, dogwalk. Open March-October. **NCC. 62T. MC.** 🐕 🔌 ♿

Banff

(1m). Banff Links Caravan Park, Banff Links, Banff, Aberdeenshire AB45 2JJ. *01261 812228.* www.aberdeen shire.gov.uk. Owner: Aberdeenshire Council. Landscape Services, Harlow Way, Inverurie AB51 4SG. Off A98 Cullen to Banff. 1m W of Banff, SP coastal route. Popular park set close to the large sandy beach of Banff Bay, popular with surfers. Newly installed children's play park next to site. Open Late March-October 31. ☆☆☆ **82T. MC. 43S.** 🐕 🔌 ♿ 🔧

(3m). Wester Bonnyton Farm Caravan Park, Gamrie, Banff, Aberdeenshire AB45 3EP. *01261 832470.* 2m E of Macduff on the B9031 and 1m off the A98, Banff to Fraserburgh road. Touring sites with hook-up facilities. Open March-October. ☆☆☆ **BH&HPA. 8T. 8MC. 2S. 16H.** 🐕 🔌 ♿ 🔧

Whitehills Caravan Park, Whitehills, Banff, Aberdeenshire AB4 2JN. *01261 861474/01888 544828.* ali@auchry. freeserve.co.uk. Owner: Mr & Mrs A Moore. 0.5m from Whitehills. Suitable location for a family holiday. Convenient for golf courses, fishing and right in the heart of castle country. Open April 1-October 31. **BH&HPA. 62S. 10H.** 🐕 🔧

Buckie

(0.25m). Findochty Caravan Park, Jubilee Terrace, Findochty, Buckie, Aberdeenshire AB56 4QA. *01542 835303.* info@findochtycaravanpark.co.uk. www.findochtycaravanpark. co.uk. Owner: Moira & Dennis Main. From Buckie 3m E on A942 on western edge of the village by the harbour. Golf,

fishing, lawn bowling, PH/restaurant and shops nearby. Situated next to rocky beaches and historic harbour. Open March 1-October 31. **25T. MC. 3S.** 🐕 🔌

Fraserburgh

Beach Esplanade, Fraserburgh, Aberdeenshire AB 12 1NS. *01346 510041.* Owner: Banff & Buchan District Council. Leisure & Recreation Dept, Banff, Aberdeenshire. Off A92. By the sea. Play area. Open last Friday March-fourth Monday October. ☆☆ **40T. 30MC. 10S.** 🐕 🔌 ♿

Esplanade Caravan Park, The Esplanade, Fraserburgh, Aberdeenshire AB43 5EU. *01346 510041.* www.aberdeen shire.gov.uk. Owner: Aberdeenshire Council. Landscape Services, Harlow Way, Inverurie AB51 4SG. Situated on the eastern side of Fraserburgh, known locally as the Broch, over-looking esplanade and large beach. Sands stretch round the bay to the Waters of Philorth and its nature reserve. Open April-October. **51T. MC. 12S.** 🐕 🔌 ♿

Huntly

(0.5m). Huntly Castle Caravan Park, The Meadow, Huntly, Aberdeenshire AB54 4UJ. *01466 794999.* enquiries@huntly castle.co.uk. www.huntlycastle.co.uk. Owner: Mr & Mrs Hugh Ballantyne. From Aberdeen on the A96 (Huntly bypass), at roundabout on outskirts of Huntly continue on A96, SP Inverness. In about 0.75m turn right, then second left, in direction of riverside. Caravan Club affiliated site. Large indoor recreation facility, including badminton, snooker, table tennis, large play area and refreshments. 5 mins walk to town. Suitable touring base for whisky, castle and coastal trails. Golf course, river fishing, swimming, shops, all within 0.5m. Open April-October. ☆☆☆☆☆ **BH&HPA. NCC. 66T. MC. 34S. 3H.** 🐕 🔌 ♿

Keith

(0.25m). Keith Caravan Park, Dunny Duff Road, Keith, Aberdeenshire AB55 3JG. *01542 882565.* S of Keith on the A96. Under new ownership, the park has undergone an upgrade recently. Toilet block refurbished. All touring pitches now served with electrics. **BH&HPA. NCC. 44T. MC. 25S. 4H.** ❂ 🐕 🔌

Kintore

(1m). Hillhead Caravan Park, Kintore, Aberdeenshire AB51 OYX. *01467 632809.* enquiries@hillheadcaravan.co.uk. www.hillheadcaravan.co.uk. Owner: Mr D G Smith & Mr A Anige. From S leave the A96 at Broomhill roundabout 3rd exit. From north stay on the A96 past Kintore (do not enter Kintore), leave at Broomhill roundabout 1st exit. Follow brown/white caravan signs on to B994. Then take second right, 3m along B994. Hillhead is 1m on right. AA 3 pennants and RAC approved. Well-equipped, quiet park. Fishing permit sold on park, golf, shop, PO, doctor nearby. Castle and whisky trails. Aberdeen city 12m, airport 6m. ☆☆☆☆ **BH&HPA. 24T. MC. 5H.** ❂ 🐕 🔌 🔧

Laurencekirk

(4m). Brownmuir Caravan Park, Fordoun, Laurencekirk, Aberdeenshire AB30 1SJ. *01561 320786.* brownmuircaravan park@talk21.com. www.brownmuircaravanpark.co.uk. Owner: Mr M B Bowers. Off A90, 4m N of Laurencekirk, 10m S of Stonehaven. At Fordoun pass village, 1m on R. Park 1m from village of Fordoun. Flat, grassy site. Children's play area. Hiking and cycling. Fishing, golf course, bowls, tennis and shops in village 1m. Open April 1-October 31. ☆☆☆ **9T. 9MC. 51S. 2H.** 🐕 ♿

(5m). Dovecot Caravan Park, Northwaterbridge, Laurencekirk, Aberdeenshire AB30 1QL. *01674 840630.* info@dovecotcaravanpark.com. www.dovecotcaravanpark.com. Owner: Mrs A Mowatt. Off A90 Dundee-Aberdeen road, 5m N of Brechin, turn off at Northwaterbridge at Edzell Woods, site 500yd on L. Sheltered park. Suitable touring base. David Bellamy Silver Conservation Award. Open April to mid-October. ✫✫✫✫ BH&HPA. 25T. MC. 40S. 1H. 🅗 🏠 ♿ 🖈

Macduff

(0.5m). Myrus Caravan Park, Macduff, Aberdeenshire AB45 3QP. Owner: Mr & Mrs J Garden. On A947. *01261 812845.* Gas. Open April 1-October 31. BH&HPA. 14T. 10MC. 30S. 6H. 🅗 🏠 🖈

Montrose

(6m). East Bowstrips Caravan Park, St Cyrus, Montrose, Aberdeenshire DD10 0DE. *01674 850328.* tully@bowstrips. freeserve.co.uk. www.ukparks.co.uk/eastbowstrips. Owner: P & G Tully. About 6m N of Montrose on A92. From S (Montrose) enter St Cyrus, pass hotel 1st L, 2nd R. From N (Aberdeen) enter St Cyrus 1st R, 2nd R. Quiet park in landscaped grounds, close to beach and nature reserve. Suitable touring centre. Fishing 1m, golf 6m. AA 4 pennants. Open April-October. ✫✫✫✫✫ BH&HPA. 30T. MC. 18S. 🅗 🏠 ♿ 🖈

Peterhead

(8m). Aden Caravan Park, Aden Country Park, Mintlaw, Peterhead, Aberdeenshire AB42 8FQ. *01771 623460.* www.aberdeenshire.gov.uk. Owner: Aberdeenshire Council. Landscape Services, Harlow Way, Inverurie AB51 4SG. On A950. Set within a woodland area with a heritage centre, which includes a working farm, restaurant and sensory garden. Open Late March-October. ✫✫✫✫✫ 73T. MC. 13S. 🅗 🏠 ♿ 🖈

Peterhead Lido Caravan Park, The Lido, Peterhead, Aberdeenshire AB42 2YP. *01779 473358.* www.aberdeen shire.gov.uk. Owner: Aberdeenshire Council. Landscape Services, Harlow Way, Inverurie AB51 4SG. Situated at the Peterhead Lido, the park is next to a busy thoroughfare overlooking the Bay of Refuge, and marina close to the maritime heritage centre, gift shop, cafeteria and play area. Open late March-October. ✫✫✫✫ 35T. 13S. 🏠 🖈

Portsoy

(0.25m). Portsoy Caravan Park, The Links, Portsoy, Aberdeenshire AB45 2RQ. *01261 842695.* www.aberdeen shire.gov.uk. Owner: Aberdeenshire Council. Landscape Services, Harlow Way, Inverurie AB51 4SG. Site overlooks Portsoy Bay, near the 17th-century harbour and village shops. Open late March-October. ✫✫✫✫ 43T. 16S. 🅗 🏠

(3m). Sandend Caravan Park, Sandend, Portsoy, Aberdeenshire AB4 2UA. *01261 842660.* sandendholi-days@aol.com. Owner: Mr B & Mrs J Winfield. 'The Old Schoolhouse', Sandend, Portsoy, Aberdeenshire. Off A98 between Cullen and Portsoy. Beside sandy beach in conservation village. Open April-October. ✫✫✫✫ NCC. 30T. 12MC. 25S. 3H. 🅗 🏠 ♿ 🖈

Rosehearty

Rosehearty Caravan Park, The Harbour, Rosehearty, Aberdeenshire AB43 7JQ. *01346 510041.* www.aberdeen shire.gov.uk. Owner: Aberdeenshire Council. Landscape Services, Harlow Way, Inverurie AB51 4SG. Situated on the seashore within the village, close to shops, hotels and services. On-site laundry and toilet/shower facilities. Open late March-October. ✫✫ 40T.

Stonehaven

Queen Elizabeth Caravan Park, Stonehaven, Aberdeenshire AB39 2RD. *01569 764041.* www.aberdeenshire.gov.uk. Owner: Aberdeenshire Council. Landscape Services, Harlow Way, Inverurie AB51 4SG. Off A92 Aberdeen to Stonehaven. The park is situated beside the village of Cowie, on the promenade next to the sports centre. Stonehaven is famous for its quaint little shops, tranquil restaurants and historic enclosed harbour. Open late March-October. ✫✫✫ 31T. 76S. 🅗 🏠 ♿ 🖈

Tarland

Camping & Caravanning Club Site - Tarland, Tarland-by-Aboyne, Aberdeenshire AB34 4UP. *01339 881388/0870 243 3331.* www.campingandcaravanning club.co.uk. Owner: Camping & Caravanning Club. Greenfields House, Westwood Way, Coventry CV4 8JH. From Aberdeen on A93 turn R in Aboyne at Strua Hotel on to B9094. After 6m take next R and then fork L before bridge, continue for 600yd, site on L. Suitable for walkers and anglers. Site is located in the quiet and pretty village of Tarland. Mountain scenery of Royal Deeside is spectacular. Non-members welcome. Special deals are available for families and backpackers. Some all-weather pitches available. Several golf courses in the area. Open March-October. ✫✫✫✫✫ 90T. 90MC. 14S. 🅗 🏠 ✎

Turriff

(10m). East Balthangie Caravan Park, East Balthangie, Cuminestown, Turriff, Aberdeenshire AB53 5XY. *01888 544261.* ebc@4horse.co.uk. www.eastbalthangie.co.uk. Owners: John & Anna Burdon. From Ellon on A948 to New Deer, road becomes B9170 to Cuminestow. Continue straight on for 2m, then turn R at the junction, SP New Byth. Park is 3.5m along this road on left-hand side. PO and shop 2m. Fresh fish and local organic veg delivered Fridays. Secure area for pet owners. Farm walk. Open March-October. 12T. 12MC. 🅗 🏠

(0.5m). Turriff Caravan Park, Station Road, Turriff, Aberdeenshire AB53 7ER. *01888 562205.* www.aberdeen shire.gov.uk. Owner: Aberdeenshire Council. Landscape Services, Harlow Way, Inverurie AB51 4SG. 0.5m from Turriff town centre off A947 Aberdeen to Banff road 9m S of Banff. Adjacent to park with children's play area, crazy golf, bowling and boating pond. Sports centre. Dogs on leads allowed. Open late March-October. ✫✫✫✫ 57T. MC. 15S. 🅗 🏠 ♿ 🖈

ANGUS

Arbroath

(1m). Elliot Caravan Site, Elliot, Arbroath, Angus. *01241 873466.* Owner: Mr R S Cargill. Davayne, Dundee Road, Arbroath, Angus DP11 2PH. On A92 Dundee to Arbroath. One small dog per van allowed. Open April 1-September 30. 10T. 6MC. 70S. 6H. 🅗 🏠 🖈

(0.5m). Red Lion Holiday Park, Dundee Road, Arbroath, Angus DD11 2PT. *01241 872038.* red_lion@btconnect.com. www.redlion-holidaypark.com. On A92 Dundee to Arbroath. Modern laundrette. Licensed bar, cafe, takeaway and children's disco. 0.5m to main shopping centre. 1m to golf course. Open March-October. 31T. 31MC. 289S. 12H. 🅗 🏠 ♿ 🖈

(0.75m). Seaton Estate Caravan Site, Arbroath, Angus DD11 5SE. *01241 874762.* seatoncaravans@btinternet.com. Owner: William Smith, John Gray and John Robertson. Follow A92 through Arbroath, turn right at Meadowbank Inn on Montrose road. Follow signs for 0.75m. Fishing, golf course, coastal walks, historial sites, sailing and boating trips, beaches. Swimming pool, sports centre nearby in Arbroath. Open March 1-October 31. ✰✰✰✰✰ **BH&HPA. NCC. 80T. 20MC. 350S. 50H.** ⌂ ✿ ⅃ ♿ ☎

Brechin

(0.5m). East Mill Road Caravan Site, East Mill Road, Brechin, Angus DD9 7EL. *01356 622810.* Owner: Mr George Murray. Trinity Caravans, Trinity, Brechin, Angus. A90 Perth to Aberdeen road, follow signs for Brechin and Montrose, about 10m N of Forfar. Laundry facilities on site. Open April-October. **40T. 10MC. 20S. 10H.** ⌂ ✿ ☎ ∅

(7m). Glenesk Caravan Park, Edzell, Brechin, Angus DD9 7YP. *01356 648565.* www.angusglens.co.uk. From A90 Aberdeen-Dundee take B966 to Edzell, 1.5m N of Edzell turn N, SP Glenesk. Park 1m from junction. Woodland site featuring a small fishing lake. Many local attractions and outdoor activities. Manager: Mr J K Gray. Open April-October. ✰✰✰ **BH&HPA. 45T. MC. 8S. 2H.** ⌂ ✿ ☎

Carnoustie

(0.5m). Woodlands Caravan Park, Newton Road, Carnoustie, Angus DD7 6HQ. *01241 854430/853246.* access concarnlc@angus.gov.co.uk. www.angus.gov.uk. Owner: Angus Council. Leisure Services, Carnoustie Leisure Centre, Links Parade, Carnoustie DD7 7JB. Take the Carnoustie turn-off from A92, turn on to Newton road just before Carnoustie and follow signs. Shops, restaurants, PO, doctors, golf course, swimming pool and leisure centre all nearby. Open mid March- mid October. ✰✰✰✰ **73T. MC. 14S.** ⌂ ✿ ☎ ♿

Forfar

(2m). Foresterseat Caravan Park, Burnside, Anroath Road, Forfar, Angus DD8 2RY. *01307 818880.* emma@ foresterseat.co.uk. www.foresterseat.co.uk. Owner: Emma Laird. Brand new park on the outskirt of Forfar. Close to golf course, fishing loch and local path network. Fully licensed restaurant on site. Views and walks. Close to historical site of the Battle of Nechantmere where Pictish stones have been found. Tourer storage also available. ✰✰✰✰ **BH&HPA. 33T. 33MC.** ⌂ ✿ ♿

(2m). Lochlands Caravan Park, Dundee Road, Forfar, Angus DD8 1XF. *01307 463621.* lochlands@btinternet.com. www. lochlands.co.uk. Turn off the A90 on to A932. After 150yd turn R on to minor road. Take immediate R into Lochlands. Easy access to touring, Glamis, Dundee, the Glens. On-site Coffee Mill and restaurant, and garden centre. Quiet, spacious site. Dogs allowed, under control at all times. All welcome. Online booking available. New amenities planned for 2006. ✰✰✰ **25T. MC.** ✿ ⌂ ✿ ♿ ☎

Lochside Caravan Park, Lochside Leisure Centre, Forfar Country Park, Forfar, Angus DD8 1BT. *01307 468917.* conforlc@angus.gov.co.uk. www.angus.gov.uk. Owner: Angus Council. Contract Services, County Buildings, Market Street, Forfar DD8 3WA. Just off A94, Perth to Aberdeen. Night halt. 3mins walk from town centre. Leisure centre on site. Social club next door to park. Swimming pool 5mins walk. Park situated on side of loch, at edge of country park. Golf and fishing close by. Local doctor on call. Open March-October. ✰✰✰ **75T. MC.** ⌂ ✿ ♿

Kirriemuir

(2m). Drumshademuir Caravan Park, Kirriemuir, Angus DD8 1QT. *01575 573284.* easson@uku.co.uk. www. drumshade muir.com. Owner: I & P Easson. Roundy Hill, By Glamis, Forfar, Angus DD8 1QT. Midway between Glamis Castle and Kirriemuir on the A928. Family-run site. Lunches, evening meals, PH. Putting. Laundry. Woodland walk. Caravan storage. AA 4 pennants. ✰✰✰✰ **BH&HPA. 80T. 80MC. 47S.** ✿ ⌂ ✿ ♿ ☎

Montrose

(12m). Gourdon Caravan Site, Gourdon, Montrose, Angus DD10 0LA. *01561 361475.* On A92. Near sea in fishing village. Shop, hotel and PH near. Open April 1-October 31. **BH&HPA. 3T. MC. 15H.** ⌂ ✿

(7m). Lauriston Caravan Park, St Cyrus, Montrose, Angus DD10 0DJ. *01674 850316.* Owner: Mr & Mrs C G Cummings. On A92. North of St Cyrus village. Open April 1-September 15. **BH&HPA. 22T. 8MC. 50S. 6H.** ⌂ ✿ ☎

(1m). Littlewood Holiday Park, Brechin Road, Montrose, Angus DD10 9LE. *01674 672973.* Owner: Mrs Denise Rennie. On A935 to the north of Montrose. Flat, grassy park with views over Montrose Basin Nature Reserve. ✰✰✰✰ **BH&HPA. 10T. MC. 37S. 6H.** ✿ ⌂ ✿

(1m). Tayock Park Homes, Brechin Road, Montrose, Angus DD10 9LE. *01674 673253.* Owner: Mr R G Wilson. W of Montrose on A935. Take A90 from Dundee, then A935 at Brechin. Holiday and residential site. Open April-October. **BH&HPA. 55S.** ⌂ ∅

(10m). Wairds Park Caravan Site, Wairds Park, Johnshaven, Montrose, Angus DD10 0EP. *01561 362395.* Owner: Wairds Park Committee. c/o End Cottage, Burn of Benholm, Montrose DD10 0HT. On A92. By the sea. Putting. Bowling. Play area. Multi-sports courts with floodlights. 0.25m to village shops and PO. Confections and refreshments sold in park reception. 6 golf courses within 20m radius. Open April 1-October 15. ✰✰✰✰ **BH&HPA. 20T. 20MC. 40S.** ⌂ ✿ ♿ ☎

ARGYLL & BUTE

Argyll

Appin Holiday Homes, Appin, Argyll, Argyll & Bute PA38 4BQ. *01631 730287.* info@appinholidayhomes.co.uk. Owner: I & S Weir. On A828, 15m south of Ballachulish Bridge. 15m north of Connel Bridge. Site on lochside with free fishing. Great hill walks. Recreation room. TV. Dinghies for hire. Caravans all fully serviced. Play area. Laundrette. Thistle Award. Open April-October. ✰✰✰✰ **BH&HPA. NCC. 8S. 8H.**

Glendaruel Caravan & Camping Park, Glendaruel, Argyll, Argyll & Bute PA22 3AB. *01369 820267.* mail@glendarUelcara vanpark.co.uk. www.glendaruelcaravanpark.co.uk. Owner: Mrs A Craig & family. Off A886. Near Kyles of Bute. 17m from Dunoon. Small, peaceful, family-run park within a 22-acre country estate. Walking, cycling and bird/wildlife watching. Thistle Award. Shop on park stocks Loch Fyne ales, range of wines, Orkney ice-cream, venison, books, maps and more. Good base for touring. Discounts arranged with various local attractions. Open April-October. ✰✰✰✰✰ **BH&HPA. 35T. MC. 27S. 1H.** ⌂ ✿ ☎

Glenfinart Caravan Park, Ardentinny, Dunoon, Argyll, Argyll & Bute PA23 8TS. *01369 810256.* From Dunoon take A815 N for 5m, turn right onto A880, after 8m park is on right opposite

SCOTLAND

Fingals Falls. Park set in the gardens of the old Glenfinart Mansion House with loch views and close to beach. Superb walking area. Open March-December. **64S. 3H.** 🛏

Glenview Caravan Park, Strontian, Loch Sunart, Argyll, Argyll & Bute PH36 4JD. *01967 402123.* glenview58@lineone.net. Owner: Sid & Shirley Farnell. On A82 take Corran Ferry across Loch Linnhe to Ardgour. Follow A861 to Strontian. Turn R at police station, site 300yd on R. Laundrette, drying room on site. Pets' corner. Shop, takeaway and doctor within 200yd. PO and petrol 0.25m. 23m from Fort William. Open March-January. ✩✩✩✩ **BH&HPA. 14T. MC. 2S. 2H. ❈ 🛏 ⌨**

West Loch Talbert Holiday Park, Escart Bay, Tarbert, Argyll, Argyll & Bute PA29 6YF. *01880 820873.* Site on left-hand side on Campbeltown road, 2m S of Tarbert. Secluded, small site with panoramic views of West Loch. Open April 1-October 31. ✩✩ **BH&HPA. 6T. 2MC. 28S. 5H.** 🛏 ⌨

Arrochar

(2m). Ardgartan Caravan & Camping Site, Forestry Commission (Forest Holidays), Arrochar, Argyll & Bute G83 7AR. *01301 702293.* fe.holidays@forestry.gsi.gov.uk. www. forestholidays.co.uk. Owner: Forestry Commission (Forest Holidays). 231 Corstorphine Road, Edinburgh EH12 7AT. On A83, Inverary to Arrochar, W of Arrochar. On the shores of Loch Long, surrounded by the scenery of the Argyll Forest Park. Brochure request line: 0131 3340066. Open March-October. ✩✩ **BH&HPA. 200T. MC.** 🛏 ⌨ ♿ 🅿

(2.5m). Caravan Club Site, River Croe, Coilessan Road, Ardgarten, Arrochar, Argyll & Bute G83 7AR. *01301 702236.* www.caravanclub.co.uk. Owner: The Caravan Club. East Grinstead Club, East Grinstead House, East Grinstead, West Sussex RH19 1UA. On A83, Inverary to Arrochar. 0.25m past Ardgarten Camp Site, turn L. After 50yd cross bridge and turn left, site entrance is 300yd on left. Small boat launching point on to Loch Long. No sanitation. Caravan Club members only. Open April-October. **114T. MC.** 🛏 ⌨

(0.3m). Glenloin House, Arrochar, Argyll & Bute G83 7AJ. *01301 702 239.* Owner: Mrs McTavish. On A83, Inverary to Arrochar. 200yd past PO behind Esso petrol station at head of Loch Long. Laundrette. Mobile snack bar. Open February 28-November 1. **5T. MC. 30S. 1H.** 🛏 ⌨ ⌨

Barcaldine

(0.5m). Camping & Caravanning Club Site - Oban, Barcaldine-by-Connel, Argyll PA37 1SG. *01631 720348/0870 243 3331.* www.campingandcaravanning club.co.uk. Owner: Camping & Caravanning Club. Greenfields House, Westwood Way, Coventry CV4 8JH. N from Connel Bridge on A828 site on right of village. Opposite Marine Resource Centre proceed through large iron gates. 13m from Oban. Conveniently placed for touring Highlands and Islands. Licensed bar on site, serves bar meals. All units accepted. Non-members welcome. Set in 4.5 acres of walled garden. Woodland walks 5 mins from site. Special deals for families and backpackers. Open March-October. ✩✩✩✩ **75T. 75MC.** 🛏 ⌨ ♿

Cairndow

(8m). Strathlachan Caravan Park, Strachur, Cairndow, Argyll & Bute PA27 8BU. *01369 860300.* On B8000. Open March-October. **95S.** 🛏 ⌨

Campbeltown

(15m). Carradale Bay Caravan Site, Carradale, Campbeltown, Argyll & Bute PA28 6QG. *01583 431665.* info@carradalebay.com. Off B842. Caravan Club affiliated site. On the wooded east coast of Kintyre, right on the sandy beach, facing the Isle of Arran. Toilet blocks, laundry facilities and vegetable preparation area. Fishing, golf, water sports and NCN cycle route nearby. Good area for walking; dog walk nearby. Peaceful off-peak. Open March-September. ✩✩✩✩ **BH&HPA. 60T. MC.** 🛏 🅿

(10m). Machribeg, Southend, Campbeltown, Argyll & Bute PA28 6RW. *01586 830249.* Owner: Mr J Barbour. Take A83 to Campbeltown then B843 for 10m to Southend. Site is on L 0.5m beyond village. Beside safe, sandy beach and 18-hole golf course. Showers and shaver points. Laundry. Payphone. Dogs allowed on leads only. No booking required. Shop and doctor's surgery 0.25m. Suitable for fishing and walking. Open Easter-September 30. **30T. 10MC. 40S. 10H.** 🛏

(5m). Peninver Sands Caravan Park, Peninver, Campbeltown, Argyll & Bute PA28 6QP. *01586 552262.* info@peninver-sands.com. www.peninver-sands.com. Owner: Mr E McCallum. Craig View, Peniver, by Campbeltown, Argyll, Argyll & Bute. On B842. Open April-October 31. ✩✩✩✩ **BH&HPA. 6T. 20S. 12H.** 🛏 🅿

Dunoon

(5m). Cot House Caravan Park, Kilmun, Dunoon, Argyll & Bute PA23 8QS. *01369 840351.* caravanpark@cothouse. fsworld.co.uk. On the A815, by south-west gateway to national park. Hard-standings for motorhomes and tourers. Open 10 months; closed November and February. ✩✩✩✩ **BH&HPA. 14T. MC. 36S. 4H.** 🛏 🅿 ⌨

(2m). Cowal Caravan Park, Victoria Road, Hunters Quay, Dunoon, Argyll & Bute PA23 8JY. *01369 704259.* On A815 Hunters' Quay to Dunoon. Look for signpost just past Western ferry terminal. Indoor swimming. Fishing, beach. Golf, sailing, boat launch, cycle hire. ✩✩✩✩ **BH&HPA. 24S. 3H. ❈** 🛏

Gairletter Caravan Park, Blairmore, Dunoon, Argyll & Bute PA23 8TP. *01369 810257.* On A880. Open March-October, and December and January. **8T. 8MC. 34S. ❈** 🛏 🅿 ♿

(2m). Hunter's Quay Holiday Village, Hunter's Quay, Dunoon, Argyll PA23 8HP. *01369 707772.* joan@drimsynie. co.uk. www.drimsynie.co.uk. Owner: Keith Campbell. Leisure centre on site, golf nearby, restaurant on site. ✩✩✩✩✩ **BH&HPA. S. H.** 🛏 ♿ ⌨ ✎

(4.5m). Invereck Countryside Holiday Park, Invereck, Sandbank, Dunoon, Argyll & Bute PA23 8QS. *01369 705544.* invereckchp@aol.com. www.caravancampingsites. co.uk. Owner: Mr Hawke. Off A815. Open April-October. **14T. 14MC. 7S. 6H.** 🛏 🅿

(9m). Loch Eck Country Lodges, Dunoon, Argyll & Bute PA23 8SG. *0800 132927.* On A815 Strachur road, 2m from Botanic Gardens. Lochside setting with views. Open March 1-October 31. **BH&HPA. 70S.** 🛏

(7m). Stratheck Country Park, Inverchapel, Loch Eck, Dunoon, Argyll & Bute PA23 8SG. *01369 840472.* enquiries@stratheck.com. www.stratheck.com. N of Dunoon on A815 next to Younger Botanic Gardens. Country club. Laundrette. Games room and games area. Play area. Fishing. Boating. Walking. Climbing etc. Highland scenery. Open March 1-January 2. ✩✩✩ **70T. 70MC. 80S. 4H.** 🛏 🅿 ⌨

Glencoe

> **(1.5m). Camping & Caravanning Club Site - Glencoe, Ballachulish, Glencoe, Argyll & Bute PA39 4LA.** *01855 811397/0870 2433331.* www.campingandcaravanning club.co.uk. Owner: Camping & Caravanning Club. Greenfields House, Westwood Way, Coventry CV4 8JH. On A82. Crianlarich to Glencoe road. Set in 40 acres. Peaceful with mountain backdrops and surrounded by forests. On site: toilets, showers, laundry, chemical toilet emptying point,, dog walk. All types of units accepted. Non-members welcome. Special deals for families and backpackers. Climbing and fishing nearby. Open April-October. ☆☆☆ **120T. 120MC.** ⊬ ☺

(0.25m). Invercoe Caravan and Camping Park, Glencoe, Argyll PH49 4HP. *01855 811210.* info@invercoe.co.uk. Owner: Iain & Lynn Brown. On B863. Thistle Award. ☆☆☆☆☆ **BH&HPA. NCC. 55T. MC. S. 5H.** ✿ ⊬ ☺ ♿ ⅃ ⌀

Helensburgh

(14m). Auchengower Caravan Park, Loch Long, Cove Kilcreggan, Helensburgh, Argyll & Bute. *01436 842517.* macmoo@anserve.com. Owner: Mr A Maconochie. Off B833 Kilcreggan to Loch Long. From Helensburgh take signposts for Coulport base (RNAD), site 2m on L after base entrance round-about. Children welcome. **30S.** ✿ ⊬ ☺

(15m). Rosneath Castle Park, Rosneath, Helensburgh, Argyll & Bute G84 0QS. *01436 831208.* enquiries@rosneath castle.demon.co.uk. www.rosneathcastle.demon.co.uk. Owner: Rosneath Castle Caravan Park Ltd. A82, then A814 for Sarelochmead and then follow signs for B833 Kilemeggan. Park is situated 1m beyond Rosneath. Water sports centre, children's fun club, PH/bistro, outdoor activity area, indoor soft play area. Open March-January. ☆☆☆☆☆ **BH&HPA. NCC. 48T. MC. 358S. 6H.** ⊬ ☺ ♿ ⅃

Inveraray

(2.5m). Argyll Caravan Park, Inveraray, Argyll & Bute PA32 8XT. *01499 302285.* enquiries@argyllcaravanpark.com. www. argyllcaravanpark.com. Owner: Duke of Argyll. Cherry Park, Inveraray. S of Inveraray. Suitable location for touring. Many places of interest within easy reach. Oban and Iona ferry 1hr drive. Open March-October. ☆☆☆☆☆ **BH&HPA. 40T. 20MC. 200S. 5H.** ⊬ ☺ ♿ ⅃

Islay

Kintra Farm Caravan Park, Kintra Beach, Port Ellen, Islay, Argyll & Bute PA42 7AT. *01496 302051.* Take unclassified road from A846 towards Oa, follow Kintra signs. Snacks, meals and takeaways. Showers. Direct access to beach. Good area for walking, birdwatching, plant and wildlife study. Port Ellen 4m. Open April-September. **T. MC.** ⊬ ♿

Isle of Mull

Shieling Holidays, Craignure, Isle of Mull, Argyll & Bute PA65 6AY. *01680 812496.* www.shielingholidays.co.uk. Owner: David & Moira Gracie. From ferry pier at Craignure turn L, in 400yd L again, follow signs. 0.5m from Craignure. On the sea with views of Ben Nevis. Showers, laundry. Short stroll to shop, pub, bistro and buses. Open April-October. ☆☆☆☆☆ **BH&HPA. 30T. 30MC. 12H.** ⊬ ☺ ♿

Loch Lomond

(8m). Ardlui Hotel & Caravan Park, Ardlui, Loch Lomond, Argyll & Bute G83 7EB. *01301 704243.* info@ardlui.co.uk. www.ardlui.co.uk. Owner: Mr D B & Mrs A E Squires. On the A82, 43m north of Glasgow. Situated on the shores of Loch Lomond, in the centre of the Loch Lomond and Trossachs National Park. 16m to Loch Lomond international golf course. ☆☆☆☆ **BH&HPA. 6T. 6MC. 77S. 5H.** ✿ ⊬ ☺ ⅃

Lochgilphead

(17m). Castle Sween Holiday Park, Achnamara, Lochgilphead, Argyll & Bute PA31 8PT. *01546 850223.* info@ellary.com. Owner: Mr Duncan H Rogers. From Lochgilphead take A816 Oban road, then B841 Crinon road at Cairnbairn to Bellonoch. Park SP from there. 15,000 acres of Scottish countryside. Lochside location with safe beaches, walking and wildlife. Restaurant. Bar. Laundrette. Bicycle hire. Slipway. Open March-October. ☆☆☆☆ **BH&HPA. 230S. 20H.** ⊬ ⅃

(11m). Leachive Caravan Park, Leachive Farm, Tayvallich, Lochgilphead, Argyll PA31 8PL. *01546 870206.* fiona@ leachive.co.uk. Owners: Mr & Mrs R MacArthur. A816 N from Lochgilphead, fork L on B841 for 3m, turn L and join B8025 to Tayvallich, site on R in village. Open April-October. **10T. 5MC. 37S. 2H.** ⊬ ☺ ♿

(0.3m). Lochgilphead Caravan Park, Bank Park, Lochgilphead, Argyll & Bute PA31 8NX. *01546 602003.* www.lochgilpheadcaravanpark.co.uk. At J of A83 and A816. Golf, swimming pool, heritage sites, fishing and walks close by. Heated toilet block, laundry and other facilities. Open March-October. ☆☆☆☆ **BH&HPA. 40T. 30MC. 30S. 10H.** ⊬ ☺ ♿

(12m). Port-na-Cloich Caravan Site, Tayvallich, Lochgilphead, Argyll & Bute. *01546 870288.* Owner: Mr D F Shaw. Off A82. Dogs allowed under strict control. Open April 1-October 31. **19S. 2H.** ⅃

Luss

(4m). Inverbeg Holiday Park, Inverbeg, Luss, Argyll & Bute G83 8PD. *01436 860267.* On A82.On Loch Lomond with private beach, good launching facilities and excellent fishing from shore. Chalets beside loch for hire. TV and games room. Play area. Family restaurant and PH 200yd. Boat trips. Co-ordinator: Elspeth Richardson. Open March-January. ☆☆☆☆ **BH&HPA. 35T. 20MC. 100S. 15H.** ⊬ ☺

Morven

Fiunary Caravan & Camping Park, Morven, Argyll PA34 5XX. *01967 421 225.* www.caravancampingsites.co.uk. Owner: Philip & Joanne Henderson. Leave A82, 8m S of Fort William. Cross Corran-Ardgour car ferry. Follow SPs to Lochaline (A884) 31m turn right on B849. 4.5 miles to site. Shop, doctor, PO 4.5m in Lochaline. Own beach. Suitable for launching small craft. Fishing and swimming locally. Forest walks from site. Convenient for Isle of Mull car ferry from Lochline 4.5m. Passenger ferry straight into Tobermory 6m. Open May-September. **20T. MC.** ⊬ ☺

Mull of Kintyre

(4.5m). The Machrihanish Caravan & Camping Park, East Trodigal, Machrihanish, Campbeltown Mull of Kintyre, Argyll PA28 6PT. *01586 810366.* steveandjacquie@mull camp.freeserve.co.uk. www.campkintyre.com. Owner: Steve & Jacquie Boyles. In Campbeltown take B843, SP Machrihanish, site on R before village. Set in a little seaside village just 0.5m walk to a good sandy beach. Privately owned site within 0.5m of the Atlantic shore with its wildlife and seals. Machrihanish Bay has 3m of sands and is next to famous classic golf course. Open March-October. **45T. 45MC. 3H.** ⊬ ☺ ♿ ⅃

SCOTLAND

Oban

(2m). Ganavan Sands Caravan Park, Ganavan Road, Oban, Argyll & Bute PA34 5TV. *01631 562179.* Owner: Mr & Mrs A Mackinnon. On entering Oban turn right at both roundabouts, keep sea on left-hand side for 1.75m park at road end. Open April-October. **80T. 60MC.** 🏕 ⬅ 🖕

(10m). Glen Gallain Caravan Park, Oban, Argyll & Bute PA34 4UU. *01852 6200.* Owner: Mrs Sandilands. A816 from Oban towards Lochgilphead, site 10m from Oban, do not turn right at B844, SP Kilninver, but carry on for 2m to Scammadale turning on left, where site can be seen on left. Suitable base for touring and walking. Fishing available. Open mid April-end October. **30T. MC.** 🏕 🖕 🖕

(8m). Highfield Touring Caravans, Highfield, 3 Kiel Croft, Benderloch, Oban, Argyll PA37 1QS. *01631 720262.* elaine@clsite.co.uk. www.clsite.co.uk. Owner: Mrs Elaine Lauder. Turn off the A828 in Benderloch village at SP for Tralee and South Shian, 5th gate on R (2nd R after restaurant). Highfield is a 7-acre, family-run croft, in a quiet country location by the sea. Suitable base base for exploring the West Highlands and the Argyll islands. Glencoe and Fort William, Inverary, Easdale, Kilmartin Glen, Lochgilphead and the Crinan Canal are all within 1hr of Highfield. Village shop/PO/garage all within 1m. Open April- end October. **10T. MC.** 🏕 🖕

(5.25m). North Ledaig Caravan Club Site, Connel, Oban, Argyll & Bute PA37 1RU. *01631 710291.* From S off A85 on to A828 SP Fort William, park is 1.5m N of Connel Bridge on L. From N off A82 on to A828 SP Connel-Oban. Park is 1m S of Benderloch on R. Caravan Club affiliated site. Members only. 30- acre park. David Bellamy Conservation Award. Toilet blocks, baby and toddler washroom and motorhome service point. Fishing, golf, watersports and NCN cycle route nearby. Good area for walking. Peaceful off-peak. Suitable for families. Open March-October. ✰✰✰✰✰ **NCC. 120T. MC.** 🏕 🖕 🖕 🖕

(2.5m). Oban Caravan & Camping Park, Gallanachmore Farm, Gallanach Road, Oban, Argyll & Bute PA34 4QH. *01631 562425.* info@obancaravanpark.com. www.obancaravanpark.com. Owner: Mr & Mrs H Jones. Follow signs to Gallanach from Oban centre roundabout. Family-run farm on seafront overlooking island of Kerrera, Area of Outstanding Natural Beauty. Showers. Laundrette. Colour brochure. Open April-end September. ✰✰✰✰ **150T. MC. 12H.** 🏕 🖕 🖕

(1.5m). Oban Divers Caravan Park, Glenshellach Road, Oban, Argyll & Bute PA34 4QJ. *01631 562755.* oban divers@tesco.net. www.obandivers.co.uk. Owner: Mr David Tye. At traffic island by tourist office, take ferry terminal exit (Albany Street). Then second left by job centre, first right, first left following 'Glenshelach' camping signs. Family-run park in quiet setting. Golf course, fishing, supermarkets nearby. Open April-October. ✰✰✰✰ **BH&HPA. 35T. MC.** 🖕 🖕 🖕

(8m). Seaview Caravan & Camping Park, Seaview, Keil Croft, Benderloch, Oban, Argyll, PA37 1QS. *01631 720360.* Owner: Violet MacKellar. A85 to Connel, cross Connel Ferry Bridge on to the A828 road, north. Site is 3m from bridge. Couples only. Shop, PO, garage under 1m. Doctor 2.5m. Open Easter-September 30. **12T. MC.** 🏕 🖕

(15m). Sunnybrae Caravan Park, Southcuan, Isle of Luing, Oban, Argyll PA34 4TU. *01852 314274.* sunnybrae-wing@btinternet.com. www.oban-holiday.co.uk. Owners: Mike & Rosy Barlow. Peaceful park on easily accessible isle of Luing. Nearest shop 2m. Suitable base for walking, cycling, diving,

wildlife, scenery. 9-hole golf course and boat trips nearby. Open February-November. ✰✰✰ **7S.** 🏕 🖉

(8m). Tralee Bay Purple Thistle Holidays, Benderloch, Oban, Argyll & Bute PA37 1QR. *01631 720255.* Owner: Mr B H Shellcock. 3m north of bridge at Connel off A828. Boat slip, fishing pond, putting green, and woodland walks. Sandy beach on site. Lodges also for hire. ✰✰✰✰ **BH&HPA. 40S. 40H.** 🏕

Tarbert

Killegruer Caravan Park, Woodend, Glenbarr, Tarbert, Argyll & Bute PA29 6XB. *01583 421355.* anne@littleson.fsnet.co.uk. Owner: Mr N Littleson. On R of A83,12m N of Campbeltown, 24m S of Tarbert, Loch Fyne. Convenient for ferry routes to Arran and Inner Hebrides. Level, grassy park overlooking safe, sandy beach. Bottled gas delivery service. Park has been upgraded to include showers and facilities for disabled visitors. Shop 1m of site. Restaurant, bar within 2m. Walking, golf, horse riding all within reasonable distance from site. Open April 1-September 30. ✰✰✰ **NCC. 20T. 5MC. 44S. 1H.** 🏕 🖕 🖕

(3m). Loch Lomond Holiday Park, Inveruglas, Tarbert, Argyll & Bute G83 7DW. *01301 704224.* enquiries@lochlomond-lodges.co.uk. www.lochlomond-caravans.co.uk. Owner: Halley's Garage Ltd. On A82 Ardlui to Tarbet. Peaceful park on lochside, suitable base for fishing and water sports, walking and touring. Open April-October and December-January (accommodation only). ✰✰✰✰✰ **NCC. 18T. MC. 72S.** 🏕 🖕 🖕

Muasdale Holiday Park, Muasdale, Tarbert, Argyll PA29 6XD. *01583 421207.* enquiries@muasdaleholidays.com. www.muasdaleholidays.com. Owners: Adrian & Alison Clements. On main A83 southern end of Muasdale village. 15m from Campbeltown. Touring park next to beach. Shop 100yd. Caravan holiday homes and tourers offer views of the Atlantic, islands and wildlife. Open Easterl-October. ✰✰✰ **BH&HPA. 10T.10MC. 8S. 8H.** 🏕 🖕

(17m). Point Sands Caravan Park, Tayinloan, Tarbert, Argyll & Bute PA29 6XG. *01583 441263.* www.pointsands.co.uk. Owner: Largie Estates. Off A83. Laundrette. Showers. Peaceful park. Safe sandy beach. Open April 1-October 31. ✰✰✰✰ **BH&HPA. NCC. 40T. MC. 65S. 5H.** 🏕 🖕 🖕 🖕

(15m). Port Ban Caravan Park, Port Ban, Kilberry, Tarbert, Argyll & Bute PA29 6YD. *01880 770224.* portban@aol.com. www.portban.com. Owner: Mrs J F Sheldrick & family. On B8024 off A83. 1m N of Kilberry. 15m S of Ardrishaig situated on the beach, with panoramic views of Islay and Jura. Family-run park with boating, tennis and other sports facilities available. Coffee bar and evening meals served during busy season. Shop on site. Fishing, golf course nearby. Kilberry Inn 1m. Open April-October. ✰✰✰ **BH&HPA. NCC. 15T. MC. 69S. 20H.** 🏕 🖕

Taynuilt

(2m). Crunachy Caravan Park, Bridge of Awe, Taynuilt, Argyll & Bute PA35 1HT. *01866 822612.* angusdouglas@freeuk.com. www.crunachy.co.uk. Owner: Angus Douglas. On the A85, Oban to Clanlarich road. 14m E of Oban. Shower, laundrette, phone, restaurant, games room and swings. Hotel/bar 300yd. Golf 2m. Fishing, walking, climbing nearby. Open March-November. **50T. 10Mc. 10S. 2H.** 🏕 🖕 🖕 🖕

AYRSHIRE (EAST)

Largs

(2.25m). South Whittlieburn Farm, Brisbane Glen, Largs, Ayrshire KA30 8SN. 01475 675881. largsbandb@southwhittlie burnfarm.freeserve.co.uk. www.SouthHound.co.uk/hotels/whittlie.html. Owners: Tom & Mary Watson. Working sheep farm NE of Largs, only 5mins from town centre. Travel about 0.5m along A78 shore road from town centre/pier, heading for Greenock, turn R at large SP for Brisbane Glen Road. Drive 2.25m, site is the second farm on left-hand side, but the only one on roadside. Fishing, hillwalking, golf course, sailing, fishing, horse riding, diving. Ferries to islands, shops, restaurants, doctor etc 2.25m. Swimming pool, theatre, putting green. ✰✰✰ **5T. 5MC.** ✿ ⚲ 🖃

New Cumnock

(2m). Glen Afton Leisure Park, Afton Road, New Cumnock, East Ayrshire KA18 4PR. 01290 332228. Owner: M & A Richardson. A76 Glasgow to Dumfries, midway. Follow sign from mini roundabout in village off New Cumnock. In picturesque valley, suitable for walkers. Fishing and golf nearby. Family PH on site. **BH&HPA. T. MC.** ✿ ⚲ 🖃 ✎

AYRSHIRE (NORTH)

Isle of Arran

Lochranza Golf Caravan and Camping Site, Lochranza, Isle of Arran, North Ayrshire KA27 8HL. 01770 830273/01770 830600. office@lochgolf.demon.co.uk. www.arran.net/lochranza. Owner: I M Robertson. In the village at N end of island, beside own superb golf course. Suitable site for golfers, birdwatchers and walkers. Climbing, hill walking, canoeing etc close by. Level, grass site. Showers. Ferry-inclusive holiday packages to Arran and Western Isles. Bottled gas sales. Open April-September inclusive. **60T. M60C.** ⚲ 🖃 & 🖃

Middleton Caravan & Camping Park, Lamlash Brodick, Isle of Arran, North Ayrshire KA27 8NN. Owner: Mr R J Middleton. Eglinton, Lamlash, Isle of Arran, North Ayrshire. Laundrette. Ironing facilities. Hair-dryers. AA 3 pennants, RAC. Open March-October. ✰✰✰ **12T. 30MC. 40S. 8H.** ⚲ 🖃

Park Avenue Caravans, Brodick Road, Lamlash, Brodick, Isle of Arran, North Ayrshire PA27 8JU. 01414 244056. Dogs allowed with residents. Open March 1-October 31. **BH&HPA. 70S.**

Kilmarnock

(2.5m). Cunninghamhead Estate, Stewarton Road, Irvine, Kilmarnock, North Ayrshire KA3 2PE. 01294 850510/07763 807990. Owner: Mr & Mrs W Laird. From Stanecastle roundabout, Irvine take B769 Stewarton road for 2.5m. Park is on left, SP at roundabout. Most services about 2m. Open April 1-September 30 for holiday vans. **BH&HPA. 30T. 12MC. 15S.** ⚲ 🖃 &

Kilwinning

(3m). Braemoor Christian Holiday Village, Torranyard, Kilwinning, North Ayrshire KA13 7RD. 01294 850286. info@braemoorchv.com. www.braemoorchv.com. 25-metre swimming pool, sauna, steamroom, jacuzzi, fitness suite, children's adventure playground. In surrounding area you will find activities that Scotland is famous for. More than 25 golf courses in a 20m radius. Fishing, rambling and historical buildings are plentiful throughout the region. Shops, doctor within 3m. Open March-October. ✰✰✰ **60S. 40H.** ⚲ &

Saltcoats

(1m). Auchenharvie Park, Saltcoats, North Ayrshire KA21 5JW. 01294 69411. Owner: Compass Leisure. Off A78 Largs or A737 Glasgow to Dalry and Saltcoats. Open March 1-October 31. **40T. 450S. 46H.** ⚲ 🖃

Sandylands Holiday Park, Auchenharvie Park, Saltcoats, North Ayrshire KA21 5JN. 0871 664 9767. sandylands.holi daypark@park-resorts.com.www.park-resorts.com. Owner: Park Resorts Ltd. 3rd Floor, Swan Court, Waterhouse Street, Hemel Hempstead, Herts HP1 1FN. From Glasgow take M77 to Prestwill airport/Kelmarnorth. Follow signs then to Irvine, then Ardrossan. Follow A78 to Stevenson. Indoor pool, water resorts programme, children's club, amusements, shops, laundrette, takeaway, family evening entertainment. Ayr racecourse. Open April-October. ✰✰✰ **BH&HPA. NCC. 700S. 40H.** ⚲ 🖃

Skelmorlie

(0.5m). Mains Caravan Park, Skelmorlie Mains, Skelmorlie, North Ayrshire PA17 5EU. 01475 520794. Owner: T A James Stirrat & Norman Stirrat. Off A78, Greenock to Largs. 4m N of Largs, SP. Open Easter-October. **BH&HPA. 12T. 8MC. 72S.** ⚲ ⚲

West Kilbride

(1m). Crosbie Towers Caravan Park, West Kilbride, North Ayrshire KA23 9PH. 01294 823028. info@crosbietowers.com. www.crosbietowers.com. Owner: Iain McClain. Quiet, woodland park with leisure and laundry facilities. Nearby access to golf, fishing, swimming, ice-skating, farm and country parks and sandy beach. Children allowed. **BH&HPA. NCC. 150S.** ⚲

AYRSHIRE (SOUTH)

Ayr

(8m). Carskeoch Caravan Park, Patna, Ayr, Ayrshire KA6 7NR. 01292 531205. Owner: Mr & Mrs W H Proctor. On A713 to Patna, site at rear of village. Licensed club. Fishing, golf, PO, doctor in 0.5m. Open March 1-October 31. **60T. 26MC. 75S.** ⚲ 🖃

(4m). Craig Tara Holiday Park, Dunure Road, Ayr, South Ayrshire KA7 4LB. 01292 265141. oewebmaster@bourne-leisure.co.uk. www.craigtaraholidaypark.com. Owner: Bourne Leisure Ltd. 1 Park Lane, Hemel Hempstead, Hertfordshire HP2 4YL. A77 towards Stranraer and 2nd R after Bankfield roundabout, S of Ayr. From Doonholm Road L at junction and R into Greenfield Avenue. At next junction L and follow Craig Tara signs. Heated indoor fun pool. Children's clubs. Day and evening entertainment. Convenience store. Laundrette. Bakery. Exclusive health suite includes indoor pool, sauna, steam room, sun bed, gym. Sports court, play area. Go karts, mini bowling, indoor crazy golf. 9-hole golf course. Odeon cinema in Ayr 4m. Open March-October. ✰✰✰✰ **BH&HPA. NCC. 29T. 880S. 300H.** ⚲ 🖃 & 🖃 ✎

(0.5m). Craigie Gardens Caravan Club Site, Craigie Road, Ayr, South Ayrshire KA8 0SS. 01292 264909. www.caravanclub.co.uk. Owner: The Caravan Club. East Grinstead House, East Grinstead, West Sussex RH19 1UA. See website for standard directions to site. Laundry. Baby and toddler washroom. Veg prep. Motorvan waste point. Calor Gas and Campingaz. Information room. Play frame plus play area. Dog walk nearby. Peaceful off-peak. Toilet block with privacy cubicles. Advance booking essential at all times. Non-members admitted. All hard-standings. Suitable for families. Beach, fishing, golf and NCN cycle route in 5m. Open March then all year. ✰✰✰✰✰ **NCC. 90T. MC.** ⚲ 🖃 &

(2m). **Crofthead Holiday Park, McNairston Road, Ayr, South Ayrshire KA6 6EN.** *01292 263516*. holidays@crofthead holidaypark.co.uk. www.croftheadholidaypark.co.uk. Owners: McCormack family. Site SP off A70. ✰✰✰ **BH&HPA. 18T. MC. 45S. 4H.** ✿ ㅓ 🐕 🖢 ⌀

(5m). **Heads of Ayr Caravan Park, Heads of Ayr, Dunure Road, Ayr, South Ayrshire KA7 4LD.** *01292 442269*. Owner: D & U Semple. On A719, Dunure to Ayr. Club. Open March-October. ✰✰✰✰ **BH&HPA. NCC. 36T. MC. 117S. 8H.** ㅓ 🐕 🖢

(6m). **Middlemuir Park, Tarbolton, Ayr, South Ayrshire KA5 5NR.** *01292 541647*. middlemuir@yahoo.co.uk. Owner: Mr T & Mrs Brough & Mr M & Mrs Severn. Off B743, Ayr to Mauchline, SP 5m from Ayr, 4m from Mauchline. Situated in the old walled gardens of Montgomerie Castle, immortalised by Robbie Burns. Open March 1-October 31. ✰✰✰ **BH&HPA. 15T. 5MC. 63S. 08H.** ㅓ 🐕

(6m). **Skeldon Caravan Park, Skeldon, Hollybush, Ayr, South Ayrshire KA6 7EB.** *01292 560502*. Owner: Mr T H Crossley. A713 from Castle Douglas, turn left at Hollybush and observe signs. West route take A713 from A77, after 6m turn right at Hollybush. Play facilities. Sheltered, scenic site on river bank, fishing available. Open April 1-September 30. **BH&HPA. 20T. 4MC. 6H.** ㅓ 🐕 🖢

(4m). **Sundrum Castle Holiday Park, Ayr, South Ayrshire KA6 5JH.** *01292 570057*. enquiries@parkdeanholidays.co.uk. www.parkdeanholidays.co.uk. Owner: Parkdean Holidays Plc. 2nd floor One Gosforth Park Way, Gosforth Business Park, Newcastle-upon-Tyne NE12 8ET. M74, J12, to A70. Park is 4m before Ayr. Indoor pool with toddlers' pool and solarium. Children's club, amusement and adventure play. Bar, food and live family entertainment. Open March-October. ✰✰✰✰ **BH&HPA. NCC. 52T. MC. 269S. 236H.** ㅓ 🐕 & 🖢

Girvan

(5m). **Ardlochan House, Maidens, Girvan, South Ayrshire.** *01655 6208/6821*. Owner: D Dunabie Caravans Ltd. On A74. Open April 1-September 30. **5T. 51S.** ㅓ

(4.5m). **Balkenna Caravan Site, Girvan Road, Turnberry, Girvan, South Ayrshire KA26 9LN.** *01655 331692*. balkenna @aol.com. www.balkenna.co.uk. Owners: Walter & Kahtleen Smith. On A77, N of Girvan. Many golf courses nearby, sea fishing. Views of Ailsa Craig and Arran. **15T. MC.** ✿ ㅓ 🐕 🖢

(8m). **Bennane Shore Holiday Park, Lendalfoot, Girvan, South Ayrshire KA26 0JG.** *01465 891233*. info@ben naneshore.com. www.bennaneshore.com. Owner: G A & S Brown. S of Girvan on A77, Stranraer to Ayr trunk road. Quiet, family park with beach frontage enjoying panoramic views across Firth of Clyde to Ailsa Craig and Kintyre Peninsula. Laundry. Boating facilities with private slipway. Sea fishing. Cliff walks. Open March-January. ✰✰✰✰ **BH&HPA. 90S. 10H.** ㅓ ⌀

(7m). **Carleton Caravan Park, Lendalfoot, Girvan, South Ayrshire KA26 0JF.** *01465 891215*. Off A77 Stranraer to Girvan at Lendalfoot village, SP. Showers. Laundry. No electric hook-ups. Open March 1-October 31. **10T. 5MC. 20S.** ㅓ

(14m). **Laggan House Leisure Park, Ballantrae, Girvan, South Ayrshire KA26 0LL.** *01465 831229*. lagganhouse@ aol.com. www.lagganhouse.co.uk. Owner: Mr & Mrs R C Bourne. Off A77, south of Ballantrae. Heated, indoor swimming pool. Licensed bar. Pool room. Showers. Sauna. Playground. Laundry. Open April 1-October 31 for tourers; open last week March-October 31 for holiday homes. ✰✰✰✰ **BH&HPA. 8T. 8MC. 80S. 12H.** ㅓ 🐕

(10m). **Queensland Holiday Park, Barrhill, Girvan, Ayrshire KA26 0PZ.** *01465 821364*. info@queenslandholidaypark.co.uk. www.queenslandholidaypark.co.uk. Owners: J & M Stewart and A & J Sensicall. From Girvan take A714, heading SE, park on R 1m before Barrhill. Peaceful, woodland park. Local fishing and golf. Suitable base for walking in Southern Upland mountains. Open March 1-October 31. ✰✰✰✰ **15T. 8MC. 38S. 3H.** ㅓ 🐕 & 🖢

(6m). **Sandhouse Caravan Park, Ardlochan Road, Maidens, Girvan, South Ayrshire KA2 69NS.** *01655 331308*. Owner: Mrs M Harper. Off A77. Open April-September. **13S.** ㅓ

(6m). **Sandy Beach Caravan Park, 25 Ardlochan Road, Maidens, Girvan, South Ayrshire KA26 9NS.** *01655 331456*. On A719, Ayr to Turnberry. 50yd from safe, sandy beach. Village location with local PO, hotel and general stores. Laundrette. Open March 1-October 31. **BH&HPA. NCC. 6T. MC. 40S.** ㅓ 🐕

Strathavon Caravan Park, Girvan, South Ayrshire. *01465 712262*. Owner: Strathavon Caravan Park Ltd. 100yd from town. Open March-October. **40T. 10MC. 162S. 5H.** 🐕 & 🖢

(3.5m). **Turnberry Holiday Park, Girvan, South Ayrshire KA26 9JW.** *01655 331288*. info@turnberryholidaypark.com. www.turnberryholiday.com. Owner: Mr R G Noon. On A77 Turnberry to Girvan Road. 400yd off main road. Surrounded by rolling hills, sandy beaches and golf courses, with an unspoilt view of Ailsa Craig and the Firth of Clyde. Open March 1-October 31. **30T. MC. 160S.** ㅓ 🐕 🖢

(9m). **Windsor Holiday Park, Barrhill, Girvan, South Ayrshire KA26 0PZ.** *01465 821355*. windsorholidaypark@barrhillgirvan. freeserve.co.uk. www.windsorholidaypark.co.uk. Owner: Mr & Mrs M Langford and Mr & Mrs A Cartwright. Situated on A714 between Newton Stewart and Girvan, 1m N of Barrhill. Peaceful site set in rolling hills and sheltered by trees. Hard-standings and level grass pitches. Many outdoor activities. Suitable base for exploring an unspoilt area. Golf, shops, swimming pool, beach within 10m. Open March 1-October 31, every weekend and two weeks at Christmas. ✰✰✰ **BH&HPA. 30T. MC. 28S.** ㅓ 🐕 & 🖢 ⌀

Maybole

(3m). **Camping & Caravanning Club Site - Culzean Castle, Culzean Castle, Maybole, South Ayrshire KA19 8JX.** *01655 760627*. www.campingandcaravan ningclub.co.uk. Owner: Camping & Caravanning Club. Greenfield House, Westwood Way, Coventry CV4 8JH. From S on A77 turn L on to A719. Site 4m on L. From N on A77 turn R on to B7023 in Maybole. After 100yd turn L, site 4m. The area has extensive views and spectacular sunsets. Non-members welcome. All types of units accepted. Site adjacent to historic castle and country park. 17m of country walks within easy access. Local attractions include sandy beaches, deer park and an aviary. Special deals available for families and backpackers. Open March-October. ✰✰✰✰ **90T. 90MC.** ㅓ 🐕 &

(4m). **Croy Bay Caravans, Croyburnfoot Park, Croy Shore, Maybole, South Ayrshire KA19 8JS.** *01292 500239*. Owner: Mr J Ferguson. Off A719. On the beach at Croy Shore. Open March-October. **10T. MC. 50S.** ㅓ 🐕 🖢

(4m). **Culzean Bay Holiday Park, Knowside, By Croyshore, Maybole, South Ayrshire KA19 8JS.** *01292 500444*. 8m S of Ayr on the A719 coast road. Open March 1-October 31. ✰✰✰✰ **BH&HPA. 15T. 10MC. 100S. 5H.** ㅓ 🐕 & 🖢

SCOTLAND

(1.5m). **The Ranch Caravan Club Site, Culzean Road, Maybole, South Ayrshire KA19 8DY.** 01655 882446. www.theranchscotland.co.uk. A77, Ayr and Maybole. In Maybole turn R on B7023. Caravan Club affiliated site. Members only. Small site with colourful rose beds and flowering shrubs. Suitable base for exploring south-west Scotland. Toilet blocks, laundry facilities and motorhome service point. Play area, swimming pool and dog walk on site. Fishing, golf and NCN cycle route nearby. Suitable for families. **NCc. 40T. MC.** ✿ ⊁ ⊞ ⅙

(4m). **The Walled Garden Caravan & Camping Park, Kilkerran, Maybole, South Ayrshire KAl9 7SL.** 01655 740323. walledgardencp@clara.co.uk. www.walledgardencp.clara.co.uk. Owner: Jim McCosh. Take B7023 from Maybole to Crosshill, proceed 200yd up Crosshill main street, then turn R to Dailly. Road joins B741; Kilkerran is to the L, 2m past Crosshill. Basic requirements and Calor Gas available, age concessions. Discounts for club members. Recreation room, carpet bowls weekly, children's play area, golf practice net, fishing, putting. Open March-October. ✩✩✩ **50T. MC.** ⊁ ⊞ ⅙

Prestwick

(2m). **Dutch House Caravan Park, Monkton, Prestwick, South Ayrshire KA9 2RA.** 01292 478285. On A77. Open March 1-October 31. ✩✩✩ **10T. 10MC. 90S.** ⊁

(1m). **Prestwick Holiday Park, Prestwick, South Ayrshire KA9 1UH.** 01292 479261. Owner: Mr & Mrs Mackay. N of Prestwick, site SP off A79. Beach. Lounge bar. Games room. Laundry. Quiet, family-run site, set between golf courses. Open March 1-October 31. ✩✩✩ **BH&HPA. NCC. 36T. 24MC. 150S. 5H.** ⊁ ⊞ ⅙ ⊾

Symington

(4m). **Dankeith Leisure Park, Dankeith, Symington, South Ayrshire.** 01563 830254. On B730, 1m from junction with A77. Open March 1-October 31. **10T. 90S.** ⊁ ⊾

Troon

(0.25m). **St Meddans Caravan Site, Low St Meddans, Troon, South Ayrshire KA10 6NS.** 01292 312957. www.ukparks.com. Owner: Mr Heron. On A759. Off No 2 Dundonald Road, in town centre. Beaches, golf course all within 5mins walk. Open March 1-October 31. **BH&HPA. 23T. 2MC.** ⊁ ⊞ ⅙

BORDERS

Cockburnspath

(1m). **Chesterfield Caravan Park, The Neuk, Cockburnspath, Borders TD13 5YH.** 01368 830459. From bypass follow signs to Abbey St Bathans. Park is about 0.5m on left from junction. Open April-October. ✩✩✩ **BH&HPA. 33T. 40MC. 40S. 1H.** ⊁ ⊞

(2m). **Peasebay Holiday Home Park, Cockburnspath, Borders TD13 5YP.** 01368 830206. www.peasebay.co.uk. Owner: Dunham Leisure Ltd. 1.5m off A1 at Cockburnspath roundabout. 22m from Berwick-upon-Tweed and 35m S of Edinburgh. 20 mins to Berwick. 10 mins to Dunbar. Surfing, fishing, close to all golf courses, shops and doctors 10 mins, PO 5 mins. Site's beach is in clean beach guide. 5 mins away from the A1. Scottish wildlife reserve adjacent to park. Open March-October. ✩✩✩✩ **BH&HPA. 35T. MC. 300S.** ⊁ ⊞ ⅙ ⊾

Duns

(6m). **Greenlaw Caravan Park, Blackadder Touring Park, Greenlaw, Duns, Borders TD10 6XX.** 01361 810341. www.greenlawcaravanpark.com. Owner: Mr C Gregg. 10m N of Coldstream and 37m S of Edinburgh on A697. SP in Greenlaw at J of A697/A6105. Riverside park with free fishing. Licensed bowling club. Shops nearby. Open Febarury 1-January 14. ✩✩✩✩ **BH&HPA. 10T. 10MC. 130S. 1H.** ⊁ ⊞

Eyemouth

Eyemouth Holiday Park, Font Road, Eyemouth, Borders TD14 5BE. 0871 664 9740. eyemouth.holidaypark@park-resorts.com. www.park-resorts.com. Owners: Park Resorts Ltd. 3rd Floor, Swan Court, Waterhouse Street, Hemel Hempstead, Herts HP1 1FN. From A1, follow signs to Eyemouth on A1107. On entering town, turn R after petrol station and L at bottom of hill into Font Rd. Family bar, lounge, laundrette, amusements, outdoor play area, children's club, family entertainment. 18-hole golf course 1m, trout fishing 2.5m. Open April-October. ✩✩✩✩ **BH&HPA. NCC. 212S. 22H.** ⊁

(2m). **Scoutscroft Holiday Centre, St Abbs Road, Coldingham, Eyemouth, Borders TD14 5NB.** 01890 771338. holidays@scoutscroft.co.uk. www.scoutscroft.co.uk. Owner: David, Margaret, John & Mark Hamilton. Melrose, St Abbs Road, Coldingham, Eyemouth, Borders. Turn off A1 on to A1107, head for St Abbs, site SP. 5mins walk to nearest shop, 5-10 mins walk to Coldingham Beach. Fishing in village, 18-hole golf course and swimming pool in Eyemouth. Dive centre on site. Slightly sloping site may not be suitable for wheelchair users. Open March 1-October 31. ✩✩✩✩✩ **BHHPA. 50T. 2MC. 120S. 20H.** ⊁ ⊞ ⅙ ⌀

Hawick

(7m). **Bonchester Bridge Caravan Park, Bonchester Bridge, Hawick, Borders TD9 8JN.** 01450 860676. Owner: Mr A Forbes. Off A68 and A7. Bar facilities at hotel nearby. AA 3 pennants. Open Easter-September. **25T. MC.** ⊁ ⊾

(2m). **Riverside Caravan Park, Hornshole Bridge, Hawick, Borders TD9 8SY.** 01450 373785. riversidehawick@supanet.com. www.riversidehawick.com. Owners: Mr & Mrs N G Atkinson. A696, Newcastle to Scottish Borders, A6088 to Hawick, from Carlisle A7 N to Hawick. Set on banks of river Teviot with free fishing. 8 acres including woods. Quiet, family-run site. Open April-October 31. ✩✩✩ **BH&HPA. 44T. MC. 55S. 7H.** ⊁ ⊞ ⅙

Innerleithen

Tweedside Caravan Park, Montgomery Street, Innerleithen, Borders EH44 6SP. 01896 831271. Owner: Linda Graham. A72, follow SPs. Surrounded by scenic hill country. Close to river Tweed. Fishing permits available. Open April 1-October 31. ✩✩✩ **30T. 30MC. 114S. 2H.** ⊞ ⅙ ⊾

Jedburgh

(1m). **Camping & Caravanning Club Site - Jedburgh, Elliot Park, Jedburgh, Borders TD8 6EF.** 01835 863393/0870 2433331. www.campingandcaravanning club.co.uk. Owner: Camping & Caravanning Club. Greenfields House, Westwood Way, coventry CV4 8JH. Off A68, north of town; SP. Close to outskirts of Jedburgh historic town on direct route in to Scotland. All types of units accepted. Some all-weather pitches. Non-members welcome. Picturesque walk by riverside to Jedburgh 1m away. Leisure centre in town, also golf and fly fishing. Special deals available for families and backpackers. Open April-October. ✩✩✩✩ **60T. 60MC.** ⊁ ⊞ ⅙

Please mention Caravan Sites 2006 when replying to advertisers

(3m). Jedwater Caravan Park, Jedburgh, Borders TD8 6PJ. *01835 869595.* jedwater@clara.co.uk. www.jedwater.co.uk. Owner: Mr N Gibson. Willowford, Camptown, Jedburgh, Borders. Off A68, S of Jedburgh. Quiet site on banks of river Ted, free fishing on site. Golf nearby. Open Easter-October. ✰✰✰✰ **BH&HPA. 30T. MC. 50S. 6H.** ♯ ☻ ⚓

(5m). Lilliardsedge Park & Golf Course, Ancrum, Jedburgh, Borders TD8 6TZ. *01835 830271.* On A68. Showers. Public phone. Licensed bars. Laundry. Tourist information. Open March 1-October 31. ✰✰✰ **BH&HPA. 40T. MC. 140S. 2H.** ♯ ☻ ⚓

Kelso

(8m). Kirkfield Caravan Park, Grafton Road, Town Yetholm, Kelso, Borders TD5 8RU. *01573 420346.* Owner: Frank Gibson. On B6352, approaching from S on A697 turn L on to B6396 for Yetholm. Garages, shop, PO in Town Yetholm. Open April 1-October 31. **25T. MC.** ♯ ☻

(1m). Springwood Caravan Park, Springwood Estate, Kelso, Borders TD5 8LS. *01573 224596.* admin@springwood. biz.www.springwood.biz. Owner: Springwood Estate. On A699. On site: play area, table tennis. Nearby: golf, cinema, swimming, pony treking, tennis. Suitable base for walking. Open March 31-October 9 for tourers; open February 24-November 11 for holiday caravans. ✰✰✰✰ **BH&HPA. 40T. 10MC. 210S.** ♯ ☻ ⚓ ⌀

Lauder

(4m). Camping & Caravanning Club Site - Lauder, Carfraemill, Oxton, Lauder, Borders TD2 6RA. *01578 750697/0870 2433331.* www.campingandcaravanning club.co.uk. Owner: Camping & Caravanning Club. Greenfields House, Westwood Way, Coventry CV4 8JH. From town of Lauder, turn R at roundabout on to A697, then L at Lodge Hotel. Site on R behind Carfraemill Hotel. 24m S of Edinburgh, close to Thirlestane Castle and a good fishing area. 4 self-catering timber chalets for hire. Non-members welcome. All types of units accepted. Set in a river valley in heart of Scottish Borders. Special deals for families and backpackers. Open March-October. ✰✰✰✰ **70T. 70MC. 4**♯ ☻ ⚓

(0.6m). Thirlestane Castle Caravan and Camping Park, Lauder, Borders TD2 6RU. *079762 31032.* maitland_carew @compuserve.com. Owner: Mr Edward Maitland-Carew. Between A68 & A697. Just outside royal burgh of Lauder, which has shops and PHs. 30m S of Edinburgh. Secluded site with views across wooded countryside and near the river. Holiday home area is being developed adjacent to touring park. Open April 1-October 1. ✰✰✰✰ **BH&HPA. NCC. 60T. MC. 20S. 1H.** ♯ ☻ ⌀

Melrose

(1m). Gibson Caravan Club Site, Gibson Park, High Street, Melrose, Borders TD6 9RY. *01896 822969.* www.caravanclub.co.uk. Owner: The Caravan Club. East Grinstead House, East Grinstead, West Sussex RH19 1UA. See website for standard directions to site. Level, peaceful site on edge of Melrose, overlooked by three hills. Non-members welcome. Shops adjacent. Motorhome service point. Toilet block with laundry. Tent campers welcome May 221-September 10. Fishing and golf 5m. Good area for walking, some hard-standings, gas, dog walk. Suitable for families. Peaceful off-peak. NCN cycle path 5m. ✰✰✰✰✰ **NCC. 60T. MC.** ✿ ♯ ☻ ⚓

Moffat

(0.25m). Camping & Caravanning Club Site - Moffat, Hammerland's Farm, Moffat, Borders DGl0 9QL. *01683 220436/0870 2433331.* www.campingandcaravan ningclub.co.uk. Owner: Camping & Caravanning Club. Greenfields House, Westwood Way, Coventry CV4 8JH. From Moffat take A708 towards Selkirk, turn R at camping sign. Turn L at Nursery. Follow club signs to site. Suitable touring base for touring Borders country. All types of units accepted. Non-members welcome. Golf and fishing nearby. 300-year-old Drumlarig Castle. Moffat has won awards for the 'Best Kept Village in Scotland'. Special deals available for families and backpackers. Open March-October. ✰✰✰✰ **180T. 180MC.** ♯ ☻ ⚓

Newcastleton

Lidalia Caravan Club Site, Old Station Yard, Moss Road, Newcastleton, Borders TD9 0RU. *01387 375819.* eddie.lidalia@freeuk.com. www.lidalia.co.uk. Members only. Small, landscaped site in an interesting village and within easy reach of shops. Toilet blocks and laundry facilities. Dog walk nearby, also fishing and golf. Good area for walking. Peaceful off-peak. **NCC. 30T. MC.** ✿ ♯ ☻ ⚓

Peebles

(0.5m). Crossburn Caravan Park, Edinburgh Road, Peebles, Borders EH45 8ED. *01721 720501.* enquiries@crossburncara vans.co.uk. www.crossburncaravans.co.uk. Owner: The Chisholm Family. On A703. Laundry. Full facilities. Games room. Play area. Open Easter or April 1-October 31. ✰✰✰✰ **BH&HPA. NCC. 40T. 40MC. 84S. 5H.** ♯ ☻ ⚓ ⌀

(1m). Rosetta Caravan & Camping Park, Rosetta Road, Peebles, Borders EH45 8PG. *01721 720770.* Owner: The Clay Family. SP all roads in Peebles. Family-owned park with golf course adjacent. Laundry, bars and bowling green. 10 minutes walk to High Street. Open April 1-October 31. ✰✰✰ **BH&HPA. NCC. 100T. 30MC. 60S. 1H.** ♯ ☻ ⚓

Selkirk

(19m). Angecroft Caravan Park, Ettrick Valley, Selkirk, Borders TD7 5JA. *01750 62355.* kevin@ettrickhall.com. www.angecroftpark.com. On B709, 4m S of Tushielaw Inn, 26m E from M6 or A74. Leave dual carriageway at Lockerbie. Peaceful holiday park with touring pitches. Open February 15-January 15. ✰✰✰ **BH&HPA. NCC. 8T. 8MC. 40S. 5H.** ♯ ☻ ⚓

(16m). Honey Cottage Caravan Park, Hope House, Ettrick Valley, Selkirk, Borders TD7 5HU. *01750 62246/015393 31291.* www.honeycottagecaravanpark.co.uk. Owner: C A & S Woof. On B709, Langholm road, and B7009 from Selkirk. B711 from Hawick, left for 1m at Tushielaw Inn on B709. Reduced facilities October to April. Shop on site. Fishing on site. Quiet site, suitable base for walking, fishing and wildlife. ✰✰✰ **40T. MC. 40S.** ✿ ♯ ☻ ⚓

(0.75m). Victoria Caravan Park, Buccleuch Road, Selkirk, Borders TD7 5DW. *01750 20897.* Owner: Scottish Borders Council. From S on A7, follow signs from Selkirk market place, from N on A7 turn R at entrance to town, SP A72 Peebles and A708 Moffat, and follow signs. From Peebles on A707 take road in to Selkirk, turn L immediately after bridge. ✰✰✰ **60T. MC.** ✿ ♯ ☻

CLACKMANNAN

Dollar

(0.5m). Riverside Caravan Park, Dollarfield, Dollar, Clackmannan FK14 7LX. *01259 742896.* info@riverside-caravanpark.co.uk. www.riverside-caravanpark.co.uk. Owner: Mr & Mrs A Small. On B913 Dollar to Dunfermline. Suitable base for hill walking, birdwatching, fishing and golf. Close to many places of interest and Knockhill racing circuit. Open April-September. BH&HPA. 30T. MC. 30S. ⌁ ◪

DUMFRIES & GALLOWAY

Annan

Galabank Caravan Site, Castlehill Gate, North Street, Annan, Dumfries & Galloway DG12 5BQ. *01556 503806.* Owner: Dumfries & Galloway Council. Community Resources (Leisure & Sport), Cotton Street, Castle Douglas. At traffic lights in Anna centre, turn on to B722, pass athletics track and site is on left. Nearby facilities include shops, PO, doctor, golf and fishing. Open May-early September. 30T. 30MC. ⌁ ◪

(4m). Queensberry Bay Caravan Park, Powfoot, Annan, Dumfries & Galloway DG12 5PU. *01461 700205.* From Annan B724, 3m on unclassified road to Powfoot 1m. Open Easter-October 31. ☆☆ BH&HPA. 80T. MC. 62S. ⌁ ◪ ⌁

Castle Douglas

Anwoth Caravan Park, Garden Street, Gatehouse-of-Fleet, Castle Douglas, Dumfries & Galloway DG7 2JU. *01557 814333.* Owners: Mr & Mrs Swalwell. In centre of Gatehouse-of-Fleet. Managed by warden. Peaceful site in Area of Outstanding Natural Beauty. Suitable touring base. Open March 1-October 31. ☆☆☆ BH&HPA. 28TMC. 42S. ⌁ ◪ ⌁

Auchenlarie Holiday Park, Gatehouse-of-Fleet, Castle Douglas, Dumfries & Galloway DG7 2EX. *01557 840251.* enquiries@auchenlarie.co.uk. www.auchenlarie.co.uk. Owners: Mr & Mrs J M Swalwell. On A 75. 5m W of Gatehouse-of-Fleet on S coast of Galloway with small sandy cove. Friendly park overlooking Wigtown Bay, with several golf courses nearby and sea and coarse fishing. Entertainment, laundrette, 3 bars with meals, games room, amusement centre, crazy golf and three play areas. AA 4 pennants. Indoor swimming pool and leisure suite, including gym, sauna, solarium, sports hall. Open March 1-October 31. ☆☆☆☆ BH&HPA. 75T. MC. 212S. 40H. ⌁ ◪ ⌁ ⌁

(5m). Barlochan Caravan Park, Palnackie, Castle Douglas, Dumfries & Galloway DG7 1PF. *01556 600256/booking 01557 870267.* whc@barlochan.co.uk. www.gillespie-leisure.co.uk. Owner: Gillespie Leisure Ltd. Brighouse Bay, Kirkcudbright, Dumfries & Galloway DG6 4TS. On A711, 2.5m SW of Dalbeattie. Friendly park overlooking Urr estuary with nearby free coarse fishing on loch. Laundrette and dishwashing. Games and TV rooms, mini-golf and play area. PH nearby. Open April 1-October 31. ☆☆☆ BH&HPA. NCC. 30T. MC. 50S. 6H. ⌁ ◪ ⌁ ⌁ ⌁

(12m). Cardoness Holiday Park, Cardoness, Gatehouse-of-Fleet, Castle Douglas, Dumfries & Galloway DG7 2EP. *01557 840288.* mark@hannay.freeserve.co.uk. Owner: Mr Mark Hannay. Off A75, Stranraer to Dumfries, on seaward side. 3m from Gatehouse of Fleet. Within 100-acre estate. 3m of sandy beaches and rocky coves. Nature trails, fishing, walks, tennis court, games room. David Bellamy Gold Conservation Award. Open April 1-October 31. BH&HPA. 6T. MC. 214S. ⌁ ◪ ⌁ ⌁

(7m). Loch Ken Holiday Park, Parton, Castle Douglas, Dumfries & Galloway DG7 3NE. *01644 470282.* www.lochkenholidaypark.freeserve.co.uk. A713 Castle Douglas to Ayr road. On the shores of the loch with sandy beach. Fishing. Cycle hire. Canoeing, boating and sailing on site. Waterskiing, sailing and golf nearby. Charge for dogs. Thistle Award. David Bellamy Gold Conservation Award. ☆☆☆☆ BH&HPA. 55T. 10MC. 19S. 11H. ✿ ⌁ ◪ ⌁ ⌁

(0.25m). Lochside Caravan & Camping Site, Lochside Park, Castle Douglas, Dumfries & Galloway DG7 1EZ. *01556 502949.* www.dumgal.gov.uk. Owner: Dumfries & Galloway Council. Community Resources (Leisure & Sport), Cotton Street, Castle Douglas, Dumfries & Galloway. Just off A75 at Castle Douglas. Located by Carlingwark Loch, Castle Douglas. Dogs on leads. Nearby facilities include doctor, PO, shops, tennis, swimming pool, golf, fishing, sailing, play area and park, boating, putting, Threave Gardens. AA 3 pennants. Open Easter to end-October. ☆☆☆ 108T. 108MC. ⌁ ◪ ⌁

(15m). Mossyard Caravan Park, Gatehouse-of-Fleet, Castle Douglas, Dumfries & Galloway DG7 2ET. *01557 840226.* enquiry@mossyard.co.uk. www.mossyard.co.uk. Owner: J McConchie & Sons. On A75, Dumfries to Stranraer, 4m beyond Gatehouse-of-Fleet, SP. Family-run park on the shores of the Fleet estuary. Suitable location for swimming, boating. Coarse fishing, swimming pool within 0.25m. Nearest village for golf and tennis 5m. Open April 1-October 31. ☆☆☆☆ BH&HPA. 15T. 20MC. 15S. 1H. ⌁ ◪ ⌁

(17m). Sandgreen Caravan Park, Gatehouse-of-Fleet, Castle Douglas, Dumfries & Galloway DG7 2DU. *01557 814351.* Off A75, Gatehouse-of-Fleet bypass. Open March 1-October 31. ☆☆ BH&HPA. 20T. MC. 185S. ⌁ ◪ ⌁

Dalbeattie

(6m). Castle Point Caravan Park, Rockcliffe, Dalbeattie, Dumfries & Galloway DG5 4QL. *01556 630248.* kee22@dial.pipex.com. http://homepage.mac.com/castle-point-site/personalpage.html. Owner: Mr J Bigham. Mansefield, Carmyllie, Angus DD11 2RA. From Dalbeattie take A710. In 5m turn right to Rockcliffe, then left after 1m. Quiet site overlooking the sea and with good views. Walks and beaches nearby. Open April- Mid October. ☆☆☆ BH&HPA. 22T. 22MC. 3S. 6H. ⌁ ◪ ⌁

Glenearly Caravan Park, Dalbeattie, Dumfries & Galloway DG5 4NE. *01556 611393.* Owners: Fred & Debbie Jardine. From Dumfries take A711 to Dalbeattie. Park entrance on right just before you enter Dalbeattie. Walking distance to shops in Dalbeattie. 6m to nearest beach. Golf courses 10mins drive. Pony trekking, mountain biking, fishing, tennis, forest walks all nearby. ☆☆☆☆ BH&HPA. 40T. MC. 57S. 2H. ✿ ⌁ ◪ ⌁

Islecroft Caravan & Camping Site, Colliston Park, Mill Street, Dalbeattie, Dumfries & Galloway DG5 4HE. *01556 612236.* Owner: Mr I & Mrs L Robertson. 11 Alpine Terrace, Dabeattie DG5 4HJ. In Dalbeattie. From A711 on to B793 in town. Take first left at The Cross into Islecroft Park. Easy access to town. Dogs on leads. Nearby: Shops, PO, doctor, tennis, golf, beaches, play area and park, paddle boats, putting. Walking, cycle tracks. Open March-October. ☆☆☆ 30T. 30MC. ⌁ ◪ ⌁

(3m). Kippford Holiday Park, Kippford, Dalbeattie, Dumfries & Galloway DG5 4LF. *01556 620636.* info@kippfordholiday park.co.uk. www.kippfordholidaypark.co.uk. Owner: C R Aston. S of Dalbeattie on A710 towards Kippford, seaside village. David Bellamy Gold Conservation Award, Touring and tenting pitches set in small groups, terraced and level with hard-standings, individually screened, on sloping ground. Thistle Award. 15mins stroll to Kippford, with 2 PHs, and coastal walk to the beach and bay. Shop, cycle hire, golf and fishing adjacent. Long-stay, group and family discounts. Open all year; bookings required for winter. ☆☆☆☆☆ **BH&HPA. NCC. 30T. 30MC. 120S. 30H.** ✿ ⊩ ◘ & ⅃

(6m). Sandyhills Bay Leisure Park, Sandyhills Bay, Dalbeattie, Dumfries & Galloway DG5 4NY. 01387 780257/Booking line 01557 870267. cs@sandyhills-bay.co.uk. www.gillespie-leisure. co.uk. Owner: Gillespie Leisure Ltd. Brighouse Bay, Kirkcudbright, Dumfries & Galloway DG6 4TS. On A710, Dumfries to Dalbeattie. Award-winning park only a few yards from beach. Coastal walks. Smugglers' cave. Showers, laundrette, dishwashing and takeaways. 18-hole golf course adjacent. Fishing, riding and eating out within walking distance. Advance bookings: 015578 70267. Facilities at Brighouse Bay site are available. Open April 1-October 31. ☆☆☆☆ **BH&HPA. NCC. 30T. 25S. 6H.** ⊩ ◘ ⅃ ⌀

Dumfries

(6m). Barnsoul Farm and Wild Life Area, Barnsoul Farm, Shawhead, Dumfries, Dumfries & Galloway DG2 9SQ. 01387 730249. barnsouldg@aol.com. www.barnsoulfarm.co.uk. Owner: A J Wight & Co. From Dumfries take A75 (Stranraer) for 6m turn R for Shawhead. At T-junction turn R then bear L, to Dunscore. Farm is 1m on L. Unspoilt site with ponds and woodlands set in well-known wildlife area. Fishing close by. Mountain bikes and Mabie Forest within 8m. David Bellamy Gold Conservation Award. AA 3 pennants. Open March-October or by appointment. ☆☆☆ **BH&HPA. 20T. 10MC. 10S. 1H.** ⊩ ◘ &

(8m). Beeswing Caravan Park, Kirgunzeon, Dumfries, Dumfries & Galloway DG2 8JL. 01387 760242. On right-hand side, 0.75m S of Beeswing on A711. Site is rural, inland, quiet and a suitable touring base. Haven for wildlife. Open March-November 1. ☆☆☆ **BH&HPA. 25T. MC. 1S. 2H.** ⊩ ◘ &

(8m). Mossband Caravan Park, Kirgunzeon, Dumfries, Dumfries & Galloway DG2 8JP. 01387 760208. Owner: G & M Dempster. Off A711. Tennis court. Play area. Open March-October. ☆☆ **15T. MC. 11S. 1H.** ◘

(5m). Mouswald Caravan Park, Mouswald Place, Dumfries, Dumfries & Galloway DG1 4JS. 01387 830226. From Gretna follow A75 past Annan. 1m past Carrutherstown take left to Mouswald. Through village, turn right before church. 0.5m to crossroads, straight across, and site 200yd on left. Bar and family room. Golf courses, riding, mountain biking nearby. Open March-October. **BH&HPA. 30T. MC. 50S. 5H.** ⊩ ◘

Newfield Caravan Park, Annan Road, Dumfries, Dumfries & Galloway DG1 3SE. 01387 750228. On A75, Carlisle to Dumfries, next to Little Chef. **20T. 5MC.** ⊩ ◘

(9m). Park of Brandedleys, Crocketford, Dumfries, Dumfries & Galloway DG2 8RG. 0845 4561760. holidays@holgates.com. www.holgates.com. Owners: Arthur Holgate & Sons Ltd. Off A75, at W end of Crocketford. Indoor and outdoor swimming pools, sauna, tennis and badminton courts, games room, recreational areas, bar and restaurant. 25 golf courses within a 20m radius. Opportunities for sea fishing, trout and salmon, as well as coarse fishing, in 20m radius. ☆☆☆☆ **BH&HPA. NCC. 65T. 40MC. 55S. 10H.** ✿ ⊩ ◘ &

(17m). Southerness Holiday Village, Southerness, Dumfries, Dumfries & Galloway DG2 8AZ. 01387 880256. enquiries@parkdeanholidays.co.uk. www.parkdeanholidays.co.uk. Owner: Parkdean Holidays Plc. 2nd Floor, One Gosforth Way, Gosforth Business Park, Newcastle-upon-Tyne NE12 8ET. Off A710. Follow Solway Coast signs from Dumfries. Modern holiday village with separate touring park catering mainly for families. Licensed club, bar meals and indoor cafe with takeaway service, heated indoor swimming pool, family entertainment, amusement centre, adventure play park. Championship golf, Pay and Play golf. Local attractions. Open March 1-October 31. ☆☆☆☆ **BH&HPA. NCC. 90T. MC. 730S. 50H.** ⊩ ◘ & ⅃

Gretna

(0.5m). Braids Caravan Park, Annan Road, Gretna, Dumfries & Galloway DG16 5DQ. 01461 337409. enquiries@thebraids caravanpark.co.uk. www.thebraidscaravanpark.co.uk. Owners: John & Isabel Scott. B721, Gretna to Annan road. Fishing information. Golf course nearby. PO, shops, doctor all within 0.75m. Bus service to Carlisle, Annan and Dumfries. 100yd from Stranraer ferry terminal. Calor Gas agency. ☆☆☆☆ **74T. MC.** ✿ ⊩ ◘ &

The Braids Caravan Park, Annan Road, Gretna, Dumfries & Galloway DG16 5DQ. 01461 337409. Owner: Mr & Mrs H Copeland & Mr J Dalgliesh. From S on A74 take A75, SP Stranraer, take 2nd left for Gretna, site on left in 500yd. AA 3 pennants, RAC appointed. ☆☆☆☆ **84T. MC. 3S.** ✿ ⊩ ◘ & ⅃

Kirkcudbright

(6m). Brighouse Bay Holiday Park, Borgue, Kirkcudbright, Dumfries & Galloway DG6 4TS. 01557 870267. whc@brig house-bay.co.uk. www.gillespie-leisure.co.uk. Owner: Gillespie Leisure Ltd. Brighouse Bay, Kirkcudbright, Dumfries & Galloway DG6 4TS. Off B727, Kirkcudbright to Borgue, or take A755 (Kirkcudbright) off A75, 2m W of Twynholm. Clear SP for 8m. Site hidden away within 1200 acres next to beach and bluebell woods. Golf and leisure club with indoor pool, toddlers' pool, steam room, jacuzzi. Also family lounge, function room, bar, bistro, games room with 10-pin easy bowl. 18-hole and 9-hole par-3 golf courses, practice area and covered driving range. Slipway, mini golf, pond canoes, nature trails, bike hire. Pony trekking. Quad bikes. Lodges also for sale and hire. ☆☆☆☆☆ **BH&HPA. NCC. 120T. 120MC. 120S. 40H.** ✿ ⊩ ◘ & ⅃ ⌀

(2.5m). Seaward Caravan Park, Dhoon Bay, Kirkcudbright, Dumfries & Galloway DG6 4TJ. 01557 331079/booking line 01557 870267. whc@seaward-park.co.uk. www.gillespie-leisure.co.uk. Owner: Gillespie Leisure Ltd. Brighouse Bay, Kirkcudbright, Dumfries & Galloway DG6 4TS. From Kirkcudbright take A755 W, then B727 to Borgue. Park, about 2.5m from Kirkcudbright. Site offers panoramic views over bay. Award-winning park. Facilities include heated outdoor pool, dishwashing, laundrette and showers. Sea angling, Beach picnic area nearby. Advance bookings: tel 01557 870267. Games and TV room, 9-hole golf course. Facilities at nearby Brighouse Bay site available for use. Scotish AA Campsite of the Year 2004. Open March 1-October 31. ☆☆☆☆ **BH&HPA. NCC. 20T. MC. 30S. 6H.** ⊩ ◘ & ⅃ ⌀

(0.5m). Silvercraigs Caravan and Camping Site, Silvercraigs Road, Kirkcudbright, Dumfries & Galloway DG6 4BT. 01557 330123. www.dumgal.gov.uk. Owner: Dumfries & Galloway Council. Community Resources (Leisure & Sport), Cotton Street, Castle Douglas, Dumfries & Galloway. In Kirkcudbright, off Silvercraigs road overlooking the town. No advance booking.

Dogs on leads. Nearby facilities include shops, PO, doctor, tennis, swimming pool, golf, museum, wildlife park, fishing, sailing, beaches, play area and park. Elevated site overlooks town of Kirkcudbright. Panoramic views of the Solway coast. AA 3 pennants. Open Easter-late October. ✰✰✰✰ **37T. 37MC.** ☝ ➤ ௸

Langholm

(0.5m). Whitshiels Caravan Site, Langholm, Dumfries & Galloway DG13 0HG. *01387 380494.* Owner: R J & C Vickers. Main A7, 0.5m N of Langholm. Showers. Telephone. Cafe on site, takeaway meals available. Chemical toilet em ptying point. Shops nearby. Open March 1-October 31. ✰✰✰ **8T. MC. 3H.** ✿ ☝ ➊ ➋

Lochmaben

(0.25m). Kirkloch Caravan Site, Kirkloch Brae, Lochmaben, Dumfries & Galloway DG11 1PZ. *01556 503806.* www.dum gal.gov.uk. Owner: Dumfries & Galloway Council. Community Resources (Leisure & Sport), Cotton Street, Castle Douglas. B709 at Lochmaben, near Lockerbie, Dumfrieshire. Enter site by Kirkloch Brae. Nearby facilities include shops, PO, doctor, golf, fishing, play area. Site is situated on the picturesque Kirkloch, in small town of Lochmaben. AA 2 pennants. Open Easter-late October. ✰✰✰ **30T. 30MC.** ☝ ➊

Lockerbie

(5m). Cressfield Caravan Park, Ecclefechan, Lockerbie, Dumfries & Galloway DG11 3DR. *01576 300702.* Leave A74 (M) at Ecclefechan, J19. Follow B7076 for 0.5m to S side of village, SP. Peaceful country park. Putting green. Sports field. Play area. Dog walk. Village amenities 0.25m. Good touring base or night halt. Golf, fishing 2m. Supermarket, cinema 5m. ✰✰✰✰✰ **20T. 20MC. 96S.** ✿ ☝ ➊ ➋

(3m). Halleaths Caravan Park, Lochmaben, Lockerbie, Dumfries & Galloway DG11 1NA. *01387 810630.* halleaths caravanpark@btopenworld.com. www.caravan-sitefinder.co.uk/ sites/2436. Owner: Gordon Hoey. From Lockerbie (M74) take A709, Lockerbie to Dumfries road. Site 0.5m on right after crossing river Annan. Kitchen area with microwave. Winter storage available. Well-sheltered site surrounded by trees. Game and coarse fishing within 1m. 5 golf courses within 9m. Open 15 March-15 November. ✰✰✰✰ **BH&HPA. 25T. MC. 65S.** ☝ ➊ ➋

(5m). Hoddom Castle Caravan Park, Hoddom, Lockerbie, Dumfries & Galloway DG11 1AS. *01576 300251.* hoddom castle@aol.com. www.hoddomcastle.co.uk. Owner: Hoddom & Kinmount Estates. Estate Office, Hoddom, Lockerbie DG11 1BE. Exit A74 M, J19, follow signs. Peaceful site part of 10,000-acre estate. Bar, restaurant, golf, tennis, fishing, nature trails on site. AA 5 pennants. Cinema, shopping centre, two 18-hole golf courses within 5m. Open April-October. ✰✰✰✰✰ **200T. MC. 44S.** ☝ ➊ ௸ ➋

(12m). King Robert The Bruce's Cave Camping & Caravan Site, Cove Farm, Kirkpatrick Fleming, Lockerbie, Dumfries & Galloway DG11 3AT. *01461 800285.* enquiries @brucescave.co.uk. www.brucescave.co.uk. Owner: Mr Andrew Ritchie, Mrs Jan Ritchie. Turn off A74 at sign Kirkpatrick Fleming, then follow all signs to Bruce's Cave. Wooded and secluded in grounds of 80-acre estate with free coarse fishing on 3m stretch of river. Restricted facilities from October 31-March 1. Shop only available in summer. Quad riding, clay pigeon shooting, paintball available nearby. BMX bikes on site. ✰✰✰✰ **NCC. 25T. 15MC. 20S. 2H.** ✿ ☝ ➊ ௸ ➋

Moffat

(2km). Craigielands Country Park, Beattock, Moffat, Dumfries & Galloway DG10 9RB. *01683 300591/300650.* Owner: Mrs Chris Harrison. J15 off new M74. Set in country estate of over 56 acres with own loch and woodland walks. Pony-trekking. One holiday caravan adapted for use by disabled people. Log cabins for sale. Yearly touring caravan plots. PH and restaurant on site. Wildlife sanctuary. **100T. 20MC. 40S. 16H.** ✿ ☝ ➊ ௸

Newton Stewart

(22km). Burrowhead Holiday Village, Tonderghie Road, Isle of Whithorn, Newton Stewart, Dumfries & Galloway DG8 8JB. *01988 500252.* Beautiful views of the Isle of Man. Indoor lesiure complex with fun slide, sauna and Jacuzzi. Play area, clubhouse and entertainment. Soft ball play area. Open March 1-October 31. ✰✰✰ **BH&HPA. NCC. 200T. 50MC. 97S. 53H.** ☝ ➊ ➋

(6m). Castle Cary Holiday Park, Creetown, Newton Stewart, Dumfries & Galloway DG8 7DQ. *01671 820264.* enquiries@castlecarypark.f9.co.uk. www.castlecary-caravans. com. Owners: Caird Leisure Ltd. Off A75. Large, heated outdoor swimming and paddling pools. Country inn with bar meals and takeaway food. Sun patio. Playground. Laundrette. Public phone. Well-stocked coarse fishing lake. Iindoor pool. Games room. Adults' snooker room. Woodland walks. Donkey park. Crazy golf. Village 0.25m for PO, shops, hotels, cafe and garage. New timber lodge development around Loch Murray. **BH&HPA. 50T. MC. 45S. 2H.** ✿ ☝ ➊ ௸ ➋

Castlewigg Caravan Park, Castlewigg, Whithorn, Newton Stewart, Dumfries & Galloway DG8 8DP. *01988 500616.* castlewigg.park@btconnect.com. www.castlewigg caravan park.co.uk. Owners: Ted & Kath Reeder. Between Sorbie and Whithorn on A746. Tranquil countryside setting. Suitable for walking, cycling, bird watching, golf and relaxation. Shops 2m. Open March 1-October 31. **BH&HPA. 6T. 5MC. 29S. 4H.** ☝ ➊

Creebridge Caravan Park, Newton Stewart, Dumfries & Galloway DG8 6AJ. *01671 402324.* www.creebridgecaravan park.com. Owner: Mr & Mrs J M Sharples. Off A75, 1m E of Newton Stewart, head for Minnigaff. Site 200yd before bridge over river. In Newton Stewart go over old bridge to Minnigaff, site 200yd on R. Quiet, secluded site. Open March 1-November 1. ✰✰✰ **BH&HPA. 25T. 6MC. 40S. 6H.** ✿ ☝ ➊

(6m). Creetown Caravan Park, Silver Street, Creetown, Newton Stewart, Dumfries & Galloway DG8 7HU. *01671 820377.* Beatrice.Mcneill@btinternet.com. www.creetown-caravans.co.uk. Owner: J & B McNeill. On A75 in village of Creetown. Toilet block. Outdoor heated swimming and paddling pools. Indoor hot-tub, games room and play area. Convenient for village amenities. Suitable touring base for south-west Scotland. Open March 1-October 31. ✰✰✰✰ **NCC. 22T. 10MC. 52S. 4H.** ☝ ➊

Drumroamin Farm Touring Site, 1 South Balfern, Kirkinner, Newton Stewart, Dumfries & Galloway DE8 9DB. *01988 840613.* enquiry@drumroamin.co.uk. www.drumroamin.co.uk. Owners: Ralph & Lesley Shell. A75 towards Newton Stewart, on to A714 towards Wigtown. Turn L on B7005, head through Bladnock, A746 through Kirkinner. Take B7004, Garlieston, turn 2nd L, site at end of lane. Rural location. Village shop and PO 1.5m. Golf course in Wigtown, book capital of Scotland. Doctors, butchers and Co-op in Wigtown. Sea and river fishing close by. Many cycle routes nearby; site also has shed for bike storage. 13m from Kirroughtree and mountain biking facilities. ✰✰✰✰ **20T. MC. 2H.** ✿ ☝ ௸ ➋

SCOTLAND

(6m). Ferrycroft Caravan Park, Creetown, Newton Stewart, Dumfries & Galloway DG8 7JS. *01671 820502.* doncook@pgen.net. Owner: Mrs B Cook. Turn off A75 into Creetown turn uphill at Clock Tower in main street and follow signs for Ferry Croft Caravan Park. Just uphill from the village of Creetown which has a grocers, butchers, PO, restaurant, hotel and crafts etc. Small, quiet site. Well situated for touring Galloway's coastline, moorlands, forests and hills. Swimming, golf, fishing and cinema within 6m. Open Easter-September 30. **3T. 3MC. 4H.** �ின ⊟

> **Garlieston Caravan Club Site, Garlieston, Newton Stewart, Dumfries & Galloway DG8 8BS.** *01988 600636.* www.caravanclub.co.uk. Owner: The Caravan Club. East Grinstead House, East Grinstead, West Sussex RH19 1UA. See website for standard directions to site. Caravan Club members only. Suitable holiday location on the Machars Peninsula. Toilet blocks, laundry facilities and motorhome service point. Good area for walking, water sports nearby. Peaceful off-peak. Site within 5mins of the beach. Open March-October. **NCC. 63T. MC.** ☆ ⊟ ⬥ ⊘

(15m). Glenluce Caravan Park, Glenluce, Newton Stewart, Dumfries & Galloway DG8 0QR. *01581 300412.* enquiries@ glenlucecaravans.co.uk. www.glenlucecaravan.co.uk. Owner: RH&RA Rankin. Take A75 Dumfries to Stranraer, leave A75 at Glenluce SP, 10m Eof Stranraer. Concealed entrance in centre of village opposite Brambles restaurant. Secluded suntrap park close to village, sea, bowling, fishing, pony trekking, golf and superb walks all within 1m. Thistle Award. Open March-October. ☆☆☆☆ **BH&HPA. 16T. 4MC. 30S. 6H.** ☆ ⊟ ⬥ ⊘ ⬥

(9m). Glentrool Holiday Park, Bargrennan, Newton Stewart, Dumfries & Galloway DG8 6RN. *01671 840280.* enquiries@ glentroolholidaypark.co.uk. www.glentroolholidaypark.co.uk. Owner: Mr & Mrs M Moore. Off A714. N of Newton Stewart. Pleasant, peaceful park in suitable situation for touring and exploring Galloway forest and hills. Horse riding, birdwatching and fishing nearby, plus off road cycle routes. Cinema, swimming pool, golf, shops, cycle hire 9m. Open March 1-October 31. ☆☆☆☆ **BH&HPA. 15T. 6MC. 22S. 3H.** ☆ ⊟ ⬥ ⬥

(18m). Kings Green Caravan Site, South Street, Port William, Newton Stewart, Dumfries & Galloway DG8 9SH. *01988 700880*Owner: Port William Community Association. Mr John Ambrose, 32 South Street, Port William, Newton Stewart DG8 9SG. On A747. Toilet block with access for disabled people. Seaside location within walking distance of Port William with shops, PHs and harbour. Many interesting places to visit, 4 golf courses within easy reach, fishing in abundance. Peaceful site with views across Luce Bay. Open March 1-October 31. **30T. MC.** ☆ ⊟ ⬥

(18m). Knock School Caravan Park, Monreith, Newton Stewart, Dumfries & Galloway DG8 8NJ. *01988 700414.* www.knockschool.com. Owner: Mrs P R Heywood. On A747, 3m S of Port William. entrance by golf course and beaches. Small, peaceful touring park. Birdwatching, archaeology and gardens locally. Golf, beaches and fishing within 5mins. Hard-standing pitches. Open Easter-September. **15T. MC.** ☆ ⊟

(12m). Monreith Sands Holiday Park, Monreith, Port William, Newton Stewart, Dumfries & Galloway DG8 9LJ. *01988 700218.* 2m east of Port William on the A747 and approximately 20 minutes drive from Newton Stewart on the A714. 300yds to sandy beach and 0.75m for golf. Open March-October. **3T. 3MC. 40S. 6H.** ☆ ⊟

(11m). Three Lochs Holiday Park, Kirkcowan, Newton Stewart, Dumfries & Galloway DG8 0EP. *01671 830304.* info@3lochs.co.uk. www.3lochs.co.uk. Owner: Holker Estates Co Ltd. Off B7027 and A75. Follow A75 until about 8m W of Newton Stewart and turn right at Dirnow crossroads and follow signs. Bottled gas. Indoor heated pool. Fishing, sailing and windsurfing. Full-size snooker room. Golf courses, leisure centre, pony trekking all nearby. Open March-October. ☆☆☆ **BH&HPA. NCC. 45T. 45MC. 100S. 10H.** ☆ ⊟ ⬥ ⬥

(18m). West Barr Farm Caravan Site, Port William, Newton Stewart, Dumfries & Galloway DG8 9QS. *01988 700367.* On A747 2m N of Port William. Small, privately owned site on Luce Bay, close to sea and 1m from village. Open April-October. **10T. MC. 30S.** ☆ ⊟

Sanquhar

(0.25m). Castleview Caravan & Camping Site, Sanquhar, Dumfries & Galloway DG4 6AX. *01659 50291.* On A76 at south (Dumfries) end of town. At Esso petrol station. Fishing, 9-hole golf course, shops, PO all nearby. Open Easter-October. **10T. 4MC. 6S.** ☆ ⬥

Southerness-on-Solway

Lighthouse Leisure, Southerness-on-Solway, Dumfries & Galloway DG2 8AZ. *01387 880277.* lighthouseleis@aol.com. www.lighthouseleisure.co.uk. Owner: C Robertson. From Drumfries, follow A710 for 20mins turn off to Southerness on L, 5mins to site. Level, lawned, family-owned park. Leisure complex with Mermaid Bar, restaurant, heated pool, sauna, gym, ten-pin bowling, amusements. Toytown. Full facilities. Close to sandy beaches and championship golf course. Open March-October. ☆☆☆ **BH&HPA. 20T. MC. 13H.** ☆ ⊟ ⬥ ⬥

Stranraer

(1m). Aird Donald Caravan Park, London Road, Stranraer, Dumfries & Galloway DG9 8RN. *01776 702025.* enquiries@ aird-donald.co.uk. www.aird-donald.co.uk. Owner: Mr H M Cassie. On A75, Newton Stewart to Stranraer. Small, sheltered site, level grass. Suitably situated for ferries to Ireland. 1m from town. Tarmac hard-standings for wet weather. ☆☆☆☆ **75T. MC.** ☆ ☆ ⊟ ⬥

(8m). Ardwell Caravan Site, Ardwell, Stranraer, Dumfries & Galloway. *01776 86249.* Owner: Ardwell Estates. Off A716. **T. 15S.** ☆

(6m). Cairnyan Caravan Park, Cairnryan, Stranraer, Dumfries & Galloway DG9 8QX. *01581 200231.* On A77, opposite P&O ferry terminal, Cairnryan. 7 chalets to let. Shop 500yd. Open April-October. ☆☆☆☆ **BH&HPA. 15T. MC. 70S. 5H.** ☆ ⊟ ⬥

(0.75m). Castle Bay Caravan Park, Portpatrick, Stranraer, Dumfries & Galloway DG9 9AA. *01776 810462.* From N take A77 Glasgow, from S take the A75 from Dumfries. Open March 1-October 31. ☆☆☆☆ **BH&HPA. 25T. 20MC. 70S. 17H.** ☆ ⊟ ⬥

(17m). Clashwhannon Caravan Site, Drummore, Stranraer, Dumfries & Galloway DG9 9QE. *01776 840374.* On A716. Bar. Restaurant. Games room. Open March-October. **5T. 4MC. 14S. 6H.** ☆ ⊟

(6m). Clayshant Holiday Park, Stoneykirk, Stranraer, Dumfries & Galloway. *01776 830278.* Owner: Mr I & T Stopford. On A715. From Dumfries follow A75 for Stranraer, turn off at SP for Drummore Road, road leads direct to site. PH on site. Manager: Carol McCreadie. Open March-October. **20T. 20MC. 45S. 2H.** ☆ ⊟

(5m). Drumlochart Caravan Park, Lochnaw, Leswalt, Stranraer, Dumfries & Galloway DG9 0RN. *01776 870232.* office@drumlochart.co.uk. www.drumlochart.co.uk. Owner: Mr S D & P R Palmer. On B7043. Heated pool. Lounge bar. Play park. Coarse fishing and boating on 10-acre loch. AA 4 pennants. Open March-October. ✩✩✩✩ **BH&HPA. 20T. 10MC. 80S. 9H.** 🛲 🖭

(7m). Galloway Point Holiday Park, Portree Farm, Portpatrick, Stranraer, Dumfries & Galloway DG9 9AA. *01776 810561.* www.gallowaypointholidaypark.co.uk. Owner: Mr & Mrs A J Mackie. Off A75, A77 S from Glasgow, A75 W from Dumfries. 1st L after 30mph on R, office at house/PH on L. Sea views. Golf, fishing and bowling nearby. Lounge bar and meals. Caravan & Camping Club listed location. RAC. David Bellamy Silver Conservation Award. Shops, PO 0.75m. Open Easter-September 30. **BH&HPA. 40T. 10MC. 80S. 3H.** 🛲 🖭

(18m). Maryport Farm Caravan Site, Drummore, Stranraer, Dumfries & Galloway. *01776 840276.* Owner: Mrs M Bailey. Off A716. Open April 1-October 31. **10T. 5MC. 30S.** 🛲

(14m). New England Bay Caravan Club Site, Port Logan, Stranraer, Dumfries & Galloway DG9 9NX. *01776 860275.* www.caravanclub.co.uk. Owner: The Caravan Club. East Grinstead House, East Grinstead, West Sussex RH19 1UA. See website for standard directions to site. Site is on the edge of Luce Bay and is landscaped into seven intimate pitching areas with sea views. Non-members and tent campers welcome. Advance booking essential bank holidays and July-August. Toilet blocks with privacy cubicles and laundry facilities. Veg prep area, gas, dog walk nearby. Motorhome service point. Games room. Play equipment. Suitable for families. Steel awning pegs required. Storage pitches, water sports and beach nearby. Peaceful off-peak. Open March-October. ✩✩✩ **NCC. 149T. MC.** 🛲 🖭 ♿

(1m). Ryan Bay Caravan Park, Innefmessan, Stranraer, Dumfries & Galloway DG9 8QP. *01776 889458.* ryanbay@hagansleisure.co.uk. www.hagansleisure.co.uk. Owners: Hagans Leisure Group. 184 Templepatrick Road, Ballyclare, Co Antrim, N Ireland BT39 0RA. Site on shore of Ryan Bay. Clubhouse. Open March-November. ✩✩ **BH&HPA. NCC. 16T. 16MC. 50S. 5H.** 🛲 🖭

(7.5m). Sandhead Caravan Park, Sandhead, Stranraer, Dumfries & Galloway DG9 9JN. *01776 830296.* Off A716. Lounge bar. Open April-October. **BH&HPA. 30T. 10MC. 70S. 6H.** 🛲 🖭 ♿ 🐕

(6m). Sands of Luce Caravan Park, Sandhead, Stranraer, Dumfries & Galloway DG9 9JR. *01776 830456.* At junction of B7084 and A716, S of Stranraer. Beside sandy beach. Beach walk to village of Sandhead. Open March 15-October 31. **BH&HPA. 50T. 10MC. 40S. 6H.** 🛲 🖭 ♿ 🐕

(7m). Sunnymeade Caravan Park, Portpatrick, Stranraer, Dumfries & Galloway DG9 8LN. *01776 810293.* info@sunnymeade98.freeserve.co.uk. A75 to Portpatrick, turn L on entering Portpatrick. Site 0.5m on L. Near beach and golf. Private fishing pond. Open April-October. **BH&HPA. 15T. 4MC. 60S. 2H.** 🛲 🖭

(4m). Wig Bay Holiday Park, Loch Ryan, Stranraer, Dumfries & Galloway DG9 0PS. *01776 853233.* On entering take A718 Kirkcolm road, right at roundabout, past garden centre. Park is on left. Heated indoor swimming pool. Play area. Bar. Games room. Laundrette. Chemical toilet emptying point. Showers. Telephone. Open March 1-October 31. ✩✩✩✩ **BH&HPA. NCC. 24T. MC. 90S.** 🛲 🖭 ♿ 🐕 ✐

Thornhill

(2m). Penpont Caravan & Camping Park, Penpont, Thornhill, Dumfries & Galloway DG3 4BH. *01848 330470.* penpont.caravan.park@ukgateway.net. www.penpontcaravanandcamping.co.uk. Owner: Mr & Mrs Van der Wielen. At north end of Thornhill take the A702 to Penpont 2m. Park is on the L just before Penpont village. Quiet, riverside park in rural setting. 5mins walk to shop, local PH and PO. Golf course 3m. River and loch fishing available locally. Open April-October. **BH&HPA. 10T. 5MC. 20S. 1H.** 🛲 🖭

(10m). Woodlea Hotel, Moniaive, Thornhill, Dumfries & Galloway DG3 4EN. *01848 200209.* mike-horley@msn-com. www.woodlea-hotel.ndo.co.uk. Owner: Mr Mike Horley. On A702 New Galloway Road, 1.5m out of Moniaive. Golf. Tennis. Bowls. Sailing. Croquet. Badminton. Play area. Pony rides. Games room. Indoor swimming pool. Sauna, restaurant, bar. Open Easter1-October 31. **8T. MC.** 🛲 🖭

Wigtown

Whitecairn Farm Caravan Park, Glenluce, Wigtown, Dumfries & Galloway DG8 0NZ. *01581 300267.* enquiries@whitecairncaravans.co.uk. www.whitecairncaravans.co.uk. Owner: Mr & Mrs Rankin. 1.5m N of Glenluce village and 2m from A75. 12m from Stranraer. Small, family-run park within easy reach of many local attractions. Fully serviced pitches for touring caravans and campers. ✩✩✩✩ **NCC. 10T. 5MC. 50S. 12H.** ✿ 🛲 🖭 ♿ ✐

DUNBARTONSHIRE (W)

Alexandria

Camping & Caravanning Club Site - Luss, Loch Lomond, Nr Glasgow, Alexandria, West Dunbartonshire G83 8NT. *01436 860658.* www.campingandcaravanningclub.co.uk. Owner: Camping & Caravanning Club. Greenfields House, Westwood Way, Coventry CV4 8JH. From Erskine Bridge take the A82 north towards Tarbet. Turn right at lodge of Loch Lomond and international camping sign. Heading S from Tarbet, take first left after site sign and lodge of Loch Lomond sign. Site is 200yd ahead. Club members' caravans and motor caravans only. On the banks of Loch Lomond with good views of Ben Lomond. Tents accepted. 12-acre park. Fishing available on site. Golf, horse riding, rock climbing and swimming pool nearby. Special deals available for families and backpackers. Open March-October. ✩✩✩✩ **45T. 45MC.** 🛲 🖭 ♿

Arrochar

(2m). Camping & Caravanning Club Site - Ardgartan, Coilessan Road, Arrochar, Dumbartonshire G83 7AR. *01301 702253/0870 2433331.* www.campingandcaravanningclub.co.uk. Owner: Camping & Caravanning Club. Greenfields House, Westwood Way, Coventry CV4 8JH. Turn off the A83 at the Forest Tourist Information Centre (TIC) and follow signs for site. Site is surrounded by scenery and wildlife, including seals, herons and eagles. Club members only. All types of units accepted. Located in 3.5 acres, with spectacular views over Loch Long and Arrochar Alps. Special deals available for families and backpackers. Open March-October. ✩✩✩ **55T. MC.** 🛲 🖭

Please mention Caravan Sites 2006 when replying to advertisers

Loch Lomond

(0.25m). Lomond Woods Holiday Park Tullichewan Balloch, Loch Lomond, West Dunbartonshire G83 8QP. *01389 755000.* lomondwoods@holiday-parks.co.uk. www.holiday-parks.co.uk. Owner: Colin & Margaret Wood. Turn R off A82, 17m N of Glasgow at roundabout SP Balloch. At next roundabout take a L following signs. Family holiday park. Play area, games room, TV lounge, laundrette. Pine lodges and caravan holiday homes also for hire. Next to 'Lomond Shores' visitor attraction. Short walk to Loch Lomond and Balloch village for Restaurants, Bars, and shops. Many local activities, including water sports, golf and fishing at Gateway to Loch Lomond National Park. ☆☆☆☆☆ **BH&HPA. 120T. 10MC. 40S. 8H. ⚡ �🛉 🚐 ⅍ ∅**

EDINBURGH

Edinburgh

Edinburgh Caravan Club Site, 35-37 Marine Drive, Edinburgh, Edinburgh EH4 5EN. *0131 3126874.* www.caravanclub.co.uk. Owner: The Caravan Club. East Grinstead House, East Grinstead, West Sussex RH19 1UA. See website for standard directions to site. Suitable holiday site. Situated to the N of the city on the Firth of Fourth, the site provides easy access to Edinburgh. Hard-standings, toilet block, laundry facilities and veg prep, play area, dog walk. Non-members and tent campers welcome. Motorhome service point. Golf and water sports nearby. Serviced pitches. Calor Gas and Campingaz. Suitable for families, beach within 5m. Zoo nearby. NCN cycle route within 5m. ☆☆☆☆☆ **NCC. 197T. ⚡ 🛉 🚐 ⅍**

(4m). Mortonhall Caravan & Camping Park, Frogston Road East, 38 Mortonhall Gate, Edinburgh, Edinburgh EH16 6TJ. *01316 641533.* mortonhall@meadowhead.co.uk. www.mead owhead.co.uk. Owner: Meadowhead Parks. Meadowhead Ltd, Charterhall, Duns, Berwickshire TD11 3RE. From city bypass leave at Lothianburn on A702, or straight on, A701, and follow signs for Mortonhall. Specimen tree arboretum on the park. Internet access, bar and restaurant, children's play areas. Golf, supermarket, dry ski slope all within 2m. Cinema and theatre 2.5m. Retail park, Ikea. Open March 11-January 5. ☆☆☆☆ **BH&HPA. 250T. MC. 20S. 19H. 🛉 🚐 ⅍ ∅**

FIFE

Anstruther

(1m). Anstruther Holiday Village, Poll Road, Cellardyke, Anstruther, Fife KY10 3JE. *01333 310484.* On A917. Club. Open March-October. **BH&HPA. 15T. 485S. 25H. 🖳**

Ashburn House Caravan Site, St Andrews Road, Crail, Anstruther, Fife KY10 3UL. *01333 450314.* Owner: A & M Ireland & Sons. On A917 Crail to St Andrews (9m). Quiet, family-run site close to town centre, harbour, golf and bowling. Open March 1-October 31. **BH&HPA. 5T. MC. 60S. 🛉 🚐**

(2m). Grangemuir Woodland Park, Pittenweem, Anstruther, Fife KY10 2RB. *01333 311213.* Owner: Grangemuir Woodland Park Ltd. Off the A917. 1m from Pittenweem. Bar and games room. Shops, PO 1m, doctor 2m. Fishing, golf nearby. Open March 1-October 31. ☆☆☆☆ **BH&HPA. 45T. 45MC. 🛉 🚐**

(0.25m). Kilrenny Mill Caravan Park, Cellardyke, Anstruther, Fife KY10 3JW. *01333 450314.* A917 coast road to Cellardyke Harbour, then 500yd along sea front. Close to shops. Outdoor leisure facilities. Panoramic views across the Firth of Forth. Open March 1-October 31. **85S. 🛉 ⅍**

(2m). St Monans Caravan Site, St Monans, Anstruther, Fife KY10 2DN. *01333 730778.* Owner: Abbeyford Caravans Ltd (Scotland). Pensarn, Abergele, Clwyd. Adjoining A917 E of St Monans. Small, quiet site beside public park, village and seaside. Open March 21-November 30. ☆☆☆ **NCC. 18T. MC. 112S. 🛉 🚐**

Crail

Balcomie Links Caravan Park, Balcomie Road, Crail, Fife KY10 3TN. *01333 450383.* balcomie-links@btconnect.com. www.ukparks.com/balcomie. Owner: V M Crockett. Off A917. Situated on the outskirts of Crail on road to golf course. Peaceful site. Hotel nearby. Laundry. Golf courses 1m. Open late March-October 31. **BH&HPA. 92S. 🛉 ∅**

Sauchope Links Caravan Park, Crail, Fife KY10 3XJ. *01333 450460.* info@sauchope.co.uk. www.sauchope.co.uk. Owner: Largo Leisure Parks Ltd. On A917. On the seashore. Heated outdoor swimming pool, games room, play area. Showers, wash basins, shaver points. Laundrette and ironing facilities. Chemical toilet emptying points. Open March-October. ☆☆☆☆☆ **50T. MC. 80S. 4H. 🛉 🚐 🖳**

Dunfermline

(2m). Fordell Gardens Caravan Park, Inverkeithing, Dunfermline, Fife KY11 5EY. *01383 413000.* tom.fordell@ ukgateway.net. Owner: Mr T Swarbrick. Fordell Gardens, Hillend, By Dunfermline, Fife KY11 7EY. From M90 take B981 to Crossgates, 2m on B981 take left on to B916 to Hillend. Park is about 500yd along B916 on left-hand side. ☆☆☆ **T. 🛉 🖳**

Elie

(2m). Shell Bay Caravan Park, Elie, Fife KY9 1AR. *01333 330283.* kateforbes@shellbay.fsnet.co.uk. Owner: Abbeyford Caravan Co (Scotland) Ltd. Pensarn, Abergele, Aberconwy & Colwyn LL22 7PW. Off A917. Lounge bar. Meals served. Laundry facilities. Private beach. Play park. Showers. Fishing and water sports. Golf courses and leisure pool nearby. Open March 21-end of November. ☆☆☆ **NCC. 120T. MC. 220S. 6H. 🛉 🚐 ⅍ 🖳**

Glenrothes

Balbirnie Park Caravan Club Site, Markinch, Glenrothes, Fife KY7 6NR. *01592 759130.* www.cara vanclub.co.uk. Owner: The Caravan Club. East Grinstead House, East Grinstead, West Sussex RH19 1UA. See website for standard directions to site. 0.5m from Markinch. Laundry. Preparation area. Motor caravan waste point. Toilet block. Playframe. Non-members welcome. Tent campers admitted. part hard-standings, part sloping. Steel awning pegs required. Gas. Information room. Dog walk nearby. Suitable for families. Peaceful off-peak. Water sports nearby. NCN cycle route wihtin 5m. Advance booking advised bank holidays and July-August. Open March-October. ☆☆☆☆ **NCC. 77T. 77MC. 🛉 🚐 ⅍**

Kennoway

(3m). Letham Feus Caravan Park, Letham, Kennoway, Fife KY8 5NT. *01333 351900.* Off A916 1.5m east of Kennoway on Kennoway-Cupar road. Open March 1-October 31. ☆☆☆ **25T. MC. 115S. 5H. 🛉 🚐 ⅍ 🖳**

Kinghorn

Kinghorn Caravan Park, Nethergate, Kinghorn, Fife. *01592 890383*. Owner: Mr J Beatson. Located in Kinghorn on seafront and near railway station. Open April 1-September 30. **6T. 103S.** ⚡ ☎

(10.5m). **Pettycur Bay Caravan Park, Kinghorn, Fife KY3 9YE**. *01592 892200*. On A921. Sea views and sandy beach. Prime tourist area close to Edinburgh, 35mins by road. No dogs in hire vans. Open March 1-October 31. **BH&HPA. 50T. 10MC. 450S. 36H.** ⛺ ⚡ ☎

Kirkcaldy

(3m). **Dunnikier Caravan Park, Dunnikier Way, Kirkcaldy, Fife KY1 3ND**. *01592 267563*. www.dunnikiercaravanpark.co.uk. Owner: Bill & Betty McIntosh. East Lodge, Dunnikier Way, Kirkcaldy, Fife. On northern outskirts of town on B981. Exit M90, J3, then take A92 to Kirkcaldy East, follow road for Kirkcaldy, take 3rd exit at roundabout and follow road for about 2m, site on left. Level pitches with grass-covered, hard-standings. 7mins walk from golf course and hotel, 5mins walk from ASDA supermarket. Country walks. Open March 1-January 31. ✰✰✰✰ **BH&HPA. NCC. 60T. 22S. 3H.** ⛺ ⚡ ☎

Leven

Leven Beach Caravan Park, North Promenade, Leven, Fife. *01333 426008*. Owner: Mr T Wallace. Direct access to sandy beach and adjoining golf course. Bar, laundry, games room. Prime tourist area. Dogs not allowed in hire caravans. Open March 1-October 31. **BH&HPA. 40T. MC. 88S. 20H.** ⛺ ⚡ ☎

Lundin Links

(1m). **Woodland Gardens Caravan & Camping Site, Blindwell Road, Lundin Links, Fife KY8 5QG**. *01333 360319*. enquiries@woodland-gardens.co.uk. www.wood land-gardens. co.uk. Owner: Mr & Mrs J D Anderson. Turn N off A915 at E end of Lundin Links. SP on A915 by international camping and caravanning signs. Suitable base for St Andrews and East Neuk of Fife. Small, quiet, family-run site. Not suitable for young children. Rural setting overlooking river Forth to Edinburgh. Open April-October. ✰✰✰✰ **20T. 20MC. 5S. 5H.** ⛺ ⚡

St Andrews

(1m). **Cairnsmill Caravan Park, Largo Road, St Andrews, Fife KY16 8NN**. *01334 473604*. cairnsmill@aol.com. www.ukparks. co.uk/cairnsmill. Owner: Kirkaldy family. On A915 Leven to St Andrews. Suitable touring base, close to a choice of golf courses and east Fife coast. Indoor heated swimming pool. Games room. Coffee bar. Fly fishing, bunkhouse. Open April-October. ✰✰✰✰ **BH&HPA. 80T. 10MC. 165S. 5H.** ⛺ ⚡ ♿ ☎

(1.5m). **Craigtoun Meadows Holiday Park, Mount Melville, St Andrews, Fife KY16 8PQ**. *01334 475959*. craigtoun@aol.com. www.craigtounmeadows.co.uk. Owner: Craigtoun Meadows Ltd. Off A91. Licensed restaurant. AA 5 pennants. Member of Best of British Holidays group. Open March 1-October 31. ✰✰✰✰✰ **BH&HPA. 61T. MC. 128S. 25H.** ⛺ ⚡ ♿ ☎ ⌀

(1m). **Kinkell Braes Caravan Site, St Andrews, Fife KY16 8PX**. *01334 474250*. Off A918 St Andrews to Crail. Lounge bar, meals served. Laundry. Play area. Games room. Showers. Holiday home adapted for disabled people for hire. Open March 21-November 30. ✰✰✰ **NCC. 100T. MC. 385S. 12H.** ⛺ ⚡ ♿ ☎

Tayport

(0.5m). **Tayport Caravan Park, Tayport, Fife DD6 9ES**. *01382 552334*. www.caravancampingsites.co.uk. Owner: Mr & Mrs R B Baillie. Tayport Links Caravan Park. Enter Tayport on B945 and

follow signs. Site by shore. Dogs on leads. Fishing, golf, forest walks, extensive beaches 5m. 15mins St Andrews, 10mins Dundee. Shops in walking distance. Surrounded by playing fields with playparks. Open March-October for tourers; March-13 January for holiday homes. ✰✰✰✰ **BH&HPA. 34T. 76S. 2H.** ⛺ ⚡ ⌀

GLASGOW

Drymen

(1.5m). **Camping & Caravanning Club Site - Milarrochy Bay, Balmaha, Drymen, Glasgow G63 OAL**. *01360 870236/0870 2433331*. www.campingandcaravanningclub.co.uk. Owner: Camping & Caravanning Club. Greenfields House, Westwood Way, Coventry CV4 8JH. A811 Balloch to Stirling road take Drymen turning in Drymen take B837 to Balmaha after 5m road turns sharply R up steep hill. Site 1.5m farther on. On east bank of Loch Lomond in heart of Rob Roy country adjacent to West Highland way. Boat hire and pleasure cruises on loch. All types of units accepted. Non-members welcome. Queen Elizabeth Forest Park, with 75,000 acres of forest, is nearby. Peaceful site. Special deals available for families and backpackers. Open March-October. ✰✰✰✰ **150T. 150MC.** ⛺ ⚡ ☎

Stepps

(0.5m). **Craigendmuir Ltd. Craigendmuir Park Business Centre, Stepps, Glasgow G33 6AF**. *0141 7792973/07833 701438*. info@craigendmuir.co.uk. www.craigendmuir.co.uk. Owner: Craigendmuir Ltd. From J11 M8 to Glasgow and from A80 follow signs for Stepps. On outskirts of Glasgow, 6m. Suitable touring base. Golf course 1.5m. Cinema, shopping centre 3m. ✰✰✰ **BH&HPA. 30T. MC. 27S. 27H.** ❀ ⛺ ⚡ ☎ ⌀

Pear Tree Caravan Site, 36 Cumbernauld Road, Stepps, Glasgow G33 6EW. *01417 791579*. Owner: Mr D H Knowles. On A80. **4T. MC.** ❀

HIGHLAND

Acharacle

(4m). **Resipole Farm Caravan & Camping Park, Loch Sunart, Acharacle, Highland PH36 4HX**. *01967 431235*. info@resipole.co.uk. www.resipole.co.uk. Owner: Mr P Sinclair. On A861. 8m W of Strontian. Laundrette. Off-licence. Pay-phone. Private slipway. Open April-October. ✰✰✰✰ **BH&HPA. 60T. 10MC. 15S. 3H.** ⛺ ⚡ ☎

Achnasheen

Camping & Caravanning Club Site - Inverewe Gardens, Inverewe Gardens, Poolewe, Achnasheen, Highlands IV22 2LF. *01445 781249/0870 2433331*. www.campingandcaravanningclub.co.uk. Owner: Camping & Caravanning Club. Greenfields House, Westwood Way, Coventry CV4 8JH. On A832, N of Poolewe, close to Inverewe Gardens and on shores of Loch Ewe. All types of units accepted. Non-members welcome. site offers mountain scenery. National Trust for Scotland organises ranger-led walks. Sea and fly fishing nearby. Seals, otters, and golden eagles. Special deals available for families and backpackers. Open March-October. ✰✰✰✰ **55T. 55MC.** ⛺ ⚡ ♿

SCOTLAND

(8m). Kinlochewe Caravan Club Site, Kinlochewe, Achnasheen, Highland IV22 2PA. *01445 760239.* www.caravanclub.co.uk. Owner: The Caravan Club. East Grinstead House, East Grinstead, West Sussex RH19 1UA. See website for standard directions to site. Small, intimate site in a peaceful position at the foot of the rugged slopes of Ben Eighe. Non-members welcome. Advance booking essential bank holidays and June-August. Toilet blocks. Laundry facilities. Motorhome service point. Good area for walking. All hard-standings, steel awning pegs required. Dog walk. Peaceful off-peak. Open March-October. ☆☆☆☆ **NCC. 56T. MC.** 🐕 🖾 &

Arisaig

(4m). Camusdarach, Arisaig, Highland PH39 4NT. *01687 450221.* camdarach@aol.com. www.camusdarach.com. Owner: Andrew & Angela Simpson. On B8008, N of Arisaig on seaward side of road near to fine sandy beaches. Traigh golf club. 6m from Mallaig, restaurants, shops and ferries to islands. Mobile shop calls. Open April-October. ☆☆☆☆ **42T.** 🐕 🖾 &

(2m). Gorton Farm Caravan Site, Gorton Farmhouse, Back of Keppoch, Arisaig, Highland PH39 4NS. *01687 450283.* Owner: Mr A Macdonald. A830 to west of Arisaig, turn left at SP 'Back of Keppoch', then 0.75m to end of road across cattle grid. Beach site with hot water, showers and shaver points. Laundry room. Pay-phone. Bottled gas. Views of Skye and isles. Wildlife. Open April 1-September 30. ☆☆☆☆ **45T. MC. 2H.** 🐕 🖾

(1.5m). Invercaimbe Caravan Site, Invercaimbe, Arisaig, Inverness-shire PH39 4NT. *01687 450375.* joycew@madasafish.com. www.invercaimbecaravansite.co.uk. On the beach. Golf nearby. Fishing and boat trips locally. **10T. 4MC. 2H.** 🐕 🖾

(2m). Portnardoran Caravan Site, Arisaig, Highland PH39 4NT. *01687 450267.* Beside sea and white sands. Laundrette. Small golf course nearby. Shops 2m. Suitable site for children. Open April 1-October 31. **31T. MC. 9S.** 🐕 🖾

(2m). Silversands Caravan Site, Arisaig, Highland. *01687 450269.* Owner: Mrs C MacDonald. Open March-October. **18T. MC. 18S.** 🐕

(1m). Skyeview Caravan Park, Arisaig, Highland PH39 4NJ. *01687 450209.* N of Arisaig, just off A830. Turn R into farm road 200yd past phone box. Hotel, bar, golf course nearby. Shops and PO within 1m. Open April-October. **15T. 5MC. 2H.** 🐕 🖾

Aviemore

(3m). Dalraddy Holiday Park, Aviemore, Highland PH22 1QB. *01479 810330.* dhp@alvie-estate.co.uk. www.alvie-estate.co.uk. Owner: Mr J D A Williamson. On B9152 (old A9). Laundrette. Play area. Licensed shop. Heated facilities block. Fishing, pony trekking and watersports. Quadbikes and 4x4s all within 2m. ☆☆☆☆ **BH&HPA. NCC30T. MC. 110S. 13H.** ❄ 🐕 🖾 & 🖾

(7m). Glenmore Caravan & Camping Site, Forestry Commission (Forest Holidays), Glenmore, Aviemore, Highland PH22 1QU. *01479 861271.* fe.holidays@forestry.gsi.gov.uk. www.forestholidays.co.uk. Owner: Forestry Commission (Forest Holidays). 231 Corstorphine Road, Edinburgh EH12 7AT. From A9 turn on to B9152, S of Aviemore. At Aviemore, turn R on to B970, keeping R at Coylumbridge. Site is 5m on. 7m from Aviemore on the

B9152 at the base of the Cairngorm mountains amid views of the Glenmore Caledonian pine forest. Close to the sandy beaches of Loch Morlich, forest walks, skiing, orienteering, water sports, fishing and guided walks. Visitor centre. Advance bookings advised Brochure request line: 01313 340066. Open December-October. ☆☆☆ **BH&HPA. 220T. MC.** 🐕 🖾 &

(0.5m). High Range Touring Caravan Park, Grampian Road, Aviemore, Highland PH22 1PT. *01479 810636.* info@highrange.co.uk. www.highrange.co.uk. Owner: Mr F Vastano. At southern end of Aviemore on the B9152 road, directly opposite the Coylumbridge B970 road leading to the Cairngorm Mountains. Situated in woodland grounds of the High Range Complex at the foot of Craigellachie Nature Reserve. 500yd from Aviemore Shopping Centre. Motel rooms, self-catering chalets, ristorante, pizzeria and bar, playground and laundrette on site. **35T. 20MC.** ❄ 🐕 🖾 &

(1.5m). Rothiemurchus Camping & Caravan Park, Coylumbridge, Aviemore, Inverness-shire PH22 1QU. *01479 812800.* lizsangster@rothiemurchus.freeserve.co.uk. www.rothic.net. Owner: Liz Sangster. From Aviemore take ski road B970, park is situated on right in 1.5m. Hard-standing touring pitches vary in size as they are laid out around trees. All pitches have 16amp electrics and TV hook-ups. New facility block. **BH&HPA. 17T. MC. 50S.** ❄ 🐕 🖾 & 🖾

Beauly

Cruivend Caravan Park, Beauly, Highland IV4 7BE. *01463 782367.* Owner: Mr K Dilks. North from Inverness to Beauly 10m on A862. Sharp left immediately after crossing bridge over river Beauly 1m before village. Hard-standings available. Play area. Laundrette. Games room. Trout loch, fishing available. Thistle Award. Open April-September. **24T. MC. 6H.** 🐕 🖾 🖾

(1m). Lovat Bridge Caravan and Camping Site, Lovat Bridge, Beauly, Highland IV4 7AY. *01463 782374/ 07770661881.* allanlymburn@beauly782.fsnet.co.uk. Owner: Allan S Lymburn. On A832, Inverness to Beauly. Set in the old Caledonian Forest next to the river Beauly. Licensed family lounge. Fishing on site. Open March-October. ☆☆☆ **40T. 40MC.** 🐕 🖾 ∅

Boat of Garten

Boat of Garten Caravan Park, Deshar Road, Boat of Garten, Inverness-shire PH24 3BN. *01479 831652.* brian gilles@totalise.co.uk. www.campgroundsofscotland.com. Owners: Brian & Maureen Gillies Off A95 Grantown to Aviemore. From A9 take A95, SP Grantown-on-Spey then follow signs for Boat of Garten. Situated in the centre of the village. Thistle Award. Fishing, golf, tennis and steam railway nearby. ☆☆☆☆ **BH&HPA. NCC. 37T. 37MC. 60S. 6H.** ❄ 🐕 🖾 & 🖾

(1m). Loch Garten Lodges & Caravan Park, Loch Garten Road, Boat of Garten, Highland PH24 3BY. *01479 831769.* tony@newtongrove.demon.co.uk. www.lochgarten.co.uk. Leave A9 immediately north of Aviemore, follow Boat of Garten signs, through village and cross river Spey, turn left on B970, first right to Tulloch. Site is on left overlooking river and Spey Valley. Aviemore 7m. Golf, fishing within 1m. Shopping 7m. ☆☆☆ **BH&HPA. 10T. MC. 20S. 4H.** ❄ 🐕 🖾 &

(2m). Osprey Caravan Park, Boat of Garten, Highland PH24 3BY. *01479 831080.* Owner: N B & H Poskitt. Off A9, on to B970 between Boat of Garten and Netheybridge. Near RSPB reserve at Loch Garten and on the bank of river Spey (fishing). Small, quiet site. Suitable base for touring. Bottled gas. Open December 1-October 31. **8H.** &

Please visit the Caravan Club website: www.caravanclub.co.uk

Caravan Sites 2006 **215**

Brora

(1.5m). Dalchalm Caravan Club Site, Brora, Highland KW9 6LP. *01408 621479*. *www.caravanclub.co.uk*. Owner: The Caravan Club. East Grinstead House, East Grinstead, West Sussex RH19 1UA. See website for standard directions to site. On east coast of Sutherland, 300yd from safe, sandy beach. Tent campers admitted. Non-members welcome. Advance booking advised June-August. Toilet blocks. Privacy cubicles. Laundry facilities. Veg prep. Motorhome service point. Golf, fishing nearby. Good area for walking. Suitable for families. Some hardstandings. Calor Gas and Campingaz. Dog walk nearby. Peaceful off-peak. Open March-October. ✰✰✰✰ NCC. 52T. MC. ⊶ ⊕ &

Caithness

Dunnet Bay Caravan Club Site, Dunnet, Thurso, Caithness, Highland KW14 8XD. *01847 821319*. www.caravanclub.co.uk. Owner: The Caravan Club. East Grinstead House, East Grinstead, West Sussex RH19 1UA. See website for standard directions to site. Suitable park for tourists who like solitude. Views of Dunnet Head, the northernmost point of mainland Britain. Toilet block, laundry facilities and motorhome service point. Fishing and water sports within 5m. Suitable for families. Non-members and tent campers welcome. Open March-October. NCC. 45T. MC. ⊶ ⊕

Inver Caravan Park, Houstry Road, Dunbeath, Caithness, Highland KW6 6EH. *01593 731441*. rhonagwillim@aol.com. www.holidayincaithness.com. Owner: Rhona Gwillim. Adjacent A9 just N of Dunbeath, 21m south west of Wick. Park entrance 40yd up road SP 'Houstry 3'. Smooth grassy site: some hard standings, dump station. Free showers, beautiful views over Dunbeath Bay. Near shop and PH/restaurant. Convenient for exploring far north or for Orkney crossings. ✰✰✰ 15T. MC. 1S. ✿ ⊶ ⊕ &

Dingwall

(5m). Black Rock Caravan Park, Evanton, Dingwall, Highland IV16 9UN. *01349 830917*. enquiries@black rockscotland.co.uk. www.blackrockscotland.co.uk. Owner: Mr & Mrs S C Macpherson. Off the A9,15m N of Inverness. Set in wooded glen on the banks of river Glass. Level, grassy and sheltered park within easy reach of west and east coasts. Showers. Play area. Telephone. Laundry. Shops nearby. Open April 1-October 31. ✰✰✰✰ BH&HPA. 67T. MC. 40S. 6H. ⊶ ⊕ &

(0.5m). Camping & Caravanning Club Site - Dingwall, Jubilee Park Road, Dingwall, Highland IVl5 9QZ. *01349 862236/0870 243 3331*. www.campingandcara vanningclub.co.uk. Owner: Camping & Caravanning Club. Greenfields House, Westwood Way, Coventry CV4 8JH. In Dingwall coming from south, take bypass and follow signs, first right down Hill Street, right at junction, left over railway bridge, then first left, SP. Suitable base for exploring the western Highlands. All types of units accepted. Non-members welcome. Site set in 6.5 acres. Millbuie Forest in the nearby Black Isle. Train excursions from Dingwall to the Kyle of Lochalsh available. Special deals available for families and backpackers. Open March-October. ✰✰✰✰ 85T. 85MC. ⊶ ⊕ &

Dornoch

(0.5m). Dornoch Caravan and Camping Park, The Links, Dornoch, Highland IV25 3LX. *01862 810423*. info@ dornochcaravans.co.uk. www.dornochcaravans.co.uk. Owner: Mr W Macrae. 19 Ross Street, Golspie, Highland. A9, 6m N of Tain. Turn right on to A949, E for 2m, entry via River Street. Adjacent to beach and golf course. Town centre 5 mins walk. Open April 1-October 24. ✰✰✰✰ BH&HPA. 125T. MC. 50S. 22H. ⊶ ⊕ & ⛍

(2.5m). Grannie's Heilan Hame Holiday Park, Embo, Dornoch, Highland IV25 3QD. *01862 810383*. enquiries@parkdean holidays.co.uk. www.parkdeanholidays.co.uk. Owner: Parkdean Holidays Plc. Drum Farm, One Gosforth Way, Gosforth Business Park, Newcastle-upon-Tyne NE12 8ET. Take A9 from Inverness northwards to Dornoch and Embo. Follow the road for Embo. Park is at the end of this road. Free indoor pool and spa bath, solarium, sauna, bar, clubhouse, entertainment/meals, tennis court, playground, games room, bowleasy mini bowling and pool. Open March-October. ✰✰✰✰ BH&HPA. NCC. 300T. MC. 143S. 140H. ⊶ ⊕ ⛍

(1.25m). Seaview Farm Caravan Park, Hilton, Dornoch, Highland IV25 3PW. *01862 810294*. Owner: Mr T R Preston. Turn left at tourist office in Dornoch. Camping and Caravanning Club listed. From Dornoch turn left at square. After 1.25m turn right at road junction by telephone box. Dogs allowed on leads. Flat site. Golf course nearby. Shops, PO, doctor in village. Open April-October. ✰✰ 16T. MC. ⊶ ⊕

Dundonnell

(8m). Badrallach D, B&B, Bothy, Cottage & Campsite, Little Loch Broom, Croft 9, Badrallach, Dundonnell, Highland IV23 2QP. *01854 633281*. michael.stott2@ virgin.net. www.badrallach.com. Owners: Mick & Ali Stott. 7m along the winding single-track road off the A832. 1m E of the Dundonnell Hotel. Lochshore site in a remote Highland setting. Bikes, boats, kites, bio-karts, kayaks for hire. Wildlife: otters, easles, red deer. ✰✰✰✰ 3T. MC. ✿ ⊶ ⊕ & ◿

Fort Augustus

(0.5m). Fort Augustus Caravan & Camping Park, Market Hill, Fort Augustus, Highland PH32 4DS. *01320 366360/01320 366618*. info@campinglochness.co.uk. www. campinglochness.co.uk. Owner: Mr Brian Clark. Beside the A82, Inverness to Fort William road, on the south side of Fort Augustus. Flat, grassy site. Situated beside golf course, open to non-members. Laundrette. Ladies' hair-dryer. Public telephone. Shops, restaurants, PHs etc within 0.5m. Open mid April-September. 50T. 50MC. ⊶ ⊕ &

Fort William

(8m). Bunree Caravan Club Site, Onich, Fort William, Highland PH33 5SE. *01855 821283*. www.caravan club.co.uk. Owner: The Caravan Club. East Grinstead House, East Grinstead, West Sussex RH19 1UA. See website for standard directions to site. On safe, sandy beach. Peaceful off-peak. Laundry room, drying room. Play area and Playframe. Toilet block with privacy cubicles. Baby and toddler washroom. Motor caravan waste point. Non-members welcome. Advance booking advised bank holidays and June-August. Recreation room. Information room. Boat launch area. Fishing from site, PH/restaurant within walking distance. Good for walking. Suitable for families. Open March-October. ✰✰✰✰✰ NCC. 99T. MC. ⊶ ⊕ &

(2.5m). Glen Nevis Caravan and Camping Park, Glen Nevis, Fort William, Highland PH33 6SX. *01397 702191.* camping @glen-nevis.co.uk. www.glen-nevis.co.uk. Owner: Glen Nevis Holidays Ltd. Off A82 at SP Glen Nevis on northern outskirts of Fort William. Site is about 2m from A82. Restaurant near site at foot of Ben Nevis. Open March 15-October 31. ✰✰✰✰✰ BH&HPA. 250T. MC. 30S. ✝ ⊞ ⚅ ⚗

(5m). Linnhe Lochside Holidays, Corpach, Fort William, Highland PH33 7NL. *01397 772376.* relax@linnhe-lochside-holidays.co.uk. www.linnhe-lochside-holidays.co.uk. Owner: Linnhe Lochside Holidays Ltd. On A830, 1m W of Corpach village. Lochside park. Pets welcome. Free fishing. 18-hole golf course, cinema 5m. PO, shops 0.5m. Open Christmas-October 31. ✰✰✰✰✰ BH&HPA. 67T. MC. 225S. 60H. ✝ ⊞ ⚅ ⚗

(2.5m). Lochy Caravan Park, Camaghael, Fort William, Highland PH33 7NF. *01397 703446.* enquiries@lochy-holiday-park.co.uk. www.lochy-holiday-park.co.uk. Owner: Ian C Brown. On A830, off A82. Laundry shop, play area, showers, toilets. Golf 0.5m, Fishing 1m. Town centre 2m. Open April-October. ✰✰✰✰ BH&HPA. 40T. 40MC. 19H. ✝ ⊞ ⚗

Fortrose

(0.5m). Camping & Caravanning Club Site - Rosemarkie, Ness Road East, Rosemarkie, Fortrose, Highlands IV10 8SE. *01381 621117/0870 2433331.* www.campingandcaravanningclub.co.uk. Owner: Camping & Caravanning Club. Greenfields House, Westwood Way, Coventry CV4 8JH. Take A832. A9 at Tore roundabout. Through Avoch, Fortrose then R at police house Down Ness Road, first L, small turning, SP for 'Golf and Caravan Site'. On shore of Black Isle in small seaside village of Rosemarkie. Non-members welcome. All types of units accepted. Coastline famous for bottlenose dolphins. Birdwatching at many local nature reserves. Inverness ony a few miles away. Special deals available for families and backpackers. Open March-October. ✰✰✰✰ 60T. 60MC. ✝ ⊞ ⚅

Gairloch

(3m). Sands Holiday Centre, Gairloch, Highland IV21 2DL. *01445 712152.* litsands@aol.com. www.highlandscaravancamp ing.co.uk. Owner: W & M Cameron. Follow A833 to Gairloch, then take B8021; site is 4m along this road. Play area. Public phone. Laundry and showers. Slipway for boats. Beach adjoining. Full facilities available May 2-mid September. Underfloor heated toilet and shower rooms. Free loch fishing for customers. Open April 1-October 15. ✰✰✰✰ BH&HPA. NCC. 160T. 50MC. 16S. 5H. ✝ ⊞ ⚅ ⚗

Grantown-on-Spey

(0.5m). Grantown-on-Spey Caravan Park, Seafield Avenue, Grantown-on-Spey, Highland PH26 3JQ. *01479 872474.* team@caravanscotland.com. www.caravanscotland.com. From town centre turn N at Bank of Scotland. Park 0.5m straight forward. Caravan Club affiliated site. Laundry, dishwashing and games room. Three chemical toilet emptying points. Motor caravan service point. Open all year except November. ✰✰✰✰✰ BH&HPA. NCC. 110T. MC. 60S. ✝ ⊞

Invergarry

(1m). Faichem Park, Ardgarry Farm, Faichem, Invergarry, Highland PH35 4HG. *01809 501226.* enquiries@ardgarry farm.co.uk. www.ardgarryfarm.co.uk. Owner: Mr J Fleming. On A87. From Invergarry travel 1m, turn R at Faichem, SP up hill on R, 600yd. Chemical toilet emptying point. Laundry and drying rooms. Showers, hair-dryers, dishwashing, cycle hire, free range eggs. Fishing, golf, walking, climbing, water sports, all nearby. Shop, hotel bar meals, garage in village 15mins walk. Open March-October. ✰✰✰✰ BH&HPA. 15T. MC. ✝ ⊞

(1m). Faichemard Farm, Invergarry, Highland PH35 4HG. *01809 501314.* dgrant@fsbdial.co.uk. www.visitscotland. com. Owner: A & D Grant. Follow signs in green writing off the A87 at Invergarry. Leave A87 1m W from junction with A82. Turn R and go past Ardgarry Farm and Faichem Park camp site, then turn R at sign 'A & D Grant'. Exclusively for adults. All pitches have own picnic tables. Telephone and laundry on site. Some individual pitches, hard-standings and hook-ups available. TOpen April 1-October 31. ✰✰✰✰ 15T. 10MC. ✝ ⊞

Inverness

(10m). Auchnahillin Caravan and Camping Park, Daviot East, Inverness, Highland IV2 5XQ. *01463 772286.* info@auchnahillin.co.uk. www.auchnahillin.co.uk. Owner: The Gibson Family. S of Inverness, off the A9, on B9154 (Moy Road). Site surrounded by hills and forest. Tranquil yet convenient for many destinations and attractions. Bar, restaurant and small shop. Full laundry facilities. Local loch for fishing. All amenities available at Inverness (7-10m). Open March-October (weather permitting). ✰✰✰✰ BH&HPA. 65T. MC. 35S. 11H. ✝ ⊞ ⚅ ⚗ ⌀

(16m). Borlum Farm Camping Park, Borlum Farm, Drumnadrochit, Inverness, Highland IV63 6XN. *01456 450220.* info@borlum.com. www.borlum.com. Owner: A D Macdonald-Haig. 1m S of Drumnadrochit on A82, Fort William road. Park 500yd on R after Lewiston. Fishing on Loch Ness. Riding centre on site. Shops 0.75m. Open March-November. ✰✰✰ BH&HPA. 15T. MC. ✝ ⊞

(0.5m). Bught Caravan & Camping Site, Bught Park, Bught Drive, Inverness, Highland IV3 5SR. *01463 236920.* pauline@invernesscaravanpark.com. www.invernesscaravan park.com. Owners: Mr J P MacDonald, Mr B MacDonald. 21 Moy Terrace, Inverness IV2 4EL. On A82, on outskirts of Inverness. Well-equipped site. Many sports facilities nearby. Walking distance to town. Open Easter-November. ✰✰✰ 60T. MC. 60S. 4S. ✝ ⊞ ⚅ ⚗

(3m). Bunchrew Caravan Park, Bunchrew, Inverness, Highland IV3 6TD. *01463 237802.* enquiries@bunchrew-cara vanpark.co.uk. www.bunchrew-caravanpark.co.uk. Owner: Mr & Mrs T M J Stevens. On A862, Beauly road. Site is in a quiet setting on the southern shore of the Beauly Firth. Situated in 20 acres of parkland. 12 Thistle Award caravans for hire. Laundrette, gas sales, licensed shop, children's day area. Grass pitches, 50 electric hook-ups. Dogs welcome but not all breeds allowed. Open March 15-December 1. ✰✰✰ BH&HPA. NCC. 125T. MC. 13S. ✝ ⊞ ⚗

(26m). Cannich Caravan & Camping, Cannich, Strathglass, Inverness, Highland IV4 7LN. *01456 415364.* enquiries@high landcamping.co.uk. www.highlandcamping.co.uk. Owner: Matthew & Fay Jones. Out of Inverness on A82 at Drumnadrochit, take A831 to Cannich. 16m from Beauly. Site situated 0.5m from village centre, where there is a shop, PH. Close to Glen Affric Nature Reserve. Highland trails for walkers and mountain bikers. Site has 24hr public telephone, laundry, play area, TV and recreation room, indoor washing-up facilities. Open December 1-October 31. ✰✰✰✰ BH&HPA. 43T. MC. 15S. 7H. ✝ ⊞ ⚅ ⌀

Culloden Moor Caravan Club Site, Newlands, Culloden Moor, Inverness, Highland IV1 5EF. *01463 790625.* www.caravanclub.co.uk. Owner: The Caravan Club. East Grinstead House, East Grinstead, West Sussex RH19 1UA. See website for signposted directions to site. Gently sloping site facing views over the Nairn Valley. Vegetable preparation area. Motorvan waste point. Playframe. Toilet block with privacy cubicles. Tent campers admitted. Non-members welcome. Advance booking advised June-August, essential July and bank holidays. Information room. Fishing. Good area for walking. Suitable for families. Local attractions include Loch Ness. Hard-standings, part sloping, laundry. Calor Gas and Campingaz. Dog walk nearby. Peaceful off-peak. Beach and NCN cycle route within 5m. Open March-January. ☆☆☆☆☆ **NCC. 97T. MC.** 🅃 🔲 &

(4m). Dochgarroch Caravan Park, Dochgarroch, Inverness, Highland IV3 6SY. *01463 861333.* On A82 Fort William road. Open April 1-September 30. **100T. MC.** 🅃 🔲 &

(16m). Highland Riding Centre, Borlum Farm, Drumnadrochit, Loch Ness, Inverness, Highland IV63 6XN. *01456 450220.* enquiries@borlum.com. www.borlum.com. Owner: Mr and Mrs A D Macdonald Haig. On A82, Fort Augustus to Inverness. 1m S of Drumnadrochit, overlooking Loch Ness. Horse riding centre on site. Working farm. Open March-November. ☆☆☆ **BH&HPA. 12T. 12MC.** 🅃 🔲

(30m). Loch Ness Caravan and Camping Park, Easter Port Clair, Invermoriston, Loch Ness, Inverness, Highland IV63 7YE. *01320 351207/351399.* bob@girvan7904.freeserve.co.uk. www.lochnesscaravancampingpark.co.uk. Owners: Bob & Liz Girvan. On A82 1.5m S of Invermoriston.Park beside Loch Ness. All vans have views, fishing allowed, permits for salmon fishing available. Large play area and lounge bar/family room with hot meals available. Laundry. Adjacent to Great Glen walk. ☆☆☆☆☆ **50T. 50MC. 6S.** ✿ 🅃 🔲 & 🔲

(0.5m). Market Hill, Fort Augustus, Loch Ness, Inverness, Highland. *01320 6360.* Owner: Mr Brian Clark. On A82. Open May-September. **50T. 50MC.** 🅃 🔲 &

(5m). Scaniport Caravan & Camping Park, Scaniport, Inverness, Highland IV2 6DL. *01463 751226.* sylviaphilip@aol.com. Owner: J Baillie Scaniport Estate. Bowlts, Chartered Surveyors, Pluscarden, By Elgin, Moray IV30 8TZ. On B862, on right-hand side of road. Secluded, small site opposite telephone box. 3.5m from village of Dores and Loch Ness. Open Easter-September. ☆☆ **BH&HPA. 30T. MC.** 🅃

(1m). Torvean Caravan Park, Glenurquhart Road, Inverness, Highland IV3 8JL. *01463 220582.* www.torvean caravanpark. co.uk. On A82 on right after crossing canal bridge. Peaceful park, overlooking golf course and canal. Laundrette. One small pet per outfit. Mobile shop. Thistle Award. Open Easter-October. ☆☆☆☆☆ **BH&HPA. NCC. 50T. MC. 10H.** 🔲 &

Isle of Skye

'Cullin View' Caravan & Campsite, Breakish, Isle of Skye, Highland IV42 8PY. *01471 822248.* Owner: Mr Archie Campbell. 6m from Kyleakin Bridge, 1.5m from Broadford. Calor Gas agents. Shop 0.25m. Open March-October. **10T. 10MC.** 🅃 &

Dunvegan Caravan Park, Dunvegan, Isle of Skye, Highland IV55 8WF. *01470 521206.* Owner: The Macleod Estate. Off A850 & A863. Open April-September. **30T. MC.** 🅃

Loch Greshornish Caravan & Camping Site, Borve, Arnisort, Edinbane, Isle of Skye, Highland IV51 9PS. *01470 582230.* info@skyecamp.com. www.skyecamp.com. Owner: Ben & Rhonda Palmer. 12m from Portree on A850, Portree to Dunvegan. 7m from Dunvegan. Nearest village 0.5m. Mountain bikes and canoes for hire. Sea fishing and coastal walking. AA 3 pennants. Open April 1-October 12. **30T.** 🅃 🔲 🔲

Staffin Caravan Site, Staffin, Portree, Isle of Skye, Highland IV51 9JX. *01470 562213.* staffin@namacleod.freeserve.co.uk. www.staffincampsite.co.uk. Owner: Mrs Norma A Macleod-Young. Off A855, Portree to Staffin, on S side of village. 16m from Portree. Fishing and hill walking locally. Quiet location overlooking Western Isles. Open March-October. ☆☆ **18T. 20MC.** 🅃 🔲 &

(1m). Torvaig Caravan & Camping Site, Portree, Isle of Skye, Highland IV51 9HU. *01478 611849.* Owner: Mr John Maclean. On A855, Staffin road, on outskirts of village of Portree. Suitable base for touring all parts of the island. Open April 1-October 20. ☆☆☆ **30T. 30MC.** 🅃 🔲

(16m). Uig Bay Caravan & Camping Site, 10 Idrigill, Uig, Isle of Skye, Highland IV15 9XU. *01470 542714.* lisa.madigan@btopenworld.com. www.uig-camping-skye.co.uk. Owner: M & L Madigan. From Portree follow A87 to Uig, past PO on L, carry on for 1m passing Caledonian MacBrayne on the right. Site is 200yd away. Fishing from bottom of site. PH 100yd. Fuel station, PO, doctors all close by. Walks. **T. MC.** ✿ 🅃 🔲 &

John O'Groats

John O'Groats Caravan Site, John O'Groats, Highland KW1 4YR. *01955 611329.* info@johnogroatscampsite.co.uk. www.johnogroatscampsite.co.uk. Owner: W & C J Steven. At end of A99 on seafront overlooking Orkney Islands. Magnificent cliff scenery 1.5m. Seal colony 4m. Harbour hotel and snack bar within 200yd. Showers, toilet for disabled people. Laundrette. Phone 100yd. PO, grocery store 600yd. Day trips by passenger ferry to Orkney. Open April 1-September 30. ☆☆☆ **90T. MC.** 🅃 🔲 &

(2m).Stroma View Souvenir Shop & Camping Site, Stroma View, John O'Groats, Highland KW1 4YC. *01955 611313.* stromadundas@aol.com. www.google.com/stromaview. Owner: Mr R G Dundas. On A836, John O'Groats to Thurso. Laundry. Electrically heated showers. Craft shop. Shaver points. Play area. Open March-October. **15T. 15MC. 2H.** 🅃 🔲 & 🔲

Kingussie

(0.5m). Kingussie Golf Club, Kingussie, Highland PH21 1LR. *01540 661600/347.* sec@kingussie-golf.co.uk. www.kingussie-golf.co.uk. Owner: Kingussie Golf Club. Off A9, Perth to Inverness. Secretary: William Baird. Open March 1-January 31. **BH&HPA. 1T. 57S. 6H.** 🅃 🔲

Kinlochleven

(3m). Caolasnacon Caravan Site, Kinlochleven, Highland PH50 4RJ. *01855 831279.* Owner: Patsy Cameron. Off A82, on to B863. Lochside location, golf course 4m. Shops, PO, doctor 3m. Open April-October. **BH&HPA. 50T. MC. 18S.** 🅃 🔲 ⌀

Kyle of Lochalsh

(8m). Ardelve Caravan Site, Dornie, Kyle of Lochalsh, Highland. *01599 555231.* Owner: Mr M Macrae. On A87. Open Easter-October. **10T. MC. 2H.** 🅃

SCOTLAND

(13m). Morvich Caravan Club Site, Inverinate, Kyle of Lochalsh, Highland IV40 8HQ. *01599 511354.* www.caravanclub.co.uk. Owner: The Caravan Club. East Grinstead House, East Grinstead, West Sussex RH19 1UA. See website for standard directions to site. 3m Shielbridge. Family holiday base. Site is on level valley floor, while all around are hills and mountains. Tent campers and non-members welcome. Advance booking essential bank holidays and June-August. Toilet blocks. Privacy cubicles. Laundry facilities. Baby washroom. Veg prep. Motorhome service point. Games room. Info room. Public transport. Fishing nearby. Good area for walking. Suitable for families. Part hard-standings, steel awning pegs required. Calor Gas and Campingaz. Dog walk nearby. Peaceful off-peak. Beach within 5m. Open March-October. ☆☆☆☆☆ **NCC. 106T. MC.** 🛏 🗗 ⅛

(3.5m). Reraig Caravan Site, Balmacara, Kyle of Lochalsh, Highland IV40 8DH. *01599 566215.* www.reraig.com. Owner: D & C H Glen-Riddell. On A87, 1.75m W of junction with A890, by Balmacara Hotel. No telephone bookings. En route to Isle of Skye, bridge 4m. Open May-September. ☆☆☆☆ **40T. MC.** 🛏 🗗 ⅛

(16m). Shiel Bridge Campsite, Shiel Bridge, Glenshiel, Kyle of Lochalsh, Highland IV40 8HW. *01599 511221.* lynne fivesisters@aol.com. Owners: John & Lynne Metcalfe. Old School House, Shiel Bridge, Glenshiel, Kyle IV40 8HW. On A87. Cafe and PO on site; PO open 8 hours week only. Fishing: sea and sea lochs, rivers and inland lochs. Open March 16-October 16 for tourers; open all year for tents. **15T. MC.** 🛏 🗗 ⅛ 🗲

Lairg

Dunroamin Caravan Park, Main Street, Lairg, Sutherland IV27 4AR. *01549 402447.* info@lairgcaravanpark.co.uk. www.lairgcaravanpark.co.uk. Owner: Margaret & Lewis Hudson. South side of A839 in village of Lairg, 300yd from Loch Shin. Perfect centre for exploring Highlands, fishing, hill-walking and water sports. Licensed restaurant and laundry on site. Pay phone. PO, banks, shops and PHs 200yd. Open April-October. ☆☆☆☆ **BH&HPA. 45T. MC. 9H.** 🛏 🗗

Grummore Caravan Club Site, Altnaharra, Lairg, Sutherland IV27 4UE. *01549 411226.* www.caravan club.co.uk. Owner: The Caravan Club. East Grinstead House, East Grinstead, West Sussex RH19 1UA. See website for standard directions to site. 2.75m from Altnaharra. Caravan Club members only. Quiet, remote site; nearest shop are 20m. Own sanitation required. Fishing, water sports and NCN cycle route nearby. Good area for walking. Peaceful off-peak. Open March-October. **NCC. 24T. MC.** 🛏 🗗

(37m). Kincraig Caravan & Camping Site, Tongue, Lairg, Sutherland, IV27 4XF. *01847 611218.* Turn off A838 into Tongue village to site. Open May-October. **15T. 15MC.** 🛏 🗗

(47m). Oldshoremore Caravan Site, Kinlochbervie, Lairg, Sutherland, IV27 4RS. *01971 521281.* A838 to Kinlochbervie, leave B801 at Kinlochbervie and continue for 2m on unclassified road to Oldshoremore. Open April-September. **11T. MC. 2S. 2H.** 🛏 🗗

Scourie Caravan & Camping Park, Harbour Road, Scourie, Lairg, Sutherland, IV27 4TG. *01971 502060.* On A894. Near Scourie village overlooking Scourie Bay. No advance bookings. Open Easter-September 30. ☆☆☆ **30T. MC.** 🛏 🗗

(5m). Woodend Caravan Site, Woodend, Achnairn, Lairg, Sutherland IV27 4DN. *01549 402248.* Owner: Mrs C M Ross. A836 from Lairg on to A838 SP. AA 3 pennants. Laundrette. Calor Gas. Campers' kitchen. Shops, PO, doctor within 5m. Golf course 14m. Open April 1-September 30. **53T. MC. 5H.** 🛏 🗗 ⅛

Lochinver

(7m). Clachtoll Caravan & Camping Site, Clachtoll, Lochinver, Highland IV27 4JD. *01571 855229.* Off the A837, 0.5m before Lochinver on to B869, about 6m to site. Children welcome. Open May-October. **60T. MC. 20S.** 🛏 ⅛

Melvich

Halladale Inn Caravan Site, Halladale Inn, Melvich, Sutherland KW14 7YJ. *01641 531 282.* mazfling@ tinyworld.co.uk. Owners: Ian & Marilyn Fling. 16m W of Thurso along A836. Small, quiet site, next door to Halladale Inn. Fine scenery and sandy beach. Suitable base for surfers, walking, birdwatching. Village shop and PO 1m. Open April 1-October 31. ☆☆☆☆ **BH&HPA. 6T.** 🛏 🗗

Nairn

(0.3m). Nairn Lochloy Holiday Park, East Beach, Nairn, Highland IV12 4PH. *01667 453764.* enquiries@parkdeanholi days.co.uk. www.parkdeanholidays.co.uk. Owner: Parkdean Holidays Plc. 2nd Floor, One Gosforth Way, Gosforth Business Park, Newcastle-upon-Tyne NE12 8ET. A1 to Edinburgh, then A9 to Inverness. Indoor heated pool, adventure play and amusements. Children's club and crazy golf. Restaurant, bar and live family entertainment. Open March-October. ☆☆☆☆ **BH&HPA. NCC. 14T. MC. 256S. 85H.** 🛏 🗗 ⅛ 🗲

Newtonmore

(3m). Invernahavon Caravan Site, Glentruim, Newtonmore, Highland PH20 1BE. *01540 673534/673219.* enquiry@inverna havon.com. Owner: Mr & Mrs H W Knox. Fernisdale, Glentruim, Newtonmore PH20 1BE. Off the A9, S of Newtownmore 10m N of Dalwhinnie. Caravan Club affiliated site. 2 golf courses within 8m, pets welcome. Fishing permits for sale from site office. Open April-October. ☆☆☆ **50T. 25MC.** 🛏 🗗 ⅛ 🗲

Spey Bridge Caravan Site, Newtonmore, Highland PH20 1BB. *01540 673275.* Take A9 north from Perth, turn on to B9150, Newtonmore road, and continue for 0.5m. Site is on the right-hand side after crossing Spey Bridge. Open Easter-October 15. **30T. MC.** 🛏

Roy Bridge

(0.3m). Bunroy Camping & Caravanning Site, Roy Bridge, Highland PH31 4AG. *01397 712332.* info@bunroycamping. co.uk. www.bunroycamping.co.uk. Owner: AD & G Markham. A82 from Fort William, on A86 at Spean Bridge, then 3m to Roy Bridge. At Stronlossit Hotel, turn right past school, follow signs for 350yd to end of road. 12m from Fort William. Peaceful site surrounded by woodland and set on the banks of the river Spean. Two hotels/restaurants and PO within a few minutes' walk. ISuitable base for touring, walking and outdoor activities. Open March 15 - October 15. ☆☆☆ **25T. MC.** 🛏 🗗

Roybridge

(2m). Inveroy Caravan Park, Inveroy, Roybridge, Highland PH31 4AQ. *01397 712275.* On the A86, 2m from Spean Bridge, 1m from Roy Bridge. Laundrette. **NCC. 14S. 7H.** ❈ 🛏 🗗

Spean Bridge

(2m). Gairlochy Holiday Park, Old Station, Gairlochy Road, Spean Bridge, Highland PH34 4EQ. *01397 712711.* theghp@talk21.com. www.theghp.co.uk. Owner: Mr Anderson. Off A82 on to B8004, at Commando Memorial, 1m N of Spean Bridge, site 1m on left and SP. Play area. Public telephone. Laundrette. Great Glen walk 0.25m away at Caledonian Canal. Free fishing on Loch Lochy. Open April-September. ✰✰✰✰ **BH&HPA. 25T. 25MC. 6S. 4H.** ⚑ ▣ ∅

Strathcarron

(23m). Applecross Camp Site, Applecross, Strathcarron, Highland IV54 8ND. *0845 1662681.* enquiries@applecross-campsite.co.uk. www.applecross.uk.com. Owner: Mr A C Goldthorpe. 8m N of Lochcarron on A896, turn left on to Applecross Road. (Bealoch-na-Ba). Applecross 11m, road not suitable for caravans. Caravans proceed on A896 for 7m, turn left, SP Applecross, 24m. In-store bakery, licensed tea room in covered garden. Open Easter-October. **BH&HPA. 60T. MC. S. 2H.** ⚑ ▣ ∅

Strathpeffer

(2m). Riverside Chalets Caravan Park, Contin, Strathpeffer, Highland IV14 9ES. *01997 421351.* Owner: Mr Finnie. On A835, junction of Ullapool to Strathpeffer to Maryburgh roads in Contin village. Quiet, riverside site. Mini market, PO next to site. Garage, golf, fishing, forest walks 2m. ✰✰ **15T. 15MC. 2S. 4H.** ✿ ⚑ ▣ ℒ

Sutherland

(1m). Pitgrudy Caravan Park, Poles Road, Dornoch, Sutherland, Highland IV25 3HY. *01862 810001.* www.pitgrudycaravanpark.co.uk. Owner: Mr G N R Sutherland. Caravan

Come and enjoy the wonderful views to the Summer Isles and mountains of North-West Scotland across picturesque Gruinard Bay

Our small, quiet Park abuts the wide, sandy beach at Laide and offers holiday caravans for hire and all facilities for tourers and tents. Ideal for walking, fishing, sailing, swimming or even just relaxing!

Please write or telephone for a copy of our brochure and price list.

Gruinard Bay Caravan Park

LAIDE, Wester Ross, IV22 2ND

Telephone/Fax: **01445 731225**

www.highlandbreaks.com

email: gruinard@ecosse.net

AA ◁

Sales, Edderton, Highland 1V19 1JY. On B9168, off A9 turn left at war memorial. Panoramic views of Dornoch Firth. Showers. Laundrette. Telephone. Play area. Thistle Award. Open April-September. ✰✰✰✰✰ **BH&HPA. NCC. 45T. 10MC. 15S. 10H.** ⚑ ▣

Sango Sands Caravan & Camping Site, Durness, Sutherland, Highland IV27 4PT. *01971 511262/511222.* keith.durness@btinternet.com. Owner: Mr Francis R M Keith. Aarhus, Durness, Sutherland, Highland IV27 4PP. Adjacent A838, overlooking Sango Bay. Cafe and restaurant, lounge bar. Gift shop. No advance bookings except for electric hook-ups. Golf course 1m. Shops, PO, doctor within 400yd. Overlooking safe, sandy beach. Open April 1-October 15. **82T. MC.** ⚑ ▣ ♿ ℒ

Tain

(2m). Dornoch Firth Caravan Park, Meikle Ferry South, Tain, Ross-shire IV19 1JX. *01862 892292.* enquiries@dornochfirth.co.uk. www.dornochfirth.co.uk. Owner: Mr W Porter. Just off A9, N of Tain, with open aspect to Dornoch Firth. Family-run park with showers and laundry facilities. Bar and restaurant adjacent. Fishing and golf nearby. Open March-November. ✰✰✰✰ **30T. MC. 20H.** ✿ ⚑ ▣

Thurso

(30m). Craigdhu Caravan Site, Bettyhill, Thurso, Highland KW14 7SP. *01641 521273.* Owner: Mr & Mrs D M Mackenzie. Dunveaden Guest House, Bettyhill, by Thurso, North Sutherlandshire. KW14 7SP. On A836 Tongue to Thurso. Shop, laundry nearby. Picturesque scenery with golden beaches, popular with botanists, geologists and birdwatchers. New swimming pool nearby. Fishing, PO and fuel pumps nearby. Open April 1-October 31. **90T. MC. 8S. 1H.** ⚑ ▣

(11m). Dunvegan Caravan Site, Reay, Thurso, Highland KW14 7RQ. *01847 811405.* Owner: J A Sutherland. On A836. Grassy, flat, sheltered site beside main road, 0.25m from sandy beach, fishing harbou and 18-hole golf course. Birdwatching and hill walks. Open May-October 30. **15T. MC.** ℒ

(0.5m). Thurso Caravan and Camping Site, Smith Terrace, Scrabster Road, Thurso, Highland KW14 7JY. *01847 894631.* Owner: Highland Council. Education Culture and Sport, Community Learning & Leisure Office, Princes Street, Thurso KW14 7DH. On A882, Thurso to Scrabster, within town boundary. Site overlooks Thurso Bay to Orkney Islands. 4.5-acre grassed park with laundry, showers, cafeteria. Surfing and sea angling nearby. Open May-September. ✰✰✰ **105T. 105MC. 10H.** ⚑ ▣ ♿

Ullapool

(3m). **Ardmair Point Caravan Site, Ardmair, Ullapool, Highland IV26 2TN.** *01854 612054.* sales@ardmair.com. www.ardmair.com. Owner: Mr Peter Fraser. Off the A835, N of Ullapool. Small site with panoramic views over the sea. Boat centre with rental facilities on site. Open May 1-October 1. ☆☆☆☆ **BH&HPA. 45T. 45MC.** ⌇ ⊕ ᵬ ⚑

Broomfield Holiday Park, Ullapool, Highland IV26 2SX. *01854 612020/664.* s.ross@broomfieldhp.com. www. broomfieldhp.com. Supermarket 5mins. Restaurants, bars, cafes, museum, leisure centre, etc. all 5mins walk from site. Open Easter-end September. ☆☆☆ **BH&HPA. 140T. MC.** ⌇ ⊕ ᵬ

Wester Ross

Gairloch Caravan and Camping Park, Strath, Gairloch, Wester Ross, Highland IV21 2BX. *01445 712373.* info@ gairlochcaravanpark.com. www.gairlochcaravanpark.com. Owner: Mr Robert Forbes. 70 St Andrews Drive, Bridge of Weir PA11 3HY. Turn west off A832 (Gairloch) on to B8021, in 0.5m turn right immediately after Millcroft Hotel, site on right. Family-run site with shower block, laundrette. Close to shops, cafe and restaurants. Chemical toilet emptying point. AA listed and graded. 70m from Inverness. Open April-October. ☆☆☆☆ **BH&HPA. 80T. 80MC. 2S. 2H.** ⌇ ⊕

> **Gruinard Bay Caravan Park, Laide, Wester Ross, Highland IV22 2ND.** *01445 731225.* gruinard@ ecosse.net. www.highlandbreaks.com. Owner: Tony & Ann Davis. On the A832, east of Laide. Gairloch 12m. Unspoilt, beachside park beside a bay, with views to mountains and islands. Open April 1-October 31. ☆☆☆ **BH&HPA. 43T. MC. 7S. 7H.** ⌇ ⊕ ⚑

Wick

(10m). **Old Hall Caravan Site, Watten, Wick, Highland.** *01955 621215.* Owner: Mr G Calder. On A882. Boats for hire. Fishing on Loch Watten and site is member of other lochs in the area; river fishing on daily permit. Open April-October for holiday homes; open all year for tourers. **7T. MC. 8S. 8H.** ⌇ ⊕

> **Riverside Caravan Club Site, Janetstown, Wick, Highland KW1 5SR.** *01955 605420.* www.caravan club.co.uk. Owner: The Caravan Club. East Grinstead House, East Grinstead, West Sussex RH19 1UA. Off A882 into Riverside Drive, site in 0.5m. River Wick runs beside site. Non-members welcome. Tent campers welcome. Toilet blocks. Laundry facilities. Veg prep. Motorhome service point. Information room. Golf, fishing, walking and water sports nearby. Calor Gas. Dog walk nearby. Peaceful off-peak. Beach within 5m. Open April-September. ☆☆☆☆ **NCC. 90T. MC.** ⌇ ⊕

INVERCLYDE

Gourock

(2m). **Cloch Caravans Holiday Park, Cloch Road, Gourock, Inverclyde PA19 1BA.** *01475 632675/634074.* ca.holt@virgin. net. www.clochcaravans.com. Owner: Miss C A Holt. On A770 Largs to Gourock. 2.5m from town of Gourock. Entrance on L. Ferry 0.5m. Station 2m. Doctor, PO 2.5m. Fishing, golf, swimming pool nearby. Bus service at park entrance. Laundry facilities available. Licensed restaurant, bar, children's play park. Wildlife. Golf, shops, swimming pool 2m. Cinema 6m. Open April 1-November 30. **BH&HPA. NCC. 165S. 20H.** ⌇ ⚑

LANARKSHIRE (NORTH)

Motherwell

(2m). **Strathclyde Country Park, 366 Hamilton Road, Motherwell, North Lanarkshire ML1 3ED.** *01698 402060.* strathclypark@northlan.gov.uk. www.northlan.gov.uk. Owner: North Lanarkshire Council. Dept. of Leisure Services, Civic Centre, Motherwell, North Lanarkshire. M74, J5. Touring site only within 1200-acre Strathclyde Country Park. Electric hook-ups and waste disposal. 24hr park security and lighting. Water sports and fun beads, guided walks, land train, beaches, play areas. Minutes from site are Innkeepers Fayre and M&D's Theme Park. Open Easter-mid October. ☆☆☆☆ **BH&HPA. NCC. 100T. MC.** ⌇ ⊕ ⚑

(7m). **Woodend Park, Mill Road, Allanton Shotts, Motherwell, North Lanarkshire.** Owner: J & J West. On A70. **T. MC.** ✿

LANARKSHIRE (SOUTH)

Biggar

(0.75)m. **Biggar Park Caravan Site, Biggar Public Park, Broughton Road, Biggar, South Lanarkshire ML12 6AZ.** *01899 220319.* Off A702. Open April 1-October 31. **12T. MC.** ⌇ ⊕

(12m). **Mount View Caravan Park, Abington, Biggar, South Lanarkshire ML12 6RW.** *01864 502808.* info@mountviewcara vanpark.co.uk. www.mountviewcaravanpark.co.uk. Owners: David & Dorothy Wightman. Old Hall Caravan Park, Capernwray, Carnforth, Lancashire LA6 1AD. M74, J13, and take A702 S into Abington Village. Follow signs along Station Road. Park is on R. Quiet site in scenic surroundings. Central location for visiting Glasgow, Edinburgh, Carlisle, Peebles, Ayr, Moffat. Suitable for overnight stops, weekends or holidays. Village shop, hotel and petrol station. Fishing and golf nearby. Open March 1-October 31. ☆☆☆☆☆ **BH&HPA. 50T. 50MC. 20S. 2H.** ⌇ ⊕ ᵬ ⌀

Mount View Caravan Park, Abington, Biggar, South Lanarkshire ML12 6RW
Quiet site set in beautiful scenery. Ideal central location for visiting Glasgow, Edinburgh, Carlisle, Peebles, Ayr, Moffat. Good for overnight stops, weekends or holidays. Holiday homes for sale and hire. Tourers, motor homes and tents welcome. Easy access being just 5 minutes from J13 off M74.
Tel: 01864 502808   www.mountviewcaravanpark.co.uk

Please visit the Caravan Club website: www.caravanclub.co.uk

SCOTLAND

Lanark

(1m). Clyde Valley Caravan Park, Kirkfield Bank Bridge, Lanark, South Lanarkshire ML11 9JW. 01555 663951. Off A73. Children allowed. Open April 1-October 31. **50T. MC. 50S.** ⛺ 🅿 ♿ ⊘

(3m). Newhouse Caravan and Camping Park, Ravensruther, Lanark, South Lanarkshire ML11 8NP. 01555 870228. new housepark@btinternet.com. www.ukparks.co.uk/ newhouse. Owner: Mrs J Seed. Off A70. Dog walk. Trout fishing on park, Open mid March-mid October. ✰✰✰✰ **BH&HPA. 40T. MC. 5S.** ⛺ 🅿 ♿ ⊾

LOTHIAN (EAST)

Aberlady

Aberlady Caravan Park, Haddington Road, Aberlady, East Lothian EH32 0PZ. 01875 870 666. Owner: Andrew Dyer. 5m from Haddington on B6137, 3m from Longniddry on A198. Quiet site, close enough to 20 golf courses, Aberlady village is a small coastal village 1m from the site with 2 hotels, a PO and a shop. Open March-October. ✰✰✰ **15T. 5MC. 2H.** ⛺ 🅿 ⊾

Dunbar

(0.5m). Belhaven Bay Caravan & Camping Park, Edinburgh Road, Dunbar, East Lothian EH42 1TU. 01368 865956. belhaven@meadowhead.co.uk. www.meadowhead.co.uk. Owner: Meadowhead Ltd., Charterhall, Duns, TD11 3RE. From A1 N or S exit at roundabout W of Dunbar. Park about 0.5m down A1087 on left side of road. From south, do not take first exit to Dunbar. Site located in the John Muir Country Park. Laundry, internet access available on the park. Children's play area. Sandy beaches nearby Thistle Award. David Bellamy Silver Conservation Award. Open March-January. ✰✰✰ **BH&HPA. NCC. 52T. 52MC. 60S. 5H.** ⛺ 🅿 ♿ ⊘

(7m). Camping & Caravanning Club Site - Barns Ness, Barns Ness, Dunbar, East Lothian EH42 1QP. 01368 863536/0870 2433331. www.campingandcaravanningclub.co.uk. Owner: Camping & Caravanning Club. Greenfields House, Westwood Way, Coventry CV4 8JH. Leaving Dunbar E on A1, turn L, SP Barns Ness, go past cement works and follow signs to site, which lies along a stretch of Berwickshire coast. Close to historic town of Dunbar. Views of coastline and sea from all pitches. All units accepted. Non-members welcome. Plenty of room for dog walking and children's ball games. Nearby 13th-century Hailes Castle. Special deals available for families and backpackers. Open March-October. ✰✰✰ **80T. 80MC.** ⛺ 🅿

THURSTON MANOR
HOLIDAY HOME PARK
INNERWICK
DUNBAR EH42 1SA
Superb heated amenities block
Full facilities - Indoor pool, bar, etc
For colour brochure telephone
AA 🔷 **01368-840643**
Visit our Website
www.thurstonmanor.co.uk

(6m). Thorntonloch Caravan Park, Innerwick, Dunbar, East Lothian. 01368 840236. thorntonloch@yahoo.co.uk. Owner: Thorntonloch Residents Association. On A1. Shop on site open at weekends. Sea fishing, right on beach. Open March 1-October 29. **10T. MC. 56S.** ⛺ 🅿 ⊾

(4m). Thurston Manor Holiday Home Park, Innerwick, Dunbar, East Lothian EH42 1SA. 01368 840643. mail@thurstonmanor.co.uk. www.thurstonmanor.co.uk. Owner: Dunham Leisure Ltd. S of Dunbar, SP from A1. Close to sea and sandy beaches. Licensed club with entertainment. Family room. Heated indoor pool, fitness centre with sauna, steam room, solarium, spa and gymnasium. Bar meals and takeaway. Private trout lake. Sea fishing and golf within 4m. Open March 1-January 8. ✰✰✰✰✰ **100T. MC. 586S. 9H.** ⛺ 🅿 ♿ ⊾

Haddington

(2.5m). The Monks Muir, Haddington, East Lothian EH41 3SB. 01620 860340. d@monksmuir.com. www.monksmuir.co.uk. Owner: Douglas & Deirdre Macfarlane. One of Scotland's oldest parks: accessible, small, tranquil, friendly and green. Set amid historic countryside, beaches and pretty villages, only 15mins from fringes of Edinburgh. ✰✰✰✰ **BH&HPA. NCC. 35T. MC. 30S. 8H.** ✿ ⛺ 🅿 ⊾

Longniddry

(1m). Gosford Gardens, Longniddry, East Lothian EH32 0PX. 01875 870487. Off A198. Advance booking essential bank holidays and July-August. **120T. MC.** ⛺ 🅿 ♿

(2.5m). Seton Sands Holiday Village, Longniddry, East Lothian EH32 0QF. 01875 814962. oewebmaster@bourne-leisure.co.uk. www.setonsandsholidayvillage.co.uk. Owner: Bourne Leisure Ltd. One Park Lane, Hemel Hempstead, Herts HP2 4YL. Take A1 to A198 slip road. Turn on to B6371 for Cockenzie, then R on to B1348. Park is 1m along on the right-hand side, SP from A1, N and S. Heated indoor swimming pool. Club. Family entertainment. Laundrette. Takeaway. Direct beach access. Mini market. Children's clubs. Amusements, multi-sports court, pool tables. Thistle Award. Welcome Host and David Bellamy Silver Conservation Award. Open April-October holidays. ✰✰✰✰ **BH&HPA. NCC. 42T. MC. 630S. 206H.** ⛺ 🅿 ♿ ⊾

Musselburgh

(1.5m). Drum Mohr Caravan Park, Levenhall, Musselburgh, East Lothian EH21 8JS. 01316 656867. bookings@drummohr.org. www.drummohr.org. Owner: Mr W Melville. E of Musselburgh between B1348 and B1361. Secluded, landscaped site on edge of countryside, yet only 20mins from Edinburgh. Good bus service to city. 5 chalets available for hire. Open March 1-October 31. ✰✰✰✰✰ **BH&HPA. NCC. 120T. 30MC. 5H.** ⛺ 🅿 ♿ ⊾

North Berwick

(1m). Gilsland Caravan Park, Grange Road, North Berwick, East Lothian EH39 5JA. 01620 892205. Owner: J B & W R McNair. Between B1347 and A198. Along Grange Road. 0.5m from swimming pool and sports centre. Golf, sailing, shopping all within 1m. Open April-October. ✰✰✰ **BH&HPA. 33T. MC. 114S.** ⛺ 🅿 ♿

(0.5m). Tantallon Caravan & Camping Park, Dunbar Road, North Berwick, East Lothian EH39 5NJ. *01620 893348.* tantallon@meadowhead.co.uk. www.meadowhead.co.uk. Owner: Meadowhead Ltd. Charterhall, Duns, Berwickshire TD11 3RE. Situated on the A198, immediately E of North Berwick. Laundry, showers. Games room, play area, 9-hole putting green. Internet access available on the park. Adjacent to Glen Golf Course. Holiday homes for disabled people available. Close to bus stop. Thistle Award. Open March-January for holiday homes; open March-October for tourers. ☆☆☆☆☆ BH&HPA. 180T. MC. 60S. 12H. 🛉 🖾 ⅄ ⅃ ⌀

(2.5m). Yellowcraig Caravan Club Site, Dirleton, North Berwick, East Lothian EH39 5DS. *01620 850217.* www.caravanclub.co.uk. Owner: The Caravan Club. East Grinstead House, East Grinstead, West Sussex RH19 1UA. See website for standard directions to site. Site has grass-covered sandy dunes, shrubs and roses creating private pitching areas. Non-members welcome. Advance booking essential bank holidays and mid July-mid August. Some hard-standings. Toilet blocks with privacy cubicles and laundry facilities. Baby/toddler washroom. Motorhome service point. Play area. Golf nearby. Suitable for families. Veg prep area. Gas. Dog walk nearby. Peaceful off peak. Beach within 5m. Open March-October. ☆☆☆☆☆ NCC. 108T. MC. 🛉 🖾 ⅄

LOTHIAN (MID)

Roslin

Slatebarns Caravan Park, Slatebarns Farm, Roslin, Mid Lothian EH25 9PU. *01314 402192.* www.slatebarns.co.uk. Owner: R & M Crawford. Follow signs to Rosslyn Chapel, past car park and site is straight ahead. Caravan Club afiliated site. 7mins walk to shops and hotels in village. Regular bus service to Edinburgh. Open April 1-October 30. ☆☆☆☆ NCC. 30T. MC. 🛉 🖾 ⅄

LOTHIAN (WEST)

East Calder

(3m). Linwater Caravan Park, West Clifton, East Calder, West Lothian EH53 0HT. *0131 3333326.* linwater@ supanet.com. www.linwater.co.uk. Owner: Jean Guinan. 10m W of Edinburgh. Take the B7030 from Newbridge, J1 of M9, and follow signs. Quiet, country park. Suitable as base for Highland Showground and Edinburgh or as stopover. Open March-October. ☆☆☆☆ BH&HPA. 60T. 60MC. 🛉 🖾 ⅄

Linlithgow

(3m). Beecraigs Caravan & Camping Site, Beecraigs Country Park, The Park Centre, Linlithgow, West Lothian EH49 6PL. *01506 844516.* mail@beecraigs.com. www. beecraigs.com. Owner: West Lothian Council. M9, J3 or J4, follow tourist signs for Beecraigs Country Park from Linlithgow. Set within Beecraigs Country Park, with miles of woodland walks, outdoor pursuit activities, fly-fishing, restaurant and visitor centre. Local shops available in Linlithgow. ☆☆☆☆ NCC. 18T. 18MC. ✿ 🛉 🖾 ⅄

(1m). Loch House Caravan Park, Loch House Farm, Linlithgow, West Lothian EH49 7RG. *01506 848283.* 16T. 16MC. ✿ 🛉 🖾

MORAY

Aberlour

(1m). Aberlour Gardens Caravan & Camping Park, Aberlour, Moray AB38 9LD. *01340 871586.* aberlourgardens@aol.com. www.aberlourgardens.co.uk. Owner: Simon & Denice Blades. Midway between Aberlour and Craigellachie, off the A95. Vehicles over 10ft 6in high use A941. Quiet, sheltered site close to river Spey and Speyside Way on the whisky trail. Shop, laundry and dishwashing facilities. and disabled/family room comprising shower, toilet, sink, baby changing table. Pets welcome. Small children's play area. Seasonal tourer pitches available. Open end March-December for tourers; open Easter-September for holiday homes. ☆☆☆☆☆ BH&HPA. 35T. MC. 30S. 2H. 🛉 🖾 ⅄ ⅃

(5m). Camping & Caravanning Club Site - Speyside, Elchies by Craigellachie, Aberlour, Moray AB38 9SL. *01340 810410/0870 243 3331.* www.campingandcaravanningclub.co.uk. Owner: Camping & Caravanning Club. Greenfields House, Westwood Way, Coventry CV4 8JH. On A941 from Elgin towards Craigellachie, turn L on to B9102 for about 3m to site. Walk along the Speyside Way or visit seaside villages. Salmon and whisky are the specialities of this area. All types of units accepted. Non-members welcome. Situated in 7 acres. Surrounding area has historic castles, National Trust properties and gardens to visit. Special deals available for families and backpackers. Open March-October. ☆☆☆☆ 75T. 75MC. 🛉 🖾 ⅄

Burghead

(0.25m). Burghead Beach Caravan Park, West Beach, Station Road, Burghead, Moray IV30 5RP. *01343 830084.* Owners: Christies (Fochabers) Ltd. The Nurseries, Fochabers, Moray IV32 7ES. NW of Elgin on the B9012. Adjacent to sandy beach and close to local facilities and shops. Open April-October. BH&HPA. 26T. MC. 60S. 🛉 🖾

Cullen

(0.25m). Cullen Bay Holiday Park, Logie Drive, Cullen, Moray AB56 4TW. *01542 840766.* enquiries@cullenbay.co.uk. www.cullenbayholidaypark.co.uk. Owner: Mr Hugh Ballantyne. Located on the NE coastal trail, overlooking Cullen Bay and the Moray coastline. Family-run park with good amenities. 10mins walk to town. Open April 1-September 30. ☆☆☆☆ BH&HPA. 40T. 20MC. 60S. 3H. 🛉 🖾 ⅄

Elgin

(5m). North Alves Caravan Park, Alves, Elgin, Moray IV30 3XD. *01343 850223.* Off A96.Turn north to site at Alves village by the school. Forres 6m. North Alves is a well-kept park with acres of grassland, 1m from beach. Several golf courses nearby. Open April 1-October 31. 40T. 40MC. 20S. 20H. 🛉 🖾 ⅃

(0.5m). Riverside Caravan Park, West Road, Elgin, Moray IV30 3UN. *01343 542813.* On Aberdeen to Inverness road on western outskirts of Elgin. Open April 1-October 31. ☆☆☆☆ 38T. MC. 31S. 🛉 🖾 ⅄ ⅃

(7m). Station Caravan Park, West Beach, Hopeman, Elgin, Moray IV30 5RU. *01343 830880.* stationcaravanpark @ talk21. com. www.stationcaravanpark.co.uk. Owner: David & Angie Steer. On NE coast 7m from Elgin, 10m from Forres follow coast road from Elgin. Laundrette and pay-phone. 5 golf courses within 10mins driving distance. Shops and doctors' surgery in village, sea and river fishing nearby. Castle and whisky trails close by. Views over Moray Firth. PHs and takeaway, food in village. Open March-November. ✰✰✰ **BH&HPA. 28T. 28MC. 70S. 10H.** 🚐 🔌

West Beach, Burghead, Elgin, Moray. *01343 835799.* Owner: Moray Council. Dept of Tech & Leisure, High Street, Elgin, Moray IU30 1BX. 9m NE of Forres on B9013. 9m NW of Elgin on B9013. Open April-September. **40T. MC. 60S. 8H.** 🚐 🔌 ♿

Fochabers

(0.5m). Burnside Caravan Park, Fochabers, Moray IV32 7ET. *01343 820511.* Owners: Christies (Fochabers) Ltd. The Nurseries, Fochabers, Moray IV32 7ES. On A96. 500yd from town. Swimming pool, sauna and spa on site. Suitable touring centre for NE Scotland. Open April 1-October 31. **BH&HPA. 44T. 20MC. 95S.** 🚐 🔌 ♿

Forres

(5m). Findhorn Sands Caravan Park, Findhorn, Forres, Moray IV36 3YZ. *01309 690324.* Owner: Calren Ltd. Off A96, at Forres roundabout to Kinloss and N at Findhorn SP at Kinloss junction, turn right at second caravan site sign leading to beach touring site. Shop, pHs, restaurants, PO 150yd. 3m to golf and doctor. Open April-October. ✰✰✰✰✰ **45T. 5MC.** 🚐 🔌 ♿ 🛒

(3.5m). Old Mill Caravan Park, Brodie, Forres, Moray IV36 2TD. *01309 641244.* admin@theoldmillbrodie.com. www.theold millbrodie.com/oldmillcaravanpark.htm. Owner: Mr & Mrs Jamieson. On A96, Forres to Nairn. Dogs allowed. Open April 1-October 31. ✰✰✰✰ **27T. MC. 45S. 18H.** N 🚐 🔌 🛒

(2m). River View Caravan Park, Mundole, Forres, Moray IV36 2TA. *01309 673932.* Owner: Overmount Ltd. On A96 and A940. Quiet, family park. Laundrette. Fishing. Children allowed. suitable base for anglers, golfers, ramblers, whisky enthusiasts and historians. Bordered by the Darnaway Forest and river Findhorn. Open April-end October. **60T. MC. 50S.** 🚐 🔌

Inverness

Camping & Caravanning Club Site - Nairn, Delnies Wood, Nairn, Inverness, MorayIV12 5NX. *01667 455281/0870 243 3331.* www.campingandcaravanning club.co.uk. Owner: Camping & Caravanning Club. Greenfields House, Westwood Way, Coventry CV4 8JH. Off the main A96, Inverness to Aberdeen road, 2m W of the town of Nairn. Look out for 'Delnies Wood' SP. Situated in wooded setting, 2m from the beach. 75 pitches set in 14 acres. Non-members welcome. Caravans, motor caravans and tents accepted. Fort George, Loch Ness and Cawdor are all worth a visit. Dolphins often seen in waters of Firth. Special deals available for families and backpackers. Open March-October. ✰✰✰ **75T. 75MC. 6S.** 🚐 🔌

Lossiemouth

(2m). East Beach Caravan Park, Seatown, Lossiemouth, Moray IV31 6JJ. *01343 545121.* Owner: Moray Council. Dept of Tech & Leisure, High Street, Elgin, Moray IV30 1BX. Situated 6.25m N of Elgin off A941. Open April-October. **32T. MC. 41S.** 🚐

(0.5m). Lossiemouth Bay Caravan Park, East Beach, Lossiemouth, Moray IV31 6NW. *01343 813980.* lossiemouth caravan@ecosse.net. wwww.lossiemouthcaravans.co.uk. Owner: Christies (Fochabers) Ltd. The Nurseries, Fochabers,

Moray IV32 7PF. Adjacent to sandy beach and close to shops and facilities at Lossiemouth. 2 golf courses 1m. Open April 1-October 31. **32T. 10MC. 108S.** 🚐 🔌 ♿

(1m). Silver Sands Leisure Park, Covesea, West Beach, Lossiemouth, Moray IV31 6SP. *01343 813262.* holidays@ silversands.freeserve.co.uk. www.travel.to/silversands. Owner: President Leisure Ltd. Covesea West Beach, Lossiemouth. On B9040. Lossiemouth to Hopeman road, Elgin 6m. On the Moray Firth with miles of beaches. Suitable location for visiting whisky distillers, castle and golf course. Facilities for all the family. Open March-October. ✰✰✰✰ **BH&HPA. NCC. 140T. MC. 168S. 45H.** 🚐 🔌 🛒

ORKNEY

Kirkwall

(0.25m). Pickaquoy Caravan and Camping Park, The Pickaquoy Centre, Muddisdale Road, Kirkwall, Orkney KW15 1LR. *01856 879900.* enquiries@pickaquoy.co.uk. www.pickaquoy.co.uk. Owner: The Pickaquoy Centre Trust. Turn R off A965 when approaching Kirkwall and follow signs. Situated on the Pickaquoy Centre Campus. Amenities' block showers. Open mid May-mid eptember. ✰✰✰ **30T. 30MC.** 🚐 🔌 ♿

Stromness

Point of Ness Camping & Caravan Site, Stromness, Orkney KW16 3DL. *01856 873535.* Owner: Orkney Islands Council. Booking to: Recreation Services Sector, Kirkwall KW15 1NY. Follow signs on leaving ferry. Grass site adjacent to shore. Open May-September. ✰✰✰ **30T. 30MC.** 🔌 ♿

PERTHSHIRE & KINROSS

Aberfeldy

(6m). Kenmore Caravan Park, Kenmore, Aberfeldy, Perthshire & Kinross PH15 2HN. *01887 830226.* info@tay mouth.co.uk. www.kenmorecaravanpark.co.uk. Owner: D Menzies & Partners. W off A9 at Ballinluig on A827, 15m to Kenmore. Family-run park, suitable base for walking, golfing, fishing etc. 9-hole golf course with bar and restaurant on site . 5 cottages available for hire. Boat hire, walking, climbing, castles, distilleries. Open March 15-November 30. ✰✰✰✰ **BH&HPA. 60T. 100S.** 🚐 🔌 ♿ 🛒

Auchterarder

Auchterarder Caravan Park. Nethercoul, Auchterarder. Perthshire PH3 1ET. *01764 663119.* info@prestonpark.co.ik. www.prestonpark.co.uk. Owners: Stuart & Susie Robertson. **23T.** ⚙ 🚐 🔌 ♿

Blairgowrie

(9m). Ballintuim Caravan Park, Ballintuim, Blairgowrie, Perthshire & Kinross PH10 7NH. *01250 886276.* Owner: Phil & Karen Clark. Bridge of Cally, Blairgowrie, Perthshire & Kinross. A93 to Bridge of Cally, then A924. Site is midway between Bridge of Cally and Kirkmichael. ✰✰✰ **BH&HPA. 16T. 10MC. 73S.** ⚙ 🚐 🔌

(1m). Blairgowrie Holiday Park, Rattray, Blairgowrie, Perthshire & Kinross PH10 7AL. *01250 876666.* blair gowrie@holiday-parks.co.uk. www.holiday-parks.co.uk. Owner:

Colin & Margaret Wood. Off A93. 1m N of Blairgowrie town centre. Follow international signs. Family-run park. Heated facilities. Laundrette. Adventure playground. Putting green. Pine lodges and caravans for hire and for sale for holidays all year round. Fishing, swimming pool locally. Shops and restaurants within 1m. 6 golf courses within 5m. ☆☆☆☆☆ **BH&HPA. 25T. 5MC. 120S. 6H.** ✿ ⚬ 🐕 ◇

(5m). Corriefodly Holiday Park, Bridge of Cally, Blairgowrie, Perthshire PH10 7JG. *01250 886236.* corriefodly@holiday-parks.co.uk. www.holiday-parks.co.uk. Owner: Colin & Margaret Wood. Follow A93, 6m N of Blairgowrie to Bridge of Cally. Turn L to Pitlochry road, at bridge and PO. Site about 100yd on L. Fishing on park grounds (charges apply). Bar, function room and games room on park. Children's play area. Laundry facilities. Golf, swimming, horse riding, walking nearby. ☆☆☆☆☆ **BH&HPA. 20T. 10MC. 120S. 3H.** ✿ ⚬ 🐕 ◇

Five Roads Caravan Park, Alyth, Blairgowrie, Perthshire PH11 8NB. *01828 632255.* steven.ewart@btopenworld.com. www.fiveroadscaravanpark.co.uk. Owner: Steven Ewart. From Blairgowrie take A926. After 4.5m turn L into site at Blackbird Inn. Site lies just outside Alyth, a small country town. Park is a small, family-run site. Inn adjacent to the park and the local shops are 0.5m away. 3 golf courses, 2 driving ranges within 1m. Local walks, fishing, pony treking, birdwatching and winter sports at Glenshee. PO, doctor, etc all within 0.5m from park. ☆☆☆☆ **BH&HPA. 20T. 6MC. 2S. 2H.** ✿ ⚬ 🐕 ⚬ 🐕 ◇

(12m). Nether Craig Caravan Park, Alyth, Blairgowrie, Perthshire & Kinross PH11 8HN. *01575 560204.* nether craig@lineone.net. www.nethercraigcaravanpark.co.uk. Owner: Peter and Pat Channon. At roundabout S of Alyth, join B954, SP Glenisla, follow caravan signs for 4m. Peaceful, family-run park. David Bellamy Gold Conservation Award. Open March 15-November 20. ☆☆☆☆☆ **BH&HPA. CaSSOA. 40T. MC.** 🐕 ⚬ 🐕 🐕

Comrie

(1m). West Lodge Caravan Park, Comrie, Perthshire PH6 2LS. *01764 670354.* www.westlodge.bravehost.com. Owner: Mr P J, E L & PP Gill. On A85 Crieff to Comrie. 4m W of Crieff. Quiet, sheltered, family-run park with showers. 10mins walk from village. Good touring centre. Calor Gas and Camping Gaz for sale. Public phone. Advance booking needed high season. Tents, motorhomes and tourers welcome. Winter tourer storage available. Good area for fishing, golf, walking, bowls. Water sports at Loch Earn. Open April 1-October 31. ☆☆☆ **BH&HPA. 10T. MC. 34S. 6H.** 🐕 ⚬ 🐕 🐕 ◇

Crieff

(1m). Braidhaugh Caravan Park, Braidhaugh South Bridgend, Crieff, Perthshire & Kinross PH7 4HP. *01764 652951.* info@braidhaugh.co.uk. www.braidhaugh.co.uk. Owner: Mr Campbell. A822 from Stirling. From Perth A85. From Lochearn A85. All hard-standings. Heated toilet block. TV hook-ups. Golfing, fishing, walking. Central location for touring Pethshire, relaxing! ☆☆☆☆ **BH&HPA. NCC. 36T. MC. 70S. 3H.** ✿ 🐕 ⚬ 🐕 🐕

(12m). Loch Earn Leisure Park, South Shore Road, St Fillans, Comrie, Crieff, Perthshire & Kinross PH6 2NL. *01764 685270.* enquiries@loch-earn.com. www.loch-earn.com. Owner: Mr P & I McCormack. Perthshire Caravan Co, Dundee Road, Errol Perth PH2 7SR. Turn L before entering St Fillans village on A85, after leaving Comrie. SP South Shore road. Bar and restaurant. Marina and water sports. Golf course, fishing nearby. Long shoreline to Loch Earn. Open end March-end October. **BH&HPA. NCC. 40T. 40MC. 230S.** 🐕 ⚬ 🐕 🐕

(7m). Riverside Caravan Park, Old Station Road, Comrie, Crieff, Perthshire & Kinross PH3 2EA. *01764 670555.* river sidescote@ukf.net. Owner: Mr D W Wilkinson. 224 Spring Bank, Hull, East Yorkshire HU3 1LU. On A85 on the twin banks of rivers Earn and Lednock. Central location. Just off the main street of Comrie Village, excellent facilities in village. Good for golf, fishing, touring, Stewart Crystal glass at Crieff. 10m from Gleneagles. Quiet par in mature grounds. Oldest whisky distillery only 6m from park. ☆☆☆☆ **BH&HPA. 135S.** 🐕 ⚬

(7m). Twenty Shilling Wood, St Fillans Road, Comrie, Crieff, Perthshire & Kinross PH6 2JY. *01764 670411.* alowe20@ aol.com. www.ukparks.co.uk/twentyshilling. Owner: Lowe family. On A85, 0.50m W of Comrie. In a national scenic area. Family-run park. Peaceful and secluded. Security gates. Shops, PO, doctor, golf, garage, fishing all within 1m. David Bellamy Gold Conservation Award. Open late March-mid October. **BH&HPA. 11T. MC. 38S.** 🐕 ⚬

Dunkeld

(1m). Inver Mill Farm Caravan Park, Inver, Dunkeld, Perthshire & Kinross PH8 0JR. *01350 727477.* invermill@ talk21.com. www.visitdunkeld.com/perthshire-caravan-park.htm. Owner: Mr & Mrs N Bryden. Turn off A9 on to A822, then immediately R to Inver, follow road for 1m past holiday home site on the L, cross bridge and take first L to park. Open end March-end October. ☆☆☆☆ **65T. MC.** 🐕 ⚬ 🐕

(1m). The Erigmore Estate, Birnam, Dunkeld, Perthshire & Kinross PH8 9XX. *01350 727236.* mandy@erigmore.co.uk. Owners: President Leisure Ltd. 12m N of Perth on A9. Indoor pool, spa bath, sauna, solarium, games room, restaurant, take-away, laundrette, lounge bar with family entertainment and adventure playground. Bike hire, tennis courts. Golf course 1m. Cinema, shopping centre 12m. Local shop 2mins away. Open March-January 7. ☆☆☆☆ **BH&HPA. NCC. 26T. 5MC. 189S. 22H.** 🐕 ⚬ 🐕

Killin

(4m). Cruachan Caravan & Camping Park, Killin, Perthshire & Kinross FK21 8TY. *01567 820302.* www.cru achanfarm. co.uk. On A827 Killin to Aberfeldy. Quiet, family-run park adjacent to farm. Highland castle. Hill and woodland walks, riding, golf, salmon and trout fishing on Loch Tay. Coffee shop, play area, gas and pay-phone. Licensed restaurant, takeway meals, packed lunches. Suitable touring base. Open mid March-October 31. ☆☆☆ **15T. 15MC. 30S. 8H.** 🐕 ⚬ 🐕 🐕

Kinloch Rannoch

(3.5m). Kilvrecht Campsite, Loch Rannoch, Kinloch Rannoch, Perthshire & Kinross PH8 0JR. *01350 727284.* hamish.murray@forestry.gsi.gov.uk. Owner: Forest Enterprise. Tay District, Inver Park, Dunkeld, Perthshire & Kinross PH8 0JR. Off B846, W of Kinnloch Rannoch on south bank of Loch Rannach. Woodland setting. Fishing nearby. Woodland wlaks. Open March-October. **45T. MC.** 🐕 ⚬

Kinross

(2.5m). Gairney Bridge Caravan & Camping Site, By Kinross, Kinross, Perthshire & Kinross KY13 9JZ. *01577 862336.* J5, M90, NE. On B996. Children welcome. Open June-September for tourers. ☆ **BH&HPA. 15T. 10MC.** ✿ 🐕 ⚬ 🐕

Turfhills Tourist Centre, Kinross, Perthshire & Kinross KY13 7NQ. *01577 63123.* Owner: Granada Motorway Services Ltd. Off A977 at J6 of M90. Petrol. Gas. Showers. Laundry room. **60T. MC. ✿ ⌁ 🐾**

Perth

(10m). Beech Hedge Caravan Park, Cargill, Perth, Perthshire & Kinross PH2 6DU. *01250 883249.* admin@beech-hedge-caravan-park.co.uk. www.beech-hedge-caravan-park.co.uk. Owners: Mr & Mrs Ritchie. On A93, Perth to Blairgowrie. N of Perth. Small, quiet site with views. Open mid March-end October. **10T. 15S. 2H. ⌁ 🔌**

(2m). Cleeve Caravan Park, Glasgow Road, Perth, Perthshire PH2 0PH. *01738 475211/2.* eross@pkc.gov.uk. Owner: Perth & Kinross Council. 3 High Street, Perth, Perthshire PH1 5JS. 750yd E of A9, M90 and Perth bypass roundabout (Broxden) on road to Perth. Open mid March-end October. ✰✰✰✰ **100T. MC. ⌁ 🔌 🐾**

(9m). Inchmartine, Inchture, Perth, Perthshire & Kinross PH14 9QQ. *01821 670212.* enquiries@perthshire-caravans.co.uk. www.perthshire-caravans.co.uk. Owner: Loch Earn Caravan Parks. On A85. Open April-October. **45T. MC. ⌁ 🔌 🐾**

(6m). St Madoes Caravan Park, St Madoes, Glencarse, Perth, Perthshire & Kinross PH2 7LZ. *01738 860244.* Owner: Mr & Mrs G M Crombie. Off A90, Perth to Dundee road. Laundry. **4T. 3MC. ✿ ⌁ 🔌**

Pitlochry

(7m). Blair Castle Caravan Park, Blair Atholl, Pitlochry, Perthshire PH18 55R. *01796 481263.* mail@blaircastlecaravan park.co.uk. www.blaircastlecaravanpark.co.uk. Owner: Blair Castle Estate Ltd. Turn off A9, 6m N of Pitlochry following signs to Blair Atholl (1m). Site in grounds of Blair Castle. Fishing, golf, bowling and pony-trekking nearby. Open March 1-November 30. ✰✰✰✰✰ **BH&HPA. NCC. 275T. 30MC. 105S. 28H. ⌁ 🔌 🐾**

(2m). Faskally Home Farm, Pitlochry, Perthshire & Kinross PH16 5LA. *01796 472007.* ehay@easynet.co.uk. www.faskally. co.uk. Owner: Mr E M R Hay. On A9 (B8019 Killiecrankie), Perth to Inverness. Bar and restaurant. Indoor heated leisure pool. Sauna, steam room and spa bath. Open March 15-October 31. ✰✰✰✰ **BH&HPA. 215T. MC. 110S. 40H. ⌁ 🔌 ⌁ 🐾**

Glengoulandie Country Park, Foss, Pitlochry, Perthshire PH16 5NL. *01887 830495.* info@glengoulandie.co.uk. www.glengoulandie.co.uk. Owners: Sandy McAdam& Craig McAdam. B846 road, 8m from Aberfeldy toward Kinloch Rannoch, on left-hand side. A deer park with Highland Cattle. A fishing loch stocked with brown trouts, a coffee shop with small range of gifts and a children's play area. Open March-October. **40S. ⌁ & 🐾 ∅**

(9m). Loch Tummel Caravan Site, Ardgualich, Pitlochry, Perthshire & Kinross. Owner: Mr N Campbell. Off A9 Perth to Inverness on B8019. **15S.**

(0.5m). Milton of Fonab Caravan Site, Bridge Road, Pitlochry, Perthshire PH16 5NA. *01796 472882.* info@fonab.co.uk. www.fonab.co.uk. Owner: Mr M F Stewart. Off A9, S of Pitlochry, on the banks of river Tummel. Mountain bike hire. 5mins walk to Pitlochry festival theatre. 1m to 18-hole golf course. Open end March-October 8. ✰✰✰✰ **BH&HPA. 150T. 25MC. 36H. ⌁ 🔌 & 🐾 ∅**

(5m). The River Tilt Park, Blair Atholl, Pitlochry, Perthshire & Kinross PH18 5TE. *01796 481467.* stuart@rivertilt. fsnet.co.uk. www.rivertilt.co.uk. Owners: Stuart & Mariss Richardson. Take B8079 off A9, SP to Blair Atholl. On banks of river Tilt, next to golf course and 100yd from town and Blair Castle. Laundrette. Refurbished, heated shower block. Calor Gas and Campingaz. New indoor heated pool. Sauna, solarium, steam room, gym and spa pool. Restaurant. David Bellamy Conservation Award. Open March-November for tourers; open all year for holiday homes. ✰✰✰✰✰ **BH&HPA. 35T. 31MC. 60S. 5H. ⌁ 🔌 ∅**

(13m). Tummel Valley Holiday Park, Tummel Bridge, Pitlochry, Perthshire PH16 5SA. *01882 634221.* enquiries@parkdeanholidays.co.uk. www.parkdeanholidays. co.uk. Owner: Parkdean Holidays Plc.2nd Floor, One Gosforth Park Way, Gosforth Business Park, Newcastle-upon-Tyne NE12 8ET. A9 to Pitlochry, then B8019 to Tummel Bridge. Indoor pool and toddlers' splash pool, solarium and sauna. Children's club and adventure play area, multi-sports court and amusement. Bar, food, and live family entertainment. Open February-January. ✰✰✰✰ **BH&HPA. NCC. 40T. MC. 173S. 159H. ⌁ 🔌 & 🐾**

St Fillans

St Fillans Caravan Park, Station Road, St Fillans, Perthshire & Kinross PH6 2NE. *01764 685274.* Owner: P & D Brown. Station House, Station Road, St Fillans, Perthshire & Kinross. Off A85, Crieff to Lochearnhead. In St Fillans turn R. Suitable base for fishing, walking, golf and water sports. Open April-October. **38S. ⌁ 🔌 🐾**

Tayside

RENFREWSHIRE

Wemyss Bay

(6m). **Wemyss Bay Holiday Home Park, Wemyss Bay, Renfrewshire. PA18 6BA.** *01475 522589.* From Glasgow follow M8 to Greenock. Take the A78 road to Wemyss Bay. Heated indoor pool, pony rides, children's clubs and family entertainment. Mini market. Laundrette. Horse riding. David Bellamy Gold Conservation Award. Thistle Award. Open April-October. ✫✫✫✫ **BH&HPA. NCC. 569S. 140H.** ♁ ☈ ☎ ∅

SHETLAND ISLANDS

Lerwick

(1.5m). **Clickimin Caravan & Camp Site, Clickimin Leisure Complex, Lochside, Lerwick, Shetland Islands ZE1 0PJ.** *01595 741000.* mail@srt.org.uk. Owners: Shetland Recreational Trust. Recently refurbished site on outskirts of Lerwick. Suitable location for touring islands. Situated next to modern leisure complex with swimming pool, leisure waters, main hall, bowls hall. Open May-October. ✫✫✫✫ **20T. 20MC. 20S.** ♁ ☎ ☈

STIRLING

Aberfoyle

(1.5m). **Cobleland Caravan & Camping Site, Forestry Commission (Forest Holidays), Aberfoyle, Stirling FK8 3UX.** *01877 382392.* fe.holidays@forestry.gsi.gov.uk. www.forestholidays.co.uk. Owner: Forestry Commission (Forest Holidays). 231 Corstorphine Road, Edinburgh, EH12 7AT. Off A81, Glasgow to Aberfoyle. In the heart of Trossachs, suitable for walking, cycling and sightseeing. Fishing nearby. Brochure request line: 0131 334 0066. Open mid March-end September. ✫✫ **BH&HPA. 135T. MC.** ♁ ☎ ☈ ☈

(3m). **Trossachs Holiday Park, Aberfoyle, Stirling FK8 3SA.** *01877 382614.* into@trossachsholidays.co.uk. www.trossachsholidays.co.uk. Owner: Joe and Hazel Norman. S of Aberfoyle on A81. Play area. TV lounge. Games room. Mountain bikes for hire. David Bellamy Gold Conservation Award. Open March 1-October 31. ✫✫✫✫✫ **BH&HPA. 45T. 40MC. 30S. 8H.** ♁ ☎ ☈

Alloa

(2m). **Auld-brig Filling Station & Caravan Site, Tullibody, Clack's, Alloa, Stirling FK10 2PF.** *01259 722684.* Owner: Mrs G Penman. Off the A907. Calor Gas on site. **BH&HPA. 2T. 2MC.** ☈ ∅

> **The Woods Caravan Club Site, Diverswell Farm, Fishcross, Alloa, Stirling FK10 3AN.** *01259 762802.* 4m from Stirling. Non-members welcome. Suitable for families. Quiet site offering panoramic views of the Ochill Hills. Toilet blocks with privacy cubicles and laundrette. Motorhome service point, vegetable preparation area. Calor Gas and Campingaz. Good area for walking, dog walk on site. Fishing, golf and NCN cycle route nearby. Open March-October **NCC. 105T. MC.** ♁ ☎ ☈

Auchenbowie

(4m). **Auchenbowie Caravan Site, Auchenbowie, Stirling FK6 6RF.** *01324 822141.* Leave M9/M80 at J9, heading S on A872 towards Derry for 0.5m, then turn right for 0.5m. Open April 1-October 31. ✫✫ **60T. MC. 10H.** ♁ ☎

Blair Drummond

> **Blair Drummond Caravan Club Site, Cuthill Brae, Blair Drummond, Stirling FK9 4UX.** *01786 841208.* www.blairdrummondcaravanpark.co.uk. Off A84, follow international caravan signs. 5m from Stirling. Members only. Site set in and around a walled garden, sheltered by mature trees and flowering shrubs. Laundry, veg prep area. Playframe. Toilet block with privacy cubicles. Motorhome waste. Gas supplies. Dog walk nearby. Suitable for families. Peaceful off-peak. NCN cycle route 5m. Advance booking advisable all times. Part hard-standings; steel awning pegs required. Blair Drummond Safari Park and Trossachs nearby. Open March-January. ✫✫✫✫ **NCC. 88T. MC.** ♁ ☎ ☈

Blairlogie

(0.5m). **Witches Craig Caravan & Camping Park, Blairlogie, Stirling FK9 5PX.** *01786 474947.* info@witchescraig.co.uk. www.witchescraig.co.uk. Owner: A & V Stephen. On A91, 3m E of Stirling. David Bellamy Gold Conservation Award and National Loo of the Year awards. Peaceful site situated below picturesque Ochil Hills. Suitable touring base. Modern facilities. Children's play park. Open April 1-October 31. ✫✫✫✫ **BH&HPA. 60T. 20MC.** ♁ ☎ ☈ ∅

Callander

(12m). **Balquhidder Braes Caravan & Camping Park, Balquhidder Station, Lochearnhead, Callander, Stirling FK19 8NX.** *01567 830293.* reastland@tiscali.co.uk. www.balquhidderbraes.co.uk. Owner: Mr & Mrs R Eastland. 1.5 from Lochearnhead take A84 Stirling road, site on left-hand side. From Strathyre, towards Lochearn 2m, site on right. Beautiful scenery. Restaurant beside site. Families welcome. Suitable touring base. Adjacent to route 7 cycleway and Rob Roy Way. Open March-November. ✫✫✫✫ **BH&HPA. 35T. 10MC. 10S. 5H.** ♁ ☎ ☈

(1m). **Callander Holiday Park, Invertrossachs Road, Callander, Stirling FK17 8HW.** *01877 330265.* tony.mower@virgin.net. Owner: Mr T Mower. Peaceful park in woodland setting. Showers. Free fishing and children's play park. Golf course, swimming pool, pony trekking, sailing all nearby. Open March 15-October 31. **BH&HPA. 120S.** ♁ ☈

(1m). **Gart Caravan Park, Stirling Road, Callander, Stirling FK17 8LE.** *01877 330002.* tony.mower@virgin.net. Owner: Mr Tony Mower. Off A84, on left. Spacious park with level grass pitches. Showers. Free fishing and children's play area. Golf, swimming pool, pony trekking, sailing nearby. Open April-October. ✫✫✫✫✫ **BH&HPA. 128T. MC. 70S.** ♁ ☎ ☈

(1m). **Keltie Bridge Caravan Park, Callander, Stirling FK17 8LQ.** *01877 330606.* stay@keltiebridge.co.uk. Owner: Cambusmore Estate. Callander, Perthshire FK17 8LJ. On A84, between Doune and Callander. Quiet riverside location, close to Callander in scenic Trossachs. Showers. Golf, sports centre 1m. Open April 1-October 31. ✫✫✫✫ **BH&HPA. 50T. 50MC. 20S.** ♁ ☎ ☈ ∅

Fintry

(1.5m). **Balgair Castle Caravan Park, Overglinns, Fintry, Stirling G63 0LP.** *01360 860283.* admin@balgaircastle.co.uk. www.balgaircastle.com. Owner: C Lamb. Riverside country park. Bar, restaurant, children's play area. Outdoor swimming pool. Open March-November. ✫✫✫✫ **BH&HPA. 63T. 140S. 10H.** ♁ ☎ ☈ ☈

Killin

(1m). Clachan Caravan Club Site, c/o Maragowan Caravan Club Site, Aberfeldy Road, Killin, Stirling FK21 8TX. *01567 820245*. www.caravanclub.co.uk. Owner: The Caravan Club. East Grinstead Club, East Grinstead House, East Grinstead, West Sussex RH19 1UA. See website for standard directions to site. Members only Several open pitching areas tucked away quietly in woodland with wild flowers. Wide range of birdlife. Own sanitation service point. Fishing, golf and NCN cycle route nearby. Dog walk on site. Good area for walking. Peaceful off-peak. Open March-October. **NCC. 45T. MC.** ♒ ⊟

Glen Dochart Caravan Park, Luib, Crianlarich, Killin, Stirling FK20 8QT. *01567 820637*. info@glendochart-caravanpark.co.uk. www.glendochart-caravanpark.co.uk. Owner: Mr McCready. Calor Gas stockist. Tennis, golf and bowling available in nearby Killin. Open March-October. ☆☆☆☆☆ **BH&HPA. 45T. MC. 40S. 3H.** ♒ ⊟ ⅏ ⅃

(2m). High Creagan Caravan Site, Killin, Stirling FK21 8TX. *01567 820449*. Owner: Mr A Kennedy. On the A827 Aberfeldy to Killin road. Open March-October. **15T. 15MC. 3H.** ♒ ⊟

(0.25m). Maragowan Caravan Club Site, Aberfeldy Road, Killin, Stirling FK21 8TN. *01567 820245*. www.caravanclub.co.uk. Owner: The Caravan Club. East Grinstead House, East Grinstead, West Sussex RH19 1UA. See website for standard directions to site. Site is a suitable family holiday base, set on one bank of the river Lochay, and within walking distance of shops and restaurants of Killin. Hard-standings. Motorhome waste point. Toilet block and laundry. Calor Gas. Veg prep. Playframe. Salmon and trout fishing. Non-members welcome. Advance booking essential bank holidays and June-August, and advised for September. Suitable for families. Privacy cubicles. Dog walk nearby. Peaceful off peak. Good area for walking, golf and NCN cycle route within 5m, water sports nearby. Open March-October. ☆☆☆☆☆ **BH&HPA. 100T. MC.** ♒ ⊟ ⅏

Rowardennan

(3m). Cashel Caravan & Camping Site, Forestry Commission (Forest Holidays), Rowardennan, Stirling G63 0AW. *01360 870234*. fe.holidays@forestry.gsi.gov.uk. www.forestholidays.co.uk. Owner: Forestry Commission (Forest Holidays). 231 Corstorphine Road, Edinburgh EH12 7AT. Off the B837, Drymen-Rowardennan road, N of Balmaha. On the shores of Loch Lomond, Cashel is suitable base for boating, cycling and walking. West Highland Way passes the site entrance. Brochure request Line: 01313 340066. Open March-October. ☆☆☆☆ **BH&HPA. 250T. MC.** ♒ ⊟ ⅏ ⅃

Strathyre

Immervoulin Caravan & Camping Park, Strathyre, Stirling FK18 8NJ. *01877 384285*. immervoulin@ freename. co.uk. www.immervoulin-caravan-camping-park.co.uk. Owner: Mr David Richards. 9m N of Callander, with clearly marked access from the A84. Situated in an area of picturesque beauty alongside the river Balvaig. Within easy walking distance of village (PO). Cycle hire on site. Canoe hire in village. Fishing on river and Loch Lubnaig. Water sports centre in Lochearnhead. Open March-October. ☆☆☆ **56T. MC.** ♒ ⊟ ⅏ ⅃

Thornhill

Mains Farm, Kippen Road, Thornhill, Stirling FK8 3QB. *01786 850605*. gsteedman@lineone.net. Owner: Mr J Steedman. From M9 J10 take A84 for 6m. Then A873 for 3m. In Thornhill village L on to B822, site on R. Five acres with scenic views, suitable touring centre for Stirling, Loch Lomond and Trossachs. Golf, tennis, swimming pool, cinema, shopping centre, all within 5-7m. Open April 1-October 31. **34T. 34MC. 2S. 2H.** ♒ ⊟ ⅏ ⅃

WESTERN ISLES

Isle of Harris

(5m). Laig House & Minch View Caravan Site, 10 Drimshadder, Isle of Harris, Western Isles HS3 3DX. *01859 511207*. Owner: Mr Angus Macdonald. 4.5m S of Tarbert on coast. Turn off A859, along the Golden Road to Drimshadder. Quiet, secluded site between loch and sea. Near village shops. Free fishing. Centrally located for touring the isles. Walking and hill climbing. Mobile shop calls weekly. Open April-October. **10T. 3MC.** ♒ ⊟

Isle of Lewis

Eilean Fraoich Camping Site, North Shawbost, Isle of Lewis, Western Isles HS2 9BQ. *01851 710504*. eilean fraoich@btinternet.com. 19m from Stornoway. Open May-October. ☆☆☆ **10T. MC.** ♒ ⊟ ⅏

Laxdale Holiday Park, 6 Laxdale Lane, Stornaway, Isle of Lewis, Western Isles HS2 0DR. *01851 703234/706966*. info@laxdaleholidaypark.com. www.laxdaleholidaypark.com. Owner: Gordon Macleod. From Stornaway ferry terminal take A857 for 1.5m, turn left just before Laxdale river, park is 100yd on left-hand side. Quiet, family-run park in peaceful, tree-lined surroundings. Modern facilities including bunkhouse. Suitable base for touring the Isles. Open March 31-October 31. ☆☆☆☆ **6T. 6MC. 6S. 4H.** ♒ ⊟ ⅏

ANGLESEY

Amlwch

(2m). Plas Eilian Caravan Park, Llaneilian, Amlwch, Anglesey LL68 9LS. *01407 830323*. Owner: Mr T A Owen. A5025 from Menai to Benllech & Amlwch. Bypass Penysarn. Turn right at filling station. Plas Eilian is next to the church. Site is close to the sea, with walks through the farm along the cliffs. Open April-October. **14T. 2MC. 2H.** ♒

(1.5m). Point Lynas Caravan Park, Llaneilian, Amlwch, Anglesey LL68 9LT. *01407 831130/01248 852423*. peter@pantysaer.freeserve.co.uk. Owner: Mr P & M Hoyland. Pant-y-Saer Caravan Park, Tynygongl, Benllech, Anglesey LL74 8SD. From Anglesey Mowers on A5025, 1.5m in seaward direction, 200yd from Porth Eilian cove. Quiet site overlooking the sea by Point Lynas, fishing, walking, swimming. Modern facilites block with laundrette, showers etc. Shops 1.5m. Golf course 3m. Open March 1-October 31. ☆☆☆☆ **BH&HPA. 12T. MC. 44S.** ♒ ⊟ ⌀

(3.5m). Pwll Coch Caravans, Lligwy Beach, Dulas, Amlwch, Anglesey LL70 9HQ. *01407 830254*. Owner: Mr R M & Mrs C E Rowlands. Red Shell Garage, Amlwch, Anglesey LL68 9NU. Off A5025, Pentraeth to Almwch, about 1m N of Moelfre. Gently sloping site with views of Lligwy Bay. 3 golf courses in area, nearest 4m. Shopping centre and cinema 15m. Open Easter-October. **BH&HPA. 85S.** ♒

(6m). Riverside Caravan Site, Llanfechell, Amlwch, Anglesey. 01407 711306. Owner: Mr R Copeland. 8m down A5025 from Valley crossroads to Llanfechell. Open March 14-October 31. **30S.** ⚫

(5m). Tyddyn Isaf Caravan Park, Lligwy Bay, Dulas, Amlwch, Anglesey LL70 9PQ. 01248 410203. enquiries@ tyddynisaf.demon.co.uk. www.tyddynisaf.demon.co.uk. Owner: Mr & Mrs Hunt. Off A5025 through Benllech up to Brynrefail village, turn right at phone box towards Lligwy beach. Private path to beach. Open March 1-October 31. ✰✰✰✰✰ **BH&HPA. 40T. 5MC. 56S.** ⚫⚫⚫⚫⚫

Beaumaris

(1.5m). Kingsbridge Caravan Park, Llanfaes, Beaumaris, Anglesey LL58 8LR. 01248 490636/07774842199. info@kings bridgecaravanpark.co.uk. www.kingsbridgecaravanpark.co.uk. Owner: Mr & Mrs A M Bate. Drive through Beaumaris, past castle, turn third L after 1.5m at first crossroads. Quiet, family park in a rural location, close to beaches, golf, fishing, walking. David Bellamy Gold Conservation Award. Open March 1-October 31. ✰✰ **BH&HPA. 48T. 4MC. 27S. 2H.** ⚫⚫⚫

Benllech Bay

Golden Sunset Holiday, Beach Road, Benllech Bay, Anglesey LL74 8SW. 01248 852345. Owner: Mr R J Hewitt. Site entrance at Benllech Bay off A5025 from Bangor, towards Amlwch. At the crossroads in Benllech. Turn R and the park is immediately on the L. Centre of village for shops, PO, doctors, tennis courts, bowls, golf. Elevated cliff-side site with views over the bay. 2 new luxury chalets also for hire. Open April-October. ✰✰ **40T. 50MC. 240S. 7H.** ⚫⚫⚫

Benllech

(1.5m). Ad Astra Caravan Park, Llangefni Road, Brynteg, Benllech, Anglesey LL78 7JH. 01248 853283. brian@brynteg53.fsnet.co.uk. www.adastracaravan.co.uk. Owner: Mrs I Iddon & Mr B Iddon. From Benllech take B5108 to California Hotel, turn L park 0.25m on R. All shops, doctor within 1.5m. Garage and golf course 0.5m. Open March 1-October 31. ✰✰✰✰✰ **BH&HPA. 12T. 12MC. 38S. 1H.** ⚫⚫⚫⚫

(0.5m). Bodafon Caravan & Camping Site, Benllech Bay, Bodafon, Benllech, Anglesey LL 74 8RU. 01248 852417. robert@bodafonpark.fsnet.co.uk. www.bodafonpark.co.uk. Owner: Mr & Mrs R G Roberts. Through the village of Benllech on A5025, site is 0.5m on L. Big yellow house. Quiet, family site near shops and beaches. Convenient for most facilities. Suitable base for touring Anglesey and Snowdonia. Golf course 5m. Beach 0.75m. Open March 1-October 31. ✰✰✰ **BH&HPA. 50T. MC. 20S.** ⚫⚫⚫

(0.5m). Pant-Y-Saer Caravan Park, Tynygongl, Benllech, Anglesey LL74 8SD. 01248 852423. peter@pantysaer. freeserve.co.uk. Owner: Moya & Peter Hoyland. Off Llangefni road, turn L along lane under Scots pine trees. Follow sign for Pant Y Saer farm. Beach 0.5m. Golf, shopping centre, doctors, PO within 1m. Coastal walks, quiet holiday park. Open March 1-January 6. **BH&HPA. 30S.** ⚫⚫

(2m). Penparc Caravan Site, Brynteg, Benllech, Anglesey. 01248 852500. Owner: Mr P Charles. On junction of the B5110 and B5108. Unlimited camping. Fishing and golf nearby. Open March 1-October 31. ✰ **17T. MC. 22S.** ⚫⚫

(2m). Penrhos Caravan Club Site, Brynteg, Benllech, Anglesey LL78 7JH. 01248 852617. www.caravanclub.co.uk. Owner: The Caravan Club. East Grinstead House, East Grinstead, West Sussex RH19 1UA. See website for standard directions to site. 5mins drive to safe, sandy beach. Close to a farm trail, bird sanctuary and sea zoo. Non-members welcome. Golf course within 5m. Play area and play equipment. Some hard-standings, part sloping. Toilet block with privacy cubicles. Laundry. Calor Gas and Campingaz, baby and toddler washroom. Motorhome service point, veg preparation area. Dog walk nearby. Water sports, good walking NCN cycle route all nearby. Suitable for families. Peaceful off-peak. Open March-October. ✰✰✰✰ **NCC. 93T. MC.** ⚫⚫⚫

(0.5m). Plas Uchaf Caravan & Camping Park, Benllech Bay, Benllech, Anglesey LL74 8NU. 01407 763012. Owner: Evans Partnership. Situated off A5025 SP on B5108. 0.5m from Benllech. Well-sheltered and level park within 1m of beach. Hot showers, hair-dryers, and dishwashing facilities. Freezers. Play area. Patio seating and tables. Dog walk. Tarmacadam roads with street lights. Tradesmen call. Open March-October. **80T. 8MC. 25S.** ⚫⚫

Brynsiencyn

(0.5m). Fron Caravan and Camping Park, Brynsiencyn, Anglesey LL61 6TX. 01248 430310. mail@froncaravanpark. co.uk. www.froncaravanpark.co.uk. Owner: Mr G & E & M Geldard. On A4080. 6.5m SW of Menai Bridge. Cross Britannia Bridge, then first slip road marked Llanfairpwllgwyn, then L on to A4080 to Brynsiencyn. Site is 0.5m beyond village on right-hand side. Laundry room. Public telephone. Gas. Hot showers. Heated outdoor swimming pool. Adventure playground. Open Easter-September 30. ✰✰✰✰ **39T. 10MC.** ⚫⚫⚫⚫

Brynteg

(0.25m). Garnedd Touring Site, Lon Bryn Mair, Brynteg, Anglesey LL78 8QA. 01248 853240. mmpicomac@aol.co.uk. www.garnedd.com. Owner: Mrs S Kirk & Mr M McCann. Take A5025 after Britannia bridge. Pass through Pentraeath and der-estriction signs, turn L on to unclassified road at layby, SP Llanbedrgoch. In 2m turn L on to B5108, 1st L. Site on R in 0.5m at orange signs. Dishwashing and laundry facilities. Winter storage available. Open March 1-October. **NCC. 20T. MC. 1S. 1H.** ⚫⚫

Cemaes Bay

(1.5m). Bryn Mechell, Llanfechell, Cemaes Bay, Anglesey LL68 0RG. Owner: Mrs V Hill. c/o Barton Park Homes, The Bungalow, Westgate, Morecambe LA3 3BA. **12S.** ✿ ⚫

Cerrigheinwen

(5m). Tregof, Bodorgan, Cerrigheinwen, Anglesey LL62 5EH. 01407 720315. Owner: Mr H W Davies. Off A5. All mod cons. Laundry. AA 3 pennants. Open April 1-October 31. **40T. 8MC.** ⚫⚫⚫

Dulas

(1m). Capel Elen, Lligwy, Dulas, Anglesey LL70 9PQ. 01248 410670. john@capelelen.co.uk. www.capelelen.co.uk. Owner: Mr & Mrs J Howl. On A5025 to village of Brynrefail, turn off opposite craft shop, park is 300yd on left-hand side. 2m from Moelfre. Fishing, coastal path, golf courses nearby. Shops, etc within 3m. Open March 1-October 31. **BH&HPA. 8T. 2MC. 45S.** ⚫⚫

Melin Rhos Caravan & Camping Site, Lligwy Bay, Dulas, Anglesey LL70 9HQ. *01248 852417.* robert@bodafonpark. fsnet.co.uk. www.bodafonpark.co.uk. Owner: R & S Roberts. Bodafon Caravan Park, Benllech, Anglesey LL74 8RU. Off A5025 Bangor to Amlwch. Turn L at Moelfre roundabout, down hill, first right. Site is at bottom of hill, before bridge. 5m from Benllech. 2m from Moelfre. Close to beach and good walks. 2m from nearest village. Golf course 5m. Open March 1-October 31. ✫✫ **30T. 30MC. 60S.** ♈ 🏥 ⌀

Minffordd, Lligwy, Dulas, Anglesey LL70 9HJ. *01248 410678.* enq@minfford-holidays.com. www.minfford-holidays.com. Owner: Mr M Hughes-Roberts. Off A5025 Benllech Bay to Amlwch. Lligwy 1m. Moelfre 2m. 6m from Amlwch. Garden park near sandy beach of Lligwy with parking alongside each caravan. Local facilities include golf, sailing, fishing, riding and sports centres. Dogs on leads by arrangement. Dragon Award and some caravans equipped for physically disabled guests. Winner 'Wales in Bloom' 2002/2003/2004. Separate field for tourers. 9-hole golf course 3m, 18-hole golf course 7m. 14m to Bangor. Open March-November. ✫✫✫✫✫ **BH&HPA. T. 10S. 5H.** ♈ 🏥 ♿

Gaerwen

(0.25m). Mornest, Pentre Berw, Gaerwen, Anglesey LL60 6HU. *01248 421725.* Owner: Miss NR & DM Jones. J7 off A55, follow signs for caravan park, 1m through village of Gaerwen. Dairy produce delivered daily. Local shops within 500yd. Winter storage arranged off site. Laundry facilities. PH/restaurant on site. Open March 1-November 30. ✫✫✫ **BH&HPA. 45T. 5MC. 15S.** ♈ 🏥

Holyhead

(2m). Bagnol Caravan Site, Ravenspoint Road, Trearddur Bay, Holyhead, Anglesey L L65 2AZ. *01407 860223.* Owner: Mr & Mrs S H Parry. Off A5, B45 to Trearddur Bay, turn left into Ravenspoint road, park 100yd on left. Site personally supervised. Open March-November. **BH&HPA. 13T. 30MC. 150S.** ♈ 🏥 ♿

(0.5m). Cliff Caravan Site, Trearddur Bay, Holyhead, Anglesey LL65 2UR. *01407 860634.* Owner: Anglesey Sales Ltd. Open March 1-October 30. **30T. MC. 100S. 5H.** ♈ 🏥

(0.5m). Gwynfair Caravan Site, Ravenspoint Road, Trearddur Bay, Holyhead, Anglesey LL65 2AX. *01407 860289.* Owner: Romward Properties Ltd. Court House, Beckford, Nr Tewkesbury, Gloucestershire GL20 7AD. Take first left after Beach Hotel, follow road to very top, site is on the left. Facilities on site include club, laundrette and showers. Open March 1-October 31. **BH&HPA. 30T. 3MC. 145S. 4H.** ♈ 🏥

▶ ▶ ▶

ty newydd

LEISURE PARK

Proprietors: Mike & Cathi

Llanbedgroch, Anglesey, Gwynedd LL76 8TZ

Tel: 01248 450677 Fax: 01248 450711

This small, select, family-run park is ideally situated for Benllech Bay with extensive views of Snowdonia. Facilities include licensed country club serving meals for the family, well-equipped shop, excellent toilet facilities, free showers, disabled toilet, baby changing room, laundry room, children's playground and games room, heated outdoor swimming pool, health centre with spa, sauna, pool, electric hook-ups and luxury fully-equipped caravans for hire. Dogs on leads are welcomed.
Sailing, water skiing, fishing, climbing, walking, 9-hole golf within 1 mile, pony trekking and safe sandy beaches are available on the island.

(9m). Penrhyn Bay Caravan Site, Penrhyn Farm, Llanwrog, Holyhead, Anglesey LL65 4YG. *01407 730496/730411.* penrhn.bay@btinternet.com. www.penrhynbay.com. Owner: E T & O Williams. A55 to Anglesey, exit 3. A5025 through Llanfachraeth, then 1st left, SP Penrhyn. Through farm to caravan park. Indoor heated swimming pool. Tennis court. Showers. Laundrette. Play area. Open Easter-end October. ✫✫✫✫ **BH&HPA. 100T. 10MC. 80S.** ♈ 🏥 ♿ 💤

(1m). Porthdafarch (South), Holyhead, Anglesey. *01407 760308.* Owner: Anglesey Caravan Parks Ltd. Off A5. Open mid March-October 31. **43S.** ♈

(10m). Sandy Beach Caravan Site, Llanfwrog, Holyhead, Anglesey LL65 4YH. *01407 730302.* sales@sandybeach.co.uk. www.sandybeach.co.uk. Owner: Mr S J Seymour Jones. A5025, after Llanfacraeth turn left and follow signs for Sandy Beach/Penrhyn. Site adjoins safe, sandy beach. Picturesque views and walks. Suitable for water sports. Licensed cafe, showers and laundry. Open April-October. **40T. 10MC. 83S. 2H.** ♈ 🏥 ♿ 💤

(3m). The Lee Caravan Park, Trearddur Bay, Ravenspoint, Holyhead, Anglesey. *01407 860485.* Owner: D E & D M Williams. Off A5. Slipway. Open March-November. **150S. 15H.** ♈ 💤

(1m). Valley of the Rocks Caravan & Camping Park, Porthdafarch Road, Treaddur Bay, Holyhead, Anglesey LL65 2LP. *01407 765787.* Owner: Anglesey Caravan Parks Ltd. Follow A55 across Anglesey to where road terminates at roundabout. 1st L at roundabout then 1st R between two PHs (The Foresters and The Angel). Follow road for about 1m until you see SP for caravan park. Turn L into site, then fork right. Reception is on L at site shop. Licensed club. 10 mins walk from beach. Toilet block. Open March-October. **11T. 14MC. 34S. 4H.** ♈ 🏥 💤

Llanbedrgoch

(0.5m). Ty Newydd Leisure Park, Brynteg Road, Llanbedrgoch, Isle of Anglesey LL76 8TZ. *01248 450677.* mike@tynewydd.com. www.tynewydd.com. Owner: Mike & Cathi Monger. Off A5025 Isle of Anglesey. Within 1m of Benllech. Club. Swimming pool. Health club. Restaurant. Golf course 0.5m. Fishing 1m. Open March-October. ✫✫✫✫ **BH&HPA. 45T. 10MC. 64S. 4H.** ♈ 🏥 ♿ 💤 ⌀

Llanfairpwll

(2m). Plas Coch Caravan & Leisure Park, Llanedwen, Llanfairpwll, Anglesey LL61 6EJ. *01248 714346.* On A4080 follow National Trust sign Plas Newydd park next estate, turn L at crossroads. 200 acres of park and farmland. 0.5m frontage on Menai Straits. Slipway. Lounge bars. Windsurfing and water skiing. Spacious tent and touring area. Several good golf courses and restaurants in area. Pitches available. Fishing, sea and freshwater, nearby. Open March 1-October 31. **50T. 20MC. 180S.** ♈ 🏥 ⌀

Marianglas

Cae Mawr Caravan Club Site, Llangefni Road, Marianglas, Anglesey LL73 8NY. *01248 853737.* www.caravanclub.co.uk. Owner: The Caravan Club. East Grinstead House, East Grinstead, West Sussex RH19 1UA. See website for standard directions to site. 2m from Benllech. Chemical toilet emptying point. No toilet block. Sea fishing and boating. Safe, sandy beaches. Non-members welcome. Golf course 5m. Motorhome waste point. Gas. Dog walk. Open March-October. **NCC. 76T. MC.** ♈ 🏥

(2m). **Home Farm Caravan Park, Marianglas, Anglesey LL73 8PH.** *01248 410614.* enq@homefarm-anglesey.co.uk. www.homefarm-anglesey.co.uk. Owner: Mr & Mrs G P Jones. On A5025. Amlwch road keep L at roundabout, 1m beyond Benllech, park is 300yd on L after church. Showers, laundrette, indoor playroom, sport games field, tennis court on site. Golf course, fishing 2m. Cinema 13m. Open April-October. ✩✩✩✩✩ **BH&HPA. 80T. 20MC. 84S.** ⊞ ⚲ & ⚑ ∅

Pigeon House Caravan Park, Marianglas, Anglesey LL73 8NY. *01248 853714.* Owners: Parciau Caravans Ltd. Off B5110 in Marianglas, 2m from Benllech. Beaches of Anglesey and mountains of Snowdonia all within easy reach. Open April 1-October 31. ✩✩✩✩ **BH&HPA. NCC. 275S.** ⊞ ⚲

Moelfre

(2m.). **Ty'n Rhos, Lligwy Bay, Moelfre, Anglesey LL72 8NL.** *01248 852417.* robert@bodafonpark.fsnet.co.uk. www.mysite-freeserve.com/bodafonpark. Owner: RG & SV Robert. Bodafon, Benllech, Anglesey LL74 8NU. Off A5025. Proceed along A5025 to Moelfre roundabout. R into Moelfre. First L by Non Design Warehouse, proceed for 2m, site is on R, 50yd passing lane leading down to Lligwy Beach. Within 0.5m of sandy beach. Washing machine and dryer available. Convenient for many facilities. Good walks nearby. AA 3 pennants. Open March-October. **30T. 10MC. 79S. 1H.** ⊞ ⚲ ∅

Newborough

(0.5m). **Awelfryn Caravan Site, Newborough, Anglesey LL61 6SG.** *01248 440230.* awelfryncp@aol.com. Owner: Mrs H Dawson. On A4080 near Llanddwyn Island. Open March 1-October 31. **12T.** ⊞ ⚲

Pentraeth

(2m). **Clai Mawr Caravan Park, Pentraeth, Anglesey LL75 8DX.** *01248 450467.* claimawr@talk21.com. Owner: Mr S N Morris. Off A5025, Bangor to Amlwch. Third turning on right after PH, The Bull. Bottle gas. Open March 1-October 31. ✩✩✩ **NCC. 8T. MC. 32S. 1H.** ⊞ ⚲ &

(0.75m). **Rhos Caravan Park, Rhos Farm, Pentraeth, Anglesey LL75 8DZ.** *01248 450214.* Owner: Mr A P Owen. On A5025 on the L after Bull Hotel. Park is 0.25m N of Pentraeth. Children's play area. Flat sheltered fields (grass and hedges). 10mins walk to Red Wharf Bay. Golf course nearby 2.5m. AA 3 pennants. Open March 15-October 30. **BH&HPA. 50T. 10MC. 66S. 6H.** ⊞ ⚲

(2.5m). **St Davids Park, Red Wharf Bay, Pentraeth, Anglesey LL75 8RJ.** *01248 852341.* paul@stdavidspark.com. www. stdavidspark.com. Owner: Ann Jones & Mary Bennett. Off A5025 Pentraeth to Benllech. Club. Children's room. Playground. Laundrette. Private beach. Slipway and boat park. Dogs allowed on residents but not on camping. Electric hook-ups for motorhomes. Open March 1-October 31. ✩✩✩✩ **BH&HPA. 130MC. 180S.** & ⚲

Rhosneigr

(0.5m). **Bodfan Farm, Rhosneigr, Anglesey LL64 5XA.** *01407 810706.* wap@llynfor.freeserve.co.uk. Owner: A Pritchard. Llynfor, Rhosneigr, Anglesey LL64 5XA. A55 to A4080, next to primary school in Rhosneigr. Quiet, family site near lake and sea. Showers, shaving points and dryers. Shops, PO, PH within 0.5m. Golf course, horse riding, tennis court, bowling green, water sports in village. Open April-September. **10T. 20MC.** ⊞ ⚲

(2m). **Plas Caravan Park, Llanfaelog, Rhosneigr, Anglesey LL63 5TU.** *01407 810234.* gail@plascaravanpark.co.uk. www.plascaravanpark.co.uk. Owner: Mal & Gail Waugh. NE of

Rhosneigr. East from Llanfaelog. Rural park within 1m of beaches. Open March-October. ✩✩✩✩ **BH&HPA. 67S.** ⊞

(0.3m). **Shore Side Caravan Park, Station Road, Rhosneigr, Anglesey LL64 5QX.** *01407 810279.* shoreside@amserve.net. www.shoresidecamping.co.uk. Owner: Mr A J Carnall. L off A55, on to the A4080, Rhosneigr road, opposite Anglesey golf club. Children welcome. Riding centre on site, panoramic views of Snowdonia. Days visits to Ireland. Local amenities include bowling green, swimming, windsurfing, fishing, tennis, plane spotters RAF valley. Restaurants and bars nearby. Park established in 1925. Open March-October. **50T. 20MC. 60S.** ⊞ ⚲

(0.5m). **Ty Hen, Station Road, Rhosneigr, Anglesey LL64 5QZ.** *01407 810331.* bernardtyhen@hotmail.com. www.tyhen. com. Owner: Mr & Mrs B J Summerfield. A55 across Anglesey, take A4080 to Rhosneigr. Entrance adjacent to railway station, near low bridge. Heated swimming pool, coarse fishing, playpark, wt/gym, sauna. Seaside Beach award. Sports, sea and coarse fishing, surfing, sub-aqua, tennis, golf and bowls all local. David Bellamy Gold Conservation Award. Open March 20-October 31. ✩✩✩ **BH&HPA. 38T. 42S. 1H.** ⊞ ⚲ &

Trearddur Bay

Tyn Rhos Camping Site, Ravenspoint Road, Trearddur Bay, Isle of Anglesey LL65 2AX. *01407 860369.* Owner: Mr D W Williams. 3m from Holyhead. A55 to J3 for Valley A5. L at lights B4545 to Trearddur Bay. L on to Ravenspoint Road. About 1m to shared entrance, take L branch. Family-run rural site with modern facilities, within minutes of seaside resort. Coastal walks, birdwatching and climbing. Water sports, from fishing to diving, local golf course and horse riding. Ferries to Ireland 3m. Local history and attractions for all tastes. Open March 1-October 31. ✩✩ **T. MC.** ⊞ ⚲ & ⚑

Tyn Towyn Caravan Park, Llon St Ffraid, Trearddur Bay, Anglesey LL65 2YS. *01407 860803.* Owner: Mr & Mrs S H Parry. Off A5 Valley Road, B454 to Trearddur Bay. On main road in centre of village overlooking the sea and main beach. 1m to golf club and leisure centre. 2m to Holyhead. Personally supervised. Open March-January. **BH&HPA. 50S.** ⊞ ∅

Tynygongl

(2m). **Bryn Awel Caravan Park, Pentraeth, Benllech Bay, Tynygongl, Anglesey LL75 8DZ.** *01248 450801.* Owner: Mr & Mrs A W Owen. On A5025. Open March 1-October 31. . **BH&HPA. 45S.** ⊞

Bwlch Holiday Park, Benllech Bay, Tynygongl, Anglesey LL74 8RF. *01248 852914.* Owners: Lloyds Caravan Sites Co Ltd. On A5025, then B5108 for 1.5m. Benllech 1m. Mains water and electricity in static caravans. Play area. Laundrette. Public phone. Showers. Open March 1-October 31. **BH&HPA. NCC. 8T. 5MC. 52S.** ⚲ ∅

BLAENAU GWENT

Tredegar

(2m). **Parc Bryn Bach, The Countryside Centre, Merthyr Road, Tredegar, Blaenau Gwent NP22 3AY.** *01495 711816.* parcbrynbach@blaenau-gwent.gov.uk. Owner: Blaenau Gwent County Borough Council. SP off A465, Heads of the Valley road. Follow signs for Parc Bryn Bach. Site nestling in woodland on 400-acre country park overlooking lake. Telephone, shower block, laundry and washing facilities in Countryside Centre, with restaurant, gift shop, tourist information and reception. Angling, water-skiing, windsurfing and other activities available on site. Suitable base for exploring Brecon Beacons and South Wales Valleys. ✫✫ **30T. MC.** ✿ ⊦ 🖰 &

BRIDGEND

Bridgend
Happy Valley Caravan Park, Wig Fach, Porthcawl, Bridgend, Bridgend CF32 0NG. *01656 782144.* Owner: Happy Valley (Porthcawl) Holiday Camps Ltd. On A4106, Bridgend to Porthcawl. 1.5m from Porthcawl. Open April 1-September 30. **BH&HPA. NCC. 60T. 20MC. 350S.** ⊦ 🖰 🗲

(2m). Kenfig Pool Caravan Park, Porthcawl, Bridgend, Bridgend CF33 4PT. *01656 740079.* Owner: Eastville Caravan Services. Off J39 M4, then B4283 via North Connelly. Site overlooks the Kenfig Pool and dunes. Set amid local nature reserve, which covers 1200 acres to the beach and Bristol Channel coast. Open March 1-November 30. **BH&HPA. 4T. MC. 75S.** ⊦ 🖰

(2m). Trecco Bay Holiday Park, Bay View Road, Porthcawl, Bridgend, Bridgend CF36 5NG. *01656 782103.* enquiries@ parkdeanholidays.co.uk. www.parkdeanholidays.co.uk. Owner: Parkdean Holidays Plc. 2nd floor One Gosforth Park Way, Gosforth Business Park, Newcastle-upon-Tyne NE12 8ET. Off M4, Bridgend to Port Talbot. 0.5m from Porthcawl. Cinema. Indoor heated fun pool. Sports and leisure centre. Licensed bars. Family entertainment centre. Bowling. Laser games. Jungle Jims. Children's clubs, 2 mins walk to beach. Dodgems. Adventure golf. Diner. Restaurant. Open February-November. ✫✫✫ **BH&HPA. NCC. 2041S. 1800H.** ⊦ & 🗲

Porthcawl
(1m). Brodawel Camping Park, Moor Lane, Nottage, Porthcawl, Bridgend CF36 3EJ. *01656 783231.* Owner: Mr M Battrick. M4 J37, along A4229 for 2m to Porthcawl, SP Moor Lane. Modern, clean site central for touring. Off-licence, games room and public telephone. Discount on weekly bookings in low season. Storage available. Blue flag beach 1m. Open April 1-October 31. **100T. 10MC.** ⊦ 🖰 & 🗲

CAERPHILLY

Bargoed
(4m). Parc Cwm Darran, Deri, Bargoed, Caerphilly CF81 9NR. *01443 875557.* honeym@caerphilly.gov.uk. www.caer philly.gov.uk. Owner: Caerphilly Country Borough Coucil. Council Offices, Pontllanfraith, Blackwood NP11 2YW. Between Deri and Fochriw on unclassified road between A469 and A465. In Parc Cwm Darran Country Park. Visitor centre, coffee shop. Circular walks, coarse fishing lake. 5m cycle track. Events throughout the year. Shop, PO 1m. Showers. Open April 1-September 30. **30T. MC.** ⊦ 🖰 &

CARDIFF

Cardiff
(0.5m). Cardiff Pontcanna Caravan Park, Pontcanna Sophia Gardens Close, Cardiff, Cardiff CF1 9JJ. *029 20398362.* www.cardiff.gov.uk. Owner: Cardiff City Council. Heath Park, Heath, Cardiff CF4 4EP. Approaching from A48 (T) take a turning into Cathedral Road and turn L in to Sophia Close. Past National Sports Centre, continue for 200yd to site. Local shops, PO, doctors, garages all within 200yd. Dogs allowed on leads. 10mins walk to city centre and Millenium Stadium. ✫✫✫ **70T. MC.** ✿ ⊦ 🖰 &

CARMARTHENSHIRE

Burry Port
(0.5m). Shoreline Caravan & Chalet Park, Burry Port, Carmarthenshire SA16 0HD. *01554 832657.* Owner: S & M Hall & Sons. Shoreline Leisure Park. Leave A484 for B4311, follow signs to harbour and caravan park. Bar. Laundrette. Showers. Playground. Family room. Regular entertainment. Cafe. Beach. Open March 1-November 30. **15T. MC. 200S.** ⊦ 🖰

Carmarthen
Ants Hill Caravan and Camping Park, Laugharne, Carmarthen, Carmarthenshire SA33 4QN. *01994 427293.* antshillcaravanpark@tiscali.co.uk. On A4066, St Clears to Laugharne. Suitable base for inland and coastal touring. Historic home town of Dylan Thomas and near the famous sands of Pendine. Clubhouse. Laundry facilities. Outdoor heated swimming pool. Play room and play area. AA 3 pennants. RAC appointed. Managers: Mr & Mrs J Downes. Open March 25-October 31. ✫✫✫ **BH&HPA. 60T. MC. 60S. 3H.** ⊦ 🖰 🗲

(14m). Broadway Caravan Park, Laugharne, Carmarthen, Carmarthenshire. *01994 427272.* Owner: Mr C Davies. On A4066. Open April 1-October 30. **6T. 6MC. 8S. 3H.** ⊦ 🖰

(1m). Pant Farm Caravan & Camping Park, Llangunnor Road, Carmarthen, Carmarthenshire SA31 2HY. *01267 235665.* Owner: H V & E Jones. Off M4 on B4300. Convenient, flat, sheltered location. Tents welcome. Walking distance to station and town. Near Botanical Garden of Wales. Shops, PO, doctor, golf course, fishing all within 1m. **30T. MC.** ✿ ⊦ 🖰 &

(10m). Pendine Sands Holiday Park, Pendine, Carmarthen, Carmarthenshire SA33 4NZ. *01994 453398.* Owner: Parkdean Holidays. 2nd Floor, One Gosforth Park Way, Gosforth Business Park, Newcastle-upon-Tyne, NE12 8ET. A40 Trunk Road from Carmarthen to St Clears. SP Pendine/Pentywyn along A4066, 8m from A40 junction. Pass through Laugharne and park reception is 5m further on right. Heated indoor swimming pool. Daytime and evening entertainment for whole family. Mini market. Bakery. Laundrette. Direct beach access. Kids clubs. Varied food choice available. David Bellamy Silver Conservation Award. Pembroke Castle, Caldy Island and a chocolate factory are all close to the park. Tenby is just 20mins drive away. Open April-October. **BH&HPA. NCC. 527S. 60H.** ⊦ 🗲

(8m). Three Rivers Leisure Park, Ferryside, Carmarthen, Carmarthenshire SA17 5TU. *01267 267270.* enquiries@ threerivershotel.co.uk. www.threerivershotel.co.uk. Owner: Mr J F Cavill. South from Pemsarm (Safeway), M4 interchange at Carmarthen, see brown Three Rivers sign on Kidwelly/Bury Port Road. 3m to Ferryside. Situated on the southern edge of Ferryside, 1 mins walk from the sea. Private health facility. Sea activities and touring base. Three-star hotel also on site. Open March 1-December 31. ✫✫✫ **BH&HPA. 41S.** ⊦ &

Clynderwen
(0.5m). Grondre Vale Holiday Park, Clynderwen, Carmarthenshire SA66 7HD. *01437 563111.* accounts@clarach.fsbusiness.co.uk. www.grondrevale.com.

WALES

Owner: Mr T Scarrott. Clarach Bay Holiday Village, Nr Aberystwyth SY23 3DT. 2ms from Narberth, On A478, Cardigan back, just off the A40. Park facilities include PH, pool, shop, showers, laundrette, games room. Local attractions: Oakwood Theme Park, Tenby, Saundersfoot, Folly Farm. Open March-November. **BH&HPA. 30T. 30MC. 80S. 4H.** ⚊☂⚏⚌

Kidwelly

Carmarthen Bay Holiday Park, Kidwelly, Carmarthenshire SA17 5HQ. *0871 664 9722.* carmarthen.bay@park-resorts.com. www.park-resorts.com. Owner: Park Resorts Ltd. 3rd Floor, Swan Court, Waterhouse Street, Hemel Hempstead, Herts HP1 1FN. M4 leave at J48. Take A4138 to Llanelli and then A484, or to B4308 to Kidwelly. Park is SP once you pass Kidwelly. Indoor pool, restaurant, takeaway, children's clubs, sports and leisure facilities, crazy golf. Open April-October. ☆☆☆ **BH&HPA. 400S. 82H.** ⚊☂⚏⚌⌀

Llanddarog

(0.5m). Coedhirion Farm Park, Llanddarog, Carmarthenshire SA32 8BH. *01267 275666.* welshfarmhouse@hotmail.com. Owner: S Evans. Just off A48. Woodland site with easy access. Near Wales Botanical garden centre. 6m from Carmarthen. Small, conveniently situated touring site. Bed and breakfast available in farmhouse. Inns, mini market, PO and hairdresser in vilage. 1m from the National Botanical Garden of Wales. **15T. 5MC.** ✿⚊☂⚏

Llandeilo

(5m). Red Dragon Inn & Caravan Park, Rhydcymerau, Llandeilo, Carmarthenshire. *01558 685527.* Owner: Red Dragon Parks. Off the A485, and on to the B4337. Coarse fishing with four pools. On-site public bar and meals available, children's room and facilities. Laundrette. Open Good Friday-October 31. **24T. MC. 6H.** ⚊☂⚏

Llandovery

(7m). Camping & Caravanning Club Site - Rhandirmwyn, Rhandirmwyn, Llandovery, Carmarthenshire SA20 0NT. *01550 760257/0870 243 3331.* www.campingandcaravanningclub.co.uk. Owner: Camping & Caravanning Club. Greenfields House, Westwood Way, Coventry CV4 8JH. From A483 in Llandovery take road SP Rhandirmwyn for 7m, turn L at PO, site is on the L before the river. From Llandovery take A483 at level crossing, turn L in 300yd by fire station signed Rhandirmwyn and continue 7m to village. Turn L at pub/PO, continue down steep hill past church for 0.5m to site on L before river bridge. Site is set in countryside. There is some spectacular countryside within easy reach of the site. The red kite, one of Britain's rarest birds, can often be seen flying above the site. There are lots of walks within easy reach of site. Non-members welcome. All units accepted. Special deals available for families and backpackers. David Bellamy Silver Conservation Award. Open March-October. ☆☆☆☆ **90T. 90MC.** ⚊☂⚏⚌

(0.5m). Erwlon Caravan & Camping Park, Llandovery, Carmarthenshire SA20 0RD. *01550 720332.* peter@erwlon. fsnet.co.uk. www.ukparks.co.uk/erwlon. Owner: Messrs Rees & Sons. On A40, Brecon to Llandovery. Set in the beautiful Towy Valley in mid-Wales. Suitable base for touring the hills and valleys of Wales. New facilities in 2005: amenity block and Superpitches. Good access. National Botanic Garden of Wales 15m. ☆☆☆ **BH&HPA. 20T. 20MC.** ✿⚊☂⚏⚌

(9m). Galltyberau, Rhandirmwyn, Llandovery, Carmarthenshire. *01550 760218.* Owner: Mr I T Williams. Site located in Upper Towy Valley. Shops, PO within 2-3m. Bird and nature reserves nearby. Fishing also available nearby. Open March-October. **20T. MC. 1H.** ⚊

Llanelli

(12m). Black Lion Caravan & Camping Park, 78 Black Lion Road, Gorslas, Cross Hands, Llanelli, Carmarthenshire SA14 6RU. *01269 845365.* blacklionsite@aol.com. www.caravansite.com. Owner: Barry G Hayes. Just off A48. Follow brown touring signs from Cross Hands (1m). Close to National Botanic Garden of Wales. Family-owned park, peaceful and well maintained. Some hard-standings. Children's play area. Caravan storage. Shops 0.5m. Caravan Club and Camping & Caravanning Club certificated. AA 3 pennants. David Bellamy Silver Conservation Award. Open April 1-September 30. ☆☆☆ **BH&HPA. 30T. MC.** ⚊☂⚏⚌

(6m). Pembrey Country Park Caravan Club Site, Pembrey, Llanelli, Carmarthenshire SA16 0EJ. *01554 834369.* www.caravanclub.co.uk. Owner: The Caravan Club. East Grinstead House, East Grinstead, West Sussex RH19 1UA. See website for standard directions to site. Set in a large country park with adventure playground and miles of sandy beaches. Non-members welcome. Advance booking essential bank holidays and school holidays.Motorhome service point. Laundry facilities. Golf, fishing and water sports nearby. Suitable for walking and for families. Some hard-standings, steel awning pegs required. Toilet block with privacy cubicles. Baby and toddler washroom. Veg prep area. Gas supplies. Play equipment. Storage pitches. Peaceful off-peak. Good walking area. NCN cycle route within 5m. Open March-January. ☆☆☆☆ **NCC. 130T. MC.** ⚊☂⚏⚌

Llangadog

(1.5m). Abermarlais Caravan Park, Llangadog, Carmarthenshire SA19 9NG. *01550 777868/777797.* www.ukparks.co.ukabermarlais. Owner: Juster & Son. 6m W of Llandovery or 6m E of Llandeilo on A40. At western end of the Brecon National Park. Showers. Suitable for a peaceful holiday in natural surroundings, own woodland. Open March 15-November 15. ☆☆☆☆ **BH&HPA. 60T. 60MC.** ⚊☂⚏⚌

(6m). Black Mountain Caravan Park, Llanddeusant, Llangadog, Carmarthenshire SA19 9YG. *01550 740217.* davidandsharon@blackmountainholidays.co.uk www.blackmountainholidays.co.uk. Owners: David Rainsley & Sharon Brooker. A40 from Brecon, follow SP Llandorery. At Trecastle turn L directly before PH, Castle coaching inn, (brown tourist sign) follow road for about 9m, turn R before Cross Inn. Showers, laundry, chemical toilet emptying point. Fishing and pony trekking close by. Part of Brecon Beacons National Park, with unique wildlife. Excellent walking country. Good base for touring mid and south Wales. RAC listed, AA 2 pennants. Cycle hire can be arranged locally. Red kite feeding station close to site (50yd), PH with good food adjacent to site. ☆☆ **BH&HPA. 10T. 10MC. 11S. 8H.** ✿⚊☂⚏⚌

Llanon

(2.5m). Brynarian Caravan Park, Cross Inn, Llanon, Carmarthenshire SY23 5NA. *01974 272231.* Owner: Mr R M & C L Hughes. Off B4337, turn towards Llanon at Cross Inn second turning on L. Play area. Showers. Laundry. Telephone for brochure. Golf, fishing nearby. Shop, restaurant, PO, garage 500yd from site. Open March 1-October 31. **BH&HPA. 20T. MC. 40S. 5H.** ⚊☂⚏

Llanwrda

(5m). Feathers Holiday Park, Llanwrda, Carmarthenshire SA19 8AY. *01550 779000.* Owner: Mr S L & F Finney. Steve Finney Caravans, Mamble, Kidderminster, Worcs DY14 9JG. Turn off A40 at Llanwrda on to A482. Follow the road for about 1.5m, site is on your left-hand side. Small river on park – own fishing rights. Close to Dolaucothi Gold Mines, 30mins from coastal resorts. Peaceful site set in rural surroundings. Open March 1-January 10. **T. MC. 30S.** 🐕

(6m). Maesbach Caravan & Camping Park, Horseshoe Valley, Ffarmers, Llanwrda, Carmarthenshire SA19 8EX. *01558 650650.* Owners: Kath & Graham Stoddart. Off A40 at Llanwrda take A482 Lampeter Road after passing Pumsaint, turn R after 1.5m for Ffarmers, follow signs. Peaceful country park, open fields views with sightings of red kites and buzzards. Showers. Washing machine, tumble dryer, chemical toilet emptying point and ice-pack freezing facilities. Rallies welcome. Wellbehaved dogs welcome. Walking routes from park. Quiet lanes for cyclists. Nearby everyday store/garage, PH, restaurant/take-away. Lampeter shops 6m. Convenient for West Wales sandy beaches, pony trekking, fishing, golf, swimming pool, Dolaucothi gold mines. Llyn Brianne reservoir. National Botanical Centre, Aberglasny Gardens, RSPB reserve and many other attractions. Open March 1-October 31. **20T. 5MC. 15S. 1H.** 🐕 🏕

(8m). Ogofau Caravan Club Site, Pumsaint, Llanwrda, Carmarthenshire SA19 8US. *01558 650365.* Adjacent to the old Roman gold mines, in the foothills of the Cambrian mountains, within a 2,500 acre estate owned and managed by the National Trust. Own sanitation required. Dog walk on site. Fishing nearby. Good area for walking. Peaceful off-peak. Open March-October. **NCC. 34T. MC.** 🐕 🏕

Penlanwen Caravan Site, Pumsaiht, Caio, Llanwrda, Carmarthenshire SA19 8RR. *01558 650667.* Owner: Mrs Rosabelle Rees. 7m NW Llandovery take A40, turn R at Llanwrda to A482 past Bridgend Inn, site signs on right-hand side. Farm site suitable for children. Pony-trekking, mountain walks, pot-holing. Guided tours of gold mine. **10T. MC.** ✿ 🐕

Springwater Lakes, Harford, Llanwrda, Carmarthenshire SA19 8DT. *01558 650788.* Owners: M & S Bexon. 4m E of Lampeter on A482. Quiet, well maintained site. Garage with convenience shop 500yd. Main shops 4m. No childrens play facilities. 4 lakes to fish on site: 1x3acre mixed coarse, 1x3acre specimen carp, 1 fly only (rainbow and browns), 1 any method rainbow trout. Open March 1-October 31. ✰✰✰✰ **BH&HPA. 20T. MC.** 🐕 🏕 ♿

Newcastle Emlyn

(2m). Afon Teifi Caravan and Camping Site, Pentre-cagal, Newcastle Emlyn, Carmarthenshire SA38 9HT. *01559 370 532.* afon.teifi@virgin.net. www.afonteifi.co.uk. Owner: Mrs S Bishop. Off A484. Quiet, riverside site. Suitable touring base for Cardigan Bay. Family-run site with playground and games room. Shop, PH and restaurant nearby. 18 hard-standings. Full facilities. Well-lit site. Open April-October. ✰✰✰ **90T. 25MC.** 🐕 🏕 ♿

(3m). Cenarth Falls Holiday Park, Cenarth, Newcastle Emlyn, Ceredigion SA38 9JS. *01239 710345.* enquiries@ cenarth-holipark.co.uk. www.cenarth-holipark.co.uk. Owner: Mr & Mrs D H G Davies. On the A484, Newcastle Emlyn to Cardigan road. Heated indoor pool and health club, bars and restaurant area. Unheated outdoor pool, open start of June till end of August. Family-run, award-winning park.

Good beaches. Lovely walks. Golf. Fishing. Shop 1m. Open March 1-December 17. ✰✰✰✰✰ **BH&HPA. 30T. 30MC. 89S. 4H.** 🐕 🏕 ♿

(1.8m). Dolbryn Camping & Caravanning, Capel Iwan Road, Newcastle Emlyn, Carmarthenshire SA38 9LP. *01239 710683.* dolbryn@btinternet.com. http://uk.geocities.com/ dolbryn@btinternet.com. Owner: Mr & Mrs D & B Spencer. Turn off on A484 in Newcastle Emlyn, SP 'Leisure Centre'. Follow camping signs, first R after garage. Peaceful site in sheltered valley. Half-hour drive to sea. Licensed bar. Play area. Open Easter-November. ✰✰ **40T. MC.** 🐕 🏕 ♿

Pontarddulais

River View Touring Park, The Dingle, Llanedi, Pontarddulais, Carmarthenshire SA4 0FH. *01269 844876.* info@riverview-touringpark.com. www.riverviewtouringpark.com. Owner: Keith Brasnett. End of M4, J49, take the A483 to Ammanford. After about 0.5m turn left into Lon-y-Felin. Site at end of road. Golf range nearby. River Gwilli along two sides of site. Plenty of wildlife and wild flowers to enjoy. Quiet site, suitable base for visiting beaches, mountains and gardens. David Bellamy Silver Conservation Award. Open March 1-January 3. ✰✰✰ **BH&HPA. 60T. MC.** 🐕 🏕 ♿ 🌿

St Clears

(3m). Afon Lodge Caravan Park, Parciau Bach, St Clears, Carmarthenshire SA33 4LG. *01994 230647.* yvonne@afon lodge.f9.co.uk. Owner: Mr & Mrs W Wiggans. From traffic lights in St Clears take road to Llanboidy, in 100yd fork right. 1.75m, first right, 0.75m first right continue for 0.25m. Quiet, secluded park in wooded valley with countryside views. Suitabletouring centre for west Wales. Open March 1-January 9. ✰✰✰ **BH&HPA. 25T. 25MC. 40S. 2H.** 🐕 🏕 🌿

Whitland

(4m). Old Vicarage Caravan Park, Red Roses, Whitland, Carmarthenshire SA34 0PE. *01834 831637.* oldvicrearoses @aol.com. Owners: Mr R Bennett & Mr B Robinson. On the A477 in Red Roses. Close to beaches and central for touring south-west Wales. Licensed club, bar meals, heated outdoor swimming pool, play area, facilities block and laundry. Separate field for ball games. Open March 1-end January. ✰✰ **BH&HPA. 17T. MC. 23S.** 🐕 🏕

CEREDIGION

Aberaeron

Aeron Coast Caravan Park, North Road, Aberaeron, Ceredigion SA46 0JF. *01545 570349.* aeroncoastcaravan park@aeron.freeserve.co.uk. www.ukparks.co.uk/aeron coast. Owner: Aeron Coast (Holidays) Ltd. 29/30 Quay Street, Carmarthen SA31 3JT. On A487, Cardigan to Aberystwyth. Filling station at entrance. 22 acres of flat, coastal parkland on edge of Aberaeron (brown signs). Filling station at entrance. Club, recreational rooms, heated swimming pool and tennis court. Families only. Children's facilities. 200yd from shops and picturesque harbour. Open March 1-October 31. ✰✰✰✰ **BH&HPA. 100T. MC. 200S.** 🐕 🏕 ♿ 🌿

(5.5m). Ffos-Helyg Caravan Park, Cilcennin, Lampeter, Aberaeron, Ceredigion SA48 8RL. *01570 471124.* ffoshelyg @hotmail.com. www.ffoshelyg.vze.com. Owner: Mrs C Williams. Off A482. Open April 1-October 31. **BH&HPA. 45S. 2H.** 🐕

(0.75m). Wide Horizons Caravan & Chalet Park, Aberaeron, Ceredigion SA46 0ET. *01545 570043.* Owner: Mr & Mrs M Parker. On A487 S of Aberaeron. 0.25m from sea with panoramic sea views. Clubhouse with lounge bar and family room. Games room. Entertainment peak periods. Laundry. Access to sea. Gas sales. Adjacent to coastal path walks. Open April 1-October 31. **BH&HPA. 90S.** ✆

Aberystwyth

(0.25m). Aberystwyth Holiday Village, Penparcau Road, Aberystwyth, Ceredigion SY23 1TH. *01970 624211.* enquiries@aberystwythholidays.co.uk. www.aberystwythholidays.co.uk. Owner: Mr R Ballard. On A487. 0.25m S of town. Near town and beach. Indoor swimming pool. 10-pin bowling centre. Shop, cafe, 2 bars entertainment. Play area. Fishing, fitness centre. Open March 1-January 10. **500T. 50MC. 200S. 30H.** ✆ ❂ ♿ ♨ ✎

(10m). Aeron View Caravan Park, Blaenpennal, Aberystwyth, Ceredigion SY23 4TW. *01974 251488.* aeronview@hotmail.com. www.aeronview.com. Owner: Mr & Mrs T N Bell. 1m off A485 Aberystwyth to Tregaron road, 4m from Tregaron. Quiet, inland site with panoramic views yet only 15mins from the sea. Suitable base for fishing, birdwatching and relaxing. Children and pets welcome. Open March 1-October 31. **BH&HPA. 4T. 4MC. 9S. 3H.** ✆

(15m). Bryn-Y-Gors Holiday Park, Pontrhydfendigaid, Aberystwyth, Ceredigion SY25 6EL. *01974 831675.* Owner: Blakemore & Co. On B4343. 0.5m out of village. Quiet holiday park set in countryside in the heart of mid-Wales. Suitable for relaxing break for people of all ages. Open March 1-October 31. **BH&HPA. 88S. 6H.** ✆ ♨

(0.5m). Brynowen Holiday Park, Borth, Aberystwyth, Ceredigion SY24 5LS. *01970 871366.* enquiries@brynowenholidaypark.co.uk. www.park-resorts.com. Owner: Park Resorts Ltd. 3rd Floor, Swan Court, Waterhouse Street, Hemel Hempstead, Herts HP1 1FN. Take the B4353 off A487 (about 4m N of Aberystwyth and 12m S of Machynlleth). The entrance to Brynowen is 100yd from the southern end of Borth seafront. Heated indoor pool. Licensed entertainment complex. Amusement arcade. Laundrette.Crazy golf. Free children's club. Entertainment for all the family. David Bellamy Gold Conservation Award. AA listed. Investor in People. Open April-October. ✩✩✩ **BH&HPA. NCC. 16T. 397S. 85H.** ✆ ❂ ♿ ♨

(4m). Clarach Bay Holiday Village, Clarach Bay, Aberystwyth, Ceredigion SY23 3DT. *01970 828277/828189.* Owner: Heatherdale Holidays Ltd. On A487. Club. Full family entertainment. Outdoor heated swimming pool. Restaurant. Fish and chip takeaway. Mini-fairground. Laundrette. Supermarket. Fishing. Tennis. Open April-October. **BH&HPA. NCC. 10T. 10MC. 215S. 40H.** ✆ ❂ ♨

(12m). Erwbarfe Farm Caravan Site, Devil's Bridge, Aberystwyth, Ceredigion SY23 3JR. *01970 890665.* Owner: G M & B E Lewis. On A4120 Ponterwyd to Devil's Bridge. Suitable base from which to tour mid-Wales. Walking, fishing, bird-watching etc. Open March-October. **20T. 10MC. 50S. 2H.** ✆ ❂

(2m). Glan-y-Mor Leisure Park, Clarach Bay, Aberystwyth, Ceredigion SY23 3DT. *01970 828900.* glanymor@sunbourne.co.uk. www.sunbourne.co.uk. Owner: W L Jones Ltd. Off A487 Machynlleth to Aberystwyth. Restaurant and takeaway. Supermarket. Amusements. Bowl and leisure centre. Licensed club. Laundrette. Showers. Fitness gym. Sauna. Steam room. Whirlpool spa. Sunbeds. Entertainment. Dogs not allowed during bank holidays and school holidays. Open March-October. ✩✩✩✩ **BH&HPA. 25T. 25MC. 160S. 60H.** ✆ ❂ ♿ ♨

(2m). Greenmeadow Caravan Holiday Home Park, Clarach Bay, Aberystwyth, Ceredigion SY23 3DT. *01970 820450.* scl@salopcaravans.co.uk. www.salopcaravans.co.uk. Owner: Salop Caravans Sites Ltd. On the A487 Machynlleth to Aberystwyth road , at Bow Street turn right between the PO and the Black Lion, SP Clarach. Follow road for 2m straight over crossroad. Well-kept park situated in a sunny elevated position, allowing panoramic views of Cardigan Bay, endless facilities close by. Open March 1-November 30. ✩✩✩✩✩ **BH&HPA. NCC. 88S.** ✆ ♿

(5m). Maes Bangor Caravan Park, Capel Bangor, Aberystwyth, Ceredigion SY23 3LT. *01970 880351.* Owner: H M, L J & R Tomkinson. On A44. Open March 1-October 31. **41S.** ✆

(1.5m). Midfield Holiday and Residential Park, Southgate, Aberystwyth, Ceredigion. SY23 4DX. *01970 612542.* enquiries@midfieldcaravanpark.co.uk. www.midfieldcaravanpark.co.uk. Owner: Mr & Mrs T B Hughes. On A4120, Aberystwyth to Devil's Bridge Road. Mainly level hilltop site with panoramic views. Public phone. Privately owned park. 0.5m to shops. Site overlooks Aberystwyth and Cardigan Bay. Open Easter-October 31. **BH&HPA. 75T. MC. 35S.** ✆ ✆

(5m). Morfa Bychan Holiday Park, Llanfarian, Aberystwyth, Ceredigion SY23 4QQ. *01970 617254.* info@hillandale.co.uk. www.hillandale.co.uk. Owner: D & D Lloyd Jones Securities Ltd. Lincomb Lock, Titton, Stourport-on-Severn, Worcestershire DY13 9QR. Off A487 southbound from Aberystwyth, first turning off A487, road unsuitable for caravans, proceed a further 2m to turning alongside radio masts. Set in over 110 acres of pastureland overlooking Cardigan Bay. Suitable location from which to explore the area. Heated swimming pool. Cinema and town 3m. Golf 4m. Open March 1-January 7. **BH&HPA. 50T. 50MC. 200S.** ✆ ❂ ♿ ♨ ✎

(2m). Ocean View Caravan Park, Clarach Bay, Aberystwyth, Ceredigion SY23 3DL. *01970 623361/ 828425.* alan@grover10. freeserve.co.uk. www.oceanviewholidays.com. Owner: Mr & Mrs Grover. Beachside, Clarach Bay, Aberystwyth, Cardiganshire. Off A487 N of Aberystwyth, turn for Clarach Bay. Follow road to beach, Ocean View is on R. Peaceful, family-run park near beach and with sea views. Suitable base for touring and beach holidays. Facilities nearby. Showers. Separate field used as dog walk. Open March 10-October 31. ✩✩✩✩ **BH&HPA. 24T. 5MC. 50S. 4H.** ✆ ❂ ♨

(5m). Pen-y-Wern Holiday Park, New Cross, Aberystwyth, Ceredigion SY23 4JT. *01974 261553.* Owner: Lomas Leisure Ltd. B4340 Trawscoed to Tregaron. Open March 1-January 9. **20T. 10MC. 85S. 6H.** ✆ ❂ ♨

(7m). Pengarreg Caravan Park, Llanrhystud, Aberystwyth, Ceredigion SY23 5DJ. *01974 202247.* iangolfmiller@aol.com. www.utowcaravans.co.uk. Owner: Mr C Miller. On A487, S of Aberystwyth, entrance opposite garage. Site situated on beach. Fishing on site. Golf 1m. PO 0.75m. Doctor 6m. Shop on site, laundry, office, licensed club, meals, children's room, 2 play areas. Hill walks.Open March 1-January 1. **BH&HPA. 50T. 8MC. 150S. 10H.** ✆ ❂ ♿ ♨ ✎

(2m). Riverside Caravan Park, Lon Glanfred, Llandre, Borth, Aberystwyth, Ceredigion SY24 5BY. *01970 820070.* Owner: Mr S J & Mrs J E South. From A487 at Bow Street, turn at Rhydepennau PH on to B4353 Llandre. Turn right 150yd past Llandre PO into Lon Glanfred. Site in 500yd. Quiet, sheltered and secluded site on banks of river Lerri. Laundrette. Hot showers. Open March 1-October 31. **BH&HPA. 22T. 20MC. 75S. 3H.** ✆ ❂ ♿ ♨

(12m). Woodlands Caravan Park, Devil's Bridge, Aberystwyth, Ceredigion SY23 3JW. *01970 890233.* wood landscp@btclick.com. www.woodlandsdevilsbridge.co.uk. Owners: Mr & Mrs Davies. 3m off A44 on A4120. Quiet, family-run site, 300yd from waterfalls. Fishing nearby, golf, tennis, horse riding 15mins drive, takeaway food and cafe on site. Mountain bike trail 3m, quiet village PH 5mins walk. Spectacular scenery. Open March 1- October 31. ✩✩ **20T. 20MC. 100S.** ☌ ▣ & ⚐

(11m). Woodlands Caravan Park, Llanon, Aberystwyth, Ceredigion SY23 5LX. *01974 202342.* Owner: Mr I Lampert. From N A487, through Llanon, R at international caravan sign. Level, secluded, tree-lined site with made-up roads. 200yd from sea. Open March 1-October 31. **BH&HPA. 40T. 40MC. 41S.** ☌ ▣ ⚐ ⌀

Borth

A Fron Caravan Park, Borth, Ceredigion SY24 5LR. *01970 611200.* Owner: Mrs E Morris. On A487. 100yds from main beach at Borth. Caravan sales and hire. Open March-October 31. **12T. 12MC. 70S. 5H.** ☌ ☌

Brynrodyn Caravan & Leisure Park, Borth, Ceredigion SY24 5NR. *01970 871472.* brynrodyn@bun.com. Owner: Mr Lloyd. On B4572 Aberystwyth to Borth. Sea views, grass sites, family park, clubhouse, play area, games room. Open March-October. ✩✩✩ **BH&HPA. 50T. 20MC. 135S. 10H.** ☌ ▣ & ⚐

(1m). Cambrian Coast Holiday Park, Borth, Ceredigion SY24 5JU. *01970 871233.* cambriancoast@sunbourne.co.uk. www. sunbourne.co.uk. Owner: W L Jones Ltd. Glan-Y-Mor Leisure Park, Clarach Bay, Aberystwyth SY23 3DT. Outdoor children's fun pool. Indoor swimming pool. Indoor and outdoor play areas. Licensed club. Restaurant facilities and takeaway. Live entertainment. Amusements. Laundrette. Dragon Award. Open March-October. ✩✩✩✩ **BH&HPA. 50T. 25MC. 144S. 25H.** ☌ ▣ & ⚐

(0.5m). Glanlerry Caravan Park, Borth, Ceredigion SY24 5LU. *01970 871413.* cath.richards.gcp@talk21.com. www.glan lerrycaravanpark.co.uk. Owner: M D & R P Richards. On B4353 between Bow St and Borth. Laundry. Bathroom. Showers. Family site only. No motor-cycles. Open March-October. **BH&HPA. 90T. MC. 100S.** ☌ ▣

Golden Sands Holiday Park, Seafront, Borth, Ceredigion SY24 5JS. *01970 871440.* Owner: Blakemore & Co. On B4353. Laundrette. Beach 50yd. Golf course adjacent. Open March-October. **BH&HPA. 60S. 20H.** ☌ ⚐

(0.5m). Pen-Y-Graig Caravan Site, Borth, Ceredigion SY24 5NR. *01970 871717.* Owner: Mr J D & Mrs W Evans. Open March 1-October 31. **85S. 1H.** ☌ ▣ &

(1m). The Mill House Caravan Park, Dol-y-bont, Borth, Ceredigion SY24 5LX. *01970 871481.* www.ukparks.co.uk/ millhousecp. Owner: Mr O J Patrick. On A487 turn west at Rhyddapenau Garage Corner (between Talybont and Bow Street) onto B4353 through Llandre. Proceed one mile. Stop under railway bridge, by white railings, then fork right into Dolybont village, first right before hump-back bridge. Quiet site, close mown grass. Fishing beside a trout stream. Open Easter-mid October. **BH&HPA. 10T. 5MC. 15S.** ☌ ▣

(3m). Ty Mawr Holiday Home Park, Ynyslas, Borth, Ceredigion SY24 5LB. *01970 871327.* Owner: P G & C C Beech. 3m north of Borth on B4353 off A487. Quiet, sheltered, level site with panoramic views of hills, nature reserve and Dovey estuary. David Bellamy Gold Conservation Award. Fishing, golf course, shops, PO, doctor all nearby. Open March-October. **BH&HPA. 12T. 50S.** ☌ ▣

Cardigan

(2.5m). Brongwyn Caravan & Touring Park, Brongwyn Mawr, Penparc, Cardigan, Ceredigion SA43 1SA. *01239 613644.* enquiries@cardiganholidays.co.uk. www.cardigan-holidays.co.uk. Owner: Mrs A Giles. On A487 Cardigan-Aberystwyth road, 2.5m south of Cardigan, turn left at crossroads in Penparc signposted Ferwig, carry on over next crossroads, after 0.5m turn right into lane, opposite blue sign. A small, peaceful park with level pitches. Indoor pool and leisure facilities available (at extra charge), laundry etc. 5mins from the market town of Cardigan and beautiful sandy beaches at Mwnt and Aberporth. Golf course, cinema, theatre, shopping centre all 3m. Ideal location for walking, fishing and golf. Open Easter-October (tourers), all year cottages. ✩✩✩ **10T. 5MC.** ☌ ▣

(6m). Caerfelin Caravan Park, Aberporth, Cardigan, Ceredigion SA43 2BY. *01239 810540.* Owner: Glyn & Sheila Bright. Off A487 to B4333 at Blaenanerch R at St Cynwyls church to park 200yd on the L. Well-sheltered about 5mins walk to sandy beaches and village. Family park. Golf, cinema 6m. Open mid March-October 31. **BH&HPA. 5T. 100S.** ☌ ▣ &

(4m). Camping Blaenwaun, Mwnt, Cardigan, Ceredigion SA43 1QF. *01239 612165.* huwdavies.mwnt@virgin.net. www.blaenwaunfarm.co.uk. Owner: H & I Davies. Follow signs for Mwnt, from Cardigan town. Quiet, family run site. Coarse fishing lake on site. Half mile from beach. Plenty of coastal walks. ✩✩✩ **20T. MC. 20S. 1H.** ❄ ☌ ▣ &

(2m). Patch Caravan Park, Gwbert on Sea, Cardigan, Ceredigion SA23 1PP. *01239 615858.* patchcardigan@ aol.com. patchcardiganpark.co.uk. Owners: Evelyn Crescent Ltd. The Grange, St Hilary, Gowbridge, Vale of Glamorgan CF71 7DP. On B4548. Peaceful site situated right on the sea shore surrounded by sand dunes. Open Easter-October. **BH&HPA. 100S.** ☌ ⚐

(14m). Troedrhiwgam Caravan Park, Llangranog, Llandyssul, Cardigan, Ceredigion. *029 20596299.* Owner: Mr G E Willams & Mrs S Evans. 17 Milton Road, Penarth, Vale of Glamorgan CF64 2SW. Off A487 Aberaeron to Cardigan. 7 miles south of New Quay. Open April 1-October 31. **2T. 2MC. 22S. 3H.** ☌

Tudu Vale Caravan Park, Llwyndafydd, Cardigan, Ceredigion SA44 6LH. Owner: Mr R Reed. Pantrhyn Farm, llwyndaefydd, Llandyssul, Ceredigion. Farmily run site, 200 yards from beach. Fishing off the rocks. Doctor 3.5 miles away New Quay. Golf 4 miles away. Horse riding on the farm. Caravans for sale. Open April-November. **10T. 5MC. 50S.** ☌ ▣

(4m). Ty-Gwyn Farm, Mwnt, Cardigan, Ceredigion SA43 1QH. *01239 614518.* Owners: M & M D Evans. Off A487 at Cardigan for Mwnt. Family-run farm site. Mwnt beach 5 minutes from site. Quiet situation. Dolphins and seals in bay. Open March-October. **20T. 5MC. 15S. 4H.** ☌ ▣

Lampeter

Hafod Brynog Caravan Park, Ystrad Aeron, Felinfach, Lampeter, Ceredigion SA48 8AE. *01570 470084.* amies@hafodbrynog.fsnet.co.uk. Owner: Mr & Mrs G Amies. On main A482 Lampeter to Aberaeron road in quiet village of Ystrad Aeron, entrance next to Brynog Arms pub. EModern shower block. Peaceful with lovely views. Ideal for coastal and inland touring or just relaxing. Walking distance to village with shops, garage, pubs. Laundrette on site. AA 3 pennants. Golf course 6m. Fishing 3m. Open April 1- September 30 for tourers; open March 1-October 31 for holiday homes. **30T. 30MC. 40S.** ⚐ ⛽

(5m). Highmead Hotel Caravan Park, Llanbyther, Lampeter, Ceredigion. *01570 480941.* Owner: Mr A L Ablett. Off A485. Fishing near. Open February-October. **8T. 2MC. 17S.** ⚐ ⛽

(5m). Moorlands Caravan Park, Llangybi, Lampeter, Ceredigion SA48 8NN. *01570 493543.* moorlands@lionram pant.co.uk. www.moorlands-caravan-park.co.uk. Owner: Valerie & Keith Edwards. Off A485 Tregaron to Lampeter. Club. Swimming pool. Play area. Golf club within walking distance. Fishing and pony-trekking nearby. Close to many places of interest including Devil's Bridge and Llyn Brianne Dam. Mountain scenery. Cardigan Bay. David Bellamy Gold Conservation Award. Open March 1-January 9. **BH&HPA. 60S. 2H.** ⚐

Llanarth

Shawsmead Caravan Club Site, Oakford, Llanarth, Ceredigion SA47 0RN. *01545 580423.* www.caravan club.co.uk. Owner: The Caravan Club. East Grinstead House, East Grinstead, West Sussex RH19 1UA. See website for standard directions to site. This site is only about 4m from the coast which is dotted with lovely bays and beaches ideal for families. Chemical closet emptying points. Mobile toilet block. Membership on site. Non-members welcome. Some hard-standings. PO in village, garage/shop 1.5 miles, fishing and golf courses nearby. Laundry, motorhome service point, veg prep area, gas, water sports nearby. Peaceful off-peak, good area for walking, beach and NCN cycle route within 5m. Open March-October. **NCC. 46T. MC.** ⚐ ⛽ ♿

Llandysul

Brynawelon Touring and Camping Park, Brynawelon, Sarnau, Llangranog, Llandysul, Ceredigion SA44 6RE. *01239 654584.* Owner: Mr J G & Mrs S L Brown. North on A487, then turn right at Sarnau Chapel crossroads. Two miles from the coast. Site 0.25m on left down lane signposted. 9 miles from Cardigan. Small, quiet, family site under personal supervision. Calor Gas available. Open Easter-September. **40T. MC. 1H.** ⚐ ⛽

(3m). Camping & Caravanning Club Site - Cardigan Bay, Llwynhelyg, Cross Inn, Llandysul, Ceredigion SA44 6LW. *01545 560029/0870 2433331.* www.camping andcaravanningclub.co.uk. Owner: Camping & Caravanning Club. Greenfields House, Westwood Way, Coventry CV4 8JH. 1m from New Quay. Left at Penrhiwgaled Arms, turn R, about 0.75m. Site on R after 250yd. Well-located site within easy reach of New Quay and Cardigan. Good coastal walks nearby. Close to beaches. Non-members welcome. All units accepted. Special deals available for families and backpackers. Open March-October. ✰✰✰✰ **90T. 90MC.** ⚐ ⛽ ♿

Dyffryn Bern Caravan Park, Penbryn Beach, Sarnau, Llandysul, Ceredigion. SA44 6RD. *01239 810900.* enquiries@dyffryn.com. www.dyffryn.com. Owner: Mr & Mrs C Atkinson. Off A487. 7m from Cardigan. Fishing lake. Conservatory cafe-bar. Open March 1-January 1 for tourers; open Easter-October 31 for hire caravans. **BH&HPA. 5T. MC. 50S. 5H.** ⚐

(12m). Gilfach Farm Caravan Site, Blaencelyn, Llangrannog, Llandysul, Ceredigion SA44 6DG. *01239 654250.* Owner: Mr G PJames. On B432 from Pentregate to Llangrannog. Open March-November. **T. MC. 150S. 10H.** ⚐

Maes Glas Caravan Park, Penbryn, Sarnau, Llandysul, Ceredigion SA44 6QE. *01239 654268.* enquiries@maesglas caravanpark.co.uk. www.maesglascaravanpark.co.uk. Owner: Mr & Mrs T Hill. Off A487 at Sarnau follow road down towards Penbryn Beach. 9m from Cardigan. Takeaway food. Games room. Peace and quiet. David Bellamy Gold Conservation Award. Dry ski slope 3m, golf course 4m, shops 9m. Open March-October. **BH&HPA. 5T. 5MC. 43S. 1H.** ⚐ ⛽ ⛽

(8m). Pantgwyn, Synod Inn, Llandysul, Ceredigion SA44 6JN. *01545 580320.* Owner: Mrs J Jones. 3-acre field on back to nature site on working dairy farm. **20T. MC.** ✿ ⚐ ⛽

(8m). Pilbach Holiday Park, Betws Ifan, Rhydlewis, Llandysul, Ceredigion SA44 5RT. *01239 851434.* heatherdale@fsbdial.co.uk. Owner: Mr Barker. Set in nearly 14 acres of land, this award-winning holiday park is surrounded by stunning countryside and close to Newquay with its picturesque harbour. The park welcomes tourers, tents, motorhomes and caravan clubs. Dragon Award. Open March 1-Mid November. ✰✰✰✰ **BH&HPA. 65T. MC. 70S. 6H.** ⚐ ⛽ ⛽

(0.5m). Rhydygalfe Caravan Park, Pontwelli, Llandysul, Ceredigion SA44 5AP. *01559 363211/362738.* Owner: D W L A G Davies. South of Llandysul on A486. Good salmon fishing close to site. Local PH and late-night shop within easy walking distance. **30T. 30MC. 5S. 3H.** ✿ ⚐ ⛽ ♿

(8m). Talywerydd Touring Caravan Park, Penbryn Sands, Sarnau, Llandysul, Ceredigion SA44 6QY. *01239 810322.* Owner: Mr & Mrs R Milka. From N or S off A487 take second Penbryn turn, site 600yd. Own tap and drain to each tourer. Heated, covered swimming pool, pitch and putt. AA 4 pennants. Open March-October. ✰✰✰✰ **BH&HPA. S.** ⚐ ⛽

Treddafydd Caravan Site, Penbryn Beach, Sarnau, Llandysul, Ceredigion SA44. *01239 654551.* Owner: Mr G & E Griffiths. Off A487 at Sarnau Church into Penbryn Beach Road, 1st L. 10m from Cardigan. Showers. Washing machine. Tumble dryer and ironing facilities. Open April-October. **10T. 3MC. 14S. 8H.** ⚐

(4m). Woodland Hideaway Park, Glynarthen, Llandysul, Ceredigion SA44 6PP. *01239 851333.* clive@woodlandhide awaypark.co.uk. www.woodlandhideawaypark.co.uk. Owner: Mr R C Passant. Off A487, on B4334, SP Rhydlewis, follow signs for Woodland Hideaway. Small, quiet park with own woodland walks. Within 5m of unspoilt sandy beaches. Laundry room. Adventure playground. Fishing, horse riding, boat trips, walking. Open March 1-October 31. ✰✰✰✰ **BH&HPA. 33S.** ⚐

Llanrhystud

(1m). Morfa Farm Caravan Park, Llanrhystud, Ceredigion SY23 5BU. *01974 202253.* morfa@morfa.net. www.morfa.net. Owner: Mr D M Morgan & Family. On A487, Aberaeron to Aberystwyth. Laundry room. Tennis court. Slipway. Telephone. Calor Gas stockist. Snooker room. Golf course 1.5m. Open April-October. **20T. 10MC. 150S. 2H.** ⚐ ⛽ ♿ ⛽

WALES

(0.25m). Penrhos Golf & Country Club, Llanrhystud, Ceredigion SY23 5AY. *01974 202999.* info@penrhosgolf.co.uk. www.penrhosgolf.co.uk. Owner: ST Teilo Ltd. Located off the A487. Laundrette. Tennis court. Leisure centre with swimming pool, sauna, steam room and fitness. 18-hole and 9-hole golf courses. Open March 1-January 6. ☆☆☆☆ **BH&HPA. 135S. 14H.** 🐾 🛁

New Quay

(1.75m). Caereithin Caravan Park, Cross Inn, New Quay, Ceredigion SA44 6LW. *01545 560624.* Owner: Mr Atkinson. A487 to Synod Inn-A486 (Newquay), 2m (Cross Inn), left at crossroads, 200yd on right. Quiet site. Open March-January. **BH&HPA. 25T. MC. 28S. 5H.** 🐾 🖾

(3m). Cwmtydu, Llwyndafydd, New Quay, Ceredigion. *01545 560494.* Owner: Mr S R Rees. Pantrhyn, Llwyndafydd, Llandyssul, Ceredigion. Off the A487 at Plwmp, 4m to Cwmtydu, site on right-hand side. 200yd from beach and small shop. Pony-trekking. Fishing from rocks. 3m from shops and PO. Golf course nearby. Open March-January. **6T. 3MC. 45S. 3H.** 🐾 🖾

(1.5m). Frondeg Caravan Park, Gilfachreda, New Quay, Ceredigion SA45 9SP. *01545 580444/07798135490.* steve hartley.cbmwc@tiscali.co.uk. Owner: S W H Hartley. Cilgraig, Gilfachreda, New Quay, Ceredigion SA45 9SP. From A487 at Llanarth take B4342 to New Quay. Turn R at crossroads after telephone box at Gilfachreda, then L at junction, 200yd on right hand side. Two miles from New Quay by road (where harbour, shops, doctor etc) or walk along the beach at low tide. Frondeg is a quiet, secluded site in a wooded valley. Dolphin watching boat trips arranged by site owner. Open April 1-October 31. **5T. 5MC. 25S.** 🐾 🖾

(0.25m). Neuadd Caravan Park, Neuadd Farm, New Quay, Ceredigion SA45 9TY. *01545 560 709.* Owners: D R Evans & W M Evans & Son. **60T. 85S.** 🐾 🖾

(1m). Ocean Heights Leisure Park, Maen-y-Groes, New Quay, Ceredigion SA45 9RL. *01545 560309.* enquiries@oceanheights.co.uk. www.oceanheights.co.uk. On A486. Indoor and outdoor swimming pool. Laundrette. Club. Arcade. Play area. Sea views. Open March 1-January 1. ☆☆☆☆ **100S.** 🐾 🛁

(2m). Pencnwc Holiday Park, Cross Inn, Llandyssul, New Quay, Ceredigion SA44 6NL. *01545 560479.* holidays@pencnwc.co.uk. www.pencnwc.co.uk. Owner: Mr I M & Mrs S J Davies. Club. Open April-October. ☆☆☆☆**BH&HPA. 100T. 50MC. 175S.** 🐾 🖾 🛁 🛁

(2.5m). Penlon Caravan Park, Cross Inn, New Quay, Ceredigion SA44 6JY. *01545 560620.* Owner: Mr Chris Willis & Miss Eleanor Bloor. On A486. Showers, laundry, chemical toilet emptying point. Games room. Play area. Open March 1-January 6. **BH&HPA. 7T. MC. 53S. 6H.** 🐾 🖾 🛁 🛁

(0.5m). Quay West Holiday Park, New Road, New Quay, Ceredigion SA45 9SE. *01545 560547.* oewebmaster@bourne-leisure.co.uk. www.quaywestholidaypark.co.uk. Owner: Bourne Leisure Ltd. One Park Lane, Hemel Hempstead, Herts HP2 4YL. Take A487 coastal trunk road from Aberystwyth or A484, then A486 from Carmarthen. Join B4342 and the park is situated on the northern side of New Quay. Cardigan Bay holiday park. Heated fun and children's pool and children's club. Daily entertainment. 3 sandy beaches. Welcome Host. David Bellamy Gold Conservation Award. Investors in People award. Open April-November. ☆☆☆☆ **BH&HPA. NCC. 612S. 170H.** 🐾 🛁 🛁

(2m). Wern Mill Camping Site, Gilfachreda, New Quay, Ceredigion SA45 9SP. *01545 580699.* Owner: Mr J B Hand. A487, Aberystwyth to Cardigan road, turn off at Llanarth to Newquay road B4342. Gilfachreda is 1.5m from Llanarth on the B4342. Tents for hire. Open Easter-October 31. ☆☆☆ **40T. 10MC.** 🐾 🖾 🛁

CONWY

Abergele

(8m). Abbeyford Holiday Camp, Bryn Road, Towyn, Abergele, Conwy LL22 9NH. *01745 334590.* info@abbeyford.com. www.abbeyford.com. Owner: Mr G Vose. Abbeyford Caravan Co Ltd, Pensarn, Abergele, Conwy LL22 7PW. Off A548, Coast Road, or A55 take Abergele turn off and follow signs for Pensarn and Rhyl. Club with regular live entertainment. Close to beach and all amenities. Open March 21-October 31. **NCC. 120S. 4H.** 🐾 🛁

(2m). Cambria Caravan Park, Towyn, Abergele, Conwy LL22 9HR. *01745 832196.* Owner: Mrs S Morris. On A548 Abergele to Prestatyn. Club and amusements. Spa and sauna. Open Easter-October. **BH&HPA. 120S. 10H.** 🐾 🖾 🖉

(10m). Caravan Site, Pen Isaf, Llangernyw, Abergele, Conwy LL22 8RN. *01745 860276.* Owner: Mr T Williams. Open March-October. **BH&HPA. 8S. 12H.** 🐾

(2m). Cosy Corner Camp, Peris Avenue, Towyn, Abergele, Conwy LL22 9HH. *01745 351874.* Owner: K H & B Jones. On A548. Dogs by permission only. Open Easter-October. **1T. 21S.** 🐾

(3m). Gaingc View, Gaingc Road, Towyn, Abergele, Conwy LL22 9HP. *01745 342957.* peter@gaingcview.fsnet.co.uk. www.gaingcviewholidaypark.co.uk. Owner: Mr & Mrs I Jones. Park is in the heart of Towyn, off Sandbank road. Only owners' dogs allowed. Open March 15-October 31. ☆☆☆☆☆ **BH&HPA. 78S. 2H.** 🛁 🖉

(3m). Happy Days Caravan Park, Towyn Road, Abergele, Conwy. *01745 350924.* Owner: Mr & Mrs A A Hodgson. Off A548. Open March 21-October 31. **BH&HPA. 315S. 100H.**

(1m). Harts Caravan Park, Pensarn, Abergele, Conwy LL22 7PY. *01745 832252.* Owner: Mr J L Hodgson. Off A548. Quiet, well-maintained site. Fully serviced caravans. One minute from beach. Suitable base for Snowdonia National Park and Rhyl. Open March-October. **120S.** 🐾 🛁 🖉

(2.5m). Henllys Farm, Towyn, Abergele, Conwy LL22 9HF. *01745 351208.* Owner: Mr B Kerfoot. On S side of A548 at Towyn. Level, sheltered site overlooking open farmland. Close to most amenities and entertainment in Towyn. Open April-October. ☆☆☆☆ **281T. MC.** 🐾 🖾 🛁

(3.5m). Hunters Hamlet Touring Caravan Park, Betws yn Rhos, Abergele, Conwy LL22 8PL. *01745 832237.* Owner: Mrs Hunter. Sirior Goch Farm, Betws yn Rhos, Abergele, Conwy. Off A55 for Abergele, then A548, Llanwrst road, for 2.75m, turn right at crossroads, Hunters Hamlet is 0.5m on left. Laundry room. Pay phone. Family bathroom. Superpitches. Open March 21-October 31. **BH&HPA. 23T. 5MC.** 🐾 🖾 🛁

(3m). Inter Leisure Parks Ltd, Towyn Road, Towyn, Abergele, Conwy LL22 9EY. *01745 832112.* Owner: Inter Leisure Parks Ltd. Situated on A548 road between Rhyl and Abergele. PH. Laundrette. Amusements. Beach. Open April 1-September 30. **330S. 20H.** 🐾

(2.5m). Kerfoots Camp, Towyn, Abergele, Conwy LL22 9HF. *01745 351208.* Owner: Mr B Kerfoot. Henllys, Towyn, Abergele LL22 9HF. On A548 at Towyn. Open March 25-end October. **BH&HPA. 253S.**

(3m). Millers Cottage Caravan Park, Gaingc Road, Towyn, Abergele, Conwy LL22 9HS. *01745 832102.* admin@millers cottage.com. www.millerscottage.com. Owner: Millers Cottage Leisure Ltd. Follow signs for Towyn from A55 expressway. At Towyn crossroads go straight across traffic lights down Sand Bank Road and L into Gaingc Road. No tourers. Family camp with large country club, children welcome. New indoor pool. Open March 21-October 30. **BH&HPA. 200S. 4H.** ⛺ 🏕 ⌀

(2.5m). Owens Caravan Park, (Gainc Bach), Towyn Road, Towyn, Abergele, Conwy LL22 9ES. *01745 353639.* Owner: The Owen Family. Rhyl to Abergele coast road. 2m from Rhyl. PO and general store opposite the site. All other amenities, shops, doctor and churches within 5mins walk. Beach 10mins walk. Open April-October. **12T. 300S.** ⛺ 🔌 ♿

(3m). Pen-y-Bryn Country Park, Roadside Delivery, Betws-yn-Rhos, Abergele, Conwy LL22 8YL. *01745 825306.* Owner: Mr J Prytherch. 0.5m NW of A548, Llanrwst to Abergele, J with B5381. Main services. Open March-January. **33S.** ⛺

(1m). Pentre Mawr Caravan Park, Queensway, Pensarn, Abergele, Conwy LL22 7RE. *01745 827462.* Owner: G J & R A Davies. Easy access to A55 main road. Close to sea and shops. All new mains services. Family -run park. Bowling green. Open March 1-November 30. ☆☆☆☆☆ **NCC. 105S.** ⛺ ⌀

(1m). Primrose Caravan Park, Peris Avenue, Towyn Road, Towyn, Abergele, Conwy LL22 9EN. *01745 342234.* Owner: Clwyd Holiday Camps Ltd. Off A548. Open March-January. ☆☆☆ **BH&HPA. 45S. 45H.** ⛺ ♿ 🏕

(2m). Roberts Caravan Park, Penrefail Cross Roads, Moelfre, Abergele, Conwy LL22 8PN. *01745 833265.* www.robertscara vanpark.co.uk. Owner: L & G Roberts. Waterloo Service Station, Penrefail Cross Roads, Moelfre, Abergele, Conwy LL22 8PN. From Abergele A548 towards Llanrwst for 2m, on to B5381 towards St Asaph; site 100yd on right. Quiet site 2m from coast. Modern facilities block. Well-stocked shop next to site. Fishing, golf, bowls nearby. Open March-October. **40T.** ⛺ 🔌 🏕

(2m). Seldon's Golden Gate Holiday Centre, Coast Road, Towyn, Abergele, Conwy LL22 9HU. *01745 833013.* enquiries @seldonsgoldengate.co.uk. www.seldonsgoldengate.co.uk. Owner: Mr R E Seldon. On A548, Abergele to Prestatyn. Club. Open March-November; 10.5-month licence also available. **T. 508S. 50H.** 🏕 ⌀

(2m). The Beach Caravan & Chalet Park, Llanddulas, Abergele, Conwy LL22 8HA. *01492 515345.* enq@thorn leyleisure.co.uk. www.thornleyleisure.co.uk. Owner: Thornley Leisure Parks. William Sutcliffe Suite, Raymond Court, Princes Drive, Colwyn Bay. Off A55. Club. Open March 1-November 30. ☆☆☆☆☆ **BH&HPA. NCC. 260S. 18H.** ⛺ 🏕

(2m). Ty Mawr Holiday Park, Towyn Road, Towyn, Abergele, Conwy LL22 9HG. *0871 664 9785.* ty.mawr@park-resorts.com. www.park-resorts.com. Owner: Park Resorts Ltd. 3rd floor Swan Court, Waterhouse Street, Hemel Hempstead, Herts HP1 1FN. Off A584, Rhyl to Abergele, about 0.25m W of Towyn. Indoor pool. Adventure playground. Mini ten-pin bowling. All-weather, multi-sports court. Children's club. Takeaway. Family entertainment day and night. Open April-October. ☆☆☆☆ **BH&HPA. NCC. 300T. MC. 428S. 80H.** ⛺ 🔌 ♿ 🏕 ⌀

(2m). Winkups Camp, Towyn Road, Towyn, Abergele, Conwy LL22 9EN. *01745 353936.* Owner: Clwyd Holiday Camps Ltd. On A548, Rhyl to Abergele. Cabaret club. Live entertainment. Supervised children's daytime activities. Supermarket. Gift shop. Cafe. Fish and chips. Open Easter-October. ☆☆ **BH&HPA. 40T. 20MC. 369S. 100H.** ⛺ 🔌 🏕

Betws-y-Coed

(1m). Cwmlanerch Caravan Park, Betws-y-Coed, Conwy LL24 0BG. *01690 710285.* www.snowdonia.org.uk. Owner: Mr J O Hughes. On B5106. Showers. Laundry. Payphone. Play area. Deep-freeze available on site. Open March 1-October 31. ☆☆☆ **16T. MC. 33S. 1H.** ⛺ 🔌

(1m). Hendre Farm Camping and Caravan Site, Betws-y-Coed, Conwy LL24 0BN. *01690 710950.* Owner: Pierce Brothers. On A5 Betws-y-Coed to Capel Curig. Showers, shaving point, washbasins and deep sink for clothes washing. Public telephone. Open March-October. **10T. MC. 23S.**

Riverside Caravan Park, Betws-y-Coed, Conwy LL24 0BA. *01690 710310.* riversidecaravanpark@btopenworld.com. Owner: R D Harrison & Son. 600yd to town. No entry to park after 9.30pm. Adjacent to golf course and river Conwy for fishing. 2 mins walk from shops, restaurants, etc. Open March 14-October 31. **BH&HPA. 40T. MC. 70S.** ⛺ 🔌 ♿

Colwyn Bay

(3m). Bron-Y-Wendon Touring Caravan Park, Wern Road, Llanddulas, Colwyn Bay, Conwy LL22 8HG. *01492 512903.* bron-y-wendon@northwales-holidays.co.uk.www.northwales-holidays.co.uk. Owner: Lawnworth Ltd (Mrs & Mrs S Dent). Leave A55 at Llanddulas (A547) interchange and follow tourist information signs to park. Award-winning park with excellent modern facilities. Welcome Host Award. All pitches have sea views and the beach is just a short walk away. Suitable base for touring holiday - Snowdonia, Llandudno and Chester are within easy reach. Colour brochure available. AA 4 pennants. ☆☆☆☆☆ **110T. 20MC.** ✿ ⊁ ◪ ⓰

(3.5m). Bryn Defaid Caravan Park, Trawscoed Road, Lysfaen, Colwyn Bay, Conwy. *01492 514670.* Owner: Mr R A Davis. 147 Oxford Road, Runcorn WA7 4PA. Open March 1-October 31. **BH&HPA. 33S.** ⊁

(1m). Seren-y-Dyffryn, Old Highway, Colwyn Bay, Conwy LL28 5YF. *01492 543131.* michaeldowling@tiscali.co.uk. Owner: Mr M T Dowling. Highway Lodge, Old Highway, Colwyn Bay, Aberconwy & Colwyn. Take Rhos-on-Sea turn off from A55. Follow signs to Mountain Zoo. Park 0.25m past zoo on left. Quiet site with views of sea and countryside. Close to most amenities. Open March 1-January 6. ☆☆☆☆ **BH&HPA. 31S.** ⊁

Conwy

(1.5m). Aberconwy Park and Country Park, Aberconwy Park, Conwy, Conwy LL32 8GA. *01492 572002.* enquiries@aberconwypark.com. www.aberconwypark.com. Owner: K J & L Houghton. Take A55, through Conwy river tunnel, take first exit (J17) following signs to Marina. Near beach and golf course. Sea view positions available. Restaurant, bar, leisure club and health spa. 24hr security. Open March 1-January 16. ☆☆☆☆☆ **BH&HPA. 350S.** ⊁ ⓰

(2m). Berthlwyd Hall Caravan and Chalet Park, Llechwedd, Conwy, Conwy LL32 8DQ. *01492 592270.* berthlwydpark@aol.com. www.berthlwydpark.co.uk. Owner: Mr R S & Mrs L H Davies. Drive into Conwy over bridge, past castle on L, turn L at mini roundabout, follow road into Gyffin, turn R at village shop, up hill and next L into Hendre Road. Follow for 1.5m, turn R for Sychnant; site is 50yd up on R. Heated swimming pool. Play area. Laundrette. Suitable base for outdoor pursuits with Snowdon National Park close by. Conwy amenities, seaside and golf nearby. Open March 1-January 14. ☆☆☆ **BH&HPA. 102S.** ⊁

(0.25m). Bryn Gynog Park, Hendre Road, Conwy, Conwy LL32 8NF. *01492 592326.* tyddynmawr@aol.com. bryngynog@bhhpa.com. Owner: Messrs D G & M E Jones. Tyddyn Mawr Farm, Rowen, Conwy, North Wales LL32 8YL. A55 expressway to Conwy, left at castle, 0.75m turn right into Mill Hill. Park 200yd on left, on Hendre Road. 2 mins walk to shops etc. On bus route and close to railway station. Near national park. On-site warden. Laundrette. Holiday farm cottages available fore hire. Views. ☆☆☆ **BH&HPA. 25S.** ✿ ⊁

(1m). Bryn Morfa Caravan Park, Bangor Road, Conwy, Conwy LL32 8DW. *01492 592402.* Owner: Houghtons Caravan & Holiday Services Ltd. On A55, Colwyn Bay to Bangor. Open March 1-January 1. **NCC. 172S.**

(1.5m). Conwy Touring Park, Trefriw Road, Conwy LL32 8UX. *01492 592856.* sales@conwytouringpark.com. www.conwytouringpark.com. Owner: Conwy Touring Park & Co. S of Conwy on B5106. Large, slate-roofed sign on L. sheltered, wooded site with splendid views. Close to beaches and Snowdonia. Special offers available. Storage facilities. Open Easter-September. ☆☆☆ **320T. 25MC.** ⊁ ◪ ⓰

Crows Nest Farm, Sychnant Pass Road, Conwy, Conwy. *01492 596058.* Owner: Miss R S Jacobson. Off A55. Open March 14-October 30. **8T. MC. 1S. 1H.** ⊁

(5m). Tyn Terfyn Touring Site, Talybont, Conwy, Conwy LL32 8YX. *01492 660525.* glentynterfyn@tinyworld.co.uk. Owner: G Turner. From Conwy Castle take B5106 for about 5m, first house on L after road sign 'Talybont'. Clean, quiet site on level ground. Suitable base for touring north Wales, castle, mountains, beaches and lakes. Open March-October. **15T.** ⊁ ◪

Corwen

(8m). Glan-Ceirw Caravan Park, Ty Nant, Corwen, Conwy LL21 0RF. *01490 420346.* glanceirwcaravanpark@tinyworld.co.uk. www.ukparks/glanceirw. Owner: Carol Godding. Between Corwen and Betws-y-Coed on A5 bordering Snowdonia National Park. Picturesque site with trout fishing. AA 3 pennants. David Bellamy Gold Conservation Award. Open March 1-October 31. ☆☆☆☆ **BH&HPA. 9T. 6MC. 29S.** ⊁ ◪

Kinmel Bay

Sunnyvale Caravan Park, The Foryd, Kinmel Bay, Conwy LL18 5AS. *01745 343584.* Owner: Mrs K C Jones. From Rhyl promenade continue towards Towyn. Cross over the Foryd Harbour bridge; the site entrance, shared with the Sunnyvale Holiday Camp, is immediately on the right. 5-acre site set in a popular seaside town with many attractions. Open March 21-October 31. **MC. 365S.** ⊁ ⛴

Llandudno

(2m). Maes Dolau Farm, Bryn Lupus Road, Llanrhos, Llandudno, Conwy. *01492 583641.* Owner: H O Proffitt. Off A546. Main services to all pitches. Booking only. Open March-January. **BH&HPA. 10T. 100S.** ⊁ ◪

(5m). Meusydd Caravan Site, Peulwys, Glan Conwy, Llandudno, Conwy LL28 5SL. *01492 580325/01248 440326.* arwel@hyddgen-freeserve.co.uk. Owner: A W Jones. Hyddgen, Llangafto, Gaerwen LL60 6LU. 0.5m off A470, 2m S of Glanconwy. Panoramic views of Conwy estuary and Snowdonia. Quiet site 2m N of Bodnant Gardens. Country walks. Open March 1-January 14. **10S.** ⊁

(3m). Tan-y-Bryn, Bryn Pydew, Llandudno, Conwy LL31 9JZ. *01492 546307.* tan-y-bryn@pydewl.fsnet.co.uk. Owner: Mr & Mrs J Hughes. Off A55. Detailed directions on request. 5mins to all amenities. Small rural tranquil site. Hard-standing for one vehicle by each static van. Open March 1-January 15. **BH&HPA. 24S.** ⊁

(3m). Tandderwen Caravan Park, Llanrhos Road, Penrhyn Bay, Llandudno, Conwy LL30 3LD. *01492 549326.* mail@tandderwen.freeserve.co.uk. www.tandderwen.freeserve.co.uk. Owner: Goldenquote Ltd. From A470 SP to Penrhyn Bay. Park on R after 1.5m. Shops, PO, doctor surgery all within 1m. Open March 17-October 31. ☆☆☆☆ **BH&HPA. 74S.**

Llandudno Junction

(3m). Forest Hills, Pabo, Llandudno Junction, Conwy LL31 9QG. *01492 581015.* Owner: Mobile Living Ltd. A55 expressway to Glanconwy Corner towards Llandudno Junction, 1st R over railway bridge. Picturesque country site south facing. Newly developed, peaceful, secluded site. Open March-January 31. **BH&HPA. 23S.** ⊁

(3m). Glan Morfa Caravan Park, Queens Road, Llandudno Junction, Conwy LL31 9NF. *01492 572563.* Owner: Mr R Jones. Plot 10, Tre Marl Industrial Estate, Llandudno Junction, Conwy LL31 9NF. Dogs allowed with park owner's permission. No children. Close to train and bus services. Open March 1-October 31. **70T. MC. 150S. 20H.** ⊁

(1m). Hendre Wen Farm, Pabo Lane, Llandudno Junction, Conwy LL31 9JE. *01492 584126.* Owner: Hendre Wen Farm Caravans. Hendre Creuddyn, Pabo Lane, Llangystennin, Llandudno Junction, Conwy LL31 9JE. A couple of minutes off A55 Expressway. Leave A55 at Llandudno and Betws-y-Coed exit, at Glan Conwy Corner. Follow signs for Llandudno Junction, at railway bridge turn sharp right into Pabo Lane. Proceed to top of lane. Calor Gas. Open March 1-October 31. **7T. 44S.** 🖰

(0.5m). Marl Farm Caravan Park, Llandudno Junction, Conwy LL31 9JA. *01492 584446.* Owner: Mrs O & Miss J M L Davies. 2 miles from Conwy and Llandudno. Park is situated just A470 between A55 and Llandudno. Go left at 2nd roundabout, left again. Entrance is on the right. All holiday homes have private gardens. 2m from Llandudno. 4 golf courses within 2m Open March 1-October 31. **BH&HPA. 11T. 62S.** 🛏 🖰

Llanrwst

(0.25m). Bodnant Caravan Park, Nebo Road, Llanrwst, Conwy Valley LL26 0SD. *01492 640248.* ermin@bodnant-caravan-park.co.uk. www.bodnant-caravan-park.co.uk. Owner: Mrs E Kerry-Jenkins. Opposite Birmingham Garage in Llanrwst, turn off A470 for B5427, SP Nebo. Park 300yd on right opposite leisure centre. Quiet, relaxed site. Landscaped park with floral features and old farm implements. Winner of 'Wales in Bloom' in 26 years. Open March 1-October 31. ✿✿✿✿ **BH&HPA. 38T. 54MC. 2S. 2H.** 🛏 🖰

Bron Derw Touring Caravan Park, Bron Derw, Llanrwst, Conwy LL26 0YT. *01492 640494.* bronderw@amserve.com. www.bronderw-wales.co.uk. Owner: Beryl Edwards. Follow A55 on to A470 for Betws-y-Coed and Llanrwst. On entering Llanrwst turn L into Parry Road, SP Llanddoged, at the T junction turn L. Then take first farm entrance, on the R, signed Bron Derw and continue up the drive until you reach the site. Family-run site in a quiet, secluded setting on the outskirts of ancient market town of Llanrwst, with its variety of shops, cafes, restaurants, swimming pool and leisure centre. Suitable location for exploring the Snowdonia mountain range and the North Wales coast. Open March-October. **15T.** 🛏 🖰 ♿

(2m). Glyn Farm Caravans, Trefriw, Llanrwst, Conwy LL27 0RZ. *01492 640442.* Owner: Mr & Mrs I W Jones. Off B5106. Turn into car park opposite Trefriw Woollen Mills. Site situated about 100yd on left within picturesque village. Dogs allowed only with tourers. Small, family-run site, central for Snowdonia and coastal resorts. Walking country. Open March-October. ✿✿✿✿ **28T. MC. 2H.** 🛏 🖰

(2m). Maenan Abbey Caravan Park, Maenan, Llanrwst, Conwy LL26 0UL. *01492 660630.* enq@thornleyleisure.co.uk. www.thornleyleisure.co.uk. Owner: Thornley Leisure Maenan Ltd. William Sutcliffe Suite, Rayminel Court, Princes Road, Colwyn Bay. On A470, N of Llanrwst. No tourers. Chalets for rent. Open March 1-November 30. ✿✿✿✿✿ **BH&HPA. NCC. 78S.** 🛏 🖰

(1.5m). Plas-Meirion Caravan Park, Gower Road, Trefriw, Llanrwst, Conwy LL27 0RZ. *01492 640247.* plasmeirion@world online.co.uk. www.4snowdoniaholidays. co.uk. Owner: Mr & Mrs C Hughes. On B5106 Conwy to Betws-y-Coed. Look out for the Woollen Mill in Trefriw, turn opposite it. Park is 200yd on left. Small, peaceful, family-run park, suitable base for touring north Wales. Open March 1-October 31. ✿✿✿✿ **BH&HPA. 5T. MC. 17S. 6H.** 🖰

Penmaenmawr

Craiglwyd Hall Caravan Park, Craiglwyd Road, Penmaenmawr, Conwy LL34 6ER. *01492 623355.* enq@thornleyleisure.co.uk. www.thornleyleisure.co.uk. Owner: Thornley Leisure Parks Ltd. William Sutcliffe Suite, Raymond Court, Princes Drive, Colwyn Bay LL29 8HT. Off A55. Club. Golf. Open March 1-November 30. ✿✿✿✿✿ **BH&HPA. 153S. 6H.** 🛏

(1.5m). Pendyffryn Hall Caravan Park and Woodlands Touring Park, Penmaenmawr, Conwy LL34 6UF. *01492 623219.* Owner: Mr & Mrs K Clarke. Situated off A55 between Conwy and Penmaenmawr. Pass through road tunnels, take first left, SP Dwygyfylchi. Site is 5th entrance on your left. 96 acres of parkland and woodlands. Short walk to the beach and the shops. Golf, fishing, sailing all nearby. Situated in Snowdonia National Park area. Open March 1-October 31. ✿✿ **25T. 80MC. 150S.** 🖰 ✐

(1m.). Tyddyn Du Touring Park, Conwy Old Road, Penmaenmawr, Conwy LL34 6RE. *01492 622300.* www.tyddyndutouringpark.co.uk. Owner: Pam Watson-Jones. Take A55 W of Conwy. Follow tourist information signs, 1st L at roundabout after Little Chef, immediate L again towards Dwygyfylchi, site entrance 200yd on R after New Legend Inn. Over-18s only. Site offers views across Conwy Bay. Suitable base for enjoying attractions of Snowdonia. Golf, riding, walking, fishing, shops and PHs nearby. Open March 22-October 31. ✿✿✿✿ **BH&HPA. 100T. MC. 6S.** 🛏 🖰 ♿

DENBIGHSHIRE

Corwen

(5m). Cilan Caravan Park, Llandrillo, Corwen, Denbighshire LL21 0SY. *01490 440440.* Owner: Barrie Attwood. Turn left off A5 (Llangollen to Bangor) at Corwen on to B4401 (Llandrillo) through village, turn right signposted Cilan Caravan Park. Play area. Telephone. Open March 1-October 31. **MC. 36S.** 🛏 🖰

(2.5m). Gaer Hyfryd Caravan Club Site, Plas Isaf, Corwen, Denbighshire LL21 0EW. *01490 412189.* pen lan5@supanet.com. Owner: Mr & Mrs D Jones. Off A5. Members only. Simple, rural, intimate site. Toilet block and laundry facilities. Play area on site and dog walk nearby. Fishing nearby, goof area for walkers. Peaceful off-peak. Open March-October. **NCC. 35T. MC.** 🛏 🖰

(4m). Hendwr Caravan Park, Llandrillo, Corwen, Denbighshire LL21 0SN. *01490 440210.* www.hendwrcaravanpark.freeserve.co.uk. Owner: J & D Hughes. Take B4401 from Corwen (A5) for 4m, site on R. Site is SP from A5 at Corwen. Laundrette. Showers. Dishwashing room. Limited facilities during winter. Fishing nearby. Good walking area. Central location for touring north and mid Wales. Open Easter/April 1-end Octoberfor tourers; open all year for owner- occupied caravans. ✿✿✿✿ **BH&HPA. 40T. MC. 87S. 4H.** 🛏 🖰 ☙

(3.5m). Llawr Bettws Caravan Park, Glanrafon, Corwen, Denbighshire LL21 0HD. *01490 460224.* david@llawrbetws.go-plus.net. Owner: Mr D M Jones. On A494, off A5, Corwen to Bala road, 2nd R after Thomas Motor Mart. Brochure by request. Gas supplies. Peaceful site in open country. Walks. Fly fishing available. Open March-November. ✿✿✿✿ **BH&HPA. 35T. 10MC. 72S. 2H.** 🛏 🖰

(5m). Y Felin Caravan Park, Llandrillo, Corwen, Denbighshire LL21 0TD. 01490 440333. Owne: Mr B T Owen. Off A5 at Corwen on B4401. Take left turn in village of Llandrillo. Shops nearby in village. Open Easter-October 31. **6T. 6MC. 20S.** ✝ ▣

Denbigh

(4.5m). Caer-Mynydd Caravan Park, Saron, Denbigh, Denbighshire LL16 4TL. 01745 550302. kathcaermynydd @aol.com. Owner: Mrs K Welch. SW of Denbigh, off A525 to Ruthin. Past comprehensive school and pool, turn R to Prion and Saron. Privately-owned park with full services. Family-run park for over 40 years. Touring base for Snowdonia. Fishing, golf and gliding nearby. Parties or groups accepted. Open March 1-October 31. **BH&HPA. 18T. 5MC. 17S. 1H.** ✝ ▣ & ▣ ∅

(2m). Eriviatt Hall, Denbigh, Denbighshire. 01745 812636. Owner: Mr T W Challoner. On A543. Open March 21-October 30. **6T. 20S.** ✝

(4m). Station House Caravan Park, Bodfari, Denbigh, Denbighshire LL16 4DA. 01745 710372. Owner: Mr R S & M R Hastings. Off A541, Denbigh to Mold road, SP Tremeirchion. On B5429, 1st house on immediate L. Walking on Offa's Dyke. Close to village shops and inns. Open April-October. ✩✩✩ **26T. MC.** ✝ ▣

Llangollen

(4.5m). Ddol Hir Caravan Park, Glyn Ceiriog, Pandy Road, Llangollen, Denbighshire LL20 7PD. 01691 718681. Owner: Mr J W Finney. Off A5 at Chirk, near Llangollen, and B4500 for 6m, site just through Glyn Ceiriog. Pandy Road is on bank of river Ceirog. Pony, trekking, quad biking, PO, shops, PHs 15mins walk. Trout fishing, mountain walks on quiet scenic riverside park. Open March 1-October 31. **BH&HPA. NCC. 25T. 25MC. 18S.** ✝ ▣

(1m). Eirianfa Riverside Holiday Park, Berwyn Road, Llangollen, Denbighshire LL20 8AB. 01978 860919. Fishing on site. White water rafting and canoeing 500yd, golf 1m. ✩✩✩ **BH*HPA. 30T.** ✿ ✝ ▣ & ▣

(1m). Ty-Ucha Farm, Maesmawr Road, Llangollen, Denbighshire LL20 7PP. 01978 860677. Owner: K Prydderch. Off A5, SP. 4-acre, quiet site. AA 3 pennants. Golf course 0.5m. Open Easter-October. **30T. 10MC.** ✝ ▣

(0.5m). Wern Isaf Caravan & Camping Park, Wern Isaf Farm, Llangollen, Denbighshire LL20 8DU. 01978 860632. wernisaf @btopenworld.com. wernisaf.supanet.com. Owners: Mr & Mrs A C Williams. Turn up hill behind Bridge End Hotel, then R into Wern Road. Site NE of Llangollen at foot of Castell Dinasbran (Crow Castle). Welcome Host Award. Good touring centre for coast and Snowdonia. Quiet scenic site with views of Dee Valley and Welsh mountains. Fishing, golf nearby, horse riding, white water rafting and many more sporting activities 0.75m from town centre. Open Easter-October. ✩✩ **BH&HPA. 20T. 6MC. 5S. 2H.** ✝ ▣ ▣

Mold

(7m). Parc Farm Caravan Park, Llanarmon-yn-lal, Griarnynd Road, Mold, Denbighshire CH7 4QW. 01824 780666. enquiries@parcfarm.co.uk. www.parcfarm.co.uk. Owner: Mr & Mrs G L Evans. Mold to Ruthin, A494 turn on to B5430. Chester to Corwen, A5104, turn on B5430. Park SP at entrance. Privately owned in rural setting, yet close to major motorways. In Clwydian Hills, with fishing, horse riding and windsurfing. Close to Offa's Dyke. Family site with indoor swimming pool, clubhouse. Golf course nearby. Gas. Tourers taken on a long-stay basis (minimum one month stay). Open March 1-January 16. ✩✩✩ **BH&HPA. 20T. 3MC. 350S.** ✝ ▣ ▣

Prestatyn

(2m). Greenacres Caravan Park, Shore Road, Gronant, Prestatyn, Denbighshire LL19 9SS. 01745 854061. info@greenacrescaravanpark.fsnet.co.uk. Owner: Mr D M Bancroft (Partner). Off A548. Golf course 2m. PH, restaurant, indoor swimming pool and children's play are on site. Open March 1-October 31. **BH&HPA. 40T. MC. 290S. 7H.** ▣ ▣

(2m). Lyons - Robin Hood Caravan Park, Coast Road, Prestatyn, Denbighshire LL18 3UU. 01745 342264. Owner: G L Mound. On A548 Prestatyn to Rhyl. Licensed club, nightly entertainment during season, lounge bar, children's disco. Bingo. Pool tables. Takeaway food. Amusement arcade and play area. Indoor heated swimming pool. Ten-pin bowling. Open March 1-January 10. **1200S.** ▣

(1m). Morfa Ddu Caravan Park, Ffordisa, Prestatyn, Denbighshire LL19 8EG. 01745 856577. Owner: Mr Bruce Meldrum. All main services. Quiet site, well hidden. Open April 1-October 31. **2T. 2MC. 30S.** ✝ ▣

(0.5m). Nant Mill Touring Caravan Park, Nant Mill Farm, Prestatyn, Denbighshire LL19 9LY. 01745 852360. nantmill touring@aol.com. www.zeropointfive.co.uk/nant_mill/ Owner: K & B L Rowley. E of Prestatyn, on A548 coast road. Beach 0.5m. Fishing, golf course, swimming, boating and horse riding all nearby. Suitable base for sightseeing in north Wales. Open March-October. ✩✩✩✩ **150T. MC.** ✝ ▣ &

(3m). Presthaven Sands Holiday Park, Shore Road, Gronant, Prestatyn, Denbighshire LL19 9TT. 01745 853343. oewebmaster@bourne-leisure.co.uk. www.presthavensands holidaypark.co.uk. Owner: Bourne Leisure Ltd. 1 Park Lane, Hemel Hempstead, Hertfordshire HP2 4YL. A55, then A5151 to Prestatyn. A548 out of Prestatyn towards Gronant. Park SP L at next set of traffic lights. 3 licensed club rooms and 1 family PH. Playground. Tennis court. Laundrette. Restaurant and takeaway. Go karts. Mini ten-pin bowling. All-weather, multi-sports court. Heated indoor and outdoor pools. Family entertainment. Beach access from park. 2 golf courses 5-10mins. Town centre 10mins. Rhyl cinema 15mins. Open March-January. ✩✩✩✩ **BH&HPA. NCC. 100T. MC. 1075S. 406H.** ✝ ▣ & ▣ ∅

(2m). St Marys Touring & Camping Park, Gronant, Prestatyn, Denbighshire LL19 9TB. 01745 853951. Owner: Meldrum Leisure. On A548 coast road, Chester to Rhyl, E of Prestatyn. Public phone. Hotel with restaurant nearby. Open Easter-October. **50T. MC.** ✝ ▣ ▣

(4m). Talacre Beach Caravan and Leisure Parks, Station Road, Talacre, Prestatyn, Denbighshire CH8 9RD. 01745 858000/0800 717707. enquiries@talacrebeach.co.uk. www. talacrebeach.co.uk. Owner: Talacre Beach Caravan Sales Ltd. No tourers. Family-run park with landscaped surroundings. Private tropical indoor pool and leisure complex, sauna fitness suite, restaurant, club, cabaret and children's entertainment. No dogs allowed in hire caravans. Open March 1-January 6. ✩✩✩✩✩ **BH&HPA. 600S. 40H.** & ▣

Tan-y-Don Caravan Park, 263 Victoria Road, Prestatyn, Denbighshire LL19 7UT. 01745 853749. parks@ban croftleisure.co.uk. www.bancroftleisure.co.uk. Owner: Bancroft Leisure. On A548 between Rhyl and Prestatyn. Family-run park near Ffrith Beach. Play area. Laundrette. Open March 1-January 10. ✩✩✩✩ **BH&HPA. NCC. 64S. 3H.**

(0.5m). The White House by the Sea, Victoria Road West, Prestatyn, Denbighshire LL19 7AP. 01745 854289. Owner: Mrs M M Jones. On A548, Rhyl to Prestatyn. Quiet park suitable for retired people. Dogs and children welcome. Gate to Ffrith Beach. Open April 1-October 31. **22H.** ✝

Rhyl

(2m). Browns Holiday Camp, Towyn, Rhyl, Denbighshire. *01745 344844*. Owner: Mr Hodgson. On A548 Rhyl to Abergele. Laundrette. Amusements. New club. Open March-October. **168S. 20H.** 🐕

(3m). Faenol Fawr XVIth Century Manor Caravan Park, Bodelwyddan, Rhyl, Denbighshire. *01745 591691*. Owner: Mr & Mrs Goddard. From Chester and east follow A55. Take exit SP Rhyl and St Asaph, turn right under flyover past Talardy Park hotel on dual carriageway towards Rhuddlan. After 1.75m turn left, SP Glan Clwyd Hospital, site on right. Restaurant. **28T. MC.** 🐕 🔌

(3m). Golden Sands Holiday Camp, Foryd Road, Kinmel Bay, Rhyl, Denbighshire LL18 5NA. *01745 343606*. bookings @goldensandsrhyl.co.uk. www.goldensandsrhyl.co.uk. From A55 leave at St Asaph and follow signs for Rhyl. Then A547 (Abergele) to first roundabout for Kinmel Bay. Follow to junction of A548 coast road and turn L. Park entrance 300yd on R at foot of stone bridge. Follow lane up side of bridge wall. Site is on beach. 2 licensed clubs. Indoor heated fun pool. Indoor play area. Amusements. Fast food takeaway. Bingo. Adventure playground. Laundrette. Rhyl with shops, cinema etc within 3m. Golf courses within 4-8m. Towyn with fair, horse trotting etc 1m. Open March 21-October 31. ✰✰✰✰ **BH&HPA. 350S. 267H.** & 🐾 ⌀

Marine Holiday Park, Cefndy Road, Rhyl, Denbighshire. *01745 345194*. Owner: A & D Goddard. Off A525. Laundrette. Take-away. Arcade. Heated indoor swimming pool. Club. Bar. Family entertainment. Secure play area. Open March 1-October 31. **460S. 100H.** & 🐾 ⌀

(1m). Oakfield Caravan Park Ltd, Kinmel Bay, Rhyl, Denbighshire LL18 5LE. *01745 342455*. oakfield@netcom.uk.co.uk. Owner: Mr I B de Gregory. On A548, Abergele to Rhyl. Fishing and golf nearby, also Asda store and local doctor. Open March 21-October 30. ✰✰✰✰ **BH&HPA. 215S.** & 🐾

(3m). Palins Holiday Park, Morfa Avenue, Kinmel Bay, Rhyl, Denbighshire LL18 5LE. *01745 342672*. Owner: Mr Ellis. On A548, Abergele to Rhyl. Indoor fun pool, family club with live nightly entertainment. Alamo Fort playground. Laundrette. Fish and chip bar. Amusement arcade and bingo. Hire shop. Dragon Award. Open Easter-end September. **22S. 30H.** 🐕 & 🐾

(3m). Pleasant View Park, Abbey Road, Rhuddlan, Rhyl, Denbighshire LL18 5RL. *01745 590282*. stuart@plvhp.fsnet.co.uk. www.pleasantviewholidaypark.com. General Manager: Stuart Young. Set in the Vale of Clwyd, adjacent to the river Clwyd and Rhuddlan Castle. Family-run park offers suitable location for visiting the many tourist attractions along the north Wales coast and Snowdonia. Open April 1-October 31. ✰✰✰ **BH&HPA. 20T. 20MC. 94S. 12H.** 🔌

(2m). Sun Valley Caravan Park, Marsh Road, Rhuddlan, Rhyl, Denbighshire LL18 5UD. *01745 590269/0831 647568*. Owner: Sunvalley Caravan Park Ltd. Off A55. St Asaph turn-off. Direction to Rhyl, next roundabout and exit, head for Rhuddlan. 100yd to left turn, site is 250yd on right. Laundrette, amusement arcade, play area, club, fishing on site. Golf, shops, swimming pools, horseriding, cycling, boat activities nearby. Open March 1-October 31. ✰✰✰✰ **BH&HPA. 190S. 10H.** 🐕 & ⌀

(1m). The Bungalow Camp, Morfa Avenue, Rhyl, Denbighshire. *01745 334897*. Owner: Ms K Rigby. Off A548. Open March 21-October 31. **BH&HPA. 21S. 12H.**

(1m). The New Pines Caravan Holiday Home & Leisure Centre, Dyserth Road, Rhyl, Denbighshire LL18 4DY. *01745 350726*. On B5119 Dyserth to Rhyl road. Swimming pool and leisure complex. Funland amusments. Supermarket. Laundrette. Family and adult entertainment venues. Lounge bar. Restaurant. Fast food outlet. Open March 1-January 10. **BH&HPA. NCC. 391S.** 🐕 & 🐾

Ruthin

Three Pigeons Caravan Site, Graigfechan, Ruthin, Denbighshire LL15 2EU. *01824 23178*. Owner: Mrs Beryl & Jim Hawley. On A525, then B5429. Showers. Family room. Country inn, bar snacks and meals. Open March-October. **10T. MC.** 🐕

(2m). Woodlands Hall Caravan Park, Llanfwrog, Ruthin, Denbighshire LL15 2AN. *01824 702066*. woodlands hall@talk21.com. www.woodlandshallcaravanpark.co.uk. Owner: Messrs R A & G J Davies. Off B5105. Country Club on site. Gas. Laundry. restaurant. Gym. Tennis court, basketball play area. Digital TV and ducted telephone points to each plot. Woodland play area. Owners only. Golf, leisure centre, supermarkets all within 2m. Manager: Mr J Ryder. Open March 1-February 14. ✰✰✰✰✰ **NCC. 200S.** 🐕 &

St Asaph

(1m). Eryl Hall, Lower Denbigh Road, St Asaph, Denbighshire LL17 0EW. *01745 582255*. Owner: Eryl Hall Ltd. On Lower Denbigh road B5381. Club, play area, laundry and showers. Shops 1m. Quiet, woodland site within easy reach of coastal towns. Open March 21-October 7. **BH&HPA. 15T. MC. 230S.** 🔌

(2m). **Penisa'r Mynydd Caravan Park, Caerwys Road, Rhuallt, St Asaph, Denbighshire LL17 0TY.** *01745 582227.* penisarmynydd@btinternet.com. Owner: Graham Dobbs. 0.5m off A55 express way. Quiet, family site. Good access, hard-standings. In open countryside with pleasant walks, including Offa's Dyke. Close to Rhyl, Prestatyn, Colwyn Bay and Llandudno. Fishing and golf close by. Shaver points. Laundrette. Open March 1-January 15. **BH&HPA. 75T. MC.** ⚓ 🔌 ♿

FLINTSHIRE

Gwespyr

(3m). **Triangle Wood Caravan Park West, Tyn-y-Morfa, Gwespyr, Flintshire CH8 9NH.** *01745 853951.* Owner: Meldrum Leisure. On A548. Open March 1-October 31. **BH&HPA. 55S.** ⚓ 🔌

Holywell

(5m). **Abbey View, Tyn-y-Morfa, Gwespyr, Holywell, Flintshire CH8 9JN.** *01745 888401/07836 289630.* Owner: P M & J P Birtles. Off A548 coast road. 3m from Prestatyn. Peaceful park. Shop 0.25m; PO, doctor's, supermarkets 3m. Fishing, golf courses 4m. Open March 1-January 14. **14S.** ⚓ ∅

Point of Ayr Holiday Park, Talacre, Holywell, Flintshire CH8 9SA. *01745 853385.* rosanna.taylor@btopenworld.com. Owner: Point of Ayr Holiday Park Ltd. SP Talacre Beach, off A548 coast road to Prestatyn (4m). 2 mins from beach. Open March 1-January 6. ✰✰✰ **BH&HPA. 15T. 364S.** ⚓ 🔌 🛒

(3m). **Sea View, Caravan Park, Gwespyr, Holywell, Flintshire CH8 9JS.** *01745 853871.* Owner: Sea View Caravan Camp (Gwespyr) Ltd. Off A548. Follow signs for Gwespyr village. Park opposite sharp left-hand bend. Open March-January. **BH&HPA. 122S.** ⚓

(3m). **Silver Birch Caravan Park, Chester Road, Tyn-Y-Morfa, Gwespyr, Holywell, Flintshire CH8 9JN.** *01745 852563/853749.* parks@bancroftleisure.co.uk. www.bancroftleisure.co.uk. Owner: Bancroft Leisure. Tan-y-Don Caravan Park, 263 Victoria Road, Prestatyn LL19 7UT. On A548, between Talacre and Gronant. 2m from Prestatyn. Family-run, landscaped park, close to beaches and suitable as touring base. Laundrette. Play area. Shop, PH, restaurant 100yds. Open March 1-January 10. ✰✰✰✰ **BH&HPA. NCC. 105S. 3H.** ⚓ ♿

(7m). **Tree Tops Caravan Park, Gwespyr, Holywell, Flintshire CH8 9JP.** *01745 560279.* maureenwalker@totalise.co.uk. www.treetopscaravanpark.co.uk. Owner: M J Walker. Off A548. 4m from Prestatyn. Woodland park. David Bellamy Gold Conservation Award. 1m from sea. Views of Dee Estuary. Open March 1-December 7. ✰✰✰✰ **BH&HPA. 158S.** ⚓ ♿

Mold

Barlow's Caravan Park, Pen-y-Cefn Road, Caerwys, Mold, Flintshire CH7 5BA. *01352 720273.* Owner: Coed Maes-Mynan Estates Ltd. Take B5122. Off A55 and A541 and follow signs. Open March 25-October 31. **NCC. T. MC. 300S.** ⚓ 🔌 🛒

(0.5m). **Caerwys Castle Caravan Park, Caerwys, Mold, Flintshire.** *01352 720748.* Owner: Caerwys Castle Camp Ltd. On A541. Open April-October. **47S.** ⚓

From Farm, Hendre, Mold, Flintshire CH7 5QW. *01352 741217.* Owner: Roberts. A541 towards Denbigh for 5m, R turn for Rhes-y-Cae, farm 3rd on R over cattle grid. Dairy farm with animals. Views of Clwydian mountains. Open April-October. **25T.** ⚓ 🔌

(3m). **Pantymwyn Caravan Park, Pantymwyn, Mold, Flintshire CH7 5EF.** *01352 740365.* Owner: Mr Gareth Rich. Erw Goed, Pantymwyn, Mold, Flintshire. Laundrette, tennis court, large playing area. Telephone plus toilet blocks. Pool room and table tennis. PO and shop within 0.5m. Open April 1-October 31. **10T. 10MC. 190S.** ⚓ 🔌

(6m). **Roberts Dyffryn Ial, Troell Yr Alun, Llanarmon-yn-Ial, Mold, Flintshire CH7 5TA.** *01824 780286.* Owner: H L & O E Roberts. Off A494 Ruthin to Mold, on B5430. Quiet, riverside site. Area of Outstanding Natural Beauty. Near country park, mountains, riding and fishing. Easy access to Chester, Snowdon National Park and coastal towns. Walking country; more than 100 footpaths. Calor Gas. Sites for couples, preferably retired. 6m from medival town Ruthin. Shopping village 1m. Golf, country park 2m. Cinema 12m. Coast 20m. Open April-October. **4T. 5MC. 18S. 3H.** 🔌

GWYNEDD

Abersoch

(1.5m). **Beach View Caravan Park, Bwlchtocyn, Abersoch, Gwynedd LL53 7BT.** *01758 712956.* Owner: Mr F Weatherby. Drive through Abersoch and Sarn Bach over crossroads. Take next L, SP Bwlchtocyn and Porthtocyn Hotel. Continue past Chapel, next L turn follow sign Porthtocyn Hotel. Park is on the L. Only 6mins from beach, fishing and all water sports. Golf course nearby. Doctor 2m; shops, garage within 2m. Open mid March-mid October. **BH&HPA. 47T. MC.** ⚓ 🔌

(0.5m). **Bryn Cethin Bach Caravan Park, Lon Garmon, Abersoch, Gwynedd LL53 7UL.** *01758 712719.* Owner: K W & M G Eyton-Jones. A499 to Abersoch, fork R at Land and Sea Garage, park 0.5m up hill on R. Laundrettes. Fishing lakes for residents. 0.5m from beach, harbour and village. Golf course 1m. Open Easter-January. ✰✰✰✰✰ **BH&HPA. 65S. 2H.** ⚓

(1m). **Caravan Site, Castellmarch, Abersoch, Gwynedd LL53 7UE.** *01758 713278.* Owner: Mr L E Jones. On A499, Pwllheli to Abersoch. Open March 1-October 31. **42S.** ⚓

(1m). **Deucoch Touring Camp Site, Sarnbach, Abersoch, Gwynedd LL53 7LD.** *01758 713293.* Owner: John & Jan Williams. Abersoch 1m. Mobile shop calls. Playground. Open March 1-October 30. ✰✰✰✰ **BH&HPA. 68T. 10MC.** ⚓ 🔌 ♿

(1m). **Green Pastures Caravan Park, Abersoch, Gwynedd LL53 7LD.** *01758 712653.* Owner: Mr P & C A Stanton. On A499 through town to Sarn Bach, turn right and follow road round for about 0.25m, turn right. Open March 1-October 31. **BH&HPA. 60S. 2H.** ⚓ 🛒

(2.5m). **Nant-y-Big Caravan Site, Nant-y-Big, Abersoch, Gwynedd LL53 7DB.** *01758 712686.* Owner: Mr J G Jones. Ceiriad, Cilan, Abersoch, Pwllheli LL53 7DB. S of Abersoch, through the village of Sarn Bach. Head for Cilan and Porth Ceiriad beach. Porth Ceiriad beach 150yd. Fishing. Golf course 1.5m. PO and shop 1m. Doctor at Abersoch village. All water sports available at Abersoch. Pony treking 1m. Open Easter-October 31. **BH&HPA. 22T. MC. 12S. 3H.** ⚓ 🔌

(1.5m). **Pant-gwyn Cottage, Sarn-Bach, Abersoch, Gwynedd.** *01758 712268.* Owner: P Thomas. Mobile shop calls. Dogs allowed on leads. Bookings taken. Open March 1-October 31. **15T. MC. 4S. 1H.** ⚓ 🔌

(1m). **Rhandir Farm, Myntho, Abersoch, Gwynedd.** *01758 712594.* Owner: Mr G Wynne-Roberts. Off A499. Open March-October. **64S.** ⚓

Please mention Caravan Sites 2006 when replying to advertisers

Sarn Farm, Sarn Bach, Abersoch, Gwynedd LL53 5BG.
01757 12144. Owner: Mr & Mrs G Jones Griffith. Site is near Abersoch village. Golf course. Beaches. Shops. Bus stop. Private road to beach. Showers. Hot water. Fridge and freezer. Open March-October. **3T. 2MC. 14S. 2H.** ⚊

(1.5m). Tal y fan Holiday Park, Abersoch, Gwynedd LL53 7UD. *01758 712140.* Owner: Haulfryn Group Ltd. The Warren, Abersoch, Pwllheli, Gwynedd LL53 7AA. A499, Pwllheli to Abersoch. Open March 1-October 31. ✰✰✰✰ **BH&HPA. NCC. 118S.** ⚊

(1m). The Warren Holiday Park, Abersoch, Gwynedd LL53 7AA. *01758 714100.* warrensales@haulfryn. co.uk. Owner: Haulfryn Group Ltd. A499, Pwllheli to Abersoch. Club. Fun pools and play area. Tennis courts. New leisure centre. Indoor pool, shop. Golf and Abersoch 2m. Open March 1-January 17. ✰✰✰✰✰ **BH&HPA. NCC. 542S.** ⚊ ⚊

(1m). Ty Newydd Farm Caravan Site, Abersoch, Gwynedd. *01758 812446.* Owner: Mr R B Jones. Open March 1-November 1. **28S.**

(0.5m). Tyn-y-Mur Camping & Touring Park, Lon Garmon, Abersoch, Gwynedd LL53 7UL. *01758 712328.* Owner: H Roberts & N Harrison. Sharp right at Land & Sea Garage on approach to Abersoch. Park 0.5m on left. Open Easter-end September. ✰✰✰✰ **BH&HPA. NCC. 40T. 10MC.** ⚊ ⚊

Amlwch

(5m). Waen Farm Caravan Park, Llanfechell, Anglesey, Amlwch, Gwynedd LL68 0RG. *01407 711561.* enquiries@ waenfarm.co.uk. www.waenfarm.co.uk. Owner: Rosemary and Bernard Murphy. 8m along A5025 from Valley crossroads. 2m to Cemaes Bay. Quiet, farmland-based site in landscape area. Seaside village nearby. Open March 1-October 31. ✰✰✰✰ **BH&HPA. 9S. 3H.** ⚊ ⚊

Bala

(5m). Bryn Gwyn Caravan & Camping Park, Llanuwchllyn, Bala, Gwynedd LL23 7UB. *01678 540687.* Owner: Mr & Mrs A P Roberts. Godre'r Aran, Llanuwchllyn, Bala, Gwynedd, N Wales. 0.5m W along Trawsfynydd road, off A494, 0.5m N of Llanuwchllyn. 1m from S end of Bala. Small, peaceful, riverside park, free fishing. Village inn within walking distance. Shop in village. Refurbished toilets. Seasonal touring caravan pitches. Dogs on leads. Open Easter-end October. **10T. 5MC. 30S.** ⚊ ⚊

(4m). Bryn Melyn Country Holiday Park, Llanderfel, Bala, Gwynedd LL23 7RA. *01678 530210.* Owner: Mr & Mrs A & B Ward. From Llangollen A5 left at Corwen on to B4401, 7m south. Suitable touring centre. Coarse fishing on park. Outdoor leisure activities, including salmon and trout fishing, nearby. Open March-January. **BH&HPA. 18T. MC. 100S. 4H.** ⚊ ⚊ ⚊

(6m). Dolhendre Caravan Park, Llanuwchllyn, Bala, Gwynedd LL23 7TD. *01678 540629.* relax@dolhendre.co.uk. www.dolhendre.co.uk. Owner: Mike & Lesley Barbet. 2m off A494, on lane SP 'Trawsfynydd 14m'. Then by phone box take right fork. Country inn and village shop within 2m. Riverside location. Fully serviced pitches. Laundry, games room, Calor Gas. Trout fishing. 2 golf courses, shops, leisure centre, lake, cinema nearby. White water rafting, horse riding, walking. David Bellamy Conservation Award. **36S.** ✿ ⚊ ⚊

Glanllyn-Lakeside Camping & Caravan Park, & Werngoch Holiday Home Caravan Park, Llanuwchllyn, Bala, Gwynedd LL23 7ST. *01678 540227/540441.* info@glanllyn. com. www. glanllyn.com. Owner: Mr E T Pugh & Mrs M W Pugh. On A494, 3m SW of Bala. Launching facilities. Lakeside location. Level parkland with extensive views of Aran, Arenig and Berwyn mountains. Central base for north and mid Wales. Open March-October. ✰✰✰✰ **BH&HPA. 84T. 50MC. 42S.** ⚊ ⚊ ⚊

(6m). Hendre Mawr Caravan Park, Llanuwchllyn, Bala, Gwynedd LL23 7UF. *01678 540658.* Owner: Mr & Mrs D A Davies. 1.5m SW of Llanuwchllyn on A494. Views of the Aran mountains. Fully-serviced pitches. Calor Gas. Adventure playground. Laundry. **BH&HPA. 49S. 3H.** ⚊

(4.5m). Palewood Holiday Park, Llanderfel, Bala, Gwynedd LL23 7RA. *01678 530212.* palewoodhp@aol.com. www.pale wood.co.uk. Owner: Mr R S Davies. M6, M54 towards Telford, then A5 towards Oswestry. Turn left on A5 to Llangollen and Corwen then left on to B4401. Site is 2m on left after Llandrillo. Small, coarse fishing lake, 34 acres of woodland. Laundrette. Public phone. Golf, water sports 5m. Shopping in Bala. Open March 1-January 14. **BH&HPA. 113S.** ⚊ ⚊

(1m). Pen-y-Garth Caravan & Camping Park, Bala, Gwynedd LL23 7ES. *01678 520485/07808 198717.* stay@penygarth. co.uk. www.penygarth.co.uk. Owner: Roger Baker. From Bala; take B4391, after 1m fork right at sign to Rhosygwaliau. Site hidden away among stunning scenery, yet close to Bala town/lake. Level, well laid-out touring and camping pitches. Wildlife. Safe for children. Open March-October. ✰✰✰✰ **BH&HPA. 30T. 5MC. 54S. 5H.** ⚊ ⚊

(0.5m). Penybont Touring & Camping Park, Llangynog Road, Bala, Gwynedd LL23 7PH. *01678 520549.* peny bont@balalake.fsnet.co.uk. www.penybont-bala.co.uk. Owner: Mr D Edwards. 0.5m from Bala, on B4391. Bala, including sailing club, 10mins walk. Modern shower block includes facilities for disabled visitors and laundry room. Calor Gas available. Open April-October. ✰✰✰✰ **BH&HPA. 35T. MC.** ⚊ ⚊ ⚊

(2.5m). Ty Isaf Caravan Site, Llangynog Road, Bala, Gwynedd LL23 7PP. *01678 520574.* Owner: Mr J D & B J Evans. Off B4391, near telephone kiosk and postbox, SE Bala. Quiet, family site with level grass. Gas sales. Showers. Games area. Fishing, golf course, shops, PO, doctor all within 2.5m. Open Easter or April 1-October 30. **30T. 5MC. 1H.** ⚊ ⚊

(4m). Tyn Cornel Camping, Frongoch, Bala, Gwynedd LL23 7NU. *01678 520759.* gates.tooth@talk21.com. www.tyncornel. co.uk. Owner: Mrs J Tooth. Take A4212 from Bala. Drive through Frongoch village, 1m beyond on L. Sharp turn over river bridge. Suitable centre for touring north Wales, water sports and fishing. Showers. New toilet/shower block opened in 2005. Riverside walk to the Celyn Reservoir and Dam from site. Open March-October. ✰✰ **BH&HPA. 37T. MC.** ⚊ ⚊ ⚊ ⚊

(3m). **Tytandderwen Caravan Park, Bala, Gwynedd LL23 7EP.** *01678 520273.* Owner: Mr R Lloyd-Davies. SE of A494. Bottled gas supplies. Open March-October 31. ✿✿✿ **BH&HPA. 10T. 10MC. 60S.** 🔥 🔌 ♿

Bangor

(3m). **Dinas Farm Camping Site, Halfway Bridge, Bangor, Gwynedd LL57 4NB.** *01248 364227.* www.dinasfarmtouring park.co.uk. Owner: M L & L E Jones. Off A5. Fishing on site - by permit only. Also 20 tents pitches available. Open March 1-October 31. **15T. 5MC.** 🔥 🔌

(1m). **Lloyds Caravan Site, Woodside, Menai Bridge Road, Bangor, Gwynedd.** *01248 362618.* Owner: J & I Lloyd. On A5122. Open March 1-October 31. **27T. MC. 53S.** 🔥

(5m). **Ogwen Bank Caravan Park & Country Club, Ogwen Bank, Bethesda, Bangor, Gwynedd LL57 3LQ.** *01248 600486.* Owner: J N Pritchard. On the A5. Set amid 12 acres of glorious woodland. Members' club with entertainment and bar snacks in main season. Children welcome. Touring pitches with own private shower, WC, washbasin, water point, and TV aerial. Laundrette. Hill walking. Open March 1-mid November. ✿✿✿ **BH&HPA. 76T. MC. 100S. H.** 🔥 🔌 ♿ 🏕

(5m). **Tros-y-Waen Holiday Farm, Pentir, Bangor, Gwynedd LL57 4EF.** *01248 364448.* Owner: Mr P W & D W Price. From B4366, at roundabout take B4547 to Llanberis, left after 0.5m. Site is 200yd on right. On working farm, quiet and central. Showers. **20T. MC.** ✿ 🔥 🏕

Barmouth

(5m). **Barmouth Bay Holiday Village, Talybont, Barmouth, Gwynedd LL43 2BJ.** *01341 247350.* www.haulfryn.co.uk. Owner: Haulfryn Group Ltd. The Warren, Abersoch, Gwynedd LL 53 7AA. Easy and scenic drive from West Midlands and North-West. From Barmouth take A496, SP Harlech, about 4.5m just before entering Talyont village, run L towards the beach, over humpback railway bridge and down to the bottom of the lane. Residents' indoor pool complex, children's play area, supermarket, laundrette. Open March 1-October 31. ✿✿✿✿ **BH&HPA. NCC. 230S.** ♿

(5m). **Benar Beach Camping & Touring Site, Talybont, Barmouth, Gwynedd LL43 2AR.** *01341 247001/247571.* Owner: Mr David Powell Jones. 5m N of Barmouth. On the seaward side of A496, midway between Barmouth and Harlech. Family site 100yd from sandy beach with dunes. Satellite and TV hook-ups. Suitable touring base for Snowdonia and mid-Wales. Access to private fishing. Open March-October. **BH&HPA. 30T. MC.** 🔥 🔌 ♿

(2m). **Caerddaniel Caravan Park, Llanaber, Barmouth, Gwynedd LL42 1RR.** *01341 280611.* enquiries@barmouth holidays.co.uk. www.barmouthholidays.co.uk. Owner: R O Williams & Son. 9 seasonal touring pitches. Dragon Award. Site adjoins sandy beach. Views and sunsets. Wayside Inn nearby with restaurant, takeaway and children's room. Walking country. 8m from Royal St David's golf course. Shops in Barmouth. Open March-November for tourers etc; open all year for owner-occupied holiday homes. ✿✿✿ **9T. 345S. 5H.** 🔥 🔌 🏕

(5m). **Dyffryn Seaside Estate, Dyffryn, Ardudwy, Barmouth, Gwynedd LL44 2HD.** *01341 247220.* Owner: Dyffryn Seaside Estate Co Ltd. On A496. Club. Dragon Award. Open March-October. **BH&HPA. 3T. 3MC. 248S. 40H.** 🔥 🔌 🏕

(1.5m). **Hendre Coed Isaf Caravan Park, Llanaber, Barmouth, Gwynedd LL42 1AJ.** *01341 280597.* enquiry@hendrecoedisaf. co.uk. www.hendrecoedisaf.co.uk. Owner: Hendre Coed Ltd. On main coastal road A496, Barmouth to Harlech. N of Barmouth. Terraced caravan pitches with views over Cardigan Bay. Pet and pet-free caravans. Club. Swimming pool. Games room. Dragon Award. Sea, mountains, golf, fishing, walks and other attractions all nearby. Open April-October. ✿✿✿✿ **BH&HPA. 93S. 6H.** 🔥 🔌

(0.5m). **Hendre Mynach Touring Caravan & Camping Park, Llanaber, Barmouth, Gwynedd LL42 1YR.** *01341 280262.* mynach@lineone.net. www.hendremynach.co.uk. Owner: Mr A R Williams. N of Barmouth on the A496, Harlech road. Suitable base for touring mid and north Wales. Heated toilet and shower blocks. Laundrette. Cafe with takeaway. Play area. Mother and baby room. 100yd from a safe, sandy beach. 2 hotels with family rooms 20mins walk. 20mins walk into Barmouth along the promenade. Pets welcome; dog walk provided. Site near to public transport. Open March 1-January 9. ✿✿✿✿ **60T. MC.** 🔥 🔌 ♿ 🏕

(4m). **Islaw'r Ffordd Caravan Park, Talybont, Barmouth, Gwynedd LL43 2AQ.** *01341 247269.* info@islawrffordd.co.uk. www.islawrffordd.co.uk. Owner: E Evans & Sons. On A496, Harlech to Barmouth. Heated indoor pool. Golf course 8m. Open March 1-December 31. ✿✿✿ **25T. 10MC. 200S. 30H.** 🔥 🔌 ♿

(4m). **Llwyn Griffri, Talybont, Barmouth, Gwynedd.** *01341 247295.* Owner: Mr Derek G Williams. Off A496. Open May-October. **25T. MC.** 🔥 🔌

(5m). **Parc Caerelwan, Talybont, Barmouth, Gwynedd LL43 2AX.** *01341 247236.* parc@porthmadog.co.uk. www.porth madog.co.uk/parc. Owners: T & V J Smedley. Off A496, Harlech to Barmouth. Turn L at 30mph sign when entering Talybont village. First caravan park on the R after the railway bridge. No tourers. Holiday home adapted for disabled users. Indoor heated swimming pool. Laundrette. Sauna, steam room, solarium, fitness room. Children's fun room. Table tennis, pool tables, golf and pony trekking close by. Pets welcome. Near 5m beach. ✿✿✿ **BH&HPA. NCC. 149S. 69H.** ✿ 🔥 🏕

(5m). **Parc Isaf Farm, Dyffryn Ardudwy, Barmouth, Gwynedd LL44 2RJ.** *01341 247447.* Owner: Mrs J Edwards. Travel from Barmouth on the A496 through the village of Talybont, then after about 0.25m there is a church on the L, a few yards on there is a right-hand turning through a pillar gateway. Site is the second farm on R. Views of Cardigan Bay. Shops, PO, sandy beach, garage within 1m. Golf, fishing, historic castle, caverns within 5m. Open March-October. **15T. 1H.** 🔥 🔌

(4m). **Rowen Caravan Park, Talybont, Barmouth, Gwynedd LL43 2AD.** *01341 242626.* holidays@rowenpark.com. Owner: Mr J L & Mrs O M Williams. Off A496, 4m Nof Barmouth on the L. Small, quiet, family-run park for families. Footpath to beach. Open April-end October. ✿✿✿✿ **BH&HPA. 35S. 27H.** 🔥 🏕 ♿

(4m). **Sarnfaen Holiday Park, Talybont, Barmouth, Gwynedd LL43 2AQ.** *01341 247241.* info@sarnfaen.co.uk. www.sarnfaen.com. Owners: R Gallimore & C Gallimore. On main A496 coast road from Barmouth L turn on entering Talybont village, over railway halt and 3rd entrance on right. Level, landscaped site, 5mins walk to sandy beach. New leisure club, heated indoor swimming pool. New adventure play area for the children. Coffee shop, games room, laundry. Dog walkOpen March 1-January 7. ✿✿✿ **BH&HPA. 109S. 30H.** 🔥 ♿ 🏕

(4m). Sunnysands Caravan Park, Talybont, Barmouth, Gwynedd LL43 2LQ. *01341 247301.* enquiries@sunny sands.co.uk. www.sunnysands.co.uk. Owner: Sunnysands Caravan Park Ltd. On the A496, Harlech to Barmouth road. Indoor pool complex. Slipway to beach. Licensed social club. Laundrette. Family amusement centre. Takeaway. Coffee shop. Children's park, shop. Leisure centre 4m. Golf course, cinema and theatre 6m. Open March 1-October 31. **BH&HPA. 25T. 25MC. 550S. 60H.** 🐕 🔌 ♿ ⚡

(5m). The Old Mill Caravan Park, Talybont, Barmouth, Gwynedd LL43 2AN. *01341 247366.* www.lokalink. co.uk/oldmillpark. Owner: M A Wild & Family. On the A496, Harlech to Barmouth road. Small, family-owned park set in wooded and landscaped grounds by the river Ysgethin with 17th-century corn mill. Open March-October. ☆☆☆☆☆ **BH&HPA. 10S. 3H.**

(2.5m). Trawsdir Touring Site, Llanaber, Barmouth, Gwynedd LL42 1RR. *01341 280999/280611.* Owner: Williams. Open March-October. **50T. MC.** 🐕 🔌 ♿

Beddgelert

(0.75m). Beddgelert Forest Camping Site, Forest Holidays, Beddgelert, Gwynedd LL55 4UU. *01766 890288.* www.forestholidays.co.uk. Owner: Forest Enterprise (Forest Holidays). 231 Corstophine Road, Edinburgh EH12 7AT. NW of Beddgelert on the A4085. 5m SW of Snowdon Forest, in a woodland environment. Suitable base from which to explore Snowdonia National Park. Brochure request: 0131 3340066. Manager: Angus Macdonald. **BH&HPA. 140T. MC.** 🐕 🔌 ♿ ⚡

Blaenau Ffestiniog

(2m). Coed y Llwyn Caravan Club Site, Gellilydan, Blaenau Ffestiniog, Gwynedd LL41 4EN. *01766 590254.* www.caravanclub.co.uk. Owner: Caravan Club. East Grinstead House, East Grinstead, West Sussex RH19 1UA. See website for standard directions to site. Caravan Club members only. Landscaped site within Snowdonia National Park. Toilet blocks. Privacy cubicles. Laundry facilities. Vegetable preparation area. Motorhome service point. Play equipment. Fishing and golf course nearby. Significant places of interest nearby. Suitable for families. Open March-October. **NCC. 104T. MC.** 🐕 🔌 ♿

(4m). Llechrwd Caravan Site, Maentwrog, Blaenau Ffestiniog, Gwynedd LL41 4HF. *01766 590240.* llechrwd@hotmail.com. www.llechrwd.co.uk. Owne: Miss N Seears. Along A496 between Blaenau Ffestiniog and Maentwrog. Quiet, family-run riverside site situated in Snowdonia National Park. Suitable centre for walking, slate mines Ffestiniog Railway and climbing. Safe beach 7m. Porthmadog 9m and Harlech 8m. Open April 1-October 31. **8T. MC. 1H.** 🐕 🔌

Caernarfon

(6m). Beach Holiday West Point, The Beach, Pontlyfni, Caernarfon, Gwynedd LL54 5ET. *01286 660400.* Owner: Mr Brian Ayers. Located off the A487 on to the A499, Caernarfon to Pwllheli road. Own beach, all water sports. TV and video. Full central heating and electric blankets. Villas for sale. Boat park and launch service available. Also sea and river fishing. Open March 1-November. ☆☆☆☆ **BH&HPA. NCC. 50S.** 🐕 ⚡ ∅

(5m). Bryn Gloch Caravan & Camping Park, Betws Garmon, Caernarfon, Gwynedd LL54 7YY. *01286 650216.* eurig@bryngloch.co.uk. www.bryngloch.co.uk. Owner: I & B Jones. On A4085, Beddgelert Caernarfon. On bank of river Gwyrfai, in the Vale of Betws. Most facilities available. Showers. 2m from Mount Snowdon. AA 4 pennants. AA Best Campsite in Wales 2005. Open January 1-October 31. ☆☆☆☆ **48T. 48MC. 4S. 15H.** ✿ 🐕 🔌 ♿ ⚡ ∅

(4m). Bryn Teg Caravan Park, Llanrug, Caernarfon, Gwynedd LL55 4RF. *01286 871374.* Owner: Thornley Holiday Parks Int. Ltd. Off A4086. Club. Heated indoor pool. Private lake. Open March-January 25. **BH&HPA. 68T. 50MC. 286S. 26H.** 🐕 🔌 ⚡

(6m). Caernarfon Bay Caravan Park, Dinas Dinlle, Caernarfon, Gwynedd LL54 5TW. *01286 830492.* caernarfon-bayhols@totalise.co.uk. Owner: Mr G K Ashurst. Off A499. Small park 50yd from beach and close to all amenities. Pets welcome. Open March 1-October 31. ☆☆☆ **18S. 5H.** 🐕 ♿ ⚡

Coed Helen Caravan Club Site, Coed Helen, Caernarfon, Gwynedd LL54 5RS. *01286 676770.* www.caravanclub.co.uk. Owner: The Caravan Club. East Grinstead House, East Grinstead, West Sussex RH19 1UA. See website for standard directions to site. Slightly sloping, open site 10mins walk from the historic town of Caernarfon. Toilet blocks, laundry facilities, vegetable preparation area, bar and dog walk nearby. Shop adjacent to the site. Fishing, golf, and NCN cycle route 5m. Suitable for families. Open March-October. **NCC. 45T.** 🐕 🔌

(1m). Coed Helen Holiday Park, Coed Helen Road, Caernarfon, Gwynedd LL54 5RT. *01286 672852.* www.haul fryn.co.uk. Owner: Haulfryn Group Ltd. The Warren, Abersoch, Pwllheli, Gwynedd LL53 7AA. On A487, 600yd from castle. Outdoor swimming pool. Residents' bar, games room. Laundrette. Open March 1-October 31. ☆☆☆ **BH&HPA. NCC. 50T. 250S.** ⚡

(0.3m). Cwm Cadnant Valley Park, Llanberis Road, Caernarfon, Gwynedd LL55 2DF. *01286 673196.* ipc@cadnant valley.co.uk. www.cwmcadnant.co.uk. Owner: DE & JP Bird. A4086, from Caernarfon to Llanberis. Site opposite school in a small, peaceful valley. 0.25m walk to town centre. Open March 14-November 3. ☆☆☆ **BH&HPA. 30T. 5MC.** 🐕 🔌 ♿

(6m). Dinlle Caravan Park, Dinas Dinlle, Caernarfon, Gwynedd LL54 5TW. *01286 830324.* enquiries@thornley leisure.co.uk. www.thornleyleisure.co.uk. Owner: Thornley Leisure Parks. Raymond Court, Princes Drive, Colwyn Bay LL28 8HT. Off A499, Pwllheli to Caernarfon. Laundrette. Licensed club. Heated swimming pool. Takeaway. Beach 300yd. Open March 1-November 30. ☆☆☆☆ **BH&HPA. 100T. 30MC. 178S. 17H.** ⌂ 🖳 ⚷

(1.5m). Glan Gwna Country Holiday Park, Caeathro, Caernarfon, Gwynedd LL55 2SG. *01286 671740.* sales@glangwna.com. www.glangwna.com. Owner: M W Jones and Family. Off A4085. Swimming pool. Club. Entertainment. Laundrette. Takeaway. Caravan Sales: 01286 671740. Riverside and parkland pitches available. Game and coarse fishing available on the park. Golf courses nearby. Open April-October for tourers; open March-January 3 for holiday homes. **70T. MC. 120S.** ⌂ 🖳 ⚷ 🏊

(.5m). Is-Helen Farm, Caernarfon, Gwynedd LL54 5RN. *01286 678497.* Owner: Mr I N Owen. Within walking distance of a golf course. fishing and sailing very close. 5mins walk to Menai Straits. Children can watch milking and feeding calves. Open March 1-October 31. ☆☆☆ **3T. 10S. 1H.** ⌂ 🖳

(7m). Llyn-y-Gele Farm Caravan Park, Pontlyfni, Caernarfon, Gwynedd LL54 5EL. *01286 660289/660283.* Owner: Mr W Vaughan-Jones. On A499. 7m S of Caernarfon, entrance 1st R by garage in Pontllyfni village. Quiet, family site near beach by private footpath. Suitable base for touring Snowdonia and Lleyn Peninsula and Anglesey. Panoramic views of Snowdonia range. Shops & PO 2m, fishing 0.25m, doctor 4m, golf 7m. AA 2 pennants and RAC listed. Open Easter-October 31. **6T. 6MC. 24S.** ⌂ 🖳

(7m). Morfa Lodge Holiday Park, Dinas Dinlle, Caernarfon, Gwynedd LL54 5TP. *01286 830205.* info@morfalodge.co.uk. www.morfalodge.co.uk. Owner: Mr D S Livingstone. Off A499, Pwllheli to Caernarfon. Club. Heated outdoor swimming pool and play equipment, shop, laundrette, toilet for disabled visitors. Showers. Dragon Award. Open March 1-October 31. ☆☆☆☆ **BH&HPA. NCC. 50T. 20MC. 150S. 20H.** ⌂ 🖳 ⚷ 🏊

(3m). Plas Gwyn Caravan Park, Plas Gwyn, Llanberis Road, Ilanrug, Caernarfon, Gwynedd LL55 2AQ. *01286 672619.* info@plasgwyn.co.uk. www.plasgwyn.co.uk. Owner: Len & Jane Hampton. Entrance off the A4086 on R, 3m from

Caernarfon, about half way to Llanberis. Gas exchange service. Shop and laundry. Caravans for hire. Bed and breakfast on request. Horse riding, golf, fishing nearby. 0.5m to shop and PO. Open March 1-October 31. ☆☆☆☆ **BH&HPA. 27T. 3MC. 18S. 5H.** ⌂ 🖳 🏊

(1.5m). Rhyd-y-Galen Caravan Park, Rhyd-y-Galen Bethel, Caernarfon, Gwynedd LL55 3PS. *01248 670110.* Owner: H M & C W Salisbury. B4366, Caernarfon to Bethel Road. Open Easter-October. **20T.** ⌂ 🖳

(2m). Riverside Camping, Seiont Nurseries, Pontrug, Caernarfon, Gwynedd LL55 2BB. *01286 678781.* brenda@ riversidecamping.freeserve.co.uk. www.riversidecamping. co.uk. Owner: Brenda Hummel. 2m from Caernarfon on right of A4086 (Caernarfon-Llanberis road). Small, sheltered site bordered by river. Located in Snowdonia within easy reach of sea and mountains. Modern toilets and separate facilities for disabled people. Children's playground. On-site: cafe/restaurant in old mill, laundrette, fishing on association water. General store and fish and chip shop 1m. Indian restaurant nearby. Open March-October. ☆☆☆☆ **20T. 5MC.** ⌂ 🖳 ⚷

(5m). Snowdon View Caravan Park, Brynrefail, Llanberis, Caernarfon, Gwynedd LL55 3PD. *01286 870349.* www.nav.to/snowdonview. Owner: Sunnysands Caravan Park Ltd. Talybont, Barmouth, Gwynedd. Off A4086, on B4547. Playground. Country tavern. Laundrette. Indoor swimming pool. Open March 1-November 1. **BH&HPA. 68T. 50MC. 170S.** ⌂ 🖳

(12m). Talymignedd Farm, Nantlle, Caernarfon, Gwynedd LL54 6BT. *01286 880374.* Owner: Mr H Jones. W of Snowdon, on the B4418 from Rhyd-ddu to Perygroes. About 2m from Rhyd-ddu. Walking, climbing and fishing on 1300 acres. Peaceful site. Open March 1-October 31. **10T. 6MC.** ⌂ 🖳

(3m). Twll Clawdd, Llanrug, Caernarfon, Gwynedd LL55 2AZ. *01286 672838.* pwd@twllclawdd.co.uk. www.twll clawdd.co.uk. Owner: Mr PW Dodd. On Caernarfon-Llanberis road. A4086. Quiet, rural surroundings within easy reach of Snowdonia (4m) and Anglesey. Calor Gas stockist. Laundrette. Showers and shaver points. Chemical toilet emptying point. Telephone. Open March 1-October 31. **40T. 10MC. 1S. 2H.** ⌂ 🖳

(3m). Tyn Rhos Farm Caravan Park, Saron, Llanwnda, Caernarfon, Gwynedd LL54 5UH. *01286 830362.* Owner: Mr W C & M J Evans. Turn R off A487, Caernarfon to Porthmadog, immediately after crossing Seiont Bridge into Pant Road, SP Saro. Site 3m on L. Showers. Golf 2.5m. Shop, PO, doctor, garage 3m. Open March-mid January. **20T. 5MC.** ⌂ 🖳

Coastal Snowdonia

300 YARDS FROM LONG SANDY BEACH

ENJOY THE BEST OF BOTH WORLDS, BETWEEN SEA AND MOUNTAINS

A "DRAGON AWARD" PARK BY THE WALES TOURIST BOARD FOR HIGH STANDARDS AND FACILITIES

Luxury Holiday Homes For Hire. All With Shower, Toilet, Fridge, Colour T.V. and Continental Quilts.

☆ **Licensed Club House**   ☆ **Electrical Hook-ups available**
☆ **Entertainment**   ☆ **Flush Toilets, Hot Showers**
☆ **Heated Swimming Pool**   ☆ **Washing-up facilities**
☆ **Games Room**   ☆ **Children's Play Area**
☆ **Tourers & Campers on level grassland** ☆ **Launderette**
☆ **Pets Welcome Under Control**

For colour brochure write or telephone:
Dinlle Caravan Park, Dinas Dinlle, Caernarfon. 01286 830 324
www.thornleyleisure.co.uk

(3m). Tyn-y-Coed Caravan Park, Llanrug, Caernarfon, Gwynedd LL55 2AQ. *01286 673565.* Owner: M & G M Williams. On RHS A4086 road to Llanberis from Caernarfon - 3 miles. Free H&C showers. Razor points. Laundry. Calor Gas. Dogs on lead only. Hotel indoor pool 0.5m. Fishing, golf course, shops, PO all within 1-3m. Open April-September. **10T. 10MC. 40S.** 🐕 🖃

(4m). Tyn-yr-Onnen Mountain Farm Caravan Park, Waunfawr, Caernarfon, Gwynedd LL55 4AX. *01286 650281.* Owner: Mr T J Griffith. Off A4085 Beddgelert road left at Waunfawr (ex-church). 200-acre working hill farm site in good hill and country walking area. Easy reach of beach, mountains and places of interest. Off beaten track with fantastic views. Animals for children to feed. Open May-October. ✰✰✰ **BH&HPA. 20T. 10MC. 3S. 3H.** 🐕 🖃 ♿ ⚑

(3m). White Tower Caravan Park, Llandwrog, Caernarfon, Gwynedd LL54 5UH. *01286 830649.* whitetower@supanet.com. www.whitetower.supanet.com. Owner: Mrs L Hulme. From Caernarfon take A487 Porthmadog road for about 0.25m, go past Tesco supermarket, straight ahead at roundabout take first R, park 3m on R. Superpitches also available. Central heated shower block for tourers. Laundrette. Club. Games room. TV room. Calor Gas sales. Heated pool, entertainment, and children's play area. Golf course 1.5m. Seasonal touring pitches available. Open March 1-January 10. ✰✰✰✰ **BH&HPA. NCC. 84T. 20MC. 54S.** 🐕 🖃 ♿ ⌀

Criccieth

(1.5m). Cae Canol Camping & Caravan Park, Criccieth, Gwynedd LL52 0NB. *01766 522351.* Owner: Mrs E W Roberts. 2m N of Criccieth via B4411. Level site, modern facilities. Electric points, golf, fishing. Lovely riverside walks within 300yd of site. Leading to Lloyd George village of LLanystumdwy. Open March-October. **20T. 20MC. 20S.** 🐕 🖃

(3m). Camping & Caravanning Club Site - Llanystumdwy, Tyddyn Sianel, Llanystumdwy, Criccieth, Gwynedd LL52 0LS. *01766 522855/0870 2433331.* www.campingandcaravanningclub.co.uk. Owner: Camping & Caravanning Club. Greenfields House, Westwood Way, Coventry CV4 8JH. From Criccieth take A497 W, 2nd right to Llanystumdwy, site on right. 1.5m from seaside resort of Criccieth. There are scenic coastal views and sandy beaches close to the site. Close to Snowdonia National Park. Pleasant walks just below the village of Llanystumdwy. All types of units accepted. Non-members welcome. Special deals available for families and backpackers. Open March-October. ✰✰✰✰ **70T. 70MC.** 🐕 🖃 ♿

(1m). Criccieth Caravan Park, Caernarfon Road, Criccieth, Gwynedd LL51 0PN. *01766 523220.* morfaddu.caravanpark@lineone.net. Owner: Mr B Meldrum. On B441, Criccieth to Caerarfon road. Located on the Lleyn Peninsula. Fishing, golf, country walks, all nearby. Open March 1-January 14. **BH&HPA. 55S.** 🐕 ⌀

(1m). Eisteddfa Caravan & Camping Park, Eisteddfa Lodge, Pentrefelin, Criccieth, Gwynedd LL52 0PT. *01766 522696.* eisteddfa@criccieth.co.uk. www.eisteddfapark.co.uk. Owner: A M & K A Leech. Come to Porthmadog and at roundabout follow A497 towards Criccieth. Follow road for 3.5m through Pentrefelin, take first R after Plasgwyn Eisteddfa. Golf course and PO 1m. Fishing lake next door. Cinema, swimming pool 3.5m. Open March 1-October 31. **50T. MC. 13S. 3H.** 🐕 🖃 ♿ ⚑

(1m). Llwyn Bugeilydd Farm, Criccieth, Gwynedd LL52 0PN. *01766 522235/07854 063192.* Owner: Robert Roberts. From A55 take A487 through Caernarfon, then just past Bryncir, turn R on to the B4411, site on L 3.5m. From Porthmadog, take A497 then turn R in Criccieth town centre on to B4411, site on R in 1m. 10mins walk to beach and shops. New shower block. Shaver and hair-dryer points. Deep sinks for laundry and washing-up with free hot water. Criccieth 18-hole golf course and also lake fishing 1.5m. Regular bus service from site main entrance. Level site with sea and mountain views, situated away from traffic noise. Dog walking field. AA 2 pennants. Open March-October. ✰✰✰✰ **30T. 5MC.** 🐕 🖃 ♿

(3.5m). Maes Meillion, LLwyn Mafon Isaf, Criccieth, Gwynedd LL52 0RE. *01766 75205.* Owner: Mr S J Jones. Open March 1-October 31. **20T. MC.** 🐕 🖃

(1m). Muriau Bach Touring Site, Rhoslan, Muriau Bach, Criccieth, Gwynedd LL52 0NP. *01766 530642.* Owner: Mr W D Roberts. On B4411. Turn off A487 onto B4411. Site is 4th on the L over a cattle grid entrance. Situated between the hills and the sea with splendid views. Quiet, family site with easy reach of places of interest. Modern facilities. Ideal centre for a holiday. Cycle track nearby. Also fishing, golf course and a choice of beaches and walks. Nearest small town is Criccieth, 3m from the site with shops, PO, doctors etc. Reduced terms for senior citizens during off peak periods. Dogs on leads. Open March 1-October 31. **20T. 20MC.** 🐕 🖃

(1m). Mynydd-Du Caravan and Camping Site, Criccieth, Gwynedd LL52 0PS. *01766 522533.* Owner: R H & E Williams. On A497. 3m W of Porthmadog, E of Criccieth on the Criccieth side of Pentrefelin. Garages, fishing and golf courses in the area. Shops, PO and doctors within 1.5m. Open April 1-October 31. **10T. MC. 12S.** 🐕 ♿

(1m). Plymouth Farm, Criccieth, Gwynedd. *01766 522327.* On A497, Pwllheli to Porthmadog. Open April 1-October 31. **16T. MC. 35S.** 🐕 🖃

(3m). Tir Llosg Riverside Caravan Site, Bryn-Efail-Isaf, Garn Dolbenmaen, Criccieth, Gwynedd. *01766 75274.* Owner: Mrs N C Jones. On B4411. Fishing. Open March-October. **10T.** 🐕

(1.5m). Trefan Farm, Criccieth, Gwynedd. Owner: Mrs G Parry. **10T.**

(1.5m). Tyddyn Cethin Caravan Park, Criccieth, Gwynedd LL52 0NF. *01766 522149.* Owner: Mr & Mrs E Cowlishaw. On B4411. Open April 1-October 31. ✰✰✰ **BH&HPA. 35T. 10MC. 40S. 2H.** 🐕 🖃

(1.25m). Tyddyn Morthwyl, Criccieth, Gwynedd L552 0NF. *01766 522115.* Owner: Mrs Trumper. Yr Hen Stabl, Tyddyn Morthwyl Campsite, Criccieth, Gwynedd LL52 0NF. On B4411. Amenities in the seaside town of Criccieth. Horse-riding and other attractions nearby.Open March 1-October 31. **10T. MC. 22S. 1H.** 🐕 🖃

Dolgellau

(5m). Craig-Wen Caravan & Touring Site, Arthog, Dolgellau, Gwynedd LL39 1BQ. *01341 250482/250900.* graig.wen@supanet.com. www.graig-wen.supanet.com. Owner: A T D & E Ameson. Between Dolgellau and Fairbourne on the A493 towards Tywyn; site on right before village of Arthog. 42-acre site reaching down to Mawddach Estuary. Facilities block. Chemical toilet emptying point. Gas bottles. Suitable base for cyclists, walkers and ramblers. Cader Idris and Fairbourne Beach 2m. Fishing, golf, shops, P(O and garages 3m. Surgery 5m. Open March 1-October 31. **10T. MC. 10S.** 🐕

(3m). Dolgamedd Caravan & Camping Park, Bontnewydd, Brithdir, Dolgellau, Gwynedd LL40 2DG. *01341 422624/ 01341 450356.* mair@dolgamedd.co.uk. www.midwalesholidays.co.uk. Owners: Tom & Mair Evans. Gwanas, Dolgellau, Gwynedd LL40 2SH. A494 from Dolgellau, travel 3m towards Bala. B4416 for Brithdir, Dolgomedd on L after bridge, beside river Wnion. 11-acre, family-run park, level and sheltered, set beside a river where camp fires are allowed. Street lights and picnic tables. Well-appointed, spacious pitches available to locate your own chosen holiday home. 3 separate fields available for tourers and campers. Swimming and fishing on site. Suitable location for birdwatching and mountain biking. Rallies welcome on site or adjacent field. Pets welcome. Open Easter or April-October 31. **BH&HPA. 15T. 5MC. 30S.** 🐾 🖭 ♿

(3m). Dolserau Uchaf, Dolgellau, Gwynedd LL40 2DE. *01341 422639.* Owner: Mr H R Jones. E of Dolgellau on A494. Open April-October 31. **20T.** 🐾 🖭

(4m). Llwyn-yr-Helm Farm, Brithdir, Dolgellau, Gwynedd LL40 2SA. *01341 450254.* On minor road 0.5m off B4416, which is a loop road from A470 to A494. Site on small working in scenic countryside. Toilet/shower block. Eggs. Suitable for walkers, country lovers and mountain bikers, also for relaxing and enjoying the views. Coast 10m. Open Easter-October. ✰✰✰ **15T. 10MC. 42S. 1H.** 🐾 🖭 ♿

(6m). Pant-y-Cae, Arthog, Dolgellau, Gwynedd LL39 1LJ. *01341 250892.* Owner: Mr & Mrs Thomas. Off A493, Towyn to Dolgellau, on road to Cregennan lakes. Fishing, horse riding, sailing, beach all nearby. Good walking and cycling country, camping on site by farmhouse. **5T. MC. 6S. 1H.** ✿ 🐾

(0.5m). Tan-y-Fron Caravan & Camping Park, Arran Road, Dolgellau, Gwynedd LL40 2AA. *01341 422638.* rowlands@ tanyfron.freeserve.co.uk. Owner: Mr E P Rowlands. Take A470 from Welshpool, turn left Dolgellau. 0.5m on left. Facilities include showers, hot and cold sinks, hair-dryers, laundry and dishwashing sinks. TV and water waste to touring caravans. Open March 1-September 30. ✰✰✰✰ **BH&HPA. 13T. MC. 20S.** 🖭

(5m). Ty'n Twll Farm, Bontddu, Dolgellau, Gwynedd LL40 2UG. *01341 430277.* Owner: Mr T A Williams. A470 to Dolgellau, turn on to A496 Barmouth road, 400yd village of Bontddu, turn sharp L inside 30mph limit. Suitable for couples or families. 2m from Mawddach trail and RSPB reserve. Open March 1-October 31. **22S. 1H.** 🐾

Dyffryn Ardudwy

Murmur-yr-Afon Touring Caravan & Camping Park, Dyffryn Ardudwy, Gwynedd LL44 2BE. *01341 247353.* mills@ murmuryrafon25.freeserve.co.uk. Owner: Mr & Mrs N E Mills. A496, coast road Barmouth to Harlech. Entrance 100yd from Bentley's garage in Dyffryn on right. Set in sheltered surroundings 1m from beach. Shop, Calor Gas and Campingaz in village, also off-licence and hotel. Open March 1-October 31. ✰✰✰✰ **30T. MC.** 🐾 🖭 ♿

Rhinog Park, Beach Road, Dyffryn Ardudwy, Gwynedd LL44 2HA. *01341 247652.* rhinogpark@countryparks.com. www. rhinogpark.co.uk. Owner: Country Parks Ltd. The Barn, Lower Cold Green, Bosbury, Ledbury HR8 1NJ. N towards Harlech from Barmouth along A496 coast road. In village, turn left down Station Road. Over level crossing past Cadwgan Hotel and entrance on right. 6m from Barmouth. 23 Lodges, 6 of which are for hire, Mountain views. Short stroll from award-winning beach. David Bellamy Conservation Award. Open March 1 - October 31. ✰✰✰✰ **BH&HPA. 25S. H.** 🐾

Fairbourne

(1m). Bwlch Gwyn Farm Caravan Park, Fairbourne, Gwynedd LL39 1BX. *01341 250107.* Owner: Mr & Mrs J M Evans. From Dolgellau follow A493 towards Fairbourne, park on left hand side. Small, quiet, farm park overlooking Mawddach Estuary and sea. 2.5m to sandy beach. Close to shops. Pony trekking. Open March 1-October 31. **BH&HPA. 10T. MC. 20S. 2H.** 🐾

Ynys Faig Camping & Caravan Site, Ynys Faig Farm, Fairbourne, Gwynedd LL38 2HQ. *01341 250648.* Owner: Mr & Mrs S C Eves. On outskirts of village. Showers. Hot and cold water. Open Easter-October 31. **30T. 20MC.** 🐾 🖭 ♿

Harlech

(4m). Barcdy Touring Caravan & Camping Park, Talsarnau, Harlech, Gwynedd LL47 6YG. *01766 770736.* anwen@barcdy.co.uk. www.barcdy.co.uk. Owner: Mrs A L Roberts. On A496 Blaenau Ffestiniog to Harlech. Bottled gas. Ideal situation for touring Snowdonia. In quiet, picturesque surroundings. Garage, PO 1m, golf course 4m. Fishing nearby (10mins walk from park). Open Easter-September 30. ✰✰✰✰ **BH&HPA. 30T. 8MC. 27S. 2H.** 🖭 🎣

(1.5m). Beach Road Caravan Park, Beach Road, Harlech, Gwynedd LL46 2UG. *01766 780328.* david@beachroadcaravans.co.uk. www.beachroadcaravans.co.uk. Owner: Mr D W Bohemia. Off A496. 75 metres along beach road, on the L hand side. Small, quiet site. Landscaped with trees and flowers. Putting green, dog walk, suitable for adults who require piece and quiet. Laundrette. Beach 5 mins walk. Royal St Davids golf course, adjacent to park. Open March-January. ✰✰✰✰ **BH&HPA. 48S. 1H.** 🐾 🖭 ♿

(2m). Llandanwg Caravan Holiday Home Park, Llandanwg, Harlech, Gwynedd LL46 2SD. *01341 241602.* llandanwgcp@aol.com. Owner: Salop Caravans Sites Ltd. Superbly kept five star park, few minutes walk from sandy beach. Two miles from historic Harlech with all its facilities. Open March 1 - November 30. ✰✰✰✰✰ **BH&HPA. NCC. 95S.** 🐾

(1m). Min-y-Don Holiday Home Park, Beach Road, Harlech, Gwynedd LL46 2UG. *01766 780286.* scl@salopcaravans.co.uk. www.salopcaravans.co.uk. Owner: Salop Caravans (Sites) Ltd. Easily accessible off the A596 coast road. Turn into Beach Road opposite Queens Hotel. Central for Snowdonia. Below Harlech Castle. 5mins walk to railway station and bus stop. Near sandy beach and St Davids golf course. Doctor 5mins walk. Laundry facilities on site. Open March-end October. **20T. 5MC. 112S.** 🐾 🖭

Pant Mawr Caravan Park, Ffordd Uchaf, Harlech, Gwynedd LL46 2SS. *01766 780226.* info@partmawrcaravans.co.uk. www.pantmawr.caravans.co.uk. Owner: Mr & Mrs R Frost. Off A496 at Llanfair or Harlech. Golf course nearby. Superb views over Lleyn peninsular and Harlech Castle. Peaceful. Open March 1-January 7. **38S.** 🐾

(0.5m). Woodland Caravan Park, Harlech, Gwynedd LL46 2UE. *01766 780419.* grace@woodlandscp.fsnet.co.uk. www.woodlandscp.fsnet.co.uk. Owner: Mr & Mrs Roberts. From Barmouth, pass golf course on left, fork right at level crossing, park is signposted. From Talsarnau at Harlech level crossing turn sharp left back on yourself. Park 200 yards on right hand side. Nearby swimming pool, beach, golf club. David Bellamy Bronze award. Shops Inns restaurants takeaway within one mile. Harlech Castle. 10m to Portmadoch, Barmouth. Open March 1-October 31. ✰✰✰✰ **BH&HPA. 18T. 18MC. 21S. 3H.** 🐾 🖭

Llanrug

(0.25m). Challoner Caravan Park, Erw Hywel Farm, Llanberis Road, Llanrug, Gwynedd LL55 2AJ. *01286 672985.* suechallcouk@supanet.com. www.suechallcouk.com. Owner: Mrs S Challoner. A4086 4m W of Llanberis and 3m E of Caernarfon. Sheltered, small, friendly, camp on farm site. Ideal for walkers and climbers. Showers. Milk and eggs. Shop close by. Close to a variety of activities. Open March-January 10. **15T. 20MC. 8S. 1H.** ⌂ ▣

Llwyngwril

(1m). Sunbeach Holiday Park, Llwyngwril, Gwynedd LL37 2QQ. *01341 250263.* www.allenscaravans.com. Owners: Allen Caravans. Wootton Hall, Wootton Wawen, Henley in Arden B95 6EE. On A493,1m S of Llwyngwril on R. 6m from Tywyn. Own beach frontage. Club with restaurant. Fishing, golfing and horse riding nearby. Bus and train service. Open February 7-January 7. **BH&HPA. NCC. 350S.** ⌂ ⅋ ▟

Merioneth

(4m). Bellaport Farm, Talybont, Nr Barmouth, Merioneth, Gwynedd LL43 2BX. *01341 247338.* Owner: Mrs Beti Roberts. Off A496, turn R at 40mph limit sign leaving Talybont village travelling north to top of lane. Barmouth 4m. 0.5m from village. Adults only. No dogs in holiday caravan. Fishing, golf course nearby. Open March-September. ✩✩✩ **20T. 5MC. 1S. 1H.** ⌂ ▣

Porthmadog

(3m). Black Rock Camping & Touring Park, Black Rock Sands, Morfa Bychan, Porthmadog, Gwynedd LL49 9YH. *01766 513919.* Owner: P Roberts. Flat 1, 9 The Firs, Bowdon, Cheshire WA14 2TG. Adjacent to 7m beach. Shop and PO 1m, leisure centre 3m. Open Easter-October. ✩✩✩ **BH&HPA. 40T. 10MC.** ⌂ ▣

(1m). Blaen Cefn, Penrhyndeudraeth, Porthmadog, Gwynedd LL48 6NA. *01766 770889/770981.* Owner: Mr Gareth Jones. Off A487. 1m to shops and pubs. Fishing on site, horse riding 4m. Open March-September. **12T. 12MC. 2S. 4H.** ⌂ ▣

(2m). Cardigan View Holiday Park, Beach Road, Morfa Bychan, Porthmadog, Gwynedd LL49 9YA. *01766 512032.* www.haulfryn.co.uk. Owner: Haulfryn Group Ltd. The Warren, Abersoch, Pwllheli, Gwynedd LL53 7AA. Turn left of Porthmadog High Street by Woolworth's. Follow signs for Morfa Bychan. Indoor swimming pool. Play area, games room. Open March 1-October 31. ✩✩✩✩ **BH&HPA. NCC. 32T. 192S.** ⌂

(2m). Garreg Goch Caravan Park, Black Rock Sands, Morfa Bychan, Porthmadog, Gwynedd LL49 9YD. *01766 512210.* Owner: Normanhurst Enterprises Ltd. 9 Burscough Street, Ormskirk, Lancashire L39 2EG. W of Portmadog. Turning for Morfa Bychan; follow this road past BP filling station, then turn left into park. Open March 1-October 31. ✩✩✩✩ **BH&HPA. 24T. 61S. 10H.** ⌂ ▣ ⅋ ▟ ⌀

(2m). Glanaber Caravan Park, Beach Road, Morfa Bychan, Porthmadog, Gwynedd LL49 9YA. *01766 512157.* Owner: I W & M E Ransley. 300yd from beach at Black Rock, near to golf links, fishing and boating. Open March-November. **BH&HPA. 55S.** ⌂

(2m). Greenacres Holiday Park, Black Rock Sands, Morfa Bychan, Porthmadog, Gwynedd LL49 9YB. *01766 514570.* oewebmaster@bourne-leisure.co.uk. www.greenacresholiday park.co.uk. Owner: Bourne Leisure Ltd. One Park Lane, Hemel Hempstead, Herts HP2 4YL. From Porthmadog High Street, turn between Woolworth's and PO towards Black Rock Sands. Carry on for about 2m.Park entrance is just the other side of Morfa Bychan, on the left-hand side. Heated indoor swimming pool. Mini market. Bakery. Laundrette. Tennis. Bowling. Pitch and putt. Children's club. Access onto Black Rock sands. Ropeworks high adventure course. Open April-November. ✩✩✩✩ **BH&HPA. NCC. 57T. MC. 927S. 212H.** ▣ ⅋ ▟

(2m). Gwyndy Caravan Park, Black Rock Sands, Morfa Bychan, Porthmadog, Gwynedd LL49 9YB. *01766 512047.* Owner: Mr M S & Mrs J Leech. In Porthmadog turn at Woolworths, 2m to Morfa Bychan, past Spar shop, turn left then second right, SP Gwyndy. Pathway to beach. Laundrette, utility room. AA listed. Golf course nearby. Open March - October. **15T. 10MC. 44S.** ▣

Ty Bricks Caravan Park, Porthmadog, Gwynedd LL49 9PP. *01766 512597.* Owner: Mr T E Jones. Small, level, quiet site, 5 mins walk from the centre of Portmadog. SAE for reply. Open March 1-October 31. **20T. 15S.** ⌂ ▣

(2.5m). Tyddyn Adi Caravan Park, Morfa Bychan, Porthmadog, Gwynedd LL49 9YW. *01766 512933.* tyddynadi @btconnect.com. www.tyddynadi.co.uk. Owner: Mr Ifor Lewis. From Porthmadoc take Morfa Bychan road; large sign on right at end of village, 400yd to site. Full facilities, TV and games room, laundrette. **20T. MC.** ✿ ⌂ ▣

(0.5m). Tyddyn Llwyn Farm Caravan & Camping Park, Morfa Bychan Road, Porthmadog, Gwynedd LL49 9UR. *01766 512205.* info@tyddynllwyn.com. www.tyddynllwyn.com. Owner: Cathrine & Peter Wright. Off A487. Turn at Woolworth's on Portnmadog High Street. Park on R side at bottom of hill. Tranquil location with level and elevated pitches. Showers. Shaver points. Laundrette. Gas bottle for sale. Hotel, bar and restaurant on site. Open March 1-October 31. ✩✩✩✩ **BH&HPA. NCC. 153T.** ⌂ ▟

Pwllheli

Aberafon Holiday Park, Nefyn, Pwllheli, Gwynedd LL53 6LL. *01758 720520.* www.haulfryn.co.uk. Owners: Haulfryn Group Ltd. The Warren, Abersoch, Pwllheli, Gwynedd LL53 7AA. From Pwllheli take A499 to Abersoch, about 1m. Turn R on to A497 to Nefyn. Through Nefyn taking Llithfaen Road, about 1m. on L. Nefyn Golf Club. Maritime Museum. Clifftop walks, fishing, sailing. **S.**

(1.5m). Abererch Sands, Pwllheli, Gwynedd LL53 6PJ. *01758 612327.* enquiries@abererch-sands.co.uk. www.aber erch-sands.co.uk. Owner: K J Dunne. On A497, Criccieth to Pwllheli. Heated indoor swimming pool. Fitness room. Play area for children. Open March 1-October 31. **BH&HPA. 70T. MC. 85S.** ⌂ ▣ ⅋ ▟

(2m). Bodfel Caravan Park, Pwllheli, Gwynedd LL53 6DW. *01758 612014.* Owner: Mr J C R Morris. Off A497. Open March 1-October 31. **BH&HPA. 20T. MC. 50S.** ⌂

(5m). Bodwrog Farm, Bodwrog, Llanbedrog, Pwllheli, Gwynedd LL53 7RE. *01758 740341.* enq@bodwrog.co.uk. www.bodwrog.co.uk. Owner: Mr D R Williams. On L of B4413, 1m from its junction with A499. Quiet, family site. Close to beaches. Sea views. New toilet/shower block.Shower and toilet for disabled people. Area for 10 tents and 10 tourers. Open Easter-end October. **10T. MC. 1H.** ⌂ ▣ ⅋

(14m). Brynffynnon Caravan Park, Rhoshirwaun, Pwllheli, Gwynedd LL53 8DS. *01758 730643.* Owner: Mr & Mrs E W Jones. 6 Tre Ddol, Sarn, Pwllheli, Gwynedd. Take the 'Whistling Sands' road off B4413. Open March 1-October 31. **15T. MC. 12H.** ⌂ ▣ ⅋

(2m). Bryngolau Caravan Park, Pwllheli, Gwynedd. *01758 813223*. Owner: Messrs H Roberts & W O Jones. Off A499. Open March 1-October 31. **BH&HPA. 39S.** ⓦ

(7m). Caer Odyn Caravan Park, Low Llan, Edern, Pwllheli, Gwynedd LL53 6YS. *01758 720846*. Owner: P Scott. Open March 1-October 31. **BH&HPA. 12T. 97S. 1H.** ⓦ 🖪

(10m). Cefn Hedog Caravan Site, Rhoshirwaun, Pwllheli, Gwynedd LL53 8HL. *01758 760443*. Owner: Mr Frank Moores. A449 west from Pwllheli. At Llanbedrog bear right on to B4413 for 5m, then right on to Whistling Sands Road. Site 100yd on right. Shower. Views, peaceful, coastal walks. 2m to shop, PO, beach. 4m to doctor. 3 golf courses within 10m. Open March-October. **5T. MC.** ⓦ

(1m). Crugan Holiday Park, Llanbedrog, Pwllheli, Gwynedd LL53 7NL. *01758 740349*. www.haulfryn.co.uk. Owner: Haulfryn Group Ltd. The Warren, Abersoch, Pwllheli, Gwynedd LL53 7AA. Off A499, between Pwllheli and Abersoch. Quiet, rural park. Open March 1-October 31. ☆☆☆☆ **BH&HPA. NCC. 100S.** ⓦ ⊘

(17m). Dwyros, Aberdaron, Pwllheli, Gwynedd. *01758 760295*. dwyroscamp@aol.com. Owner: Mr G A Jones. B 4413 into Aberdaron, turn right on bridge, site 0.25m on right. Level site overlooking Aberdaron bay, with its two islands, and only five mins walking distance from the village and beach. Site offers panoramic views of this Area of Outstanding Natural Beauty. Open April 1-October 30. **30T. 30MC. 6S.** ⓦ 🖪

(1m). Gimblet Rock Holiday Park, Outer Harbour, Pwllheli, Gwynedd LL53 5AY. *01758 612770*. www.haulfryn.co.uk. Owner: Haulfryn Group Ltd. The Warren, Abersoch, Pwllheli, Gwynedd. Coming into Pwllheli on A499, turn L at the Railway Station. Turn L into the housing estate and drive through boatyards on to the park. Residents' Club, children's play area. Park overlooks Pwllheli marina. Caravans for sale. Open March 1-October 31. ☆☆☆☆ **BH&HPA. NCC. 131S.** ⓦ ⊘

(3m). Hafan y Mor Holiday Park, Pwllheli, Gwynedd LL53 6HX. *01758 704516*. oewebmaster@bourne-leisure.co.uk. www.hafanymorholidaypark.co.uk. Owner: Bourne Leisure Ltd. 1 Park Lane, Hemel Hempstead, Herfordshire HP2 4YL. M54 to Telford, A5 past Oswestry and Llangollen. Take A494 to Bala, at traffic lights turn R following signs for Porthmadog, then SP for Criccieth and Pwllheli. Park is 3m on your L. Heated indoor swimming pool. Daytime and evening entertainment for all the family, convenience store. Bakery, laundrette. Direct beach access. Views of Snowdonia. Children's clubs. All-weather, multi-sports court. Open March-November. ☆☆☆☆ **BH&HPA. NCC. 644S. 177H.** ⓦ 🖢

(1m). Hendre Caravan Park, Efailnewydd, Pwllheli, Gwynedd LL53 8TN. *01758 613416/612793*. Owner: Mr A M Jones. On A497 to Nefy, turn left at Efailnewydd on to B4415, site 100yd. Country site in easy reach of safe beaches and shops. Some vacancies. 18-hole golf course 2m. Village shop, PO within walking distance. Open March 1-October 31. **BH&HPA. 20T. MC. 120S.** ⓦ 🖪

(4m). Penyberth Caravan Park, Penrhos, Pwllheli, Gwynedd. *01758 612581*. Owner: Mr O W Owen. Pen-y-Bont, Llangian, Pwllheli, Gwynedd. On A499, Abersoch to Pwllheli. Families only. Open March 1-October 31. **102T. MC. 250S. 6H.** ⓦ 🖪 & 🖢

(9m). Pistyll Caravan Park, Pistyll, Nefyn, Pwllheli, Gwynedd. *01758 720480*. Owner: Mr Brian & Mrs Anwen Owens. Laundry room. Open March-October. **28S.** ⓦ

(3.5m). Refail Touring & Camping Park, Llanbedrog, Pwllheli, Gwynedd LL53 7NP. *01758 740511*. refail.llanbedrog @ukonline.co.uk. Owner: Mrs C Evans. Follow A499 from Pwllhei. At Llanbedrog turn R on to B4413, SP 'Refail'. Site 200yd on R. Sheltered, family park with views, excellent facilities and easy access. Sandy beach, shops, PHs, bistro and restaurant 5mins walk. Seasonal touring pitches. Open Easter-October 31. ☆☆☆☆☆ **33T. MC.** ⓦ 🖪 &

(5m). The Willows Camping & Caravan Park, Mynytho, Abersoch, Pwllheli, Gwynedd LL53 7RW. *01758 740850/ 740140*. tedoutten@compuserve.com. www.abersoch.co.uk. Owner: Mr W V Outten. Turn right off A499 at Llanbedrog on to B4413. 30mph sign at Mynytho turn right. Site on left within 0.25m, pass 1st Bryntirion sign. 2m N of Abersoch. Families and couples only. Site in peaceful surroundings. 4 acres of camping fields. 1.5-acre fishing lake. Children's play area. Toilets, showers. Birdwatching. Outstanding views of Snowdonia and Cardigan Bay. Shop, PO within 0.25m. PHs, restaurants nearby. **BH&HPA. 20T. 20MC.** ✿ ⓦ 🖪 ⃝

(18m). Tir Glyn Caravan Park, Tir Glyn, Aberdaron, Pwllheli, Gwynedd LL53 8DA. *01758 760248*. www.aberdaronlink. co.uk. Owner: Mr J Roberts. 0.5m from shops. Aberdaron to Uwchmynydd road, B4413, first L turn, site 0.25m. Above Fisherman's Cove. Dogs on leads. All pitches located around the outside of the field. Open May-October. **30T. MC. 1S.** ⓦ 🖪

(10m). Towyn Farm, Tudweiliog, Pwllheli, Gwynedd. *01758 770600*. Owner: Mr W W Owen. Situated on the N coast of the Lleyn Peninsula. A499 from Caernarfon, A497 from Porthmadog. Flat site with shower. 200yd safe, sandy beach. Pub with bar meals 10mins walk. Open March 1-October 31. **12T. MC.** ⓦ 🖪

(4m). Trallwyn Hall Caravan Park, Four Crosses (Y Ffor), Pwllheli, Gwynedd. *01758 713223*. Owner: Victoria Williams-Ellis. 22 Northchurch Road, London N1 4EH. On A499. Rural park set within 600-acre estate. Sea and mountain views. Open March 1-January 31. **34S.** ⓦ

(12m). Ty Mawr Caravan Park, Bryncroes, Pwllheli, Gwynedd LL53 8EH. *01248 351537/01758 730535*. www.tymawr-caravan-park.co.uk. Owner: Mr Roy Jones. 11 Goleufryn, Penrhos, Bangor, Gwynedd LL57 2LY. On B4413 ,about 1.5m beyond Sarn Meillteryn. Within easy reach of numerous glorious beaches such as Whistling Sands, Penllech etc. Open April 1-October 31. ☆☆☆☆ **15T. MC.** ⓦ 🖪 &

(6m). Ty-Hir, Mynytho, Pwllheli, Gwynedd LL53 7RR. *01758 740539*. Owner: Mr J H Williams. On B4413. Fishing and golf course nearby. Shops, PO and doctor within 0.5m. Open March 1-October 31. **10T. 5MC. 15S.** ⓦ 🖪

(3m). Tyddyn Heilyn Caravan Park, Tyddyn Heilyn Farm, Chwilog, Pwllheli, Gwynedd LL53 6SW. *01766 810441*. Owner: T E & Mrs L Hughes Jones. From A497 to B4354 and at village of Chwilog, before pub turn right in between houses opposite Povey the butcher's. 1.5m along road, 2nd site, signed. Scenic 10m walks passing through this farmland, overlooking Cardigan Bay. Snowdonia scenery. Birdwatching – coastal and country birds. Within easy reach of shops, good eating places and PHs. Near 2 fishing rivers and lakes, riding school, ample good golf, miles safe cycle tracks. Site level and shaded. Open February-January. **BH&HPA. 9T. 12MC. 19S. 2H.** ⓦ 🖪

(10m). Tyn Llan Caravan Park, Tudweiliog, Pwllheli, Gwynedd LL53 8NB. Owner: Mr R L & H Jones. From Liverpool/Manchester area A55 to Bangor. A487 to Caernarvon A499 towards Pwllheli. B4417 to Tudweiliog. No tourers. Sea views. Path from site, through fields to beach. All services except gas. Local shop, PH. Golf course 5m. Cinema, shopping centre 10m. Open March 1-October 31. **31S.** 🛒 &

(4m). Wern Newydd Tourer Park, Llanbedrog, Pwllheli, Gwynedd LL53 7PG. *01758 740220.* office@wern-newydd.co. uk. www.wern-newydd.co.uk. Owner: Mrs M L Valentine. Turn R off A499 (Pwllheli-Abersoch) in Llanbedrog on to B4413, SP Aberdaron, continue through village, past the PO on the R, then take first turning R on to unclassified road. Site entrance on the R in 700yd. Peaceful site. 15mins walk to the beach, 5mins to village. Good eating places, shops, PHs, etc. Mobile shop visits in high season. Open March-October. ✰✰✰ **BH&HPA. NCC. 30T.** 🛒 🖾

(4m). Wernol Caravan Park, Chwilog, Pwllheli, Gwynedd LL53 6SW. *01766 810506.* catherine@wernol.com. www. wernol.com. Owner: Mrs C Jones. From Portmadog (A497), turn R on to B4354, 1m to Chwilog. Turn R in Chwilog opposite butcher's shop (blind turning). Park 1m on R. Free coarse fishing lake. Country walks. 5 golf courses within 12m radius. 1m to village shop and country PH. 4m marina at Pwllheli. Cycle route. Open March-January. ✰✰✰✰ **BH&HPA. 70S. 5H.** 🛒

Woodland Caravan Park, Botwnnog, Nr Abersoch, Pwllheli, Gwynedd LL53 8RG. *01248 671235/07780 813965.* gwionw@aol.com. Owner: Mr Gwion Williams. Y Gragen, Lon Pencei, Abersoch, Gwynedd LL53 7AU. Off B4413, 4.5m from Abersoch. Children's play area, wash room with washing machine and dryer. Golf course, sailing/boating 5m. Nearest village 1m. Public footpaths. Open March-October. **BH&HPA. 29S.** 🛒 ⌀

Tywyn

Cwmrhwyddfor Camp Site, Talyllyn, Tywyn, Gwynedd LL36 9AJ. *01654 761286/380.* Owner: Mr T D Nutting. On A487, 6m from Dolgellau at bottom of Talyllyn Pass. White house on right at foot of Cader Idris mountain. Showers, shaver points, chemical toilet emptying point. Electric hook-ups. Tents also accepted. Within easy reach sea. Easy access. Suitable base for walking. Fishing in stream. Craft shops. Pony trekking, golf, shop nearby. Hotel and cafe in walking distance. Open March 1-end October. Open all year for tents. **25T. 5MC.** ✿ 🐕 🖾

(5.5m). Glanywern, Dysefin Farm, Llanegryn, Tywyn, Gwynedd LL36 9TH. *01654 782247.* Owner: Mr B Roberts. 3m E of the village of Llanegryn by Bird Rock. Showers and toilet facilities. Fishing, golf course nearby. Shops 6m. Open April-October 31. **20T. MC. 1H.** 🛒 🖾

(2m). Llwyn-Teg Caravan Park, Bryncrug, Tywyn, Gwynedd LL36 9NU. *01654 710416.* Owner: Mr & Mrs G Jenkins. On A493, Dolgellau to Tywyn, 200yd from junction with B4405. In village of Bryncrug. Notourers or motor caravans. Shop nearby. All caravans connected to all services. Fully modernised. Laundry. Beach, shopping centre 2m. Golf 5m. Open February 1-October 31. ✰✰✰✰✰ **BH&HPA. 24S.** 🛒 &

Neptune Hall and Caravan Park, The Promenade, Tywyn, Gwynedd LL36 0DL. *01654 710432/01654 710343.* Owner: Messrs B R & R F Tunnadine. Off A493. Dogs allowed if kept under control. No dogs in hire caravans. Club on site. Open 1week before Easter-October 31. **5T. MC. 280S. 3H.** 🖿

(0.25m). Pall Mall Farm Caravan Park, Tywyn, Gwynedd LL36 9RU. *01654 710384/710591.* Owner: Mr & Mrs M L Vaughan & Mr R Vaughan. On A493. New leisure centre. Play area. Bed and breakfast. Open Easter-October. **30T. 10MC. 46S.** 🛒 🖾

(5m). Peniarth Caravan Park, Llanegryn, Tywyn, Gwynedd LL36 9UD. *01654 710101.* www@wynne.co.uk. Owner: William Williams-Wynne. Site just outside village of Llanegryn on the Bird Rock road and 5m from the popular resort of Tywyn. Golf course at Aberdovey. River running through Peniarth Estate for fishing. No club, no amusements, no noise. Private fishing. Open March-October. **BH&HPA. 25S.** 🛒

(0.5m). Penllyn Caravan Park Ltd, Neptune Road, Tywyn, Gwynedd LL36 0DP. *01654 710416.* Owner: Mr G Jenkins. Llwynteg, Bryncrug, Tywyn, Gwynedd LL36 9NU. Situated off Neptune road, Tywyn. No tourers or motor caravans. Updated site with all services to caravans. Situated on seafront at Tywyn. Shops, cinema 0.5m. Golf 3m. Open February-November. **BH&HPA. 60S.** 🛒 &

(3m). Tynllwyn Caravan & Camping Park, Bryncrug, Tywyn, Gwynedd LL36 9RD. *01654 710370.* ppspsmc@aol.com. www.tynllwyncaravanpark.co.uk. Owner: Mr & Mrs P L McEvoy. Off A493. Small, family-run site. Telephone, laundry, play area. Talyllyn narrow-gauge steam railway runs past site. Open March-October. ✰✰✰ **BH&HPA. NCC. 18T. MC. 56S. 6H.** 🛒 🖾 🖿

(4m). Waenfach Caravan Site, Llanegryn, Tywyn, Gwynedd LL36 9SB. *01654 710375.* Owner: Mr & Mrs Davies. Off A493. Beautiful views on working farm. Spacious amenities block with laundry facilities. Public phone. Deep freeze. Dogs under control. Shops 1m; doctor, hospital, PO in Tywyn. Sea and river fishing, golf course 5m. Open Easter-October 31. **10T. MC. 46S.** 🛒 🖾

(3m). Woodlands Holiday Park Ltd, Bryncrug, Tywyn, Gwynedd LL36 9UH. *01654 710471.* On B4405. Club. Swimming pool. Mobile shop calls. Open Easter-October 31. ✰✰✰✰ **BH&HPA. 20T. MC. 122S.** 🛒 🖾

(1m). Ynysmaengwyn Holiday Park, Tywyn, Gwynedd LL36 9RY. *01654 710684.* rita@ynysmaengwyn.freeserve.co.uk. www. ynysmaengwyn.co.uk. Owner: Mr & Mrs Blunden. On A493. Open April 1-October 31. ✰✰✰✰ **NCC. 20T. MC. 115S.** 🛒 🖾 &

(1m). Ysguboriau Farm Caravan Park, Tywyn, Gwynedd LL36 9RY. *01654 710321.* Owner: Mrs Gwenda Jones. On A493, Dolgellau to Tywyn. Near sea and mountains and Talyllyn narrow-gauge railway. Free fishing. Open week before Easter-October 31. **30T. 5MC. 140S.** 🛒 🖾

MERTHYR TYDFIL

Merthyr Tydfil

(4m). Grawen Caravan & Camping Park, Cwm-Taff, Cefn-Coed, Merthyr Tydfil, Merthyr Tydfil CF48 2HS. *01685 723740.* grawen.touring@virgin.net. www.walescaravanand camping.com. Owner: Mrs F Pugh. On A470. Brecon Beacons road 2m from A465. Picturesque forest, mountain and reservoir walks close to site in clean fresh air with easy access. A wealth of history in the town and valleys. 30 tent pitches also available. Open April-October. ✰✰✰ **BH&HPA. NCC. 15T. 10MC.** 🛒 🖾 🖿

MONMOUTHSHIRE

Abergavenny

(3m). Aberbaiden Caravan and Camping Park, Gilwern, Abergavenny, Monmouthshire NP7 0EF. *01873 830157.* Owner: Powell Bros. Just off A465 at Gilwern roundabout. Situated in National Park, 9 acres of part woodland, grass pitches and hard-standings. Wash basins. Pony trekking and boating, swimming and golf all about 2m. Very close to Brecon Beacons and Black Mountains. Open April 1-October 31. **15T. 15MC. 12S. 1H.** 🐕 🛍

(6m). Clydach Gorge Caravan & Campsite, Station Road, Clydach, Abergavenny, Monmouthshire NP3 6XB. *01633 644856.* Owner: Monmouthshire County Council. Planning & Economic Dept., Country Hall, Cwmbran. SP off Heads of the Valleys road, A465, between Abergavenny and Brynmawr. Showers. Chemical toilet emptying point. Open April-September. **25T. MC.** 🐕 🖃

(5.25m). Pandy Caravan Club Site, Pandy, Abergavenny, Monmouthshire NP7 8DR. *01873 890370.* www.caravanclub.co.uk. Owner: Caravan Club. East Grinstead House, East Grinstead, West Sussex RH19 1UA. See website for standard directions to site. Level site with views of the Black Mountains. Non-members welcome. Advance booking essential, some hardstandings. Toilet blocks. Privacy cubicles. Laundry facilities. Veg prep. Motorhome service point. Golf, fishing nearby. Good area for walking. Gas supplis. Dog walk. Peaceful off peak. NCN cycle route within 5m. Open March-October. ✰✰✰ **NCC. 53T. MC.** 🐕 🖃 ♿

(7m). Pontkemys Caravan & Camping Park, Pontkemys, Chainbridge, Abergavenny, Monmouthshire NP7 9DS. *01873 880688.* info@pontkemys.com. www.pontkemys.com. Owners: Bryan & Rose Jones. 4m from Usk. On B4598 to Abergavenny. M4, J24, N on A449, or from M5/M50/A40, S on A449 to Usk. PH 300yd, golf course 400yd. Usk Valley walk 300yd. Dogs charged for. Dog walk area. Booking advisable, some hardstandings. Open March-October. ✰✰✰ **45T. MC.** 🐕 🖃 ♿ 🛍

(2m). Pyscodlyn Farm Camping & Caravan Site, Llanwenarth Citra, Abergavenny, Monmouthshire NP7 7ER. *01873 853271.* pyscodlyn.farm@virgin.net. www.pyscodlyn caravanpark.com. Owner: K. T. Davies. W of Abergavenny on A40 to Brecon. Suitable baase for exploring Black Mountains and Brecon Beacons National Park. Fishing tickets available for river Usk. Golf and pony trekking nearby. Open April 1-October 31. ✰✰✰ **BH&HPA. 60T. MC. 1H.** 🐕 🖃

(5m). Rising Sun, Pandy, Abergavenny, Monmouthshire NP7 8DL. *01873 890254.* Owner: Owen & Mandy Price. Off A465. Bar/restaurant. Bar food. Hot and cold showers. Children's play area. **25T. MC.** ❖ 🐕 🖃

Monmouth

(3m). Bridge Caravan Park, Dingestow, Monmouth, Monmouthshire NP25 4DY. *01600 740241.* info@bridgecaravan park.co.uk. www.bridgecaravanpark.co.uk. Owner: S Holmes. SP from Abergavenny junction of A449 trunk road. In the heart of the Vale of Usk and Wye Valley, next to the river Trothy. Fishing available to all visitors. Woodland background. Open Easter-October. ✰✰✰ **42T. 8MC. 3H.** 🐕 🖃 ♿ 🛍

(2m). Glen Trothy Caravan and Camping Park, Mitchel Troy, Monmouth, Monmouthshire NP25 4BD. *01600 712295.* enquiries@glentrothy-co.uk. www.glentrothy.co.uk. Owner: H & M Y Price. SW Monmouth, off new A40. On edge of Wye Valley and Forest of Dean. Good facilities. Play area. Free brochure. Open March 1-October 31. ✰✰✰ **BH&HPA. 84T. MC.** 🖃 ♿

(1m). Kings Orchard Caravan Site, Mansons Cross, Withy Lane, Monmouth, Monmouthshire NP25 5LF. *01600 714186.* mhoaten@aol.com. Owner: Mr M H Oaten. Off A466. Open March 31-October 31. ✰✰✰ **6S.** 🐕

(0.5m). Monmouth Caravan Park, Rockfield Road, Monmouth, Monmouthshire NP5 3BA. *01600 714745.* mail@monmouthcaravanpark.co.uk. www.monmouthcaravan park.co.uk. Owner: Mr & Mrs Brown. Family-run park. New facilities' block and clubhouse. Fishing. 0.25m on B4233 Rockfield Road, just past fire and ambulance station. Open March 1-January 5. ✰✰✰✰ **BH&HPA. 50T. 10MC. 2H.** 🐕 🖃 ♿ 🛍

(6m). Pen-Y-Van Chalet Park, The Narth, Monmouth, Monmouthshire NP25 4AG. Owner: Mr & Mrs R Hearne. 3 Greenacres Park, Coalpit Heath, S Glos BS36 2UB. Chepstow 12m. Open April 1-October 31. **BH&HPA. 12S.** 🐕

NEATH & PORT TALBOT

Port Talbot

(6m). Afan Argoed Countryside Centre, Afan Forest Park, Cynonville, Port Talbot, Neath & Port Talbot SA13 3HG. *01639 850564.* Owner: Neath & Port Talbot County Borough Council. On A4107, exit 40 off M4. Dogs allowed under strict control. Bread and milk delivered. 850446. Caravan Club listed. Open April-October. **10T. MC.** 🐕 ♿

NEWPORT

Coedkernew

Tredegar House Country Park Caravan Club Site, Coedkernew, Newport NP10 8TW. *01633 815600.* www.caravanclub.co.uk. Owner: The Caravan Club. East Grinstead House, East Grinstead, West Sussex RH19 1UA. See website for standard directions to site. 7-acre site located within 1m of the M4 and is only 7m from Cardiff. Adventure playground adjacent. Toilet blocks. Privacy cubicles. Laundry facilities. Veg prep. Motorhome service point. Fishing and golf nearby. Non-members and tent campers welcome. Some hardstandings. Gas supplies. Dog walk nearby. Open March-December. ✰✰✰✰ **NCC. 82T. MC.** 🐕 🖃 ♿

Crosskeys

(2m). Cwmcarn Forest Drive Campsite, Nantcarn Valley, Cwmcarn, Crosskeys, Newport NP11 7FA. *01495 272001.* cwmcarn-vc@caerphilly.gov.uk. www.caerphilly.gov.uk/visiting. J28 M4-A467 to Crosskeys and follow signs for site. Sited at entrance to Cwmcarn Forest Drive Tourist attraction. Shower block. Telephone on site. Laundry facilities. Fishing nearby. Visitor centre with coffee shop and gift shop. Mountain bike trail and bike wash. New downhill track opened in summer 2005. ✰✰✰✰ **37T. MC.** ❖ 🐕 🖃 ♿

PEMBROKESHIRE

Amroth

(1.25m). Pendeilo Leisure Park, Amroth, Pembrokeshire SA67 8PR. *01834 831259.* pendeiloholidays@aol.com. www.pendeilo.co.uk. Owner: NJ & CM Clark. Pendeilo Villa, Amroth, Pembrokeshire. Off A477. At Llanteg, in the direction of Tenby, turn left at Murco garage. Park isabout 1m on the right. Heated pool, play area and laundrette. Well-behaved dogs welcome. Dragon Award. Pub/restaurant 10 mins walk. Open March 1-October 31. ✰✰✰✰✰ **BH&HPA. 43S. 12H.** 🐕 ♿ 🛍

Clynderwen

(2m). Glancleddau Farm, Glancleddau, Clynderwen, Pembrokeshire SA66 7JF. *01437 563368.* Owner: A M G Llewellin. Modern farmhouse with 1.5m private salmon and seatrout fishing. Llys-y-fron Country Park with all amenities including trout fishing 5m. Oakwood adventure park 5m, Preseli mountains and views and near beaches. Bottled gas. Open March-October. **MC. 2H.**

(0.5km). Gower Villa Caravan Park, Gower Villa Lane, Clynderwen, Pembrokeshire SA66 7NL. *01437 563859.* richard.payler@talk21.com. www.gowervillatouringpark.com. Owner: Mr & Mrs R Payler. From Narberth A478 towards Cardigan in Clunderwen village, first R after Farmer Association store. Quiet location off private lane: 400yd to shops, PH and petrol station. Toilet block. Level grass, some hard-standings, rally field available. Suitable base for touring SW Wales. Open March 1-December 4. ✰✰✰✰ **BH&HPA. 59T. MC.** 🐾 🕿 &

Trefach Caravan Park, Mynachlogddu, Clynderwen, Pembrokeshire SA66 7RU. *01994 419225.* trefach@ bigfoot.com. www.trefach.co.uk. Owner: O & D Enterprises. Off A478. 3.5m from Crymych. 18-acre country site. Central to all Pembrokeshire, ideal for exploring by foot, car or horseback. Heated swimming pool. Play room. Restaurant. Bar. Fishing nearby. Open March-January 6. ✰✰✰ **BH&HPA. 20T. MC. 50S. 4H.** 🐾 🕿 &

Dinas Cross

(5m). Dinas Cross Country Club, The Old Rectory, Dinas Cross, Pembrokeshire SA42 0UN. *01348 811260.* Owner: Mr & Mrs Hall. On A487 Cardigan to Fishguard. Sea views, many beaches. Pub. Restaurant. Club. Heated pool. Laundry. Cottages for hire. Open March 1-January 11. ✰✰✰✰✰ **126S.** 🐾 &

Fishguard

(3m). Fishguard Bay Caravan & Camping Park, Garn Gelli, Fishguard, Pembrokeshire SA65 9ET. *01348 811415.* enquiries@fishguardbay.com. www.fishguardbay. com. Owner: C N & L Harries. Take A487 Fishguard to Cardigan road. Turning on your L. Well signposted. Games/pool room, children's play area. TV common room. Laundrette. Cinema, town and swimming pool 3m. Golf course 5m. Open March-December. ✰✰✰✰ **BH&HPA. 20T. 20MC. 50S. 11H.** 🐾 🕿 🕿

(0.25m). Fishguard Holiday Park, Greenacres, Fishguard, Pembrokeshire SA65 9JH. *01348 872462.* www.howells leisure.co.uk. Owner: Howells Leisure. Off A40, Haverfordwest to Fishguard road. Club. Nightly entertainment. Swimming pool. Takeaway. Short breaks and weekly stays. Just a few mins walk into town. Open March-November. ✰✰✰✰ **BH&HPA. 74S. 60H.** 🐾 & 🕿

(1.5m). Gwaun Vale Touring Park, Llanychaer, Fishguard, Pembrokeshire SA65 9TA. *01348 874698.* margaret.harris@ talk21.com. Owner: Mrs Margaret Harris. From Fishguard take B4313, SP Llanychaer and Gwaun Valley. Park 1.5m on R. Local PH 0.5m. Laundrette. Telephone. Play area. Dog walk. Gas. Fishing, boating, swimming, coast and mountain walks and Irish ferry within 2m. Clean, unspoilt beaches. Open March 1-October 31. ✰✰✰✰ **BH&HPA. 30T. 4MC.** 🐾 🕿 🕿

(1m). Tregroes Park, Fishguard, Pembrokeshire SA65 9QF. *01348 872316.* Owner: Mr Hugh Williams. Club house. Hot water, showers. Playground. Attractive country site. Horse riding, fishing, boating nearby. Beach 1m. Open April-October. ✰✰ **45T. MC.** 🐾 🕿

Haverfordwest

(8m). Brandy Brook Camping and Caravan Site, Rhyndaston, Haycastle, Haverfordwest, Pembrokeshire SA62 5PT. *01348 840272.* Owner: Mr F M Rowe. A487 from Haverfordwest to Roch Motel. SP at the right-hand turn. Secluded, quiet site in a remote natural valley. Open Easter-October. **BH&HPA. 6T. 33S.** 🐾 🕿

Camping & Caravanning Club Site - St Davids, Dwr Cwmwdig, Berea, St David's, Haverfordwest, Pembrokeshire SA62 6DW. *01348 831376/0870 243 3331.* www.campingandcaravanningclub.co.uk. Owner: Camping & Caravanning Club. Greenfields House, Westwood Way, Coventry CV4 8JH. From Fishguard on A487 after Croesgoch, fork R. Follow 'Abereiddy' signs. Site is 300yd W of crossroads. 5m from St David's. Site is set in 4 acres with 40 pitches accepting all units. Chocks needed as all pitches are sloping. Very convenient for the coast, being 0.5m by footpath from Aber-eiddy. Site is located in rural setting 1m from the Heritage coast and close to Britain's smallest cathedral city. Non-members welcome. Fishing 1m. Special deals available for families and backpackers. Open April-October. ✰✰✰✰ **40T. 40MC.** 🐾 🕿

(7m). Cove Holiday Park, Howelston, Little Haven, Haverfordwest, Pembrokeshire SA62 3UU. *01305 821284/01437 781818.* Owner: Totemplant Ltd. c/o Cove Park, Pensylvanna Road, Portland, Dorset DT5 1HT. Off B4327. Overlooking St Brides Bay and one mile from Little Haven. Showers. Washbasins and clothes' washing sinks. Shaver points. Hair-dryer. Calor Gas and Campingaz. Freezing facilities. Dishwashing sink. Payphone on site. Full serviced pitches available. Open April-September. ✰✰✰ **6T. 40MC. 60S. 10H.** 🐾 🕿

(5m). Creampots Touring Caravan and Camping Park, Broadway, Broad Haven, Haverfordwest, Pembrokeshire SA62 3TU. *01437 781776.* www.creampots.co.uk. Owner: Christine & Wayne Ashford. Havenway Broadway, Broad Haven, Haverfordwest SA62 3TU. From Haverfordwest take B4341 Broad Haven road. At Broadway turn left, SP Milford Haven. Park is second on the right. Quiet, level site with heated facilities. Convenient for touring, beaches, coastal path, watersports and bird sanctuaries. Open March-October. ✰✰✰✰✰ **60T. MC. 1H.** 🐾 🕿 &

(7m). Hasguard Cross Caravan Park, Hasguard Cross, Haverfordwest, Pembrokeshire SA62 3SL. *01437 781443.* hasguard@aol.com. www.hasguardcross.co.uk. Owner: D & K James. B4327 out of Haverfordwest. After 7m, turn right to Little Haven. Site entrance 200yd on right-hand side. Children allowed. ✰✰✰✰ **BH&HPA. 25T. MC. 35S. 7H.** ✿ 🐾 🕿

(18m). Hendre Eynon, St David's, Haverfordwest, Pembrokeshire SA62 6DB. *01437 720474.* www.ukparks. co.uk/hendreeynon. Owner: Mr & Mrs I Jamieson. 2m NE of St David's on unclassified road to Llanrhian. Simple style on a working farm with superb facilities. Two perimeter pitching fields with sheltering trees. Suitable for walkers, birdwatchers and botanists. Open April 1-October 1. ✰✰✰ **BH&HPA. 50T. 10MC.** 🐾 🕿 &

(12m). Llangungar Fach Caravan Site, Solva, Haverfordwest, Pembrokeshire. *01437 721202.* Owner: Mr D Vaughan. On A487, Haverfordwest to St David's. Open March-October. **T. 20MC. 50S. 2H.** 🐾 🕿

WALES

(17m). Lleithyr Farm & Bron-y-Garn Caravan Park, Whitesands, St David's, Haverfordwest, Pembrokeshire SA62 6PR. *01437 720245.* james@lleighyr.catchtrust.org. www.whitesands-stdavids.co.uk. Owner: Mrs I H James. Off A487. Haverfordwest 17m, St David's 1.5m. Open March 1-January 6. ☆☆☆ **30T. 15MC. ⚑ 🚲 & 🔋**

(7m). Newgale Beach Holiday Park, Roch, Haverfordwest, Pembrokeshire SA62 6AS. *01437 710675.* Owner: Mathew Baker Caravans Ltd. Off A487. From Newgale take coast road to Nolton Haven, park 0.5m 2nd turn on left. Cafe near. Newgale Beach frontage. Open March-November. **BH&HPA. NCC. 15T. 55S. ⚑ 🚲**

(12m). Nine Wells Caravan & Camping Park, Nine Wells, Solva, Haverfordwest, Pembrokeshire SA62 6UH. *01437 721809.* Owner: N D Bowie. Ocean Heights, St Brides View, Solva, Haverfordwest SA62 6TB. From Haverfordwest take A487 SP St Davids, go through Solva. After 0.5m SP to Nine Wells, 5mins walk down National Trust valley to footpath and sea. Fishing, sailing, boating and beaches nearby. PO, village shops, pubs and restaurants in Solva. Pembrokeshire coastal footpath nearby. Open Easter-September. **14T. 16S. ⚑ 🚲**

(6m). Nolton Bay Caravan Park, Nolton Haven, Haverfordwest, Pembrokeshire SA62 3NH. *01437 710263.* caravans@noltonhaven.com. Owner: Jim & Joyce Canton. A487 from Haverfordwest. At Newgale turn off S to Nolton Haven. 100yd inland from Nolton Haven beach. 100yd from sandy beach. Village PH. Good sea fishing. Pony riding. Open March 1-January 10. **BH&HPA. 25S. 5H. ⚑**

(6m). Nolton Cross Caravan Site, Nolton, Haverfordwest, Pembrokeshire SA62 3NP. *01437 710701.* helen@noltoncross-holidays.co.uk. www.noltoncross-holidays.co.uk. Owner: Mr P G Thomas. Off A487 St David's to Haverfordwest, 1.5m from coast overlooking St Brides Bay. Coarse fishing lake on site. Open March 1-January 9. ☆☆☆ **BH&HPA. 15T. MC. 30S. 8H. ⚑ 🚲**

(12m). Park Hall Caravan Park, Penycwm, Haverfordwest, Pembrokeshire SA62 6LS. *01437 721606.* Owner: E R & H M Harries. Off A487 Haverfordwest to St David's. Turn right at SP for Royal Signals Cawdor Barracks, then first left. Site 1m from A487. Near coastal path, beaches, walks. Golf course. Open March-October. **BH&HPA. 40T. 10MC. 120S. ✿ ⚑ &**

(17m). Prendergast Caravan Site, Trefin, Haverfordwest, Pembrokeshire SA62 5AJ. *01348 831368.* Owner: Mr A Jenkins. 8m NE of St Davids. Via A487 to Trefin, SP. N for 1m to site. 0.25m from beach. Open April-October. ☆☆☆ **6T. 6MC. 12H. 🚲**

(6.5m). Redlands Touring Caravan & Camping Park, Hasguard Cross, Nr Little Haven, Haverfordwest, Pembrokeshire SA62 3SJ. *01437 781300.* info@redlands camping.co.uk. www.redlandstouring.co.uk. Owner: Trevor & Jenny Flight. On B4327, 6.5m SW of Haverfordwest. Do not approach via Broad Haven. 5 acres of open grassland. Pets welcome. Convenient base for Pembrokeshire holidays. Close to beaches and famous coastal path. Open March-December. ☆☆☆☆ **BH&HPA. 64T. MC. ⚑ 🚲 🔋**

(15m). Rhosson Ganol, St David's, Haverfordwest, Pembrokeshire SA62 6PY. *01437 720361.* Owner: HJ & EM Griffiths. On A487. St David's 1m. Open Easter-October. **BH&HPA. 6T. MC. 30S. ⚑**

(4m). Scamford Caravan Park, Scamford, Keeston Camrose, Haverfordwest, Pembrokeshire SA62 6HN. *01437 710304.* holidays@scamford.com. www.scamford.com. Owner: RJ & CC White. Off A487. Small, quiet, country park near sandy

beaches and coastal path. Play area. Warm welcome from resident owners: Richard and Christine. Open March 1-October 31. ☆☆☆☆ **BH&HPA. 5T. 5MC. 25H. ⚑ 🚲**

(5m). South Cockett Touring Caravan & Camping Park, Broadway, Little Haven, Haverfordwest, Pembrokeshire SA62 3TU. *01437 781296/781760.* esmejames@hotmail.co.uk. www.southcockett.co.uk. Owner: Mrs E R James. Take B4341 from Haverfordwest, turn L at official caravan and camping sign. Site 300yd on R. Shop 1m. Showers. Laundrette. Hot water to basins. Freezer pack service. Calor Gas and Campingaz stocked. Open Easter-October. **73T. MC. ⚑ 🚲**

(15m). Torbant Caravan Park, Croesgoch, Haverfordwest, Pembrokeshire SA62 5JN. *01348 831261.* www.torbant. co.uk. Owners: Mrs L R Parker & Miss S L Parker. On A487. Halfway between St David's and Fishguard. Laundry. Games room. Heated swimming pool. Play area. Open March 1-January 10. ☆☆☆☆☆ **BH&HPA. 90S. ⚑**

(14m). Tretio Touring Caravan & Camping Park, St David's, Haverfordwest, Pembrokeshire SA62 6DE. *01437 781600/ 720270.* info@tretio.com. www.tretio.com. Owner: Bryn & Phil Rees. Mountain Farm, Broadway, Broadhaven, Haverfordwest, Pembrokeshire SA62 3HU. Off B3283. St David's 3m. On leaving St David's keep left at St David's rugby ground and continue straight for 3m until sign pointing right. Park 300yd. Park is located in Pembrokeshire Nationa Park. 0.25m off coast road and 0.5m to coastal path, panoramic views. 4.5-acre 9-hole pitch and putt course. PO, doctors, shops available in St David's, 3m. 1.5m to nearest beach. Open March-October. ☆☆☆ **10T. MC. 30S. 3H. ⚑ 🚲 & 🔋**

Kilgetty

Croft Holiday Park, Reynalton, Kilgetty, Pembrokeshire SA68 0PE. *01834 860315.* enquiries@croftholidaypark.com. www.croftholidaypark.com. Owner: Mr C H Pendleton, Mr V C Pendleton & Mrs A Pendleton. Off A40. On A478 follow brown signs for 'Croft Park' from Templeton. David Bellamy Silver Conservation Award. Dragon Award. Licensed clubhouse. Playground. Laundrette. Restaurant. Takeaway. Fishing, horse riding 3m. Shops 4m. Golf 5m. Cinema 8m. Open March-November. ☆☆☆☆ **BH&HPA. 50T. MC. 90S. 5H. ⚑ 🚲 & 🔋**

(1m). Ryelands Caravan Park, Ryelands Lane, Kilgetty, Pembrokeshire SA68 0UY. *01834 812369.* Owner: D H Jenkins. Turn R off A477 kilgetty bypass (St Clears-Pembroke) at roundabout on to A478 (Narberth) at next roundabout turn R, in 0.5m pass railway bridge turn L into Ryelands Lane, park 0.75m on R. Most amenities available at Kilgetty. Fishing, golf course, Oakwood 5m away. Open March 1-October 30. **30T. MC. ⚑ 🚲**

(0.75m). Stone Pitt, Begelly, Kilgetty, Pembrokeshire SA68 0XE. *01834 811086.* Owner: Mr P E Holland. Situated in Belgelly village, private drive on A478 by public telephone box. 6 acres, mainly level site with secluded pleasant walks. Hot/cold Showers. Mini-laundrette. All hard-standings with water drains. Peak booking advisable. Open March 1-January 9. ☆☆ **BH&HPA. 55T. MC. ⚑ 🚲 & 🖉**

Milford Haven

(4m). Sandy Haven Caravan & Camp Site, Herbrandston, Milford Haven, Pembrokeshire SA73 3AL. *01646 698844/695209 - late July/Aug).* Owner: Sandy Haven Caravan Site Ltd. 13 Hamilton Terrace, Milford Haven, Pembrokeshire SA73 2AL. Turn left at Taberna Inn in village, follow road down to beach. Close to all Pembrokeshire attractions: Skomer

Marine Reserve, castles etc. Suitable for families, coastal walkers. In Pembrokeshire Coast National Park. Waterside location. Fishing, boating, skiing, golf, riding all close by. Sandy beaches and estuary. Wonderful for birdlife. Open April-August. ☆☆☆ **2T. MC. 20S.** ⊁

Narbeth

(1m). Allensbank Holiday Park, Providence Hill, Narberth, Pembrokeshire SA67 8RF. *01834 860243.* Owner: Harrison Stevens. A478 main N Tenby road. Open Easter-September. ☆☆☆ **BH&HPA. 11T. MC. 6S. 12H.** ⊁ ⊟

(3.5m). Derwenlas Caravan Park, Clynderwen, Narberth, Pembrokeshire SA66 7SU. *01437 563504.* Owner: Mr & Mrs Rowland. Off the A478. Open April-September. **4T. 4MC. 19S.** ⊁ ⊟

Golden Grove Leisure Park, Pleasant Valley, Stepaside, Narberth, Pembrokeshire SA67 8LN. *01834 812464.* **T. MC. S.** ⊁ ⊟ ⅃

(5m). Little Kings Park, Ludchurch, Narberth, Pembrokeshire SA67 8PG. *01834 831330.* www.littlekings.co.uk. Owner: Messrs. R J & C W Blake. From the A477 turn left towards Amroth and Wiseman's Bridge, take first turn right, SP Ludchurch, park is 0.25m on the left-hand side. Games room. Laundry facilities. Residents' bar and restaurant adjoining sun patio and covered heated pool. Open Easter-September. ☆☆☆☆ **BH&HPA. 66T. 66MC. 15H.** ⊁ ⊟ & ⅃

(4m). Llandissilio Caravan Park, Clynderwen, Narberth, Pembrokeshire. *01437 563408.* Owner: Mrs P Bucknell. On A478. New indoor heated swimming pool with bar, sauna and spa. Open Easter-November. ☆☆☆ **BH&HPA. 30T. 5MC. 20S. 10H.** ⊁ ⊟ ⅃

(4m). Llandre Farm, Egremont, Clynderwen, Narberth, Pembrokeshire. *01437 563215.* Owner: Mrs S B Thomas. Caerelwyn, Llandissilio, Clynderwen, Pembrokeshire. On the B4313 Fishguard to Narberth road. Open March 1-October 1. **22S.** ⊁ ⊟

(7m). New Park, Landshipping, Narberth, Pembrokeshire SA67 8BG. *01834 891284.* Owner: E & C A Jones. From Eturn left off A40 at Canaston Bridge on to A4075, turn right at Canaston Bowls towards Martletwy Landshipping, after 2m turn right, after 200yd turn left. Entrance on left within 0.5m. Fishing and sailing on river Cleddau 1m. Tranquil countryside retreat. Horse riding, theme park and ten-pin bowling 3m. Golf course 12m, cinema 14m. Open March 1-January 9. **BH&HPA. 5T. MC. 30S. 3H.** ⊁ ⊟

(0.5m). Noble Court Holiday Park, Redstone Road, Narberth, Pembrokeshire SA67 7ES. *0183 4 861908.* enquiries@noblecourtholidaypark.com. www.noblecourtholidaypark.com. Owner: Celtic Holiday Parks Ltd. Located off the A40, on the B4313 road, N of Narberth and 0.5m S of the A40. Club. Heated swimming pool, coarse fishing. Shops 0.5m. David Bellamy Silver Conservation Award. Open March 1-October 31. ☆☆☆☆ **BH&HPA. 92T. 2MC. 60S.** ⊁ ⊟ &

Oakland Caravan Park, Summerhill, Amroth, Narberth, Pembrokeshire SA67 8NS. *01834 811051.* plank@so1506.f9.co.uk. www.caravancampingsites.co.uk/pembrokeshire. Owner: Mr & Mrs D Plank. 1.5m off A477 towards Wiseman's Bridge. 1m from Amroth, 2.5m from Saundersfoot. Kilgetty 3m. Small, quiet, family park. 1m from beaches. Upgraded to high

standard. Sandy beach, food shop, PHs, restaurants, takeaway foods all 1m. Indoor heated pool and golf course 6m. Open March 1-January 9. **22S. 2H.** ⊘

Pinewood Caravan Park, Wisemans Bridge, Narberth, Pembrokeshire SA67 8NU. *01834 811082.* Owner: Les & Gwen Grecian. Park is located 1.5 miles from Saundersfoot. Just 300 yards from the beach. Small, peaceful, family-run park adjacent to the Pembrokeshire coastal path. Dragon Award. No tourers and no tents allowed. Open Easter-October. ☆☆☆☆☆ **BH&HPA. 8H.** ⊘

(5m). Pleasant Valley Caravan Park, Wiseman's Bridge, Narberth, Pembrokeshire SA67 8NY. *01834 813631/812462.* Owner: O M Cooke. Off the A477 between Amroth and Saundersfoot. A quiet, secluded site just 3 mins walk from beach with a PH. Free car parking. Open March-November. **7T. 3MC. 45S. 6H.** ⊁ ⊟ ⅃

(1m). Redford Caravan Park, Princes Gate, Narberth, Pembrokeshire SA67 8TD. *01834 860251.* Owner: Mr M & A Gateley. On B4314. Pool. Club. Open March 1-October 31. **50T. 6MC. 75S. 15H.** ⊁ ⊟ ⅃

(10m). Rosebush Caravan Park, Rhoslwyn, Rosebush, Narberth, Pembrokeshire SA66 7QT. *01437 532206/0831 223166.* Owner: Mr G Williams. On the B4313, B4329 1m away. Boating. Coarse fishing. Adults only. Open March 25-October 31. **BH&HPA. 45T. 5MC. 15S.** ⊁ ⊟ ⅃

(6m). Starre Gorse Caravan Site, Stepaside. Pleasant Valley, Narberth, Pembrokeshire SA67 8LR. *01834 812428.* Owner: Mr W J G Hughes. Off A477. Heated swimming pool. Open March-October. **75S. 25H.** ⊁ ⅃

The Dingle, Jesse Road, Narberth, Pembrokeshire SA67 7DP. *01834 860482.* Owner: Mrs R Owen & Sons. Laundry. Showers. Clubhouse. Play area. Oakwood 4m and nearest beach 6m. Shop nearby. Open March-October. **26T. 4MC. 30S. 2H.** ⊁ ⊟

(2m). Wood Office Caravan Park, Cold Blow, Narberth, Pembrokeshire SA67 8RR. *01834 860565.* Owner: Mrs Morgan. Parkis located on the B4315. Close to Oakwood Park, Folly Farm and Heron's Brook. Central located for touring the area. A flat site. Open Easter-October 1. **45T. MC. 45S.** ⊁ ⊟ ⅃

(2m). Woodland Vale Caravan Park, Ludchurch, Narberth, Pembrokeshire SA67 8JE. *01834 831319.* info@woodlandvale.com. www.woodlandvale.com. Owner: Mr T Scarrott. Clarach Bay Holiday Village, Nr Aberystwyth SY23 3DT. Off A40 and A477. Park facilities include indoor swimming pool complex, club, pool, games room, live entertainment, meals available, laundrette, shop, showers. Local attractions: Oakwood Theme Park, Tenby, Saundersfoot, Folly Farm and others. Open February-November. **BH&HPA. 30T. 80S. 4H.** ⊁ ⊟ ⅃ ⊘

Newport

Newport Bay Caravan Parklands, The Parrog, Newport, Pembrokeshire SA42 0XN. *01348 811220.* www.matthewbakercaravans.co.uk. Owner: Matthew Baker Caravans. Dinas Cross, Newport, Pembrokeshire. Parrog Road is a direct lead-off the A487, which runs through Newport town, park 400yd farther on. Open March 1-November 7. **BH&HPA. NCC. 69S. H.** ⊁

Pembroke

(2.5m). Freshwater East Caravan Club Site, Trewent Hill, Freshwater East, Pembroke, Pembrokeshire SA71 5LJ. 01646 672341. www.caravanclub.co.uk. Owner: The Caravan Club. East Grinstead House, East Grinstead, West Sussex RH19 1UA. See website for standard directions to site. Within the Pembrokeshire Coast National Park. Part sloping, information room, dog walk nearby. 2 toilet blocks. Privacy cubicles. Laundry facilities. Veg prep. Motorhome waste point. Hard-standings. Calor Gas and Campingaz. Play area. Non-members and tent campers welcome. Do not tow to the beach. Fishing and water sports. Good area for walking. Suitable for families. Peaceful off peak. NCN cycle route 5m. Open March-October. ✰✰✰✰✰ NCC. 130T. MC. ⛟ ⛆ ⛆ ⛆

(3m). Upper Portclew Touring Site, Freshwater East, Pembroke, Pembrokeshire SA71 5LA. 01646 672112. Owner: Mrs M A Phillips. Carmarthen, turn left. Milton to Lamphey, 7m E. Site on right before village. PO and shops 1.5m, Lamphey. Fishing on beach, rocks. Doctors 3m, Pembroke. Golf course 6m, Tenby 10m. Open May-September. 5T. 20MC. ⛟ ⛆

(1m). Windmill Hill Caravan Park, Windmill Hill Farm, Pembroke, Pembrokeshire SA71 5BT. 01646 682392. wjgibby@btopenworld.com. Owner: Jay & Jenny Gibby. Situated 1 mile south of Pembroke town on the B4319. Close to the Pembrokeshire National Park with its beaches. 5 mins from the ferry terminal to Ireland. Modern toilets and showers on the park. Open March-October. 30T. 10MC. ⛟ ⛆

Saundersfoot

(5m). Beachdean Leisure Park, Reynalton, Kilgetty, Saundersfoot, Pembrokeshire SA68 0PE. 01834 891643. info@beachdeanholidays.co.uk. www.beachdeanholidays.co.uk. Owner: Mr & Mrs J Thomas. Take the A477 to Kilgetty, then the A478 towards Narberth turn sharp left at Boar's Head, Templeton for Reynalton. Peaceful, tranquil park in pleasant rural surroundings. Floral display. Open March 1-October 31. ✰✰✰✰✰ BH&HPA. 45S. 6H. ⛟ ⛆

(3m). Blackmoor Farm, Ludchurch, Amroth, Saundersfoot, Pembrokeshire SA67 8PG. 01834 831242. ltecornth@aol.com. www.infozone.com.hk/blackmoorfarm. Owner: Mr & Mrs Cornthwaite. Off A477 2.5m from Amroth. Small, select family park on own 36-acre farm. Near beautiful beaches at Amroth, Saundersfoot and Tenby. Peaceful surroundings, safe for children, free donkey rides. Games and laundry room. Open April-September. ✰✰✰✰✰ BH&HPA. 06S. 6H. ⌀

(0.75m). Bonville's Court Caravan Park, Weighbridge Office, off Ridgeway, Saundersfoot, Pembrokeshire SA69 9NA. 0370 801503. Owner: Mr W J Davies. A40 from Carmarthen to St Clears, then A477 to Kilgetty roundabout, take Tenby to Saundersfoot road for 0.75m, follow Saundersfoot sign on B4316 via Ridgeway Road, park is 0.5m on right. Laundrette. Open March 1-November 30. BH&HPA. 10T. MC. 48S. 6H. ⛟ ⛆

(1.5m). Brickyard Holiday Home Park, Wiseman's Bridge, Saundersfoot, Pembrokeshire SA69 9AX. 01834 813500/811500. Owner: Hean Castle Estate. Leisure Dept CS2000, Hean Castle Estate Office, Saundersfoot, Pembrokeshire, SA69 9AL. Follow A478 towards Tenby, turn left on to B4316 to Saundersfoot, left at police station and follow road to Wiseman's Bridge, entrance 100yd on the right. Seafront, terraced site overlooking Carmarthen Bay. All enquiries to estate office. Open April 1-October 31. BH&HPA. 48S.

(2m). Mill House Caravan Park, Pleasant Valley, Stepaside, Saundersfoot, Pembrokeshire SA67 8LN. 01834 812069. holiday@millhousecaravan.co.uk. www.millhousecaravan.co.uk. Owner: Simon & Amanda Wood. 13m W St Clears A477. Turn L for Stepaside, first L and first L for Pleasant Valley. Site 0.5m on L. Family site next to old watermill. 15mins walk to beach, coast path and PH. Hard-standings, TV and electricity included. Dragon Award. Open March-October. ✰✰✰✰ BH&HPA. 8T. 1MC. 15S. 6H. ⛟ ⛆

(1.5m). Moreton Farm Leisure Park, Moreton, Saundersfoot, Pembrokeshire SA69 9EA. 01834 812016. moretonfarm@btconnect.com. www.moretonfarm.co.uk. Owner: Nixon Ltd. On A478, Kilgetty to Tenby, 3.5m. Saundersfoot 1.5m. Set in peaceful surroundings. Modern facilities. Pine lodges and cottages. Bed linen provided. Play area. Open March 1-November 1. ✰✰✰✰ BH&HPA. 20T. MC. 12H. ⛆ ⛆ ⛆

(1m). Moysland Farm Camping Site, Narberth Road, Saundersfoot, Pembrokeshire SA69 9DS. 01834 812455. Owner: Mrs V Rawson and Mrs M J Humphries. On A478 at junction of Sandy Hill Lane. 2m N of Tenby. Showers. Owner on site. Supervision at all times. Booking essential. Open July-September. 3T. 14MC. ⛟ ⛆

(0.75m). Saundersfoot Bay Leisure Park, Saundersfoot, Pembrokeshire SA69 9DG. 01834 812284. enquiries@saundersfootbay.co.uk. www.saundersfootbay.co.uk. Manager: Mr Gavin Steer. 0.75m from Saundersfoot towards Tenby on coastal side of B4316. Award-winning park with panoramic sea views. Laundrette. Dogs allowed by arrangement. Past winner of Calor Gas 'Best Caravan Park in Britain' award. Golf course, angling, cinema, horse riding, sailing, indoor swimming pool, all within 3m. Beach 0.75m. Open March-October. ✰✰✰✰✰ BH&HPA. 180S. 22H. ⛟ ⛆

(1m). Sunnyvale Holiday Park, Valley Road, Saundersfoot, Pembrokeshire SA69 9BT. 01348 872462. www.howellsleisure.co.uk. Owner: Howells Leisure. Greenacres, Fishguard SA65 9JH. Take A478 towards Tenby. 3m from Tenby. Enter Pentlepoir. Pass Murco petrol station on R, take next left into Valley Road. Park 150yd down on left-hand side. Club. Nightly entertainment. Heated indoor swimming pool. Open March-October. ✰✰✰✰ BH&HPA. 47T. 3MC. 53S. 53H. ⛟ ⛆ ⛆ ⌀

The Scar Holiday Home Park, Frances Road, Saundersfoot, Pembrokeshire SA69 9AH. 01834 810181. Owner: Hean Castle Estate. Hean Castle Estate Office, Saundersfoot, Pembrokeshire SA69 9AL. From Kilgetty bypass follow A478 towards Tenby, turn left on to B4316 to Saundersfoot, turn left at police station, entrance 100yd on left. Quiet, secluded park divided in sections by hedge banks and mature trees. 250yd from village centre. All enquiries to estate office. Open April 1-October 30. BH&HPA. 79S. 10H. ⛟ ⌀

(1m). White Gate Caravan Park, Pleasant Valley, Stepaside, Saundersfoot, Pembrokeshire SA67 8NY. 01834 811543. info@whitegatecaravanpark.co.uk. www.whitegatecaravanpark.co.uk. Owner: Alyson & Peter Hicks. 26 Mayfield Acres, Kilgetty SA68 0UW. Off A477, at L turn for Wiseman's Bridge. Follow road through Stepaside and take lower road into Pleasant Valley. Close to Saundersfoot and coastal path. Small, select park set in peaceful wooded valley, only 400yd from beach. No pets. Dragon Award. Open March-October. ✰✰✰✰✰ BH&HPA. 8H. ⌀

(0.75m.). Windy Hill Holiday Park, Sardis, Saundersfoot, Pembrokeshire SA67 8JX. 01834 812766. Owner: Elizabeth Maddox. Turn right off the A477. SP Kilgetty, then take first left, 150yd, into Sardis Road. Site is about 0.75m on your right. Park

---

Please visit the Caravan Club website: www.caravanclub.co.uk

is set on high level overlooking some 60 square miles of countryside, some of which is in the Pembrokeshire Coast National Park. Launderette and children's play area on site. Shopping is only 0.75m at Kilgetty with about 12 shops and a Co-op supermarket, garage and PO. Doctor at Saundersfoot 1.25m. Golf courses, fishing, theme parks, wildlife parks, all within 5m. Beaches 1m. Open Easter-mid October. **30T. 15MC. 2S.** ⚕ 🅮

Zealand Holiday Home Park, Saundersfoot, Pembrokeshire SA69 9GA. *01834 813500/811500.* Owner: Hean Castle Estate. Leisure Dept CS2000, Hean Castle Estate Office, Saundersfoot, Pembrokeshire SA69 9AL. From Kilgetty bypass follow A478 towards Tenby, turn left on to B4316 to Saundersfoot, turn left at police station, site entrance 100yd on left via Scar Holiday Home Park. Quiet, well-sheltered park 400yd from village centre. All enquiries to estate office. Open April 1-October 31. **BH&HPA. 56S.**

St David's

(0.5m). Caerfai Bay Caravan & Tent Park, St David's, Pembrokeshire SA62 6QT. *01437 720274.* info@caerfaibay. co.uk. Owner: Mr & Mrs I E Panton. Off A487 Haverfordwest to St David's, in St David's at Visitor Centre near Grove Hotel, park at end of road on the right. Panoramic sea views. Seaside award. Bathing beach 200yd, adjacent to Pembrokeshire coastal path and numerous local outdoor pursuits. Laundrette. Showers. AA 3 pennants. Shops 0.75m, golf 2m. Open March-mid November. ✩✩✩✩ **BH&HPA. 28T. 15MC. 32S. 8H.** ⚕ 🅮 ♿

(1.5m). Lleithyr Meadow Caravan Club Site, Whitesands, St David's, Pembrokeshire SA62 6PR. *01437 720401.* www.caravanclub.co.uk. Owner: The Caravan Club. East Grinstead House, East Grinstead, West Sussex RH19 1UA. See website for standard directions to site. Holiday site nestling by three headlands of the Pembrokeshire coast. Toilet block. Privacy cubicles. Laundry facilities. Veg prep. Information room. Shop adjacent. Gas supplies. Motorhome waste point. Play equipment. Non-members welcome. Fishing, golf and water sports nearby. Good area for walking. Dog walk nearby. Beach and NCN cycle route within 5m. Open March-October. ✩✩✩✩ **NCC. 120T. MC.** ⚕ 🅮 ♿ ▨

(9m). Mabws Bridge Residential & Leisure Home Park, Mathry, St David's, Pembrokeshire SA62 5JB. *01348 831466.* Owner: S & M Hall Leisure Ltd. Dinas Country Club, Dinas Cross, Nr Newport, Pembs SA42 0UN. St David's (9m) to Fishguard Road (4m) A487. Small, family-owned park in a tranquil, rural setting offering a secure and peaceful environment to all home owners. Laundry. Disabled facilities, showers, hardstanding surfaces and heated swimming pool. Children and pets allowed. Retired and semi-retired home owners. Rallies welcome. Open March 1-January 10. ✩✩✩✩ **40T. 40MC. 30S. 2H.** ✳ ⚕ 🅮 ♿ ▨

Tenby

(5m). Buttyland Touring Caravan and Tent Park, Manorbier, Tenby, Pembrokeshire SA70 7SN. *01834 871278.* buttyland@tesco.net. www.buttyland.co.uk. On A4139, Pembroke to Tenby. Open Easter-October. **35T. 15MC.** ⚕ 🅮 ♿

(2.5m). Crackwell Holiday Park, Penally, Tenby, Pembrokeshire SA70 7RX. *01834 842688.* crackwelltenby@ aol.com. Owner: Mr M Thomas. Belgrave Hotel, The Esplanade, Tenby, Pembrokeshire SA70 7DU. A40 from Carmarthen, follow A4139 from Tenby 2.5m on right-hand side. Level pitches. Superpitches for tourers available. Friendly local staff. 24hr

telephone answering service. Laundrette. Small convenience shop. Play area. Families only. Coastal path, beaches and all leisurely pursuits nearby. Open April 1-October 31. **BH&HPA. 75T. 25MC. 50S. 20H.** ⚕ 🅮 ▨ ▨

(4.5m). Cross Park Holiday Centre, Broadmoor, Kilgetty, Tenby, Pembrokeshire SA68 0RS. *01834 811244.* www.newhorizonsholidays.co.uk. Owner: Mr & Mrs M A Whitehouse. New Horizons Holidays. Continue on A477, 1m W of Kilgetty. Turn right at Cross Inn, park 250yd on left. Picturesque family park with excellent facilities, showbar with nightly entertainment, children's club, heated indoor swimming pool, shop, games room. Open March-December. ✩✩✩✩ **BH&HPA. 35T. 15MC. 85S. 25H.** ⚕ 🅮 ♿ ▨ ▨

(4m). Hazelbrook Caravan Park, Sageston, Milton, Tenby, Pembrokeshire SA70 8SY. *01646 651351.* www.hazelbrook caravanpark.co.uk. Owner: A P Sole. Off A477, on to B4318 at Sageston roundabout; site is 20yd on the R. Quiet, family site. Hard and grass-standings. Free showers. Shop. Laundry and ironing facilities. Games room. Good for coast and country holidays. Open March 1-January 9. **70T. 10MC. 50S. 20H.** ⚕ 🅮 ▨

(1m). Kiln Park Holiday Centre, Marsh Road, Tenby, Pembrokeshire SA70 7RB. *01834 844126.* oewebmaster@ bourne-leisure.co.uk. www.kilnparkholidaycentre.com. Owner: Bourne Leisure Ltd. One Park Lane, Hemel Hempstead, Herts HP2 4YL. Follow A477/A478 to Tenby for about 6m. Follow caravan/camping signs to Penally. Kiln Park is 0.5m on your L. 2 show bars. Heated indoor fun pool complex. Spa bath, sauna. Laundrette. Arcade. Cafe and takeaway food. Mini market. Petrol station. Direct beach access. Family entertainment. Pitch and putt, tennis courts, mini bowling, bouncy castle, play area. 2 golf courses within 5mins drive. Oakwood Theme Park 15mins. Cinema in Tenby. Open March-November. ✩✩✩✩ **BH&HPA. NCC. 60T. 15MC. 710S. 84H.** ⚕ 🅮 ♿ ▨ ▨

(10m). Lawrenny Quay Caravan Site, Lawrenny Quay, Lawrenny, Kilgetty, Tenby, Pembrokeshire SA68 0PR. *01646 651439/212.* Owner: Lawrenny Yacht Station. Off A4075. Water's edge hotel accommodation, yachtsmen's and fishermen's bars. Showers. Petrol, diesel station, moorings swinging and pontoons. Chandlery. Open March 1-December 31. **30T. MC. 50S.** ⚕ 🅮

(2m). Lydstep Beach Holiday Resort, Lydstep Haven, Tenby, Pembrokeshire SA70 7SB. *01834 871874.* oewebmaster@ bourne-leisure.co.uk. www.lydstepbeachholidayresort.com. Owner: Bourne Leisure Ltd. One Park Lane, Hemel Hempstead, Herts HP2 4YL. A40 then A478 to Tenby. Take A4139 SP Penally. Passing Kiln Park on your L follow main road for nearly 3m and park entrance is on L. Owners lounge, bar, snooker room, spa bath, gym, sun beds, steam room, family entertainment, private bay with boat launch, seaviews, shops and restaurants. Fishing, golf all nearby. Open March-January. ✩✩✩✩ **BH&HPA. NCC. 464S.** ⚕ ♿ ▨ ▨

(5m). Manorbier Bay Holiday Park, Manorbier, Tenby, Pembrokeshire SA70 7SR. *01834 871235.* www.manorbier bay.com. Owner: Mr & Mrs H B Farr. On A4139, Pembroke to Tenby. 1m from beach. Laundrette. Showers. Play area. Park located within Pembrokeshire country park area. Bar on site. Shop, PO 10mins walk to village of Manorbier, 0.25m. Open March 1-October 31. **BH&HPA. 19T. MC. 66S. 2H.** ⚕ 🅮

Manorbier Country Park, Station Road, Manorbier, Tenby, Pembrokeshire SA70 7SN. *01834 871952.* Owner: Mr Bob Mcharg. From Tenby follow A4139 towards Pembroke. Road widens with chapel on right, take right hand turn for Manorbier-Newton Station, park 300yds on left. Heated indoor pool. Rail staion nearby. Bottle gas supplies. Swimming pool. Laundry. Facilities block. Selection of sporting activities nearby. Open March 1-October 31. ☆☆☆☆☆ NCC. 35T. 101S. 50H. 🖸 & 🖳

(4m). Masterland Farm, Broadmoor, Kilgetty, Tenby, Pembrokeshire SA68 0RH. 01834 813298. bonsermasterland@aol.com. www.ukparks.co.uk/masterland. Owner: Mrs Davies. A477 to Broadmoor, turn right at Cross Inn, after 300yd turn R for park. Ideal for beaches and touring, all modern facilities. Baby bathroom. Bar and restaurant. Games and TV room. Booking advisable at peak times. Open February 28-January 9. ☆☆☆ BH&HPA. 38T. MC. 🐕 🖸 ⌀

(6m). Meadow House Holiday Park, Amroth, Tenby, Pembrokeshire SA67 8NS. 01834 812438. Owner: Treatcourt Ltd. 6m NE of Tenby. From Tenby take A478. After 3.5m turn R on to A477, turn R again at sign Amroth and Wisemans Bridge. From St Clears on A477 for 10m, after Stage Coach Inn turn L at sign. 1m from beach. Indoor swimming pool. Open March-October. BH&HPA. 70T. MC. 150S. 🖸 ⌀

(4m). Milton Bridge Caravan Park, Milton, Tenby, Pembrokeshire SA70 8PH. 01646 651204. milton-bridge@tiscali.co.uk. Owner: Mr & Mrs K Gouldsbrough. Directly off the A477 at Milton, SP for Cosheston. Showers. Laundrette. Small, peaceful, family-run park set in national park on river estuary. Convenient for visiting Pembroke's numerous attractions. Open March 1-October 31. BH&HPA. 15T. 23S. 🐕 🖸

(3m). New Minerton Leisure Park, Devonshire Drive, St Florence, Tenby, Pembrokeshire SA70 8RH. 01646 651461. Owner: Country Leisure Properties. From Kilgetty roundabout, follow A477 to Pembroke at Sageston, turn L on B4318 to Tenby and Manor House Wildlife Park. Devonshire Drive is opposite Manor House Park. Club. Heated pool. Fishing lake. All-weather bowling green. Golf course within 3m. Open March 1-January 10. BH&HPA. 164S. 🐕 ⌀

North Cliff Caravan Park, North Cliff, Tenby, Pembrokeshire SA70 8AU. 01834 843526. Owner: Mr F & Mrs J Hodgkinson. Take left fork after passing 'Welcome to Tenby' sign on A478 into Narberth Road, at bottom of road turn left into The Croft, park at top of road. Nearest site to beach and town. Winter tel. 01782 303527. Open Easter-September. 15H. 🐕

(6m). Park Farm Caravans, Manorbier, Tenby, Pembrokeshire SA70 7SU. 01834 871273. Owner: Mr G Thomas. Guydor, Lamphey, Pembroke SA71 5NW. Take A4139 W from Tenby for about 6m, take second turning for Manorbier, after 200yd turn right. Footpath to beach 0.5m, through wooded valley past 14th-century castle. Quiet, family site. Open April-October. BH&HPA. 12T. 10MC. 70S. 🐕 🖸 🖳

(2m). Rowston Holiday Park, New Hedges, Tenby, Pembrokeshire SA70 8TL. 01834 842178. andrea@rowston-hp.freeserve.co.uk. www.rowston-holiday-park.co.uk. Owner: Mr D C Ormond. Follow signs for New Hedges through village mini-market on right, park is second turning on left. Flat to sloping park with sea views. Open April 1-October 31. BH&HPA. 110T. MC. 133S. 12H. 🐕 🖸

(1m). Rumbleway Caravan Park, New Hedges, Tenby, Pembrokeshire SA70 8TR. 01834 845155. Owner: Mr V G Lawrence. On A478, Cardigan to Tenby, on New Hedges by-pass. Club. The Retreat PH on site, food supplied. Heated outdoor pools, play area, amusement arcade, laundrette and facilities block. Open April-October. BH&HPA. 75T. MC. 130S. 15H. 🖸 & 🖳

(1.5m). The Lodge Farm Caravan Site, New Hedges, Tenby, Pembrokeshire SA70 8TH. 01834 842468. info@lodgefarmtenby.fsworld.co.uk. Owner: Mr & Mrs S J Weaver. On A478 Narberth to Tenby. Flat site. Some touring pitches have sea views. Laundrette. Club and games room. Takeaway food. AA 2 pennants. Sports. Fishing from private beach. Shops/PO 200yd from site entrance. Garage 50yd from entrance. Animal attractions. Children's play area. Open March-October. BH&HPA. 65T. MC. 40S. 🐕 🖸 🖳

(3.5m). Trefalun Park, Devonshire Drive, St Florence, Tenby, Pembrokeshire SA70 8RD. 01646 651514. trefalun@aol.com. www.trefalunkpark.co.uk. Owner: Alan Higgs. W of St Florence, Devonshire Drive is off B4318 opposite Manor House Wildlife Park. Club, swimming pool and fishing lake at adjoining park. Mains water and drainage pitches available. Golfing and horse riding available within walking distance of park. Open April-October. ☆☆☆☆☆ BH&HPA. 60T. 5MC. 10S. 5H. 🐕 🖸 &

(3m). Trevayne Caravan Park, Saundersfoot, Tenby, Pembrokeshire SA69 9DL. 01834 813402. Owner: Mr D L Reed. Off A478, Narberth to Tenby. 15mins walk from New Hedges village. Newly-built block of showers, toilets and washing facilities. Open April 1-October 30. BH&HPA. 80T. 20MC. 80S. 🐕 🖸 &

(6m). Tudor Glen Caravan Park, Jameston, Manorbier, Tenby, Pembrokeshire SA70 7SS. 01834 871417. info@tudorglencaravanpark.co.uk. www.tudorglencaravanpark.co.uk. Owner: V J Stevens & Sons. On A4139, Tenby to Pembroke. Family site. No groups. 1m from Manorbier Beach and Pembrokeshire coastal path. Golf at Tenby, with its beaches, 5m away. Open March 1-October 31. ☆☆☆☆ BH&HPA. 30T. 3MC. 20S. 🖸 🖳

(1m). Well Park, Tenby, Pembrokeshire SA70 8TL. 01834 842179. enquiries@wellparkcaravans.co.uk. www.wellparkcaravans.co.uk. Owner: Mr D J Nash. On right-hand side of main A478 Tenby road. 1m before reaching Tenby. Dragon Award. Family-run park convenient for beaches and touring Pembrokeshire coast. Laundrette. Games room. Licensed bar. Wales in Bloom Award. Golf course nearby. 4mins walk to shops, PO. Doctors 1m. Open April-October. ☆☆☆☆☆ BH&HPA. 40T. 10MC. 42S. 6H. 🐕 🖸

(3m). Whitewell Caravan Park, Lydstep Beach, Tenby, Pembrokeshire SA70 7RY. 01834 871569. Owners: Brian & Diane Kelly. Off A4139, Tenby to Manorbier. Campers' bar. Club. Footpath to Lydstep beach. Theme and adventure park, golf course nearby. Open Easter-October. 20T. 20MC. 50S. 🐕 🖸 🖳

(0.75m). Windmills Caravan Park, Narberth Road, Tenby, Pembrokeshire SA70 8TJ. 01834 842200. www.camping-tenby.co.uk. On A478. Near Tenby, L turn. 0.75m Tenby with lovely sea views. Open Easter-October. 8T. 10MC. 15S. 🐕 🖸

(1.5m). Wood Park Caravans, New Hedges, Tenby, Pembrokeshire SA70 8TL. 01834 843414. info@woodpark.co.uk.www.woodpark.co.uk.Owner: Mrs E M Hodgkinson. At roundabout, 2m N of Tenby, take A478, then second R and R again. Family park with licensed bar, games room, laundrette, facilities block. Small dogs only allowed, except Easter week, spring bank holiday week and school holidays. Open Easter-end September. ☆☆☆☆ BH&HPA. 40T. MC. 90S. 35H. 🖸

Whitland

(3m). Pantglas Farm Caravan Park, Tavernspite, Whitland, Pembrokeshire SA34 ONS. 01834 831618. steve@pantglasfarm.com. www.pantglasfarm.com. Owner: Steve & Alison Bolas. On A477, Tenby to Pembroke. Turn right, Red Roses to

WALES

Tavernspite. Take the middle road at village pump, Pantglas 800 yd on left. Quiet, family-run, rural park. Play area. Near Amroth, Saundersfoot and Tenby. Caravan storage. Open Easter-October. ☆☆☆☆ **BH&HPA. 81T. 5MC.** 🐕 🏢 ⚲ ⚱

(6m). South Caravan Holiday Park, Tavernspite, Whitland, Pembrokeshire SA34 0NL. *01834 831451/651/586.* Owner: Mrs E James & Mr I H James. On B4314. 85 metres SW of St Clears and 2.75m S of Whitland. From St Clears take A477 to Red Roses, turn R for 1.25m to Tavernspite. Indoor heated swimming pool. Club. Bar meals. Takeaway food. Laundrette. Coarse fishing on site. Golf course 5m. Open April-October. **BH&HPA. 45T. 45MC. 115S.** 🐕 🏢

POWYS

Brecon

(4.5m). Aberbran Caravan Club Site, Aberbran, Brecon, Powys LD3 9NH. *01874 622424.* www.caravanclub.co.uk. Owner: The Caravan Club. East Grinstead House, East Grinstead, West Sussex RH19 1UA. See website for standard directions to site. On edge of Brecon Beacons National Park. Non-members welcome. Chemical toilet emptying point. Advance booking essential. Shipping length of outfit required due to size limitation of some pitches. No toilet block. Hard-standings. Gas. Dogwalk. Fishing and golf nearby. Good area for walking. Open March-October. **NCC. 24T.** 🐕 🏢

(8m). Anchorage Caravan Park, Bronllys, Brecon, Powys LD3 0LD. *01874 711246.* www.ukparks.co.uk/anchorage. Owner: J A & B M Powell & Sons. On A438, between Brecon and Hay-on-Wye. Nr Brecon Beacons. SAE for brochure. High standard park with panoramic views. Childrens play area, PO, hairdresser's, laundrette, TV room. Golf course, cinema 8m. Open all year for tourers; open Easter-end October for holiday homes. ☆☆☆☆ **BH&HPA. 60T. 10MC. 83S.** ✿ 🐕 🏢 ⚲ ⚱

(1m). Bishops Meadow Caravan Park, Hay Road, Brecon, Powys LD3 9SW. *01874 622051/622392.* enquiries@bishopsmeadow.co.uk. www.bishops-meadow.co.uk. Owner: Mrs D E Perry & family. Situated on the B4602 about 1m from the town centre. Views of the Brecon Beacons from the park. Restaurant is open all day. Friendly lounge bar. Heated outdoor swimming pool. Play area. Dogs' excercise area. Open March 1-October 31. ☆☆☆☆ **80T. MC.** 🐕 🏢 ⚲ ⚱

LLYNFI HOLIDAY PARK
Llangorse Lake, Brecon Beacons, Wales, LD3 7TR

A flat, well-sheltered camping and caravan park at Llangorse Lake in the Brecon Beacons National Park. An ideal centre for touring South and Mid-Wales. Own boating facilities. All amenities with bar and heated pool. Seasonal sites available for caravans. Holiday homes for sale.

Write for reservation and brochure

(SAE please) or telephone
Llangorse (01874) 658 283
Fax: (01874) 658 575
www.btinternet.com/brianstrawford/
brian.strawford@btinternet.com

(1.5m). Brynich Caravan Park, Brynich, Brecon, Powys LD3 7SH. *01874 623325.* holidays@brynich.co.uk. www.brynich.co.uk. Owner: Mr & Mrs C R & A M Jones. Brynich, Brecon, Powys LD3 7SH. East of Brecon. Located on the A470 200 yards from the A40-A470 roundabout. Award-winning, family-run park with panoramic views of the Brecon Beacons. Two immaculately clean, fully equipped amenity blocks including baby and disabled rooms. Play area, adventure playground and recreation field. Relaxing brookside walks and dog exercise field. Easy access, large level pitches with short grass. Off-licence. Restaurant adjoining site. Children's soft indoor play facility next door. Open March 20-October 29. ☆☆☆☆☆ **BH&HPA. 130T. MC.** 🐕 🏢 ⚲ ⚱

(15m). Dan-yr-Ogof The National Showcaves for Wales, Abercrave, Glyntawe, Brecon, Powys SA9 1GJ. *01639 730284.* ashford@showcaves.co.uk. www.showcaves.co.uk. Midway between Brecon and Swansea on the A4067 and within the Brecon Beacons National Park. Bordered by mountain river in Brecon Beacons National Park. Ski slope. Suitable walking area. Warden: A C Price. Dogs on leads at all times. Open Easter-October 31. **30T. MC.** 🐕 🏢

(6m). Lakeside Caravan Park, Llangorse, Brecon, Powys LD3 7TR. *01874 658226.* holidays@lakeside.zx3.net. www.lakeside-holidays.net. Owner: R P B & W P Davies. Off A40 at Bwlch, then B4560 to Llangorse. SP to Llangorse lake and common. AA 3 pennants. David Bellamy Silver Conservation Award. Clubhouse. Cafe, activity centre and PHs nearby. Riding, climbing centres 1m. Indoor swimming pool, golf course, cinema, gliding, shop/market town within 6m. Open March-October. ☆☆☆☆ **BH&HPA. 20T. 10MC. 92S. 10H.** 🐕 🏢 ⚲ ⚱

(6m). Llynfi Holiday Park, Llangorse, Brecon, Powys LD3 7TR. *01874 658283.* brian.strawford@btinternet.com. www.llynfi.com. Owner: Mr B & J Strawford. Off B4560. Park is on flat, secluded and grassy in the Brecon Beacons National Park. Langorse lake a short walk. Heated pool, licensed bar and all facilities. Open April-October. ☆☆☆ **BH&HPA. 30T. 15MC. 108S.** 🐕 🏢

(10m). Mill Field Caravan Park, Three Cocks, Brecon, Powys LD3 0SL. *01497 847381.* Owner: Mr D A Lewis. Midway between Brecon and Hay-on-Wye on the A438, two-acre, flat field. Cafe, shop, petrol station and village PH adjoining. Calor Gas and Camping Gaz. **18T. MC.** ✿ 🐕 ⚱

(3m). Pencelli Castle Caravan & Camping Park, Pencelli, Brecon, Powys LD3 7LX. *01874 665451.* caravan@pencelli-castle.co.uk. www.pencelli-castle.co.uk. Owner: Mr & Mrs G Rees. On B4558 off A40. SE of Brecon. Peaceful, countryside park in the heart of Brecon Beacons National Park. Luxurious shower block. Within walking distance of highest peaks. Adjoining Brecon Canal. Village PH 150yd. Bike hire. On bus route. ☆☆☆☆☆ **BH&HPA. 40T. 40MC.** ✿ 🏢 ⚲ ⚱

(8m). Riverside International Caravan & Camping Park, Talgarth, Brecon, Powys LD3 0HL. *01874 711320.* www.riversideinternational.co.uk. Owner: Mr & Mrs Gorman. On A479. Licensed restaurant. Games room. Heated indoor swimming pool. Leisure complex, Gym, sauna, jacuzzi. Laundrette. Bathroom. Public phone. Takeaway service. Fishing on site. Ideal for cycling and walking. AA 3 pennants. Open Easter-October 31. ☆☆☆☆ **BH&HPA. 85T. MC.** 🏢 ⚲

Builth Wells

(4m). Fforest Fields, Hundred House, Builth Wells, Powys LD1 5RT. *01982 570406.* office@fforestfields.co.uk. www.fforestfields.co.uk. Owner: Mr & Mrs G T Barstow. Easy access off A481, 0.5m from Hundred House village. Peaceful, level mown site straddling a mountain stream. Hard-standings. Clean, modern facilities with free showers. Laundry. Dogs welcome. Lovely forest and moorland walks direct from site, excellent for bird-watching. PH and village store 0.5m. Open April-October 31. ✰✰✰✰ **BH&HPA. 40T. 20MC.** ⊁ ◘

(6m). Irfon River Caravan Park, Upper Chapel Road, Garth, Builth Wells, Powys LD4 4BH. *01591 620310.* 500yd S of Garth on B4519, W of Builth Wells. Nestling between the Eppynt and Cambrian mountains. A quiet, family-run park, on the banks of the river Irfon with trout fishing. Suitable for touring mid Wales. Open Easter-October. ✰✰✰✰ **BH&HPA. 12T. 12MC. 47S.** ⊁ ◘ &

Rhosgoch Holiday Park, Rhosgoch, Builth Wells, Powys LD2 3JB. *01497 851253.* Owner: Mrs V Baylis. Off A438 or B4594. 5m from Hay-on-Wye. No tourers and no motoro caravans. Golf and pony-trekking nearby. Small dogs only and on leads. Caravans occasionally for sale and pitch available for siting vans. 5m to shops, doctor, PO. Open March 1-October 31. **BH&HPA. 16S.** ⊁

(8m). Riverside Caravan Park, Llangammarch Wells, Builth Wells, Powys LD4 4BY. *01591 620465.* Owner: Mr & Mrs B Smith. From Builth Wells take A483 and second L turn in Garth SP Llangammarch Wells 2m. Peaceful park with surrounding mountain views, many places of interest locally. Modern facilities. Shop nearby. Laundry room, barbecue area with large gazebo. Hard-standing, lawned and riverside pitches; all-year tourer storage. Large safe play area. Fishing. Open April-October. **BH&HPA. 15T. 16MC. 12S. 1H.** ⊁ ◘

Churchstoke

(3m). Mellington Hall, Holiday Home Park, Churchstoke, Powys SY15 6HX. *01588 620011.* info@mellingtonhallcaravan park.co.uk. www.mellingtonhallcaravanpark.co.uk. Owner: Mr Alistair Evans. Leave A489, 1.5m W of Churchstoke, on to B4385 to Mellington. Fishing on site. Dog exercise area. Peace and tranquility. Rare trees planted around 300 acres of lush parkland. Bar and restaurant facilities. **BH&HPA. 30T. 30MC. 95S.** ✿ ⊁ ◘ &

Crickhowell

(4m). Cwmdu Caravan and Camping Site, Crickhowell, Powys NP8 1RU. *01874 730441.* Owner: Mrs O M Farr. On A479. Shop. Gas. Showers. Suitable base for exploring national park. Quiet location. Walking on Black Mountains from site. Open March-October. **50T. 10MC. 27S.** ⊁ ◘

Riverside Caravan & Camping Park, New Road, Crickhowell, Powys NP8 1AY. *01873 810397.* Owner: Miss R Price. Between A40 and B4558. Level, grassy site with new improved shower block. Canal nearby. Town 5mins walk. Mountain walks. Restaurant 200yd. No single-sex groups, hang or paragliders. Adults only, over-18s. Open March 1-October 31. **BH&HPA. 25T. 10MC. 20S.** ⊁ ◘

Hay-on-Wye

(1.5m). Forest Park Caravan Site, Clyro, Hay-on-Wye, Powys HR3 5SG. *01497 820156.* forestcaravans@aol.com. Owner: Mr & Mrs G Terry. 0.5m from Clyro, on the Painscastle road. Toilet/showers for touring and tents. Washing/drying machines. 2 golf courses (0.5 - 2m). Shops in Hay-on-Wye, local general store in Clyro. **BH&HPA. 25T. 3MC. 28S. 4H.** ✿ ⊁ ◘

(6.5m). Penlan Caravan Park, Brilley, Hay-on-Wye, Powys HR3 6JW. *01497 831485.* peter@penlan.org.uk. www.penlan caravanpark.co.uk. Owner: Mr & Mrs P Joyce. Situated 0.5m from Kington along road to Whitney-on-Wye, 4.5m SW of Kington. A small, secluded site with views, peace and space. National Trust farm. Advanced notice of arrival essential. Brochure available. Open Easter-October 31. ✰✰✰✰ **12T. MC.** ⊁ ◘

Llanbrynmair

(1m). Badgers Glade Park, Llanbrynmair, Powys SY19 7DU. *01650 521622/580.* Owner: David Cullen. On main A470,17m from Newtown, 9m from Machynlleth. Open end of February-October 31. **20T. MC. 85S. 10H.** ⊁ ◘ &

(1m). Cringoed Caravan & Camping Park, The Birches, Llanbrynmair, Powys SY19 7DR. *01650 521237.* cringoedcar avan.park@virgin.net. Owner: Mr Paul & Mrs Sue Mathers. The Birches, Cringoed, Llanbrynmair, Powys. Turn off A470 at Llanbrynmair on the B4518 for 1m. By river Twymyn. New facilities' block and laundry room. Suitable base for touring mid Wales with its many attractions, including castles, slate mines and the Alternative Technology Centre. Golf course and shoping at Machynlleth 5m. Site nestle besides the river Twymyn with breathtaking scenery. Open March 7-January 7. ✰✰✰✰ **BH&HPA. NCC. 35T. MC. 35S. 2H.** ⊁ ◘

Gwern-y-Bwlch Caravan Club Site, Llanbrynmair, Powys SY19 7EB. *01650 521351.* www.caravanclub. co.uk. Owner: The Caravan Club. East Grinstead House, East Grinstead, West Sussex RH19 1UA. See website for standard directions to site. Site, located in Mid Wales between Snowdonia and Montgomeryshire, offers mountain views. Chemical toilet emptying point. Calor Gas and Campingaz. Shop 1.5m. Non-members are welcome. No toilet block. Some hard-standings. Good area for walking. Dog walk. Open April-October. **NCC. 38T. MC.** ⊁ ◘

Llandinam

(1m). Gellidywyll Caravan Park, Llandinam, Powys SY17 5BJ. *01686 688361.* Owner: Mr R J Rees. On A470 Caersws to Llandinam. The park has all mains services. Local attractions include the Clywedog and Elan reservoirs with sailing and fishing, two local leisure centres, a golf course on the next farm and a local clay pigeon shooting centre. Open Easter-October 31. **2T. MC. 80S.** ⊁

Llandrindod Wells

(10m). Bryn-Ithon Caravan Park, Llananno, Llanbister, Llandrindod Wells, Powys LD1 6TR. *01597 840231.* Owner: Mr G G Hughes. 0.5m N of Llanbister, SP at junction 200yd. Midway between Newtown and Llandrindod Wells on the A483. Rambling. Calor Gas. Fishing. 1 hour from coast. Shop. 5m. Elan Valley 12m. Open March 1-October 31. **10T. MC. 24S.** ⊁ &

(10m). Brynithon Caravan Park, Llanbister, Llandrindod Wells, Powys LD1 6TR. *01597 840231.* Owner: G G Hughes. Midway between Newtown and Llandrindod Wells off the A483. Small, quiet site set in scenic surroundings. 10 mins walk from village where you find a shop and PO. Good walking area with lovely views across the Ithon Valley. Good site for the Royal Welsh Show (Builth Wells) or the Victorian Festival (Llandrindod Wells). Open March 1-October 31. **5T. 25S.** ⊁ &

(3m). Dalmore Caravan Park, Howey, Llandrindod Wells, Powys LD1 5RG. *01597 822483.* Owner: Mr Brian Thorpe. Off A483, 3m S of Llandrindod Wells and 4m N of Builth Wells, top of the hill. Small, select, well maintained park with level, terrace pitches and panoramic views second to none. All facilities, suitable for retired visitors. Golf, fishing, cinema, bowls, shopping all within 3. 2 Pubs serving meals within 1.5m. Members of Welsh Tourist Board, AA & Camping & Caravan Club. Open March-October. ☆☆☆ **20T. MC. 20S. 1H.** 🔌

(3m). Disserth Caravan & Camping Park, Disserth, Howey, Llandrindod Wells, Powys LD1 6NL. *01597 860277.* m.hobbs@virgin.net. www.disserth.com. Owner: Mike & Ann Hobbs. 1m off A483 Llandrindod Wells to Builth Wells, by Disserth Church between Howey and Newbridge-on-Wye. Level, sheltered pitches in peaceful riverside setting. Ideal touring centre. Licensed bar, free hot showers and dishwashing. Fishing on site. Shops, golf 3m. Cinema 6m. AA 3 pennants. Open March 1-October 31. **BH&HPA. 30T. 5MC. 20S. 1H.** 🔌 & 🐾

(6m). Nantymynach Caravan Site, Nantmel, Llandrindod Wells, Powys LD1 6EW. *01597 810491.* Owner: Mr L G Price. Off A44. Cross gates to Rhayader, turn L at sign Doldowlod also sign Nantymynach caravan & camping park. Open Easter-November. **10T. 10MC. 20S.** ✿ 🐾

(5m). Rhiw Villa, Hundred House, Llandrindod Wells, Powys LD1 5RY. *01982 570352.* Owner: Mr W R Williams. Off A481. Open April 1-September 30. **2T. MC. 17S.** 🐾

(3m). The Park Motel Caravan Park, Crossgates, Llandrindod Wells, Powys LD1 6RF. *01597 851201.* Owner: Laura, Steve McNulty & Family. On A44. 3-acres. Licensed lounge bar with TV. Restaurant. Hot showers. Swimming pool. Games room. Play area. Open March-October. ☆☆☆ **BH&HPA. 13T. 5MC. 19S. 4H.** 🐾 🔌 & 🐾

(7m). The Pines Caravan Park, Pine Lodge, Doldowlod, Llandrindod Wells, Powys LD1 6NN. *01597 810068.* info@pinescaravanpark.co.uk. www.pinescaravanpark.co.uk. Owner: Mr & Mrs R E Goulding. 3.5m S of Rhayader on A470 to Builth Wells. Shop. Gas. Pub and restaurant adjacent. Near Elan Valley reservoirs and Red Kite Centre. Excellent birdwatching and walking. David Bellamy Gold Conservation Award. Swimming pool 4m. Golf course 8m. Cinema 9m. Open March 1-October 31. **BH&HPA 30S. 3H.** 🐾

Llanfyllin

(1m). Parc Lletyreos Caravan Park, Llanfyllin, Powys SY22 5HU. Owner: E A O Evans. Caeaugwynedd, Llanfyllin, Powys SY22 5HU. On B4391. All caravans must have mains sewerage. Open Easter-Christmas. **11S.**

Llangammarch Wells

(2m). The Coppins Caravan Park, Cefn Gorwydd, Llangammarch Wells, Powys LD4 4DP. *01591 610625.* phil&julie@thecoppins.freeserve.uk. Owner: Mr & Mrs P R Eyers. A483 to Llanwrtyd Wells. Follow signs for Cefn Gorwydd. At Celn Gorwydd crossroads, follow signs towards Tirabad; Coppins is 200 yards on left. Peaceful, rural mid-Wales. Small family run caravan park with outstanding views. Suitable for couples. Walking and cycling from park. Fishing, horse-riding, golf nearby. Local shops, chemist and doctor's surgery 2 miles. Open February-December. ☆☆☆☆ **BH&HPA. 24S. 3H.** 🐾

Llangynog

(0.5m). Henstent Caravan Touring Park, Llangynog, Powys SY10 0EP. *01691 860479.* henstent@mac.com. www.homepage.mac.com/henstent. Owner: Dean & Melanie Morris. Off B4391. From A5 follow signs for Bala. Small

peaceful family run park set in the beautiful Tanat Valley, enjoying spectacular mountain views and frontage to the river Tanat. Rural location popular with bird watchers and walkers. Two excellent inns nearby serving reasonably priced quality meals and snacks. Open March 1-October 31. 12 months' licence for tourers available by application. **BH&HPA. 25T. 25MC. 40S.** 🐾 🔌

Minafon Caravan Park, Llangynog, Powys SY10 0EX. *01691 860204.* deal@tinyworld.co.uk. www.virtual-shropshire. co.uk/parcfarm. Owner: Messrs G E & M R Deal. Boncyn, Meifod, Powys SY22 6HP. On B4391. Open Easter-end October. **25S.** 🐾

Llanidloes

(0.5m). Clywedog (Riverside) Holiday Home Park, Llanidloes, Powys SY18 6NE. *01686 412682.* clywedog park@aol.com. www.clywedogpark.co.uk. Owner: T D & C A Onions. From Llanidloes take the B4518, SP for Llynclywedog. Site is 0.75m on the left-hand side. Laundry. Golf, sailing, sports centre, fishing and Clywedog Dam are all nearby. Satellite TV. Within walking distance of Llanidloes town centre (15 mins). Open March-January. **88S.** 🐾

(0.8m). Dol-llys Caravan Park, Dol-llys Farm, Llanidloes, Powys SY18 6JA. *01686 412694.* Owner: Mr O S Evans. From roundabout on A470 in Llanidloes take B4569. Past hospital. Fork right and site is first on right. Campers' kitchen. Fishing in river Severn. Play area. Fishing, golf course, PO, doctor and sports centre all within 1m. Open April-October. **20T. 5MC.** 🐾 🔌

(0.5m). Dulas Caravan Site, Llanidloes, Powys. *01686 412862.* Owner: Mr Rowlands and Evans. Sww-y-Buarth, Lower Glandulas, Llanidloes, Powys SY18 6RE. On A470. Small, family farm site. Local fishing available. Next to sports centre. Open Easter-October 31. **3T. MC. 6S. 4H.** 🐾

(1.5m). Leylands Caravan Park, Dolwen, Llanidloes, Powys SY18 6LQ. *01686 412668.* Owner: Mr & Mrs T Bebb. On A470. Small, family-run park. Open February 1-October 31 and two weeks at Christmas. ☆☆☆☆☆ **84S.** 🐾 ⌀

Llansantffraid

(6m). Trederwen Caravan Site, Llansantffraid, Powys SY22 6SY. *01691 828784.* Owner: Mr Ashton. On B4393. Open Easter or April 1-October 31. **T. MC. 179S.** 🐾

(2m). Vyrnwy Caravan Park, Minafon, Llansantffraid, Powys SY22 6SY. *01691 828217.* Owner: Mr D C Roberts. 1.5m from A483. Oswestry 6m, at crossroads turn right on to the B4393 for 1.5m. Open April 1-October 31. **30T. 10MC. 148S.** 🐾 🔌

LLanwddyn

(1m). Fronheulog Caravan Park, Lake Vyrnwy, LLanwddyn, Powys SY10 0NN. *01691 870362.* Owner: Mr & Mrs Neil Jones. On B4393. 2m on right-hand side before Lake Vyrnwy. Quiet site with breathtaking views. Sorry we do not cater for children, but pets are welcome. 0.5m local shop, RSPB reserves, tea rooms and gift shops. Suitable for walkers and birdwatchers. Open April 1-October 31. **12T. 6MC. 36S.** 🐾

(2m). Hen Efail Caravan Park, Lake Vyrnwy, Llanwddyn, Powys S10 0NL. *01691 870694.* Owner: Mr Bebb. Small secluded park, bordering on to the Dyfnont Forest. Ideal for walkers and bird watching. Open February 1-October 31. ☆☆☆☆☆ **BH&HPA. 69S.** 🐾 ⌀

Llanymynech

(0.75m). Tanat Caravan Park, Carreghofa Lane, Llanymynech, Powys SY22 6LH. *01691 831536/07860 349746.* ian@hall440. freeserve.co.uk. www.tanatcaravanpark.co.uk. Owner: Mr I W Hall & Mrs C L Hall. Llanymynech is on the A483 approximately halfway between Oswestry and Welshpool. At the crossroads in the village centre turn right on the B4393 signposted for Llansantffraid, after about 350yds turn right into Carreghofa Lane, park is about 1.5m. Facilities include: launderette, children's play area, public telephone, games room, fishing on private stretch of river. Golf course nearby. Open March 1-December 31. **120S.** ⚑

Machynlleth

(8m). Bryn Uchel Caravan Park, Cwmllinau, Machynlleth, Powys SY20 9PE. *01650 511441.* Owner: Mr & Mrs H E Davies. On A470 between Cemaes Road and Mallwyd round-about. Open March-October. **BH&HPA. 102S.** ⚑

(4m). Cefn Crib Caravan Park, Pennal, Machynlleth, Powys. *01654 75239.* Owner: Messrs G & G J Rowlands. On A493 Aberdovey to Machynlleth. Open March 1-October 31. **10T. MC. 42S.**

(12m). Celyn Brithion Caravan & Camping Park, Dinas Mawddwy, Machynlleth, Powys SY20 9LP. *01650 531344.* celyn.brithion@btopenworld.com. www.celynbrithion.co.uk. Owner: Mr & Mrs Turnbull. On A458 Shrewsbury to Barmouth. Situated on the A470 between Dolgellau and Machynlleth. 4 hotels with bar and restaurant facilities all nearby. Garage and village shop with adjoining cafe. Mill shop and cafe close by. Open March 1-October 31. **8T. MC. 14S.** ⚑ 🅿

(5m). Dovey Valley Caravan & Camping Park, Llanwrin, Machynlleth, Powys SY20 8QJ. *01650 511501/ 07718892498.* Owner: Mr C Taylor. 8a Old Market Street, Thetford IP24 2EQ. Off A489. NE to B4404 and follow signs. Small site, forest and mountain walking. Half hour to beach at Aberdovey. Coarse fishing, clay shooting on site. Golf 6m. Main shopping 6m. PO, village shop, doctor 1m. Holiday letting in barn conversion and modern 4 bed chalet. Open Easter-October. **40T. 10MC. 56S. 5H.** ⚑ 🅿 ♿

(1m). Garth Holiday Park, Garth Road, Machynlleth, Powys SY20 8HQ. *01584 881126.* enquiries@garthholidaypark.co.uk. www.garthholidaypark.co.uk. Owners: E&M Leisure Parks Ltd, Blake Horse Farm Caravan Park, Eastham, Tenbury Wells, WR15 8NS. Off A489. In Machynlleth turn R between hospital and chip shop, R again behind hospital and follow Garth Road. Fishing river. Hotel on site. Plus 13 log cabins sold and 2 new for sale. Shops, sports centre, swimming pool, golf, horse riding nearby. David Bellamy Gold Conservation Award for last 8 years. Open March 1-January 15 for holiday caravans; open all year for cabins. **BH&HPA. 115S.** ⚑ ♿

(2m). Morben Isaf Touring & Home Park, Derwenlas, Machynlleth, Powys SY20 8SR. *01654 781473.* Owner: Bywater Leisure Parks Ltd. On A487 Aberystwyth Road. Estuary park suitable for walking, fishing, birdwatching, golfing etc. 10 mins for beautiful sandy beach. Open March 1-October 31. ☆☆☆☆☆ **BH&HPA. NCC. 26T. 10MC. 60S.** ⚑ 🅿 ♿

(5m). Mynachdy, Aberhosan, Site A, Machynlleth, Powys. *01654 702188.* Owner: J G & A L Jones. Open April 1-October 31. **T. MC. 25H.** ⚑

(9m). Ty Craig Holiday Park, Llancynfelin, Machynlleth, Powys SY20 8PU. *01970 832339.* Owner: Mr RJ & MB Rhodes. On B4353, near Borth. 1m from Junction with A497 at Treir-Ddol. Quite, secluded site. Golf course nearby. Shops, doctors, PO within 3m. Open March 1-January 10. **BH&HPA. 15T. 30S. 5H.** ⚑ 🅿

(10m). Tynypwll Caravan & Camping Site, Dinas Mawddwy, Machynlleth, Powys SY20 9JF. *01650 531326.* Owner: M & I Pugh. Take A470 at Mallwyd for 1m, turn right by second garage for Dinas Mawddwy. Turn right by 'Red Lion' on the corner, site 200 yards on left. Fishing. PO, shops within 0.5m. Scenery and walks. **10T. MC. 60S. 1H.** ⚑ 🅿

(2m). Warren Parc, Penegoes, Machynlleth, Powys SY20 8NN. *01654 702054.* warrenparc@hotmail.com. Owner: Mr & Mrs N A Warren-Kyle. 2m from Machynlleth on A489. Open March 1-October 31. ☆☆☆☆ **BH&HPA. 100S. 2H.** ⚑ ♿

Montgomery

(2m). Argae Hall Caravan Park, Garthmyl, Montgomery, Powys SY15 6RU. *01686 640216.* Owner: Mr & Mrs Jones. A483 from Welshpool to Newtown then the B4385 to Montgomery. On the banks of the river Severn with free fishing. Hot showers. Launderette. Chemical toilet disposal point. Playroom. Putting green. PH and club, food, enter-tainment. Open April 1- October 31 and two weeks at Christmas; open 48 hours per week for rest of year. **30T. 30MC. 112S.** ✿ ⚑ 🅿

(2.5m). Bacheldre Water Mill, Church Stoke, Montgomery, Powys SY15 6TE. *01588 620489.* info@ bacheldremill.co.uk. www.bacheldremill.co.uk. Owner: Mrs H Jay. W out of Churchstoke on A489 after 2m turn L SP Bacheldre Mill. Small, secluded site with 25 level, grass pitches, most with hook-ups. Toilet/showers facilities all inclusive. Open Easter-October. ☆☆☆☆ **BH&HPA. 25T. MC.** ⚑ 🅿 ⛽

(2m). Caerhowel Caravan and Camping Site, Caerhowel Cottage, Caerhowel, Montgomery, Powys. *01686 668598.* Owner: Mr & Mrs W A Bengry. From Welshpool take A483, turn left at Garthmyl for Forden, site near Lion Hotel. Open March-October. **28T. MC.** ⚑

(3m). Daisy Bank Touring Caravan Park, Snead, Montgomery, Powys SY15 6EB. *01588 620471.* j.spurgeon @tesco.net. www.daisy-bank.co.uk. Owner: J Spurgeon & C Wheeler. Situated on the A489 between Lydham and Churchstoke. 3m NW Bishop's Castle. 2m E of Churchstoke. Individual drainage. Showers. TV hook-up. Fenced off dog walk. Fantastic views across the Camlad Valley. Adults-only park. All pitches fully serviced. ☆☆☆☆☆ **BH&HPA. 55T. MC.** ✿ ⚑ 🅿 ♿

(3m). Foggy Bottom, Churchstoke, Montgomery, Powys SL15 6SP. *01588 620079.* www.foggybottom.co.uk. Situated on the mid Wales/Shropshire border, 1m W of Churchstoke. Perfect setting for fishing, walking, riding and golf. Launderette and games room facility. Open March-January. **BH&HPA. 50S.** ⚑

Newtown

(2m). Glandulas Caravan Holiday Home Park, Glandulas Farm, Newtown, Powys SY16 4HZ. *01686 626532.* Owner: Mrs G E J Jerman. W of Newtown on the A489. Suitable base for discovering mid-Wales and the west coast. Convenient for walking and fishing. Golf course and leisure centre within 1m. Shops, post office, doctor and cottage hospital within 2m, also theatre and cinema. Open March 1-January 14. ☆☆☆☆☆ **BH&HPA. 45S.** ⚑ ♿

(8m). Gwernydd Hall Holiday Park, New Mills, Newtown, Powys SY16 3NW. *01686 650236.* Owner: Stokes & Co. Off A483 Welshpool to Newtown. Open March 1-November 30. ☆☆☆☆ **BH&HPA. 5T. 120S.** ⚑ 🅿

WALES

(8m). Penddol Caravan Park, Carno, Newtown, Powys SY17 5JP. *01686 420259.* Quiet and peaceful. Heated swimming pool. Bowling green. children's playground. Fishing nearby. Open March 1-November 30. **BH&HPA. 45S.** ⴲ

(7m). Tynycwm Camping & Caravan Site, Aberhafesp, Newtown, Powys SY16 3JF. *01686 688651/07711 497424.* Owner: Mr Dilwyn Richards. Follow A489 to Caersws, then turn right on the B4569 signposted Aberhafesp. At first crossroads straight over the B4568 ignoring sign for Aberhafesp, at second crossroads turn left signposted Bwlchygarreg. Farm and site 1m on right. Quiet site on hill farm, scenic walks over the hills. Pony trekking, fishing, golf, nearest village 3 miles. Open May 1-October 31. **50T. MC. 4S.** ⴲ ⴲ

(4m). Ye Olde Smithy Caravan Park, Abermule, Newtown, Powys. *01584 711280.* info@bestparks.co.uk. Owner: Mr A Jones. Westbrook, Little Hereford, Ludlow, Shropshire. Leave A483 and enter village of Abemule. Turn down lane opposite village shop and PO. Very well run and very pretty garden like park all pitches are fully services and hard-standings. On banks of river Severn with 0.5m fishing, new toilet and shower block. Local shop wihin 300yd. Open March 1-November 30. **BH&HPA. 30T. 30MC. 55S.** ⴲ ⴲ ⴲ ⴲ ⴲ

Oswestry

Glendower Caravan Park, Llangynog, Oswestry, Powys SY10 0EX. *01691 860304.* info@glendowerpark.co.uk. www.glendowerpark.co.uk. Owner: Mr & Mrs D Scarborough. On B4391 to Bala. Library/book exchange. Washing/drying facilities. Crown Green Bowling, 2 good PHs in village and shop 3m away. Open March 1-November 30th. ✰✰✰✰ **44S.** ⴲ ⴲ

Penybontfawr

(0.25m). Parc Farm Caravan Site, Penybontfawr, Powys SY10 0PD. *01691 860204.* deal@tinyworld.co.uk. www.virtual-shropshire.co.uk/parcfarm. Owner: Mr & Mrs G E Deal. Boncyn, Meifod, Powys SY22 6HP. On B4391. Open Easter-end October. **15T. 15MC. 65S. 4H.** ⴲ ⴲ

Presteigne

(2m). Norton Manor Country Estate, Norton, Presteigne, Powys LD8 2EG. *01625 585343/0790 1816064.* Owner: Barrs Parks Ltd. Wizard Country Park, Bradford Lane, Nether Alderley, Macclesfield, Cheshire SK10 4UE. In the grounds of a large manor. Fishing and shooting on park. Acres of woodland for walking. Private bus service twice weekly. Golf courses 5 and 8m. **189S.** ⴲ ⴲ ⴲ ⴲ

(1m). Rockbridge Park, Presteigne, Powys LD8 2NF. *01547 560300/0797 7588731.* dustinrockbridge@hotmail.com. Owner: Mr R M Deakins. On B4356 W of Presteigne. Small, tranquil park in wonderful scenery. Near Offa's Dyke. Open April 1-September. **BH&HPA. 21T. 10MC.** ⴲ ⴲ ⴲ

The Old Station Caravan Site, New Radnor, Presteigne, Powys LD8 2SS. *07917 846508.* info@oldstationcaravanpark.co.uk. www.oldstationcaravanpark.co.uk. Owners: Mr & Mrs J Roe. 12 Banley Drive, Kington, Herefordshire HR5 3FD. On A44, 6m from Kington, on L 50yd before New Radnor. Schedule to re-open at Easter 2006. Under new ownership. New toilet block, showers and laundry. Situated on old railway station, old station buildings converted to holiday lets with original features retained. Open April-October. **12T. MC. 16S. 3H.** ⴲ ⴲ ⴲ

Walton Court Farm, Walton, Presteigne, Powys LD8 2PY. *01544 350259.* Owner: Mr E Price. On A44. 3m from Kington. In beautiful unspoilt countryside. 3m from Kington. Close to Offas Dyke. Footpathand PH nearby. **10T. 5MC. S. 10H.** ⴲ ⴲ ⴲ

Rhayader

(3m). Doldowlod Caravan Club Site, Llandrindod Wells, Rhayader, Powys LD1 6NN. *01597 810409.* Caravan Club affiliated site. Members only. Medium-size, level site of considerable charm and quiet beauty. Own sanitation required. Motorhome service point. Good area for walking, dog walk on site. Fishing and NCN cycleroute nearby. Quiet and peaceful off-peak. Open March-October. **50T. MC.**

(0.5m). Gigrin Farm Caravan Site, South Street, Rhayader, Powys LD6 5BL. *01597 810243.* kites@gigrin.co.uk. www.gigrin.co.uk. Owner: Eithel Pugh Powell. Sof Rhayader. Just off the A470. Bryafon Country House - meals 100 yards. Exellent TV/reception. Red Kite centre and nature trail open all year. Feeding Red Kites at 2 o'clock GMT, daily. Bottled gas. Dogs on leads. **15T. MC.** ⴲ ⴲ ⴲ ⴲ ⴲ

Wyeside Caravan Park, Llangurig Road, Rhayader, Powys LD6 5LB. *01597 810183.* info@wyesidecamping.co.uk. www.wyesidecamping.co.uk. Owner: Mr K Brumwell. On the outskirts of Rhayader on the A470. On the banks of the river Wye. Excellent facilities on site and in town. 3m Elan Valley. Colour brochure available. Open March-November. ✰✰✰✰ **20T. 20MC. 40S. 2H.** ⴲ ⴲ ⴲ

Welshpool

(5m). Bank Farm Caravan Park, Middletown, Welshpool, Powys SY21 8EJ. *01938 570526.* gill@bankfarmcaravans.fsnet.co.uk. www.bankfarmcaravans.co.uk. Owner: Mr & Mrs D Corfield. On the A458 Shrewsbury to Welshpool road. Family run park with beautiful views, part flat, part sloping. Open March-October. ✰✰✰✰ **BH&HPA. 20T. 5MC. 31S. 1H.** ⴲ ⴲ ⴲ

(11m). Baxter Mill, Llanfair Caereinion, Welshpool, Powys. *01938 810990.* Owner: Jackie Morgan. Open March 1-October 31. **40S.** ⴲ

(15m). Carmel Caravan Park, Tynewydd, Cefn Coch, Llanfair Caereinion, Welshpool, Powys SY21 0AJ. *01938 810542.* www.carmelcaravanpark.com. Owner: Mr T K Robinson. Take A458 from Welshpool to Llanfair Caereinion. Turn left over bridge into town centre. Follow signs to Cefn Coch turn left before Inn, follow park signs for 2m. Fishing on site, golf course 6m. Shops, PO and doctor within 5m. Open March-November 1. ✰✰✰ **BH&HPA. 40T. 8MC. 149S.** ⴲ ⴲ ⴲ

(12m). Cefn Coch Caravan Park, Cefn Coch, Welshpool, Powys SY21 0AE. *01938 810247/810289.* Owner: Mr & Mrs Oliver & Sons. Open Easter-mid October. **BH&HPA. 2T. 4MC. 60S. 4H.** ⴲ

(2m). Derwen Mill Holiday Park, Guilsfield, Welshpool, Powys SY21 9PH. *01938 554365.* Owners: Steven & Tesni Jones. From Welshpool town centre, follow Dolgellau signs until you reach roundabout by steam railway, then take A490 towards Llanfyllin for 2.5m, turn right on to B4392, SP for Guilsfield, 0.5m turn right after Derwen Garden Centre. Golf 0.5m; 2m town centre with shops, restaurants, cinema, etc. Open February-December for holiday caravans; open all year for lodges. **BH&HPA. 54S.** ⴲ ⴲ

(8m). Fir View Caravan Park, Llangnyiew, Meifod, Welshpool, Powys SY21 0LT. *01938 810575.* Off A495. 3m S of Meifod, only one hour from Birmingham and 1.5 hours from Manchester and Liverpool. Forest setting. Clubhouse. Heated outdoor swimming pool (with leisure complex). Children's playground. Open March-November. **BH&HPA. 120S.** ⴲ

(6m). Henllan Caravan Park, Llangyniew, Welshpool, Powys SY21 9EJ. *01938 810554.* sue@henllancp.fsnet.co.uk. www.henllancaravanpark.co.uk. Owner: Mrs Sue Evans. Off A458 Welshpool to Dolgellau. Situated on meadowland adjoining river Banwy. Pitch and putt course. Club. Bottled gas available. Fishing. Club/restaurant on park, play area. Open March 1-December 31. **BH&HPA. NCC. 6T. 10MC. 66S. 1H.** 🛏 🔌

Hidden Valley, Maesmawr, Welshpool, Powys SY21 9DF. *01938 850300.* phil@hvcp.co.uk. www.hvcp.co.uk. Owner: Mr P A Jones. on B4392, left at Hardings Garden Centre, off the A490 Welshpool to Llanfylin Road. Heated swimming pool. Trout fishing. Tennis courts. Farm walks. Golf. Open March 1-October 31. ☆☆☆☆ **BH&HPA. 120S.** 🛏 🔌

(7m). Maes-yr-Afon Caravan Park, Berriew, Welshpool, Powys SY21 8QB. *01686 640587.* Owner: Mr J Metcalf. A483 Welshpool to Newtown branch to Berriew on B4390 then SP direct to park. Fishing. Play area. Showers. Open March-October. ☆☆☆☆ **10T. 10MC. 60S.** 🛏 🔌

(3m). Moat Farm, Manafon, Welshpool, Powys SY21 8BL. *01686 87372.* Owner: Mr K Lewis. Dogs allowed on leads. Well lit site. **15T. 138S.** 🛏 🔌

(10m). Neuadd Bridge Caravan & Chalet Park, Llanfair Caereinion, Welshpool, Powys SY21 0HX. *01938 810245.* www.nbcp.co.uk. Owner: Mr & Mrs D H Neville. On A458. 10 miles west of Welshpool, just past the village of Llanfair Caereinion and on the junction of the A495. Digital sky TV, and BT telephone lines to every pitch. Play area, laundry, putting and bowling greens. Golf, fishing, sailing, shops, walking, cinema. Open March 1-December 31. **BH&HPA. 146S.** 👤 🔌

(6m). Pen-y-Pentre Caravan Park, Llangyniew, Welshpool, Powys SY21 0JT. *01938 810397.* rogermorgan@ penpentre. sagehost.co.uk. Owner: Mr & Mrs R F Morgan. 6m W of Welshpool, 0.5m off A458 at JB4382 and B4389. Quiet country park with full services to all caravans. Fishing 1m. Golf course 3m. Open March 1-December 31. **BH&HPA. 35S.** 🛏

River Meadow Holiday Centre, Minffordd, Llangadfan, Welshpool, Powys SY21 0PL. *01938 820277.* Owner: Mr & Mrs T A Mills. Open March-October. **NCC. 20T. MC. 50S. 1H.** 🛏

(17m). Riverbend Caravan Park, Llangadfan, Llanfair Caereinion, Welshpool, Powys SY21 0PP. *01938 820356.* info@hillandale.co.uk. www.hillandale.co.uk. Owners: D & D Lloyd Jones Securities Ltd. t/a Hillandale Caravans, Lincomb Lock, Stouport on Severn, Worcs DY13 9QR. On A458 Welshpool to Dolgellau, turn left in village of Llangadfan immediately before Cann Office Hotel. Level riverside touring field with extensive private fishing. Shop 200yd, PH 100yd, golf, poney trekking nearby. Only short drive to the coast. **BH&HPA. 50T. MC. 90S.** ✿ 🛏 🔌

(1.5m). Severn Caravan and Camping Park, Kilkewydd, Forden, Welshpool, Powys SY21 8RT. *01938 580238.* Owner: J M & M G Oliver. Off A490. Hot showers. Play area. Horse riding. Fishing and boating. Open April 1-October 31. **20T. 20MC. 86S.** 🛏 🔌 👤

(8m). Tan-y-Fridd Caravan Park, Llangyniew, Llanfair Caereinion, Welshpool, Powys. *01938 810575.* Off A495 3m south of Meifod. 1 hour from Birmingham and 1.5 hours from Manchester and Liverpool. Quiet and peaceful park. Forest walks. Heated swimming pool. Tennis court. Clubhouse.Open April 1-October 30. **BH&HPA. 59S.** 🛏

(18m). Twin Rivers Caravan Park, Foel, Welshpool, Powys SY21 0NS. *01938 820516.* Owner: Mr Gordon Kendrick.

Positioned on the banks of the rivers Banwy and Twrch just off main A458 road from Welshpool at Foel. 14-acres pretty, landscaped, family park. Heated outdoor swimming pool, fishing, golf, boating, horse riding etc. Gas supplies on site. Open March 1-November 30. **BH&HPA. 30T. 3MC. 125S.** 🛏 🔌 👤

Valley View Holiday Home Park, Pentrebeirdd, Welshpool, Powys SY21 9DL. *01938 500265.* Off A490. Outdoor and indoor swimming pools. Pony trekking. Games room. Beach within walking distance. Children. Dogs. **BH&HPA. 145S.** 👤 🧳 ⌀

RHONDDA CYNON TAFF

Aberdare

(0.75m). Dare Valley Country Park, Aberdare, Rhondda Cynon Taff CF44 7RG. *01685 874672.* Owner: Rhondda Cynon Taff County Borough Council. Follow signs from town centre. Small site set in 500 acres of parkland. Two lakes, riding centre, miles of waymarked footpaths and cafeteria on site. Suitable base for visiting the Gower coast, Brecon Beacons etc. Open January 3-December 23. **BH&HPA 25T. MC.** 🛏 🔌 👤

SWANSEA

Gower

Three Cliffs Bay Caravan Site, North Hills Farm, Penmaen, Gower, Swansea SA3 2HB. *01792 371218.* www.threecliffs bay.co.uk. Owner: D G & J M Beynon. A4118 from Swansea (9m). Site SP in village of Penmaen. Open April-October 31. ☆☆☆☆ **20T. MC.** 🛏 🔌 🧳

Gowerton

Gowerton Caravan Club Site, Pont-y-Cob Road, Gowerton, Swansea SA4 3QP. *01792 873050.* www.caravanclub.co.uk. Owner: The Caravan Club. East Grinstead House, East Grinstead, West Sussex RH19 1UA. See website for standard directions to site. Non-members welcome. Hard-standings. Toilet blocks. Privacy cubicles. Laundry facilities. Veg Prep. Motorhome service point. Gas. Playframe. Dog walk. Storage. Peaceful off-peak. Good area for walking, NCN cycle route within 5m. Gower Peninsula beaches. Open March-October. ☆☆☆☆ **NCC. 130T. MC.** 🛏 🔌 👤

Llangennith

(17m). Hillend Caravan Park, Hillend, Llangennith, Swansea SA3 1JD. *01792 386204.* Owner: Hillend Caravan Park Ltd. Adjacent to Rhosilli Bay. 13 acres camping. No bookings. SAE for information. Open Easter or April 1-November 30. **25MC. 256S.** ⚓

Llanrhidian

Llanrhidian Holiday Park, Llanrhidian, Swansea SA3 1EU. *01792 391083/390678.* Owner: A F & G E Richards. Leave M4 at J47 then via Gorseinon. Gowerton to Penclawdd then 5m, park is on left-hand side on the Gower coast. 40-acre wooded grass park. Family room. Swimming pool. Laundrette. Adventure playground. Playroom. Snooker room. Bar. Open March 1-January 10. **220T. MC. 197S.** ⚓ ⚓ ⚓

Oxwich

Greenway Holiday Park, Oxwich, Swansea SA3 1LY. *01792 390220.* Owner: Mr & Mrs Mead. On A4118. About 15m from Swansea. Showers. Laundry. Swimming pool. Bars. Children's adventure playground. Open March-December. **BH&HPA. MC. 100S. 30H.** ⚓ ⚓

Oxwich Camping Park, Oxwich, Swansea SA3 1LS. *01792 390777.* Owner: Mrs C A Discombe. Take A4118 from Swansea, turn L at Oxwich SP, after 1m turn R, park 0.25m on the R. A quiet, secluded, family park in the heart of the Gower Peninsula, 8m from Killay. Heated swimming pool, hot showers. Village amenities, shop, restaurant, beach in Oxwich village. Open April-September. ☆☆☆ **180MC.** ⚓

Port Eynon

Highfields Holiday Park, Port Eynon, Swansea SA3 1NN. *01792 390286.* Owner: Mr & Mrs Bernard Edwards. Showers. Well-equipped mini-market with off licence. Takeaway meals. Laundry facilities. Three minutes' walk from safe sandy beach. Situated in an Area of Outstanding Natura Beauty. Open April 1-October 31. **BH&HPA. 112T. MC. 137S. 4H.** ⚓ ⚓ ⚓

(1m). Horton Farm, Horton, Port Eynon, Swansea SA3 1LB. *01792 390256.* Owner: Mr J B Munby. **151S.**

(14m). Newpark Holiday Park, Port Eynon, Swansea SA3 1NP. *01792 390292.* Owner: Mrs Newland. On A4118. Uninterrupted views over bay. Showers, laundry. Play area and games room. Open April-October. ☆☆ **BH&HPA. 112T. 40MC. 14H.** ⚓ ⚓ ⚓

Rhossilli

(1m). Pitton Cross Caravan & Camping Park, Rhossilli, Swansea SA3 1PL. *01792 390593.* roger@pittoncross.co.uk. www.pittoncross.co.uk. Owner: Mr Roger Button. From Swansea - A4118 to Scurlage 16m, turn right signposted Rhossili, we are 2m on L. Level site 1m from coast. Walking, sea fishing, surfing, bird-watching nearby. Off-peak discounts for over-50s. Open February-November. ☆☆☆ **50T. 10MC.** ⚓ ⚓ ⚓ ⚓

Swansea

(15m). Bank Farm Leisure Park, Horton, Gower, Swansea, Swansea SA3 1LL. *01792 390228/390452.* bankfarm leisure@aol.com. www.bankfarmleisure.co.uk. Owner: E Richards & Co. A4118 for Port Eynon, left turn for Horton 1m after Scurlage, site entrance on right. 16m from Swansea. Superb views overlooking Port Eynon Bay. Showers. Swimming pool. Licensed bar and coffee bar, play area, Calor Gas. Open March 1-November 14. ☆☆☆ **NCC. 230T. MC. 100S.** ⚓ ⚓ ⚓ ⚓

(6m). Blackhills Caravan Park, Blackhills Road, Fairwood Common, Swansea, Swansea SA2 7JN. *01792 207065/0850 207065.* Owner: Blackhills Leisure (Gower) Ltd. Off A4118, Swansea to Port Eynon. Off-licence. Gas. Main dealers for Cosalt, Willerby, Carnaby. Open March-November. **120S. 22H.** ⚓ ⚓

(17m). Broughton Farm Caravan Park, Broughton Farm, Llangennith, Swansea, Swansea SA3 1JP. *01792 386213.* www.bfcltd.co.uk. Owner: Broughton Farm Caravan Park. Broughton Farm, Llangennith, Swansea SA3 1JP. M4, J47, via Gowerton, B4295 Llanrhidian to Llangennith, SP. Open March 1-November 15. ☆☆☆☆ **BH&HPA. NCC. 250S.** ⚓ ⚓

(4m). Riverside Caravan Park, Ynysforgan Farm, Morriston, Swansea, Swansea SA6 6QL. *01792 775587.* Owner: Mr Brian & Mrs Y Parker. J45 of M4, direct access to caravan park from roundabout under motorway. Showers. Chemical toilet disposal point. Laundry room. Gas supplies. Picnic and barbecue area. Licensed club. Indoor swimming pool on site. Children welcome. Dogs allowed by arrangement. ☆☆☆ **CaSSOA. 120T. 10MC.** ✿ ⚓ ⚓ ⚓ ⚓

VALE OF GLAMORGAN

Barry

(5m). Fontygary Holiday Park, Rhoose, Barry, Vale of Glamorgan CF62 3ZT. *01446 710386.* Owner: Fontygary Holiday Parks Ltd. On B4265 Llantwit Major to Rhoose. Club. Indoor leisure complex includes cabaret lounge, bars, indoor heated swimming pool and health club. Off-licence. Open March 1-January 6. ☆☆☆ **400S. 50H.** ⚓ ⚓ ⚓

(1.5m). Vale Touring Caravan Park, Port Road (West), Barry, Vale of Glamorgan CF62 3BT. *01446 719311.* royphillips@one-tel.com. www.valetouringcaravanpark.uk. Owner: Mrs A Phillips. On R of A4226 Barry to Rhoose. From M4 J33 follow signs for Cardiff Airport. Shaver points. 100yd from hotel. Good entrance to park, 6 metres wide, off the A4050 road. Open March-December. ☆☆ **40T. MC.** ⚓ ⚓

Cowbridge

(3m). Llandow Touring Caravan Park, Llandow, Cowbridge, Vale of Glamorgan CF7 7PB. *01446 794527.* enquiries@llandowcaravanpark.com. www.llandowcaravanpark.com. Owner: A & S Evans. Marcross Farm, Marcross, Llantwit Major, Vale of Glamorgan. Exit M4 at junction 33 to Cardiff Airport. Take A48 to Cowbridge-Bridgend, bypass Cowbridge, first left to B4268 (Llantwit Major), keep on this road until brown signs. Sheltered, secluded park set in the Vale of Glamorgan. Seasonal touring pitches. Caravan storage. Open February 1-December 1. ☆☆☆☆ **BH&HPA. CaSSOA. 70T. 30MC.** ⚓ ⚓ ⚓ ⚓

Llantwit Major

(0.5m). Acorn Camping & Caravanning, Hamlane South, Llantwit Major, Vale of Glamorgan CF611RP. *01446 794024.* info@acorncamping.co.uk. www.campingandcaravansites.co.uk. Owner: Derek & Sandra Bradley. M4 to J33 follow signs to Cardiff Airport then to Llantwit Major on B4265. Follow signs to site from Llantwit Major. About 1m from the beach in the Glamorgan Heritage coast. One caravan suitable for disabled people's use. Hard-standings and serviced pitches available. Open February 1-December 8. ☆☆☆☆ **BH&HPA. 40T. 10MC. 15S. 4H.** ⚓ ⚓ ⚓ ⚓

Penarth

(2m). The Bay Caravan Park, St Marys Well Bay, Lavernock, Penarth, Vale of Glamorgan CF64 5XS. *029 20707512.* baycar avanpark@aol.com. Owner: Hamlett Enterprises Ltd. Ystrad Court, Ystradowen, Cowbridge, Vale of Glamorgan CF7 7TN. On B4267, Barry to Penarth. Indoor swimming pool, clubhouse, family lounge, children's room, barbecue, laundry, tennis courts. Shop. Open February 1-November 30. ✰✰✰ **BH&HPA. 270S. 14H.** 📖 ⅋ 🛆 ∅

WREXHAM

Bwlchgwyn

(0.5m). Cae Adar Farm, Cae Adar, Bwlchgwyn, Wrexham LL11 5UE. *01978 757385.* Owner: Mr E Evans. On A525, Wrexham to Ruthin. 5m W of Wrexham. Open April-October. **12T. 12MC.** 📖 🚂

Chirk

(0.5m). Lady Margaret's Park Caravan Club Site, Chirk, Wrexham LL14 5AA. *01691 777200.* www.caravan club.co.uk. Owner: The Caravan Club. East Grinstead House, East Grinstead, West Sussex RH19 1UA. See website for directions to site. Members only. Wooded parkland site adjacent to Chirk Castle; many other castles and historic sites close by. Some hard-standings. Steel awning pegs required. Toilet blocks. Privacy cubicles. Laundry facilities. Baby and toddler washroom. Veg prep. Motorhome service point. Calor Gas and Campingaz. Play equipment. Good area for walking. Suitable for families. Open March-January. **NCC. 106T. MC.** 📖 🚂 ⅋

Eyton

(0.5m). The Plassey Touring Caravan & Leisure Park, Eyton, Wrexham LL13 0SP. *01978 780277.* enquiries@theplassey. co.uk. www.theplassey.co.uk. Owner: Mr J S Brookshaw. Bangor-on-Dee exit (B5426) off A483 Chester-Oswestry bypass. 2.5m on L. Multi-award winning park with many amenities including: 9-hole golf course, swimming pool, badminton courts, table tennis, sauna and sunbed, restaurant, coffee shop, retail shops, craft workshops, tuition in ceramics, daily classes, adventure playground , garden centre, hairdresser, beauty salon, and Craft Centre open all year. Open March 1-November 8. ✰✰✰✰✰ **BH&HPA. 100T. 20MC.** 📖 🚂 ⅋ 🛆

Ruabon

(5m). James Caravan Park, Ruabon, Wrexham LL14 6DW. *01978 820148.* ✰✰✰ **30T. 10MC.** ✿ 📖 🚂 ⅋

ANTRIM

Antrim

(1m). Sixmilewater Caravan Park, Lough Road, Antrim, Co Antrim BT41 4DQ. *028 9446 4963.* info@antrim.gov.uk. www.antrim.gov.uk/caravanpark. Owner: Antrim Borough Council. Development and Leisure Services, The Steeple, Antrim BT41 1BJ. Follow SP for Antrim Forum/Lough Shore Park and turn off Dublin Road (A26) on to Lough Road. Close to the shores of Lough Neagh, in an area steeped in history and with many attractions and activities for the holidaymaker to enjoy. Touring caravans, motor caravans and tents accepted. Facilities include modern toilet and shower block and fully equipped laundry. TV lounge and games room due to open at Easter 2006. Open Easter-end October. ✰✰✰✰ **NCC. 18T. 18MC.** 📖 🚂 🛆

Ballycastle

(5m). Ballypatrick Forest, 155 Cushendell Road, Ballycastle, Co Antrim. *01265 762301.* Owner: Department of Agriculture. On the A2. 5m forest drive offering views of Ballycastle and Rathlin Island. **11T. 2MC.** ✿ 📖

(0.5m). Fair Head Caravan Park, 13 White Park, Ballycastle, Co Antrim BT54 6HA. *01265 762077.* Owner: Lex Fleck. Situated on the Causeway coast. Giant's Causeway 2m. Open March 17-October 31. **12T. 140S.** 📖 🚂 🛆

Silvercliffs Holiday Park, 21 Clare Road, Causeway Coast, Ballycastle, Co Antrim BT54 5DB. *028 20762550.* silvercliffs@hagansleisure.co.uk. www.hagansleisure.co.uk. Owner: Hagans Leisure Group. 184 Templepatrick Road, Ballyclare, Co Antrim, N Ireland BT39 0RA. From the A26, take the A44 to Ballycastle. Go straight through Ballycastle and turn L at Marine Court Hotel roundabout, taking you to North Street and on to Clare Road. Park is 0.5m on righthand side. Situated in elevated position, the site commands views over Ballycastle Bay. Just a 20mins drive from the Giant's Causeway. Suitable touring base base from which to explore Northern Ireland's Causeway Coastand glens. Facilities include indoor heated pool, play area and a traditional bar with live entertainment. Open March-November. ✰✰ **BH&HPA. NCC. 80T. 80MC. 300S. 47H.** 📖 🚂 🛆

NORTHERN IRELAND

Ballymena

(1.8m). Cushendall Caravan Site, 62 Coast Road, Cushendall, Ballymena, Co Antrim BT44 0GW. *028 2177 1699/028 2176 1254.* Owner: Moyle District Council. 7 Mary Street, Ballcastle, Antrim. On A2. 25m from Larne ferry heading north, enjoying the picturesque Glens of Antrim on your journey. Open Easter-end September. **25T. 4MC. 64S.** 🐾 ⅋

(14m). Glenariff Forest Park, 98 Glenariff Road, Glenariff, Ballymena, Co Antrim BT44 0QX. *028 2566 2873/028 2175 8232.* Owner: Department of Agriculture. On A43, Ballymena to Waterfoot road. Free entry to Forest Park for all customers. ✩✩ **20T. 5MC.** ✿ 🐾 ⍤ ⅋

Private Caravan Site, Ash Vale, Lemanalary, Carnlough, Ballymena, Co Antrim. *01574 885685.* Owner: Mr R McAlister. 0.25m from Cannlough. Park licensed for 35 caravans or homes. Dogs allowed under control. Bottled gas supplies. Mobile shop calls at site. Open April-September. **T. MC. SH.** 🐾

Ballymoney

(4m). Drumaheglis Marina & Caravan Park, 36 Glenstall Road, Ballymoney, Co Antrim BT53 7QN. *028 2766 6466.* helen.neill@ballymoney.gov.uk. www.ballymoney.gov.uk. Well SP from the A26 Ballymoney to Coleraine Road. Caravan Club affiliated site. Non-members and tent campers welcome. Award-winning park is one of the new with access to the lower river Bann. Toilet blocks, laundry facilities and motorhome service point. Playground and play area on site. Suitable for families. Fishing, golf and water sports nearby. Open March-October. ✩✩✩✩✩ **53T. MC.** 🐾 ⍤ ⅋

Bushmills

Portballintrae Holiday Home Park, Ballaghmore Avenue, Portballintrae, Bushmills, Co Antrim BT57 8RX. *028 2073 1478/028 7082 4644.* Owner: Rubane Investments Ltd. From Belfast M2 and A26 to Ballymoney, B62 and B17 to Bushmills, B145 to Portballintrae. SP at site entrance and junction of A2 and B145. Calor Gas available. Telephone on site. 3 golf courses within 6m. Sea angling within 1m. Open March-November. ✩✩ **NCC. 34T. 5MC. 150S.** 🐾 ⍤ ⅋

Larne

Brown's Bay Caravan Park, Brown's Bay, Islandmagee, Larne, Co Antrim. *01574 260088.* Follow signs to Carrickfergus from Larne and take turn for Islandmagee along B90. Head north past power station. Site overlooks lighthouse. Open Easter-September. **29T. MC.** 🐾 ⍤

(3.5m). Carnfunnock Country Park, Drains Bay, Coast Road, Larne, Co Antrim BT40 2QG. *028 2827 0541/028 28260088.* carnfunnock@btconnect.com. www.larne.gov.uk/carnfunnock. html. Owner: Larne Borough Council. Smiley Buildings, Victoria Road, Larne, Co Antrim BT40 1RU. On A2 coast road, N of Larne between Drains Bay and Ballygally. Situated on the Antrim coast within 473 acres of parkland. Attractions include walled garden, miniature railway, orienteering, children's adventure playground, golf activities, maze, woodland walks, picnic/bbq areas, modern visitor centre with gift and coffee shop. Open St Patrick's day-end November. ✩✩✩ **28T. MC.** 🐾 ⍤ ⅋ ⅃

(0.5m). Curran Court Caravan Park, 131 Curran Road, Larne, Co Antrim BT40 1BD. *028 2827 3797/3203.* Owner: Crawford Leitch. 84-86 Curran Road, Larne BT40 1BU. From town centre follow signs for leisure centre. Park opposite hotel and beside putting and bowling greens. 0.5m from ferry terminal and most amenities. Open April-September. ✩✩ **30T.** 🐾 ⍤ ⅋ ⍤ ⅃

(12m). The Ranch Caravan Park, 93 Mullaghboy Road, Islandmagee, Larne, Co Antrim BT40 3TR. *01960 382441.* Owner: Mr M Russell. On B150, turn off A2 for Islandmagee, follow signs for Mullaghboy and Portmuck. Open April 1-October 31. **BH&HPA. 5T. 5MC. 63S.** 🐾 ⍤ ⅃

Portrush

(0.5m). Blairs Caravans Ltd, 29 Dhu Varren, Portrush, Co Antrim BT56 8EW. *028 70822760.* Owner: T D Blair. On coast road between Portrush and Portstewart. Caravan accessory shop. 200yd from beach and 9-hole golf course 1.25m. Royal Portrush championship links 1m, Giant's Causeway 7m. Open April 1-October 31. **NCC. 25T. MC. 115S.** 🐾 ⍤

Hilltop Holiday Park, 60 Loguestown Road, Portrush, Co Antrim BT56 8PD. *028 70823537/822237.* Owner: Mr T Blair. 29 Dhu-Varren, Portrush BT56 8EW. Located on the A29, Coleraine to Portrush road. Play area. Hard-standings. Laundry facilities. Open April 1-November 2. **NCC. 50T. 20MC. 330S. 10H.** 🐾 ⍤

(1m). Skerries Holiday Park, 126 Dunluce Road, Portrush, Co Antrim BT56 8NB. *028 70822531.* Owner: D J Locuhart Ltd. Ballycastle Road, Coleraine BT52 2DY. On A2, Bushmills to Portrush coast road. Play area. Tennis courts. Open April 1-October 31. **70T. 20MC. 780S.** 🐾 ⍤ ⅃

ARMAGH

Lurgan

(2m). Kinnego Marina Caravan Park, Kinnego Marina, Oxford Island, Lurgan, Co Armagh BT66 6WJ. *028 3832 7573/028 3831 2400.* kinnego.marina@craigavon.gov.uk. Owner: Craigavon Borough Council, Leisure Department. Off roundabout 10, M1 Lurgan, down the embankment road to Oxford Island 0.25m. Park is on the shores of lough and nature reserve. Open April-End October. ✩✩ **10T. 10MC.** 🐾 ⍤ ⍤ ⅃

Markethill

(1m). Gosford Forest Park, 7 Gosford Demesne, Gosford Forest Park, Markethill, Armagh, Co Armagh BT60 1GD. *028 3755 1277/028 37552169(peak times).* Owner: Department of Agriculture & Rural Development (Forestry). Take A28 from Armagh 6m. A28 from Newry 11m. Hard-standing pitches Picnic and barbecue areas. Function hall with basic kitchin heating, chairs and tables. Horse riding routes. Waymarked trails. Guided tours (bookable), orienteering routes, special events (arranged by permit). Heritage, poultry and rare breeds collection. ✩✩✩ **50T. 5MC.** ✿ 🐾 ⍤ ⅃

DOWN

Ballywalter

(2m). Rosebank Caravan Site, 199 Whitechurch Road, Ballywalter, Co Down BT22 2JZ. *028 42758211.* Owner: Mr W Hopes. On the A2, 3m from Millisle. Level, grassy site beside sandy beach. Open April-October. **NCC. 6T. 6MC. 80S.** 🐾 ⍤

Castlewellan

(0.5m). Castlewellan Forest Park, The Grange, Castlewellan, Co Down BT31 9BO. *028 4377 8664.* Owner: Department of Agriculture. Dundonald House, Belfast BT4 3SB. Contact Head Forester. ✩✩✩ **81T. MC.** ✿ 🐾 ⍤ ⅃

Please mention Caravan Sites 2006 when replying to advertisers

Downpatrick

(7m). Castle Ward, Strangford, Downpatrick, Co Down. *028 44 881680*. Owner: The National Trust. Rowallane, Saintfield, Ballynahinch BT24 7LH. NE of Downpatrick, 1.5m W of Strangford village on an A25. Shower block. Situated within National Trust estate on the shores of Strangford Lough. Close to historic buildings and Area of Outstanding Natural Beauty. Open Easter-September 30. **26T.** 🐕 🔌 ♿

(1m). Coney Island Caravan Camp, Ardglass, Downpatrick, Co Down BT30 7UH. *01396 841448*. Owner: Mr C Braniff. Open Good Friday-November 15. **6T. 6MC. 94S.** 🗎

(6m). Minerstown Caravan Park, Minerstown, Downpatrick, Co Down BT30 8LR. *01396 85527*. Owner: Coastline Caravans Ltd. Open April 1-November 15. **15T. 160S.** 🐕

Kilkeel

(4m). Chestnutt Caravan Park, 3 Grange Road, Cranfield West, Kilkeel, Co Down BT34 4LJ. *028 4176 2653*. Off A2. Follow signs for Cranfield beach. Adjacent to award-winning Cranfield beach. Fast food outlet and games room on park. Open March 17-October 31. ✰✰✰✰✰ **BH&HPA. 20T. MC. 240S. 10H.** 🐕 🔌 ♿ 🗎

(20m). Sandilands Caravan Site, 30 Cranfield Road, Cranfield East, Kilkeel, Co Down BT34 4LQ. *028 4176 3634/029 4176 2653*. Owner: Mr & Mrs F Chestnut. On C365. Superpitches for tourers. Private beach. Open mid March-end October. ✰✰✰✰ **22T. 5MC. 200S.** 🐕

(3.5m). The Original Cranfield Caravan Park, 123 Cranfield Road, Cranfield East, Kilkeel, Co Down BT34 4LJ. *028 4176 2572*. Owner: Jim & Sandra Chestnutt. Off A2, 3.5m from Kilkeel fishing village,18m from Newry, along sea front.18-hole golf course, fishing, and pony-trekking nearby. New toilets and showers for disabled people. Open March-end October. ✰✰✰✰✰ **BH&HPA. 54T. MC. 200S.** 🐕 🔌 ♿ 🗎

Killy Leagh

(1m). Camping & Caravanning Club Site - Delamont Country Park, Down Patrick Road, Killy Leagh, Co Down BT30 9TZ. *028 4482 1833/0870 243 3331*. www.campingandcaravanningclub.co.uk. Owner: The Camping & Caravanning Club. Greenfields House, Westwood Way, Coventry, CV4 8JH. Off A22 1m S of Killyleagh and 4m N of Down Patrick. About 1 hour from Belfast ferry and 1.5 hours from port of Larne. Located in an Area of Outstanding Natural Beauty; plenty of walks, picnic areas, birdwatching, Victorian walled garden and children's playground. Sea fishing off Ardglass; coarse and game fishing. Other local activities include walking, cycling, golf, horse riding. Non-members welcome. All types of units accepted. Some Superpitches available. Special deals available for families and backpackers. David Bellamy Silver Conservation Award. Open March-October. ✰✰✰✰✰ **63T. 63MC.** 🐕 🔌 ♿

Newcastle

Bay View Caravan Park, Castle Lane, Dundrum, Newcastle, Co Down. *01396 75344*. Owner: Mr R S McCall. Shop nearby. March 15-October 31. **BH&HPA. 71S.** 🐕

Bonny's Newcastle Trailer Park, 82 Tullybrannigan Road, Newcastle, Co Down BT33 0PD. *01396 722351*. Owner: Mrs D Carr. Proceed along Newcastle main street, turn right at Donard Park. Entrances to hundreds of acres of forest walks 1m. **NCC. 50T. MC. 430S.** 🐕 🔌 🗎

(0.5m). Bonny's Sunnyholme, 33 Castlewellan Road, Newcastle, Co Down BT33 0JY. *01396 722739*. Owner: Mrs D Carr. On main Castlewellan to Newcastle road. Beside Burrendale Hotel. New barbecue and children's play area. Open March-November. **BH&HPA. 30T. 10MC. 250S.** 🐕 🔌 🗎

Boulevard Caravan Park, 114 Dundrum Road, Newcastle, Co Down. *01846 638336/01396 722130*. Owner: Mr E F & M Crawford. 386 Upper Ballynahinch Road, Lisburn, Co Antrim BT27 6XL. 10 mins from town. Open March-October. **NCC. 15T. MC. 144S.** 🐕 🔌 🗎

(2m). Bryansford Caravan Park, 1 Bryansford Village, Newcastle, Co Down BT33 0PT. *028 43724017*. Owner: Mr T Walsh. Open April 1-October 31. **9T. 97S.** ❄ 🐕 🗎 ✎

(2m). Lazy B J Ranch, Dundrum Road, Newcastle, Co Down BT33 0LW. *01396 723533*. Owner: Mr & Mrs P Bonny. 2m outside Dundrum on left-hand side of the main Belfast to Newcastle Road. Open Easter-October. **40T. MC. 43S. 4H.** 🐕 🔌 🗎

Murlough Caravan Site, Lower Newcastle, Newcastle, Co Down. *01396 723184/722288*. Owner: Mr J & Mrs Truesdale. 180 Dundrum Road, Newcastle, County Down. On main Belfast road. Open March 17-October 17. **30T. 4MC. 81S.** 🐕 🔌

(2m). Tollymore Forest Park Caravan Site, 176 Tullybranigan Road, Newcastle, Co Down BT33 0PW. *028 4372 2428*. Owner: Department of Agriculture. Dundonald House, Belfast BT4 3SB. 32m S of Belfast, SP from Newcastle. Inquiries to Head Forester. ✰✰✰ **100T. MC.** ❄ 🐕 🔌 🗎

(1m). Windsor Holiday Park, 138 Dundrum Road, Newcastle, Co Down BT33 0LN. *028 43723367*. windsor@hagansleisure.co.uk. www.hagansleisure.co.uk. Owner: Hagans Leisure Group. 184 Templepatrick Road, Ballyclare, Co Antrim, N Ireland BT39 0RA. On A24. Tranquil park situated within walking distance of the popular holiday resort of Newcastle, with its sandy beaches and championship golf course. Open mid March-end October. ✰✰ **BH&HPA. NCC. 36T. MC. 100S. 5H.** 🐕 🔌 🗎

(0.5m). Woodcroft Caravan Park, 104 Dundrum Road, Newcastle, Co Down BT33 0QS. *028 437 22284*. Owner: Paul & Tracey Magowan. Grassy, level, quiet, famliy-run site. Open March 17-October 12. **BH&HPA. 39T. MC. 108S.** 🐕 🔌 ♿

Newry

Annalong Caravan Park, 38 Kilkeel Road, Annalong, Newry, Co Down BT34 4JJ. *028 4176 2653*. Owner: Chestnutt Caravans. On A2, in the centre of village. Park gently slopes to sea, with touring pitches on seafront. Golf 6m. Shopping centre, cinema 20m. Open mid March 17-end October. ✰✰✰✰✰ **BH&HPA. 12T. MC. 160S.** 🐕 🔌 ♿ ✎

(2.5m). Leestone Caravan Park, Leestone Road, Maghereagh Kilkeel, Newry, Co Down BT34 4NW. *01693 762567*. Owner: Mr J McKibbin. Off A2, N of Kilkeel on Kilkeel-Newcastle road. Open April-October. **20T. 5MC. 150S. 10H.** 🐕 🔌 🗎

Newtownards

(13m). Ballyhalbert Caravan Park, 96-98 Shore Road, Ballyhalbert, Newtownards, Co Down BT22 1BJ. *028 4275 7555*. Owner: 57 Developments Ltd. Take the A2 from Bangor and travel S on peninsula. Park is on right on entering Ballyhalbert village. Recreation hall, games room, cafe, laundrette and play area. Open March-January 5. **NCC. 20T. 5MC. 400S.** 🐕 ♿ 🗎

(7m). Ballywhiskin Caravan & Camping Park, 216 Ballywalter Road, Millisle, Newtownards, Co Down BT21 2LY. *028 91862262.* admin@ballywhiskincaravanandcamping.com.www.ballywhiskincaravanandcamping.com. Owner: Roy & Hilda Butler. From Newtownwards take B172 E to Millisle, turn R on A2 towards Ballywalter, site on the R. Open weekends during winter. Hard-standings and laundry facilities. Situated close to beach. Small animal farm on site. Playing field and play park. Children welcome. Within easy reach of many places of interest. Golf, horse riding, tennis, swimming pool, shopping centre, cinema all available within 7m. Open April-October. ✿✿✿ **BH&HPA. 17T. 10MC. 169S.** 🛈 🌐 🏪

(9m). Happyvale Caravan Park, 112 Ballywalter Road, Millisle, Newtownards, Co Down. *028 9186 1457.* Owner: Mr J Magill. Open Easter-October. **4T. 56S.**

(15m). Kirkistown Caravan Park, 55 Main Road, Cloughy, Newtownards, Co Down BT22 1JB. *028 42771183.* Owner: Mr Peter Marsden. Off A2. Level, free-draining site. Newly contructed, heated facilities block. Sandy beach. Play park. Windsurfing and golf course adjacent. **NCC. 40T. 5MC. 90S.** ✿ 🛈 🌐 ♿

Rockmore Park, 150 Whitechurch Road, Ballywalter, Newtownards, Co Down BT22 2JZ. *028 4275 8342.* Owner: Mr Hugh Warnock. 1 mile from Ballywalter on right-hand side, on Millisle Road. 3rd caravan site. Adjacent to sandy beach. Fishing, golf 1m. Open March-October. **10T. MC. 10S.** 🛈 ♿

(8m). Seaview Caravan Park, 1 Donaghadee Road, Millisle, Newtownards, Co Down BT22 2BY. *028 91861248.* www.seaviewcaravansales.com. Owner: Mr D Colwell. On A2. Open April 1-October 30. **40T. MC. 276S.** 🛈 🌐

Portaferry

Exploris Touring Caravan Park, Exploris Aquarium, The Rope Walk, Castle Street, Portaferry, Co Down BT22 1NZ. *028 4272 8610/028 4272 8062.* Small site in the grounds of Exploris. 5 mins walk from centre of Portaferry. Open Easter-September. ✿✿✿ **12T. 12MC.** 🛈 🌐 ♿ 🏪

(4.5m). Silver Bay Caravan Park, 15 Ardminnan Road, Portaferry, Co Down BT22 1QJ. *028 42771321.* info@ardminnan.com. Owner: Mr J Gowan & Mrs I Gowan. On A20. From Belfast to Newtownards, Grey Abbey, Kircubbin and take B173 to Cloughey. Site is about 1m along coast road. Safe beach. Bar/restaurant. Horse riding. 50-acre, 9-hole golf links. Shop, PO in Cloughey 1m. Doctor in Portaferry. Open week before Easter-October 31. **10T. 4MC. 154S.** 🛈 🌐

FERMANAGH

Enniskillen

(8m). Blaney Caravan Park, Blaney, Enniskillen, Co Fermanagh BT93 7ER. *028 68641634.* info@blaneycaravanpark.com. www.blaneycaravanpark.com. Owner: Mr David B Bailey. From Enniskillen on A46 to Belleek. Hard-standings and waste hook-ups for touring caravans. **24T. MC. 10S.** ✿ 🛈 🌐 ♿ 🏪

Fermanagh

Lough Melvin Holiday Centre, Main Street, Garrison, Fermanagh, Co Fermanagh BT93 4FG. *01365 658142/02868 658142.* Owner: c/o S Rooney. Located in the village of Garrison. On the shores of Loch Meluin, famous for the Gillaroo Trout. 2mins walk to shops, PO, PHs and restaurants. ✿✿✿ **9T. MC.** ✿ 🛈 🌐 ♿

Irvinestown

(5m). Castle Archdale Caravan Park, Lisnarick, Irvinestown, Co Fermanagh BT94 1PP. *028 68621588.* Owner: David Mahon. Rosculban, Kesh, Co Fermanagh. 10m from Enniskillen, off B82, Enniskillen to Kesh Road. On shore of Lower Lough Erne. In Castle Archdale Country Park. Restaurant, takeaway, playpark, pony-trekking cycle hire and ferry to White Island. Open April 1-October 31. **NCC. 58T. MC. 136S. 12H.** 🛈 🌐 ♿ 🏪

Kesh

(2m). Lakeland Caravan Park, Drumrush, Boa Island Road, Kesh, Co Fermanagh BT93 1AD. *028 68631578.* mail@drumrush.co.uk. www.drumrush.co.uk. Owner: Joan & Lisa Armstrong. Dogs on leads only welcome. Licensed bar and restaurant on site. 10-bedroom guesthouse. Play park for children, tennis court. On shores of Lough Erne, water sports centre on shore. ✿✿✿✿ **NCC. 35T. 10MC. 1H.** ✿ 🛈 🌐 ♿

Lisnaskea

(3m). Share Holiday Village, Smith's Strand, Lisnaskea, Co Fermanagh BT92 2EQ. *028 6772 2122.* celia@sharevillage.org. www.sharevillage.org. Owner: Discovery 80 Ltd (Share). From A4, main Belfast to Enniskillin road, turn off at Maguirebridge, go through to Lisnaskea, take B127 to Derrylin, Share Centre is 4m on right. Share Holiday village is a residential, outdoor activity centre with mostl facilities. Purpose built for use by people wih disabilities and able-bodied people. Canoeing, sailing, archery, climbing wall and arts activities. Indoor swimming pool with ramped access. Coffee shop and takeaway. Shops, PO doctor 3m. Open Easter-Halloween. ✿✿✿ **13T. 6MC.** 🌐 ♿ 🏪

LONDONDERRY

Coleraine

(6m). Castlerock Holiday Park, 24 Sea Road, Castlerock, Coleraine, Co Londonderry BT51 4TN. *028 7084 8381.* Owner: Bonalston Caravans Ltd. Take A2 from Coleraine. Laundry. Playground. Poolroom. Open Ester-October. **NCC. 20T. 5MC. 210S. 10H.** 🛈 🌐

(7m). Springwell Caravan Site, Springwell Forest, Dunhill Road, Coleraine, Co Londonderry. On A37 (T). Maximum stay 7 nights. Forest touring site permit holders only. Temporary permits available from the District Forest office, given 3 days notice: tel 015047 62547. **12T. MC.** ✿ 🛈

Limavady

(12m). Benone Tourist Complex, 53 Benone Avenue, Magilligan, Limavady, Co Londonderry BT49 0LQ. *028 7775 0555.* Owner: Limavady Borough Council. 7 Connell Street, Limavady BT49 0HA. Situated on coast road about 9m from Coleraine. Complex includes 9-hole, par-3 golf course and golf practice range. Outdoor heated splash pool. 4 tennis courts. Bowling green. Modern activity play area. Events programme and cafe opened during July and August. Seasonal shop available. ✿✿✿✿ **100T. 100MC.** ✿ 🛈 🌐 ♿

(7m). Golden Sands Caravan Park, 26a Benone Avenue, Magilligan, Limavady, Co Londonderry BT49 0LQ. *028 7775 0324.* Owner: J & S Walls. Benone Avenue, Limavady, Co Londonderry. Dogs allowed only at manager's discretion. Open March-October 31. **BH&HPA. 100T. 10MC. 300S. 8H.** 🛈 🌐 🏪

Moneymore

(1m). Springhill Caravan Park, 20 Springhill Road, Moneymore, Co Londonderry BT45 7NG. *028 86748210.* On B18, Moneymore to Coagh. Gift shop in season. **20T. MC.** ✿ ♿

Portrush

(2m). Carrick-Dhu Holiday Park, 12 Ballyreagh Road, Portrush, Co Antrim BT40 1BD. *028 7082 3712/028 7035 2181.* Owner: Coleraine Borough Council. On A2, Portrush to Portstewart. Open April 1-October 6. **BH&HPA. 45T. 45MC. 419S. 7H.** ✴ 🖰 ⌂ 🗲

Portstewart

(1.5m). Juniper Hill Caravan Park, 70 Ballyreagh Road, Portstewart, Co Londonderry BT55 7PT. *028 7083 2023/028 7035 2181.* Owner: Coleraine Borough Council. On A2, Portrush to Portstewart. Open April 1-October 1. ☆☆☆ **75T. 40MC. 405S.** ✴ 🗲

(1m). Portstewart Caravan Park, 30A Burnside Road, Portstewart, Co Londonderry BT55 7SW. *01265 833308.* Owner: O'Neills Caravan Sales Ltd. 80 Mill Road, Portstewart, Co Londonderry. Take A2 from Coleraine, on approach to Portstewart, turn left at first roundabout into Burnside Road, park 500yd on left. Open Easter-October. **NCC. 92S.** ✴

TYRONE

Clogher

(1.5m). Clogher Valley Country Caravan Park, 9 Fardnoss Road, Clogher, Co Tyrone BT76 0HG. *028 8554 8932.* Owner: Sydney & Olive Somerville. 52 Favour Royal Road, Aughna Cloy, Co Tyrone BT69 6BR. 0.3m off A4 between Clogher and Fivemiletown. 50m west of Belfast towards Enniskillen. Forest and river walks. Fishing. Open mid March-end October. ☆ **BH&HPA. NCC. 30T. 20MC. 10S. 3H.** ✴ 🖰 🗲

Dungannon

(1m). Dungannon Park, Moy Road, Dungannon, Co Tyrone BT71 6DY. *028 8772 7327.* dungannonpark@utvinternet.com. Owner: Dungannon & South Tyrone Borough Council. SP off the A29. Fishing, barbecue area, play area, tennis courts. Located within a 70-acre public park, overlooking a rainbow trout, 12 acre lake. More than 1.5m of walks to be explored at your leisure through mature woodland with a panoramic view of the Tyrone countryside from the heights of Nunnery Hill. Open March-October. ☆☆☆☆ **12T. 12MC.** ✴ 🖰 ⌂

Fivemiletown

(0.5m). Round Lake Caravan Park, Murley Road, Fivemiletown, Co Tyrone BT75 0QS. *028 8776 7259/028 8772 7327.* dungannonpark@utvinternet.com. Owner: Dungannon & South Tyrone Borough Council. Circular Road, Dungannon, Co Tyrone BT71 6DT. Site is on the Fintona Road, set beside the Round Lake. Visitor centre and play area. Lakeside walks. 10mins walk from village, shops and restaurants. Busy market village atmosphere. Site is staffed on a part-time basis, with attendance mornings and evenings. Open March-October. ☆☆ **12T. 12MC.** ✴ 🖰 ⌂

Please remember to mention *Caravan Sites 2006* when you contact any sites listed in this guide, or when you respond to any advertisements.

CAVAN

Virginia

(3m). Lough Ramor Caravan & Camping Park, Ryefield, Virginia, Co Cavan. *00 353 1 837 1717.* 0.3m off N3 route, S of Virginia on the scenic shores of Lough Ramor. Hard-standing pitches with electrical supply points. Toilet block. Fishing and boating. Shops, PHs and restaurants nearby. Open May-end September. **10T. MC.** ✴ 🖰 ⌂

CLARE

Carrigaholt

Rahona Lodge Caravan Park, Carrigaholt, Co Clare. *00 353 65 9058186.* Open March-end October. **T. MC.**

Corofin

Corofin Village Camping & Caravan Park, Main Street, Corofin, Co Clare. *00 353 65 6837683.* corohost@iol.ie. From Ennis follow N85 and R476. From Galway City follow N18 towards Gort, then R460 via Kilmacduagh to Corofin. Sheltered site with games room and laundrette. Walking and cycling. Fishing lakes nearby. Open April-September. **T. MC.** ✴ 🖰 ⌂

Doolin

(0.5m). Nagle's Doolin Camping & Caravan Park, Doolin, Co Clare. *00 353 65 7074458.* ken@doolincamping.com. www. doolincamping.com. From Lisdoonvarna go towards Cliff of Moher, turn R for Doolin and follow signs to Doolin Pier. Site located beside Doolin Pier. Only with 15 hard-standings. Can accommodate touring vans and camper vans on the grass . Overlooked by the Cliffs of Moher and just a short walk from three of Ireland's most famous PHs, with traditional music nightly. Excellent restaurants, Lahinch Seaworld and heated swimming pool nearby. Shop open from June 1 to end of August. Pitch and putt 200yd from site. Open April 1-September 30. **NCC. 62T. MC. 1H.** ✴ 🖰 ⌂ 🗲

Riverside Caravan & Camping Park, Doolin, Co Clare. *00 353 65 7074314.* joan@oconnorsdoolin.com. www.oconnors doolin.com. Owners: Joan & Pat O'Connor. From Lisdoonvarna go towards Cliffs of Moher (N67), turn R for Doolin. Go straight at main crossroads in centre of Doolin. Park is situated over Aille River Bridge on left-hand side of road, behind O'Connors bed and breakfast guesthouse. Situated in the centre of Doolin within 5mins walk from PHs, shops and restaurants. Local attractions in areatrips to Aran Islands, coastal walks, potholing, Ailwee Caves, pony trekking, river and sea fishing, pitch and putt, bicycle hire. Open May-September. **NCC. T. MC.** ✴ 🖰 ⌂ 🗲

Kilkee

Cunningham's Holiday Park, Kilkee, Co Clare. *00 353 61 451009.* Open June-end September. **T.**

Green Acres Caravan Park, Doonaha, Kilkee, Co Clare. *00 353 65 9057011.* SP off N67 road between Kilrush and Kilkee, or direct, 5mins from Kilkee. Family-run park in a quiet and secluded setting on the shores of the river Shannon. Spectacular coastal views, lovely beaches. Suitable base for walking. Dolphin watch nearby. Open April-September. **T. MC.** ✴ 🖰 ⌂

Killaloe

(2.5m). Lough Derg Holiday Park, Killaloe, Co Clare. *00 353 61 376777.* info@loughderg.net. www.loughderg.net. From Dublin, Limerick Road, N7, N from Nenagh, follow signs for Killaloe/Ballina. Family-owned and family-run site situated in the scenic Shannon Valley, on shores of Lough Derg. Amenities include provisions shop, restaurant, takeaway food, games room and laundry room. Boating, angling, golf course, activity centre locally. Open mid May-mid September. **32T. MC.** 🐕🗲♿🗲

Kilrush

Aylevarroo Caravan & Camping Park, Kilrush, Co Clare. *00 353 65 51102.* Open May-mid September. **T. MC.**

Lahinch

Lahinch Camping & Caravan Park, Lahinch, Co Clare. *00 353 65 81424.* 200yd S of Lahinch on coast road. Quiet, family-run park supervised at all times. Great variety of traditional pubs, craft shops, music shop and restaurants in village. Beach renowned for surf. Walks by sea. Championship golf course. Open May-end September. **20T. MC.** 🐕🗲

Miltown Malbay

Lahiff's Caravan & Camping, Spanish Point, Miltown Malbay, Co Clare. *00 353 65 84006.* Open April-end September. **T. MC.**

Mountshannon

(1.3m). Lakeside Holiday Park, Mountshannon, Co Clare. *00 353 61 927225.* lakesidecamping@eircom.net. www.lakeside ireland.com. Straight through Mountshannon, on Portumna Road. First turn R, SP. This natural lakeside water sport park is located on the shores of Lough Derg. Dogs allowed except during July and August. Amenities include tennis, boat hire, soccer pitch, table tennis, swimming and fishing. Pitch and Putt, cafe/bistro, bicycle hire, pony riding for children, golf course, PHs and shops available within 2m. Open May-October. **17T. MC. 10S. 8H.** 🐕🗲

CORK

Ballymacoda

(2m). Sonas Caravan Park, Ballymacoda, Co Cork. *00 353 24 98132/00 353 24 98960.* sonas-camping@yahoo.co.uk. www. sonascamping.ie. Owner: C Riordon. From Cork take N25 to Castlemartyr, just over bridge in village, take R632 to Ladysbridge, Turn left in middle of village for Ballymacoda. Follow direction signs from Ballymacoda to Sonas. From Rosslake, take N25 to Youphall, 1.25m past town take R633 to Ballymacoda. Park is set in an unspoilt, rural, birdwatching area, with direct access to the beach. Facilities include shop, play and TV rooms, full laundry, tennis court, volleyball and football pitch. Open May 1-mid September. **13T. MC.** 🐕🗲♿🗲

Bantry

Dunbeacon Caravan & Camping Park, Durrus, Bantry, Co Cork. *00 353 27 62851.* clemnjula@eircom.net. Owners: J Walton and Cairns. From Bantry take R591 to Durrus. After Durrus, continue on this road for another 3m; site is on the left-hand side. Family-run, secluded site with views overlooking Dunmanus Bay. Suitable base for touring west Cork. PHs, restaurants, fishing, water sports, walking and archaeological sites nearby. Open Easter-October. **7T. 7MC.** 🐕🗲

(4m). Eagle Point Camping, Ballylickey, Bantry, Co Cork. *00 353 27 50630.* eaglepointcamping@eircom.net. www.eagle pointcamping.com. N71 Cork to Blandon, R586 Bandon to Bantry. N71 Bantry to Glengarriff. Entrance opposite EMO Petrol station. Caravan Club affiliated site. 20 acre park covering an entire penisula, surrounded by mountain ranges and overlooking Bantry Bay. Toilet block and laundry facilities.

Playground on site. Good area for walking, golf and water sports nearby. Suitable for families. Peaceful off-peak. Open April-September. **NCC. 125T. MC.** 🐕🗲♿🗲

Blarney

(1.5m). Blarney Caravan & Camping Park, Stone View, Blarney, Co Cork. *00 353 21 4516519.* con.quill@camping-ire land.ie. www.blarneycaravanpark.com. Owner: C Quill. N25 take N8 towards Cork City. From N8 take sign for north ring road/Limerick, N20 then Blarney R617. SP from Blarney Esso filling station. Set in countryside, spacious, well sheltered and well landscaped, personally supervised giving a high standard of cleanliness and security. 18-hole pitch and putt course on site. Shops, restaurants, PHs within Blarney. Coarse/game fishing nearby. Open March 15-October 31. **40T. MC.** 🐕🗲♿🗲

Clonakilty

Desert House Caravan & Camping Park, Coast Road, Clonakilty, Co Cork. *00 353 23 33331.* From Cork N71 to Bandon and Clonakilty. Park is SP at roundabout in Clonakilty. Family-run park. Small touring park situated on a dairy farm overlooking Clonakilty Bay. Nearby model village, water sports, tennis, golf, pitch and putt, fishing, bird watching, sandy beaches. Open Easter and May-September. **14T. MC.** 🐕🗲

Fermoy

Blackwater Valley Caravan & Camping Park, Mallow, Killarney Road, Fermoy, Co Cork. *00 353 25 32147.* black watervalley.caravanpark@eircom.net.Owners: Mr & Mrs Ryan. We are on N72 from Rosslare to Killarney. 200yd from Fermoy town on Killarney road and N8 Cork-Dublin road. Family-run park on banks of river Blackwater. Fishing on site. Within easy reach golf course, pitch and putt, pony trekking, cinema and youth centre. 200yd from shops, restaurants and PHs. Adjacent to Fermoy town park with swimming pool, leisure centre and playground. Member of Irish Caravan Council: graded 3 stars. Open March 15-October 31. **10T.** 🐕🗲♿🗲

Glengarriff

Dowlings Caravan & Camping Park, Castletownbere Road, Glengarriff, Co Cork. *00 353 27 63154.* Park is located 1m out of Glengariff, on Castletownbere Road, R572. Situated between the mountains and the sea, 400yd from Glengarriff Harbour. Forest walks, angling, swimming, mountain climbing, orienteering, sailing and golf all nearby. Site open (June-September), play area, games room, TV, laundry service, takeaway (July-August), bar, traditional Irish music and singing nightly. Open Easter-October 31. **25T. MC.** 🐕🗲♿🗲

Kinsale

Garrettstown House Holiday Park, Kinsale, Co Cork. *00 353 21 4778156.* 6m from Kinsale R600. Through Ballinspittle village, past school and football pitch on main road to beach. Set in grounds of 18th-century estate, park provides numerous facilities for families in high season. Blue Flag beach 0.5m. Open May-mid September. **20T. MC.** 🐕🗲♿🗲

Skibbereen

Barleycove Holiday Park, Crookhaven, Skibbereen, Co Cork. *00 353 28 35302/00 353 21 4346466.* Owners: Kenneally's Caravans Ltd. Mobile Home Hire, Bishopstown, Cork. N71 Cork to Bandon, R589 Bandon to Bantry. R591 to Crookhaven just before Bantry. Beaches, scenery and walks. Tennis courts, pitch and putt, bicycle hire, children's club, baby-sitting, indoor/outdoor games, barbecue area, takeaway/cafe, mini market. Horse riding, golf, wind-surfing, fishing boat trips nearby. Open Easter and May-mid September. **35T.** 🗲♿🗲

Please mention Caravan Sites 2006 when replying to advertisers

(0.5m). **The Hideaway Camping & Caravan Park, Skibbereen, Co Cork.** *00 353 28 22254/33280.* the_hideaway @oceanfree.net. Owners: Stephen & Helen Keohane. On R596 to Castletownsend. Family-run park in a suitable location for touring the south-west. Rural setting, only 10mins walk to Skibbereen town. Ford, VW, Honda and Hyundai garages in Skibbereen. Birdwatching, golf course nearby. Ferries to islands of Cape Clear and Sherkin available from Baltimore. Liddle and supermarkets in Skibbereen. Open Easter-end September. **35T. 25MC.** ⊶ ⊖ ♿

DONEGAL

Ballyshannon

Lakeside Centre Caravan & Camping Park, Belleek Road, Ballyshannon, Co Donegal. *00 353 719852822.* erneent@ eir com.net. www.donegalbay.com. From Ballyshannon take N3 for Belleek. Site is on the left-hand side after about 0.5m. Overlooks the waters of Assaroe Lake. Well-serviced and fully supervised modern site. Shops, PHs, restaurants, take-aways, leisure and entertainment facilities available in Ballyshannon. Facilities for rallies or groups, meetings; function room available for hire. Open March-September. ✩✩✩✩ **60T. 60MC.** ⊶ ⊖ ♿

Downings

Casey's Caravan & Camping Park, Downings, Co Donegal. *00 353 74 55301.* rosapenna@eircom.net. Casey's is situated on the edge of Sheephaven Bay in the fishing village of Downings, 25m from Letterkenny. Shops, PHs and a hotel are all within 200yd. Safe, sandy beach nearby. Open April-September. **10T. MC.** ⊶ ⊖ ⚑

Portsalon

Knockalla Caravan & Camping Park, Portsalon, Co Donegal. *00 353 74 59108/53213.* Owners: C & H Doherty. Situated near Portsalon on the Knockalla Coast Road, overlooking Ballymastocker Bay. Miles of safe, sandy beach. Local amenities include golf, pitch and putt, angling, mountain climbing, walks. Open March-September. **90T. MC.** ⊶ ⊖ ⚑

DUBLIN

Dublin

(5m). **Camac Valley Tourist Caravan & Camping Park, Naas Road, Clondakin, Dublin 22, Co Dublin.** *00 353 1 464 0644.* info@camacvalley.com. www.camacvalley.com. Owner: Dennis Brennan. M50 motorway, exit at J9 and take N7 S, in direction Cork. Award-winning park. Groups and rallies well catered for in spacious park, while the individual hard-standings are private and pleasant. ✩✩✩✩ **113T. MC.** ❀ ⊶ ⊖ ♿

Rush

North Beach Caravan & Camping Park, North Beach, Rush, Co Dublin. *00 353 1 8437131.* info@northbeach.ie. www.north beach.ie. Owners: Anthony & Ann McNally. From S: N1, M1, M50. Leave N1 to R at Esso filling station N of Swords, turn R at Lusk. Along Rush main street, L at SP for North Beach, 50yd down road. Turn R at next sign for North Beach. Family-owned, family-run site. Picturesque, peaceful, secure location beside Irish Sea. Rural surroundings. 200yd frontage and direct access to sandy beach safe for swimming, water sports and fishing. Walking distance to supermarket, shops, restaurant, PO. Open April 1-September 30. **64T. MC.** ⊶ ⊖

GALWAY

Clifden

(6m). **Acton's Beachside Caravanning & Camping, Gallach, Streamstown Point, Clifden, Co Galway.** *00 353 9544036.* Owner: Christopher Acton. Located W of Clifden, adjacent Omey Island, near Claddaghduff village. Site set on a peninsula within a natural heritage area. Sea and beach frontage. Panoramic views. Riding, golf nearby, diving, water-skiing, dolphin watching, fishing, boating, hill and beach walking. Open April-October. **8T. 8MC.** ⊖ ♿

Galway City

Ballyloughane Caravan & Camping Park, Ballyloughane Beach, Renmore, Galway City, Co Galway. *00 353 91 755338/752029.* galwcamp@iol.ie. From Dublin/Limerick: 4.5m from Oranmore (N6 West). At first roundabout approaching city take exit SP 'Merlin Park/Renmore/Mervue'. Second turn left after Merlin Park Hospital/stores at Dawn Dairies. Quiet, family-run touring park supervised with high standard of security. Situated beside sandy beach with panoramic views of Galway Bay and less than 3m from city centre. Supermarket, laundrette, newsagent within 200yd. **25T. MC** ⊶ ⊖

Renvyle

Connemara Caravan & Camping Park, Lettergesh, Renvyle, Co Galway. *00 353 95 43406.* Owner: Willie Laffey. 5m S of Leenane, turn right off the main Westport/Clifden road (5m to site). Within 3m: salmon/sea trouts/sea angling, mountain climbing, windsurfing, canoeing, diving, golf, horse riding. Restaurants, PHs, shop, PO, laundrette, mobile bank, Irish traditional music. Dolphins often seen from site. Open May-September. **10T. MC.** ⊖ ⚑

Spiddal

Spiddal Caravan & Camping Park, Spiddal, Co Galway. *00 353 91 553372/558960.* paircsaoire@eircom.net. 10m from Spiddal village in Connemara Gaeltacht. Turn right at SP in centre of village. Galway City and Salthill 10m. Gaelic-speaking park. Nearest park to the Aran Islands. Scenic walks, beaches, aqua sports. Craft village. Irish music/PHs. Modern toilet block, fully serviced hard-standing, playground, indoor play area, laundry, showers. Open mid March-mid October. **25T. MC.** ⊶ ⊖

KERRY

Ballyheigue

Casey's Caravan & Camping Park, Main Street, Ballyheigue, Co Kerry. 00 353 66 7133195. Ballyheigue village. 10m from Tralee heading towards Kerry Head. Halfway up the Main Street on the right-hand side. Family-run park. All amenities. Exit to main street with shops, supermarkets, PO, takeaway food and pubs. 9-hole golf course open to green fees. Water sports on beach. Hill walking. Open May-September. **14T. MC.** 🐾 🅥

Caherdaniel

(1.2m). Glenbeg Caravan & Camping Park, Caherdaniel, Co Kerry. 00 353 66 9475182. glenbeg@eircom.net. Located on the Ring of Kerry Road, approx. 31m from Kenmare, 18m from Caherciveen. Adjacent to fine sandy beach. Park fronted by a sheltered cove in the Kenmare bay, a good location for water sports' enthusiasts. Suitable base for hill walkers, horse riding, visiting historic sites. Restaurants, PHs and a hotel located within walking distance. Open April 15-October 7. **59T.** 🐾 🅥 ♿

(1m). Wave Crest Caravan Park, Glenbeg, Caherdaniel, Co Kerry. 00 353 66 9475188. wavecrest@eircom.net. www.wave crestcamping.com. Located on the main Ring of Kerry Road, 30m from Kenmare and 20m from Cahirciveen. Park overlooks Kenmare Bay. Safe sandy beaches and water sports available. Within 3m surfing, boat trips to nearby islands, deep sea fishing trips, swimming and diving. Open March 15-October 15. **55T. MC.** 🐾 🅥 🇿

Cahirciveen

(0.5m). Mannix Point Camping and Caravan Park, Cahirciveen, Co Kerry. 00 353 66 9472806. mortimer@camp ingkerry.com. www.campinginkerry.com. Owner: Mortimer Moriarty. Located on the coast, 300yd off N70 Ring of Kerry Road, 0.5m W of town centre. Site open out of season by prior arrangement. Site is surrounded on three sides by mountains and faces the Atlantic islands of Valentia and Beginish to the south-west. Nearby attractions include water sports, diving, climbing, walks, horse riding, sea, river and sea fishing, bird-watching, golf, pitch and putt. Art galleries, potteries, PHs and restaurants. Supermarket 500yd. Traditional music and dancing. Open March 15-October 1. **42T. MC.** 🐾 🅥

Castlegregory

Anchor Caravan Park, Castlegregory, Co Kerry. 00 353 66 7139157. anchorcaravanpark@eircom.net. www.caravanparks ireland.net. 12m from Tralee, on Tralee-Dingle coast road. SP from Camp junction. Sheltered park with direct access to a sandy beach and safe bathing. Games room, TV room, playgrounds, laundry facilities, hot showers available on site. Nearby attractions include golf, fishing, water sports, restaurants, bars, supermarkets, hotel and takeaway. Open Easter-September 30. **30T. MC.** 🐾 🅥

Dingle

(1m). Ballintaggart House Budget Accommodation, Racecourse Road, Dingle, Co Kerry. 00 353 66 9151454. info@dingleaccommodation.com. www.dingleaccommodation. com. Owners: Paddy Fenton. Located on the right as you approach Dingle Town by the Tralee to Dingle road, the N86. Site is situated in the grounds of a 1703 hunting lodge close to Dingle town, overlooking the bay and with easy access to beaches and rock climbing site at Doonshean. Shop and garage 0.5m. Fishing, golf, hill walking and beaches nearby. Open May-September 30. **18T. MC.** 🐾 🅥 ♿

Kenmare

(3.5m). Ring of Kerry Caravan & Camping Park, Kenmare, Co Kerry. 00 353 64 41648. info@kerrycamping.com. www.kerry camping.com. Owner: Catherine Gibbons. Take the Sneem/Ring of Kerry road. Site established over 20 years. Views of Kenmare Bay. Suitable base for touring the Ring of Kerry, Beara and Dingle peninsulas. PHs, restaurants, crafts, galleries in Kenmare. Golf, quad biking, diving, walks all available nearby. Open April 1-September 30. **25T. MC.** 🐾 🅥 🇿

Killarney

(2m). Donoghues White Villa Farm Caravan & Camping ParkKillarney-Cork Road (N22), Killarney, Co Kerry. 00 353 6420671/6432456. killarneycaravanpark@eircom.net. www.killarney caravanpark.com. Owners: O'Donoghue Family. Located E of Killarney on the N22, Killarney-Cork road. Park entrance is 500yd E of N22/N72 junction. Sheltered, peaceful touring park. Park is bordered by a wood of oak and holly trees. Farm walks to river Flesk (fishing), National farm museum and original traditional Irish cottage. Ideal touring base for Ring of Kerry, Dingle and Beara Peninsulas. Daily coach tours from caravan park arranged. Golf 2m, shopping village 1.2m, PH 0.5m. Taxi and bus service (request bus stop at park entrance). Self-catering apartments for rent. Open April 1-October 3. **24T. 24MC.** 🐾 🅥 ♿

(1m). Fleming's White Bridge Caravan & Camping Park, White Bridge, Ballycasheen Road, Killarney, Co Kerry. 00 353 64 31590. info@killarneycamping.com. www.killarney camping.com. Moira & Hillary Fleming. 300yd off N22 Cork Road. East of Killarney. Caravan Club affiliated. 3 modern sanitation blocks, shop open daily June1-September 1, tourist information, 2 laundries, games room, TV lounge, sports field, fishing on site, bicycle hire and dog walks. Golf, cinema, shopping centre within 1m; 3m. Open April 13-October 15 and October 26-30. ✪✪✪✪ **92T. 6H.** 🐾 🅥 🇿 ⌀

(1m). Flesk Muckross Caravan & Camping Park, Muckross Road, Killarney, Co Kerry. 00 353 64 31704. info@camping killarney.com. www.campingkillarney.com. On N71 road to Kenmare. Follow signs for national park and lakes. Next door to Glen Eagle Hotel. 7-acre park is situated at the gateway to 25,000 acres of Killarney's parklands and lakes. At the start of the Kerry way, walking/cycle path from site to national park and lakes. Other facilities include bakery, cafe, take-away, hotel rooms, bar, restaurant, laundry, adults room, bike hire, etc. Open end March-end September. **36T. MC.** 🐾 🅥 ♿ 🇿

(5m). Fossa Caravan & Camping Park, Fossa, Killarney, Co Kerry. 00 353 64 31497. fossaholidays@eircom.net. www. camping-holidaysireland.com. From Cork and Mallow, J of N22/N72, continue towards Killarney town. At the top of the hill take second exit off the first roundabout, follow road till second roundabout, take third exit, (all the time following road signs for the N72 Ring of Kerry/Killorglin/Cahirciveen/Dingle road). Continue for about 3.5m. Fossa is the second park on the R. Family-run park set in wooded area, in the village of Fossa, overlooking the MacGillycuddy Reeks and just 5mins walk from Lough Leane. Graded 4 stars. Open end March-end September. **62T. MC.** 🐾 🅥 ♿ 🇿

Ring of Kerry

Glenross Caravan & Camping Park, Glenbeigh Village, Ring of Kerry, Co Kerry. 00 353 66 9768451/64 31590. glenross@eir com.net. www.killarneycamping.com. Owner: Joan Fleming. From Killarney/Killorglin take the N70 towards Glenbeigh. Park is on the R just before entering village. 6m from Killorglin. Caravan Club affiliated site. Views of Rossbeigh Beach. Suitable touring base for Dingle and Killarney. Popular venue for watersports, fishing, horse riding, walking, mountain climbing. Bicycle hire. An associate site of Fleming's White Bridge, Killarney, discount for staying at both parks. Open April 28-September 26. ✰✰✰✰ **18T. 18MC. 40S. 6H.** 🐕 🔌

Goosey Island Campsite, Sneem, Ring of Kerry, Co Kerry. *00 353 64 45577.* washer@oceanfree.net. Park is in the centre of Sneem village on the Ring of Kerry. New development, situated on the banks of the Sneem river. Good location for walkers. Open April 15-October 15. **15T. MC.** 🐕 🔌 &

(1m). West's Caravan Park, Killarney Road, Killorglin, Ring of Kerry, Co Kerry. *00353 66 9761240.* enquiries@westcaravans.com. Owner: Liam & Linda West. From Killorglin take the main Killarney Road and after 1m West's Caravan Park will be on your right-hand side. Suitable location for touring Killarney, Dingle, mountains, beaches, golf and peninsulas. Overlooking Ireland's highest mountain, on banks of river. Tennis, game fishing, play area, laundry etc on park. PHs and food nearby. 8 golf courses within 8m, sea fishing 15m. Ferry inclusive holiday packages. Mobile home available for hire short term, weekly or long stay. Open Easter-October. **BH&HPA. 10T. 10MC. 60S. 54H.** 🐕 🔌

Tralee

(1m). Tralee Bayview Mobile Home and Touring Caravan Park, Killeen, Tralee, Co Kerry. *00 353 66 7126140.* bayviewtralee@eircom.net. On Main Tralee-Abbeydorney-Ballybunion Road. Secluded, tree-lined site registered with the Irish Tourist Board for more than of 20 years. Sports centre, heated pool, table tennis, pitch and putt all nearby. Refurbished laundry/drying area. Upgraded shower and toilet facilities. Open May-October. **18T. MC. 5S.** 🐕 🔌 & 🛒

Woodlands Caravan & Camping Park, Dan Spring Road, Tralee, Co Kerry. *00 353 66 7121235.* wdlands@eircom.net. www.camping-ireland.ie. Owners: Mike & Martina McDonneill. From N21, N22 turn L at roundabout after McDonalds and follow signs. From N69 follow for Dingle until Tralee Marina, turn L, continue straight through a roundabout at Aqua Dome for 200yd. Park is located on a 16-acre parkland setting just a 10mins walk from the centre of Tralee town, connected by bridge to the Aqua Dome. Graded 4 stars. Golf, bowling, sea angling, diving, horse riding, sailing, windsurfing all available locally. Open mid March-end September. **85T. MC.** 🐕 🔌 & 🛒

KILDARE

Athy

Forest Farm Caravan & Camping Park, Dublin Road, Athy, Co Kildare. *00 353 507 31231.* forestfarm@eircom.net. 3m from Athy Heritage town on Dublin road, N78, 38m from Dublin. Family-run park on 140-acre working farm. Surrounded by mature trees, beech and evergreen. Recently opened and finished to a high standard. Fishing on river Barrow and Grand Canal in Athy. Bicycles for hire. **32T. MC.** ✿ 🐕 🔌

KILKENNY

Bennettsbridge

(2m). Nore Valley Caravan & Camping Park, Bennettsbridge, Co Kilkenny. *00 353 7727229.* norevalleypark@eircom.net. www.norevalleypark.tripod.com. Owners: Samuel & Isobel Harper. From Kilkenny R700 to Bennettsbridge, just before bridge turn R at sign. Site on an open farm. Patrons have access to farm and children are encouraged to assist in animal feeding.

River walk through farm and woodland. Crazy golf, poolroom, play area, pedal Go-Karts and trailer rides. Bicycles for hire. Swimming, fishing, canoeing, golf, horse riding within 10m. Open March-October. **30T. MC. 4S.** 🐕 🔌 & 🛒

Kilkenny

(1m). Tree Grove Caravan & Camping Park, Danville House, Kilkenny, Co Kilkenny. *00 353 56 7770302.* treecc@iol.ie. Site located after roundabout on R700, in the direction of New Ross. Conveniently located for touring medieval Kilkenny and south-east. Horse riding, fishing, golf and other outdoor pursuits within easy access of park. Golf clubs, bikes for hire. Free and unlimited showers, sheltered eating area. Open March-November. **12T. MC.** 🐕 🔌 &

LIMERICK

Adare

(2.5m). Adare Camping & Caravanning Park, Adare, Co Limerick. *00 353 61 395376.* dohertycampingadare@eircom.net. www.adarecamping.com. Owner: H & M Doherty. From Limerick N20/N21 for Tralee. Stay on N21 through Adare. Take L for R519 for Ballingarry and follow camp signs. Relaxing atmosphere, sheltered boundaries. Play area for children separate from parking area. Local amenities include old abbeys, churches, fishing, golf, pitch and putt, horse riding, bicycle hire, restaurants etc. Hot spa and campers' kitchen. Open March-September. **28T. MC.** 🐕 🔌 & 🛒

Kilcornan

(1.8m). Coillte Forest Park, Curragh Chase Caravan & Camping Park, Kilcornan, Co Limerick. *00 353 61 396349.* eileen.okeeffe@coillte.ie. www.coillte.ie. Owners: Coillte (Irish Forestry Board). From Limerick city take N69 coast road for 15m SW towards Foynes. Tranquil setting providing walkways, lake, wildlife. Within the forest are the ruins of Curragh Chase House, the 18th-century home of poet Aubrey DeVere. Children's play area. Open May-September. **50T. MC.** 🐕 🔌 🛒

LOUTH

Dundalk

Gyles Quay Caravan & Camping Park, Dundalk, Co Louth. *00 353 42 9376262.* 16km from Dundalk. Travel 2m on the Dundalk/Newry Road. Turn right on to coast road, travel 65m and turn right at SP for Gyles Quay. PH on site. Golf, fishing, mountain climbing, wind surfing all within 3m. Live entertainment. Open May-September. **13T. MC.** 🐕 🔌 🛒

MAYO

Achill Island

Keel Sandybanks Caravan & Camping Park, Keel, Achill Island, Co Mayo. *00 353 9490 32288.* info@achillcamping.com. www.achillcamping.com. Owners: Mr John Nestor. Belcarra, Castlebar, Co Mayo, Ireland. From Castlebar (Co Mayo) to Achill Sound via Newport. Take R319 to Keel (8km). Park is adjacent to Keel Beach, on L as you enter village. Bridged-linked to mainland Mayo, Achill Island offers scenic beauty and a range of holiday opportunities unequalled anywhere. From Keel, explore west of Ireland or enjoy boating, angling, sailboard lessons, surfing, mountain walking and golfing. Outdoor playing area for children. Graded 4 stars. Open end May-early September. **42T. 30MC. 13S. 10H.** 🐕 🔌 & 🛒

Seal Caves Caravan & Camping Park, The Strand, Dugort, Achill Island, Co Mayo. 00 353 9843262. N59 to Achill Sound. R319 to Bunacurry Junction, turn R, 3m to Valley Cross Roads, turn L 2.5m to Dugort Beach. Set in scenic and sheltered part of the island. Two Blue Flag beaches, seal caves, megalithic tombs, deserted village. Nightly entertainment locally and in nearby villages. 7 nights for the price of 6. Fishing 0.5m; golf course 3.5m; garage 4m; PO, doctor 5m; supermarkets 7.5m. Open April 1-September 30. **20T. MC.** 🛏 🖭 🖫

Ballina

(2m). Belleek Caravan & Camping Park, Ballina, Co Mayo. 00 353 96 71533. lenahan@belleekpark.com. 300yd off the Ballina to Killala Road, R314. Sheltered and tranquil location with full facilities. Salmon fishing in river Moy. Nearby historical sites, Blue Flag beaches, 18-hole golf, deep sea angling and all leisure activities. All amenities in town of Ballina. Open all year by arrangement. **NCC. 32T. MC.** 🐕 🖭 🖫

Castlebar

(8km). Carra Caravan & Camping Park, Belcarra, Castlebar, Co Mayo. 00 353 9032054. post@mayoholidays.com. www.horsedrawn.mayonet.com. From Castlebar follow N84 towards Ballinrobe. Cross the railway bridge and turn left for Belcarra, 5m. Horse-drawn caravan holidays and country walks are a speciality from this quiet, family-run park in Mayo's award-winning 'Tidiest Village'. Shops, PHs, bike hire, fishery all within 200yd. Open June-September. **10T. 3MC.** 🛏 🖫

(7m). Carrowkeel Camping & Caravan Park, Ballyvary, Castlebar, Co Mayo. 00 353 9490 31264. carrowkeelpark@eir com.net. Owner: Alex Peters. Take N5, Castlebar to Dublin. Carrowkeel Park is SP on your L. Suitably located for walking, cycling, touring and (salmon) fishing. Facilities include an on-site shop with tourist information, clubhouse with open fire, live entertainment in high season. Games room and outdoor play area for children. Open April-Setpember. **28T. MC.** 🛏 🖭 🖫

Cong

(1.25m). Cong Caravan & Camping Park, Lisloughrey, Quay Road, Cong, Co Mayo. 00 353 949546089. info@quietman-cong.com. www.quietman-cong.com. Owners: Gerry & Margaret Collins. From Cong, go out on the Galway Road, past Ashford Castle entrance gates. Take next right, park is on your right after cemetery. Fishermen's paradise with rods and boats available and plentiful supply of lakes, rivers and underground streams. Laundrette, children's playground, boat rental and shop on site. Bike rental. Mini golf themed on fairytales and nursery rhymes next door at The Quietman. Nightly Film show for residents in mini cinema. Pony trekking and falconry nearby. Forest walks, caving. **40T. MC.** ✿ 🛏 🖭 🖫

Knock

Knock Caravan & Camping Park, Claremorris Road, Knock, Co Mayo. 00 353 9488100. info@knock-shrine.ie. www.knock-shrine.ie. At Knock roundabout take (N17) Claremorris/Galway Road for 1m, the park is located on the L. Caravan Club affiliated site Suitable base for touring Mayo and the west of Ireland. Toilet blocks, laundry facilities and motorhome service point. TV rooms and play area. Dog walk nearby. Good area for walking. Fishing nearby. Peaceful off-peak. Open March-October. **NCC. 58T. MC.** 🛏 🖭 &

Louisburgh

Old Head Forest Caravan & Camping Park, Old Head, Louisburgh, Co Mayo. 00 353 876486885. N60 to Westport. Road R335 to Louisburgh. Old Head is 12m from Westport. Turn right at Old Head crossroad. Park 350yd to left-hand side. In woodland surroundings, located at edge of Old Head prehistoric woods on shores of Clew Bay. Old Head has a pier and slipway with lifeguard on duty. Wide range of outdoor pursuits at local adventure centres. Open June-September. **20T. MC.** 🛏 🖭 🖫

Westport

(2m). Parkland Caravan & Camping Park, Westport House & Country Park, Westport, Co Mayo. 00 353 9827766. camping@westporthouse.ie. www.westporthouse.ie. On main Westpott-Louisburgh road, R335. Turn right at Westport Quay. Within 3m: 18-hole golf course, deep-sea angling on Clew Bay, pony trekking, restaurants, PHs, dancing. Within easy driving distance: sandy beaches, salmon and sea-trout fishing, sailing and mountain climbing. Open May-September. **40T. MC**🖭

OFFALY

Clonmacnoise

(10m). The Glebe Caravan & Camping Park, Clonfanlough, Clonmacnoise, Co Offaly. 00 353 90 6430277. info@glebe caravanpark.ie. www.glebecaravanpark.ie. Owners: Noel & Vivienne Holmes. Clonfanlough is 3m E of Clonmacnoise, about half way between Ballinahown and Shannonbridge. Site SP at turning off Clonmacnoise Road. Award winning, family-run park offering modern facilities in unspoilt rural setting near from the famous site of Clonmacnoise. Many local attractions. Suitable base for touring the midlands of Ireland or as a peaceful, relaxing stopover on your journey. Open Easter-mid October. **15T. MC.** 🛏 🖭 & 🖫

Tullamore

Green Gables Caravan & Camping Park, Geashill, Tullamore, Co Offaly. 00 353 50643760. ggcp@iol.ie. Geashill is on the R420 between Tullamore and Portarlington. Quiet, family-run park in Geashill village. PHs and shops alongside, offers a good base for touring. Suitable for walking, cycling, fishing, horse riding, birdwatching, garden visits, golf or just relaxing. Nearby canal, peatlands, fine monuments. Open Easter-September. **30T. MC.** 🛏 🖭 & 🖫

ROSCOMMON

Athlone

(3m). Hodson Bay Caravan & Camping Park, Athlone, Co Roscommon. 00 353 90292448. On N61, from the western part of Athlone travel north for 3m, turn right at sign for Hodson Bay. On shores of Lough Ree in centre of Ireland with boating, fishing, swimming available. Hotel, marina and 18-hole golf course 500yd. Cruiser trips on lake nearby. Open June-September. **19T. MC.** 🖭

Ballaghderreen

(3.7m). Willowbrook Caravan & Camping Park, Kiltybranks, Ballaghderreen, Co Roscommon. 00 353 949861307. info@willowbrookpark.com. www.willowbrookpark.com. Owners: Dave & Lin Whitfield. Take R293 from Ballaghderreen towards Castlerea/Ballyhaunis, then R325 over the bridge and bear left for 1m, turn right at site SP, park is 500yd along road. Family-run park set in the Lung Valley. Unspoiled landscape suitable for relaxing holiday. Toilet for disabled visitors. Tuck shop. On-site activities include: archery, kayaking, coarse fishing. Tennis courts and 9-hole golf course nearby. **10T. MC. 1H.** ✿ 🛏 🖭

Boyle

(2m). **Lough Key Caravan & Camping Park, Lough Key Forest Park, Boyle, Co Roscommon.** *00 353 719662212/ 719662363.* seamus.duignan@coillte.ie. www.coillte.ie. Owners: Coillte Teo - The Irish Forestry Board. On the N4 National Primary Route. Set in the surroundings of the 800-acre Lough Key Forest Park on the shores of Lough Key, on the river Shannon. Many activities to enjoy on site. Miles of forest walks and trails. Coarse fishing, fly fishing available. Range of entertainment (restaurants, bars, traditional music), arts, crafts, shopping, golf and much more provided locally. Open March-September. **52T. MC.** ⊮ ⊕ ⚡

Knockroghery

Gailey Bay Caravan & Camping Park, Knockroghery, Co Roscommon. *00 353 90361058.* From Athlone or Roscommon, take turn nearest railway station. 1.5m off the T34, about 6m from Roscommon town and 13m from Athlone. Family-run, self-contained holiday park on the shores of Lough Rea, where truly peaceful waters flow. Located in an area steeped in culture and heritage and suitable for sailing, fishing and water sports. Open April-October. **12T. MC.** ⊮ ⊕ ⚡

SLIGO

Easkey

Atlantic 'N' Riverside Caravan & Camping Park, Easkey, Co Sligo. *00 353 9649001.* atlanticriverside@yahoo.com. 26m W of Sligo off the main Sligo/Ballina road. Park is in the centre of Easkey village; customers should call in to the PO. Family-run park bordering Easkey River (salmon and trout fishing). 5mins walk from the Atlantic for surfing, canoeing, sea-fishing, bird watching and nature walks. Shops, PHs, restaurant, takeaway foods, bicycle hire and buses all within walking distance. Open March-September. **19T. MC.** ⊮ ⊕ ⚐ ⚡

Enniscrone

Atlantic Caravan Park, Enniscrone, Co Sligo. *00 353 9636132.* A long-established, family holiday resort. Adjacent to 3m golden beach. 18-hole golf course, fishing, pony trekking all nearby. Open April-October. **50T. MC.**

Riverstown

Lough Arrow Touring Caravan Park, Ballynary, Riverstown, Co Sligo. *00 353 719666018.* latp@eircom.net. www.rock viewhotel.ie/campsite. Owners: Terry & Mary Wilson. S on N4: L at Castlebaldwin. Follow signs to site. N on N4: first R past Boyle turning, follow signs to site. Registered with Bord Failte and Irish Caravan Council. Adults only. Site located on lough shore. Boat hire. Nearest shop 3m. Fishing adjacent and within 5m (several lakes). Three golf courses within 8m. Pub adjacent. Open April 1-October 31. **30T.** ⊮ ⊕ ⚐

Rosses Point

Greenlands Caravan & Camping Park, Rosses Point, Co Sligo. *00 353 719177113.* noelineha@eircom. Owner: Noeline Cogan. Cairns Hill, Sligo. 5m W of Sligo on R29 off N15. Family site with direct access to two safe beaches. Golf beside the site. Sailing club at 100yd. Views of mountains and sea all around. All the attractions of the area are within a short drive. Hotel, restaurants shop at 500yd. AA 4 pennants. Open March-September. **100T. MC.** ⊮ ⊕ ⚐

Strandhill

Strandhill Caravan & Camping Park, Strandhill, Co Sligo. *00 353 7168111.* On N59, 5m W of Sligo. Site is on airport road, at Strandhill Beach. Mecca for surfers. Flat sands of Culleenamore, more suitable for family fun, are just 1m away. Golf is 500yd, shops, PHs and restaurants within 100yd. Pitches on grass and hard-standings. Open April-September. **65T. MC.** ⊮ ⊕ ⚐

TIPPERARY

Cahir

(6m). **The Apple Caravan & Camping Park, Moorstown, Cahir, Co Tipperary.** *00 353 5241459.* con@theapplefarm.com. www.theapplefarm.com. Located about 300yd off the main Waterford/Limerick road (N24), between Clonmel (5.5m) and Cahir (4m). Our friendly site is located on an award-winning fruit farm. You will be welcome to wander round the orchards, try some of the farm-pressed apple juice and help yourself to a few strawberries or raspberries when in season. On-site facilities: free access to tennis courts and rackets, unlimited hot water, spring water for drinking and large indoor area. Open May-September. **16T. MC.** ⊕ ⚐

Clogheen

Parsons Green Caravan & Camping Park, Clogheen, Co Tipperary. *00 353 5265290.* kathleennoonan@oceanfree.net. www.clogheen.com. Take R668 from Cahir and Lismore. Take R655 from Clonmel R655 from Mitchelstown. Small, family-run park, centrally situated for touring the whole of the south of Ireland. On-site facilities include garden and river walks, pet field, farm museum, takeaway, coffee shop, playground, pony, boat rides, picnic area, tennis and basketball court. Golf, fishing, hill-walking nearby. **20T. MC.** ✿ ⊮ ⊕

Glen of Aherlow

Ballinacourty House Caravan & Camping Park, Glen of Aherlow, Co Tipperary. *00 353 6256559/00 353 877807307.* info@camping.ie. www.camping.ie. Owners: The Stanley family. At traffic lights in Tipperary Town turn L and follow signs for Glen Hotel. Take next R after Glen Hotel 0.5m next R (watch out for hairpin bends and steep incline). Family-run park in tranquil surroundings. Table tennis, tennis court, children's playground and mini golf on site. Horse riding, fishing, golf, swimming pool all available locally. Open April-September. **50T. MC.** ⊮ ⊕ ⚡

Glen of Aherlow Caravan & Camping Park, Newtown, Glen of Aherlow, Co Tipperary. *00 353 6256555.* rdrew@ eircom.net. www.tipperarycamping.com. Owners: George and Rosaline Drew. Caravan Club affiliated site. Spectacular scenery. Toilet blocks and laundry facilities. TV and games room. Dog walk on site. Good area for walking and golf nearby. Peaceful off-peak. **NCC. T. MC.** ✿ ⊮ ⊕ ⚐

Roscrea

(1.5m). **Streamstown Caravan & Camping Park, Streamstown, Roscrea, Co Tipperary.** *00 353 50521519.* streamstowncaravanpark@eircom.net. www.elyocarroll.com. From Roscrea take R491 to Shinrone for 1m. Park is SP. Park is set on a dairy farm, in quiet, landscaped surroundings. Good standard amenities and a relaxing atmosphere are guaranteed. 5 nights for the price of 4. Local activities include: horse riding, golf, historical sites, fishing, hill walking. Open April-October. **14T. MC.** ⊮ ⊕ ⚐

WATERFORD

Dungarvan

Bayview Caravan & Camping Park, Ballinacourty, Dungarvan, Co Waterford. *00 353 5845345/5842296.* bayview@cablesurf.com. From Dungarvan turn S off N25 on to Gold Coast Road and follow signs to park. Gold Coast Golf and Leisure Centre, restaurant, bar, swimming pool, all 200yd from park. Other amenities in area: angling, sailing, water-skiing, swimming, tennis, etc. Two 18-hole golf courses within 2m. Open April-October. **26T. MC.** ⌂ ⚑ ⚐ ♿

(3.5m). Casey's Caravan & Camping Park, Clonea, Dungarvan, Co Waterford. *00 353 5841919.* Follow SP off N25. From Dungarvan town take R675 coast road follow SP. Direct access to beach. Top facilities include playground, TV room, games room, crazy golf, telephone, shop adjacent to park. Fishing, sailing and sail-boarding. Three golf courses in the area. Open April-September. **284T. MC.** ⚐

Tramore

Newtown Cove Caravan & Camping Park, Tramore, Co Waterford. *00 353 51 381979/381121.* info@newtowncove.com. www.newtowncove.com. Owners: John & Sarah Good. From Tramore on R675 Coast Road to Dungarvan: 0.5m from town turn L at the top of the second hill, before roundabout. Family-run park, in a peaceful setting, well sheltered. On-site children's playground, TV and games rooms, shop, laundry. 400yd from sea swimming and fishing. 18-hole golf course. Open May-September. **40T. MC. 56S.** ⌂ ⚐

WESTMEATH

Multyfarnham

Lough Derravaragh Caravan & Camping Park, Multyfarnham, Co Westmeath. *00 353 4471500.* camping@iol.ie. Owner: Paul Smith. On N4 between Mullingar and Longford, take road to Multyfarnham and follow signs to Derravaragh/Donore. Set in 38 acres of mature wooded foreshore. Fishing with boat and engine hire. Golf courses, horse riding, dog racing, forest walks, historic sites, castles and PHs are all nearby. Open March-September; open rest of year by appointment. **23T. MC.** ⌂ ⚑ ⚐

WEXFORD

Ballaghkeen

(4m). The Trading Post, The Ballagh, Ballaghkeen, Co Wexford. *00 353 5327368.* info@wexfordcamping.com. www.wexfordcamping.com. Owner: Patrick Power. From Wexford take R741 for 8.5m. The Trading Post service station and camper park is on your L. Facilities include TV room, laundrette, barbecue area, children's play area, service station deli and fourcourt shop. Pub, golf courses, sandy beach all nearby. Open April-September. **14T. MC.** ⌂ ⚑ ⚐ ♿

New Ross

Ocean Island Caravan & Camping Park, Fethard On Sea, New Ross, Co Wexford. *00 353 51 397148.* Set in a tranquil location within easy walking distance of sandy beaches, horse riding, pony trekking, fishing, swimming, par-3 golf nearby, children's outdoor playground. Shop, games room, laundry open July and August only. Open Easter-Setpember. **10T. MC.** ⌂ ⚑ ♿ ⚐

Rosslare

(5.5m). St Margarets Beach Caravan & Camping Park, Our Lady's Island, Rosslare, Co Wexford. *00 353 5331169.* stmarg@indigo.ie. Owner: Kathryn Traynor. N25 to Tagoat, then follow signs to L for Lady's Island/Carne. Continue for 1m. After St Iver's Bar turn L, continue for 1m, SP. Nature preserve and bird sanctuary nearby. Adjacent to Wexford coastal path and miles of safe sandy beach. Family-run site; owners live on site. Open March-October. **10T. MC.** ⌂ ⚐ ⚑

Wexford

Ferrybank Camping & Caravan Park, Ferrybank, Wexford, Co Wexford. *00 353 44378/43274.* wexfordcorporation@wexfordcorp.ie. www.wexfordcorp.ie. 5mins walk across bridge on seafront on R741. On seafront overlooking town and harbour. Heated indoor swimming pool and shop attached. Golf, fishing, surfing, sailing, Blue Flag beaches and tennis within easy reach. Open Easter-September. **54T. MC.** ⌂ ⚑ ♿ ⚐

WICKLOW

Donard

Moat Farm Caravan & Camping Park, Donard, Co Wicklow. *00 353 45404727.* moatfarm@ireland.com. Owner: E & N Allen. From Dun Laoghaire follow signs for N4 and N7, then on to N81. 9m S of Blessington, turn L at Old Toll House PH. See signs. Park is 1m from here. Small, quiet, family-run park in a rural setting, 1mins' walk from the village. Modern, fully serviced park. 20 tent pitches also available. Golf, fishing, pony trekking within easy reach. Good walking country. Suitable touring base. Open March-September. **20T. MC.** ⌂ ⚑ ⚐ ♿

Rathdrum

Avonmore Riverside Caravan & Camping Park, Rathdrum, Co Wicklow. *00 353 40446080.* info@avonmoreriverside.com. www.avonmoreriverside.com. Owner: L Taylor. From Dublin N11 to Rathnew, then R752. From Rosslare, N11 to Arklow, then R752. Quiet site on banks of Avonmore river and on edge of Wicklow Mountains. 10mins walk from village PHs, shops and restaurants. Trout fishing on site. Open Easter-September. **10T. MC.** ⌂ ⚑ ⚐ ♿

Redcross Village

River Valley Caravan & Camping Park, Redcross Village, Co Wicklow. *00 353 40441647.* info@rivervalleypark.ie. www.rivervalleypark.ie. Owner: Mrs V Williams. From Dublin N11 S, continue for 30m, passing Beehive PH on L, continue for another 2m to Lil Doyle's PH on R, turn for Redcross. Site in village 3m. Caravan Club affiliated site. No dogs allowed during July and August. Scenic surroundings. Suitable touring base. Golf, walking, trails, horse riding, water sports, shore and fresh water angling. Restaurant and bar. Open March-September. **NCC. 80T. MC. 40S.** ⌂ ⚑ ♿ ⚐ ✎

Roundwood

Roundwood Caravan & Camping Park, Roundwood, Co Wicklow. *00 353 12818163.* info@dublinwicklowcamping.com. www.dublinwicklowcamping.com. Owners: Jim McCormack, Fergus Brennan. Off N11. From Dublin and Dun Laoghaire turn R at Kilmacanogue from Rosslare, L at Ashford village. Fully developed park in heart of Wicklow Mountains, in quaint village of Roundwood, overlooking Vartry Lakes and Forest. Shops, PHs, restaurants, markets and entertainment within 5mins stroll. Mountain and forest walks. Golf, fishing, equestrian sports nearby. Open May-September. **31T. MC.** ⌂ ⚑ ⚐

index to advertisers

from the publishers of *Caravan*

www.caravanmagazine.co.uk

Motor Caravan

www.motorcaravanmagazine.co.uk

WHAT HOLIDAY Caravan

PARK HOME & HOLIDAY CARAVAN

www.phhc.co.uk

index to advertisers

Please visit the Caravan Club website: www.caravanclub.co.uk